.NET and COM: The Complete Interoperability Guide

Adam Nathan

SAMS

201 West 103rd St., Indianapolis, Indiana, 46290 USA

.NET and COM: The Complete Interoperability Guide

Copyright © 2002 by Sams Publishing

International Standard Book Number: 0-672-32170-x

Library of Congress Catalog Card Number: 2001093566

Printed in the United States of America

First Printing: January 2002

04   03   02   01   4   3   2   1

Trademarks

Warning and Disclaimer

EXECUTIVE EDITOR
Shelley Kronzek

DEVELOPMENT EDITOR
Anne Marie Walker

MANAGING EDITOR
Matt Purcell

PROJECT EDITOR
Andy Beaster

COPY EDITORS
Ned Snell
Katie Robinson

INDEXER
Ginny Bess

PROOFREADERS
Kay Hoskin
Plan-It Publishing

TECHNICAL EDITORS
Dave Mortenson
Bob Willer

TEAM COORDINATOR
Pamalee Nelson

INTERIOR DESIGNER
Anne Jones

COVER DESIGNER
Aren Howell

PAGE LAYOUT
Susan Geiselman
Rebecca Harmon
Cheryl Lynch
Michelle Mitchell

Contents at a Glance

Introduction   **1**

Part I   **Background**

1   Introduction to the .NET Framework   **13**

2   Bridging the Two Worlds—Managed and Unmanaged Code   **47**

Part II   **Using COM Components in .NET Applications**

3   The Essentials for Using COM in Managed Code   **77**

4   An In-Depth Look at Imported Assemblies   **139**

5   Responding to COM Events   **201**

6   Advanced Topics for Using COM Components   **247**

7   Modifying Interop Assemblies   **323**

Part III   **Using .NET Components in COM Applications**

8   The Essentials for Using .NET Components from COM   **379**

9   An In-Depth Look at Exported Type Libraries   **425**

10   Advanced Topics for Using .NET Components   **459**

Part IV   **Designing Great .NET Components for COM Clients**

11   .NET Design Guidelines for Components Used by COM Clients   **497**

12   Customizing COM's View of .NET Components   **539**

13   Exposing .NET Events to COM Clients   **591**

14   Implementing COM Interfaces for Binary Compatibility   **627**

Part V   **Designing Great COM Components for .NET Clients**

15   Creating and Deploying Useful Primary Interop Assemblies   **683**

16   COM Design Guidelines for Components Used by .NET Clients   **715**

17   Implementing .NET Interfaces for Type Compatibility   **739**

Part VI   **Platform Invocation Services (PInvoke)**

18   The Essentials of PInvoke   **771**

19   Deeper Into PInvoke and Useful Examples   **809**

Part VII   Advanced Topics

    20   Custom Marshaling **879**

    21   Manually Defining COM Types in Source Code **957**

    22   Using APIs Instead of SDK Tools **1039**

Part VIII   Comprehensive Examples

    23   Writing a .NET Arcade Game Using DirectX **1105**

    24   Writing .NET Visualizations for Windows Media Player **1195**

Part IX   Appendices

    A   `System.Runtime.InteropServices` Reference **1249**

    B   SDK Tools Reference **1375**

    C   `HRESULT` to .NET Exception Transformations **1399**

    D   .NET Exception to `HRESULT` Transformations **1415**

    E   PInvoke Definitions for Win32 Functions **1431**

    F   Glossary **1487**

       Index **1497**

Contents

Introduction   1

PART I   Background

1   Introduction to the .NET Framework   13
    What Is .NET? 14
        The .NET Framework 15
    Features of the .NET Framework 16
        Version Resiliency (The End of DLL Hell) 16
        Trivial Deployment 19
        Fine-Grained Security 20
        Platform Neutrality 21
    Concepts Important for This Book 22
        Assemblies 22
        Metadata 26
        Reflection 26
        Custom Attributes 28
    Languages and Tools 33
        C# 34
        Visual Basic .NET 38
        C++ 42
        IL Assembler (ILASM) 45
        IL Disassembler (ILDASM) 45
    Conclusion 46

2   Bridging the Two Worlds—Managed and Unmanaged Code   47
    Managed Code Versus Unmanaged Code 48
        Goals of Unmanaged Code Interaction 48
        How Can Using Unmanaged Code Be Secure? 49
    How Unmanaged Code Interacts with Managed Code 49
        Platform Invocation Services (PInvoke) 49
        Mixed-Mode Programming Using Managed
            Extensions to C++ 50
        Java User Migration Path to .NET (JUMP to .NET) 51
        COM Interoperability 51
    Unmanaged Code Isn't Always the Answer 72
    Conclusion 72

Part II   Using COM Components in .NET Applications

3   The Essentials for Using COM in Managed Code   77

Referencing a COM Component in Visual Studio .NET 78

Referencing a COM Component Using Only the .NET
   Framework SDK 81

Example: A Spoken `Hello, World` Using the Microsoft
   Speech API 83

The Type Library Importer 84

   Interop Assemblies 84

   Primary Interop Assemblies 86

Using COM Objects in ASP.NET Pages 90

   Example: Using ADO in ASP.NET 92

   Using COM+ Components 96

An Introduction to Interop Marshaling 96

Common Interactions with COM Objects 99

   Creating an Instance 99

   Calling Methods and Properties on a COM Object 101

   Releasing a COM Object 109

   Casting to an Interface (`QueryInterface`) 110

   Error Handling 112

   Enumerating Over a Collection 114

   Passing the Right Type of `Object` 115

   Late Binding and By-Reference Parameters 119

Using ActiveX Controls in .NET Applications 120

   Referencing an ActiveX Control in Visual Studio .NET 121

   Referencing an ActiveX Control Using Only the .NET
      Framework SDK 122

   Example: A Simple Web Browser 123

Deploying a .NET Application That Uses COM 126

Example: Using Microsoft Word to Check Spelling 127

Conclusion 137

4   An In-Depth Look at Imported Assemblies   139

Converting the Library 141

Converting COM Data Types 143

   Combining Several Types in One 145

   Complex Types 152

Converting Methods and Properties 162

   Methods 162

   Properties 171

   Special DISPIDs 173

Converting Interfaces 177

Converting Classes 179

    Coclass Interfaces and Parameter/Field Replacement 180

    The RCW Class 182

Converting Modules 187

Converting Structures 189

Converting Unions 191

Converting Enumerations 193

Converting Typedefs 194

Converting ActiveX Controls 196

Conclusion 199

5   Responding to COM Events   201

Callbacks in .NET 202

    Callback Interfaces 202

    Delegates 204

    Events 208

Callbacks in COM 214

Handling COM Events in Managed Code 218

    The Raw Approach 218

    Type Library Importer Transformations 222

    Using the Event Abstraction 224

    Lazy Connection Point Initialization 227

    Connectable Objects You Don't Instantiate 229

Handling ActiveX Control Events in Managed Code 235

    ActiveX Importer Transformations 235

    Using ActiveX Events 240

Conclusion 245

6   Advanced Topics for Using COM Components   247

Do-It-Yourself Marshaling 248

    C# Unsafe Code Versus `System.Runtime.InteropServices` APIs ..250

    Examples of Manipulating `IntPtr` Types 258

Threading and Apartments 275

    Threading in COM Versus Threading in .NET 275

    Choosing Your Apartment State in a .NET Application 277

    Callbacks from a COM Object to a .NET Object 282

Troubleshooting an `InvalidCastException` 289

    `QueryInterface` Failure 290

    Casting to an RCW Class 295

Garbage Collection 299

Securing Unmanaged Calls 304

Using COM+ and DCOM Objects 309

Inheriting from COM Classes 311
Debugging into COM Components 315
Monitoring Performance 320
Conclusion 321

7   Modifying Interop Assemblies   323
How to Change an Assembly's Contents 325
IL Assembler Syntax 328
    Data Types 332
    Passing Parameters 334
    MarshalAsAttribute Syntax 334
Changing Data Types 340
Exposing Success HRESULTs 342
Arrays 348
    Exposing SAFEARRAYs Differently 348
    Adding Size Information to C-Style Arrays 349
Custom Attributes 351
    Changing Attribute Contents 354
    Marking Classes as Visual Basic Modules 356
    Adding Back helpstring Information 358
    Adding Custom Marshalers 364
    Adding DISPIDs 366
    Adding Back IDL Custom Attributes 371
Adding Methods to Modules 372
Conclusion 374

Part III   Using .NET Components in COM Applications

8   The Essentials for Using .NET Components from COM   379
A Sample .NET Component 380
Using a .NET Component in Visual Basic 6 382
Using a .NET Component in Unmanaged Visual C++ 385
Using a .NET Component in Unmanaged JScript 388
Assembly Registration 390
The Type Library Exporter 394
.NET Class Interfaces 397
Interacting with a .NET Object 399
    Creating a .NET Object 399
    Calling Members on a .NET Object 400
    Getting Rich Error Information 403
    Enumerating Over a Collection 415
Deploying a COM Application That Uses .NET 415
Hosting Windows Forms Controls in Internet Explorer 417
Conclusion 422

9   An In-Depth Look at Exported Type Libraries   425

Converting the Assembly 426

Converting .NET Data Types 429

Converting Members 434

    Methods 434

    Properties 441

    Fields 444

    Events 446

Converting Interfaces 447

Converting Classes 449

Converting Value Types 452

Converting Enumerations 453

Conclusion 457

10   Advanced Topics for Using .NET Components   459

Avoiding Registration 460

    Hosting the Common Language Runtime 460

    Using the `ClrCreateManagedInstance` API 468

Hosting Windows Forms Controls in Any

    ActiveX Container 471

Working Around COM-Invisibility 477

Using Reflection to Invoke Static Members 482

Handling .NET Events 488

Unexpected Casing in Type Libraries 489

Advanced Shutdown Topics 492

Conclusion 493

Part IV   Designing Great .NET Components for COM Clients

11   .NET Design Guidelines for Components Used by
COM Clients   497

Naming Guidelines 499

    Names to Avoid 500

    Namespaces and Assembly Names 502

    Case Insensitivity 503

Usage Guidelines 506

    Interfaces Versus Classes 506

    Interfaces Versus Custom Attributes 508

    Properties Versus Fields 510

    Using Overloaded Methods 511

    Using Constructors 513

    Using Enumerations 514

    Choosing the Right Data Types 516

Reporting Errors 520
    Defining New Exception Types 520
    General Guidelines 523
Exposing Enumerators to COM 524
Versioning 527
    Library Identifiers (LIBIDs) 529
    Class Identifiers (CLSIDs) 530
    Interface Identifiers (IIDs) 531
Deployment 532
Testing Your Component from COM 535
Conclusion 537

12 Customizing COM's View of .NET Components   539

Customizing Data Types 540
    `MarshalAsAttribute` Basics 541
    Customizing Arrays 549
    Detecting Incorrect Use of `MarshalAsAttribute` 552
    Customizing Data Flow 553
Customizing Structure Layout 554
Exposing Class Interfaces 556
Using Visual Basic .NET's `ComClassAttribute` 560
Making APIs Invisible to COM 562
Customizing Registration 565
    Choosing Your Own ProgID 566
    Adding Arbitrary Registration Code 567
Providing Your Own GUIDs 574
Providing Your Own DISPIDs 574
Controlling Interface Derivation 578
Returning a Specific `HRESULT` 579
Disabling Type Library Marshaling of .NET Interfaces 580
Creating Multi-Cultured Methods 582
Using Optional Parameters in Any Language 583
Exposing .NET Objects As COM+ Objects 584
Conclusion 586

13 Exposing .NET Events to COM Clients   591

Exposing Events Without Using Extra CLR Support 592
Exposing Events Using Extra CLR Support 598
    Using `ComSourceInterfacesAttribute` 598
    Defining a Source Interface 600
    The `Phone` Example Revisited 602
    Visual Basic .NET's `ComClassAttribute` 605
    Design Guidelines 608

Example: Handling a .NET Windows Form's Events from COM 611
    The .NET Event Source 611
    The COM Event Sink 623
  Conclusion 626

14 Implementing COM Interfaces for Binary Compatibility   627
  Getting Interface Definitions 628
  Binary Compatibility with Visual Basic 6 Classes 629
  Example: Implementing Office XP Smart Tag Interfaces 634
    Running the Example Using Visual Studio .NET 646
    Running the Example Using Only the .NET
      Framework SDK 650
  Interface Implementation Shortcuts in Visual Studio .NET 650
  Common Problems When Implementing COM Interfaces 653
    Parameterized Properties 653
    Interface Inheritance 654
    Returning Specific HRESULTs 656
  COM Interfaces with Default CCW Implementations 657
    IUnknown 657
    IDispatch 659
    IMarshal 672
    IProvideClassInfo 673
    ISupportErrorInfo 674
    IConnectionPointContainer 675
    IObjectSafety 676
  COM Interfaces Bridged to Different .NET Types 678
  Conclusion 679

Part V Designing Great COM Components for .NET Clients

15 Creating and Deploying Useful Primary Interop Assemblies   683
  Primary Interop Assembly or Brand New Assembly? 684
  Creating a Primary Interop Assembly 686
    Generating a Strong Name 686
    Handling References to Other Type Libraries 687
    Naming the Output Assembly 690
    Customizing the Metadata 693
  Deploying and Registering a Primary Interop Assembly 694
  Writing IDL That Produces Good Type Libraries 697
    Referencing External Types 698
    Defining Classes 702
    Defining Structures, Enums, and Unions 707
    Using Constants Appropriately 709

Avoiding Ignored Constructs 710
Registering the Type Library 711
What About ActiveX Controls? 712
Conclusion 713

16   COM Design Guidelines for Components Used by
     .NET Clients   715
General Guidelines 716
Using Array Parameters 717
Use SAFEARRAYs 717
Use Zero Lower Bounds 719
Use Single-Dimensional Arrays 719
Issues with VARIANT Parameters 720
Reporting Errors 720
Reserve Failure HRESULTs for Exceptional Circumstances 721
Don't Return Success HRESULTs Other than S_OK 721
Set Additional Error Information 722
Adjusting Certain COM-Specific Idioms 729
Passing a Pointer to Anything 729
Passing Type Information 730
Passing Error Information 731
Managing Limited Resources 731
Threading and Apartment Guidelines 733
Providing Self-Describing Type Information 734
Naming Guidelines 734
Performance Considerations 735
Conclusion 738

17   Implementing .NET Interfaces for Type Compatibility   739
Class Interfaces 741
Interface Inheritance 743
Considerations for Visual C++ Programmers 747
Example: Implementing IDisposable to Clean Up Resources 750
Considerations for Visual Basic 6 Programmers 759
Example: Implementing IFormattable to Customize ToString ..761
Example: Implementing IHashCodeProvider and IComparer
to Use a COM Object as a Hashtable Key 764
Conclusion 767

Part VI   Platform Invocation Services (PInvoke)

18   The Essentials of PInvoke   771
Using PInvoke in Visual Basic .NET 773
Using PInvoke in Other .NET Languages 776

Choosing the Right Parameter Types 778
    Strings 782
    Arrays 792
Customizing `Declare` and `DllImportAttribute` 795
    Choosing a Different Function Name 796
    Customizing the Behavior of Strings 796
    Changing the "Exact Spelling" Setting 799
    Choosing a Calling Convention 799
    Customizing Error Handling 800
Conclusion 807

19 Deeper Into PInvoke and Useful Examples   809
Callbacks 810
    Using Delegates as Function Pointers 811
    Invoking Unmanaged Function Pointers in Managed Code 818
Passing Structures 821
    Customizing Structures with Custom Attributes 829
    Using Formatted Classes 839
    The Structure Inspector 844
Handling Variable-Length Structures and Signatures 847
Using C# Unsafe Code 849
Guarding Against Premature Garbage Collection 852
    The `System.GC.KeepAlive` Method 861
    The `System.Runtime.InteropServices.HandleRef`
      Value Type 861
Choosing the DLL Location or Name Dynamically 863
Example: Responding Immediately to Console Input 865
Example: Clearing the Console Screen 868
Example: Using `CoCreateInstanceEx` to Activate Remote
    COM Objects 871
Conclusion 875

Part VII Advanced Topics

20 Custom Marshaling   879
Transforming Types Without Custom Marshaling 882
Custom Marshaling Architecture 895
    The Custom Marshaler 896
    The Consumers 898
    The Adapter Objects 901
Marshalers, Marshalers, Marshalers! 913
    Example: Marshaling Between .NET and COM Fonts 914
    Example: Marshaling Between `System.IO.Stream` and
      `IStream` 923

Example: Marshaling With Arrays 943
Example: Providing Deterministic Release of Resources 947
Limitations 952
Conclusion 953

21   Manually Defining COM Types in Source Code   957
Using SDK Tools for Support 960
Manually Defining COM Interfaces 962
Important Custom Attributes 963
IUnknown-Only Interfaces 964
Dual Interfaces 975
Dispinterfaces 982
Interface Inheritance 984
Working With Language Limitations 988
Handy Customizations 998
Manually Defining Coclass Interfaces and Event Types 1003
Manually Defining COM Structures 1019
Manually Defining COM Enums 1022
Manually Defining COM Classes 1022
Defining Classes the Simple Way 1024
Defining Classes the Hard Way 1029
Avoiding the Balloon Effect 1033
Conclusion 1036

22   Using APIs Instead of SDK Tools   1039
Generating an Assembly from a Type Library 1040
Creating a Dynamic Assembly 1042
Getting a Primary Interop Assembly 1047
Saving the Dynamic Assembly 1048
Generating a Type Library from an Assembly 1050
Creating a Dynamic Type Library 1050
Saving the Dynamic Type Library 1055
Registering and Unregistering Assemblies 1056
Installing and Uninstalling Serviced Components 1059
Example: Using the APIs in an Interactive Application 1061
The Importer 1069
The Exporter 1083
The Registrar 1092
The COM+ Installer 1097
The Windows Forms Client 1100
Conclusion 1101

Part VIII   Comprehensive Examples

23   Writing a .NET Arcade Game Using DirectX   1105

The User's Perspective 1106

The Programmer's Perspective 1108

DirectX Interaction 1112

The Game Class 1119

Sounds and Pictures 1133

Layers 1150

Screens 1155

The Actors 1157

Using the Game Class 1166

E-mail Attack—The Advanced Version 1171

Conclusion 1194

24   Writing .NET Visualizations For Windows Media Player   1195

The COM Visualization API 1197

The `Render` Method 1199

Other Methods 1200

Creating a .NET Visualization API 1201

The `IWMPEffects` Interface 1202

Supporting Structs and Enums 1204

The `Visualization` Class 1208

Using the .NET Visualization API 1224

A Simple Visualization 1224

The Wizard Visualization 1227

The Colorful Visualization 1231

The Dancing Cat Visualization 1235

Conclusion 1243

Part IX   Appendices

A   `System.Runtime.InteropServices` Reference   1249

The `System.Runtime.InteropServices` Namespace 1250

The `ArrayWithOffset` Value Type 1252

The `AssemblyRegistrationFlags` Enumeration 1254

The `AutomationProxyAttribute` Custom Attribute 1254

The `BIND_OPTS` Value Type 1255

The `BINDPTR` Value Type 1255

The `CALLCONV` Enumeration 1255

The `CallingConvention` Enumeration 1255

The `CharSet` Enumeration 1256

The `ClassInterfaceAttribute` Custom Attribute 1256

The `ClassInterfaceType` Enumeration 1257

The CoClassAttribute Custom Attribute 1258
The ComAliasNameAttribute Custom Attribute 1258
The ComConversionLossAttribute Custom Attribute 1258
The ComEventInterfaceAttribute Custom Attribute 1258
The COMException Exception 1259
The ComImportAttribute Pseudo-Custom Attribute 1260
The ComInterfaceType Enumeration 1260
The ComMemberType Enumeration 1261
The ComRegisterFunctionAttribute Custom Attribute 1261
The ComSourceInterfacesAttribute Custom Attribute 1261
The ComUnregisterFunctionAttribute Custom Attribute 1262
The ComVisibleAttribute Custom Attribute 1262
The CONNECTDATA Value Type 1263
The CurrencyWrapper Class 1263
The DESCKIND Enumeration 1264
The DESCUNION Value Type 1264
The DispatchWrapper Class 1264
The DispIdAttribute Custom Attribute 1265
The DISPPARAMS Value Type 1266
The DllImportAttribute Pseudo-Custom Attribute 1266
The ELEMDESC Value Type 1267
The ErrorWrapper Class 1267
The EXCEPINFO Value Type 1268
The ExporterEventKind Enumeration 1268
The ExtensibleClassFactory Class 1269
The ExternalException Exception 1271
The FieldOffsetAttribute Pseudo-Custom Attribute 1271
The FILETIME Value Type 1272
The FUNCDESC Value Type 1272
The FUNCFLAGS Enumeration 1272
The FUNCKIND Enumeration 1273
The GCHandle Value Type 1273
The GCHandleType Enumeration 1277
The GuidAttribute Custom Attribute 1278
The HandleRef Value Type 1278
The ICustomAdapter Interface 1280
The ICustomFactory Interface 1281
The ICustomMarshaler Interface 1281
The IDispatchImplAttribute Custom Attribute 1282
The IDispatchImplType Enumeration 1283
The IDLDESC Value Type 1283
The IDLFLAG Enumeration 1283

The `IMPLTYPEFLAGS` Enumeration 1283

The `ImportedFromTypeLibAttribute` Custom Attribute 1284

The `ImporterEventKind` Enumeration 1284

The `InAttribute` Pseudo-Custom Attribute 1284

The `InterfaceTypeAttribute` Custom Attribute 1285

The `InvalidComObjectException` Exception 1286

The `InvalidOleVariantTypeException` Exception 1286

The `INVOKEKIND` Enumeration 1287

The `IRegistrationServices` Interface 1287

The `ITypeLibConverter` Interface 1287

The `ITypeLibExporterNameProvider` Interface 1288

The `ITypeLibExporterNotifySink` Interface 1289

The `ITypeLibImporterNotifySink` Interface 1289

The `LayoutKind` Enumeration 1290

The `LCIDConversionAttribute` Custom Attribute 1290

The `LIBFLAGS` Enumeration 1291

The `Marshal` Class 1292

The `MarshalAsAttribute` Pseudo-Custom Attribute 1342

The `MarshalDirectiveException` Exception 1344

The `ObjectCreationDelegate` Delegate 1345

The `OptionalAttribute` Pseudo-Custom Attribute 1345

The `OutAttribute` Pseudo-Custom Attribute 1346

The `PARAMDESC` Value Type 1347

The `PARAMFLAG` Enumeration 1347

The `PreserveSigAttribute` Pseudo-Custom Attribute 1347

The `PrimaryInteropAssemblyAttribute` Custom Attribute 1348

The `ProgIdAttribute` Custom Attribute 1349

The `RegistrationServices` Class 1349

The `RuntimeEnvironment` Class 1351

The `SafeArrayRankMismatchException` Exception 1352

The `SafeArrayTypeMismatchException` Exception 1352

The `SEHException` Exception 1353

The `STATSTG` Value Type 1353

The `StructLayoutAttribute` Pseudo-Custom Attribute 1354

The `SYSKIND` Enumeration 1354

The `TYPEATTR` Value Type 1355

The `TYPEDESC` Value Type 1355

The `TYPEFLAGS` Enumeration 1355

The `TYPEKIND` Enumeration 1355

The `TYPELIBATTR` Value Type 1356

The `TypeLibConverter` Class 1356

The `TypeLibExporterFlags` Enumeration 1357

The `TypeLibFuncAttribute` Custom Attribute 1358

The `TypeLibFuncFlags` Enumeration 1358

The `TypeLibImporterFlags` Enumeration 1358

The `TypeLibTypeAttribute` Custom Attribute 1359

The `TypeLibTypeFlags` Enumeration 1359

The `TypeLibVarAttribute` Custom Attribute 1359

The `TypeLibVarFlags` Enumeration 1359

The `UCOMIBindCtx` Interface 1360

The `UCOMIConnectionPoint` Interface 1360

The `UCOMIConnectionPointContainer` Interface 1360

The `UCOMIEnumConnectionPoints` Interface 1360

The `UCOMIEnumConnections` Interface 1361

The `UCOMIEnumMoniker` Interface 1361

The `UCOMIEnumString` Interface 1361

The `UCOMIEnumVARIANT` Interface 1361

The `UCOMIMoniker` Interface 1362

The `UCOMIPersistFile` Interface 1363

The `UCOMIRunningObjectTable` Interface 1363

The `UCOMIStream` Interface 1364

The `UCOMITypeComp` Interface 1364

The `UCOMITypeInfo` Interface 1365

The `UCOMITypeLib` Interface 1366

The `UnknownWrapper` Class 1366

The `UnmanagedType` Enumeration 1367

The `VARDESC` Value Type 1368

The `VarEnum` Enumeration 1369

The `VARFLAGS` Enumeration 1370

The `System.Runtime.InteropServices.CustomMarshalers`
Namespace 1370

The `EnumerableToDispatchMarshaler` Class 1370

The `EnumeratorToEnumVariantMarshaler` Class 1371

The `ExpandoToDispatchExMarshaler` Class 1371

The `TypeToTypeInfoMarshaler` Class 1372

The `System.Runtime.InteropServices.Expando` Namespace 1372

B   SDK Tools Reference   1375

`TLBIMP.EXE` 1376

`/asmversion` 1377

`/delaysign` 1377

`/keycontainer` 1377

`/keyfile` 1378

`/out` 1378

`/namespace` 1379

```
/primary ..........................................................................1379
/publickey ......................................................................1379
/reference ......................................................................1380
/strictref .......................................................................1380
/sysarray ........................................................................1380
/unsafe ..........................................................................1380
/nologo ..........................................................................1381
/silent ..........................................................................1381
/verbose .........................................................................1381
/help and /? .....................................................................1381
```
TLBEXP.EXE 1382
```
/names ...........................................................................1383
/out .............................................................................1384
/nologo ..........................................................................1384
/silent ..........................................................................1384
/verbose .........................................................................1384
/help and /? .....................................................................1384
```
REGASM.EXE 1385
```
/codebase ........................................................................1386
/regfile .........................................................................1386
/registered ......................................................................1387
/tlb  ............................................................................1387
/unregister ......................................................................1389
/nologo ..........................................................................1389
/silent ..........................................................................1389
/verbose .........................................................................1390
/help and /? .....................................................................1390
```
AXIMP.EXE 1390
```
/delaysign .......................................................................1391
/keycontainer ....................................................................1391
/keyfile .........................................................................1392
/out .............................................................................1392
/publickey .......................................................................1392
/source ..........................................................................1393
/nologo ..........................................................................1393
/silent ..........................................................................1393
/verbose .........................................................................1393
/help and /? .....................................................................1393
```
REGSVCS.EXE 1394
```
/appname .........................................................................1394
/c   .............................................................................1395
/componly ........................................................................1395
/exapp ...........................................................................1395
```

/extlb 1395

/fc 1395

/noreconfig 1395

/parname 1395

/reconfig 1396

/tlb 1396

/u 1396

/nologo 1396

/quiet 1396

/help and /? 1396

C   **HRESULT to .NET Exception Transformations**   **1399**

D   **.NET Exception to HRESULT Transformations**   **1415**

E   **PInvoke Definitions for Win32 Functions**   **1431**

GDI32.DLL 1433

KERNEL32.DLL 1442

OLE32.DLL 1461

SHELL32.DLL 1470

USER32.DLL 1472

F   **Glossary**   **1487**

    Index   **1497**

Foreword

Working on the Common Language Runtime (CLR) for the past three-and-a-half years has been a fantastic opportunity. It's not often that you get the chance to work on a project where you can forget about the past and design an exciting new set of technologies from the ground up, uninhibited by the constraints of maintaining backward compatibility.

The CLR offers a fresh solution to the problems developers face in building and using reusable components and deployable applications. It's an entirely new architecture aimed squarely at simplifying the development and deployment process. In designing the CLR we took the opportunity to step back and look at the process of writing reusable components using COM today. We examined the problems people had with things like reference counting, apartments, and registration, and we looked at the aspects of the model that made building COM components complicated. One of the primary design goals in building the CLR was to eliminate that complexity. In short, it was time to make programming fun again.

COM was nothing short of revolutionary when it was first introduced. It provided a standard mechanism with which developers could build reusable components. Most developers like to forget about the pre-COM days, when linking to static DLL exports was about as close as you could get to reusability. Over the years, the popularity of COM has grown enormously, to the point where today, just about every application that provides any level of extensibility does so using COM. But as features were added, the complexity of COM has grown. After nearly ten years of COM enhancements, that complexity reached the point where it began to seriously impede developer productivity.

In some ways, COM is like your 1994 Ferrari. When you first sat in the driver's seat, you thought it was the greatest, but after a few years, the novelty wore off, and all you focus on is that rattle under the hood and the grinding in the transmission when you try to shift into third gear. After programming with COM for several years, joining the CLR team was like an opportunity to build a new Ferrari, with cool new features that promised to make driving fun again. We had the talent, we had the resources, and we had a 1994 Ferrari sitting in the garage for reference. Most importantly, we had management-level support to build the best darn Ferrari we possibly could. There was only one catch—not everyone could afford a new Ferrari, and even those who could were sometimes a bit skeptical of all the new features. After all, most of the older models were still working pretty well, as long as you stayed out from under the hood.

Surprisingly, some people were actually interested in buying parts of the new Ferrari to use in older models rather than buying a whole new car. And believe it or not, some people loved the old-style Ferrari so much they even wanted to put old parts on the new cars. It seemed that no matter how cool the new model was, there was always someone asking, "Will I be able to take that transmission and put it in my '94 Ferrari?" Here we were designing this fabulous new machine, and all people could think about was backward compatibility. (Well, that may not be exactly how it went, but it's not far off.)

Faced with these requests for compatibility, we formed the Interoperability team within the CLR, whose role it was to build a bi-directional bridge between COM and .NET. Wherever possible, we ignored compatibility constraints in designing the features of the CLR so that we could use the best possible design. Once the feature was designed, the Interop team was faced with the task of bridging the features between .NET and COM. In most cases, the Interop team was able to build the bridge without affecting the initial design. In rare cases (such as enumerations), the interoperability constraints forced us to change the original design for better backward compatibility.

Designing, building and testing this Interop bridge was no small task. It required talented people who had both COM and .NET expertise. Of those involved, Adam Nathan, author of this book, was one of the most talented and important players. Adam joined the team early in the process as a member of the Interop test team. If you had access to the RAID database we use to track bugs, you'd find that Adam has filed a whopping 2022 bugs since the project started (and he's not done yet). That's more bugs than anyone else on the entire team. These weren't trivial bugs, and an amazing 1873 of them were resolved "fixed." Getting a bug fixed is the equivalent of a base hit for a tester; if Adam played for the Seattle Mariners, he'd be batting .926 (that's even better than Ichiro). Equally impressive is how few bugs Adam opened that were resolved "by design"—only 44 bugs, or two percent of the total. From a program manager's perspective, Adam is the kind of test developer you wish you could have on your team.

On top of that, Adam has made numerous contributions to the design of Interop. There was more than one occasion when Adam pointed out flaws in the design that sent developers and program managers back to the garage with their tails between their legs. Consider that Adam did all of this while writing this book in his spare time—during his first year of marriage—and I think you'll agree that he's truly an authority when it comes to COM Interop and the CLR. I know of no one who could have done a finer job writing this book than Adam.

Dennis Angeline

Lead Program Manager

Microsoft .NET Common Language Runtime

About the Author

Adam Nathan is a software design engineer on Microsoft's .NET Common Language Runtime Quality Assurance team. Taking on the role of an external software developer, Adam has worked to ensure the quality and usability of COM Interoperability for over two years. He has participated in the design decisions that have shaped the product from its beginnings, and thus is able to give a unique perspective when explaining this complex technology to the reader. Adam is also a coauthor of *ASP.NET: Tips, Tutorial, and Code*.

Adam has served on a panel of .NET experts, provided technical assistance during hands-on labs, and helped to prepare demonstrations at the Microsoft Professional Developers Conferences in 2000 and 2001. He has seen where developers of all skill levels frequently struggle with COM Interoperability and Platform Invocation Services, and regularly provides technical assistance on .NET mailing lists. Adam received an honors B.S. degree in Computer Science at Cornell University, Ithaca, New York.

Dedication

To my high school sweetheart, best friend, and beautiful bride, Lindsay.

Acknowledgments

First and foremost, I thank my wife, Lindsay, from the bottom of my heart. Taking on the project of writing such a large book during our first year of marriage was not an easy decision to make, and perhaps not a wise one, considering what a time-consuming project this ended up becoming! Almost a calendar full of holidays, both of our birthdays, and even our one-year anniversary passed by, and all the while I was writing. Yet through it all, Lindsay remained inhumanly patient and understanding while I toiled through the evenings and late nights that I should have been spending with her. She shared most of the worst parts about writing a book without receiving most of the benefits. Toward the end, when the schedule was extra-hectic, she even helped me put together Appendix E and translated some of my hand-drawn diagrams to electronic form! Lindsay, please accept this (and our new kitten Shadow!) as my sincere apology. I love you.

It amazes me how little decisions you make throughout life can cause quite an impact years later. One of these small decisions of mine was to take on a certain independent study project while I was a student at Cornell University, which exposed me to Microsoft's Component Object Model. I'd like to thank my project advisor, Werner Vogels, for introducing me to COM, a technology that ended up guiding the direction of my career!

There are lots of wonderful people at Microsoft I'd like to thank, and I'll list their names at the risk of forgetting someone. First, I thank my managers, Chris Waldron and Kory Srock, for their support. I thank Mahesh Prakriya for his initial communication with Sams Publishing, making it possible for me to write this book. Also, lots of thanks belong to David Mortenson (who took on the huge job of being a technical editor), Dan Takacs, Sonja Keserovic, Scott Wadsworth, and Matt Lyons for reviewing drafts of some chapters. I'd also like to thank Kevin Ransom and Jian Lee, who have given helpful input. I also thank Bob Willer, who doesn't work at Microsoft but jumped in midway through the project and did a great job as a second technical editor.

I'd like to thank the great people at Sams for their incredible patience in dealing with an author who doesn't seem to know the meaning of the word "deadline"! They gave me the freedom to spend way too much time writing and revising in order to produce the highest quality chapters possible. I'd like to thank Shelley Kronzek, Anne Marie Walker, Andy Beaster, Katie Robinson, Ned Snell, and all the people whom I didn't get to work with directly. I greatly appreciate all of your hard work.

I thank all of my family and friends for their encouragement and entertainment throughout the past year. Finally, I thank you, the reader, for picking up a copy of this book!

Tell Us What You Think!

As the reader of this book, *you* are our most important critic and commentator. We value your opinion and want to know what we're doing right, what we could do better, what areas you'd like to see us publish in, and any other words of wisdom you're willing to pass our way.

As an Executive Editor for Sams, I welcome your comments. You can fax, e-mail, or write me directly to let me know what you did or didn't like about this book—as well as what we can do to make our books stronger.

Please note that I cannot help you with technical problems related to the topic of this book, and that due to the high volume of mail I receive, I might not be able to reply to every message.

When you write, please be sure to include this book's title and author as well as your name and phone or fax number. I will carefully review your comments and share them with the author and editors who worked on the book.

Fax: 317-581-4770

E-mail: feedback@samspublishing.com

Mail: Shelley Kronzek, Executive Editor
             Sams Publishing
             201 West 103rd Street
             Indianapolis, IN 46290 USA

Introduction

Welcome to *.NET and COM: The Complete Interoperability Guide*. First, to avoid any unsatisfied customers, let me make clear that this is not a book about domain names for Web sites! This is a book about two technologies that enable software developers to leverage existing software while taking advantage of the Microsoft .NET platform: *COM Interoperability* (often abbreviated as *COM Interop*), and *Platform Invocation Services* (often shortened to *Platform Invoke*, or simply *PInvoke*). Without them, widespread adoption of the Microsoft .NET platform would not be growing as quickly as it has been, because developers of .NET software projects would essentially be forced to start from scratch.

In observing the history of the .NET platform, from its initial announcement at the Microsoft Professional Developers Conference in the summer of 2000, to its two subsequent beta releases, to its 1.0 release at the beginning of 2002, I've seen many software developers ask *a lot* of questions about COM Interoperability and PInvoke! These are complex technologies, and they are especially important to understand as software developers evaluate what to do with large bodies of existing software. Interoperating with existing software is one of the first .NET topics a developer should master, because a pure .NET world can't begin overnight (if at all). Even if you're starting a new .NET software project from scratch, chances are that you'll need to take advantage of interoperability somewhere—whether you need to use APIs exposed by the operating system or by third-party components.

I've seen other .NET books dedicate a chapter or two to COM Interoperability and/or PInvoke. These chapters sometimes provide a nice introduction to the technologies, but real-world applications almost never behave as nicely as canonical examples. Instead, they often require techniques that just can't be covered in one or two chapters. Since I started working on the COM Interoperability team over two and a half years ago, I've always believed that an entire book on .NET's interoperability services would be a must-have for the development community. Nobody else has stepped up to the challenge, so I went ahead and wrote it!

It was very hard for me to come up with a concise title for this book and still convey the broad array of topics covered. Let me explain the motivation behind the final title (chosen with the help of Shelley Kronzek). The ".NET and COM" part should be obvious, but the subtitle is chosen for the following reasons:

- **Complete**—COM Interoperability and Platform Invocation Services are large topics, and this is a large book. I've made every effort to make this book as comprehensive as possible. It ended up being twice as long as I originally anticipated (and took me twice as long to write it), but I wanted to ensure that this book deserved to be described as "complete." So I kept writing until the entire story was told.

- **Interoperability**—Although the title doesn't mention Platform Invocation Services, this book is about general interoperability with existing software. The focus of the book is with COM Interoperability, but I believe that this book also serves as a complete reference for Platform Invocation Services, a technology that doesn't necessarily involve COM.
- **Guide**—I wanted this book to be more than just a reference, but one that guides you step-by-step through the nuances, and one with an abundance of code examples. This includes some fun examples toward the end of the book, including a .NET arcade game! In addition, I wanted to capture and explain *why* these technologies are designed the way they are, something a plain reference book might not bother covering.

Who Should Read This Book?

This book is for anyone wanting to leverage existing pre-.NET software with .NET applications or components. I don't expect you to know anything about .NET in advance, but the more background in .NET you have (and experience with one .NET language), the better off you'll be. Most of the book assumes familiarity with either "raw COM" or COM through Visual Basic 6, but its concepts are explained in enough detail such that you should still get a lot out of the book without in-depth prior knowledge. Even if you (gasp!) don't care about COM, you should still be able to get a lot out of Part VI and Appendix E, because they are targeted for reusing any existing software in .NET, even if it has nothing to do with COM.

To summarize, by reading this book, you learn how to:

- Leverage existing software (COM-based or not) in new .NET applications.
- Plug new .NET components into an existing COM architecture, taking advantage of .NET's many features rather than continuing to program the COM way.
- Design your software to work well in both .NET and COM-based surroundings.
- Call any unmanaged APIs (such as Win32 functions) in any .NET language.
- Interoperate with COM+ and DCOM objects, as well as ActiveX controls.

If there's one thing abundant in this book, it's source code examples! .NET examples are provided in C#, Visual Basic .NET, and Visual C++ .NET, and should be easy to reproduce in any .NET language. Although most examples are printed in one language, every one is available for download from this book's Web site in both C# and Visual Basic .NET, where applicable. COM Interoperability and PInvoke are language-independent at the core, but this book highlights features in all three languages that add value to interoperability in their own unique ways (and may guide your decision of which .NET language to use when interoperability is needed).

COM examples are provided in Visual C++ (version 6 or 7), IDL, and Visual Basic 6, to help the readers whose only exposure to COM is through Visual Basic. Throughout the book, special considerations for Visual Basic COM components are given. Many source code examples in these COM-based languages are also available for download.

Software Requirements

This book targets the final release of version 1.0 of the Microsoft .NET Framework and its Software Development Kit (SDK), and version 7.0 of Microsoft Visual Studio .NET.

The only software required—besides Microsoft Windows—is the freely downloadable .NET Framework SDK, available at `msdn.microsoft.com`. This book explains not only how to accomplish every task using nothing other than the free SDK, but also how to accomplish the tasks using Visual Studio .NET. If you already have Visual Studio .NET—the ultimate development tool providing the rapid application development (RAD) experience for developing .NET applications—you'll appreciate the extra content covering some of its features as they relate to the examples.

Some of the examples in this book use Microsoft COM-based technologies to demonstrate concepts in a realistic setting. Most of these are freely downloadable, such as the Microsoft Speech SDK, the Windows Media Player SDK, and the Microsoft DirectX SDK. Downloading instructions appear with the examples. A few examples use Microsoft Office, but having this software is not required to understand the concepts.

How This Book is Organized

This book is organized in nine parts. The heart of the book is Parts II through V, which cover all angles of the COM Interoperability picture. With COM Interoperability, there are two basic directions of interaction: a .NET component calling a COM component and a COM component calling a .NET component. Parts II and III cover the client side of both directions for the application developer, and parts IV and V cover the server side of both directions for the component developer. This organization is summarized in the following diagram:

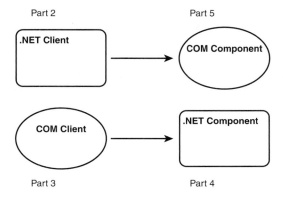

FIGURE IN.1

A conceptual overview of Parts II-V.

This picture is a simplification, because it does not mean that the topics covered only apply to simple client/server interaction; the "clients" pictured could actually be components themselves in a long chain of a multi-tiered application. Regardless of an application's structure or what pieces of an application are made up of .NET and COM components, the themes remain the same unless called out otherwise in these chapters.

Material specific to COM+ components can be found in the following places:

- Using COM+ components in .NET applications—Chapter 6
- Custom attributes for writing .NET serviced components—Chapter 12
- Programmatically installing .NET components in the COM+ Component Services Explorer—Chapter 22
- Manually installing .NET components in the COM+ Component Services Explorer—Appendix B

Here's a summary of all nine parts of the book:

Part I. Background

Besides containing the obligatory overviews of the .NET Framework and COM, this part of the book covers a handful of concepts that are especially important for the remainder of the book.

- Chapter 1, "Introduction to the .NET Framework," explains the .NET Framework's and Common Language Runtime's position in the broad .NET initiative, and pays special attention to two .NET features: reflection and custom attributes. The chapter ends with an overview of C#, Visual Basic .NET, and Visual C++ .NET, the three .NET languages given focus in this book.
- Chapter 2, "Bridging the Two Worlds—Managed and Unmanaged Code," is an overview of .NET interoperability services, introducing the four main mechanisms for leveraging existing code in .NET applications: Platform Invocation Services, Mixed-Mode Programming in Visual C++ .NET, Java User Migration Path to .NET (JUMP to .NET), and last but not least, COM Interoperability.

Part II. Using COM Components in .NET Applications

This is the largest part of the book, and it covers the topics that most .NET developers need to know first.

- Chapter 3, "The Essentials for Using COM in Managed Code," covers the information necessary to use most COM components and ActiveX controls and most of their APIs in .NET applications.

- Chapter 4, "An In-Depth Look at Imported Assemblies," explains exactly how COM type information gets translated into .NET type information. This chapter arms you with the knowledge to handle the fact that the source code required to use COM components in a .NET language sometimes doesn't resemble the source code using them in COM-based languages (and perhaps the examples in COM components' .NET-unaware documentation).

- Chapter 5, "Responding to COM Events," discusses the .NET and COM event models, how the Common Language Runtime integrates these two disparate mechanisms, and how to respond to events raised by COM components and ActiveX controls.

- Chapter 6, "Advanced Topics for Using COM Components," covers a handful of advanced topics, including debugging, troubleshooting common problems, DCOM, security, threading models, do-it-yourself marshaling, and more.

- Chapter 7, "Modifying Interop Assemblies," discusses how to use .NET Framework SDK tools to disassemble, modify, and reassemble components containing the .NET view of COM APIs. This is sometimes necessary to make COM components usable in .NET, and other times it's a big help in improving their ease of use.

Part III. Using .NET Components in COM Applications

This part of the book covers tasks that are the opposite of the tasks covered in Part II. Using .NET components in a COM-based language is not as common as using COM components in a .NET language, but is still a topic of great importance.

- Chapter 8, "The Essentials for Using .NET Components from COM," is the opposite of Chapter 3. This chapter explains the information necessary to use most .NET components in COM applications. It also demonstrates how to host .NET components and Windows Forms controls inside Internet Explorer and write script that uses them.

- Chapter 9, "An In-Depth Look at Exported Type Libraries," is the opposite of Chapter 4 and explains exactly how .NET type information gets translated into COM type information. Using .NET APIs in COM often differs significantly from using them in .NET languages. Since it's unlikely that most .NET components will be documented from COM's perspective, this chapter fills in the gaps and removes the need for such documentation.

- Chapter 10, "Advanced Topics for Using .NET Components," the opposite of Chapter 6, covers the advanced topics of using .NET components in COM applications. This includes tricks for using .NET APIs that are supposed to be invisible to COM, using .NET components without registration, using reflection to invoke static members, and some advanced shutdown-related APIs exposed by the Common Language Runtime.

Part IV. Designing Great .NET Components for COM Clients

This part of the book complements Part II, focusing on the .NET components that might be used by COM clients.

- Chapter 11, ".NET Design Guidelines for Components Used by COM Clients," explains how to design your .NET components while keeping the ease-of-use for potential COM clients in mind, so your clients won't have to buy a copy of this book to figure out how to use the components from COM!

- Chapter 12, "Customizing COM's View of .NET Components," covers the long list of custom attributes provided by COM Interoperability, so you can customize the way your .NET components are exposed to COM. It also introduces custom attributes provided by .NET Enterprise Services that enable you to take advantage of component services available for COM+ objects.

- Chapter 13, "Exposing .NET Events to COM Clients," discusses how to take extra steps to ensure that any events you raise can be handled naturally from COM. Unless you follow the procedures explained in this chapter, .NET events are essentially unusable from COM's perspective.

- Chapter 14, "Implementing COM Interfaces for Binary Compatibility," discusses binary compatibility, and the subtleties that can arise when .NET classes implement COM interfaces. It also discusses the interfaces automatically implemented when .NET components are exposed to COM, and how to customize their behavior.

Part V. Designing Great COM Components for .NET Clients

This part of the book complements Part III, focusing on the COM components that might be used by .NET clients.

- Chapter 15, "Creating and Deploying Useful Primary Interop Assemblies," discusses ways of creating and distributing type information for existing COM components that maximize their use in .NET. It also discusses cosmetic changes that greatly improve a COM component's .NET usability with minimal impact.

- Chapter 16, "COM Design Guidelines for Components Used by .NET Clients," is analogous to Chapter 11, and explains how to design new COM components (or redesign old ones) so they can be used seamlessly as if they were "pure" .NET components.

- Chapter 17, "Implementing .NET Interfaces for Type Compatibility," is analogous to Chapter 14, and discusses the subtleties and limitations (especially for Visual Basic 6 users) in writing COM classes that implement .NET interfaces.

Part VI. Platform Invocation Services (PInvoke)

This part of the book serves as a complete reference for Platform Invocation Services.

- Chapter 18, "The Essentials of PInvoke," covers the basic use of PInvoke in C# and Visual Basic .NET. It instructs how to create correct PInvoke signatures and how to customize them, as well as the data type transformations that must be understood in order to be successful.
- Chapter 19, "Deeper Into PInvoke and Useful Examples," covers a handful of important topics such as callbacks, structure marshaling, interaction with garbage collection, and C# unsafe code. It also includes several examples using Win32 APIs to accomplish common tasks that are not possible with .NET Framework APIs alone.

Part VII. Advanced Topics

These chapters cover advanced topics in COM Interoperability used in both directions of COM and .NET interaction.

- Chapter 20, "Custom Marshaling," describes how to write a custom marshaler that controls how COM types are exposed to .NET, and vice-versa.
- Chapter 21, "Manually Defining COM Types in Source Code," shows how to create the same type definitions emitted by the type library importer in any high-level .NET language. It also covers ways to customize and improve upon these definitions.
- Chapter 22, "Using APIs Instead of SDK Tools," covers a handful of APIs that enable you to programmatically do the same tasks done by several of the .NET Framework SDK tools, and ends with source code for a large graphical application that takes advantage of all these APIs.

Part VIII. Comprehensive Examples

This is the fun part of the book, containing the full source code for two large examples that use COM Interoperability and Platform Invocation Services. Although the examples are meant to be entertaining, the same concepts can be applied to more serious business applications.

- Chapter 23, "Writing a .NET Arcade Game Using DirectX," is a large example of using COM in a .NET application to create a video game. This example demonstrates the concepts of Part II, Part VI, and Chapter 21.
- Chapter 24, "Writing .NET Visualizations for Windows Media Player," is an example of writing .NET components to be used by a COM client that knows nothing about .NET, all to the beat of some music in Windows Media Player. This example demonstrates the concepts of Part IV and Chapter 21.

Part IX. Appendices

- Appendix A, "System.Runtime.InteropServices Reference," covers every type and member in the System.Runtime.InteropServices namespace in depth and in alphabetical order.

- Appendix B, "SDK Tools Reference," describes the COM Interoperability-related command-line utilities that ship with the .NET Framework SDK, and all of their options.

- Appendix C, "HRESULT to .NET Exception Transformations," contains a list that completely defines how HRESULT values (COM error codes) are transformed into .NET exception types. For convenience, the list appears twice—sorted by HRESULT values and sorted by exception name.

- Appendix D, ".NET Exception to HRESULT Transformations," is the opposite of Appendix C and contains a list that displays how exception types defined in the .NET Framework are exposed to COM as HRESULT values. For convenience, the list appears twice—sorted by HRESULT values and sorted by exception name.

- Appendix E, "PInvoke Definitions for Win32 Functions," contains a list of PInvoke method signatures that, once you define any necessary parameter types, enables a .NET program to call just about any Win32 API appearing in one of five core Windows DLLs—KERNEL32.DLL, GDI32.DLL, OLE32.DLL, SHELL32.DLL, and USER32.DLL.

- Appendix F, "Glossary," defines common terms used throughout this book.

Conventions Used in This Book

To bring special attention to certain material in a chapter, or to make some material easier to follow, the following special elements appear in this book:

- FAQ sidebars
- Digging Deeper sidebars
- Tips
- Cautions

FAQ

FAQ (Frequently Asked Question) sidebars present questions readers might have regarding the subject matter in particular spots in the book—then they provide concise answers to those questions.

DIGGING DEEPER

Digging Deeper sidebars present advanced or more detailed information on a subject than is provided in the text surrounding them. Think of Digging Deeper material as stuff you can look into if you're curious, but can ignore if you're not.

TIP

Tips are bits of information that can help you in real-world situations. They often offer shortcuts or alternative approaches to make a task easier, quicker, or safer.

CAUTION

Cautions alert you to an action or condition that can lead to an unexpected or unpredictable result—such as a loss of data—and tell you how to avoid or fix the results.

This book also uses various typesetting styles to distinguish between explanatory and instructional text and text you enter:

- Onscreen messages, program code, commands, filenames, and URLs appear in a special `monospaced` font.
- *Placeholders*—words that you replace with actual code—are indicated with `monospace italic`.
- Some lines of code may appear in `monospace bold`, for emphasis.

For more information, please visit the book's Web site at `http://www.samspublishing.com`. Type 067232170x in the Search box and click Search.

Background

PART
I

IN THIS PART

1 Introduction to the .NET Framework   13

2 Bridging the Two Worlds—Managed and
Unmanaged Code   47

Introduction to the .NET Framework

IN THIS CHAPTER

- What Is .NET?   14
- Features of the .NET Framework   16
- Concepts Important for This Book   22
- Languages and Tools   33

This chapter presents the .NET Framework, giving a high-level, medium-level, and hands-on introduction to its main features. If you're already familiar with the .NET Framework, treat this chapter as a brief refresher to ensure that you're familiar with .NET concepts that are important for the remainder of this book.

What Is .NET?

Microsoft .NET is a broad initiative that is meant to revolutionize the way applications are written. The Internet is at the center of this revolution, with focus on loosely coupled Web services. These Web services are based on XML (Extensible Markup Language), and can be discovered on the Internet using the Simple Object Access Protocol (SOAP). XML is a standardized, self-describing data format that is the key to communication across heterogeneous systems. You can think of XML Web services simply as components or Application Programming Interfaces (APIs) exposed on a Web site rather than a DLL residing on your own computer.

The goal of .NET is to make computers easier to use and more flexible with higher-quality software that is faster to produce and easier to maintain. (Sounds good, doesn't it?) Don't let the name fool you—.NET isn't solely about the Net. Although .NET enables new kinds of applications to be written, traditional Windows applications that have nothing to do with the Internet can benefit enormously from .NET. The .NET platform consists of the following four pieces:

- Infrastructure and tools—The .NET Framework, Visual Studio .NET, .NET Enterprise Servers, and Windows .NET. The .NET Framework and Visual Studio .NET are the portions of .NET discussed in this book. The .NET Enterprise Servers include Exchange, SQL Server, Commerce Server, Application Center, BizTalk Server, and many more.

- Services—These are components that expose a wide range of functionality over the Internet, collectively known as .NET My Services. .NET My Services is based on XML, uses SOAP over HTTP or DIME (Direct Internet Message Encapsulation) for data interchange between clients and servers, and uses .NET Passport technology for user authentication. Microsoft provides a number of core services (such as .NET Documents and .NET Calendar), but anyone can develop their own services that use the .NET My Services infrastructure.

- User experience—An updated user interface that enables user-friendly computing on many different devices.

- Device software—Applications that enable smart Internet-enabled clients to take advantage of XML Web services.

The .NET revolution isn't happening overnight. At the time of writing, only the "Infrastructure and tools" portion of .NET has non-beta products available.

The .NET Framework

The .NET Framework is the focus of this book and the core of .NET. It enables the creation of all sorts of applications, whether tightly coupled or loosely coupled, Web-based or not. Specifically, the .NET Framework is comprised of the following pieces:

- The Common Language Runtime (CLR)
- Core class libraries
- ASP.NET
- Windows Forms
- Web Forms
- Classes for graphics, network access, data access, and more

Although technically not part of the framework, several programming languages that are built on the .NET Framework are included not only in the .NET Framework Software Development Kit (SDK), but with the .NET Framework redistributable package to support ASP.NET's on-the-fly compilation.

DIGGING DEEPER

For shorthand, documentation often refers to *.NET* when it really means the *.NET Framework*. This book (including its title!) is no exception. Just to be clear, for the rest of this book, the terms *.NET*, *.NET Framework*, and *managed* (a term discussed in Chapter 2, "Bridging the Two Worlds—Managed and Unmanaged Code") can be considered synonyms.

The Common Language Runtime (CLR)

What exactly is a *runtime*? You might have heard of the Microsoft C Runtime Library (MSVCRT.DLL) or the Visual Basic Runtime (such as MSVBVM60.DLL). A runtime, short for *runtime environment*, is a component that provides execution services for programs. In other words, a *runtime* is needed at *run time* for programs to function. For instance, a program written in Visual Basic cannot run on a computer without the Visual Basic Runtime installed.

So, as the name suggests, the Common Language Runtime is an execution environment for multiple languages—any programming language that targets the .NET Framework. Because components written in multiple languages targeting the .NET Framework share the same execution environment, they can interact in powerful ways. For example, a Visual Basic .NET class can inherit from a class written in C#. Thanks to the CLR, language choice is largely a personal preference that has little effect on the performance or capabilities of the software produced. Languages built on top of the .NET Framework are often called *managed languages* or *.NET languages*, and the compilers are often called *managed compilers* or *.NET compilers*.

The Common Language Specification (CLS)

Because .NET languages have the infrastructure to interact with each other seamlessly, yet each language may choose to implement its own unique features, Microsoft has established a Common Language Specification that defines a subset of functionality that all .NET languages should support. (It also defines conventions that should be followed.) This way, component writers can guarantee that their components will work seamlessly from C#, Visual Basic .NET, COBOL, Perl, Eiffel, or any other .NET language that honors the CLS, by restricting their public APIs to the subset of features defined by the CLS. Such a component is said to be *CLS-compliant*. CLS restrictions apply only to public types and their public or protected members, parameters, and return types. Internally, components can do whatever they want and still be considered CLS-compliant.

Examples of features in the CLS (that languages must support) are strings, integers, enumerations, and arrays. Examples of features not in the CLS are unsigned integers, optional parameters, and pointers. Thus, you should avoid writing public methods with features such as optional parameters because you can't count on every language supporting them. Some compilers can optionally check the CLS-compliance of your code, so you don't have to become familiar with the rules and examine your code manually. Also, rest assured that most of the APIs that Microsoft exposes in the .NET Framework are CLS-compliant.

Features of the .NET Framework

The .NET Framework has many features that make it a simple, productive, and powerful environment enabling rapid application development. These features include tight language integration, automatic memory management (garbage collection), rich class libraries, services for debugging and profiling, and much more. This section focuses on the following important features:

- Version resiliency
- Trivial deployment
- Fine-grained security
- Platform neutrality

Version Resiliency (The End of DLL Hell)

If you've done any software development, you're probably painfully aware of the versioning problem with shared components. Typically called *DLL Hell*, it's a widely known problem that continues to infest software, plaguing users with fragile applications that can break whenever the system state is changed—most notably installation or uninstallation of any software. One of the main goals of the .NET Framework is to eliminate DLL Hell, enabling robust applications that are immune to external changes.

What Exactly Is DLL Hell?

DLL Hell is made possible by multiple applications sharing the same component. The ability for multiple applications to reuse existing components can be a good thing—it enables programmers to use existing, well-tested functionality rather than writing new and potentially buggy code. Furthermore, multiple applications that share the same component (rather than statically linking to a library) also save disk space and memory, and reduce download time.

The problem with this is applications that share the same component are exposed to problems caused by changes to the physical files. A setup program could incorrectly overwrite a DLL, or it could install a completely different DLL in the same shared directory (such as the Windows System32 directory) that happens to have the same filename. Installation could also fail to update necessary DLLs if they are locked by another application. Although these scenarios are possible, malfunctioning setup programs are not typically the source of DLL Hell.

Instead, problems mostly occur when a component is "correctly" replaced with a newer version. The application whose setup program replaced the component works fine, but existing applications that used the older version might break. This problem can manifest as random performance problems, crashes, or other incorrect behavior. To make the problem worse, there are no easy ways to pinpoint its cause. If the problem can be tracked down to a new version of a DLL, you could replace the new DLL with an older version. However, this would likely cause problems with the application you recently installed that requires the newer component. Because you can have only one copy of the DLL, you're stuck. This is DLL Hell.

Why do new DLLs cause problems? It's practically impossible for any new version of a component that is *supposed* to be backward compatible to be 100% compatible. New features and bug fixes can change some of the component's semantics in subtle ways. Component authors don't know what kinds of assumptions clients make (intentionally or not) that aren't "in the contract." For example, programs can rely on memory leaks, incorrect return values, or the timing and order of operations. These can be considered bugs in the client applications, but regardless of fault, the end user pays the price.

Note that Windows, starting with Windows 2000 and Windows 98 Second Edition, combats DLL Hell with some support for side-by-side components and a technique known as *DLL/COM redirection*. This support enables you to "privatize" a DLL by copying it in your local directory and carefully following rules about registration and unregistration. This can be helpful, but does not completely solve the problems of DLL Hell. Windows 2000 also introduced system file protection that prevents initially installed DLLs in the System32 directory from being replaced without lots of extra effort.

The .NET Framework Solution

The .NET Framework solution to DLL Hell balances the benefits of sharing with the benefits of isolation. Programs that work initially can continue to work forever, even in a constantly changing environment. To accomplish this, developers can ensure that their applications always use the same components the applications were built and tested with, but they also have the freedom to use upgraded components when it's safe to do so. The .NET Framework also provides the means to diagnose and fix problems caused by upgraded components.

For component writers, sharing in .NET is an explicit decision rather than a default behavior. This is unlike the pre-.NET world in which any component placed in a system directory or registered in the Windows Registry is instantly globally available. Although isolated components cannot be affected by changes to other applications, they lack the benefits of sharing. Of course, many components (such as the ones Microsoft supplies in the .NET Framework) must be shared to be useful. In the .NET Framework, even shared components don't necessarily cause client applications to suffer from the problems discussed earlier. That is because the .NET Framework supports two concepts that put an end to software fragility:

- Side-by-side components
- Version policy

Side-By-Side Components

Rather than forcing developers to replace an older component with one that is supposed to be backward compatible, support for side-by-side components means that multiple versions can safely exist at the same time. The .NET Framework enables multiple versions of a component to run simultaneously on the same computer or even in the same process. Thus, applications that were built and tested using version 1.5 of a component can continue to use version 1.5, and applications that were built and tested using version 2.7 can use version 2.7.

Each .NET Framework component is self-describing, including information on which versions of dependent components it was built with. The Common Language Runtime uses this information to determine which version of a component to load when multiple versions exist side-by-side. Having the capability to use side-by-side components has two implications for component authors:

- You no longer need to worry about maintaining backward compatibility because installing a new version of the component doesn't mean that older applications will break. Attempting to remain as backward compatible as possible is still a good idea, however, if you want clients to upgrade to your new version.

- You must take special care when accessing global data or resources because you must be prepared for a scenario in which multiple versions of your component are trying to access resources at the same time. Fortunately, the .NET Framework provides mechanisms (such as isolated storage) to make this easier.

DIGGING DEEPER

The Common Language Runtime, although not a .NET component, supports multiple versions of itself coexisting side-by-side in a similar fashion. If it didn't support this, every .NET application could still suffer versioning problems caused by changes to the underlying runtime.

With side-by-side components, applications can use the same components they were built and tested with, and DLL Hell is no longer a factor. The problem with always using the same components is that applications can't easily evolve. If a component is updated with a critical bug fix due to a security flaw, or re-released with significant performance improvements, every client application would need to be recompiled and redistributed to take advantage of the fixes. To eliminate this problem, the .NET Framework has version policy.

Version Policy

A *version policy* enables a developer or administrator to configure which versions of components should be used on the end user's machine *after the application has been deployed*. Policies can be changed at any time for an entire machine (*machine policy*), a single component (*publisher policy*), or for a single client application (*application policy*). Thus, applications get the benefits of using shared components, but can be individually rolled back to their original state if problems occur. This removes the need to privatize a DLL or statically link to a library.

Some examples of version policies are

- Bind to the exact version with which applications were built. This is the safest policy (and therefore called *safe mode*) but applications won't pick up any bug fixes.

- Redirect requests for a certain version (or a range of versions) to a new specific version. The idea here is that later "compatible" versions of a component can be shipped with such a policy. If the component breaks its compatibility promise, the user or administrator has the power to roll back problematic client applications so they use an earlier version.

Therefore, the .NET Framework places the power and flexibility in the hands of client applications or administrators to manage the components used. Each computer can be easily configured and re-configured to get the right balance of sharing and isolation.

Trivial Deployment

Because .NET applications and components are self-describing, the .NET Framework doesn't require you to place any information in the Windows Registry. Thus, in many scenarios, installing an application is as simple as copying files, and uninstalling it is as simple as deleting the files. In addition, because components and applications can be isolated or shared side-by-side, deployment in the .NET Framework is often called *zero-impact deployment* or *xcopy deployment* (as in the xcopy command, which is a more powerful form of copy). Sometimes deployment via copy or xcopy commands isn't sufficient, so the .NET Framework supports code downloading via cab files as well as Windows Installer packages. Note that the isolation and side-by-side features also mean that rebooting is no longer necessary during installation because you aren't replacing files that are used by running applications. This ease in deployment is critical to a Web-centric future, but is also great news for traditional applications.

Fine-Grained Security

Computer users have become used to essentially an all-or-nothing mindset when it comes to security and running software. The operating system can restrict access to many parts of the computer depending on the identity of the user, but programs that a user runs have the same privileges as the user herself. Because most users don't write the software they run, they can't know if the software is buggy or malicious. This problem has become well known with the epidemic of e-mail viruses. Users must decide whether they trust a piece of software or not before they attempt to run it. This fact of life becomes apparent when you visit a Web site with ActiveX controls and you're presented with dialog boxes like the one shown in Figure 1.1.

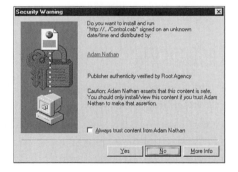

FIGURE 1.1

A typical security warning displayed by Internet Explorer when attempting to visit a Web site with an ActiveX control.

The .NET Framework has two security mechanisms to remedy the security problems of the pre-.NET world:

- Code access security
- Role-based security

Code Access Security

To address the reality that trustworthy users often run untrustworthy code, code access security is based on assigning permissions to *code*—not users—based on evidence. The evidence consists of the origin of the code (such as the local machine, the intranet zone, the Internet zone), the publisher, whether or not the code is verifiably type-safe, and more. Furthermore, code access security can catch software attempting to do something it doesn't have permission to do at run time. Therefore, just because a program executes doesn't mean it has the same level of access as the user.

The .NET Framework defines permissions and permission sets, but user-defined ones can be added. Security policy can be configured by an administrator, deciding which code groups have which permissions. A program can demand that its clients have certain permissions or request three kinds of permissions for itself: minimum, optional, and refused. *Minimum permissions* must be granted in order to execute; *optional permissions* are ones that code can use to provide additional (but not required) functionality; and *refused permissions* are ones that code never wants to be granted. The last one might sound strange, but it's the principle of least privilege in action. To prevent malicious activity caused by other programs exploiting bugs in your code (known as a luring attack), it's good practice to refuse permissions that you know you don't require. Requesting permissions is optional, but it can be useful if you don't want your component to run in a semi-trusted state for which you have to handle run-time errors caused by insufficient permissions.

Role-Based Security

The role-based security mechanism provided by the .NET Framework is closer to the kind of security seen prior to the .NET Framework. In this scheme, permissions are granted to users and roles (groups of users). These users and roles can be based on Windows accounts or on custom identities unrelated to the operating system. As with code access security, the .NET Framework's role-based security is extensible.

Platform Neutrality

Compilers that produce .NET applications do not emit platform-specific code, with the exception of Visual C++ .NET. Instead, compilers produce *Microsoft Intermediate Language*, often called *MSIL* or simply *IL*. At run time or installation time, the IL is compiled into platform-specific code so that it can be executed. This compilation is done using a just-in-time compiler (JIT) that is part of the Common Language Runtime. IL is not interpreted—native code is always executed. Because of this technology, .NET applications will be able to run without recompilation on any operating system that contains an implementation of the Common Language Infrastructure (CLI). The CLI is a specification being standardized by ECMA, an international standards organization. The CLR is the Microsoft implementation of the CLI.

Therefore, you can look forward to writing code for your 32-bit desktop computers that will also work on 64-bit computers, small devices, and other operating systems in addition to Windows. Not every part of the .NET Framework will be available on all platforms, but the output of ECMA's standardization work will be a subset of functionality that you can count on to be available everywhere. This book is solely based on the 32-bit Windows implementation of the .NET Framework, although some considerations are given to help you avoid non-portable code.

Concepts Important for This Book

This section introduces, in more technical detail, the concepts that enable the features of the .NET Framework just discussed. An understanding of these concepts is important for getting the most out of this book.

- Assemblies
- Metadata
- Reflection
- Custom attributes

Assemblies

An assembly is a self-describing logical component. Assemblies are units of deployment, units of security, units of versioning, and units of scope for the types contained within. Assemblies are the key to the deployment and versioning features of the .NET Framework, so you can reread the earlier sections and replace the word *component* with *assembly*.

Although an assembly is typically one executable or one DLL, it could be made up of multiple files. These files could be anything—modules, pictures, Web pages, and so on. The main reason for creating a multi-file assembly is to enable the downloading of pieces of the assembly as needed, rather than downloading the entire assembly at once. Also, a multi-file assembly is the only built-in way to use multiple languages in the same assembly, because some .NET compilers can produce modules that can be linked together.

An assembly must contain a manifest describing its contents, and usually contains MSIL, resources, and metadata describing the types contained in the assembly. A manifest can contain the following information:

- A simple name
- A four-part version number of the form *Major.Minor.Build.Revision*
- A culture, such as Dutch (nl) or Korean (ko)
- The publisher's public key

- A list of files that make up the assembly
- A list of dependent assemblies, including each assembly's name, version, culture, and public key (if applicable)
- Permission requests
- Exported types
- Resources

The first four items make up the identity or "name" of an assembly, and only the first two items are required. In this book, assemblies are identified by only their simple name unless the additional parts of the name are relevant to the discussion. Notice that an assembly name and the filename containing the manifest are independent. In most cases, an assembly's simple name must be the filename without its three-letter extension.

A frequent source of confusion for beginners is that an assembly name and a namespace are two independent concepts. An assembly can contain types with multiple namespaces (or no namespace), and a single namespace can appear in multiple assemblies. That said, most assemblies contain a single namespace that matches the assembly name or multiple namespaces that begin with the assembly's name. A good example is the `System.Web` assembly, which contains the namespaces `System.Web`, `System.Web.Caching`, `System.Web.Compilation`, `System.Web.Configuration`, and many more. Notable exceptions are the `mscorlib` and `System` assemblies, both of which contain members with the namespaces `System`, `System.Diagnostics`, `System.IO`, `System.Security.Permissions`, and `System.Threading`. Therefore, remember that it's never enough to know only a type's namespace in order to use it—you must also know (and reference) the correct assembly.

The `mscorlib` assembly, in addition to being the only assembly in the .NET Framework with a funny-looking name, contains the core library of the .NET Framework. This assembly must always be referenced for basic functionality. Whenever a type name is mentioned in the book, you can assume that it's defined in the `mscorlib` assembly unless specified otherwise. In contrast to `mscorlib`, the `System` assembly contains additional basic functionality that is often needed but not considered as fundamental as the APIs in `mscorlib`.

Strong Names

An assembly can be given a unique name when the publisher includes its public cryptographic key in the manifest. An assembly name that includes a public key is said to have a *strong name* or *shared name*. In addition, by digitally signing an assembly using a public and *private* key, a publisher can protect an assembly from tampering. Digitally signing an assembly stores a cryptographic hash of the contents of each file in the assembly. The contents of the hashes are verified at run time to ensure that the assembly has not been corrupted or tampered with. Cryptographic key pairs can be generated using the Strong Name Tool (`SN.EXE`) provided in the .NET Framework SDK.

Signing is done at compilation time, but because developers typically don't have immediate access to their company's private key, the .NET Framework supports *partially signed assemblies*. Partially signed assemblies contain the public key in the manifest, but don't contain hashes of the file contents (for which the private key is needed). When you're ready to deploy your application, you can complete the signature with the private key as a final step. For this to work, you can set a development-time security policy that allows for this weaker condition.

It's important to note that strong names and digital signing in this context are not the same as giving an Authenticode digital signature with the File Signing Tool (`SIGNCODE.EXE`, also in the .NET Framework SDK). Strong names by themselves have no inherent trust associated with them. Authenticode signatures work with certificates that have associated trust. Because these are independent concepts, assemblies can and should be given both strong names and Authenticode signatures.

Global Assembly Cache

The Global Assembly Cache (sometimes referred to as the GAC) is a machine-wide repository for assemblies that are shared by multiple applications. Whereas application-private assemblies are stored in directories local to the client application, shared assemblies must be installed in the cache. Installation can be done by dragging and dropping a file into the cache directory, using the .NET Management tool, using the Global Assembly Cache Utility (`GACUTIL.EXE`), or using an installation package that is aware of the GAC. The user performing the installation must have administrative rights, and assemblies installed in the cache must have a strong name.

The cache is found in the `Windows\Assembly` (or `WinNT\Assembly`) directory. Thanks to a Windows shell extension, the Global Assembly Cache looks like a magical directory where assemblies live side-by-side, shown in Figure 1.2. If you browse the directory from a command prompt, you'll see how the GAC is really structured. The cache in the figure contains versions 1.0, 1.5, and 3.0 of the `MyComponent` assembly. Whereas the first two versions are culture-neutral, version 3.0 has three cultures installed: American English, French, and Korean.

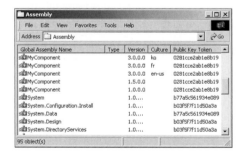

FIGURE 1.2

The Global Assembly Cache, as viewed in Windows Explorer.

FAQ: **How is the Global Assembly Cache different from any other global directory with shared components, such as the `System32` directory?**

Although the GAC is conceptually a flat directory with a list of components, it does not have the DLL Hell-enabling characteristics of the `System32` directory. Because multiple versions of the same assembly can live side-by-side, and each assembly is guaranteed to have a unique name, there can be no problems due to name or version conflicts. Furthermore, the assemblies in the GAC can be configured with versioning and security policies. The files in the `System32` directory can't be configured for customized behaviors.

Referencing Assemblies

To use types in other assemblies from your own application, you must reference the assemblies containing the types. Within the Visual Studio .NET Integrated Development Environment (IDE), this is usually done from the dialog displayed by choosing the `Project`, `Add Reference` menu item, or by right-clicking the `References` branch of the `Solution Explorer`, as shown in Figure 1.3.

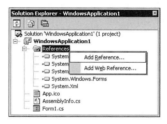

FIGURE 1.3

Adding a reference to another assembly in Visual Studio .NET's Solution Explorer.

Visual C++ .NET projects don't reference assemblies by using the Solution Explorer, but by a statement in source code. Also, be aware that different Visual Studio .NET project types reference different assemblies by default. For example, a C# Windows Application project references `System`, `System.Data`, `System.Drawing`, `System.Management`, `System.Windows.Forms`, and `System.Xml`. Outside Visual Studio .NET, the C# and Visual Basic .NET compilers reference assemblies from the command line. The end of this chapter describes how to reference assemblies in each language by using the command-line compilers.

Metadata

Any assemblies with type definitions contain corresponding type information describing them. This information is called *metadata* (data about data). All .NET compilers emit both IL and metadata when creating assemblies. The Common Language Runtime uses an assembly's metadata at compile time when other assemblies reference and use its types, and at run time in order to load classes and provide its execution services.

Metadata provides the raw language-neutral representation of .NET types. It contains rich information, including type names, inheritance relationships, visibility, and any other attributes that can be specified in source code. Almost no information is lost when converting definitions in source code to definitions in metadata. Therefore, metadata is fundamental to the tight integration of languages using Common Language Runtime.

Metadata is also extensible, as described in the "Custom Attributes" section.

Reflection

Reflection is the process of programmatically obtaining type information. Programs can dynamically inspect ("reflect upon") the metadata for any assemblies, dynamically instantiate objects and invoke members, and even emit metadata dynamically (a technology called *Refection Emit*). Reflection provides late binding facilities like COM's IDispatch and IDispatchEx interfaces, type inspection like COM's ITypeInfo and ITypeInfo2 interfaces, and much more.

Reflection can be done using the System.Type class and several APIs in the System .Reflection namespace (in the mscorlib assembly). The C# code in Listing 1.1 demonstrates how to use reflection to find types in an assembly and dynamically invoke its members.

LISTING 1.1   C# Code Demonstrating Reflection

```
 1: using System;
 2: using System.Reflection;
 3:
 4: class UsingReflection
 5: {
 6:   public static void Main(String [] args)
 7:   {
 8:     if (args.Length < 1)
 9:     {
10:       Console.WriteLine("You must specify an assembly name.");
11:       return;
12:     }
13:
```

LISTING 1.1   Continued

```
14:      Assembly a = null;
15:
16:      try
17:      {
18:        // Load the assembly from a filename
19:        a = Assembly.LoadFrom(args[0]);
20:        Console.WriteLine("Assembly: " + a.GetName());
21:      }
22:      catch (Exception e)
23:      {
24:        Console.WriteLine ("Could not load the assembly: " + e.Message);
25:        return;
26:      }
27:
28:      // Enumerate over the types in the assembly
29:      foreach (Type t in a.GetTypes())
30:      {
31:        try
32:        {
33:          Console.Write("Attempting to create " + t.FullName + "...");
34:
35:          // Create an instance.
36:          // This fails if there's no public default constructor.
37:          object o = Activator.CreateInstance(t);
38:
39:          Console.WriteLine(" Succeeded.");
40:
41:          // Enumerate over the methods in the type
42:          foreach (MethodInfo method in t.GetMethods())
43:          {
44:            // Look for methods with no parameters
45:            if (method.GetParameters().Length == 0)
46:            {
47:              Console.Write("Invoking " + method.Name + "...");
48:              object returnValue = method.Invoke(o, null);
49:              Console.WriteLine(" Succeeded and returned " + returnValue);
50:            }
51:          }
52:        }
53:        catch (Exception e)
54:        {
55:          Console.WriteLine(" Failed (" + e.GetType().ToString() + ").");
56:        }
57:      }
58:    }
59: }
```

Line 19 loads an assembly whose filename is passed as a command-line parameter. The loop beginning on Line 29 checks each type contained inside and attempts to instantiate it, which succeeds if the type has a public default constructor. Lines 42–51 examine all of the type's methods, and for each one that has no parameters, Line 48 dynamically invokes the method. Run this code at your own risk, because an assembly containing a public parameter-less FormatDisk method could have disastrous consequences!

The output of the program in Listing 1.1 begins as follows when run on the System.Drawing assembly:

```
Assembly: System.Drawing, Version=1.0.3300.0, Culture=neutral,
➥PublicKeyToken=b03f5f7f11d50a3a
Attempting to create ThisAssembly... Succeeded.
Invoking GetHashCode... Succeeded and returned 1
Invoking ToString... Succeeded and returned ThisAssembly
Invoking GetType... Succeeded and returned ThisAssembly
Attempting to create AssemblyRef... Succeeded.
Invoking GetHashCode... Succeeded and returned 43
Invoking ToString... Succeeded and returned AssemblyRef
Invoking GetType... Succeeded and returned AssemblyRef
```

Custom Attributes

Types can have predefined attributes such as "public" or "sealed," but the .NET Framework allows you to invent and use your own attributes, such as "stable" or "blue" or "last updated 5 days ago." Such user-defined attributes are called *custom attributes* (or often just *attributes*), and .NET languages have intuitive syntax for using them. The following C# class uses a "description" attribute:

```
[Description("Represents a user's bank account")] // custom attribute
public class Account
{
    ...
}
```

Custom attributes are stored in metadata, so applications can use reflection to find custom attributes and react to them appropriately. You might not be impressed by the previous example because you could accomplish the same thing by implementing an IDescription interface with a Description property or by deriving from a base class with a virtual Description property. The neat thing about custom attributes, however, is that they can be placed on *anything*—methods, properties, fields, parameters, return values, structures, assemblies, modules, and more. Custom attributes are used throughout the .NET Framework for many purposes. You'll see that custom attributes play a crucial role in the later parts of this book.

Writing Your Own Custom Attribute

A custom attribute is simply a public class that derives from System.Attribute. The recommended convention is to end every attribute class name with Attribute to make its intent as clear as possible. Fortunately C#, Visual Basic .NET, and Visual C++ .NET all allow you to omit the Attribute portion of a custom attribute's name when applying the attribute to save typing and improve readability.

An attribute's public fields and writable properties act like its constructors' optional named parameters when the attribute is applied. Listing 1.2 implements a KeywordAttribute that can be used to mark APIs with searchable keywords, similar in spirit to how Web pages are marked with keywords to be picked up by search engines. An intelligent class library browser can make use of these attributes and provide the user with searching functionality.

LISTING 1.2   A Custom Attribute Written in C#

```
1: using System;
2:
3: [AttributeUsage(AttributeTargets.All, AllowMultiple=true)]
4: public class KeywordAttribute : Attribute
5: {
6:   private string keyword;
7:   private int relevance;
8:
9:   // Constructor - called when the attribute is applied
10:   public KeywordAttribute(string word)
11:   {
12:     this.keyword = word;
13:     this.relevance = 5;
14:   }
15:
16:   // Read-only property to get the keyword
17:   public virtual string Keyword
18:   {
19:     get { return keyword; }
20:   }
21:
22:   // Property to get/set the relevance
23:   public virtual int Relevance
24:   {
25:     get { return relevance; }
26:     set { relevance = value; }
27:   }
28: }
```

The custom attribute has a required piece—the word—enforced by the constructor, and an optional piece—a relevance value that defaults to the value 5—enabled by the writable public property.

Notice the custom attribute placed on the KeywordAttribute class. This is the System.AttributeUsageAttribute class, which should be used by all custom attributes to indicate what elements they can be applied to. Valid target elements are specified using the System.AttributeTargets enumeration. The choices for AttributeTargets are Assembly, Class, Constructor, Delegate, Enum, Event, Field, Interface, Method, Module, Parameter, Property, ReturnValue, Struct, and All. Values can be combined using the bitwise-OR operator (| in C# and C++, Or in Visual Basic .NET).

The AttributeUsageAttribute class has two boolean properties that can optionally be set using the named parameter syntax. An Inherited property indicates whether the attribute automatically appears on derived types (from reflection's point of view). The default is true. An AllowMultiple property indicates whether multiple instances of the attribute can be placed on the same element. The default is false because this is rarely desired. KeywordAttribute sets this to true because we want the ability to apply multiple keywords to the same element.

Using a Custom Attribute

Language-specific custom attribute syntax is covered toward the end of this chapter in the "C#", "Visual Basic .NET", and "C++" sections, but the following code snippet is a C# interface that applies the KeywordAttribute that was just defined:

```
[Keyword("application"), Keyword("app"), Keyword("program",Relevance=2)]
public interface IApplication
{
  [Keyword("animated", Relevance=10), Keyword("movie"), Keyword("picture")]
  void EnableAnimations();

  [Keyword("exit"), Keyword("shutdown"), Keyword("close"), Keyword("kill")]
  void Quit();

  [Keyword("title")]
  string Caption { get; set; }

  [Keyword("parent"), Keyword("owner")]
  string Creator { get; set; }
}
```

Retrieving a Custom Attribute

Writing a program that looks for custom attributes and acts on them is pretty simple, thanks to reflection. Listing 1.3, an updated version of Listing 1.1, searches all the types and members in the input assembly for KeywordAttributes. If it finds any, it displays them to the console.

LISTING 1.3 Using Reflection to Discover Custom Attributes

```
 1: using System;
 2: using System.Reflection;
 3:
 4: class UsingReflection
 5: {
 6:   public static void Main(String [] args)
 7:   {
 8:     if (args.Length < 1)
 9:     {
10:       Console.WriteLine("You must specify an assembly name.");
11:       return;
12:     }
13:
14:     Assembly a = null;
15:
16:     try
17:     {
18:       // Load the assembly from a filename
19:       a = Assembly.LoadFrom(args[0]);
20:       Console.WriteLine("Assembly " + a.GetName());
21:     }
22:     catch (Exception e)
23:     {
24:       Console.WriteLine("Could not load the assembly: " + e.Message);
25:       return;
26:     }
27:
28:     // Enumerate over the types in the assembly
29:     foreach (Type t in a.GetTypes())
30:     {
31:       try
32:       {
33:         KeywordAttribute [] attributes;
34:
35:         // Check for the KeywordAttribute on the type
36:         attributes = (KeywordAttribute [])
37:           t.GetCustomAttributes(typeof(KeywordAttribute), true);
38:
39:         PrintKeywords(t.ToString(), attributes);
40:
41:         // Enumerate over the members in the type
42:         foreach (MemberInfo member in t.GetMembers())
43:         {
44:           // Check for the KeywordAttribute on the member
45:           attributes = (KeywordAttribute [])
46:             member.GetCustomAttributes(typeof(KeywordAttribute), true);
```

LISTING 1.3   Continued

```
47:
48:              PrintKeywords(t.ToString() + "." + member.Name, attributes);
49:          }
50:        }
51:        catch (Exception e)
52:        {
53:          Console.WriteLine(" Failed (" + e.GetType().ToString() + ").");
54:        }
55:      }
56:    }
57:
58:    public static void PrintKeywords(string element,
59:      KeywordAttribute [] attributes)
60:    {
61:      Console.WriteLine(">> " + element);
62:
63:      foreach (KeywordAttribute a in attributes)
64:      {
65:       Console.WriteLine("   keyword = " + a.Keyword +
66:         " (" + a.Relevance + ")");
67:      }
68:    }
69: }
```

This code must be compiled with Listing 1.2 for the definition of KeywordAttribute. If run on an assembly containing the previously defined IApplication interface, the output of the code in Listing 1.3 is

```
>> IApplication
   keyword = program (2)
   keyword = app (5)
   keyword = application (5)
>> IApplication.set_Creator
>> IApplication.get_Creator
>> IApplication.set_Caption
>> IApplication.get_Caption
>> IApplication.Quit
   keyword = exit (5)
   keyword = close (5)
   keyword = kill (5)
   keyword = shutdown (5)
>> IApplication.EnableAnimations
   keyword = movie (5)
   keyword = animated (10)
```

```
    keyword = picture (5)
>> IApplication.Caption
    keyword = title (5)
>> IApplication.Creator
    keyword = owner (5)
    keyword = parent (5)
```

Pseudo-Custom Attributes

Several of the custom attributes defined by the .NET Framework are known as *pseudo-custom attributes*. These attributes are used just like regular custom attributes in source code, but are treated specially by the CLR. Rather than persisting the information as a regular custom attribute, pseudo-custom attributes are represented by custom reserved bits in metadata, just as modifiers like `public` or `virtual` have reserved bits. Pseudo-custom attributes are not extensible—there's a predefined list. For the most part, you shouldn't care whether an attribute is a pseudo-custom attribute. The unfortunate consequence of pseudo-custom attributes is that they can't be discovered using the standard reflection technique (`GetCustomAttributes`) shown in Listing 1.3. Some can be discovered through other APIs, specific to each pseudo-custom attribute. The `System.Runtime.InteropServices` chart on the inside front cover indicates pseudo-custom attributes with italics.

Languages and Tools

Now that you've read about the high-level features of the .NET Framework and seen details about the technologies involved, it's time to give you hands-on introductions to some languages and tools included in the .NET Framework SDK.

Several languages target the .NET Framework, and the three discussed in this book are Visual C# .NET (often abbreviated to just C#), Visual Basic .NET (VB .NET), and Visual C++ .NET (often abbreviated to just C++). C# is geared toward developers with a C++ or Java background, Visual Basic .NET is best for rapid application development, and C++ is for developers who need the most flexibility at the expense of productivity. In this section, you'll look at some syntax for each language and see `Hello, World` examples. In Chapter 3, "The Essentials for Using COM in Managed Code," you'll use COM to turn each example into a spoken "Hello, World"!

These three languages support the subset of functionality required by the CLS, but each language has some noticeable feature differences. For example:

- C# supports XML documentation and *unsafe code* that uses pointers, but doesn't support optional parameters or default values.

- Visual Basic .NET supports late binding without using reflection syntax, but doesn't support unsigned types or operator overloading.

- Visual C++ .NET supports writing unmanaged code intertwined with managed code, discussed in Chapter 2, "Bridging the Two Worlds—Managed and Unmanaged Code."

In future versions of these languages, the differences between them are bound to increase. In addition, each language has differing degrees of features inside Visual Studio .NET. For example, Visual Basic .NET projects have the best IntelliSense and background-compilation support, whereas Visual C++ .NET projects provide the most flexibility in customizing compilation options.

> **Tip**
>
> The command-line compilers and tools presented in this section (and throughout the book) are included in your computer's path if you've installed the .NET Framework SDK. If you've installed Visual Studio .NET, however, they are not included in your path by default. Instead, you can run these utilities from a Visual Studio .NET command prompt by selecting Microsoft Visual Studio .NET, Visual Studio .NET Tools, Visual Studio .NET Command Prompt from the Windows Start menu. In this command prompt window, the directories containing the SDK utilities are included in the PATH environment variable.

C#

C# is the language that fits in the .NET Framework most naturally because it was designed alongside the .NET Framework and carries no legacy. Although the assemblies that comprise the .NET Framework, such as mscorlib, System.Xml, System.Drawing, and so forth, could have been written in just about any .NET languages (because they are CLS-compliant for the most part), most were written in C#.

By default, the command-line compiler implicitly references the mscorlib assembly, and possibly more depending on whether the compiler is configured to use the global csc.rsp file that references additional assemblies. Additional assemblies can be referenced at the command line by using the /reference (or /r for short) option with the filename containing the assembly manifest.

C# has a using statement that is often used to enable shorter syntax. You can employ using with any namespace so that you don't have to preface every member with the namespace it lives in (as long as there are no ambiguities). Note that the using statement is optional and works only for assemblies that are already referenced. Within a Visual Studio .NET project, several assemblies and namespaces may be implicitly referenced and used depending on the project type.

> **TIP**
>
> The most common mistake for C# beginners is to assume that `using` is sufficient for referencing types because it happens to work for types in the implicitly referenced `mscorlib` assembly. The fact that a namespace such as `System` can span multiple assemblies also adds to this confusion. Just remember that `using` is an optional syntactic shortcut, but referencing an assembly containing the types you wish to use is always required.

C# has built-in keywords that serve as aliases for the core data types in the `System` namespace (and `mscorlib` assembly). These are listed in Table 1.1.

TABLE 1.1   C# Keywords and Their Corresponding .NET Framework Data Types

C# Data Type	System Data Type
object	System.Object
string	System.String
decimal	System.Decimal
bool	System.Boolean
char	System.Char
byte	System.Byte
sbyte	System.SByte
short	System.Int16
int	System.Int32
long	System.Int64
ushort	System.UInt16
uint	System.UInt32
ulong	System.UInt64
float	System.Single
double	System.Double

There is no difference in the code produced whether you use the alias or the "real" `System` type.

Hello, C# World

Here is the C# version of Hello, World:

```
using System; // Shortcut to avoid typing System.Console
public class Class1
{
  public static void Main()
  {
    Console.WriteLine("Hello, C# World!");
  }
}
```

To run this using Visual Studio .NET:

1. Create a new C# console application by selecting File, New, Project and then selecting Console Application under the Visual C# Projects folder.
2. Replace the code in Class1.cs with the previously shown code.
3. Run it by selecting the Debug, Start menu item.

To run this using only the .NET Framework SDK:

1. Type the code into a file called Class1.cs, and save it.
2. From a command prompt, type

   csc Class1.cs

3. Now run Class1.exe from the command prompt.

Custom Attribute Syntax

Custom attributes are placed in square brackets. The following code uses DllImportAttribute, setting its EntryPoint property using the named parameter syntax:

```
[DllImport("kernel32.dll", EntryPoint="MessageBox")]
```

Multiple custom attributes can be placed in a single pair of square brackets, delimited by commas. Parentheses can be left off altogether when calling a default constructor (one with no parameters). Listing 1.4 shows the syntax for many uses of the following custom attribute that can be placed on anything:

```
[AttributeUsage(AttributeTargets.All, AllowMultiple=true)]
public class ExampleAttribute : Attribute {}
```

LISTING 1.4   Putting the ExampleAttribute Custom Attribute on All Kinds of Targets in C#

```
1: // Attribute on assembly, placed at the top of a source file
2: [assembly:Example]
3: // Attribute on module, placed at the top of a source file
```

LISTING 1.4 Continued

```
 4: [module:Example]
 5:
 6: [Example] // Attribute on class
 7: public class Class1
 8: {
 9:    [Example] // Attribute on constructor
10:    public Class1() { ... }
11:
12:    [Example] // Attribute on method
13:    public void MyMethod1([Example] int i) { ... } // Attribute on parameter
14:
15:    [return:Example] // Attribute on return value
16:    public int MyMethod2() { ... }
17:
18:    [Example] // Attribute on property
19:    public string MyProperty
20:    {
21:      [return:Example] // Attribute on return value for accessor method
22:      get { ... }
23:      [param:Example] // Attribute on parameter for accessor method
24:      set { ... }
25:    }
26: }
27:
28: [Example] // Attribute on struct
29: public struct MyStruct
30: {
31:    [Example] // Attribute on field
32:    public int MyField;
33: }
34:
35: [Example] // Attribute on delegate
36: public delegate int MyDelegate1();
37:
38: [return:Example] // Attribute on delegate's return value
39: public delegate int MyDelegate2();
40:
41: [Example] // Attribute on enum
42: public enum MyEnum
43: {
44:    One,
45:    Two
46: }
47:
48: [Example, Example, Example] // Multiple attributes on interface
49: public interface MyInterface
```

LISTING 1.4   Continued

```
50: {
51:   [Example] // Attribute on event
52:   event MyDelegate1 MyEvent;
53: }
```

Visual Basic .NET

Visual Basic .NET (VB .NET) is the successor to Visual Basic 6. Because the language is now based on the Common Language Runtime, Visual Basic .NET has great new features available to any .NET language: multithreading, inheritance, rich APIs, and much more. In addition, the language is now fully integrated into the Visual Studio .NET IDE and has a fully functional command-line compiler. There are a handful of areas outside the CLS that Visual Basic .NET supports but C# doesn't, and vice-versa. For instance, although Visual Basic .NET supports non-default parameterized properties (C# does not), it doesn't support custom attributes with System.Object parameters.

For programmers familiar with Visual Basic 6, the downside to Visual Basic .NET is that it isn't completely compatible. To ensure that Visual Basic .NET programs interoperate well with other .NET languages, some changes were made to clean up the language. Additional changes were made to address common complaints and misunderstandings among Visual Basic programmers. Some examples are

- The code Dim a, b, c, d as String now declares four Strings rather than three Variants and a String
- Arguments are now passed by-value by default
- Parentheses are now required when calling methods
- The Let, Set, and LSet statements are no longer supported
- Default properties are no longer supported (unless they have parameters)

The Visual Basic .NET compiler also optionally performs more strict type-checking that can be enabled with the Option Strict On directive.

By default, the compiler implicitly references two assemblies: mscorlib and Microsoft.VisualBasic. Additional assemblies can be referenced at the command line by using the /reference (or /r for short) option with the filename containing the assembly manifest. Visual Basic .NET's Imports statement functions like C#'s using statement. The statement is optional and only enables shorter syntax in the source file; it "imports" a *name*, not an *assembly*. Within a Visual Studio .NET project, several assemblies and namespaces may be implicitly referenced and used depending on the project type.

DIGGING DEEPER

There's one subtle difference between Visual Basic .NET's `Imports` statement and C#'s `using` statement: `Imports` works with namespace prefixes. Using `System.Runtime.Remoting.ObjectHandle` as an example, a VB .NET program could have the line:

```
Imports System.Runtime
```

then successfully use the identifier `Remoting.ObjectHandle` elsewhere in the file. In C#, you cannot break-up namespaces in such a fashion; either the entire namespace must be listed with a `using` statement, or the entire namespace must be used as a prefix to any types from the namespace.

Like C#, Visual Basic .NET has built-in keywords that serve as aliases for the core data types in the `System` namespace, listed in Table 1.2.

TABLE 1.2   Visual Basic .NET Keywords and Their Corresponding .NET Framework Data Types

Visual Basic .NET Data Type	System Data Type
Object	System.Object
String	System.String
Decimal	System.Decimal
Boolean	System.Boolean
Char	System.Char
Byte	System.Byte
Short	System.Int16
Integer	System.Int32
Long	System.Int64
Single	System.Single
Double	System.Double

Hello, Visual Basic .NET World

Here is the Visual Basic .NET version of `Hello, World`:

```
Imports System ' Shortcut to avoid typing System.Console
Public Module Module1
  Public Sub Main()
```

```
    Console.WriteLine("Hello, Visual Basic .NET World!")
  End Sub
End Module
```

To run this using Visual Studio .NET:

1. Create a new Visual Basic .NET console application by selecting File, New, Project and then selecting Console Application under the Visual Basic Projects folder.

2. Replace the code in Module1.vb with the previously shown code.

3. Run it by selecting the Debug, Start menu item.

To run this using only the .NET Framework SDK:

1. Type the code into a file called Module1.vb, and save it.

2. From a command prompt, type

   vbc Module1.vb

3. Now run Module1.exe from the command prompt.

Custom Attribute Syntax

Custom attributes are placed in angle brackets. The following code uses DllImportAttribute, setting its EntryPoint property using the named parameter syntax:

```
<DllImport("kernel32.dll", EntryPoint:="MessageBox")>
```

Multiple custom attributes can be placed in a single pair of angle brackets, delimited by commas. Parentheses can be left off altogether when calling a default constructor. Listing 1.5 shows the syntax for many uses of the same ExampleAttribute that can be placed on anything:

```
<AttributeUsage(AttributeTargets.All, AllowMultiple:=True)> _
Public Class ExampleAttribute
    Inherits Attribute
End Class
```

LISTING 1.5   Putting the ExampleAttribute Custom Attribute on All Kinds of Targets in Visual Basic .NET

```
1: ' Attribute on assembly, placed at the top of a source file
2: <Assembly:Example>
3: ' Attribute on module, placed at the top of a source file
4: <Module:Example>
5:
6: <Example> Public Class Class1 ' Attribute on class
7:   <Example> Public Sub New() ' Attribute on constructor
8:     ...
```

LISTING 1.5   Continued

```
 9:    End Sub
10:
11:    <Example> Public Sub MyMethod1() ' Attribute on method
12:       ...
13:    End Sub
14:
15:    Public Sub MyMethod2(<Example> s As String) ' Attribute on parameter
16:       ...
17:    End Sub
18:
19:    ' Attribute on return value
20:    Public Function MyMethod3() As <Example> String
21:       ...
22:    End Function
23:
24:    ' Attribute on property and another attribute on
25:    ' return value for get accessor method
26:    <Example> Public Property MyProperty As <Example> String
27:       Get
28:          ...
29:       End Get
30:
31:       ' Attribute on parameter for accessor method
32:       Set (<Example> Value As String)
33:          ...
34:       End Set
35:    End Property
36: End Class
37:
38: <Example> Public Structure MyStruct ' Attribute on struct
39:    <Example> Public MyField As Integer ' Attribute on field
40: End Structure
41:
42: ' Attribute on delegate
43: <Example> Public Delegate Function MyDelegate1() as Integer
44: ' Attribute on delegate's return value
45: Public Delegate Function MyDelegate2() as <Example> Integer
46:
47: <Example> Public Enum MyEnum ' Attribute on enum
48:    One
49:    Two
50: End Enum
51:
52: ' Multiple attributes on interface
```

LISTING 1.5   Continued

```
53: <Example, Example, Example> Public Interface MyInterface
54:   <Example> Event MyEvent() ' Attribute on event
55: End Interface
```

C++

Visual C++ .NET has *managed extensions* that enable you to write code that compiles to MSIL and makes use of the .NET Framework. This capability means that C++ programmers can take advantage of features such as automatic memory management and self-describing objects. To avoid noncompliance with C++ standards, all the new .NET Framework-related keywords begin with double underscores, such as __gc, __interface, and __delegate. The result is a usually odd-looking syntax to those first introduced to the managed extensions (or even to those using them for quite some time!), but the capabilities of Visual C++ .NET are quite powerful.

Unlike C# and Visual Basic .NET, assemblies are referenced in source code with a #using statement (and the filename containing the assembly manifest) that acts much like an #include statement. Furthermore, no assemblies are implicitly referenced. This means that any program using managed extensions must have

```
#using <mscorlib.dll>
```

at the top of a source file. The equivalent of C#'s using statement and Visual Basic .NET's Imports statement is using namespace. As with Imports in VB .NET, using namespace works with namespace prefixes in addition to entire namespaces.

Using some of C++'s data types can be equivalent to some data types in the System namespace, as shown in Table 1.3.

TABLE 1.3   C++ Keywords and Their Corresponding .NET Framework Data Types

C++ Data Type	System Data Type
bool	System.Boolean
wchar_t	System.Char
char	System.Byte
signed char	System.SByte
short	System.Int16
int or long	System.Int32
__int64	System.Int64

TABLE 1.3   Continued

C++ Data Type	System Data Type
unsigned short	System.UInt16
unsigned int or unsigned long	System.UInt32
unsigned __int64	System.UInt64
float	System.Single
double	System.Double

Hello, C++ World

Here is the C++ version of Hello, World:

```
#using <mscorlib.dll>    // Required to take advantage of the .NET Framework
using namespace System; // Shortcut to avoid typing System::Console
void main()
{
  Console::WriteLine(S"Hello, C++ World!");
};
```

The S indicates that the string literal is a System::String.

To run this using Visual Studio .NET:

1. Create a new C++ application by selecting File, New, Project and then selecting Managed C++ Application under the Visual C++ Projects folder.
2. Replace the code in *ProjectName*.cpp with the previously shown code.
3. Run it by selecting the Debug, Start menu item.

To run this using only the .NET Framework SDK:

1. Type the code into a file called HelloWorld.cpp, and save it.
2. From a command prompt, type

   cl /CLR HelloWorld.cpp

3. Now run HelloWorld.exe from the command prompt.

Custom Attribute Syntax

As in C#, custom attributes are placed in square brackets. The following code uses DllImportAttribute, setting its EntryPoint property using the named parameter syntax:

```
[DllImport("kernel32.dll", EntryPoint="MessageBox")]
```

Multiple custom attributes can be placed in a single pair of square brackets, delimited by commas. Parentheses can be left off altogether when calling a default constructor. Listing 1.6

shows the syntax for many uses of the same `ExampleAttribute` that can be placed on anything:

```
[AttributeUsage(AttributeTargets::All, AllowMultiple=true)]
public __gc class ExampleAttribute : public Attribute {};
```

LISTING 1.6   Putting the `ExampleAttribute` Custom Attribute on All Kinds of Targets in C++

```
 1: #using <mscorlib.dll>
 2: // Assembly containing definition of ExampleAttribute
 3: #using <Chapter1.dll>
 4: // Shortcut to avoid typing System::String
 5: using namespace System;
 6: // Attribute on assembly, placed at the top of a source file
 7: [assembly:Example];
 8: // Attribute on module, placed at the top of a source file
 9: [module:Example];
10:
11: [Example] // Attribute on class
12: public __gc class Class1
13: {
14:   public:
15:
16:   [Example] // Attribute on constructor
17:   Class1() { ... }
18:
19:   [Example] // Attribute on method
20:   void MyMethod1([Example] String* s) { ... } // Attribute on parameter
21:
22:   [returnvalue:Example] // Attribute on return value
23:   int MyMethod2() { ... }
24:
25:   [returnvalue:Example] // Attribute on return value for accessor method
26: __property String* get_MyProperty() { ... }
27:   // Attribute on parameter for accessor method
28: __property void set_MyProperty([Example] String* s) { ... }
29: };
30:
31: [Example] // Attribute on struct
32: public __gc struct MyStruct
33: {
34:   [Example] // Attribute on field
35:   int MyField;
36: };
37:
```

LISTING 1.6   Continued

```
38: [Example] // Attribute on delegate
39: public __delegate int MyDelegate1();
40:
41: [returnvalue:Example] // Attribute on delegate's return value
42: public __delegate int MyDelegate2();
43:
44: [Example] // Attribute on enum
45: public __value enum MyEnum
46: {
47:   One,
48:   Two
49: };
50:
51: [Example, Example, Example] // Multiple attributes on interface
52: public __gc __interface MyInterface
53: {
54:   [Example] // Attribute on event
55:   __event MyDelegate1* MyEvent;
56: };
```

IL Assembler (ILASM)

ILASM can be considered a tool, but it's also a language compiler just like the others. ILASM takes source code consisting of raw MSIL and low-level metadata descriptions as input and produces assemblies or modules. The easiest way to see this MSIL and metadata syntax is to take any assembly and use the IL Disassembler to produce an IL text file. Programming in IL Assembler's language is analogous to programming in assembly code. It's not as easy as using a high-level language, but it provides the most power and flexibility (and is still higher-level than true assembly code). The IL Assembler utility is named ILASM.EXE, and can be automatically found in your path from a Visual Studio .NET command prompt or from a regular command prompt if you've installed the .NET Framework SDK.

IL Disassembler (ILDASM)

ILDASM is a very handy utility whether or not you have Visual Studio .NET. Although it can produce a text file, its default behavior is to present a graphical view of the contents of an assembly—not just MSIL as the name implies, but metadata, too. ILDASM shows a hierarchical view of the metadata much like Visual Studio .NET's object browser, but double-clicking any member displays a separate window containing its MSIL implementation. Another useful feature is to display all the metadata in a single window by pressing Ctrl+M. The IL Disassembler utility is named ILDASM.EXE, and can be automatically found in your path from a

Visual Studio .NET command prompt or from a regular command prompt if you've installed the .NET Framework SDK.

Conclusion

This chapter presented a general overview of the .NET Framework, highlighting some useful features that any software developer can appreciate:

- Version resiliency
- Trivial deployment
- Fine-grained security
- Platform neutrality

You also learned about specific features of the .NET Framework that are important to developers who are learning to use the technology:

- Assemblies
- Metadata
- Reflection
- Custom attributes

Finally, you took a quick look at some .NET Framework languages and tools that are used in this book. Although this chapter is by no means a comprehensive overview of the .NET Framework, it should be a great starting point for those getting their feet wet and all you really need to know to understand most concepts presented in the book. Other .NET specifics, such as garbage collection, events, debugging, and so forth, are explained in later chapters when they become relevant.

Bridging the Two Worlds— Managed and Unmanaged Code

IN THIS CHAPTER

- Managed Code Versus Unmanaged Code   48
- How Unmanaged Code Interacts with Managed Code   49
- Unmanaged Code Isn't Always the Answer   72

This chapter explains how and why managed code and unmanaged code interact, and introduces the interoperability technologies that are the subject of this book. It also provides an overview of COM, relating it to the .NET Framework and highlighting important differences between the two programming models.

Managed Code Versus Unmanaged Code

Throughout this book (and much documentation), the terms *unmanaged code* and *managed code* are used. See the following "Frequently Asked Question" sidebars for an explanation of what is meant by these terms. C#, Visual Basic .NET, and C++ with Managed Extensions all produce managed code. Visual Basic 6 and plain C++, on the other hand, produce unmanaged code.

FAQ: What is managed code?

Managed code requires the execution environment of the Common Language Runtime (CLR). Compilers emit managed code as MSIL, the intermediate language described in Chapter 1, "Introduction to the .NET Framework." The reason for the name is that the code is managed by the CLR and objects are allocated from heaps managed by the CLR.

FAQ: What is unmanaged code?

Unmanaged code does not use nor require the execution environment of the Common Language Runtime. Unmanaged code is outside the reach of the CLR's security system, garbage collector, and other services.

Goals of Unmanaged Code Interaction

The .NET Framework enables interaction with unmanaged code in a few different ways. Using the features described in this chapter, you don't have to build managed applications from scratch. Instead, you can still build applications using all the great functionality that current software components provide. Because .NET is a new technology, a lot of functionality doesn't exist natively. Examples of this are voice recognition, advanced 3D graphics, and an endless number of other areas. This isn't a problem for .NET applications, however, because any previous unmanaged implementations can still be used by managed code.

Besides enabling numerous components to be a part of a .NET developer's toolbox, interoperability is great news for anyone who has *written* such software components using pre-.NET technology. Unmanaged components aren't suddenly obsolete with the arrival of .NET because managed clients can still use them. There's often no need to port existing software because it still functions in this new world of .NET, but interoperability services also enable gradual migration of unmanaged components into the managed world if you do wish to migrate unmanaged code to take advantage of new .NET features.

How Can Using Unmanaged Code Be Secure?

Because managed code can interact with unmanaged code (which, by definition, is outside the control of the .NET Framework's security system), there must be a restriction on calling unmanaged code. Otherwise, a malicious assembly can simply call out to unmanaged code to do its dirty work. This restriction is in the form of an *unmanaged code permission*. Thus, no managed components can execute unmanaged code unless they are granted this permission. Although technically not the same as full trust, permission to run unmanaged code is really the same thing in practice because unmanaged code's capabilities are only limited by forces outside the .NET Framework (such as the security provided by the operating system).

How Unmanaged Code Interacts with Managed Code

Four technologies exist that enable the interaction between unmanaged and managed code:

- Platform Invocation Services (PInvoke)
- Mixed-Mode Programming Using Managed Extensions to C++
- Java User Migration Path to .NET (JUMP to .NET)
- COM Interoperability

Platform Invocation Services (PInvoke)

Many programs expose APIs as static entry points in a dynamic link library (DLL). For example, the Win32 API consists of static entry points in modules such as KERNEL32.DLL, USER32.DLL, GDI32.DLL, and ADVAPI32.DLL. To continue using such APIs in managed code, the Common Language Runtime has a feature called Platform Invocation Services, or PInvoke for short. PInvoke enables the following two actions:

- Calling entry points in unmanaged DLLs
- Passing function pointers to unmanaged code for callbacks

Unmanaged C++ code accomplishes this functionality using the LoadLibrary and GetProcAddress APIs. Visual Basic 6 exposes this using the Declare statement.

PInvoke works by having a method declaration in managed code marked with a special custom attribute (System.Runtime.InteropServices.DllImportAttribute). This attribute contains a string with the name of the DLL that contains the exported function. Visual Basic .NET supports the same Declare syntax as Visual Basic 6, but uses PInvoke as the underlying mechanism.

Here is the canonical example of C# code that uses PInvoke to access a commonly used method in the Win32 API:

```
using System;
using System.Runtime.InteropServices; // For DllImportAttribute

public class HelloWorld
{
  [DllImport("user32.dll")]
  public static extern
    int MessageBox(IntPtr hWnd, string text, string caption, int type);

  public static void Main()
  {
    // Call the unmanaged MessageBox method, just for demonstration.
    MessageBox(IntPtr.Zero, "Hello, World!", "Caption", 0);
  }
}
```

Often, there isn't a need to call the common Win32 APIs in managed code because there are equivalent managed APIs in the .NET Framework that you can call without the security restrictions associated with calling unmanaged code. In this example, you can call the managed System.Windows.Forms.MessageBox.Show method, defined in the System.Windows.Forms assembly, instead.

Using the Win32 API might be handy when porting existing code to a managed language, or necessary if wanted features aren't exposed in the equivalent managed APIs. PInvoke is also useful for your own DLLs, or for DLLs that don't already have equivalent functionality available in managed APIs. PInvoke is covered in Part VI, "Platform Invocation Services."

Mixed-Mode Programming Using Managed Extensions to C++

Unlike Visual Basic .NET, which changed from Visual Basic 6 to fit solely into the .NET Framework, Visual C++ .NET hasn't removed or changed anything in the language. Instead, managed extensions have been added. The result is a pretty slick and powerful way to write interacting managed and unmanaged code—even in the same source file! If you compile any existing C++ code with the Visual C++ .NET compiler's /CLR switch, MSIL is produced instead of all native code and the program still works the same way at run time. There's no good reason to do this unless you change or add to the code, but at this point you can reference assemblies and call any managed APIs. The following code is an update to the "Hello, World" C++ example in Chapter 1, combining the worlds of managed and unmanaged code:

```
#using <mscorlib.dll> // Reference an assembly
#include <stdio.h>    // Include a header file
void main()
{
  printf("Hello, Unmanaged World!\n");
  System::Console::WriteLine(S"Hello, Managed World!");
};
```

This is sometimes called mixed-mode programming, referring to the mixing of managed and unmanaged code. Using the language's new keywords (such as __gc), existing code can gradually take advantage of more and more features from the .NET Framework. The price of the power to mix managed and unmanaged code is that the Visual C++ .NET compiler produces code that is not verifiably type safe (checked by the Common Language Runtime), so additional security constraints apply.

Note that this language-specific feature differs from the language-neutral PInvoke and the soon-to-be-introduced COM Interoperability features because it involves recompiling and updating source code. However, developers might find this an easy way of introducing managed interfaces to existing C++ components (which helps cross-language interoperability if they don't already expose COM interfaces). You'll see some mixed-mode programming in action in Chapter 20, "Custom Marshaling."

Java User Migration Path to .NET (JUMP to .NET)

JUMP to .NET is the preferred migration path for Java (and Visual J++) programs to enter the .NET world. The first part of JUMP to .NET is Microsoft Visual J# .NET, a Java-language development tool that plugs into Visual Studio .NET and includes upgrade tools for Visual J++ 6.0 projects. Visual J# .NET is in a beta release at the time of writing. The second part of JUMP to .NET is a utility that converts Java source code into C# source code.

COM Interoperability

I've saved COM Interoperability for last because it's the most complicated of the technologies presented, and because it's the main focus of this book. Commonly referred to as *COM Interop*, it provides a bridge between COM and the .NET Framework. More concretely, it enables the use of COM components from managed code and the use of .NET components from COM.

So, what exactly *is* COM Interoperability? It's made up of three parts:

- Core services provided by the Common Language Runtime. The CLR provides the infra-structure that enables .NET components to communicate with COM components, and vice-versa. This core functionality is at the root of other features in the .NET Framework, such as support for ActiveX controls and support for COM+ services.

- A handful of APIs. Many features of COM Interoperability work without any additional COM-specific coding in .NET applications. However, there is an Interop API (classes, custom attributes, and so on) in the `mscorlib` assembly with the namespace `System.Runtime.InteropServices`. The `Runtime` portion of the namespace indicates that these APIs interact with services provided by the Common Language Runtime. There are other COM-specific types and methods in other namespaces, such as: `System`, `System.Windows.Forms` (for APIs related to ActiveX controls), and `System.EnterpriseServices` (for APIs related to COM+ services).

- Tool support. In order for COM Interoperability to work, certain tasks often need to be performed to produce type information, or to ensure proper registration. The .NET Framework SDK provides some essential programs (tools) that can be used from the command line to carry out the necessary tasks. These tools are described throughout the book and summarized in Appendix B, "SDK Tools Reference." In addition to the tools provided by the SDK, you can think of Visual Studio .NET as the ultimate tool for pulling together tons of functionality, and combining it into one seamless experience. Visual Studio .NET has built-in support for making COM Interoperability so seamless that you might not even realize COM is involved (if you're lucky). One good example is that ActiveX controls can be dropped onto a Windows Form or an ASP.NET page just as if they were managed controls.

FAQ: Is COM dead?

This was, understandably, one of the most frequently asked questions when the .NET initiative was first announced. The answer is no, COM is not *yet* dead, and some of the themes of COM programming may never die. First, COM technology is built into such a large number of applications (including many parts of the Windows operating system) that it can safely be said that COM is physically going to be around for awhile. Second, the ideas of interface-based programming and reusable software components that are central to COM are still thriving in the .NET Framework.

Thanks to the Common Language Runtime's COM Interoperability services, COM objects can participate in the .NET Framework just like any other objects. A consequence of this is that any .NET language (such as C#) is now a great tool for writing COM objects! Furthermore, the component services introduced in COM+ are the exact same component services powering the .NET Framework. Thus, the integration of COM is needed for core .NET functionality, not just backward compatibility. It's likely that future versions of the .NET Framework will depend less on COM and COM+ for a variety of services, but such a transition would not affect the usefulness of existing COM and COM+ components. If you're writing new software components, you should go with .NET, but your investment in COM components is not wasted.

Goals of COM Interoperability

The goals of unmanaged code interaction (described earlier) also apply to COM Interoperability, which has another important goal worth mentioning: programming model consistency.

As described later in this chapter, the programming models of COM and the .NET Framework differ greatly. To simplify communication between COM objects and .NET objects, the Common Language Runtime masks these differences. Thus, a COM object is not only usable from managed code, but often usable *the same way* you would use a .NET object. Rather than calling CoCreateInstance and checking for HRESULTs, you can use the new operator and catch exceptions. Similarly, COM clients don't need to learn any new tricks to use .NET components. They can be used just like COM objects—calling CoCreateInstance, QueryInterface, and so forth. Therefore, COM components don't need to be redesigned to avoid appearing antiquated or hard-to-use in the .NET world, and .NET components can be used by unmodified COM components written well before .NET came along.

Note that COM Interoperability works at the binary level. This ensures the capability to expose .NET types that are compatible with COM's expectations, and vice-versa. This does not mean that the source code involved in creating such types looks anything like it does in unmanaged languages. Much of that capability depends on the programming language you use.

About COM

This section contains the obligatory overview of COM. If you're familiar with COM, you should still read the comparisons to the .NET Framework to get a clear picture of the hurdles COM Interoperability overcomes. If your exposure to COM is only through pre-.NET versions of Visual Basic, don't worry too much about these details. Throughout the book, necessary COM concepts are explained in both VB terms and in "raw" terms.

COM, which made its debut in the early 1990s as the technology powering OLE 2.0, is described in Microsoft's documentation as follows: "COM is a platform-independent, distributed, object-oriented system for creating binary software components that can interact. COM is the foundation technology for Microsoft's OLE (compound documents) and ActiveX (Internet-enabled components) technologies, as well as others." Like the .NET Framework, COM is not a programming language, but a language-independent framework for creating components. More specifically, COM is a specification for a binary standard that defines how objects can interact, and is also a library containing low-level APIs.

Distributed COM (DCOM), introduced in 1996, enhanced COM by enabling components on different computers to communicate. With Windows 2000 came the arrival of COM+, the evolution of Microsoft Transaction Server (MTS) and COM. COM+ provides built-in services (such as security, object pooling, and transaction management) so that it becomes much easier to write scalable enterprise applications.

COM classes, also known as coclasses (the "co" is short for COM), must implement interfaces to expose functionality. The interface that every COM object must implement, and the root of all COM interfaces, is IUnknown. The types that COM exposes are typically written or presented in Interface Definition Language (IDL), whose syntax is based on an older language called Object Definition Language (ODL). The IDL representation of IUnknown is the following:

```
[
  object,
  uuid(00000000-0000-0000-C000-000000000046),
  pointer_default(unique)
]
interface IUnknown {
  HRESULT QueryInterface([in] GUID* riid, [out, iid_is(riid)] void** ppvObj);
  unsigned long AddRef();
  unsigned long Release();
};
```

IUnknown's methods enable clients to manipulate the object's reference count and ask the object what interfaces it implements.

Many objects implement IDispatch to enable dynamic method invocation (also referred to as late binding), whose IDL definition is shown here:

```
[
  object,
  uuid(00020400-0000-0000-C000-000000000046),
  pointer_default(unique)
]
interface IDispatch : IUnknown {
  HRESULT GetTypeInfoCount([out] unsigned int* pctinfo);
  HRESULT GetTypeInfo([in] unsigned int itinfo, [in] unsigned long lcid,
    [out] void** pptinfo);
  HRESULT GetIDsOfNames([in] GUID* riid,
    [in, size_is(cNames)] char** rgszNames, [in] unsigned int cNames,
```

```
    [in] unsigned long lcid, [out, size_is(cNames)] long* rgdispid);
  HRESULT Invoke([in] long dispidMember, [in] GUID* riid,
    [in] unsigned long lcid, [in] unsigned short wFlags,
    [in] DISPPARAMS* pdispparams, [out] VARIANT* pvarResult,
    [out] EXCEPINFO* pexcepinfo, [out] unsigned int* puArgErr);
};
```

Clients can call the methods of IDispatch to get type information and invoke members by name. COM components typically store and deploy type information in the form of type libraries. Type libraries are explained in more detail in the upcoming "Type Information" section.

Useful COM Utilities

The following utilities, included in the Windows Platform SDK, are widely used in COM development. If you have Visual Studio, you have these tools. Otherwise, they can be downloaded from MSDN Online (http://msdn.microsoft.com). It's a good idea to familiarize yourself with these tools if you haven't already.

- OLE/COM Object Viewer (OLEVIEW.EXE). This tool can, among other things, display the contents of a type library in IDL notation. This capability can be very useful and is used throughout the book. Visual Studio .NET lists this utility on its Tools menu. To view a type library, you can pass the name of the file containing it as a command-line parameter, for example:

  oleview stdole2.tlb

  A type library can also be selected by clicking View TypeLib on the File menu or toolbar. Figure 2.1 shows what viewing a type library looks like using OLEVIEW.EXE.

- MIDL.EXE and MKTYPLIB.EXE. These two utilities can compile an IDL or ODL text file to a binary type library. MIDL.EXE is preferred, and considered a replacement for MKTYPLIB.EXE.

- REGSVR32.EXE. This necessary utility registers and unregisters COM components in the Windows Registry. Because registration needs to be done on any computer (not just a developer's machine), this tool is shipped with the Windows operating system.

- REGEDIT.EXE and REGEDT32.EXE. These utilities, which enable viewing and editing of the Windows Registry, are also shipped with Windows. Figures that display the registry throughout this chapter use REGEDIT.EXE.

Differences Between COM and the .NET Framework

The .NET Framework can be considered an evolution of COM—taking the same high-level goals, but making them easier to accomplish and better suited for an Internet-centric world. Both of these frameworks focus on building reusable components that can communicate regardless of the programming language used to create them. Despite the similarities, the details of the two technologies are quite different. We'll now examine some of these differences, focusing on the following:

- Programming Model
- Type Information
- Identity
- Locating Components
- Type Compatibility
- Versioning
- Type Safety
- Error Handling
- Object Lifetime

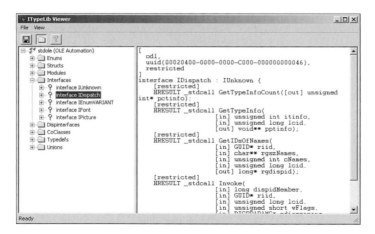

FIGURE 2.1

*The OLE/COM Object Viewer (*OLEVIEW.EXE*) displaying the contents of a type library.*

Another important difference—threading models—is discussed in Chapter 6, "Advanced Topics for Using COM Components." The result of all these differences is that the .NET Framework is simpler than COM. Although simplicity is in the eye of the beholder, I believe that if a survey were conducted using developers who were forced to become proficient in both COM programming and .NET programming, the results would clearly favor the .NET Framework.

> ### DIGGING DEEPER
>
> If you're a Visual Basic 6 programmer, you might not be convinced by some upcoming comparisons. VB6 hides many of the details of COM to reduce the learning curve and provide the same kind of simple, productive environment provided by the .NET Framework. Thus, VB6 programmers typically don't have to worry about GUIDs (Globally Unique Identifiers), HRESULTs (COM error codes), IUnknown pointers, and much more. The difference with the .NET Framework, however, is that now much of the simplicity is built into the system rather than built into a language. Besides being good news for .NET language designers, who benefit from the simplicity, this means that VB .NET is more powerful than previous versions of Visual Basic (as it doesn't have to limit functionality by hiding ugly details). In the end, having simplicity baked into the system provides a better user experience. For example, a VB6 application can crash if it's using a COM component that has been modified in some harmful way, such as a changed method signature. If a VB .NET application encounters the same situation, a much clearer MissingMethodException is thrown.

Programming Model

The .NET Framework and COM are both object-oriented models. COM's status of being truly object oriented has been the subject of debates, due to its lack of implementation inheritance. However you define what it means to be object oriented, I think it's safe to say that COM is object oriented enough for practical purposes. The .NET Framework model is much richer, however.

COM deals primarily with interfaces, although Visual Basic 6 makes the exact opposite seem true. It is only through interfaces that you can invoke methods and properties of COM objects. Coclasses are non-descript entities that you create just to ask for certain interfaces. COM supports single interface inheritance, but not implementation inheritance (that is, class inheritance). Instead, COM enables implementation reuse via aggregation and containment. Containment is an easy concept, in which one object simply delegates work to a second object contained inside. Aggregation is a powerful and more complex mechanism, which enables an outer object to expose the implementation of an inner object without delegating to the inner object on a call-by-call basis.

The .NET Framework type system has interfaces, but COM has *three kinds* of interfaces:

- IUnknown-only interfaces—Interfaces that don't support IDispatch (sometimes called custom interfaces)

- Dispinterfaces—Interfaces whose members can only be called through the IDispatch interface

- Dual interfaces—Interfaces can be both called directly and accessed through IDispatch

The .NET Framework is object-based, so implementing interfaces is no longer a requirement for cross-component communication. Unlike COM, multiple interface inheritance and single implementation inheritance are supported. Classes can have all sorts of methods: static (Shared in VB .NET), instance, virtual (CanInherit in VB .NET), and even overloaded methods. Besides methods, classes can have properties, fields, events (all of which are first class members), and even constructors with any number of arguments. .NET classes and members can also have various levels of visibility (such as public, protected, and private). None of this is possible in COM. All these features have been available in programming languages (such as C++) for years, but the .NET Framework extends all these concepts to the component level. So, objects written in any .NET language can take advantage of these rich features.

Type Information

Type information—the description of classes, interfaces, and more—is an important part of both COM and the .NET Framework. In COM, type information can be stored in many forms. It's commonly stored in a language-specific fashion (such as C++ header files or IDL files). More common, however, is the language-neutral representation of COM type information, known as a *type library*. Although type library viewers often present the information in IDL syntax, a type library contains binary information describing COM interfaces and coclasses that the author chooses to expose.

DIGGING DEEPER

It seems strange to talk about IDL files as a language-specific form of type information since the original purpose of using IDL with COM was to provide a language-neutral representation of COM types. In reality, however, IDL files are only directly used in C++ projects since they aren't consumable by any other major language. Type libraries, on the other hand, can be consumed by Visual C++, Visual Basic, and even Visual J++ programs.

Creating a type library for a COM component is optional, and it might be a separate file (such as MSHTML.TLB), or it might be embedded in a DLL as a resource (as in MSXML.DLL). Coclasses state a subset of interfaces that they implement—not necessarily all of them. For example, although coclasses authored in Visual Basic 6 always implement ISupportErrorInfo, the type libraries produced by VB6 don't bother listing this interface in coclass statements. COM components written in VB6 have predictable type information, but type libraries created from other sources (such as `MIDL.EXE`) can contain plenty of tricks because COM doesn't enforce the correctness of the information. The result is that you can't count on type information being correct, complete, or even available.

A COM object's type information, if available, can be obtained programmatically via the `ITypeInfo` interface (or the `ITypeInfo2` interface, which was later created to enable access to extended information). There are a host of other interfaces related to the discovery of type information (such as `ITypeLib`, `ITypeLib2`, `ITypeComp`, and `IRecordInfo`).

As introduced in the preceding chapter, type information has only one form in the .NET Framework: metadata. Unlike type information in COM, it is always available, complete, and accurate for every single component. It's so complete that even private types and members are visible in metadata (something that makes a few people uneasy when they discover it for their own components). Any .NET compiler (even C++) must produce and consume metadata directly, so there's no type information in separate files (like an IDL file) to mess around with.

The ubiquity and completeness of metadata is the source of much of the power in the .NET Framework. The CLR never has to ask an object if it supports an interface (as in COM's `IUnknown.QueryInterface`), or ask an object to construct itself (as in COM's class factories). Instead, it can consume and inspect the object's metadata to provide these services without executing user-written code. Similarly, late binding can be performed without requiring objects to provide the functionality themselves (contrary to COM's `IDispatch` interface).

Type information can be obtained and manipulated programmatically using `System.Type`, which can be considered the managed equivalent of COM's `ITypeInfo` interface. The other classes and interfaces that are used to access type information live in the `System.Reflection` namespace.

Identity

It's important to give a unique identity to classes and interfaces that you share with others. You could name a component "Brad's Super-Fast Hashtable" and be reasonably sure that your users will never install another application that exposes something with the same name. However, there are probably a good number of software developers named Brad, and someday one of those people might ship a component with this exact name. COM and the .NET Framework have two different methods of providing developers with an easy way to give their components and types unique names.

In COM, classes and interfaces have human friendly names such as `WebBrowser` and `ISupportErrorInfo`, but their *real* names are 128-bit numbers known as UUIDs (Universally Unique Identifiers) or more often GUIDs (Globally Unique Identifiers) since it's easier to pronounce. To make GUIDs as readable as possible (which isn't easy for a 128-bit number!), they are typically shown in a segmented hexadecimal format known as *registry format*:

`ECEBEC7C-C62F-4279-85E7-B799BACAA24A`

COM developers can generate GUIDs using the CoCreateGuid API in OLE32.LIB to generate a number that, with a very high degree of certainty, is a unique value. Prior to Windows 2000, the CoCreateGuid algorithm used the current date and time plus the MAC address of the computer's network card to generate the value. Nowadays, GUID generation is based on a cryptographic pseudo-random number generator. Rather than calling CoCreateGuid directly, developers often use the GUIDGEN.EXE graphical utility or the UUIDGEN.EXE command-line utility (which ship with the Windows Platform SDK), or they rely on Visual Studio to automatically generate GUIDs in COM-related projects.

DIGGING DEEPER

Although GUIDs are rarely used in managed code, they can still be useful for generating unique identifiers. The CoCreateGuid API is exposed in the .NET Framework as the static System.Guid.NewGuid method.

GUIDs are given many other names, depending on what they are describing. These names are

- CLSID (Class Identifier)—Identifies a class
- IID (Interface Identifier)—Identifies an interface
- LIBID (Library Identifier)—Identifies a type library
- AppID (Application Identifier)—Identifies an application (used by DCOM)

In all cases, these identifiers are nothing more than 128-bit GUIDs.

Thus, when a COM client requests an instance of the "Brad's Super-Fast Hashtable" class, it calls COM's standard instantiation method (CoCreateInstance) to request an instance of the class with a CLSID of ECEBEC7C-C62F-4279-85E7-B799BACAA24A. Because referring to types by these ugly GUIDs isn't very human friendly, classes often have another identifier known as a ProgID (Programmatic Identifier). A ProgID is simply a string that contains a nice name, which *should* be unique if everyone follows recommended conventions, but there's no guarantee of uniqueness. ProgIDs are commonly seen in Visual Basic 6 code when calling VB's CreateObject method:

```
Dim o as Object
Set o = CreateObject("BradCo.SuperFastHashtable")
```

In the .NET Framework, there are no separate identifiers tacked onto types. A type is uniquely identified by its name (usually including a namespace) plus the identity of the assembly containing the type.

As explained in Chapter 1, an assembly is uniquely identified by a simple name, version, culture, and public key token. Thus, every single type has an associated version, culture, and public key token. The public key token is what ensures uniqueness. Whereas every other piece of assembly identity can easily conflict with other assemblies (much like with ProgIDs in COM), no two assemblies produced by different publishers should ever have the same public key token. As for conflicts between assembly or type names when the public key token is identical, it is the responsibility of the individual publisher that owns the public key to choose names wisely.

DIGGING DEEPER

It is possible to "spoof" an assembly's public key token in your own partially signed assembly, and take on its identity. This malicious act is comparable to purposely using someone else's GUID for your own type in COM. For assemblies, however, the .NET Framework security system can detect this malicious act because the malicious assembly writer can't completely sign it without the original publisher's private key.

People often refer to a fully qualified type name as a name that includes its namespace; but the fully, fully qualified type name that guarantees uniqueness is called an assembly-qualified type name. Current .NET languages (excluding IL Assembler) don't have syntax to declare assembly-qualified type names. The compilers find the assembly containing each type via referenced assemblies. (This means that you can't declare and use two different type names that differ only in their assembly identities in the same compilation unit.) The relationship between fully qualified type names and assembly-qualified type names is reminiscent of the relationship between ProgIDs and CLSIDs. One noticeable difference is that the type names are the actual names rather than additional identifiers, and assembly identity is mostly human readable.

The following C# code demonstrates how to obtain a fully qualified name, as well as an assembly-qualified name, for a given type using `System.Type`'s `AssemblyQualifiedName` property:

```
// Print the fully-qualified type name (the same name used in source code)
Console.WriteLine(typeof(System.Collections.Hashtable));

// Print the assembly-qualified type name, contains additional information
Console.WriteLine(typeof(System.Collections.Hashtable).AssemblyQualifiedName);
```

This code gives the following output:

```
System.Collections.Hashtable
System.Collections.Hashtable, mscorlib, Version=1.0.3300.0,
➥Culture=neutral, PublicKeyToken=b77a5c561934e089
```

The format of an assembly-qualified name is *TypeName, AssemblyName*. As seen in the previous example, an assembly name is a comma-delimited list of its defining characteristics.

Locating Components

The identities for COM and .NET components contain no information about their physical location in the file system. A GUID is just a number, and an assembly name (although closely resembling a filename) is not a filename, nor does it provide location information. Thus, both COM and the .NET Framework have a mechanism for finding a component from a type's identity.

COM components must be registered in the Windows Registry to be instantiated. The various identifiers described earlier can be listed under various keys of the `HKEY_CLASSES_ROOT` registry hive, as shown:

CLSIDs	HKEY_CLASSES_ROOT\CLSID\{*CLSID*}
IIDs	HKEY_CLASSES_ROOT\Interface\{*IID*}
LIBIDs	HKEY_CLASSES_ROOT\TypeLib\{*LIBID*}
ProgIDs	HKEY_CLASSES_ROOT*ProgID*
AppIDs	HKEY_CLASSES_ROOT\AppId\{*AppID*}

Rather than manually typing the appropriate registry entries, developers frequently use one of several tools available to register and unregister COM components. The most common means of registration and unregistration is the `REGSVR32.EXE` utility, described in the "Useful COM Utilities" section.

When a COM client wants to create an instance of a class by calling `CoCreateInstance`, COM checks the registry values under the key for the specified CLSID. These registry values tell COM the name and location of the executable or DLL that needs to be loaded to activate the class. Figure 2.2 shows typical registry entries found under a CLSID key.

FIGURE 2.2
Typical Windows Registry entries for a CLSID, displayed with REGEDIT.EXE.

Depending on the registry entries and on the client's request, COM looks for the component one of the following ways:

- in the same process as the client (an *inproc server*)
- in an EXE running in a separate process (an *outproc server*)
- in an EXE running on a different machine (a *remote server*)

ProgIDs are stored in the Windows Registry as a means to look up the corresponding CLSID. This can be seen in Figure 2.3.

FIGURE 2.3
Typical Windows Registry entries for a ProgID.

Registered LIBIDs are used by Visual Basic 6 (and Visual Studio .NET) to provide a list of components that can be referenced in your project. The entries under the LIBID point to a file containing the type library, which is not necessarily the same file containing any implementation. In addition, interfaces are often registered with entries that point to special marshaling classes. These classes implement proxies that are used whenever interface pointers are marshaled across context boundaries. Chapter 6 describes these classes in more detail.

With all these registry entries (and more) pointing to files scattered around the file system, COM's registration process is fairly brittle. If files are moved without updating the corresponding registry entries, programs break. It's also easy to pollute the registry with entries for programs that no longer exist. I can't tell you how many entries are in my computer's registry for sample COM components that I've written and forgotten to unregister!

In the .NET Framework, the Windows Registry is not used for locating components. When a client needs to instantiate a class in a given assembly, the .NET Framework looks for the assembly in either the Global Assembly Cache (GAC), the local directory, or some other location specified by a configuration file. This means that if private applications don't need to share components, they can simply place all the relevant files in the same directory, and everything works. This is refreshingly simple compared to COM, in which registration is always required.

When components need to be shared, they should be installed in the Global Assembly Cache. When COM programmers first hear this, they often think: Wait a minute! Isn't this just the Windows Registry all over again? The answer is no. Just as the GAC is an improvement over a shared directory such as System32 for storing components, it's also an improvement over the Windows Registry for locating components.

FAQ: Why is the Global Assembly Cache any better than the Windows Registry?

One important difference is that the Windows Registry is a multipurpose and fairly generic information store. It's extremely difficult, if not impossible, to understand the entire contents of your computer's registry. The Global Assembly Cache, on the other hand, has one purpose: storing assemblies. The main problem with the Windows Registry is that it can get stale, cluttered, and polluted pretty easily. For instance, COM-related registry entries have paths to files, but if a file is moved or deleted, the registry has incorrect information (unless the culprit knows about this dependency and remembers to update the registry). The Global Assembly Cache, however, can't have out-of-date information about assemblies because the assemblies are actually *stored* inside the cache! There is almost no disconnected information that can become stale.

Type Compatibility

In the world of COM, programming languages have their own type systems and runtime environments. Communication between such components is accomplished through COM's binary standard. It is this binary compatibility that enables COM to be language neutral. The downfall is that COM has its own type system—requiring either additional work for languages, or additional work for programmers, to transform data appropriately.

The .NET Framework isn't considered a binary standard, but rather a *type standard*, because components communicate using the Common Language Runtime's type system. Each .NET language's type system *is* the CLR type system. This means that regardless of which managed language you use, a String is a String, an Object is an Object, and so on.

Versioning

Versioning is the process of evolving the contract exposed by a component. As future versions are released, you might want to add (or even remove/rename) members of classes, interfaces, and more. Making these changes without causing grief to your clients can be tricky, but the .NET Framework was designed with these needs in mind.

In COM, type libraries are associated with a two-part version number (*Major.Minor*). This allows for side-by-side versions of a type library to be listed in the registry. Figure 2.4 shows registry entries for multiple versions of the Visual Basic for Applications (VBA) type library (2.1, 4.0, 5.0, and 6.0).

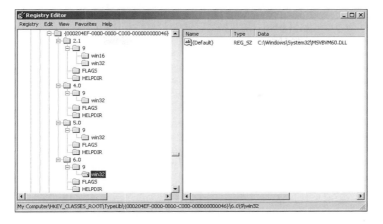

FIGURE 2.4
Typical Windows Registry entries for multiple versions of the same type library.

There's nothing very dynamic about type libraries and version numbers—this is just a way of organizing them. In fact, COM developers often assign brand new LIBIDs to later versions of the same component's type library.

ProgIDs also have a versioning scheme. There are actually two types of ProgIDs: version-dependent and version-independent. Version-dependent ProgIDs look just like version-independent ProgIDs with an extra period and a version number. Clients can use a version-dependent ProgID (if it exists) to obtain a specific version, or use the version-independent ProgID to get the current version, as defined by a key in the registry. In Visual Basic 6 code, this looks like the following:

```
' Give me the current version of the Word.Application object
Set o = CreateObject("Word.Application")

' Give me version 8
Set o = CreateObject("Word.Application.8")

' Give me version 9
Set o = CreateObject("Word.Application.9")
```

Figure 2.5 shows how multiple ProgIDs are organized in the registry.

Versioning does not apply to a COM interface. Interfaces, when defined, must always stay the same. Removing or changing members obviously breaks clients that invoke or implement such members. Adding members breaks clients that implement the interface. Therefore, any updates to an interface must be done to a new interface with a different IID, so it has a completely different identity as far as COM is concerned. As for coclasses, they can safely be modified to implement additional interfaces.

FIGURE 2.5

Typical Windows Registry entries for version-dependent and version-independent ProgIDs.

Unlike the situation in COM, versioning is one of the central themes of the .NET Framework. As you've seen in the preceding chapter, multiple versions of an assembly can live side-by-side in the Global Assembly Cache (much like multiple versions of a type library can live side-by-side in the registry). One big difference is that an administrator can specify a versioning policy on a machine-wide or application-by-application basis, deciding which applications should use which versions of components. Because of this, it's fairly painless to install a new version of a shared .NET component, tell all your applications to switch to the new version, and roll back the change for any application that breaks because of unexpected incompatibilities.

Thanks to the dynamic binding performed by the Common Language Runtime, classes can add and rearrange members without breaking clients. Interfaces still can't be changed without breaking clients, although an interface's members can safely be rearranged (unlike interfaces in COM).

Type Safety

Type-safe code, as defined in .NET Framework documentation, is well-behaved code that can only access memory it is allowed to access. Unmanaged code is not type safe, and there are no general mechanisms to prove that unmanaged code never accesses memory it shouldn't inside a given process. Managed code, on the other hand, is often type safe. As mentioned in the preceding chapter, the .NET Framework security system is capable of giving code guaranteed to be type safe a higher level of trust. For example, type safety is the key to carefully executing downloaded code—ensuring that malicious activity cannot be performed by playing tricks with memory. Besides preventing malicious activity, type safety in programming languages can increase developer productivity by catching a broader class of bogus operations at compile time rather than run time.

Error Handling

Reporting and receiving errors is a programming fact of life. COM and the .NET Framework have standard methods of reporting errors, and these methods are significantly different.

The COM way of error handling is checking integral status codes, called HRESULTs (also called SCODEs in "ancient" times), returned by members. These status codes are 32 bits long and segmented into 4 portions, detailed in the following list:

- The most significant bit is called the severity bit. Failure is indicated by a "1" and success or a non-fatal warning is indicated by a "0".
- There are 4 reserved bits following the severity bit.
- Next, there are 11 bits comprising the facility code, which represents the source responsible for the failure. The facility code acts like a category that determines the meaning of the remaining bits.
- The remaining 16 bits describe the warning or error.

HRESULT values are typically called failure HRESULTs or success HRESULTs based on the value of the severity bit. Components that define new HRESULTs should document them so that clients can interpret the codes they might receive.

A proper unmanaged C++ client should check the value of the returned HRESULT after every method call, which can be cumbersome. On the other hand, Visual Basic 6 provides a nice abstraction for an HRESULT in its global Err object. When a failure HRESULT is returned, Visual Basic 6 raises an error, eliminating the need to check for failure after every action. Another nice thing about the Err object is that it has several properties (such as Description), which can give user-friendly information about the cause of the error rather than just a cryptic number. This extra information, when available, can also be obtained in unmanaged C++ via the IErrorInfo interface, demonstrated in Chapter 8, "The Essentials for Using .NET Components from COM." Checking to see if COM objects support this interface and using this extra information is significantly more work than simply checking the HRESULT value, so C++ clients often don't bother and instead suffer with the lack of rich error information.

In the .NET Framework, on the other hand, errors are communicated to clients via exceptions. Of course, nothing prevents a die-hard HRESULT fan from returning error codes rather than throwing exceptions in methods that he defines and implements. Typically, this is not done, however, due to the ease and built-in support for throwing and catching exceptions. There is no standard mechanism for the same kind of nonerror notifications that success HRESULTs provide in COM.

The great thing about exceptions is that rich error information is easy to obtain. Like VB6's Err object, exceptions contain many properties, which in turn contain the extra information. Unlike the Err object, however, exceptions are extensible. By deriving from System.Exception, you can define your own exception class with any number of properties, methods, and so forth. Another great aspect of exception handling is that different types of errors are distinguished by the type name of the exception object (something human readable, such as `System.OutOfMemoryException`), instead of an error code. The one unfortunate aspect of exceptions is that throwing one is expensive in terms of performance. As the name implies, they should be reserved for exceptional situations. Thus, managed APIs often indicate failure by returning a null object where a valid instance is expected. An example of this is the `System.Type.GetType` method. If this method can't obtain the type specified in the string parameter, it fails by returning a null `Type`. (If you don't like this behavior, it also has an overload with a boolean `throwOnError` parameter that makes it throw an exception to indicate failure instead.) Another example is C#'s as keyword, which (besides confusing VB programmers who use As completely differently) enables you to perform a cast operation and not throw an `InvalidCastException` on failure. Instead, failure causes the target object to be null.

Object Lifetime

The lifetime of an object refers to the time it remains in memory—from creation to destruction. The rules of object lifetime are another major difference between COM and the .NET Framework.

In COM, an object is responsible for managing its own lifetime and determining when to delete itself. An object is able to determine this through its reference count. Because all objects must implement the `IUnknown` interface, clients of any COM object call `IUnknown.AddRef` to increment the reference count when obtaining an interface pointer. Likewise, clients call `IUnknown.Release` to decrement the reference count when finished with an interface pointer. When the object's reference count reaches zero, it is free to self-destruct. Because an object is typically destroyed as soon as a user is finished with it, COM objects are typically written to release any resources at the time of destruction (such as files or database connections).

Because Visual Basic 6 hides `IUnknown` and its methods from programmers, the Visual Basic runtime handles reference counting for you, based on the scope of the variable containing an interface pointer. If waiting for Visual Basic to call `IUnknown.Release` is problematic, you can tell VB to call it at a specific time by setting the object's reference equal to `Nothing`.

In the .NET Framework, programmers no longer need to perform the mundane and error-prone task of reference counting, nor do they need to deal with the hard problems it can cause (such as breaking cycles). That's because the .NET Framework uses garbage collection to manage object lifetime. Rather than requiring each object to maintain a reference count and destroy itself, the Common Language Runtime tracks the usage of an object and frees it when it is no longer in use. The important difference, of course, is that the object isn't always freed as soon as the last client is finished using it. It's freed at some undetermined point afterward when the garbage (i.e. memory) is collected. This means that setting an object reference equal to `Nothing` in VB .NET no longer immediately releases the object, as it did in VB6.

Because an object might not be released soon after a client is finished with it, the practice of releasing resources at destruction time is not a good idea in the .NET Framework. Instead, resource-holding classes typically implement System.IDisposable, which has a Dispose method that clients should call explicitly when finished with the object. Such classes also typically call Dispose in their finalizers (just in case the user forgot to call it).

DIGGING DEEPER

The practice of implementing a finalizer and a Dispose method that do the same thing is a common practice for .NET objects that hold resources. If a client of the object forgets to call Dispose when finished, resources are "leaked" when the object is collected unless there's a finalizer that does the work of Dispose. Therefore, the finalizer serves as a safety net to guard against careless clients. Although releasing resources at finalization isn't ideal (since they may be held much longer than necessary), it's better than not releasing them at all.

In addition, to avoid having the clean-up code called twice in the case when the client remembers to call Dispose, Dispose should call GC.SuppressFinalize so the finalizer isn't invoked during garbage collection.

How COM Interoperability Works

You've now seen the multitude of differences in the details of these two technologies, and might be wondering how COM Interoperability is able to bridge these two worlds. The answer lies in wrapper objects, which give COM objects the illusion that they're interacting with other COM objects and give .NET objects the illusion that they're interacting with other .NET objects. A wrapper object produced for a COM object and consumed by .NET clients is called a Runtime-Callable Wrapper (RCW), where *runtime* refers to the Common Language Runtime. The wrapper object produced for a .NET object and consumed by COM clients is called a COM-Callable Wrapper (CCW).

To maintain object identity, each COM instance is wrapped by a single RCW, and each .NET instance is wrapped by a single CCW. These wrappers are responsible for handling the transitions between COM and .NET (such as data marshaling, exception handling, object lifetime, and much more). Most of the time, all this works without additional coding. You can create an instance of a wrapper using familiar object-creation syntax, and the wrapper internally creates the real object. You can call members on a wrapper and the real object's members get called appropriately. The .NET Framework SDK provides utilities that generate type information for the wrappers (either a type library describing CCWs, or an assembly with metadata describing RCWs) and a utility that handles registration of either kind of wrappers. These utilities are discussed throughout the book, and listed in Appendix B, "SDK Tools Reference." Let's now take a closer look at these two types of wrappers.

Runtime-Callable Wrapper (RCW)

When using a COM object in managed code, you aren't talking to the object directly. Instead, you're interacting with an RCW. An RCW acts as a proxy to the COM object, and looks just like any other .NET object. The wrapper forwards calls to the original object through its exposed interfaces. This enables managed code to be written that uses COM objects in a seamless way, as pictured in Figure 2.6. In this figure, you can see that IUnknown and IDispatch are not exposed to the .NET clients. The result is that these clients never need to know about the COM way of reference counting and late binding. They can stick to the world of garbage collection and reflection that they're used to.

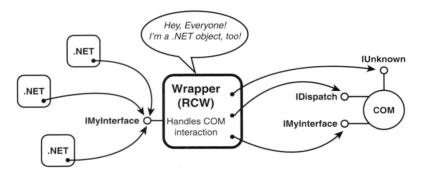

FIGURE 2.6
.NET clients calling methods on a wrapper object that hides the complexity of COM.

The bridging of data marshaling, exception handling, and more is covered in subsequent chapters. Right now let's look at how object lifetime is handled when the two worlds interact. To prevent managed clients of a COM object from engaging in reference counting, an RCW's lifetime is controlled by garbage collection (just like any other managed object). Each RCW caches interface pointers for the COM object it wraps, and internally performs reference counting on these interface pointers. When an RCW is collected, its finalizer calls IUnknown. Release on all its cached interface pointers. Thus, a COM object is guaranteed to be alive as long as its RCW is alive. The .NET Framework also provides an API that can be used to force the Release calls at a specific time, rather than waiting for garbage collection to occur. This is described in the following chapter.

If the RCW has associated metadata available, the RCW looks much like the original coclass. It has a similar type name and contains members of its implemented interfaces. But if no metadata exists for an RCW, it looks like a generic RCW type with the odd name

`System.__ComObject` (an internal class in the `mscorlib` assembly). Chapter 6, "Advanced Topics for Using COM Components," contains more information about how this happens and what you can do about it.

COM-Callable Wrapper (CCW)

When using a .NET object in COM, you aren't talking to the object directly. Instead, you're interacting with a CCW. A CCW acts as a proxy to the managed object and looks just like any other COM object. The wrapper forwards calls to the original object through its exposed members. This enables managed components to be written that can plug into existing COM applications that don't know anything about .NET, as pictured in Figure 2.7. In this figure, you can see that a CCW implements standard COM interfaces such as `IDispatch`, `IProvideClassInfo`, and many more (besides the required `IUnknown` interface). The result is that the objects are easier to use for COM clients that take advantage of these interfaces.

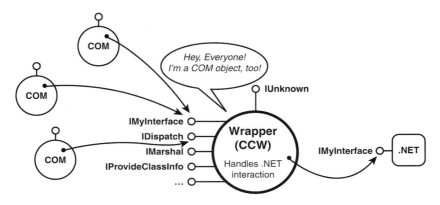

FIGURE 2.7
COM clients calling methods on a wrapper object that looks just like another COM object.

Again, focusing on object lifetime, the CCW is not a managed class and thus is not controlled by garbage collection. It is reference counted just like any other COM object. Each CCW holds a reference to the .NET object it wraps. When the CCW's reference count reaches zero, it destroys itself and releases the inner reference, making the managed object eligible for garbage collection. Thus, a .NET object is guaranteed to be alive as long as its CCW is alive.

Everything that a .NET component exposes to .NET clients might not be available to COM clients. Besides the fact that certain functionality is always off-limits to COM clients (such as parameterized constructors), authors of .NET components can pick and choose any subset of functionality to make off-limits for COM clients. This is discussed further in Part III, "Using .NET Components in COM Applications," but the short story is that the usefulness of a CCW varies greatly depending on the design of the .NET component.

Unmanaged Code Isn't Always the Answer

Although interaction with unmanaged code can work fairly seamlessly, in this book you see that it's not always as easy as interaction with managed code. Besides trickier deployment, security constraints, and possible performance penalties; APIs that were designed specifically for the pre-.NET environment don't always work as cleanly in the managed world. Thus, keep in mind that managed APIs might already exist for the functionality provided by COM components you want to use. The downside is that there's usually a learning curve for any new APIs. The choice is yours, thanks to unmanaged code interoperability. If you don't want to learn the new data access model in the .NET Framework, go ahead and use the exact same ADO model you're familiar with. Table 2.1 (which is by no means an exhaustive list) displays some commonly used unmanaged technologies, along with the namespaces and physical modules (each of which happens to be a single-file assembly) containing .NET APIs with similar functionality.

TABLE 2.1 Some Common Unmanaged Technologies, and Where to Find Managed APIs with Similar Functionality

Technology	Related Functionality	
	Namespace	*Filename*
ActiveX Data Objects (ADO)	System.Data	System.Data.dll
Active Directory	System.DirectoryServices	System.Directory Services.dll
Collaborative Data Objects (CDO, CDONTS, CDOSYS)	System.Web.Mail	System.Web.dll
MSXML	System.Xml	System.Xml.dll
Win32 - Graphics	System.Drawing	System.Drawing.dll
Win32 - Windows	System.Windows.Forms	System.Windows.Forms.dll
Windows Management Instrumentation(WMI)	System.Management	System.Management.dll

Conclusion

This chapter ends Part I, "Background," with an overview of how unmanaged code can be utilized in the .NET Framework and the importance of this interaction. After all, without the capability to interact with unmanaged code, it's unlikely that the .NET Framework would catch on very quickly. Again, the technologies enabling this are:

- Platform Invocation Services (PInvoke)
- Mixed-Mode Programming Using Managed Extensions to C++
- Java User Migration Path to .NET (JUMP to .NET)
- COM Interoperability

You should now understand the main ways in which COM differs from the .NET Framework, and how wrappers are used to bridge these differences.

The following chapter begins Part II, "Using COM Components in .NET Applications," which delves into the specifics of using COM objects in managed code. Because Visual Basic 6 hides many details of COM, the way managed code is written to interact with COM components is similar to the way VB6 code is written. Due to underlying differences (such as garbage collection versus reference counting), however, the similar syntax can be misleading. Programmers need to learn some new tricks to use COM objects effectively, and that's what Part II of this book is all about.

The list of components consists of type libraries that are registered in the Windows Registry (under HKEY_CLASSES_ROOT\TypeLib). Each name displayed is the contents of the library's helpstring attribute, or the library name if none exists. To add a reference to a type library that isn't listed, click Browse... and select the file. This registers the type library, so the next time it is listed in the dialog. You should double-click Microsoft Speech Object Library in the list to try the upcoming example.

3. Click the OK button.

DIGGING DEEPER

It may surprise you to learn that the list of assemblies on the Add Reference dialog's .NET tab is obtained from the Windows Registry, not from the Global Assembly Cache. The GAC is not meant to be used at development time, so Visual Studio .NET uses the registry to find places in the file system to search for assemblies.

To add your own assemblies to the list, you can add a new subkey under the HKEY_LOCAL_MACHINE\SOFTWARE\Microsoft\.NETFramework\AssemblyFolders key (or the same key under HKEY_CURRENT_USER) with any name, such as "My Company". Its default value should be set to the name of a directory, such as "C:\Program Files\My Company\". Any assemblies (with a .dll extension) that reside in this directory are loaded and listed with its assembly name, or the string inside its System.Reflection.AssemblyTitleAttribute custom attribute if it exists.

If adding the reference succeeded, a SpeechLib reference appears in the References section of the Solution Explorer window, shown in Figure 3.2.

Reference to the COM Component

FIGURE 3.2

The Solution Explorer after a reference has been added.

You can use the Object Browser (by clicking View, Other Windows, Object Browser) to view the contents of the SpeechLib library, as shown in Figure 3.3.

FIGURE 3.3
Browsing the type information for a COM component.

Referencing a COM Component Using Only the .NET Framework SDK

Now, let's look at how to accomplish the same task using only the .NET Framework SDK. The following example uses the .NET Framework Type Library to Assembly Converter (TLBIMP.EXE). This utility is usually just called the type library importer, which is what TLBIMP stands for. As mentioned in Chapter 1, if you've installed Visual Studio .NET but still want to run the SDK tools, you may have to open a Visual Studio .NET command prompt to get the tools in your path.

The steps for referencing a COM component without Visual Studio .NET are:

1. From a command prompt, run TLBIMP.EXE on the file containing the desired type library, as follows (replacing the path with the location of SAPI.DLL on your computer):

   ```
   TlbImp "C:\Program Files\Common Files\Microsoft Shared\Speech\sapi.dll"
   ```

   This example command produces an assembly in the current directory called SpeechLib.dll because SpeechLib is the name of the input library (which can be seen by opening SAPI.DLL using the OLEVIEW.EXE utility). A lot of warnings are produced when running TLBIMP.EXE, but you can ignore them.

2. Reference the assembly just as you would any other assembly, which depends on the language. Using the command-line compilers that come with the SDK, referencing an assembly is done as follows:

C# (from a command prompt):

```
csc HelloWorld.cs /r:SpeechLib.dll
```

Visual Basic .NET (from a command prompt):

```
vbc HelloWorld.vb /r:SpeechLib.dll
```

Visual C++ .NET (in source code):

```
#using <SpeechLib.dll>
```

After TLBIMP.EXE has generated the assembly, you can browse its metadata using the IL Disassembler (ILDASM.EXE) by typing the following:

```
ildasm SpeechLib.dll
```

The name *IL Disassembler* is a little misleading because it's really useful for browsing metadata, which is separate from the MSIL. As shown in Figure 3.4, most SpeechLib methods don't even contain MSIL because the methods are empty implementations that forward calls to

the original COM component. This can be seen by double-clicking on member names.

FIGURE 3.4

Using the IL Disassembler as an object browser.

ILDASM.EXE gives you much more information than the object browser in Visual Studio .NET, including pseudo-custom attributes. The information in the windows that appear when you double-click on items is explained in detail in Chapter 7, "Modifying Interop Assemblies."

Example: A Spoken `Hello, World` Using the Microsoft Speech API

Once you've either referenced the Microsoft Speech Object Library in Visual Studio .NET, or run the `TLBIMP.EXE` utility on `SAPI.DLL`, you're ready to write the code that uses this COM component. This can be done with these two steps:

1. Type the following code either in a Visual Studio .NET project or in your favorite text editor.

   The C# version (`HelloWorld.cs`):

   ```
   using SpeechLib;
   class Class1
   {
     static void Main()
     {
       SpVoice voice = new SpVoice();
       voice.Speak("Hello, World!", SpeechVoiceSpeakFlags.SVSFDefault);
     }
   }
   ```

   The Visual Basic .NET version (`HelloWorld.vb`):

   ```
   Imports SpeechLib
   Module Module1
     Sub Main()
       Dim voice as SpVoice
       voice = new SpVoice()
       voice.Speak("Hello, World!")
     End Sub
   End Module
   ```

   The C++ version (`HelloWorld.cpp`):

   ```
   #using <mscorlib.dll>  // Required for all managed programs
   #using <SpeechLib.dll> // The assembly created by TLBIMP.EXE
   using namespace SpeechLib;
   void main()
   {
     SpVoice* voice = new SpVoiceClass();
     voice->Speak("Hello, World!", SpeechVoiceSpeakFlags::SVSFDefault);
   };
   ```

   Because Visual C++ .NET projects do not provide a mechanism for referencing COM components, `TLBIMP.EXE` needs to be used to create `SpeechLib.dll` regardless of whether or not you use Visual Studio .NET.

2. Compile and run the code (and listen to the voice). Feel free to have some more fun with the Speech API. You'll find that interacting with it is easy after you've gotten this far.

Notice the differences between the C#, Visual Basic .NET, and C++ versions of the same program. For example, the C# and C++ calls to Speak use two parameters but the same call in VB .NET has just one parameter. That's because the second parameter is optional, yet C# and C++ do not support optional parameters. Instead, a value must always be passed. Also notice that the C++ program instantiates SpVoiceClass instead of SpVoice as the others do. In this case, the C# and VB .NET compilers are doing some extra work behind-the-scenes to enable the user to work with a class that has the same name as the original COM coclass. More information about this extra work is given in the next chapter, "An In-Depth Look at Imported Assemblies."

The Type Library Importer

COM components such as the Microsoft Speech API expose type information using type libraries, but .NET compilers (excluding Visual C++ .NET) don't understand type libraries. They only understand .NET metadata as a source of type information. Therefore, the key to making a COM component readily available to the .NET world is a mechanism that takes a type library and produces equivalent metadata. The Common Language Runtime's execution engine contains this functionality, which is called the *type library importer*.

The term *type library importer* was introduced previously when describing TLBIMP.EXE, but the type library importer is exposed in other ways as well. In fact, when you add a reference to a COM component in Visual Studio .NET, you are really invoking the type library importer. This creates a new assembly, and this assembly—not the type library—is what your project is *really* referencing. This assembly (SpeechLib.dll in the previous example) is the same file that would have been generated by TLBIMP.EXE. It's always a single file with a .dll extension, and is placed in a directory specific to your project when generated by Visual Studio .NET.

Interop Assemblies

An assembly produced by the type library importer is known as an *Interop Assembly* because it contains definitions of COM types that can be used from managed code via COM Interoperability. The metadata inside an Interop Assembly enables .NET compilers to resolve calls, and enables the Common Language Runtime to generate a Runtime-Callable Wrapper (RCW) at run time.

You can think of importing a type library as providing a second view of the same COM component—one for unmanaged clients and another for managed clients. This relationship is shown in Figure 3.5.

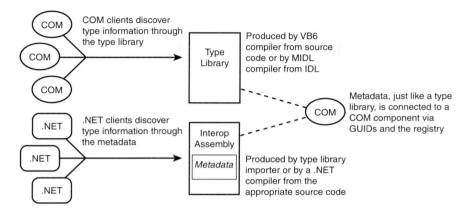

FIGURE 3.5

Two views of the same COM component.

The actual implementation of the COM component remains in the original COM binary file(s). In other words, nothing magical happens to transform unmanaged code into the MSIL produced by a .NET compiler. Unlike normal assemblies, which contain an abundance of both metadata and MSIL, Interop Assemblies consist mostly of metadata. The signatures have special custom attributes and pseudo-custom attributes that instruct the CLR to delegate calls to the original COM component at run time.

3

THE ESSENTIALS
FOR USING COM
IN MANAGED CODE

There are three ways of using the type library importer to create an Interop Assembly:

- Referencing a type library in Visual Studio .NET.
- Using TLBIMP.EXE, the command-line utility that is part of the .NET Framework SDK.
- Using the TypeLibConverter class in the System.Runtime.InteropServices namespace.

All three of these methods produce the exact same output, although each option gives more flexibility than the previous one. TLBIMP.EXE has several options to customize the import process, but Visual Studio .NET doesn't expose these customizations when referencing a type library. Using TLBIMP.EXE to precisely mimic the behavior of Visual Studio .NET when it imports a type library, you'd need to run it as follows:

```
TlbImp InputFile /out:Interop.LibraryName.dll /namespace:LibraryName /sysarray
```

where *InputFile* is the file containing the type library (such as SAPI.DLL) and *LibraryName* is the name found inside the type library that can be viewed with OLEVIEW.EXE (such as SpeechLib). All of TLBIMP.EXE's options are covered in Appendix B, "SDK Tools Reference."

The TypeLibConverter class enables programmatic access to type library importing, and has one additional capability when compared to TLBIMP.EXE—importing an in-memory type library. The use of this class is demonstrated in Chapter 22, "Using APIs Instead of SDK Tools."

Some of the transformations made by the type library importer are non-intuitive. For example, every COM class (such as SpVoice) is converted to an *interface*, then an additional class with the name *ClassName*Class (such as SpVoiceClass) is generated. More information about this transformation is given in the next chapter, "An In-Depth Look at Imported Assemblies," but this is why SpVoiceClass had to be used in the C++ Hello, World example. The C# and VB .NET compilers perform a little magic to enable instantiating one of these special interfaces such as SpVoice, and treats it as if you're instantiating SpVoiceClass instead.

Whereas the process of converting type library information to metadata is called *importing*, and the process of converting metadata to type library information is called *exporting*. Type library export is introduced in Chapter 8, "The Essentials for Using .NET Components from COM."

> **TIP**
>
> Although TLBIMP.EXE has several options that Visual Studio .NET doesn't allow you to configure within the IDE, you can reference an Interop Assembly in two steps in order to gain the desired customizations within Visual Studio .NET. First, produce the Interop Assembly exactly as you wish using TLBIMP.EXE. Then, reference this assembly within Visual Studio .NET using the .NET tab instead of the COM tab. Simply browse to the assembly and add it to your project, just as you would add any other assembly.

Everything so far assumes that a type library is available for the COM component you want to use. For several existing COM components, this is simply not the case. If the COM component has one or more IDL files, you could create a type library from them using the MIDL compiler. (Unfortunately, there's no such tool as IDLIMP that directly converts from IDL to .NET metadata.) As mentioned previously in Figure 3.5, however, .NET compilers can produce the same kind of metadata that the type library importer produces, so you can create an Interop Assembly directly from .NET source code. This advanced technique is covered in Chapter 21, "Manually Defining COM Types in Source Code." An easy solution to a lack of type information is to perform late binding, if the COM objects you wish to use support the IDispatch interface. See the "Common Interactions with COM Objects" section for more information.

Primary Interop Assemblies

The previously described process of generating Interop Assemblies has an undesirable side effect due to the differences in the definition of identity between COM and the .NET Framework. Therefore, extra support exists to map .NET and COM identities more appropriately.

In COM, a type is identified by its GUID. It doesn't matter where you get the definition; if the numeric value of the GUID is correct, then everything works. You might find a common COM interface (such as IFont) defined in ten different type libraries, rather than each library referencing the official definition in the OLE Automation type library (STDOLE2.TLB). This duplication doesn't matter in the world of COM.

On the other hand, if ten different *assemblies* each have a definition of IFont, these are considered ten unrelated interfaces in managed code simply because they reside in different assemblies. The containing assembly is part of a managed type's identity, so it doesn't matter if multiple interfaces have the same name or look identical in all other respects.

This is the root of the identity problem. Suppose ten software companies write .NET applications that use definitions in the OLE Automation type library (STDOLE2.TLB). Each company uses Visual Studio .NET and adds a reference to the type library, causing a new assembly to be generated called stdole.dll. Each company digitally signs the assemblies that comprise the application, including the stdole Interop Assembly, as shown in Figure 3.6.

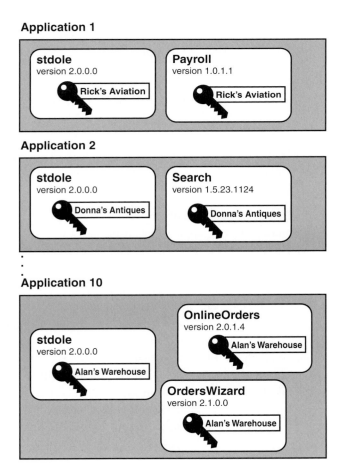

FIGURE 3.6

Applications from ten different companies—each using their own Interop Assembly for the OLE Automation type library.

Now imagine a user's computer with all ten of these programs installed. One problem is that the Global Assembly Cache is cluttered with Interop Assemblies that have no differences except for the publisher's identity, shown in Figure 3.7. The difference in publishers can be seen as differences in the public key tokens.

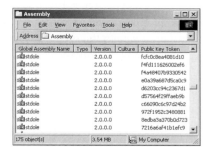

FIGURE 3.7

The opposite of DLL Hell—a cluttered Global Assembly Cache with multiple Interop Assemblies for the same type library.

Even if all these Interop Assemblies aren't installed in the GAC, the computer could be cluttered in other places, such as local application directories. This is the opposite of DLL Hell—application isolation taken to an extreme. There is no sharing whatsoever, not even when it's safe for the applications to do so.

Besides clutter, the main problem is that none of these applications can easily communicate as they could if they were unmanaged COM applications. If the Payroll assembly from Figure 3.6 exposes a method with an IFont parameter and the Search assembly wants to call this, it would try passing a stdole.IFont signed by Donna's Antiques. This doesn't work because the method expects a stdole.IFont signed by Rick's Aviation. As far as the CLR is concerned, these are completely different types.

What we really want is a single managed identity for a COM component's type definitions. Such "blessed" Interop Assemblies do exist, and are known as *Primary Interop Assemblies* (PIAs). A Primary Interop Assembly is digitally signed by the publisher of the original COM component. In the case of the OLE Automation type library, the publisher is Microsoft. A Primary Interop Assembly is not much different from any other Interop Assembly. Besides being digitally signed by the COM component's author, it is marked with a PIA-specific custom attribute (System.Runtime.InteropServices.PrimaryInteropAssemblyAttribute), and usually registered specially.

Figure 3.8 shows what the ten applications would look like if each used the Primary Interop Assembly for the OLE Automation Type Library rather than custom Interop Assemblies.

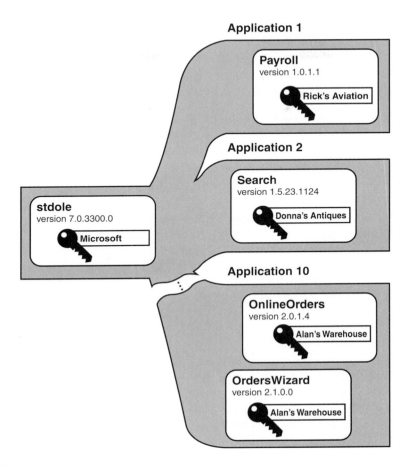

FIGURE 3.8

Applications from ten different companies—each using the Primary Interop Assembly for the OLE Automation type library.

Nothing forces .NET applications to make use of a PIA when one exists. The notion of Primary Interop Assemblies is just a convention that can be used by tools, such as Visual Studio .NET, to help guide software developers in the right direction by referencing common types.

To make use of Primary Interop Assemblies, adding a reference to a type library in Visual Studio .NET is a little more complicated than what was first stated. Visual Studio .NET tries to avoid invoking the type library importer if at all possible, since it generates a new assembly with its own identity. Instead, Visual Studio .NET automatically adds a copy of a PIA to a project's references if one is registered for a type library that the user references on the COM tab of

3

the Add Reference dialog. (A copy of an assembly is just as good as the original, since the internal assembly identity is the same.) The TLBIMP.EXE utility, on the other hand, simply warns the user when attempting to create an Interop Assembly for a type library whose PIA is registered on the current computer; it still creates a new Interop Assembly. TLBIMP.EXE does make use of registered PIAs for dependent type libraries, described in the next chapter.

As Primary Interop Assemblies are created for existing COM components, they will likely be available for download from MSDN Online or component vendor Web sites. At the time of writing, no PIAs other than the handful that ship with Visual Studio .NET exist.

DIGGING DEEPER

It's possible to work around the identity problem caused by multiple Interop Assemblies without a notion of Primary Interop Assemblies. Due to the way in which COM interfaces are handled by the CLR, it's possible to cast from a COM interface definition in one assembly to a COM interface definition in another assembly if they have the same IID. (This does not work for regular .NET interfaces.) It's also possible to convert from a COM class defined in one assembly to a COM class defined in another assembly using the Marshal.CreateWrapperOfType method. Nothing enables converting between instances of duplicate structure definitions, but a structure's fields could be copied one-by-one.

But Primary Interop Assemblies have another important use. Interop Assemblies often need modifications, such as the ones shown in Chapter 7 to be completely usable in managed code. When you have a PIA with such customizations registered on your computer, you can benefit from these customizations simply by referencing the type library for the COM component you wish to use inside Visual Studio .NET. For example, the PIA for Microsoft ActiveX Data Objects (ADO), which ships with Visual Studio .NET, contains some customizations to handle object lifetime issues. If you created your own Interop Assembly for ADO using TLBIMP.EXE, you would not benefit from these customizations.

The process of creating and registering Primary Interop Assemblies is discussed in Chapter 15, "Creating and Deploying Useful Primary Interop Assemblies."

Using COM Objects in ASP.NET Pages

As in ASP pages, COM objects can be created in ASP.NET Web pages with the <object> tag. Using the <object> tag with a runat="server" attribute enables the COM object to be used in server-side script blocks. The <object> tag can contain a class identifier (CLSID) or programmatic identifier (ProgID) to identify the COM component to instantiate. The following code illustrates how to create an instance of a COM component using a CLSID:

```
<object id="MyObject" runat="server"
    classid="e2d9b696-86ce-45d3-8fc6-fb5b90230c11"
/>
```

And the following code illustrates how to create an instance of a COM component using a ProgID:

```
<object id="MyObject" runat="server"
    progid="Excel.Chart"
/>
```

These two COM-specific techniques use late binding and do not require Interop Assemblies in order to work. However, the ASP.NET <object> tag can also be used with a class attribute to instantiate .NET objects or COM objects described in an Interop Assembly. This can be used as follows:

```
<object id="recset" runat="server"
    class="ADODB.RecordsetClass, ADODB, Version=7.0.3300.0, Culture=neutral,
➡PublicKeyToken=b03f5f7f11d50a3a"
/>
```

The class string contains an assembly-qualified class name, which has the *ClassName*, *AssemblyName* format. The assembly name could be just an assembly's simple name (such as ADODB or SpeechLib) if the assembly is not in the Global Assembly Cache. This is known as *partial binding* since the desired assembly isn't completely described. Assemblies that may reside in the Global Assembly Cache, however, must be referenced with their complete name, as shown in the preceding example. (Version policy could still be applied to cause a different version of the assembly to be loaded than the one specified.) As with the C++ Hello, World example, the Class suffix must be used with the class name.

Interop Assemblies used in ASP.NET pages should be placed with any other assemblies, such as in the site's \bin directory.

ASP.NET also provides several ways to create COM objects inside the server-side script block:

- Using Server.CreateObject
- Using Server.CreateObjectFromClsid
- Using the new Operator

The Server.CreateObject method should be familiar to ASP programmers. Server.CreateObject is a method with one string parameter that enables you to create an object from its ProgID. The following code illustrates how to create an instance of a COM component using Server.CreateObject in Visual Basic .NET:

```
Dim connection As Object
connection = Server.CreateObject("ADODB.Connection")
```

The `Server.CreateObjectFromClsid` method is used just like `Server.CreateObject` but with a string representing a CLSID.

Again, these are two COM-specific mechanisms that use late binding. To take advantage of an Interop Assembly, you could use the `new` operator as in the `Hello, World` examples or use an overload of the `Server.CreateObject` method. This overload has a `Type` object parameter instead of a string. To use this method, we can obtain a `Type` object from a method such as `System.Type.GetType`, which is described in the "Common Interactions with COM Objects" section.

> **TIP**
>
> Using `Server.CreateObject` with a `Type` object obtained from `Type.GetType` or using the `<object>` tag with the `class` attribute is the preferred method of creating a COM object in an ASP.NET page. Besides giving you the massive performance benefits of early binding, it supports COM objects that rely on `OnStartPage` and `OnEndPage` notifications as given by classic ASP pages (whereas the `New` keyword does not).

Example: Using ADO in ASP.NET

To demonstrate the use of COM components in an ASP.NET Web page, this example uses one of the most widely used COM components in ASP—Microsoft ActiveX Data Objects, or *ADO*.

> **TIP**
>
> The functionality provided by ADO is available via ADO.NET, a set of data-related classes in the .NET Framework. Using these classes in the `System.Data` assembly is the recommended way to perform data access in an ASP.NET Web page.
>
> However, because a learning curve is involved in switching to a new data-access model, you may prefer to stick with ADO. Thanks to COM Interoperability, you can continue to use these familiar COM objects when upgrading your Web site to use ASP.NET.

Listing 3.1 demonstrates using the ADO COM component in an ASP.NET page by declaring two ADO COM objects with the `<object>` tag.

LISTING 3.1   Traditional ADO Can Be Used in an ASP.NET Page Using the Familiar
`<object>` Tag

```
1: <%@ Page aspcompat=true %>
2: <%@ Import namespace="System.Data" %>
3: <script language="VB" runat="server">
4: Sub Page_Load(sender As Object, e As EventArgs)
5:   Dim strConnection As String
6:   Dim i As Integer
7:
8:   ' Connection string for the sample "pubs" database
9:   strConnection = _
10:    "DRIVER={SQL Server};SERVER=(local);UID=sa;PWD=;DATABASE=pubs;"
11:
12:   Try
13:     ' Call a method on the page's connection object
14:     connection.Open(strConnection)
15:   Catch ex as Exception
16:     Response.Write("Unable to open connection to database.  " + ex.Message)
17:   End Try
18:
19:   Try
20:     ' Set properties and call a method on the page's recordset object
21:     recordset.CursorType = 1 ' 1 = ADODB.CursorTypeEnum.adOpenKeyset
22:     recordset.LockType = 3   ' 3 = ADODB.LockTypeEnum.adLockOptimistic
23:     ' 2 = ADODB.CommandTypeEnum.adCmdTable
24:     recordset.Open("titles", connection, , , 2)
25:   Catch ex as Exception
26:     Response.Write("Unable to open recordset.  " + ex.Message)
27:   End Try
28:
29:   Dim table As DataTable
30:   Dim row As DataRow
31:
32:   ' Create a DataTable
33:   table = New DataTable()
34:
35:   ' Add the appropriate columns
36:   For i = 0 to recordset.Fields.Count - 1
37:     table.Columns.Add(New DataColumn(recordset.Fields(i).Name, _
38:       GetType(String)))
39:   Next
40:
41:   ' Scan through the recordset and add a row for each record
42:   Do While Not recordset.EOF
43:     row = table.NewRow()
```

LISTING 3.1   Continued

```
44:
45:      ' Look at each field and add an entry to the row
46:      For i = 0 to recordset.Fields.Count - 1
47:        row(i) = recordset.Fields(i).Value.ToString()
48:      Next
49:
50:      ' Add the row to the DataTable
51:      table.Rows.Add(row)
52:
53:      recordset.MoveNext()
54:    Loop
55:
56:    ' Update the DataGrid control
57:    dataGrid1.DataSource = New DataView(table)
58:    dataGrid1.DataBind()
59:
60:    ' Cleanup
61:    recordset.Close()
62:    connection.Close()
63: End Sub
64: </script>
65:
66: <html><title>Using ADO in ASP.NET</title>
67:    <body>
68:      <form runat=server>
69:        <asp:DataGrid id="dataGrid1" runat="server"
70:          BorderColor="black"
71:          GridLines="Both"
72:          BackColor="#ffdddd"
73:        />
74:      </form>
75:      <object id="connection" runat="server"
76:        progid="ADODB.Connection"/>
77:      <object id="recordset" runat="server"
78:        progid="ADODB.Recordset"/>
79:    </body>
80: </html>
```

The `<%@ Page aspcompat=true %>` directive in Line 1 is explained in Chapter 6, "Advanced Topics for Using COM Components." The important part of Listing 3.1 is Lines 75–78, which declare the two COM objects used in the ASP.NET page via ProgIDs. The HTML portion of the page contains one control—the DataGrid control. This data grid will hold the information that we obtain using ADO.

Inside the `Page_Load` method, Lines 9–10 initialize a connection string for the sample database (pubs) in the local machine's SQL Server. You may need to adjust this string appropriately to run the example on your computer. Lines 21–24 use a few "magic numbers"—hard-coded values that represent various ADO enumeration values mentioned in the code's comments. If you use the Primary Interop Assembly for ADO, then you can reference the actually enum values instead.

After creating a new `DataTable` object in Line 33, we add the appropriate number of columns by looping through the `Fields` collection. On Line 37, each column added is given the name of the current field's `Name` property, and the type of the data held in each column is set to the type `String`. The `Do While` loop starting in Line 42 processes each record in the `Recordset` object. Once `Recordset.EOF` is true, we've gone through all the records. With each record, we create a new row (Line 43), add each of the record's fields to the row (Lines 46–48), and add the row to the table (Line 51). Each string added to a row is the current field's `Value` property. `ToString` is called on the `Value` property in Line 47, in case the data isn't already a string. In Lines 57–58, we associate the `DataTable` object with the page's `DataGrid` control and call `DataBind` to display the records. Finally, Lines 61–62 call `Close` on the two ADO objects to indicate that we're finished with them.

Figure 3.9 displays the output of Listing 3.1 as shown in a Web browser.

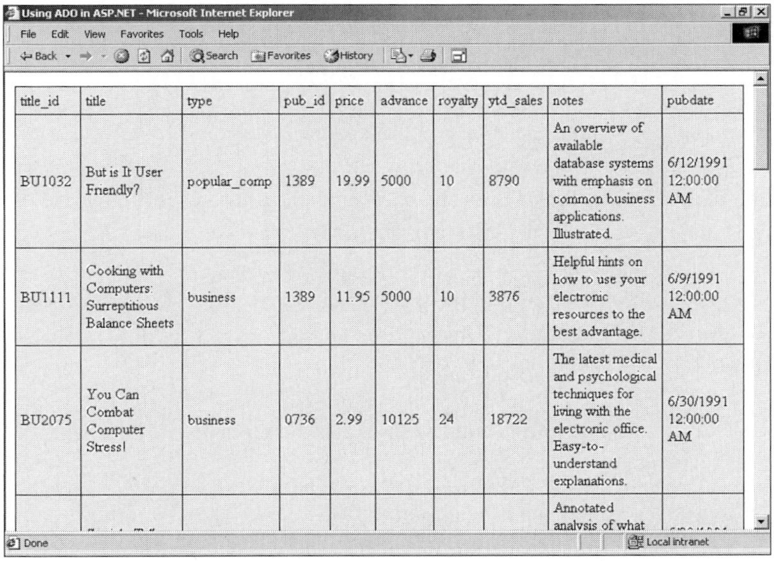

FIGURE 3.9
The output of Listing 3.1 when viewed in a Web browser.

Using COM+ Components

Just like COM components, COM+ components—formerly Microsoft Transaction Server (MTS) components—can be used in an ASP.NET application. However, due to differences between the ASP and ASP.NET security models, using COM+ components in an ASP.NET application might require changing their security settings.

If you get an error with a message such as "Permission denied" when attempting to use COM+ components, you should be able to solve the problem as follows:

1. Open the `Component Services` explorer.
2. Under the `Component Services` node, find the COM+ application you wish to use, right-click on it, and select `Properties`.
3. Go to the `Identity` tab and change the account information to a brand new local machine account.
4. At a command prompt, run `DCOMCNFG.EXE`, a tool that lets you configure DCOM settings (such as security) for your COM+ application.
5. Go to the `Default Security` tab and click the `Edit Default…` button in the `Default Access Permissions` area.
6. Add the new user created in Step 3.
7. Restart Internet Information Services (IIS).

An Introduction to Interop Marshaling

When calls are made from managed code to unmanaged code (or vice-versa), data passed in parameters needs to be converted from one representation to another. These conversions are described in the next chapter. The process of packaging data to be sent from one entity to another is known as *marshaling*. In COM, marshaling is done when sending data across context boundaries such as apartments, operating system processes, or computers. (Apartments are discussed in Chapter 6.) To differentiate the marshaling performed by the CLR from COM marshaling, the process of marshaling across unmanaged/managed boundaries is known as *Interop marshaling*.

COM marshaling often involves extra work for users, such as registering a type library to be used by the standard OLE Automation marshaler or registering your own proxy/stub DLL to handle marshaling for custom interfaces that can't adequately be described in a type library. Interop marshaling, on the other hand, is handled transparently in a way that's usually sufficient by a CLR component known as the *Interop Marshaler*. The metadata inside an Interop Assembly gives the Interop Marshaler the information it needs to be able to marshal data from .NET to COM and vice-versa.

Interop marshaling is completely independent of COM marshaling. COM marshaling occurs externally to the CLR, just as in the pre-.NET days. If COM marshaling is needed due to a call to a COM component occurring across contexts, Interop marshaling occurs either before or after COM marshaling, depending on the order of data flow. One direction of COM marshaling and Interop marshaling is pictured in Figure 3.10.

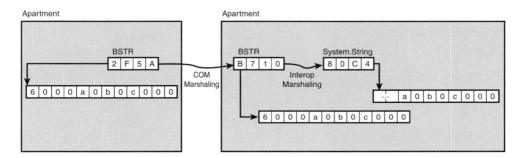

FIGURE 3.10
The relationship between Interop marshaling and COM marshaling.

In this diagram, a COM component returns a COM string type known as a BSTR to a .NET application calling it. BSTR is a pointer to a length-prefixed Unicode string. The pictured string contains "abc" and has a four-byte length prefix that describes the string as six bytes long. (The extra zeros appear in memory because each Unicode character occupies two bytes.) The calling .NET object happens to be in a different apartment, so standard COM marshaling copies the string to the caller's apartment. See Chapter 6 for controlling what kind of apartment a .NET application runs in when using COM Interoperability.

Once the BSTR has been marshaled by a standard COM mechanism, the Interop Marshaler is responsible for copying the data to a .NET string instance (System.String). Although .NET strings are also Unicode and length-prefixed, they have additional information stored in their prefix. Hence, a copy must be made between these two bitwise-incompatible entities. This new System.String instance can then be returned to the .NET caller (after the Interop Marshaler calls SysFreeString to destroy the BSTR). The CLR and the Interop Marshaler don't know or care that COM marshaling has occurred before it performed Interop Marshaling, as long as the unmanaged data is presented correctly in the current context. If an interface pointer were being passed from one apartment to the next and the interface did not have an appropriate COM marshaler registered for it, the call would fail just as it would in a pure COM scenario.

Many data types, such as strings, require copying from one internal representation to another during an Interop transition. When such data types are used by-reference, the Interop

Marshaler provides copy-in/copy-out behavior rather than true by-reference semantics. Several common data types, however, have the same managed and unmanaged memory representations. A data type with the same managed and unmanaged representation is known as *blittable*. The blittable .NET data types are:

- `System.SByte`
- `System.Int16`
- `System.Int32`
- `System.Int64`
- `System.IntPtr`
- `System.Byte`
- `System.UInt16`
- `System.UInt32`
- `System.UInt64`
- `System.UIntPtr`
- `System.Single`
- `System.Double`
- Structs composed only of the previous types
- C-style arrays whose elements are of the previous types

In version 1.0 of the CLR, the Interop Marshaler *pins* and directly exposes managed memory to unmanaged code for any blittable types. (Pinning is discussed in Chapter 6.) By taking advantage of a common memory representation, the Interop Marshaler copies data only when necessary and therefore exhibits better performance when blittable types are used. This implementation detail can show up in more ways than performance, however. For example, copying data in or out of an Interop call can be suppressed by custom attributes, but for blittable types these same custom attributes have no effect because the original memory is always directly exposed to the method being called. Chapter 12, "Customizing COM's View of .NET Components," discusses these custom attributes and their relationship to blittable data types.

You can customize the behavior of the Interop Marshaler in two ways:

- Changing the metadata inside Interop Assemblies to change the way the Interop Marshaler treats data types. This technique is covered in Chapter 6.
- Plugging in your own custom marshaler, as discussed in Chapter 20, "Custom Marshaling."

Common Interactions with COM Objects

Interacting with types defined inside an Interop Assembly often feels just as natural as interacting with .NET types. There are some additional options and subtleties, however, and they're discussed in this section.

Creating an Instance

Creating an instance of a COM class can be just like creating an instance of a .NET class. The Hello, World example showed the most common way of creating a COM object—using the new operator. At run time, after the metadata is located, the class's ComImportAttribute pseudo-custom attribute tells the Common Language Runtime to create an RCW for the class, and to construct the COM object by calling CoCreateInstance using the CLSID specified in the class's GuidAttribute.

DIGGING DEEPER

When instantiating an RCW, the exact CoCreateInstance call that the new operator maps to is as follows, in C++ syntax:

```
CoCreateInstance(clsid, NULL, CLSCTX_SERVER, IID_IUnknown, (void**)&punk);
```

The CLSCTX_SERVER flag means that the object could be created in-process, out-of-process, or even on a remote computer (using DCOM), depending on how the coclass is registered.

If you need to modify the behavior of this call, you could alternatively call CoCreateInstance or CoCreateInstanceEx yourself using Platform Invocation Services (PInvoke). This technique is shown in Chapter 19, "Deeper Into PInvoke and Useful Examples."

Not all coclasses are creatable, however. Instances of noncreatable types can only be obtained when returned from a method or property. The object's RCW is created as soon as you obtain a COM object in this way.

Alternatives to the new Operator

There are other ways to create a COM object, some of which don't even require metadata for the COM object. In Visual Basic 6, you can avoid the need to reference a type library by calling CreateObject and passing the object's ProgID (a string). In the .NET Framework, you can avoid the need to reference an Interop Assembly by using the System.Type and System.Activator classes.

Creating an object in this alternative way is a two-step process:

1. Get a `Type` instance so that we can create an instance of the desired class. This can be done three different ways, shown here in C# using the Microsoft Speech `SpVoice` class:

   - `Type t = Type.GetTypeFromProgID("SAPI.SpVoice");`
   - `Type t = Type.GetTypeFromCLSID(new Guid("96749377-3391-11D2-9EE3-00C04F797396"));`
   - `Type t = Type.GetType("SpeechLib.SpVoiceClass, SpeechLib, Version=5.0.0.0, Culture=neutral, PublicKeyToken=null");`

2. Create an instance of the type (shown in C#):

   ```
   Object voice = Activator.CreateInstance(t);
   ```

In step 1, the goal of all three techniques is to return a `Type` instance whose `GUID` property is set to the CLSID of the COM object we want to create. The first technique obtains the CLSID indirectly from the registry by using the class's ProgID. Most COM classes are registered with ProgIDs (which doesn't necessarily match the type name qualified with the library name, as in this example) so calling `GetTypeFromProgID` is a popular option. The second technique passes the CLSID directly, which should be reserved for COM objects without a ProgID due to its lack of readability.

Whereas the first two techniques don't require an Interop Assembly (which is great for COM objects that aren't described in a type library), the third technique of using `Type.GetType` does require one at run time. That's because the string passed to `Type.GetType` represents a .NET type whose metadata description must be found and loaded in order for the call to succeed. The format for the string is the same as the string used with the `class` attribute for an `<object>` tag in an ASP.NET page:

ClassName, AssemblyName

Step 2 creates an instance of the COM object and assigns it to an `Object` variable. With this variable, you could call members in a late bound fashion, shown in the "Calling Methods and Properties on a COM Object" section. Or, if you compiled the program with metadata definitions of interfaces that the COM object implements, you could cast the object to such an interface. In the `SpVoice` example, you could do the following:

```
SpVoice voice = (SpVoice)Activator.CreateInstance(t);
```

However, if you compile with a metadata definition of `SpVoice`, then you might as well instantiate the object using `new`.

> ### DIGGING DEEPER
>
> `Type.GetTypeFromProgID` and `Type.GetTypeFromCLSID` have overloads that accept a string parameter with a server name. This enables COM objects to be created on a specified remote computer even if they are registered to also be creatable locally. Chapter 6 has more information.

For backwards compatibility with Visual Basic 6, you can still call `CreateObject` in Visual Basic .NET. Calling this method with a ProgID does the same thing as calling `Type.GetTypeFromProgID` followed by `Activator.CreateInstance`. (As with any .NET APIs, this can be called from other languages as well. `CreateObject` is simply a static method on the `Interaction` class inside the `Microsoft.VisualBasic` assembly.)

Detecting Errors

The most common error when attempting to create a COM object is due to the class not being registered (meaning that the CLSID for the class doesn't have an entry under `HKEY_CLASSES_ROOT\CLSID` in the Windows Registry). When an error occurs during object creation, a `COMException` (defined in `System.Runtime.InteropServices`) is thrown. When calling one of the three `Type.GetType…` methods, however, failure is indicated by returning a null `Type` object unless you call the overloaded method with a boolean `throwOnError` parameter.

Because the goal of calling `Type.GetTypeFromCLSID` is to return a `Type` instance with the appropriate GUID, and because the desired GUID is passed directly as a parameter, the implementation of `Type.GetTypeFromCLSID` doesn't bother checking the Windows Registry. Instead, it always returns a `Type` instance whose `GUID` property is set to the passed-in CLSID. Therefore, failure is not noticed until you attempt to instantiate the class using the returned `Type` instance.

Calling Methods and Properties on a COM Object

When you have metadata for the COM object, calling methods is no different from calling methods and properties on a .NET object (as shown in the `Hello, World` example):

```
voice.Speak("Hello, World!", SpeechVoiceSpeakFlags.SVSFDefault);
```

There is one thing to note about properties and C#. Sometimes COM properties aren't supported by C# because they have by-reference parameters or multiple parameters. (C# does support properties with multiple parameters, also known as *parameterized properties*, if they are also default properties.) In such cases, C# doesn't allow you to call these properties with the normal property syntax, but *does* allow you to call the accessor methods directly. An example of this can be seen with the Microsoft SourceSafe 6.0 type library, which has the following property defined on the IVSSDatabase interface (shown in IDL):

```
[id(0x00000008), propget]
HRESULT User([in] BSTR Name, [out, retval] IVSSUser** ppIUser);
```

In C#, this property must be called as follows:

```
user = database.get_User("Guest");
```

Attempting to call the User property directly would cause compiler error CS1546 with the following message:

```
Property or indexer 'User' is not supported by the language; try directly
calling accessor method 'SourceSafeTypeLib.VSSDatabase.get_User(string)'.
```

In Visual Basic .NET, this same property can be used with regular property syntax:

```
user = database.User("Guest")
```

If you don't have metadata for the COM object (either by choice or because the COM object doesn't have a type library), you must make late-bound calls, as the compiler has no type definitions. In Visual Basic .NET, this looks the same as it did in Visual Basic 6 (as long as you ensure that Option Strict is turned off):

```
Imports System
Module Module1
  Sub Main()
    Dim t as Type
    Dim voice as Object
    t = Type.GetTypeFromProgID("SAPI.SpVoice")
    voice = Activator.CreateInstance(t)
    voice.Speak("Hello, World!")
  End Sub
End Module
```

This can simply be compiled from the command line as follows, which does not require the SpeechLib Interop Assembly:

```
vbc HelloWorld.vb
```

Because the type of voice is System.Object, the Visual Basic .NET compiler doesn't check the method call at compile time. It's possible that a method called Speak won't exist on the voice object at run time or that it will have a different number of parameters (although we know otherwise), but all failures are reported at run time when using late binding.

In C#, however, the equivalent code doesn't compile:

```
using System;

class Class1
{
```

DON'T DO THIS

```
static void Main()
{
  Type t = Type.GetTypeFromProgID("SAPI.SpVoice");
  object voice = Activator.CreateInstance(t);

  // Causes compiler error CS0117:
  // 'object' does not contain a definition for 'Speak'
  voice.Speak("Hello, World!", 0);
}
}
```

DON'T DO THIS

That's because the type of voice is System.Object and there's no method called Speak on this type. The only way to make a late-bound call in C# is to use the general .NET feature of reflection, introduced in Chapter 1. Therefore, the previous C# example can be changed to:

```
using System;
using System.Reflection;

class Class1
{
  static void Main()
  {
    Type t = Type.GetTypeFromProgID("SAPI.SpVoice");
    object voice = Activator.CreateInstance(t);
    object [] args = new Object[2];
    args[0] = "Hello, World!";
    args[1] = 0;
    t.InvokeMember("Speak", BindingFlags.InvokeMethod, null, voice, args);
  }
}
```

When reflecting on a COM object using Type.InvokeMember, the CLR communicates with the object through its IDispatch interface. Different binding flags can be used to control what kind of member is invoked. Internally, which binding flag is chosen affects the wFlags parameter that the CLR passes to IDispatch.Invoke. These binding flags are:

- BindingFlags.InvokeMethod. The CLR passes DISPATCH_METHOD, which indicates that a method should be invoked.

- BindingFlags.GetProperty. The CLR passes DISPATCH_PROPERTYGET, which indicates that a property's get accessor (propget) should be invoked.

- BindingFlags.SetProperty. The CLR passes DISPATCH_PROPERTYPUT | DISPATCH_PROPERTYPUTREF, which indicates that either a property's set accessor (propputref) or let accessor (propput) should be invoked. If the property has both of these accessors, it's up to the object's IDispatch implementation to decide which to invoke.

- BindingFlags.PutDispProperty. The CLR passes DISPATCH_PROPERTYPUT, which indicates that a property's let accessor (propput) should be invoked.
- BindingFlags.PutRefDispProperty. The CLR passes DISPATCH_PROPERTYPUTREF, which indicates that a property's set accessor (propputref) should be invoked.

For more information about COM properties, see Chapter 4.

When you don't have metadata for a COM object, the amount of information that you can get through the reflection API is limited. In addition (unlike .NET objects), not all COM objects support late binding because COM objects might not implement IDispatch. If you try to use Type.InvokeMember with such a COM object, you'll get an exception with the message:

```
The COM target does not implement IDispatch.
```

For these types of objects, having metadata definitions of the types and using different reflection APIs (such as MemberInfo.Invoke) is a must because late binding isn't an option.

DIGGING DEEPER

When reflecting on a COM object that is defined in an Interop Assembly, you can use reflection APIs such as MemberInfo.Invoke even if the object doesn't support IDispatch. All of the reflection APIs except Type.InvokeMember call through a COM object's v-table unless the interface you're invoking on happens to be a dispinterface.

If you're reflecting on a COM object that has no metadata, Type.InvokeMember is just about the only reflection functionality you can make use of. For example, calling Type.GetMethods on such an object returns the methods of the generic System.__ComObject class rather than the COM object's methods. Without metadata, there is no way to enumerate a COM object's methods using reflection.

Using Optional Parameters

Optional parameters, commonly used in COM components, are parameters that a caller might omit. Optional parameters enable callers to use shorter syntax when the default values of parameters are acceptable, such as the second parameter of the Speak method used previously.

Optional Parameters in COM

In IDL, a method with optional parameters looks like this:

```
HRESULT PrintItems([in, optional] VARIANT x, [in, optional] VARIANT y);
```

In Visual Basic 6, this method might be implemented as follows:

```
Public Sub PrintItems(Optional ByVal x as Variant, Optional ByVal y as Variant)
  If Not IsMissing(x) Then ReallyPrint x
  If Not IsMissing(y) Then ReallyPrint y
End Sub
```

The VARIANT type can represent a missing value (meaning that the caller didn't pass anything). A missing value can be determined in VB6 using the built-in IsMissing method, and can be determined in unmanaged C++ by checking for a VARIANT with type VT_ERROR and a value equal to DISP_E_PARAMNOTFOUND (defined in winerror.h):

```
//
// MessageId: DISP_E_PARAMNOTFOUND
//
// MessageText:
//
//  Parameter not found.
//
#define DISP_E_PARAMNOTFOUND             _HRESULT_TYPEDEF_(0x80020004L)
```

Non-VARIANT types can also be optional if they have a default value, demonstrated by the following method:

IDL:

```
HRESULT AddItem([in, optional, defaultvalue("New Entry")] BSTR name,
  [in, optional, defaultvalue(1)] short importance);
```

Visual Basic 6:

```
Public Sub AddItem(Optional ByVal name As String = "New Entry",
  Optional ByVal importance As Integer = 1)
```

For parameters with default values, the method implementer doesn't check for a missing value because if the caller didn't pass a value, it looks to the method as if the caller passed the default value.

Optional Parameters in the .NET Framework

Optional parameters also exist in the .NET Framework, although support for them is not required by the CLS. This means that you can't count on taking advantage of optional parameters in all .NET languages—C# being a prime example. Because C# does not support optional parameters, it can become frustrating to use COM objects that make heavy use of them.

FAQ: Why doesn't C# support optional parameters?

The C# designers decided not to support optional parameters because their implementation has the unfortunate consequence of emitting the default value into the caller's MSIL instructions as if the caller passed the value in source code. For example, in Visual Basic .NET, viewing the IL produced for the following method call

```
list.AddItem()
```

reveals that the code produced is equivalent to the code that would be produced if the programmer had written

```
list.AddItem("New Entry", 1)
```

This could result in versioning headaches if a future version of a component changes the default values because the values are hard-coded in the client. One could argue that a component shouldn't change default values as they are part of a contract with a client. One could also argue that it doesn't matter if the default values change because the clients still get the same behavior for the values they're passing in. If the component *did* want clients to switch to a new default, however, it couldn't be achieved without recompiling every client. Besides, C# prefers to be explicit to avoid any confusion. The recommended alternative to achieve the same effect as optional parameters when designing .NET components is to use method overloading. So, a C# programmer should define the following methods to get the same functionality as the earlier AddItem method:

```
public void AddItem()
{
  AddItem("New Entry", 1);
}
public void AddItem(string name)
{
  AddItem(name, 1);
}
public void AddItem(short importance)
{
  AddItem("New Entry", importance);
}
public void AddItem(string name, short importance)
{
  // Real implementation
}
```

This encapsulates the default values in the component's implementation. Note that method overloading isn't possible in COM because each method on an interface must have a unique name.

The type library importer preserves the optional marking on parameters in the metadata that it produces. So, optional parameters in COM look like optional parameters to the .NET languages that support them. In Visual Basic .NET, for example, calling a COM method with optional parameters works the same way as it does in Visual Basic 6, as demonstrated in the Visual Basic .NET Hello, World example.

Behind the scenes, the VB .NET compiler fills in each missing parameter with either the default value or a System.Type.Missing instance if no default value exists. When passed to unmanaged code, the CLR converts a System.Type.Missing type to COM's version of a missing type—a VT_ERROR VARIANT with the value DISP_E_PARAMNOTFOUND. You could explicitly pass the Type.Missing static field for each optional parameter, but this isn't necessary as the VB .NET compiler does it for you. In languages like C#, however, passing Type.Missing can be useful for "omitting" a parameter.

Consider the following method, shown in both IDL and Visual Basic 6:

IDL:

```
HRESULT AddAnyItem([in, optional, defaultvalue("New Entry")] VARIANT name,
  [in, optional, defaultvalue(1)] VARIANT importance);
```

Visual Basic 6:

```
Public Sub AddAnyItem(Optional ByVal name As Variant = "New Entry",
  Optional ByVal importance As Variant = 1)
```

This method can be called in Visual Basic .NET the following ways, which are all equivalent:

- `list.AddAnyItem()`
- `list.AddAnyItem("New Entry")`
- `list.AddAnyItem(, 1)`
- `list.AddAnyItem("New Entry", 1)`
- `list.AddAnyItem(Type.Missing, Type.Missing)`
- `list.AddAnyItem("New Entry", Type.Missing)`
- `list.AddAnyItem(Type.Missing, 1)`

Because the C# compiler ignores the optional marking in the metadata, only the last four ways of calling AddAnyItem can be used in C#.

For non-VARIANT optional parameters, C# programs must explicitly pass a default value to get the default behavior. That's because the compiler won't allow you to pass `Type.Missing` where a string is expected, for example. If you're not sure what the default value for a parameter is, view the type library using OLEVIEW.EXE or the corresponding metadata using ILDASM.EXE. The metadata for the AddAnyItem method is shown here:

```
.method public newslot virtual instance void
  AddAnyItem([in][opt] object  marshal( struct) name,
             [in][opt] object  marshal( struct) importance)
  runtime managed internalcall
{
  .custom instance void [mscorlib]
    System.Runtime.InteropServices.DispIdAttribute::.ctor(int32) =
    ( 01 00 00 00 03 60 00 00 )
  .param [1] = "New Entry"
  .param [2] = int16(0x0001)
} // end of method IList::AddItem
```

But there's one more wrinkle for C# programmers—optional VARIANT parameters that are passed by-reference. As discussed in the next chapter, a VARIANT passed by-reference looks like `ref object` in C#. Thus, you can't simply pass `Type.Missing` or `ref Type.Missing` because it's a static field. You need to pass a reference to a variable that has been set to `Type.Missing`. For example, to call the following method from the Microsoft Word type library:

```
VARIANT_BOOL CheckSpelling(
  [in] BSTR Word,
  [in, optional] VARIANT* CustomDictionary,
  [in, optional] VARIANT* IgnoreUppercase,
  [in, optional] VARIANT* MainDictionary,
  [in, optional] VARIANT* CustomDictionary2,
  [in, optional] VARIANT* CustomDictionary3,
  [in, optional] VARIANT* CustomDictionary4,
  [in, optional] VARIANT* CustomDictionary5,
  [in, optional] VARIANT* CustomDictionary6,
  [in, optional] VARIANT* CustomDictionary7,
  [in, optional] VARIANT* CustomDictionary8,
  [in, optional] VARIANT* CustomDictionary9,
  [in, optional] VARIANT* CustomDictionary10);
```

you need the following silly-looking C# code:

```
object missing = Type.Missing;
result = msWord.CheckSpelling(
  word,              // Word
  ref missing,       // CustomDictionary
  ref ignoreUpper,   // IgnoreUppercase
  ref missing,       // AlwaysSuggest
  ref missing,       // CustomDictionary2
  ref missing,       // CustomDictionary3
  ref missing,       // CustomDictionary4
  ref missing,       // CustomDictionary5
  ref missing,       // CustomDictionary6
  ref missing,       // CustomDictionary7
  ref missing,       // CustomDictionary8
  ref missing,       // CustomDictionary9
  ref missing);      // CustomDictionary10
```

It's ugly, but it works. This sometimes comes as a surprise because people don't often think of [in] VARIANT* in IDL as being passed by-reference, as there's no [out] flag.

Releasing a COM Object

The Common Language Runtime handles reference counting of COM objects, so there is no need to call IUnknown.AddRef or IUnknown.Release in managed code. You simply create the object using the new operator, or one of the other techniques discussed, and allow the system to take care of releasing the object.

Leaving it up to the CLR to release a COM object can sometimes be problematic because it does not occur at a deterministic time. Once you're finished using an RCW, it becomes eligible for garbage collection but does not actually get collected until some later point in time. And the wrapped COM object doesn't get released until the RCW is collected.

Sometimes COM objects require being released at a specific point during program execution. If you need to control exactly when the Runtime-Callable Wrapper calls `IUnknown.Release`, you can call the static (`Shared` in VB .NET) `Marshal.ReleaseComObject` method in the `System.Runtime.InteropServices` namespace. For a COM object called `obj`, this method can be called in Visual Basic .NET as follows:

```
Dim obj As MyCompany.ComObject
...
' We're finished with the object.
Marshal.ReleaseComObject(obj)
```

`Marshal.ReleaseComObject` has different semantics than `IUnknown.Release`—it makes the CLR call `IUnknown.Release` on every COM interface pointer it wraps, making the instance unusable to managed code afterwards. Attempting to use an object after passing it to `ReleaseComObject` raises a `NullReferenceException`. See Chapter 6 for more information about eagerly releasing COM objects.

| **TIP** | |

In Visual Basic 6, a COM object could be immediately released by setting the object reference to `Nothing` (null):

```
Set comObj = Nothing
```

In managed code, however, setting an object to `Nothing` or null only makes the original instance *eligible* for garbage collection; the object is not immediately released. For COM objects, this can be accomplished by calling `ReleaseComObject` instead of or in addition to the previous line of code. For both .NET and COM objects, this can be accomplished by calling `System.GC.Collect` and `System.GC.WaitForPendingFinalizers` after setting the object to `Nothing` or null.

Casting to an Interface (`QueryInterface`)

In COM, calling `QueryInterface` is the way to programmatically determine whether an object implements a certain interface. The equivalent of this in .NET is casting. (In Visual Basic .NET, casting is done with either the `CType` or `DirectCast` operators.)

When attempting to cast a COM type to another type, the CLR calls `QueryInterface` in order to ask the object if the cast is legal, unless the type relationship can be determined from metadata. Because COM classes aren't required to list all the interfaces they implement in a type library, a `QueryInterface` call might often be necessary. Figure 3.11 diagrams what occurs when a COM object (an RCW) is cast to another type in managed code. There's more to the story than what is described here, however, which is indicated with the ellipses in the figure. Chapter 5, "Responding to COM Events," will update this diagram with the complete sequence of events.

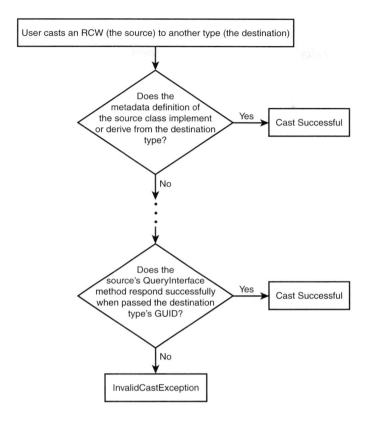

FIGURE 3.11
Casting a COM object to another type in managed code.

This relationship between casting and `QueryInterface` means that an `InvalidCastException` is thrown in managed code whenever a `QueryInterface` call fails. When using COM components, however, an `InvalidCastException` can be thrown in other circumstances that don't involve casting. Chapter 6 discusses some of the common problems that cause an `InvalidCastException`.

The following code snippets illustrate how various unmanaged and managed languages enable coercing an instance of the `SpVoice` type to the `ISpVoice` interface:

Unmanaged C++:

```cpp
IUnknown* punk = NULL;
ISpVoice* pVoice = NULL;
...
HRESULT hresult = punk->QueryInterface(IID_ISpVoice, (void**)&pVoice);
```

Visual Basic 6:

```
Dim i as ISpVoice
Dim v as SpVoice
...
Set i = v
```

C#:

```
ISpVoice i;
SpVoice v;
...
i = (ISpVoice)v;
```

Visual Basic .NET:

```
Dim i as ISpVoice
Dim v as SpVoice
...
i = CType(v, ISpVoice)
```

Because casting a COM object is like calling QueryInterface, COM objects should not be cast to a *class* type; they should only be cast to an *interface*. Not all COM objects expose a mechanism to determine what their class type is; the only thing you can count on is determining what interfaces it implements. However, because the names that represent classes in COM (such as SpVoice) now represent interfaces, casting to one of these special interfaces works. It results in a QueryInterface call to the class's default interface. What does not always work is casting a COM object to a type that's represented as a class in metadata, such as SpVoiceClass.

Error Handling

As mentioned in the preceding chapter, the COM way of error handling is to return a status code called an HRESULT. To bridge the gap between the two models of handling errors, the CLR checks for a failure HRESULT after an invocation and, if appropriate, throws an exception for managed clients to catch. The type of the exception thrown is based on the returned HRESULT, and the contents of the exception can contain customized information if the COM object sets additional information via the IErrorInfo interface. The translation between IErrorInfo and a .NET exception is covered in Chapter 16, "COM Design Guidelines for Components Used by .NET Clients." The exception types thrown by the CLR for various HRESULT values are listed in Appendix C, "HRESULT to .NET Exception Transformations."

In .NET, the type of an exception is often the most important aspect of an exception that enables clients to programmatically take a course of action. Although the CLR transforms some often-used HRESULTs (such as E_OUTOFMEMORY) into system-supplied exceptions (such as

System.OutOfMemoryException), many COM components define and use custom HRESULTs. Unfortunately, such HRESULTs cannot be transformed to nice-looking exception types by the CLR. There are two reasons for this:

- Appropriate exception types specific to custom HRESULT values would need to be defined somewhere in an assembly.
- The CLR would need a mechanism for transforming arbitrary HRESULT values into arbitrary exception types, and there's no way to provide this information. In other words, the HRESULT transformation list in Appendix C is nonextensible.

Any unrecognized failure HRESULT is transformed to a System.Runtime.InteropServices. COMException. This is probably one of the most noticeable seams in the nearly seamless interoperation of COM components. COMExceptions have a public ErrorCode property that contains the HRESULT value, making it possible to check exactly which HRESULT caused this generic exception. This is demonstrated by the following Visual Basic .NET code:

```
Try
  Dim msWord As Object = new Word.Application()
Catch ex as COMException
  If (ex.ErrorCode = &H80040154)
    MessageBox.Show("Word is not registered.")
  Else
    MessageBox.Show("Unexpected COMException: " + ex.ToString())
  End If
Catch ex as Exception
  MessageBox.Show("Unexpected exception: " + ex.ToString())
End Try
```

Other exception types typically don't have a public member that enables you to see the HRESULT, but every exception *does* have a corresponding HRESULT stored in a protected property, called HResult. The motivation is that in the .NET Framework, checking for error codes should be a thing of the past, and replaced by checking for the type of exception.

DIGGING DEEPER

There is usually no need to check the HRESULT value inside an arbitrary exception, but it is possible by calling the System.Runtime.InteropServices.Marshal. GetHRForException method. It can also be done using the System.Runtime.InteropServices.ErrorWrapper class, but that isn't its intent.

> **CAUTION**
>
> COM methods may occasionally change the data inside by-reference parameters before returning a failure HRESULT. When such a method is called from managed code, however, the updated values of any by-reference parameters are not copied back to the caller before the .NET exception is thrown. This effect is only seen with non-blittable types because any changes that the COM method makes to by-reference blittable types directly change the original memory.

All this discussion overlooks the fact that an HRESULT doesn't just represent an error code. It can be a nonerror status code known a success HRESULT, identified by a severity bit set to zero. Success HRESULTs other than S_OK (the standard return value when there's no failure) are used much less often than failure HRESULTs, but can show up when using members of widely used interfaces. One common example is the IPersistStorage.IsDirty method, which returns either S_OK or S_FALSE, neither of which is an error condition.

HRESULTs are hidden from managed code, so there's no way to know what HRESULT is returned from a method or property unless it causes an exception to be thrown. One could imagine a SuccessException being thrown whenever a COM object returns an interesting success HRESULT, but throwing an exception slows down an application and thus should be reserved for exceptional situations. Chapter 7 demonstrates a way to expose HRESULTs in imported signatures in order to handle success HRESULTs.

Enumerating Over a Collection

Thanks to the transformations performed by the type library importer, enumerating over a collection exposed by a COM object is as simple as enumerating over a collection exposed by a .NET object. This occurs as long as the COM collection is exposed as a member with DISPID_NEW_ENUM that returns an IEnumVARIANT interface pointer, as discussed in the next chapter.

The following is a Visual Basic .NET code snippet that demonstrates enumeration over a collection exposed by the Microsoft Word type library. More of this is shown in the example at the end of this chapter.

```
Dim suggestions As SpellingSuggestions
Dim suggestion As SpellingSuggestion
suggestions = msWord.GetSpellingSuggestions("errror")

' Enumerate over the SpellingSuggestions collection
For Each suggestion In suggestions
  Console.WriteLine(suggestion.Name)
Next
```

Passing the Right Type of Object

When COM methods or properties have VARIANT parameters, they look like System.Object types to managed code. Passing the right type of Object so that the COM component sees the right type of VARIANT is usually straightforward. For example, passing a managed Boolean means the component sees a VARIANT containing a VARIANT_BOOL (a Boolean in VB6), and passing a managed Double means the component sees a VARIANT containing a double.

The tricky cases are the managed data types that have multiple unmanaged representations. Some common types used in COM no longer exist in the .NET Framework: CURRENCY, VARIANT, IUnknown, IDispatch, SCODE, and HRESULT. Therefore, as discussed further in Chapter 4, .NET Decimal types can be used to represent COM CURRENCY or DECIMAL types, .NET Object types can be used to represent COM VARIANT, IUnknown, or IDispatch types, and .NET integers can be used to represent COM SCODE or HRESULT types. If a COM signature had a CURRENCY parameter, you could simply pass a Decimal when early-binding to the corresponding method described in an Interop Assembly. The CLR would automatically transform it to a CURRENCY because the type library importer decorates such parameters a custom attribute that tells the CLR what the unmanaged data type is. With a VARIANT parameter, however, there needs to be some way to control whether the type passed looks like a DECIMAL (VT_DECIMAL) or a CURRENCY (VT_CY) to the COM component, and this information is not captured in the signature.

The solution for using a single .NET type to represent multiple COM types lies in some simple wrappers (not to be confused with RCWs or CCWs) defined in the System.Runtime. InteropServices namespace. There is a wrapper for each basic type that doesn't exist in the managed world:

- CurrencyWrapper   Used to make a Decimal look like a CURRENCY type when passed inside a VARIANT.
- UnknownWrapper   Used to make an Object look like an IUnknown interface pointer when passed inside a VARIANT.
- DispatchWrapper   Used to make an Object look like an IDispatch interface pointer when passed inside a VARIANT.
- ErrorWrapper   Used to make an integer or an Exception look like an SCODE when passed inside a VARIANT.

Listing 3.2 shows C# code that demonstrates how to use these wrappers to convey different VARIANT types when calling the following GiveMeAnything method (shown in its unmanaged and managed representations):

IDL:

```
HRESULT GiveMeAnything([in] VARIANT v);
```

Visual Basic 6:

```
Public Sub GiveMeAnything(ByVal v As Variant)
```

C#:

```
public virtual void GiveMeAnything(Object v);
```

LISTING 3.2   Using `CurrencyWrapper`, `UnknownWrapper`, `DispatchWrapper`, and `ErrorWrapper` to Convey Different `VARIANT` Types

```
Decimal d = 123.456M;
int i = 10;
Object o = ...

// Pass a VARIANT with type VT_DECIMAL (Decimal)
comObj.GiveMeAnything(d);

// Pass a VARIANT with type VT_CY (Currency)
comObj.GiveMeAnything(new CurrencyWrapper(d));


// Pass a VARIANT with type VT_UNKNOWN
comObj.GiveMeAnything(new UnknownWrapper(o));

// Pass a VARIANT with type VT_DISPATCH
comObj.GiveMeAnything(new DispatchWrapper(o));

// Pass a VARIANT with whatever the type of the object is.
// For example, a String results in type VT_BSTR, and an object like
// System.Collections.Hashtable results in type VT_DISPATCH.
comObj.GiveMeAnything(o);


// Pass a VARIANT with type VT_I4 (long in IDL, Short in VB6)
comObj.GiveMeAnything(i);

// Pass a VARIANT with type VT_ERROR (SCODE)
comObj.GiveMeAnything(new ErrorWrapper(i));

// Pass a VARIANT with type VT_ERROR (SCODE)
// using the value of the exception's internal HRESULT.
comObj.GiveMeAnything(new ErrorWrapper(new StackOverflowException()));
```

> **CAUTION**
>
> The Interop Marshaler never creates wrapper types such as `CurrencyWrapper` when marshaling an unmanaged data type to a managed data type; these wrappers work in one direction only. Combined with the copy-in/copy-out semantics of by-reference parameters passed across an Interop boundary, this fact can cause behavior that sometimes surprises people. If you pass a `CurrencyWrapper` instance by-reference to unmanaged code (via a parameter typed as `System.Object`), it becomes a `Decimal` instance after the call even if the COM object did nothing with the parameter.

Table 3.1 summarizes what kind of instance can be passed as a `System.Object` parameter in order to get the desired VARIANT type when marshaled to unmanaged code. When early binding to a COM object, these only apply when the parameter type is `System.Object`, because otherwise these types would not be marshaled as VARIANTs.

TABLE 3.1 .NET Types and Their Marshaling Behavior Inside VARIANTs

Type of Instance	VARIANT *Type*
null (Nothing in VB .NET)	VT_EMPTY
System.DBNull	VT_NULL
System.Runtime.InteropServices.CurrencyWrapper	VT_CY
System.Runtime.InteropServices.UnknownWrapper	VT_UNKNOWN
System.Runtime.InteropServices.DispatchWrapper	VT_DISPATCH
System.Runtime.InteropServices.ErrorWrapper	VT_ERROR
System.Reflection.Missing	VT_ERROR with value DISP_E_PARAMNOTFOUND
System.String	VT_BSTR
System.Decimal	VT_DECIMAL
System.Boolean	VT_BOOL
System.Char	VT_U2
System.Byte	VT_U1
System.SByte	VT_I1
System.Int16	VT_I2
System.Int32	VT_I4
System.Int64	VT_I8
System.IntPtr	VT_INT

TABLE 3.1   Continued

Type of Instance	VARIANT *Type*
System.UInt16	VT_U2
System.UInt32	VT_U4
System.UInt64	VT_U8
System.UIntPtr	VT_UINT
System.Single	VT_R4
System.Double	VT_R8
System.DateTime	VT_DATE
Any Array	VT_... | VT_ARRAY
System.Object or other .NET classes	VT_DISPATCH

An array of strings appears as VT_BSTR | VT_ARRAY, an array of doubles appears as VT_R8 | VT_ARRAY, and so on. The VT_I8 and VT_U8 VARIANT types listed in Table 3.1 are not supported prior to Windows XP. Also, notice that in version 1.0 the Interop Marshaler does not support VARIANTs with the VT_RECORD type (used for user-defined structures).

TIP

Because null (Nothing) is mapped to an "empty object" (a VARIANT with type VT_EMPTY) when passed to COM via a System.Object parameter, you can pass new DispatchWrapper(null) or new UnknownWrapper(null) to represent a null object. This maps to a VARIANT with type VT_DISPATCH or VT_UNKNOWN, respectively, whose pointer value is null.

DIGGING DEEPER

The conversions in Table 3.1 are based on the type code that each type's IConvertible implementation returns from its GetTypeCode method. Therefore, any .NET object that implements IConvertible can control how it gets marshaled inside a VARIANT. For example, an object that returns a type code equal to TypeCode.Double is marshaled as a VT_R8 VARIANT.

Late Binding and By-Reference Parameters

Previous code examples have shown how to late bind to a COM component using either reflection or Visual Basic .NET late binding syntax. Table 3.1 and the use of wrappers such as `CurrencyWrapper` are also important for late binding because all parameters are packaged in VARIANTs when late binding to a COM component. One remaining issue that needs to be addressed is the handling of by-reference parameters.

When late binding to .NET members (or members defined in an Interop Assembly), the metadata tells reflection whether a parameter is passed by value or by reference. When late binding to COM members via `IDispatch` (using `Type.InvokeMember` in managed code), however, the CLR has no way to know which parameters must be passed by value and which must be passed by reference. Because all parameters are packaged in VARIANTs when late binding to a COM component, a by-reference parameter looks like a VARIANT whose type is bitwise-ORed with the VT_BYREF flag.

Reflection and the VB .NET late binding abstraction choose different default behavior when late binding to COM members—Visual Basic .NET passes all parameters *by reference* by default, but `Type.InvokeMember` passes all parameters *by value* by default!

Changing the default behavior in the VB .NET case is easy. As in earlier versions of Visual Basic, you can surround an argument in extra parentheses to force it to be passed by value:

```
Dim s As String = "SomeString"
' Call COM method via late binding
' The String parameter is passed by-reference (VT_BSTR | VT_BYREF)
comObj.SomeMethod(s)

' Call COM method again via late binding
' The String parameter is passed by-value (VT_BSTR)
comObj.SomeMethod((s))
```

Changing the default behavior with `Type.InvokeMember` is not so easy. To pass any parameters by reference, you must call an overload of `Type.InvokeMember` that accepts an array of `System.Reflection.ParameterModifier` types. You must pass an array with only a single `ParameterModifier` element that is initialized with the number of parameters in the member being invoked. `ParameterModifier` has a default property called `Item` (exposed as an indexer in C#) that can be indexed from 0 to *NumberOfParameters*-1. Each element in this property must either be set to true if the corresponding parameter should be passed by reference, or false if the corresponding parameter should be passed by value. This is summarized in Listing 3.3, which contains C# code that late binds to a COM object's method and passes a single string parameter first by reference and then by value.

LISTING 3.3   Using `System.Reflection.ParameterModifier` to Pass Parameters to COM with the `VT_BYREF` Flag

```
using SomeComLibrary;
using System.Reflection;

public class LateBinding
{
  public static void Main()
  {
    SomeComObject obj = new SomeComObject();

    object [] args = { "SomeString" };

    // Initialize a ParameterModifier with the number of parameters
    ParameterModifier p = new ParameterModifier(1);
    // Set the VT_BYREF flag on the first parameter
    p[0] = true;
    // Always create an array of ParameterModifiers with a single element
    ParameterModifier [] mods = { p };

    // Call the method via late binding.
    // The parameter is passed by reference (VT_BSTR | VT_BYREF)
    obj.GetType().InvokeMember("SomeMethod", BindingFlags.InvokeMethod, null,
      obj, args, mods, null, null);

    // Call the method again using the simplest InvokeMember overload
    // The parameter is passed by value (VT_BSTR)
    obj.GetType().InvokeMember("SomeMethod", BindingFlags.InvokeMethod, null,
      obj, args);
  }
}
```

Using `ParameterModifier` is only necessary when reflecting using `Type.InvokeMember` because all other reflection methods use metadata that completely describes every parameter in the member being called. Note that there is no built-in way to pass an object to COM that appears as a VARIANT with the type `VT_VARIANT | VT_BYREF`. Additionally, in an early bound call, there is no way to pass a VARIANT with the `VT_BYREF` flag set without resorting to do-it-yourself marshaling techniques described in Chapter 6.

Using ActiveX Controls in .NET Applications

The terms *ActiveX control* and *COM component* are often used interchangeably, but in this book an ActiveX control is a special kind of COM component that supports being hosted in an

ActiveX container. Such objects typically implement several interfaces such as IOleObject, IOleInPlaceObject, IOleControl, IDataObject, and more. They are typically registered specially as a control (as opposed to a simple class) and are marked with the [control] IDL attribute in their type libraries. They also usually have a graphical user interface.

The .NET equivalent of ActiveX controls are Windows Forms controls. Just as it's possible to expose and use COM objects as if they are .NET objects, it's possible to expose and use ActiveX controls as if they are Windows Forms controls. First we'll look at the process of referencing an ActiveX control in Visual Studio .NET, then how to do it with a .NET Framework SDK utility. Finally, we'll look at an example of hosting and using the control on a .NET Windows Form. For these examples, we'll use the WebBrowser control located in the Microsoft Internet Controls type library (SHDOCVW.DLL).

Referencing an ActiveX Control in Visual Studio .NET

If you referenced the Microsoft Internet Controls type library as you would any other type library, then the WebBrowser class could only be used like an ordinary object; you wouldn't be able to drag and drop it on a form. Using ActiveX controls as Windows Forms controls requires these steps:

1. Start Visual Studio .NET and create either a new Visual Basic .NET Windows application or a Visual C# Windows application. The remaining steps apply to either language.

2. Select Tools, Customize Toolbox… from the menu, or right-click inside the Toolbox window and select Customize Toolbox… from the context menu. There are two kinds of controls that can be referenced: COM Components and .NET Framework Components. The default COM Components tab shows a list of all the registered ActiveX controls on the computer. This dialog is shown in Figure 3.12.

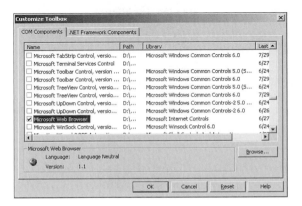

FIGURE 3.12
Adding a reference to an ActiveX control in Visual Studio .NET.

3. Select the desired control, then click the OK button.

If these steps succeeded, then an icon for the control should appear in the Toolbox window. Select it and drag an instance of the control onto your form just as you would with any Windows Forms control. At this point, at least two assemblies are added to your project's references—an Interop Assembly for the ActiveX control's type library (and any dependent Interop Assemblies), and an *ActiveX Assembly* that wraps any ActiveX controls inside the type library as special Windows Forms controls. This ActiveX Assembly always has the same name as the Interop Assembly, but with an Ax prefix. Figure 3.13 shows these two assemblies that appear in the Solution Explorer window when referencing and using the WebBrowser ActiveX control.

The ActiveX Assembly

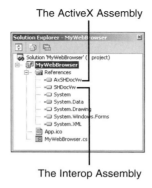

The Interop Assembly

FIGURE 3.13

The Solution Explorer after an ActiveX control has been added to a Windows Form.

Referencing an ActiveX Control Using Only the .NET Framework SDK

Now, let's look at how to accomplish the same task using only the .NET Framework SDK. The following example uses the .NET ActiveX Control to Windows Forms Assembly Generator (AXIMP.EXE), also known as the ActiveX importer. This utility is the TLBIMP.EXE of the Windows Forms world, and can be used as follows:

1. From a command prompt, type the following (replacing the path with the location of SHDOCVW.DLL on your computer):

   AxImp C:\Windows\System32\shdocvw.dll

   This produces both an Interop Assembly (SHDocVw.dll) and ActiveX Assembly (AxSHDocVw.dll) for the input type library in the current directory. Unlike TLBIMP.EXE, AXIMP.EXE does not search for the input file using the PATH environment variable.

2. Reference the ActiveX Assembly just as you would any other assembly, which depends on the language. Depending on the nature of your application, you might also have to reference the Interop Assembly, the `System.Windows.Forms` assembly, and more.

The Interop Assembly created by `AXIMP.EXE` is no different from the one created by `TLBIMP.EXE`. If a Primary Interop Assembly for the input type library is registered on the current computer, `AXIMP.EXE` references that assembly rather than generating a new one.

If no ActiveX control can be found in an input type library, `AXIMP.EXE` reports:

`AxImp Error: Did not find any registered ActiveX control in '…'.`

In order for `AXIMP.EXE` to recognize a COM class as an ActiveX control, it must be registered on the current computer with the following registry value:

`HKEY_CLASSES_ROOT\CLSID\{CLSID}\Control`

Being marked in the type library with the `[control]` attribute is irrelevant.

Example: A Simple Web Browser

Now that we know how to generate and reference an ActiveX Assembly that wraps an ActiveX control as a Windows Forms control, we'll put together a short example that uses an ActiveX control in managed code. Listing 3.4 demonstrates the use of the `WebBrowser` control to create a simple Web browser application, pictured in Figure 3.14. Parts of the listing are omitted, but the complete source code is available on this book's Web site.

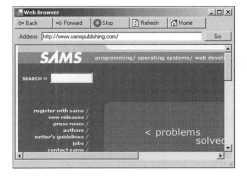

FIGURE 3.14
The simple Web browser.

LISTING 3.4   `MyWebBrowser.cs`. Using the `WebBrowser` ActiveX Control in C#

```
1: using System;
2: using SHDocVw;
```

LISTING 3.4 Continued

```
 3: using System.Windows.Forms;
 4:
 5: public class MyWebBrowser : Form
 6: {
 7:   ...
 8:   object m = Type.Missing;
 9:
10:   // Constructor
11:   public MyWebBrowser()
12:   {
13:     // Required for Windows Form Designer support
14:     InitializeComponent();
15:     // Start on the home page
16:     axWebBrowser1.GoHome();
17:   }
18:
19:   // Clean up any resources being used
20:   protected override void Dispose( bool disposing )
21:   {
22:     if (disposing)
23:     {
24:       if (components != null)
25:       {
26:         components.Dispose();
27:       }
28:     }
29:     base.Dispose(disposing);
30:   }
31:
32:   // Required method for Designer support
33:   private void InitializeComponent()
34:   {
35:     ...
36:     this.axWebBrowser1 = new AxSHDocVw.AxWebBrowser();
37:     ...
38:     ((System.ComponentModel.ISupportInitialize)
39:       (this.axWebBrowser1)).BeginInit();
40:     ...
41:     this.axWebBrowser1.OcxState = ((System.Windows.Forms.AxHost.State)
42:       (resources.GetObject("axWebBrowser1.OcxState")));
43:     ...
44:     ((System.ComponentModel.ISupportInitialize)
45:       (this.axWebBrowser1)).EndInit();
46:     ...
```

LISTING 3.4 Continued

```
47:    }
48:
49:    [STAThread]
50:    static void Main()
51:    {
52:      Application.Run(new MyWebBrowser());
53:    }
54:
55:    // Called when one of the toolbar buttons is clicked
56:    private void toolBar1_ButtonClick(object sender,
57:      ToolBarButtonClickEventArgs e)
58:    {
59:      if (e.Button.Text == "Back")
60:      {
61:        try { axWebBrowser1.GoBack(); }
62:        catch {}
63:      }
64:      else if (e.Button.Text == "Forward")
65:      {
66:        try { axWebBrowser1.GoForward(); }
67:        catch {}
68:      }
69:      else if (e.Button.Text == "Stop")
70:      {
71:        axWebBrowser1.Stop();
72:      }
73:      else if (e.Button.Text == "Refresh")
74:      {
75:        axWebBrowser1.CtlRefresh();
76:      }
77:      else if (e.Button.Text == "Home")
78:      {
79:        axWebBrowser1.GoHome();
80:      }
81:    }
82:
83:    // Called when "Go" is clicked
84:    private void goButton_Click(object sender, System.EventArgs e)
85:    {
86:      axWebBrowser1.Navigate(navigateBox.Text, ref m, ref m, ref m, ref m);
87:    }
88: }
```

Line 8 declares a `Missing` instance used for optional parameters in Line 86. The constructor in Lines 11–17 first calls the standard `InitializeComponent` method to initialize the form's user interface, then calls `GoHome` on the ActiveX control to browse to the user's home page.

Lines 33–47 contain a few of the lines inside `InitializeComponent` that relate to the ActiveX control. Although the class is called `WebBrowser`, the class created by the ActiveX importer always begins with an `Ax` prefix. Therefore, Line 36 instantiates a new `AxWebBrowser` object. Lines 56–81 contain the event handler that gets called whenever the user clicks on one of the buttons across the top of the form. Whenever the `Back` and `Forward` buttons are clicked, the `GoBack` and `GoForward` methods are called, respectively. Because these methods throw an exception if there is no page to move to, any exception is caught and ignored. This is not the ideal way to implement these buttons, but it will have to wait until Chapter 5.

Notice that Line 75 calls a method called `CtlRefresh`, although the original `WebBrowser` control doesn't have such a method. What happens here is that any class created by the ActiveX importer ultimately derives from `System.Windows.Forms.Control`, and this class already has a property called `Refresh`. To distinguish members of the ActiveX control from members of the wrapper's base classes, the ActiveX importer places a `Ctl` prefix (which stands for *control*) on any members with conflicting names. The `AxWebBrowser` class has many other renamed members due to name conflicts—`CtlContainer`, `CtlHeight`, `CtlLeft`, `CtlParent`, `CtlTop`, `CtlVisible`, and `CtlWidth`.

Finally, Lines 84–87 call the ActiveX control's `Navigate` method when the user clicks the `Go` button.

Deploying a .NET Application That Uses COM

Deploying a .NET application that uses COM components is not quite as simple as deploying a .NET application that doesn't. Besides satisfying the requirements of the .NET Framework, you must satisfy the requirements of COM. This means registering the COM component(s) in the Windows Registry on the user's machine, just as you would have if no managed code were involved. This is usually accomplished by running `REGSVR32.EXE` on each COM DLL. It might also be necessary to register type libraries, which adds additional registry entries for interfaces. If you're relying on a component being installed (such as the Microsoft Speech SDK), no additional work is necessary, except the supplied installation.

Unless you late bind to the COM components and only create COM types via ProgID or CLSID, you also need to deploy metadata for the COM components you use. This is no different from managed types because metadata is needed at compile time and at run time. It sometimes seems like more of a burden for COM types, however, because the metadata resides in an

Interop Assembly separate from the file containing the implementation. These should be installed just like other assemblies, either in the Global Assembly Cache and/or in an application-specific directory.

You should avoid deploying Interop Assemblies for COM components you didn't author if Primary Interop Assemblies already exist. If you need to create Primary Interop Assemblies for your own COM components, see Chapter 15.

Example: Using Microsoft Word to Check Spelling

To end the chapter, let's apply everything we've learned to a larger example. This example application is a very simple word processor, shown in Figure 3.15, which uses Microsoft Word for its spellchecker functionality. The user can type inside the application, and then click the Check Spelling button. Each misspelled word (according to Microsoft Word) is highlighted in red and underlined. At any time, the user can right-click a word and choose from a list of correctly spelled replacements supplied by Microsoft Word. The application also gives an option to ignore words with all uppercase letters. When selected, such a word isn't ever marked as misspelled, and alternate spellings aren't suggested when right-clicking it.

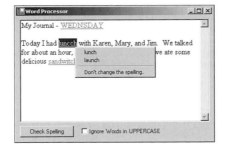

FIGURE 3.15
The example word processor.

The code, shown in C# in Listing 3.5, demonstrates the use of by-reference optional parameters, error handling with COM objects, and enumerating over a collection. The C# version is shown because calling the methods with optional parameters requires extra work. The Visual Basic .NET version on this book's Web site looks much less messy when calling these methods.

To compile or run this example, you must have Microsoft Word on your computer. The sample uses Word 2002, which ships with Microsoft Office XP. If you have a different version of Word installed, it should still work (as long as you use the appropriate type library instead of the one mentioned in step 2).

If you have Visual Studio .NET, here are the steps for creating and running this application:

1. Create a new Visual C# Windows Application project.

2. Add a reference to `Microsoft Word 10.0 Object Library` using the method explained at the beginning of this chapter.

3. View the code for `Form1.cs` in your project, and change its contents to the code in Listing 3.5. One way to view the code is to right-click on the filename in the `Solution Explorer` window and select `View Code`.

4. Build and run the project.

Otherwise, if all you have is the .NET Framework SDK, you can perform the following steps:

1. Create and save a `Form1.cs` file with the code in Listing 3.5. The Windows Forms code inside `InitializeComponent` is omitted, but the complete source code is available on this book's Web site.

2. Use `TLBIMP.EXE` to generate an Interop Assembly for the Microsoft Word type library as follows:

    ```
    TlbImp "C:\Program Files\Microsoft Office\Office10\msword.olb"
    ```

    The path for the input file may need to change depending on your computer's settings. If a PIA for the Word type library is available, you should download it from MSDN Online and use that instead of running `TLBIMP.EXE`.

3. Compile the code, referencing all the needed assemblies:

    ```
    csc /t:winexe Form1.cs /r:Word.dll /r:System.Windows.Forms.dll
    ➥/r:System.Drawing.dll /r:System.dll
    ```

4. Run the generated executable.

LISTING 3.5   `Form1.cs`. Using Microsoft Word Spell Checking in C#

```
 1: using System;
 2: using System.Drawing;
 3: using System.Windows.Forms;
 4:
 5: public class Form1 : Form
 6: {
 7:    // Visual controls
 8:    private RichTextBox richTextBox1;
 9:    private Button button1;
10:    private CheckBox checkBox1;
11:    private ContextMenu contextMenu1;
12:
13:    // Required designer variable
```

LISTING 3.5   Continued

```
14:    private System.ComponentModel.Container components = null;
15:
16:    // The Word application object
17:    private Word.Application msWord;
18:
19:    // Two fonts used to display normal words and misspelled words
20:    private Font normalFont = new Font("Times New Roman", 12);
21:    private Font errorFont = new Font("Times New Roman", 12,
22:      FontStyle.Underline);
23:
24:    // Objects that need to be passed by-reference when calling Word
25:    private object missing = Type.Missing;
26:    private object ignoreUpper;
27:
28:    // Event handler used for the ContextMenu when
29:    // the user clicks on spelling suggestions
30:    private EventHandler menuHandler;
31:
32:    // Constructor
33:    public Form1()
34:    {
35:      // Required for Windows Form Designer support
36:      InitializeComponent();
37:      menuHandler = new System.EventHandler(this.Menu_Click);
38:    }
39:
40:    // Called when the form is loading.  Initializes Microsoft Word.
41:    protected override void OnLoad(EventArgs e)
42:    {
43:      base.OnLoad(e);
44:
45:      try
46:      {
47:        msWord = new Word.Application();
48:
49:        // Call this in order for GetSpellingSuggestions to work later
50:        msWord.Documents.Add(ref missing, ref missing, ref missing,
51:          ref missing);
52:      }
53:      catch (System.Runtime.InteropServices.COMException ex)
54:      {
55:        if ((uint)ex.ErrorCode == 0x80040154)
56:        {
57:          MessageBox.Show("This application requires Microsoft Word " +
```

LISTING 3.5   Continued

```
58:                 "to be installed for spelling functionality.  " +
59:                 "Since Word can't be located, the spelling functionality " +
60:                 "is disabled.", "Warning");
61:             button1.Enabled = false;
62:             checkBox1.Enabled = false;
63:         }
64:         else
65:         {
66:           MessageBox.Show("Unexpected initialization error.  " +
67:             ex.Message + "\n\nDetails:\n" + ex.ToString(),
68:             "Unexpected Initialization Error", MessageBoxButtons.OK,
69:             MessageBoxIcon.Error);
70:           this.Close();
71:         }
72:       }
73:     catch (Exception ex)
74:     {
75:       MessageBox.Show("Unexpected initialization error.  " + ex.Message +
76:         "\n\nDetails:\n" + ex.ToString(),
77:         "Unexpected Initialization Error", MessageBoxButtons.OK,
78:         MessageBoxIcon.Error);
79:       this.Close();
80:     }
81:   }
82:
83:   // Clean up any resources being used
84:   protected override void Dispose(bool disposing)
85:   {
86:     if (disposing)
87:     {
88:       if (components != null)
89:       {
90:         components.Dispose();
91:       }
92:     }
93:     base.Dispose(disposing);
94:   }
95:
96:   // Required method for Designer support
97:   private void InitializeComponent()
98:   {
99:     ...
100:   }
101:
```

LISTING 3.5 Continued

```
102:    // The main entry point for the application
103:    [STAThread]
104:    public static void Main()
105:    {
106:      Application.Run(new Form1());
107:    }
108:
109:    // Checks the spelling of the word contained in the string argument.
110:    // Returns true if spelled correctly, false otherwise.
111:    // This method ignores words in all uppercase letters if checkBox1
112:    // is checked.
113:    private bool CheckSpelling(string word)
114:    {
115:      ignoreUpper = checkBox1.Checked;
116:
117:      // Pass a reference to Type.Missing for each
118:      // by-reference optional parameter
119:
120:      return msWord.CheckSpelling(word, // Word
121:        ref missing,                    // CustomDictionary
122:        ref ignoreUpper,                // IgnoreUppercase
123:        ref missing,                    // AlwaysSuggest
124:        ref missing,                    // CustomDictionary2
125:        ref missing,                    // CustomDictionary3
126:        ref missing,                    // CustomDictionary4
127:        ref missing,                    // CustomDictionary5
128:        ref missing,                    // CustomDictionary6
129:        ref missing,                    // CustomDictionary7
130:        ref missing,                    // CustomDictionary8
131:        ref missing,                    // CustomDictionary9
132:        ref missing);                   // CustomDictionary10
133:    }
134:
135:    // Checks the spelling of the word contained in the string argument.
136:    // Returns a SpellingSuggestions collection, which is empty if the word
137:    // is spelled correctly.
138:    // This method ignores words in all uppercase letters if checkBox1
139:    // is checked.
140:    private Word.SpellingSuggestions GetSpellingSuggestions(string word)
141:    {
142:      ignoreUpper = checkBox1.Checked;
143:
144:      // Pass a reference to Type.Missing for each
145:      // by-reference optional parameter
```

LISTING 3.5   Continued

```
146:
147:     return msWord.GetSpellingSuggestions(word,  // Word
148:       ref missing,                              // CustomDictionary
149:       ref ignoreUpper,                          // IgnoreUppercase
150:       ref missing,                              // MainDictionary
151:       ref missing,                              // SuggestionMode
152:       ref missing,                              // CustomDictionary2
153:       ref missing,                              // CustomDictionary3
154:       ref missing,                              // CustomDictionary4
155:       ref missing,                              // CustomDictionary5
156:       ref missing,                              // CustomDictionary6
157:       ref missing,                              // CustomDictionary7
158:       ref missing,                              // CustomDictionary8
159:       ref missing,                              // CustomDictionary9
160:       ref missing);                             // CustomDictionary10
161:   }
162:
163:   // Called when the "Check Spelling" button is clicked.
164:   // Checks the spelling of each word and changes the font of
165:   // each misspelled word.
166:   private void button1_Click(object sender, EventArgs e)
167:   {
168:     try
169:     {
170:       // Return all text to normal since
171:       // underlined spaces might be left behind
172:       richTextBox1.SelectionStart = 0;
173:       richTextBox1.SelectionLength = richTextBox1.Text.Length;
174:       richTextBox1.SelectionFont = normalFont;
175:
176:       // Beginning location in the RichTextBox of the next word to check
177:       int index = 0;
178:
179:       // Enumerate over the collection of words obtained from String.Split
180:       foreach (string s in richTextBox1.Text.Split(null))
181:       {
182:         // Select the word
183:         richTextBox1.SelectionStart = index;
184:         richTextBox1.SelectionLength = s.Length;
185:
186:         // Trim off any ending punctuation in the selected text
187:         while (richTextBox1.SelectionLength > 0 &&
188:           Char.IsPunctuation(
189:           richTextBox1.Text[index + richTextBox1.SelectionLength - 1]))
```

LISTING 3.5   Continued

```
190:          {
191:            richTextBox1.SelectionLength--;
192:          }
193:
194:          // Check the word's spelling
195:          if (!CheckSpelling(s))
196:          {
197:            // Mark as incorrect
198:            richTextBox1.SelectionFont = errorFont;
199:            richTextBox1.SelectionColor = Color.Red;
200:          }
201:          else
202:          {
203:            // Mark as correct
204:            richTextBox1.SelectionFont = normalFont;
205:            richTextBox1.SelectionColor = Color.Black;
206:          }
207:
208:          // Update to point to the character after the current word
209:          index = index + s.Length + 1;
210:        }
211:      }
212:      catch (Exception ex)
213:      {
214:        MessageBox.Show("Unable to check spelling.  " + ex.Message +
215:          "\n\nDetails:\n" + ex.ToString(), "Unable to Check Spelling",
216:          MessageBoxButtons.OK, MessageBoxIcon.Error);
217:      }
218:    }
219:
220:    // Called when the user clicks anywhere on the text.  If the user
221:    // clicked the right mouse button, this determines the word underneath
222:    // the mouse pointer (if any) and presents a context menu of
223:    // spelling suggestions.
224:    private void richTextBox1_MouseDown(object sender, MouseEventArgs e)
225:    {
226:      try
227:      {
228:        if (e.Button == MouseButtons.Right)
229:        {
230:          // Get the location of the mouse pointer
231:          Point point = new Point(e.X, e.Y);
232:
233:          // Find the index of the character underneath the mouse pointer
```

3

THE ESSENTIALS
FOR USING COM
IN MANAGED CODE

LISTING 3.5   Continued

```
234:          int index = richTextBox1.GetCharIndexFromPosition(point);
235:
236:          // Length of the word underneath the mouse pointer
237:          int length = 1;
238:
239:          // If the character under the mouse pointer isn't whitespace,
240:          // determine what the word is and display spelling suggestions
241:
242:          if (!Char.IsWhiteSpace(richTextBox1.Text[index]))
243:          {
244:            // Going backward from the index,
245:            // figure out where the word begins
246:            while (index > 0 && !Char.IsWhiteSpace(
247:              richTextBox1.Text[index-1])) { index--; length++; }
248:
249:            // Going forward, figure out where the word ends,
250:            // making sure to not include punctuation except for apostrophes
251:            // (This works for English.)
252:            while (index + length < richTextBox1.Text.Length &&
253:              !Char.IsWhiteSpace(richTextBox1.Text[index + length]) &&
254:              (!Char.IsPunctuation(richTextBox1.Text[index + length]) ||
255:              richTextBox1.Text[index + length] == Char.Parse("'"))
256:              ) length++;
257:
258:            // Now that we've found the entire word, select it
259:            richTextBox1.SelectionStart = index;
260:            richTextBox1.SelectionLength = length;
261:
262:            // Clear the context menu in case
263:            // there are items on it from last time
264:            contextMenu1.MenuItems.Clear();
265:
266:            // Enumerate over the SpellingSuggestions collection
267:            // returned by GetSpellingSuggestions
268:            foreach (Word.SpellingSuggestion s in
269:              GetSpellingSuggestions(richTextBox1.SelectedText))
270:            {
271:              // Add the menu item with the suggestion text and the
272:              // Menu_Click handler
273:              contextMenu1.MenuItems.Add(s.Name, menuHandler);
274:            }
275:
276:            // Display special text if there are no spelling suggestions
277:            if (contextMenu1.MenuItems.Count == 0)
```

LISTING 3.5   Continued

```
278:              {
279:                  contextMenu1.MenuItems.Add("No suggestions.");
280:              }
281:              else
282:              {
283:                  // Add two more items whenever there are spelling suggestions.
284:                  // Since there is no event handler, nothing will happen when
285:                  // these are clicked.
286:                  contextMenu1.MenuItems.Add("-");
287:                  contextMenu1.MenuItems.Add("Don't change the spelling.");
288:              }
289:
290:              // Now that the menu is ready, show it
291:              contextMenu1.Show(richTextBox1, point);
292:            }
293:          }
294:        }
295:      catch (Exception ex)
296:      {
297:        MessageBox.Show("Unable to give spelling suggestions.  " +
298:            ex.Message + "\n\nDetails:\n" + ex.ToString(),
299:            "Unable to Give Spelling Suggestions", MessageBoxButtons.OK,
300:            MessageBoxIcon.Error);
301:      }
302:    }
303:
304:    // Called when a spelling suggestion is clicked on the context menu.
305:    // Replaces the currently selected text with the text
306:    // from the item clicked.
307:    private void Menu_Click(object sender, EventArgs e)
308:    {
309:      // The suggestion should be spelled correctly,
310:      // so restore the font to normal
311:      richTextBox1.SelectionFont = normalFont;
312:      richTextBox1.SelectionColor = Color.Black;
313:
314:      // Obtain the text from the MenuItem and replace the SelectedText
315:      richTextBox1.SelectedText = ((MenuItem)sender).Text;
316:    }
317: }
```

3

THE ESSENTIALS
FOR USING COM
IN MANAGED CODE

Line 17 declares the Application object used to communicate with Microsoft Word, and Lines 20–21 define the two different fonts that the application uses—one for correctly spelled words and one for misspelled words. Line 25 defines a `Missing` instance that is used for accepting the default behavior of optional parameters. It's defined as a `System.Object` due to C#'s requirement of exact type matching when passing by-reference parameters. The `ignoreUpper` variable in Line 26 tracks the user's preference about checking uppercase words, and the `menuHandler` delegate in Line 30 handles clicks on the context menu presented when a user right-clicks. Events and delegates are discussed in Chapter 5.

The `OnLoad` method in Lines 41–81 handles the initialization of Microsoft Word. If Word isn't installed, it displays a warning message and simply disables spell checking functionality rather than ending the entire program. The `CheckSpelling` method in Lines 113–133 returns true if the input word is spelled correctly, or false if it is misspelled (according to Word's own `CheckSpelling` method). The `GetSpellingSuggestions` method in Lines 140–161 returns a `SpellingSuggestions` collection returned by Word for the input string. These `CheckSpelling` and `GetSpellingSuggestions` methods wrap their corresponding Word methods simply because the original methods are cumbersome with all of the optional parameters that must be dealt with explicitly.

The `button1_Click` method in Lines 166–218, which is called when the user clicks the `Check Spelling` button, enumerates over every word inside the `RichTextBox` control and calls `CheckSpelling` to determine whether to underline each word. The `richTextBox1_MouseDown` method in Lines 224–302 determines if the user has right-clicked on a word. If so, it dynamically builds a context menu with the collection of spelling suggestions returned by the call to `GetSpellingSuggestions` in Line 269. The `Menu_Click` method in Lines 307–316 is the event handler associated with any misspelled words displayed on the context menu. When the user clicks a word in the menu, this method is called and Line 315 replaces the original text with the corrected text.

Microsoft Word is an out-of-process COM server, meaning that it runs in a separate process from the application that's using it. You can see this process while the example application runs by opening Windows Task Manager and looking for `WINWORD.EXE`.

Using Windows Task Manager, here's something you can try to see exception handling in action:

1. Start the example application.

2. Open Windows Task Manager by Pressing `Ctrl+Alt+Delete` (and, if appropriate, clicking the `Task Manager` button) and end the `WINWORD.EXE` process, as shown in Figure 3.16. The exact step depends on your version of Windows, but there should be a button marked either `End Process` or `End Task`.

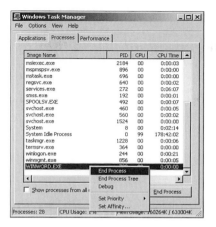

FIGURE 3.16
Ending the WINWORD.EXE process while the client application is still running.

3. Although the server has been terminated, the client application is still running. Now press the Check Spelling button on the example application.

4. Observe the dialog box that appears, which is shown in Figure 3.17. This is the result of the catch statement in the button1_Click method.

FIGURE 3.17
Handling a COMException caused by a failure HRESULT.

Conclusion

This chapter discussed a bunch of topics that are essential for using COM components in .NET applications. In this chapter, you've seen how to reference COM components via Interop Assemblies generated by the type library importer. Primary Interop Assemblies were also introduced, so you should understand why they should be used whenever possible instead of generating your own Interop Assemblies.

You've also seen the main ways to create a COM object:

With metadata:	`new` or `Type.GetType` + `Activator.CreateInstance`
Without metadata:	`Type.GetTypeFromProgID` or `Type.GetTypeFromCLSID` + `Activator.CreateInstance`

You've also seen how to invoke a COM object's methods via its v-table, or by late binding. The next chapter examines Interop Assemblies in detail so you can gain a better understanding on what to expect when using any COM objects in managed code, and how it differs from using them in COM-based languages.

An In-Depth Look at Imported Assemblies

IN THIS CHAPTER

- Converting the Library   141
- Converting COM Data Types   143
- Converting Methods and Properties   162
- Converting Interfaces   177
- Converting Classes   179
- Converting Modules   187
- Converting Structures   189
- Converting Unions   191
- Converting Enumerations   193
- Converting Typedefs   194
- Converting ActiveX Controls   196

Chapter 3, "The Essentials for Using COM in Managed Code," demonstrated how using a COM component in a .NET application can be just like using a .NET component after you've generated an Interop Assembly. Similarly, it showed how using an ActiveX control can be just like using a Windows Forms control after you've generated an ActiveX Assembly. With the help of the component's documentation and Visual Studio .NET's IntelliSense feature, perhaps many COM components and ActiveX controls can be used without an in-depth understanding of the contents of these assemblies and their relation to the original type libraries. However, it is often necessary to gain a deeper understanding of the type library importer and the ActiveX importer. After all, most COM components are documented from the perspective of an unmanaged C++ or Visual Basic 6 (VB6) user!

This chapter describes in depth the behavior of both the type library importer and the ActiveX importer. Each element that can be found in a type library (classes, interfaces, methods, properties, and so on) is discussed, one at a time. Although using types in an Interop Assembly often feels like using the same types in Visual Basic 6, metadata in an assembly and type information in a type library are quite different. Therefore, it's best to think of the generated metadata as a transformation of the type library, containing .NET definitions of the original COM types. These .NET definitions serve as type information for the Runtime-Callable Wrappers (RCWs) used at run time.

Rather than containing large examples, this chapter contains several short code listings that demonstrate each transformation. Because both metadata and type library information are stored as binary data, examples need to be shown in representative languages. Most COM examples are shown in Visual Basic 6 and Interface Definition Language (IDL) syntax, and most .NET examples are shown in C# and Visual Basic .NET syntax.

As mentioned in the previous chapter, the type information in an Interop Assembly tells the Interop Marshaler how to marshal data to and from the corresponding COM component. The metadata that the type library importer produces is not much different from the metadata found in any .NET component. It is simply decorated with custom attributes and pseudo-custom attributes that signal that special treatment from the CLR is required. The importer knows how to produce metadata type definitions that correspond to the Interop Marshaler's rules for converting unmanaged types to managed types. The Interop Marshaler is not general-purpose, but it is somewhat flexible. Thus, the designers of the type library importer have made some choices about how the metadata should look in situations with more than one possibility. In other words, the type definitions can be manually altered and still work without problems. The process of customizing the Interop Assembly is covered in Chapter 7, "Modifying Interop Assemblies."

Converting the Library

There is a one-to-one mapping between a type library and an Interop Assembly. The Interop Assembly always contains metadata for all the types in one type library. If the input type library references and uses types from additional type libraries, the importer automatically generates an additional assembly for each referenced type library.

> **CAUTION**
>
> In order for the type library importer to automatically generate additional Interop Assemblies for dependent type libraries, the dependent type libraries must be registered. This is necessary because type libraries are referenced via Library IDs (LIBIDs), and the Windows Registry is the only mechanism capable of locating them. If Primary Interop Assemblies are registered for dependent type libraries, they will be referenced automatically by the imported assembly.

The generated Interop Assembly is always a single-file assembly. When created by TLBIMP.EXE, the default assembly name is equal to the library name, and the default filename is equal to the library name plus .dll. When created inside Visual Studio .NET, the assembly name and filename are Interop.*LibraryName* and Interop.*LibraryName*.dll, respectively. In either case, all the types inside the assembly reside in a single namespace equal to the library name.

The library name is not necessarily the filename of the file containing the type library. In Visual Basic 6 it's known as the project name, and in IDL it's the name of the library statement (highlighted in the following IDL code):

```
[
  uuid(C866CA3A-32F7-11D2-9602-00C04F8EE628),
  version(5.0),
  helpstring("Microsoft Speech Object Library")
]
library SpeechLib
{
  importlib("stdole2.tlb");
  ...
  coclass SpVoice {
    [default] interface ISpeechVoice;
    interface ISpVoice;
    [default, source] dispinterface _ISpeechVoiceEvents;
  };
  ...
};
```

As you saw in Chapter 3, an Interop Assembly called `SpeechLib.dll` is generated with types such as `SpeechLib.SpVoice` for a type library containing this information. Using the library name as a namespace should feel natural to VB6 programmers because these same names serve a similar purpose in VB6 code.

CAUTION

Sometimes COM components have a library name that is the same as the filename containing the type library. This is quite common for components authored in Visual Basic 6, because the default behavior of the IDE makes them the same (for example, `Project1`). An example of this can be seen by running `TLBIMP.EXE` on the Microsoft XML type library (`MSXML.DLL`) from the same directory in which it resides on your computer:

```
C:\windows\system32>TlbImp MSXML.dll
```

For this situation, `TLBIMP.EXE` gives the following message:

```
TlbImp error: Output file would overwrite input file
```

The solution is to have `TLBIMP.EXE` place the output file in a different directory and/or choose a different name for the output file using the `/out` option:

```
TlbImp MSXML.dll /out:Interop.MSXML.dll
```

```
TlbImp MSXML.dll /out:C:\MyApplication\MSXML.dll
```

Be extremely careful with the `/out` option, however, because the name you choose for the filename will also become the namespace associated with all the type definitions contained within (minus the `.dll` extension, of course). The bad thing about this is whatever case you use—`msxml`, `MsXmL`, `MSXML`, and so on—will become the case of the namespace. To avoid this confusion, you should set the namespace independently of the output filename by using the `/namespace` option.

The output assembly, like all assemblies, has a four-part version number (*Major.Minor.Build. Revision*). Type libraries have a two-part version number (*Major.Minor*), so the assembly produced has the version *Major.Minor*.0.0. The culture of the assembly is always marked as neutral, and it doesn't have a strong name unless it was produced using the `TLBIMP.EXE` strong-naming options described in Chapter 15, "Creating and Deploying Useful Primary Interop Assemblies." In Visual Studio .NET, the `General` property page for Visual C# projects enables users to select a key file or key container used to give Interop Assemblies a strong name. These options are labeled `Wrapper Assembly Key File` and `Wrapper Assembly Key Name`. If you decide to use one of these options, be sure to do it *before* referencing the COM components! This option is not available to Visual Basic .NET or Visual C++ .NET projects. The reasoning for this is that you should attempt to find a Primary Interop Assembly for a COM component you wish to use (which is already strong-named) rather than giving it your own strong name.

Now that we've covered the properties of the output assembly, we'll look in depth at how the contents of the assembly are produced, based on the input type library. Because everything in a type library is implicitly public (otherwise it would simply be omitted from the type information), every type and member is public in the output assembly.

Converting COM Data Types

A type library is typically filled with data types used as method or property parameters, fields of structures, and so on. Every data type occurrence in a type library is converted to an equivalent data type in the Interop Assembly's metadata. Table 4.1 lists the transformations done by the type library importer. Each COM data type is shown in two representations: IDL and Visual Basic 6. The .NET type is shown as the language-neutral system type. Keep in mind what the system type means in your language of choice, shown in Chapter 1, "Introduction to the .NET Framework." For example, although System.Int16 can be used in any .NET language, it is typically referred to by the alias short. (When compiled, short becomes System.Int16 in MSIL.)

CAUTION

When browsing type libraries, OLEVIEW.EXE doesn't display the COM DECIMAL type correctly, showing wchar_t instead.

TABLE 4.1   COM Data Types are Converted to .NET Data Types with Similar Semantics

IDL Type	VB6 Type	.NET Type
char	N/A	System.SByte
short	Integer	System.Int16
int, long, HRESULT, and SCODE	Long	System.Int32
int64	N/A	System.Int64
unsigned char	Byte	System.Byte
unsigned short	N/A	System.UInt16
unsigned int and unsigned long	N/A	System.UInt32
uint64	N/A	System.UInt64
float	Single	System.Single
double	Double	System.Double
BSTR, LPSTR, and LPWSTR	String	System.String
VARIANT_BOOL	Boolean	System.Boolean

TABLE 4.1   Continued

IDL Type	VB6 Type	.NET Type
DATE	Date	System.DateTime
GUID	N/A	System.Guid
DECIMAL	N/A	System.Decimal
CURRENCY	Currency	System.Decimal
VARIANT	Variant	System.Object
IUnknown*	Unknown	System.Object
IDispatch*	Object	System.Object
void*	Any	System.IntPtr
IDispatchEx*	IDispatchEx	System.Runtime.InteropServices.Expando.IExpando
IEnumVARIANT*	IEnumVARIANT	System.Collections.IEnumerator
ITypeInfo*	ITypeInfo	System.Type

This table is accurate for data types used as parameters, but the conversions are sometimes slightly different for data types used as fields of structures. This is discussed in the "Converting Structures" section later in the chapter.

The IDL data types in Table 4.1 represent the OLEVIEW.EXE IDL representation of data types contained in a type library (with the exception of DECIMAL). However, IDL can contain a variety of distinct types for the same type library type. Thus, some information can be lost when creating a type library from IDL.

TIP

Because IDL files or documentation for COM components might refer to some data types not mentioned in Table 4.1, it's helpful to know how these additional types look inside a type library. For example:

- boolean and small become char
- wchar_t becomes unsigned short
- hyper and __int64 become int64
- [string] char* becomes LPSTR
- [string] wchar_t* becomes LPWSTR
- byte becomes unsigned char
- unsigned hyper and unsigned __int64 become uint64

Combining Several Types in One

In Table 4.1 you can see that, as in the conversion from IDL to a type library, distinct type library types can become a single data type in .NET. This continual loss of information is pictured in Figure 4.1.

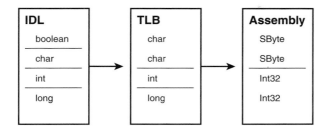

FIGURE 4.1

Information about data types can be lost when moving from an IDL definition to a type library definition, and when moving from a type library definition to a metadata definition.

As mentioned in the previous chapter, some common types used in COM no longer exist in the .NET Framework: CURRENCY, VARIANT, IUnknown, IDispatch, SCODE, and HRESULT. With the exception of HRESULT versus SCODE, the original type library type isn't *lost* when converted to metadata, just hidden in a pseudo-custom attribute called MarshalAsAttribute (commonly abbreviated as MarshalAs). MarshalAsAttribute (described further in Chapter 12, "Customizing COM's View of .NET Components") has a constructor with an UnmanagedType parameter. UnmanagedType is an enumeration in System.Runtime.InteropServices that defines the range of types found in a type library.

> **DIGGING DEEPER**
>
> If you open the mscorlib assembly in the IL Disassembler, you can see that System.Currency and System.Variant types do exist in the .NET Framework! These are non-public types, however, and thus cannot be used.

Each potentially ambiguous .NET type that the importer produces (Int32, Decimal, String, and Object) is marked with MarshalAsAttribute. The following sections look more closely at these types, explaining the rationale behind their removal from the .NET Framework, and why the COM types are mapped to .NET types the way they are.

VARIANT, IUnknown*, and IDispatch*

The root of all COM interfaces is IUnknown. For any class to be considered a COM object, it must implement at least IUnknown. (All COM objects written in Visual Basic 6 implement IUnknown; it's just hidden from the programmer.) For these reasons, an occurrence of IUnknown* in COM has a role like the System.Object type in the .NET Framework, which can be used to represent a reference to any type. It's not quite that simple in COM, however, because base types (like integers and strings) are not COM objects and can't implement interfaces. So, IUnknown* really means a pointer to any *interface*.

COM also has a VARIANT type that can contain anything: interface pointers, base types (such as integers), or even user-defined structures. Because a System.Object instance can *be* any type, and a VARIANT instance can *contain* any type, a mapping between these two is natural.

IDispatch is an interface that is implemented by most COM objects to support late binding, although it's not required the way IUnknown is. IDispatch doesn't exist in the managed world, because every .NET object automatically has the late binding functionality of IDispatch through reflection mechanisms. Because every .NET object supports late binding, there is also a pretty strong relationship between IDispatch* (a pointer to an interface that supports late binding) and System.Object (a reference to an object that supports late binding). Note that Visual Basic 6 has an Object type that really means IDispatch*.

Rather than carrying forward a distinction between these generic types in .NET, they have all been merged into the single System.Object type. By default, a System.Object in a managed signature is assumed to be a VARIANT in COM. If it's supposed to represent IUnknown* or IDispatch*, the type in the signature must be marked with MarshalAsAttribute and the appropriate UnmanagedType values. Listing 4.1 demonstrates this by showing the transformation of three method signatures from VB6/IDL to metadata, as viewed by C# and Visual Basic .NET. The type library importer would actually mark the parameter of the VariantParameter method with MarshalAs(UnmanagedType.Struct) (which means VARIANT) but this is omitted from the listing because it's the default behavior for Object parameters.

LISTING 4.1   The COM View and the .NET View of the Same Methods with VARIANT, IUnknown*, and IDispatch* Parameters

---

`UNMANAGED`

Visual Basic 6:

```
Public Sub VariantParameter(ByVal var As Variant)

Public Sub IUnknownParameter(ByVal unk As IUnknown)

Public Sub IDispatchParameter(ByVal disp As Object)
```

LISTING 4.1 Continued

IDL:

```
HRESULT VariantParameter([in] VARIANT var);

HRESULT IUnknownParameter([in] IUnknown* unk);

HRESULT IDispatchParameter([in] IDispatch* disp);
```

MANAGED

C#:

```
public virtual void VariantParameter(Object var);

public virtual void IUnknownParameter(
  [MarshalAs(UnmanagedType.IUnknown)] Object unk);

public virtual void IDispatchParameter(
  [MarshalAs(UnmanagedType.IDispatch)] Object disp);
```

Visual Basic .NET:

```
Public Overridable Sub VariantParameter(ByVal var As Object)

Public Overridable Sub IUnknownParameter( _
  <MarshalAs(UnmanagedType.IUnknown)> ByVal unk As Object)

Public Overridable Sub IDispatchParameter( _
  <MarshalAs(UnmanagedType.IDispatch)> ByVal disp As Object)
```

> **TIP**
>
> `MarshalAsAttribute` is always marked on signatures; not on the use of such signatures. Therefore, you never need to use or be aware of the existence of `MarshalAsAttribute` when calling members of COM objects in managed code. The type library importer takes care of the necessary custom attribute markings for you.

The `void*` type is commonly used in C++ to represent a pointer to anything, so you might expect this to also be converted to `System.Object`. As you can see in Table 4.1, it's converted to `System.IntPtr`, an integer with the size of a pointer. This conversion must be done because the memory pointed to by the `void*` can be absolutely anything. So, there can be no standard mechanism to transform it into a `System.Object`. Fortunately, `VARIANT` or `IUnknown*` are typically used in COM methods instead of `void*`. So, what can you do with a `System.IntPtr` type in managed code? This is covered in Chapter 6, "Advanced Topics for Using COM Components."

> | **TIP**
> |
> | The .NET type System.IntPtr is not a pointer to an integer, but an integer *of size pointer*, just as System.Int16 is an integer of size 16 bits and System.Int32 is an integer of size 32 bits. This is like the Win32 INT_PTR type. It is typically used to hold a pointer to an object, because the size of an object's address changes depending on the underlying platform (for example, 32 or 64 bits).

CURRENCY and DECIMAL

COM has separate types for CURRENCY and DECIMAL, but the .NET Framework has no public System.Currency type, only System.Decimal. A separate currency type in .NET was eliminated because the Decimal type can represent anything that COM's CURRENCY type can represent. Thus, .NET applications use the System.Decimal type for storing currency values. Because of this, it's natural for DECIMAL in COM to become System.Decimal, and for CURRENCY in COM to become System.Decimal marked with the MarshalAsAttribute pseudo-custom attribute. Listing 4.2 shows the transformation.

LISTING 4.2 The COM View and the .NET View of the Same Methods with DECIMAL and CURRENCY Parameters

`UNMANAGED`

Visual Basic 6:

```
' The DECIMAL type is not supported in VB6.

Public Sub CurrencyParameter(ByVal money As Currency)
```

IDL:

```
HRESULT DecimalParameter([in] DECIMAL number);

HRESULT CurrencyParameter([in] CURRENCY money);
```

`MANAGED`

C#:

```
public virtual void DecimalParameter(Decimal number);

public virtual void CurrencyParameter(
  [MarshalAs(UnmanagedType.Currency)] Decimal money);
```

LISTING 4.2   Continued

Visual Basic .NET:

```
Public Overridable Sub DecimalParameter(ByVal number As Decimal)

Public Overridable Sub CurrencyParameter( _
  <MarshalAs(UnmanagedType.Currency)> ByVal money As Decimal)
```

BSTR, LPSTR, and LPWSTR

BSTR (basic string), LPSTR (pointer to string), and LPWSTR (pointer to wide-character string) are three distinct types used to represent a string in unmanaged code, so they all become System.String in metadata. This is consistent with Visual Basic 6, in which all three of these type library types are treated as a String. So, what's the difference between them?

- BSTR, which stands for either *basic string* or *binary string*, is the most commonly used string type in COM. It contains Unicode characters and is prefixed with its length. Because the length of the string is always known, a BSTR can contain embedded null characters. String types authored in Visual Basic 6 are BSTRs.

- LPSTR is a pointer to an array of ANSI characters. The end of the string is marked with a null character. Although less commonly used in COM than a BSTR, an LPSTR is more convenient to use in unmanaged C++ code.

- LPWSTR is a pointer to an array of Unicode characters, with the end marked by a null character. The *W* stands for *wide*, because each Unicode character consumes twice as much memory as an ANSI character (two bytes instead of one).

Listing 4.3 shows the transformation with these three types of strings. The type library importer would actually mark the parameter of the BStrParameter method with MarshalAs(UnmanagedType.BStr) but this is omitted from the listing because it's the default behavior for String parameters.

LISTING 4.3   The COM View and the .NET View of the Same Methods with a Variety of String Parameters

`UNMANAGED`

Visual Basic 6:

```
' The LPSTR and LPWSTR types cannot be defined in VB6.

Public Sub BStrParameter(ByVal text As String)
```

IDL:

```
HRESULT LPStrParameter([in] LPSTR text);
```

LISTING 4.3   Continued

```
HRESULT LPWStrParameter([in] LPWSTR text);

HRESULT BStrParameter([in] BSTR text);
```

MANAGED

C#:

```csharp
public virtual void LPStrParameter(
  [MarshalAs(UnmanagedType.LPStr)] string text);

public virtual void LPWStrParameter(
  [MarshalAs(UnmanagedType.LPWStr)] string text);

public virtual void BStrParameter(string text);
```

Visual Basic .NET:

```vb
Public Overridable Sub LPStrParameter( _
  <MarshalAs(UnmanagedType.LPStr)> ByVal text As String)

Public Overridable Sub LPWStrParameter( _
  <MarshalAs(UnmanagedType.LPWStr)> ByVal text As String)

Public Overridable Sub BStrParameter(ByVal text As String)
```

If a COM method has an LPSTR or LPWSTR parameter treated as an [in, out] buffer, the importer still represents it as a by-value System.String, which is not appropriate because a .NET string is immutable. Using the techniques described in Chapters 6 and 7, you could change the parameter to a System.IntPtr type instead and use it in an appropriate way.

SCODE and HRESULT

The SCODE and HRESULT types don't exist in the .NET Framework, so they become 32-bit integers in managed code (again, with the MarshalAsAttribute pseudo-custom attribute).

> ## FAQ: What is an SCODE and how does it differ from an HRESULT?
>
> An SCODE (which stands for *status code*) is a number that describes an error or warning. On 16-bit platforms, an SCODE was used as a step to creating an HRESULT, but on 32-bit platforms, SCODE and HRESULT are just different names for the exact same thing. There are still subtle differences when using these types; for example, an SCODE is a valid type to store in a VARIANT (using the variant type VT_SCODE), but an HRESULT is not (using the variant type VT_HRESULT). Because there is no value in preserving the distinction between these types in managed code, they are indicated by the more general UnmanagedType.Error enumeration value when imported to an Interop Assembly.

You saw in the preceding chapter that the HRESULT return values are hidden in managed signatures, just as in Visual Basic 6. Thus, this transformation mainly comes into play with HRESULT and SCODE parameters. It's rare to see such a thing, but Listing 4.4 provides an example.

LISTING 4.4   The COM View and the .NET View of the Same Methods with SCODE and HRESULT Parameters

`UNMANAGED`

IDL:

```
HRESULT SCodeParameter([in] SCODE scode);

HRESULT HResultParameter([in] HRESULT hr);
```

`MANAGED`

C#:

```
public virtual void SCodeParameter(
  [MarshalAs(UnmanagedType.Error)] int scode);

public virtual void HResultParameter([MarshalAs(UnmanagedType.Error)] int hr);
```

Visual Basic .NET:

```
Public Overridable Sub SCodeParameter( _
  <MarshalAs(UnmanagedType.Error)> ByVal scode As Integer)

Public Overridable Sub HResultParameter( _
  <MarshalAs(UnmanagedType.Error)> ByVal hr As Integer)
```

Unlike with the previously examined types, MarshalAsAttribute is mainly for informational purposes when used with UnmanagedType.Error, as the data is still just marshaled as a 32-bit number.

FAQ: If HRESULTs are really unsigned integers, why are they represented as *signed* integers in managed code?

The type library importer attempts to generate CLS-compliant code whenever possible so that the type definitions can be usable by any .NET language. Unsigned integers are not in the CLS, and Visual Basic .NET doesn't support them. Although the importer converts plain unsigned integers into the non-CLS-compliant System.UInt32, converting HRESULTs to signed integers is consistent with the CLS-compliant Exception class (which stores its corresponding HRESULT as a signed integer).

4

AN IN-DEPTH LOOK AT IMPORTED ASSEMBLIES

Complex Types

Data types in a type library can be more complex than the basic ones listed in Table 4.1, such as user-defined classes, interfaces, structs, or an array of any other type. Each complex type is converted to a corresponding .NET complex type, and these are covered throughout the rest of this chapter. The transformation for the use of these types as parameters or fields is usually simple: With two exceptions, an occurrence of any unmanaged type *X*, *Y*, or *Z* as a parameter or field is transformed into the managed type *X*, *Y*, or *Z*. One exception is the set of types listed in Table 4.1. The other exception is for default interfaces that are only implemented by one class inside a type library. More about this is discussed in the "Converting Classes" section.

In this section, we're first going to take a look at what happens to three special interface types (listed in Table 4.1) that don't abide by the typical rules. After this, we examine array types.

IDispatchEx, IEnumVARIANT, and ITypeInfo Interface Pointers

Occurrences of IDispatchEx*, IEnumVARIANT*, and ITypeInfo*, which represent pointers to standard COM interfaces (like IUnknown* and IDispatch*), are converted to different .NET types with similar semantics in the managed world. These COM interfaces have the following semantics:

- IDispatchEx. This obscure and poorly documented interface is an extension to IDispatch that, besides enabling dynamic invocation, enables dynamic addition and removal of members. The .NET equivalent interface is IExpando. IDispatchEx is mainly used by unmanaged scripting languages, such as JScript, and IExpando is mainly used by managed scripting languages, such as JScript .NET.

- IEnumVARIANT. This interface provides the means to enumerate over a collection of VARIANTs. It is almost identical to IEnumerator, the .NET interface that provides the means to enumerate over a collection of Objects. Thus, IEnumVARIANT* parameters and fields are transformed into IEnumerator types.

- ITypeInfo. Using this interface is the standard COM way to programmatically view an object's type information. The managed analog to this interface is the System.Type class, the gateway to reflection.

The transformation of IDispatchEx*, IEnumVARIANT*, and ITypeInfo* parameters and fields to IExpando, IEnumerator, and Type parameters and fields, respectively, are essential in making COM objects seamlessly usable in .NET. That's because .NET applications are designed to use these new types for the same common tasks. If using a COM collection in managed code required calling methods on IEnumVARIANT, many .NET clients would need to have separate code to deal with .NET collections and COM collections (not to mention an extra step to determine whether it's dealing with a pure .NET object or a COM object)!

The `IEnumVARIANT` to `IEnumerator` transformation is part of what enables `foreach` in C# and `For Each` in VB .NET to work on a COM object (as demonstrated in the preceding chapter), because these language constructs call the methods of `IEnumerator`. The other part that makes this work is covered later in this chapter, in the "Special DISPIDs" section.

DIGGING DEEPER

The transformations of `IDispatchEx*`, `IEnumVARIANT*`, and `ITypeInfo*` are done using custom marshaling (covered in Chapter 20, "Custom Marshaling"). This minor implementation detail has two effects:

- The transformed types in the Interop Assembly are marked with `MarshalAsAttribute` in such a way as to make the custom marshaling work.
- It's possible to get the raw COM data type if you really want to use it by taking advantage of an interface called `ICustomAdapter`. See Chapter 20 for more information.

Listing 4.5 demonstrates the transformation for an `IEnumVARIANT*` parameter, which assumes that the `System.Runtime.InteropServices.CustomMarshalers` namespace is being used/imported in addition to `System.Runtime.InteropServices`, and also that the `CustomMarshalers` assembly that ships with the .NET Framework is being referenced.

LISTING 4.5 `IEnumVARIANT*` Parameters are Transformed to `IEnumerator` Types Providing the Same Enumeration Semantics in a .NET-Centric Manner

---

UNMANAGED

Visual Basic 6:

```
Public Sub EnumeratorParameter(ByVal enum As IEnumVARIANT)
```

IDL:

```
HRESULT EnumeratorParameter([in] IEnumVARIANT* enum);
```

MANAGED

C#:

```
public virtual void EnumeratorParameter(
  [MarshalAs(UnmanagedType.CustomMarshaler,
  MarshalTypeRef=typeof(EnumeratorToEnumVariantMarshaler))] IEnumerator e);
```

LISTING 4.5 Continued

Visual Basic .NET:

```
Public Overridable Sub EnumeratorParameter( _
  <MarshalAs(UnmanagedType.CustomMarshaler, _
   MarshalTypeRef:=GetType(EnumeratorToEnumVariantMarshaler))> _
  ByVal e As IEnumerator);
```

Arrays

The transformation of COM arrays from a type library to .NET metadata is an interesting topic because it's filled with limitations and gotchas. First, we'll take a look at the most common type of array, a SAFEARRAY. Then we'll look at a handful of array representations that are lumped into a category known as *C-style arrays*. A C-style array is simply a pointer to a type, and that type happens to be the first element of an array (a contiguous sequence of types in memory). To differentiate a pointer to a single instance from a pointer to the beginning of an array, IDL contains a plethora of attributes that describe the pointer: length_is, size_is, first_is, last_is, and max_is. (There's even a min_is attribute, but this is never used on Microsoft platforms!) Different combinations of these attributes affect the way the array is classified, as described in the following sections.

SAFEARRAYS

In COM, an array is typically represented as a SAFEARRAY type. A SAFEARRAY is a self-describing array that can contain any type capable of being placed in a VARIANT. It can have any number of dimensions—each with distinct upper and lower bounds. A SAFEARRAY is the same as Visual Basic 6's array type.

The default importer behavior when encountering SAFEARRAYs differs depending on whether you use TLBIMP.EXE or Visual Studio .NET. When referencing a type library in Visual Studio .NET, the IDE effectively runs TLBIMP.EXE with its /sysarray option. This means that every occurrence of a SAFEARRAY is converted to a System.Array type. System.Array is the base class of all .NET arrays, and is flexible enough to represent anything a SAFEARRAY can represent (multiple dimensions and custom bounds for each dimension).

The problem with System.Array is that it's more cumbersome to use in the current .NET languages than more specific array types (reminiscent of using SAFEARRAYs in unmanaged C++). Elements of a System.Array must be accessed via methods such as GetValue and SetValue. Furthermore, the type of a System.Array's elements is not known at compile time, so you lose a degree of strong typing when using these generic arrays.

TIP

> If you're interacting with a COM object whose imported members use System.Array types, the easiest way to get and set array elements is to first cast the System.Array type to a more specific array, such as int[,] in C#. Casting a System.Array works for arrays of any type or dimension (as long as you're casting it to the same kind of array) but does not work for an array with any non-zero lower bounds in C#, Visual Basic .NET, or C++. This limitation exists simply because these languages don't natively support arrays with non-zero lower bounds, so there's no matching array type to which you can cast the System.Array!

Suppose that a Visual Basic 6 COM object has a method called ReturnArray that returns a two-dimensional SAFEARRAY. In C#, it could be used as a generic System.Array as follows:

```
Array a = comObj.ReturnArray();

// Don't assume anything about the lower bounds, but assume
// we're dealing with a 2-D array.
for (int i = a.GetLowerBound(0); i <= a.GetUpperBound(0); i++)
{
  for (int j = a.GetLowerBound(1); j <= a.GetUpperBound(1); j++)
  {
    a.SetValue((int)a.GetValue(i, j) * 2, i, j);
  }
}
```

For a simple case such as this, there are better alternatives such as using foreach to access each element of the array regardless of the number of dimensions. However, the methods of System.Array are used just to demonstrate what dealing with the generic Array type might look like.

If we know that both dimensions have a zero lower bound, however, we could cast it to a more specific array type and interact with that instead:

```
int [,] a = (int [,]) comObj.ReturnArray();

// We know the lower bounds must be zero if the cast succeeded.
for (int i = 0; i < a.GetLength(0); i++)
{
  for (int j = 0; j < a.GetLength(1); j++)
  {
    a[i,j] = a[i,j] * 2;
  }
}
```

Because `System.Array` types can be a hassle to use, `TLBIMP.EXE` provides a choice for how `SAFEARRAY`s should be imported into an Interop Assembly. If you use the `/sysarray` option from a command prompt, the behavior matches Visual Studio .NET. If you don't use the `/sysarray` option and accept the default command-line behavior, all `SAFEARRAY`s are imported as *one-dimensional* arrays with a zero lower bound. The importer can't do anything more appropriate because `SAFEARRAY`s don't describe their bounds or rank in a type library—only the type of their elements.

If a COM component only uses `SAFEARRAY`s that are single-dimensional and have a lower bound of zero, the default `TLBIMP.EXE` behavior works great. For such components that don't already have a Primary Interop Assembly, it's a good idea to use `TLBIMP.EXE` from a command prompt and reference the output assembly in Visual Studio .NET rather than referencing the type library directly in Visual Studio .NET. This way, you can eliminate the use of `System.Array` in the imported signatures.

Of course, if a COM component intends to communicate with either multi-dimensional `SAFEARRAY`s or `SAFEARRAY`s with non-zero lower bounds, the default `TLBIMP.EXE` transformation would not be acceptable. .NET clients would be prevented from passing anything other than a 1-D zero-lower-bound array by the compiler, and COM clients would be prevented from passing anything other than a 1-D zero-lower-bound array by an exception thrown by the Interop Marshaler.

The `/sysarray` option in `TLBIMP.EXE` is a crude switch that affects how every array in a type library is presented to the .NET world. If you desire more fine-grained control, or want certain arrays to be imported as multi-dimensional arrays with a fixed rank, see Chapter 7.

CAUTION

Although version 1.0 of the Interop Marshaler does not support marshaling `VARIANT`s containing structures (UDTs), marshaling `SAFEARRAY`s of structures is supported when passed as a parameter. There's an important limitation to this support, however: Any structure used as `SAFEARRAY` elements must be described in a registered type library, *and* must be marked with a GUID in the original type library! All UDTs defined in Visual Basic 6 are marked with GUIDs, but several COM components do not mark their structs with GUIDs.

A quick way to see whether a struct can be marshaled in a `SAFEARRAY` is to call `Marshal.GetITypeInfoForType`, passing the type of the imported value type inside an Interop Assembly. If this succeeds, then it can be marshaled inside a `SAFEARRAY` successfully. If not, then one workaround is to modify the type library containing the structure definition using `OLEVIEW.EXE` to get an IDL representation, and using `MIDL.EXE` to compile an updated IDL file to a new type library.

Fixed-Length Arrays

Fixed-length arrays (or more simply, fixed arrays) don't use any of the aforementioned IDL attributes that are typically used with C-style arrays. Instead, a constant array capacity is simply specified in its declaration (shown here in IDL):

```
HRESULT 1DFixedArrayParameter([in] double arr[10]);
```

```
HRESULT 2DFixedArrayParameter([in] double arr[2][5]);
```

Method signatures with fixed-length arrays cannot be authored in Visual Basic 6, but can be called correctly from a Visual Basic 6 program. The type library importer preserves fixed-length arrays in metadata by using a variation of `MarshalAsAttribute` with an additional `SizeConst` property set to the constant value. For parameters, the importer marks fixed arrays with `UnmanagedType.LPArray` (pointer to an array) and for fields of structures, the importer marks fixed arrays with `UnmanagedType.ByValArray` (all the elements are embedded in the structure).

The .NET array that corresponds to a fixed array is a flattened, one-dimensional version of the original array in row-major order. Unlike the case for SAFEARRAYs, this flattening transformation is done to accommodate an Interop Marshaler limitation rather than a limitation in type library expressiveness. The Interop Marshaler simply doesn't support fixed-length arrays with more than one dimension in Version 1.0. Listing 4.6 demonstrates the transformation of fixed-length arrays for both parameters and fields.

LISTING 4.6 The COM View and the .NET View of the Same Fixed-Length Arrays

`UNMANAGED`

IDL:

```
typedef [uuid(8A8997DF-E100-4416-B63C-BE50D20B6B51)]
struct HasFixedArrays
{
  double arr1[10];
  double arr2[2][5];
} HasFixedArray;

HRESULT FixedArrayParameter1D([in] double arr[10]);

HRESULT FixedArrayParameter2D([in] double arr[2][5]);
```

VB6 (as seen in the VB6 object browser):

```
Public Type HasFixedArrays
  arr1(0 To 9) As Double
  arr2(0 To 1, 0 To 4) As Double
End Type
```

LISTING 4.6   Continued

```
Sub FixedArrayParameter1D(arr(0 To 9) As Double)

Sub FixedArrayParameter2D(arr(0 To 1, 0 To 4) As Double)
```

| MANAGED |

C#:

```
[Guid("8A8997DF-E100-4416-B63C-BE50D20B6B51")]
public struct HasFixedArrays
{
  [MarshalAs(UnmanagedType.ByValArray, SizeConst=10)]
  public double [] arr1;
  [MarshalAs(UnmanagedType.ByValArray, SizeConst=10)]
  public double [] arr2;
}

public virtual void FixedArrayParameter1D(
  [MarshalAs(UnmanagedType.LPArray, SizeConst=10)] double [] arr);

public virtual void FixedArrayParameter2D(
  [MarshalAs(UnmanagedType.LPArray, SizeConst=10)] double [] arr);
```

Visual Basic .NET:

```
<Guid("8A8997DF-E100-4416-B63C-BE50D20B6B51")> _
Public Structure HasFixedArrays
  <MarshalAs(UnmanagedType.ByValArray, SizeConst:=10)> _
  Public arr1() As Double
  <MarshalAs(UnmanagedType.ByValArray, SizeConst:=10)> _
  Public arr2() As Double
End Structure

Public Overridable Sub FixedArrayParameter1D( _
  <MarshalAs(UnmanagedType.LPArray, SizeConst:=10)> ByVal arr() As Double)

Public Overridable Sub FixedArrayParameter2D( _
  <MarshalAs(UnmanagedType.LPArray, SizeConst:=10)> ByVal arr() As Double)
```

Varying Arrays

Varying arrays look similar to fixed-length arrays, but enable you to pass only a contiguous slice of the array. This is sometimes a handy optimization in COM, especially when calls must be marshaled across process or computer boundaries. The size and location of the slice is specified at run time with separate parameters. These parameters contain the number of elements in the transmitted slice and the index of the first element. The relationship between the array parameter and these special parameters is indicated with the IDL length_is and first_is attributes, demonstrated in the following IDL signatures:

```
HRESULT VaryingArrayParameter1(
  [in, length_is(length)] double arr[256], [in] long length);

HRESULT VaryingArrayParameter2(
  [in, length_is(length), first_is(start)] double arr[256],
  [in] long length, [in] long start);

HRESULT VaryingArrayParameter3(
  [in, length_is(10), first_is(5)] double arr[256]);
```

The expression inside `length_is` indicates the number of elements in the array slice, and the expression inside `first_is` indicates the index of the first element in the slice. If `first_is` is not specified, the first element of the slice is the first element of the array (index 0). The expressions inside the `length_is` and `first_is` attribute statements could be constants, parameters, or mathematical expressions. As with fixed-length arrays, however, the array's capacity must be specified at compile time.

DIGGING DEEPER

An alternative to specifying `length_is` would be to use the `last_is` IDL attribute to specify the last (highest) index of the slice in the array. Therefore, specifying a `length_is` of *x* would be equivalent to specifying a `last_is` equal to `first_is` + *x*. The choice of `length_is` versus `last_is` is purely a cosmetic one.

Hopefully the discussion of all these IDL attributes was enlightening, but the bad news is that none of these attributes are present in a type library. Type libraries weren't designed to hold this information. If you create a type library from an IDL file containing varying arrays, they end up looking just like plain old fixed-length arrays. This can be verified by opening the type library using OLEVIEW.EXE, where the previous signatures would look like the following:

```
HRESULT VaryingArrayParameter1([in] double arr[256], [in] long length);

HRESULT VaryingArrayParameter2(
  [in] double arr[256], [in] long length, [in] long start);

HRESULT VaryingArrayParameter3([in] double arr[256]);
```

Because the type library importer uses a type library as input, and not an IDL file, it has no idea that these arrays were meant to be associated with special semantics. The `length` parameter in this example is a good hint for a human observer, but it's meaningless to the importer. Thus, such parameters are imported as regular fixed-length array parameters representing the entire array.

4

AN IN-DEPTH LOOK AT IMPORTED ASSEMBLIES

Conformant Arrays

The *conformance* of an array is its capacity. A *conformant array* is therefore an array with a dynamic capacity. This is in contrast to a varying array, which is a dynamic slice of a fixed-capacity array. Conformant arrays can have any capacity specified at run time in a separate size parameter. The relationship between the array parameter and size parameter is indicated by the IDL size_is attribute. (The expression inside size_is contains the number of elements in the array.)

As with the other IDL array-related attributes, size_is cannot appear in a type library. The result of this is that the type library importer sees such a parameter as a pointer to a single instance, not an array of any kind. The conversion for conformant arrays is demonstrated in Listing 4.7. The ConformantArray2D IDL signature uses size_is to mark the capacity of each dimension in the two-dimensional array. There are many permutations of size_is with multi-dimensional arrays, but the example shown is a common usage.

Listing 4.7 The .NET View of Conformant Arrays is Quite Different from the COM View Due to Limitations in the Expressiveness of Type Libraries

UNMANAGED

IDL:

```
HRESULT 1DConformantArray([in, size_is(count)] double *arr, [in] long count);

HRESULT 2DConformantArray([in, size_is(count1, count2)] double **arr,
  [in] long count1, [in] long count2);
```

MANAGED

C#:

```
public virtual void 1DConformantArray(ref double arr, int count);

public virtual void 2DConformantArray(System.IntPtr arr,
  int count1, int count2);
```

Visual Basic .NET:

```
Public Overridable Sub 1DConformantArray(ByRef arr As Double, ByVal count As
Integer)

Public Overridable Sub 2DConformantArray(ByVal arr As System.IntPtr,
  ByVal count1 As Integer, ByVal count2 As Integer)
```

DIGGING DEEPER

The arrays in Listing 4.7 are written as simple pointers to `double` in IDL. Often, one of the following notations is used instead to clearly show that the parameter is an array (shown here for a one-dimensional array):

```
double arr[]
```

```
double arr[*]
```

However, no matter which notation is used, such a parameter still looks like a simple pointer inside a type library.

The imported `ConformantArray1D` method is only usable if you plan to always pass one element. Obviously, this almost never suffices. The workaround is to change the method signature manually, as demonstrated in Chapter 7. You might be wondering what happened to the array parameter of `ConformantArray2D`. It is covered in the "Methods" section of this chapter, but the quick answer is that multiple levels of indirection cause it to be transformed as a raw pointer (`System.IntPtr`).

DIGGING DEEPER

As with `length_is`, `size_is` has an alternative attribute for those who would rather specify a maximum index—`max_is`. Setting `size_is` to *x* is the same as setting `max_is` to *x*–1. As with `length_is` and `last_is`, the choice of `size_is` versus `max_is` is cosmetic.

Conformant Varying Arrays

As the name suggests, conformant varying arrays combine the properties of varying arrays with the properties of conformant arrays, enabling you to pass a dynamically sized slice of a dynamic-capacity array! In other words, you can use `size_is` (or `max_is`), `length_is` (or `last_is`), and `first_is` all at the same time. In COM documentation, conformant varying arrays are often called *open arrays*. Conformant varying arrays often look like the following in IDL:

```
HRESULT ConformantVaryingArrayParameter(
  [in, size_is(capacity), length_is(filled)] double *arr,
  [in] long capacity, [in] long filled);
```

Although all the array examples have been marked `[in]` only, conformant varying arrays can be useful when the array and `length_is` parameter are both marked `[in, out]`. This enables a caller to allocate an array and communicate to the method how large it is. Then, the method can return to the caller how many elements of the array it filled in with data.

This should no longer be surprising to you, but because none of the relevant IDL attributes appear in a type library, the type library importer sees conformant varying arrays as simple pointers (just as it does for any conformant array). Chapter 7 demonstrates how to make conformant varying arrays look like conformant arrays. Unfortunately, the "varying" functionality is not supported by the Interop Marshaler, so the entire array must always be passed.

Converting Methods and Properties

COM interfaces have two types of members: methods and properties. These members contain parameters and return types that are transformed into managed data types (according to the list presented in Table 4.1), but the members themselves also go through some transformations.

Methods

A managed signature produced for a type library's method looks very similar to the same method's signature in Visual Basic 6. Much of this is due to the conversion that hides each method's HRESULT. In this section we're going to look at the handful of transformations done for a method. There are four areas of focus:

- Hiding the HRESULT
- By-Value versus By-Reference
- [in] versus [out] versus [in, out]
- Parameter Arrays

An important thing to notice is that in COM methods, a variety of oddities that aren't usable from Visual Basic 6 can now be used in Visual Basic .NET (just as they can be in any .NET language).

Hiding the HRESULT

COM methods typically return an HRESULT and can have a special [out, retval] parameter that represents the real return value. As in VB6, an HRESULT return value is hidden and an [out, retval] parameter becomes the return value (if it exists) in a .NET signature. This is demonstrated in Listing 4.8.

LISTING 4.8   The COM View and the .NET View of the Same Simple Methods—One with [out, retval] and One Without

UNMANAGED

Visual Basic 6:

```
Public Sub SetName(ByVal name As String)
```

LISTING 4.8 Continued

```
Public Function GetName() As String
```

IDL:

```
HRESULT SetName([in] BSTR name);
HRESULT GetName([out, retval] BSTR name);
```

MANAGED

C#:

```
public virtual void SetName(string name);

public virtual string GetName();
```

Visual Basic .NET:

```
Public Overridable Sub SetName(ByVal name As String)

Public Overridable Function GetName() As String
```

Because the HRESULT (used to communicate failure) is removed from the signature, exceptions are thrown by the RCW wrapping the COM object to indicate failure.

Although it's rare, sometimes COM methods don't return HRESULTs. For such methods, the type library importer doesn't do any kind of return value transformation. Thus, the signature is preserved in managed code and marked with a special pseudo-custom attribute: PreserveSigAttribute. Such methods can't be defined in Visual Basic 6, but an example defined in IDL is shown in Listing 4.9.

LISTING 4.9 The COM View and the .NET View of a Method That Doesn't Return an HRESULT

IDL:

```
BSTR GetName();
```

C#:

```
[PreserveSig] public virtual String GetName();
```

Visual Basic .NET:

```
<PreserveSig> Public Function GetName() As String
```

4

AN IN-DEPTH LOOK
AT IMPORTED
ASSEMBLIES

DIGGING DEEPER

Users of Interop Assemblies don't typically notice the custom attributes that the importer places on types and members, and there's no reason to. These custom attributes, such as `PreserveSigAttribute`, exist for the benefit of the Interop Marshaler, so it can marshal the data correctly without also requiring a type library to be present. For example, the methods in Listings 4.8 and 4.9 are called the exact same way in managed code (shown here in C#):

```
string name = obj.GetName();
```

If you want to see all the attributes that the type library importer places on items in an Interop Assembly, you can view it using `ILDASM.EXE` or the Visual Studio .NET object browser. Be aware, however, that pseudo-custom attributes (such as `PreserveSigAttribute` and `MarshalAsAttribute`) appear in IL in ways other than typical custom attributes and cannot be seen in the Visual Studio .NET object browser. See Chapter 7 to learn how to detect the presence of pseudo-custom attributes in IL Assembler syntax.

By-Value Versus By-Reference

In Visual Basic 6, parameters can be marked by-reference (`ByRef`) or by-value (`ByVal`). This designation is preserved in the imported .NET signature. In IDL terms, parameters with an extra level of indirection (an extra *) become by-reference parameters; otherwise they're passed by value. This is shown in Listing 4.10.

LISTING 4.10   The COM View and the .NET View of the Same Methods with By-Value and By-Reference Parameters

---

`UNMANAGED`

Visual Basic 6:

```
Public Sub Strings(ByVal byvalue As String, ByRef byreference As String)

Public Sub Interfaces(ByVal byvalue As Object, ByRef byreference As Object)
```

IDL:

```
HRESULT Strings([in] BSTR byvalue, [in, out] BSTR* byreference);

HRESULT Interfaces([in] IDispatch* byvalue, [in, out] IDispatch** byreference);
```

LISTING 4.10   Continued

MANAGED

C#:

```csharp
public virtual void Strings(string byvalue, ref string byreference);

public virtual void Interfaces(
  [MarshalAs(UnmanagedType.IDispatch)] Object byvalue,
  [MarshalAs(UnmanagedType.IDispatch)] ref Object byreference);
```

Visual Basic .NET:

```vbnet
Public Overridable Sub Strings(ByVal byvalue As String, ByRef byreference As _
  String)

Public Overridable Sub Interfaces( _
  <MarshalAs(UnmanagedType.IDispatch)> ByVal byvalue As Object, _
  <MarshalAs(UnmanagedType.IDispatch)> ByRef byreference As Object)
```

> **TIP**
>
> Parameters of interface types are always interface *pointers*, so they always have at least one level of indirection. Thus, for parameters of interface types, `*` means ByVal and `**` means ByRef.

Parameters with more than one extra level of indirection (***, or more, for interface types and **, or more, for other types) cannot be converted to their corresponding managed types because .NET doesn't have the notion of a reference to a by-reference parameter. Therefore, any such types are converted to System.IntPtr types containing the raw pointer values. Chapter 6 demonstrates what useful tasks you can accomplish with IntPtr types in managed code. Visual Basic 6 can't define such parameters, but Listing 4.11 has an example originating in IDL.

LISTING 4.11   The COM View and the .NET View of Parameters With More Than One Extra Level of Indirection

UNMANAGED

IDL:

```
HRESULT DontTryThisAtHome([in, out] BSTR** one, [in, out] IUnknown*** two);
```

4

AN IN-DEPTH LOOK AT IMPORTED ASSEMBLIES

LISTING 4.11   Continued

```
MANAGED
```

C#:

```
public virtual void DontTryThisAtHome(IntPtr one, IntPtr two);
```

Visual Basic .NET:

```
Public Overridable Sub DontTryThisAtHome(ByVal one As IntPtr, _
  ByVal two As IntPtr)
```

TLBIMP.EXE emits a warning such as the following whenever encountering a type that it converts to `System.IntPtr`:

```
TlbImp warning: At least one of the arguments for '…' can not be marshaled
by the runtime marshaler.  Such arguments will therefore be passed as a pointer
and may require unsafe code to manipulate.
```

Furthermore, the importer sometimes marks such members with the `ComConversionLossAttribute` custom attribute. This custom attribute is for informational purposes only, and is meant to indicate imported entities whose description loses fidelity compared to the information in the original type library.

These warnings and custom attributes can be safely ignored. Although they may shake your confidence in the ability of COM Interoperability to handle the COM component, using `IntPtr` parameters in managed code is not very difficult. One misleading aspect of these warnings is that `TLBIMP.EXE` even emits them when converting `void*` to `IntPtr`, which is the best thing it could possibly emit (that is also CLS compliant)!

DIGGING DEEPER

`void**` is an exception to the rule that parameters with more than one extra level of indirection are converted to `System.IntPtr`. `void*` is already transformed to a `System.IntPtr` (because both types describe a blind pointer to random memory), so `void**` is transformed to a *by-reference* `System.IntPtr` parameter. Note that `void***`, `void****`, and the like are transformed as a simple `System.IntPtr` for the same reason any other type is. (Hopefully, you'll never need to use COM objects with such types, however!)

FAQ: The first time I run TLBIMP.EXE, I get several warnings, but when I run it subsequent times on the same input file, I get fewer warnings (or none)! Why does this happen?

TLBIMP.EXE automatically imports any dependent type libraries if it can't find an Interop Assembly to satisfy the reference. The reference can be satisfied by a registered Primary Interop Assembly, an Interop Assembly in the current directory, or an Interop Assembly specified at the command-line with /reference.

The first time you import a type library that causes dependent type libraries to be imported, TLBIMP.EXE reports warnings for *all* the type libraries it imports. If you run TLBIMP.EXE again without deleting all the assemblies it may have created, it won't bother re-importing the dependent type libraries because they will be found in the current directory. Therefore, any warnings that occurred for the dependent assemblies are no longer displayed.

[in] Versus [out] Versus [in, out]

In IDL syntax, a method's parameters are almost always marked with an attribute that indicates the direction of data flow: [in], [out], or [in, out]. (The Microsoft IDL compiler, MIDL, treats parameters with no directional attribute as [in].) These attributes have the following meaning:

- [in]—The data is marshaled from caller to callee.
- [out]—The data is marshaled from callee to caller.
- [in, out]—The data is marshaled in both directions.

Although a parameter with an extra level of indirection is often marked [in, out] in IDL, it could also be marked just [in] or just [out]. Parameters without a level of indirection cannot be marked as [out] or [in, out] because the callee would have no means of allocating its memory. These attributes don't affect whether a parameter is by-reference or by-value in the corresponding managed signature, so the IDL signatures in Listing 4.12 produce almost the same results as the Strings method in Listing 4.10.

4

CAUTION

The distinction between in-out-ness of a parameter and by-ref-ness of a parameter is often a source of confusion, especially for a common usage of in-only VARIANT pointers. This was seen in the preceding chapter, in which parameters of the CheckSpelling method in the Microsoft Word type library became by-reference Objects. However, using [in] VARIANT* instead of [in] VARIANT in COM is typically done as a performance optimization, not as an indication of by-reference behavior (otherwise it would be marked [in, out]).

> Another reason that the VARIANT/Object transformation is special is that VARIANT is a structure (a value type), but System.Object is a reference type. VARIANT is the only type for which the type library importer performs this value/reference transformation.

LISTING 4.12   The COM View and the .NET View of Methods with In-Only and Out-Only By-Reference Parameters

`UNMANAGED`

IDL:

```
HRESULT Strings1([in] BSTR byvalue, [in] BSTR* byreference);

HRESULT Strings2([in] BSTR byvalue, [out] BSTR* byreference);
```

`MANAGED`

C#:

```
public virtual void Strings1(string byvalue, ref string byreference);

public virtual void Strings2(string byvalue, out string byreference);
```

Visual Basic .NET:

```
Public Overridable Sub Strings1(ByVal byvalue As String, _
  ByRef byreference As String)

Public Overridable Sub Strings2(ByVal byvalue As String, _
  ByRef byreference As String)
```

Notice the difference in the C# signatures from Listing 4.10. C# treats out-only parameters separately from regular by-reference parameters with its out keyword. With out, C# enforces the fact that you can't initialize the variable passed to the method before calling it. The signature with the in-only, by-reference parameter doesn't visibly affect the C# signature, and neither permutation visibly affects the Visual Basic .NET signature.

DIGGING DEEPER

The various combinations of [in] and [out] are, in fact, preserved in imported .NET signatures as pseudo-custom attributes. Technically, they should be shown in all the managed code listings in this chapter, but are omitted for simplicity. Programmers calling the methods usually don't notice these attributes, but they can make a difference in the behavior seen at run time (just as they would in completely unmanaged applications). The signatures in Listing 4.12 technically look like the following, with InAttribute and OutAttribute:

C#:

```
public virtual void Strings1([In] String byvalue,
  [In] ref String byreference);

public virtual void Strings2([In] String byvalue,
  out String byreference);
```

Visual Basic .NET:

```
Public Overridable Sub Strings1(<[In]> ByVal byvalue As String, _
  <[In]> ByRef byreference As String)

Public Overridable Sub Strings2(<[In]> ByVal byvalue As String, _
  <Out> ByRef byreference As String)
```

From a metadata perspective, C#'s out keyword is the same as [Out] ref.

Parameter Arrays

A *parameter array* is a special type of array parameter. Such an array parameter doesn't look like an array to the caller of a method that uses one. Instead, the method appears to take an arbitrary number of arguments that don't need to be stuffed into an array. Visual Basic's ParamArray keyword enables this special calling syntax. It looks like the following in Visual Basic 6:

```
' Method with a ParamArray
Public Sub ParamArrayParameter(ParamArray arr() As Variant)
  ...
End Sub

Public Sub Main
  ' Invoking the method with any number of arguments
  ParamArrayParameter 1
  ParamArrayParameter 1, 2, 3
  ParamArrayParameter "a", "b", 3, "d", 7.2
End Sub
```

From the callee's point of view, the caller has passed an array; and from the caller's point of view, the method accepts any number of arguments. In the first call of the preceding example, the method sees an array with one element containing the number 1. In the last case, the method sees an array with five elements containing strings and numbers. A parameter array must be a one-dimensional array and must be the last parameter listed.

In IDL, parameter arrays are indicated with a [vararg] attribute, which stands for "variable number of arguments." Parameter arrays also exist in the .NET Framework, so the type library importer is able to preserve this feature in Interop Assemblies. The importer accomplishes this by placing a System.ParamArrayAttribute custom attribute on the parameter in question. .NET compilers can then choose to look for this attribute to interpret the array as a parameter array. Parameter arrays are not in the CLS, so any .NET language that doesn't support them simply sees them as a regular array parameter. Parameter arrays are marked with ParamArray in VB .NET (as in Visual Basic 6) and with params in C#. The parameter array transformation is shown in Listing 4.13.

> ## CAUTION
>
> Parameter arrays in Visual Basic 6 methods are not useful as parameter arrays in .NET because Visual Basic 6 enforces that arrays marked with ParamArray are passed by-reference. VB .NET and C#, on the other hand, only recognize an array as a parameter array if it's passed by value! Still, the importer marks all parameter arrays with the ParamArrayAttribute in case any .NET language comes along that supports by-reference parameter arrays.

LISTING 4.13 The COM View and the .NET View of a Method with a Parameter Array

`UNMANAGED`

Visual Basic 6:

```
' Cannot specify by-value parameter array in VB6.

Public Sub ByRefParamArrayParameter(ParamArray arr() As Variant)
```

IDL:

```
[vararg]
HRESULT ByValParamArrayParameter([in] SAFEARRAY(VARIANT) arr);

[vararg]
HRESULT ByRefParamArrayParameter([in, out] SAFEARRAY(VARIANT)* arr);
```

`MANAGED`

C#:
```
public virtual void ByValParamArrayParameter(params object [] arr);

// The [ParamArray] attribute is present in metadata, but ignored by C#
public virtual void ByRefParamArrayParameter(ref object [] arr);
```

LISTING 4.13   Continued

Visual Basic .NET:

```
Public Overridable Sub ByValParamArrayParameter( _
  ByVal ParamArray arr() As Object)

' The <ParamArray> attribute is present in metadata, but ignored by VB .NET
Public Overridable Sub ByRefParamArrayParameter(ByRef arr() As Object)
```

Properties

Properties in COM consist of one, two, or three methods grouped together. In IDL, a property with all three methods looks like this:

```
[id(0x68030000), propget]
HRESULT Data([out, retval] VARIANT* pRetVal);
[id(0x68030000), propput]
HRESULT Data([in] VARIANT var);
[id(0x68030000), propputref]
HRESULT Data([in] VARIANT var);
```

What distinguishes these methods from regular methods are the propget, propput, and prop-putref markings. In unmanaged C++ or Visual Basic 6, implementing a property is simply a matter of implementing these methods, which are commonly referred to as *accessor methods*. In Visual Basic 6, the Data property shown previously might be implemented as follows:

```
Private varData As Variant

' The "getter" is the [propget] method
Public Property Get Data() As Variant
  If IsObject(varData) Then
    Set Data = varData
  Else
    Let Data = varData
  End If
End Property

' The "letter" is the [propput] method
Public Property Let Data(ByVal v As Variant)
  Let varData = v
End Property

' The "setter" is the [propputref] method
Public Property Set Data(ByVal v As Variant)
  Set varData = v
End Property
```

4

AN IN-DEPTH LOOK
AT IMPORTED
ASSEMBLIES

So, what is the purpose of properties? Although implementing properties feels just like implementing methods, properties enable clients to use a simpler syntax than method calls, which provides a nice abstraction. In Visual Basic 6, these methods can't be called directly. Instead, the propget method is called when the client gets the value, as follows:

```
d = chart.Data
```

The propput is called when the client puts (or sets) the value, as follows:

```
chart.Data = 5
```

or

```
Let chart.Data = 5
```

The propputref is called when the client puts an object reference, as follows:

```
Set chart.Data = MyObject
```

A COM property can implement any subset of these three methods, and usually doesn't implement all three.

A .NET property typically has one or two accessor methods: a getter and a setter, used like propget and propput, respectively. Although C#, Visual Basic .NET, and managed C++ code doesn't support the creation of properties with more methods, .NET metadata supports an arbitrary number of accessor methods (known as *other accessors*). Whereas a COM property is just a group of methods with extra attributes, metadata has a notion of a property as a separate element distinct from the accessor methods. A property lists its accessor methods, seen here for the Data property in raw IL Assembler syntax:

```
.property object Data()
{
  .get instance object TypeName::get_Data()
  .set instance void TypeName::set_Data(object)
  .other instance void TypeName::let_Data(object)
}
```

This notation means that the property's get accessor is implemented by a method called get_Data, the property's set accessor is implemented by a method called set_Data, and it has an other accessor with the name let_Data.

The type library importer performs the following steps to transform a COM property to a .NET property:

1. A .NET property is created with the same name as the COM property.
2. A propget method, if it exists, is converted to a get accessor method with the name get_*PropertyName*.

3. A `propputref` method, if it exists, is converted to a set accessor method with the name `set_PropertyName`.

4. A `propput` method, if it exists, is converted to a set accessor method with the name `set_PropertyName`, as long as the property doesn't also have a `propputref` method.

5. If a property has both `propput` and `propputref` methods, the `propput` becomes an other accessor with the name `let_PropertyName`.

No current .NET languages have special syntax to call additional accessors, so clients can just call the `let_PropertyName` accessor explicitly as a regular method.

CAUTION

A common mistake is made when porting code that calls a let accessor from Visual Basic 6 to Visual Basic .NET. The source of the problem is that the typical VB6 syntax for invoking a *let* accessor is identical to the VB .NET syntax for invoking a *set* accessor! Fortunately, the problem only arises in the rare cases when properties implement all three accessors: Get, Set, and Let. To illustrate, the following VB6 code uses the ADO (ActiveX Data Objects) `Recordset.ActiveConnection` property:

```
var = recset.ActiveConnection        ' Get

recset.ActiveConnection = "..."       ' Let

Set recset.ActiveConnection = conn ' Set
```

This translates into the following Visual Basic .NET code:

```
' Get: the same familiar syntax.
var = recset.ActiveConnection

' Set: the same as the old Let syntax!
recset.ActiveConnection = "..."

' Let: much different syntax than before!
recset.let_ActiveConnection(conn)
```

If you accidentally call a set accessor when you mean to call a let accessor, unexpected behavior can occur at run time. The error usually manifests as an exception, but it depends on the property's implementation.

Special DISPIDs

A DISPID, short for *dispatch identifier*, is a number assigned to methods and properties of an interface derived from `IDispatch`, which is used to identify them during late binding. DISPIDs are listed in IDL using the `id` attribute, which we saw in the IDL snippet from the last section:

```
[id(0x68030000), propget]
HRESULT Data([out, retval] VARIANT* pRetVal);
[id(0x68030000), propput]
HRESULT Data([in] VARIANT var);
[id(0x68030000), propputref]
HRESULT Data([in] VARIANT var);
```

Notice that property accessors must share the same DISPID value, but each method and group of property accessors must have distinct numbers. DISPIDs on members in a type library are preserved in metadata with the DispIdAttribute, so the CLR can use them when late binding to a COM object. In addition, two special DISPID values that have significance in the world of COM cause the type library importer to make additional transformations. These values are 0 and –4, and are commonly called DISPID_VALUE and DISPID_NEWENUM, respectively.

DISPID_VALUE (0)

A member with a DISPID equal to 0 is considered a *default member*. This is the mechanism that enables Visual Basic 6 to support default properties. For instance, in the case of an object obj with a default property Text, the two lines of VB6 code are equivalent:

```
obj.Text = "My Text"
```

```
obj = "My Text"
```

By checking for a DISPID equal to 0, the importer can transform default members in COM to default members in .NET. The .NET way of indicating a default member is to place a System.Reflection.DefaultMemberAttribute on the class or interface containing the member, so that's what the importer does. (Rather than an attribute on the member itself, this attribute contains the name of the default member in a string property.) .NET languages look for this attribute to determine which member, if any, can be treated specially as the default.

Because the syntax for using default properties can be confusing (as in the last example, where it looks as if obj itself is being set to My Text), Visual Basic .NET and C# only support special syntax for default properties that have one or more parameters. These are known as *parameterized properties*, and C# calls them *indexers*. Thus, a default property Text that has an integer parameter can be accessed as follows:

Visual Basic .NET:

```
obj.Text(2) = "My Text"
```

```
obj(2) = "My Text"
```

C#:

```
obj[2] = "My Text";
```

C# won't even permit you to call an indexer by name. It forces you to use the shorter syntax, which can cause some confusion if you don't realize that the COM property you're trying to call is a default member. .NET languages are free to ignore default members and treat them just like regular members, which is what C# and VB .NET do if the default member is either a property with no parameters, or a method.

DIGGING DEEPER

Using reflection, you can always take advantage of default members regardless of whether the language recognizes a member as default. Reflection enables you to pass an empty string for the name of the default member, rather than having to type it. So, the following two lines of C# code are equivalent for a default method called DefaultMethod:

```
obj.GetType().InvokeMember("", BindingFlags.InvokeMethod,
  null, obj, null);

obj.GetType().InvokeMember("DefaultMethod", BindingFlags.InvokeMethod,
  null, obj, null);
```

As you can see, this isn't much of a shortcut because there's already a lot to type, but the support is there if you want to use it.

DISPID_NEWENUM (–4)

A member with a DISPID equal to –4 is found on a collection interface. This special member, often called NewEnum, returns an interface that enables clients to enumerate objects in a collection (for example, the For Each statement in Visual Basic 6). When you add a collection class to a VB6 project, it contains a hidden interface with the DISPID_NEWENUM member, as follows:

```
[id(-4), propget, hidden]
HRESULT NewEnum([out, retval] IUnknown** pRetVal);
```

IUnknown is used so that a variety of enumeration interfaces can be accommodated. However, earlier in this chapter we saw that the most commonly used COM enumeration interface is called IEnumVARIANT. Thus, the following signature is also valid for DISPID_NEWENUM:

```
HRESULT NewEnum([out, retval] IEnumVARIANT** pRetVal);
```

Whereas VB6 looks for a member with a DISPID of –4 to enable For Each, VB .NET and C# look for a method called GetEnumerator. Thus, the conversion of IEnumVARIANT types to IEnumerator isn't enough to make foreach/For Each work on a COM object in .NET. This is because the .NET interface would have a member with the original name (such as NewEnum) rather than the required GetEnumerator method. Therefore, the importer transforms appropriate members with a DISPID of –4 to methods called GetEnumerator. An appropriate member is either a method or a `propget` accessor method that returns an `HRESULT` and has a single `IUnknown**` or `IEnumVARIANT**` [out, retval] parameter. The `GetEnumerator` method produced looks like the following:

C#:

```
public IEnumerator GetEnumerator();
```

Visual Basic .NET:

```
Public Function GetEnumerator() As IEnumerator
```

(It also marks the `IEnumerator` types with `MarshalAsAttribute` to indicate custom marshaling to an `IEnumVARIANT` interface, but this isn't required because `IEnumerator` always marshals to `IEnumVARIANT`.) These transformations enable .NET clients to naturally enumerate over COM objects in a natural way, just as the author had intended for COM clients.

The type library importer does one more thing: It indicates that the managed class containing `GetEnumerator` implements `System.Collections.IEnumerable`, an interface whose only method is `GetEnumerator`. This is done because, although VB .NET and C# check for enumeration capability by looking for the `GetEnumerator` method name, the official way for a class to expose an enumerator (according to the CLS) is to implement `IEnumerable`. Thus, by marking the class as implementing this interface, the type library importer ensures that any CLS-compliant .NET language can still enumerate over COM collections in a natural way.

DIGGING DEEPER

The reason that the C# and VB .NET compilers check for a `GetEnumerator` method, rather than simply checking for the `IEnumerable` interface, is to enable strongly typed enumerations. Class authors can take advantage of this by having their `GetEnumerator` method return a type that's more specialized than the generic `IEnumerator` interface (for example, one that has a `Current` property of a specific type, such as `String` or `DateTime`, rather than `Object`). See `System.Collections.Specialized.StringCollection` in the `System` assembly for an example of this. Although checking for a special method name might sound bizarre, it's similar to checking for a special DISPID in COM, which enables the member to return either `IEnumVARIANT` or a more specialized type, such as `IEnumString` or `IEnumUnknown`.

Converting Interfaces

When you understand the transformations done for data types, methods, and properties, there's not much more to know about an interface. Each COM interface becomes a .NET interface containing the transformed methods. The imported interface is marked with several custom attributes, depending on characteristics of the interface, but the two required custom attributes are GuidAttribute and ComImportAttribute. GuidAttribute contains the interface's IID (interface identifier) listed in the type library, and ComImportAttribute indicates that the interface was originally defined as a COM interface that's been imported into metadata.

One subtle aspect of imported interfaces involves inheritance. Both COM and .NET have interface inheritance, and the inheritance relationships are preserved in metadata—excluding IUnknown and IDispatch. Any COM interface that directly derives from IUnknown or IDispatch becomes a .NET interface that doesn't derive from any interface. Instead, information about whether the original COM interface extends from IUnknown or IDispatch is captured in a custom attribute (InterfaceTypeAttribute). A COM interface that directly derives from another interface (besides IUnknown and IDispatch) becomes a .NET interface that continues to derive from that other interface. This is pictured in Figure 4.2.

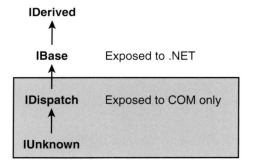

FIGURE 4.2
Interface inheritance hierarchies are preserved in .NET metadata up to, but not including, the IDispatch *and/or* IUnknown *interfaces.*

Listing 4.14 demonstrates interface inheritance and its transformation to .NET interfaces, using two famous COM interfaces: IProvideClassInfo and IProvideClassInfo2.

LISTING 4.14   Two COM Interfaces and Their Transformation to .NET Interfaces

UNMANAGED

IDL:

```
[
  object,
  uuid(B196B283-BAB4-101A-B69C-00AA00341D07),
  pointer_default(unique)
]
interface IProvideClassInfo : IUnknown
{
  HRESULT GetClassInfo([out] ITypeInfo ** ppTI);
};

[
  object,
  uuid(A6BC3AC0-DBAA-11CE-9DE3-00AA004BB851),
  pointer_default(unique)
]
interface IProvideClassInfo2 : IProvideClassInfo
{
  HRESULT GetGUID([in] DWORD dwGuidKind, [out] GUID *pGUID);
};
```

MANAGED

C#:

```
[
  ComImport,
  InterfaceType(ComInterfaceType.InterfaceIsIUnknown),
  Guid("B196B283-BAB4-101A-B69C-00AA00341D07")
]
public interface IProvideClassInfo
{
  void GetClassInfo(out ITypeInfo ppTI);
}

[
  ComImport,
  InterfaceType(ComInterfaceType.InterfaceIsIUnknown),
  Guid("A6BC3AC0-DBAA-11CE-9DE3-00AA004BB851")
]
public interface IProvideClassInfo2 : IProvideClassInfo
{
  void GetClassInfo(out ITypeInfo ppTI);
  void GetGUID(uint dwGuidKind, out Guid pGUID);
}
```

The surprising part about the importer's transformation is that any base interface methods (GetClassInfo in Listing 4.14) are duplicated on the .NET definition of the derived interface. The type library importer always adds methods from all base interfaces (except IUnknown and IDispatch) to a derived interface in order to preserve the COM interface's v-table layout. In this case, when a .NET client calls the GetGUID method on the IProvideClassInfo2 interface, it is simply calling slot 5 on the interface v-table of the COM object (the second method of the interface plus the three IUnknown methods). The InterfaceTypeAttribute shown in the listing tells the CLR what the first methods of the v-table are (for example, just three slots for IUnknown, or seven slots for IUnknown plus IDispatch). However, all other methods in the v-table must be present in the interface definition.

This is a subtle difference for .NET clients and doesn't usually affect the programmer's use of the interface. For example, whether or not IProvideClassInfo2 directly defines a method called GetClassInfo, managed code could still call it on an IProvideClassInfo2 variable due to the inheritance relationship.

It's rare, but depending on the layout of the COM interface, the .NET definition of an interface might contain extra funny-looking methods, with names beginning with _VtblGap. These are used to fill what are known as *v-table gaps*—extra spaces between methods in the v-table. You can simply ignore these methods.

Converting Classes

The transformations done by the type library importer for COM classes are the source of the most confusion for users of Interop Assemblies. Most of the transformations were not done in beta versions of the CLR, but were added due to customer feedback that using COM components in .NET languages was not as easy as it was in Visual Basic 6. Now, the behavior of the type library importer makes the straightforward use of COM components very simple in C# or Visual Basic .NET. However, if you start to dig into the metadata produced by the type library importer, things can get confusing really quickly.

Classes in COM (called *coclasses* in IDL and *class modules* in VB6) do not have members that can be called directly. They just have a list of interfaces implemented, which is shown here in IDL for a class in the Microsoft Speech API:

```
[
  uuid(5FB7EF7D-DFF4-468A-B6B7-2FCBD188F994),
  helpstring("SpMemoryStream Class")
]
coclass SpMemoryStream {
  [default] interface ISpeechMemoryStream;
  interface ISpStream;
};
```

An instance of a class is obtained from a separate class, known as a class factory. After a client has an instance of the class, a client's only communication is through interfaces that the object implements. Of course, Visual Basic 6 hides all these details from the programmer, so COM objects can be created with New and it appears as if members of the default interface (ISpeechMemoryStream in this example) can be invoked directly on class types.

To provide a similar abstraction to what Visual Basic 6 provides, the type library importer performs the following steps when encountering a coclass:

1. Create a .NET *interface* with the same name as the coclass. This interface, known as a *coclass interface*, has no members itself but derives from the coclass's default interface. This interface is marked with the same IID as the default interface.

2. Create a .NET *class* with the same name as the coclass plus a Class suffix. This class represents the RCW, and is described in "The RCW Class."

3. If the coclass's default interface is defined in the same type library as the coclass, and if it's not listed as being implemented by any other coclass in the type library, replace any parameters and fields of the default interface type with the coclass interface type created in step 1.

The importer does additional work when a coclass lists source interfaces (used in event handling) but this is discussed in Chapter 5, "Responding to COM Events."

Coclass Interfaces and Parameter/Field Replacement

If it weren't for additional support from the C# and VB .NET compilers, the previously-listed transformations would mean that whenever you wanted to instantiate a coclass called XYZ, you'd need to instantiate a .NET class called XYZ**Class**! And this is exactly what happens in Visual C++ .NET, seen in Chapter 3's Hello, World example.

To avoid the confusion of dealing with renamed classes, C# and VB .NET enable you to write code that appears to *instantiate a coclass interface*! That's right, you can do the following in C#, for example, even though the .NET SpMemoryStream type is really an interface:

```
SpMemoryStream ms = new SpMemoryStream();
```

During compilation, the C# compiler pretends that you instead wrote the following line of code:

```
SpMemoryStream ms = new SpMemoryStreamClass();
```

In order to make this work, the type library importer marks all coclass interfaces with the CoClassAttribute custom attribute from the System.Runtime.InteropServices namespace. Therefore, the imported SpMemoryStream interface from the preceding example looks like the following in C# syntax:

```
[
  ComImport,
  Guid("EEB14B68-808B-4ABE-A5EA-B51DA7588008"),
  CoClass(typeof(SpMemoryStreamClass))
]
public interface SpMemoryStream : ISpeechMemoryStream
{
}
```

The C# and VB .NET compilers accept code that appears to instantiate an interface as long as the interface is marked with CoClassAttribute. The compilers simply swap the interface with the type stored in the interface's CoClassAttribute. You can call members of the default interface directly on the instantiated type (since the coclass interface derives from the default interface), or you can cast to non-default interfaces in order to call their members.

So what do all these strange importer transformations and compiler magic buy us? By effectively duplicating a coclass's default interface with the name of the class, .NET clients are lead to believe that they are invoking members on the class directly, as in Visual Basic 6. COM classes authored in Visual Basic 6 have hidden default interfaces beginning with an underscore that many users aren't even aware of. Therefore, these transformations shield users from dealing with these previously hidden interfaces in C# or VB .NET code.

An equally important part of this transformation is step 3, in which default interface parameters and fields are replaced with coclass interfaces to present .NET clients with effectively the same interface but with a nicer name. Because of the confusion this replacement can cause when it's not desired, this is only done if there's a high degree of certainty that the default interface is deeply tied to the class that implements it. Therefore, if the default interface is not in the same type library as the coclass implementing it, or if it's listed as being implemented by more than one coclass in the same type library, any parameters and fields of the default interface type are left as the raw interface type in .NET signatures.

To understand the benefit of this parameter/field replacement, consider ActiveX Data Objects (ADO) and its widely-used Recordset coclass. The result of step 3 means that a VB6 COM object that returns a Recordset instance still appears to return a Recordset coclass interface in managed code. If you opened the COM component's type library in OLEVIEW.EXE, however, you'd see that it *really* returns a _Recordset interface pointer—the hidden default interface for the Recordset coclass. Interacting with this previously-hidden interface would be confusing for programmers used to Visual Basic 6.

Another nice side effect of these transformations is that programmers often have the urge to cast a returned COM object to its class type, but this cannot succeed in general. RCWs can only reliably be cast to *interfaces* that they implement. When a .NET programmer casts an RCW to a coclass interface, however, he may think he's casting to a class type but in fact he's simply casting to the object's default interface, which is the desired behavior!

Finally, these transformations make event handling on returned COM objects work seamlessly. This mechanism is described in the following chapter.

> **CAUTION**
>
> Whenever you need to interact with an RCW's class in any way other than using the new operator in C# or VB .NET, you must remember to include the Class suffix! Nothing else recognizes the CoClassAttribute custom attribute. Besides other .NET languages, this includes language-neutral mechanisms such as reflection. Anywhere you need to provide a string with a class's name, as in calling Type.GetType or when using ASP.NET, omitting the Class suffix means that the type you specify will be treated as a regular .NET interface.

The RCW Class

The .NET classes generated by the type library importer accurately represent the RCWs fabricated by the CLR. These are rarely used directly in C# or Visual Basic .NET programs, but it can be helpful to understand their characteristics. The type library importer does three things when creating these classes:

- Adds a constructor
- Adds members of all implemented interfaces
- Adds events for all source interfaces

Besides these transformations, the .NET class might have a System.Reflection. DefaultMemberAttribute custom attribute or implement System.Collections.IEnumerable depending on whether it has methods with special DISPIDs, as described earlier in this chapter. These two actions happen based *only* on members of the default interface. Similarly, DispIdAttributes are only added to members of the class that belong to the default interface. To take advantage of default members or enumerators on non-default interfaces, clients must cast the class type to the specific interface type.

Adding a Constructor

The .NET class is given a public default constructor (that is, a constructor with no parameters), unless the coclass is marked as [noncreatable] in the type library. The constructor enables the creation of the COM object by using the built-in syntax of the managed language, and ends up being called when a C# or VB .NET programmer writes code that appears to instantiate a coclass interface. The constructor call results in a CoCreateInstance call at run time.

If a class is marked [noncreatable], it cannot be instantiated. Instead, an internal (Family in VB .NET) default constructor is generated. This means that the constructor could only be called within the Interop Assembly, making it off-limits to any code. Instances of classes that cannot be created must obtained by calling APIs that return them.

Adding Members of Implemented Interfaces

The importer creates the appropriate metadata that enables all .NET languages to invoke members of *all* implemented interfaces (not just the default interface) directly on the class. Of course, this excludes any interfaces that the coclass doesn't list as being implemented in the original type library. This way, using RCWs for coclasses that implement multiple interfaces feels no different from using any other .NET class.

This action of adding multiple interface members to a single class isn't perfect due to conflicts that might arise in member names. If a class implements multiple interfaces that have a member with the same name *and same parameters*, it renames members on the class. If members with conflicting names had different parameters, then they are simply treated as overloaded methods and their names are left alone.

Name conflicts are resolved by prefixing member names with the interface name and an underscore. This is done to all duplicated names, except for one "winning" interface's member that gets to keep its original name. Members on the default interface always win, followed by the order in which the interfaces appear in the type library's coclass statement. Listing 4.15 illustrates this process.

LISTING 4.15   A COM Class That Implements Several Interfaces, and the .NET Class Produced by the Type Library Importer

IDL:

```
[
  uuid(BE919067-81D8-4F1D-A9DD-78E4F11863A7),
  helpstring("Baby musical robot with built-in VCR")
]
coclass Robot
{
  [default] interface IBaby;
  interface IVideoRecorder;
  interface IMusician;
};

[...]
interface IBaby : IUnknown
{
```

LISTING 4.15 Continued

```
  HRESULT Eat([in] BSTR food);
  HRESULT Cry();
  HRESULT Play([in] BSTR game);
};

[...]
interface IVideoRecorder : IUnknown
{
  HRESULT Stop();
  HRESULT Rewind();
  HRESULT Play();
  HRESULT FastForward();
};

[...]
interface IMusician : IUnknown
{
  HRESULT Play([in] BSTR song);
  HRESULT Stop();
  HRESULT ChooseInstrument([in] BSTR instrument);
};
```

C#:

```
[...]
public class RobotClass : IBaby, IVideoRecorder, IMusician
{
  public virtual void Eat(string food);
  public virtual void Cry();
  public virtual void Play(string game);
  public virtual void Stop();
  public virtual void Rewind();
  public virtual void Play();
  public virtual void FastForward();
  public virtual void IMusician_Play(string song);
  public virtual void IMusician_Stop();
  public virtual void ChooseInstrument(string instrument);
}
```

The C# representation is approximate, as the exact metadata produced by the importer for a class can't be produced in C# source code. The members on RobotClass in Listing 4.15 are necessary to distinguish, for example, which Play action you want the robot to perform (playing like a baby, a video recorder, or a musician). Notice that the Play method corresponding to the IVideoRecorder interface is not renamed because it has a signature that's distinct from the other two Play methods.

DIGGING DEEPER

If IVideoRecorder happened to have a member called IMusician_Play, the importer would create a method called IMusician_Play_2 when adding the members of IMusician. The general fall-back technique when resolving name conflicts is to append an underscore and a unique number to the conflicting name.

The name changing process should look familiar to Visual Basic 6 programmers because pre-fixing member names with *InterfaceName_* is required when implementing an interface member. As all these name conversions only occur on a class, you can still cast an RCW class to an interface to call any of the methods with their original names.

The "Converting Interfaces" section explained that the importer adds base interface members to derived interfaces. This normally doesn't matter to .NET clients, except that it has an unfortunate side effect whenever a coclass implements both a base and a derived interface. This is somewhat common, and can be seen in the WebBrowser coclass from the Microsoft Internet Controls type library (SHDOCVW.DLL in your system32 directory):

```
[
  uuid(8856F961-340A-11D0-A96B-00C04FD705A2),
  helpstring("WebBrowser Control"),
  control
]
coclass WebBrowser {
    [default] interface IWebBrowser2;
    interface IWebBrowser;
    [default, source] dispinterface DWebBrowserEvents2;
    [source] dispinterface DWebBrowserEvents;
};
```

The WebBrowser coclass implements IWebBrowser and IWebBrowser2, an interface that ultimately derives from IWebBrowser, as shown in the following IDL:

```
[...]
interface IWebBrowser : IDispatch {
    [id(0x00000064),
      helpstring("Navigates to the previous item in the history list.")]
    HRESULT GoBack();
    [id(0x00000065),
      helpstring("Navigates to the next item in the history list.")]
    HRESULT GoForward();
    ...plus many more members
};
```

```
[...]
interface IWebBrowserApp : IWebBrowser {
   ...
};

[...]
interface IWebBrowser2 : IWebBrowserApp {
   ...
};
```

This pattern of implementing a base and derived interface is typically done so that older clients (who only know about the original IWebBrowser interface) can still query for this interface, and newer clients (who are aware of IWebBrowser2) can take advantage of its extra functionality.

The imported WebBrowserClass class contains the methods of each of the three imported interfaces that it implements. Because the managed definition IWebBrowser2 contains all IWebBrowser's methods (GoBack, GoForward, and so forth), the class ends up with two copies of each of these methods! Each method of IWebBrowser gets a modified name (IWebBrowser_GoBack, IWebBrowser_GoForward, and so forth) because each method of the default IWebBrowser2 interface is added to WebBrowserClass first. WebBrowserClass doesn't end up with any duplicated members belonging to IWebBrowserApp because the coclass doesn't list it as an implemented interface. All these extra members may be annoying when using object browsers or IntelliSense, but they can be ignored.

Adding Events for Source Interfaces

The type library importer does its most complicated transformation when it encounters source interfaces listed in a coclass statement. Source interfaces are not implemented by the class, but can be invoked by the class to report events. A source interface is marked [source] in IDL, as seen in the WebBrowser coclass presented earlier:

```
[
  uuid(8856F961-340A-11D0-A96B-00C04FD705A2),
  helpstring("WebBrowser Control"),
  control
]
coclass WebBrowser {
    [default] interface IWebBrowser2;
    interface IWebBrowser;
    [default, source] dispinterface DWebBrowserEvents2;
    [source] dispinterface DWebBrowserEvents;
};
```

The transformation for source interfaces is covered in Chapter 5.

Converting Modules

Type libraries can have modules that contain global methods and/or constants. These are equivalent to what Visual Basic 6 calls standard modules in referenced COM components.

DIGGING DEEPER

Although modules in referenced COM components are used like standard modules in Visual Basic 6, standard modules in VB6 projects do not get placed in the generated type library.

Because .NET doesn't intrinsically have a notion of modules, the type library importer turns modules into sealed .NET classes. (In VB .NET terms, this is equivalent to a `NotInheritable` class.) For each type library module, a .NET class is created that contains the constants as public static fields. Unfortunately, methods in type library modules are omitted in the .NET classes that are produced. Listing 4.16 demonstrates the conversion for two modules, which are defined in the DirectX 8 for Visual Basic type library.

TIP

A module's methods can be added to the imported .NET class manually using PInvoke. For more information, see Chapter 7 and Part VI, "Platform Invocation Services."

LISTING 4.16   IDL Representation of Two Modules, and Their Transformation Shown in C#

`UNMANAGED`

IDL:

```
[
  dllname("dx8vb.dll")
]
module D3DCOLORAUX {
  [entry(0x60000000), helpcontext(0x000150b5)]
  long _stdcall D3DColorRGBA([in] short r, [in] short g, [in] short b,
    [in] short a);
  [entry(0x60000001), helpcontext(0x000150b3)]
  long _stdcall D3DColorARGB([in] short a, [in] short r, [in] short g,
    [in] short b);
```

LISTING 4.16   Continued

```
[entry(0x60000002), helpcontext(0x000150b6)]
long _stdcall D3DColorXRGB([in] short r, [in] short g, [in] short b);
[entry(0x60000003), helpcontext(0x000150b4)]
long _stdcall D3DColorMake([in] single r, [in] single g, [in] single b,
  [in] single a);
};

[
  dllname("<no entry points>")
]
module DINPUT8STRINGCONSTANTS {
  const BSTR DIPROP_AUTOCENTER      = "diprop_autocenter";
  const BSTR DIPROP_AXISMODE        = "diprop_axismode";
  const BSTR DIPROP_BUFFERSIZE      = "diprop_buffersize";
  const BSTR DIPROP_CALIBRATIONMODE = "diprop_calibrationmode";
  const BSTR DIPROP_DEADZONE        = "diprop_deadzone";
  const BSTR DIPROP_RANGE           = "diprop_range";
  const BSTR DIPROP_SATURATION      = "diprop_saturation";
  const BSTR DIPROP_KEYNAME         = "diprop_keyname";
  const BSTR DIPROP_SCANCODE        = "diprop_scancode";
};
```

MANAGED

C#:

```
public class DINPUT8STRINGCONSTANTS
{
  public static const string DIPROP_AUTOCENTER      = "diprop_autocenter";
  public static const string DIPROP_AXISMODE        = "diprop_axismode";
  public static const string DIPROP_BUFFERSIZE      = "diprop_buffersize";
  public static const string DIPROP_CALIBRATIONMODE
    = "diprop_calibrationmode";
  public static const string DIPROP_DEADZONE        = "diprop_deadzone";
  public static const string DIPROP_RANGE           = "diprop_range";
  public static const string DIPROP_SATURATION      = "diprop_saturation";
  public static const string DIPROP_KEYNAME         = "diprop_keyname";
  public static const string DIPROP_SCANCODE        = "diprop_scancode";
};
```

Notice that the D3DCOLORAUX module in Listing 4.16 isn't even imported, because it only has methods.

Converting Structures

A struct in a type library, known as a *user-defined type* (*UDT*) in Visual Basic 6, becomes a value type in metadata. Value types are known as structs in C# and structures in VB .NET. Most of the .NET Framework's primitive types are value types (such as all the integral types: `System.Int...`, `System.UInt...`, `System.Decimal`, `System.DateTime`, `System.Double`, and so on). Besides the value types, two *reference* types that are often considered primitive types are `System.Object` and `System.String`.

Value types are used to efficiently represent small instances whose contents represent their identity. (For example, two integer objects containing the value 5 should be treated as identical objects.) In .NET, the differences between value types and any other types (known as *reference types*) are:

- They are allocated on the stack rather than a garbage-collected heap.
- They can never be null.
- They are always sealed.
- The contents of a value type parameter cannot be changed unless passed by reference.

Value types are more expressive than COM structs because they can contain methods. Thus, every value type created by the type library importer is relatively simple. Each field in the unmanaged struct is transformed to a public field in the managed value type, as shown in Listing 4.17.

LISTING 4.17   A Simple Struct Shown in Visual Basic 6 and IDL, and Then in C# and VB .NET

UNMANAGED

Visual Basic 6:

```
Public Type RECT
  Left As Long
  Top As Long
  Right As Long
  Bottom As Long
End Type
```

IDL:

```
typedef [uuid(1196C224-8B6C-4D94-AD87-F6AF18A27F21)]
struct tagRECT
{
  long Left;
```

LISTING 4.17   Continued

```
    long Top;
    long Right;
    long Bottom;
} RECT;
```

MANAGED

C#:

```csharp
[Guid("1196C224-8B6C-4D94-AD87-F6AF18A27F21")]
public struct RECT
{
    public int Left;
    public int Top;
    public int Right;
    public int Bottom;
}
```

Visual Basic .NET:

```vb
<Guid("1196C224-8B6C-4D94-AD87-F6AF18A27F21")> _
Public Structure RECT
    Public Left As Integer
    Public Top As Integer
    Public Right As Integer
    Public Bottom As Integer
End Structure
```

The data types making up the fields of a struct are converted to .NET data types, just as they are when appearing as method parameters. The main difference is that value type fields with an extra level of indirection are converted to a `System.IntPtr`. Thus, the fields lose their type identity one level of indirection sooner because there's no such thing as a by-reference field.

Another noticeable difference is that `VARIANT_BOOL` fields (`Boolean` in VB6) are imported as 16-bit integer fields rather than the expected `Boolean` fields. This is done for historical reasons, because beta versions of the Interop Marshaler did not support marshaling `Boolean` fields. This marshaling is now supported, but you would need to change an Interop Assembly using the technique described in Chapter 7 in order to take advantage of such marshaling. If you encounter an `Int16` field that represents a `VARIANT_BOOL`, you must be familiar with `VARIANT_BOOL`'s internal representation to be able to use it correctly. In other words, you must treat -1 as true and 0 as false.

> **DIGGING DEEPER**
>
> Types and members in type libraries can contain several attributes that don't have meaning in .NET, such as `restricted` or `hidden`. These attributes are stored in three custom attributes, which the type library importer emits when appropriate:
>
> - `TypeLibTypeAttribute`. Contains the attributes set on types: classes, interfaces, structs, enums, and so on.
> - `TypeLibFuncAttribute`. Contains the attributes set on an interface's method or property.
> - `TypeLibVarAttribute`. Contains the attributes set on fields of structures.
>
> Using reflection, you can programmatically extract this information from Interop Assemblies in case it has special meaning for your application.

Converting Unions

A union is a special kind of struct containing several fields at the same offset in memory. IDL makes a distinction between two types of unions: encapsulated and nonencapsulated. These use IDL attributes (such as `switch_type` and `switch_is`), but none of this information, nor the distinction between the two types of unions, is captured inside a type library. In a type library, a union looks almost identical to a struct.

Because fields of a union overlap, unions are useful in COM for providing different views of the exact same data. Unions don't exist in the pure .NET world, so unmanaged unions are imported as regular value types. However, the type library importer places a few custom attributes on the imported value type to preserve the union's memory layout in the .NET definition. This is demonstrated in Listing 4.18 for a union defined in the Microsoft HTML Object Library (`MSHTML.TLB` in your `system32` directory).

LISTING 4.18 An Unmanaged Union Is Converted to a .NET Value Type with Custom Attributes to Indicate the Unique Memory Layout

UNMANAGED

IDL (as viewed by OLEVIEW):

```
typedef union tag__MIDL_IWinTypes_0009
{
  long hInproc;
  long hRemote;
} __MIDL_IWinTypes_0009;
```

LISTING 4.18 Continued

MANAGED

C#:

```csharp
[StructLayout(LayoutKind.Explicit)]
public struct __MIDL_IWinTypes_0009
{
  [FieldOffset(0)] public int hInproc;
  [FieldOffset(0)] public int hRemote;
}
```

Visual Basic .NET:

```vb
<StructLayout(LayoutKind.Explicit)> _
Public Structure __MIDL_IWinTypes_0009
  <FieldOffset(0)> Public hInproc As Integer
  <FieldOffset(0)> Public hRemote As Integer
End Structure
```

The importer uses a pair of pseudo-custom attributes, defined in System.Runtime.
InteropServices, to preserve the memory layout of the union in the value type definition:
StructLayoutAttribute and FieldOffsetAttribute. StructLayoutAttribute uses a value of
the LayoutKind enumeration to specify what kind of memory layout the value type uses. The
importer marks unions with LayoutKind.Explicit, indicating that every field of the struct is
marked with a byte offset. This byte offset, specified with FieldOffsetAttribute, is the number of bytes between the beginning of the structure in memory and the beginning of the field. In
Listing 4.18, you can see that each field of a union is marked with the same zero offset, meaning that the fields all point to the same location in memory. This is the only way to define a
union in .NET.

> **CAUTION**
>
> If a union contains a field that is a pointer to a type, the imported value type is given
> *no* fields whatsoever. Using such value types in managed code requires advanced
> techniques, such as C# unsafe code, demonstrated in Chapter 6.

The importer marks all value types that don't represent unions with StructLayoutAttribute
and the LayoutKind.Sequential value, but Listing 4.17 omitted this attribute for simplicity
(and because it's the default behavior in C# and VB .NET). See Chapter 19, "Deeper Into
PInvoke and Useful Examples," for more information about structure layout.

Converting Enumerations

An enumeration (commonly called an enum, and not to be confused with enumerating over a collection) is a set of constants of the same integral type, grouped under a common name. There's no significant difference between managed and unmanaged enums, so one is easily converted to the other, as shown in Listing 4.19.

LISTING 4.19   An Unmanaged Enum and a Managed Enum Are Both a Simple Set of Constants

`UNMANAGED`

Visual Basic 6:

```
Public Enum Day
  Sunday    = 0
  Monday    = 1
  Tuesday   = 2
  Wednesday = 3
  Thursday  = 4
  Friday    = 5
  Saturday  = 6
End Enum
```

IDL:

```
typedef [uuid(A6B79FB5-4E04-487A-86FC-33E52C5716E6)]
enum {
  Sunday    = 0,
  Monday    = 1,
  Tuesday   = 2,
  Wednesday = 3,
  Thursday  = 4,
  Friday    = 5,
  Saturday  = 6
} Day;
```

`MANAGED`

C#:

```
[Guid("A6B79FB5-4E04-487A-86FC-33E52C5716E6")]
public enum Day
{
  Sunday    = 0,
  Monday    = 1,
  Tuesday   = 2,
  Wednesday = 3,
```

4

AN IN-DEPTH LOOK AT IMPORTED ASSEMBLIES

LISTING 4.19   Continued

```
   Thursday  = 4,
   Friday    = 5,
   Saturday  = 6
}
```

Visual Basic .NET:

```
<Guid("A6B79FB5-4E04-487A-86FC-33E52C5716E6")> _
Public Enum Day
   Sunday    = 0
   Monday    = 1
   Tuesday   = 2
   Wednesday = 3
   Thursday  = 4
   Friday    = 5
   Saturday  = 6
End Enum
```

The main difference between managed and unmanaged enums is their use, not their definitions. In most .NET languages, you must qualify managed enum members with the name of the enum (for example, typing Day.Sunday instead of just Sunday in the previous listing).

Converting Typedefs

IDL can have type definitions (typedefs) that give an alternative name, or alias, to a type. The OLE Automation type library (STDOLE2.TLB in your system32 directory) contains many widely used typedefs, such as the following:

```
typedef [uuid(66504301-BE0F-101A-8BBB-00AA00300CAB), public]
unsigned long OLE_COLOR;
```

This means that OLE_COLOR is really nothing more than an unsigned long, but methods and properties can use OLE_COLOR parameters to represent colors because the alias makes the intent more obvious. For example, the Visual Basic 6 property browser presents a color chooser for properties of type OLE_COLOR, so users aren't directly exposed to the numeric representation.

There are no typedefs in the managed world, so the importer does not create a managed definition of typedefs such as OLE_COLOR. It does, however, do something special when encountering a signature that uses a typedef, such as:

```
HRESULT SetColor([in] OLE_COLOR color);
```

which becomes the following signature in C#:

```
void SetColor ([ComAliasName("stdole.OLE_COLOR")] uint color);
```

Because there is no managed definition of OLE_COLOR, the parameter is left as the real type. Rather than losing the information that the COM object treats the number as an OLE_COLOR, however, the importer marks the parameter with a custom attribute, called ComAliasNameAttribute. It's not quite as convenient (and not quite as obvious that it should be a color in object browsers, unless they show custom attributes), but you can still check for aliases and take action.

You might be wondering why the type library importer doesn't convert OLE_COLOR types to System.Drawing.Color types because the conversion seems as natural as converting DATE to System.DateTime. That would be nice, but the type library importer restricts itself to converting base types to the core types defined in the mscorlib assembly. However, the type library exporter, described in detail in Chapter 9, "An In-Depth Look at Exported Type Libraries," does the reverse conversion from System.Drawing.Color to OLE_COLOR.

TIP

If you're faced with calling COM methods in managed code that use OLE_COLOR parameters, note that there are two sets of methods in the .NET Framework that convert between a System.Drawing.Color instance and an OLE_COLOR:

- System.Drawing.ColorTranslator.ToOle and System.Drawing.ColorTranslator.FromOle.
- System.Windows.Forms.AxHost.GetOleColorFromColor and System.Windows.Forms.AxHost.GetColorFromOleColor.

Both sets of methods do the same thing, although I prefer the latter methods because they represent OLE_COLOR as an unsigned integer, which matches the types produced by the type library importer. Therefore, the SetColor method shown previously could be called as follows in C#:

```
comObj.SetColor(AxHost.GetOleColorFromColor(Color.BurlyWood));
```

For typedefs of structures or enumerations, the type library importer creates two versions of the same type but with two different names. For example, the Microsoft Smart Tag SDK defines the following typedef and enum pair in its type library (shown in IDL):

```
typedef [public]
__MIDL___MIDL_itf_mstag_0000_0001 IF_TYPE;

typedef enum {
  IF_TYPE_CHAR = 1,
  IF_TYPE_SINGLE_WD = 2,
```

```
IF_TYPE_REGEXP = 4,
IF_TYPE_PARA = 8,
IF_TYPE_CELL = 16
} __MIDL___MIDL_itf_mstag_0000_0001;
```

The Interop Assembly corresponding to this type library contains an enumeration named IF_TYPE and another enumeration named __MIDL___MIDL_itf_mstag_0000_0001. Fortunately, any signatures that use the typedef (IF_TYPE) are imported as signatures that use the value type with the matching name.

Converting ActiveX Controls

ActiveX controls are coclasses that are typically marked with the IDL control attribute (as seen in the familiar WebBrowser coclass from the Microsoft Internet Controls type library):

```
[
  uuid(8856F961-340A-11D0-A96B-00C04FD705A2),
  helpstring("WebBrowser Control"),
  control
]
coclass WebBrowser {
    [default] interface IWebBrowser2;
    interface IWebBrowser;
    [default, source] dispinterface DWebBrowserEvents2;
    [source] dispinterface DWebBrowserEvents;
};
```

The control attribute is optional. As discussed in Chapter 3, the official indicator that a COM class is an ActiveX control is the presence of the following registry value:

```
HKEY_CLASSES_ROOT\CLSID\{clsid}\Control
```

Chapter 3 also introduced a separate mechanism, specific to Windows Forms, that creates an ActiveX Assembly. This enables the control to be treated just like a Windows Forms control. Because this is separate from the type library importer, the importer treats a coclass, such as WebBrowser, no differently than any other coclass. The corresponding .NET class in the Interop Assembly can be used as a regular class, and should be used if you don't require extra functionality specific to ActiveX controls.

Thus, each ActiveX control definition can appear in three forms:

1. The *coclass* refers to the original definition of the class in a type library.

2. The *raw class* refers to the .NET class definition generated by the type library importer.

3. The *control class* refers to the .NET class definition generated by the ActiveX importer with special behavior specific to ActiveX and Windows Forms controls.

So, what exactly does the ActiveX importer produce in the ActiveX Assembly, and how does it relate to the Interop Assembly produced by the type library importer? The steps of the ActiveX importer can be summarized as follows:

1. If a Primary Interop Assembly isn't registered for the input type library, invoke the type library importer on the input type library to generate the Interop Assembly and any dependent Interop Assemblies. These assemblies are no different from the ones that would have been produced by any other means, such as running `TLBIMP.EXE`.

2. For each coclass registered as an ActiveX control, create a control class with the name Ax*ClassName* that derives from `System.Windows.Forms.AxHost`, and place it in an assembly called Ax*LibraryName*.

3. Add a public default constructor to each control class that constructs the base `AxHost` class by passing the CLSID of the corresponding coclass.

4. Add members of each coclass's default interface to each control class definition. This is in contrast to the type library importer, which adds the methods of all implemented interfaces to the raw class definition. Any methods or properties that conflict with members on base classes (such as `AxHost`) are given a `Ctl` prefix. Any events that conflict with members on base classes are given an `Event` suffix. Be aware that some properties might be added to the control class as raw accessor methods that can't be used with property syntax without modifications.

5. For any properties or methods that *return* a type marked with `ComAliasName("stdole.OLE_COLOR")`, convert the type to a `System.Drawing.Color` type. This enables COM color properties to be treated as .NET color properties (in the Visual Studio .NET property browser, for example). This transformation is not done for method parameters.

6. For any properties or methods that *return* an `IFont` or `IFontDisp` interface, convert the type to `System.Drawing.Font`. Similarly, convert `IPicture` to `System.Drawing.Image`. This enables COM fonts and COM images to be treated as .NET fonts and .NET images. As with `System.Drawing.Color`, these transformations are not done for method parameters.

7. Make any control classes implement `System.Collections.IEnumerable` if the corresponding raw class implements it. Besides this interface, no other interfaces are listed as being implemented by the control class besides interfaces implemented by the `AxHost` base class. (Not even the default COM interface that the control class effectively implements is listed as an implemented interface, due to potential changes in member signatures.)

8. Add some members to each control class to handle events and underlying plumbing.

9. Add additional types to the ActiveX Assembly to enable event handling in the Windows Forms style.

> **TIP**
>
> Because the AXIMP.EXE utility has a /source option to generate C# source code, you can clearly see what the contents of an ActiveX Assembly are (the result of the previous nine steps), and you can customize it for your purposes.

> **TIP**
>
> A .NET control class does not directly wrap a COM object as an RCW does. If you're using a control class in managed code but want to interact with the corresponding RCW instead, call the control's GetOcx method to obtain the desired object. GetOcx is defined on the System.Windows.Forms.AxHost class and inherited by all control classes. This needs to be done if you require casting the RCW to a non-default interface.

Steps 8 and 9 are covered in Chapter 5. The members added in step 4 are similar to the members that appear on the raw class, except no pseudo-custom attributes and almost no regular custom attributes are placed on the control class. The rationale is that the ActiveX importer does only what's necessary to make ActiveX controls appear as Windows Forms controls—no more and no less.

> **DIGGING DEEPER**
>
> The attentive reader might be wondering how pseudo-custom attributes can be omitted from a control class's members because pseudo-custom attributes (such as MarshalAsAttribute and PreserveSigAttribute) can be essential for properly interacting with COM methods. The answer is that the control classes created by the ActiveX importer don't directly call unmanaged code. Instead, the implementation of each member calls the member on a private field called ocx, defined as the coclass's default interface. This interface's definition, located in the Interop Assembly created by the type library importer, has all the necessary attributes to handle the call to the COM component correctly.

Conclusion

This chapter covered all the details of how .NET type information is generated from COM type information. These transformations are the key to COM objects being easily usable in .NET applications without requiring extensive modifications. Of course, the transformations work best for components that follow COM guidelines and conventions. For example, components that use a custom enumeration scheme, or custom data types that serve the same purpose as standard ones, cannot be transformed as nicely. (Such components would be hard to use from Visual Basic 6, so they should be quite rare.)

As you read the rest of this book, you may find yourself referring back to this chapter for a variety of reasons. For example, the importer's behavior is important if you ever want to

- Modify the type information produced by the type library importer (Chapter 7, "Modifying Interop Assemblies").
- Write your own type information manually instead of using the type library importer (Chapter 21, "Manually Defining COM Types in Source Code").
- Design COM components that may be used in .NET applications (Part V, "Designing Great COM Components for .NET Clients").

In this chapter, you also saw some of the ways in which a type library is less descriptive than IDL files. Chapter 7 demonstrates how to "add back" the missing information. I often get asked about why the type library importer omits a certain type or certain information from an Interop Assembly, and the reason is almost always that the information is not in the type library to begin with. For example, types defined in an IDL file outside of a `library` block do not get placed in a type library unless used by other types *inside* the `library` block. Viewing an input type library with `OLEVIEW.EXE` is the best way to understand its contents.

FAQ: Why are Interop Assemblies created from type libraries, even though they contain less information than IDL files?

There are three main reasons for this:

- Many more COM components have a type library and no IDL file than those that have an IDL file and no type library. For example, any COM component written in Visual Basic has a type library only.

- Reliable tools exist to create a type library from an IDL file (such as MIDL), but there is no official tool for reliably creating IDL from a type library. OLEVIEW.EXE is a useful type library viewer, but it is not a commercial-strength IDL generator.

- COM components are often deployed with a type library, but rarely with an IDL file. A good reason for this is that programs written in any Visual Studio 6 language can directly use type libraries (even Visual C++ with its #import statement), but they can't directly use IDL.

A tool that converts IDL to .NET metadata could be written to take advantage of extra information in an IDL file (mainly for arrays), but it would be a daunting task, combining the work of MIDL.EXE with the work of TLBIMP.EXE. Fortunately, as you'll see in Chapter 7, postprocessing the output of TLBIMP.EXE is a much easier task.

Responding to COM Events

IN THIS CHAPTER

- Callbacks in .NET   202
- Callbacks in COM   214
- Handling COM Events in Managed Code   218
- Handling ActiveX Control Events in Managed Code   235

In both COM and .NET, events play a central role in bi-directional communication. *Bi-directional communication* refers to the paradigm in which clients call into components, which in turn call back into clients. In graphical user interfaces, for example, bi-directional communication is natural because clients of user interface objects such as buttons, check boxes, and tabs wish to be notified when the human user changes their states. Besides graphical applications, callback functionality is commonly used for asynchronous processing when a method has a lot of work to do, or used to let clients insert their own logic inside a method's algorithm. For example, the caller of a sorting algorithm could be called back whenever two objects in a collection need to be compared, so the client can customize the algorithm to suit its needs.

The title of this chapter is overly simplified because, strictly speaking, COM doesn't have built-in events like .NET does. Instead, COM components often use a standard *connection points* protocol, described in this chapter, that tools like Visual Basic 6 are able to conceal in an abstraction of events. The developers of COM Interoperability went to great lengths to make "events" in COM be exposed as .NET events, but some aspects of this support are not intuitive to people encountering it for the first time. This chapter tells you everything you need to know about handling a COM component's events in managed code.

Callbacks in .NET

Although arguably less convoluted than COM's bi-directional conventions, the subject of bi-directional communication in .NET can often cause confusion. Before jumping into the topic of how COM events are exposed to .NET, it helps to understand the .NET callback mechanisms. This section briefly covers the three main mechanisms for implementing callback behavior in .NET applications:

- Passing an interface instance
- Passing a delegate
- Hooking up to events

Callback Interfaces

In the "callback interfaces" approach, a member can be defined with an interface parameter on which it calls members, perhaps on the same thread or perhaps on a different thread. With this scheme, any client object can simply implement the interface then pass itself (or an instance of another object implementing the interface) to the member. This is demonstrated with a contrived example in Listing 5.1.

LISTING 5.1   Using an Interface to Provide Callback Functionality in .NET

```csharp
 1: using System;
 2:
 3: public interface IChatRoomDisplay
 4: {
 5:   void DisplayMessage(string text);
 6:   void UserJoined(string user);
 7:   void UserLeft(string user);
 8: }
 9:
10: public class ConsoleDisplay : IChatRoomDisplay
11: {
12:   public void DisplayMessage(string text)
13:   {
14:     Console.WriteLine("MESSAGE: " + text);
15:   }
16:
17:   public void UserJoined(string user)
18:   {
19:     Console.WriteLine("JOINED: " + user);
20:   }
21:
22:   public void UserLeft(string user)
23:   {
24:     Console.WriteLine("LEFT: " + user);
25:   }
26: }
27:
28: public class ChatRoomClient
29: {
30:   public static void Main()
31:   {
32:     IChatRoomDisplay display = new ConsoleDisplay();
33:     ChatRoomServer server = new ChatRoomServer();
34:     ...
35:     server.Run(display);
36:     ...
37:   }
38: }
39:
40: public class ChatRoomServer
41: {
42:   public void Run(IChatRoomDisplay display)
43:   {
44:     ...
```

LISTING 5.1   Continued

```
45:      // The callback
46:      if (display != null) display.DisplayMessage(text);
47:      ...
48:   }
49: }
```

Lines 3–8 define a callback interface—IChatRoomDisplay—that is used by the Run method in Lines 42–48. The ConsoleDisplay class in Lines 10–26 implements the three callback methods and acts as the callee when ChatRoomServer.Run calls its DisplayMessage method.

This pattern of callback interfaces is used in several places in the .NET Framework. For example, an object implementing System.Collections.IComparer can be passed to System.Array.Sort or System.Array.BinarySearch for callback purposes. A class type could be used in a method signature for callbacks rather than an interface, but this is usually undesirable because it limits the types of objects that can be passed in.

Delegates

Whereas an interface is a contract for a collection of methods, a delegate is a contract for a single method. Delegates are often referred to as type-safe function pointers because they represent a reference to any method with a signature that matches the delegate definition—whether it's an instance method or static method (Shared in Visual Basic .NET).

Delegates can be used for callbacks on a method-by-method basis rather than using an interface with potentially several members (such as IChatRoomClient and its three methods). Besides supporting bi-directional communication at the granularity of methods, delegates also enable *multicasting* of callbacks. This means that multiple delegates can be combined together such that what appears to be a single callback to the callback initiator is actually a method invocation on every one of a list of methods.

A delegate is declared like a method with no body plus an extra keyword:

C#:

```
delegate void DisplayMessage(string text);
```

Visual Basic .NET:

```
Delegate Sub DisplayMessage(text As String)
```

C++:

```
__delegate DisplayMessage(String* text);
```

When compiled to metadata, delegates are represented as classes deriving from
System.Delegate or the derived System.MulticastDelegate class (for multicast delegates).
All delegates defined in C#, Visual Basic .NET, or C++ are emitted as multicast delegates.
Because delegates are types just like classes or interfaces, they can appear outside a type defin-
ition or inside as a nested type. Listing 5.2 updates the callback example from Listing 5.1
using delegates.

LISTING 5.2   Using Delegates to Provide Callback Functionality in C#

```
 1: using System;
 2:
 3: // The delegates
 4: public delegate void DisplayMessage(string text);
 5: public delegate void UserJoined(string user);
 6: public delegate void UserLeft(string user);
 7:
 8: public class Display
 9: {
10:   public void ConsoleMessage(string text)
11:   {
12:     Console.WriteLine("MESSAGE: " + text);
13:   }
14:
15:   public void AnnoyingMessage(string text)
16:   {
17:     System.Windows.Forms.MessageBox.Show("MESSAGE: " + text);
18:   }
19: }
20:
21: public class ChatRoomClient
22: {
23:   public static void Main()
24:   {
25:     Display display = new Display();
26:     ChatRoomServer server = new ChatRoomServer();
27:     DisplayMessage one = new DisplayMessage(display.ConsoleMessage);
28:     DisplayMessage two = new DisplayMessage(display.AnnoyingMessage);
29:     DisplayMessage both = one + two;
30:     ...
31:     server.Run(both);
32:     ...
33:   }
34: }
35:
```

LISTING 5.2 Continued

```
36: public class ChatRoomServer
37: {
38:   public void Run(DisplayMessage display)
39:   {
40:     ...
41:     // The callback
42:     if (display != null) display(text);
43:     ...
44:   }
45: }
```

Lines 4–6 define three delegates replacing the single interface from Listing 5.1. In this example, the Display class chooses to provide two methods matching only one delegate—DisplayMessage. Because an implementation for UserJoined or UserLeft is not required by this version of the ChatRoomServer.Run method, the class doesn't have to bother with them. Lines 27 and 28 create two delegates by passing the function name with a given instance to the delegate's constructor. The C# compiler treats delegate construction specially, hiding the fact that a delegate's constructor requires an instance and a function pointer. In C++, you have to instantiate a delegate as follows:

```
DisplayMessage* one = new DisplayMessage(display, &Display::ConsoleMessage);
DisplayMessage* two = new DisplayMessage(display, &Display::AnnoyingMessage);
```

Line 29 creates a third delegate by adding the previous two. This provides multicasting behavior so the call to the delegate in Line 42 invokes both the ConsoleMessage and AnnoyingMessage methods (in no guaranteed order). Often, the += and -= operators are used with multicast delegates in order to add/subtract a new delegate from an existing one.

Listing 5.3 demonstrates the same code that uses delegates from Listing 5.2, but in Visual Basic .NET rather than C#.

LISTING 5.3 Using Delegates to Provide Callback Functionality in Visual Basic .NET

```
 1: Imports System
 2:
 3: ' The delegates
 4: Public Delegate Sub DisplayMessage(ByVal text As String)
 5: Public Delegate Sub UserJoined(ByVal user As String)
 6: Public Delegate Sub UserLeft(ByVal user As String)
 7:
 8: Public Class Display
 9:   Public Sub ConsoleMessage(ByVal text As String)
10:     Console.WriteLine("MESSAGE: " & text)
```

LISTING 5.3   Continued

```
11:    End Sub
12:
13:    Public Sub AnnoyingMessage(ByVal text As String)
14:      System.Windows.Forms.MessageBox.Show("MESSAGE: " & text)
15:    End Sub
16: End Class
17:
18: Module ChatRoomClient
19:    Sub Main()
20:      Dim display As New Display()
21:      Dim server As New ChatRoomServer()
22:      Dim one As DisplayMessage = AddressOf display.ConsoleMessage
23:      Dim two As DisplayMessage = AddressOf display.AnnoyingMessage
24:      Dim both As DisplayMessage = both.Combine(one, two)
25:      ...
26:      server.Run(both)
27:      ...
28:    End Sub
29: End Module
30:
31: Public Class ChatRoomServer
32:    Public Sub Run(ByVal display As DisplayMessage)
33:      ...
34:      ' The callback
35:      If (Not display Is Nothing) Then display(text)
36:      ...
37:    End Sub
38: End Class
```

Lines 4–6 define the three delegates, and Lines 8–16 contain the Display class with two methods that match the signature of DisplayMessage. Lines 22 and 23 create two delegates by simply using the AddressOf keyword before the name of each method. Lines 22 and 23 could have been replaced with the following longer syntax:

```
Dim one As DisplayMessage = _
  New DisplayMessage(AddressOf display.ConsoleMessage)
Dim two As DisplayMessage = _
  New DisplayMessage(AddressOf display.AnnoyingMessage)
```

but the shorter version used in the listing is preferred.

Line 24 creates the both delegate by combining the previous two. Visual Basic .NET doesn't support overloaded operators (such as + used in Listing 5.2), but calling Delegate.Combine

5

has the same effect as adding two delegates in C#. Similarly, calling `Delegate.Remove` has the same effect as subtracting one delegate from another in C#.

Events

Events are a layer of abstraction over multicast delegates. Whereas delegates are types, events are first class *members* of types just like methods, properties, and fields. An event member is defined with a multicast delegate type, representing the "type" of event, or the signature that any handlers of it must have, for example:

C#:

```
// The delegate
public delegate void DisplayMessageEventHandler(string text);
// The event
public event DisplayMessageEventHandler DisplayMessage;
```

Visual Basic .NET:

```
' The delegate
Public Delegate Sub DisplayMessageEventHandler(text As String)
' The event
Public Event DisplayMessage As DisplayMessageEventHandler
```

C++:

```
// The delegate
public: __delegate DisplayMessageEventHandler(String* text);
// The event
public: __event DisplayMessageEventHandler* DisplayMessage;
```

By convention, delegates representing event handler signatures are given an `EventHandler` suffix. Visual Basic .NET further simplifies event definitions by enabling you to specify a delegate signature directly in the event definition:

```
Public Event DisplayMessage(text As String)
```

In this case, the compiler emits a delegate with the name `DisplayMessageEventHandler`, nested in the class containing the event.

Just as a property is typically just an abstraction over a private field of the same type with get and/or set accessors, an event, by default, is an abstraction over a private field of the same delegate type with two accessors called *add* and *remove*. These two accessor methods expose the delegate's `Combine` (+) and `Remove` (-) functionality, respectively, and nothing else.

A consequence of the event's corresponding delegate field being private is that it can only be invoked—and therefore the event can only be raised—by the class defining the event, even if the event member is public. This is the reason classes with events often define protected On*EventName* methods that raise an event, so derived classes can raise them too.

FAQ: Why would I define a .NET class with events instead of simply using delegates?

Encapsulation is the reason to use events rather than only delegates in .NET applications. Because the only delegate functionality exposed to other classes is adding and removing delegates to the invocation list, the user of an event cannot reassign the delegate field to another instance and thereby disconnect any other event handlers hooked up to the delegate. For a Windows Form, for example, a C# client is prevented from incorrectly doing the following:

```
// Anyone else listening to the Resize event is disconnected
myForm.Resize = new EventHandler(Resize);
```

and must do the following instead:

```
myForm.Resize += new EventHandler(Resize);
```

Another good reason to use events is so clients can take advantage of built-in support in the Visual Studio .NET IDE. For example, events of Windows Forms controls can be exposed in the property and event browser for easy event handler hookup.

An interesting difference between defining events and defining properties is that an event's accessors and the private field being used by the accessors are all emitted by default in C# and Visual Basic .NET. In C#, you can opt to explicitly define these accessors in case you want to implement the event in an alternative way, but the default behavior is almost always sufficient. To get a clear picture of what an event definition really means, here's how you could define everything explicitly in C# and get the same behavior as the `DisplayMessage` event definitions shown previously:

```
// Private delegate field
private DisplayMessageEventHandler displayMessage;

// Public event with explicit add/remove accessors
public event DisplayMessageEventHandler DisplayMessage
{
  [MethodImpl(MethodImplOptions.Synchronized)]
  add { displayMessage += value; }
  [MethodImpl(MethodImplOptions.Synchronized)]
  remove { displayMessage -= value; }
}
```

The `MethodImplAttribute` pseudo-custom attribute is used with the `Synchronized` value to ensure that multiple threads can't execute these accessors simultaneously.

Listing 5.4 continues the example from the previous three listings, but this time using events instead of callback interfaces or just delegates.

LISTING 5.4   Using Events to Provide Callback Functionality in C#

```
 1: using System;
 2:
 3: // The delegates
 4: public delegate void DisplayMessageEventHandler(string text);
 5: public delegate void UserJoinedEventHandler(string user);
 6: public delegate void UserLeftEventHandler(string user);
 7:
 8: public class Display
 9: {
10:   public void ConsoleMessage(string text)
11:   {
12:     Console.WriteLine("MESSAGE: " + text);
13:   }
14:
15:   public void AnnoyingMessage(string text)
16:   {
17:     System.Windows.Forms.MessageBox.Show("MESSAGE: " + text);
18:   }
19: }
20:
21: public class ChatRoomClient
22: {
23:   public static void Main()
24:   {
25:     Display display = new Display();
26:     ChatRoomServer server = new ChatRoomServer();
27:     server.DisplayMessage += new
28:       DisplayMessageEventHandler(display.ConsoleMessage);
29:     server.DisplayMessage += new
30:       DisplayMessageEventHandler(display.AnnoyingMessage);
31:     ...
32:     server.Run();
33:     ...
34:     server.DisplayMessage -= new
35:       DisplayMessageEventHandler(display.ConsoleMessage);
36:     server.DisplayMessage -= new
37:       DisplayMessageEventHandler(display.AnnoyingMessage);
38:   }
39: }
40:
41: public class ChatRoomServer
42: {
```

LISTING 5.4 Continued

```
43:    // The events
44:    public event DisplayMessageEventHandler DisplayMessage;
45:    public event UserJoinedEventHandler UserJoined;
46:    public event UserLeftEventHandler UserLeft;
47:
48:    public void Run()
49:    {
50:       ...
51:       // The callback
52:       if (DisplayMessage != null) DisplayMessage(text);
53:       ...
54:    }
55: }
```

This listing starts the same as Listing 5.2, but with the delegates renamed with an
EventHandler suffix. ChatRoomServer now has three event members defined in Lines 44–46,
each one using one of the three delegate types. ChatRoomClient adds two delegates to the
DisplayMessage event (Lines 27–30) and removes them when it's finished listening to the
events (Lines 34–37). Line 52, by invoking the delegate, causes the event to be raised so both
ConsoleMessage and AnnoyingMessage are executed.

FAQ: What do I use on the right side of the -= operator when unhooking an event handler? How could subtracting a new delegate instance possibly unhook the instance that was added?

Unhooking an event handler is an odd-looking operation because a new delegate
instance is usually what gets subtracted rather than the delegate instance that was
originally added. For example:

```
// Hook up the event handler
server.DisplayMessage +=
  new DisplayMessageEventHandler(display.ConsoleMessage);
...
// Unhook the event handler
server.DisplayMessage -=
  new DisplayMessageEventHandler(display.ConsoleMessage);
```

It turns out that the implementation of Delegate.Add and Delegate.Remove disre-
gards delegate *instances*; all that's important is the object instance and function
passed to a delegate's constructor. Therefore, it's not necessary to store a delegate
instance you've added in order to remove it later, and the delegate subtraction code
in Listing 5.4 is correct.

In Visual Basic .NET, hooking and unhooking an event handler to an event is done using `AddHandler` and `RemoveHandler` statements, respectively, rather than `+=` and `-=`. Raising an event must be done with a `RaiseEvent` statement. Listing 5.5 demonstrates this by updating Listing 5.4 to Visual Basic .NET.

LISTING 5.5   Using Events to Provide Callback Functionality in Visual Basic .NET

```vb
 1: Imports System
 2:
 3: Public Class Display
 4:   Public Sub ConsoleMessage(ByVal text As String)
 5:     Console.WriteLine("MESSAGE: " & text)
 6:   End Sub
 7:
 8:   Public Sub AnnoyingMessage(ByVal text As String)
 9:     System.Windows.Forms.MessageBox.Show("MESSAGE: " & text)
10:   End Sub
11: End Class
12:
13: Module ChatRoomClient
14:   Sub Main()
15:     Dim display As New Display()
16:     Dim server As New ChatRoomServer()
17:     AddHandler server.DisplayMessage, AddressOf display.ConsoleMessage
18:     AddHandler server.DisplayMessage, AddressOf display.AnnoyingMessage
19:     ...
20:     server.Run()
21:     ...
22:     RemoveHandler server.DisplayMessage, AddressOf display.ConsoleMessage
23:     RemoveHandler server.DisplayMessage, AddressOf display.AnnoyingMessage
24:   End Sub
25: End Module
26:
27: Public Class ChatRoomServer
28:   Public Event DisplayMessage(ByVal text As String)
29:   Public Event UserJoined(ByVal user As String)
30:   Public Event UserLeft(ByVal user As String)
31:
32:   Public Sub Run()
33:     ...
34:     ' The callback
35:     RaiseEvent DisplayMessage(text)
36:     ...
37:   End Sub
38: End Class
```

The combination of delegate-less event definitions in Lines 28–30 and delegate-less event hookup using AddHandler and RemoveHandler in Lines 17–18 and 22–23 means that Visual Basic .NET programmers often don't need to be aware of the existence of delegates to use events. The compiler hides all of the underlying delegate details. The RaiseEvent statement in Line 35 handles the null check before invoking the event's delegate, which had to be performed explicitly in C#. So if the DisplayMessage event had no handlers attached, Line 35 would have no effect.

As with Visual Basic 6, Visual Basic .NET enables the use of a WithEvents keyword to make the use of events even easier than in Listing 5.5. Listing 5.6 demonstrates how to use WithEvents in Visual Basic .NET.

LISTING 5.6   Using the WithEvents Shortcut in Visual Basic .NET

```
 1: Imports System
 2:
 3: Module ChatRoomClient
 4:   Dim WithEvents server As New ChatRoomServer()
 5:
 6:   Sub Main()
 7:     ...
 8:     server.Run()
 9:     ...
10:   End Sub
11:
12:   Public Sub ConsoleMessage(ByVal text As String) _
13:     Handles server.DisplayMessage
14:     Console.WriteLine("MESSAGE: " & text)
15:   End Sub
16:
17:   Public Sub AnnoyingMessage(ByVal text As String) _
18:     Handles server.DisplayMessage
19:     System.Windows.Forms.MessageBox.Show("MESSAGE: " & text)
20:   End Sub
21: End Module
22:
23: Public Class ChatRoomServer
24:   Public Event DisplayMessage(ByVal text As String)
25:   Public Event UserJoined(ByVal user As String)
26:   Public Event UserLeft(ByVal user As String)
27:
28:   Public Sub Run()
29:     ...
30:     ' The callback
31:     RaiseEvent DisplayMessage(text)
```

LISTING 5.6 Continued

```
32:     ...
33:    End Sub
34: End Class
```

When you declare a class or module variable using WithEvents (Line 4), any of the class's or module's event handler methods are automatically added and removed to the instance when appropriate. Event handler methods are identified with the Handles keyword, seen in Lines 13 and 18. The Handles keyword in Line 13 states that the ConsoleMessage method is an event handler for the server object's DisplayMessage event. Similarly, the Handles keyword in Line 18 states that AnnoyingMessage is also an event handler for the server object's DisplayMessage event. The appropriate AddHandler and RemoveHandler functionality is handled automatically by the compiler.

Callbacks in COM

In COM, three callback mechanisms are analogous to the .NET mechanisms:

- Passing an interface instance
- Passing a function pointer
- Using connection points (events in Visual Basic 6)

Using callback interfaces in COM is the exact same idea as using callback interfaces in .NET. It tends to be a fairly common pattern, especially for C++-authored COM components, because using connection points adds complexity for both ends of the communication channel. Chapter 6, "Advanced Topics for Using COM Components," has an example of a DirectX COM object that uses a callback interface. Function pointers are a precursor to delegates. Because they aren't commonly used in COM and aren't important for this chapter, there's no need to cover them any further. Using unmanaged function pointers in managed code is covered in Chapter 19, "Deeper Into PInvoke and Useful Examples."

Connection points are the COM equivalent of .NET events. Connection points are really just a general protocol for setting up and using interface callbacks. The generic nature of the protocol enables tools like Visual Basic 6 to abstract it inside event-like syntax. Notice the difference here—.NET events are based on delegates for method-level granularity whereas COM events are really based on interfaces (collections of methods).

The terminology for describing connection points in COM is notoriously confusing, so here's an attempt to sort out the terms before describing the interfaces and protocol:

- The object causing an event to be raised is called the *source*, also known as a *connectable object*. This was the ChatRoomServer class in Listings 5.4, 5.5, and 5.6. This is clearer than calling it something like a "server" because bi-directional communication causes clients to sometimes be servers and servers to sometimes be clients!

- The object handling ("listening to") events is called the *sink*. This was the Display class in Listings 5.4 and 5.5 because it contained the implementation that was being called from the source.

- The callback interface that is implemented by the sink and called by the source is called a *source interface*, or sometimes called an *outgoing interface*. This was the IChatRoomDisplay interface in Listing 5.1.

- For each source interface that the source calls back upon, the object doing the actual callbacks is called a *connection point*. Every connection point corresponds exactly to one source interface.

- A sink object being attached to a connection point (from passing it a callback interface) is considered a *connection*.

The source interface is really the focus of the connection point protocol, and is nothing more than a callback interface. To Visual Basic 6 programs, source interfaces appear to behave like a collection of events. Through a series of initialization steps, the sink (or an object using the sink) passes the sink-implemented interface pointer to the source so it can call back on the interface to simulate events. The part that often confuses people is that the source coclass usually lists source interfaces in its coclass statement marked with the IDL [source] attribute. For example, a coclass representing the ChatRoomServer class from Listing 5.1 might look like the following:

```
[
  uuid(0002DF01-0000-0000-C000-000000000046)
]
coclass ChatRoomServer {
  [default] interface IChatRoomServer;
  [default, source] dispinterface IChatRoomDisplay;
};
```

This does not mean that the ChatRoomServer class *implements* IChatRoomDisplay; it doesn't. Instead, it's simply expressing that it supports calling back members of the IChatRoomDisplay interface when an instance is passed to it using the connection points protocol. Listing source interfaces is the way for a COM class to advertise to type library consumers such as Visual Basic 6 that the class "has events." This is analogous to .NET classes defining public event members. In any coclass's list of source interfaces, one is always considered the default, just as with implemented interfaces. The default source interface is the only one accessible as a collection of events in Visual Basic 6 programs.

DIGGING DEEPER

> The `IChatRoomDisplay` source interface in the previous coclass definition was marked as a dispinterface because that's the only kind of source interface that Visual Basic 6 can expose as events. For this reason, source interfaces are almost always defined to be dispinterfaces. (This is also the default behavior for source interfaces generated by the ATL wizard in Visual C++.) Note that this is not a restriction of the connection points protocol, nor is it required for COM Interoperability.

At run time, the `[source]` markings in a type library are meaningless; COM classes advertise that they support events by implementing an interface called `IConnectionPointContainer` *and* by returning connection point objects via this interface. This interface has two methods—`EnumConnectionPoints` and `FindConnectionPoint`.

`EnumConnectionPoints` can be called to discover all the connection points and their source interfaces supported by the object. This method returns an `IEnumConnectionPoints` interface, which provides methods to enumerate over the collection of connection points, each of which is represented as an `IConnectionPoint` interface.

`FindConnectionPoint` enables a client to ask for a specific connection point identified by an IID of a source interface. This is extremely similar to `QueryInterface`, but in this case a client asks what source interfaces the object calls rather than what interfaces the object implements. If successful, an `IConnectionPoint` interface is returned.

Connection point objects (which implement `IConnectionPoint`) are provided by the connectable object, representing a collection of events. Just as a .NET event has `add` and `remove` accessors that enable clients to hook and unhook event handler delegates, `IConnectionPoint` has `Advise` and `Unadvise` methods that enable clients to hook and unhook a callback interface pointer as follows:

- A client calls `Advise` with an `IUnknown` pointer to itself, then `Advise` passes back an integral "cookie" that uniquely identifies the connection. The callback object being passed to `Advise` must implement the appropriate source interface.

- When the client is finished listening to events, it can call `Unadvise` with the cookie value obtained from `Advise` to notify the connectable object.

`IConnectionPoint` has a few additional methods that enable enumerating of connections, obtaining the IID of a connection point's source interface, or obtaining a connection point's container, but they aren't important for this discussion.

Figure 5.1 illustrates the steps of the connection points protocol in a typical scenario. The sink object is traditionally the client object that initiates the connections, waits to receive event notifications, then terminates the connections when finished. The first four steps comprise the initialization phase, similar to hooking up event handlers in .NET. Step 5 represents the period of time when any "events are raised"—the source object calls back on the sink object's source interface whenever appropriate. Finally, Step 6 terminates the connection. In this illustration, the object that sets up the connection point communication *is* the sink object, but often this client might *contain* one or more sink objects, much like the source object contains one or more connection points.

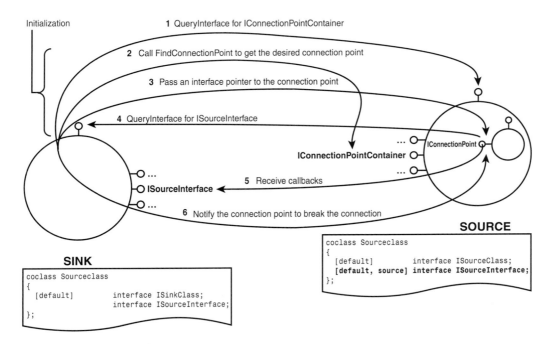

FIGURE 5.1

Connection points summarized.

The connection point infrastructure doesn't prevent multicasting of events, but this needs to be managed manually by the connectable objects, just as it could be done with callback interfaces. For example, a connectable object could enumerate through its list of connections and call each sink object's method one-by-one.

Handling COM Events in Managed Code

Now that we've covered how callback functionality commonly appears in .NET and COM applications, it's time to examine how to handle callbacks from COM in .NET applications. As mentioned in the previous section, handling unmanaged callback interfaces and function pointers in managed code is demonstrated in Chapters 6 and 19. In addition, the details of implementing COM interfaces in managed code are covered in Chapter 14, "Implementing COM Interfaces for Binary Compatibility," because this falls under the realm of writing .NET components for COM "clients." So let's move on to connection points.

First, we'll briefly look at the raw approach of using connection points in managed code. This approach works, but it doesn't leverage any of COM Interoperability's event-specific support. Then, we'll look at the transformations made by the type library importer related to events, and the behavior they enable.

The Raw Approach

Suppose that you want to use the `InternetExplorer` coclass defined in the Microsoft Internet Controls type library (`SHDOCVW.DLL`), which is defined as follows:

```
[
  uuid(0002DF01-0000-0000-C000-000000000046),
  helpstring("Internet Explorer Application.")
]
coclass InternetExplorer {
  [default] interface IWebBrowser2;
  interface IWebBrowserApp;
  [default, source] dispinterface DWebBrowserEvents2;
  [source] dispinterface DWebBrowserEvents;
};
```

Also suppose that you want to handle "events" raised from its default source interface. Following the steps explained in the last section, you could interact with connection points the same way you would in unmanaged C++ code. The .NET Framework provides .NET definitions of all the connection point interfaces in the `System.Runtime.InteropServices` namespace, although renamed with a `UCOM` prefix (which stands for *unmanaged COM*). Listing 5.7 demonstrates how this could be done in C#.

CAUTION

The code in Listing 5.7 is *not* the recommended way to handle COM events in managed code, because it doesn't take advantage of built-in event-specific Interop support discussed in the "Type Library Importer Transformations" section. When you have an Interop Assembly with these transformations, you can use events in a more natural fashion.

LISTING 5.7   Using Raw Connection Points in C# to Handle Internet Explorer Events

```
 1: using System;
 2: using SHDocVw;
 3: using System.Runtime.InteropServices;
 4:
 5: public class BrowserListener : DWebBrowserEvents2
 6: {
 7:   private UCOMIConnectionPoint icp;  // The connection point
 8:   private int cookie = -1;           // The cookie for the connection
 9:
10:   public BrowserListener()
11:   {
12:     InternetExplorer ie = new InternetExplorer();
13:
14:     // Call QueryInterface for IConnectionPointContainer
15:     UCOMIConnectionPointContainer icpc = (UCOMIConnectionPointContainer)ie;
16:
17:     // Find the connection point for the
18:     // DWebBrowserEvents2 source interface
19:     Guid g = typeof(DWebBrowserEvents2).GUID;
20:     icpc.FindConnectionPoint(ref g, out icp);
21:
22:     // Pass a pointer to the host to the connection point
23:     icp.Advise(this, out cookie);
24:
25:     // Show the browser
26:     ie.Visible = true;
27:     ie.GoHome();
28:   }
29:
30:   ~BrowserListener()
31:   {
32:     // End the connection
33:     if (cookie != -1) icp.Unadvise(cookie);
34:   }
35:
36:   // Event handlers for all of the source interface's methods
37:
38:   public void DownloadBegin()
39:   {
40:     Console.WriteLine("DownloadBegin");
41:   }
42:
43:   public void NavigateComplete2(object pDisp, ref object URL)
44:   {
```

LISTING 5.7 Continued

```
45:        Console.WriteLine("NavigateComplete2: " + URL);
46:    }
47:
48:    public void OnQuit()
49:    {
50:        Console.WriteLine("OnQuit");
51:
52:        // End the connection
53:        icp.Unadvise(cookie);
54:        cookie = -1;
55:
56:        Environment.Exit(0);
57:    }
58:
59:    public void OnStatusBar(bool StatusBar)
60:    {
61:        Console.WriteLine("OnStatusBar: " + StatusBar);
62:    }
63:
64:    ...
65:
66:    public static void Main()
67:    {
68:        BrowserListener host = new BrowserListener();
69:
70:        // Keep the program running while Internet Explorer is open
71:        Console.WriteLine("*** Press Enter to quit ***");
72:        Console.Read();
73:    }
74: }
```

A Primary Interop Assembly (PIA) for SHDOCVW.DLL does not exist at the time of writing, so this listing references a standard Interop Assembly, which can be generated by running the following from a command prompt:

```
tlbimp shdocvw.dll /namespace:SHDocVw /out:Interop.SHDocVw.dll
```

The BrowserListener class implements the DWebBrowserEvents2 source interface because it's acting as a sink object that will be passed to the connection point. Therefore, all of the source interface's methods must be implemented in Lines 38–64. For brevity, only four such methods are shown, but the complete source code is available on this book's Web site. Each method implementation prints the "event" name to the console plus some additional information, if applicable, passed in as parameters to the method.

The constructor in Lines 10–28 instantiates the `InternetExplorer` coclass then does the connection point initialization described in the previous section. First, it obtains a reference to the `InternetExplorer` object's `IConnectionPointContainer` interface by casting the object to `UCOMIConnectionPointContainer` in Line 15. Line 19 retrieves the IID for the source interface corresponding to the desired connection point, and Line 20 calls `FindConnectionPoint` to retrieve an `IConnectionPoint` instance for the IID.

> **TIP**
>
> `System.Type`'s `GUID` property is a handy way to obtain the GUID for any COM type with a metadata definition. An instance of the object isn't needed because you can obtain the desired type object by using `typeof` in C#, `GetType` in Visual Basic .NET, or `__typeof` in C++.

Line 23 calls `UCOMIConnectionPoint.Advise`, which sends a reference to the sink object to the connection point and gets a cookie in return. The cookie is used when calling `Unadvise` in the finalizer on Line 33 or in the `OnQuit` event handler on Line 53. Line 54 sets the cookie value to -1 so `Unadvise` isn't called twice when the user closes Internet Explorer before closing our example application.

The result of running the program in Listing 5.7 is shown in Figure 5.2. The console window logs all events occurring from the user's actions inside the launched Internet Explorer window.

FIGURE 5.2

Running the program in Listing 5.7.

5

RESPONDING TO
COM EVENTS

That's all there is to manually performing event handling using connection points in managed code. Of course, the previous listing undoubtedly seems unacceptable to Visual Basic 6 programmers. This approach has the following problems:

- It's obvious that we're dealing with a COM object, because the connection point protocol is foreign to .NET components.
- Using connection points isn't as easy as the event abstraction provided by Visual Basic 6.
- All of the source interface methods had to be implemented, even if we only cared about a handful of the events.

To solve these problems, the type library importer produces several types to expose connection points as standard .NET events. These types are discussed in the next section.

Type Library Importer Transformations

To expose connection points as .NET events, the type library importer does a lot of extra work besides the usual transformations. Every time the type library importer encounters an interface listed with the [source] attribute, it creates some additional types:

- *SourceInterfaceName*_Event—An interface just like the source interface but with .NET event members instead of plain methods. Each event is named the same as its corresponding method on the source interface and has a delegate type with the same signature as its corresponding source interface method. This is commonly referred to as an *event interface*. Such an interface's name typically looks unusual because source interfaces usually have an Events suffix, resulting in a name with an Events_Event suffix.
- *SourceInterfaceName*_*MethodName*EventHandler—A delegate corresponding to a single method on the source interface. The delegate has the same signature as the source interface's corresponding method. Such a delegate is generated for every source interface method.
- *SourceInterfaceName*_EventProvider—A private class that implements the *SourceInterfaceName*_Event interface, handling the interaction with the connection point inside the events' implementation.
- *SourceInterfaceName*_SinkHelper—A private sink class that implements the source interface. These objects are passed to the COM object's IConnectionPoint.Advise method and receive the callbacks, as in Listing 5.7.

The private event provider class obtains the COM object's connection point container and the appropriate connection point, and the private sink helper class implements the source interface, so managed code that uses the importer-generated events is insulated from any connection point interaction. These types work the same way even if multiple coclasses share the same source interface(s). The sink helper effectively transforms an entire interface into independent methods that can be selectively used on a method-by-method basis. Visual Basic 6 provides a similar abstraction with its dynamic sink object, discussed in Chapter 13, "Exposing .NET Events to COM Clients."

DIGGING DEEPER

> The event provider and sink helper classes are the only types generated by the type library importer that contain a managed code implementation. Viewing these types using ILDASM.EXE, you can see the IL instructions that differentiate these types from the others.

To help make using the events as seamless as possible, an imported class and its coclass interface are also affected when a coclass lists at least one source interface in its type library. The .NET class type (such as InternetExplorerClass for the previous example) implements the event interface for each one of the coclass's source interfaces. As with its regular implemented interfaces, any name conflicts caused by multiple source interfaces with same-named members are handled by renaming conflicting members to *InterfaceName_MemberName*. Unfortunately, in this case *InterfaceName* corresponds to the importer-generated event interface name and not the original source interface. So, in the case of a name conflict, the event gets the odd-looking name *SourceInterfaceName_Event_SourceInterfaceMethodName*.

CAUTION

> Name conflicts in classes that support multiple source interfaces can be quite common, resulting in really long event member names. For example, it's a common practice to implement multiple source interfaces where one interface is a later version of another, duplicating all of its methods and adding a few more. The InternetExplorer coclass does this with its DWebBrowserEvents2 and DWebBrowserEvents source interfaces (although each interface has members that the other does not). This results in the .NET InternetExplorerClass type having event members such as StatusTextChange and DWebBrowserEvents_Event_ StatusTextChange.
>
> Another common example of name conflicts occurs between methods and events. It's common to have a Quit method and a Quit event, for instance. For these conflicts, the .NET method gets the original name and the .NET event gets the decorated name such as DWebBrowserEvents_Event_Quit.
>
> Fortunately, C# and Visual Basic .NET programs usually don't use the importer-generated class types directly due to the abstraction provided for coclass interfaces. These renamed members are mostly noticeable for C++ programmers or for users of an object browser.

The coclass interface (such as `InternetExplorer`, in the previous example) derives from the event interface corresponding to the *default* source interface, but no others. This is consistent with the fact that a coclass interface only derives from its default interface and no other interfaces implemented by the original coclass. Therefore, the event members can be used directly on these types.

> **CAUTION**
>
> In version 1.0 of the CLR, the type library importer doesn't properly handle type libraries containing a class that lists a source interface defined in a separate type library. One workaround is to edit the type library by extracting an IDL file using a tool like OLEVIEW.EXE, modifying the IDL, then compiling a new type library to import using MIDL.EXE. In IDL, you could either omit the source interface from the coclass's interface list, or you could redefine the interface in the same type library.

Using the Event Abstraction

Now that you've seen all the extra types that the type library importer creates for connectable COM objects, it's time to use them. Listing 5.8 is an update to the C# code in Listing 5.7, using the recommended .NET event abstraction rather than dealing with connection point interfaces.

LISTING 5.8 Using .NET Events in C# to Handle Internet Explorer Events

```
 1: using System;
 2: using SHDocVw;
 3:
 4: public class BrowserListener
 5: {
 6:   private InternetExplorer ie;
 7:
 8:   public BrowserListener()
 9:   {
10:     ie = new InternetExplorer();
11:
12:     // Hook up event handlers to the events we care about
13:     ie.DocumentComplete += new
14:       DWebBrowserEvents2_DocumentCompleteEventHandler(DocumentComplete);
15:     ie.ProgressChange += new
16:       DWebBrowserEvents2_ProgressChangeEventHandler(ProgressChange);
17:     ie.TitleChange += new
18:       DWebBrowserEvents2_TitleChangeEventHandler(TitleChange);
19:
20:     // Events corresponding to the non-default source interface:
```

LISTING 5.8   Continued

```
21:      ((DWebBrowserEvents_Event)ie).WindowResize += new
22:        DWebBrowserEvents_WindowResizeEventHandler(WindowResize);
23:      ((DWebBrowserEvents_Event)ie).Quit += new
24:        DWebBrowserEvents_QuitEventHandler(Quit);
25:
26:      // Show the browser
27:      ie.Visible = true;
28:      ie.GoHome();
29:    }
30:
31:    public void DocumentComplete(object pDisp, ref object URL)
32:    {
33:      Console.WriteLine("DocumentComplete: " + URL);
34:    }
35:
36:    public void ProgressChange(int Progress, int ProgressMax)
37:    {
38:      Console.WriteLine("ProgressChange: " + Progress +
39:        " out of " + ProgressMax);
40:    }
41:
42:    public void TitleChange(string Text)
43:    {
44:      Console.WriteLine("TitleChange: " + Text);
45:    }
46:
47:    public void WindowResize()
48:    {
49:      Console.WriteLine("WindowResize");
50:    }
51:
52:    public void Quit(ref bool Cancel)
53:    {
54:      Console.WriteLine("Quit");
55:      Environment.Exit(0);
56:    }
57:
58:    public static void Main()
59:    {
60:      BrowserListener listener = new BrowserListener();
61:
62:      // Keep the program running while Internet Explorer is open
63:      Console.WriteLine("*** Press Enter to quit ***");
64:      Console.Read();
65:    }
66: }
```

5

RESPONDING TO
COM EVENTS

Notice that the `System.Runtime.InteropServices` namespace is not needed in this listing. That's usually a good sign that the use of COM Interoperability is seamless in the example. Lines 13–24 hook up the class's event handlers to only the events we desire to handle. This is in contrast to Listing 15.7, in which we needed to implement every method of the `DWebBrowserEvents2` source interface. The trickiest thing about handling COM events is knowing the names of the corresponding delegates (although Visual Studio .NET's IntelliSense solves this problem) because, for example, Visual Basic 6 programmers moving to C# are likely being exposed to the source interface names for the first time. Visual Basic .NET helps a great deal in this regard because the programmer doesn't need to know about the delegate names.

Whereas Lines 13–18 attach event handlers to events that correspond to the default source interface (`DWebBrowserEvents2`), Lines 21–24 attach event handlers to events that correspond to the second source interface (`DWebBrowserEvents`). Because the `InternetExplorer` coclass interface only derives from the default event interface (`DWebBrowserEvents2_Event`), it's necessary to explicitly cast the variable to the other event interface implemented by the class (`DWebBrowserEvents_Event`). If this approach doesn't appeal to you, the alternative is to declare the `ie` variable as the class type instead of the coclass interface, so you can take advantage of its multiple interfaces without casting. For example, changing Lines 6–10 to:

```
 6:    private InternetExplorerClass ie;
 7:
 8:    public BrowserListener()
 9:    {
10:      ie = new InternetExplorerClass();
```

means that Lines 21–24 could be changed to:

```
21:      ie.WindowResize += new
22:        DWebBrowserEvents_WindowResizeEventHandler(WindowResize);
23:      ie.DWebBrowserEvents_Event_Quit += new
24:        DWebBrowserEvents_QuitEventHandler(Quit);
```

The `WindowResize` event can now be handled without casting, but the drawback to using the class type is that member names might be renamed to avoid conflicts with member from other interfaces. In this case, the `InternetExplorer` class already has a `Quit` method, so the `Quit` event must be prefixed with its event interface name.

Hooking up event handlers to events corresponding to non-default source interfaces is pretty easy when you consider what would need to be done in Listing 5.7 to achieve the same effect using the raw approach. Besides implementing the `DWebBrowserEvents2` source interface and its 27 methods, the class would need to also implement the `DWebBrowserEvents` source interface and its 17 methods, many of which are identical to `DWebBrowserEvents` methods. Furthermore, the class would need to call `FindConnectionPoint` for both source interfaces, call `Advise` for both, store two cookie values, and call `Unadvise` for both.

This listing doesn't bother with unhooking the event handlers, because this is handled during finalization and there's no compelling reason to unhook them earlier. To see exactly how the importer-generated types wrap connection point interaction, see Chapter 21, "Manually Defining COM Types in Source Code."

Lazy Connection Point Initialization

When providing event support, the CLR always calls FindConnectionPoint as late as possible; in other words, the first time a source interface's method has a corresponding event to which a handler is being added. After that, subsequent event handler additions corresponding to the same source interface can be handled by the sink helper object without communicating with the COM connection point.

In Listing 5.8, Line 13 provokes a FindConnectionPoint call for DWebBrowserEvents2, and Line 21 provokes a FindConnectionPoint call for DWebBrowserEvents. This "lazy connection point initialization," besides saving some work if all or some of an object's connection points are never used, can be critical for COM objects requiring some sort of initialization before its connection points are used.

The need for extra initialization besides that which is done by instantiation (CoCreateInstance) is not a common occurrence, but the COM-based Microsoft Telephony API (TAPI), introduced in Windows 2000, has an example of such an object. The Microsoft TAPI 3.0 Type Library (contained in TAPI3.DLL in your Windows system directory) defines a TAPI class with Initialize and Shutdown methods. Initialize must be called after instantiating a TAPI object but before calling any of its members. Similarly, Shutdown must be the last member called on the object. The TAPI class supports a source interface with a single method called Event that represents all events raised by the object.

When using this TAPI type in .NET, you must take care not to use any of its event members before calling its Initialize method. This way, TAPI's IConnectionPointContainer. FindConnectionPoint method won't be called until after the object has been initialized. Attempting to hook up event handlers before the object is ready results in a non-intuitive exception thrown.

When using the Visual Basic .NET-specific WithEvents and Handles support to respond to events, you can't take advantage of the lazy connection point initialization. This is because instantiating a WithEvents variable in Visual Basic .NET effectively calls AddHandler at that time to attach any methods that use the Handles statement. Therefore, declaring a TAPI type using WithEvents in Visual Basic .NET and implementing an event handler for it causes instantiation to fail. The workaround for this is to manually call AddHandler after Initialize, rather than using the language's WithEvents support. This is demonstrated in Listing 5.9.

LISTING 5.9   The Ordering of Event Hookup Can Sometimes Make a Difference

Event hookup on instantiation:

```
1: Imports System
2: Imports TAPI3Lib
3:
4: Module Module1
5:
6:   Private WithEvents t As TAPI
7:
8:   Sub Main()
9:     t = New TAPI() ' Error! Connection points aren't ready!
10:     t.Initialize() ' Now they are but the hookup was already attempted
11:     ...
12:     t.Shutdown()
13:   End Sub
14:
15:   Public Sub t_Event(TapiEvent As TAPI_EVENT, pEvent As Object) _
16:     Handles t.Event
17:     Console.WriteLine("Handling event " + TapiEvent)
18:   End Sub
19: End Module
```

Lazy event hookup:

```
1: Imports System
2: Imports TAPI3Lib
3:
4: Module Module1
5:
6:   Private t As TAPI
7:
8:   Sub Main()
9:     t = New TAPI()
10:     t.Initialize() ' Connection points are now ready
11:     AddHandler t.Event, AddressOf t_Event
12:     ...
13:     RemoveHandler t.Event, AddressOf t_Event
14:     t.Shutdown() ' The TAPI object is now "dead"
15:   End Sub
16:
17:   Public Sub t_Event(TapiEvent As TAPI_EVENT, pEvent As Object)
18:       Console.WriteLine("Handling event " + TapiEvent)
19:   End Sub
20: End Module
```

This listing uses the Microsoft TAPI 3.0 Type Library, which can be referenced in Visual Studio .NET or created by running `TLBIMP.EXE` on `TAPI3.DLL`. The first version of the code is the straightforward approach for Visual Basic .NET programmers, but it fails due to attempting to setup connection points before `Initialize` is called. The second version of the code has the workaround—calling `AddHandler` yourself after calling `Initialize` and likewise calling `RemoveHandler` before calling `Shutdown`.

Connectable Objects You Don't Instantiate

You've now seen that using event members on a COM class you instantiate is usually straight-forward. If you're using the coclass interface type, you can directly use any event members on the default source interface, or cast to one of the importer-generated event interfaces the class implements to use non-default event members. If you're using the RCW class directly (such as `InternetExplorerClass`), then all event members can be used directly without casting, although some of the event names may be prefixed with its source interface name if there are conflicts.

Sometimes you want to use event members on an object you didn't instantiate, such as an object returned to you from a method call. There are four main possibilities for such a situation:

- Scenario 1—A .NET signature returns a coclass interface type that supports events. At run time, the returned instance is wrapped in the strongly-typed RCW with the specific class type (such as `InternetExplorerClass`).

- Scenario 2—A .NET signature returns a coclass interface type that supports events. At run time, the returned instance is wrapped in the generic RCW (`System.__ComObject`).

- Scenario 3—A .NET signature returns a regular interface type or `System.Object` type, but you know that the instance returned will support events. At run time, the returned instance is wrapped in the strongly typed RCW with the specific class type (such as `InternetExplorerClass`).

- Scenario 4—A .NET signature returns a regular interface type or `System.Object` type, but you know that the instance returned will support events. At run time, the returned instance is wrapped in the generic RCW (`System.__ComObject`).

The wrapping of returned COM objects is what differentiates scenario 1 versus scenario 2, and scenario 3 versus scenario 4. When the returned object is defined as the coclass interface type in the .NET signature, the returned object is always wrapped in the strongly typed RCW unless the same instance has previously been wrapped in with the generic `System.__ComObject` type. When the returned object is defined as any other interface or `System.Object`, the returned object is always wrapped in `System.__ComObject` unless the object implements `IProvideClassInfo` and its Interop Assembly has been registered.

In scenario 1, any members on the event interface corresponding to the class's default source interface can be used directly. For example:

C#:

```
// GiveMeInternetExplorer returns an InternetExplorer coclass interface
InternetExplorer ie = obj.GiveMeInternetExplorer();
ie.DocumentComplete += new
  DWebBrowserEvents2_DocumentCompleteEventHandler(DocumentComplete);
```

Visual Basic .NET:

```
' GiveMeInternetExplorer returns an InternetExplorer coclass interface
Dim ie As InternetExplorer = obj.GiveMeInternetExplorer()
AddHandler ie.DocumentComplete, AddressOf DocumentComplete
```

This can be done because the coclass interface contains all the events from the default source interface via inheritance.

Any members on event interfaces corresponding to non-default source interfaces can be obtained with a simple cast. For example:

C#:

```
// GiveMeInternetExplorer returns an InternetExplorer coclass interface
InternetExplorer ie = obj.GiveMeInternetExplorer();
((DWebBrowserEvents_Event)ie).WindowResize += new
  DWebBrowserEvents_WindowResizeEventHandler(WindowResize);
```

Visual Basic .NET:

```
' GiveMeInternetExplorer returns an InternetExplorer coclass interface
Dim ie As InternetExplorer = obj.GiveMeInternetExplorer()
AddHandler CType(ie.DocumentComplete, DWebBrowserEvents_Event), _
  AddressOf DocumentComplete
```

This casting should seem natural, because the strongly typed RCW implements the entire set of event interfaces corresponding to all of its source interfaces. Another option would be to cast to the instance's class type (`InternetExplorerClass`) and use all event members directly, but this isn't recommended because it wouldn't work for scenario 2 and it's not always easy to know which scenario applies to your current situation.

The code example suggesting that the `InternetExplorer` coclass interface is returned is used just for demonstration purposes. In reality, the importer alone never produces such a signature with coclass interface parameter replacement because the `InternetExplorer` coclass's default interface (`IWebBrowser2`) is listed as implemented by four coclasses in the Microsoft Internet Controls type library. For many other examples (or hand-tweaked Interop Assemblies), returning a coclass interface that supports events can be quite common.

Scenario 2 behaves just like scenario 1 from the programmer's perspective, as long as you don't attempt to cast the returned object to a class type. Any events corresponding to the default source interface can be used directly on the coclass interface type, and the returned object can be cast to any additional importer-generated event interfaces.

Scenarios 3 and 4 always require a cast because the type returned has no explicit relationship to an interface or class with event members. For example:

C#:

```csharp
// GiveMeABrowser returns an IWebBrowser2 interface or System.Object
InternetExplorer ie = (InternetExplorer)obj.GiveMeABrowser();

// Use an event corresponding to the default source interface
ie.DocumentComplete += new
  DWebBrowserEvents2_DocumentCompleteEventHandler(DocumentComplete);

// Use an event corresponding to a non-default source interface
((DWebBrowserEvents_Event)ie).WindowResize += new
  DWebBrowserEvents_WindowResizeEventHandler(WindowResize);
```

Visual Basic .NET:

```vbnet
' GiveMeABrowser returns an InternetExplorer coclass interface
Dim ie As InternetExplorer = CType(obj.GiveMeABrowser(), InternetExplorer)

' Use an event corresponding to the default source interface
AddHandler ie.DocumentComplete, AddressOf DocumentComplete

' Use an event corresponding to a non-default source interface
AddHandler CType(ie.DocumentComplete, DWebBrowserEvents_Event), _
  AddressOf DocumentComplete
```

5

RESPONDING TO
COM EVENTS

Regardless of how you obtain a COM object that supports events, hooking up handlers to its event members is only a cast away (as long as a metadata definition of the event interface is available).

FAQ: What can I do if the COM object I want to use raises events but doesn't list the appropriate source interface in its coclass definition?

If the COM object you're using has omitted this information from its type library, then the type library importer doesn't know that it should create the event-related types. Without these types, you can always fall back to the raw connection points method demonstrated in Listing 5.7. Otherwise, the easiest thing might be editing the type library by using OLEVIEW.EXE to extract IDL, adding the source interface, then compiling a new type library to import using MIDL.EXE. Or, refer to Chapter 21 which demonstrates how to perform the event transformations done by the type library importer in any .NET language.

If you step back and think about scenarios 2 and 4, you might wonder how casting the System.__ComObject instance to an event interface could possibly work. The metadata for the System.__ComObject type does not claim to implement any interfaces, and calling the COM object's QueryInterface with a request for an event interface would fail because the COM object knows nothing about these .NET-specific interfaces.

The "magic" that makes the cast succeed is nothing other than a custom attribute. Every event interface created by the type library importer is marked with the ComEventInterfaceAttribute custom attribute, which contains two Type instances. The first Type represents the .NET definition of the source interface to which the event interface belongs. The second Type represents the event provider class that implements the event members.

When performing a cast from a COM object (an RCW) to an event interface, the CLR uses the information in this custom attribute to hook up all the pieces. As long as the COM object implements IConnectionPointContainer and responds successfully to a FindConnectionPoint call with the IID of the source interface listed in the ComEventInterfaceAttribute custom attribute, the cast succeeds. Otherwise, the cast fails with an InvalidCastException.

This event interface behavior is the area omitted from Figure 3.11 in Chapter 3, "The Essentials for Using COM in Managed Code." Figure 5.3 updates this diagram with a full description of what happens when you attempt to cast an RCW to any type.

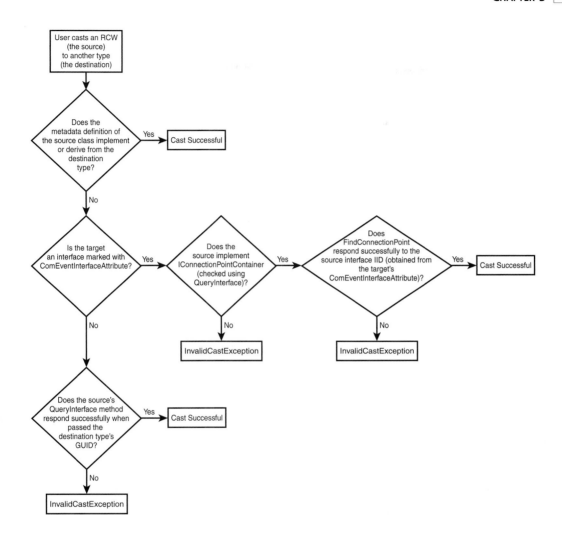

The process of casting a COM object (Runtime-Callable Wrapper): The full story.

Listing 5.10 adds a twist to the previous examples of handling events from the
`InternetExplorer` type. Here, we attach event handlers to the object's `Document` property.

LISTING 5.10   Hooking Up Event Handlers to Objects We Don't Instantiate

```
1: using System;
2: using SHDocVw;
3: using mshtml;
4:
```

LISTING 5.10   Continued

```
 5: public class WebBrowserHost
 6: {
 7:   private InternetExplorer ie;
 8:
 9:   ...
10:
11:   public void Document_MouseOver()
12:   {
13:     Console.WriteLine("MouseOver");
14:   }
15:
16:   public bool Document_Click(IHTMLEventObj pEvtObj)
17:   {
18:     Console.WriteLine("Click: " + pEvtObj.x + ", " + pEvtObj.y);
19:     return true;
20:   }
21:
22:   public void DocumentComplete(object pDisp, ref object URL)
23:   {
24:     Console.WriteLine("DocumentComplete");
25:
26:     ((HTMLDocumentEvents_Event)ie.Document).onmouseover += new
27:       HTMLDocumentEvents_onmouseoverEventHandler(Document_MouseOver);
28:     ((HTMLDocumentEvents2_Event)ie.Document).onclick += new
29:       HTMLDocumentEvents_onclickEventHandler(Document_Click);
30:   }
31:   ...
32: }
```

The omitted parts of this example are the same as the code shown in Listing 5.8. Besides referencing an Interop Assembly for the Microsoft Internet Controls type library, this listing also
references the Primary Interop Assembly for the Microsoft HTML Object Library
(MSHTML.TLB) for definitions of IHTMLEventObj, HTMLDocumentEvents_Event, and
HTMLDocumentEvents2_Event.

Lines 26–29 hook up event handlers to two of the events supported by the
InternetExplorer.Document property. Document is defined as a generic System.Object, but
we know that the instance is always an HTMLDocument type. (The property was likely defined
as such to avoid a dependency on the large MSHTML type library.) Therefore, the property
can be cast to any event interfaces implemented by the .NET HTMLDocumentClass type. The
onmouseover event corresponds to the HTMLDocument coclass's default source interface
(HTMLDocumentEvents) whereas the onclick event corresponds to a second source interface
(HTMLDocumentEvents2).

The listing could have cast the Document property to the HTMLDocument coclass interface, for example:

```
HTMLDocument doc = (HTMLDocument)ie.Document;
```

Ordinarily, this would enable the use of the default event interface's event members directly but in this case it wouldn't because the HTMLDocument interface, via inheriting the coclass's default DispHTMLDocument interface, has properties with the same names as every event! To disambiguate between the onmouseover property and the onmouseover event, you'd need to cast to the HTMLDocumentEvents_Event interface anyway.

This example doesn't unhook its event handlers from the ie.Document object, but it's a good idea to do so as soon as you're finished with the current document because this might occur well before garbage collection.

Handling ActiveX Control Events in Managed Code

As discussed in the previous two chapters, the ActiveX importer produces its own classes that wrap coclasses representing ActiveX controls as Windows Forms controls. If an ActiveX Assembly didn't also contain some extra transformations for events, then the AxHost-derived wrapper classes that you can host in a Windows Forms control would not appear to have any events. Therefore, the ActiveX importer must clearly do some transformations as well. These transformations, and their use, are covered in this section.

ActiveX Importer Transformations

Just as classes generated by the type library importer contain event members when the coclass lists an interface marked with the IDL [source] attribute, classes generated by the ActiveX importer also contain event members. However, only event members corresponding to the default source interface are created. Any non-default source interfaces are ignored. Name conflicts are handled by appending an Event suffix to applicable event names.

Besides the additions made to the AxHost-derived classes (more of which are shown in the next listing), the ActiveX importer creates some additional types every time it encounters a coclass listing a source interface:

- *SourceInterfaceName_MethodName*EventHandler—A delegate, one for each method on the default source interface (excluding methods that have no parameters, which use the System.EventHandler delegate). Unlike the delegates created by the type library importer, these signatures *do not* match the signatures of methods in the source interface. Instead, the delegate signature always has two parameters to (almost) match the convention used by all delegates in Windows Forms. The first parameter is a System.Object type named sender. The second parameter, named e, is a type described next in the list.

- *SourceInterfaceName_MethodName*Event—A class with a public field representing each parameter of a source interface method. One of these classes exists for each method on the source interface that has one or more arguments. This is the second e parameter used in each delegate signature, but fails to conform to .NET guidelines in two ways: the class does not derive from System.EventArgs and it does not have an EventArgs suffix.

- Ax*CoClassName*EventMulticaster—A public sink class that implements the source interface. This serves a similar role as the sink helper class generated by the type library importer.

No event interfaces are generated because the Ax*CoClassName* class is always used directly. There's also no separate event provider class because that functionality is merged into the Ax*CoClassName* class.

DIGGING DEEPER

The reason a separate event provider class is generated by the type library importer is that classes marked with the ComImportAttribute pseudo-custom attribute cannot contain any implementation. None of the classes in an ActiveX Assembly are marked with this attribute because they don't directly represent COM types.

Listing 5.11 shows snippets of C# code inspired by the code obtained by running the ActiveX importer on the file containing the Microsoft Internet Controls type library, for example:

```
aximp C:\Windows\System32\shdocvw.dll /source
```

This type library contains the WebBrowser control introduced in Chapter 3:

```
[
  uuid(8856F961-340A-11D0-A96B-00C04FD705A2),
  helpstring("WebBrowser Control"),
  control
]
coclass WebBrowser {
  [default] interface IWebBrowser2;
  interface IWebBrowser;
  [default, source] dispinterface DWebBrowserEvents2;
  [source] dispinterface DWebBrowserEvents;
};
```

The WebBrowser coclass has the same two source interfaces as the InternetExplorer coclass used throughout this chapter, so you can easily compare how events are handled with imported ActiveX controls to how they are handled with plain imported coclasses.

LISTING 5.11 Some of the Types and Members Generated by the ActiveX Importer for Event Support

```
 1: [AxHost.ClsidAttribute("{8856f961-340a-11d0-a96b-00c04fd705a2}")]
 2: [DesignTimeVisibleAttribute(true)]
 3: [DefaultProperty("Name")]
 4: public class AxWebBrowser : AxHost
 5: {
 6:   private SHDocVw.IWebBrowser2 ocx;
 7:   private AxWebBrowserEventMulticaster eventMulticaster;
 8:   private AxHost.ConnectionPointCookie cookie;
 9:   ...
10:   public event System.EventHandler DownloadBegin;
11:   public event DWebBrowserEvents2_CommandStateChangeEventHandler
12:     CommandStateChange;
13:   ...
14:   protected override void CreateSink()
15:   {
16:     try
17:     {
18:       this.eventMulticaster = new AxWebBrowserEventMulticaster(this);
19:       this.cookie = new AxHost.ConnectionPointCookie(this.ocx,
20:         this.eventMulticaster, typeof(SHDocVw.DWebBrowserEvents2));
21:     }
22:     catch (System.Exception) {}
23:   }
24:
25:   protected override void DetachSink()
26:   {
27:     try {
28:       this.cookie.Disconnect();
29:     }
30:     catch (System.Exception) {}
31:   }
32:   ...
33:   internal void RaiseOnDownloadBegin(object sender, System.EventArgs e)
34:   {
35:     if (this.DownloadBegin != null)
36:       this.DownloadBegin(sender, e);
37:   }
38:
39:   internal void RaiseOnCommandStateChange(object sender,
40:     DWebBrowserEvents2_CommandStateChangeEvent e)
41:   {
42:     if (this.CommandStateChange != null)
43:       this.CommandStateChange(sender, e);
```

5

**RESPONDING TO
COM EVENTS**

LISTING 5.11   Continued

```
44:   }
45:   ...
46: }
47: ...
48: public delegate void DWebBrowserEvents2_CommandStateChangeEventHandler(
49:   object sender, DWebBrowserEvents2_CommandStateChangeEvent e);
50:
51: public class DWebBrowserEvents2_CommandStateChangeEvent
52: {
53:   public int command;
54:   public bool enable;
55:
56:   public DWebBrowserEvents2_CommandStateChangeEvent(
57:     int command, bool enable)
58:   {
59:     this.command = command;
60:     this.enable = enable;
61:   }
62: }
63: ...
64: public class AxWebBrowserEventMulticaster : SHDocVw.DWebBrowserEvents2
65: {
66:   private AxWebBrowser parent;
67:
68:   public AxWebBrowserEventMulticaster(AxWebBrowser parent)
69:   {
70:     this.parent = parent;
71:   }
72:   ...
73:   public virtual void DownloadBegin()
74:   {
75:     System.EventArgs downloadbeginEvent = new System.EventArgs();
76:     this.parent.RaiseOnDownloadBegin(this.parent, downloadbeginEvent);
77:   }
78:
79:   public virtual void CommandStateChange(int command, bool enable)
80:   {
81:     DWebBrowserEvents2_CommandStateChangeEvent commandstatechangeEvent =
82:       new DWebBrowserEvents2_CommandStateChangeEvent(command, enable);
83:     this.parent.RaiseOnCommandStateChange(this.parent,
84:       commandstatechangeEvent);
85:   }
86:   ...
87: }
```

The snippets of the `AxWebBrowser` class shown focus on two events and their supporting types and members—`DownloadBegin` and `CommandStateChange`. Lines 10–12 define the two events. Because the `DownloadBegin` source interface method has no parameters, the simple `System.EventHandler` delegate is used rather than defining a new `DWebBrowserEvents2_DownloadBeginEventHandler` delegate with the exact same signature. The `CommandStateChange` source interface method does have parameters, so a specific delegate type is used with this event.

The `CreateSink` and `DetachSink` methods in Lines 14–31 connect and disconnect the connection point for the object's default source interface. `CreateSink` is invoked when the control's `System.ComponentModel.ISupportInitialize.EndInit` implementation is called, as is done inside the Visual Studio .NET-generated `InitializeComponent` method when a Windows Forms control is dragged onto a form in the designer. `DetachSink` is invoked inside the control's `IDisposable.Dispose` implementation. Keep this in mind in case you're using an ActiveX control that's picky about when its default connection point is used (as in the TAPI example earlier in the chapter). If some custom initialization routine must be called first, you'd need to insert a call to it somewhere in-between the control's instantiation and the call to `EndInit`, which would unfortunately be inside the designer-generated `InitializeComponent` method that you're not supposed to touch.

The `RaiseOn...` methods, one per event, are defined in Lines 33–44 so that the event multicaster class, defined later, has access to raising the events. Lines 48–62 contain the pair of delegate and quasi-`EventArgs` class for the event that doesn't use the standard `System.EventArgs` delegate. Besides not having the `EventArgs` suffix and not deriving from `System.EventArgs`, the event argument classes generated by the ActiveX importer have another oddity that goes against .NET conventions—every field name is lowercase, even if the original parameters in the source interface method were uppercase (as were `Command` and `Enable`). The constructor in Lines 56–61 simply provides a convenient means for setting all of the class's fields.

TIP

To minimize confusion when using types generated by the ActiveX importer and to conform to .NET guidelines, it might be a good idea to modify the types produced. This can easily be done using `AXIMP.EXE`'s `/source` option to generate C# source code for the ActiveX assembly. Before compiling the generated source, you can rename the `...Event` classes to `...EventArgs` classes, perhaps capitalize the public fields of these classes, and make them derive from `System.EventArgs`. Another user-friendly change would be to rename the delegate types from *SourceInterfaceName_MethodName*EventHandler to simply *MethodName*EventHandler as long as the name doesn't conflict with others.

When compiling source code generated from `AXIMP.EXE`, you'll need to reference the corresponding Interop Assembly, `System.Windows.Forms.dll`, and `System.dll`.

Finally, the `AxWebBrowserEventMulticaster` class in Lines 64–87 is the event sink that implements the default source interface, receives the callbacks, and raises the .NET event to anyone who may be listening.

> **TIP**
>
> Besides renaming types, you can take advantage of ActiveX importer-generated source code to make changes that can add functionality. A good example of this would be to add the code necessary to handle non-default source interfaces just as the default source interface is currently handled.

Using ActiveX Events

To conclude this chapter, we'll update the Web Browser example from Listing 3.4 in Chapter 3 with event support. We'll not only fix the behavior of the `Back` and `Forward` buttons to be implemented the way the ActiveX control intended, but add a history list and a log of all events. The final product is pictured in Figure 5.4.

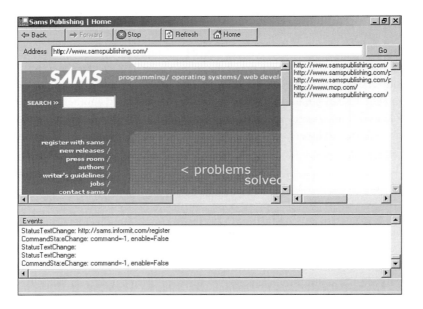

FIGURE 5.4
The event-enabled .NET Web browser.

Inside Visual Studio .NET, the easiest way to add event handlers to an event is to click on the Events lightning bolt in the property browser, then double-click on any events you wish to handle. An empty method signature and the appropriate event hooking and unhooking code are then emitted for you. Figure 5.5 displays the events for the WebBrowser control. When displayed in categorized mode, the events originating from COM can easily be identified because they fall under the Misc category and have no description in the lower pane.

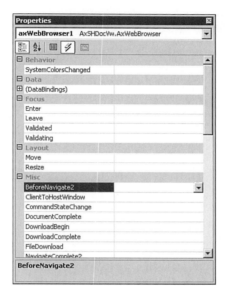

FIGURE 5.5
The Visual Studio .NET property browser showing events.

Listing 5.12 shows the important parts of the source code for the updated example. The full source code is available in C# and Visual Basic .NET on this book's Web site.

LISTING 5.12   Using Events on a Hosted ActiveX Control

```
 1: using System;
 2: using SHDocVw;
 3: using AxSHDocVw;
 4: using System.Windows.Forms;
 5:
 6: public class MyWebBrowser : Form
 7: {
 8:   private System.ComponentModel.IContainer components;
 9:   private AxWebBrowser axWebBrowser1;
10:   ...
```

LISTING 5.12   Continued

```
11:    // Used for any optional parameters
12:    private object m = Type.Missing;
13:
14:    public MyWebBrowser()
15:    {
16:      // Required for Windows Form Designer support
17:      InitializeComponent();
18:      axWebBrowser1.GoHome();
19:    }
20:    ...
21:    private void InitializeComponent()
22:    {
23:      ...
24:      axWebBrowser1.StatusTextChange += new
25:        DWebBrowserEvents2_StatusTextChangeEventHandler(
26:        axWebBrowser1_StatusTextChange);
27:      axWebBrowser1.CommandStateChange += new
28:        DWebBrowserEvents2_CommandStateChangeEventHandler(
29:        axWebBrowser1_CommandStateChange);
30:      axWebBrowser1.TitleChange += new
31:        DWebBrowserEvents2_TitleChangeEventHandler(
32:        axWebBrowser1_TitleChange);
33:      axWebBrowser1.NavigateComplete2 += new
34:        DWebBrowserEvents2_NavigateComplete2EventHandler(
35:        axWebBrowser1_NavigateComplete2);
36:      axWebBrowser1.ProgressChange += new
37:        DWebBrowserEvents2_ProgressChangeEventHandler(
38:        axWebBrowser1_ProgressChange);
39:      ...
40:    }
41:    ...
42:    private void axWebBrowser1_CommandStateChange(object sender,
43:      DWebBrowserEvents2_CommandStateChangeEvent e)
44:    {
45:      eventList.Items.Add("CommandStateChange: command=" + e.command +
46:        ", enable=" + e.enable).EnsureVisible();
47:
48:      if (e.command == (int)CommandStateChangeConstants.CSC_NAVIGATEBACK)
49:      {
50:        // Toggle the state of the "Back" button
51:        toolBar1.Buttons[0].Enabled = e.enable;
52:      }
53:      else if (e.command ==
54:        (int)CommandStateChangeConstants.CSC_NAVIGATEFORWARD)
55:      {
```

LISTING 5.12 Continued

```
56:         // Toggle the state of the "Forward" button
57:         toolBar1.Buttons[1].Enabled = e.enable;
58:     }
59: }
60: ...
61: private void axWebBrowser1_NavigateComplete2(object sender,
62:   DWebBrowserEvents2_NavigateComplete2Event e)
63: {
64:   navigateBox.Text = e.uRL.ToString();
65:   historyList.Items.Add(e.uRL);
66:   eventList.Items.Add("NavigateComplete2: " + e.uRL).EnsureVisible();
67: }
68: ...
69: private void axWebBrowser1_ProgressChange(object sender,
70:   DWebBrowserEvents2_ProgressChangeEvent e)
71: {
72:   progressBar1.Maximum = e.progressMax;
73:   progressBar1.Value = e.progress;
74:   eventList.Items.Add("ProgressChange: " + e.progress + " out of " +
75:     e.progressMax).EnsureVisible();
76: }
77: ...
78: private void axWebBrowser1_StatusTextChange(object sender,
79:   DWebBrowserEvents2_StatusTextChangeEvent e)
80: {
81:   statusBar1.Text = e.text;
82:   eventList.Items.Add("StatusTextChange: " + e.text).EnsureVisible();
83: }
84:
85: private void axWebBrowser1_TitleChange(object sender,
86:   DWebBrowserEvents2_TitleChangeEvent e)
87: {
88:   this.Text = e.text;
89:   eventList.Items.Add("TitleChange: " + e.text).EnsureVisible();
90: }
91: ...
92: private void toolBar1_ButtonClick(object sender,
93:   ToolBarButtonClickEventArgs e)
94: {
95:   if (e.Button.Text == "Back")
96:   {
97:       axWebBrowser1.GoBack();
98:   }
99:   else if (e.Button.Text == "Forward")
100:      {
```

LISTING 5.12   Continued

```
101:             axWebBrowser1.GoForward();
102:         }
103:         else if (e.Button.Text == "Stop")
104:         {
105:           axWebBrowser1.Stop();
106:         }
107:         else if (e.Button.Text == "Refresh")
108:         {
109:           axWebBrowser1.CtlRefresh();
110:         }
111:         else if (e.Button.Text == "Home")
112:         {
113:           axWebBrowser1.GoHome();
114:         }
115:     }
116:
117:     private void goButton_Click(object sender, System.EventArgs e)
118:     {
119:         axWebBrowser1.Navigate(navigateBox.Text, ref m, ref m, ref m, ref m);
120:     }
121: }
```

The first difference between this listing and the corresponding listing in Chapter 3 is in Lines 24–38. This shows a sampling of some of the events being handled. This code is automatically generated by Visual Studio .NET when double-clicking on events in the property browser.

Lines 42–90 show all of the interesting events that do something other than add information to the log. The implementation of the CommandStateChange event handler in Lines 42–59 first adds some information to the eventList log, which is a ListView control. Then, it toggles the state of either the Back or Forward button based on the information passed into the event. The NavigateComplete2 event handler in Lines 61–67 updates the TextBox control with the current URL and adds it to the history list, a ListBox control. Notice how the lowercase transformations done by the ActiveX importer produces a funny looking field called uRL!

The ProgressChange event handler in Lines 69–76 uses the passed-in information to control the form's ProgressBar control, and the StatusTextChange event handler in Lines 78–83 updates the form's StatusBar control with the passed-in text. Finally, the TitleChange event handler in Lines 85–90 updates the form's caption with the title of the current Web page.

The updated toolBar1_ButtonClick implementation now simply calls the methods corresponding to each button's action. The calls to GoBack and GoForward no longer need to be wrapped inside exception handling because the user shouldn't be able to click these buttons when there are no more pages in the list. (If an exception were to occur, it would be a problem that we'd want to know about.)

Conclusion

The goal of this chapter was to explain how to handle events raised by COM components (including ActiveX controls) when they use the connection points protocol. The complement to this chapter is Chapter 13, which covers the opposite direction in which a .NET component is the event source and a COM component is the event sink.

In either case, this type of bi-directional communication is sometimes called *tightly coupled events*. Although the event source has no knowledge of the event sinks that are listening, every event sink must have prior knowledge about the event source. In a *loosely coupled events* system, as in COM+, an event sink can receive event notifications from event sources that it's not even aware of.

FAQ: I've hooked up a .NET event handler to a COM event but it never gets raised when it's supposed to! What's going on?

The likely cause of this is that an exception occurs when the COM source attempts to call a method on the source interface, but the COM object "swallows" the failure HRESULT returned rather than reporting it. This can actually be a fairly common occurrence for two reasons:

- Most source interfaces are dispinterfaces.
- By default, value types (UDTs) cannot be passed as parameters when late binding across the managed/unmanaged boundary.

The significance of the source interface being a dispinterface is that when the COM event source calls back upon any event sink, it is forced to perform late binding through the IDispatch interface. The Interop Marshaler does not support marshaling VARIANTs with the VT_RECORD type, discussed further in the next chapter, which is exactly what value type parameters become when passed to a method invoked through IDispatch. The Interop Marshaler throws an exception when this is attempted. One way to fix such a problem is to mark the importer-generated sink helper class with the IDispatchImplAttribute custom attribute and the value IDispatchImplType.CompatibleImpl. This custom attribute is described in Chapter 14, "Implementing COM Interfaces for Binary Compatibility," and modifying importer-generated classes is the topic of Chapter 7, "Modifying Interop Assemblies." If you own the COM component, you could instead change the source interface to a dual interface, although this prevents Visual Basic 6 clients from working properly.

Another cause of events not being raised to managed code is a COM object that calls `QueryInterface` for `IDispatch` rather than the specific source interface during Step 4 of Figure 5.1. Because the importer-generated sink helper classes are non-public, they do not successfully respond to such a query. For example, various events from Microsoft Excel, Microsoft Outlook, and Microsoft PowerPoint cannot be sinked in .NET applications without changing the sink helper classes generated by the type library importer to be public instead of private using the techniques introduced in Chapter 7 (or using a PIA that contains such customizations).

In addition to this issue, Microsoft PowerPoint 2002 has a dual source interface—`EApplication`—whose members are not marked with DISPIDs. This causes event handling in .NET applications to fail because the CLR cannot properly handle incoming invocations via DISPIDs without the proper DISPIDs present in the metadata description of the dual source interface. Although not available at the time of writing, a PIA for Microsoft PowerPoint should solve this problem by containing an updated interface definition with DISPIDs.

Occasionally, failure to source events can occur when the COM event source passes an invalid `VARIANT`. This causes the invocation on the .NET sink helper to throw an `InvalidOleVariantTypeException`. The `BeforeNavigate2` event, used in the examples throughout this chapter, is one such event that runs into this problem!

Advanced Topics for Using COM Components

IN THIS CHAPTER

- Do-It-Yourself Marshaling   248
- Threading and Apartments   275
- Troubleshooting an `InvalidCastException` 289
- Garbage Collection   299
- Securing Unmanaged Calls   304
- Using COM+ and DCOM Objects   309
- Inheriting from COM Classes   311
- Debugging into COM Components   315
- Monitoring Performance   320

The previous three chapters covered a lot of information that should help you use most COM components within .NET components and applications, especially if the author of the COM component has produced a customized Primary Interop Assembly. This chapter focuses on a handful of advanced topics that should help you use *any* COM components in .NET:

- Do-it-yourself marshaling
- Threading and apartments
- Troubleshooting an `InvalidCastException`
- Garbage collection
- Securing unmanaged calls
- Using COM+ and DCOM objects
- Inheriting from COM classes
- Debugging into COM components
- Monitoring performance

Do-It-Yourself Marshaling

The Interop Marshaler knows what to do only by examining a .NET signature described in metadata. Often, the metadata created by the type library importer needs to be modified to work around limitations of the importer or of the marshaler itself. Chapter 7, "Modifying Interop Assemblies," describes *how* to change signatures created by the type library importer, but this section describes what kind of signature changes can be beneficial. What I call "do-it-yourself marshaling" is different from what's considered *custom marshaling*, which uses the same kind of do-it-yourself marshaling encapsulated inside a custom marshaling class. Custom marshaling is described in Chapter 20, "Custom Marshaling."

The data type typically involved in "do-it-yourself marshaling" is `System.IntPtr`, a CLS-compliant type that can be used to represent a pointer to anything (in other words, `void*`), because it's a value that's the size of a pointer. For `IntPtr` types, the Interop Marshaler does nothing more than expose the value, just as it would for any other integral type. There's nothing intrinsic to `IntPtr` that makes it contain the value of a pointer; it's just a good use of the type because it's always the correct size for the underlying platform. Therefore, when a pointer to a COM data type is passed as a `System.IntPtr`, managed code gets a chance to manipulate and use the COM data type's raw memory representation without the marshaler's intervention. COM-style marshaling still happens if and when appropriate, as shown in Figure 6.1, an update to Figure 3.10 in Chapter 3, "The Essentials for Using COM in Managed Code."

Advanced Topics for Using COM Components

CHAPTER 6

249

6

ADVANCED TOPICS
FOR USING COM
COMPONENTS

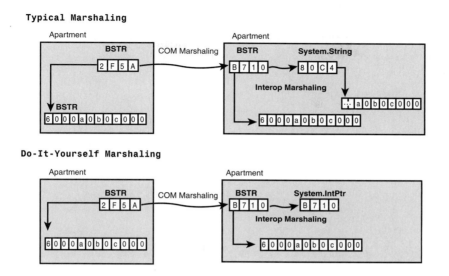

FIGURE 6.1

Interop marshaling depends upon the metadata signature.

The first case represents typical Interop Marshaling, for which a pointer to a `BSTR` containing "abc" is marshaled as a reference to a `System.String` type. The only difference in the second case is that the parameter in the .NET signature is `System.IntPtr`. In this case, the raw pointer to the COM-marshaled `BSTR` is exposed to managed code. Although it isn't too compelling to work with raw `BSTR` types in managed code because .NET strings can express the same information (and have tons of manipulation methods), this can be a great technique for types such as `VARIANT` for which the Interop Marshaler doesn't handle all possible varieties. Or, it can become a necessary technique for COM objects that expose parameters as `void*` types that would have otherwise been able to be marshaled automatically had their type information been more specific.

The primary means for manipulating `System.IntPtr` types as if they are pointers is the `Marshal` class in the `System.Runtime.InteropServices` namespace and its many members. This chapter uses just a handful of its methods in the examples, but the `Marshal` class and all of its members are described in Appendix A, "`System.Runtime.InteropServices` Reference."

As mentioned in Chapter 4, "An In-Depth Look at Imported Assemblies," whenever the type library importer encounters a parameter or return type that it can't marshal, it emits the following warning:

```
At least one of the arguments for 'MemberName' can not be marshaled by the
runtime marshaler. Such arguments will therefore be passed as a pointer and
may require unsafe code to manipulate.
```

For example, when importing the DirectX 7 for Visual Basic Type Library (DX7VB.DLL), the importer emits 18 such warnings. Seventeen of these are simply due to a void* argument in a method signature, which is really marshaled correctly by the Interop Marshaler given the limited type information.

Passing an argument "as a pointer" simply means using the System.IntPtr type. The term "unsafe code" refers to the C# feature to use pointer syntax inside members or code blocks marked with the unsafe keyword. The text is a bit misleading because the signatures produced by the importer never have pointer types so they aren't instantly usable by C# unsafe code without at least a cast from the IntPtr type to something like void*. Furthermore, C# unsafe code is never *required* to manipulate such types; the same manipulations can be performed in any language using the CLS-compliant APIs in System.Runtime.InteropServices, as described in the next section.

C# Unsafe Code Versus System.Runtime.InteropServices APIs

C# unsafe code is a great feature for performing direct memory manipulation in a way that's natural to C and C++ programmers (with some limitations). In the heated language wars that are often verbally fought between C# and VB .NET zealots, I commonly hear that "C# has unsafe code, but VB .NET doesn't." It's important to understand, however, that you can do just about anything that's possible with C# unsafe code in any .NET language thanks to two classes in the System.Runtime.InteropServices namespace—Marshal and GCHandle. The syntax isn't always as readable and almost never as concise as using pointers, but the memory manipulations are the same.

> **TIP**
>
> Whenever using C# unsafe code, it not only must be used inside a class, member, or block marked unsafe, but you must use the /unsafe option when compiling the code using the command-line compiler. Inside Visual Studio .NET, this can be done by selecting Configuration Properties, Build on your Visual C# .NET project's property page, then setting Allow unsafe code blocks to True.

> **DIGGING DEEPER**
>
> C# unsafe code requires unmanaged code permission just as the APIs in System.Runtime.InteropServices do because a malicious program using unsafe code would have the power to do "unsafe things" by directly accessing memory outside the bounds of type safety.

Advanced Topics for Using COM Components

CHAPTER 6

251

6

ADVANCED TOPICS
FOR USING COM
COMPONENTS

The following is a list of ten features enabled by C# unsafe code and instructions for accomplishing the same functionality in any language (shown in Visual Basic .NET) using the interoperability APIs:

- Declaring and using pointer types (like `byte*`, `int*`, and so on). This can effectively be done in any language by declaring the type as `IntPtr`.

  C# Unsafe Code:

  ```
  byte* ptrToByte;
  ```

  Language-Neutral Approach:

  ```
  Dim ptrToByte As IntPtr
  ```

- Pointer indirection (such as `*ptr`), also known as dereferencing a pointer. This can also be accomplished with several of `Marshal`'s methods, such as `ReadByte`, `ReadInt16`, `ReadInt32`, `ReadInt64`, and `ReadIntPtr`.

  C# Unsafe Code:

  ```
  byte* ptrToByte = ...;
  byte b = *ptrToByte;
  ```

  Language-Neutral Approach:

  ```
  Dim ptrToByte As IntPtr = ...
  Dim b As Byte = Marshal.ReadByte(ptrToByte)
  ```

  Obtaining a pointer to a variable (the ellipses in the previous code) is discussed in the "Obtaining the Address of Value Types" section after this list.

- Pointer member access (using `ptr->member` as a shortcut for `(*ptr).member`). This can also be accomplished with several of `Marshal`'s methods, such as `ReadByte`, `ReadInt16`, `ReadInt32`, `ReadInt64`, `ReadIntPtr`. Examples of using these methods are shown in "Examples of Manipulating `IntPtr` Types" section.

- C-like array pointer syntax (so `ptr[i]` means `*(ptr + i)`). With `Marshal.Copy`, you could copy a pointer to a C-style array to a .NET array, but to avoid copying you must use `Marshal.Read...` and `Marshal.Write...` rather than array syntax in languages other than C#.

  C# Unsafe Code:

  ```
  public unsafe void FillArray(byte* ptr, int count, byte value)
  {
    for (int i = 0; i < count; i++) ptr[i] = value;
  }
  ```

  Language-Neutral Approach:

  ```
  Public Sub FillArray(ptr As IntPtr, count As Integer, value As Byte)
    Dim i As Integer
    For i = 0 To count-1
  ```

```
    Marshal.WriteByte(ptr, i, value)
  Next i
End Sub
```

- Obtaining the address of value types (like &someInteger). Without C# unsafe code, this can't be done cleanly, but there are workarounds, discussed after this list in the "Obtaining the Address of Value Types" section.

- Pointer arithmetic on all pointer types except for void* (the +, -, ++, and -- operators). This is only directly possible with C# unsafe code. IntPtr types must be converted to other integers before arithmetic can be done.

  C# Unsafe Code:

  ```
  byte* ptrToByte = ...;
  byte* newPtr = ptrToByte + 10;
  ```

  Language-Neutral Approach:

  ```
  Dim ptrToByte As IntPtr = ...
  ' This only works on 32-bit platforms due to calling IntPtr.ToInt32
  Dim newPtr = New IntPtr(ptrToByte.ToInt32() + 10)
  ```

- Pointer comparison (the ==, !=, >, <, >=, and <= operators). In contrast, IntPtr supports the equality and inequality operators, but any other comparisons must be done by converting IntPtr types to other integers first. In Visual Basic .NET, IntPtr types cannot be compared with = or <> because the language doesn't support overloaded operators. Instead, you can call the IntPtr.op_Equality or IntPtr.op_Inequality methods.

  C# Unsafe Code:

  ```
  if (ptrToByte != newPtr) ...
  ```

  Visual Basic .NET:

  ```
  If (IntPtr.op_Inequality(ptrToByte, newPtr)) ...
  ```

- Obtaining the size, in bytes, of value types using the sizeof keyword. This is similar to Marshal.SizeOf but it reports the *managed* size of an instance, not the *unmanaged* size. Plus, it can only be used on value types, not on reference types with structure layout. This is explained in more depth after this list.

- Pinning a reference type using the fixed statement so a pointer to it can be used directly without its physical location on the GC heap changing. This can be done in any language using the GCHandle class in the System.Runtime.InteropServices namespace. The following silly example demonstrates how to treat a .NET string as a character array without having to allocate a separate array (as String.ToCharArray does).

  C# Unsafe Code:

  ```
  string s = "abcdefg";
  // Pin the string to a fixed location
  ```

Advanced Topics for Using COM Components

CHAPTER 6

253

6

ADVANCED TOPICS
FOR USING COM
COMPONENTS

```csharp
fixed (char* ptr = s)
{
  // Print each character on a separate line, up to the first null
  for (int i = 0; ptr[i] != '\0'; i++)
  {
    Console.WriteLine(ptr[i]);
  }
}
```

Language-Neutral Approach:

```vb
Dim s As String = "abcdefg"
Dim handle As GCHandle
Try
  ' Pin the string to a fixed location
  handle = GCHandle.Alloc(s, GCHandleType.Pinned)
  Dim ptr As IntPtr = handle.AddrOfPinnedObject()

  ' Print each character on a separate line, up to the first null
  Dim i As Integer = 0
  While (Marshal.ReadInt16(ptr, i) <> 0)
    Console.WriteLine(Convert.ToChar(Marshal.ReadInt16(ptr, i)))
    i = i + 2
  End While
Finally
  If (handle.IsAllocated) Then handle.Free()
End Try
```

TIP

Notice that when treating a .NET string as a character array, the character index is incremented by one each iteration in C# unsafe code. On the other hand, in Visual Basic .NET, the index must be incremented by two each time. When calculating offsets using IntPtr types, you must always specify the number in bytes (in this case, 2 bytes for a Unicode character). In contrast, when doing pointer arithmetic in C# unsafe code, the offset is automatically multiplied by the size of the pointed-to data.

- Allocating memory on something other than a GC heap using the stackalloc keyword. The Marshal class doesn't provide a way to allocate memory on the stack, but does provide methods such as AllocCoTaskMem and AllocHGlobal for allocating memory on heaps not managed by the .NET garbage collector.

> **Tip**
>
> Pinning an object in a garbage-collected heap is necessary when doing something with its memory address, because the .NET garbage collector is free to move the physical location of an object at any time. For instance, it compacts objects when "holes" appear in memory. Although regular object references don't need any special treatment to account for the moveable nature of .NET objects, pointers are a different story. If an object moves while you are using a static memory address, you may end up manipulating memory that doesn't belong to the object you thought it did.
>
> Because pinning objects interferes with the garbage collector's operation, too much pinning for long periods of time can significantly reduce the performance of your application. Therefore, make `fixed` statements as small as possible and free any allocated GCHandle instances as early as possible. In addition, allocating a GCHandle should be done inside a `try` block and freeing it should be done inside a `finally` block, so an exception won't prevent proper clean-up. The `fixed` statement implicitly has the same sort of `try...finally` semantics so you don't need to worry about ensuring unpinning when using it.

Now let's examine two of the list items a little closer:

- Obtaining the address of value types
- Obtaining the size of types

Obtaining the Address of Value Types

Using C# unsafe code, obtaining the address of a value type is simple:

```
int x = 5;
int* address = &x;
```

or:

```
int x = 5;
IntPtr address = new IntPtr(&x);
```

The & operator works on blittable types, or other primitive types such as `bool` or `char`, plus structs containing fields of these primitive types.

Without C# unsafe code, you can accomplish the same thing using the GCHandle class to pin the instance. Pinning can be done to an object on a GC heap, so this technique actually operates on the boxed form of a value type. This isn't very natural, unlike the case for reference types that already exist on the GC heap, but it can be done as follows in Visual Basic .NET:

Advanced Topics for Using COM Components

CHAPTER 6

255

6

ADVANCED TOPICS
FOR USING COM
COMPONENTS

```
Dim x As Integer = 5
Dim box As Object = x
Dim handle As GCHandle
Try
   handle = GCHandle.Alloc(box, GCHandleType.Pinned)
   Dim address As IntPtr = handle.AddrOfPinnedObject()
   ...
Finally
   If (handle.IsAllocated) Then handle.Free()
End Try
x = CInt(box)
```

Notice how an `Object` variable named box is explicitly declared and assigned back to the integer x after the call. Passing a value type like x directly to `GCHandle.Alloc` would not give the desired results because it would be operating on a temporary boxed object that has no relation to the original value type.

This combination of boxing a value type and pinning carries a lot of overhead for the simple action of getting an address of a value type. Often, a better solution is to allocate memory using `Marshal.AllocHGlobal` or `Marshal.AllocCoTaskMem` because these methods return the desired `IntPtr` value containing the address of the memory. For example:

```
Dim address As IntPtr = IntPtr.Zero
Try
   ' Allocate four bytes of memory
   address = Marshal.AllocHGlobal(Marshal.SizeOf(GetType(Int32)))
   ' Initialize the value
   Marshal.WriteInt32(address, 5)
   ...
Finally
   If IntPtr.op_Inequality(address, IntPtr.Zero) Then
      Marshal.FreeHGlobal(address)
   End If
End Try
```

Obtaining the Size of Types

You might guess that C#'s `sizeof` keyword (used with the name of a type) and the `Marshal` class's `SizeOf` method (which has a `System.Type` parameter) do the same thing. You'd be wrong. (It's okay; I was fooled too.) This incorrect assumption is easy to make, especially considering the error message given by the C# compiler when attempting to use `sizeof` outside of an unsafe block:

```
error CS0233: sizeof can only be used in an unsafe
  context (consider using System.Runtime.InteropServices.Marshal.SizeOf)
```

In short, C#'s sizeof reports the *managed size* of a type (in bytes), whereas Marshal.SizeOf reports the *unmanaged size* of a type (also in bytes). The unmanaged size of a type is the size of whatever unmanaged type a managed type would be marshaled to by the Interop Marshaler. When non-blittable types are involved, the managed and unmanaged sizes can be different.

As a demonstration, consider the following value type defined in C#:

```
public struct HowBigAmI
{
  public char un;
  public char deux;
  public char trois;
}
```

The following C# code prints the size of the value type using both techniques. The results are shown in the comments:

```
Console.WriteLine(sizeof(HowBigAmI));               // Prints 8
Console.WriteLine(Marshal.SizeOf(typeof(HowBigAmI)));  // Prints 3
```

Why such a big difference? In .NET, the char type is a Unicode character, which occupies two bytes. So, you might expect sizeof to return 6, but the size of the structure ends up being eight bytes. That's because the official contract for sizeof states that it returns the total size that would be occupied by each element in an array of the type in question, including any padding. In this case, two bytes of padding are added to the end of the value type.

Each character field, however, is marshaled to unmanaged code as a one-byte ANSI character. This is due to the fact that all value types defined in C# are implicitly marked with the following pseudo-custom attribute:

```
[StructLayout(LayoutKind.Sequential, CharSet=CharSet.Ansi)]
```

No padding is done for the unmanaged struct, so the unmanaged size of HowBigAmI is 3 bytes (one byte per character).

CAUTION

Never use Marshal.SizeOf to determine the "real size" of a managed type, because the results can be misleading. Just think of Marshal.SizeOf as "Marshal.UnmanagedSizeOf". An appropriate use of Marshal.SizeOf is to fill a struct's "size field" when passing it to unmanaged code. An example of this is shown in Chapter 19, "Deeper Into PInvoke and Useful Examples."

Furthermore, you should never use Marshal.SizeOf with the System.Char type to determine the current platform's character size—use

Advanced Topics for Using COM Components

CHAPTER 6

257

6

ADVANCED TOPICS
FOR USING COM
COMPONENTS

Marshal.SystemDefaultCharSize instead. This is because Marshal.SizeOf always reports 1 for the size of the System.Char type regardless of platform due to an extremely subtle reason. It reports the size of the System.Char value type in the mscorlib assembly, which has a single character field. Because the definition of System.Char is marked with CharSet.Ansi, the structure would have a size of 1 byte if marshaled to unmanaged code as a plain struct (just as HowBigAmI would have a size of 3 bytes). But because the System.Char type is treated specially as a character primitive type, it is never passed as a plain struct to unmanaged code. By default, character parameters and return types are marshaled as 2-byte Unicode characters, and character fields in a structure are marshaled depending on the structure's character set. Note that doing sizeof(char) in C# unsafe code always returns 2 regardless of platform because .NET characters are always Unicode.

Another difference between the two size-taking techniques is the set of types for which you're allowed to discover the size. You can use sizeof on any types that you could take the address of (using &): blittable types plus primitive types like char and bool, and any value types composed only of these blittable or primitive types. Marshal.SizeOf is a little more flexible because it doesn't return the true managed size; it can be used on any type that would be successfully marshaled to unmanaged code as a structure. This includes reference types with struct layout. So, for the following redefined HowBigAmI type:

```
[StructLayout(LayoutKind.Sequential, CharSet=CharSet.Ansi)]
public class HowBigAmI
{
  public char un;
  public char deux;
  public char trois;
}
```

sizeof(HowBigAmI) fails to compile with the message:

```
Cannot take the address or size of a variable of a managed type ('HowBigAmI')
```

because it looks like any other reference type from .NET's perspective. However, Marshal.SizeOf still returns 3 because it looks like the same HowBigAmI struct to unmanaged code.

DIGGING DEEPER

A nice property of sizeof is that it's faster than using Marshal.SizeOf. For all the primitive types—sbyte, byte, short, ushort, int, uint, long, ulong, char, float, double, and bool—the sizeof expression is replaced with a constant value when compiled. (This is still true when the corresponding mscorlib types are used, such as System.Int32, and so on.) For non-primitive types, the sizeof expression corresponds to an MSIL instruction called sizeof. Although evaluated at run time (or perhaps JIT time), it's still faster than a Marshal.SizeOf call. But remember that in many cases this is comparing apples and oranges because the two techniques have different semantics.

Examples of Manipulating `IntPtr` Types

Now let's look at five examples in which manipulating IntPtr types commonly needs to be done. These are:

- *struct***
- C-style array fields
- By-reference value types that could be null
- VARIANTs containing structures
- SAFEARRAYs containing VARIANTs containing structures

*struct***

A COM parameter that is a reference to a reference to a structure is a classic example of a case for which the type library importer produces an IntPtr type, losing information from the original signature. The problem for the importer is that there's no such thing as a reference to a by-reference parameter in the .NET world. It could produce a signature literally with *struct*** because the .NET type system *does* have a notion of pointers (as in C# unsafe code or C++) but this signature would not be CLS-compliant. As an important example, it would not be useable from Visual Basic .NET.

The following method from the IDirectoryObject interface in the ActiveDS Type Library (ACTIVEDS.TLB) has a *struct*** parameter, because _ads_attr_info is defined as a structure:

```
HRESULT _stdcall GetObjectAttributes(
  [in] LPWSTR* pAttributeNames,
  [in] unsigned long dwNumberAttributes,
  [out] _ads_attr_info** ppAttributeEntries,
  [out] unsigned long* pdwNumAttributesReturned);
```

Advanced Topics for Using COM Components

CHAPTER 6

259

6

ADVANCED TOPICS
FOR USING COM
COMPONENTS

Therefore, the importer produces the following signature (in C# syntax):

```csharp
public virtual void GetObjectAttributes(
  [In, MarshalAs(UnmanagedType.LPWStr)] ref string pAttributeNames,
  uint dwNumberAttributes,
  IntPtr ppAttributeEntries,
  out uint pdwNumAttributesReturned);
```

DIGGING DEEPER

The `ppAttributeEntries` parameter that gets imported as an `IntPtr` type is actually also marked with the `OutAttribute` custom attribute because the original parameter is marked as such. However, the `InAttribute` and `OutAttribute` directional pseudo-custom attributes have no effect on the marshaling of by-value `IntPtr` types, so `[Out]` is omitted from the example.

This method allocates memory for the `ppAttributeEntries` structure returned via the third parameter, and because its original definition is marked as out-only we know that it's safe to pass a null pointer to the method. (In `System.IntPtr` terms, a "null pointer" means `IntPtr.Zero`.) The method actually returns an *array* of _ads_attr_info structures, but for this example we'll assume it's returning a 1-element array for simplicity. The example in the "C-Style Array Fields" section shows what to do when you've got a pointer to an array of structures.

TIP

A null pointer appears as an `IntPtr` type with the value of 0. The easiest way to initialize an `IntPtr` to null is to set it to the static `IntPtr.Zero` field, which is simply an `IntPtr` instance with the value of 0. Similarly, comparing an `IntPtr` to `IntPtr.Zero` is the easiest way to check if it's null. You *could* use the expression new `IntPtr(0)` but its intent isn't as clear.

The default importer behavior of transforming *struct*** to an `IntPtr` type is unfortunate, because it only works when the callee doesn't wish to change the address of the pointer being pointed to. For instance, you might believe you could call the `GetObjectAttributes` method using the following C# code:

```
IntPtr ppStruct = IntPtr.Zero;

// ppStruct cannot change from IntPtr.Zero
// because it's just a by-value integral type
obj.GetObjectAttributes(ref names, 1, ppStruct, out attributes);

// The remaining code doesn't work because ppStruct is still IntPtr.Zero:

// Dereference the pointer to get a single level of indirection
IntPtr pStruct = Marshal.ReadIntPtr(ppStruct);
// Copy the data from the pointer-to-struct
_ads_attr_info theStruct = (_ads_attr_info)Marshal.PtrToStructure(
  pStruct, typeof(_ads_attr_info));
```

DON'T DO THIS

But this won't work because the passed-in `ppStruct` value cannot change because it's just a by-value integer. It would still have the value `IntPtr.Zero` despite the fact that the callee tried to pass back the address of the memory it allocated. To fix this, we must use the techniques described in Chapter 7 to convert the outermost pointer to a reference. In other words, the by-value `IntPtr` representing a pointer-to-pointer-to-struct becomes a by-reference `IntPtr` representing a simple pointer-to-struct. Here, we'll just focus on how to do everything except the signature editing, leaving it for the next chapter, so this section's example assumes that the `GetObjectAttributes` method has the following .NET signature (shown in C# syntax):

```
public virtual void GetObjectAttributes(
  [In, MarshalAs(UnmanagedType.LPWStr)] ref string pAttributeNames,
  uint dwNumberAttributes,
  out IntPtr pAttributeEntries,
  out uint pdwNumAttributesReturned);
```

DIGGING DEEPER

In C#, `out IntPtr` is much different from `[Out] IntPtr`, because the former is a shortcut for saying `[Out] ref IntPtr`.

The tricky part of do-it-yourself marshaling is that you have to be cognizant of who allocates memory, who is supposed to free it, and how memory is allocated and freed. Usually the Interop Marshaler handles this for you, although it only works correctly for memory allocated and freed by the COM task memory allocator. However, when you effectively bypass the marshaler (by making it think it's passing a simple integer for which it does no extra work), the responsibility is on your shoulders. In this case, the documentation for `GetObjectAttributes` states that the caller must free the memory for the returned array by calling the `FreeADsMem` API, a static entry point exposed by `ACTIVEDS.DLL`.

The following C# code demonstrates how to call the updated GetObjectAttributes method:

```
IntPtr ptr = IntPtr.Zero;
try
{
  obj.GetObjectAttributes(ref names, 1, out ptr, out attributes);
  // Copy the data from the pointer-to-struct
  _ads_attr_info theStruct = (_ads_attr_info)Marshal.PtrToStructure(
    ptr, typeof(_ads_attr_info));
  // Now use theStruct just like any .NET value type
  ...
}
finally
{
  // Free the memory allocated by GetObjectAttributes
  if (ptr != IntPtr.Zero) FreeADsMem(ptr);
}
```

First, the method is called passing a null pointer. After the call, Marshal.PtrToStructure can be called to fill a new instance of the _ads_attr_info type with the data from the instance pointed to by ptr. In the finally block, we free the memory using FreeADsMem, as the documentation instructs. To be able to call FreeADsMem from managed code, we need to define a PInvoke signature for it, for example:

```
[DllImport("activeds.dll")]
static extern bool FreeADsMem(IntPtr pMem);
```

PInvoke is discussed in Part VI, "Platform Invocation Services (PInvoke)."

If you wanted to *implement* IDirectoryObject in managed code, you could implement the updated GetObjectAttributes method as follows in C#:

```
public virtual void GetObjectAttributes(
  [In, MarshalAs(UnmanagedType.LPWStr)] ref string pAttributeNames,
  uint dwNumberAttributes,
  out IntPtr pAttributeEntries,
  out uint pdwNumAttributesReturned)
{
  // For simplicity, assume we want to return a 1-element array
  pAttributeEntries = AllocADsMem(Marshal.SizeOf(typeof(_ads_attr_info)));

  // Create a new value type
  _ads_attr_info newStruct = new _ads_attr_info();
  // Fill the struct's fields with data
  newStruct.pszAttrName = "AttrName";
  ...
```

```
// Copy the data to the struct allocated in unmanaged memory
Marshal.StructureToPtr(newStruct, pAttributeEntries, false);
}
```

To comply with the documented behavior of GetObjectAttributes, memory is allocated using AllocADsMem rather than using Marshal.AllocCoTaskMem or Marshal.AllocHGlobal. Again, this requires a PInvoke signature:

```
[DllImport("activeds.dll")]
static extern IntPtr AllocADsMem(int cb);
```

After the fields of the new struct are set with the usual syntax, the data is copied to the unmanaged memory using Marshal.StructureToPtr. The last parameter, for which false is passed, determines whether any memory for reference type fields in the struct living in unmanaged memory should be freed before overwriting it with the contents of the value type. For example, if the pszAttrName string field were pointing to a valid string in the unmanaged copy of the structure, we'd want to free it by passing true for the third parameter. In this case, because the field is set to null in the freshly-allocated unmanaged memory, we pass false.

C-Style Array Fields

Another example in which the type library importer creates an IntPtr type is for structs containing a C-style array field. The ADS_FAXNUMBER structure, also in the Active DS Type Library and shown here in IDL syntax, is such a structure:

```
typedef [public] __MIDL___MIDL_itf_ads_0000_0013 ADS_FAXNUMBER;

typedef struct tag__MIDL___MIDL_itf_ads_0000_0013 {
  LPWSTR TelephoneNumber;
  unsigned long NumberOfBits;
  unsigned char* Parameters;
} __MIDL___MIDL_itf_ads_0000_0013;
```

This is imported as follows (in C# syntax):

```
[ComConversionLoss]
public struct ADS_FAXNUMBER
{
  [MarshalAs(UnmanagedType.LPWStr)] string TelephoneNumber;
  uint NumberOfBits;
  IntPtr Parameters;
}
```

To make use of the elements in this array, Marshal.Copy can be used to extract the elements and create a new .NET array with the same data. In Visual Basic .NET, this looks like the following:

```
Dim n As ADS_FAXNUMBER
Dim i As Integer
n = obj.ReturnFaxNumber()

' Create a new .NET array of the appropriate length
Dim byteArray(arrayLength-1) As Byte
' Copy the data pointed to by the IntPtr value
Marshal.Copy(n.Parameters, byteArray, 0, arrayLength)

For i = 0 To arrayLength
  Console.WriteLine(byteArray(i))
Next i
```

As is always the case with C-style arrays, the length of the array must be known through some external means, such as a separate parameter. In this example, an imaginary `arrayLength` variable is assumed to contain this information.

To avoid the potentially slow operation of copying a large chunk of data pointed to by an `IntPtr` to a .NET instance, the `Marshal` class provides several reading and writing methods that enable you to work with the data directly. So, the previous example could be changed as follows:

```
Dim n As ADS_FAXNUMBER
Dim i As Integer
n = obj.ReturnFaxNumber()

' Directly use the returned "pointer"
For i = 0 To arrayLength
  Console.WriteLine(Marshal.ReadByte(n.Parameters, i))
Next i
```

This can be useful if you're interested in only a small number of elements of a large array. For this example, however, calling `Marshal.ReadByte` for every element of the array is slower than calling `Marshal.Copy` once, because every call requires a transition into unmanaged code. As described in Chapter 16, "COM Design Guidelines for Components Used by .NET Clients," minimizing the number of transitions between managed and unmanaged code can significantly improve performance. Replacing several calls to unmanaged code within a loop with a single larger call outside the loop is a great way to do this.

If you need to create a type to be passed via an `IntPtr`, you often need to allocate unmanaged memory (memory not on a GC heap) using a method of the `Marshal` class as follows:

```
Dim n As ADS_FAXNUMBER
Dim ptr As IntPtr = IntPtr.Zero
Dim byteArray(arrayLength-1) As Byte
n = New ADS_FAXNUMBER()
```

```
...
Try
  ptr = Marshal.AllocCoTaskMem(Marshal.SizeOf(GetType(Byte)) * arrayLength)
  ' Copy the .NET array to the allocated unmanaged memory
  Marshal.Copy(byteArray, 0, ptr, arrayLength)
  n.Parameters = ptr
  ...
Finally
  If IntPtr.op_Inequality(ptr, IntPtr.Zero) Then Marshal.FreeCoTaskMem(ptr)
End Try
```

Again, methods exist to avoid copying data in the managed to unmanaged direction. In the previous example, `Marshal.WriteByte` could have been used to avoid creating a .NET array in the first place. Notice the use of `Marshal.SizeOf` to determine how many bytes of unmanaged memory need to be allocated.

By-Reference Value Types That Could Be Null

Sometimes a COM object has a parameter that's a pointer to a value type for which null (`Nothing` in VB .NET) is a valid thing to pass. A common example of this can be seen with COM's `IStream` interface and its `Read` method, shown here in IDL syntax:

```
HRESULT Read([out, size_is(cb), length_is(*pcbRead)] void *pv,
  [in] ULONG cb, [out] ULONG *pcbRead);
```

In unmanaged code, if you pass a valid pointer to a `ULONG` type, the method returns the number of bytes read. If you pass a null pointer, it doesn't bother giving you the information. Such a method gets imported as follows:

```
public virtual void Read(IntPtr pv, uint cb, out uint pcbRead);
```

But in .NET, value types cannot be null, nor can you pass null when a reference to any type (value type or reference type) is required. When calling such a method in managed code, you'd never be able to pass null, which is usually not a huge loss. For `IStream.Read`, you could call it as follows in C# and simply ignore the returned integer if you don't care about the value:

```
uint pcbRead;
stream.Read(pv, cb, out pcbRead);
```

The situation is worse if you need to implement such a COM method in managed code, however. If a COM object calls your `Read` implementation and passes a null pointer for the third parameter, an exception is thrown at run time. This is not correct behavior because the method's documentation states that it's okay to pass null. To fix this, you can use the techniques in Chapter 7 to change the by-reference integer to an `IntPtr` parameter to get the following .NET signature:

```
public virtual void Read(IntPtr pv, uint cb, IntPtr pcbRead);
```

This method can now be called in C# by doing the following to pass null:

```
// Pass a "null pointer"
stream.Read(pv, cb, IntPtr.Zero);
```

or the following to pass a valid pointer:

```
IntPtr ptr = IntPtr.Zero;
try
{
  // Allocate an integer so we can pass its pointer
  ptr = Marshal.AllocHGlobal(Marshal.SizeOf(typeof(Int32)));
  stream.Read(pv, cb, ptr);
  // Extract the returned value
  int value = Marshal.ReadInt32(ptr);
  ...
}
finally
{
  if (ptr != IntPtr.Zero) Marshal.FreeHGlobal(ptr);
}
```

Furthermore, the Read method can now be implemented as follows, which works even if a COM object passes a null pointer:

```
public virtual void Read(IntPtr pv, uint cb, IntPtr pcbRead)
{
  ...
  if (pcbRead != IntPtr.Zero)
    Marshal.WriteInt32(pcbRead, someNumber);
}
```

> **TIP**
>
> There's another way to solve the problem of by-reference value types that could be null so that you don't have to resort to using the Marshal class to manipulate IntPtr types. In the Stream.Read example, rather than defining the by-reference integer as an IntPtr you can define it as an *array* of integers:
>
> ```
> public virtual void Read(IntPtr pv, uint cb,
>   [Out, MarshalAs(UnmanagedType.LPArray)] int [] pcbRead);
> ```
>
> (In this case, OutAttribute isn't strictly necessary because integers are blittable.) You can pass null for such a parameter because arrays are reference types. To pass a valid integer by-reference, simply pass a one-element array. When implementing such a method, checking for null is straightforward, and extracting the by-reference value is done simply as pcbRead[0]! The only downside to this approach is the potential confusion caused by users of the method that don't understand why the parameter is an array.

VARIANTs **Containing Structures**

The next example works with a signature containing a pointer to a VARIANT, which gets imported as a by-reference System.Object parameter. Usually this is the desired behavior, but not when the VARIANT must contain a structure (UDT), also known as a VARIANT with the VT_RECORD type (because *record* is another term for structure). This is problematic for two reasons:

- There is no way to pass a VT_RECORD VARIANT to COM via a System.Object type. The Interop Marshaler exposes boxed value types and reference types with struct layout as VT_DISPATCH VARIANTs (or VT_UNKNOWN, when appropriate) so a COM object can't treat it like a structure or even access its fields directly; it could only call its methods such as GetType or ToString. (A .NET-aware COM client could use reflection, however, to extract the field values!) Attempting to pass a boxed value type to a COM component expecting a structure usually results in an exception, such as a "Type Mismatch" COMException from VB6 components.

- There is no way for a COM object to return a VT_RECORD VARIANT to managed code via a System.Object type. This applies to return values as well as by-reference Object parameters. When a COM object attempts to do so, the Interop Marshaler throws an ArgumentException with the following message:

  The method returned a VT_RECORD Variant, which is not supported by Interop.

This message should really say that it's not *naturally* supported by the Interop *Marshaler*, because you can get this to work, as this section demonstrates. Using the techniques in Chapter 7, we can change such a by-reference Object parameter to an IntPtr type in order to take VARIANT marshaling into our own hands. Again, we'll just focus on how to do everything except the signature editing, leaving it for the next chapter.

Suppose we have a Visual Basic 6 COM component (an ActiveX DLL project) with the following code inside a class module named Class1:

```
Type RECT
  Left As Long
  Top As Long
  Right As Long
  Bottom As Long
End Type

Public Sub FillRect(ByRef v As Variant)
  Dim r As RECT
  r.Left = 0
  r.Top = 0
```

Advanced Topics for Using COM Components

CHAPTER 6

267

6

ADVANCED TOPICS
FOR USING COM
COMPONENTS

```
      r.Right = Screen.Width
      r.Bottom = Screen.Height
      v = r
End Sub
```

When running the type library importer on the compiled DLL and its embedded type library, we get the following signature (in C# syntax):

```
public virtual void FillRect(ref object v);
```

We've already established that such a signature is unusable from managed code. It runs into the previously mentioned second scenario because it doesn't do anything with the incoming VARIANT, but it attempts to pass one to a .NET client. Assume that, using the techniques discussed in Chapter 7, the signature is changed to look like the following:

```
public virtual void FillRect(IntPtr v);
```

Listing 6.1 demonstrates how to use the updated signature in C#. See Chapter 7 for instructions on how to modify the Interop Assembly containing the FillRect definition, which is required in order to compile this listing.

DIGGING DEEPER

Alternatively, the signature could have been redefined as:

```
public virtual void FillRect(ref Variant v);
```

where Variant is the user-defined structure in Listing 6.1. This makes it easier to use than in Listing 6.1, but would either require the definition of the Variant structure inside the Interop Assembly or require it to reference to the assembly defining it.

LISTING 6.1   Performing Manual VARIANT Marshaling in C#

```
 1: using System;
 2: using System.Reflection;
 3: using System.Runtime.InteropServices;
 4: using ComObject;
 5:
 6: public struct Variant
 7: {
 8:    public ushort vt;
 9:    public ushort wReserved1;
10:    public ushort wReserved2;
11:    public ushort wReserved3;
12:    public IntPtr pvRecord;
13:    public IntPtr pRecInfo;
```

Listing 6.1 Continued

```
14: }
15:
16: [
17:   ComImport,
18:   Guid("0000002F-0000-0000-C000-000000000046"),
19:   InterfaceType(ComInterfaceType.InterfaceIsIUnknown)
20: ]
21: public interface IRecordInfo
22: {
23:   void RecordInit(IntPtr pvNew);
24:   void RecordClear(IntPtr pvExisting);
25:   void RecordCopy(IntPtr pvExisting, IntPtr pvNew);
26:   Guid GetGuid();
27:   string GetName();
28:   uint GetSize();
29:   UCOMITypeInfo GetTypeInfo();
30:   object GetField(IntPtr pvData,
31:     [MarshalAs(UnmanagedType.LPWStr)] string szFieldName);
32:   IntPtr GetFieldNoCopy(IntPtr pvData, [MarshalAs(UnmanagedType.LPWStr)]
33:     string szFieldName, ref object pvarField);
34:   void PutField(uint wFlags, IntPtr pvData, [MarshalAs(
35:     UnmanagedType.LPWStr)] string szFieldName, [In] ref object pvarField);
36:   void PutFieldNoCopy(uint wFlags, IntPtr pvData, [MarshalAs(
37:     UnmanagedType.LPWStr)] string szFieldName, [In] ref object pvarField);
38:   void GetFieldNames(IntPtr pcNames, [In, Out] string [] rgBstrNames);
39:   [PreserveSig]
40:   bool IsMatchingType(IRecordInfo pRecordInfo);
41:   [PreserveSig]
42:   IntPtr RecordCreate();
43:   void RecordCreateCopy(IntPtr pvSource, ref IntPtr ppvDest);
44:   void RecordDestroy(IntPtr pvRecord);
45: }
46:
47: public class VT_RECORDWorkaround
48: {
49:   [DllImport("oleaut32.dll", PreserveSig=false)]
50:   private static extern IntPtr
51:     GetRecordInfoFromTypeInfo(IntPtr pTypeInfo);
52:
53:   public static void Main()
54:   {
55:     Class1 obj = new Class1();
56:
57:     Variant v = new Variant();
58:
```

LISTING 6.1   Continued

```
59:     // Create an IRecordInfo instance
60:     IntPtr ptr = GetRecordInfoFromTypeInfo(
61:       Marshal.GetITypeInfoForType(typeof(RECT)));
62:     IRecordInfo info = (IRecordInfo)Marshal.GetObjectForIUnknown(ptr);
63:
64:     // Initialize the Variant
65:     v.vt = (ushort)VarEnum.VT_RECORD; // VT_RECORD = 36
66:     v.pvRecord = info.RecordCreate();
67:     v.pRecInfo = ptr;
68:
69:     GCHandle handle = new GCHandle();
70:
71:     try
72:     {
73:       // Pin the boxed value type just so we can get the address
74:       handle = GCHandle.Alloc(v, GCHandleType.Pinned);
75:
76:       // Call the COM object's method expecting a pointer to a Variant
77:       obj.FillRect(handle.AddrOfPinnedObject());
78:     }
79:     finally
80:     {
81:       if (handle.IsAllocated) handle.Free();
82:     }
83:
84:     // Convert the VT_RECORD Variant to the wrapped value type
85:     object o = new RECT();
86:     VT_RECORDToStructure(v, ref o);
87:     RECT r = (RECT)o;
88:
89:     Console.WriteLine(
90:       r.Left + " " + r.Top + " " + r.Right + " " + r.Bottom);
91:   }
92:
93:   public static void VT_RECORDToStructure(Variant v, ref Object o)
94:   {
95:     if (v.vt != (ushort)VarEnum.VT_RECORD)
96:       throw new ArgumentException("Incorrect VARIANT type");
97:
98:     IRecordInfo info =
99:       (IRecordInfo)Marshal.GetObjectForIUnknown(v.pRecInfo);
100:
101:     if (info.GetName() != o.GetType().Name)
102:     {
```

LISTING 6.1 Continued

```
103:        throw new ArgumentException("Variant name '" + info.GetName() +
104:          "' doesn't match object name '" + o.GetType().Name + "'.");
105:      }
106:
107:      // Copy every field's data, thanks to reflection
108:      foreach (FieldInfo fi in o.GetType().GetFields())
109:      {
110:        fi.SetValue(o, info.GetField(v.pvRecord, fi.Name));
111:      }
112:    }
113: }
```

Lines 1–4 list the System namespace for the IntPtr type; System.Reflection for the generic VARIANT-to-Object transformation done at the end of the listing; System.Runtime. InteropServices for a handful of custom attributes, the Marshal and GCHandle classes, and more; and ComObject is the namespace containing the Visual Basic 6 class—Class1—with the FillRect method.

Lines 6–14 contain a definition of the raw COM VARIANT structure, simplified for our specific use of the type. The real definition has two unions: one that shares all 16 bytes with a DECIMAL field named decVal, and one that shares the 8 bytes occupied by pvRecord and pRecInfo with 39 other fields so you can view the data as an integer or a date or a boolean, and so on. This definition is entirely usable regardless of the type of VARIANT because the IntPtr types can be manipulated however you'd like; the field names are just biased toward using the structure with the VT_RECORD type. The structure implicitly has sequential layout, required by all structs marshaled to unmanaged code, because this is the default behavior in C# (as well as in VB .NET and C++).

> **CAUTION**
>
> If you attempt to define a COM structure such as Variant in any other language than C#, VB .NET, or C++, check to see if your compiler automatically emits value types with sequential layout. (This can be checked using ILDASM.EXE.) When in doubt, always mark a value type to be used from unmanaged code with the StructLayoutAttribute custom attribute and its LayoutKind.Sequential value.
>
> Also, Variant is a keyword in Visual Basic .NET, so you'd want to define the structure with a different name (such as RawVariant) if using it in VB .NET.

Advanced Topics for Using COM Components

CHAPTER 6

271

6

ADVANCED TOPICS
FOR USING COM
COMPONENTS

Lines 16–45 define the IRecordInfo COM interface manually, necessary for the kind of raw interaction with VT_RECORD VARIANTs that the rest of the listing does. Instructions for manually defining COM interfaces are given in Chapter 21, "Manually Defining COM Types in Source Code," so the definition won't be explained here.

FAQ: What is the IRecordInfo interface?

Although hidden by Visual Basic 6, IRecordInfo is the COM interface that makes it possible to pass structures inside a VARIANT type. Because *record* is another term for a structure, you can think of it as "IStructInfo". Information about all types in a type library can be extracted from the ITypeInfo interface, but IRecordInfo provides extra information specific to structs. The IRecordInfo interface has reflection-like methods for getting and setting fields, plus several methods (similar to those that exist for VARIANTs) that initialize, clear, copy, create, and destroy structures.

When passing a VARIANT with type VT_RECORD, the VARIANT contains two pointers—one to the structure itself and one two an IRecordInfo implementation describing the structure. Both are necessary because the reflection-like methods of IRecordInfo require that you pass in an instance of the structure. This is unlike the analogous .NET System.Type because is always corresponds to a certain instance.

Lines 49–51 define a PInvoke signature for the GetRecordInfoFromTypeInfo method exposed by OLEAUT32.DLL. Lines 57–74 prepare the Variant object to be passed to the FillRect method. Although the COM method doesn't actually do anything with the incoming instance, it must appear to be a valid VT_RECORD VARIANT. First, Lines 60 and 61 use the GetRecordInfoFromTypeInfo to get an OLE Automation-supplied implementation of IRecordInfo. This method requires an ITypeInfo pointer for a structure, which is obtained using Marshal.GetITypeInfoFromType. To convert the returned IntPtr to an IRecordInfo interface pointer, Line 62 calls Marshal.GetObjectForIUnknown. This method treats the passed-in IntPtr type as an IUnknown pointer, and constructs an RCW for the object. When the returned Object type is cast to IRecordInfo, a QueryInterface call is performed by the RCW, as usual.

Now that we've obtained an IRecordInfo instance, Lines 65–67 initialize the Variant type appropriately. Its type, stored in the vt field, is set to VT_RECORD using the VarEnum enumeration defined in System.Runtime.InteropServices. Its pRecInfo field is set to the IntPtr representing a pointer to the IRecordInfo implementation, and its pvRecord field is set to a new instance of RECT obtained by calling the IRecordInfo implementation's RecordCreate method.

Line 74 pins the boxed Variant only to get the address of the value type to pass as the IntPtr parameter to FillRect. As discussed in the previous section, this could have been accomplished by allocating the memory for the Variant instance on a non-GC heap using Marshal.AllocCoTaskMem or Marshal.AllocHGlobal, or by taking advantage of C# unsafe code and doing the following inside an unsafe block:

```
IntPtr addrOfVariant = new IntPtr(&v);
```

Line 77 calls the COM object's method with the address of the Variant, so Line 81 unpins the object by calling the GCHandle's Free method. Notice that the unpinning is done as soon as possible so the impact to the garbage collector is minimized. Because the FillRect method fills the RECT instance returned via the by-reference parameter with data, Lines 89–90 print its contents. But first the IntPtr parameter needs to be converted to a RECT type; the opposite of the conversion done before the call. This is done by the VT_RECORDToStructure method defined in Lines 93–112, a general-purpose method that works for any type of struct inside a VT_RECORD Variant. This can be done using the power of reflection plus the reflection-like methods in IRecordInfo.

Line 95 checks to make sure that the incoming Variant does indeed have the VT_RECORD type, then Lines 98–99 extract the IRecordInfo instance from the Variant. Lines 101–105 do one last sanity check, making sure that the name of the struct represented by the IRecordInfo and the name of the .NET type match. Finally, Lines 108–111 enumerate through the fields of the boxed value type and use FieldInfo.SetValue to set each field to the value obtained by IRecordInfo.GetField.

SAFEARRAYs Containing VARIANTs Containing Structures

You can run into the same marshaler limitations when a COM object uses SAFEARRAYs of
VARIANTs for which the VARIANT type must be VT_RECORD. If treated as a .NET array of
System.Object types, attempting to pass an array of boxed value types suffers from the same
ArgumentException described in the previous section. One could imagine defining and using a
raw SAFEARRAY structure in managed code just as we used a raw VARIANT structure, such as
defining the following in C#:

```
public struct SafeArray
{
  ushort cDims;
  ushort fFeatures;
  uint cbElements;
  uint cLocks;
  IntPtr pvData;
  IntPtr rgsabound;
}
```

But this often isn't necessary if the COM object passes or returns a *pointer* to a SAFEARRAY,
because the IntPtr value representing a pointer to a SAFEARRAY can be passed directly to several SAFEARRAY APIs provided by OLE Automation and obtainable via PInvoke. Listing 6.2
shows an example of using these APIs to print the contents of a SAFEARRAY containing
VARIANTs with type VT_RECORD that each contain a POINT structure. In this example, the COM
object has a method called ReturnPtrToSafeArray that returns a pointer to the SAFEARRAY.
The source code for this method is available from the book's Web site. The Variant type and
VT_RECORDToStructure method from Listing 6.1 are referenced here.

LISTING 6.2 Performing Manual SAFEARRAY Marshaling in C#

```
1: using System;
2: using System.Runtime.InteropServices;
3:
4: public class SafeArrayManipulation
5: {
6:   // The second parameter of this signature is customized for the
7:   // single-dimensional array case.  For general use, rgIndices should be
8:   // defined as an array: int [] rgIndices
9:   [DllImport("oleaut32.dll", PreserveSig=false)]
10:   extern static IntPtr SafeArrayGetElement(IntPtr psa, ref int rgIndices);
11:
12:   [DllImport("oleaut32.dll", PreserveSig=false)]
13:   extern static int SafeArrayGetLBound(IntPtr psa, uint nDim);
14:
15:   [DllImport("oleaut32.dll", PreserveSig=false)]
16:   extern static int SafeArrayGetUBound(IntPtr psa, uint nDim);
```

LISTING 6.2   Continued

```
17:
18:    public static void Main()
19:    {
20:      SomeComObject obj = new SomeComObject();
21:      IntPtr psa = obj.ReturnPtrToSafeArray();
22:
23:      // Get the SAFEARRAY bounds
24:      int lBound = SafeArrayGetLBound(psa, 1);
25:      int uBound = SafeArrayGetUBound(psa, 1);
26:
27:      for (int i = lBound; i <= uBound; i++)
28:      {
29:        // Extract a pointer to the element
30:        IntPtr ptr = SafeArrayGetElement(psa, ref i);
31:        // Copy the data from the pointer to a new Variant instance
32:        Variant v = (Variant)Marshal.PtrToStructure(ptr, typeof(Variant));
33:        // Convert the VT_RECORD Variant to the wrapped value type
34:        object o = new POINT();
35:        VT_RECORDWorkaround.VT_RECORDToStructure(v, ref o);
36:        POINT p = (POINT)o;
37:        // Finally, print the element
38:        Console.WriteLine(p.x + " " + p.y);
39:      }
40:    }
41: }
```

> **TIP**
>
> Listings 6.1 and 6.2 use COM methods that pass or return a pointer to a VARIANT or a pointer to a SAFEARRAY. Often, these types are passed directly rather than with a level of indirection. In these cases, the parameters would have to be changed to be the corresponding structure types rather than System.IntPtr. Chapter 7 describes how to change a parameter such as a by-value Object inside an Interop Assembly to a Variant value type like the one defined in Listing 6.1.

As mentioned in Chapter 5, "Responding to COM Events," late binding to methods with structure parameters is problematic because the nature of late binding means that all parameters are automatically passed in VARIANTs. Structure parameters must be passed as VT_RECORD VARIANTs when late binding, causing the same failures from the Interop Marshaler. If the parameters in questions are *pointers* to structures, you can change them to be IntPtr types and use the same kind of techniques demonstrated in this chapter.

Advanced Topics for Using COM Components

CHAPTER 6

275

6

ADVANCED TOPICS
FOR USING COM
COMPONENTS

For dispinterfaces, which by definition only support late binding, the situation is even worse. In managed code, you cannot invoke members that use by-value UDT parameters directly on dispinterfaces. If such parameters are not pointers but instead by-value structs, there's no way to change the .NET definition of a dispinterface signature to make it work with the built-in late binding support. That's because a structure of some sort must be passed to the member (except for the unlikely case in which the struct is small enough that a primitive type like int or long could be passed in its place). One alternative would be to manually write a .NET IDispatch definition that uses raw VARIANT types as in Listing 6.1, cast the object implementing the dispinterface to IDispatch, then call IDispatch.Invoke yourself with raw VARIANT structures that you fill appropriately. In this case, you must perform all the same work that you would have to do in unmanaged C++ code.

Threading and Apartments

COM's threading models and various apartment types have always been a source of great confusion. Fortunately, .NET no longer has a notion of apartments or different kinds of threads. (.NET has its own new and often-confusing concepts such as application domains, but that's another story.) Threading is yet another area in which COM Interoperability does a lot of work to bridge two disparate models. In this section, we'll look at the following topics in threading:

- Threading in COM versus threading in .NET
- Choosing your apartment state in a .NET application
- Callbacks from a COM object to a .NET object

Threading in COM Versus Threading in .NET

In .NET, objects can be accessed by any number of threads at any time. This means that class authors must take on the responsibility of protecting internal state from getting corrupted due to concurrent access and also ensure that all methods are reentrant. This is known as being *threadsafe*. Or, class authors should document when their classes are not threadsafe so clients don't attempt to use the same instance from multiple threads. Examples of this can be seen throughout the .NET Framework. For instance, Windows Forms classes are not threadsafe, so they provide a mechanism (Control.Invoke) to facilitate using the classes from multiple threads. As another example, System.Collection.Hashtable supports multiple concurrent readers but only one writer at a time for performance reasons. But if you want to support multiple concurrent writers, you can call its Synchronized method to obtain a threadsafe wrapper to the original Hashtable.

The .NET Framework has several mechanisms to manage concurrency, such as the Monitor and Mutex classes in the System.Threading namespace. (C#'s lock statement implicitly uses Monitor.Enter and Monitor.Exit.) The System.Runtime.Remoting.Contexts class has a

`SynchronizationAttribute` custom attribute for Remoting purposes. In addition, any method can be marked as requiring synchronization using the little-known `System.Runtime.CompilerServices.MethodImplAttribute` custom attribute with the `MethodImplOptions.Synchronized` value, as shown in the previous chapter.

Writing threadsafe code is not an easy task, so COM has the notion of *apartments* to protect programs that rely on thread affinity and to isolate programmers who don't want to worry about concurrency issues. An apartment is a logical process that contains one or more running threads, used to group together objects that have the same threading requirements. Every COM object lives inside exactly one apartment.

There are three kinds of apartments:

- Single-Threaded Apartments (STAs) only contain one thread and zero or more COM objects. Any process can contain zero or more STAs.
- Multi-Threaded Apartments (MTAs) contain one or more threads and zero or more COM objects. A process can only contain zero or one MTA.
- Neutral Apartments (NAs), introduced with COM+, contain no threads; just COM objects. A process can only contain zero or one NA.

Every thread must "enter" an apartment before instantiating or using COM objects. This occurs when a program initializes the COM library by calling `CoInitialize` or `CoInitializeEx`. Calling `CoInitialize(NULL)` or `CoInitializeEx(NULL, COINIT_APARTMENT_THREADED)` means that the current thread enters an STA (making it an *STA thread*), whereas calling `CoInitializeEx(NULL, COINIT_MULTITHREADED)` means that the current thread enters an MTA (making it an *MTA thread*). There's no such thing as an "NA thread" because NAs never contain threads.

COM objects that are in-process servers advertise their threading model requirements using the Windows Registry. The `ThreadingModel` registry value under the `HKEY_CLASSES_ROOT\CLSID\{CLSID}\InProcServer32` key contains a string that can be set to:

- `Apartment`—Indicates that the COM object must be created in an STA.
- `Free`—Indicates that the COM object must be created in an MTA.
- `Both`—Indicates that the COM object can be created in any type of apartment: an STA, MTA, or NA. (The value is called `Both` because it existed before NAs were invented. As if COM threading models weren't confusing enough already!)
- `Neutral`—Indicates that the COM object must be created in an NA.
- `Single`—Indicates that the COM object must be created in the "main STA," the first STA created in the process. This exists only for legacy reasons, from the time before COM had threading models and each process could only have one thread. It's also the default behavior if no `ThreadingModel` value exists.

With this information, `CoCreateInstance` instantiates the COM objects in the appropriate apartment.

So what's the value in having all these rules with threading models and apartment types? As mentioned earlier, the main motivation is to have the notion of a single-threaded atmosphere (an STA) to enable rapid application development free from the complexities of multithreading. Many COM components live in STAs, including any authored in Visual Basic 6 (with the exception of `ActiveX EXE` projects) or with Microsoft Foundation Classes (MFC). By default, COM objects created using the Visual C++ ATL wizard live in STAs as well. Such components are called *apartment-threaded components*, and are the easiest kind to write because they live in a sheltered world.

A COM object living in an STA (which has the `Single` or `Apartment` threading model) can only be called by the thread that created the object. To make such an object usable from COM objects living in an MTA or other STAs, any calls from different threads are synchronized with a queue used by the original thread. On Windows, COM uses the Windows message queue. Therefore, any STA thread must have a Windows message loop.

A COM object that lives in an MTA, on the other hand, can be called by multiple threads concurrently just like .NET objects. Such components are called *free-threaded components* and must handle synchronization themselves. Although more difficult to write correctly, free-threaded components can achieve high performance because they can be called from multiple threads without incurring the cost of COM marshaling. Any calls crossing from one apartment to another are more expensive than intra-apartment calls due to proxy/stub marshaling and a thread switch, so COM clients should attempt to live in the same apartment as the COM objects they use whenever possible. Objects registered as `Both` make this task easier, as the in-process server always gets created in the same apartment as the creator.

The neutral apartment was introduced to help avoid performance problems when cross-apartment calls are required. Because an NA has no threads, COM objects living an NA (also known as *neutral components*) are always called on the same thread doing the calling, whether an MTA thread or an STA thread. The result is a lightweight proxy that does not require a thread switch. Neutral components must still worry about synchronization just like free-threaded components.

Choosing Your Apartment State in a .NET Application

When using COM components in a .NET client application, the CLR must initialize the COM library at some point before the first COM object is instantiated. By default, the CLR calls `CoInitializeEx` as follows:

```
CoInitializeEx(0, COINIT_MULTITHREADED)
```

This means that .NET threads are MTA threads by default. This has the following implications for using apartment-threaded COM components from managed code:

- Some COM objects requiring an STA may simply be unusable if you attempt to call them from an MTA thread. For example, Microsoft Collaboration Data Objects (CDO) has a `Session` class that returns an error in such a situation. Deadlocks are also possible in this scenario, depending on the two components.

- Because the COM object would be created in a separate apartment, COM attempts to set up a proxy to marshal the calls from one thread to another. Even if a proxy can be created (which can sometimes require extra registration of a proxy/stub DLL), performance suffers due to the extra work involved.

Therefore, it's desirable to have control over the apartment that a .NET component resides in. This can be done by putting one of two custom attributes on your .NET application's entry point (the `Main` method):

- `System.STAThreadAttribute`—Instructs the CLR to initialize COM with `CoInitializeEx(NULL, COINIT_APARTMENT_THREADED)`, so the current thread is an STA thread.

- `System.MTAThreadAttribute`—Instructs the CLR to initialize COM with `CoInitializeEx(NULL, COINIT_MULTITHREADED)`, so the current thread is an MTA thread.

CAUTION

Be mindful of the threading requirements of any COM object you use in managed code so you can avoid cross-apartment COM marshaling. Cross-apartment marshaling may not work if the COM interfaces you're calling on don't have a proxy/stub marshaler registered, or you may experience poor performance due to the extra marshaling.

This behavior is not specific to .NET but is true for plain COM clients and servers as well. The difference is that you may be used to developing in an STA world (using Visual Basic 6, MFC, the default ATL behavior, and so on) but switching to a language like C# places you in an MTA world by default.

Failure due to unmarshalable interfaces manifests as an `InvalidCastException`, but other kinds of failures can result from incompatible threading models, such as a `COMException` with the message, "An internal error occurred in a remote procedure call (RPC)." When using ActiveX controls wrapped as Windows Forms controls, a `System.Threading.ThreadStateException` is thrown during object construction if the current thread is not an STA thread.

Using `STAThreadAttribute` looks like the following in C#:

```
[STAThread]
public static void Main(string [] args)
{
  ...
}
```

The CLR always waits to initialize COM until it's needed, so in theory this custom attribute has no effect if COM Interoperability is never used. It turns out, however, that the CLR internally uses COM when starting up so COM is always initialized by the time the first line of code inside `Main` is run.

TIP

The Visual Basic .NET compiler automatically emits the `STAThreadAttribute` on an application's entry point (`Sub Main`) to more closely match the apartment-threaded nature of Visual Basic 6. To override this behavior, you can use `MTAThreadAttribute`. In any other language, MTA behavior is the default, overridable using `STAThreadAttribute`. Visual Studio .NET marks the `Main` method with `STAThreadAttribute` by default in Visual C# Windows Application and Console Application projects.

In an ASP.NET page, you can accomplish the same thing as using `STAThreadAttribute` in a standalone application by using the following directive at the top of the `.aspx` page:

```
<%@ Page aspcompat=true %>
```

This is known as turning on *ASP Compatibility Mode*. As with any .NET applications, the threads used by ASP.NET have an MTA apartment state by default. Using ASP Compatibility Mode forces the page to run on an STA thread instead.

ASP.NET's built-in instantiation mechanisms—`Server.CreateObject`, `Server.CreateObjectFromClsid`, and the `<object>` tag (with `runat="server"`)—check to see if you're instantiating an apartment-threaded COM object on an ASP.NET page that isn't running in ASP Compatibility Mode, but only if you're creating the object via ProgID or CLSID. If the object's threading requirements aren't compatible with the thread's apartment state, instantiation fails. ASP.NET makes this check for three reasons:

- Almost all COM objects used in ASP pages are apartment-threaded.
- Using an apartment-threaded COM component can be dangerous or poor-performing without `aspcompat=true`.
- A COM component's threading requirements aren't obvious unless you check the registry, and ASP.NET developers are unlikely to do so.

The non-ASP.NET-specific instantiation mechanisms do not enforce such a requirement.

> **CAUTION**
>
> The `aspcompat=true` directive is supported only in ASP.NET Web pages (`.aspx` files), not in XML Web services (`.asmx` files).

What if you're writing a .NET component that is used by a .NET application whose entry point you don't control? You can still control the initialization of COM, but only on a thread that hasn't yet been initialized. This can be done by obtaining the current thread instance (assuming the current thread has not been initialized) and setting its `ApartmentState` property. The `Thread.ApartmentState` property can be set to one of the following values in the `System.Threading.ApartmentState` enumeration:

- `STA`—An STA thread, running inside a single-threaded apartment.
- `MTA`—An MTA thread, running inside a multithreaded apartment.

The enumeration also has an `Unknown` value that represents an apartment state has not yet been chosen, which means that COM has not yet been initialized. Because COM gets initialized during program startup, this state is never seen on the main thread (nor can it be set programmatically).

Once a thread's `ApartmentState` has been chosen, you cannot change it. Attempting to set a thread's `ApartmentState` property never throws an exception, but attempting to change it from a state other than `Unknown` silently fails.

In order to set a thread's `ApartmentState` property successfully, you must do it on a new thread because the main thread's apartment state was chosen when COM gets initialized during process startup. This is demonstrated by the odd-behaving C# code:

```
using System;
using System.Threading;

public class ThreadingModels
{
  public static void Main()
  {
    Thread.CurrentThread.ApartmentState = ApartmentState.STA;
    // The next line prints "MTA"!
```

DON'T DO THIS

```
    Console.WriteLine(Thread.CurrentThread.ApartmentState);
  }
}
```

Because the default MTA behavior was chosen during startup, setting `ApartmentState` to an STA thread has no effect. The code should have marked `Main` with `STAThreadAttribute` instead. The implicit `STAThreadAttribute` emitted by the Visual Basic .NET compiler causes the reverse odd behavior:

```
Imports System
Imports System.Threading

Public Module ThreadingModels
  Public Sub Main()
    Thread.CurrentThread.ApartmentState = ApartmentState.MTA
    ' The next line prints "STA"!
    Console.WriteLine(Thread.CurrentThread.ApartmentState.ToString())
  End Sub
End Module
```

🚫 DON'T DO THIS

The following code demonstrates the correct way to set the `ApartmentState` property, by using a brand new thread that has not been initialized:

```
using System.Threading;

public class ThreadingModels
{
  public void CalledOnMTAThread()
  {
    Thread t = new Thread(new ThreadStart(CalledOnSTAThread));
    t.ApartmentState = ApartmentState.STA;
    t.Start();
    ...
  }

  private void CalledOnSTAThread()
  {
    ...
  }
}
```

DIGGING DEEPER

When creating and starting a new thread, it's a good practice to set the thread's `ApartmentState` property before starting the thread. This was done in the previous code example, although removing the following line in `CalledOnMTAThread`:

```
t.ApartmentState = ApartmentState.STA;
```

and adding the following line at the beginning of `CalledOnSTAThread`:

```
Thread.CurrentThread.ApartmentState = ApartmentState.STA
```

would accomplish the same thing. The confusing part about the apartment state of new threads is that new threads do in fact begin in the `Unknown` apartment state (as long as it was not set before the thread started), yet its `ApartmentState` property is set to the `MTA` enumeration value. Until the apartment state is actually set, however, the apartment state could become either `STA` or `MTA` at the time that COM is initialized.

Callbacks from a COM Object to a .NET Object

Callbacks from a COM object in .NET applications are a source of much confusion because the behavior does not match the rules of COM. In the previous section, you saw that when managed code calls members of a COM object, the same rules of threads and apartments apply. If the COM object lives in an STA, any calls from MTA threads are marshaled appropriately so the COM object remains in its world of thread affinity.

But, in the other direction, no such thread or context switch occurs. Even if you've marked your .NET object as created on an STA thread, COM components (or .NET components, for that matter) are able to call you on multiple threads. A managed thread's apartment state only affects the instantiation of COM objects, not of .NET objects. If you're expecting a managed callback method to be called on a certain thread, you're responsible for getting to the right thread yourself before calling the code with the thread affinity.

Unlike most COM objects, there is no way to force .NET objects to live in an STA. .NET objects are always exposed to COM in a context-agile fashion, effectively as if they aggregate the free-threaded marshaler (FTM). This is because a design goal of .NET is to avoid thread affinity wherever possible. The result is that no .NET components can assume that they will only be called on one thread.

Advanced Topics for Using COM Components

CHAPTER 6

283

6

ADVANCED TOPICS
FOR USING COM
COMPONENTS

> **TIP**
>
> There's an exception to the rule that all .NET components may be called by multiple threads. The `System.EnterpriseServices.ServicedComponent` class and any subclasses strictly act as COM objects. This means that if a `ServicedComponent` or derived type is created on an STA thread, all calls from COM objects *and even .NET objects* are always marshaled to the original thread.

Listing 6.3 shows Visual Basic .NET code using DirectX that receives a callback on a separate MTA thread despite the fact that the main thread is implicitly an STA thread. In this case, attempting to call members of a COM object created on the main thread fails because the `DirectMusicPerformance` interface being called upon cannot be marshaled across apartment boundaries (due to no proxy/stub marshaler being registered for the interface). The equivalent code works without errors in Visual Basic 6 because all code is executed on the same STA thread.

LISTING 6.3   Visual Basic .NET Code with COM Callbacks on a Separate Thread

```
 1: Imports System
 2: Imports System.Windows.Forms
 3: Imports DxVBLib
 4:
 5: Public Class Form1
 6:   Inherits Form
 7:   Implements DirectXEvent
 8:
 9:   Dim performance As DirectMusicPerformance
10:
11:   ' Callback method (called on a different thread)
12:   Private Sub DXCallback(eventid As Integer) _
13:     Implements DirectXEvent.DxCallBack
14:
15:     Dim msg As DMUS_NOTIFICATION_PMSG
16:
17:     Try
18:       ' Fails since DirectMusicPerformance is not marshalable
19:       performance.GetNotificationPMSG(msg)
20:     Catch ex as Exception
21:       MessageBox.Show(ex.ToString())
```

LISTING 6.3   Continued

```
22:     End Try
23:   End Sub
24:
25:   ' Constructor
26:   Public Sub New()
27:     MyBase.New
28:
29:     Dim directX As DirectX7 = new DirectX7()
30:
31:     ' Set up the music
32:     performance = directX.DirectMusicPerformanceCreate()
33:     performance.Init(Nothing, 0)
34:     performance.SetPort(-1, 4)
35:     Dim loader As DirectMusicLoader = directX.DirectMusicLoaderCreate()
36:     Dim segment As DirectMusicSegment
37:     segment = loader.LoadSegment("heartland2.sgt")
38:     Dim style As DirectMusicStyle = loader.LoadStyle("heartlnd.sty")
39:
40:     ' Set up the callback
41:     performance.AddNotificationType( _
42:       CONST_DMUS_NOTIFICATION_TYPE.DMUS_NOTIFY_ON_MEASUREANDBEAT)
43:     Dim notification As Integer = directX.CreateEvent(Me)
44:     performance.SetNotificationHandle(notification)
45:
46:     ' Begin playing the music
47:     performance.PlaySegment(segment, 0, 0)
48:   End Sub
49:
50:   Public Shared Sub Main()
51:     Application.Run(new Form1())
52:   End Sub
53: End Class
```

To compile this listing, you must reference System.Windows.Forms.dll, System.dll, and
DxVBLib.dll, an Interop Assembly for the DirectX 7 for Visual Basic Type Library
(DX7VB.DLL) generated by the type library importer. This program requires two files from the
DirectX SDK, which can be downloaded from MSDN Online, to be copied to the same direc-
tory. These are heartland.sty and heartland2.sgt, two files that enable music to be played.
(Any pair of .sty and .sgt files will do, as long as you change the filenames in the listing.)
They can be located with the samples installed by the SDK, in the folder containing media
such as pictures and sounds.

This code represents a blank Windows Form that uses DirectX (specifically, DirectMusic) to play a song. Every time the song's measure or beat changes, the form receives a callback. The callback interface is called `DirectXEvent`, and its single method is called `DXCallback`. Lines 12–23 implement the `DXCallback` method, but first we'll look at the form's constructor in Lines 26–48.

Line 29 instantiates the `DirectX7` object, which serves like a class factory for the many objects available from DirectX. Lines 32–38 initialize the music using "segment" and "style" files available from the DirectX SDK. Line 32 is important because it marks the creation of the `performance` object, an object that implements the `DirectMusicPerformance` interface. The object returned is apartment-threaded, and because the main thread is an STA thread, it enters the current apartment.

Lines 41–44 setup the callback by, among other things, passing a reference to itself to `DirectX7.CreateEvent`, which expects an object implementing `DirectXEvent`. The `DirectMusicPerformance` object supports several kinds of callbacks, and you can select which ones you're interested in by calling `AddNotificationType` with appropriate enumeration values. Line 42 specifies that we're only interested in callbacks when the music's measure or beat changes. Line 47 begins playing the music asynchronously. Control returns immediately to the main thread, at which point the Windows message loop idly runs inside `Application.Run` on Line 51.

When the callbacks occur on a new thread, Line 19 attempts to call a member of the `performance` COM object, which causes the following exception:

```
System.InvalidCastException: QueryInterface for interface
➡DxVBLib.DirectMusicPerformance failed.
    at DxVBLib.DirectMusicPerformance.GetNotificationPMSG
➡(DMUS_NOTIFICATION_PMSG& message)
    at Form1.DXCallback(Int32 eventid)
```

You could manually register an appropriate proxy/stub marshaler for the `DirectMusicPerformance` interface to make Listing 6.3 run correctly, but Listing 6.4 will demonstrate a Visual Basic .NET source solution instead.

DIGGING DEEPER

You could prove to yourself that `DXCallback` is called on a different thread by displaying the current thread's hash code inside `DXCallback` and inside `Form1`'s constructor (by calling `System.Threading.Thread.CurrentThread.GetHashCode`). `GetHashCode` is the official means of obtaining a stable and unique identifier for a .NET thread. A thread's hash code is guaranteed to be unique across all application domains, although it has no relation to the underlying operating system's thread ID.

Notice that the implementation of DXCallback catches the exception and displays a message box with its contents. Had it not done that, the call to GetNotificationPMSG would have appeared to silently fail. That's because the InvalidCastException thrown would propagate to DXCallback's caller, and that caller is some COM object inside DirectX. This COM object happens to ignore any failure HRESULTs returned by DXCallback implementations, so the exception gets silently "swallowed." This is reasonable behavior for the DirectX COM object because it has no great way to report such an error.

CAUTION

Be careful about exceptions thrown from .NET methods called back from COM. If the method appears to silently fail, chances are the exception is being caught by the COM Interop layer and the resultant failure HRESULT is being ignored by the COM caller. This behavior is especially non-intuitive for Visual Basic 6 developers, because the VB6 runtime directly raises the error rather than letting it propagate up the call stack.

Fortunately, you can configure the Visual Studio .NET debugger to behave like the Visual Basic 6 IDE and trap the exception before letting it propagate to the caller. Follow these steps to make the debugger trap most .NET exceptions:

1. Select Debug, Exceptions… from the menu.

2. Highlight Common Language Runtime Exceptions and then select Break into the debugger inside the box labeled When the exception is thrown:.

3. Click OK.

The subset of .NET exceptions to which these changes apply depends on the settings of the subnodes of Common Language Runtime Exceptions. The debugger behavior for each exception type can be configured individually or configured to inherit the parent node settings.

Listing 6.4 updates the VB .NET code from Listing 6.3 with some threading constructs to handle the multi-apartment issues with the unmarshalable interface. The idea here is to use the System.Threading.ManualResetEvent class so the callback thread can signal the thread that created the performance object when callbacks occur. The original thread can then execute the original callback implementation, then wait for the next signal. An easier hack would have been to derive the Form1 class from System.EnterpriseServices.ServicedComponent to inherit its COM-like threading behavior, but then the class wouldn't be able to derive from System.Windows.Form, because .NET doesn't support multiple implementation inheritance.

LISTING 6.4   Visual Basic .NET Code to Make COM Callbacks Run on the Right Thread

```
1: Imports System
2: Imports System.Windows.Forms
3: Imports System.Threading
4: Imports DxVBLib
5:
6: Public Class Form1
7:    Inherits Form
8:    Implements DirectXEvent
9:
10:    Dim performance As DirectMusicPerformance
11:    Dim mre As ManualResetEvent
12:    Shared t As Thread
13:
14:    ' Callback method (called on a third thread)
15:    Private Sub DXCallback(eventid As Integer) _
16:      Implements DirectXEvent.DxCallBack
17:      Try
18:        mre.Set()
19:      Catch ex as Exception
20:        MessageBox.Show(ex.ToString())
21:      End Try
22:    End Sub
23:
24:    ' Constructor
25:    Public Sub New()
26:      MyBase.New
27:      t = New Thread(New ThreadStart(AddressOf Run))
28:      t.ApartmentState = ApartmentState.STA
29:      t.Start()
30:    End Sub
31:
32:    ' A second thread that creates the COM objects
33:    ' and does the work of the callback
34:    Private Sub Run
35:      Dim directX As DirectX7 = new DirectX7()
36:
37:      ' Set up the music
38:      performance = directX.DirectMusicPerformanceCreate()
39:      performance.Init(Nothing, 0)
40:      performance.SetPort(-1, 4)
41:      Dim loader As DirectMusicLoader = directX.DirectMusicLoaderCreate()
42:      Dim segment As DirectMusicSegment
43:      segment = loader.LoadSegment("heartland2.sgt")
44:      Dim style As DirectMusicStyle = loader.LoadStyle("heartlnd.sty")
45:
```

LISTING 6.4   Continued

```
46:      ' Set up the callback
47:      performance.AddNotificationType( _
48:        CONST_DMUS_NOTIFICATION_TYPE.DMUS_NOTIFY_ON_MEASUREANDBEAT)
49:      Dim notification As Integer = directX.CreateEvent(Me)
50:      performance.SetNotificationHandle(notification)
51:
52:      ' Initialize ManualResetEvent to an unsignaled state
53:      mre = New ManualResetEvent(False)
54:
55:      ' Begin playing the music
56:      performance.PlaySegment(segment, 0, 0)
57:
58:      While True
59:        mre.WaitOne()
60:        SameThreadCallback()
61:        mre.Reset()
62:      End While
63:    End Sub
64:
65:    ' Callback implementation that runs on the second thread
66:    Private Sub SameThreadCallback
67:      Dim msg As DMUS_NOTIFICATION_PMSG
68:      ' Calling on DirectMusicPerformance succeeds when called
69:      ' on the same thread the object was created on
70:      performance.GetNotificationPMSG(msg)
71:    End Sub
72:
73:    Public Shared Sub Main()
74:      Application.Run(new Form1())
75:      t.Abort()
76:    End Sub
77: End Class
```

This listing begins by adding the System.Threading namespace to the list of imported namespaces. This time, in Form1's constructor (Lines 25–30), a second thread is started to create all the COM objects and the main thread waits inside Application.Run on Line 74. This is done because the thread that creates the COM object is going to have to wait for callback notifications in a loop. If the main UI thread were the one waiting, the Windows Form would be non-responsive to user input. So, the second thread is started in Line 29, which executes the Run method. The second thread's apartment state needs to be set to STA in Line 28 for the sake of instantiating the apartment-threaded DirectMusicPerformance object in Line 38, otherwise the CLR's internal QueryInterface call would fail. Unlike the main thread in Visual Basic .NET programs, freshly created threads always have an uninitialized apartment state that becomes `ApartmentState.MTA` unless you explicitly set it otherwise.

The implementation of `Run` is the same as the previous listing's constructor until Line 53, where the `ManualResetEvent` instance is initialized to an unsignaled state. After kicking off the playing of music in Line 56, this second thread enters an infinite loop. Inside this loop, it waits for the `ManualResetEvent` instance to be signaled, calls the `SameThreadCallback` method, then resets the `ManualResetEvent` instance so it waits again at the beginning of the next loop iteration. `SameThreadCallback` is defined in Lines 66–71, and does the work that was originally intended for the `DXCallback` method. To prevent this thread from keeping the process running infinitely, Line 75 aborts it once the Windows Form has been closed (causing control to leave the `Application.Run` method).

The `DXCallback` method in Lines 15–22 now must only call `ManualResetEvent.Set` to signal to the correct thread that a callback has occurred.

> **CAUTION**
>
> You can't escape multithreading in the .NET Framework. For example, a class's finalizer is always invoked by the CLR on a separate finalizer thread. If you're called on a separate thread, you better handle it appropriately. This can be a huge issue when attempting to migrate Visual Basic 6 code to Visual Basic .NET when using COM interfaces that don't support cross-context marshaling. As Listings 6.3 and 6.4 demonstrate, the code required can be substantially different.

Troubleshooting an `InvalidCastException`

On the surface, there are two main causes for an `InvalidCastException` thrown when using COM objects:

- `QueryInterface` failure
- Casting to an RCW class

Both of these causes, and their underlying causes, are discussed in the following sections. These discussions exclude the obvious causes for an `InvalidCastException`, such as casting an object to an interface that it simply does not implement.

DIGGING DEEPER

There could actually be a third cause to a COM-related `InvalidCastException`: any COM member that returns the `E_NOINTERFACE` HRESULT. As shown in Appendix C, "HRESULT to .NET Exception Transformations," this HRESULT value is always transformed to this exception type. However, very few COM members besides `QueryInterface` return this HRESULT value, so this case should rarely be seen in practice.

`QueryInterface` Failure

An `InvalidCastException` caused by a `QueryInterface` failure can happen when you're casting an RCW to a COM interface, or when you're simply trying to call a method on an RCW with no casting involved. It often seems weird when the simple act of calling a COM object causes an `InvalidCastException`, but it happens because the CLR calls `QueryInterface` the first time you attempt to call a method on an interface that doesn't match the type of the object you're calling the method on. For example, calling a method directly on a strongly typed RCW class (one with a `Class` suffix) provokes a `QueryInterface` call:

```
// Calls QueryInterface for only IUnknown:
WebBrowserClass wb = new WebBrowserClass();
// Calls QueryInterface for IWebBrowser2 before calling the method:
wb.GoHome();
```

Declaring types as interfaces causes `QueryInterface` calls to be done earlier:

```
// Calls QueryInterface for IWebBrowser2:
IWebBrowser2 wb = new WebBrowserClass();
// Simply calls the method:
wb.GoHome();
```

The CLR sometimes calls `QueryInterface` in other non-casting situations as well, such as if a COM object is used from a different STA thread or context.

Any `InvalidCastException` caused by a failed `QueryInterface` call has the following message:

```
QueryInterface for interface InterfaceName failed.
```

It can often be difficult to determine the cause of a `QueryInterface` failure, but there are four common sources that people run into:

Advanced Topics for Using COM Components

CHAPTER 6

291

6

ADVANCED TOPICS
FOR USING COM
COMPONENTS

- Incompatible apartments and lack of marshaling support
- Non-reflexive IUnknown implementations
- Type library errors
- Recompiling VB6 projects without binary compatibility

Incompatible Apartments and Lack of Marshaling Support

If your managed code is running inside in a different apartment than the failing COM object's apartment, the interface target type must be able to be marshaled from one apartment to the other. As discussed in the previous section, this is COM marshaling—not Interop marshaling— and is no different from when no managed code is involved. If the target interface is unmarshalable, then a cross-apartment QueryInterface call always fails. This problem shows up often in .NET applications because several COM objects require running in an STA, whereas .NET threads are MTA threads by default. We also saw that this problem can occur due to callbacks on new threads, regardless of the apartment state.

The simplest solution is to change the threading behavior of your managed code to run in an STA thread by default, as discussed in the previous section. When both components are in the same apartment, no COM marshaling is required to make the QueryInterface call succeed.

Another solution is to make the interface marshalable from one apartment to another. This can be done by registering a proxy/stub DLL using the Windows Registry value HKEY_CLASSES_ROOT\Interface\{*IID*}\ProxyStubClsid32 set to the proxy/stub marshaler's CLSID. If all of an interface's members use OLE Automation-compatible parameters, and if the interface is marked with the IDL oleautomation attribute, then its type library can usually be registered to cause the standard OLE Automation marshaler to be registered for the interface. This is called *type library marshaling*, because the OLE Automation marshaler uses the information in the interface's type library definition to determine how to marshal the interface. If the interface is not marked with the oleautomation attribute but its members use only OLE Automation-compatible parameters, you could manually register OLE Automation's type library marshaler (with CLSID 00000320-0000-0000-C000-000000000046) and hope for the best.

For Visual Basic 6 and ATL components, running REGSVR32.EXE on the DLL usually registers the embedded type library in addition to the standard COM registration. Opening a type library with OLEVIEW.EXE also registers the type library.

> **CAUTION**
>
> When using ATL COM components, you may sometimes be surprised to learn that interfaces that should have a registered proxy/stub marshaler (generated by MIDL) do not. When using the Visual C++ 6 ATL COM Wizard and selecting `Allow merging of proxy/stub code`, the default behavior does not properly register the proxy/stub DLL required for cross-context COM marshaling. The generated `dlldatax.c` file does not get built with the project's output. To fix this, do the following:
>
> 1. Right-click on the `dlldatax.c` file in the `FileView` window and select `Settings…`.
> 2. On the `General` tab, uncheck `Exclude file from build`.
> 3. On the `C/C++` tab, choose the `Precompiled Headers` category and select `Not using precompiled headers`.
> 4. Click `OK` to accept these changes.

Regardless of whether you make the COM interface marshalable across contexts, marking the .NET component with the same threading model as the COM component is a good idea, because it provides the best performance by avoiding this extra marshaling. If you can't change the threading model of your .NET component (either because you don't control the entry point or perhaps because you use Windows Forms controls) and if registering a proxy/stub interface marshaler is too difficult, consider the technique of starting a new thread to call and use a COM component, as shown in the previous section.

Non-Reflexive IUnknown Implementations

The rules of COM dictate that any `IUnknown.QueryInterface` implementation must be transitive, symmetric, and reflexive. However, errors in COM objects can occasionally occur that breaks some of these rules. The reflexive behavior is critical for COM Interoperability because the CLR calls `QueryInterface` on any incoming COM object before wrapping it in an RCW to ensure that it supports the interface that the signature claims the instance supports. For example, suppose a COM method signature is defined as:

```
IMoniker GiveMeAMoniker();
```

The object returned by `GiveMeAMoniker` must respond successfully to a `QueryInterface` call for `IMoniker`; otherwise, an `InvalidCastException` occurs from the failed `QueryInterface` call. This check is done by the CLR to avoid subtle incorrect run-time behavior caused by incorrect signatures or COM objects that don't follow the rules of COM. This strictness is especially handy for catching errors when manually defining your own type information for COM components, described in Chapter 21.

> **Caution**
>
> Visual Basic 6 does not check that an object implements the interface given in its parameter/return type declaration, which is why so many of these types of problems surface for the first time with .NET. The CLR is a stricter COM client than Visual Basic 6, and isn't as forgiving when a COM object breaks the rules of COM. The most vulnerable COM objects are ones authored in C++ (because you have more power to make mistakes) and primarily used in Visual Basic 6 (because it's so forgiving).

This problem used to plague the `NameList` type in SQL Distributed Management Objects (SQLDMO), a part of Microsoft SQL Server 2000, before its first service pack was released in July 2001. Without the service pack, the following C# code fails with an `InvalidCastException`, because querying the returned object for the `NameList` interface (the signature's return type) fails:

```
SQLDMO.Application app = new SQLDMO.Application();
SQLDMO.NameList list = app.ListAvailableSQLServers();
```

As with any `QueryInterface` failure, you should be able to reproduce it in unmanaged C++:

```
SQLDMO::NameList* list1;
SQLDMO::NameList* list2;
// The call works fine...
hr = app->ListAvailableSQLServers(&namelist);
...
// ...but the QueryInterface call fails:
hr = list1->QueryInterface(__uuidof(SQLDMO::NameList), (void**)list2);
```

> **Tip**
>
> Attempting to reproduce a `QueryInterface` failure in unmanaged C++ code is a great way to isolate the problem and convince yourself that COM Interoperability is not (directly) responsible for the failure. Just be sure that you're accurately imitating managed code interaction, such as initializing COM with the appropriate threading model.

Besides waiting for a fix to the COM object, there's not much you could do to fix this type of problem unless you can find another interface on which to invoke members. If you changed the metadata signature's return type to represent `IUnknown` rather than a specific interface (which would be `System.Object` marked with `MarshalAs(UnmanagedType.IUnknown)`), then the call would succeed, assuming that the object responds successfully to a `QueryInterface` call to `IUnknown`. But to call the members of the returned object, you'd need to late bind using `Type.InvokeMember`, and this would only work if the returned object happened to implement `IDispatch`. Changing a signature in this way is discussed in Chapter 7.

Type Library Errors

The same sort of failed `QueryInterface` problems can happen when a COM component's type library simply contains errors. The DirectX for Visual Basic 8.0 type library had a few such problems in version 8.0a (fixed in later releases), which caused unexpected `InvalidCastExceptions` to be thrown in managed code. For example, the `Direct3DDevice8` interface was given the following IID in its type library definition:

7385E4DF-8FE8-41D5-86B6-D7B48547B6CF

However, the "same" interface in the C++ header file (`IDirect3DDevice8` in d3d8.h) has an IID that differs by one digit:

7385E5DF-8FE8-41D5-86B6-D7B48547B6CF

The object can be queried successfully for the interface represented by the second GUID, but not the first one. Therefore, when the CLR asks the COM object whether it implements 7385E4DF-8FE8-41D5-86B6-D7B48547B6CF, it returns E_NOINTERFACE because it doesn't recognize the IID. If the `QueryInterface` call instead passed the correct 7385E5DF-8FE8-41D5-86B6-D7B48547B6CF value, the COM object would return S_OK and everything would proceed as expected.

Of course, the incorrect IID in the type library does not affect Visual Basic 6 programs (the intended audience of the type library). The next chapter shows how to change the generated Interop Assembly's IID for this interface to work around such a problem.

Recompiling VB6 Projects Without Binary Compatibility

Because there's no way to control the GUIDs assigned to classes and interfaces generated by the Visual Basic 6 compiler, the VB6 IDE provides the option to compile a project with *binary compatibility*. This works by telling VB6 the file containing a previously compiled type library with which you want your recompiled component to be compatible. The classes and interfaces generated on recompilation are given the same CLSIDs and IIDs as they had in the previous version. This is critical if you don't want to break COM clients of your component that don't have the luxury of being recompiled with your new type library.

If you recompile a Visual Basic 6 ActiveX DLL project without using binary compatibility, existing COM clients and .NET clients alike often experience failed `QueryInterface` calls. If the clients attempt to instantiate one of your VB6 classes, the CLSID change might not be noticeable if the old CLSID is still registered. But attempting to make the same `QueryInterface` call for the VB6 class interface will fail due to the changed IID.

If you can't revert your VB6 component back to its old CLSIDs and IIDs, you'll need to re-import an Interop Assembly (assuming that .NET clients use it) and recompile any .NET clients with the new Interop Assembly.

Casting to an RCW Class

Casting a COM object (an RCW) to a class type is really no different from casting a .NET object to a class type, in that the class's metadata is the sole determining factor of whether or not the cast succeeds. If the object's class type—the type you'd get by calling its `GetType` method—either *is* the destination type or *derives from* the destination type, the cast succeeds. Otherwise, the cast fails with an `InvalidCastException` and the generic message "Specified cast is not valid."

The reason that casting COM objects to class types can fail when you don't expect it to is that it's not always obvious what the type of the source instance is. When instantiating the object yourself using your language's `new` keyword, the type of the instance is the strongly-typed RCW class. But when an instance of a COM object is returned to you, via a method's return type or a by-reference parameter, its type may not be what you expect. The reason for this is that COM objects are always passed/returned as interface pointers. In "pure COM," you don't know exactly what the type of the object you're dealing with is; you can only discover what interfaces it supports via `QueryInterface`. This excludes COM objects that implement `IProvideClassInfo` or some other custom interface that enables a user to retrieve a CLSID and therefore discover the class type.

If the CLR cannot determine the type of a COM object, then it has no choice but to use an RCW of the generic `System.__ComObject` type (an internal type inside the `mscorlib` assembly) when presenting a COM object to managed code. This `__ComObject` type is the source of casting confusion, because the programmer expected the type to be a strongly-typed class that the instance really is. The problem is that just because you know the real type of a COM object doesn't mean that the CLR has the same semantic information (or metadata for the desired type) to wrap it as such. Attempting to cast a `System.__ComObject` type to a class type will always fail unless the target type happens to be one of its public base classes—`System.Object` or `System.MarshalByRefObject`. This is because the metadata for `__ComObject` is static and has no relationship with any other classes.

The CLR uses several tricks, however, to avoid wrapping a COM object with the `System.__ComObject` type whenever possible. For one thing, if the type library importer replaced a parameter, field, or return type with a coclass interface type, then it has essentially made the assertion that the COM instance *is* a certain coclass. In this case, the CLR wraps the returned instance in a strongly-typed RCW using the .NET class type specified in the coclass interface's `CoClassAttribute` custom attribute unless the same COM instance (with the same `IUnknown` pointer address) has previously been wrapped in a different type, likely `System.__ComObject`.

If the static type of a returned COM instance (the type in the metadata signature) is not a coclass interface, then the CLR attempts to discover the class type of the COM object by asking if it implements the `IProvideClassInfo` COM interface. This classic interface is implemented by many COM objects (including any authored in Visual Basic 6) to provide a means of discovering what class a COM object really is. This interface has a single method—`GetClassInfo`—that return's the COM object's CLSID. This isn't quite enough information for the CLR, however, because it ultimately needs a .NET class type with which to wrap the COM object.

To get a .NET class type that corresponds to a CLSID, the CLR checks for the presence of two Windows Registry values under the `HKEY_CLASSES_ROOT\CLSID\{clsid}\InprocServer32` key:

```
Assembly="AssemblyName, Version=…, Culture=…, PublicKeyToken=…"
Class="NamespaceQualifiedClassName"
```

With this information, the CLR can wrap the COM object with the class specified in the registry, as long as it can load the specified assembly. This means that the assembly mentioned in the registry must be in the Global Assembly Cache, the application directory, or anywhere such that calling `Assembly.Load` with the `Assembly` value's string would succeed (because that's essentially what the runtime is doing). Or, there could be a third value alongside the other two, pointing to the location of the assembly; for example:

```
CodeBase=file:///C:/MyApplication/MyAssembly.dll
```

If this value is present, then the assembly will be loaded from the specified location (essentially like `Assembly.LoadFrom`), but only if it can't be found through the normal loading procedure.

Rest assured that you don't have to manually add these registry keys to enable this behavior. The Assembly Registration utility in the .NET Framework SDK (`REGASM.EXE`) adds the `Assembly` and `Class` entries for you when it's run on an Interop Assembly. It also has a `/codebase` option for adding the `CodeBase` value for every class. This utility is usually used when exposing non-Interop assemblies to COM, covered in Chapter 8, "The Essentials for Using .NET Components from COM," but it does the job here as well.

Therefore, COM objects returned to you whose static type is something other than a coclass interface (which would be either some other interface or `System.Object`), are wrapped with the strongly-typed RCW class if the object implements `IProvideClassInfo` *and* if the Interop

Advanced Topics for Using COM Components

CHAPTER 6

297

6

ADVANCED TOPICS
FOR USING COM
COMPONENTS

Assembly containing the strongly-typed RCW class definition is registered appropriately. All Primary Interop Assemblies are usually registered using REGASM.EXE, so it's likely that you'll see this nicer wrapping behavior with types defined in PIAs. If, for some reason, the CLR is unable to load the assembly or find the class specified in the registry, it silently falls back to using the __ComObject wrapper type.

DIGGING DEEPER

There's one subtle behavior to registering Interop Assemblies using REGASM.EXE that's worth pointing out. Because REGASM.EXE is primarily designed for exposing .NET classes to COM clients, it only registers COM-creatable classes—ones with a public default constructor in their metadata representation. Therefore, only coclasses that aren't marked as noncreatable in its type library end up with these extra values in the registry. (Non-creatable coclasses often don't even have their CLSID listed under HKEY_CLASSES_ROOT\CLSID in the registry because in COM this is used for instantiation only.)

This is unfortunate because noncreatable coclasses almost certainly show up in methods that return an instance of the class, otherwise the class wouldn't be defined in the first place. To enable such classes to be wrapped in the strongly-typed RCW when their static type is something other than its coclass interface, you'd need to add the Assembly and Class (and CodeBase, if applicable) registry values manually. This is pretty easy to do with the combination of reflection and the .NET registry APIs in the Microsoft.Win32 namespace, although left as an exercise for the reader.

CAUTION

It was mentioned in Chapter 3, but it's worth mentioning again: *Never* cast a COM object to a class type because you don't know for sure when it will succeed and when it will fail. The Class suffix on imported classes is meant to discourage casting to such a type. You can access all of the objects functionality by casting to any implemented interface or any event interface instead.

Changing the Type of the RCW

If you're not happy with the type that a COM object was wrapped with—you either got System.__ComObject when you desire a strongly-typed RCW, or got the wrong strongly-typed RCW due to an overzealous coclass interface transformation—you can change it using the Marshal.CreateWrapperOfType method in the System.Runtime.InteropServices namespace.

One major benefit of having a strongly-typed RCW instance rather than `System.__ComObject` (besides being able to invoke members on all of its interfaces without casting) is that you can use the entire reflection API to get the information you'd expect. With a `System.__ComObject` type, the only useful thing you can do is call `Type.InvokeMember`.

`CreateWrapperOfType` takes an existing RCW and the type you want it to be wrapped in and returns the new wrapper object. For example, if you have an instance of a COM object called `oldObj` with type `OldWrapper`, you can change its wrapper to the `NewWrapper` type as follows:

C#:

```
NewWrapper newObj = (NewWrapper)Marshal.CreateWrapperOfType(oldObj,
  typeof(NewWrapper))
```

Visual Basic .NET:

```
Dim newObj As NewWrapper = CType(Marshal.CreateWrapperOfType(oldObj, _
  GetType(NewWrapper)), NewWrapper)
```

C++:

```
NewWrapper* newObj = (NewWrapper*)Marshal::CreateWrapperOfType(oldObj,
  __typeof(NewWrapper))
```

The instance passed as the first parameter must be an RCW (which means it either is a `System.__ComObject` instance or derived from one), and the type passed as the second parameter must be an RCW type (which means it's marked with the `ComImportAttribute` pseudo-custom attribute).

This method won't let you convert one wrapper to another arbitrarily. Instead, it succeeds only if the source instance responds successfully when the CLR calls its `QueryInterface` implementation for *every interface* listed as implemented by the target type, with the exception of importer-generated event interfaces. (What makes these event interfaces exempt is that they're marked as "COM-invisible," a concept that's introduced in Chapter 8.) Therefore, the `CreateWrapperOfType` algorithm applies the logic of "If it looks like a duck, walks like a duck, and smells like a duck, it must be a duck!" If the source object doesn't pass this test, `CreateWrapperOfType` fails with an `InvalidCastException` and the message "Source object can not be converted to the destination type because it does not support all the required interfaces."

The important drawback to using `CreateWrapperOfType` is that it loses the identity of the COM object. In other words, a second .NET instance—a second RCW—wraps the same COM object. Therefore, the following C# code:

Advanced Topics for Using COM Components

CHAPTER 6

299

6

ADVANCED TOPICS
FOR USING COM
COMPONENTS

```
NewWrapper newObj = (NewWrapper)Marshal.CreateWrapperOfType(oldObj,
  typeof(NewWrapper))

if (newObj == oldObj)
  Console.WriteLine("Objects are the same.");
else
  Console.WriteLine("Objects are not the same.");
```

would print "Objects are not the same." This counters the normal behavior (described in Chapter 2) that every COM object has exactly one RCW.

DIGGING DEEPER

> Besides using `CreateWrapperOfType`, there are two other cases in which a COM object's identity is not maintained in .NET. One is when custom marshaling is used, which is described in Chapter 20. The other is when a proxy to a coclass that already has an RCW is returned to managed code, because there's no efficient way for the CLR to determine that it's the same object as the original coclass.
>
> Otherwise, every time an interface pointer for a given COM component is passed into managed code *in the same context or apartment*, it gets wrapped with the same RCW.

Garbage Collection

Chapter 3 introduced the issue that the garbage-collected world of .NET exhibits different behavior than the reference counted world of COM. These differences can cause problems when using COM objects that must be released at specific points in a program. The need for this can be driven by performance concerns, or by semantics of an object model that require certain objects to be released at certain times. `Marshal.ReleaseComObject` was introduced as a way to deterministically release COM objects when called.

To understand how `Marshal.ReleaseComObject` works, you should understand that COM objects wrapped in RCWs are not reference-counted based on the number of .NET clients. Instead, any COM interface obtained through an RCW has its reference count incremented *once*. When the RCW is garbage collected, its finalizer calls `IUnknown.Release` on every cached interface pointer. `Marshal.ReleaseComObject` simply performs this release step when called rather than during the RCW's finalization. Although the RCW might still be alive on a GC heap, attempting to use it throws a `NullReferenceException`. If multiple .NET clients use the same RCW and one of the clients calls `ReleaseComObject`, the RCW is no longer usable to *any* .NET clients.

> ### DIGGING DEEPER
>
> In version 1.0 of the .NET Framework, calling `System.GC.SuppressFinalize` on an RCW has no effect. The underlying COM object still gets released upon finalization unless `Marshal.ReleaseComObject` has already been called.

There are two important things to remember when using `Marshal.ReleaseComObject`:

- Be aware of any intermediate RCWs created when using an RCW. You may have to call `ReleaseComObject` more than once to clean up everything without waiting for garbage collection.

- When calling `ReleaseComObject` on multiple objects that are dependent on each other, be sure to release them in the correct order. For example, ADO requires that you release a `Recordset` instance before releasing its corresponding `Connection` instance.

Usually calling `ReleaseComObject` once does the trick for releasing the wrapped COM object because an RCW's reference count is typically set to 1. However, an RCW's reference count gets incremented every time the same COM interface pointer is passed from unmanaged to managed code. It's rare that this occurs more than once, but to be absolutely sure that calling `ReleaseComObject` releases the underlying COM object, you'd need to call `ReleaseComObject` in a loop until the returned reference count reaches zero.

Unlike typical reference count values returned by `IUnknown.AddRef` and `IUnknown.Release`, you *can* count on the value returned by `ReleaseComObject` to be reliable. Once the count reaches zero, the CLR is guaranteed to release all of the COM object's interface pointers that the CCW holds onto.

Sometimes, due to custom marshaling, you may think you're interacting with an RCW but you're actually interacting with a special .NET object instead. This can happen when COM enumerator objects implementing `IEnumVARIANT` are exposed as .NET enumerator objects implementing `IEnumerator`. Calling `ReleaseComObject` on such an instance would not work, since it's not an RCW. Chapter 20 demonstrates this and shows a solution.

Another popular option to release COM objects immediately is to do it the .NET way: calling `System.GC.Collect` followed by `System.GC.WaitForPendingFinalizers`. If you've finished using RCWs and they are eligible for collection, these two calls will not only release the wrapped COM objects but also the RCWs themselves. This is sometimes the only option if you've created RCWs that you don't store in variables (as can happen if you're calling an object's property's property). The problem with using `GC.Collect` is that it's not always obvious when .NET objects are considered to be eligible for collection, as demonstrated by the following code snippets.

Let's look at some simple demonstrations with Microsoft PowerPoint 2002, which gets installed with Microsoft Office XP, to better understand the effects of garbage collection when using COM objects. On a computer with Office XP (or just PowerPoint 2002), the upcoming four code snippets can be run by placing them inside the `Main` method in a C# file that looks like the following:

```csharp
using System;
using PowerPoint;
using Microsoft.Office.Core;

public class Client
{
  public static void Main()
  {
    ...
  }
}
```

This can be compiled as follows using the C# command-line compiler:

```
csc client.cs /r:PowerPoint.dll /r:Office.dll
```

Or, to compile debuggable code, you can instead type:

```
csc client.cs /r:PowerPoint.dll /r:Office.dll /debug
```

The referenced DLLs (`PowerPoint.dll` and `Office.dll`) can be created by running `TLBIMP.EXE` on the `MSPPT.OLB` file found in the `Program Files\Microsoft Office\Office10` directory then placing them in the same directory as your C# client.

All of the following code snippets create a new PowerPoint `Application` object, set its `Visible` property so we can see the application after it's created, then call `Application.Quit` to close the application. The PowerPoint application does not shut down if any of its objects are still being referenced by the client application, so this is an easy way to see when COM objects get released in a variety of scenarios.

The first code snippet causes PowerPoint to exit properly, so you only see a quick flash for the moment that the application is visible:

```csharp
Application app = new Application();
app.Visible = MsoTriState.msoTrue;
app.Quit();
```

```
Console.WriteLine("Press Enter to exit...");
Console.ReadLine();
```

The call to `Console.ReadLine` is present simply to keep the managed client alive; it simulates other work done by the client application. This is necessary because the PowerPoint application always exits once the managed client process terminates because all COM references get released (unless the client is forcibly shut down with `Ctrl+C`).

Next, we add a single line to the previous code that stores the object returned by Application's `Presentations` property in a local variable:

```
Application app = new Application();
Presentations pres = app.Presentations;
app.Visible = MsoTriState.msoTrue;
app.Quit();

Console.WriteLine("Press Enter to exit...");
Console.ReadLine();
```

This single line of code causes the PowerPoint application to remain open after `Quit` has been called! The COM object wrapped by the `pres` RCW has not been released because nothing provoked garbage collection. One way to get the expected behavior would be to force release by calling `Marshal.ReleaseComObject`:

```
Application app = new Application();
Presentations pres = app.Presentations;
app.Visible = MsoTriState.msoTrue;
app.Quit();

// This causes the PowerPoint application to exit:
System.Runtime.InteropServices.Marshal.ReleaseComObject(pres);

Console.WriteLine("Press Enter to exit...");
Console.ReadLine();
```

However, one might attempt to use `GC.Collect` instead to indirectly release the COM object as a side-effect of garbage collection. (This is desirable if other COM objects have been created that were not stored in variables.) This would look like the following:

```
Application app = new Application();
Presentations pres = app.Presentations;
app.Visible = MsoTriState.msoTrue;
app.Quit();

// Attempt to collect the pres instance
GC.Collect();
GC.WaitForPendingFinalizers();
```

Advanced Topics for Using COM Components

CHAPTER 6

303

6

ADVANCED TOPICS
FOR USING COM
COMPONENTS

```
Console.WriteLine("Press Enter to exit...");
Console.ReadLine();
```

This code exhibits unintuitive behavior. If compiled with a debug configuration (the /debug option for the command-line C# compiler), the PowerPoint application does not exit immediately, but if compiled without debugging information (the default for the command-line C# compiler), the PowerPoint application *does* exit immediately. When compiled with /debug, the pres instance is still considered "alive" due to the way that the JIT compiler tracks local variables, which differs between debuggable code and non-debuggable code.

Therefore, the only surefire way to ensure that an object gets collected by a call to GC.Collect is to first exit the method that declares the variable (assuming that nobody has a reference to the object to keep it alive). But exiting a method might not be as easy as it sounds; simple methods are sometimes inlined by the JIT compiler. In such cases, you may think you're exiting a method when looking at source code, but at run time you really aren't. If you're concerned about inlining, you can mark a method with System.Runtime.CompilerServices.MethodImplAttribute and its MethodImplOptions.NoInlining value to prevent it from happening.

Listing 6.5 demonstrates this final technique using the objects from Microsoft PowerPoint's imported type library. When running the code in this listing, the PowerPoint application always exits promptly regardless of compiler options.

LISTING 6.5   Ensuring That All PowerPoint RCWs Are Collected When Finished Using Them So the Application Exits Promptly

```
 1: using System;
 2: using PowerPoint;
 3: using Microsoft.Office.Core;
 4: using System.Runtime.CompilerServices;
 5:
 6: public class Client
 7: {
 8:   [MethodImpl(MethodImplOptions.NoInlining)]
 9:   public static void DoWorkWithPowerPoint()
10:   {
11:     Application app = new Application();
12:     Presentations pres = app.Presentations;
13:     app.Visible = MsoTriState.msoTrue;
14:     app.Quit();
15:   }
16:
17:   public static void Main()
18:   {
```

LISTING 6.5   Continued

```
19:      DoWorkWithPowerPoint();
20:
21:      // The app and pres instances will now be collected
22:      GC.Collect();
23:      GC.WaitForPendingFinalizers();
24:
25:      Console.WriteLine("Press Enter to exit...");
26:      Console.ReadLine();
27:  }
28: }
```

DIGGING DEEPER

Although this section focuses on forcing early garbage collection, it's sometimes necessary to prevent premature garbage collection. This is often necessary when using PInvoke to avoid intermittent bugs that are really hard to catch. Chapter 19 discusses the problem and its solutions.

Securing Unmanaged Calls

Code-access security is an important part of any .NET application. Unmanaged code is outside the reach of the .NET security system, so if unmanaged code executes it can do whatever the operating system allows it to (based on the identity of the user who runs the code). This could include formatting your hard drive, sending e-mail messages on your behalf, or other nasty things. Fortunately, by default, all calls to COM objects are secure because they require everyone in the call stack to have *unmanaged code permission*. This permission is one of a handful of .NET security permissions that are generally regarded as "full trust" because so much can be done by code with these permissions. (Other such permissions include *reflection permission* and *serialization permission*.) In the default .NET security policy, applications that run from the local computer have unmanaged code permission granted to them, but applications running from the intranet or Internet zones do not.

If you believe that your interactions with unmanaged code can't be abused in an unintended and harmful way, you may wish to *assert* unmanaged code permission to enable your code to be run in an environment without this permission. As long as the client of your component trusts *your* component, you can assert permissions to prevent the CLR from checking farther down the call stack. (If non-trusted components could assert permissions, there would be no point to having permissions at all.) Chapter 3, for example, used Microsoft Word for spell-checking functionality. It's pretty reasonable to assume that the act of checking spelling is a "safe" operation, so a user of Word's `Application` object could assert unmanaged code permission as follows:

```
[
  SecurityPermission(SecurityAction.Assert,
  Flags=SecurityPermissionFlag.UnmanagedCode)
]
public bool IsMisspelled(string word)
{
  // This should be a safe operation
  return msWord.CheckSpelling(word, ref missing, ref missing, ref missing,
    ref missing, ref missing, ref missing, ref missing, ref missing,
    ref missing, ref missing, ref missing, ref missing);
}
```

If the assembly containing the `IsMisspelled` method is marked with `AllowPartiallyTrustedCallersAttribute` from the `System.Security` namespace, and if the computer's policy is set such that this assembly is trusted, then the addition of `SecurityPermissionAttribute` makes it possible for code without any permissions to call `IsMisspelled`.

CAUTION

Be very careful when asserting any permissions, and when using `AllowPartiallyTrustedCallersAttribute`. Every use of these mechanisms adds a risk of exposing a security hole, violating the trust your component has been given. Remember that calling unmanaged code is secure by default. Programs get into trouble only when trying to be more accommodating or trying to gain the best possible performance by doing things such as asserting unmanaged code permission.

Rather than using the all-or-nothing approach to permissions, you may wish to provide a more granular permission requirement so your component can run in a semi-trusted environment. For example, despite the fact that file I/O classes use unmanaged code (Win32 APIs) to do the bulk of their work, they can require just *file I/O permission* to perform file I/O rather than unmanaged code permission. This can be achieved with the coding pattern of demanding one permission while asserting another. For example, the following code assumes that a new permission type called `DictionaryPermission` has been created, and uses it to restrict access to `IsMisspelled` to those who are allowed to look in a dictionary:

```
[
  SecurityPermission(SecurityAction.Assert,
  Flags=SecurityPermissionFlag.UnmanagedCode)
```

```
]
public bool IsMisspelled(string word)
{
   // Demand permission to access a dictionary
   new DictionaryPermission().Demand();

   return msWord.CheckSpelling(word, ref missing, ref missing, ref missing,
      ref missing, ref missing, ref missing, ref missing, ref missing,
      ref missing, ref missing, ref missing, ref missing);
}
```

Another security concept that's important and easy to misunderstand is known as a *link demand*. This type of demand checks only a member's immediate caller for a required permission. With a link demand, the caller's permissions are checked once during *link time* (another name for when the called method is just-in-time compiled), or during "JIT time." A link demand can be placed on a member, or on a type to affect all of the type's members except a static class constructor. (When an assembly isn't marked with AllowPartiallyTrustedCallersAttribute, every public member of a strong-named assembly is already implicitly marked with a link demand for full trust.) The following Visual Basic .NET code demonstrates making a link demand for unmanaged code permission:

```
<SecurityPermissionAttribute(SecurityAction.LinkDemand, _
 Flags:=SecurityPermissionFlag.UnmanagedCode)> _
Public Sub UnsafeOperation()
   ...
End Sub
```

Link demands are performed independently of the run-time stack walking performed for regular demands. By making a link demand for a certain permission rather than a regular demand, you can realize substantial performance improvements. However, link demands must be used carefully because it makes code susceptible to *luring attacks*. A luring attack refers to untrusted malicious code using trusted code to act on its behalf and do something damaging.

The reason link demands are important to understand for interoperability scenarios is that every member of the Marshal class and every member of the GCHandle class (except the IsAllocated property) in the System.Runtime.InteropServices namespace is marked with a link demand for unmanaged code permission to boost performance at the expense of security. The result is that care must be used with these APIs to prevent exposing a security hole in your own assembly, if it allows partially-trusted callers. The following C# code exposes a method that wraps Marshal.PtrToStringBSTR to provide the same behavior of creating a new .NET string from the contents of a BSTR:

```
// If this is a trusted method that allows partially-trusted callers,
// a client could trick it into doing something malicious
```

Advanced Topics for Using COM Components

CHAPTER 6

307

6

ADVANCED TOPICS
FOR USING **COM**
COMPONENTS

```
public string StringFromBSTR(IntPtr ptr)
{
  return Marshal.PtrToStringBSTR(ptr);
}
```

DON'T DO THIS

If this is a public member of a trusted component that has unmanaged code permission and allows partially-trusted callers, it opens up a security hole. Because `Marshal.PtrToStringBSTR` only performs a link demand for unmanaged code permission, any caller of `StringFromBSTR` doesn't require any sort of permission to execute its code. A malicious caller could then trick `StringFromBSTR` to read and return data from any random spot in memory by passing an `IntPtr` type with a random value, and discover information that it should not have access to. To prevent this from happening, the method should either demand unmanaged code permission, or perform a faster link demand and "pass the buck" to its caller:

```
// Guard against malicious callers without unmanaged code permission
[SecurityPermissionAttribute(SecurityAction.LinkDemand,
 Flags=SecurityPermissionFlag.UnmanagedCode)]
public string StringFromBSTR(IntPtr ptr)
{
  return Marshal.PtrToStringBSTR(ptr);
}
```

The link demand could alternatively be placed on the class containing the `StringFromBSTR` method.

CAUTION

If you use `AllowPartiallyTrustedCallersAttribute`, be very careful whenever you call a member that performs a link demand, so you don't expose dangerous functionality to untrusted callers of your strong-named component. The most widely used examples of members that perform a link demand are those of the `System.Runtime.InteropServices.Marshal` class.

Members that perform a link demand should say so in their documentation, but as in many cases where documentation isn't adequate, the IL Disassembler (`ILDASM.EXE`) can come to the rescue. Any methods using a link demand have a `.permissionset linkcheck` statement in their disassembly information displaying what kind of permission is being demanded. Figure 6.2 shows what this looks like for one of the `Marshal.Copy` overloads. You can see the text representation of the link demand on the right-hand side of the window.

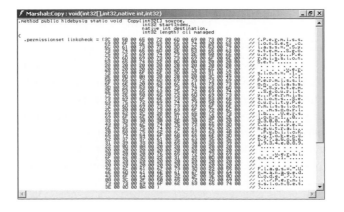

FIGURE 6.2
A link demand displayed in the IL Disassembler.

One last topic regarding unmanaged code and security is a custom attribute called
System.Security.SuppressUnmanagedCodeSecurityAttribute. This custom attribute can be
marked on a class, interface, or method, to turn off the security stack walk that checks for
unmanaged code permission at run time. A link demand for unmanaged code permission
occurs in its place.

Although it's tempting to use this custom attribute to increase performance, you should avoid
it. Besides making code vulnerable to luring attacks, it has an interesting side effect. When an
interface is marked with SuppressUnmanagedCodeSecurityAttribute, it requires that the
caller have unmanaged code permission even if it's implemented by a .NET class (meaning no
unmanaged code is involved). Without this custom attribute, unmanaged code permission
would only be required if the interface is implemented by a COM object.

The type library importer can optionally produce Interop Assemblies with the
SuppressUnmanagedCodeSecurityAttribute custom attribute on all the types within.
TLBIMP.EXE exposes this as its /unsafe option. When using this option, any user of such an
Interop Assembly must take great care to encapsulate the use of the Interop Assembly so that it
doesn't permit its callers to do too much without the appropriate permissions. Because an
Interop Assembly contains all public types and members for other assemblies to make use of,
an author of an "unsafe" Interop Assembly can't limit who can use and misuse the assembly.
This is why TLBIMP.EXE's /unsafe option is not recommended, and should never be used
when creating a PIA.

Using COM+ and DCOM Objects

Both COM+ objects and DCOM objects can be used from managed code just like COM objects. All the standard COM Interoperability features apply, and there isn't any additional built-in support for using such objects besides two methods for invoking DCOM objects on remote computers—Type.GetTypeFromProgID and Type.GetTypeFromCLSID.

Both Type.GetTypeFromProgID and Type.GetTypeFromCLSID have four overloads, two of which contain a string parameter that specifies a server name. This specifies the server on which the remote object should be created when you call Activator.CreateInstance using the Type object returned from either of these methods. This looks like the following in C#:

```
Type t = Type.GetTypeFromProgID("MyProgID", "MyComputerName");
Object o = Activator.CreateInstance(t);
```

Visual Basic .NET's CreateObject method can also be used for the same purpose:

```
Dim o As Object = CreateObject("MyProgID", "MyComputerName")
```

Internally, creating an object in this fashion calls CoGetClassObject with the CLSCTX_REMOTE_SERVER flag and a COSERVERINFO structure whose pwszName field is set to a server name. This is standard DCOM, so all the standard rules apply. If you register the COM object appropriately on both computers (including a registered type library or registered proxy/stub DLL on the client machine necessary for COM marshaling), then everything should work just as it does from a COM client.

One easy way to set up a remote COM object is to install it as a COM+ object in the Component Services explorer. This can be done as follows on the server computer:

1. Select Component Services from the Administrative Tools item on the Windows Control Panel.
2. Choose the Component Services, Computers, My Computer, COM+ Applications node under the Console Root.
3. Right-click on COM+ Applications and select New, Application.
4. Follow the wizard to create an empty application.
5. Under the node for your empty application, right click on the Components folder and select New, Component.
6. Follow the wizard to add your COM component.

Now that the server computer is set up, you can register the COM component and its type library on the client machine (assuming that the COM component's interfaces use type library marshaling).

An alternative way to create a remote object using DCOM is to simply use the new keyword, for example (in C#):

```
Object o = new MyClass();
```

Because the CLR calls CoCreateInstance with the CLSCTX_SERVER flag (which is a combination of CLSCTX_INPROC_SERVER, CLSCTX_LOCAL_SERVER, and CLSCTX_REMOTE_SERVER) in this situation, you can force new to create the COM object remotely as long as it's registered appropriately on the client machine to point to the remote machine.

If you require the security and MultiQI features of CoCreateInstanceEx when creating remote COM objects, you'll need to use PInvoke to call this method directly. An example of this is shown in Chapter 19. No built-in methods in the .NET Framework expose the functionality of CoCreateInstanceEx.

CAUTION

On some versions of Windows (before Windows XP or before Windows 2000 with Service Pack 3), calling CoGetClassObject with CLSCTX_REMOTE_SERVER attempts to create the COM object *locally* before attempting to create it remotely. This incorrect behavior can therefore been seen when using Type.GetTypeFromProgID, Type.GetTypeFromCLSID, or VB .NET's CreateObject on such operating systems when a COM class is registered on the client machine such that it could successfully be created locally. A workaround on these operating systems is to call CoCreateInstanceEx directly via PInvoke in your .NET client.

DCOM can be used for communication between .NET and COM components (in either direction), or even between two .NET components when they both expose themselves as COM objects. However, .NET Remoting is the preferred means of cross-process and cross-machine communication. Just as it's easy to use DCOM from .NET applications, it's easy to communicate with a remote COM object using .NET Remoting. Figure 6.3 displays this scenario. It demonstrates two .NET applications communicating with the same remote COM object. One uses DCOM, and the other uses SOAP via .NET Remoting.

Once you create an Interop Assembly for a COM component, you can publish it just as you would any other assembly to be used with .NET Remoting. This diagram is a simplification, because the top client likely references a local version of the Interop Assembly in order to cast the object returned by Activator.CreateInstance to interfaces that the COM object implements. Similarly, the bottom client requires a local copy of the Interop Assembly in order to use .NET Remoting. For more information about .NET Remoting, consult the .NET Framework SDK documentation.

Advanced Topics for Using COM Components

CHAPTER 6

311

6

ADVANCED TOPICS
FOR USING COM
COMPONENTS

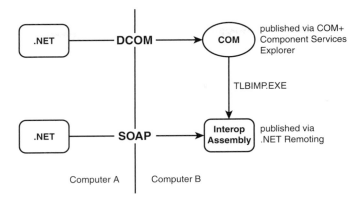

FIGURE 6.3
Communicating with a remote COM object using DCOM or using SOAP.

Creating new .NET objects that act like COM+ objects themselves can be done by creating a
serviced component—a class that derives from System.EnterpriseServices.
ServicedComponent. The behavior of such a class is controlled with a variety of custom attributes listed in Chapter 12, "Customizing COM's View of .NET Components."

Inheriting from COM Classes

At first glance of this section's title, you might think, "Why on earth would I want to inherit
from a COM class? I barely want to use inheritance with .NET classes." Still, this feature
exists, and has some interesting properties.

As mentioned in Chapter 2, "Bridging the Two Worlds—Managed and Unmanaged Code,"
COM doesn't have a notion of inheritance. Instead, implementation reuse is achieved through
containment or aggregation. In an interesting mix of the COM and .NET programming models,
it is possible for a .NET class to derive from an RCW in a limited fashion. Internally, deriving
from a COM class uses aggregation to provide the illusion of inheritance.

DIGGING DEEPER

If you derive from a COM object that doesn't support aggregation, the CLR performs
blind containment. This is strongly discouraged, so you should attempt to derive only
from COM objects that support aggregation.

If you were not familiar with the renaming done by the type library importer with classes and coclass interfaces, your first attempt might be to derive from the coclass interface, such as ADO's `Recordset`:

```
public class CustomRecordset : Recordset
{
    ...
}
```

This is *not* inheritance, however; it's simply implementing an interface. It's more apparent in a language like Visual Basic .NET which distinguishes between implementing an interface and deriving from a class (with `Implements` and `Inherits` keywords), but in C# or C++ the previous code can be misleading. In Visual Basic .NET, it would look as follows:

```
Public Class CustomRecordset
  Implements Recordset
  ...
End Class
```

Still, implementing a coclass interface usually fulfills the same need as inheritance would, because COM objects should always be passed via interface parameters anyway. The downside to implementing a coclass interface means that you must implement all of its members, *including* any event members from the default event interface that the coclass interface might be deriving from.

Deriving from a COM class instead looks like the following:

C#:

```
public class CustomRecordset : RecordsetClass
{
    ...
}
```

Visual Basic .NET:

```
Public Class CustomRecordset
  Inherits RecordsetClass
  ...
End Class
```

Using inheritance, however, doesn't turn out to be a much better option. When deriving from an RCW, the CLR has a little-known rule that if you override *any* members that correspond to a COM interface, you must override *all* of that interface's members. Unfortunately, no .NET compilers enforce this rule. The result for single-interface COM classes is that you end up with the same requirement of implementing all of the class's members (except for event members from the event interface), but without the compiler support to guide you.

> **Caution**
>
> When defining a .NET class that derives from a COM class (the strongly typed RCW), make sure that you override all members of an interface if you override any of them. Failure to do so causes a `TypeLoadException` to be thrown at run time with the message, "Types extending from COM objects should override all methods of an interface implemented by the base COM class."
>
> There are a handful of easy ways to check for a `TypeLoadException`. One way would be to run the .NET Framework PE Verifier utility (`PEVERIFY.EXE`) that comes with the SDK. When running this tool on an assembly with such a class, you'd get the following error:
>
> ```
> [IL]: Error:  [token …] Type load failed.
> ```
>
> The message isn't very descriptive, but if you run the Assembly Registration Utility (`REGASM.EXE`) or simply write code that instantiates your incorrectly derived class, you'll get the exception with the descriptive message.

This limitation may seem to make using inheritance with COM classes useless, but it's reasonable considering that COM classes were not designed to be inherited from. For example, COM classes can't expose protected members that expose internal state that may be needed by derived classes, so what are the chances that overriding `Recordset.Open` alone could perform differently than the base `Open` method and still work seamlessly with the interface's other members? Implementing inheritance correctly is hard enough for classes *designed* to be inherited from; imagine how hard it would be to implement inheritance with a base class whose designers never imagined it being derived from! By overriding all the methods in an interface, you're effectively re-implementing it. If you really only wanted to affect a handful of methods (such as logging when `Open` and `Save` are called before calling the base `Open` and `Save` methods), overriding all the other interface members to simply call their corresponding base members isn't too much of a hassle.

Another limitation of deriving from COM classes is that some .NET languages may not support defining some signatures that appear in COM interfaces, yet you'd need to define them in order to override them. For example, Visual Basic .NET does not support defining properties with by-reference parameters (although you can *call* such properties), so a Visual Basic .NET class cannot derive from a COM class and override a property with by-reference parameters. These language limitations are discussed in Chapter 21.

An interesting option is available to derived .NET classes, and that is the ability to control how the base class is instantiated. This can be done with a delegate defined with the same signature as `ObjectCreationDelegate` in the `System.Runtime.InteropServices` namespace. The delegate signature has a `System.IntPtr` parameter called `aggregator` and returns a `System.IntPtr` type. The `aggregator` parameter represents the `pUnkOuter` parameter that would be passed to `CoCreateInstance`, and the returned `IntPtr` should be a pointer to an `IUnknown` interface, just like what `CoCreateInstance` would return.

To "register" the delegate so it's called during class construction, it must be passed to the static `ExtensibleClassFactory.RegisterObjectCreationCallback` method, also in the `System.Runtime.InteropServices` namespace. There are two important guidelines for calling this method:

1. `RegisterObjectCreationCallback` must be called inside the class's *class constructor*, also known as a *static initializer*. This is a constructor marked `static` in C# and C++ or `Shared` in VB .NET that gets executed once before the first instance of the class is created.

2. `RegisterObjectCreationCallback` may only be called once per class type.

Also, in version 1.0 of the CLR, the delegate passed to `RegisterObjectCreationCallback` must correspond to an instance method rather than a static method.

By registering an appropriate delegate, the Runtime-Callable Wrapper will invoke this custom method instead of calling `CoCreateInstance` to instantiate the base COM class. The base object can be instantiated however you like—as a singleton object, with a COM moniker, on a remote machine, from the running object table (ROT), and so on. So even if you never override any of the base class's members, using this callback mechanism can still provide useful behavior that overrides the behavior of `new`.

> **TIP**
>
> Deriving from an RCW simply to control instantiation rather than overriding members is a slick way to hide a potentially complex activation scheme within a client's use of the `new` keyword. The base COM object, however, must behave correctly when aggregated for this to work.

The following C# code demonstrates the use of `ExtensibleClassFactory.RegisterObjectCreationCallback` to plug in a `CustomCreateInstance` method that replaces `CoCreateInstance` and uses a moniker to create the base COM object.

```csharp
public class MyDerivedClass : MyCoClass
{
```

Advanced Topics for Using COM Components

CHAPTER 6

315

6

ADVANCED TOPICS
FOR USING COM
COMPONENTS

```
// Class constructor
public static MyDerivedClass()
{
  MyDerivedClass c = new MyDerivedClass();
  ExtensibleClassFactory.RegisterObjectCreationCallback(
    new ObjectCreationDelegate(c.CustomCreateInstance));
}

public IntPtr CustomCreateInstance(IntPtr aggregator)
{
  object o = Marshal.BindToMoniker("...");
  return Marshal.GetIUnknownForObject(o);
}
}
```

Debugging into COM Components

Visual Studio .NET has a feature called *mixed-mode debugging*, with which you can debug COM Interoperability calls from managed code into unmanaged code—or vice-versa—all from within the same IDE. This functionality is not available in the .NET Framework SDK debugger (CORDBG.EXE).

To be able to step into the source code of a COM component (or .NET component, for that matter) you need two items:

- The source code for the component
- A *program database file* (with the extension .pdb) that provides the debugger with extra information needed to debug the program and associate machine code statements with lines of source code

Any Visual C++ programs compiled using the Debug configuration automatically have a .pdb file available. For Visual Basic 6 programs, you need to perform an extra step because .pdb files are not generated by default. To create one, open the Visual Basic 6 project you wish to make debuggable in the Visual Basic 6 IDE and perform the following steps:

1. Select *ProjectName* Properties… from the Project menu inside the Visual Basic 6 IDE.
2. Click on the Compile tab.
3. Check the Create Symbolic Debug Info option, then click the OK button. (See Figure 6.4.)
4. Recompile the project (Make *FileName*… on the File menu).

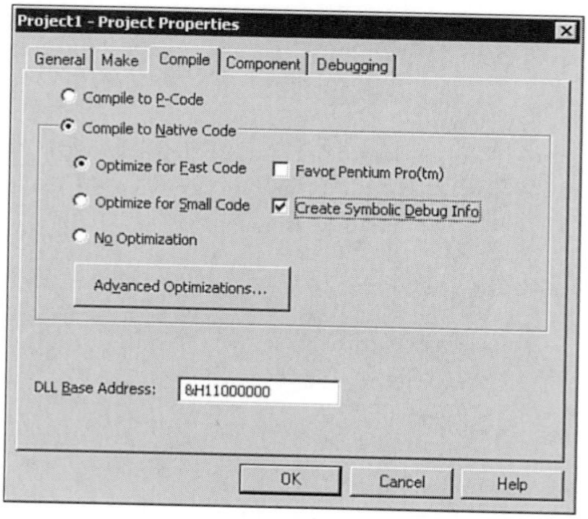

FIGURE 6.4

Creating a debuggable Visual Basic 6 COM component.

Once you have a COM component that can be debugged, simply leave the .pdb file alongside the unmanaged DLL to which it belongs. Visual Studio .NET will be able to find it there.

The trick to debugging programs that use COM Interoperability is that the Visual Studio .NET debugger does not enable stepping into unmanaged code by default. Instead, you need to explicitly enable mixed-mode debugging. This functionality is disabled by default because it makes the debugger run more slowly than it would otherwise. Interestingly enough, the procedure for turning on the functionality is different for Visual C#, Visual Basic, and Visual C++ projects!

To enable this feature, do the following inside Visual Studio .NET:

1. Right-click on the project name in the Solution Explorer, and select `Properties` from the menu.

2. Select `Debugging` under the `Configuration Properties` folder.

3. Choose your next setting based on the language you use:

   - For Visual C# projects, set `Enable Unmanaged Debugging` to `True`.
   - For Visual Basic projects, check `Unmanaged code debugging`.
   - For Visual C++ projects, set the `Debugger Type` to `Mixed`.

These three actions are displayed in Figures 6.5, 6.6, and 6.7.

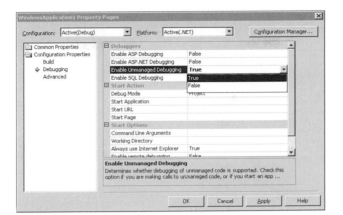

FIGURE 6.5
Enabling mixed-mode debugging in a Visual C# .NET project.

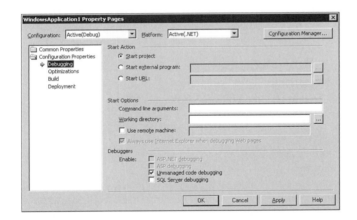

FIGURE 6.6
Enabling mixed-mode debugging in a Visual Basic .NET project.

> **TIP**
>
> Be sure to enable mixed-mode debugging when you want to step from managed code into unmanaged code! Otherwise, the debugger won't stop at unmanaged breakpoints and silently refuses to honor your request to step into an unmanaged member, stepping over it instead.

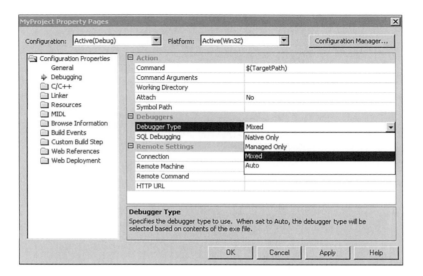

FIGURE 6.7

Enabling mixed-mode debugging in a Visual C++ .NET project.

That's all there is to it! Now you can use the Visual Studio .NET debugger as you normally would, and seamlessly step into COM components. Figure 6.8 shows someone stepping from a C# application into a Visual Basic 6 COM component. Notice the call stack, with the VB6 stack frame marked with the language BASIC.

> **CAUTION**
>
> Visual Basic 6 doesn't always generate complete debug information, especially for local variables. As a result, it's common to see incorrect or incomplete information in the Visual Studio .NET debugger's Locals window when debugging VB6 components, such as variables named unnamed_var1 instead of the real variable names.

> **CAUTION**
>
> There are a few limitations to the mixed-mode debugging support. The result is that sometimes you'll need to set breakpoints to stop the debugger in places where the "stepping" operation doesn't work as expected. The limitations are:

Advanced Topics for Using COM Components

CHAPTER 6

319

6

ADVANCED TOPICS
FOR USING COM
COMPONENTS

- Stepping from one thread to another is not supported. This means that attempting to step into a call on an STA COM component from an MTA thread or an MTA COM component from an STA thread acts like a "step over" operation because one thread must be marshaled to the other. To work around this, you could simply set a breakpoint inside the COM call and the debugger will stop on it.

- The complete call stack may not always be shown when it consists of both managed and unmanaged stack frames. In particular, unmanaged frames can sometimes be missing. In the rare cases when this happens, stepping across a missing unmanaged frame from managed code can produce the wrong results. To work around this, you can set a breakpoint and jump to it rather than stepping one line at a time.

- Property evaluation in debugger windows can be extra slow. To avoid this, you can tell the debugger to not evaluate properties. This is a good idea, anyway, for all applications, because a debugger evaluating a property with side effects can produce incorrect behavior in the application you're debugging. For any project type, you can turn this off as follows:

  1. Choose Options from the Tools menu.

  2. Select General under the Debugging folder.

  3. Uncheck Allow property evaluation in variables windows.

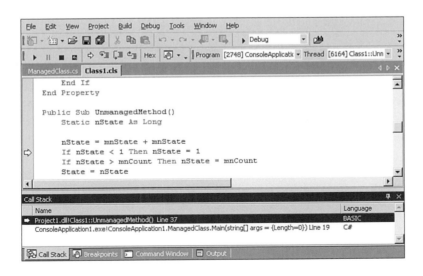

FIGURE 6.8

Stepping into a Visual Basic 6 COM component inside Visual Studio .NET.

RPC debugging is not enabled by default, even for unmanaged-only projects. To enable it, do the following:

1. Choose `Options` from the `Tools` menu.
2. Select `Native` under the `Debugging` folder.
3. Check `RPC debugging`.

Monitoring Performance

To create software with top-notch performance, it's important to understand how processing time is being spent when the application runs. For programmers new to the .NET Framework and COM Interoperability, understanding your application's run-time performance profile is critical, because it's easy to inadvertently use a poor-performing approach. To help obtain such information, NT-based versions of Windows have a System Monitor in which applications that expose *performance objects* can be monitored while they are running. This utility can display information using line graphs, bar charts, and other displays, so it can be a great tool for understanding performance problems such as bottlenecks in your application.

The .NET Framework exposes several performance objects that can be used with the System Monitor, including one specifically for interoperability. Every performance object has one or more *performance counters*, individual data values being tracked over time, such as "number of bytes in the GC heaps," or "number of classes loaded."

The interoperability performance object contains the following performance counters, listed here with their displayed names:

- `# of CCWs`—The number of COM-Callable Wrappers (CCWs) currently active. With this counter, you can see how many .NET objects are currently being used from COM.
- `# of marshalling` [sic]—The number of times marshaling occurs across the managed/unmanaged boundary in either direction. This counter doesn't show the times when the marshaling overhead is small enough for the marshaling stubs to become inlined. (Stubs are pieces of code that perform the marshaling.) This counter applies to both COM Interoperability and PInvoke.
- `# of Stubs`—The number of stubs that have been created by the CLR to perform marshaling, either in a COM Interoperability or PInvoke call.
- `# of TLB exports / sec`—This counter is never used.
- `# of TLB imports / sec`—This counter is never used.

To view these performance counters, available on a system-wide or per-process basis, use the following steps on Windows 2000, Windows XP, or subsequent operating systems:

Advanced Topics for Using COM Components

CHAPTER 6

321

6

ADVANCED TOPICS
FOR USING COM
COMPONENTS

1. Run PERFMON.EXE at a command prompt.
2. Right-click on the list at the bottom of the right-hand pane and select Add Counters..., or click on the button at the top with the plus icon.
3. Select the desired counters from the .NET CLR Interop performance object. This dialog is pictured in Figure 6.9.

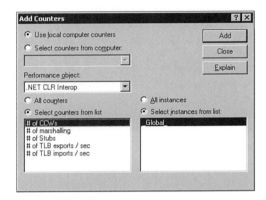

FIGURE 6.9
Selecting interoperability performance counters.

The .NET Framework also provides several performance counter APIs in the System.Diagnostics namespace, enabling you to create your own performance counters and use any performance counters programmatically. Consult the .NET Framework documentation for more information about performance counters.

Conclusion

This chapter rounds out this book's coverage of using COM components in .NET applications. The only chapter remaining in Part II, mentioned several times in this chapter, focuses on the task of modifying Interop Assemblies using tools provided by the .NET Framework SDK. Although this chapter only contained one Frequently Asked Question, all of the material covered answers several FAQs that appear time and time again when developers get serious about using COM components in managed code. Hopefully, this information will come in handy as you take on the adventure for yourself.

Modifying Interop Assemblies

IN THIS CHAPTER

- How to Change an Assembly's Contents   325
- IL Assembler Syntax   328
- Changing Data Types   340
- Exposing Success HRESULTs   342
- Arrays   348
- Custom Attributes   351
- Adding Methods to Modules   372

We've seen in previous chapters that an Interop Assembly produced by the type library importer might not always be appropriate for the COM component you wish to use. This chapter describes a relatively easy way to modify the metadata inside an Interop Assembly to suit your needs. You'll see examples of the types of changes that can be made, and the types of changes that typically need to be made. Such changes are desirable or even necessary for a variety of reasons, which fall into three main categories:

- Limitations of type library expressiveness. For example, the type library importer can't do a sensible conversion for C-style arrays because they look no different inside a type library than a pointer to a single type. Furthermore, the type library contains no information about the size for such arrays.

- Limitations of the importer. Examples of this are ignoring methods in a type library module, always hiding an HRESULT return type, and ignoring IDL custom attributes.

- Errors or omissions in the type library. This is the most rare of the three categories, but sometimes type libraries can contain errors that affect proper behavior or they may omit useful types. This, of course, isn't the fault of the type library importer—if you put garbage in, you get garbage out.

This chapter is different from the others in that we're going to look at several small examples that focus on taking advantage of two important tools in the .NET Framework SDK—the IL Assembler (ILASM.EXE) and the IL Disassembler (ILDASM.EXE). We'll be looking at mostly "raw metadata" as shown by ILDASM.EXE and understood by ILASM.EXE, rather than at signatures in higher-level languages like C#, Visual Basic .NET, and C++.

Modifying an Interop Assembly isn't the only way to work around limitations in the type library importer—you could write the types and signatures manually in a higher-level language. This technique works even when you don't have a type library, and can be handy for more complex modifications. Whereas defining the type information in a higher-level language is an optional and advanced technique covered in Chapter 21, "Manually Defining COM Types in Source Code," the technique of modifying an Interop Assembly produced by the importer is easier and often necessary for ease of use in .NET applications. Hence, we cover this topic now in Part II rather than in Part VII, "Advanced Topics."

> **TIP**
>
> None of the techniques in this chapter are necessary for customizing behavior specific to an ActiveX Assembly produced by this ActiveX Control importer. That's because the AXIMP.EXE utility makes it easy with its /source command-line option. This option generates C# source code that can be customized as you see fit. Since the ActiveX Assembly depends on an Interop Assembly, however, customizations may still need to be done to dependent assemblies.

Hopefully the COM component you wish to use in managed code already has a Primary Interop Assembly (PIA) with any necessary customizations made by its author. If you wrote the COM component, then following the techniques in this chapter helps you create a good PIA. For more information about creating PIAs, see Chapter 15, "Creating and Deploying Useful Primary Interop Assemblies."

How to Change an Assembly's Contents

Any time you want to modify the contents of an assembly, there are three fundamental steps to follow:

1. Disassemble the assembly, and output its contents to a text file (typically given a .il extension). This can be done with ILDASM.EXE as follows:

   ```
   ildasm MyAssembly.dll /out:MyAssembly.il
   ```

2. Change the contents of the text file (sometimes called an *IL file*) using your favorite text editor. The rest of this chapter gives examples of how to make specific changes, highlighting any changes you'll likely want to make.

3. Reassemble the assembly, using the updated text file as the source code. This can be done with ILASM.EXE as follows:

   ```
   ilasm /dll MyAssembly.il
   ```

These steps are pictured in Figure 7.1.

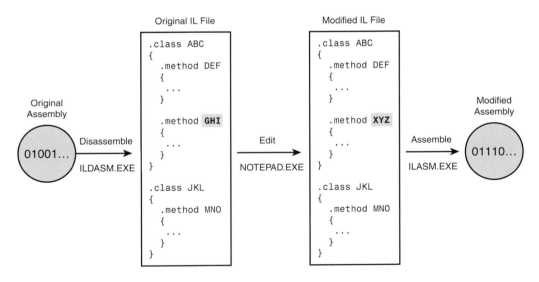

FIGURE 7.1

The IL Disassembler and IL Assembler, when used together, enable easy modifications of binary assembly files.

This technique can be leveraged in COM Interoperability by using an Interop Assembly produced by the type library importer in step 1.

Caution

If you plan to double-check your changes to an assembly by disassembling the modified assembly created in step 3 and comparing the resultant text file to the text file created in step 1, you'll find that comparing the two text files isn't so easy. Many differences often appear between two such semantically equivalent files because the order in which ILDASM.EXE emits multiple custom attributes on the same element varies. Because Interop Assemblies are filled with custom attributes, many meaningless differences show up when performing this check due to attribute re-ordering.

An Interop Assembly always contains an unmanaged resource with the Win32 file version information (the information seen when viewing its properties in Windows Explorer) copied from the original type library file. Therefore, when disassembling an Interop Assembly, ILDASM.EXE prints out something like:

```
// WARNING: Created Win32 resource file MyAssembly.res
```

To include this same unmanaged resource information in the modified assembly, you can use the /resource command-line switch on ILASM.EXE. Thus, step 3 should really be the following when working with Interop Assemblies (or any assemblies with an embedded unmanaged resource):

```
ilasm /dll MyAssembly.il /resource:MyAssembly.res
```

Digging Deeper

ILDASM.EXE's /resource option is only necessary (and only works) for embedding a single unmanaged resource file (which typically has a .res extension). When disassembling and reassembling an assembly with *managed resources*, the files emitted by ILDASM.EXE are automatically picked up by ILASM.EXE as long as they are kept in the same directory. Of course, an Interop Assembly generated by the type library importer never contains managed resources.

For a demonstration of using managed resources in a .NET application, see Chapter 24, "Writing .NET Visualizations for Windows Media Player."

This whole process of taking an assembly apart and putting it back together might sound like a scary thing to do (or a major hack), but it's really not that bad when you see how it's done.

FAQ: What stops a malicious person from using the IL Disassembler and the IL Assembler to modify assemblies in a harmful way?

In short, the .NET Framework security system. For any fully-signed strong-named assembly, a cryptographic key pair helped to produce an embedded hash of its contents. If a single bit (literally) of the assembly has changed since it was signed, the change is detected by the CLR and the assembly will not be loaded. To enable "legal" changing of a strong-named assembly, ILASM.EXE has command-line signing options. Thus, if (and only if) you have access to the original cryptographic key pair, you can modify a signed assembly without causing security violations. There is no protection mechanism for assemblies without a strong name, so anyone could modify them using the previous steps.

Just as TLBIMP.EXE has command-line options for digitally signing an Interop Assembly (covered in Chapter 15, "Creating and Deploying Useful Primary Interop Assemblies"), ILASM.EXE has a command-line option for digitally signing the "re-engineered" assembly. If your key pair resides in a file called MyKey.snk, you can use the /key option as follows:

```
/key:MyKey.snk
```

This is the same as using TLBIMP.EXE's /keyfile option. If your key pair resides in a container called MyContainer, you can use the /key option with the @ symbol as follows:

```
/key:@MyContainer
```

This is the same as using TLBIMP.EXE's /keycontainer option.

To summarize, the complete sequence of steps for modifying an Interop Assembly are typically:

1. Generate the original Interop Assembly:

   ```
   TlbImp MyTypeLib.tlb /out:MyAssembly.dll
   ```

2. Disassemble the Interop Assembly:

   ```
   ildasm MyAssembly.dll /out:MyAssembly.il
   ```

3. Change the contents of the text file.

4. Reassemble the assembly, giving it a strong name and including the unmanaged resources:

   ```
   ilasm /dll MyAssembly.il /resource:MyAssembly.res /keyfile:MyKey.snk
   ```

There's no need to digitally sign the original Interop Assembly if you're immediately going to disassemble and reassemble it. As long as you digitally sign the assembly produced by the IL Assembler, the result is the same whether the original one was signed or not.

> **TIP**
>
> The IL Assembler produces a lot of output when assembling an IL file, reporting each class it assembles along the way. Because of this, any warnings or errors that are reported can get scrolled off the screen by the time the assembler finishes, leaving you with the following frustrating message:
>
> ```
> *****FAILURE*****
> ```
>
> To have ILASM.EXE only report errors and warnings, use its /quiet option, as follows:
>
> ```
> ilasm /dll /quiet MyAssembly.il /resource:MyAssembly.res
> /keyfile:MyKey.snk
> ```

> **CAUTION**
>
> When performing the final step of assembling the modified assembly, do not change the name of the output file to anything other than the original assembly filename. If you want to save the original assembly, you should move or rename it before performing this final step. The reason is that the assembly's filename should match its simple assembly name, which appears inside the IL file you're assembling.
>
> If you renamed the output file and still had the original assembly in the same directory, the original one might be used by clients, even if you recompiled them while referencing your renamed assembly. That's because only the assembly reference gets persisted into client assemblies, and at run time your modified assembly could be ignored if its filename didn't match the assembly name.
>
> If you want to change the output filename, you also must change the assembly's name inside the IL file and be sure to recompile any clients of your assembly so they reference the new name.

IL Assembler Syntax

Before looking at how to change the information in the IL text file, let's look at what you can expect to see inside the file. The contents are sometimes referred to as "raw IL," but that term is a little misleading. An assembly contains both metadata (describing the types and signatures) and IL (the source code containing the actual implementation). Furthermore, although Interop

Assemblies contain IL for managed event-related members, there's never a compelling reason to change this IL. For Interop Assemblies, the importance is in the metadata. Because the contents of the IL file use a syntax recognized and assembled (or compiled) by ILASM.EXE, we'll refer to this as IL Assembler syntax. Listing 7.1 displays snippets of the IL file for the Microsoft Word Interop Assembly. The contents were generated by running TLBIMP.EXE on the MSWORD.OLB file that ships with Office XP, then using ILDASM.EXE.

LISTING 7.1   Snippets of Word.il, the File Produced by ILDASM.EXE for Microsoft Word's Interop Assembly

```
 1: //  Microsoft (R) .NET Framework IL Disassembler.  Version 1.0.3300.0
 2: //  Copyright (C) Microsoft Corporation 1998-2001. All rights reserved.
 3:
 4: .assembly extern mscorlib
 5: {
 6:   .publickeytoken = (B7 7A 5C 56 19 34 E0 89 )               // .z\V.4..
 7:   .ver 1:0:3300:0
 8: }
 9: .assembly extern Office
10: {
11:   .ver 2:2:0:0
12: }
13: .assembly extern VBIDE
14: {
15:   .ver 5:3:0:0
16: }
17: .assembly Word
18: {
19:   .custom instance void [mscorlib]System.Runtime.InteropServices.
20: ImportedFromTypeLibAttribute::.ctor(string) =
21:   ( 01 00 04 57 6F 72 64 00 00 )                    // ...Word..
22:   .custom instance void [mscorlib]System.Runtime.InteropServices.
23: GuidAttribute::.ctor(string) =
24:   ( 01 00 24 30 30 30 32 30 39 30 35 2D 30 30 30 30   // ..$00020905-0000
25:     2D 30 30 30 30 2D 63 30 30 30 2D 30 30 30 30 30   // -0000-c000-00000
26:     30 30 30 30 30 34 36 00 00 )                      // 0000046..
27:   .hash algorithm 0x00008004
28:   .ver 8:2:0:0
29: }
30: .module Word.dll
31: // MVID: {1187CCAE-A004-47A6-96BA-D7661EFE46D8}
32: .imagebase 0x00400000
33: .subsystem 0x00000003
34: .file alignment 4096
35: .corflags 0x00000001
36: // Image base: 0x031b0000
37: //
```

LISTING 7.1   Continued

```
38: // ============== CLASS STRUCTURE DECLARATION ==================
39: //
40: .namespace Word
41: {
42:   .class public auto ansi sealed WdMailSystem
43:         extends [mscorlib]System.Enum
44:   {
45:   } // end of class WdMailSystem
46:
47:   Many more declarations here...
48: } // end of namespace Word
49:
50: // ===========================================================
51:
52:
53: // ============== GLOBAL FIELDS AND METHODS ==================
54:
55:
56: // ===========================================================
57:
58:
59: // ============== CLASS MEMBERS DECLARATION ==================
60: //   note that class flags, 'extends' and 'implements' clauses
61: //          are provided here for information only
62:
63: .namespace Word
64: {
65:   .class public auto ansi sealed WdMailSystem
66:         extends [mscorlib]System.Enum
67:   {
68:     .field public specialname rtspecialname int32 value__
69:     .field public static literal valuetype Word.WdMailSystem
70:       wdNoMailSystem = int32(0x00000000)
71:     .field public static literal valuetype Word.WdMailSystem
72:       wdMAPI = int32(0x00000001)
73:     .field public static literal valuetype Word.WdMailSystem
74:       wdPowerTalk = int32(0x00000002)
75:     .field public static literal valuetype Word.WdMailSystem
76:       wdMAPIandPowerTalk = int32(0x00000003)
77:   } // end of class WdMailSystem
78:
79:   Many more declarations here...
80: } // end of namespace Word
81:
82: //*********** DISASSEMBLY COMPLETE ********************
83: // WARNING: Created Win32 resource file Word.res
```

The first thing to notice at the beginning of the IL file is the C++-style comments beginning with //. Lines 4–16 list the assemblies referenced by the current one in the three .assembly extern blocks. Each block contains all information necessary to identify the assembly, such as its name, version number, and public key token (for strong-named assemblies). Every Interop Assembly has a reference to the mscorlib assembly, and the Microsoft Word Interop Assembly also references VBIDE and Office for additional types.

Lines 17–29 contain a .assembly block with the same sort of information for the current Word assembly. In this block, Interop Assemblies always contain an ImportedFromTypeLibAttribute custom attribute containing the type library name and a GuidAttribute custom attribute containing the LIBID. The syntax of custom attributes is explained in more depth later in the "Custom Attributes" section. Lines 30–36 list information for the current module, which we never need to worry about.

Line 40 begins a section of the IL file containing declarations of all types in the assembly, not including their members. All types appear in a .namespace block which contains all the types in the Word namespace. The listing omits all but one class, which happens to be an enumeration. In IL Assembler syntax, this looks like a regular class that derives from System.Enum.

Line 53 marks a section for global fields and methods, which imported Interop Assemblies do not contain. Line 63 begins the declaration of the members and implementation of any types. The declarations of classes (such as the one in Lines 42–45) are repeated in order to associate members with their containing types. The IL Assembler associates these duplicate definitions with the previous ones by type name only, so if the definition of WdMailSystem in Lines 65–77 said private instead of public or omitted the fact that it derives from System.Enum, it would have no effect as long as the initial class declaration was not changed.

Looking at the members of WdMailSystem in Lines 65–77, we see four values (represented as static fields of the class): 0, 1, 2, and 3. Every managed enum has a value__ field hidden by higher-level languages that contains the current value for each instance of the enum. The remaining members are omitted from the listing, so Line 80 marks the end of the Word namespace and Lines 82–83 add any ILDASM.EXE warning messages to the end of the file as comments.

TIP

Do you want to combine multiple assemblies into one? ILASM.EXE supports specifying a list of files at the command line, and compiles them all into the same single-file assembly. These input files could be the result of running ILDASM.EXE on several separate assemblies. The only special requirement is that there can only be one .assembly block in all the files to specify the output assembly's name, version, and so on, so

> you'd need to delete all but one in the input files. You can still have multiple
> .assembly extern blocks for referencing external assemblies (and you can even have
> duplicate references without consequences).
>
> This same technique could be used to create a single-file assembly whose source code
> was originally written in multiple languages, such as C# and Visual Basic .NET.

In an Interop Assembly, only the event-related members generated by the importer (discussed in Chapter 5, "Responding to COM Events") contain IL instructions. Here's an example of the IL Assembler syntax for the constructor (indicated with .ctor) for the ApplicationEvents_SinkHelper class that appears in the Interop Assembly from Listing 7.1:

```
.method assembly specialname rtspecialname
        instance void  .ctor() cil managed
{
  // Code size       24 (0x18)
  .maxstack  4
  IL_0000:  ldarg     0
  IL_0004:  call      instance void [mscorlib]System.Object::.ctor()
  IL_0009:  ldarg     0
  IL_000d:  ldc.i4    0x0
  IL_0012:  stfld     int32 Word.ApplicationEvents_SinkHelper::m_dwCookie
  IL_0017:  ret
} // end of method ApplicationEvents_SinkHelper::.ctor
```

Data Types

Chapter 1, "Introduction to the .NET Framework," listed the aliases for each of the primitive System types in C#, VB .NET, and C++. Table 7.1 shows what the same System types look like in IL Assembler syntax.

TABLE 7.1 The IL Assembler Types That Correspond to the Fundamental System Types in the mscorlib Assembly

System Data Type	IL Assembler Data Type
System.Object	object
System.String	string
System.Decimal	valuetype [mscorlib]System.Decimal
System.Boolean	bool
System.Char	char
System.Byte	unsigned int8

TABLE 7.1 Continued

System Data Type	IL Assembler Data Type
System.SByte	int8
System.Int16	int16
System.Int32	int32
System.Int64	int64
System.IntPtr	native int
System.UInt16	unsigned int16
System.UInt32	unsigned int32
System.UInt64	unsigned int64
System.UIntPtr	native unsigned int
System.Single	float32
System.Double	float64

Notice that unlike C#, VB .NET, and C++, the IL Assembler has keywords for the size-agnostic `IntPtr` and `UIntPtr` types. If you're wondering about the funny looking syntax for expressing `System.Decimal`, IL Assembler doesn't have a keyword for the `System.Decimal` type. Instead, the syntax shown is the syntax used for any user-defined type.

This syntax for user-defined data types begins by classifying the type as a value type (with the `valuetype` keyword) or as a reference type (with the `class` keyword). It then specifies the assembly's simple name in square brackets, followed by the type name qualified with its namespace. The assembly name inside the square brackets must match one of the names listed in the file's `.assembly extern` statements, otherwise the type cannot be found. The Microsoft Word Interop Assembly from Listing 7.1 uses one type from the VBIDE assembly—the `_VBProject` interface. You can find this in a few places of the IL file as the following:

```
class [VBIDE]VBIDE.VBProject
```

The assembly also uses many types in the `Office` assembly; for example:

```
class [Office]Microsoft.Office.Core.Assistant
```

TIP

Don't get confused by the word `class` in an IL file. In IL Assembler syntax, this is any kind of reference type—even an interface. An interface is treated as a special type of class.

> ## DIGGING DEEPER
>
> IL Assembler has unique syntax for nested types:
>
>   OuterType/InnerType
>
> For example, a parameter whose type is the `ObjectCollection` type nested inside `System.Windows.Forms.ListBox` is expressed as follows:
>
>   class System.Windows.Forms.ListBox/ObjectCollection

Passing Parameters

Whereas by-reference parameters are indicated with `ref` in C# and `ByRef` in VB .NET, the IL Assembler notation for a by-reference parameter is an ampersand (&) after the type name. (Pointers, as in C# unsafe code, are represented as * after the type name.) Thus, the `Quit` method on the `Word._Application` interface, which has three by-reference object parameters, looks like the following:

```
.method public hidebysig newslot virtual abstract
instance void  Quit([in][opt] object&  marshal( struct) SaveChanges,
                    [in][opt] object&  marshal( struct) OriginalFormat,
                    [in][opt] object&  marshal( struct) RouteDocument
                  ) runtime managed internalcall
{
  .custom instance void [mscorlib]
    System.Runtime.InteropServices.DispIdAttribute::.ctor(int32) =
      ( 01 00 51 04 00 00 00 00 )                      // ..Q.....
} // end of method _Application::Quit
```

Notice the `[in]` and `[opt]` markings. These correspond to the `InAttribute` and `OptionalAttribute` pseudo-custom attributes. The `OutAttribute` pseudo-custom attribute is denoted similarly with `[out]`. In IL Assembler syntax, these attributes always go directly in front of the type name. Every parameter in an Interop Assembly usually has at least one of these attributes because parameters in a type library are usually marked with the `[in]` and/or `[out]` IDL attributes.

MarshalAsAttribute Syntax

Besides `InAttribute`, `OutAttribute`, and `OptionalAttribute`, another pseudo-custom attribute that is used throughout an Interop Assembly is `MarshalAsAttribute`. In IL Assembler, this looks like `marshal(type)`, as shown in the following signature for the `Item` method of the `FontNames` class:

```
.method public hidebysig newslot virtual abstract
        instance string
        marshal( bstr)
        Item([in] int32 Index) runtime managed internalcall
{
  .custom instance void [mscorlib]
    System.Runtime.InteropServices.DispIdAttribute::.ctor(int32) =
      ( 01 00 00 00 00 00 00 00 )
} // end of method FontNames::Item
```

The `marshal` keyword, when used, appears as follows:

- Between the type name and variable name when applied to a parameter, for example:

  ```
  .method public hidebysig newslot virtual abstract
              instance void  MyMethod(string  marshal( bstr) s) cil managed
  ```

- Immediately before the type name when applied to a field, for example:

  ```
  .field public  marshal( bstr) string MyField
  ```

- Between the return type name and method name when applied to a return value, as seen previously in the `FontNames.Item` method.

For each possible `UnmanagedType` value that can exist inside `MarshalAsAttribute`, IL Assembler has a special keyword. The syntax for each value is shown in Table 7.2. The meaning of each of the `UnmanagedType` enumeration values is explained in Chapter 12, "Customizing COM's View of .NET Components." The important ones for this chapter are explained as they are used.

TABLE 7.2 Every Value Used with `MarshalAsAttribute` Corresponds to Custom IL Assembler Syntax

Attribute Value	IL Assembler Syntax
MarshalAs(UnmanagedType.AnsiBStr)	marshal(ansi bstr)
MarshalAs(UnmanagedType.AsAny)	marshal(as any)
MarshalAs(UnmanagedType.Bool)	marshal(bool)
MarshalAs(UnmanagedType.BStr)	marshal(bstr)
MarshalAs(UnmanagedType.ByValArray, SizeConst=100)	marshal(fixed array [100])
MarshalAs(UnmanagedType.ByValTStr, SizeConst=100)	marshal(fixed sysstring [100])
MarshalAs(UnmanagedType.Currency)	marshal(currency)

TABLE 7.2   Continued

Attribute Value	IL Assembler Syntax
MarshalAs(UnmanagedType. CustomMarshaler, MarshalTypeRef=typeof(*T*))	marshal(custom ("*T*", ""))
MarshalAs(UnmanagedType.Error)	marshal(error)
MarshalAs(UnmanagedType.FunctionPtr)	marshal(method)
MarshalAs(UnmanagedType.I1)	marshal(int8)
MarshalAs(UnmanagedType.I2)	marshal(int16)
MarshalAs(UnmanagedType.I4)	marshal(int32)
MarshalAs(UnmanagedType.I8)	marshal(int64)
MarshalAs(UnmanagedType.IDispatch)	marshal(idispatch)
MarshalAs(UnmanagedType.Interface)	marshal(interface)
MarshalAs(UnmanagedType.IUnknown)	marshal(iunknown)
MarshalAs(UnmanagedType.LPArray)	marshal([])
MarshalAs(UnmanagedType.LPStr)	marshal(lpstr)
MarshalAs(UnmanagedType.LPStruct)	marshal(lpstruct)
MarshalAs(UnmanagedType.LPTStr)	marshal(lptstr)
MarshalAs(UnmanagedType.LPWStr)	marshal(lpwstr)
MarshalAs(UnmanagedType.R4)	marshal(float32)
MarshalAs(UnmanagedType.R8)	marshal(float64)
MarshalAs(UnmanagedType.SafeArray)	marshal(safearray)
MarshalAs(UnmanagedType.Struct)	marshal(struct)
MarshalAs(UnmanagedType.SysInt)	marshal(int)
MarshalAs(UnmanagedType.SysUInt)	marshal(unsigned int)
MarshalAs(UnmanagedType.TBStr)	marshal(tbstr)
MarshalAs(UnmanagedType.U1)	marshal(unsigned int8)
MarshalAs(UnmanagedType.U2)	marshal(unsigned int16)
MarshalAs(UnmanagedType.U4)	marshal(unsigned int32)
MarshalAs(UnmanagedType.U8)	marshal(unsigned int64)
MarshalAs(UnmanagedType.VariantBool)	marshal(variant bool)
MarshalAs(UnmanagedType.VBByRefStr)	marshal(byvalstr)

There are two special cases to point out—UnmanagedType.LPArray and UnmanagedType. SafeArray. UnmanagedType.LPArray means that the parameter it is attached to is a C-style array in the unmanaged signature. It can be used in conjunction with an ArraySubType named parameter set to a value of the UnmanagedType enumeration. This *sub type* is the type of the array's elements. The IL Assembler syntax for using UnmanagedType.LPArray with the ArraySubType is [] appended to whatever the type for ArraySubType is. For example, the following in C#:

```
[MarshalAs(UnmanagedType.LPArray, ArraySubType=UnmanagedType.Currency)]
```

is equivalent to the following in IL Assembler:

```
marshal(currency[])
```

If no ArraySubType parameter is specified (as in Table 7.2), the Interop Marshaler uses the default unmanaged type that corresponds to the managed array's element type.

UnmanagedType.SafeArray means that the parameter it is attached to is a SAFEARRAY in the unmanaged signature. It can be used in conjunction with a SafeArraySubType named parameter set to a value of the VarEnum enumeration, also defined in the System.Runtime.InteropServices namespace. Just like ArraySubType, SafeArraySubType specifies the type of the array's elements. For example, specifying the following in Visual Basic .NET:

```
<MarshalAs(UnmanagedType.SafeArray, SafeArraySubType:=VarEnum.VT_CY)>
```

is equivalent to the following in IL Assembler:

```
marshal(safearray currency)
```

> **CAUTION**
>
> In version 1.0 of the .NET Framework, Decimal array parameters marked with SafeArraySubType equal to VT_CY don't correctly marshal as a SAFEARRAY with CURRENCY elements in both directions. Such a SAFEARRAY can be marshaled from COM to .NET (via a return type marked with marshal(safearray currency)) but any attempt to pass a .NET Decimal array to COM via such a parameter fails with a SafeArrayTypeMismatchException. If you require passing CURRENCY SAFEARRAYs across the Interop boundary, you'll need to resort to do-it-yourself marshaling, described in Chapter 6, "Advanced Topics for Using COM Components."

The reason that the named parameter requires a separate enumeration is that a SAFEARRAY's element type is a VARIANT type represented by a subset of the VarEnum enumeration. The element type of a C-style array, on the other hand, can be just about anything represented by the UnmanagedType enum.

Just as the IL Assembler has special syntax for the values of the UnmanagedType enumeration, it has special syntax for the values of the VarEnum enumeration. Only about half of the values of VarEnum are valid when describing the type of a SAFEARRAY, but for completeness all the values are listed in Table 7.3 with the corresponding IL Assembler syntax. These words or symbols should be placed immediately after safearray, as in the previous safearray currency case.

TABLE 7.3   Every Value of the SafeArraySubType Named Parameter Used with MarshalAsAttribute Corresponds to Custom IL Assembler Syntax

SafeArraySubType *Value*	*IL Assembler Syntax*
VarEnum.VT_ARRAY	[ ]
VarEnum.VT_BLOB	blob
VarEnum.VT_BLOB_OBJECT	blob_object
VarEnum.VT_BOOL	bool
VarEnum.VT_BSTR	bstr
VarEnum.VT_BYREF	&
VarEnum.VT_CARRAY	carray
VarEnum.VT_CF	cf
VarEnum.VT_CLSID	clsid
VarEnum.VT_CY	currency
VarEnum.VT_DATE	date
VarEnum.VT_DECIMAL	decimal
VarEnum.VT_DISPATCH	idispatch
VarEnum.VT_EMPTY	*blank space*
VarEnum.VT_ERROR	error
VarEnum.VT_FILETIME	filetime
VarEnum.VT_HRESULT	hresult
VarEnum.VT_I1	int8
VarEnum.VT_I2	int16
VarEnum.VT_I4	int32
VarEnum.VT_I8	int64
VarEnum.VT_INT	int

TABLE 7.3 Continued

SafeArraySubType *Value*	*IL Assembler Syntax*
VarEnum.VT_LPSTR	lpstr
VarEnum.VT_LPWSTR	lpwstr
VarEnum.VT_NULL	null
VarEnum.VT_PTR	*
VarEnum.VT_R4	float32
VarEnum.VT_R8	float64
VarEnum.VT_RECORD	record
VarEnum.VT_SAFEARRAY	safearray
VarEnum.VT_STORAGE	storage
VarEnum.VT_STORED_OBJECT	stored_object
VarEnum.VT_STREAM	stream
VarEnum.VT_STREAMED_OBJECT	streamed_object
VarEnum.VT_UI1	unsigned int8
VarEnum.VT_UI2	unsigned int16
VarEnum.VT_UI4	unsigned int32
VarEnum.VT_UI8	unsigned int64
VarEnum.VT_UINT	unsigned int
VarEnum.VT_UNKNOWN	iunknown
VarEnum.VT_USERDEFINED	userdefined
VarEnum.VT_VARIANT	variant
VarEnum.VT_VECTOR	vector
VarEnum.VT_VOID	void

Some of the values are meant to be bitwise-ORed with others, such as VarEnum.VT_BYREF. The IL Assembler syntax for doing this is simply appending one to the other. For example, the following in C#:

```
[MarshalAs(UnmanagedType.SafeArray,
    SafeArraySubType=(VarEnum.VT_CY | VarEnum.VT_BYREF))]
```

looks like the following in IL Assembler:

```
marshal(safearray currency&)
```

That ends our whirlwind tour of IL Assembler syntax, except for the syntax of custom attributes, which is covered in the upcoming "Custom Attributes" section. To get a better feel of what IL Assembler syntax looks like, disassemble any assembly and peruse the contents of the IL file produced.

> **TIP**
>
> If you don't know how to represent a higher-level language construct in IL Assembler syntax, the easiest way to find out is to write a small program that contains this construct in a higher-level language, then open the compiled assembly and inspect it with `ILDASM.EXE`.

Changing Data Types

Now it's time to look at some of the useful changes one can make to the IL file for an Interop Assembly before reassembling it. Once you understand how to represent the various data types in IL Assembler, swapping them (as allowed by the Interop Marshaler) should be easy.

For example, the previous chapter used an example for which an `IntPtr` parameter needed to be changed to a by-reference or out-only `IntPtr` parameter. This could be accomplished by changing the following signature:

```
.method public hidebysig newslot virtual abstract
   instance void  GetObjectAttributes(
      [in] string&  marshal( lpwstr) pAttributeNames,
      unsigned int32 dwNumberAttributes,
      native int ppAttributeEntries,
      [out] unsigned int32& pdwNumAttributesReturned
   ) runtime managed internalcall {}
```

to:

```
.method public hidebysig newslot virtual abstract
   instance void  GetObjectAttributes(
      [in] string&  marshal( lpwstr) pAttributeNames,
      unsigned int32 dwNumberAttributes,
      [out] native int& ppAttributeEntries,
      [out] unsigned int32& pdwNumAttributesReturned
   ) runtime managed internalcall {}
```

The ampersand makes it by-reference, and the [out] makes it out-only (out IntPtr in C#). Another Chapter 6 example required changing a by-reference integer to an `IntPtr` type. This can be done by changing:

Modifying Interop Assemblies

CHAPTER 7

341

7

MODIFYING
INTEROP
ASSEMBLIES

```
.method public hidebysig newslot virtual abstract
  instance void  Read(native int pv,
    unsigned int32 cb,
    [out] unsigned int32& pcbRead
  ) runtime managed internalcall {}
```

to:

```
.method public hidebysig newslot virtual abstract
  instance void  Read(native int pv,
    unsigned int32 cb,
    native int pcbRead
  ) runtime managed internalcall {}
```

The Chapter 6 example that required changing a by-reference System.Object parameter to an IntPtr type to perform manual VARIANT marshaling could be accomplished by changing:

```
.method public hidebysig newslot virtual abstract
  instance void  FillRect(
    [in][out] object&  marshal( struct) v
  ) runtime managed internalcall {}
```

to:

```
.method public hidebysig newslot virtual abstract
  instance void  FillRect(
    native int v
  ) runtime managed internalcall {}
```

The [in] and [out] attributes aren't necessary on by-value IntPtr types because the Interop Marshaler doesn't do any marshaling besides passing the integral value.

Changing the IntPtr in the previous signature to a void* type to be used by C# unsafe code would look like the following:

```
.method public hidebysig newslot virtual abstract
  instance void  FillRect(
    void* v
  ) runtime managed internalcall {}
```

No kind of unsafe marking is necessary; designating code in such a way is enforced by the C# compiler but does not exist at the MSIL level.

Another change you could make is to take advantage of marshaling support that bridges OLE_COLOR and System.Drawing.Color. The importer creates a signature like the following for a method with an OLE_COLOR parameter:

```
.method public hidebysig newslot virtual abstract instance void
  GiveMeAColor([in] unsigned int32 c) runtime managed internalcall
{
```

```
.custom instance void [mscorlib]
  System.Runtime.InteropServices.DispIdAttribute::.ctor(int32) =
    ( 01 00 00 00 03 60 00 00 )                          // .....`..
.param [1]
.custom instance void [mscorlib]
  System.Runtime.InteropServices.ComAliasNameAttribute::.ctor(string) =
    ( 01 00 10 73 74 64 6F 6C 65 2E 4F 4C 45 5F 43 4F   // ...stdole.OLE_CO
      4C 4F 52 00 00 )                                   // LOR..
}
```

Because the Interop Marshaler supports it, this parameter could be changed to use
`System.Drawing.Color` as follows:

```
.method public hidebysig newslot virtual abstract instance void
  GiveMeAColor([in] valuetype [System.Drawing]System.Drawing.Color c)
  runtime managed internalcall
{
  .custom instance void [mscorlib]
    System.Runtime.InteropServices.DispIdAttribute::.ctor(int32) =
      ( 01 00 00 00 03 60 00 00 )                        // .....`..
}
```

as long as you also reference the `System.Drawing` assembly:

```
.assembly extern System.Drawing
{
  .publickeytoken = (B0 3F 5F 7F 11 D5 0A 3A )           // .?_....:
  .ver 1:0:3300:0
}
```

Exposing Success HRESULTs

With the metadata produced by the type library importer, there is no way for a .NET client to
distinguish between any success HRESULTs returned by a COM method because no exception is
thrown. By altering metadata signatures, you can expose the HRESULT return value to .NET
clients so the exact value can always be checked.

> **CAUTION**
>
> A side effect of exposing an HRESULT return value is that the value always needs to be
> checked whether it's a success code or an error code. In essence, exposing the HRESULT
> return value "turns off" the mapping of HRESULTs to .NET exceptions. Calling such a
> method never causes an exception to be thrown unless something external to the
> method causes it (such as StackOverflowException).

Modifying Interop Assemblies

CHAPTER 7

343

7

MODIFYING
INTEROP
ASSEMBLIES

For an example of altering a signature to expose the HRESULT return value, let's look at two methods in the Microsoft Word Interop Assembly—Documents.Add and _Application.Quit. These signatures are displayed in Listing 7.2.

LISTING 7.2   Metadata Definitions of Documents.Add and _Application.Quit Produced by the Type Library Importer

Documents.Add:

```
 1: .method public hidebysig newslot virtual abstract
 2:   instance class Word.Document
 3:   marshal( interface)
 4:   Add([in][opt] object&  marshal( struct) Template,
 5:       [in][opt] object&  marshal( struct) NewTemplate,
 6:       [in][opt] object&  marshal( struct) DocumentType,
 7:       [in][opt] object&  marshal( struct) Visible
 8:      ) runtime managed internalcall
 9: {
10:   .custom instance void [mscorlib]
11:     System.Runtime.InteropServices.DispIdAttribute::.ctor(int32) =
12:     ( 01 00 0E 00 00 00 00 00 )
13: } // end of method Documents::Add
```

_Application.Quit:

```
 1: .method public hidebysig newslot virtual abstract
 2:   instance void  Quit([in][opt] object&  marshal( struct) SaveChanges,
 3:                       [in][opt] object&  marshal( struct) OriginalFormat,
 4:                       [in][opt] object&  marshal( struct) RouteDocument
 5:                      ) runtime managed internalcall
 6: {
 7:   .custom instance void [mscorlib]
 8:     System.Runtime.InteropServices.DispIdAttribute::.ctor(int32) =
 9:     ( 01 00 51 04 00 00 00 00 )                        // ..Q.....
10: } // end of method _Application::Quit
```

You should recognize both of these methods from the spell checker example in Chapter 3, "The Essentials for Using COM in Managed Code." Although they don't return success HRESULTs other than S_OK, they serve as instructive examples because one managed signature returns void whereas the other returns an object. Documents is an interface, and because none of the coclasses in Word's type library claim to implement it, its signature only shows up once in the Interop Assembly. On the other hand, the type library's Application coclass lists _Application as one of the interfaces it implements, so the Quit signature occurs twice in the Interop Assembly: inside the _Application interface and inside the ApplicationClass class.

> **TIP**
>
> When changing a signature in an Interop Assembly, remember to change the definition in the interface and any class that implements the interface. Failure to update all occurrences of the same signature in the same way usually results in a TypeLoadException, but could instead produce subtle incorrect behavior depending on the type of change.
>
> If you're changing the signature for an imported event's delegate (which can only be done in limited scenarios), there are at least four places to change: the source interface method, the generated delegate's Invoke signature, the sink helper's method (since it implements the source interface), and the call to the delegate's Invoke method inside the sink helper implementation.

Three metadata changes must be made when transforming a signature to expose its HRESULT return value:

1. If the return type is not void, add a by-reference parameter to the end of the parameter list with the type of the return value. This can be given any name that doesn't conflict with the other parameter names. Be sure to move any custom attributes (pseudo or otherwise) that are applied to the return type to the new parameter. If the return type is void, you can skip this whole step.

2. Change the return type of the method to int32, and mark it with marshal(error) to indicate that the integer is really an HRESULT type.

3. To make these signature changes work, the signature must be marked with preservesig to indicate that the metadata signature preserves the "raw" unmanaged signature. The preservesig keyword corresponds to the PreserveSigAttribute pseudo-custom attribute.

The transformed versions of the two Word signatures are shown in Listing 7.3.

LISTING 7.3   Metadata Definitions of Documents.Add and _Application.Quit After Making Manual Changes to Expose HRESULT Return Values

Documents.Add:

```
1:  .method public hidebysig newslot virtual abstract
2:      instance int32
3:      marshal(error)
4:      Add([in][opt] object&  marshal( struct) Template,
5:          [in][opt] object&  marshal( struct) NewTemplate,
```

LISTING 7.3 Continued

```
 6:         [in][opt] object&  marshal( struct) DocumentType,
 7:         [in][opt] object&  marshal( struct) Visible,
 8:         [out] class [Word]Word._Document& marshal(interface) retVal
 9:         ) runtime managed internalcall preservesig
10: {
11:    .custom instance void [mscorlib]
12:      System.Runtime.InteropServices.DispIdAttribute::.ctor(int32) =
13:        ( 01 00 0E 00 00 00 00 00 )
14:        } // end of method Documents::Add
```

_Application.Quit:

```
 1: .method public hidebysig newslot virtual abstract
 2:    instance int32 marshal(error)
 3:    Quit([in][opt] object&  marshal( struct) SaveChanges,
 4:         [in][opt] object&  marshal( struct) OriginalFormat,
 5:         [in][opt] object&  marshal( struct) RouteDocument
 6:         ) runtime managed internalcall preservesig
 7: {
 8:    .custom instance void [mscorlib]
 9:      System.Runtime.InteropServices.DispIdAttribute::.ctor(int32) =
10:        ( 01 00 51 04 00 00 00 00 )                    // ..Q.....
11: } // end of method _Application::Quit
```

You could make the int32 return type an unsigned int32 instead, but it's a good idea to stick with int32. You should already know the two reasons for this: the unsigned int32 type isn't in the CLS (and unusable from VB .NET) and the COMException class exposes its HRESULT as an int32 type. The marshal(error) is not really necessary, because it's only useful when late binding to a method with SCODE parameters. It's a good idea to use it, however, just for informational purposes.

Listing 7.4 shows what a .NET client might look like if using the original Microsoft Word Interop Assembly, and what the same client might look like if using the modified Interop Assembly.

LISTING 7.4 Two Versions of a C# Client—One That Uses the Original Assembly and One That Uses the Assembly with Modifications from Listing 7.3

Using the original assembly:

```
1: using System;
2:
3: public class UseWord
4: {
```

LISTING 7.4   Continued

```
 5:   public static void Main()
 6:   {
 7:     object missing = Type.Missing;
 8:
 9:     try
10:     {
11:       Word.Application msWord = new Word.Application();
12:       Word._Document doc = msWord.Documents.Add(ref missing, ref missing,
13:         ref missing, ref missing);
14:
15:       Console.WriteLine("Added the document '" + doc.FullName + "'.");
16:
17:       msWord.Quit(ref missing, ref missing, ref missing);
18:     }
19:     catch (Exception ex)
20:     {
21:       Console.WriteLine("Unexpected error: " + ex.ToString());
22:     }
23:   }
24: }
```

Using the modified assembly:

```
 1: using System;
 2:
 3: public class UseWord
 4: {
 5:   public static bool FAILED(int hr)
 6:   {
 7:     return (hr < 0);
 8:   }
 9:
10:   public static void Main()
11:   {
12:     object missing = Type.Missing;
13:     Word.Application msWord = null;
14:     try
15:     {
16:       msWord = new Word.Application();
17:     }
18:     catch (Exception ex)
19:     {
20:       Console.WriteLine("Unexpected error: " + ex.ToString());
21:       return;
22:     }
23:
```

LISTING 7.4   Continued

```
24:        int hr = 0; // S_OK
25:        Word._Document doc;
26:
27:        hr = msWord.Documents.Add(ref missing, ref missing, ref missing,
28:          ref missing, out doc);
29:        if (FAILED(hr))
30:        {
31:          Console.WriteLine("Unexpected error: 0x" + hr);
32:          return;
33:        }
34:
35:        try
36:        {
37:          Console.WriteLine("Added the document '" + doc.FullName + "'.");
38:        }
39:        catch (Exception ex)
40:        {
41:          Console.WriteLine("Unexpected error: " + ex.ToString());
42:          return;
43:        }
44:
45:        hr = msWord.Quit(ref missing, ref missing, ref missing);
46:        if (FAILED(hr))
47:          Console.WriteLine("Unexpected error: 0x" + hr);
48:    }
49: }
```

The first version of the client contains nothing new. The three main actions—instantiating the Application object, adding a document, and calling Quit—are all done within the try...catch block because they all throw exception on failure. This is not the case in the second code snippet. Notice the definition of FAILED in Lines 5–8 of the second client. This method is used like the FAILED macro prevalent in unmanaged C++ programs, returning true for any failure HRESULT and false for any success HRESULT. For a signed integer, if the severity bit is set then the number is less than zero.

Lines 29 and 46 call the FAILED method to check for success or failure in lieu of exception handling. On failure, Lines 31 and 47 print the value of the HRESULT return value. The _Document interface "returned" by the Add method now shows up as an out parameter in C#, as can be seen in Lines 27 and 28. No additional error information (such as a message) is automatically available, but could be obtained via a PInvoke call to the Windows GetErrorInfo API, or by calling Marshal.ThrowExceptionForHR (in System.Runtime.InteropServices) with the returned HRESULT. This method internally calls GetErrorInfo to populate the thrown exception with information.

Another option for creating an Interop Assembly with exposed HRESULT return types is to copy a type library and modify it before running the importer. In the IDL file (which you may have to obtain by running OLEVIEW.EXE on the type library), simply change each method's HRESULT return type to an int or long type. Now create a new type library by running MIDL.EXE or MKTYPLIB.EXE on the new IDL file. Running the type library on this modified type library produces an Interop Assembly full of methods marked with PreserveSigAttribute. The only thing missing from the Interop Assembly is the marshal(error) marking on the int return types, but we already know that this doesn't really matter. If you decide to try this, make sure that you're changing a *copy* of the type library then throwing it out after running the type library importer.

TIP

Marking a method with PreserveSigAttribute can be useful for more than just exposing success HRESULTs. If a COM object exposes information from an error object via customized interfaces (in other words, implementing an interface like IAdditionalErrorInfo in addition to IErrorInfo on an object passed to SetErrorInfo), then marking methods with PreserveSigAttribute is necessary to prevent the CLR from calling GetErrorInfo and swallowing the custom error object when a failure HRESULT is returned. After calling such a method marked with PreserveSigAttribute, managed code could then make a PInvoke call to GetErrorInfo, cast the returned object to a .NET definition of your customized interface (as in IAdditionalErrorInfo), then extract the desired information. When error objects only expose information via IErrorInfo, then changing signatures to use PreserveSigAttribute is not required because all the information (except the GUID returned from IErrorInfo.GetGUID) is copied to members of the .NET exception thrown by the CLR.

Arrays

Chapter 4, "An In-Depth Look at Imported Assemblies," outlined all the different types of arrays and the problems when attempting to use the metadata produced by the type library exporter. We'll look at the two main types of arrays separately—SAFEARRAYs and C-style arrays.

Exposing SAFEARRAYs Differently

A SAFEARRAY parameter, which looks like the following in a type library:

```
SAFEARRAY(long)
```

is either transformed into a single-dimensional array with a lower bound of zero (int32[] in IL Assembler syntax) or to a generic System.Array type (class [mscorlib]System.Array in IL Assembler syntax) so it can be used as a multi-dimensional array or as an array with non-zero lower bounds. The importer generates System.Array types for all SAFEARRAYs by default in Visual Studio .NET (or with the /sysarray option with TLBIMP.EXE).

It's sometimes helpful to have more fine-grained control over the transformation of SAFEARRAYs in metadata, deciding on a case-by-case basis. The change you can make to a single array parameter depends on how the array is used. If you know the number of dimensions of the array will always be the same and each dimension has a lower bound of zero, define it as *type*[] but place commas inside the brackets. The number of dimensions is one more than the number of commas, so whereas:

```
int32[]
```

is a one-dimensional array,

```
int32[,]
```

is a two-dimensional array,

```
int32[,,]
```

is a three-dimensional array, and so on.

If the number of dimensions can vary or if non-zero lower bounds are used, then the array type should be defined as the generic System.Array defined in the mscorlib assembly. This looks like the following:

```
class [mscorlib]System.Array
```

The mscorlib assembly is always referenced in an Interop Assembly, so no additional work is needed besides changing the parameter.

Adding Size Information to C-Style Arrays

As discussed in Chapter 4, C-style arrays look no different than a pointer to a single instance in a type library. Thus, a C-style array parameter looks like a by-reference type, for a method such as the following unmanaged C++ method:

```
STDMETHODIMP CArrayClass::ArrayParameter(long *a, long size)
{
  for (int i = 0; i < size; i++)
    printf("a[%d] = %d\n", i, a[i]);

  return S_OK;
}
```

The corresponding signature would look like the following in IL Assembler syntax:

```
.method public hidebysig newslot virtual abstract
  instance void  ArrayParameter([in] int32& a,
                                [in] int32 size) runtime managed internalcall
{
  .custom instance void
    [mscorlib]System.Runtime.InteropServices.DispIdAttribute::.ctor(int32)
    = ( 01 00 01 00 00 00 00 00 )
} // end of method IArrayClass::ArrayParameter
```

Such a signature should be changed to a simple one-dimensional zero-lower-bound array as follows:

```
.method public hidebysig newslot virtual abstract
  instance void  ArrayParameter([in] int32[] marshal([+1]) a,
                                [in] int32 size) runtime managed internalcall
{
  .custom instance void
    [mscorlib]System.Runtime.InteropServices.DispIdAttribute::.ctor(int32)
    = ( 01 00 01 00 00 00 00 00 )
} // end of method IArrayClass::ArrayParameter
```

The rule for converting this array is to simply replace & with [ ], and mark the parameter with a variation of marshal([ ]). This attribute specifies that the array is a C-style array (UnmanagedType.LPArray) and is necessary so the marshaler doesn't treat the parameter as a SAFEARRAY. If the signature contains a parameter with the size of the array, this information should be added to the managed signature using MarshalAsAttribute's SizeParamIndex named parameter. This value, valid only with UnmanagedType.LPArray, can be set to the index of the parameter (counting from zero) containing the size of the array. That is why the previous signature has:

```
marshal([+1])
```

This odd-looking syntax is equivalent to:

```
<MarshalAs(UnmanagedType.LPArray, SizeParamIndex:=1)>
```

in Visual Basic .NET. The plus sign distinguishes the number as a parameter index rather than the number of elements in the array. Using the SizeParamIndex feature is only supported on by-value array parameters, and the parameter containing the size must be a by-value integral parameter. If you have a signature that uses a by-reference size parameter or a by-reference C-style array, you should convert the array parameter to be an IntPtr (native int) type instead. (If the array has more than one level of indirection, you should pass the IntPtr as a by-reference parameter.)

DIGGING DEEPER

The size information marked with `SizeParamIndex` is only used by the Interop Marshaler when transforming an unmanaged array to a managed array. The size of any array allocated in managed code is known, thus no additional information is required. Because this feature can only be used on by-value arrays, marking a signature with this size information is only really necessary when implementing a method with such a signature in managed code that will be called by unmanaged code. If you don't specify this, your managed method will always see an array with one element when called from a COM client.

See Chapter 14, "Implementing COM Interfaces for Binary Compatibility," for more information about implementing COM interfaces in managed code.

The client for the previous transformed signature could look like the following in C#:

```
int [] a = {1, 2, 3, 4, 5};
ArrayClass o = new ArrayClass();
o.ArrayParameter(a, a.Length);
```

TIP

The easiest way to use a multi-dimensional C-style array in managed code is to define the signature just as you would for a one-dimensional C-style array. You can then treat it as a "flattened" array, with a length equal to the sum of all of its elements across all dimensions.

There's no support for defining C-style arrays as multi-dimensional in metadata because `UnmanagedType.LPArray` only works with one `SizeParamIndex` value and/or one `SizeConst` value. There's no way to specify individual sizes of multiple dimensions.

There's no way to express varying array functionality (passing only a slice of the C-style array) in a managed signature, unless you replace it with an `ArrayWithOffset` type. See Appendix A, "`System.Runtime.InteropServices` Reference," for information about this value type.

Custom Attributes

Some of the earlier examples showed custom attributes in IL Assembler syntax. Unlike pseudo-custom attributes, which each have their own syntax, all real custom attributes are structured as follows:

```
.custom instance void AttributeName::.ctor() = ( contents )
```

Unlike C#, Visual Basic .NET, and C++, you must not leave off the `Attribute` suffix from the name. Chapter 1 showed where to place custom attributes in C#, VB .NET, and C++ programs using an `ExampleAttribute` custom attribute. Listing 7.5 shows the placement of this attribute on all target types, but this time in IL Assembler syntax. Some of these are never seen in Interop Assemblies (for example the importer doesn't put any custom attributes on a module and never generates fields), but all are shown in the listing for your information.

LISTING 7.5 The Placement of the `ExampleAttribute` Custom Attribute on Any Type of Target Using IL Assembler Syntax

On an assembly:

```
.assembly MyAssembly
{
  .custom instance void ExampleAttribute::.ctor() = ( 01 00 00 00 )
  ...
}
```

On a module:

```
.module MyModule.dll
.custom instance void ExampleAttribute::.ctor() = ( 01 00 00 00 )
```

On a class:

```
.class public auto ansi beforefieldinit MyClass
       extends [mscorlib]System.Object
{
  .custom instance void ExampleAttribute::.ctor() = ( 01 00 00 00 )
  ...
}
```

On a struct:

```
.class public sequential ansi sealed beforefieldinit MyStruct
       extends [mscorlib]System.ValueType
{
  .custom instance void ExampleAttribute::.ctor() = ( 01 00 00 00 )
  ...
}
```

On a method:

```
.method public hidebysig newslot virtual abstract
  instance void MyMethod() cil managed
{
```

Modifying Interop Assemblies

CHAPTER 7

353

7

MODIFYING
INTEROP
ASSEMBLIES

LISTING 7.5   Continued

```
.custom instance void ExampleAttribute::.ctor() = ( 01 00 00 00 )
...
}
```

On a parameter:

```
.method public hidebysig instance void MyMethod(string s,
  int32 i, float64 d) cil managed
{
  ... custom attributes on the method go here
  .param [1] // Applied to first parameter
  .custom instance void ExampleAttribute::.ctor() = ( 01 00 00 00 )
  .param [3] // Applied to third parameter
  .custom instance void ExampleAttribute::.ctor() = ( 01 00 00 00 )
  ...
}
```

On a return value:

```
.method public hidebysig instance void MyMethod(string s) cil managed
{
  ... custom attributes on the method go here
  .param [0] // Return value is treated like a 0th parameter
  .custom instance void ExampleAttribute::.ctor() = ( 01 00 00 00 )
  ...
}
```

On a property:

```
.property instance string MyProperty()
{
  .custom instance void ExampleAttribute::.ctor() = ( 01 00 00 00 )
  ...
}
```

On an event:

```
.event [mscorlib]System.EventHandler MyEvent
{
  .custom instance void ExampleAttribute::.ctor() = ( 01 00 00 00 )
  ...
}
```

On a delegate:

```
.class public auto ansi sealed MyDelegate
      extends [mscorlib]System.MulticastDelegate
{
```

LISTING 7.5   Continued

```
  .custom instance void ExampleAttribute::.ctor() = ( 01 00 00 00 )
  ...
}
```

On an enumeration:

```
.class public auto ansi sealed MyEnum
       extends [mscorlib]System.Enum
{
  .custom instance void ExampleAttribute::.ctor() = ( 01 00 00 00 )
  ...
}
```

On an interface:

```
.class interface public abstract auto ansi MyInterface
{
  .custom instance void ExampleAttribute::.ctor() = ( 01 00 00 00 )
  ...
}
```

On a field:

```
.field private int32 myField
.custom instance void ExampleAttribute::.ctor() = ( 01 00 00 00 )
```

Now that you've seen what custom attributes look like wherever they appear, let's look at how to make some custom attribute modifications to make Interop Assemblies work better.

Changing Attribute Contents

How do you know what an attribute's contents should look like (such as the 01 00 00 00 in the previous examples)? As pictured in Figure 7.2, custom attribute contents always start with 01, followed by four bytes containing the size of the remaining data. This data could be a number, a boolean value (where 01 is true and 00 is false) or Unicode characters comprising a string. After the data, four bytes typically end the custom attribute to specify the number of named properties or fields that the attribute contains. This explains why a custom attribute with no additional data, such as ExampleAttribute, has the contents of 01 00 00 00. The count of named properties or fields is optional, so it might not always be present.

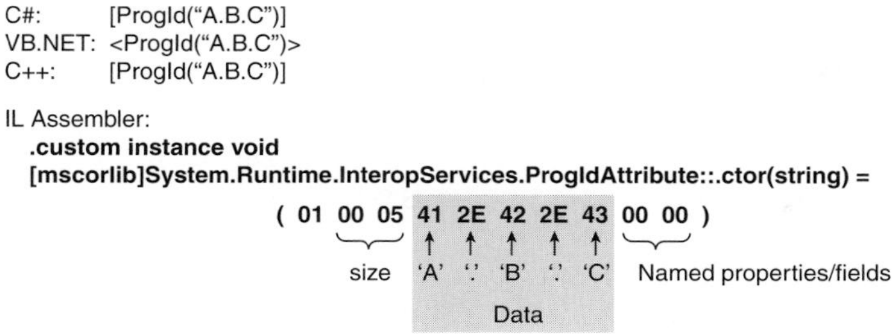

```
C#:       [ProgId("A.B.C")]
VB.NET:   <ProgId("A.B.C")>
C++:      [ProgId("A.B.C")]
```

IL Assembler:
> **.custom instance void**
> **[mscorlib]System.Runtime.InteropServices.ProgIdAttribute::.ctor(string) =**

(01 00 05 **41 2E 42 2E 43** 00 00)

size · 'A' '.' 'B' '.' 'C' · Named properties/fields

Data

FIGURE 7.2
Custom attribute contents are comprised of three parts and are shown as hexadecimal digits in IL Assembler syntax.

When an input type library contains incorrect information, fixing it in metadata might require you to change a custom attribute's contents. The previous chapter mentioned a problem in the original DirectX 8 for Visual Basic type library, in which the Direct3DDevice8 interface was marked with this IID:

7385E4DF-8FE8-41D5-86B6-D7B48547B6CF

instead of the correct one:

7385E5DF-8FE8-41D5-86B6-D7B48547B6CF

To make such a change in metadata, you simply need to find the definition of Direct3DDevice8 in its IL file:

```
.class interface public abstract auto ansi import Direct3DDevice8
{
  .custom instance void [mscorlib]
    System.Runtime.InteropServices.GuidAttribute::.ctor(string) =
    ( 01 00 24 37 33 38 35 45 34 44 46 2D 38 46 45 38   // ..$7385E4DF-8FE8
      2D 34 31 44 35 2D 38 36 42 36 2D 44 37 42 34 38   // -41D5-86B6-D7B48
      35 34 37 42 36 43 46 00 00 )                      // 547B6CF..
  .custom instance void [mscorlib]
    System.Runtime.InteropServices.ComConversionLossAttribute::.ctor() =
    ( 01 00 00 00 )
  .custom instance void [mscorlib]
    System.Runtime.InteropServices.InterfaceTypeAttribute::.ctor(int16) =
    ( 01 00 01 00 00 00 )
  ...
}
```

Then change the first 34 (the hexadecimal value representing the "4" character in GuidAttribute's string) to 35 (the value representing "5"). Making this change looks like the following:

```
.class interface public abstract auto ansi import Direct3DDevice8
{
  .custom instance void [mscorlib]
    System.Runtime.InteropServices.GuidAttribute::.ctor(string) =
    ( 01 00 24 37 33 38 35 45 35 44 46 2D 38 46 45 38    // ..$7385E5DF-8FE8
      2D 34 31 44 35 2D 38 36 42 36 2D 44 37 42 34 38    // -41D5-86B6-D7B48
      35 34 37 42 36 43 46 00 00 )                       // 547B6CF..
  .custom instance void [mscorlib]
    System.Runtime.InteropServices.ComConversionLossAttribute::.ctor() =
    ( 01 00 00 00 )
  .custom instance void [mscorlib]
    System.Runtime.InteropServices.InterfaceTypeAttribute::.ctor(int16) =
    ( 01 00 01 00 00 00 )
  ...
}
```

Of course, updating the comment containing the IID's string representation is not necessary. You'd see it updated automatically if you later disassembled the modified Interop Assembly.

Marking Classes as Visual Basic Modules

As explained in Chapter 4, although type libraries can have both modules and coclasses, the .NET Framework combines these into the single notion of a class. Visual Basic .NET, however, has the notion of a module that can contain static (shared) members. In metadata, a VB .NET module is simply a class with a custom attribute—`Microsoft.VisualBasic.CompilerServices. StandardModuleAttribute` defined in the `Microsoft.VisualBasic` assembly.

All you need to do to turn any class in an Interop Assembly into a module is to mark it with this attribute. Because members of modules can be used in VB .NET without being qualified by the module name (as in Visual Basic 6), this is a nice alteration to make to classes that were originally type library modules. For an example, let's look at the `DINPUT8STRINGCONSTANTS` class in the DirectX 8 Interop Assembly (imported from `DX8VB.DLL`):

```
.class public abstract auto ansi DINPUT8STRINGCONSTANTS
       extends [mscorlib]System.Object
{
  .field public static literal  marshal( bstr) string DIPROP_AUTOCENTER =
"diprop_autocenter"
  .field public static literal  marshal( bstr) string DIPROP_AXISMODE =
"diprop_axismode"
  .field public static literal  marshal( bstr) string DIPROP_BUFFERSIZE =
"diprop_buffersize"
  .field public static literal  marshal( bstr) string DIPROP_CALIBRATIONMODE =
```

```
"diprop_calibrationmode"
  .field public static literal  marshal( bstr) string DIPROP_DEADZONE =
"diprop_deadzone"
  .field public static literal  marshal( bstr) string DIPROP_RANGE =
"diprop_range"
  .field public static literal  marshal( bstr) string DIPROP_SATURATION =
"diprop_saturation"
  .field public static literal  marshal( bstr) string DIPROP_KEYNAME =
"diprop_keyname"
  .field public static literal  marshal( bstr) string DIPROP_SCANCODE =
"diprop_scancode"
} // end of class DINPUT8STRINGCONSTANTS
```

DINPUT8STRINGCONSTANTS is a module in the original type library, so Visual Basic 6 clients can refer to DIPROP_AUTOCENTER rather than the more cumbersome DINPUT8STRINGCONSTANTS. DIPROP_AUTOCENTER. To mark this as a VB .NET module, add the following text:

```
.class public abstract auto ansi DINPUT8STRINGCONSTANTS
        extends [mscorlib]System.Object
{
  .custom instance void [Microsoft.VisualBasic]
   Microsoft.VisualBasic.CompilerServices.StandardModuleAttribute::.ctor()
   = ( 01 00 00 00 )
  .field public static literal  marshal( bstr) string DIPROP_AUTOCENTER =
"diprop_autocenter"
  .field public static literal  marshal( bstr) string DIPROP_AXISMODE =
"diprop_axismode"
  .field public static literal  marshal( bstr) string DIPROP_BUFFERSIZE =
"diprop_buffersize"
  .field public static literal  marshal( bstr) string DIPROP_CALIBRATIONMODE =
"diprop_calibrationmode"
  .field public static literal  marshal( bstr) string DIPROP_DEADZONE =
"diprop_deadzone"
  .field public static literal  marshal( bstr) string DIPROP_RANGE =
"diprop_range"
  .field public static literal  marshal( bstr) string DIPROP_SATURATION =
"diprop_saturation"
  .field public static literal  marshal( bstr) string DIPROP_KEYNAME =
"diprop_keyname"
  .field public static literal  marshal( bstr) string DIPROP_SCANCODE =
"diprop_scancode"
} // end of class DINPUT8STRINGCONSTANTS
```

The data inside the custom attribute—01 00 00 00—indicates that the attribute has no parameters. One more addition is needed for the previous change to work. We need to add a reference to the `Microsoft.VisualBasic` assembly, otherwise `ILASM.EXE` would give the following error when reassembling the IL file:

```
DxVBLibA.il(8532) : error — Undefined assembly ref 'Microsoft.VisualBasic'
```

To add a reference to the assembly, add the following `.assembly extern` block in the same location as the other `.assembly extern` blocks, for example after the reference to `mscorlib`:

```
.assembly extern mscorlib
{
  .publickeytoken = (B7 7A 5C 56 19 34 E0 89 )          // .z\V.4..
  .ver 1:0:3300:0
}
.assembly extern Microsoft.VisualBasic
{
  .publickeytoken = (B0 3F 5F 7F 11 D5 0A 3A )          // .?_....:
  .ver 7:0:3300:0
}
```

The `.publickeytoken`, and `.ver` values must correspond to the desired version of the `Microsoft.VisualBasic` assembly. The easiest way to get this information is to disassemble an assembly that references it. If you don't know of any, it's trivial to create one that does. Compiling any simple Visual Basic .NET program automatically references the assembly.

That's all there is to it. Of course, this change only benefits VB .NET clients. Other languages ignore this VB-specific attribute and see such classes as regular classes whose static members still need to be qualified with the class name. Also, because the type library importer only preserves a module's constants and not its methods, no .NET clients are able to call a module's methods. In the "Adding Methods to Modules" section, you'll see a way to fix this.

Adding Back `helpstring` Information

One of the sorely missed pieces of type library information that is not preserved in an Interop Assembly is the contents of IDL `helpstring` attributes. The `helpstring` attribute can be found on anything in a type library, and contains a description of the item it's attached to. For example, the Microsoft Internet Controls type library (`SHDOCVW.DLL`) defines the following `ISearch` interface with documentation in these attributes:

```
[
  odl,
  uuid(BA9239A4-3DD5-11D2-BF8B-00C04FB93661),
  helpstring("Enumerated Search"),
  hidden,
  dual,
  oleautomation
]
```

```
interface ISearch : IDispatch {
    [id(0x60020000), propget, helpstring("Get search title")]
    HRESULT Title([out, retval] BSTR* pbstrTitle);
    [id(0x60020001), propget, helpstring("Get search guid")]
    HRESULT Id([out, retval] BSTR* pbstrId);
    [id(0x60020002), propget, helpstring("Get search url")]
    HRESULT URL([out, retval] BSTR* pbstrUrl);
};
```

Here the `helpstring` attributes provide (arguably) helpful descriptions of the interface and each one of its properties. Clients like Visual Basic 6 can use these strings to display helpful information. You can see this information in the Visual Basic 6 property browser and object browser.

The closest equivalent to the IDL `helpstring` attribute in the .NET world is `System.ComponentModel.DescriptionAttribute`. Visual Studio .NET uses this attribute to display helpful information in its property and event browser. Although `DescriptionAttribute` is meant for properties and events, it's marked with `AttributeUsage(AttributeTargets.All)`. Thus, we can apply this attribute to anything in an Interop Assembly—using it wherever the `helpstring` attribute exists on the corresponding element in the type library. It's a time-consuming task to do this manually for large assemblies, but can be done nonetheless to provide built-in documentation.

FAQ: Why doesn't the type library importer save the `helpstring` contents in `DescriptionAttribute` automatically?

`DescriptionAttribute` isn't quite the same thing as `helpstring`. For one thing, `DescriptionAttribute` is really meant for Windows Forms controls unlike the universally-used `helpstring`. Whereas `helpstring` contains a localized string (one that can adapt to the current user's locale), `DescriptionAttribute` contains a simple string. For this reason, and to avoid bloating an Interop Assembly's metadata, the importer ignores `helpstring` attributes in the type library.

Adding `DescriptionAttributes` manually isn't hard, but generating the right contents manually can be tedious because the strings must be expressed as a list of hexadecimal Unicode values. Probably the easiest way to get each attribute's contents is to write each attribute with each string in a higher-level language, compile a temporary assembly that you can disassemble, then copy the attributes in IL Assembler syntax.

For example, the following temporary C# source:

```
using System.ComponentModel;
[Description("Enumerated Search")]
public interface ISearch {}
```

gives us the necessary syntax for ISearch's helpstring after compiling it and disassembling the assembly:

```
.custom instance void [System]
  System.ComponentModel.DescriptionAttribute::.ctor(string) =
  ( 01 00 11 45 6E 75 6D 65 72 61 74 65 64 20 53 65    // ...Enumerated Se
    61 72 63 68 00 00 )                                // arch..
```

Listing 7.6 contains the original metadata produced by the type library importer for the ISearch interface, and Listing 7.7 shows how to modify the metadata to add in DescriptionAttributes with the type library's helpstring information.

LISTING 7.6   Original Metadata Produced for the ISearch Interface in the Microsoft Internet Controls Type Library

```
 1: .class interface public abstract auto ansi import ISearch
 2: {
 3:   .custom instance void [mscorlib]
 4:   System.Runtime.InteropServices.TypeLibTypeAttribute::.ctor(int16) =
 5:   ( 01 00 50 10 00 00 )                               // ..P...
 6:   .custom instance void [mscorlib]
 7:   System.Runtime.InteropServices.GuidAttribute::.ctor(string) =
 8:   ( 01 00 24 42 41 39 32 33 39 41 34 2D 33 44 44 35   // ..$BA9239A4-3DD5
 9:     2D 31 31 44 32 2D 42 46 38 42 2D 30 30 43 30 34   // -11D2-BF8B-00C04
10:     46 42 39 33 36 36 31 00 00 )                      // FB93661..
11:
12:   .method public hidebysig specialname virtual abstract
13:           instance string get_Title() runtime managed internalcall
14:   {
15:     .custom instance void [mscorlib]
16:     System.Runtime.InteropServices.DispIdAttribute::.ctor(int32) =
17:     ( 01 00 00 00 02 60 00 00 )                        // .....`..
18:   } // end of method ISearch::get_Title
19:
20:   .method public hidebysig specialname virtual abstract
21:           instance string get_Id() runtime managed internalcall
22:   {
23:     .custom instance void [mscorlib]
24:     System.Runtime.InteropServices.DispIdAttribute::.ctor(int32) =
25:     ( 01 00 01 00 02 60 00 00 )                        // .....`..
26:   } // end of method ISearch::get_Id
27:
```

LISTING 7.6 Continued

```
28:    .method public hidebysig specialname virtual abstract
29:            instance string get_URL() runtime managed internalcall
30:    {
31:      .custom instance void [mscorlib]
32:      System.Runtime.InteropServices.DispIdAttribute::.ctor(int32) =
33:      ( 01 00 02 00 02 60 00 00 )                          // .....`..
34:    } // end of method ISearch::get_URL
35:
36:    .property string Title()
37:    {
38:      .custom instance void [mscorlib]
39:      System.Runtime.InteropServices.DispIdAttribute::.ctor(int32) =
40:      ( 01 00 00 00 02 60 00 00 )                          // .....`..
41:      .get instance string SHDocVw.ISearch::get_Title()
42:    } // end of property ISearch::Title
43:
44:    .property string Id()
45:    {
46:      .custom instance void [mscorlib]
47:      System.Runtime.InteropServices.DispIdAttribute::.ctor(int32) =
48:      ( 01 00 01 00 02 60 00 00 )                          // .....`..
49:      .get instance string SHDocVw.ISearch::get_Id()
50:    } // end of property ISearch::Id
51:
52:    .property string URL()
53:    {
54:      .custom instance void [mscorlib]
55:      System.Runtime.InteropServices.DispIdAttribute::.ctor(int32) =
56:      ( 01 00 02 00 02 60 00 00 )                          // .....`..
57:      .get instance string SHDocVw.ISearch::get_URL()
58:    } // end of property ISearch::URL
59: } // end of class ISearch
```

LISTING 7.7 Metadata for the `ISearch` Interface with Added `DescriptionAttributes`

```
1: .assembly extern System
2: {
3:    .publickeytoken = (B7 7A 5C 56 19 34 E0 89 )          // .z\V.4..
4:    .ver 1:0:3300:0
5: }
6: ...
7: .class interface public abstract auto ansi import ISearch
8: {
```

LISTING 7.7   Continued

```
 9:    .custom instance void [System]
10:    System.ComponentModel.DescriptionAttribute::.ctor(string) =
11:    ( 01 00 11 45 6E 75 6D 65 72 61 74 65 64 20 53 65   // ...Enumerated Se
12:      61 72 63 68 00 00 )                               // arch..
13:    .custom instance void [mscorlib]
14:    System.Runtime.InteropServices.TypeLibTypeAttribute::.ctor(int16) =
15:    ( 01 00 50 10 00 00 )                               // ..P...
16:    .custom instance void [mscorlib]
17:    System.Runtime.InteropServices.GuidAttribute::.ctor(string) =
18:    ( 01 00 24 42 41 39 32 33 39 41 34 2D 33 44 44 35   // ..$BA9239A4-3DD5
19:      2D 31 31 44 32 2D 42 46 38 42 2D 30 30 43 30 34   // -11D2-BF8B-00C04
20:      46 42 39 33 36 36 31 00 00 )                      // FB93661..
21:
22:    .method public hidebysig specialname virtual abstract
23:            instance string get_Title() runtime managed internalcall
24:    {
25:      .custom instance void [mscorlib]
26:      System.Runtime.InteropServices.DispIdAttribute::.ctor(int32) =
27:      ( 01 00 00 00 02 60 00 00 )                       // .....`..
28:    } // end of method ISearch::get_Title
29:
30:    .method public hidebysig specialname virtual abstract
31:            instance string get_Id() runtime managed internalcall
32:    {
33:      .custom instance void [mscorlib]
34:      System.Runtime.InteropServices.DispIdAttribute::.ctor(int32) =
35:      ( 01 00 01 00 02 60 00 00 )                       // .....`..
36:    } // end of method ISearch::get_Id
37:
38:    .method public hidebysig specialname virtual abstract
39:            instance string get_URL() runtime managed internalcall
40:    {
41:      .custom instance void [mscorlib]
42:      System.Runtime.InteropServices.DispIdAttribute::.ctor(int32) =
43:      ( 01 00 02 00 02 60 00 00 )                       // .....`..
44:    } // end of method ISearch::get_URL
45:
46:    .property string Title()
47:    {
48:      .custom instance void [System]
49:      System.ComponentModel.DescriptionAttribute::.ctor(string) =
50:      ( 01 00 10 47 65 74 20 73 65 61 72 63 68 20 74 69  // ...Get search ti
51:        74 6C 65 00 00 )                                // tle..
52:      .custom instance void [mscorlib]
```

LISTING 7.7   Continued

```
53:        System.Runtime.InteropServices.DispIdAttribute::.ctor(int32) =
54:        ( 01 00 00 00 02 60 00 00 )                    // .....`..
55:        .get instance string SHDocVw.ISearch::get_Title()
56:    } // end of property ISearch::Title
57:
58:    .property string Id()
59:    {
60:      .custom instance void [System]
61:      System.ComponentModel.DescriptionAttribute::.ctor(string) =
62:      ( 01 00 0F 47 65 74 20 73 65 61 72 63 68 20 67 75   // ...Get search gu
63:        69 64 00 00 )                                 // id..
64:      .custom instance void [mscorlib]
65:      System.Runtime.InteropServices.DispIdAttribute::.ctor(int32) =
66:      ( 01 00 01 00 02 60 00 00 )                    // .....`..
67:      .get instance string SHDocVw.ISearch::get_Id()
68:    } // end of property ISearch::Id
69:
70:    .property string URL()
71:    {
72:      .custom instance void [System]
73:      System.ComponentModel.DescriptionAttribute::.ctor(string) =
74:      ( 01 00 0E 47 65 74 20 73 65 61 72 63 68 20 75 72   // ...Get search ur
75:        6C 00 00 )                                    // l..
76:      .custom instance void [mscorlib]
77:      System.Runtime.InteropServices.DispIdAttribute::.ctor(int32) =
78:      ( 01 00 02 00 02 60 00 00 )                    // .....`..
79:      .get instance string SHDocVw.ISearch::get_URL()
80:    } // end of property ISearch::URL
81: } // end of class ISearch
```

First, a reference to the System assembly needed to be added in Lines 1–5 because that's the assembly containing System.ComponentModel.DescriptionAttribute.

Notice that the attributes were only added to the interface and its properties, not their associated accessor methods. Because the accessor methods are usually hidden from any IDE that may take advantage of DescriptionAttribute information, there's no point in marking them. Adding all of this information manually for an entire assembly can be quite time-consuming, so writing a program to scan a type library and add these attributes might be in order for those serious about adding them.

Adding Custom Marshalers

Custom marshaling is an advanced topic discussed in Chapter 20, "Custom Marshaling." The bottom line is that you can write a custom marshaler to transform any COM interface type into any .NET reference type when used as a parameter, field, or return type. The problem with the custom marshaling mechanism is that the managed signature must be marked as using a custom marshaler. The type library importer only recognizes a handful of built-in custom marshalers, and there's no standard mechanism to plug-in your own. As a result, the disassemble/reassemble technique must be used to apply user-defined custom marshalers to types in an Interop Assembly.

For an example, let's look at the DirectX 7 for Visual Basic type library. In this type library the DirectDrawSurface7 interface has the following SetFont method:

```
HRESULT _stdcall SetFont([in] IFont* font);
```

This looks like the following in an IL file:

```
.method public hidebysig newslot virtual abstract
  instance void  SetFont([in] class DxVBLib.IFont  marshal( interface) font)
  runtime managed internalcall
{
} // end of method DirectDrawSurface7::SetFont
```

DIGGING DEEPER

Notice that the IFont type in the DirectDrawSurface7.SetFont signature is defined in the DxVBLib namespace and in the same assembly, despite the fact that IFont is a famous COM interface defined in the OLE Automation type library (STDOLE2.TLB). This is an occurrence of the classic identity problem with .NET and COM. The IFont interface is redefined in the type library and works just fine for COM clients because its IID matches the IFont IID defined elsewhere. For .NET clients, however, this IFont interface is incompatible with the official IFont interface.

Although the DxVBLib.IFont type is different from the official IFont, it doesn't matter for most custom marshaling scenarios. Had the official IFont definition been used, the SetFont signature would look like:

```
.method public hidebysig newslot virtual abstract
  instance void  SetFont([in] class [stdole]stdole.IFont  marshal(
interface) font)
  runtime managed internalcall
{
} // end of method DirectDrawSurface7::SetFont
```

Changing signatures to reference official type definitions in Primary Interop Assemblies rather than duplicate type definitions is a great modification, and should be done if you're creating your own PIA.

Let's assume that there's a special custom marshaler class called `FontMarshaler` contained in the namespace `MyCompany.CustomMarshalers` in an assembly called `MyCustomMarshalers` that can transform any COM `IFont` type into the .NET `System.Drawing.Font` type. (An example of writing such a class is shown in Chapter 20.) This custom marshaler can be applied to the signature by changing it to something like the following:

```
.method public hidebysig newslot virtual abstract
   instance void  SetFont([in] class [System.Drawing]System.Drawing.Font
   marshal(custom("MyCompany.CustomMarshalers.FontMarshaler, MyCustomMarshalers,
➡ Version=1.0.0.0, Culture=neutral, PublicKeyToken=e1a867530915b145", "")) font)
        runtime managed internalcall
{
} // end of method DirectDrawSurface7::SetFont
```

The first string inside `marshal(custom(…))` must contain the fully-qualified type name and the complete assembly identity. It's okay to completely change the type of the parameter, because the custom marshaler class is invoked at run time to handle the transformation between the new type and the original type. For a transformation such as this, you'd need to add a reference to the `System.Drawing` assembly at the top of the IL file so the definition of `System.Drawing.Font` could be found. For example, this might look like:

```
.assembly extern System.Drawing
{
  .publickeytoken = (B0 3F 5F 7F 11 D5 0A 3A )                // .?_....:
  .ver 1:0:3300:0
}
```

The type library importer only marks `IEnumVARIANT` and `IDispatchEx` types as marshaled with a custom marshaler, as mentioned in Chapter 4. If you don't like this behavior, perhaps because of performance concerns, you could remove the custom marshaler marking by replacing, for example:

```
System.Collections.IEnumerator marshal(custom(
"System.Runtime.InteropServices.CustomMarshalers.EnumeratorToEnumVariant,
➡ CustomMarshalers, Version=1.0.3300.0, Culture=neutral,
➡ PublicKeyToken=b03f5f7f11d50a3a", ""))
```

with simply:

```
[stdole]stdole.IEnumVARIANT
```

and adding a reference to the `stdole` Primary Interop Assembly if one doesn't already exist.

> **CAUTION**
>
> Removing custom marshaler usage in an Interop Assembly is not recommended, because custom marshalers help enable COM components to behave as .NET clients expect. In addition, every custom marshaler that the type library importer uses provides a mechanism for communicating with the original COM interface (such as IEnumVARIANT). This is discussed in Chapter 20.

Adding DISPIDs

Chapter 5 described a source interface in the Microsoft PowerPoint 2002 type library that does not mark its members with DISPIDs. To handle these events using an Interop Assembly generated by the type library importer, each member of the PowerPoint.EApplication interface should be marked with the DISPID that PowerPoint uses to call each member. Listing 7.8 shows an updated interface with all the correct DISPIDs. If a PIA for this type library is made available, it should already contain this customization.

LISTING 7.8   Manually Added DISPIDs for the EApplication Interface in the Microsoft PowerPoint Interop Assembly

```
 1: .class interface public abstract auto ansi import EApplication
 2: {
 3:    .custom instance void [mscorlib]
 4:    System.Runtime.InteropServices.GuidAttribute::.ctor(string) =
 5:    ( 01 00 24 39 31 34 39 33 34 43 32 2D 35 41 39 31    // ..$914934C2-5A91
 6:      2D 31 31 43 46 2D 38 37 30 30 2D 30 30 41 41 30    // -11CF-8700-00AA0
 7:      30 36 30 32 36 33 42 00 00 )                       // 060263B..
 8:    .custom instance void [mscorlib]
 9:    System.Runtime.InteropServices.TypeLibTypeAttribute::.ctor(int16) =
10:    ( 01 00 00 10 00 00 )
11:
12:    .method public hidebysig newslot virtual abstract
13:      instance void  WindowSelectionChange([in] class PowerPoint.Selection
14:        marshal( interface) Sel) runtime managed internalcall
15:    {
16:      .custom instance void [mscorlib]
17:      System.Runtime.InteropServices.DispIdAttribute::.ctor(int32) =
18:      ( 01 00 D1 07 00 00 00 00 )
19:    } // end of method EApplication::WindowSelectionChange
20:
21:    .method public hidebysig newslot virtual abstract
22:      instance void  WindowBeforeRightClick([in] class PowerPoint.Selection
```

LISTING 7.8 Continued

```
23:        marshal( interface) Sel, [in][out] bool& Cancel)
24:        runtime managed internalcall
25:    {
26:      .custom instance void [mscorlib]
27:      System.Runtime.InteropServices.DispIdAttribute::.ctor(int32) =
28:      ( 01 00 D2 07 00 00 00 00 )
29:    } // end of method EApplication::WindowBeforeRightClick
30:
31:    .method public hidebysig newslot virtual abstract
32:      instance void  WindowBeforeDoubleClick([in] class PowerPoint.Selection
33:        marshal( interface) Sel, [in][out] bool& Cancel)
34:        runtime managed internalcall
35:    {
36:      .custom instance void [mscorlib]
37:      System.Runtime.InteropServices.DispIdAttribute::.ctor(int32) =
38:      ( 01 00 D3 07 00 00 00 00 )
39:    } // end of method EApplication::WindowBeforeDoubleClick
40:
41:    .method public hidebysig newslot virtual abstract
42:      instance void  PresentationClose([in] class PowerPoint.Presentation
43:        marshal( interface) Pres) runtime managed internalcall
44:    {
45:      .custom instance void [mscorlib]
46:      System.Runtime.InteropServices.DispIdAttribute::.ctor(int32) =
47:      ( 01 00 D4 07 00 00 00 00 )
48:    } // end of method EApplication::PresentationClose
49:
50:    .method public hidebysig newslot virtual abstract
51:      instance void  PresentationSave([in] class PowerPoint.Presentation
52:        marshal( interface) Pres) runtime managed internalcall
53:    {
54:      .custom instance void [mscorlib]
55:      System.Runtime.InteropServices.DispIdAttribute::.ctor(int32) =
56:      ( 01 00 D5 07 00 00 00 00 )
57:    } // end of method EApplication::PresentationSave
58:
59:    .method public hidebysig newslot virtual abstract
60:      instance void  PresentationOpen([in] class PowerPoint.Presentation
61:        marshal( interface) Pres) runtime managed internalcall
62:    {
63:      .custom instance void [mscorlib]
64:      System.Runtime.InteropServices.DispIdAttribute::.ctor(int32) =
65:      ( 01 00 D6 07 00 00 00 00 )
66:    } // end of method EApplication::PresentationOpen
```

LISTING 7.8   Continued

```
 67:
 68:    .method public hidebysig newslot virtual abstract
 69:      instance void  NewPresentation([in] class PowerPoint.Presentation
 70:      marshal( interface) Pres) runtime managed internalcall
 71:    {
 72:      .custom instance void [mscorlib]
 73:      System.Runtime.InteropServices.DispIdAttribute::.ctor(int32) =
 74:      ( 01 00 D7 07 00 00 00 00 )
 75:    } // end of method EApplication::NewPresentation
 76:
 77:    .method public hidebysig newslot virtual abstract
 78:      instance void  PresentationNewSlide([in] class PowerPoint.Slide
 79:      marshal( interface) Sld) runtime managed internalcall
 80:    {
 81:      .custom instance void [mscorlib]
 82:      System.Runtime.InteropServices.DispIdAttribute::.ctor(int32) =
 83:      ( 01 00 D8 07 00 00 00 00 )
 84:    } // end of method EApplication::PresentationNewSlide
 85:
 86:    .method public hidebysig newslot virtual abstract
 87:      instance void  WindowActivate([in] class PowerPoint.Presentation
 88:      marshal( interface) Pres, [in] class PowerPoint.DocumentWindow
 89:      marshal( interface) Wn) runtime managed internalcall
 90:    {
 91:      .custom instance void [mscorlib]
 92:      System.Runtime.InteropServices.DispIdAttribute::.ctor(int32) =
 93:      ( 01 00 D9 07 00 00 00 00 )
 94:    } // end of method EApplication::WindowActivate
 95:
 96:    .method public hidebysig newslot virtual abstract
 97:      instance void  WindowDeactivate([in] class PowerPoint.Presentation
 98:      marshal( interface) Pres, [in] class PowerPoint.DocumentWindow
 99:      marshal( interface) Wn) runtime managed internalcall
100:    {
101:      .custom instance void [mscorlib]
102:      System.Runtime.InteropServices.DispIdAttribute::.ctor(int32) =
103:      ( 01 00 DA 07 00 00 00 00 )
104:    } // end of method EApplication::WindowDeactivate
105:
106:    .method public hidebysig newslot virtual abstract
107:      instance void  SlideShowBegin([in] class PowerPoint.SlideShowWindow
108:      marshal( interface) Wn) runtime managed internalcall
109:    {
110:      .custom instance void [mscorlib]
```

LISTING 7.8 Continued

```
111:      System.Runtime.InteropServices.DispIdAttribute::.ctor(int32) =
112:      ( 01 00 DB 07 00 00 00 00 )
113:    } // end of method EApplication::SlideShowBegin
114:
115:    .method public hidebysig newslot virtual abstract
116:      instance void SlideShowNextBuild([in] class PowerPoint.SlideShowWindow
117:      marshal( interface) Wn) runtime managed internalcall
118:    {
119:      .custom instance void [mscorlib]
120:      System.Runtime.InteropServices.DispIdAttribute::.ctor(int32) =
121:      ( 01 00 DC 07 00 00 00 00 )
122:    } // end of method EApplication::SlideShowNextBuild
123:
124:    .method public hidebysig newslot virtual abstract
125:      instance void SlideShowNextSlide([in] class PowerPoint.SlideShowWindow
126:      marshal( interface) Wn) runtime managed internalcall
127:    {
128:      .custom instance void [mscorlib]
129:      System.Runtime.InteropServices.DispIdAttribute::.ctor(int32) =
130:      ( 01 00 DD 07 00 00 00 00 )
131:    } // end of method EApplication::SlideShowNextSlide
132:
133:    .method public hidebysig newslot virtual abstract
134:      instance void  SlideShowEnd([in] class PowerPoint.Presentation
135:      marshal( interface) Pres) runtime managed internalcall
136:    {
137:      .custom instance void [mscorlib]
138:      System.Runtime.InteropServices.DispIdAttribute::.ctor(int32) =
139:      ( 01 00 DE 07 00 00 00 00 )
140:    } // end of method EApplication::SlideShowEnd
141:
142:    .method public hidebysig newslot virtual abstract
143:    instance void  PresentationPrint([in] class PowerPoint.Presentation
144:    marshal( interface) Pres) runtime managed internalcall
145:    {
146:      .custom instance void [mscorlib]
147:      System.Runtime.InteropServices.DispIdAttribute::.ctor(int32) =
148:      ( 01 00 DF 07 00 00 00 00 )
149:    } // end of method EApplication::PresentationPrint
150:
151:    .method public hidebysig newslot virtual abstract
152:      instance void  SlideSelectionChanged([in] class PowerPoint.SlideRange
153:      marshal( interface) SldRange) runtime managed internalcall
154:    {
```

LISTING 7.8   Continued

```
155:        .custom instance void [mscorlib]
156:        System.Runtime.InteropServices.DispIdAttribute::.ctor(int32) =
157:        ( 01 00 E0 07 00 00 00 00 )
158:      } // end of method EApplication::SlideSelectionChanged
159:
160:    .method public hidebysig newslot virtual abstract
161:        instance void  ColorSchemeChanged([in] class PowerPoint.SlideRange
162:        marshal( interface) SldRange) runtime managed internalcall
163:    {
164:        .custom instance void [mscorlib]
165:        System.Runtime.InteropServices.DispIdAttribute::.ctor(int32) =
166:        ( 01 00 E1 07 00 00 00 00 )
167:      } // end of method EApplication::ColorSchemeChanged
168:
169:    .method public hidebysig newslot virtual abstract
170:        instance void  PresentationBeforeSave([in] class
171:        PowerPoint.Presentation marshal( interface) Pres,
172:        [in][out] bool& Cancel) runtime managed internalcall
173:    {
174:        .custom instance void [mscorlib]
175:        System.Runtime.InteropServices.DispIdAttribute::.ctor(int32) =
176:        ( 01 00 E2 07 00 00 00 00 )
177:      } // end of method EApplication::PresentationBeforeSave
178:
179:    .method public hidebysig newslot virtual abstract
180:        instance void  SlideShowNextClick([in] class
181:        PowerPoint.SlideShowWindow  marshal( interface) Wn,
182:        [in] class PowerPoint.Effect  marshal( interface) nEffect)
183:        runtime managed internalcall
184:    {
185:        .custom instance void [mscorlib]
186:        System.Runtime.InteropServices.DispIdAttribute::.ctor(int32) =
187:        ( 01 00 E3 07 00 00 00 00 )
188:      } // end of method EApplication::SlideShowNextClick
189: } // end of class EApplication
```

TIP

As mentioned in Chapter 5, another metadata change that can be important to event handling is turning the private sink helper classes generated by the type library importer into public classes. This helps whenever an event source calls QueryInterface

Modifying Interop Assemblies

CHAPTER 7

371

7

MODIFYING
INTEROP
ASSEMBLIES

for `IDispatch` on the sink object returned via `IConnectionPoint.Advise`. The change can be done by changing a class like the following:

```
.class private auto ansi sealed ApplicationEvents_SinkHelper
  extends [mscorlib]System.Object
  implements Outlook.ApplicationEvents
```

to:

```
.class public auto ansi sealed ApplicationEvents_SinkHelper
  extends [mscorlib]System.Object
  implements Outlook.ApplicationEvents
```

Adding Back IDL Custom Attributes

Type library attributes such as `restricted` or `noncreatable` are stored in the three attributes `TypeLibTypeAttribute`, `TypeLibFuncAttribute`, and `TypeLibVarAttribute`, depending on what they're applied to. IDL has its own extensible custom attributes, however, that are ignored by the type library importer.

An IDL custom attribute has the following format:

```
[custom(guid, value)]
```

Unlike a .NET custom attribute, which is uniquely identified by its assembly, namespace, and name, IDL custom attributes are uniquely identified by a GUID. The *value* portion contains the attribute's data—anything that can fit inside a `VARIANT`.

If you use COM components that make use of these custom attributes and would like to preserve them in Interop Assemblies, you could define your own .NET custom attribute that can contain this information. In C#, such an attribute might look like the following:

```
using System;

[AttributeUsage(AttributeTargets.All)]
public class IdlCustomAttribute : Attribute
{
  private object value;
  private Guid guid;

  public IdlCustomAttribute(Guid guid, object value)
  {
    this.guid = guid;
    this.value = value;
  }
```

```
public object Value { get { return value; } }
public Guid Name { get { return guid; } }
}
```

Instances of this attribute could then be sprinkled throughout a disassembled Interop Assembly wherever the IDL custom attributes existed in the original type library. Of course, because there's no official universally recognized attribute that plays this role, doing this has limited applications.

Adding Methods to Modules

Because the type library importer ignores methods in any type library module, adding these methods to an Interop Assembly manually is often desirable. This can be done as follows:

1. If the module only contains methods (in other words, no constants) then the class needs to be added to the metadata because the importer skips it altogether. If the module contains any constants, the class is already present in the metadata and you can skip this step.

2. Mark the class as a Visual Basic module, as shown earlier in the "Marking Classes as Visual Basic Modules" section. This isn't necessary, but nice for VB .NET clients.

3. Add each method to the class. Because a module's methods are static entry points into a DLL, this uses PInvoke technology, covered in Part VI of this book. Therefore, the details of creating the appropriate method signatures won't be covered here.

Listing 7.9 shows the definition of a module in the DirectX 8 for Visual Basic type library with four methods. Listing 7.10 shows what the corresponding .NET class would look like if the class and its methods were manually added to the Interop Assembly.

LISTING 7.9   The IDL Definition of D3DCOLORAUX, a Module in the DirectX 8 for Visual Basic Type Library

```
 1: [
 2:   dllname("dx8vb.dll")
 3: ]
 4: module D3DCOLORAUX {
 5:   [entry(0x60000000), helpcontext(0x000150b5)]
 6:   long _stdcall D3DColorRGBA([in] short r, [in] short g, [in] short b,
 7:     [in] short a);
 8:   [entry(0x60000001), helpcontext(0x000150b3)]
 9:   long _stdcall D3DColorARGB([in] short a, [in] short r, [in] short g,
10:     [in] short b);
11:   [entry(0x60000002), helpcontext(0x000150b6)]
12:   long _stdcall D3DColorXRGB([in] short r, [in] short g, [in] short b);
```

Modifying Interop Assemblies

CHAPTER 7

373

7

MODIFYING
INTEROP
ASSEMBLIES

LISTING 7.9   Continued

```
13:    [entry(0x60000003), helpcontext(0x000150b4)]
14:    long _stdcall D3DColorMake([in] single r, [in] single g,
15:      [in] single b, [in] single a);
16: };
```

LISTING 7.10   The Hand-Crafted Metadata Definition of D3DCOLORAUX from Listing 7.9

```
.class public abstract auto ansi D3DCOLORAUX
  extends [mscorlib]System.Object
{
  .custom instance void [Microsoft.VisualBasic]
    Microsoft.VisualBasic.CompilerServices.StandardModuleAttribute::.ctor()
    = ( 01 00 00 00 )

  .method public hidebysig static pinvokeimpl("dx8vb.dll"
    as "VB_D3DColorRGBA" winapi)
  int32  D3DColorRGBA([in] int16 r, [in] int16 g, [in] int16 b,
                      [in] int16 a) cil managed preservesig
  {
  }
  .method public hidebysig static pinvokeimpl("dx8vb.dll"
    as "VB_D3DColorARGB" winapi)
  int32  D3DColorARGB([in] int16 a, [in] int16 r, [in] int16 g,
                      [in] int16 b) cil managed preservesig
  {
  }
  .method public hidebysig static pinvokeimpl("dx8vb.dll"
    as "VB_D3DColorXRGB" winapi)
  int32  D3DColorXRGB([in] int16 r, [in] int16 g,
                      [in] int16 b) cil managed preservesig
  {
  }
  .method public hidebysig static pinvokeimpl("dx8vb.dll"
    as "VB_D3DColorMake" winapi)
  int32  D3DColorMake([in] float32 r, [in] float32 g, [in] float32 b,
                      [in] float32 a) cil managed preservesig
  {
  }
} // end of class D3DCOLORAUX
```

Conclusion

After reading this chapter, you should be armed with the necessary techniques to handle whatever Interop Assemblies the type library importer might throw at you. Any changes you make must adhere to the rules of the CLR and the Interop Marshaler. The type library importer knows how to generate "correct" metadata, despite the fact that it may not suit your needs. If you change it to suit your needs, be sure you stay within the rules.

With all these modifications to metadata and a compiler (ILASM) much less restrictive than higher-level languages, how do you know if you make mistakes or break the rules? Fortunately, many mistakes are caught by ILASM when attempting to reassemble the IL file. Other errors can show up at run time when loading a type or calling a modified member, depending on the nature of the change. Common exceptions thrown for metadata changed in an inappropriate way are TypeLoadException, InvalidCastException, and MarshalingDirectiveException. The best advice to avoid such mistakes is to follow the guidelines in this chapter and be careful. Save an original copy of the type library and/or Interop Assembly (in a different directory or with a different name) just in case things go wrong.

> **TIP**
>
> The .NET Framework PE Verifier (PEVERIFY.EXE) ships with the .NET Framework SDK and can be run on modified assemblies to detect errors that the IL Assembler would not detect. This utility detects unverifiable code, which can easily be a result of an incorrect modification to an Interop Assembly. The type library importer almost never produces unverifiable code on its own.

> **DIGGING DEEPER**
>
> You might notice that disassembling and reassembling an assembly without making any changes can produce a slightly larger file. Because ILASM.EXE is a single-pass compiler, it may emit type references for types in the same assembly (that already have a type definition, or *TypeDef*) as if they were in a different one. These redundant type references are harmless, but add to the size of the binary file. These type references don't show up in the IL file, but can be seen in the advanced metadata view by pressing Ctrl+M when ILDASM.EXE is open in graphical mode.

Remember that using ILDASM.EXE and ILASM.EXE to modify an assembly isn't always the only option. If you're starting with IDL file to generate a type library, it's easiest just to modify the original source so the type library and the Interop Assembly contain the appropriate information. If starting with a type library, you could obtain an IDL representation from a tool like OLEVIEW.EXE (with the caveats mentioned in Chapter 4), modify it, then compile it (with MIDL.EXE or MKTYPLIB.EXE). Such techniques mainly serve as alternatives for the following sections of this chapter, because they rely on the type library importer exhibiting the desired behavior:

- Changing data types (for the most part)
- Changing attribute contents
- Adding DISPIDs

Sometimes modifying the type library might be easier for those people familiar with the MIDL compiler and all of its switches. Plus, as long as the IDL correctly reflects your COM component, you can be sure that the metadata you get from the type library importer is correct. For COM novices who just want to get the component working, modifying the assembly is usually much easier.

Another change that could either be made to the input type library or the output assembly is to add helpful types that were excluded from the original type library. Sometimes types such as enums can be useful for a COM component's APIs but are defined in a C++ header file rather than a type library. In this case, it's often easy to paste the C++ type definition into a temporary C# file, make minor syntax changes, then compile and disassemble it. This disassembled definition can then be inserted in your Interop Assembly.

When changes must be made to work around limitations of type library expressiveness or the importer's conversion process, then you have no choice but to modify the assembly. This applies to most of this chapter's sections, which described:

- Exposing success HRESULTs (to some extent)
- Exposing SAFEARRAYs differently
- Adding size information to C-style arrays
- Marking classes as Visual Basic modules
- Adding back helpstring information
- Adding custom marshalers
- Adding back IDL custom attributes
- Adding methods to modules

7

MODIFYING INTEROP ASSEMBLIES

CAUTION

Visual Studio .NET users should be extra careful when modifying an Interop Assembly because there may be multiple copies of it under your project folder. For example, there could be one in a Debug folder, a Release folder, and also a separate bin folder. Make sure that you replace all of the original Interop Assemblies with your new one.

Using .NET Components in COM Applications

IN THIS PART

8 The Essentials for Using .NET Components from COM   379

9 An In-Depth Look at Exported Type Libraries 425

10 Advanced Topics for Using .NET Components 459

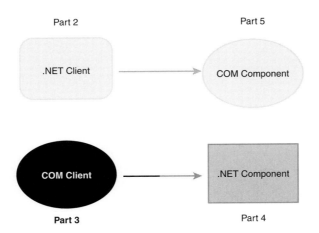

The Essentials for Using .NET Components from COM

IN THIS CHAPTER

- A Sample .NET Component   380
- Using a .NET Component in Visual Basic 6   382
- Using a .NET Component in Unmanaged Visual C++   385
- Using a .NET Component in Unmanaged JScript   388
- Assembly Registration   390
- The Type Library Exporter   394
- .NET Class Interfaces   397
- Interacting with a .NET Object   399
- Deploying a COM Application That Uses .NET   415
- Hosting Windows Forms Controls in Internet Explorer   417

It's time to switch gears and take our first glimpse at the other half of COM Interoperability—.NET components and the COM clients that use them. This chapter is structured similarly to Chapter 3, "The Essentials for Using COM in Managed Code."

First, we look at three quick examples—using a .NET component in a Visual Basic 6 application, in an unmanaged Visual C++ application (version 6.0 or 7.0), and from unmanaged script. After that, we examine some important concepts related to the exposure of .NET components to COM, then cover the basic interactions that can be done with .NET components from unmanaged code.

A Sample .NET Component

For the first examples of using a .NET component in COM applications, we'll use a simple .NET class written in C#, shown in Listing 8.1.

LISTING 8.1 StringValidator.cs. A Simple .NET Class We'll Use from COM Clients

```
 1: using System.Text.RegularExpressions;
 2: using System.Reflection;
 3:
 4: [assembly:AssemblyKeyFile("KeyFile.snk")]
 5:
 6: public class StringValidator
 7: {
 8:   public bool IsPhoneNumber(string s)
 9:   {
10:     return Regex.IsMatch(s,
11:       @"^(((\(\d{3}\)( )?)|(\d{3}( |\-)))\d{3}\-\d{4})$");
12:   }
13:
14:   public bool IsZipCode(string s)
15:   {
16:     return Regex.IsMatch(s, @"^((\d{5})|(\d{5}\-\d{4}))$");
17:   }
18:
19:   public bool IsSSN(string s)
20:   {
21:     return Regex.IsMatch(s, @"^\d{3}\-\d{2}\-\d{4}$");
22:   }
23: }
```

To compile this code, first generate a key file using the .NET Framework Strong Name Utility (SN.EXE) as follows:

```
sn -k KeyFile.snk
```

Then use the C# command-line compiler as follows, in the same directory as `KeyFile.snk`:

```
csc /t:library StringValidator.cs /r:System.dll
```

Line 4 uses the assembly-level `AssemblyKeyFileAttribute` custom attribute to give the `StringValidator` assembly a strong name. This makes it easy to globally share the assembly with COM clients.

This `StringValidator` class uses a single .NET regular expression API (`Regex.IsMatch`) available in the `System.Text.RegularExpressions` namespace in the `System` assembly. (If you're not familiar with regular expressions, then just trust that these methods do what they claim to do.)

`IsPhoneNumber` returns true if the input string represents a U.S. phone number; false otherwise. It accepts numbers in the following form, where *n* is a digit:

nnn nnn-nnnn

nnn-nnn-nnn

(nnn) nnn-nnnn

(nnn)nnn-nnnn

`IsZipCode` returns true if the input string represents a U.S. zip code; false otherwise. It accepts five-digit zip codes (*nnnnn*) or nine-digit zip codes (*nnnnn-nnnn*). `IsSSN` returns true if the input string represents a Social Security number (*nnn-nn-nnnn*) and false otherwise.

8

USING .NET COMPONENTS FROM COM

TIP

Notice the strings prefixed with @ in Lines 11, 16, and 21 in Listing 8.1. These are called *verbatim string literals*. Such a string is processed verbatim, meaning no escape characters are recognized—except for two quotes ("") representing one ("). Verbatim string literals can even span multiple lines, such as:

```
string s = @"Line 1
Line 2
Line 3 with a ""quoted"" word";
```

Verbatim string literals in C# are much like string literals in Visual Basic except for the fact that they can span multiple lines. Verbatim string literals are quite handy for strings that contain several backslashes, such as regular expressions, Windows directory names, or Windows Registry key names. With regular strings, every backslash would need to be escaped with an additional backslash.

Using a .NET Component in Visual Basic 6

We'll briefly run through the steps of using a .NET component in Visual Basic 6 in this section, saving detailed explanations for the remainder of the chapter after these first three examples. To use the StringValidator class from Visual Basic 6, do the following:

1. Register the assembly using the .NET Framework Assembly Registration Utility (REGASM.EXE) as follows:

   ```
   regasm StringValidator.dll /tlb
   ```

   The /tlb option creates and registers a type library with the name StringValidator.tlb.

2. Start Visual Basic 6 and create a new project, such as a Standard EXE project.

3. Add a reference to the desired type library by selecting Project, References… from the menu. This dialog was first shown in Figure 3.1 (in Chapter 3) but is shown again in Figure 8.1, highlighting the entry for our StringValidator type library.

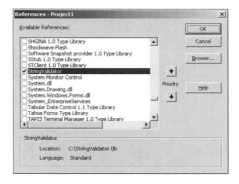

FIGURE 8.1

The Visual Basic 6 References dialog.

TIP

Often, type libraries for .NET assemblies do not contain a library-level helpstring to describe their contents, so they appear in the Visual Basic 6 References list with their simple assembly name (with underscores replacing periods). For example, the StringValidator assembly appears in the list simply as StringValidator. Other assemblies, such as mscorlib, customize their description with the System.Reflection. AssemblyDescriptionAttribute custom attribute. Therefore, the mscorlib.tlb type library appears in the list as Common Language Runtime Library. Don't confuse this

> with the `Common Language Runtime Execution Engine 1.0 Library` entry, a type library that describes COM types exposed by the CLR execution engine for advanced users such as CLR hosts (discussed in Chapter 10, "Advanced Topics for Using .NET Components").

4. Click the `OK` button. If adding the reference succeeds, the type library's contents appear in the Visual Basic 6 object browser, shown in Figure 8.2. You can access the object browser by selecting `View`, `Object Browser` from the menu or by pressing `F2`. Notice that none of `StringValidator`'s methods appears in the object browser. Similarly, when you try to use the class, you won't get any help from IntelliSense. This is expected because `StringValidator` exposes an auto-dispatch class interface, discussed in the ".NET Class Interfaces" section.

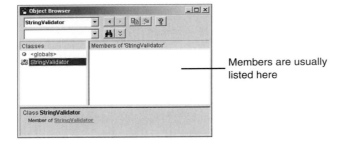

Members are usually listed here

FIGURE 8.2

The Visual Basic 6 object browser.

5. Install the assembly into the Global Assembly Cache (GAC) using the .NET Framework Global Assembly Cache Utility (`GACUTIL.EXE`) as follows:

```
gacutil -i StringValidator.dll
```

The reason we gave `StringValidator` a strong name in Listing 8.1 was so that we could install it in the GAC, because the GAC allows only strong-named assemblies to be installed.

6. Create three `TextBox` controls on the Visual Basic 6 form called `PhoneText`, `ZipText`, and `SSNText`, and a button named `SubmitButton`. The source code for this is on this book's Web site, but the form is pictured in Figure 8.3.

7. Place the code in Listing 8.2 inside the form's code window, then select `Run`, `Start` or press `F5` to run the program. You can then try out each of the three methods by typing in text and pressing the submit button.

8

USING .NET COMPONENTS FROM COM

FIGURE 8.3

The Visual Basic 6 client form.

Listing 8.2 contains the code for the Visual Basic 6 COM client that uses the `StringValidator` class.

LISTING 8.2   Visual Basic 6 Code Using a .NET Class

```
 1: Private Sub SubmitButton_Click()
 2:   Dim validator As StringValidator.StringValidator
 3:   Set validator = New StringValidator.StringValidator
 4:
 5:   If (Not validator.IsPhoneNumber(PhoneText)) Then _
 6:     MsgBox "'" + PhoneText + "' is not a valid phone number.", , "Error"
 7:
 8:   If (Not validator.IsZipCode(ZipText)) Then _
 9:     MsgBox "'" + ZipText + "' is not a valid zip code.", , "Error"
10:
11:   If (Not validator.IsSSN(SSNText)) Then _
12:     MsgBox "'" + SSNText + "' is not a valid social security number.", ,
"Error"
13:
14: End Sub
```

Notice that the code to create and use the .NET object is no different from code to create and use a COM object. The `validator` variable must be declared as `StringValidator.StringValidator` rather than just `StringValidator` simply because the library name matches the class name. Had the assembly been compiled with a different filename, this would not have been necessary.

The calls on the `validator` variable end up being late-bound calls via `IDispatch` even though nothing in the code indicates it. This takes advantage of the fact that Visual Basic 6 allows you to call non-existent members on dual interfaces (such as the empty auto-dispatch interface implemented by the `StringValidator` coclass), and transparently handles it with calls to `IDispatch.GetIDsOfNames` and `IDispatch.Invoke`.

Using a .NET Component in Unmanaged Visual C++

The steps for using a .NET component in unmanaged Visual C++ code are shorter than the steps for Visual Basic 6 because referencing a type library is done in source code. (If you tried out the example in the previous section, you can skip the first two steps here.) To use the StringValidator assembly in unmanaged C++ code, you should do the following:

1. Register the assembly using the .NET Framework Assembly Registration Utility (REGASM.EXE) as follows:

   ```
   regasm StringValidator.dll /tlb
   ```

   The /tlb option creates and registers a type library with the name StringValidator.tlb.

2. Install the assembly into the Global Assembly Cache (GAC) using the .NET Framework Global Assembly Cache Utility (GACUTIL.EXE) as follows:

   ```
   gacutil -i StringValidator.dll
   ```

3. Create a new Visual C++ project with the code from Listing 8.3.

Listing 8.3 contains unmanaged C++ code that uses the StringValidator class as if it were a COM class.

LISTING 8.3 Unmanaged Visual C++ Code Using a .NET Class

```
 1: #define _WIN32_DCOM
 2: #include <stdio.h>
 3: #include <wtypes.h>
 4:
 5: // Reference the type library for the StringValidator assembly
 6: #import "StringValidator.tlb" no_namespace named_guids raw_interfaces_only
 7:
 8: int main(int argc, char* argv[])
 9: {
10:   IUnknown* pUnk = NULL;
11:   IDispatch* pDisp = NULL;
12:   HRESULT hresult;
13:
14:   // Initialize COM
15:   hresult = CoInitializeEx(NULL, COINIT_MULTITHREADED);
16:   if (FAILED(hresult))
17:   {
18:     printf("ERROR: Cannot initialize COM: 0x%x\n", hresult);
19:     return -1;
```

LISTING 8.3   Continued

```
20:    }
21:
22:    // Instantiate the .NET StringValidator class
23:    hresult = CoCreateInstance(CLSID_StringValidator, NULL,
24:      CLSCTX_INPROC_SERVER, IID_IUnknown, (void **)&pUnk);
25:    if (FAILED(hresult))
26:    {
27:      printf("ERROR: Cannot create object: 0x%x\n", hresult);
28:      return -1;
29:    }
30:
31:    // Get the IDispatch interface
32:    hresult = pUnk->QueryInterface(IID_IDispatch, (void**)&pDisp);
33:    if (FAILED(hresult))
34:    {
35:      printf("ERROR: Cannot obtain the IDispatch interface pointer: 0x%x\n",
36:        hresult);
37:      pUnk->Release();
38:      return -1;
39:    }
40:
41:    pUnk->Release();
42:
43:    // Get the DISPID for the IsZipCode method
44:    OLECHAR* name = L"IsZipCode";
45:    DISPID dispid;
46:    hresult = pDisp->GetIDsOfNames(IID_NULL, &name, 1, GetUserDefaultLCID(),
47:      &dispid);
48:    if (FAILED(hresult))
49:    {
50:      printf("ERROR: GetIDsOfNames failed: 0x%x\n", hresult);
51:      pDisp->Release();
52:      return -1;
53:    }
54:
55:    // Initialize the IsZipCode parameter
56:    VARIANT args[1];
57:    VariantInit(&args[0]);
58:    args[0].vt = VT_BSTR;
59:    args[0].bstrVal = SysAllocString(L"90210");
60:    DISPPARAMS params = { args, NULL, 1, 0 };
61:
62:    // Invoke the IsZipCode method
63:    VARIANT result;
```

LISTING 8.3   Continued

```
64:   VariantInit(&result);
65:
66:   hresult = pDisp->Invoke(dispid, IID_NULL, GetUserDefaultLCID(),
67:     DISPATCH_METHOD, &params, &result, NULL, NULL);
68:   if (FAILED(hresult))
69:   {
70:     printf("ERROR: Invoke failed: 0x%x\n", hresult);
71:   }
72:   else
73:   {
74:     if (result.boolVal == VARIANT_TRUE)
75:       printf("The input string is a valid zip code.\n");
76:     else
77:       printf("The input string is not a valid zip code.\n");
78:   }
79:
80:   // Free the string and release the IDispatch pointer
81:   VariantClear(&args[0]);
82:   pDisp->Release();
83:
84:   CoUninitialize();
85:   return 0;
86: }
```

Line 6 imports `StringValidator`'s type library using the Visual C++ #import statement and a few directives that make its use easier:

- `no_namespace`—Doesn't enclose the type library types in a separate namespace. Without this, they would be in a namespace equal to the library name.
- `named_guids`—Defines constants for the LIBID, IIDs, and CLSIDs. These have the form `LIBID_LibraryName`, `IID_InterfaceName`, and `CLSID_CoclassName`.
- `raw_interfaces_only`—Suppresses Active Template Library (ATL) smart pointers and wrappers that expose failure `HRESULT`s as C++ exceptions.

You'll either need to ensure that `StringValidator.tlb` is in the same path as the C++ project or change the string in Line 6 appropriately. Line 15 initializes COM, and Lines 23–24 instantiate the COM-Callable Wrapper (CCW) for the `StringValidator` class using the familiar `CoCreateInstance` function. The `CLSID_StringValidator` constant is defined thanks to using `named_guids` with the #import statement. An `IDispatch` pointer is obtained via `QueryInterface` in Line 32.

Lines 46–47 retrieve the DISPID for the `IsZipCode` method so it can be used in a call to `IDispatch.Invoke`.

> **CAUTION**
>
> Never hard-code DISPIDs in your C++ code, especially if they aren't described in the interface's type library definition. Instead, always call `IDispatch.GetIDsOfNames` before calling `IDispatch.Invoke` at least once for a given instance to obtain the DISPID for the desired member's name. DISPIDs for members obtained via an auto-dispatch class interface (explained in the ".NET Class Interfaces" section) are not guaranteed to stay the same from one version of a .NET class to another. Plus, authors of .NET classes may inadvertently change their CLR-generated DISPIDs from one version of a component to the next if they don't fully understand their interactions with COM.

Lines 56–60 prepare the string parameter to pass to the `IsZipCode` method, and Lines 66–67 call `IDispatch.Invoke`. If the call succeeds, Line 74 checks to see whether the return value is true or false and prints an appropriate message. Because the returned VARIANT contains a VARIANT_BOOL type, VARIANT_TRUE represents true (with a value of –1), and VARIANT_FALSE represents false (with a value of 0).

> **CAUTION**
>
> When calling a member via `IDispatch.Invoke` that has more than one parameter, the array of parameters inside the DISPPARAMS structure must be passed in reverse order. This is the way all `IDispatch` implementations must behave, and is not specific to .NET.

Using a .NET Component in Unmanaged JScript

Using a .NET component in unmanaged JScript is not much different from using it in Visual Basic 6. (If you tried out either of the previous two examples, you can skip the first two steps here.) To use the `StringValidator` assembly in unmanaged JScript, you should do the following:

1. Register the assembly using the .NET Framework Assembly Registration Utility (`REGASM.EXE`) as follows:

   ```
   regasm StringValidator.dll /tlb
   ```

   The `/tlb` option creates and registers a type library with the name `StringValidator.tlb`.

2. Install the assembly into the Global Assembly Cache (GAC) using the .NET Framework Global Assembly Cache Utility (GACUTIL.EXE) as follows:

```
gacutil -i StringValidator.dll
```

3. Create a text file called Client.js with the code such as the following:

```
var validator = new ActiveXObject("StringValidator")
validator.IsZipCode("16146")
```

4. Run the script using Windows Script Host from a command prompt as follows:

```
wscript Client.js
```

or simply:

```
Client.js
```

And that's all there is to it. The JScript code creates the .NET object via its registered ProgID using ActiveXObject, then calls its IsZipCode method which internally uses the CCW's IDispatch implementation. Using the .NET object from VBScript works the same way.

By always being forced to late bind, unmanaged script can encounter limitations of the IDispatch implementations of .NET objects. For example, the default IDispatch implementation exposed for .NET objects does not enable COM clients to call members with user-defined value type (UDT) parameters. These limitations, and others, are discussed in Chapter 14, "Implementing COM Interfaces for Binary Compatibility."

Once registered, .NET objects can be created and used in script embedded in a Web page just like COM objects are used. The following Web page demonstrates the use of the StringValidator class, created using the <object> tag and its CLSID:

```html
<html>
  <script>
    function CheckZipCode()
    {
      result.value = validator.IsZipCode(t.value)
    }
  </script>
  <body>
    <object
      id="validator" classid="clsid:4EB55600-64CF-30EC-8616-9B6D3FA24EC2">
    </object>
    <br><input type="text" id="t">
    <input type="button" id="b" value="Zip Code?" onclick="CheckZipCode()">
    <br><input type="text" id="result"> Result
  </body>
</html>
```

When any .NET class is registered, a CLSID is automatically generated if the class doesn't choose its own via a custom attribute in source code. (Furthermore, this CLSID doesn't change as long as the class or its containing assembly doesn't change.) To figure out the CLSID for any .NET class, you could search in the Windows Registry or use REGASM.EXE's /regfile option. This option generates a file that displays the entries that would be added to the registry if REGASM.EXE is run without this option. For the StringValidator assembly, this can be done as follows:

```
regasm StringValidator.dll /regfile
```

This generates a StringValidator.reg file that contains the desired CLSID in entries such as the following:

```
[HKEY_CLASSES_ROOT\StringValidator\CLSID]
@="{4EB55600-64CF-30EC-8616-9B6D3FA24EC2}"
```

When using this option, no registration occurs, so you'll still want to run REGASM.EXE without the /regfile option. REGASM.EXE is covered further in the "Assembly Registration" section and Appendix B, "SDK Tools Reference."

> **CAUTION**
>
> The registration files generated by REGASM.EXE are for informational purposes only. They do not necessarily contain all of the registry entries that would be added by registering an assembly with REGASM.EXE, for reasons described in Chapter 12, "Customizing COM's View of .NET Components." Furthermore, the InProcServer32 default values contained in these files do not properly escape the backslashes in the path. Using this file for registration (by running REGEDIT.EXE on the file, for example) would add empty InProcServer32 default values to the registry, causing activation of any .NET object described inside to fail.

.NET objects can be used from unmanaged script without any registration, however, and with many other benefits compared to ActiveX controls. This is accomplished with a new form of the <object> tag, and is covered in the "Hosting Windows Forms Controls in Internet Explorer" section.

Assembly Registration

Before using a .NET class from a COM client, as done in Listings 8.2 and 8.3 and the script examples, it must be registered in the Windows Registry. There are three easy ways to register an assembly so that it can be used by COM clients:

- Using the Register for COM Interop project option in Visual Studio .NET (Visual C# and Visual Basic .NET projects only).

- Using REGASM.EXE, a command-line utility that is part of the .NET Framework SDK and .NET Framework redistributable package.

- Using the RegistrationServices class in the System.Runtime.InteropServices namespace.

All three of these techniques do the same registration, but each option gives more flexibility than the previous one. The first option is covered in Chapter 11, ".NET Design Guidelines for Components Used by COM Clients," because this would be used by the developer of the .NET component, not the COM client. REGASM.EXE was used in the earlier example, and all of its options are covered in Appendix B. REGASM.EXE is included on any computer that has just the .NET Framework redistributable package, because registration is a task that needs to be done on an end user's computer. The RegistrationServices class gives you the ability to register an in-memory assembly. The use of this class is demonstrated in Chapter 22, "Using APIs Instead of SDK Tools."

When used with no options, REGASM.EXE adds the following registry entries for each coclass in a regular assembly (in other words, not an imported Interop Assembly):

```
HKEY_CLASSES_ROOT\ProgID\[default]="NamespaceQualifiedClassName"
HKEY_CLASSES_ROOT\ProgID\CLSID\[default]="{CLSID}"
HKEY_CLASSES_ROOT\CLSID\{CLSID}\[default]="NamespaceQualifiedClassName"
HKEY_CLASSES_ROOT\CLSID\{CLSID}\Implemented Categories\
➡ {62C8FE65-4EBB-45E7-B440-6E39B2CDBF29}
HKEY_CLASSES_ROOT\CLSID\{CLSID}\InprocServer32\[default]=
➡ "WindowsSystemDirectory\mscoree.dll"
HKEY_CLASSES_ROOT\CLSID\{CLSID}\InprocServer32\Assembly="FullAssemblyName"
HKEY_CLASSES_ROOT\CLSID\{CLSID}\InprocServer32\Class=
➡ "NamespaceQualifiedClassName"
HKEY_CLASSES_ROOT\CLSID\{CLSID}\InprocServer32\RuntimeVersion="Version"
HKEY_CLASSES_ROOT\CLSID\{CLSID}\InprocServer32\ThreadingModel="Both"
HKEY_CLASSES_ROOT\CLSID\{CLSID}\ProgId\[default]="ProgID"
```

When used with its /tlb option, as done in the StringValidator example, REGASM.EXE creates and registers a type library. (Creating type libraries for assemblies is discussed in the next section, "The Type Library Exporter.") The type library registration performed by REGASM.EXE is the same as calling the OLE Automation LoadTypeLibEx API with the REGKIND_REGISTER flag; it is not specific to .NET. See Appendix B for the entries that standard COM type library registration adds to the Windows Registry.

Notice that the default value for the InprocServer32 key is set to the filename of MSCOREE.DLL, a component of the CLR execution engine, rather than the filename of the assembly. In MSCOREE.DLL, the CLR exposes a DllGetClassObject entry point that creates class factories for CCWs.

8

USING .NET
COMPONENTS
FROM COM

When this `DllGetClassObject` method is called, the CLR checks the `Class` value registered under the passed-in CLSID to determine which .NET class needs to be instantiated. If the assembly containing the class is not already loaded, the CLR loads the assembly specified with the `Assembly` value the same way that it would for a .NET client application. This means that the assembly must be placed somewhere where the CLR can find it. For example, it could be placed in the Global Assembly Cache (GAC), in the same directory as the client executable, or somewhere specified in a configuration file. The `StringValidator` assembly used at the beginning of the chapter was given a strong name and installed in the GAC. This is the recommended approach because all assemblies are effectively shared once registered in the Windows Registry, and the GAC is where shared assemblies should be stored.

TIP

Installing assemblies in the Global Assembly Cache gives the best performance compared to any other location. The GAC is the first place the assembly resolver searches when loading an assembly. Furthermore, the CLR validates an assembly's digital signature when it is *installed* in the GAC. For assemblies not in the GAC, the CLR must validate the signature every time an assembly is *loaded*.

CAUTION

When running a compiled Visual Basic 6 COM client outside the VB6 IDE, the executable directory is simply the directory containing the compiled client executable. In this scenario, an assembly could be placed in the same directory and used by the COM client without problems. When running a Visual Basic 6 COM client *within* the VB6 IDE, however, the executable directory becomes the directory containing Visual Basic itself—`VB6.EXE`. Clearly you don't want to make a habit of copying assemblies to the directory containing `VB6.EXE`, so using an alternative, such as installing the assembly in the GAC, works well.

A similar situation occurs when using .NET objects from unmanaged script. If you run the script using the Windows Script Host, the executable directory is the directory containing `WSCRIPT.EXE`. Placing assemblies in the same directory as the script files does not help the CLR find them.

Failure to place an assembly in an appropriate place is the Number One cause for errors when people first attempt to use .NET objects from COM clients. We're accustomed to COM objects getting registered with their path and filename, but assemblies are different. Figure 8.4 shows what this common error looks like from a Visual Basic 6 project. The failure manifests as a `TypeLoadException`, so COM clients see the HRESULT `COR_E_TYPELOAD` (0x80131522).

FIGURE 8.4
Failure to load an assembly from a Visual Basic 6 project.

FAQ: What does the HRESULT 0x80131522 mean (or any other HRESULT beginning with 0x8013)?

0x8013522 is COR_E_TYPELOAD, the HRESULT corresponding to System.TypeLoadException. This is frequently caused by attempting to instantiate a .NET class that's registered but whose assembly is not in a location that can be found by the CLR's assembly resolver.

All .NET HRESULTs have the facility value FACILITY_URT (URT stands for *universal runtime*), which is 13. Therefore, all .NET failure HRESULTs begin with 0x8013. Check Appendix D, ".NET Exception to HRESULT Transformations," for the list of what .NET exception was likely thrown to cause any such HRESULT.

Developers sometimes view the process of giving an assembly a strong name and installing it in the GAC as too laborious, especially when the assembly is still being developed and constantly being changed. REGASM.EXE has a shortcut that enables you to place an assembly wherever you'd like and have it be found and loaded without the help of configuration files. This shortcut is its /codebase option. When using this, REGASM.EXE places an additional entry for each coclass registered, for example:

```
HKEY_CLASSES_ROOT\CLSID\{CLSID}\InprocServer32\CodeBase=
➥ file:///C:/…/MyAssembly.dll
```

With this value registered, the CLR can locate assemblies anywhere in the file system. Or, the CodeBase value could even be a URL! In this case, the assembly is automatically downloaded on demand.

The CodeBase value is only used as a hint, however. If an assembly can be found in the usual places, then it gets loaded as if the CodeBase value doesn't exist. Configuration files aside, the GAC is searched first, then the local directory, and finally the CodeBase value if it exists. If you're familiar with the System.Reflection.Assembly class, then you can think of CodeBase as enabling an Assembly.LoadFrom call after a failed call to Assembly.Load. Be aware that this search order differs from regular .NET applications. If a .NET application uses a configuration file that specifies a `CodeBase` value, then the GAC is searched first, followed by the `CodeBase`, followed by the local directory.

If you use `/codebase` on an assembly without a strong name (which is the simplest and quickest way to enable the use of .NET components from COM), `REGASM.EXE` emits the following warning:

```
RegAsm warning: Registering an unsigned assembly with /codebase can cause
your assembly to interfere with other applications that may be installed on
the same computer. The /codebase switch is intended to be used only with
signed assemblies. Please give your assembly a strong name and re-register it.
```

> **CAUTION**
>
> Using `/codebase` to register an assembly without a strong name should only be done for testing purposes. Ordinarily, private assemblies should reside in the same directory or a subdirectory of an application, but `/codebase` enables you to circumvent this rule. If multiple applications have assemblies without strong names that contain types with the same names, subtle incorrect behavior can occur by the wrong types getting loaded.

The `/codebase` option is intended for developer scenarios, rather than for use by applications distributed to end users. Using a codebase hint is often a handy shortcut when registering .NET objects to be used within the Visual Basic 6 IDE or from Windows Script Host. When registered with a `CodeBase` value, assemblies can be found even if they are not in the GAC or in the directory containing `VB6.EXE` or `WSCRIPT.EXE`.

The Type Library Exporter

Although registering an assembly is required for standard COM usage, creating a type library for an assembly is optional. Type libraries aren't required to use .NET objects from COM, because you could perform late binding (or hand-craft an appropriate IDL file for C++ clients) just as you could for a COM object without a type library. Type libraries, however, are usually desired because they make .NET types readily available to COM applications with minimal effort. The mechanism that creates a type library describing types in a .NET assembly is known as the *type library exporter*. The type library exporter is the inverse of the type library importer; it takes an assembly as input and produces a standalone type library (a `.tlb` file) as output.

An exported type library contains definitions of COM-Callable Wrappers (CCWs). The term *exported class* is synonymous with a CCW. As with type library importing, none of the implementation of a .NET component is translated to unmanaged code; the appropriate type definitions in metadata are simply translated to COM type definitions. Unlike Interop Assemblies, exported type libraries (or *Interop Type Libraries*) usually work "out of the box" because the input metadata is rich enough to tell the exporter everything it needs to know to produce the appropriate signatures.

There are four ways to use the type library exporter to generate a type library:

- Using the `Register for COM Interop` project option in Visual Studio .NET (Visual C# and Visual Basic .NET projects only).
- Using `REGASM.EXE`, a command-line utility that is part of the .NET Framework SDK and .NET Framework redistributable package, with its `/tlb` option.
- Using `TLBEXP.EXE`, a command-line utility that is part of the .NET Framework SDK.
- Using the `TypeLibConverter` class in `System.Runtime.InteropServices`.

All four of these methods produce the exact same type library by default, although each option gives more flexibility than the previous one. Again, the first option is covered in Chapter 11. The second option of using `REGASM.EXE` was done in the `StringValidator` example. `TLBEXP.EXE`, the third option, is a utility analogous to `TLBIMP.EXE`, and its sole purpose is to export a type library; it does no registration. All of its options are covered in Appendix B. The `TypeLibConverter` class gives you the ability to export a type library from an in-memory assembly, and also gives you the chance to perform customizations before saving the type library. The use of this class is demonstrated in Chapter 22.

8

USING .NET COMPONENTS FROM COM

> **TIP**
>
> The following sequence of commands:
>
> ```
> tlbexp MyAssembly.dll
> regasm MyAssembly.dll
> ```
>
> is *not* equivalent to the following command:
>
> ```
> regasm MyAssembly.dll /tlb
> ```
>
> because the latter registers the type library that gets exported. Type library registration is useful for having the type library appear in lists, such as Visual Basic 6's `References` dialog, and also necessary for cross-context COM marshaling. Therefore, using the `TLBEXP.EXE` utility is often not necessary.

Some assemblies, such as `mscorlib`, ship with type libraries. Such type libraries should always be used rather than exporting new ones because they may contain customizations.

FAQ: I used TLBEXP.EXE (or REGASM.EXE with its /tlb option), but the type library it created is empty (or missing a lot of the types). What's wrong with the type library exporter?

Nothing is wrong; it's just doing what it's told to do. .NET types, members, or even entire assemblies have the option of marking themselves as *COM-invisible* using System.Runtime.InteropServices.ComVisibleAttribute. This means the following:

- A COM-invisible type is never exported to a type library.
- A COM-invisible class, in addition to not being exported, is not registered and only responds successfully to QueryInterface calls for interfaces that are not marked COM-invisible (plus standard COM interfaces implemented by the CCW except for IDispatch).
- A COM-invisible member cannot be called directly by a COM client. It isn't exported, it's omitted from the v-table exposed to COM, and it's not accessible via late-bound IDispatch access.
- A COM-invisible assembly's types are all COM-invisible by default.

Most assemblies in the .NET Framework are marked entirely COM-invisible, such as System.Xml.dll, System.Web.dll, and many more. If you run the following:

```
tlbexp System.Xml.dll
```

then a type library called System.Xml.tlb is produced that looks like the following when viewed in OLEVIEW.EXE:

```
[
  uuid(82CF3206-FF1E-37F8-BF64-1AD5D9A2BFF4),
  version(1.0),
  helpstring("System.Xml.dll"),
  custom(90883F05-3D28-11D2-8F17-00A0C9A6186D, "System.Xml,
➥ Version=1.0.3300.0, Culture=neutral, PublicKeyToken=b77a5c561934e089")
]
library System_Xml
{
    // TLib :      // Forward declare all types defined in this typelib
};
```

Of course, this type library is useless. Other .NET Framework assemblies, such as System.Drawing.dll and System.Windows.Forms.dll, expose only a subset of types to COM so their exported type libraries are much smaller than you might expect. In fact, the System.Text.RegularExpressions.Regex class used in Listing 8.1 is COM-invisible, which is why its functionality had to be exposed indirectly via the StringValidator class. The `mscorlib` assembly is the only core .NET Framework assembly that is entirely COM-visible.

To check if an entire assembly is marked COM-invisible, you can open it in the IL Disassembler (`ILDASM.EXE`) and check for `ComVisibleAttribute` set to false (`10 00 00 00 00` in the attribute constructor) inside the assembly manifest:

```
.custom instance void [mscorlib]System.Runtime.InteropServices.
➥ ComVisibleAttribute::.ctor(bool) = ( 01 00 00 00 00 )
```

However, individual types can override the assembly-wide setting, so just because the manifest contains the attribute set to false doesn't mean that the exported type library will be empty. Therefore, it's best to simply export a type library and see what you get.

Chapter 10 shows some tricks to make COM-invisible types usable from COM (despite the wishes of their authors), and Chapter 12 discusses how and why assemblies make types and members invisible to COM.

.NET Class Interfaces

Classes defined in Visual Basic 6 have automatic class interfaces that expose their members. CCWs for .NET classes usually implement automatic class interfaces, too. Such class interfaces aren't exactly the same as VB6 class interfaces, but are essentially the same idea.

Sometimes a CCW does not implement a class interface for its corresponding .NET class. For example, the `TypeLibConverter` coclass (representing `System.Runtime.InteropServices.TypeLibConverter`) implements a real .NET interface (`ITypeLibConverter`) as its default interface:

```
[
  uuid(F1C3BF79-C3E4-11D3-88E7-00902754C43A),
  version(1.0),
  custom(0F21F359-AB84-41E8-9A78-36D110E6D2F9,
    "System.Runtime.InteropServices.TypeLibConverter")
]
coclass TypeLibConverter {
  interface _Object;
  [default] interface ITypeLibConverter;
};
```

Whether a .NET class exposes its own class interface is controlled with a custom attribute explained in Chapter 12.

If a CCW does implement a class interface, it is always the default interface. This is important for Visual Basic 6 clients because the default interface determines which members appear to belong to the class type. There are two kinds of class interfaces a CCW could expose:

- An auto-dispatch class interface. This is the most common, because it is the default behavior for .NET classes (as seen with the `StringValidator` class in Listing 8.1). Such a class interface is easily identifiable by the fact that it's a dual interface whose definition contains no members. By calling its inherited `IDispatch` members, you can late bind to public members of the class and its base classes (except for members marked as COM-invisible). This was demonstrated in Listings 8.2 and 8.3 and the script examples, and looks no different than using an auto-dual interface in VB6—except that you don't get IntelliSense for the members.

- An auto-dual class interface. This dual interface contains all the public COM-visible members of the class and its base classes. These are the same members that can be invoked on an auto-dispatch class interface; the only difference is that type information for these members is available in the exported type library, and COM clients can v-table bind to the members rather than being restricted to late binding.

The "auto" in both of these names refers to the fact that the CLR automatically fabricates these class interfaces at run time. Here's what the auto-dispatch class interface for the `StringValidator` class from Listing 8.1 looks like in its exported type library (as seen in `OLEVIEW.EXE`):

```
[
  odl,
  uuid(C286EFF2-D7C4-3712-B8EE-BC7A7F84A823),
  hidden,
  dual,
  oleautomation,
  custom(0F21F359-AB84-41E8-9A78-36D110E6D2F9, "StringValidator")
]
interface _StringValidator : IDispatch {
};
```

CCWs always implement interfaces that are implemented by the corresponding .NET class's base classes, and this includes class interfaces if the base classes expose them. Because `System.Object` exposes a class interface (`_Object`) and every .NET class derives from `System.Object`, every exported .NET class lists `_Object` as an implemented interface. This can be seen in the definition of the exported `StringValidator` coclass (as seen in `OLEVIEW.EXE`):

```
[
  uuid(4EB55600-64CF-30EC-8616-9B6D3FA24EC2),
  version(1.0),
  custom(0F21F359-AB84-41E8-9A78-36D110E6D2F9, "StringValidator")
]
```

```
coclass StringValidator {
  [default] interface _StringValidator;
  interface _Object;
};
```

FAQ: **Why do .NET classes force COM clients to make late bound calls to its members by default by calling through "empty" interfaces?**

The reason type information for class interface members isn't exposed by default is that exposing it would not be safe for versioning. Authors of .NET classes can freely add members in a later version, but this can easily break COM clients dependent on the layout of a class interface. By restricting COM clients to late binding by default, COM clients don't care if an interface layout changed or members were added anywhere, as long as existing members were not renamed or removed.

The reason that the exporter generates empty IDispatch-derived interfaces named _CoclassName rather than simply exposing IDispatch as a coclass's default interface is to preserve the identity of the .NET class types. For example, if a COM class implements a .NET interface with a member containing a MyClass parameter, COM treats the parameter as MyClass's default interface (_MyClass). When exposing this COM class to .NET, the type library importer can match up the _MyClass parameter in the COM object's type library to the original MyClass .NET definition. This is enabled by a special IDL custom attribute on the _MyClass interface definition that contains a reference to the .NET MyClass definition and its assembly.

Rather than exposing class interfaces, COM-friendly .NET components should define and implement real interfaces whose members can be accessed through a v-table. This is discussed further in Chapter 12.

Interacting with a .NET Object

Just as in using a COM object from managed code looks like using a .NET object, using a .NET object from unmanaged code looks like using a COM object, because you're really interacting with a CCW. This section provides an overview of the common interactions you can perform with a .NET object through its CCW.

Creating a .NET Object

Listings 8.2 and 8.3 and the script examples demonstrated that .NET objects can be created just like COM objects. All CCWs support aggregation, and implement several well-known COM interfaces, discussed in Chapter 14.

The one major limitation with object creation is that only .NET classes with public default constructors can be instantiated by a COM client via CoCreateInstance. COM has no built-in way to create an object and pass parameters simultaneously. Instead, a COM client could instantiate a *different* .NET object that has a public default constructor (like a factory object) and call a member that returns the desired instance. The object's CCW is created as soon as you obtain a .NET object this way.

Because .NET classes with public default constructors are registered with ProgIDs by default, they can also be created using them. For example, in Visual Basic 6:

```
Dim o As Object
Set o = CreateObject("StringValidator")
If o.IsZipCode("16146") Then ...
```

This approach of using CreateObject then late binding in Visual Basic 6 is handy because it doesn't require a type library to be referenced. This technique can be valuable for COM objects that don't have a type library, but because a type library can be obtained for any assembly by simply running the type library exporter, it's no longer as important.

Calling Members on a .NET Object

The next chapter, "An In-Depth Look at Exported Type Libraries," discusses the transformations performed by type library exporter, and this helps to understand how to call members of a CCW. In this section, we'll briefly touch on some common surprises or limitations that face COM developers attempting to call members of a .NET object:

- Any .NET signatures that are exposed to COM with by-value UDT or by-value SAFEARRAY parameters cannot be called by Visual Basic 6 clients. This is no different than if a COM object exposed such parameters, and is an unfortunate limitation of Visual Basic 6. .NET arrays are passed by-value much more often than by-reference, and are exposed as SAFEARRAYs by default.

- System.Object types are exposed as VARIANT types by default. This can seem a little unnatural in C++ when you want to pass an interface pointer, but all you need to do is create a VARIANT with type VT_UNKNOWN or VT_DISPATCH and set its punkVal or pdispVal member to your interface pointer:

```
VARIANT obj;
VariantInit(&obj);
obj.vt = VT_UNKNOWN;
obj.punkVal = pMyInterfacePointer;
pMyInterfacePointer->AddRef();
```

- .NET fields and properties are both exposed as COM properties. When using #import in Visual C++, raw property accessors can be accessed via names such as get_*PropertyName*, put_*PropertyName*, or putref_*PropertyName*. The ATL wrappers have names such as Get*PropertyName*, Put*PropertyName*, or PutRef*PropertyName* by default. The put_ and Put prefixes often catch programmers by surprise because set_ or Set would seem more natural for .NET property setters.

- Static members (Shared in VB .NET) are not directly exposed to COM. If you require calling such members, the easiest workaround is to write some managed code that wraps calls to static members inside instance members. Chapter 10 demonstrates a different workaround that uses reflection from unmanaged C++. .NET classes can choose to expose static members via late binding, but this is rarely done. Chapter 14 has the details.

- ToString methods are exported as *properties*. Furthermore, they are marked as default properties for classes that don't already have a default member. This odd-sounding transformation is done mainly for the benefit of Visual Basic 6, so you can "print an object" as follows:

```
Dim s As New StringValidator.StringValidator
MsgBox s
```

This displays "StringValidator", the result of StringValidator.ToString, because the default property is implicitly invoked.

- .NET *class interfaces* contain members inherited from base classes, but .NET *interfaces* are not exposed with members of their base interfaces. Instead, all exported .NET interfaces derive directly from IUnknown or IDispatch and only contain the members directly defined on them. To be able to call members on base .NET interfaces, a COM client must call QueryInterface for the desired interface.

Besides these items, .NET overloaded methods are a highly-visible annoyance when used from COM. COM interfaces cannot have overloaded methods, because each member's name must be unique. To account for this, the names of overloaded methods are decorated when exposed to COM in order to avoid name conflicts. The first overloaded method emitted in metadata (which should be the first method listed in source code, but this ultimately depends on the .NET compiler) gets to keep its name, but the remaining overloaded methods are given a suffix of _2, _3, and so on.

When calling an overloaded method, you need to figure out which method name to use based on the signatures in a type library. This isn't possible when late binding to an auto-dispatch class interface, however, because the signatures don't appear in an exported type library. For example, the System.Text.StringBuilder class has 19 public Append methods. These are exposed to COM as Append, Append_2, ..., Append_19, but they are not accessible via anything other than the empty _StringBuilder auto-dispatch class interface. Rather than figuring out

8

USING .NET
COMPONENTS
FROM COM

which `Append` method has which decorated name by trial and error, you can perform the following steps:

1. Open the assembly containing the overloaded methods (in this case, `mscorlib.dll`) in the IL Disassembler (`ILDASM.EXE`).

2. On the `View` menu, make sure that `Show Public` is the only one of the `Show...` options checked. Non-public overloads don't affect exported names.

3. On the `View` menu, make sure that `Sort by name` is not checked. We need to see the exact order that the members appear in metadata, because that is how the exporter processes the signatures.

4. Open the node for the class containing the overloaded methods you wish to check. The first one listed gets to keep its name when exposed to COM; the second one gets the `_2` suffix, and so on.

Figure 8.5 demonstrates this process for `System.Text.StringBuilder` and its `Append` overloads.

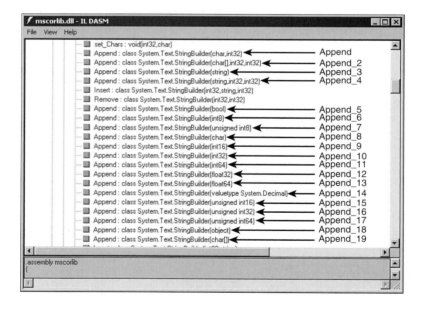

FIGURE 8.5

Using the IL Disassembler to view overloaded methods in the order processed by the type library exporter.

> **CAUTION**
>
> Calling overloaded members of a .NET object is a little dangerous, because authors of .NET components may inadvertently add an overloaded method in the middle of the component's existing overloaded methods or change the ordering of the overloaded methods. Such a change would change the methods' names exposed to COM and likely break any COM clients using them. (.NET clients don't notice, because the signatures and names all look the same to them.)
>
> Authors of .NET components should not allow this to happen, but the safest action for the paranoid COM developer is to wrap all calls to overloaded methods in *managed code* that exposes them to COM using customized method names.

Getting Rich Error Information

.NET exceptions are exposed as COM HRESULTs because COM components are accustomed to handling errors this way. But seeing a returned error code such as 0x80131522 is not nearly as user-friendly as seeing a TypeLoadException thrown with a descriptive message. Fortunately, additional information from a thrown exception is available to COM clients.

For example, suppose the following Visual Basic 6 code attempts to use the System.Collections.Stack class in an invalid way:

```
Dim s As New Stack
' Attempt to pop an element off an empty stack
s.Pop
```

It's illegal to call Pop on an empty Stack, so doing this in a .NET language would result in a System.InvalidOperationException thrown with the message "Stack empty." Sure enough, running the previous code in Visual Basic 6 results in a run-time error with a dialog box containing the HRESULT for InvalidOperationException (0x80131509) but also the exception's message. This is pictured in Figure 8.6.

To run this code, you must reference mscorlib.tlb in your Visual Basic 6 project, which appears as Common Language Runtime Library in the References dialog. You must also register the mscorlib assembly as follows because it is not registered by default:

```
regasm mscorlib.dll
```

If mscorlib has not been registered, attempting to create an instance of a class defined inside it returns the REGDB_E_CLASSNOTREG failure HRESULT (0x80040154). Don't use REGASM.EXE's /tlb option because it already ships with a type library, and don't use the /codebase option because the CLR doesn't need a codebase hint in order to find mscorlib.dll.

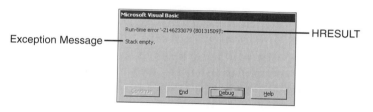

FIGURE 8.6

A .NET exception's message is displayed by Visual Basic 6 when an error occurs.

So how is the Visual Basic 6 IDE able to display a .NET exception message, because it pre-dates .NET? The answer is that a CCW makes common exception information available through standard COM mechanisms. The mechanisms differ depending on whether you're late binding (such as calling Stack.Pop through its class interface) or v-table binding. Visual Basic 6 hides these mechanisms from the programmer, but we can see them in unmanaged C++ code.

> **TIP**
>
> Rich error information is always available for failure HRESULTs caused by .NET exceptions. You should make it a habit to use the techniques described in this section to extract this information (at least the exception's message) whenever an error occurs. Some COM examples in this book don't perform this extra step for the sake of brevity.

Late Binding in Unmanaged C++

Listing 8.4 demonstrates how to get error information besides an HRESULT from an invalid call to Stack.Pop in unmanaged C++. Because the Stack class doesn't implement an interface exposing the Pop method nor does it expose a class interface with type information, we must perform late binding. The rich error information is obtained by passing an EXCEPINFO structure to IDispatch.Invoke. (EXCEPINFO stands for *exception information*.)

LISTING 8.4   Unmanaged C++ Code That Obtains Rich Error Information When Late Binding

```
1: #define _WIN32_DCOM
2: #include <stdio.h>
3: #include <wtypes.h>
4:
5: // Reference the type library for mscorlib
```

LISTING 8.4   Continued

```
6:  #import "c:\\Windows\\Microsoft.NET\\Framework\\vn.n.nnnn\\mscorlib.tlb"
7:  ➥no_namespace named_guids raw_interfaces_only
8:
9:  int main(int argc, char* argv[])
10: {
11:   IUnknown* pUnk = NULL;
12:   IDispatch* pDisp = NULL;
13:   HRESULT hresult;
14:
15:   // Initialize COM
16:   hresult = CoInitializeEx(NULL, COINIT_MULTITHREADED);
17:   if (FAILED(hresult))
18:   {
19:     printf("ERROR: Cannot initialize COM: 0x%x\n", hresult);
20:     return -1;
21:   }
22:
23:   // Instantiate the System.Collections.Stack class
24:   hresult = CoCreateInstance(CLSID_Stack, NULL, CLSCTX_INPROC_SERVER,
25:     IID_IUnknown, (void **)&pUnk);
26:   if (FAILED(hresult))
27:   {
28:     printf("ERROR: Cannot create object: 0x%x\n", hresult);
29:     return -1;
30:   }
31:
32:   // Get the IDispatch interface
33:   hresult = pUnk->QueryInterface(IID_IDispatch, (void**)&pDisp);
34:   if (FAILED(hresult))
35:   {
36:     printf("ERROR: Cannot obtain IDispatch pointer: 0x%x\n", hresult);
37:     pUnk->Release();
38:     return -1;
39:   }
40:
41:   pUnk->Release();
42:
43:   // Get the DISPID for the Pop method
44:   OLECHAR* name = L"Pop";
45:   DISPID dispid;
46:   hresult = pDisp->GetIDsOfNames(IID_NULL, &name, 1,
47:     GetUserDefaultLCID(), &dispid);
48:   if (FAILED(hresult))
49:   {
```

LISTING 8.4   Continued

```
50:        printf("ERROR: GetIDsOfNames failed: 0x%x\n", hresult);
51:        pDisp->Release();
52:        return -1;
53:    }
54:
55:    // Invoke the Pop method
56:    VARIANT result;
57:    VariantInit(&result);
58:    DISPPARAMS params = { NULL, NULL, 0, 0 };
59:    EXCEPINFO excepInfo;
60:
61:    hresult = pDisp->Invoke(dispid, IID_NULL, GetUserDefaultLCID(),
62:      DISPATCH_METHOD, &params, &result, &excepInfo, NULL);
63:    if (FAILED(hresult))
64:    {
65:      printf("ERROR: Invoke failed:          0x%x\n", hresult);
66:      if (hresult == DISP_E_EXCEPTION)
67:      {
68:        printf("HRESULT returned by Stack.Pop: 0x%x\n", excepInfo.scode);
69:        printf("Exception Source:              %S\n", excepInfo.bstrSource);
70:        printf("Exception Message:             %S\n",
71:          excepInfo.bstrDescription);
72:        printf("HelpFile:                      %S\n",
73:          excepInfo.bstrHelpFile);
74:        printf("HelpContext:                   %d\n",
75:          excepInfo.dwHelpContext);
76:
77:        if (excepInfo.bstrSource != NULL)
78:          SysFreeString(excepInfo.bstrSource);
79:        if (excepInfo.bstrDescription != NULL)
80:          SysFreeString(excepInfo.bstrDescription);
81:        if (excepInfo.bstrHelpFile != NULL)
82:          SysFreeString(excepInfo.bstrHelpFile);
83:      }
84:    }
85:
86:    // Release the IDispatch pointer
87:    pDisp->Release();
88:
89:    CoUninitialize();
90:    return 0;
91: }
```

Lines 6–7 import the type library for the mscorlib assembly. (You should replace the path for this file as appropriate for your computer's settings.)

TIP

When referencing mscorlib.tlb using #import in a Visual C++ 6 application, the following warning might be emitted by the compiler, depending on your settings:

```
mscorlib.tlh(6946) : warning C4146:
➥ unary minus operator applied to unsigned type, result still unsigned
```

In a Visual C++ 7 application, you may get the following warnings instead:

```
Listing8_4.cpp(6) : warning C4278: 'ReportEvent': identifier in type
library
➥ 'path\mscorlib.tlb' is already a macro; use the 'rename' qualifier
Listing8_4.cpp(6) : warning C4278: 'ReportEvent': identifier in type
library
➥ 'path\mscorlib.tlb' is already a macro; use the 'rename' qualifier
```

These warnings stem from the mscorlib.tlh file produced by the Visual C++ type library importer, which contains C++ definitions of types described in the imported type library. (TLH stands for *type library header*.)

You can safely ignore such warnings, or disable them by placing a #pragma directive *before* the #import statement. For example, to disable warning C4146, you could do the following:

```
#pragma warning( disable : 4146 ) // Turns off warning 4146
```

You could then restore the default handling of the warning after the #import statement as follows:

```
#pragma warning( default : 4146 )
```

8

**USING .NET
COMPONENTS
FROM COM**

The CCW for the System.Collections.Stack class is instantiated in Lines 24–25 using CoCreateInstance, and an IDispatch pointer is obtained via QueryInterface in Line 33. Alternatively, we could have obtained a _Stack interface pointer, but IDispatch is just as good because we can only call the inherited IDispatch methods on _Stack anyway.

Lines 46–47 call GetIDsOfNames to retrieve the DISPID for Stack.Pop, and Lines 61–62 invoke the method. Notice that a reference to an EXCEPINFO structure declared in Line 59 is passed as the second-to-last parameter to Invoke. If the Invoke call fails with the DISP_E_EXCEPTION HRESULT, then the member was invoked but it returned a failure HRESULT. The failure HRESULT that the member returned and additional information can be extracted from the fields of the passed-in EXCEPINFO structure, but only when Invoke returns DISP_E_EXCEPTION. Therefore, Line 66 checks to see if the call fails with this HRESULT then proceeds to display the failure information in Lines 68–75.

The output of running this code is:

```
ERROR: Invoke failed:          0x80020009
HRESULT returned by Stack.Pop: 0x80131509
Exception Source:              mscorlib
Exception Message:             Stack empty.
HelpFile:                      (null)
HelpContext:                   0
```

The first HRESULT is DISP_E_EXCEPTION, and the second HRESULT is COR_E_INVALIDOPERATION, the HRESULT for System.InvalidOperationException, found in Appendix D.

The EXCEPINFO structure has the following fields, which contain the following information when a .NET exception is thrown:

- wCode—Always set to 0.

- wReserved—Always set to 0.

- bstrSource—A string set to the contents of the exception's Source property.

- bstrDescription—A string set to the contents of the exception's Message property.

- bstrHelpFile—A string set to the contents of the exception's HelpLink property. If the HelpLink string ends with # followed by a number, only the string contents before the # are copied.

- dwHelpContext—Set to 0, unless the exception's HelpLink string ends with # followed by a number. In this case, dwHelpContext is set to that number.

- pvReserved—Always null.

- pfnDeferredFillIn—Always null.

- scode—The value of the exception's HResult property.

TIP

If the HRESULT returned by IDispatch.Invoke is not DISP_E_EXCEPTION (0x80020009), then the failure either occurred before or after the member was invoked. Failure before invocation can be caused by problems such as a wrong number of parameters or wrong parameter types. If the HRESULT returned is DISP_E_PARAMNOTFOUND or DISP_E_TYPEMISMATCH, then the index of the parameter causing the error is returned via Invoke's last parameter if a reference to a valid unsigned integer is passed. Failure after invocation can be caused by attempting to marshal invalid by-reference data types or return values back to unmanaged code.

When late binding, there's no way to extract additional information about the .NET exception thrown besides what is exposed via EXCEPINFO. For example, the exception's StackTrace and InnerException properties can't be read without an intermediate .NET object that catches the exception and exposes the information in a custom fashion.

V-Table Binding in Unmanaged C++

When v-table binding to a COM object, extra error information can be obtained by using the GetErrorInfo API to get an IErrorInfo interface pointer. IErrorInfo is defined as follows (in IDL):

```
interface IErrorInfo: IUnknown
{
  HRESULT GetGUID([out] GUID *pguid);
  HRESULT GetSource([out] BSTR *pbstrSource);
  HRESULT GetDescription([out] BSTR *pbstrDescription);
  HRESULT GetHelpFile([out] BSTR *pbstrHelpFile);
  HRESULT GetHelpContext([out] DWORD* pdwHelpContext);
}
```

Calling GetErrorInfo works only when the member that was invoked called SetErrorInfo before returning a failure HRESULT (which is done by all CCWs when a .NET member throws an exception). To indicate whether a COM object calls SetErrorInfo on failure, it can implement the ISupportErrorInfo interface. This interface has a single method— InterfaceSupportsErrorInfo—which returns S_OK if the object uses rich error information (for the interface implementation corresponding to an IID passed to the method) or S_FALSE if it does not.

All CCWs implement this interface and return S_OK from InterfaceSupportsErrorInfo, so this check is not strictly necessary if you know you're interacting with a .NET object. Similar to the EXCEPINFO structure in the previous example, the members of IErrorInfo return the following information when used for a .NET exception:

- GetGUID—Always returns GUID_NULL, a GUID set to all zeros. This is supposed to return the IID of the interface that defines the HRESULT, but .NET exceptions don't have such a notion.
- GetSource—Returns a string set to the contents of the exception's Source property.
- GetDescription—Returns a string set to the contents of the exception's Message property.
- GetHelpFile—Returns a string set to the contents of the exception's HelpLink property. If the HelpLink string ends with # followed by a number, only the string contents before the # are copied.
- GetHelpContext—Returns 0, unless the exception's HelpLink string ends with # followed by a number. In this case, GetHelpContext returns that number.

An exciting thing about obtaining an IErrorInfo interface pointer after a .NET exception is thrown is that the object returned by GetErrorInfo that implements IErrorInfo *is the .NET exception object*! This means that .NET-aware COM clients can successfully query for any COM-visible interface implemented by the exception or any of its COM-visible class interfaces, such as _Exception (the class interface for System.Exception), and call its members to get additional information.

TIP

.NET exception objects implement IErrorInfo when exposed to COM. Therefore, when a .NET exception is thrown toward a COM client and becomes a failure HRESULT, the CLR calls SetErrorInfo with the exception object so it can be retrieved by a COM client that calls GetErrorInfo.

Using QueryInterface to obtain an _Exception interface is useful, because it's an auto-dual class interface, so its members can be called without late binding. From _Exception, you can discover things such as the exception's stack trace, inner exception, or exception type. For exceptions that define their own members, such as System.IO.FileNotFoundException and its FileName property, using its most-derived class interface (_FileNotFoundException) enables COM clients to get this custom data. Most of the time, this requires late binding, because it's rare for a .NET exception to implement an interface exposing such information or exposing a class interface that isn't auto-dispatch.

Unfortunately, the .NET exception object cannot be accessed in Visual Basic 6 because the Err object that is raised is not the same object as the one implementing IErrorInfo. Instead, it is a separate object that has been initialized with the information from the object implementing IErrorInfo, and the original object is discarded by the Visual Basic 6 runtime.

Listing 8.5 demonstrates how to get the usual rich error information from IErrorInfo and then how to get .NET-specific error information from _Exception. To provoke an exception, this listing calls the RemoveAt method on an empty System.Collections.ArrayList instance. Because RemoveAt is defined on the IList interface implemented by ArrayList, we can call it without late binding.

LISTING 8.5   Unmanaged C++ Code That Obtains Rich Error Information When V-table Binding

```
1: #define _WIN32_DCOM
2: #include <stdio.h>
3: #include <wtypes.h>
```

LISTING 8.5 Continued

```
 4:
 5: #import "c:\\Windows\\Microsoft.NET\\Framework\\vn.n.nnnn\\mscorlib.tlb"
 6:➡no_namespace named_guids raw_interfaces_only
 7:
 8: int main(int argc, char* argv[])
 9: {
10:   IUnknown* pUnk = NULL;
11:   IList* pList = NULL;
12:   ISupportErrorInfo* pSuppErrInfo = NULL;
13:   IErrorInfo* pErrInfo = NULL;
14:   _Exception* pException = NULL;
15:   _Type* pType = NULL;
16:   HRESULT hresult;
17:
18:   // Initialize COM
19:   hresult = CoInitializeEx(NULL, COINIT_MULTITHREADED);
20:   if (FAILED(hresult))
21:   {
22:     printf("ERROR: Cannot initialize COM: 0x%x\n", hresult);
23:     return -1;
24:   }
25:
26:   // Instantiate the System.Collections.ArrayList class
27:   hresult = CoCreateInstance(CLSID_ArrayList, NULL, CLSCTX_INPROC_SERVER,
28:     IID_IUnknown, (void **)&pUnk);
29:   if (FAILED(hresult))
30:   {
31:     printf("ERROR: Cannot create object: 0x%x\n", hresult);
32:     return -1;
33:   }
34:
35:   // Get the IList interface
36:   hresult = pUnk->QueryInterface(IID_IList, (void**)&pList);
37:   if (FAILED(hresult))
38:   {
39:     printf("ERROR: Cannot obtain the IList interface pointer: 0x%x\n",
40:       hresult);
41:     pUnk->Release();
42:     return -1;
43:   }
44:
45:   hresult = pList->RemoveAt(1);
46:   if (FAILED(hresult))
47:   {
```

LISTING 8.5 Continued

```
48:        printf("ERROR: RemoveAt failed: 0x%x\n\n", hresult);
49:
50:        // Check if the object supports extended error information
51:        hresult = pList->QueryInterface(IID_ISupportErrorInfo,
52:          (void**)&pSuppErrInfo);
53:        if (SUCCEEDED(hresult))
54:        {
55:          hresult = pSuppErrInfo->InterfaceSupportsErrorInfo(IID_IList);
56:          if (hresult == S_OK)
57:          {
58:            // Attempt to get the IErrorInfo pointer
59:            hresult = GetErrorInfo(0, &pErrInfo);
60:            if (SUCCEEDED(hresult))
61:            {
62:              BSTR source = NULL;
63:              BSTR description = NULL;
64:              BSTR helpFile = NULL;
65:              unsigned long helpContext;
66:
67:              hresult = pErrInfo->GetSource(&source);
68:              if (SUCCEEDED(hresult)) printf("Source:        %S\n\n",
69:                source);
70:
71:              hresult = pErrInfo->GetDescription(&description);
72:              if (SUCCEEDED(hresult)) printf("Description:   %S\n\n",
73:                description);
74:
75:              hresult = pErrInfo->GetHelpFile(&helpFile);
76:              if (SUCCEEDED(hresult)) printf("HelpFile:      %S\n\n",
77:                helpFile);
78:
79:              hresult = pErrInfo->GetHelpContext(&helpContext);
80:              if (SUCCEEDED(hresult)) printf("HelpContext:   %d\n\n",
81:                helpContext);
82:
83:              if (source != NULL) SysFreeString(source);
84:              if (description != NULL) SysFreeString(description);
85:              if (helpFile != NULL) SysFreeString(helpFile);
86:
87:              // Call members of the .NET exception object
88:              BSTR stackTrace = NULL;
89:              BSTR toString = NULL;
90:              BSTR exceptionTypeName = NULL;
```

LISTING 8.5 Continued

```
 91:
 92:             hresult = pErrInfo->QueryInterface(IID__Exception,
 93:              (void**)&pException);
 94:          if (SUCCEEDED(hresult))
 95:          {
 96:            hresult = pException->get_StackTrace(&stackTrace);
 97:            if (SUCCEEDED(hresult)) printf("Stack Trace:      %S\n\n",
 98:              stackTrace);
 99:
100:            hresult = pException->get_ToString(&toString);
101:            if (SUCCEEDED(hresult)) printf("ToString:         %S\n\n",
102:              toString);
103:
104:            hresult = pException->GetType(&pType);
105:            if (SUCCEEDED(hresult))
106:            {
107:              hresult = pType->get_ToString(&exceptionTypeName);
108:              if (SUCCEEDED(hresult)) printf("Exception Type: %S\n\n",
109:                exceptionTypeName);
110:            }
111:
112:            if (toString != NULL) SysFreeString(toString);
113:            if (stackTrace != NULL) SysFreeString(stackTrace);
114:            if (exceptionTypeName != NULL)
115:              SysFreeString(exceptionTypeName);
116:          }
117:        }
118:      }
119:    }
120:  }
121:
122:  // Release interface pointers
123:  if (pUnk != NULL) pUnk->Release();
124:  if (pList != NULL) pList->Release();
125:  if (pSuppErrInfo != NULL) pSuppErrInfo->Release();
126:  if (pErrInfo != NULL) pErrInfo->Release();
127:  if (pException != NULL) pException->Release();
128:  if (pType != NULL) pType->Release();
129:
130:  CoUninitialize();
131:  return 0;
132: }
```

Lines 5–6 import `mscorlib.tlb`, just as in the previous listing. The `raw_interfaces_only` directive is important to prevent ATL from turning the failed HRESULT from the call to `IList.RemoveAt` into a C++ exception.

The CCW for the `ArrayList` is instantiated in Lines 27–28 and the `IList` interface pointer is obtained in Line 36. Line 45 contains the call to `RemoveAt` that intentionally fails. Once it fails, Lines 51–56 ensure that the object supports rich error information in its `IList` implementation by calling `QueryInterface` to obtain an `ISupportErrorInfo` interface pointer then checking for S_OK returned by `InterfaceSupportsErrorInfo` for IID_IList. As mentioned earlier, this is really not necessary because all CCWs implement this interface and return S_OK from `InterfaceSupportsErrorInfo`, but it's done here for completeness.

Line 59 calls the `GetErrorInfo` API to obtain an `IErrorInfo` pointer, and Lines 67–81 print the information obtained from it (skipping `GetGUID` because it returns GUID_NULL). This is as far as .NET-unaware COM clients will go, but Lines 92–93 call `QueryInterface` for IID__Exception (the IID for the `_Exception` interface) so the program can print more information specific to the .NET exception. Lines 96–98 print the string returned by the exception's `StackTrace` property, and Lines 100–102 print the string returned by the exception's `ToString` method (exported as a `ToString` property). Line 104 calls `_Exception`'s `GetType` method (inherited from `System.Object`) to get an `_Type` interface pointer, the class interface for `System.Type`. On this interface pointer, Line 107 calls its `ToString` property to print the name of the exception's type.

The output of running this code is

```
ERROR: RemoveAt failed: 0x80131502

Source:         mscorlib

Description:    Index was out of range. Must be non-negative and less than
➥ the size of the collection.
Parameter name: index

HelpFile:       (null)

HelpContext:    0

Stack Trace:       at System.Collections.ArrayList.RemoveAt(Int32 index)

ToString:       System.ArgumentOutOfRangeException: Index was out of range.
➥ Must be non-negative and less than the size of the collection.
Parameter name: index
   at System.Collections.ArrayList.RemoveAt(Int32 index)

Exception Type: System.ArgumentOutOfRangeException
```

Enumerating Over a Collection

Thanks to the transformations done by the type library exporter, enumerating over a collection exposed by a .NET object is as simple as enumerating over a collection exposed by a COM object. The For Each statement in Visual Basic 6 works on a .NET collection because a GetEnumerator method is exposed with DISPID_NEW_ENUM (a DISPID equal to –4) and appears to return an IEnumVARIANT interface. The unmanaged C++ code to enumerate over a collection isn't very pretty, but here's a snippet of Visual Basic 6 code that proves that .NET enumerators are exposed in the fashion familiar to COM:

```
Dim list As New ArrayList
Dim v As Variant

list.Add 1
list.Add 2
list.Add 3
list.Add 4

For Each v In list
  MsgBox v
Next
```

Running this code, which must be done inside a project referencing mscorlib.tlb for the definition of ArrayList, produces four message boxes that display "1", "2", "3", "4", in that order. As with any COM client that uses types from the mscorlib assembly, you must be sure that the assembly has been registered with REGASM.EXE before running it.

Deploying a COM Application That Uses .NET

Correctly deploying a COM application that uses .NET components is not quite as simple as deploying a COM application that doesn't. Besides satisfying the requirements of COM, you must satisfy the requirements of the .NET Framework.

The best place to install assemblies used by COM is in the Global Assembly Cache (GAC). Because they get registered globally in the Windows Registry, they become shared components from COM's perspective even if they were intended to be used privately. Besides registering assemblies on target computers, you might also need to export type libraries and register them on target computers if your application depends on cross-context COM marshaling. If you are developing the .NET components being used by your COM clients, see Chapter 11 for more information about deploying .NET components and considerations that need to be made regarding the versioning of your components.

Speaking of versioning, the side-by-side nature of the CLR has an interesting side effect for COM clients that use multiple .NET components. Every COM-creatable class in every assembly gets registered with a `RuntimeVersion` value that can affect what version of the CLR is loaded when it's instantiated by a COM client. Suppose a single COM application uses two .NET classes, A and B, each from a different assembly. It's conceivable that each class is registered with a different version of the CLR (once more than one version of the CLR exists). Each process can only have one CLR loaded, so if the two .NET objects are created in the same process, a single version of the CLR must be chosen.

The version of the CLR that gets loaded is affected only by the registry entry accompanying the *first* .NET class to be activated. With this behavior, the loaded CLR version could appear to randomly change from one program execution to another, based on the order that program events occur that cause the classes to be loaded. This is pictured in Figure 8.7, in which the loaded version of the CLR is determined by which button a user clicks first in a hypothetical COM application.

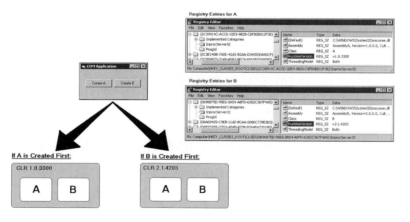

FIGURE 8.7

The CLR version loaded is determined by the first .NET class instantiated.

Hopefully, the version of the CLR that gets loaded doesn't make one bit of difference to your application's behavior. Still, it's possible that a later version of the CLR could have a bug or incompatibility that affects your application, and users might encounter the problem only at certain times, due to the seemingly random behavior of choosing which CLR gets loaded. .NET applications don't exhibit this non-deterministic behavior, because the CLR is loaded from the start when the client application is managed.

To prevent this behavior, COM applications that use multiple .NET components should be deployed with a configuration file that specifies the desired version of the CLR. That's right—

.NET configuration files work with unmanaged executables as well as managed executables! When MSCOREE.DLL is loaded as the in-process COM server, it checks for an appropriate configuration file with the appropriate contents before checking the RuntimeVersion registry value to determine which version of the CLR to load. A configuration file overrides anything specified by RuntimeVersion registry keys, so it provides consistency in the face of multiple runtimes.

For an unmanaged executable named MyApp.exe, you should create a configuration file called MyApp.exe.config with contents such as the following:

```xml
<?xml version="1.0"?>
<configuration>
  <startup>
    <requiredRuntime version="v1.0.3300"/>
  </startup>
</configuration>
```

This configuration file must be in the same directory as MyApp.exe. For more information about .NET configuration files, such as using them for Web applications, consult the .NET Framework SDK documentation.

Hosting Windows Forms Controls in Internet Explorer

Chapter 3 demonstrated that exposing ActiveX controls as Windows Forms controls is supported by the .NET Framework and fairly easy to accomplish thanks to the ActiveX Importer. The reverse action of exposing Windows Forms controls as ActiveX controls is *not* supported (although it was in Beta 1 of the .NET Framework). It's still possible to expose Windows Forms controls as general-purpose ActiveX controls, but you must do so at your own risk. Chapter 10 describes how to do this. What *is* supported is hosting Windows Forms controls in Internet Explorer (versions 5.0 and later), as long as the client computer has the .NET Framework installed (at least the redistributable package). In fact, any .NET objects can be hosted in this manner, but this section focuses specifically on Windows Forms controls.

FAQ: How are Windows Forms controls hosted in a Web page better than ActiveX controls?

Windows Forms controls have the following advantages over ActiveX controls:

- No COM registration is required. The Windows Registry is not used to locate and activate Windows Forms controls hosted in Internet Explorer, so no global computer state is modified.

> - Windows Forms controls are safe. The user or administrator can decide how much a control is allowed to do thanks to the CLR's code access security. If a control attempts to do something it isn't allowed to do, it is stopped via a security exception. With an ActiveX control, you are presented with a dialog and forced to either not run it at all or give it full trust to do whatever it desires.
>
> - Pieces of controls can be downloaded on demand. Dependent modules and assemblies don't need to be downloaded until the control requires them to be loaded. By partitioning your control into several assemblies, or by creating a multi-module assembly, you can display your control's initial user interface without waiting for the entire control to download.
>
> - Windows Forms controls run in isolation. By being restricted to the Assembly Download Cache (different from the GAC), downloaded controls cannot affect other applications on your computer.
>
> A negative aspect to using Windows Forms controls on a Web site is that they require at least the .NET Framework redistributable package on the client machine. Until the .NET Framework is as ubiquitous as Internet Explorer, Web sites need to provide alternative functionality for clients without the .NET Framework.

Web pages can use Windows Forms controls with the `<object>` tag and special syntax that looks like the following:

```
<object classid="URL/AssemblyFileName#FullyQualifiedClassName"></object>
```

For example:

```
<object id="myControl"
  classid="http:MyAssembly.dll#Chapter8.MyControl"
  height="200"
  width="200">
  <param name="Text" value="My Control">
</object>
```

By default, the control's fore color, back color, and font are inherited from the Web page's HTML. The `<param>` tags can be used to set properties of the control; name specifies the property's name and value specifies the value you're setting it to. Any .NET class can be instantiated in this manner, even ones without a user interface. The object created is a CCW, just as in all the previous interactions with .NET objects.

.NET objects created with this `<object>` tag syntax are fully scriptable by COM-aware script languages such as VBScript or JScript as if they are ActiveX controls. This is because all CCWs created in this fashion implement a COM interface called IObjectSafety in such a way to mark themselves as safe for scripting. This is safe to do because Internet Explorer hosts the Web page in an application domain with permissions appropriate to the zone of its URL (such as "Internet Zone"). This application domain acts as a *sandbox* that isolates the code such that it can't perform tasks that aren't allowed. Strong-named .NET components must be marked with AllowPartiallyTrustedCallersAttribute, introduced in Chapter 6, "Advanced Topics for Using COM Components," to be hosted in a Web page.

CAUTION

A problematic aspect of Windows Forms controls hosted in Internet Explorer is that if you want script to respond to .NET events by hooking up event handlers, the Windows Forms control must be granted unmanaged code permission. This is necessary because when the control fires an event, the transition from the managed event source to the unmanaged event sink requires the permission. But by granting unmanaged code permission to a control, you lose the security advantage over ActiveX controls, because it would no longer be running in a semi-trusted state.

In addition, creating a Windows Forms control that exposes events in a way that COM understands is not trivial. Chapter 13, "Exposing .NET Events to COM Clients," covers this topic.

Listing 8.6 contains C# source code for a simple Windows Forms control called LabeledTextBox. This control combines two existing controls—Label and TextBox—because these simple controls are often used together. LabeledTextBox exposes two properties for setting the text of either sub-control.

LISTING 8.6   A Simple Windows Forms Control

```
 1: using System.Windows.Forms;
 2: using System.Security;
 3:
 4: [assembly:AllowPartiallyTrustedCallersAttribute]
 5:
 6: public class LabeledTextBox : UserControl
 7: {
 8:    private System.Windows.Forms.TextBox textBox1;
 9:    private System.Windows.Forms.Label label1;
10:    private System.ComponentModel.Container components = null;
11:
12:    public LabeledTextBox()
13:    {
14:      // This call is required by the Windows.Forms Form Designer
```

8

USING .NET
COMPONENTS
FROM COM

LISTING 8.6   Continued

```
15:      InitializeComponent();
16:    }
17:
18:    public string LabelText
19:    {
20:      get { return label1.Text; }
21:      set { label1.Text = value; }
22:    }
23:
24:    public string TextBoxText
25:    {
26:      get { return textBox1.Text; }
27:      set { textBox1.Text = value; }
28:    }
29:
30:    // Clean up any resources being used
31:    protected override void Dispose(bool disposing)
32:    {
33:      if (disposing)
34:      {
35:        if (components != null)
36:          components.Dispose();
37:      }
38:      base.Dispose(disposing);
39:    }
40:
41:    // Required method for Designer support
42:    private void InitializeComponent()
43:    {
44:      this.textBox1 = new System.Windows.Forms.TextBox();
45:      this.label1 = new System.Windows.Forms.Label();
46:      this.SuspendLayout();
47:
48:      this.textBox1.Anchor = ((System.Windows.Forms.AnchorStyles.Top |
49:          System.Windows.Forms.AnchorStyles.Bottom)
50:        | System.Windows.Forms.AnchorStyles.Right);
51:      this.textBox1.Location = new System.Drawing.Point(112, 0);
52:      this.textBox1.Multiline = true;
53:      this.textBox1.Name = "textBox1";
54:      this.textBox1.Size = new System.Drawing.Size(144, 20);
55:      this.textBox1.TabIndex = 0;
56:      this.textBox1.Text = "TextBox";
57:
58:      this.label1.Anchor = (((System.Windows.Forms.AnchorStyles.Top |
59:          System.Windows.Forms.AnchorStyles.Bottom)
```

LISTING 8.6 Continued

```
60:            | System.Windows.Forms.AnchorStyles.Left)
61:            | System.Windows.Forms.AnchorStyles.Right);
62:        this.label1.Name = "label1";
63:        this.label1.Size = new System.Drawing.Size(112, 20);
64:        this.label1.TabIndex = 1;
65:        this.label1.Text = "Label";
66:        this.label1.TextAlign = System.Drawing.ContentAlignment.MiddleRight;
67:
68:        this.Controls.AddRange(new System.Windows.Forms.Control[] {
69:          this.label1, this.textBox1});
70:        this.Name = "LabeledTextBox";
71:        this.Size = new System.Drawing.Size(256, 20);
72:        this.ResumeLayout(false);
73:    }
74: }
```

Listing 8.7 contains a simple Web page that hosts the LabeledTextBox control, with some unmanaged JScript code that interacts with it.

LISTING 8.7 Hosting and Scripting a Windows Forms Control in a Web Page

```
1: <html>
2:   <script>
3:     function SetValues()
4:     {
5:       theControl.LabelText = "Name";
6:       theControl.TextBoxText = "Lindsay";
7:     }
8:   </script>
9:   <body onload="SetValues()">
10:     <object id="theControl" classid="LabeledTextBox.dll#LabeledTextBox">
11:     </object>
12:   </body>
13: </html>
```

To run this example, you should create a new virtual directory using Internet Information Services (IIS) and place the Windows Forms control and the HTML document inside it. The virtual directory's execution permissions must be set to Scripts only rather than Scripts & Executables. You might need to modify the classid string used with the <object> tag depending on the location of the physical assembly file.

Figure 8.8 shows the result of viewing the Web page from Listing 8.7.

FIGURE 8.8

A Windows Forms control hosted in a Web page.

Using unmanaged script to interact with .NET objects that are created with this custom <object> tag syntax has its limitations. Besides the limitation of calling members with UDT parameters (mentioned in the "Using a .NET Component in Unmanaged JScript" section), and besides the security restrictions preventing event handling from untrusted script, JScript and VBScript code cannot pass an instance of a .NET object as a parameter whose type is a class other than System.Object or System.MarshalByRefObject. This is because the scripting engine wraps all CCWs inside another COM object, so when such an object is passed back to managed code, it looks like a System.__ComObject instance (a generic COM object). Parameters that are defined as primitive types or interfaces are usable, but attempting to call a member with a parameter that's a Hashtable or ArrayList, for example, fails as a type mismatch.

Conclusion

This chapter introduced the steps involved in writing COM applications that use .NET components, some of the related common issues and problems, and some good practices, such as getting rich error information accompanying failure HRESULTs and shipping configuration files with your client executables. The importance of taking advantage of rich error information can't be stressed enough for unmanaged C++ clients. It greatly simplifies the debugging process.

Exposing Windows Forms controls as ActiveX controls was covered for the one scenario officially supported—hosting them in Internet Explorer using a new activation scheme that's very un-COM-like. Chapter 10 examines Windows Forms controls again to show what else we can do with them that's not officially supported.

Because COM is often an afterthought (or a "neverthought") for authors of .NET components, using them in COM applications can often be unnatural. You've seen some examples of unnatural behavior in this chapter (such as odd names for overloaded methods or being forced to late bind), and will see more in the next two chapters. These problems can be more common and more serious in this direction than the reverse direction of using COM components in .NET applications. The reason for this is that the CLR bends over backwards to make existing COM components work as naturally as possible, because most were written before .NET existed. The CLR isn't as zealous about making all .NET constructs and patterns useable from COM, however. Authors of .NET components can be given advice to make their components COM-friendly (the subject of Part IV), and have the power to fix their APIs that are hard to use for COM clients at the time that they are first designed. Therefore, .NET developers have little excuse for creating components that are hard to use from COM!

An In-Depth Look at Exported Type Libraries

IN THIS CHAPTER

- Converting the Assembly   426
- Converting .NET Data Types   429
- Converting Members   434
- Converting Interfaces   447
- Converting Classes   449
- Converting Value Types   452
- Converting Enumerations   453

The previous chapter demonstrated how using a .NET component in a COM application can be just like using a COM component, and how type libraries can be created for any .NET component simply by running `TLBEXP.EXE` (or `REGASM.EXE` with its `/tlb` option). In many cases, using the exported type definitions may be self-explanatory, but it is often necessary to gain a deeper understanding of the type library exporter. Even if the author of the .NET component considered the needs of COM users when designing the APIs, it's unlikely that they are documented from the perspective of an unmanaged C++ or Visual Basic 6 user.

This chapter describes the behavior of the type library exporter in depth. Each element that can be found in an assembly is discussed, one element at a time, in a way that's similar to Chapter 4, "An In-Depth Look at Imported Assemblies." As with Chapter 4, this chapter contains several short code listings that demonstrate each transformation. Because both metadata and type library information are stored as binary data, examples need to be shown in representative languages. Most COM examples are shown in Visual Basic 6 and IDL syntax, and most .NET examples are shown in C# and Visual Basic .NET syntax.

The elements that the type library exporter produces—coclasses, interfaces, methods, properties, and so on—are not much different than the elements found in any type library. The exporter knows how to produce type definitions that correspond to the Interop Marshaler's rules for converting managed types to unmanaged types. These exported type library definitions serve as type information for the COM-Callable Wrappers (CCWs) used at run time. Unlike Interop Assemblies, however, exported type information is not *used* by the Interop Marshaler at run time; the marshaler always bases its work on metadata definitions.

Converting the Assembly

There is a one-to-one mapping between an assembly and a type library. A single exported type library always contains the appropriate definitions for an entire assembly, even if the assembly consists of multiple files. If the input assembly uses types from additional assemblies in any exported signatures, the exporter automatically generates an additional type library for each referenced assembly. These dependent assemblies must be able to be located when the exporter runs—for example, in the Global Assembly Cache or the current directory.

The generated type library has the name *AssemblyName*`.tlb`, where *AssemblyName* is the assembly's simple name, unless a different output name is chosen. The most important aspect of the output type library is not its filename, however, but its identity. Type libraries are identified by the following information:

- Library Identifier (LIBID)
- Version
- Locale Identifier (LCID)

If the input assembly isn't marked with a `GuidAttribute` custom attribute that chooses a LIBID, the exporter chooses a LIBID based on the input assembly's simple name, version, and public key. This ensures that assemblies differing by any of this information results in a different LIBID. It also ensures that an assembly's LIBID remains constant as long as its identity (not counting locale) remains the same.

The exporter uses the assembly's major and minor version numbers to form the two-part type library version number, unless the major and minor version numbers are both set to zero. In this case, the exported type library is given the version 1.0 because some OLE Automation APIs don't work properly with a type library version of 0.0. This means that assemblies with version numbers differing only by build or revision numbers end up with the same type library version. Fortunately, the type libraries would still have different identities because their LIBIDs would be different.

The exported type library's locale identifier (LCID) is set to the default value of zero for assemblies with a neutral culture. For assemblies marked with the `System.Reflection.AssemblyCultureAttribute` pseudo-custom attribute, the LCID is based on the culture. Every culture has an associated LCID, which can be discovered using `System.Globalization.CultureInfo`'s `LCID` property, for example:

```
// Print the LCID for the French-Canadian culture
Console.WriteLine(new CultureInfo("fr-ca").LCID);
```

A type library's LCID can't be seen when viewed using `OLEVIEW.EXE`, but can be seen when the type library is registered, since its location is registered under the following key:

```
HKEY_CLASSES_ROOT\TypeLib\{LIBID}\MajorVersion.MinorVersion\LCID\win32
```

Although not part of a type library's identity, the library name is important to clients because Visual C++ and Visual Basic treat it like a namespace. The library name is *always* the input assembly's simple name, even if a different output filename is chosen. However, an assembly's name can contain many characters that are not legal as a type library name, such as periods. Because periods are quite common in assembly names, the exporter converts all periods to underscores. For example, a type library exported for the `System.Windows.Forms` assembly has the name `System_Windows_Forms`. Any other special characters (like dollar signs or plus signs) are left alone, but .NET languages (other than IL Assembler) don't allow them in assembly names anyway.

Although the importer discards library-level helpstrings when creating Interop Assemblies, the exporter marks the `library` statement with a helpstring for any assemblies marked with the `System.Reflection.AssemblyDescriptionAttribute` custom attribute, using the attribute's string contents.

Therefore, an assembly containing the following custom attributes in C# source code (perhaps in an `AssemblyInfo.cs` file, as generated by Visual Studio .NET):

```
using System.Reflection;
[assembly:AssemblyDescription("A sample assembly")]
[assembly:AssemblyVersion("2.0.300.5")]
```

results in the following exported type library (shown in IDL syntax):

```
[
  uuid(C85E9A02-706C-3E4E-B4E3-34216CF30C0C),
  version(2.0),
  helpstring("A sample assembly"),
  custom(90883F05-3D28-11D2-8F17-00A0C9A6186D,
➡ "ChapterNine, Version=2.0.300.5, Culture=neutral, PublicKeyToken=null")
]
library ChapterNine
{
  ...
};
```

DIGGING DEEPER

Notice the IDL custom attribute identified with the GUID `90883F05-3D28-11D2-8F17-00A0C9A6186D` that appears in all exported type libraries. This attribute contains a string representation of the input assembly's full name. The type library importer makes use of this attribute, so any new type libraries that reference an exported type library are imported as Interop Assemblies that reference the *original* dependent assemblies. In other words, it preserves the identity of assemblies in their exported type libraries. This action of importing a type library that references type libraries exported from .NET assemblies is discussed in Chapter 17, "Implementing .NET Interfaces for Type Compatibility."

The IDL custom attribute also instructs the type library importer to not attempt to produce an assembly for such a type library because this means that the type library was exported from an assembly. You can think of this custom attribute like an "ExportedFromAssembly" custom attribute, the reverse of `ImportedFromTypeLibAttribute` in `System.Runtime.InteropServices`.

That covers the properties of the output type library. Now we'll look in depth at how the contents of the type library are produced based on the input assembly.

Converting .NET Data Types

This section covers the data type transformations done by the type library exporter for parameters and return values, and fields of structures. Table 9.1 lists the transformations. These transformations also help summarize the Interop Marshaler's rules for marshaling .NET types to COM types. As in Chapter 4, each .NET type is shown as the language-neutral type. Keep in mind how the .NET type is typically used in your language of choice (such as int instead of System.Int32). Each COM data type is shown in two representations: IDL and Visual Basic 6.

The Unknown types listed under the "VB6 Type" column is not a real data type in Visual Basic 6, but simply what its object browser shows for IUnknown parameters. This table is a little more complicated than the reverse table in Chapter 4, since .NET data types can be marked with the MarshalAsAttribute pseudo-custom attribute to change their marshaling behavior and therefore their representation in a type library, discussed in Chapter 12, "Customizing COM's View of .NET Components." The UnmanagedType values listed represent values inside this attribute. For any data types whose default export/marshaling behavior differs depending on whether they are used as a parameter (including return types) or as a field in an exported structure, both default behaviors are listed separately.

TABLE 9.1 .NET Data Types Are Converted to COM Data Types with Similar Semantics

.NET Type	*IDL Type*	*VB6 Type*
System.SByte	char	N/A
System.Int16	short	Integer
System.Int32	long	Long
with UnmanagedType.Error	HRESULT	Long
System.Int64	int64	N/A
System.IntPtr	long	Long
System.Byte	unsigned char	Byte
System.Char		
default for parameters	unsigned short	N/A
default for struct fields (CharSet.Ansi)	unsigned char	Byte
default for struct fields (CharSet.Unicode)	unsigned short	N/A
with UnmanagedType.U1	unsigned char	Byte
with UnmanagedType.U2	unsigned short	N/A

TABLE 9.1   Continued

.NET Type	IDL Type	VB6 Type
System.UInt16	unsigned short	N/A
System.UInt32	unsigned long	N/A
with UnmanagedType.Error	HRESULT	Long
System.UInt64	uint64	N/A
System.UIntPtr	unsigned long	N/A
System.Single	single	Single
System.Double	double	Double
System.Boolean		
default for parameters	VARIANT_BOOL	Boolean
default for struct fields	long	Long
with UnmanagedType.Bool	long	Long
with UnmanagedType.I1	unsigned char	Byte
with UnmanagedType.U1	unsigned char	Byte
with UnmanagedType.VariantBool	VARIANT_BOOL	Boolean
System.DateTime	DATE	Date
System.Guid	GUID	N/A
System.Decimal		
default	DECIMAL	N/A
with UnmanagedType.Currency	CURRENCY	Currency
System.String		
default for parameters	BSTR	String
default for struct fields	LPSTR	String
with UnmanagedType.LPStr	LPSTR	String
with UnmanagedType.LPWStr	LPWSTR	String
with UnmanagedType. CustomMarshaler	long	Long
System.Text.StringBuilder	LPSTR	String
with UnmanagedType.LPStr	LPSTR	String
with UnmanagedType.LPWStr	LPWSTR	String
with UnmanagedType. CustomMarshaler	IUnknown*	Unknown

TABLE 9.1 Continued

.NET Type	IDL Type	VB6 Type
System.Object		
default for parameters	VARIANT	Variant
default for struct fields	IUnknown*	Unknown
with UnmanagedType.IUnknown	IUnknown*	Unknown
with UnmanagedType.IDispatch	IDispatch*	Object
with UnmanagedType.Struct	VARIANT	Variant
with UnmanagedType. CustomMarshaler	IUnknown*	Unknown
with UnmanagedType.Interface	IUnknown*	Unknown
SomeInterface	*SomeInterface**	*SomeClassOr- Interface*
with UnmanagedType. CustomMarshaler	IUnknown*	Unknown
SomeClass	*DefaultInterface**	*SomeClass*
with UnmanagedType. CustomMarshaler	IUnknown*	Unknown
SomeFormattedClass	*SomeStruct**	ByRef *SomeUDT*
with UnmanagedType. CustomMarshaler	IUnknown*	Unknown
SomeDelegateClass		
default for parameters	*DefaultInterface**	*SomeDelegateClass*
default for struct fields	int	Long
with UnmanagedType.FunctionPtr	int	Long
with UnmanagedType. CustomMarshaler	IUnknown*	Unknown
SomeValueType	*SomeStruct*	*SomeUDT*
SomeEnum		
with 32-bit underlying type	*SomeEnum*	*SomeEnum*
with any other underlying type	*underlying type*	*underlying type*
array of *SomeType*		
default for parameters	SAFEARRAY(*SomeType*)	*SomeType*()
with UnmanagedType.ByValArray	*SomeType*[*size*]	*SomeType*(0 To size-1)
with UnmanagedType.LPArray	(parameters only)	*SomeType**

9

EXPORTED TYPE
LIBRARIES

TABLE 9.1   Continued

.NET Type	IDL Type	VB6 Type
SomeType		
with UnmanagedType.SafeArray	SAFEARRAY(SomeType)	SomeType()
with UnmanagedType. CustomMarshaler	long	Long

> **CAUTION**
>
> Notice that the exporter treats System.IntPtr, System.UIntPtr, string and array types marked with UnmanagedType.CustomMarshaler, and delegates marked with UnmanagedType.FunctionPtr as int and long data types. This works fine on 32-bit platforms, but such types really represent a platform-sized pointer. If you're concerned with the exported type library being useable as-is on any platform, you should alter the type library (using tools like OLEVIEW.EXE and MIDL.EXE) to change these ints and longs to void* types.

Table 9.1 assumes that the data types are all COM-visible. Otherwise, COM-invisible reference types are exported as IUnknown* and COM-invisible value types are not exported at all, causing members exposing them to be skipped.

> **CAUTION**
>
> Unfortunately, a COM-invisible enum parameter is treated just like any other value type. Rather than being replaced with its (COM-visible) underlying type, the member exposing the enum does not get exported at all.

Besides the transformations with and UnmanagedType.CustomMarshaler, UnmanagedType.FunctionPtr, most of the transformations in the table should be self-explanatory. Boolean types are sometimes exported as the long type to represent the Win32 BOOL type. Both are 32-bit types, but BOOL can't be expressed in a type library. System.Char fields of a struct are exported (and marshaled) depending on the structure's character set, which is ANSI by default in C#, Visual Basic .NET, and Visual C++ .NET. See Chapter 19, "Deeper Into PInvoke and Useful Examples," for more information about structures and their character sets. When arrays are exported, their element type may differ based on a MarshalAsAttribute marking that uses SafeArraySubType or ArraySubType, described in Chapter 12.

CAUTION

In version 1.0 of the CLR, arrays of characters are not exported correctly when marked with `UnmanagedType.ByValArray` and used as fields of structures with the character set `CharSet.Auto`. Such a character array field is correctly exported as an array of `unsigned char` or `unsigned short` types if the structure has an ANSI or Unicode character set, respectively. However, with a platform-dependent character set, such a field is exported as an array of `void` types. You should avoid platform-dependent character sets in types exported to a type library, anyway, because the character set of the computer on which the type library is exported may not match the character set of the computer on which a client of the type library is running.

The *SomeFormattedClass* table entry requires an explanation. A *formatted class* or *formatted reference type* is a class that is marked with structure layout using `StructLayoutAttribute`. Such a reference type gets exported to COM the same way a value type does, but with an extra level of indirection. This means that a formatted class's fields are exposed to COM, but no methods, properties, or events are. Chapter 19 shows an example of defining and using a formatted class.

CAUTION

Although the type library exporter converts a structure's array fields to SAFEARRAYs by default, the Interop Marshaler only supports marshaling SAFEARRAYs as parameters or return types in version 1.0. Therefore, .NET array fields are only exported in a useable way if marked with the `MarshalAsAttribute` pseudo-custom attribute, covered in Chapter 12.

The exporter only generates three possible kinds of arrays—SAFEARRAYs, fixed-length C-style arrays, and pointers to C-style arrays. There's no distinction to be made about varying, conformant, or conformant varying since these can't be expressed in a type library.

Although multidimensional arrays are supported via COM Interoperability, arrays of arrays are not. This means types expressed with [][] in C#. Members using such array types are never exported.

Converting Members

Although COM interfaces have only two types of members (methods and properties), .NET types can have methods (including overloaded methods), properties, fields, and events. Therefore, the type library exporter, following the contract of the Interop Marshaler, performs many different transformations to fit rich .NET object models into the less expressive world of COM.

Although the transformations specific to each member type are discussed in the following sections, one action done by the exporter applies to all member types in a dual interface or dispinterface— choosing DISPIDs. The exporter assigns default DISPIDs, starting with 0x60020000 if none are explicitly assigned. Any default members (such as indexers in C#), which are indicated by the System.Reflection.DefaultMemberAttribute in metadata, are given DISPID 0 (DISPID_VALUE) unless another member is explicitly assigned that DISPID. DISPIDs can be chosen by the author of .NET members by using the DispIdAttribute custom attribute, described in Chapter 12.

Methods

There are six main transformations done by the type library exporter to make .NET method signatures usable and familiar to COM clients:

- Exposing an HRESULT
- Handling [in] versus [out] versus [in, out]
- Handling Overloaded Methods
- Converting ToString
- Converting GetEnumerator
- Converting Parameter Arrays

Exposing an HRESULT

Unless marked with PreserveSigAttribute, a .NET method is transformed so that a return value, if it exists, becomes an [out, retval] parameter, and an HRESULT is returned. This is demonstrated in Listing 9.1.

LISTING 9.1   The .NET View and the COM View of the Same Simple Methods

MANAGED

C#:

```
public void SetName(String name);

public String GetName();
```

LISTING 9.1   Continued

```
[PreserveSig] public int ReturnInt();

[PreserveSig] [return:MarshalAs(UnmanagedType.Error)]
public int ReturnHResult();
```

Visual Basic .NET:

```
Public Sub SetName(name As String)

Public Function GetName() As String

<PreserveSig> Public Function ReturnInt() As Integer

<PreserveSig> Public Function ReturnHResult() _
  As <MarshalAs(UnmanagedType.Error)> Integer
```

`UNMANAGED`

Visual Basic 6:

```
Public Sub SetName(ByVal name As String)

Public Function GetName() As String

Public Function ReturnInt() As Long

Public Sub ReturnHResult()
```

IDL:

```
HRESULT SetName([in] BSTR name);

HRESULT GetName([out, retval] BSTR name);

long ReturnInt();

HRESULT ReturnHResult();
```

> **TIP**
>
> To see the transformations in Listing 9.1 and the other listings in this chapter for yourself, you'd need to either define the signatures on an interface or on a class marked with the custom attribute `ClassInterface(ClassInterfaceType.AutoDual)` to see the signatures in the exported library. Otherwise, members of a class are not exposed in the exported auto-dispatch class interfaces. `ClassInterface (ClassInterfaceType.AutoDual)` should only be used for testing purposes, however.

9

EXPORTED TYPE
LIBRARIES

In the cases where `PreserveSigAttribute` isn't used, the returned `HRESULT` value is always `S_OK` unless an exception is thrown during the execution of the method. In that case, an `HRESULT` value corresponding to the exception is returned. Appendix D, ".NET Exception to `HRESULT` Transformations," describes these transformations.

Handling `[in]` Versus `[out]` Versus `[in, out]`

When representing parameters of .NET methods as parameters of a COM method, the type library exporter does the following:

- By-value reference type parameters are marked `[in]`. The only exception to this rule is the `System.Text.StringBuilder` type because it's frequently used as an in/out buffer. See Chapter 18, "The Essentials of PInvoke," for more details. All by-value reference type parameters have one level of indirection except for the reference types listed in the next bullet point.

- By-value value type parameters, strings (when exported as `BSTR`), arrays (when exported as `SAFEARRAY`), `System.Object` (when exported as `VARIANT`), and types marshaled as `void*` that are represented as `int` or `long` (shown previously in Table 9.1), are always marked `[in]` and have no levels of indirection.

- All by-reference parameters are marked [in, out] and have one additional level of indirection than they do in the by-value case.

- Pointers to types (as used with C# unsafe code) are exported just like by-reference parameters, but can have extra levels of indirection if the .NET parameter is a pointer to a pointer, and so on. Calling such methods from COM works only when the parameters point to blittable types.

These rules are demonstrated in Listing 9.2.

LISTING 9.2   The .NET View and the COM View of the Same Methods with By-Value and By-Reference Parameters

MANAGED

C#:

```
public void Strings(String byvalue, ref String byreference);

public void Arrays(int [] byvalue, ref int [] byreference);

public void ValueTypes(double byvalue, ref double byreference);

public void ReferenceTypes(ICloneable byvalue, ref ICloneable byreference);
```

LISTING 9.2   Continued

Visual Basic .NET:

```
Public Sub Strings(ByVal byvalue As String, ByRef byreference As String)

Public Sub Arrays(ByVal byvalue As Integer(), ByRef byreference As Integer())

Public Sub ValueTypes(ByVal byvalue As Double, ByRef byreference As Double)

Public Sub ReferenceTypes(ByVal byvalue As ICloneable, _
  ByRef byreference As ICloneable)
```

`UNMANAGED`

Visual Basic 6:

```
Public Sub Strings(ByVal byvalue As String, ByRef byreference As String)

' VB6 doesn't support the by-value SAFEARRAY used by the Arrays method

Public Sub Interfaces(ByVal byvalue As Object, ByRef byreference As Object)

Public Sub ReferenceTypes(ByVal byvalue As ICloneable, _
  ByRef byreference As ICloneable)
```

IDL:

```
HRESULT Strings([in] BSTR byvalue, [in, out] BSTR* byreference);

HRESULT Arrays([in] SAFEARRAY(long) byvalue,
  [in, out] SAFEARRAY(long)* byreference);

HRESULT ValueTypes([in] double byvalue, [in, out] double* byreference);

HRESULT ReferenceTypes([in] ICloneable* byvalue,
  [in, out] ICloneable** byreference);
```

9

EXPORTED TYPE
LIBRARIES

CAUTION

The fact that reference types are marked and marshaled as [in] by default rather than [in, out] is often unintuitive for .NET programmers when these reference types have layout (as with formatted classes or arrays). This causes only "in" behavior to be observed with Interop marshaling for non-blittable types or COM marshaling across contexts. On the other hand, when managed code calls a managed method with a reference type parameter, "in, out" behavior is always observed. See Chapter 18 for more information.

Chapter 12 shows how a parameter can be marked with either `InAttribute` or `OutAttribute` (or both) to change its exported (and, in some cases, marshaling) behavior. If either of the attributes is present, the exporter always does exactly what the attributes dictate even if it doesn't make sense (such as marking a by-value integer with `[out]`). This transformation is illustrated in Table 9.2.

TABLE 9.2   Export Behavior Controlled by `InAttribute` and `OutAttribute`

Attributes on Parameter	Exported IDL Attributes
InAttribute	[in]
OutAttribute	[out]
InAttribute + OutAttribute	[in, out]

Handling Overloaded Methods

A canonical example of .NET being more expressive than COM is overloaded methods. Although a .NET class or interface can have multiple methods with the same name (as long as each method's parameters are different), COM interfaces cannot. As mentioned in the previous chapter, the exporter accounts for this by renaming all but the first method by appending _2, _3, and so on, demonstrated in Listing 9.3 with methods exported for `System.AppDomain`.

LISTING 9.3   The .NET View and the COM View of the Same Overloaded Methods

```
MANAGED
```

C#:

```
public int ExecuteAssembly(string assemblyFile, Evidence assemblySecurity);

public int ExecuteAssembly(string assemblyFile);

public int ExecuteAssembly(string assemblyFile, Evidence assemblySecurity,
    string [] args);
```

Visual Basic .NET:

```
Public Overloads Function ExecuteAssembly(assemblyFile As String, _
    assemblySecurity As Evidence) As Integer

Public Overloads Function ExecuteAssembly(assemblyFile As String) As Integer

Public Overloads Function ExecuteAssembly(assemblyFile As String, _
    assemblySecurity As Evidence, args() As String) As Integer
```

LISTING 9.3 Continued

`UNMANAGED`

Visual Basic 6:

```
Public Function ExecuteAssembly(ByVal assemblyFile As String, _
  ByVal assemblySecurity As Evidence) As Integer

Public Function ExecuteAssembly_2(ByVal assemblyFile As String) As Integer

' VB6 doesn't support the by-value SAFEARRAY used by ExecuteAssembly_3
```

IDL:

```
[id(0x6002002b)]
HRESULT ExecuteAssembly([in] BSTR assemblyFile,
  [in] _Evidence* assemblySecurity, [out, retval] long* pRetVal);

[id(0x6002002c),
  custom(0F21F359-AB84-41E8-9A78-36D110E6D2F9, "ExecuteAssembly")]
HRESULT ExecuteAssembly_2([in] BSTR assemblyFile, [out, retval] long* pRetVal);

[id(0x6002002d),
  custom(0F21F359-AB84-41E8-9A78-36D110E6D2F9, "ExecuteAssembly")]
HRESULT ExecuteAssembly_3([in] BSTR assemblyFile,
  [in] _Evidence* assemblySecurity, [in] SAFEARRAY(BSTR) args,
  [out, retval] long* pRetVal);
```

The extra IDL custom attribute on the `ExecuteAssembly_2` and `ExecuteAssembly_3` methods helps the CLR match the renamed exported members to the original overloads.

Converting `ToString`

If a .NET class has no default member and no member marked with a DISPID of zero, its `ToString` method inherited from `System.Object` is transformed into a property get accessor with a DISPID equal to zero. This transformation is done so it is treated as a default property in COM. As seen in the previous chapter, treating `ToString` as a default property is pretty natural in Visual Basic 6, especially when you want to "print an object" as if it's a string. This transformation can be seen when viewing `_Object`, the class interface for `System.Object`, in Listing 9.4.

LISTING 9.4 The `_Object` Class Interface

```
[
  odl,
  uuid(65074F7F-63C0-304E-AF0A-D51741CB4A8D),
  hidden,
  dual,
  nonextensible,
```

9

EXPORTED TYPE
LIBRARIES

LISTING 9.4   Continued

```
oleautomation,
custom(0F21F359-AB84-41E8-9A78-36D110E6D2F9, "System.Object")
]
interface _Object : IDispatch {
  [id(00000000), propget, custom(54FC8F55-38DE-4703-9C4E-250351302B1C, 1)]
  HRESULT ToString([out, retval] BSTR* pRetVal);
  [id(0x60020001)]
  HRESULT Equals([in] VARIANT obj, [out, retval] VARIANT_BOOL* pRetVal);
  [id(0x60020002)]
  HRESULT GetHashCode([out, retval] long* pRetVal);
  [id(0x60020003)]
  HRESULT GetType([out, retval] _Type** pRetVal);
};
```

Interestingly enough, any method called ToString, regardless of its signature, is transformed into a property get accessor but not necessarily with a DISPID equal to zero. This method-to-property transformation cannot be suppressed. The extra IDL custom attribute with the GUID 54FC8F55-38DE-4703-9C4E-250351302B1C identifies these exported property get accessors as methods on the .NET side, so the importer handles this transformation correctly when importing a coclass that implements an exported interface with a ToString member. This scenario is the topic of Chapter 17.

Converting GetEnumerator

If a .NET type defines a GetEnumerator method that has no parameters and returns a System.Collections.IEnumerator type, the exporter gives it a DISPID equal to –4 (DISPID_NEWENUM) and transforms the IEnumerator type to the COM IEnumVARIANT interface:

C#:

```
public IEnumerator GetEnumerator();
```

IDL:

```
[id(0xfffffffc)]
HRESULT GetEnumerator([out, retval] IEnumVARIANT** pRetVal);
```

This is done to make .NET enumerators work seamlessly as COM enumerators, as demonstrated in the previous chapter.

Converting Parameter Arrays

Similar to type library import, the exporter converts .NET parameter arrays to COM parameter arrays, but only if the type of the array is System.Object. This is a requirement of COM, which states that the IDL [vararg] attribute is only valid for a SAFEARRAY with VARIANT elements. This transformation is demonstrated in Listing 9.5.

LISTING 9.5   The COM View and the .NET View of Methods with Parameter Arrays

`MANAGED`

C#:

```
public void ObjectParamArray(params object [] arr);

public void StringParamArray(params string [] arr);
```

Visual Basic .NET:

```
Public Sub ObjectParamArray(ParamArray arr() As Object)

Public Sub StringParamArray(ParamArray arr() As String)
```

`UNMANAGED`

IDL:

```
[vararg] HRESULT ObjectParamArray([in] SAFEARRAY(VARIANT) arr);

HRESULT StringParamArray([in] SAFEARRAY(BSTR) arr);
```

> **CAUTION**
>
> An exported method with a parameter array (marked with `[vararg]`) is unusable from Visual Basic 6 since the language requires that parameter arrays be passed by-reference despite the fact that Visual Basic .NET requires parameter arrays to be passed by value. However, unlike the reverse problem when exposing VB6 parameter arrays to Visual Basic .NET, you can't even treat the parameter array as a regular array parameter—the method is simply unusable!

You cannot define a .NET parameter array as by-reference as an attempt to appease Visual Basic 6 clients. The C# compiler gives error CS1661 ("The params parameter cannot be declared as ref or out") and the Visual Basic .NET compiler gives error BC30667 ("ParamArray parameters must be declared 'ByVal'").

Properties

The transformations done for properties during export aren't nearly as complicated as the transformations done during import, since normal .NET properties only have one or two accessors. (And if a .NET property has more accessors, such as one written using the IL Assembler, these extra accessors are just treated like regular methods.) The rules are as follows:

- Get accessors are exported as get accessors (`propget`).
- Set accessors are exported as set accessors (`propputref`) if the type of the .NET property is a reference type, excluding strings and arrays.
- Set accessors are exported as let accessors (`propput`) if the type of the .NET property is a value type, string, or array.

Listing 9.6 illustrates these rules.

LISTING 9.6   The COM View and the .NET View of Properties

```
MANAGED
```

C#:

```csharp
public int IntProperty { get; set; }

public string StringProperty { get; set; }

public ISerializable InterfaceProperty { get; set; }

public object ObjectProperty { get; set; }

public int [] ValueTypeArrayProperty { get; set; }

public SomeClass [] ReferenceTypeArrayProperty { get; set; }
```

Visual Basic .NET:

```vbnet
Public Property IntProperty As Integer

Public Property StringProperty As String

Public Property InterfaceProperty As ISerializable

Public Property ObjectProperty As Object

Public Property ValueTypeArrayProperty As Integer()

Public Property ReferenceTypeArrayProperty As SomeClass()
```

```
UNMANAGED
```

Visual Basic 6:

```vb
Public Property Get IntProperty() As Long
Public Property Let IntProperty(ByVal RHS As Long)
```

LISTING 9.6   Continued

```
Public Property Get StringProperty() As String
Public Property Let StringProperty(ByVal RHS As String)

Public Property Get InterfaceProperty() As ISerializable
Public Property Set InterfaceProperty(ByVal RHS As ISerializable)

Public Property Get ObjectProperty() As Variant
Public Property Set ObjectProperty(ByVal RHS As Variant)

' ByVal array types aren't supported in VB6
```

IDL:

```
[id(0x60020000), propget]
HRESULT IntProperty([out, retval] long* pRetVal);
[id(0x60020000), propput]
HRESULT IntProperty([in] long pRetVal);

[id(0x60020002), propget]
HRESULT StringProperty([out, retval] BSTR* pRetVal);
[id(0x60020002), propput]
HRESULT StringProperty([in] BSTR pRetVal);

[id(0x60020004), propget]
HRESULT InterfaceProperty([out, retval] ISerializable** pRetVal);
[id(0x60020004), propputref]
HRESULT InterfaceProperty([in] ISerializable* pRetVal);

[id(0x60020006), propget]
HRESULT ObjectProperty([out, retval] VARIANT* pRetVal);
[id(0x60020006), propputref]
HRESULT ObjectProperty([in] VARIANT pRetVal);

[id(0x60020008), propget]
HRESULT ValueTypeArrayProperty([out, retval] SAFEARRAY(long)* pRetVal);
[id(0x60020008), propput]
HRESULT ValueTypeArrayProperty([in] SAFEARRAY(long) pRetVal);

[id(0x6002000A), propget]
HRESULT ReferenceTypeArrayProperty(
  [out, retval] SAFEARRAY(_SomeClass*)* pRetVal);
[id(0x6002000A), propput]
HRESULT ReferenceTypeArrayProperty([in] SAFEARRAY(_SomeClass*) pRetVal);
```

9

EXPORTED TYPE
LIBRARIES

The parameters of the exported property accessors don't have names, which is why a program like OLEVIEW.EXE might name them pRetVal, whereas Visual Basic 6 names them RHS.

The implication of these property transformations is that you can't define a .NET System.Object property and have it behave exactly like a VARIANT property as defined in Visual Basic 6, because VB6 generates all three accessors. To write .NET types that behave exactly like existing COM types, you should follow the techniques described in Chapter 14, "Implementing COM Interfaces for Binary Compatibility."

Fields

In COM, only structs have fields, but in .NET both value types and reference types can have fields. When a struct is exported for a .NET value type or formatted reference type, .NET fields simply become COM fields. But when a class interface is exported for a class with fields, the fields are converted into properties. The rules for this are simple:

- Any field is exposed with a get accessor (propget) and a let accessor (propput) regardless of data type, unless marked as read-only.
- If the field is marked as read-only (readonly in C# and ReadOnly in VB .NET), only a get accessor (propget) is exported.

Listing 9.7 illustrates these rules.

LISTING 9.7   The COM View and the .NET View of Fields Exported as Properties

MANAGED

C#:

```
public int IntField;

public string StringField;

public ISerializable InterfaceField;

public object ObjectField;

public int [] ValueTypeArrayField;

public SomeClass [] ReferenceTypeArrayField;

public readonly int ReadOnlyField;
```

Visual Basic .NET:

```
Public IntField As Integer

Public StringField As String

Public InterfaceField As ISerializable
```

LISTING 9.7   Continued

```
Public ObjectField As Object

Public ValueTypeArrayField As Integer()

Public ReferenceTypeArrayField As SomeClass()

Public ReadOnly ReadOnlyField As Integer
```

UNMANAGED

Visual Basic 6:

```
Public Property Get IntField() As Long
Public Property Let IntField(ByVal RHS As Long)

Public Property Get StringField() As String
Public Property Let StringField(ByVal RHS As String)

Public Property Get InterfaceField() As ISerializable
Public Property Let InterfaceField(ByVal RHS As ISerializable)

Public Property Get ObjectField() As Variant
Public Property Let ObjectField(ByVal RHS As Variant)

' ByVal array types aren't supported in VB6

Public Property Get ReadOnlyField() As Long
```

IDL:

```
[id(0x60020000), propget]
HRESULT IntField([out, retval] long* pRetVal);
[id(0x60020000), propput]
HRESULT IntField([in] long pRetVal);

[id(0x60020002), propget]
HRESULT StringField([out, retval] BSTR* pRetVal);
[id(0x60020002), propput]
HRESULT StringField([in] BSTR pRetVal);

[id(0x60020004), propget]
HRESULT InterfaceField([out, retval] ISerializable** pRetVal);
[id(0x60020004), propput]
HRESULT InterfaceField([in] ISerializable* pRetVal);

[id(0x60020006), propget]
HRESULT ObjectField([out, retval] VARIANT* pRetVal);
[id(0x60020006), propput]
HRESULT ObjectField([in] VARIANT pRetVal);
```

9

EXPORTED TYPE
LIBRARIES

LISTING 9.7   Continued

```
[id(0x60020008), propget]
HRESULT ValueTypeArrayField([out, retval] SAFEARRAY(long)* pRetVal);
[id(0x60020008), propput]
HRESULT ValueTypeArrayField([in] SAFEARRAY(long) pRetVal);

[id(0x6002000A), propget]
HRESULT ReferenceTypeArrayField([out, retval] SAFEARRAY(_SomeClass*)* pRetVal);
[id(0x6002000A), propput]
HRESULT ReferenceTypeArrayField([in] SAFEARRAY(_SomeClass*) pRetVal);

[id(0x6002000C), propget]
HRESULT ReadOnlyField([out, retval] long* pRetVal);
```

This transformation is similar to fields defined in Visual Basic 6, which are actually exposed as COM properties.

DIGGING DEEPER

> Because .NET interfaces do not contain fields, the field-to-property transformations in Listing 9.7 can only be seen in a type library with auto-dual class interfaces. Fields can still be invoked as properties when late binding to an auto-dispatch class interface, however.

Events

Strictly speaking, there's no such thing as an "event" in COM. Therefore, when an interface for a class contains an event member, the exporter exposes its two accessor methods for adding and removing event handlers. This is shown in Listing 9.8.

LISTING 9.8   The COM View and the .NET View of an Event

MANAGED

C#:

```
public event TimerEventHandler Timer
```

Visual Basic .NET:

```
Public Event Timer
```

LISTING 9.8   Continued

UNMANAGED

Visual Basic 6:

```
Public Sub remove_Timer(ByVal obj As TimerEventHandler)
Public Sub add_Timer(ByVal obj As TimerEventHandler)
```

IDL:

```
[id(0x60020004)]
HRESULT remove_Timer([in] _TimerEventHandler* obj);
[id(0x60020005)]
HRESULT add_Timer([in] _TimerEventHandler* obj);
```

The next chapter explains why these methods are not very useful to COM clients wishing to hookup event handlers. Chapter 13, "Exposing .NET Events to COM Clients," explains how authors of .NET APIs can expose events to COM in a more natural way.

Converting Interfaces

Converting public, COM-visible .NET interfaces to COM interfaces is straightforward once you understand the member conversions just discussed. The exporter produces three kinds of interfaces—those that don't derive from IDispatch (IUnknown-only interfaces), dual interfaces, and dispinterfaces. All .NET interfaces are dual unless marked otherwise with the InterfaceTypeAttribute discussed in Chapter 12. Like LIBIDs, exported interfaces are given automatically-generated IIDs if the .NET definitions aren't marked with GuidAttribute custom attributes.

Any types exported to a type library—interfaces, classes, structures, enums—are given their simple .NET type names that exclude their namespaces. If the same assembly contains multiple public types with the same name but in separate namespaces, each exported type name becomes *Namespace_TypeName* to avoid duplicate definitions. (This renaming is still done even if only one of the conflicting types is exported due to the others being marked COM-invisible.) As with assembly names being converted to library names, any periods in the namespace (or :: in Visual C++ .NET) are converted to underscores.

As with importing, there's a subtle aspect to exporting interfaces that derive from other interfaces. When exporting an inheritance hierarchy of .NET interfaces, the resultant COM interfaces appear as unrelated "slices," containing only the members defined directly on them. This is shown in Listing 9.9.

9

EXPORTED TYPE
LIBRARIES

LISTING 9.9   The C# Representation of Two Interfaces Related by Inheritance, and the IDL Representation of the Exported Interfaces

`MANAGED`

```csharp
namespace System.Collections
{
  public interface IEnumerator
  {
    bool MoveNext();
    object Current { get; }
    void Reset();
  }

  public interface IDictionaryEnumerator : IEnumerator
  {
    object Key { get; }
    object Value { get; }
    DictionaryEntry Entry { get; }
  }
}
```

`UNMANAGED`

```idl
[
  odl,
  uuid(496B0ABF-CDEE-11D3-88E8-00902754C43A),
  version(1.0),
  dual,
  oleautomation,
  custom(0F21F359-AB84-41E8-9A78-36D110E6D2F9,
    "System.Collections.IEnumerator")
]
interface IEnumerator : IDispatch {
  [id(0x60020000)]
  HRESULT MoveNext([out, retval] VARIANT_BOOL* pRetVal);
  [id(0x60020001), propget]
  HRESULT Current([out, retval] VARIANT* pRetVal);
  [id(0x60020002)]
  HRESULT Reset();
};

[
  odl,
  uuid(35D574BF-7A4F-3588-8C19-12212A0FE4DC),
  version(1.0),
  dual,
```

LISTING 9.9 Continued

```
oleautomation,
custom(0F21F359-AB84-41E8-9A78-36D110E6D2F9,
  "System.Collections.IDictionaryEnumerator")
]
interface IDictionaryEnumerator : IDispatch {
  [id(0x60020000), propget]
  HRESULT key([out, retval] VARIANT* pRetVal);
  [id(00000000), propget]
  HRESULT value([out, retval] VARIANT* pRetVal);
  [id(0x60020002), propget]
  HRESULT Entry([out, retval] DictionaryEntry* pRetVal);
};
```

Because both interfaces derive directly from IDispatch, a COM user can't directly call a member like MoveNext directly on an IDictionaryEnumerator type. Instead, a C++ client must call IUnknown.QueryInterface to get an IEnumerator interface pointer, and a Visual Basic 6 client must declare a new variable of type IEnumerator and set the reference of the IDictionaryEnumerator type to it (causing a QueryInterface call).

FAQ: Why isn't the inheritance of .NET interfaces preserved when exported as COM interfaces?

From the CLR's perspective, .NET interfaces don't *really* inherit from one another as COM interfaces do, although high-level .NET languages provide these semantics. Therefore, exporting them as individual "slices" faithfully represents their true CLR representation. A benefit of this interface slicing is that COM users of the derived interface are not affected if members are added to a base interface (which should never really be done anyway), because the v-table for the derived interface remains unchanged. The exporter and Interop Marshaler could have instead constructed v-tables that preserve the semantics of interface inheritance, but this would have required a standard translation of .NET's multiple interface inheritance to COM's single interface inheritance.

9

Converting Classes

Public COM-visible .NET classes are exported as coclasses (unless they are formatted classes). Because coclasses themselves don't have members, a class interface is often generated and implemented by the coclass. An automatically-generated class interface always has the name _CoclassName and is always marked as dual, but by default lists no members since they can only be invoked via late binding.

So, rather than listing members, coclasses in a type library list interfaces that they implement (although usually not all interfaces). A coclass exported from a .NET class lists all the public COM-visible interfaces that the corresponding .NET class implements, all the public COM-visible interfaces implemented by its base classes, plus any class interfaces exposed for the class or its base classes. An exported coclass is marked with the IDL [noncreatable] attribute if the .NET class doesn't have a public default constructor or is marked as abstract (MustInherit in VB .NET), so COM clients know that they can't attempt to create an instance of it. Listing 9.10 demonstrates the transformation from .NET classes to COM classes. Besides the class interfaces, each coclass lists _Object as an implemented interface since that's the class interface for the .NET classes' System.Object base class.

LISTING 9.10 Two .NET Classes and Their Exported IDL Coclass Representation

MANAGED

C#:

```
public class SomeClass
{
  ...
}

public class SomeNonCreatableClass
{
  // Private constructor
  private EmptyNonCreatableClass() {}
  ...
}
```

Visual Basic .NET:

```
Public Class SomeClass
  ...
End Class

Public Class SomeNonCreatableClass
  ' Private constructor
  Private Sub New()
  End Sub
  ...
End Class
```

LISTING 9.10   Continued

`UNMANAGED`

IDL:

```
[
  uuid(A36749B0-4B9D-383C-9801-8DC5BD66A707),
  version(1.0),
  custom(0F21F359-AB84-41E8-9A78-36D110E6D2F9, "SomeClass")
]
coclass SomeClass {
  [default] interface _SomeClass;
  interface _Object;
};

[
  uuid(B3DADFC4-E315-32B6-AE09-6E329BD5F194),
  version(1.0),
  noncreatable,
  custom(0F21F359-AB84-41E8-9A78-36D110E6D2F9, "SomeNonCreatableClass")
]
coclass SomeNonCreatableClass {
  [default] interface _SomeNonCreatableClass;
  interface _Object;
};
```

DIGGING DEEPER

Modules in Visual Basic .NET are represented as classes with a private default constructor in metadata, so any such modules are exported as non-creatable coclasses to COM.

Whenever a formatted .NET class is converted to a struct, the exporter issues a warning because it might catch users of the exported type library by surprise. The transformation for a formatted class is the same as the transformation for a value type, described in the next section.

9

EXPORTED TYPE
LIBRARIES

Converting Value Types

Value types are exported as structs (UDTs) in a type library. Although value types can contain methods—even implement interfaces—only its fields are exposed to COM since type library structs don't have the same capabilities. As listed in Table 9.1, data types exported as fields of structs undergo different conversion rules than data types exported as parameters or return types. Listing 9.11 shows an example.

LISTING 9.11 Two .NET Classes and Their Exported IDL Coclass Representation

MANAGED

C#:

```csharp
public struct Entry
{
  public object Value;
  private string name;
  public string GetName() { return name; }
  public void SetName(string desiredName) { name = desiredName; }
}
```

Visual Basic .NET:

```vbnet
Public Structure Entry
  Public Value As Object
  Private name As String
  Public Function GetName() As String
    GetName = name
  End Function
  Public Sub SetName(desiredName As String)
    name = desiredName
  End Sub
End Structure
```

UNMANAGED

Visual Basic 6:

```vb
Public Type Entry
  Value As Unknown
  name As String
End Type
```

LISTING 9.11   Continued

IDL:

```
typedef [uuid(2E868727-AEED-3FDC-978B-2D7AF384FE9F), version(1.0),
  custom(0F21F359-AB84-41E8-9A78-36D110E6D2F9, "Entry")]
struct tagEntry {
  IUnknown* Value;
  LPSTR name;
} Entry;
```

In this contrived example, notice how the methods are omitted from the COM structs. Also notice that private fields are exposed just like public fields! There is no way to hide fields of a structure from COM, either via .NET visibility or attempting to restrict COM visibility, since to COM a structure's layout is critical for proper operation. In many cases, the problems caused by lack of a value type's methods being exposed to COM are mitigated by the fact that the underlying non-public representation can be directly manipulated.

The type library exporter generates a union instead of a plain struct for any .NET types marked with StructLayout(LayoutKind.Explicit) whose fields are all marked with a memory offset of zero.

> **CAUTION**
>
> If any value types are marked with StructLayout(LayoutKind.Auto), the exporter silently treats them the same as value types with sequential layout. However, attempting to use such structs in COM may fail in subtle ways because the CLR is free to rearrange the layout at any time. You can check what kind of layout a .NET value type has by opening its assembly with the IL Disassembler (ILDASM.EXE) and looking at the first entry under the value type's node. It will either say auto, sequential, or explicit, the first of which should never be used from unmanaged code.

Converting Enumerations

Converting .NET enumerations to COM enumerations is not as straightforward as the reverse. One complication is that enums defined in a type library can only have a 32-bit underlying type, whereas .NET enums can have any integral underlying type. For any .NET enumeration, regardless of underlying type, the exporter creates a 32-bit enumeration with the same values. If an enum has a 64-bit underlying type, however, *and* it contains at least one value that doesn't fit in 32 bits, type library export fails with a message like the following:

```
Type library exporter encountered an error while processing
➥ 'BigEnum.BigValue, MyAssembly'. Error: The enum member
➥ BigEnum.BigEnum_BigValue has a value which can not be expressed
➥ as a 32-bit integer. Type library enum members must be 32-bit integers.
```

It would be incorrect for .NET signatures with non-32-bit enum parameters to be exported as COM signatures with enum parameters, since the exported enums are 32-bit. Therefore, any such parameters are exported as their underlying types instead. This transformation is listed in Table 9.1 at the beginning of the chapter. Because the enumeration type might still appear in the type library, COM clients can still use it to convert to and from the integral values passed as parameters.

A second complication involves the name of enumeration members. Every enum member is named *EnumName_MemberName* rather than just *MemberName*. These transformations are demonstrated in Listing 9.12, including the transformations done when enums are used as parameters.

LISTING 9.12   The C# Representation of Enumerations and Enumeration Parameters, and the IDL Representation of These Exported Types

```
MANAGED
public enum PrimaryColors : byte
{
  Red,
  Yellow,
  Blue
}

public enum Months : short
{
  January,
  ...
  December
}

public enum Difficulties : ushort
{
  Easy,
  Medium,
  Hard
}

public enum WeekDays
{
  Sunday,
  ...
```

LISTING 9.12   Continued

```
  Saturday
}

public enum Speeds : uint
{
  Slow,
  Medium,
  Fast
}

public enum Status : long
{
  Error,
  Warning,
  Information
}

public interface IUseEnums
{
  void SetPrimaryColor(PrimaryColors color);
  void SetMonth(Months month);
  void SetDifficulty(Difficulties difficulty);
  void SetWeekDay(WeekDays day);
  void SetSpeed(Speeds speed);
  void SetStatus(Status status);
}
```

`UNMANAGED`

```
typedef [uuid(0BDB3946-42AB-331B-87ED-8C2EE221955C), version(1.0),
  custom(0F21F359-AB84-41E8-9A78-36D110E6D2F9, "PrimaryColors")]
enum {
  PrimaryColors_Red = 0,
  PrimaryColors_Yellow = 1,
  PrimaryColors_Blue = 2
} PrimaryColors;

typedef [uuid(FA9B5260-818C-381A-949E-4373F3783FF5), version(1.0),
  custom(0F21F359-AB84-41E8-9A78-36D110E6D2F9, "Months")]
enum {
  Months_January = 0,
  ...
  Months_December = 11
} Months;
```

9

EXPORTED TYPE
LIBRARIES

LISTING 9.12   Continued

```
typedef [uuid(E7E8B8DF-6062-41CD-AAC7-98B9CA229343), version(1.0),
  custom(0F21F359-AB84-41E8-9A78-36D110E6D2F9, "Difficulties")]
enum {
  Difficulties_Easy = 0,
  Difficulties_Medium = 1,
  Difficulties_Hard = 2
} Difficulties;

typedef [uuid(EFBE16C4-DE2B-3D70-B2D6-0993C085A241), version(1.0),
  custom(0F21F359-AB84-41E8-9A78-36D110E6D2F9, "WeekDays")]
enum {
  WeekDays_Sunday = 0,
  ...
  WeekDays_Saturday = 6
} WeekDays;

typedef [uuid(2B5597AF-03EE-3CC6-A27F-E7DFEA99C1D3), version(1.0),
  custom(0F21F359-AB84-41E8-9A78-36D110E6D2F9, "Speeds")]
enum {
  Speeds_Slow = 0,
  Speeds_Medium = 1,
  Speeds_Fast = 2
} Speeds;

typedef [uuid(2EB33C9A-149A-3251-9E34-4878BB98C6B3), version(1.0),
  custom(0F21F359-AB84-41E8-9A78-36D110E6D2F9, "Status")]
enum {
  Status_Error = 0,
  Status_Warning = 1,
  Status_Information = 2
} Status;

[
  odl,
  uuid(B00611B8-68A0-34DB-83C6-00FCE34D9808),
  version(1.0),
  dual,
  oleautomation,
  custom(0F21F359-AB84-41E8-9A78-36D110E6D2F9, "IUseEnums")
]
interface IUseEnums : IDispatch {
  [id(0x60020000)]
  HRESULT SetPrimaryColor([in] unsigned char color);
  [id(0x60020001)]
```

LISTING 9.12   Continued

```
HRESULT SetMonth([in] short month);
[id(0x60020002)]
HRESULT SetDifficulty([in] unsigned short difficulty);
[id(0x60020003)]
HRESULT SetWeekDay([in] WeekDays day);
[id(0x60020004)]
HRESULT SetSpeed([in] Speeds speed);
[id(0x60020005)]
HRESULT SetStatus([in] int64 Status);
};
```

Notice that the exported SetWeekDay and SetSpeed methods use the exported WeekDays and Speeds enumerations, but the other methods' parameters are replaced with the non-32-bit underlying types.

FAQ: Why are .NET enum member names decorated with the enum name when exported to a type library?

It might seem unnecessary for the type library exporter to change the name of enum members because any member name conflicts can be handled by the user qualifying the member name with the enum name. For example, if the previous enum member names were left alone, the ambiguous Medium could be qualified as Difficulties.Medium versus Speeds.Medium in Visual Basic 6 or Difficulties::Medium versus Speeds::Medium in C++ and the non-ambiguous members could be used simply as Monday or Blue rather than WeekDays_Monday or Colors_Blue.

However, a type library containing multiple enums with the same member name does not work well when used in unmanaged Visual C++. The C++ #import directive promotes all enum members to the same namespace so duplicated member names in separate enums produce compile-time errors for unmanaged Visual C++ clients. (MIDL doesn't even let you create a type library with multiple enums with the same-named member, although Visual Basic 6 allows it.) The result is that all COM clients must suffer with slightly more verbose enum member names.

Conclusion

This chapter covered all the major details of how COM type information is generated from .NET type information. These transformations are the key to .NET objects being easily usable in COM applications without requiring special effort on the part of the .NET programmer.

With the type library exporter, a COM client can see interfaces, coclasses, structs, enums, and unions representing .NET entities. The exporter never produces type library modules or typedefs.

This chapter is a complement to Part IV, which is all about designing .NET components so that they are exposed to COM in the most natural way possible. The exporter's transformations are meant to work best for components that follow .NET guidelines and conventions, but you've seen cases where typical .NETisms like overloaded methods and event members don't get exposed nicely by default.

Advanced Topics for Using .NET Components

IN THIS CHAPTER

- Avoiding Registration   460

- Hosting Windows Forms Controls in Any ActiveX Container   471

- Working Around COM-Invisibility   477

- Using Reflection to Invoke Static Members 482

- Handling .NET Events   488

- Unexpected Casing in Type Libraries   489

- Advanced Shutdown Topics   492

Just as Chapter 6, "Advanced Topics for Using COM Components," focused on a handful of advanced topics for using COM components in .NET applications, this chapter focuses on a handful of advanced topics for using .NET components in COM applications. These topics include

- Avoiding registration
- Hosting Windows Forms controls in any ActiveX container
- Working around COM-invisibility
- Using reflection to invoke static members
- Handling .NET events
- Unexpected casing in type libraries
- Advanced shutdown topics

Avoiding Registration

The standard mechanisms for using .NET components in COM applications require the registration of the .NET components just as if they were COM components. In the .NET world of xcopy deployment, avoiding this registration is desirable. For example, Chapter 8, "The Essentials for Using .NET Components from COM," demonstrated that running Windows Forms Controls in Internet Explorer requires no registration. Two approaches can be used with *any* COM application to avoid the registration of .NET components:

- Hosting the Common Language Runtime (CLR)
- Using the ClrCreateManagedInstance API

Hosting the Common Language Runtime

The CLR supports being hosted inside an application that controls its behavior. The host application is responsible for creating application domains, creating objects, and running managed user code. For example, the .NET Framework ships with a CLR host used by ASP.NET and a CLR host used by Internet Explorer (which enables the creation of .NET objects using the new <object> tag syntax without registration). It's also unmanaged hosting code that initializes the CLR in traditional .NET console or Windows applications.

The CLR provides a *hosting API* that consists of static entry points in MSCOREE.DLL, plus COM classes and interfaces described in MSCOREE.TLB. The centerpiece of these APIs is the CorRuntimeHost coclass, which implements the following COM interfaces:

- ICorRuntimeHost—Provides control of core services such as threads and application domains.
- IGCHost—Provides control of garbage collection.

- `ICorConfiguration`—Enables the configuration of debugging and garbage collection.

- `IValidator`—Enables validation of an assembly, to determine whether it contains unverifiable code. Note that this is a completely different interface than the .NET `System.Web.UI.IValidator` interface!

- `IDebuggerInfo`—Enables a host to discover if a debugger is currently attached to the process.

Listing 10.1 demonstrates Visual Basic 6 code that makes use of the hosting API to create and use a `System.Collections.SortedList` instance from the `mscorlib` assembly. Unlike the use of `mscorlib` types in Chapter 8, the `mscorlib` assembly does not need to be registered with `REGASM.EXE` in order for the code in the listing to run.

LISTING 10.1   Hosting the CLR and Using .NET Objects in a Visual Basic 6 COM Client

```
1: Dim host As CorRuntimeHost
2: Dim domain As AppDomain
3:
4: ' Initialize the CLR
5: Set host = New CorRuntimeHost
6: host.Start
7: host.GetDefaultDomain domain
8:
9: ' Create an instance in the default domain
10: Dim sl As SortedList
11: Set sl = _
12:    domain.CreateInstance("mscorlib", "System.Collections.SortedList").Unwrap
13:
14: ' Use it normally
15: sl.Add "Advanced", "Advanced"
16: sl.Add "Topics", "Topics"
17: sl.Add "for", "for"
18: sl.Add "Using", "Using"
19: sl.Add ".NET", ".NET"
20: sl.Add "Components", "Components"
21:
22: Dim list As IEnumerable
23: Set list = sl.GetValueList
24:
25: ' Enumerate through the sorted list of values
26: Dim s As String
27: Dim v As Variant
28: For Each v In list
29:    s = s + v + " "
30: Next
31: MsgBox s
32: host.Stop
```

This code can be inserted in a Visual Basic 6 project that references MSCOREE.TLB ("Common Language Runtime Execution Engine 1.0 Library") and MSCORLIB.DLL ("Common Language Runtime Library"). MSCOREE.TLB contains the definition of CorRuntimeHost and MSCORLIB.DLL contains the definition of AppDomain, SortedList, and IEnumerable.

Lines 1–7 contain the code to initialize the CLR and get a reference to the default application domain. Alternatively, the CorBindToRuntimeEx API exported by MSCOREE.DLL could have been used to load the CLR into a process, but instantiating the CorRuntimeHost coclass is easier—especially for Visual Basic 6 programs.

Lines 11–12 create an instance of the System.Collections.SortedList class in the mscorlib assembly using AppDomain.CreateInstance. This method returns a System.Runtime. Remoting.ObjectHandle instance, so its Unwrap method must be called in order to obtain a reference to the desired instance. The returned instance is a COM-Callable Wrapper, just like the one that would be returned using the techniques in Chapter 8.

DIGGING DEEPER

System.AppDomain has three overloads of CreateInstance, but only one can be called from Visual Basic 6 due to the use of by-value array parameters, which VB6 does not support. For each overload of CreateInstance, AppDomain also has a corresponding CreateInstanceAndUnwrap method that returns the desired instance directly rather than returning an ObjectHandle that requires unwrapping. These CreateInstanceAndUnwrap methods are not exposed to COM, however, because AppDomain's default interface does not include them.

Lines 15–20 add the words from this chapter's title to the list, using the same string for each item's key and value since the code is interested in sorting the words alphabetically. Line 23 calls SortedList.GetValueList to get an IList reference, Lines 28–30 enumerate over the list and append each value to a string, then Line 31 prints the value in a message box. The resulting string is ".NET Advanced Components for Topics Using." Finally, Line 32 calls CorRuntimeHost's Stop method because we're finished with it. If we were finished with an application domain other than the default domain, we would call the CorRuntimeHost. UnloadDomain at this point. The default application domain cannot be unloaded, however.

Notice that although SortedList.GetValueList returns an IList interface, Line 22 declares the returned type as an IEnumerable variable. IList derives from IEnumerable, but the For Each statement in Line 28 would not work if list were declared as an IList type instead. This is due to the fact that interface inheritance is not exposed to COM, as discussed in the previous chapter. Had `GetValueList` returned a .NET class type that implements `IList` (exposed as a class interface), the return type could be declared as the class type in Visual Basic 6 and `For Each` would work since class interfaces contain inherited members.

The assembly name passed as the first parameter to `AppDomain.CreateInstance` must be a complete specification if the assembly is to be loaded from the Global Assembly Cache, for example:

```
System, Version=1.0.3300.0, Culture=neutral, PublicKeyToken=b77a5c561934e089
```

The `mscorlib` assembly is the only exception to this rule. (Private assemblies, however, can be loaded with a partial specification.) The string that specifies the assembly name is case-insensitive, but the string that specifies the type name is case-sensitive (and must be qualified with its namespace). Figure 10.1 demonstrates the error raised from Listing 10.1 if the type name was given in an incorrect case. You should recognize the HRESULT value as `COR_E_TYPELOAD` (from `System.TypeLoadException`).

Figure 10.1

Error raised with incorrect use of `Activator.CreateInstance`.

Listing 10.2 demonstrates hosting code similar to Listing 10.1, but in unmanaged C++. This listing takes advantage of an `AppDomain.CreateInstance` overload (exported as `CreateInstance_3`) to instantiate a .NET object using a *parameterized constructor*! This example creates a `System.Collections.ArrayList` instance with its constructor that accepts an initial capacity.

Listing 10.2   Hosting the CLR and Using .NET Objects in an Unmanaged Visual C++ COM Client

```
1: #define _WIN32_DCOM
2: #include <stdio.h>
3: #include <wtypes.h>
4:
5: // Reference the two necessary type libraries
6: #import "path\\mscoree.tlb" no_namespace named_guids raw_interfaces_only
7: #import "path\\mscorlib.tlb" no_namespace named_guids raw_interfaces_only
8:
```

LISTING 10.2   Continued

```
 9: IUnknown* pUnk = NULL;
10: IUnknown* pUnk2 = NULL;
11: ICorRuntimeHost* pHost = NULL;
12: _AppDomain* pDomain = NULL;
13: _ObjectHandle* pHandle = NULL;
14: IDispatch* pDisp = NULL;
15:
16: BSTR asmName;
17: BSTR typeName;
18: VARIANT arrayList;
19: VARIANT param;
20:
21: void Cleanup()
22: {
23:   pHost->Stop();
24:   if (pUnk) pUnk->Release();
25:   if (pUnk2) pUnk2->Release();
26:   if (pDisp) pDisp->Release();
27:   if (pHandle) pHandle->Release();
28:   if (pDomain) pDomain->Release();
29:   if (pHost) pHost->Release();
30:   if (asmName) SysFreeString(asmName);
31:   if (typeName) SysFreeString(typeName);
32:   VariantClear(&param);
33:   VariantClear(&arrayList);
34:   CoUninitialize();
35: };
36:
37: int main(int argc, char* argv[])
38: {
39:   HRESULT hresult;
40:
41:   // Initialize COM
42:   hresult = CoInitializeEx(NULL, COINIT_MULTITHREADED);
43:   if (FAILED(hresult))
44:   {
45:     printf("ERROR: Cannot initialize COM: 0x%x\n", hresult);
46:     Cleanup();
47:     return -1;
48:   }
49:
50:   // Initialize the CLR
51:   hresult = CoCreateInstance(CLSID_CorRuntimeHost, NULL,
52:     CLSCTX_INPROC_SERVER, IID_IUnknown, (void **)&pUnk);
```

LISTING 10.2   Continued

```
53:    if (FAILED(hresult))
54:    {
55:      printf("ERROR: Cannot create host object: 0x%x\n", hresult);
56:      Cleanup();
57:      return -1;
58:    }
59:
60:    // Get the ICorRuntimeHost interface
61:    hresult = pUnk->QueryInterface(IID_ICorRuntimeHost, (void**)&pHost);
62:    if (FAILED(hresult))
63:    {
64:      printf("ERROR: Cannot get ICorRuntimeHost interface pointer: 0x%x\n",
65:        hresult);
66:      Cleanup();
67:      return -1;
68:    }
69:
70:    // Start the host
71:    hresult = pHost->Start();
72:    if (FAILED(hresult))
73:    {
74:      printf("ERROR: Cannot start host: 0x%x\n", hresult);
75:      Cleanup();
76:      return -1;
77:    }
78:
79:    // Get the default domain
80:    hresult = pHost->GetDefaultDomain(&pUnk2);
81:    if (FAILED(hresult))
82:    {
83:      printf("ERROR: Cannot get default domain: 0x%x\n", hresult);
84:      Cleanup();
85:      return -1;
86:    }
87:
88:    // Get the _AppDomain interface
89:    hresult = pUnk2->QueryInterface(IID__AppDomain, (void**)&pDomain);
90:    if (FAILED(hresult))
91:    {
92:      printf("ERROR: Cannot get _AppDomain interface pointer: 0x%x\n",
93:        hresult);
94:      Cleanup();
95:      return -1;
96:    }
97:
```

10

ADVANCED TOPICS FOR USING .NET COMPONENTS

LISTING 10.2 Continued

```
 98:    // Strings for CreateInstance_3
 99:    asmName = SysAllocString(L"mscorlib");
100:    typeName = SysAllocString(L"System.Collections.ArrayList");
101:
102:    // Create a 1D array with one integer element
103:    SAFEARRAY* psa = SafeArrayCreateVector(VT_VARIANT, 0, 1);
104:    VariantInit(&param);
105:    param.vt = VT_I4;
106:    param.lVal = 128;
107:    LONG index = 0;
108:
109:    hresult = SafeArrayPutElement(psa, &index, &param);
110:    if (FAILED(hresult))
111:    {
112:      printf("ERROR: Cannot set SAFEARRAY element: 0x%x\n", hresult);
113:      Cleanup();
114:      return -1;
115:    }
116:
117:    // Create an instance of ArrayList using a parameterized constructor
118:    hresult = pDomain->CreateInstance_3(asmName, typeName, VARIANT_TRUE,
119:      BindingFlags_Default, NULL, psa, NULL, NULL, NULL, &pHandle);
120:    if (FAILED(hresult))
121:    {
122:      printf("ERROR: Cannot create instance: 0x%x\n", hresult);
123:      Cleanup();
124:      return -1;
125:    }
126:
127:    // Unwrap the ArrayList instance inside the ObjectHandle
128:    VariantInit(&arrayList);
129:    hresult = pHandle->Unwrap(&arrayList);
130:    if (FAILED(hresult))
131:    {
132:      printf("ERROR: Could not unwrap object handle: 0x%x\n", hresult);
133:      Cleanup();
134:      return -1;
135:    }
136:
137:    // Get the IDispatch interface so we can call the Capacity property
138:    hresult = arrayList.punkVal->QueryInterface(IID_IDispatch,
139:      (void**)&pDisp);
140:    if (FAILED(hresult))
141:    {
```

LISTING 10.2   Continued

```
142:        printf("ERROR: Could not get IDispatch interface pointer: 0x%x\n",
143:          hresult);
144:      Cleanup();
145:      return -1;
146:    }
147:
148:    // Get the DISPID for the Capacity property
149:    OLECHAR* name = L"Capacity";
150:    DISPID dispid;
151:    hresult = pDisp->GetIDsOfNames(IID_NULL, &name, 1, GetUserDefaultLCID(),
152:      &dispid);
153:    if (FAILED(hresult))
154:    {
155:      printf("ERROR: GetIDsOfNames failed: 0x%x\n", hresult);
156:      Cleanup();
157:      return -1;
158:    }
159:
160:    // Invoke the Capacity property
161:    VARIANT result;
162:    VariantInit(&result);
163:    DISPPARAMS params = { NULL, NULL, 0, 0 };
164:
165:    hresult = pDisp->Invoke(dispid, IID_NULL, GetUserDefaultLCID(),
166:      DISPATCH_PROPERTYGET, &params, &result, NULL, NULL);
167:    if (FAILED(hresult))
168:    {
169:      printf("ERROR: Invoke failed: 0x%x\n", hresult);
170:      Cleanup();
171:      return -1;
172:    }
173:
174:    printf("ArrayList Capacity: %d\n", result.lVal);
175:
176:    Cleanup();
177:    return 0;
178: };
```

As with Listing 10.1, this listing references two .NET type libraries: MSCOREE.TLB and
MSCORLIB.TLB. The *path*s used in Lines 6 and 7 are two different directories, and vary based
on your computer's settings.

> **TIP**
>
> Although `MSCOREE.DLL` resides in the Windows system directory (for example, `C:\Windows\system32`), `MSCOREE.TLB` resides in the .NET Framework folder where assemblies such as `MSCORLIB.DLL` exist. For example, such a folder may look as follows:
>
>   C:\Windows\Microsoft.NET\Framework\v1.0.3300\

Lines 51–52 instantiate the `CorRuntimeHost` class, Line 71 calls its `Start` method, and Line 80 calls its `GetDefaultDomain` method, as was done in Listing 10.1 (but with much fewer lines of code). The difference here is in Lines 118–119, which call the `CreateInstance` overloaded method that's exposed to COM as `CreateInstance_3`. `_AppDomain` is a real .NET interface exposed as a dual interface, so the `CreateInstance_3` method can be called without using `IDispatch`. The array of parameters to pass to this method is prepared in Lines 103–115. This array contains a single integer element with the value 128, representing the desired initial capacity of the `ArrayList` instance.

After the object has been instantiated, Line 129 calls `Unwrap` on the returned `ObjectHandle`. Then, to prove that the `ArrayList` was created with an initial capacity of 128, Lines 138–172 handle all the steps necessary to invoke the get accessor for the object's `Capacity` property. This involves querying for `IDispatch` (since the property is not defined on any .NET interface), retrieving the DISPID for the property (Lines 149–158), then invoking using that DISPID (Lines 161–172). Finally, Line 174 prints the capacity value, so running this program prints the following to the console:

```
ArrayList Capacity: 128
```

> **TIP**
>
> By hosting the runtime and calling `_AppDomain::CreateInstance_3` in unmanaged C++, a COM client can instantiate .NET objects using a parameterized constructor.

Using the `ClrCreateManagedInstance` API

`MSCOREE.DLL` exports a static entry point called `ClrCreateManagedInstance` that enables unmanaged code to create .NET objects without writing any code to host the CLR. This method is declared in `MSCOREE.IDL`, which ships with the .NET Framework SDK. This file simply echoes the declaration to `MSCOREE.H`, which looks like the following:

```
STDAPI ClrCreateManagedInstance(LPCWSTR pTypeName, REFIID riid,
  void **ppObject);
```

This method works much like `CoCreateInstance`, but with a string representing a .NET class rather than a CLSID representing a COM class. The string passed as `pTypeName` must be an assembly-qualified class name unless the class is defined in the `mscorlib` assembly. The `riid` parameter is the IID of the interface to be returned, and the `ppObject` parameter is the returned interface pointer. As with `CoCreateInstance`, `IID_IUnknown` is often passed for the `riid` parameter. COM-visibility rules are enforced with the object returned from this method, as when hosting the CLR in the previous two listings. That's because you interact with the same CCWs you'd be using with standard COM Interoperability.

Listing 10.3 demonstrates the use of `ClrCreateManagedInstance` in unmanaged C++ code to instantiate a `System.CodeDom.CodeObject` object then call its `UserData` property via late binding. As with the previous two listings, no registration is required for this code to work.

LISTING 10.3   Using `ClrCreateManagedInstance` to Create and Use .NET Objects from COM Without Registration

```
 1: #define _WIN32_DCOM
 2: #include <stdio.h>
 3: #include <wtypes.h>
 4:
 5: // The header file that declares ClrCreateManagedInstance
 6: #include "path\\mscoree.h"
 7:
 8: IDispatch* pDisp = NULL;
 9: IUnknown* pUnk = NULL;
10: VARIANT result;
11:
12: void Cleanup()
13: {
14:   if (pUnk) pUnk->Release();
15:   if (pDisp) pDisp->Release();
16:   VariantClear(&result);
17:   CoUninitialize();
18: };
19:
20: int main(int argc, char* argv[])
21: {
22:   HRESULT hresult;
23:
24:   // Initialize COM
25:   hresult = CoInitializeEx(NULL, COINIT_MULTITHREADED);
26:   if (FAILED(hresult))
```

LISTING 10.3 Continued

```
27:  {
28:    printf("ERROR: Cannot initialize COM: 0x%x\n", hresult);
29:    Cleanup();
30:    return -1;
31:  }
32:
33:  // Create an instance of the System.CodeDom.CodeObject class
34:  hresult = ClrCreateManagedInstance(L"System.CodeDom.CodeObject, System,
35: ➥Version=1.0.3300.0, Culture=neutral, PublicKeyToken=b77a5c561934e089",
36:    IID_IUnknown, (void**)&pUnk);
37:  if (FAILED(hresult))
38:  {
39:    printf("ERROR: Could not create instance: 0x%x\n", hresult);
40:    Cleanup();
41:    return -1;
42:  }
43:
44:  // Get the IDispatch interface so we can call the UserData property
45:  hresult = pUnk->QueryInterface(IID_IDispatch, (void**)&pDisp);
46:  if (FAILED(hresult))
47:  {
48:    printf("ERROR: Could not get IDispatch interface pointer: 0x%x\n",
49:      hresult);
50:    Cleanup();
51:    return -1;
52:  }
53:
54:  // Get the DISPID for the UserData property
55:  OLECHAR* name = L"UserData";
56:  DISPID dispid;
57:  hresult = pDisp->GetIDsOfNames(IID_NULL, &name, 1, GetUserDefaultLCID(),
58:    &dispid);
59:  if (FAILED(hresult))
60:  {
61:    printf("ERROR: GetIDsOfNames failed: 0x%x\n", hresult);
62:    Cleanup();
63:    return -1;
64:  }
65:
66:  // Invoke the UserData property
67:  VariantInit(&result);
68:  DISPPARAMS params = { NULL, NULL, 0, 0 };
69:
70:  hresult = pDisp->Invoke(dispid, IID_NULL, GetUserDefaultLCID(),
```

LISTING 10.3   Continued

```
71:      DISPATCH_PROPERTYGET, &params, &result, NULL, NULL);
72:    if (FAILED(hresult))
73:    {
74:      printf("ERROR: Invoke failed: 0x%x\n", hresult);
75:      Cleanup();
76:      return -1;
77:    }
78:
79:    Cleanup();
80:    return 0;
81: };
```

Line 6 includes MSCOREE.H, whose location depends on your computer's settings. For a Visual Studio .NET user, the file resides in the Program Files\Microsoft Visual Studio .NET\FrameworkSDK\include directory. The code must be linked with MSCOREE.LIB to resolve the ClrCreateManagedInstance call. Visual Studio .NET users can find this file in the Program Files\Microsoft Visual Studio .NET\FrameworkSDK\Lib directory.

In this example, no type libraries needed to be referenced, but if you need to reference MSCORLIB.TLB in addition to including MSCOREE.H, you should use #import's exclude directive as follows:

```
#import "path\\mscorlib.tlb" no_namespace named_guids
➥ raw_interfaces_only exclude("IObjectHandle")
```

This is needed because the IObjectHandle interface is defined in both MSCOREE.H and MSCORLIB.TLB.

Line 25 initializes COM, which is strictly not necessary because the call to ClrCreateManagedInstance initializes COM if it isn't already. Lines 34–36 call ClrCreateManagedInstance with the assembly-qualified string for System.CodeDom.CodeObject. Line 45 queries for the IDispatch interface so we can late bind to the object, and Lines 55–77 handle the invocation of the UserData property.

Hosting Windows Forms Controls in Any ActiveX Container

Before delving into this section, I want to make it clear that the only supported ActiveX container for hosting .NET Windows Forms is Internet Explorer. And there's a good reason for this—almost every ActiveX container behaves slightly differently and causes incompatibilities for the controls being hosted. Windows Forms controls are tuned and tested for Internet Explorer, and hosting them in any other ActiveX container may not completely work. This is why there is no automatic support for exposing Windows Forms controls as generic ActiveX controls.

That said, it is possible to use Windows Forms controls as ActiveX controls for any container (such as a Visual Basic 6 form) *at your own risk*. The only additional work that enables this is the addition of some Windows Registry keys and values. These additions are outlined in the following steps:

1. Under `HKEY_CLASSES_ROOT\CLSID\{clsid}`, where *clsid* is the CLSID of the Windows Forms control class, add a subkey named `Control`.

2. Under `HKEY_CLASSES_ROOT\CLSID\{clsid}\Implemented Categories`, add a subkey named `{40FC6ED4-2438-11CF-A3DB-080036F12502}`. This GUID is `CATID_Control`, the COM component category that identifies the class as an ActiveX control. Unlike Step 1, this is optional but could be useful for some ActiveX containers.

3. Under `HKEY_CLASSES_ROOT\CLSID\{clsid}`, add a subkey named `MiscStatus`. This key's default value should be set to a value of bitwise-ORed members of the `OLEMISC` enumeration, described after these steps.

4. Under `HKEY_CLASSES_ROOT\CLSID\{clsid}`, add a subkey named `TypeLib`. This key's default value should be set to the LIBID of the type library exported for the assembly containing the Windows Forms control.

5. Under `HKEY_CLASSES_ROOT\CLSID\{clsid}`, add a subkey named `Version`. This key's default value should be set to the two-part version of the type library exported for the assembly containing the Windows Forms control, such as "1.0".

If you don't add the `TypeLib` and `Version` subkeys, and if the exported type library is not registered, Visual Basic 6 does not show the control on the `Control` tab of its `Components` dialog.

The `OLEMISC` enumeration, whose values must be used with the `MiscStatus` subkey, is defined in the Windows Platform SDK as shown in Listing 10.4.

LISTING 10.4   The `OLEMISC` Enumeration Used When Registering ActiveX Controls

```
 1: typedef enum tagOLEMISC
 2: {
 3:   OLEMISC_RECOMPOSEONRESIZE = 1,
 4:   OLEMISC_ONLYICONIC = 2,
 5:   OLEMISC_INSERTNOTREPLACE = 4,
 6:   OLEMISC_STATIC = 8,
 7:   OLEMISC_CANTLINKINSIDE = 16,
 8:   OLEMISC_CANLINKBYOLE1 = 32,
 9:   OLEMISC_ISLINKOBJECT = 64,
10:   OLEMISC_INSIDEOUT = 128,
11:   OLEMISC_ACTIVATEWHENVISIBLE = 256,
```

LISTING 10.4   Continued

```
12:    OLEMISC_RENDERINGISDEVICEINDEPENDENT = 512,
13:    OLEMISC_INVISIBLEATRUNTIME = 1024
14:    OLEMISC_ALWAYSRUN = 2048,
15:    OLEMISC_ACTSLIKEBUTTON = 4096,
16:    OLEMISC_ACTSLIKELABEL = 8192,
17:    OLEMISC_NOUIACTIVATE = 16384,
18:    OLEMISC_ALIGNABLE = 32768,
19:    OLEMISC_SIMPLEFRAME = 65536,
20:    OLEMISC_SETCLIENTSITEFIRST = 131072,
21:    OLEMISC_IMEMODE = 262144,
22:    OLEMISC_IGNOREACTIVATEWHENVISIBLE = 524288,
23:    OLEMISC_WANTSTOMENUMERGE = 1048576,
24:    OLEMISC_SUPPORTSMULTILEVELUNDO = 2097152
25: } OLEMISC;
```

The various values of the enumeration are described in the Platform SDK documentation (available on MSDN Online) but a sensible `MiscStatus` value for Windows Forms controls is `OLEMISC_RECOMPOSEONRESIZE | OLEMISC_INSIDEOUT | OLEMISC_ACTIVATEWHENVISIBLE | OLEMISC_SETCLIENTSITEFIRST` (131457). You could also include flags such as `OLEMISC_ ACTSLIKEBUTTON` or `OLEMISC_ACTSLIKELABEL`, depending upon the nature of your control.

Listing 10.5 contains portions of an update to the `LabeledTextBox` control from Listing 8.6 in Chapter 8, to perform the five registration steps listed previously. It does this with the use of custom registration functions that are invoked by `REGASM.EXE`. See Chapter 12, "Customizing COM's View of .NET Components," for more information about custom registration functions.

LISTING 10.5   The `LabeledTextBox` Control That Registers Itself As a Generic ActiveX Control

```
 1: using System;
 2: using System.Security;
 3: using Microsoft.Win32;
 4: using System.Windows.Forms;
 5: using System.Runtime.InteropServices;
 6:
 7: [assembly:AllowPartiallyTrustedCallersAttribute]
 8:
 9: public class LabeledTextBox : UserControl
10: {
11:    private System.Windows.Forms.TextBox textBox1;
12:    private System.Windows.Forms.Label label1;
13:    private System.ComponentModel.Container components = null;
14:
15:    // Custom Registration Function
```

10

ADVANCED TOPICS
FOR USING .NET
COMPONENTS

LISTING 10.5   Continued

```
16:    [ComRegisterFunction]
17:    private static void ComRegisterFunction(Type t)
18:    {
19:      RegistryKey key = Registry.ClassesRoot.OpenSubKey("CLSID\\" +
20:        t.GUID.ToString("B"), true);
21:      // Step 1
22:      key.CreateSubKey("Control");
23:      // Step 2
24:      key.CreateSubKey(
25:        "Implemented Categories\\{40FC6ED4-2438-11CF-A3DB-080036F12502}");
26:      // Step 3
27:      key.CreateSubKey("MiscStatus").SetValue("", "131457");
28:      // Step 4
29:      key.CreateSubKey("TypeLib").SetValue("",
30:        Marshal.GetTypeLibGuidForAssembly(t.Assembly).ToString("B"));
31:      // Step 5
32:      string version = t.Assembly.GetName().Version.Major.ToString() +
33:        "." + t.Assembly.GetName().Version.Minor.ToString();
34:      if (version == "0.0") version = "1.0";
35:      key.CreateSubKey("Version").SetValue("", version);
36:      key.Close();
37:    }
38:
39:    // Custom Unregistration Function
40:    [ComUnregisterFunction]
41:    private static void ComUnregisterFunction(Type t)
42:    {
43:      try
44:      {
45:        Registry.ClassesRoot.DeleteSubKeyTree(
46:          "CLSID\\" + t.GUID.ToString("B"));
47:      }
48:      // Ignore exception thrown if key doesn't exist
49:      catch (ArgumentException) {}
50:    }
51:
52:    public LabeledTextBox()
53:    {
54:      // This call is required by the Windows.Forms Form Designer
55:      InitializeComponent();
56:    }
57:
58:    public string LabelText
59:    {
60:      get { return label1.Text; }
61:      set { label1.Text = value; }
```

Listing 10.5   Continued

```
62:    }
63:
64:    public string TextBoxText
65:    {
66:      get { return textBox1.Text; }
67:      set { textBox1.Text = value; }
68:    }
69:
70:    // Clean up any resources being used
71:    protected override void Dispose(bool disposing)
72:    {
73:      ...
74:    }
75:
76:    // Required method for Designer support
77:    private void InitializeComponent()
78:    {
79:      ...
80:    }
81: }
```

Lines 32–35 handle the type library version number specially because it doesn't equal *Major.Minor* if the assembly version number is 0.0. For the omitted parts of the listing, check out this book's Web site or the corresponding listing in Chapter 8.

The following steps can be performed to host a Windows Forms control on a Visual Basic 6 form:

1. Register the assembly containing the Windows Forms control as follows:

   `regasm LabeledTextBox.dll /tlb /codebase`

   Using the /codebase option is the easiest way to get your assembly found from within the Visual Basic 6 IDE, but you could alternatively do something like giving the assembly a strong name and installing it into the Global Assembly Cache. During this step, the ComRegisterFunction method defined in Lines 13–34 of Listing 10.5 is invoked by REGASM.EXE to add the registry entries specific to ActiveX controls.

2. Open a new Visual Basic 6 project such as a Standard EXE project.

3. Right-click on the Toolbox window and select Components....

4. Select the name of the control, such as LabeledTextBox, then press OK. This dialog is shown in Figure 10.2.

5. Drag the control onto the form, as shown in Figure 10.3.

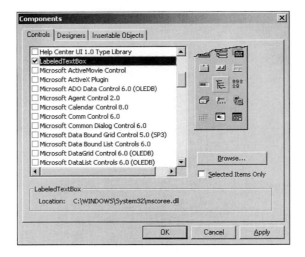

FIGURE 10.2

Selecting a Windows Forms control registered as an ActiveX control in Visual Basic 6.

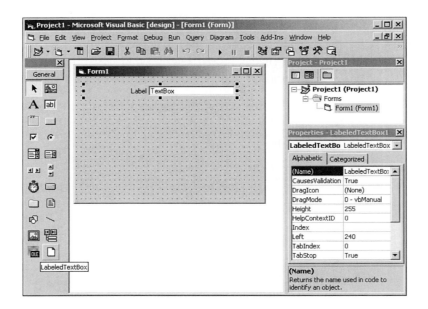

FIGURE 10.3

Dragging a Windows Forms control onto a Visual Basic 6 form.

From this point, you may have mixed results in getting such an application to work correctly, because this kind of interaction is not supported.

Working Around COM-Invisibility

Although .NET types and members are sometimes made invisible to COM, there's ultimately nothing a .NET component author can do to prevent the use of functionality from COM if it's publicly available to .NET components. Anyone can write a COM-visible .NET component that acts as an intermediate layer between .NET and COM components. This layer can easily expose COM-invisible .NET functionality to COM by routing calls from the COM component to the .NET component.

But exposing COM-invisible functionality to COM is often easier than explicit delegation. As you know, a .NET class interface contains the members of base classes. More precisely, it contains the public COM-visible members of base classes. This behavior doesn't take into consideration the COM-visibility of classes themselves, so public members of a COM-invisible base class become visible in a derived class's class interface unless the members are individually marked as being COM-invisible. Listing 10.6 demonstrates this often-unexpected behavior. This listing uses two custom attributes—ComVisibleAttribute and ClassInterfaceAttribute—which are explained in Chapter 12.

LISTING 10.6   Tricks with COM-Visibility and Inheritance

C#:

```csharp
using System.Runtime.InteropServices;

// Interface inheritance

[ComVisible(false)]
public interface IAmInvisibleToCom
{
  void SomeMethod();
}

public interface IAmVisibleToAll : IAmInvisibleToCom
{
}

// Class inheritance

[ComVisible(false)]
public class ClassForManagedEyesOnly
{
```

LISTING 10.6 Continued

```
  public void SomeMethod() {}
}

// Expose type information for the class interface
// so we can see what members it contains
[ClassInterface(ClassInterfaceType.AutoDual)]
public class ClassVisibleToAll : ClassForManagedEyesOnly
{
}
```

Exported Type Library:

```
[
  odl,
  uuid(735D3585-2865-3D19-AFD1-F49DB7F31903),
  version(1.0),
  dual,
  oleautomation,
  custom(0F21F359-AB84-41E8-9A78-36D110E6D2F9, "IAmVisibleToAll")
]
interface IAmVisibleToAll : IDispatch {
};


[
  odl,
  uuid(161A4787-9BF8-39BC-A274-D36F51F42D9C),
  hidden,
  dual,
  nonextensible,
  oleautomation,
  custom(0F21F359-AB84-41E8-9A78-36D110E6D2F9, "ClassVisibleToAll")
]
interface _ClassVisibleToAll : IDispatch {
  [id(00000000), propget, custom(54FC8F55-38DE-4703-9C4E-250351302B1C, 1)]
  HRESULT ToString([out, retval] BSTR* pRetVal);
  [id(0x60020001)]
  HRESULT Equals([in] VARIANT obj, [out, retval] VARIANT_BOOL* pRetVal);
  [id(0x60020002)]
  HRESULT GetHashCode([out, retval] long* pRetVal);
  [id(0x60020003)]
  HRESULT GetType([out, retval] _Type** pRetVal);
  [id(0x60020004)]
  HRESULT SomeMethod();
};
```

Although the `IAmVisibleToAll` *interface* that derives from a COM-invisible interface doesn't contain the base method (as usual), the `ClassVisibleToAll` *class* contains the COM-invisible base class's `SomeMethod` method. Had the `SomeMethod` method been directly marked with `ComVisible(false)`, it would not appear in class interfaces for derived classes.

This inheritance behavior, which can seem strange at first glance, can come in handy whenever you want to expose classes to COM that derive from COM-invisible classes. For example, consider the following vanilla Windows Form written in Visual Basic .NET:

```
Imports System.Windows.Forms

Public Class ComVisibleForm
  Inherits Form
End Class
```

Although `System.Windows.Forms.Form` is a COM-invisible class, this simple `ComVisibleForm` class can be instantiated from COM, and most of the methods of `Form` can be invoked via late binding. For example, a Visual Basic 6 client could do something like:

```
Dim f As Object
Set f = New ComVisibleForm
f.Text = "Late binding doesn't look too bad in VB6!"
f.BorderStyle = 2 'FormBorderStyle.Fixed3D
f.Show
```

The `ComVisibleForm` coclass looks like the following in the type library, with the empty `_ComVisibleForm` class interface making the base `Form` methods available via late binding:

```
[
  uuid(9A0D1EDF-B7B0-353A-8069-5E75EABF8F19),
  version(1.0),
  custom(0F21F359-AB84-41E8-9A78-36D110E6D2F9, "ComVisibleForm")
]
coclass ComVisibleForm {
  [default] interface _ComVisibleForm;
  interface _Object;
  interface IComponent;
  interface IDisposable;
};
```

If the base methods were COM-invisible by default, the derived class would have to either override each method or provide separate methods that call each base class method. Instead, this only needs to be done for methods that have COM-invisible parameter types. To get a feel for the methods that can be invoked on the `ComVisibleForm` class interface, you could mark the class with `ClassInterfaceType.AutoDual` and export a type library. This technique is described in Chapter 12. Listing 10.7 shows what the beginning of this extremely long class

interface looks like (truncated for brevity). Note that exporting such a type library causes
TLBEXP.EXE to complain about several methods because you're now exposing methods with
COM-invisible value type parameters. These originally COM-invisible methods are defined in
the base classes in the System.Windows.Forms assembly.

LISTING 10.7   The Beginning of a Class Interface for the ComVisibleForm Class That
Derives from System.Windows.Forms.Form

```
[
  odl,
  uuid(6BE782C9-DD90-3BC6-A565-1EE9E0BD28F6),
  hidden,
  dual,
  nonextensible,
  oleautomation,
  custom(0F21F359-AB84-41E8-9A78-36D110E6D2F9, ComVisibleForm)
]
interface _ComVisibleForm : IDispatch {
  [id(00000000), propget, custom(54FC8F55-38DE-4703-9C4E-250351302B1C, 1)]
  HRESULT ToString([out, retval] BSTR* pRetVal);
  [id(0x60020001)]
  HRESULT Equals(
                  [in] VARIANT obj,
                  [out, retval] VARIANT_BOOL* pRetVal);
  [id(0x60020002)]
  HRESULT GetHashCode([out, retval] long* pRetVal);
  [id(0x60020003)]
  HRESULT GetType([out, retval] _Type** pRetVal);
  [id(0x60020004)]
  HRESULT GetLifetimeService([out, retval] VARIANT* pRetVal);
  [id(0x60020005)]
  HRESULT InitializeLifetimeService([out, retval] VARIANT* pRetVal);
  [id(0x60020006)]
  HRESULT CreateObjRef(
                  [in] _Type* requestedType,
                  [out, retval] IDispatch** pRetVal);
  [id(0x60020007), propget]
  HRESULT Site([out, retval] ISite** pRetVal);
  [id(0x60020007), propputref]
  HRESULT Site([in] ISite* pRetVal);
  [id(0x60020009)]
  HRESULT add_Disposed([in] IDispatch* value);
  [id(0x6002000a)]
  HRESULT remove_Disposed([in] IDispatch* value);
  [id(0x6002000b)]
  HRESULT Dispose();
  [id(0x6002000c), propget]
  HRESULT Container([out, retval] IContainer** pRetVal);
  [id(0x6002000d), propget]
  HRESULT AllowDrop([out, retval] VARIANT_BOOL* pRetVal);
  [id(0x6002000d), propput]
  HRESULT AllowDrop([in] VARIANT_BOOL pRetVal);
  [restricted] void Missing22();
  [restricted] void Missing23();
  [id(0x60020011), propget]
  HRESULT BackColor([out, retval] OLE_COLOR* pRetVal);
  [id(0x60020011), propput]
  HRESULT BackColor([in] OLE_COLOR pRetVal);
  ...
```

Members of System.Object (_Object)

Members of MarshalByRefObject

Members of Component (the IComponent and IDisposable interfaces)

Members of Control

Gaps for methods removed due to COM-invisible value type parameters

For overloaded methods that end up with mangled names (such as `Invoke_2`, `Invalidate_6`, and so on), a COM-friendly Windows Form should expose methods with unique names in the derived class that call the base methods so COM doesn't have to. This technique is also useful for members that can't be called from COM due to COM-invisible value type parameters. For example, the `Form` class has an `Anchor` property (inherited from the base `Control` class) of type `AnchorStyles`, a COM-invisible enumeration. By providing a different property, say `MyAnchor`, using the underlying type of the enumeration instead, the same functionality could be exposed to COM. For example:

```
Imports System.Windows.Forms

Public Class ComVisibleForm
  Inherits Form

  ' MyAnchor delegates to the base Anchor property
  Public Property MyAnchor As Integer
    Get
      Return MyBase.Anchor
    End Get
    Set
      Value = MyBase.Anchor
    End Set
  End Property
End Class
```

The best choice, as explained in the following chapter, would be to define an interface with exactly the methods you want to expose to COM, say `IForm`, and use that as the default interface.

DIGGING DEEPER

The CLR ensures that COM-invisible interfaces and members are not directly used by COM at run time. However, the CLR does not enforce that COM-invisible classes cannot be instantiated by COM clients. Instead, a .NET class marked as COM-invisible simply means that it doesn't get registered and it doesn't get exported to a type library. Therefore, by manually registering a .NET class with the appropriate CLSID, you can enable a COM-invisible .NET class to be directly instantiated via `CoCreateInstance` (`New` in Visual Basic 6)! This only works if the class has a public default constructor. Furthermore, you can only query for COM-visible interfaces and invoke COM-visible members.

Determining what the CLSID for a .NET class would be if it were registered is easy; in managed code, get a `Type` that represents the COM-invisible class and call the `GUID` property to see the CLSID value. For example, in C#:

```
Console.WriteLine(typeof(ComInvisibleClass).GUID);
```
This property returns what would be the CLSID for `ComInvisibleClass` if it were COM-visible.

Using Reflection to Invoke Static Members

Reflecting over .NET objects in unmanaged code is fairly simple, even in unmanaged C++, because many of the important reflection classes expose auto-dual class interfaces (such as `_Type` and `_MemberInfo`). Using reflection from COM can be useful for discovering metadata that does not get exported to type libraries. It's also great for invoking static members, which do not get directly exposed to COM.

The process of invoking static members on a given CCW instance is straightforward. First, you call the `GetType` instance method on the class interface for `System.Object` (`_Object`) to get a `System.Type` instance that represents the original instance. Then, you can call `InvokeMember` on the `_Type` interface with the appropriate binding flags for invoking the static member. Besides the binding flags that specify the member type (method, property, or field) and visibility, the binding flags should include `Static` and `FlattenHierarchy`. The latter flag is necessary if the static member is defined on a base class of the current type rather than directly on the type.

However, static members often appear on classes for which an instance can never be obtained. Widely used examples of such classes are `Marshal` in the `System.Runtime.InteropServices` namespace, `Activator` in the `System` namespace, or `Console` in the `System` namespace. These classes serve as containers for static members, so they don't have any public constructors, nor do any members return instances of them.

Fortunately, it's still possible to invoke static members on such classes by taking advantage of `_Type`, the class interface for `System.Type`. Because static members can be invoked via reflection without a corresponding instance, all we need to obtain is the *type* for the class containing a static member rather than an instance of the class. To call any static member *M* on any type *T*, you can perform the following steps:

1. Create any .NET object, and query for the `_Object` interface from its CCW.

2. Call `_Object.GetType` to get a `System.Type` instance.

3. Call `_Type.GetType`, which is the instance method inherited from `System.Object`, to get another `System.Type` instance. This time, however, the `Type` instance represents the `System.Type` type instead of the original type.

4. Call `InvokeMember` on the second `Type` instance with the appropriate binding flags to call the static `System.Type.GetType` method. Pass the name of *T*, qualified with its assembly name if necessary, as the parameter to `GetType`.

5. Extract the `_Type` interface pointer from the `VARIANT` returned by `InvokeMember`. This represents *T*, so call `InvokeMember` on this interface with the appropriate binding flags, passing the name of *M* to invoke the desired static method.

Listing 10.8 performs these steps in unmanaged C++ and demonstrates using them with two static members in the `mscorlib` assembly: `System.Console.ReadLine` and `System.AppDomain.CurrentDomain`. Unfortunately, it's not possible to do this in Visual Basic 6 because `Type.InvokeMember` uses by-value array parameters, which are not supported in VB6.

LISTING 10.8   Using Reflection to Invoke Any Static .NET Members

```
 1: #define _WIN32_DCOM
 2: #include <stdio.h>
 3: #include <wtypes.h>
 4:
 5: #import "path\\mscorlib.tlb" no_namespace named_guids raw_interfaces_only
 6:
 7: HRESULT InvokeStaticMember(BSTR typeName, BSTR memberName,
 8:   BindingFlags memberType, SAFEARRAY* parameters, VARIANT* retVal)
 9: {
10:   HRESULT hresult;
11:   IUnknown* pUnk = NULL;
12:   _Object* pObj = NULL;
13:   _Type* pType = NULL;
14:   _Type* pTypeOfType = NULL;
15:   _Type* pDesiredType = NULL;
16:   VARIANT typeNameParam;
17:   VARIANT getTypeRetVal;
18:   VARIANT nullObject;
19:   SAFEARRAY* psa;
20:   LONG index;
21:   BSTR getTypeName = SysAllocString(L"GetType");
22:
23:   VariantInit(&typeNameParam);
24:   VariantInit(&getTypeRetVal);
25:   VariantInit(&nullObject);
26:
27:   // Instantiate a dummy class just so we can get a System.Type instance
28:   hresult = CoCreateInstance(CLSID_Object, NULL,
29:     CLSCTX_INPROC_SERVER, IID_IUnknown, (void **)&pUnk);
```

LISTING 10.8 Continued

```
30:    if (FAILED(hresult)) goto cleanup;
31:
32:    // Get the _Object interface so we can call GetType
33:    hresult = pUnk->QueryInterface(IID__Object, (void**)&pObj);
34:    if (FAILED(hresult)) goto cleanup;
35:
36:    // Call _Object.GetType
37:    hresult = pObj->GetType(&pType);
38:    if (FAILED(hresult)) goto cleanup;
39:
40:    // Call the instance Type.GetType method (inherited from Object)
41:    // in order to get the type for System.Type rather than the type for
42:    // System.Object
43:    hresult = pType->GetType(&pTypeOfType);
44:    if (FAILED(hresult)) goto cleanup;
45:
46:    // Prepare a 1-element array containing the passed-in type name
47:    // to pass to the static Type.GetType method
48:    psa = SafeArrayCreateVector(VT_VARIANT, 0, 1);
49:    typeNameParam.vt = VT_BSTR;
50:    typeNameParam.bstrVal = typeName;
51:    index = 0;
52:    hresult = SafeArrayPutElement(psa, &index, &typeNameParam);
53:    if (FAILED(hresult)) goto cleanup;
54:
55:    // Invoke the static Type.GetType method using reflection on the
56:    // type for System.Type in order to get the desired type
57:    nullObject.vt = VT_EMPTY;
58:    hresult = pTypeOfType->InvokeMember_3(getTypeName,
59:      (BindingFlags)(BindingFlags_InvokeMethod | BindingFlags_Public |
60:      BindingFlags_Static | BindingFlags_FlattenHierarchy), NULL,
61:      nullObject, psa, &getTypeRetVal);
62:    if (FAILED(hresult)) goto cleanup;
63:
64:    // Get the _Type interface so we can call the static InvokeMember
65:    // method on the desired type to invoke the desired static member
66:    hresult = getTypeRetVal.punkVal->QueryInterface(IID__Type,
67:      (void**)&pDesiredType);
68:    if (FAILED(hresult)) goto cleanup;
69:
70:    // Invoke the desired static member
71:    pDesiredType->InvokeMember_3(memberName, (BindingFlags)(memberType |
72:      BindingFlags_Public | BindingFlags_Static |
73:      BindingFlags_FlattenHierarchy), NULL, nullObject, parameters,
```

LISTING 10.8   Continued

```
74:        retVal);
75:     if (FAILED(hresult)) goto cleanup;
76:
77: cleanup:
78:     if (pUnk) pUnk->Release();
79:     if (pObj) pObj->Release();
80:     if (pType) pType->Release();
81:     if (pTypeOfType) pTypeOfType->Release();
82:     if (pDesiredType) pDesiredType->Release();
83:     if (getTypeName) SysFreeString(getTypeName);
84:     SafeArrayDestroy(psa);
85:     VariantClear(&typeNameParam);
86:     VariantClear(&getTypeRetVal);
87:     VariantClear(&nullObject);
88:
89:     return hresult;
90: };
91:
92: int main(int argc, char* argv[])
93: {
94:     HRESULT hresult;
95:     VARIANT retVal;
96:     _AppDomain* pDomain = NULL;
97:     BSTR typeName1, typeName2, memberName1, memberName2, directory;
98:
99:     // Initialize COM
100:    hresult = CoInitializeEx(NULL, COINIT_MULTITHREADED);
101:    if (FAILED(hresult))
102:    {
103:      printf("ERROR: Cannot initialize COM: 0x%x\n", hresult);
104:      return -1;
105:    }
106:
107:    VariantInit(&retVal);
108:
109:    // -----------------------------------------
110:    // Example 1: Calling System.Console.ReadLine
111:    // -----------------------------------------
112:
113:    typeName1 = SysAllocString(L"System.Console");
114:    memberName1 = SysAllocString(L"ReadLine");
115:
116:    printf("Type in something followed by Enter: ");
117:
118:    hresult = InvokeStaticMember(typeName1, memberName1,
```

LISTING **10.8**   Continued

```
119:      BindingFlags_InvokeMethod, NULL, &retVal);
120:    if (FAILED(hresult))
121:    {
122:      printf("ERROR: Invocation failed: 0x%x\n", hresult);
123:      return -1;
124:    }
125:
126:    wprintf(L"You typed: '%s'\n", retVal.bstrVal);
127:
128:    // -------------------------------------------------
129:    // Example 2: Calling System.AppDomain.CurrentDomain
130:    // -------------------------------------------------
131:
132:    typeName2 = SysAllocString(L"System.AppDomain");
133:    memberName2 = SysAllocString(L"CurrentDomain");
134:
135:    hresult = InvokeStaticMember(typeName2, memberName2,
136:      BindingFlags_GetProperty, NULL, &retVal);
137:    if (FAILED(hresult))
138:    {
139:      printf("ERROR: Invocation failed: 0x%x\n", hresult);
140:      return -1;
141:    }
142:
143:    // Get the _AppDomain interface from the returned IUnknown pointer
144:    hresult = retVal.punkVal->QueryInterface(IID__AppDomain,
145:      (void**)&pDomain);
146:    if (FAILED(hresult))
147:    {
148:      printf("ERROR: Could not get _AppDomain interface pointer: 0x%x\n",
149:        hresult);
150:      return -1;
151:    }
152:
153:    // Call the BaseDirectory property on the _AppDomain instance
154:    pDomain->get_BaseDirectory(&directory);
155:    wprintf(L"Base directory of the current domain: '%s'\n", directory);
156:
157:    CoUninitialize();
158:    return 0;
159:  };
```

The *path* in Line 5 must be replaced with the location of MSCORLIB.TLB on your computer, which can vary according to your settings. Step 1 is performed in Lines 28–34. System.Object is chosen as the dummy object to instantiate, so CLSID_Object (which is defined thanks to using the #import statement in Line 5) is passed to CoCreateInstance. Step 2 is performed in Lines 37–38, and step 3 is performed in Lines 43–44.

Lines 48–53 create a single-element SAFEARRAY containing the passed-in type name. This is passed to the Type.InvokeMember call in Lines 58–61, which is step 4. This step demonstrates the invocation of a static method (GetType) on a class for which we've got an instance (System.Type). Notice that the simplest overload of Type.InvokeMember is exposed to COM as InvokeMember_3! Also notice that the SAFEARRAY passed to InvokeMember_3 contains a VARIANT rather than directly containing a BSTR. That's because Type.InvokeMember expects an array of System.Object instances, so passing an array of strings would be a type mismatch.

TIP

To pass a null object to a .NET parameter exposed as a VARIANT, pass a VARIANT with its vt field set to VT_EMPTY. Listing 10.8 does this for the target parameter of _Type.InvokeMember_3.

Step 5 is performed in Lines 66–75. Lines 66–67 extract the IUnknown pointer from the returned VARIANT and query for the _Type interface. Lines 71–74 call InvokeMember_3 on this interface with the passed-in member name, member type, and parameters. The returned object is stored in the retVal variable, which is accessible to the caller of InvokeStaticMember.

This five-step procedure is pretty lengthy in unmanaged C++, but the same code would look as follows in C#:

```
Object o = new Object();
Type t = o.GetType();
Type typeOfType = t.GetType();
Type desiredType = (Type)typeOfType.InvokeMember("GetType",
  BindingFlags.InvokeMethod | BindingFlags.Static | BindingFlags.Public |
  BindingFlags.FlattenHierarchy, null, null, new object[]{typeName});
return desiredType.InvokeMember(memberName, memberType | BindingFlags.Static |
  BindingFlags.Public | BindingFlags.FlattenHierarchy, null, null, parameters);
```

Lines 113–126 demonstrate the static invocation functionality with the System.Console.ReadLine method, and Lines 132–155 demonstrate it with the System.AppDomain.CurrentDomain property.

10

ADVANCED TOPICS FOR USING .NET COMPONENTS

CAUTION

Using reflection in unmanaged script has a limitation in version 1.0 of the CLR: .NET members with enum parameters cannot be invoked. COM clients can invoke .NET members with enum parameters via v-table binding, late binding via IDispatch, and v-table binding to reflection APIs (such as Type.InvokeMember), but not when late binding via IDispatch to reflection APIs (a sort of double-late binding). Unmanaged script falls into the last category when explicitly using reflection, so it runs into this limitation.

Handling .NET Events

By default, .NET events cannot be handled (or *sinked*) by COM components without extra managed code that handles the events and then communicates with COM. Listing 10.9 demonstrates how events are exposed to COM by listing the 14 members that get exported for the seven events of _AppDomain, the default interface for System.AppDomain.

LISTING 10.9   Exported Methods for the Seven Events Exposed by the _AppDomain Interface

```
 1: [id(0x60020007)]
 2: HRESULT add_DomainUnload([in] _EventHandler* value);
 3: [id(0x60020008)]
 4: HRESULT remove_DomainUnload([in] _EventHandler* value);
 5: [id(0x60020009)]
 6: HRESULT add_AssemblyLoad([in] _AssemblyLoadEventHandler* value);
 7: [id(0x6002000a)]
 8: HRESULT remove_AssemblyLoad([in] _AssemblyLoadEventHandler* value);
 9: [id(0x6002000b)]
10: HRESULT add_ProcessExit([in] _EventHandler* value);
11: [id(0x6002000c)]
12: HRESULT remove_ProcessExit([in] _EventHandler* value);
13: [id(0x6002000d)]
14: HRESULT add_TypeResolve([in] _ResolveEventHandler* value);
15: [id(0x6002000e)]
16: HRESULT remove_TypeResolve([in] _ResolveEventHandler* value);
17: [id(0x6002000f)]
18: HRESULT add_ResourceResolve([in] _ResolveEventHandler* value);
19: [id(0x60020010)]
20: HRESULT remove_ResourceResolve([in] _ResolveEventHandler* value);
21: [id(0x60020011)]
22: HRESULT add_AssemblyResolve([in] _ResolveEventHandler* value);
```

Listing 10.9   Continued

```
23: [id(0x60020012)]
24: HRESULT remove_AssemblyResolve([in] _ResolveEventHandler* value);
25: [id(0x60020013)]
26: HRESULT add_UnhandledException(
27:   [in] _UnhandledExceptionEventHandler* value);
28: [id(0x60020014)]
29: HRESULT remove_UnhandledException(
30:   [in] _UnhandledExceptionEventHandler* value);
```

Because COM interfaces have no notion of events, each event member is exported as a pair of accessor methods—add_*EventName* and remove_*EventName*. These correspond to the event accessors introduced in Chapter 5, "Responding to COM Events."

Just as .NET clients invoke these accessors (with different syntax, such as += or AddHandler) to hook and unhook event handlers, a COM client could theoretically call add_*EventName* to hook up an event handler and remove_*EventName* to unhook an event handler. The problem is that a COM client has no good way to pass a correct argument to any of these methods. Each accessor method must be passed an instance of a .NET delegate, so the only way to pass it such a type is to write some managed code that can create a .NET delegate and pass it to COM. (Passing a COM object implementing a class interface such as _EventHandler does not work, as discussed in Chapter 17, "Implementing .NET Interfaces for Type Compatibility.") COM clients can't directly instantiate delegates because they don't have public default constructors. You could get around this limitation by using the CLR hosting technique described in the "Hosting the Common Language Runtime" section, but attempting to set up a delegate from unmanaged code is tricky without writing some managed code.

Chapter 13, "Exposing .NET Events to COM Clients," describes how .NET components can expose their events to COM using the familiar connection point protocol. If this is done, then COM clients can handle events the same way that they always have—by implementing source interfaces.

Unexpected Casing in Type Libraries

Identifiers in type libraries sometimes have different casing than what you might expect. For example, the names of exported methods or properties are sometimes lowercase, whereas their corresponding .NET members have uppercase names. Listing 10.10 demonstrates this phenomenon for _MemberInfo, an auto-dual class interface exported for System.Reflection. MemberInfo. Although the .NET MemberInfo class has a Name property, the _MemberInfo interface has a name property.

Listing 10.10   The Class Interface for `System.Reflection.MemberInfo` Has a Property
Called `name` Rather Than `Name`

```
 1: interface _MemberInfo : IDispatch
 2: {
 3:   [id(00000000), propget, custom(54FC8F55-38DE-4703-9C4E-250351302B1C, 1)]
 4:   HRESULT ToString([out, retval] BSTR* pRetVal);
 5:   [id(0x60020001)]
 6:   HRESULT Equals([in] VARIANT obj, [out, retval] VARIANT_BOOL* pRetVal);
 7:   [id(0x60020002)]
 8:   HRESULT GetHashCode([out, retval] long* pRetVal);
 9:   [id(0x60020003)]
10:   HRESULT GetType([out, retval] _Type** pRetVal);
11:   [id(0x60020004), propget]
12:   HRESULT MemberType([out, retval] MemberTypes* pRetVal);
13:   [id(0x60020005), propget]
14:   HRESULT name([out, retval] BSTR* pRetVal);
15:   [id(0x60020006), propget]
16:   HRESULT DeclaringType([out, retval] _Type** pRetVal);
17:   [id(0x60020007), propget]
18:   HRESULT ReflectedType([out, retval] _Type** pRetVal);
19:   [id(0x60020008)]
20:   HRESULT GetCustomAttributes([in] _Type* attributeType,
21:     [in] VARIANT_BOOL inherit, [out, retval] SAFEARRAY(VARIANT)* pRetVal);
22:   [id(0x60020009)]
23:   HRESULT GetCustomAttributes_2([in] VARIANT_BOOL inherit,
24:     [out, retval] SAFEARRAY(VARIANT)* pRetVal);
25:   [id(0x6002000a)]
26:   HRESULT IsDefined([in] _Type* attributeType, [in] VARIANT_BOOL inherit,
27:     [out, retval] VARIANT_BOOL* pRetVal);
28: };
```

What causes this to happen? Type libraries, like Visual Basic, are case-insensitive. More specifically, identifiers in a type library (class names, method names, parameter names, and so on) are stored in a case-insensitive table. Once one case of an identifier is added to the table (such as `name`), any later occurrences of the identifier, regardless of case, are not added to the table (such as `Name`). This situation is pictured in Figure 10.4.

Instead of each occurrence of a `name` identifier in the type library having its original case, all occurrences point to the same entry in the table. The first casing encountered wins, and all subsequent occurrences match that case in the output type library. For Listing 10.10, countless methods defined in `mscorlib.tlb` before the `_MemberInfo` interface have a parameter called `name`. For example, the `IResourceWriter.AddResource` method is exported before `MemberInfo` and has such a parameter, so the all-lowercase version wins.

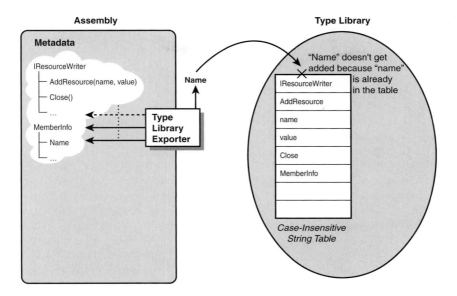

FIGURE 10.4

Type libraries store identifiers in a case-insensitive table, so the first case emitted by the exporter becomes the only case.

This phenomenon has nothing to do with .NET or with type library exporting. It's simply a characteristic of type libraries, and can happen even when you create a type library from an IDL file that has the same identifier with conflicting cases. The type library exporter, however, has a mechanism to help manage this case-insensitivity issue. Appendix B, "SDK Tools Reference," describes how to control the exported case of identifiers using TLBEXP.EXE's /names option.

TIP

The #import statement in Visual C++ can be used with a rename directive to change any identifier found in a type library to something else. Therefore, the rename directive can be used to handle unexpected case changes. For example, if you do the following in an unmanaged C++ application, it will appear as if _MemberInfo has a property called Name:

```
#import <mscorlib.tlb> rename("name", "Name")
```

Of course, it also means that methods like IResourceWriter.AddResource are given a parameter called Name, but that casing change won't affect the use of such methods. The rename directive replaces every occurrence of the first string with the second string, and can be specified multiple times for multiple string replacements.

> The rename directive can also be used with substrings of identifier names, so it can be useful for renaming the Get, Put, and PutRef prefixes that are automatically added to property accessors to avoid name conflicts with other members. For example:
>
> ```
> #import <mylibrary.tlb> rename("Get", "Get_")
> ```

Advanced Shutdown Topics

MSCOREE.DLL exports two functions related to process shutdown that can be useful for unmanaged applications that use .NET objects:

- CoEEShutDownCOM
- CorExitProcess

Calling CoEEShutDownCOM forces the CLR to release all interface pointers it holds onto inside RCWs. This method usually doesn't need to be called, but can be necessary if you're running leak-detection code or somehow depend on all interface pointers being released before process termination. It has no parameters and a void return type. If used, it should be one of the last calls an application makes before shutting down. To use this function in C++, include COR.H and link with MSCOREE.LIB. COR.H can be found in the same directory as MSCOREE.H, introduced earlier in the chapter.

CorExitProcess performs an orderly shutdown of the CLR, including the finalization of any .NET objects that have not yet been finalized, and exits the process with the passed-in error code. It has the following signature, from its C++ header file:

```
void STDMETHODCALLTYPE CorExitProcess(int exitCode);
```

In managed applications, the finalizers for any objects used almost always get invoked at some time before the process shuts down. An exceptional situation must occur to prevent the finalizers of all objects from running. For example, if an object's finalizer doesn't appear to be making progress, the CLR is free to terminate it early. Also, if managed code forces process shutdown with a PInvoke call to ExitProcess, the CLR doesn't have a chance to run any cleanup code such as invoking objects' finalizers.

When an *unmanaged* application uses .NET objects, however, the chance of finalizers getting run before the process shuts down is much less. Unmanaged process termination does not force finalizers to be run, unless the application uses a .NET-aware runtime such as version 7 of the Visual C++ runtime. The simple action of normally exiting an unmanaged Visual C++ 7 program enforces graceful shutdown of the CLR, but exiting an unmanaged Visual C++ 6 program (or Visual Basic 6 program) terminates the process abruptly. Graceful shutdown doesn't occur automatically because, without a call to `CorExitProcess`, the CLR is only notified that the process is shutting down from `DllMain`'s process detach notification. The loader lock is held at this point, so there is no way that finalization code can safely run.

Therefore, sophisticated COM clients need to call `CorExitProcess` in order for finalization to occur at shutdown as expected. To use this function in C++, include `MSCOREE.H` and link with `MSCOREE.LIB`.

If you're using .NET objects that hold onto non-memory resources, you'll want to dispose of the objects as soon as you're finished using them rather than waiting for garbage collection or process shutdown by calling their `IDisposable.Dispose` method (assuming the objects follow the convention of implementing `IDisposable`). A `Dispose` method typically does the same work as an object's finalizer, but suppresses finalization since the cleanup work is already performed when a client remembers to call it.

FAQ: Why doesn't the CLR call `Dispose` on a .NET object that implements `IDisposable` once the CCW's reference count reaches zero?

`IDisposable.Dispose` should be called when a .NET object is no longer being used by any clients—managed or unmanaged. If `Dispose` were called when a CCW's reference count reached zero, then any managed clients that were still holding onto a reference to the object would fail the next time they attempted to use it.

Therefore, the same mechanism for eagerly releasing a .NET object applies to COM clients as well as .NET clients; if the object implements `IDisposable`, call `Dispose` when you're finished using it. Otherwise, simply making a CCW's reference count reach zero with calls to `IUnknown.Release` only makes the .NET object *eligible* for collection. Its time of destruction remains non-deterministic.

Chapter 20, "Custom Marshaling," demonstrates a way to change the behavior of CCWs to call `IDisposable.Dispose`, so existing COM clients that don't call `Dispose` can still benefit from this behavior.

Conclusion

This chapter completes this book's coverage of using .NET components in COM applications. If you're writing a new client application or investing a lot of development effort in an existing COM client, you should seriously consider writing the client with a .NET language instead. A .NET client doesn't require registration of any .NET components being used, can naturally make use of static members or events, doesn't have the same problems with case-sensitivity or

10

ADVANCED TOPICS
FOR USING .NET
COMPONENTS

overloaded methods (in most .NET languages), doesn't require special treatment when shutting down a process, and so on. And, as demonstrated in Part II, "Using COM Components in .NET Applications," a .NET application can work naturally with COM components as well as .NET components!

The next chapter begins Part IV, "Designing Great .NET Components for COM Clients," which focuses on the .NET side of the same COM client/.NET server direction of COM Interoperability. By designing .NET components that follow these guidelines, you'll prevent COM clients from encountering some of the issues covered in this chapter.

FAQ: Can I use a .NET executable (.EXE) as an out-of-process COM server?

It's possible to indirectly use any .NET executable or DLL as an out-of-process COM server, but not without extra work. It doesn't matter whether your .NET component is packaged as an .EXE file or a .DLL file, because MSCOREE.DLL is always registered as the in-process server. But with proper registration (not done by REGASM.EXE) and an appropriate host executable (such as DLLHOST.EXE), it's possible to set up an out-of-process COM server that encapsulates the in-process server. This is no different than for standard in-process COM components.

Out-of-process behavior is typically accomplished by creating a new COM+ server application (as opposed to a library application, which runs in-process) containing the desired .NET or COM component. See Appendix B for a description of REGSVCS.EXE, a utility that installs .NET components into the COM+ Component Services explorer.

Designing Great .NET Components for COM Clients

IN THIS PART

11 .NET Design Guidelines for Components Used by COM Clients   497

12 Customizing COM's View of .NET Components   539

13 Exposing .NET Events to COM Clients   591

14 Implementing COM Interfaces for Binary Compatibility   627

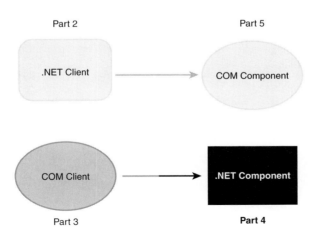

.NET Design Guidelines for Components Used by COM Clients

IN THIS CHAPTER

- Naming Guidelines   499

- Usage Guidelines   506

- Reporting Errors   520

- Exposing Enumerators to COM   524

- Versioning   527

- Deployment   532

- Testing Your Component from COM   535

This chapter begins Part IV, "Designing Great .NET Components for COM Clients" in which we look at the process of writing .NET components that might be exposed to COM clients. Two kinds of .NET components fall into this category:

- Components designed primarily with .NET clients in mind, for which ease of use from COM is an added bonus
- Components specifically written for COM clients, because writing a COM component in a .NET language is often easier than writing it in a non-.NET language (especially unmanaged C++)

This chapter focuses mostly on the first type of .NET component, covering general design decisions that affect both .NET and COM users of your class library. Chapters 12 and 13 focus on customizations that affect only COM users. Chapter 14, "Implementing COM Interfaces for Binary Compatibility," focuses on the second type of .NET component, describing how to achieve binary compatibility with existing COM clients by implementing COM interfaces.

FAQ: How do I write a COM component in a .NET language such as C# or Visual Basic .NET?

Any .NET component is automatically a COM component, as demonstrated in Part III, "Using .NET Components in COM Applications." The main difference between .NET components used as COM components and traditional COM components is that .NET DLLs do not export four entry points that traditional in-process COM servers export:

- DllCanUnloadNow
- DllGetClassObject
- DllRegisterServer
- DllUnregisterServer

Instead, the CLR execution engine (MSCOREE.DLL) exports these and is registered as the in-process server, acting on the assembly's behalf. For this reason, some people don't consider .NET components to be true COM components, just components that can act like COM components. Either way, the fact remains that you don't need to do anything special to write a COM component in any .NET language; no additional code or custom attributes are necessary to expose .NET components to the world of COM.

Part III demonstrated that exposing a .NET component to COM is easy to do, but designing it to be "COM-friendly" is much harder. The .NET Framework gives a lot of flexibility to API designers, and that's great, but it also makes it easier for developers to make bad choices. To help steer software developers and architects in the right direction, the .NET Framework SDK documentation contains a section entitled `Design Guidelines for Class Library Developers`, found under the `Reference` section in the `.NET Framework` topic. These guidelines promote (among other things) consistency, predictability, and ease-of-use from any .NET language.

This chapter focuses on these .NET design guidelines in the context of usability from COM, to promote ease-of-use from any .NET *or COM* language. Whereas some of the documented .NET guidelines work well for COM clients, and some don't affect COM clients, others greatly reduce your COM usability. The goal of this chapter's guidelines is to help you improve your class library's usability from COM without sacrificing any ease of use for .NET clients.

> **TIP**
>
> Occasionally, authors who aren't concerned about designing COM-friendly .NET components (or who want to discourage the use of their class libraries from COM clients) make their entire assembly COM-invisible. Doing this is discussed in Chapter 12, "Customizing COM's View of .NET Components." However, as you've seen in Part III, COM-invisible APIs can cause a lot of confusion for your users. It's often an unnecessary limitation to impose on your users, making otherwise usable APIs unusable from COM without workarounds.

Naming Guidelines

The .NET Framework documentation gives extensive naming guidelines in order to make your APIs predictable, easy to search, and easy to understand with minimal documentation. These guidelines cover casing, word forms (nouns for types versus verbs for members), and word choice (for example, avoiding abbreviations). For the most part, COM clients aren't affected by your name decisions any differently than .NET clients, but this section discusses a few special considerations to keep in mind.

Any .NET naming guidelines in the SDK documentation that are not given attention in this section either coincide with making a .NET type COM-friendly or don't have any effect. For example, the naming guideline to not give enumeration members a common prefix or an `Enum` suffix works well for COM clients because they see enumeration members almost identically—`FileAccess.Read` (in C# and VB .NET) or `FileAccess::Read` (in C++) versus `FileAccess_Read` in the exported type library.

Names to Avoid

The .NET guidelines warn against using identifiers that conflict with common keywords in any .NET language, such as the VB .NET keywords AddHandler or For. (Of course, this is hard to do as the set of .NET languages continues to grow.) When considering COM clients, the set of words to avoid expands slightly. For example, it would be unwise to give a public member the name of a COM data type such as BSTR, VARIANT, or IUnknown since it would wreak havoc with unmanaged C++ COM clients.

Fortunately, it's unlikely that you'd want to use any "COM keywords" as names of .NET APIs because most of them don't make sense outside the context of COM. Remember that for any names that should be avoided, any variations differing in case should be avoided, too. This is for the benefit of case-insensitive languages like VB .NET or the case-insensitive type libraries that are exposed to COM clients.

DIGGING DEEPER

Most languages have a mechanism for using types and members whose names conflict with keywords. Therefore, defining types and members with keyword names doesn't necessarily block the use of your APIs from certain languages. For example, Visual Basic enables you to surround a keyword-named identifier with square brackets, C# enables you to precede the identifier with the @ symbol, and Visual C++ lets you rename type library identifiers with the #import statement's rename directive. Still, this doesn't avoid the fact that such names can end up being confusing and cumbersome for your users!

You should also avoid creating member names that conflict with the names of the IUnknown or IDispatch interfaces' methods. These are:

- QueryInterface
- AddRef
- Release
- GetTypeInfoCount
- GetTypeInfo
- GetIDsOfNames
- Invoke

Because all .NET classes and interfaces have IUnknown's methods when exposed to COM and most classes and interfaces have IDispatch's methods, user-defined members with these names are exposed to COM with different names to avoid name collisions. Although it's unlikely that you'd name a method GetIDsOfNames, it's not far-fetched to want to create a method called Release or Invoke. It is okay, however, to define member names that *contain* these words, such as ReleaseHandler or InvokeMember.

As explained in Chapter 9, "An In-Depth Look at Exported Type Libraries," the type library exporter appends an underscore and a unique number to disambiguate your methods with the same name. So the following Visual Basic .NET interface:

```
Public Interface ISlingshot
  Sub Load()
  Sub Release()
End Interface
```

is exposed to COM as follows (in IDL syntax):

```
[
  ...
]
interface ISlingshot : IDispatch {
  [id(0x60020000)]
  HRESULT Load();
  [id(0x60020001), custom(0F21F359-AB84-41E8-9A78-36D110E6D2F9, "Release")]
  HRESULT Release_2();
};
```

Requiring COM clients to call a Release_2 method, which likely would not be mentioned in ISlingshot's .NET-focused documentation, does not provide a great user experience.

DIGGING DEEPER

In the .NET Framework class libraries, only System.Runtime.InteropServices.Marshal has a Release method. It's static, however, so the method is never exposed as Release_2.

Invoke is another story, with several occurrences throughout the .NET Framework. Many of them are COM-invisible, so they usually aren't exposed to COM either.

Something else to avoid, which may not be obvious, is a property with a given name (let's say *Prop*) if a method already exists on the current type or any base types with the name Get*Prop* or Set*Prop*. Why? Because, by default, the Visual C++ type library importer (invoked by the

#import statement) creates accessor methods for properties prefixed with "Get" and "Set." Therefore, an interface with such a property/method pair causes a name collision (albeit for unmanaged Visual C++ clients only), forcing the client to use additional directives with the #import statement to avoid the duplicate names.

> **CAUTION**
>
> Any .NET class that exposes an auto-dual class interface should avoid readable properties called Type or HashCode. The accessor methods generated for COM clients by Visual C++ (GetType or GetHashCode) would conflict with the methods with the same name from System.Object that are already defined on every class interface.

Namespaces and Assembly Names

A .NET namespace doesn't have significance to COM clients, because exported type names don't include a namespace unless name conflicts occur, as explained in Chapter 9. What *is* significant is the library name, which is often used like a namespace in Visual Basic 6 code or unmanaged Visual C++ code. Because the type library exporter creates the library name from the assembly's simple name, it's important to choose a sensible assembly name.

So, how do you choose an assembly's simple name? The C#, VB .NET, and C++ compilers set this name to the name of the DLL (minus the file extension). For multi-file assemblies, the compilers choose the name of the DLL containing the manifest. The convention for choosing a DLL name (a project name in Visual Studio .NET) is to match the namespace of the types contained within. If the assembly contains multiple namespaces, the name chosen is usually the longest common prefix of the namespaces. Therefore, although .NET namespaces don't affect COM clients directly, they usually affect them indirectly by influencing the choice of assembly name.

The recommended assembly name/namespace has the form of:

CompanyName.TechnologyName

Such as, perhaps:

SamsPublishing.Books.DotNet.DotNetAndCom.Chapter11

Be aware, however, that dots (periods) are illegal in a library name, so the type library exporter converts them to underscores when constructing a library name from an assembly name. The previous assembly name would result in a library name that looks like:

SamsPublishing_Books_DotNet_DotNetAndCom_Chapter11

Therefore, you might consider choosing a short assembly name without periods for the benefit of COM clients but using longer period-delimited namespaces for the benefit of .NET clients.

Case Insensitivity

Chapter 10, "Advanced Topics for Using .NET Components," demonstrated the problems that arise when differently cased identifiers in an assembly's public APIs are exported to a case-insensitive type library. Consider this section a reminder to avoid using the same identifier with a different case as much as possible.

If you follow the .NET guidelines of always using Pascal casing (uppercase first letter, as in "PascalCasing") for public types and members, then you never have to worry about case conflicts among the type and member names exposed to COM. Parameter names can cause problems, however, because the guidelines recommend using camel casing (lowercase first letter, as in "camelCasing"). Therefore, it's somewhat likely that any large assembly contains the same identifier as a lowercase parameter name somewhere and a capital type or member name somewhere else. Listing 11.1 demonstrates this with two C# interfaces that follow the .NET naming guidelines, but are exported with undesirable behavior due to the conflicting IsVisible and isVisible identifiers.

LISTING 11.1   .NET Interfaces with Conflicting Capitalization of the Same Identifier

C#:

```
1: public interface IControl
2: {
3:   void ChangeState(bool isVisible, bool isEnabled);
4: }
5: public interface ITreeNode
6: {
7:   bool IsVisible { get; set; }
8: }
```

Inside Exported Type Library:

```
 1: [
 2:   ...
 3: ]
 4: interface IControl : IDispatch {
 5:   [id(0x60020000)]
 6:   HRESULT ChangeState(
 7:     [in] VARIANT_BOOL isVisible,
 8:     [in] VARIANT_BOOL isEnabled);
 9: };
10:
```

LISTING 11.1   Continued

```
11: [
12:   ...
13: ]
14: interface ITreeNode : IDispatch {
15:   [id(0x60020000), propget]
16:   HRESULT isVisible([out, retval] VARIANT_BOOL* pRetVal);
17:   [id(0x60020000), propput]
18:   HRESULT isVisible([in] VARIANT_BOOL pRetVal);
19: };
```

Notice that the name of the property changed from ITreeNode.IsVisible on the .NET side to ITreeNode.isVisible on the COM side since IControl.ChangeState's isVisible parameter was emitted first by the C# compiler. Once isVisible is placed in the type library's case-insensitive table, the same entry is used for both the isVisible parameter and the IsVisible property. This can be pretty confusing for COM users looking at documentation for the .NET types. Had ITreeNode been emitted before IControl, the property's name would be preserved and ChangeState's parameter would be renamed to IsVisible. This would be more desirable than the parameter name changing since COM clients likely wouldn't even notice the parameter name change. For this trivial example, switching the order of interface definitions in the source code would do just this.

> **CAUTION**
>
> Besides parameters of public members, beware of private fields of value types! Since these are exposed to COM just like public fields yet are typically named with camel casing, the effects of these names are just as dangerous as the effects of parameter names!

Controlling the case of exported identifiers by re-arranging source code is not practical or even possible for large projects. When compiling multiple source files, the order that they are processed can be unpredictable, even changing based on the fully qualified path names of the source files! The result is that the simple action of re-compiling your assembly can potentially change COM's view of your APIs, causing compilation errors (for C++ clients; not case-insensitive VB6 clients) if a COM client is recompiled with your new exported type library! Adding new classes or members to your assembly increases the chances that the case of your exported APIs will change! To prevent making inadvertent API changes, you should create a "names file" and use it with TLBEXP.EXE's /names option. This is described in Appendix B, "SDK Tools Reference."

CAUTION

If you're developing an application with managed and unmanaged pieces, you can encounter a situation in which the cases of exported types or members oscillate regularly and cause unmanaged C++ compilation errors! You should consider using a names file with the type library exporter, but using the `rename` directive with the unmanaged C++ `#import` statement can hide these undesirable effects, as discussed in Chapter 10.

DIGGING DEEPER

It should be obvious that type and member names changing case can break COM clients on re-compilation. However, you can rest assured that normal COM clients can't be broken by such name changes when they aren't recompiled.

V-table binding doesn't rely on names; just virtual function table slots. When COM clients late bind to .NET components using the `IDispatch` interface, the names passed into `Invoke` are case-insensitive, so a case change can't matter. When COM clients late bind to .NET components using the `IDispatchEx` interface (which is possible for .NET classes implementing `IReflect` or `IExpando`), its `InvokeEx` method supports case-sensitive member invocation. However, the managed implementation should be based on .NET names, not the names that are exported in a type library. For more about the `IDispatchEx` interface, refer to Chapter 14.

Another course of action would be to avoid the name conflicts in the first place by renaming conflicting types, members, or parameters. Don't switch parameter names to use pascal casing or type/member names to use camel casing because doing so would look non-standard to .NET clients. On the other hand, naming an `IsVisible` property as something like `Visible` instead can prevent these problems without impacting .NET clients.

TIP

The problems caused by non-deterministic casing of exported identifiers are serious enough to warrant writing a little utility that scans your assemblies for case conflicts, and either generates a names file to use when exporting a type library or notifies you so you can change the conflicting names. Such a program could easily be written with the help of reflection. Or, using the type library exporter APIs described in Chapter

22, "Using APIs Instead of SDK Tools," you could create a smart exporter that gives the casing of type and member names priority over the casing of parameter names.

If you end up using a names file, be sure to ship the exported type library with your application so your users don't attempt to export one that does not have the desired casing!

Keep in mind that these case-sensitivity problems are not specific to COM Interoperability. Standard C++ COM components can run into the same problems when creating a type library with the same identifiers in multiple cases.

Usage Guidelines

Whereas the previous section focused on the names used in your .NET class libraries, this section focuses on the usage of types and members, regardless of their names. For example, static members (Shared in VB .NET) should either be avoided or accompanied with instance members that accomplish the same tasks because static members aren't naturally exposed to COM.

First we'll look at some tradeoffs involved in choosing when to use classes, when to use interfaces, when to use custom attributes, and so on. Then we'll drill down into specific concerns that arise when using overload methods, parameterized constructed, and enumerations.

Interfaces Versus Classes

As you know, COM is based on interfaces. All APIs are exposed via interfaces, and all parameters are either primitive types, structures, or interfaces; never classes. (The classes you can define and use as parameters in Visual Basic 6 are really hiding an interface/coclass pair, so you end up with the same design considerations as defining an interface.) With .NET, however, you can choose how much you want to involve interfaces in your public APIs.

The .NET guidelines recommend using classes instead of interfaces. The motivation behind this recommendation is that APIs that use class types heavily are generally considered to be easier to use than APIs that use interface types heavily. Also, an abstract class (MustInherit in VB .NET) is more flexible than an interface from a versioning perspective. A non-abstract member could be added to an abstract class without breaking existing derived classes. Adding a member to an interface, however, would break any existing classes implementing the interface because they would no longer implement all the members.

Implementation inheritance is touted as an easy way to get a stock implementation that can be customized as you see fit, but this is often difficult without intimate knowledge about the class's implementation. In COM, the same pattern can be achieved with interface implementation plus delegation. A COM class can implement a large interface and selectively implement methods. For methods whose implementation the class wants to "inherit," it can simply call methods on another object that already implements the interface.

The heavy use of classes can be seen throughout the .NET Framework APIs. For example:

- Remote objects that need to be marshaled by reference must derive from the `System.MarshalByRefObject` class.
- Web services must derive from the `System.Web.Services.WebService` class.
- Windows Forms must derive from the `System.Windows.Forms.Form` class.
- Web Forms must derive from the `System.Web.UI.Page` class.
- Serviced components must derive from the `System.EnterpriseServices.ServicedComponent` class.

In a world without multiple implementation inheritance, however, relying too much on class types can put unintended constraints on clients. For example, it's impossible to have a Windows Form class that is also a serviced component. Had the requirements instead been "Windows Forms must implement the `IForm` interface, serviced components must implement the `IServicedComponent` interface," and so on, this restriction would not exist because any class can implement an arbitrary number of interfaces. A more realistic limitation can be seen with the `System.Windows.Forms.MainMenu` class. This class is used as the type of the `System.Windows.Forms.Form.Menu` property, yet many of `MainMenu`'s methods necessary for customizing its drawing behavior are not virtual (`Overridable` in VB .NET). The result is that you can't plug in your own custom-drawn menu object as a Windows Form's menu. Had the `Menu` property been an `IMainMenu` interface, there would be no roadblock to doing this.

Therefore, even without COM in the picture, you should use interface types rather than class types for parameters, properties, and fields of public or protected APIs in case someone wants to plug in objects that can't derive from the class you defined. For COM-friendly .NET components, communicating via interface types is always preferred over class types. When interfaces are available, COM clients don't need to rely on invoking thru CLR-generated class interfaces. These class interfaces are either slower to use due to forced late binding or they don't version well.

Furthermore, a COM object implementing a .NET interface can be passed to a .NET method expecting an interface parameter. From the .NET perspective, every COM object is a Runtime-Callable Wrapper (RCW) that either is the `System.__ComObject` type or a type that derives from it, and that class derives from `System.MarshalByRefObject` which derives from

`System.Object`. This means that a COM object can only be passed as a parameter to a .NET method if the signature expects either an interface or one of the classes in the RCW's inheritance hierarchy (`Object`, `MarshalByRefObject`, `__ComObject`, or the type itself).

The point to remember is that although COM's role in your applications may be fading away, the role of interfaces is just as important as always. If you define an interface as well as a class that implements the interface, COM clients can make use of the interface when such objects are passed to COM, yet .NET clients can mostly ignore the interface and use the class directly.

> **TIP**
>
> When defining classes, define a corresponding interface for the class to implement and always use the interface type rather than the class type in any method, property, field, or event definitions. This provides maximum flexibility for both .NET and COM users of your APIs.
>
> A great example of such a class/interface pair exists in the `System` assembly: `System.ComponentModel.Component` and `System.ComponentModel.IComponent`. The .NET Framework has well over 100 methods with an `IComponent` parameter, such as `System.Windows.Forms.Design.PictureBoxDesigner.Initialize`:
>
> ```
> public void Initialize(IComponent component);
> ```
>
> At the same time, the .NET Framework has no methods with a `Component` parameter. Therefore, there's no limit on the types of classes (even COM classes) that can be passed in as long as they implement the `IComponent` interface.

Interfaces Versus Custom Attributes

The .NET guidelines advise against using interfaces as "empty markers." This means that you shouldn't define an empty interface to mark a class with a certain characteristic, for example (in C#):

```
public interface IRestricted {}

public class C : IRestricted
{
  ...
}
```

After all, this is what custom attributes are for! In .NET APIs, it's more natural to define a `RestrictedAttribute` custom attribute and mark the class with this.

With a class that implements IRestricted, clients determine whether an object is classified as "restricted" by casting the type to the interface and seeing whether or not it fails. (Thanks to operators like C#'s as, a failed cast does not have to incur the expense of an InvalidCastException.) With a class marked with a RestrictedAttribute custom attribute, a .NET client can check for the RestrictedAttribute with code like the following (in C#):

```
public bool IsRestricted(Object o)
{
  object [] attributes = o.GetType().GetCustomAttributes(
    typeof(RestrictedAttribute), true);

  if (attributes.Length > 0)
    return true;
  else
    return false;
}
```

Custom attribute retrieval requires more code and is slower than a cast, but it's standard practice in the .NET Framework. Note that true is passed for the GetCustomAttributes inherit parameter because this matches the inherited behavior of an interface, but it only has an effect if the custom attribute is defined to enable inheritance.

The choice between marking a class with a custom attribute or having it implement an interface is also present when the attribute or interface must contain members. For example, the KeywordAttribute custom attribute defined in Chapter 1, "Introduction to the .NET Framework," could instead be defined as the following interface if you only wanted to use it on classes:

```
public interface IKeywordProvider
{
  string [] GetKeywords();
  int [] GetRelevanceFactors();
}
```

There are two disadvantages for COM clients when .NET components use custom attributes rather than interfaces:

- Custom attributes don't appear in exported type libraries, so they can't be retrieved in a fashion familiar to COM clients. The exporter makes no attempt to bridge .NET custom attributes to IDL custom attributes.

- Inspecting a custom attribute's member from COM involves late binding unless the custom attribute class implements an interface or exposes an auto-dual class interface. Besides the significantly worse performance compared to a simple QueryInterface call and method calls through a v-table, late binding from unmanaged C++ code is cumbersome.

Therefore, you might want to consider defining and implementing interfaces before going overboard with marking your classes with custom attributes, especially if you need more than a simple marker. There are actually a few examples of empty marker interfaces in the .NET Framework where you would have expected a custom attribute (such as System.Web. IHttpHandler in the System.Web assembly) but ironically they are all COM-invisible. Of course, if you need to mark elements such as parameters or methods with extra information, custom attributes are the only choice.

> ### TIP
>
> To make custom attribute retrieval more COM-friendly for custom attributes with members, have your attribute classes implement interfaces exposing its members. That way, COM clients don't have to use late binding to retrieve the attribute's data. So, if you decide to mark a class with a custom attribute rather than having it implement an interface, define the interface with these members anyway so the attribute class can implement it!
>
> For the KeywordAttribute example in Chapter 1, this technique would look like the following:
>
> ```
> using System;
>
> public interface IKeyword
> {
>   string Keyword { get; }
>   int Relevance { get; set; }
> }
>
> [AttributeUsage(AttributeTargets.All, AllowMultiple=true)]
> public class KeywordAttribute : Attribute, IKeyword
> {
>   // Implementation is identical to Listing 1.2.
>   ...
> }
> ```
>
> It's a good idea not to end the interface name with "Attribute" since it might confuse users to believe that the interface is itself a custom attribute.

Properties Versus Fields

The .NET guidelines recommend the use of properties rather than public fields. Although properties incur some overhead, they version more gracefully than fields because a property's implementation can be changed in a compatible way. To change the behavior of a field, you'd need to convert it to a property first but that's not a compatible change. Although the client source code may look the same for accessing an object's field and accessing an object's property, they are two entirely different actions at the MSIL level.

Although fields of .NET classes are exposed as COM properties, this does not mean that changing between properties and fields is a compatible change for COM clients. They are when a COM client late binds by name (without saving the property's DISPID) but the layout of the class interface changes. When exposing an auto-dual class interface for a .NET class, any public fields become COM properties at the *end* of the interface. For this reason, too, public fields should be avoided when exposing an auto-dual class interface because the order of members in source code doesn't faithfully represent the order of the interface that COM clients may rely on.

The guidelines also recommend using read-only static fields or constants rather than properties for global constant values. For example (in C#):

```
public struct Byte
{
  public const byte MinValue = 0;
  public const byte MaxValue = 25;
  ...
}
```

Keep in mind, however, that such static fields are not directly accessible from COM, whereas properties that expose these values would be.

Using Overloaded Methods

The .NET guidelines recommend the use of overloaded methods to define different methods with the same semantics, or to provide clients with a variable number of arguments. In addition, the guidelines recommend using overloaded methods instead of optional parameters because optional parameters are not in the CLS (so languages like C# don't have to support them). That is why, for example, `System.Reflection.Assembly` doesn't define a single `GetType` method that looks like the following (in VB .NET syntax):

```
Public Function GetType( _
  name As String, _
  Optional throwOnError As Boolean = False, _
  Optional ignoreCase As Boolean = False _
) As System.Type
```

but rather three overloads to achieve the same combinations of invocations:

```
Overloads Public Function GetType( _
  name As String _
) As Type
```

```
Overloads Public Function GetType( _
  name As String, _
  throwOnError As Boolean _
) As Type

Overloads Public Function GetType( _
  name As String, _
  throwOnError As Boolean, _
  ignoreCase As Boolean _
) As Type
```

Indeed, the use of overloaded methods is pervasive in the .NET Framework. Unfortunately, as you've seen in Chapter 8, "The Essentials for Using .NET Components from COM," overloaded methods are not permitted in COM, so the renamed methods exposed to COM are not COM-friendly. The previous GetType methods on the exported Assembly class interface are exported to a type library as follows (in Visual Basic 6 syntax):

```
Public Function GetType_2( _
  ByVal name As String _
) As Type

Public Function GetType_3( _
  ByVal name As String, _
  ByVal throwOnError As Boolean _
) As Type

Public Function GetType_4( _
  ByVal name As String, _
  ByVal throwOnError As Boolean, _
  ByVal ignoreCase As Boolean _
) As Type
```

Notice that even the first method has _2 appended because all the GetType methods are overloads of System.Object.GetType, which also appears on the _Assembly interface. Besides looking unfamiliar to COM clients following the Assembly class's documentation, the situation is even worse when such methods are on classes that don't expose them on an interface with type information. When late binding, COM clients may end up guessing what the name of the overloaded method is they're invoking by trial and error, unless they use an assembly browser like ILDASM.EXE that can show the exact order in which the overloaded methods are defined by the class. In addition, overloaded methods present a problem for versioning that's discussed in the upcoming "Versioning" section.

Versioning headaches alone should discourage you from using overloaded methods. But besides versioning, choosing whether or not to use overloaded methods usually involves a tradeoff between ease of use for .NET clients and ease of use for COM clients. Here are some guidelines:

- Consider changing overloaded methods to regular methods with similar names. `Assembly.GetType` is probably not a good candidate for this (or I'm not imaginative enough), but the three methods could be called `GetTypeCaseSensitive`, `GetTypeCaseInsensitive`, `FastGetTypeCaseSensitive`, `FastGetTypeCaseInsensitive`. (The "Fast" could refer to the faster act of returning null on failure rather than throwing an exception.) However, these names are long and strange-looking for all clients (.NET or COM)!

- If you're primarily concerned with Visual Basic clients (VB .NET on the .NET side and VB6 on the COM side), favor optional parameters on a single method rather than over-loaded methods. This is beneficial because all clients see the original method name. In the worst case, clients that don't support optional parameters simply can't omit any arguments. Be aware, however, of the versioning concerns with optional parameters outlined in Chapter 3, "The Essentials for Using COM in Managed Code."

- Although the guidelines tell you to avoid reserved parameters because an overloaded method can always be added later, you might want to consider limited use of reserved parameters if it's likely that more functionality will need to be added at a later date.

- If you must use overloaded methods, try to make the most commonly used overload the first one listed so most COM clients won't have to use the overloads with mangled names. (This is also good for IntelliSense in Visual Studio .NET so it shows the most commonly used overload first.)

> **TIP**
>
> Using overloaded methods, but making the most common one defined first, is the choice made throughout the .NET Framework. Therefore, choosing this pattern for your APIs has the benefit of consistency with the framework.

Using Constructors

You must define a public default constructor (one with no parameters) if you plan to make your class creatable from COM. Therefore, if you plan to create parameterized constructors, be sure to also expose the same functionality through a public default constructor coupled with members that enable the user to set the same state that would have been set with the constructor parameters.

Notice that in C#, Visual Basic .NET, and C++, the compiler supplies an empty public default constructor if you don't define any constructors. If you *do* add any constructors yourself, then the compiler no longer supplies one implicitly. Listing 11.2 demonstrates this situation.

LISTING 11.2   Writing COM-Creatable Classes and Non-COM-Creatable Classes in C#

```csharp
public class A
{
  // COM-creatable since it implicitly
  // has a public default constructor
}

public class B
{
  // Not COM-creatable since it doesn't
  // have a public default constructor

  public B(int b) {}
}

public class C
{
  // COM-creatable since it explicitly
  // has a public default constructor

  public C() {}
  public C(int c) {}
}
```

Using Enumerations

The .NET guidelines recommend the use of enumerations (enums) for strongly-typed parameters, properties, fields, and so on. This remains a good practice when COM clients are involved, with one exception. As mentioned in the previous chapter, unmanaged script clients are unable to invoke .NET members with enum parameters via reflection in version 1.0 of the CLR. Still, in most cases, rather than defining static constants in your class, such as (in C#):

```csharp
public const int DAYOFWEEK_SUNDAY = 0;
public const int DAYOFWEEK_MONDAY = 1;
public const int DAYOFWEEK_TUESDAY = 2;
public const int DAYOFWEEK_WEDNESDAY = 3;
public const int DAYOFWEEK_THURSDAY = 4;
public const int DAYOFWEEK_FRIDAY = 5;
public const int DAYOFWEEK_SATURDAY = 6;
```

you should define an enumeration:

```
public enum DayOfWeek
{
    Sunday = 0,
    Monday = 1,
    Tuesday = 2,
    Wednesday = 3,
    Thursday = 4,
    Friday = 5,
    Saturday = 6,
}
```

(And in this case, don't even bother defining it because the canonical DayOfWeek enumeration already exists in the System namespace.) Enums are natural for .NET clients because they are widely used in .NET Framework APIs, and they are natural for most COM clients because the alternative of using constants would not be exposed to COM.

Another guideline for defining enums is to use a 32-bit integer as the underlying type. This is the default behavior for enums defined in C#, VB .NET, and C++, but it's possible in all these languages to define enumerations with a different base type, such as a 64-bit integer:

C#:

```
public enum ManyFlags : long
{
    ...
}
```

Visual Basic .NET:

```
Public Enum ManyFlags As Long
    ...
End Enum
```

C++:

```
public __value enum ManyFlags : System::Int64
{
    ...
};
```

Increasing the size of the enum from 32 bits would be necessary if defining an enumeration with more than 32-bit flags. However, such enumerations pose a problem for COM since an enumeration in a type library always has a 32-bit underlying type. As discussed in Chapter 9, parameters, return types, and fields of non-32-bit enum types are exported as their underlying types. The enums themselves are still exported as long as its values fit inside 32 bits, but they can't be used directly in exported signatures. Therefore, avoid defining enumerations with base types other than a 32-bit integer because doing so eliminates most of the benefit of using enums in the first place from COM's perspective.

> **TIP**
>
> An enumeration consisting of more than 32 bit flags can most likely be re-factored to multiple enumerations. Such an action could be used to avoid enumerations based on types that are too big for type libraries.

Choosing the Right Data Types

The kind of data types you choose to use in your public methods, properties, and fields is critical to ensuring smooth interaction with COM. The next chapter focuses on customizing COM's view of data types with `MarshalAsAttribute`, but here we'll briefly look at some general data type guidelines.

Using OLE Automation Compatible Types

The most important guideline is to make your classes and interfaces OLE Automation compatible by restricting your public signatures to using only OLE Automation compatible data types. That's right, you should still be concerned with OLE Automation compatibility of .NET types when interaction with COM is likely!

A COM interface is considered OLE Automation compatible if it is derived from `IDispatch` or `IUnknown` (as all exported .NET interfaces are), marked with the `[oleautomation]` attribute (as all exported .NET interfaces are), and all of its members are OLE Automation compatible.

A COM member is considered OLE Automation compatible if it has the STDCALL calling convention (on 32-bit platforms, which all exported .NET members do have), if its return type is `HRESULT`, `SCODE`, or `void`, and if its parameter types are all from a subset of data types. These data types, in their .NET form, are listed in Table 11.1. These types can be used as by-value or by-reference parameters and still be considered OLE Automation compatible.

TABLE 11.1   .NET Data Types That Are Marshaled as OLE Automation Compatible Data Types

.NET Data Types
`System.Boolean` (when marshaled as `VARIANT_BOOL`)
`System.Byte`
`System.Drawing.Color`

TABLE 11.1   Continued

.NET Data Types
System.DateTime
System.Decimal (when marshaled as CURRENCY)
System.Double
System.Int16
System.Int32
System.IntPtr
System.Object (when marshaled as VARIANT, IUnknown, or IDispatch)
System.Single
System.String (when marshaled as BSTR)
Enums with a System.Int32 or System.Int16 underlying type
Arrays of the preceding types (when marshaled as SAFEARRAY)

For .NET data types that can be marshaled to more than one COM data type, Table 11.1 points out which of the COM types are OLE Automation compatible. Again, marshaling customizations are covered in the next chapter. Although SAFEARRAYs are OLE Automation compatible, Visual Basic 6 clients can't consume methods with by-value SAFEARRAY parameters, so you might want to avoid those as much as possible.

Why should your .NET types be OLE Automation compatible, anyway? It's important for .NET classes because by default they are only accessed from COM via IDispatch, so parameters and return types must be able to be stored inside a VARIANT. However, VARIANTs can contain several types that aren't OLE Automation compatible, such as unsigned integers. It's most important that .NET interfaces (including class interfaces) are OLE Automation compatible because the exported interfaces use the OLE Automation type library marshaler for COM marshaling across apartment, thread, or process boundaries.

Chapter 6, "Advanced Topics for Using COM Components," explained that COM objects that aren't OLE Automation-compatible work fine across apartments in managed code as long as an appropriate marshaler is registered for the appropriate interfaces. Similarly, using .NET objects that aren't OLE Automation-compatible can work fine across apartments as long as an appropriate marshaler is registered to perform the customized COM marshaling. The "Disabling Type Library Marshaling of .NET Interfaces" section in the next chapter describes how an ambitious .NET developer can accomplish this. Fortunately, because .NET classes are registered with the Both threading model value, COM marshaling can often be avoided when .NET components are used in-process, making the need for OLE Automation compatibility less important.

> **TIP**
>
> Besides COM marshaling concerns, it's a good idea to use OLE Automation compatible data types for the sake of Visual Basic COM clients. The CLS guidelines help by excluding unsigned integers, but you should also avoid publicly exposing types like `System.Guid` or `System.Decimal` (without using `MarshalAsAttribute` to turn it into the `CURRENCY` type) because they can't be consumed in Visual Basic 6.

Avoiding Pointers

Rather than exposing parameters that are pointers to types, use by-reference parameters. In other words, do this in a C# interface:

```
void UpdateTime(ref DateTime t);
```

rather than:

```
unsafe void UpdateTime(DateTime* t);
```

DON'T DO THIS

Although the signature in an exported type library looks the same for both cases, shown below in IDL, the two signatures behave much differently:

```
HRESULT UpdateTime([in, out] DATE* t);
```

Exposing pointers to COM is not a good idea because the Interop Marshaler only does a shallow copy of the data being pointed to. This means that passing pointers across the Interop boundary only works as you might expect for blittable types like integers, floats, and doubles.

Avoiding public signatures with pointer types is a good idea in .NET anyway, since pointers are not in the CLS and languages like Visual Basic .NET would not be able to consume your APIs.

> **TIP**
>
> Always prefer defining by-reference parameters rather than using pointers. Besides being better for .NET clients, the Interop Marshaler is designed for them.

Avoiding Nested Arrays

Nested arrays, also known as *jagged arrays*, are simply arrays of arrays. Nested arrays are not supported in COM Interoperability. Note that nested arrays are not the same as multi-dimensional arrays, which are supported. Nested arrays provide the flexibility of non-rectangular storage, but multi-dimensional arrays should be favored in your public APIs so COM clients can be supported.

To summarize, define methods as follows:

C#: `void ProcessData(int [,] data)`

VB .NET: `Sub ProcessData(data(,) As Integer)`

rather than the COM-unusable alternative:

C#: `void ProcessData(int [][] data)`

VB .NET: `Sub ProcessData(data()() As Integer)`

DON'T DO THIS

Avoiding User-Defined Value Types

Due to the COM Interoperability limitations with VARIANTs containing the VT_RECORD type, user-defined value types (UDTs) should be avoided as much as possible in APIs that might be exposed to COM. This means avoiding exposing generic System.Object types that could contain value types, since COM clients would be forced to access the value type thru a VARIANT. Even exposing a value type as its exact type is bad for COM clients that late bind, because parameters are packed into VARIANTs. Chapter 14 discusses a workaround for the late binding scenario, however, by customizing the IDispatch implementation exposed to COM. Late binding aside, by-value UDT parameters can't be
consumed by Visual Basic 6 clients when v-table binding, so that's another good reason to avoid them.

If you do decide to define and use your own value types, avoid defining fields that are reference types such as arrays or classes other than Object. Such fields can't be marshaled unless marked with MarshalAsAttribute appropriately, as discussed in Chapter 19, "Deeper Into PInvoke and Useful Examples." Also, keep in mind that because only a value type's instance fields are exposed to COM (whether public or not), none of the properties and methods you might define are directly available to COM.

DIGGING DEEPER

When defining value types, it's important to remember that private fields are exposed to COM. This fact can affect the use of common obfuscation techniques. The process of obfuscation, when applied to software, means obscuring internal details such that the software's usage is unaffected, but the software is much harder to reverse-engineer. If you decide to scramble the names of your non-public types and members, you could be scrambling part of the public API from COM's perspective!

Reporting Errors

When it comes to reporting errors, the .NET guidelines provide good information that coincides with being COM-friendly. Two particularly important guidelines are to throw exceptions for error conditions, and to favor throwing pre-defined exception types rather than inventing your own kind of exception. As always, there are some additional considerations to think about to make your use of exceptions provide the best experience for COM clients.

Defining New Exception Types

Defining a new exception type can be useful when you provide additional information that clients can act on programmatically. For example, System.Runtime.InteropServices could define a ClassNotRegisteredException type with a Clsid property of type Guid that contains the CLSID corresponding to the class that isn't registered. Catching a ClassNotRegisteredException and checking its Clsid property would be much handier than catching a COMException, checking if the ErrorCode property returns 0x80040154 (REGDB_E_CLASSNOTREG), then parsing the CLSID string from the Message property. However, new exception types can be overkill if most users have no need to take different programmatic action. This is why such a ClassNotRegisteredException doesn't exist—most users would not want to attempt anything more than displaying a message about this type of error.

When defining a new exception type that might be thrown to a COM client, choosing a value for its protected HResult property is critical because this value becomes an HRESULT in the unmanaged world that identifies the exception type. Choosing a unique value is recommended so COM clients can easily identify the unique exception type. As demonstrated in Chapter 8, "The Essentials for Using .NET Components from COM," a non-Visual Basic COM client can always discover the exact type of exception thrown by calling _Object.GetType on the object obtained from the IErrorInfo interface pointer, but this isn't something many COM clients are likely to do.

DIGGING DEEPER

When defining new HRESULT values, the rules of COM dictate that you must choose something of the form 0x8004*nnnn* unless you work for Microsoft. The most significant bit is set to indicate that the value represents an error, and the facility code of 4 (FACILITY_ITF) represents error codes resulting from non-Microsoft interfaces. The final 16 bits (represented by *nnnn*) must be a number greater than 512 (0x200).

Creating a hierarchy of exceptions can be valuable for your .NET users, but it doesn't mean much to COM clients. If every exception type defines its own HRESULT value, then these error codes have no real connection that enables them to be grouped as a unit. Therefore, exception designers sometimes share HRESULT values with similar exceptions so a COM client can "catch" a set of exception types all at once. The most common form of this is simply inheriting the HRESULT value from your base exception class. For example, if you define a handful of exceptions that derive from System.ApplicationException that don't override ApplicationException's HResult property, a COM client could always handle any application-defined errors the same way (such as printing the exception's message) simply by checking for the single HRESULT belonging to ApplicationException (0x80131600). Inheriting the base exception class's HRESULT is often done unintentionally, because the author might not have even been aware of the HResult property that could have been overridden or didn't fully understand the consequences.

TIP

When defining a new exception type, remember to perform the following actions so the exception can be transported from one machine to another:

- Mark the exception with the System.SerializableAttribute custom attribute
- Implement a deserialization constructor, which looks like the following in C#:
  ```
  public MyException(SerializationInfo info, StreamingContext context)
  ```
- Implement the System.Runtime.Serialization.ISerializable interface if your exception type contains its own fields

These steps have nothing to do with COM Interoperability, but they're important for .NET exceptions and easy to forget.

User-defined exceptions have an undesirable aspect for applications that make more than one transition between managed and unmanaged code in a given call stack. As discussed in Chapter 3, many user-defined errors from COM objects appear as a COMException in managed code. This happens because the CLR has a list of HRESULTs that are transformed into specific exceptions, and there's no way to add to the list. Therefore, any unrecognized HRESULT, even if originating from a .NET exception, becomes a COMException. Figure 11.1 depicts a .NET exception being thrown from a .NET component and caught by another .NET component. If there's a COM component in the middle that propagates the error from server to client, the exception transforms into a COMException.

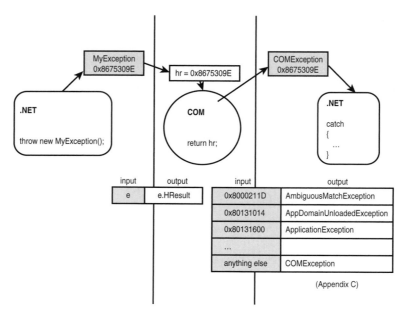

FIGURE 11.1

When passing from .NET to COM to .NET, any exception not in the CLR's list morphs into a COMException.

Fortunately, other exception information (such as the ever-important message) is preserved, but the type of the exception is not. Appendix C, "HRESULT to .NET Exception Transformations," contains the complete list illustrated in the figure. In general, it's best to avoid user-defined exceptions and use exceptions whose types are familiar to .NET clients and whose HRESULT values are familiar to COM clients.

CAUTION

If you examine the list of HRESULT to exception transformations in Appendix C, you'll notice that the HRESULTs are comprised of well-known COM HRESULTs plus HRESULTs defined by the .NET exceptions in the mscorlib assembly. This means that no exceptions defined elsewhere in the .NET Framework are preserved when passing through a COM layer. Treat the list of exceptions in Appendix C as your "play book" of exceptions that should be thrown whenever possible rather than exceptions not in the list.

General Guidelines

Besides avoiding user-defined exceptions, here are some general do's and don'ts for using exceptions in COM-friendly .NET components:

- Try to fit as much information as possible into an exception's `Message`, `HelpLink`, and `Source` properties because this information is natural to obtain from COM using `IErrorInfo` (or the global `Err` object in Visual Basic 6). Although the other members (like `InnerException` or user-defined members) can be accessible from COM, existing COM clients that are unaware of .NET may be designed to perform intelligent actions based on the standard information.

- Don't overuse inner exceptions. Any COM clients that aren't .NET-aware (for instance, the Visual Basic 6 IDE) would only display the information for the outermost exception because that's the only error they would be aware of.

- Throw exceptions for errors rather than returning error codes. Although returning error codes looks natural to COM (as long as the method is marked with the `PreserveSigAttribute`), such APIs are not natural to use in .NET.

- If you're intent on returning error codes rather than throwing exceptions, be sure to mark such a method with the `PreserveSigAttribute` so your return value is treated as the return value from COM's perspective. Otherwise, COM clients would have two different error codes to worry about when calling your method. Be sure that your returned error codes respect the COM standard for `HRESULT`s.

- Avoid returning null (`Nothing` in VB .NET) rather than throwing an exception to indicate failure. Returning null for common error cases is recommended by the .NET guidelines and done in some common .NET Framework APIs. Although it's compelling to not throw an exception on failure in situations in which the failure may occur frequently (for performance reasons), this behavior can be very confusing to COM clients. Why? Because COM clients see `S_OK` returned whenever an exception isn't thrown, so it may mistakenly lead COM clients to believe the call succeeded when it really did not.

TIP

Many .NET Framework methods that return null on failure have an overload with a boolean `throwOnError` parameter, giving clients the choice of fast failure versus easily noticeable failure. If you feel that it's necessary to provide a method that returns null on failure, consider adding the throw-on-error overload, but list that definition first in source code. Assuming that your compiler respects the ordering when emitting metadata, you'll encourage COM clients to call the version that fails more naturally for them since the throw-on-error overload would have the original method name, whereas the method that returns null on failure would be decorated with the _2 suffix.

Exposing Enumerators to COM

One of the topics discussed by the .NET guidelines is choosing when to expose arrays and when to expose collections. Indeed, an array is a type of collection, but the difference here is whether all elements are handed out at once or if elements are obtained one-at-a-time through calls into your component. Exposing a collection can be useful, for example, to provide read-only access to the elements of a non-public array. The trade-off for .NET and COM interaction is that returning an array is a single method call that crosses the managed/unmanaged boundary, but the call can be expensive if the CLR must marshal a large array with non-blittable elements. On the other hand, returning a collection can result in many method calls across the Interop boundary (especially if the client inspects every element of the collection), but each method call could involve much less marshaling. Usually exposing arrays to COM clients yields better performance.

If you want to expose an enumerator on a .NET type, the official technique is to implement `System.Collections.IEnumerable`. `IEnumerable` has a single `GetEnumerator` method that returns an `IEnumerator` interface, which enumerates over generic `Object` types. C#'s `foreach` statement and VB .NET's `For Each` statement actually work with *any* method called `GetEnumerator` that takes no parameters and returns an object with a `MoveNext` method and a readable `Current` property. This enables *strongly typed enumerations*, because the types being enumerated can be made more specific for better performance.

COM clients expect an enumerator type to be returned by a member marked with DISPID –4. This enumerator type is usually the `IEnumVARIANT` interface (COM's equivalent of `IEnumerator`) but can be more specific types as well.

COM Interoperability handles .NET collections in a way such that the design that's natural for .NET also fits in well for COM. For starters, the `IEnumerator` type is always exposed to COM as `IEnumVARIANT`. In addition, the definition of `IEnumerable` marks its `GetEnumerator` method with a custom attribute so it's exported with a DISPID equal to –4. This means that the `IEnumerable` interface is exported as follows (as seen by running `OLEVIEW.EXE` on `mscorlib.tlb`):

```
[
  odl,
  uuid(496B0ABE-CDEE-11D3-88E8-00902754C43A),
  version(1.0),
  dual,
  oleautomation,
  custom(0F21F359-AB84-41E8-9A78-36D110E6D2F9,
"System.Collections.IEnumerable")
]
```

```
interface IEnumerable : IDispatch
{
    [id(0xfffffffc)]
    HRESULT GetEnumerator([out, retval] IEnumVARIANT** pRetVal);
};
```

The 0xfffffffc value is hexadecimal for –4. Therefore, any class that implements IEnumerable or an interface derived from IEnumerable can be used as an enumerator naturally from COM.

The support doesn't stop there, however. Any class or interface exposed to COM that has a GetEnumerator method with the proper format is assigned a DISPID of –4 unless a different member is already explicitly marked with that DISPID. The "proper format" is a method with no parameters, a return type of IEnumerator, and with the name of GetEnumerator (although any case will do). This means that the following .NET interface:

```
public interface INonStandardCollection
{
  IEnumerator GetEnumerator();
}
```

is exported to COM as:

```
[
  ...
]
interface INonStandardCollection : IDispatch
{
  [id(0xfffffffc)]
  HRESULT GetEnumerator([out, retval] IEnumVARIANT** pRetVal);
};
```

Since strongly-typed GetEnumerator methods aren't automatically marked with DISPID –4 when exposed to COM, you should mark such methods with this DISPID explicitly using DispIdAttribute. This is demonstrated in Listing 11.3.

LISTING 11.3 Marking a Strongly-Typed GetEnumerator Method with the DispIdAttribute Is Recommended to Properly Expose an Enumerator to COM

C#:

```
using System.Collections;
using System.Runtime.InteropServices;

public interface IBadStronglyTypedCollection
{
  IDictionaryEnumerator GetEnumerator();
}
```

LISTING 11.3   Continued

```
public interface IGoodStronglyTypedCollection
{
  [DispId(-4)]
  IDictionaryEnumerator GetEnumerator();
}
```

In the Exported Type Library (IDL syntax):

```
[
  ...
]
interface IBadStronglyTypedCollection : IDispatch {
    [id(0x60020000)]
    HRESULT GetEnumerator([out, retval] IDictionaryEnumerator** pRetVal);
};


[
  ...
]
interface IGoodStronglyTypedCollection : IDispatch {
    [id(0xfffffffc)]
    HRESULT GetEnumerator([out, retval] IDictionaryEnumerator** pRetVal);
};
```

A typical pattern used by .NET classes is to explicitly implement IEnumerable to provide the standard enumerator when the client calls on the IEnumerable type, while defining a public GetEnumerator method with a strongly-typed enumerator returned. To be COM-friendly, the DispIdAttribute should be applied to the strongly-typed GetEnumerator, as shown in the following C# code:

```
 1: using System.Collections;
 2: using System.Runtime.InteropServices;
 3:
 4: public class EnumerableObject : IEnumerable
 5: {
 6:   private Hashtable table;
 7:
 8:   ...
 9:
10:   // Explicitly-implemented GetEnumerator
11:   IEnumerator IEnumerable.GetEnumerator()
12:   {
13:     return table.Values.GetEnumerator();
14:   }
15:
```

```
16:    // Strongly-typed GetEnumerator
17:    [DispId(-4)]
18:    public IDictionaryEnumerator GetEnumerator()
19:    {
20:      return table.GetEnumerator();
21:    }
22: }
```

By using the IEnumerable interface, COM clients can get the standard IEnumVARIANT interface back by invoking the member with DISPID –4. When calling methods on the class via late binding, invoking the member with DISPID –4 gives back the IDictionaryEnumerator interface. Had the attribute not been applied in Line 17, no enumerator would be exposed on the class type from COM's perspective.

TIP

When defining a collection class, always implement the IEnumerable interface. When adding a strongly-typed GetEnumerator method, mark it with the DispIdAttribute custom attribute to give it a DISID equal to –4.

Versioning

A .NET class library author can make certain changes to her assembly so that .NET clients built with a previous version can switch to using the updated version without experiencing problems. This process of safely evolving a component in compatible ways is known as *versioning*.

Besides changing implementation, an assembly's public APIs can sometimes be changed in ways that don't break existing .NET clients. This includes:

- Adding types
- Adding members to enums (without affecting existing values)
- Adding members to classes
- Reordering types in source code
- Reordering enum members in source code (without affecting existing values)
- Reordering class, value type, or interface members in source code

It should be obvious that removing or changing public or protected members would break any .NET clients that currently use them. Although adding members to an interface doesn't affect .NET clients that call its members, it would break any .NET clients that attempt to *implement* the interface because it would no longer implement the entire interface. So even in the pure .NET world, adding members to an interface should never be done.

The default behavior of COM Interoperability enables a class library author to make almost all of the same kinds of changes to an assembly without breaking COM clients. The allowable changes are slightly more restrictive when COM clients are involved, so it's important to understand what kind of changes you can make and still be compatible. Here are changes you can make that are compatible for both .NET and COM clients:

- Adding types
- Adding members to enums (without affecting existing values)
- Adding members to classes marshaled as reference types that don't expose an auto-dual class interface (with an exception for overloaded methods)
- Reordering types in source code
- Reordering enum members in source code (without affecting existing values)
- Reordering members in source code for classes marshaled as reference types that don't expose an auto-dual class interface (with an exception for overloaded methods)

The one noticeable difference is that members of interfaces or types marshaled as structs should *never* be rearranged once you've shipped an assembly. Such a change won't affect .NET clients but completely breaks COM clients that rely on interface or structure layout.

Adding or reordering methods of classes that don't expose auto-dual class interfaces is mostly safe because the class's members are either not directly accessible from COM or accessible only via late binding. As long as COM clients don't cache DISPIDs (which can change when members are reordered or added), late binding by member names continues to work as classes evolve. The reason .NET classes are given auto-dispatch class interfaces by default is to prevent COM clients from depending on DISPIDs that may change. The next chapter describes how to enable the different kinds of class interfaces.

CAUTION

Due to the way overloaded methods are handled, there's an important exception to two of the changes that are otherwise compatible for .NET and COM clients. Because the method names exposed to COM (with _2, _3, and so on) are determined by the ordering of the overloads, rearranging overloaded methods or adding a new overload before the last existing overload causes the method names to change from COM's perspective! This is why using overloaded members can be dangerous. Although it might be tempting to rearrange them, perhaps sorted by how frequently they're used so IntelliSense behaves nicer, never rearrange them once you've shipped your assembly!

Besides auto-dispatch class interfaces that insulate COM clients from evolving classes, the key to COM Interoperability's default versioning behavior lies in the automatically generated GUIDs for .NET types. Authors of .NET types don't need to think about generating unique GUIDs and decorating types with them since GUIDs are no longer used for identification in the strictly-.NET world. COM clients still require GUIDs in order to use your types, but fortunately the CLR generates them for .NET types on demand. Furthermore, the GUIDs are generated in such a way that provides COM clients with a versioning experience consistent with .NET clients. The rules of generating these automatic GUIDs are explained in the next few sections, which discuss LIBIDs, CLSIDs, and IIDs. The next chapter describes how to choose your own GUIDs if you want more control.

With all of the automatically-generated GUIDs, you can rest assured that they won't conflict with GUIDs generated by the existing `CoCreateGuid` API used by all standard tools.

Library Identifiers (LIBIDs)

Recall that when a type library is registered, its location is placed under the following registry key:

`HKEY_CLASSES_ROOT\TypeLib\{LIBID}\Major.Minor\LCID\win32`

The algorithm that automatically generates a LIBID for a type library exported from an assembly ensures that each distinct assembly produces a type library that can be registered independently of any others.

To do this, a unique LIBID is generated based on a hash of three of the four parts of an assembly's identity—name, public key, and version. An assembly's culture does not affect the LIBID because this information is preserved in a type library's locale identifier (LCID), and it's possible to register multiple type libraries with the same LIBID but different locales. The same is true for a type library version number, so why does the assembly version number affect the LIBID? Because an assembly's four-part version number can express more values than a type library's two-part version number. Therefore, having a LIBID that changes along with the assembly's version number is the only way to distinguish between type libraries for two assemblies that are identical except for build and revision numbers. Two otherwise-identical assemblies with version numbers 1.0.0.0 and 1.0.9.23 can be registered independently under:

`HKEY_CLASSES_ROOT\TypeLib\{LIBID1}\1.0\LCID\win32`

and

`HKEY_CLASSES_ROOT\TypeLib\{LIBID2}\1.0\LCID\win32`

Class Identifiers (CLSIDs)

The unique CLSIDs generated are based on a hash of a fully-qualified class name and the identity of the assembly containing the class. This ensures that classes with different identities in the .NET world always have different identities in COM by default. As with the generation of LIBIDs, only three fourths of an assembly's identity is used as input for calculating CLSIDs. Therefore, two classes differing only by culture would have the same CLSIDs, but assembly cultures are intended to be used for satellite assemblies containing resources; not code. The same rules for CLSIDs apply to GUIDs generated for delegates, structs, and enums.

The fact that a class's members don't affect its automatically generated CLSID makes member additions or reordering a compatible change for COM clients. But the CLSID only remains the same as long as the assembly's version number doesn't change. If you do change the version number, publisher policy can redirect requests for the older assembly to the newer assembly as long as the older assembly is still registered. Figure 11.2 illustrates this situation.

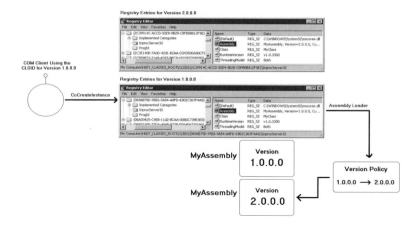

FIGURE 11.2

COM objects built with assembly version 1.0.0.0 can still work with assembly version 2.0.0.0.

CAUTION
By default, every Visual Studio .NET project uses the AssemblyVersionAttribute custom attribute to give the assembly a version of "1.0.*". The wildcard has the effect of producing a different assembly version number each time the project is compiled. This behavior does not work well with the automatically generated LIBIDs and CLSIDs because it causes them to change each time you re-compile the project! This causes any COM clients to fail unless they are recompiled with the newer version of

the assembly, unless you also bother with publisher policy each time. Plus, if you register your assembly each time, you can pollute your registry with multiple entries pretty quickly. To solve this problem, you should change the value of `AssemblyVersionAttribute` (in `AssemblyInfo.cs`, `AssemblyInfo.vb`, or `AssemblyInfo.cpp`, depending on the project language) to a stable number that doesn't use a wildcard.

Interface Identifiers (IIDs)

An IID that is generated for a .NET interface is based on a hash of its fully-qualified name plus the signatures of all the interface's members that are exposed to COM. This means that changing or adding methods to an interface gives it a new IID because an interface should never be changed without changing its identity.

Unlike CLSIDs or LIBIDs, the interface's assembly identity does not affect IID generation. It's critical for versioning that IIDs don't change based on an assembly's version number. Consider the scenario pictured in Figure 11.2. The COM client believes it's using version 1.0.0.0 of the assembly, and may query for several interfaces exposed in that assembly's exported type library. To be compatible, version 2.0.0.0 of the assembly must contain the same classes and interfaces, but if the interfaces' IIDs would have changed, then the COM client's `QueryInterface` calls would have failed.

One subtlety to the IID generation rule is that the names of an interface's members don't play a role in the IID generation. This means that you could change the order of an interface's methods, and if the list of signatures still looked the same (ignoring member names), the IID would not change. For example, changing a C# interface definition from:

```
public interface ITrafficLight
{
  void Go();
  void Stop();
  void Yield();
}
```

to:

```
public interface ITrafficLight
{
  void Stop();
  void Yield();
  void Go();
}
```

would not affect .NET clients but would break COM clients in subtle ways since they could still get the "same" interface but calling its methods by v-table offsets now does something entirely different. The moral of the story, mentioned earlier, is that you should never, ever reorder members!

Because assembly identity does not factor into IID calculations, unrelated interfaces in separate assemblies released by separate publishers can end up with the same IID if they have the same fully-qualified name and the same "shape." Although this is an unlikely occurrence (even more unlikely than conflicting ProgIDs in COM), it can make unregistration of an exported type library dangerous since there's a possibility that an interface will be unregistered that is needed by a separate application for COM marshaling. One way to avoid this situation is to give your interfaces explicit IIDs, as explained in the next chapter, and take on the responsibility of ensuring that your interface definitions never change.

Deployment

When deploying an assembly that might be used by COM clients, it's a good idea to register it with REGASM.EXE so clients don't have to perform the registration. This would be like registering a COM component with REGSVR32.EXE when deploying it. You may also want to deploy and register a type library, generated using REGASM.EXE's /tlb option.

CAUTION

The side-by-side and versioning capabilities of .NET components work well with COM clients, *as long as all versions of the components remain registered*. That's because COM clients built with an older version of an assembly can only be redirected to a newer version if the older version's registry entries are still in the Windows Registry (shown in Figure 11.2).

Imagine that you install a COM application that uses version 1.0 of assembly *X*, and then install version 2.0 of assembly *X* that includes publisher policy to redirect requests for version 1.0 to version 2.0. You might be tempted to uninstall version 1.0 if the COM application still works correctly with version 2.0. However, if *X*'s uninstallation program unregisters *X*, then doing so breaks the COM application because the CLSIDs it uses in CoCreateInstance calls are no longer registered. Similarly, if *X* has a type library that was originally registered but now unregistered, necessary registry entries for marshaling interfaces may have been removed, since IIDs remain fixed across assembly versions.

To summarize, unregistration poses the following dangers if you uninstall version 1.0 after installing version 2.0:

- Unregistered IIDs break COM marshaling of interfaces.
- Unregistered CLSIDs break COM instantiation of classes from 1.0. If other COM clients attempt to instantiate classes from 2.0, it still works unless the .NET component used `GuidAttribute` to keep CLSIDs fixed from one version to the next.

If you instead install the COM application with version 1.0 of *X*, then uninstall version 1.0 *before* installing version 2.0, unregistration causes the following problems:

- IIDs are still registered, so COM marshaling is not broken.
- Unregistered CLSIDs break COM instantiation of classes from 1.0, unless the .NET component used `GuidAttribute` to keep CLSIDs fixed from one version to the next. If other COM clients attempt to instantiate classes from 2.0, it still works.

You can even run into trouble if you install the COM application with version 1.0 of *X*, then install version 2.0, then uninstall *version 2.0*. This causes the following problems:

- Unregistered IIDs break COM marshaling of interfaces.
- CLSIDs for version 1.0 are still registered, unless the .NET component used `GuidAttribute` to keep CLSIDs fixed from one version to the next. Therefore, COM instantiation of classes from 1.0 still works if the .NET component used the CLSIDs auto-generated by the CLR.

Therefore, you should be conservative with unregistration of assemblies and their type libraries, because it can have disastrous effects for COM clients dependent on these registry entries.

.NET assemblies should usually be given a strong name, and the best place to install assemblies that may be used by COM clients is the Global Assembly Cache. Besides the fact that assemblies in the GAC are loaded faster than assemblies elsewhere, relying on a file path using the `CodeBase` mechanism is more fragile. If you do decide to register a `CodeBase` pointing to the location of your assembly, be sure that your assembly has a strong name in order to prevent it from interfering with other .NET applications.

Visual Studio .NET exposes the functionality of `REGASM.EXE` in Visual C# and Visual Basic .NET projects via the `Register for COM Interop` project setting. Figure 11.3 shows this option for a Visual C# project, and Figure 11.4 shows this option for a Visual Basic .NET project. You can reach these dialogs by right-clicking on your project in the Solution Explorer and choosing `Properties`, but it's only enabled for class library projects.

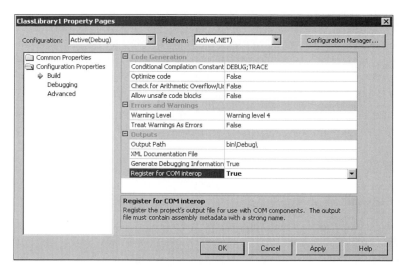

FIGURE 11.3

The Register for COM Interop option in a Visual C# project.

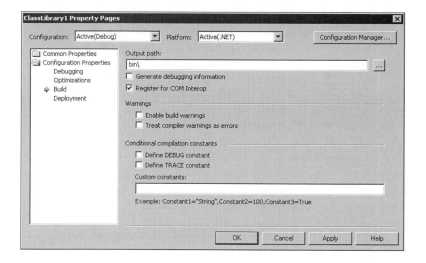

FIGURE 11.4

The Register for COM Interop option in a Visual Basic .NET project.

> **CAUTION**
>
> Using Visual Studio .NET's `Register for COM Interop` option is equivalent to doing the following from a command prompt:
>
>   regasm MyProject.dll /tlb /codebase
>
> Although the property page shown in Figure 11.3 states that the registration can only be done for strong-named assemblies, this is not enforced in any Visual Studio .NET project type. Because the `/codebase` option is used, you may want to avoid the use of `Register for COM Interop` altogether, or at least ensure that your assembly has a strong name.

Testing Your Component from COM

Obviously, the more testing you can do to exercise your .NET component from COM, the better. For those who don't want to invest a lot of time in doing this, there are a few simple tasks that should be done to give your class library a COM-focused sanity check:

- Run `REGASM.EXE` on your assemblies to ensure that no errors or warnings occur.

- Run `REGASM.EXE` on your assemblies with the `/regfile` option in order to understand exactly what gets registered for the assemblies.

- Run `TLBEXP.EXE` on your assemblies to ensure that no errors or warnings occur when exporting type libraries. (Or decide whether or not you're willing to accept the conditions explained by the warnings.)

- View the type libraries produced by `TLBEXP.EXE` in a viewer like `OLEVIEW.EXE` to get a handle on what your APIs look like to COM clients. It's this step in which you're likely to find the most surprises, such as renamed members due to conflicts, case-insensitivity effects, and members that you may not have realized were exposed or hidden.

- After running `REGASM.EXE` on your assemblies, open `OLEVIEW.EXE` and locate your classes in the tree view under `Object Classes, Grouped by Component Category, .NET Category`. By expanding the node for a class, `OLEVIEW.EXE` attempts to instantiate it. If it succeeds, it calls `IUnknown.QueryInterface` on your object for every registered interface on the machine and lists the interfaces the instantiated object implements. This is a quick yet very useful test to make sure that your objects can be successfully instantiated and the expected interfaces can be obtained, as pictured in Figure 11.5. (However, it's possible that more interfaces than just the ones listed can be obtained since not all interfaces are necessarily registered.) If you can't find the class you're looking for after running

REGASM.EXE, make sure that it's marked as public in the assembly and has a public default constructor. Although failure can occur from an exception thrown within your object's constructor, 99% of the failures are due to HRESULT 0x80131552—a type load exception caused by not being able to locate the assembly listed in the registry. Unless you drop your assemblies in the same directory as OLEVIEW.EXE (only temporarily for test purposes, of course), you should either run REGASM.EXE with the /codebase option or install the assemblies into the Global Assembly Cache to make them loadable from OLEVIEW.EXE.

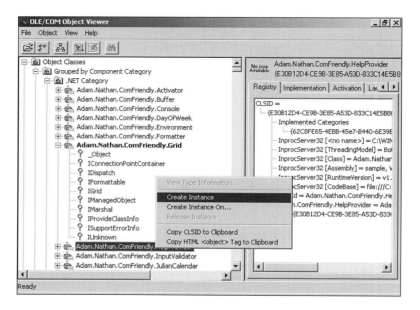

FIGURE 11.5
Using OLEVIEW.EXE *to test your .NET components from COM.*

This is just about all you can do besides sitting down and writing some code to test your class library from COM. (Unless, of course, you already have some mechanism for automated COM component testing.) Visual Basic 6 is a good environment to use for writing some quick tests that use your .NET components.

Conclusion

COM Interoperability was designed to make common .NET practices exposed as common COM practices. Just because HRESULTs and pointers are used in COM APIs doesn't mean that you should continue using them in .NET APIs exposed to COM. However, as this chapter shows, there's a limit to how much COM Interoperability can or will do.

Although .NET components can be exposed to COM with no extra work needed by the component developer, and although the CLR and its COM Interoperability tools choose sensible default behavior, there are still many special considerations to keep in mind if there's a possibility for your components to be used by COM clients.

The main lessons, in a nutshell, are:

- Don't create APIs that rely on parameterized constructors.
- Don't create APIs that rely on static members.
- Don't create APIs that rely on non-field members in value types.
- Don't create APIs that rely on nested arrays.
- Think twice before using overloaded methods.
- Don't forget the benefits of interface-based programming.
- Throw exception types defined in the mscorlib assembly.

The key to all of the advice in this chapter is to make your class libraries more COM-friendly while sacrificing as little as possible all the benefits that the published .NET guidelines give to .NET clients. Rather than trying to completely avoid COM-unfriendly elements like static members, providing COM-friendly alternatives can appease both worlds as long as it doesn't clutter your APIs with two ways to accomplish everything. By understanding the limitations and interactions when COM clients attempt to use your .NET APIs, you can make more informed decisions about your design.

Customizing COM's View of .NET Components

IN THIS CHAPTER

- Customizing Data Types   540
- Customizing Structure Layout   554
- Exposing Class Interfaces   556
- Using Visual Basic .NET's `ComClassAttribute`   560
- Making APIs Invisible to COM   562
- Customizing Registration   565
- Providing Your Own GUIDs   574
- Providing Your Own DISPIDs   574
- Controlling Interface Derivation   578
- Returning a Specific `HRESULT`   579
- Disabling Type Library Marshaling of .NET Interfaces   580
- Creating Multi-Cultured Methods   582
- Using Optional Parameters in Any Language   583
- Exposing .NET Objects as COM+ Objects   584

The Common Language Runtime (CLR) provides reasonable default behavior when exposing .NET components to COM. This default behavior is safe in the face of versioning, and almost always matches what a COM client expects to see. The result is that .NET component authors *mostly* don't need to know or care whether some of their clients may live in the unmanaged neighborhood. COM-specific modifications to .NET components are sometimes necessary, however. This chapter discusses the many ways to tune and customize a .NET component to get the exact behavior you want in the COM world.

The lesson of this chapter is that customization is done with custom attributes. COM Interoperability is one of the areas of the .NET platform that makes the most use of custom attributes, with a whopping 30 attributes in the `System.Runtime.InteropServices` namespace. These custom attributes enable the developer to customize everything from data marshaling to registration by providing extra information to the Interop Marshaler and tools like `REGASM.EXE`. Specifically, this chapter examines the following customizations:

- Customizing data types
- Customizing structure layout
- Exposing class interfaces
- Using Visual Basic .NET's `ComClassAttribute`
- Making APIs invisible to COM
- Customizing registration
- Providing your own GUIDs
- Providing your own DISPIDs
- Controlling interface derivation
- Returning a specific `HRESULT`
- Disabling type library marshaling of .NET interfaces
- Creating multi-cultured methods
- Using optional parameters in any language
- Exposing .NET objects as COM+ objects

Customizing Data Types

As discussed in previous chapters, the way in which data types are exposed to COM can be customized with `MarshalAsAttribute`, `InAttribute`, and `OutAttribute`. These attributes affect the behavior of the Interop Marshaler, and can affect what the types look like in an exported type library depending on the change. This section examines the following topics:

- MarshalAsAttribute basics
- Customizing arrays
- Detecting incorrect use of MarshalAsAttribute
- Customizing data flow

MarshalAsAttribute Basics

MarshalAsAttribute can be marked on parameters, return types, and fields. To customize a property's type, you must place the attribute on the get accessor's return type and set accessor's parameter, for example:

C#:

```csharp
public Decimal Amount
{
  [return: MarshalAs(UnmanagedType.Currency)]
  get { ... }
  [param: MarshalAs(UnmanagedType.Currency)]
  set { ... }
}
```

Visual Basic .NET:

```vb
Public Property Amount As <MarshalAs(UnmanagedType.Currency)> Decimal
  Get
    ...
  End Get
  Set (<MarshalAs(UnmanagedType.Currency)> ByVal Value As Decimal)
    ...
  End Set
End Property
```

C++:

```cpp
[returnvalue:MarshalAs(UnmanagedType::Currency)]
__property Decimal get_Amount() { ... }
__property void set_Amount([MarshalAs(UnmanagedType::Currency)] Decimal value)
{ ... }
```

> **CAUTION**
>
> Version 7.0 of the Visual C++ .NET compiler has a bug that makes it impossible to mark a property get accessor's return value with MarshalAsAttribute. If you attempt to apply the attribute to the get accessor's return value, the compiler places it on the set accessor's parameter instead (if one exists)!

MarshalAsAttribute has a required parameter that is a value of the UnmanagedType enumeration, as well as a handful of named parameters that can or must be used with certain values. Table 12.1 lists every value of the UnmanagedType enumeration along with how to use it with MarshalAsAttribute—what data types you can place it on, what it means, and what MarshalAsAttribute options are used with it. The emphasized rows contain values that can be used to change the default behavior of COM Interoperability. The values in the other rows never need to be used with COM signatures, but could be used to make default behavior explicit.

> **TIP**
>
> It often isn't necessary to mark parameters with MarshalAsAttribute because every possible parameter type has default marshaling behavior, as demonstrated by Table 9.1 in Chapter 9, "An In-Depth Look at Exported Type Libraries." Become familiar with the default behavior so you don't end up littering your signatures with unnecessary custom attributes. Besides slightly increasing the size of your metadata, overuse of MarshalAsAttribute can decrease the readability of your code.

TABLE 12.1 Every UnmanagedType Value Used with MarshalAsAttribute, Types on Which Each is Valid When Using COM Interoperability, and Each Value's Meaning

Enum Value	Types Valid On	Meaning
UnmanagedType.AnsiBStr	**System.String**	**A BSTR with ANSI characters (rarely used).**
UnmanagedType.AsAny	Nothing	Valid for PInvoke only.
UnmanagedType.Bool	**System.Boolean**	**4-byte value for which false is zero and true is non-zero. This is the Win32 BOOL type.**
UnmanagedType.BStr	System.String	A BSTR (String in VB6), the default COM view of a string type.
UnmanagedType.ByValArray	**Array fields in value types**	**An array with a fixed number of elements. Must be used with MarshalAsAttribute's SizeConst setting. Can also be used with the ArraySubType setting to override the default element type.**

TABLE 12.1 Continued

Enum Value	Types Valid On	Meaning
UnmanagedType.ByValTStr	System.String fields in value types	A character array with a fixed number of elements. Must be used with MarshalAsAttribute's SizeConst setting. The characters can be ANSI or Unicode, depending on the CharSet value of the containing value type.
UnmanagedType.Currency	System.Decimal	A CURRENCY type.
UnmanagedType.CustomMarshaler	Any reference type	Allows a user to plug in a special marshaler that must be specified using either MarshalAsAttribute's MarshalTypeRef or MarshalType setting. Can also be used with MarshalAsAttribute's Cookie setting to provide the marshaler with extra information.
UnmanagedType.Error	System.Int32, System.UInt32	An HRESULT value.
UnmanagedType.FunctionPtr	System.Delegate or a type derived from it	An integer that can be used as a C-style function pointer.
UnmanagedType.I1	System.SByte, System.Boolean	A one-byte signed integral value. Can be used to transform a boolean value into a one-byte C-style bool, for which 1 means true and 0 means false.
UnmanagedType.I2	System.Int16	A two-byte signed integral value.
UnmanagedType.I4	System.Int32	A four-byte signed integral value.
UnmanagedType.I8	System.Int64	An eight-byte signed integral value.
UnmanagedType.IDispatch	System.Object	An IDispatch pointer (Object in VB6).
UnmanagedType.Interface	Any reference type	The exact interface type or the default interface if applied to a class type. When applied to System.Object, it's the same as UnmanagedType.IUnknown.

TABLE 12.1 Continued

Enum Value	Types Valid On	Meaning
`UnmanagedType.IUnknown`	`System.Object`	An `IUnknown` pointer.
`UnmanagedType.LPArray`	An array type	A pointer to the first element in a C-style array. Can be used with `MarshalAsAttribute`'s `SizeParamIndex` and/or `SizeConst` settings to specify the length of the array. Can also be used with the `ArraySubType` setting to override the default element type.
`UnmanagedType.LPStr`	`System.String,` `System.Text.` `StringBuilder`	A null-terminated ANSI string.
`UnmanagedType.LPStruct`	Nothing	Valid for PInvoke only.
`UnmanagedType.LPTStr`	Nothing	Valid for PInvoke only.
`UnmanagedType.LPWStr`	`System.String,` `System.Text.` `StringBuilder`	A null-terminated Unicode string.
`UnmanagedType.R4`	`System.Single`	A four-byte floating point value.
`UnmanagedType.R8`	`System.Double`	An eight-byte floating point value.
`UnmanagedType.SafeArray`	Any array type	A `SAFEARRAY`. This is the default behavior for .NET array parameters, but can be used with `MarshalAsAttribute`'s `SafeArraySubType` setting to override the default element type.
`UnmanagedType.Struct`	`System.Object`	A `VARIANT`.
`UnmanagedType.SysInt`	`System.IntPtr`	A platform-sized signed integral value.
`UnmanagedType.SysUInt`	`System.UIntPtr`	A platform-sized unsigned integral value.
`UnmanagedType.TBStr`	`System.String`	A `BSTR` with platform-dependent characters (rarely used).

TABLE 12.1 Continued

Enum Value	Types Valid On	Meaning
UnmanagedType.U1	**System.Byte,** **System.Boolean**	**A one-byte unsigned integral value. Can be used to transform a boolean value into a one-byte C-style `bool`, for which 1 means true and 0 means false.**
UnmanagedType.U2	System.UInt16	A two-byte unsigned integral value.
UnmanagedType.U4	System.UInt32	A four-byte unsigned integral value.
UnmanagedType.U8	System.UInt64	An eight-byte unsigned integral value.
UnmanagedType.VariantBool	**System.Boolean**	**A `VARIANT_BOOL` type (Boolean in VB6).**
UnmanagedType.VBByRefStr	System.String	Used by VB .NET for PInvoke.

DIGGING DEEPER

The Visual C++ .NET compiler implicitly marks all `bool` types with `MarshalAs(UnmanagedType::U1)` because this represents a C-style boolean value. Therefore, you must explicitly mark `bool` parameters with `MarshalAs(UnmanagedType::VariantBool)` in C++ to get such types exported and marshaled as `VARIANT_BOOL` types.

See Part VI, "Platform Invocation Services," for explanations of the `UnmanagedType` values that can't be used with COM Interoperability. Some of the values (such as `UnmanagedType.Interface`) that aren't very useful for COM Interoperability can be useful for PInvoke. Although `UnmanagedType.ByValTStr` can be used with COM Interoperability, you can't export a signature that uses this value to a type library, because a type library can't capture the notion of a platform-dependent character set.

> **CAUTION**
>
> Use caution when exposing `System.Text.StringBuilder` parameters to COM with version 1.0 of the CLR. When a string allocated in unmanaged code is marshaled to a `StringBuilder`, the Interop Marshaler only copies 32 bytes of the string (32 ANSI characters or 16 Unicode characters). See Chapter 18, "The Essentials of PInvoke," for more information about `StringBuilder`.

`MarshalAsAttribute`, like the other custom attributes in `System.Runtime.InteropServices`, has an `Inherited` property set to false. Therefore, the attribute must be explicitly marked everywhere to get the marshaling behavior you'd expect. If you write a class that implements an interface with methods that use `MarshalAsAttribute`, no .NET compilers enforce that you place the same attributes on the implemented method signature. This is because the method, with or without such attributes, works the same way for .NET clients. Such methods, of course, look different from a COM perspective. Thus, if you don't mark the attribute everywhere, COM clients could see different behavior depending on whether they call through your interface or your class (through its class interface). Listing 12.1 shows source code that makes the mistake of not marking the `GiveMoney` signature with `UnmanagedType.Currency` everywhere it's used. `ClassInterfaceAttribute` is used to make the type information for class interfaces visible, as explained in the "Exposing Class Interfaces" section. Listing 12.2 shows the interface definitions that would be in an exported type library.

LISTING 12.1   Incorrect C# Source Code in Which Not Every Occurrence of the Same Signature Is Marked with the Same `MarshalAsAttribute`

```
 1: using System;
 2: using System.Runtime.InteropServices;
 3:
 4: [assembly:ClassInterface(ClassInterfaceType.AutoDual)]
 5:
 6: public interface IDonate
 7: {
 8:   void GiveMoney([MarshalAs(UnmanagedType.Currency)] Decimal amount);
 9: }
10:
11: public class Philanthropist : IDonate
12: {
13:   // UnmanagedType.Currency is omitted for demonstration
14:   public virtual void GiveMoney(Decimal amount) { ... }
15: }
16:
```

LISTING 12.1 Continued

```
17: public class Humanitarian : Philanthropist
18: {
19:   public override void GiveMoney(
20:     [MarshalAs(UnmanagedType.Currency)] Decimal amount) { ... }
21: }
```

LISTING 12.2 The Contents of the Type Library Exported from the Assembly Whose Source is in Listing 12.1

```
 1: [
 2:   odl,
 3:   uuid(61544550-7E59-3E4F-8933-3B4D0B55C3CA),
 4:   version(1.0),
 5:   dual,
 6:   oleautomation,
 7:   custom(0F21F359-AB84-41E8-9A78-36D110E6D2F9, "IDonate")
 8: ]
 9: interface IDonate : IDispatch {
10:   [id(0x60020000)]
11:   HRESULT GiveMoney([in] CURRENCY amount);
12: };
13:
14: [
15:   uuid(60698795-8BCB-34F0-9828-C2AE1B2AFA4F),
16:   version(1.0),
17:   custom(0F21F359-AB84-41E8-9A78-36D110E6D2F9, "Philanthropist")
18: ]
19: coclass Philanthropist {
20:   [default] interface _Philanthropist;
21:   interface _Object;
22:   interface IDonate;
23: };
24:
25: [
26:   uuid(49E87883-A9FD-355C-B597-A80299F9A1A6),
27:   version(1.0),
28:   custom(0F21F359-AB84-41E8-9A78-36D110E6D2F9, "Humanitarian")
29: ]
30: coclass Humanitarian {
31:     [default] interface _Humanitarian;
32:     interface _Philanthropist;
33:     interface _Object;
34:     interface IDonate;
35: };
36:
```

LISTING 12.2   Continued

```
37: [
38:   odl,
39:   uuid(544A0C79-B279-334E-92FF-3B05BFD5C7F3),
40:   hidden,
41:   dual,
42:   nonextensible,
43:   oleautomation,
44:   custom(0F21F359-AB84-41E8-9A78-36D110E6D2F9, "Philanthropist")
45: ]
46: interface _Philanthropist : IDispatch {
47:   [id(00000000), propget, custom(54FC8F55-38DE-4703-9C4E-250351302B1C, 1)]
48:   HRESULT ToString([out, retval] BSTR* pRetVal);
49:   [id(0x60020001)]
50:   HRESULT Equals(
51:     [in] VARIANT obj,
52:     [out, retval] VARIANT_BOOL* pRetVal);
53:   [id(0x60020002)]
54:   HRESULT GetHashCode([out, retval] long* pRetVal);
55:   [id(0x60020003)]
56:   HRESULT GetType([out, retval] _Type** pRetVal);
57:   [id(0x60020004)]
58:   HRESULT GiveMoney([in] DECIMAL amount);
59: };
60:
61: [
62:   odl,
63:   uuid(FD19F48A-D547-36DB-885C-E2E88D999A83),
64:   hidden,
65:   dual,
66:   nonextensible,
67:   oleautomation,
68:   custom(0F21F359-AB84-41E8-9A78-36D110E6D2F9, "Humanitarian")
69: ]
70: interface _Humanitarian : IDispatch {
71:   [id(00000000), propget, custom(54FC8F55-38DE-4703-9C4E-250351302B1C, 1)]
72:   HRESULT ToString([out, retval] BSTR* pRetVal);
73:   [id(0x60020001)]
74:   HRESULT Equals([in] VARIANT obj, [out, retval] VARIANT_BOOL* pRetVal);
75:   [id(0x60020002)]
76:   HRESULT GetHashCode([out, retval] long* pRetVal);
77:   [id(0x60020003)]
78:   HRESULT GetType([out, retval] _Type** pRetVal);
79:   [id(0x60020004)]
80:   HRESULT GiveMoney([in] CURRENCY amount);
81: };
```

In the resulting type library, notice that `IDonate`'s `GiveMoney` method and `_Humanitarian`'s `GiveMoney` method have the expected `CURRENCY` type (Lines 11 and 80), yet `_Philanthropist`'s `GiveMoney` signature has a `DECIMAL` parameter (Line 58) because `MarshalAsAttribute` was omitted on the `Philanthropist` class. All of these signatures can be used from COM without error, but it presents unmanaged code with inconsistencies. Plus, for this example, the `_Philanthropist.GiveMoney` method can't be called from a Visual Basic 6 client because VB6 doesn't support `DECIMAL` types. Whenever you use `Decimal` types representing money in .NET signatures, it's a good idea to mark them with `UnmanagedType.Currency` so COM clients can use them naturally.

> **CAUTION**
>
> When marking types with `MarshalAsAttribute`, be sure to mark every occurrence of the signature. For example, if the signature appears in an interface, you should place the attribute in the interface's signature as well as the signature in any classes that implement it.

Customizing Arrays

When exposing array fields or parameters to COM, there are three `UnmanagedType` values that can be used: `ByValArray`, `LPArray`, and `SafeArray`. Only `ByValArray` is supported for fields, and only `LPArray` and `SafeArray` are supported for parameters.

`UnmanagedType.ByValArray` must be used with `MarshalAsAttribute`'s `SizeConst` named parameter so the Interop Marshaler knows how many array elements to marshal in either direction. When using `UnmanagedType.LPArray`, it's important to either use `MarshalAsAttribute`'s `SizeConst` named parameter or `SizeParamIndex` named parameter so the Interop Marshaler knows how many elements to marshal for arrays allocated in unmanaged code. Whereas `SizeConst` can be set to the number of array elements to be marshaled, `SizeParamIndex` can be set to the zero-based index of the parameter that contains the number of array elements at run time. The array parameter marked with `MarshalAsAttribute` and the size parameter indicated by `SizeParamIndex` must both be passed by-value, so the `SizeParamIndex` mechanism is not as flexible as IDL's `size_is`.

`MarshalAsAttribute`'s `ArraySubType` named parameter can be set to an `UnmanagedType` value, but not all of the enumeration's values are valid. For instance, an element type of `UnmanagedType.LPArray` isn't allowed. If no element type is specified, the default unmanaged representation of the managed array element type is assumed. Therefore, the element type only needs to be specified for cases like making an array of `Object` types looking like an array of `IDispatch` types rather than an array of `VARIANT`s.

> ## DIGGING DEEPER
>
> With `UnmanagedType.LPArray`, it's actually possible to use *both* `SizeConst` and `SizeParamIndex` together, as follows:
>
> ```
> void ArrayMethod(
>   [MarshalAs(UnmanagedType.LPArray, SizeParamIndex=1, SizeConst=10)] int
> [] x,
>   int count);
> ```
>
> This means that, when called from unmanaged code, the marshaler treats the array as having count + 10 elements. In IL Assembler syntax, this signature looks like the following:
>
> ```
> .method public hidebysig newslot virtual abstract instance void
>   ArrayMethod(int32[] marshal([10 + 1]) x, int32 count) cil managed
> ```

When defining new .NET APIs, exposing arrays as SAFEARRAYs is the preferred method. You should keep this default behavior unless you're especially concerned about unmanaged C++ clients, for whom dealing with SAFEARRAYs can be cumbersome. Although arrays are exposed as SAFEARRAYs by default, you can use `UnmanagedType.SafeArray` along with the `SafeArraySubType` named parameter to customize the type of the array's elements. In fact, this is the only valid `MarshalAsAttribute` named parameter you can use with `UnmanagedType.SafeArray` (besides `SafeArrayUserDefinedSubType`, described later). For example, `SizeConst` and `SizeParamIndex` aren't valid because all of the array size information is stored inside the SAFEARRAY structure. `SafeArraySubType`, when used, must be set to a value of the `System.Runtime.InteropServices.VarEnum` enumeration. Although it has 44 values (in order to stay faithful to the unmanaged definition of this famous enumeration), only a subset of them are valid for a SAFEARRAY's element type. Table 12.2 lists the valid values of `VarEnum` when setting the value of `SafeArraySubType`. As in Table 12.1, values that change default marshaling behavior are emphasized.

TABLE 12.2 Valid Values Describing SAFEARRAY Element Types

Enum Value	Valid With Types	Meaning
VarEnum.VT_BOOL	System.Boolean	VARIANT_BOOL types.
VarEnum.VT_BSTR	System.String	BSTR types.
VarEnum.VT_CY	**System.Decimal**	**CURRENCY types.**
VarEnum.VT_DATE	System.DateTime	DATE types.
VarEnum.VT_DECIMAL	System.Decimal	DECIMAL types.
VarEnum.VT_DISPATCH	**System.Object**	**IDispatch interface pointers.**

Customizing COM's View of .NET Components

CHAPTER 12

551

12

COM'S VIEW
OF .NET
COMPONENTS

TABLE 12.2 Continued

Enum Value	Valid With Types	Meaning
VarEnum.VT_ERROR	**System.Int32, System.UInt32**	**HRESULT values.**
VarEnum.VT_I1	**System.SByte, System.Boolean**	**One-byte signed integral values. Can be used to transform boolean elements into one-byte C-style bool types, for which 1 means true and 0 means false.**
VarEnum.VT_I2	System.Int16	Two-byte signed integral values.
VarEnum.VT_I4	System.Int32	Four-byte signed integral values.
VarEnum.VT_I8	System.Int64	Eight-byte signed integral values.
VarEnum.VT_INT	**System.Int32**	**Two- or four-byte integral values.**
VarEnum.VT_LPSTR	**System.String, System.Text.StringBuilder**	**Null-terminated ANSI strings.**
VarEnum.VT_LPWSTR	**System.String, System.Text.StringBuilder**	**Null-terminated Unicode strings.**
VarEnum.VT_R4	System.Single	Four-byte floating point values.
VarEnum.VT_R8	System.Double	Eight-byte floating point values.
VarEnum.VT_RECORD	types exported as structures	Structures (UDTs).
VarEnum.VT_UI1	**System.Byte, System.Boolean**	**One-byte unsigned integral values. Can be used to transform boolean values into one-byte C-style bool types, for which 1 means true and 0 means false.**
VarEnum.VT_UI2	System.UInt16	Two-byte unsigned integral values.
VarEnum.VT_UI4	System.UInt32	Four-byte unsigned integral values.
VarEnum.VT_UI8	System.UInt64	Eight-byte unsigned integral values.
VarEnum.VT_UINT	**System.UInt32**	**Two- or four-byte unsigned integral values.**
VarEnum.VT_UNKNOWN	**System.Object**	**IUnknown interface pointers.**
VarEnum.VT_VARIANT	System.Object	VARIANT types.

Table 12.2 leaves out one important option. Any of the VarEnum values in the table can be used as a SafeArraySubType when placing MarshalAs(UnmanagedType.SafeArray, …) on a System.Array type. Using UnmanagedType.SafeArray on System.Array enables the exposure of this generic array type as a specific type of SAFEARRAY rather than an _Array class interface. By default, System.Array is exposed as a SAFEARRAY of VARIANTs, so every VarEnum value except for VarEnum.VT_VARIANT changes the default marshaling behavior in this case.

> **CAUTION**
>
> In version 1.0 of the CLR, using MarshalAs(UnmanagedType.SafeArray, VarEnum.VT_CY) on an array of Decimal types does not work as expected, causing the Interop Marshaler to fail with a SafeArrayTypeMismatchException. To work around this, you could use do-it-yourself marshaling with IntPtr, as described in Chapter 6, "Advanced Topics for Using COM Components."

MarshalAsAttribute has another array-related named parameter: SafeArrayUserDefinedSubType. This can be used with UnmanagedType.SafeArray only when SafeArraySubType is set to VarEnum.VT_RECORD, VarEnum.VT_DISPATCH, or VarEnum.VT_UNKNOWN. It is set to a Type object to represent the array's element type. This is only useful when the marked data type is the generic System.Array, to be able to expose a SAFEARRAY to COM with an arbitrary rank or non-zero lower bounds.

Detecting Incorrect Use of MarshalAsAttribute

Because MarshalAsAttribute is a pseudo-custom attribute, it is treated differently at compile time than regular custom attributes. The benefit is that, unlike regular custom attributes, more error-checking than usual is available at compile time. You won't get compile-time errors for using an UnmanagedType value that isn't appropriate for the data type it's attached to, but you will get compilation errors for the following mistakes:

- Placing MarshalAsAttribute on a target it doesn't belong on (like a property or assembly).
- Using MarshalAsAttribute with an UnmanagedType value only allowed on fields (such as ByValTStr) on a parameter or return type.
- Using MarshalAsAttribute named parameters that can't be used with the UnmanagedType value, or omitting a named parameter that's necessary with the UnmanagedType value.
- Giving values for any MarshalAsAttribute parameters outside the valid range.

Such a compile-time error in C# might look like the following:

```
error CS0647: Error emitting
'System.Runtime.InteropServices.MarshalAsAttribute'
        attribute -- 'SizeConst is required for a fixed string.'
```

Other errors, such as putting an `UnmanagedType` value on an unrelated type, can be caught by the type library exporter. For example, running `TLBEXP.EXE` on an assembly containing a method which has `MarshalAs(UnmanagedType.BStr)` on a `Decimal` parameter gives the following warning:

```
Type library exporter warning processing 'MyClass.MyMethod(decimalParameter),
MyAssembly'.  Warning: The method or field has an invalid
ELEMENT_TYPE/NATIVE_TYPE combination.
```

`ELEMENT_TYPE` refers to the .NET data type, and `NATIVE_TYPE` refers to the `UnmanagedType` value. Unfortunately, such warnings are not seen during type library export when using the `Register for COM Interop` inside Visual Studio .NET.

Whereas some errors are caught during compilation and some are caught during type library export, some errors in using `MarshalAsAttribute` are simply ignored! Therefore, it is important to be careful when marking types with `MarshalAsAttribute`.

CAUTION

Mismatches in `SafeArraySubType` values and the types they're applied on are not caught as errors by compilers nor the type library exporter. For example, you could mark a managed array of double types with `MarshalAs(UnmanagedType.SafeArray, SafeArraySubType=VarEnum.VT_BSTR)` and the exporter happily produces a type library signature with an array of strings. Such errors can cause bad run-time problems, so be sure to follow the rules in Table 12.2 to avoid making these mistakes.

Customizing Data Flow

Using `MarshalAsAttribute` isn't the only way to customize the behavior of a parameter. You can also use two more custom attributes—`InAttribute` and `OutAttribute`—to customize the direction of data flow. These attributes affect data flow across managed/unmanaged boundaries the same way that IDL's `[in]` and `[out]` attributes do. See Chapter 4, "An In-Depth Look at Imported Assemblies," for descriptions of their behavior.

By default, by-value parameters (except for `StringBuilder` types) are treated as `[In]`, by-reference parameters are treated as `[In, Out]` and out-only parameters (as defined by C#) are treated as `[Out]`. `OutAttribute` is often used on a by-reference parameter to simulate C#'s out keyword in other .NET languages. InAttribute and OutAttribute are often used together on by-value array or formatted class parameters to get the in/out behavior that most people expect. InAttribute alone can be used on a by-reference parameter to suppress outward marshaling as a performance optimization, when appropriate.

> ### CAUTION
>
> Visual Basic .NET requires that you either use the full name of the InAttribute custom attribute or surround In with square brackets (for example, <[In]>) because In is a keyword. This doesn't apply to the OutAttribute custom attribute, however, because Out is not a keyword.

Customizing Structure Layout

You've seen that user-defined value types are exported as structures in a type library. Unlike in the managed world, however, the exact memory layout of a structure is important to COM. This layout can be customized using StructLayoutAttribute. StructLayoutAttribute requires that you specify a member of the LayoutKind enumeration. This can be one of three values:

- LayoutKind.Auto. The CLR chooses how to arrange the fields in the structure. This should never be used when interacting with unmanaged code, because the memory layout chosen is unpredictable.

- LayoutKind.Sequential. The fields are arranged sequentially, in the order they appear in source code. This is the default in C#, Visual Basic .NET, and C++.

- LayoutKind.Explicit. The fields are arranged using byte offsets specified by the user on each field using a second custom attribute: FieldOffsetAttribute.

StructLayoutAttribute also enables you to optionally set additional information, such as CharSet, which affects how string and character fields are marshaled. The following C# struct demonstrates the use of CharSet:

```
[StructLayout(LayoutKind.Sequential, CharSet=CharSet.Unicode)]
public struct MyStruct
{
  string Field1;
  [MarshalAs(UnmanagedType.ByValTStr, SizeConst=256)] string Field2;
}
```

String fields (such as `Field1`) are by default treated as `LPSTR` or `LPWSTR`, based on the `CharSet` value of the containing struct. C#, Visual Basic .NET, and C++ assume an ANSI character set by default. When marked with `UnmanagedType.ByValTStr`, the string is either a buffer of ANSI or Unicode characters, also depending on the `CharSet` value. Thus, the previous value type gets exported to COM as follows:

```
struct tagMyStruct
{
  LPWSTR Field1;
  unsigned short Field2[256];
} MyStruct;
```

> **TIP**
>
> Using `LayoutKind.Explicit`, you can create a union in managed code! Simply mark each field with the same offset of zero. For example:
>
> ```
> [StructLayout(LayoutKind.Explicit)]
> public struct MyStruct
> {
>    [FieldOffset(0)] short Field1;
>    [FieldOffset(0)] int Field2;
>    [FieldOffset(0)] long Field3;
> }
> ```
>
> This causes each field to overlap in the same memory location. Reference types (such as classes and arrays) and primitive types are not allowed to overlap.

These attributes are critical when trying to define all sorts of existing Win32 structures, but when defining .NET value types, you should stick to the default behavior as much as possible to avoid confusion. The most important point is that, when defining .NET value types, marking them with `LayoutKind.Sequential` or `LayoutKind.Explicit` make them usable from COM. With automatic layout, exported structs look just fine in a type library, but attempting to use them from COM causes run-time errors. Fortunately, the default layout for value types defined in C#, VB .NET, and C++ is sequential, so nothing special needs to be done to make value types COM-friendly in these languages.

DIGGING DEEPER

Despite the fact that the C#, Visual Basic .NET, and C++ compilers emit value types with an implicit LayoutKind.Sequential, not all .NET languages may follow this convention. Therefore, be sure that value types are marked appropriately for your language if exposure to unmanaged code is a possibility. StructLayoutAttribute is a pseudo-custom attribute, so you can see the layout and character set described directly in type definitions in IL Assembler syntax. For example:

```
.class public auto ansi sealed beforefieldinit AutoStructWithAnsiCharSet
       extends [mscorlib]System.ValueType

.class public explicit unicode sealed beforefieldinit
ExplicitStructWithUnicodeCharSet
       extends [mscorlib]System.ValueType

.class public sequential autochar sealed beforefieldinit
SequentialStructWithAutoCharSet
       extends [mscorlib]System.ValueType
```

Exposing Class Interfaces

Chapter 8, "The Essentials for Using .NET Components from COM," introduced the notion of a *class interface*—an interface generated by the CLR that provides access to public members of the class (including members from base classes) for COM clients. The behavior of class interfaces exposed to COM is controlled with ClassInterfaceAttribute. This attribute has one required parameter that is a value of the ClassInterfaceType enumeration. The values are the following:

- ClassInterfaceType.AutoDispatch. An empty-looking class interface is generated with the name _ClassName that derives from IDispatch. COM clients must call the class's members through IDispatch's Invoke method. This is the default setting.

- ClassInterfaceType.None. No class interface is generated. With this setting, only the members of implemented interfaces (and the members of any interfaces or class interfaces exposed for base classes) can be invoked from COM. The first listed interface becomes the default interface that can be invoked late-bound through IDispatch. (Depending on the compiler and the situation, this "first" interface might not always be the first one listed in source code.) If a class marked with ClassInterfaceType.None doesn't implement any interfaces, the default interface available to COM clients is _Object, the auto-dual class interface for System.Object. Any interfaces (including class interfaces) from base classes are still exposed to COM, unless every class in the inheritance chain is marked with ClassInterfaceType.None.

- `ClassInterfaceType.AutoDual`. A dual class interface is generated that exposes type information for the same members that could be invoked in an auto-dispatch class interface. This is the most convenient option for clients, but also the most dangerous for the owner of the component. Choosing this limits the kinds of modifications that can be made to the class without breaking COM clients in the future.

DIGGING DEEPER

Several of the custom attributes in `System.Runtime.InteropServices`, such as `ClassInterfaceAttribute`, have two constructors—one that takes an enumeration value and one that takes a plain 16-bit integer. The constructor with a 16-bit integer is used by the type library importer, but should be avoided in your own code. Both work the same way, but using the constructor with an enum produces more readable code that's less error-prone.

`ClassInterfaceAttribute` can be marked on classes or assemblies. Placing the attribute at the assembly level is a shortcut for placing it on every class in the assembly. Furthermore, the assembly-level `ClassInterfaceAttribute` setting can be overridden on a class-by-class basis by marking individual classes with `ClassInterfaceAttribute` and a different `ClassInterfaceType` value. This pattern is frequently used with the custom attributes in `System.Runtime. InteropServices`.

Why are auto-dispatch class interfaces exposed to COM by default? Because the exported type library contains no type information for auto-dispatch class interface members, unmanaged clients cannot (easily) cache DISPIDs or depend on interface layout. This is great because the ordering of members and their DISPIDs can easily change if .NET component authors are not careful. With the default setting, almost any class updates that are compatible for .NET clients are also compatible for COM clients, as discussed in the previous chapter.

Auto-dual class interfaces, on the other hand, are useful in a controlled environment, but can present problems in the face of versioning. Because COM interfaces are tied to the layout of their methods, adding members to anywhere but the end of a class would cause early-bound COM clients to end up calling different members than they thought they were, most likely resulting in a crash. Even adding members at the end of a class is catastrophic for derived classes that expose an auto-dual class interface, because any derived class members are pushed later in the v-table! Real .NET interfaces exposed to COM don't have this problem because they don't include the base members of .NET interfaces in the v-table.

Adding new members to a class or rearranging its members cannot adversely affect COM clients that late bind to auto-dispatch class interfaces, with one exception. As mentioned in the previous chapter, the exception to the version-safety of auto-dispatch class interfaces is overloaded methods, whose name decorations (_2, _3, and so on) can change based on the order they appear. Adding or moving method overloads is dangerous for COM clients. For the following class:

```
public class C
{
  // COM client can call this as "OverloadedMethod"
  public void OverloadedMethod() { ... }

  // COM client can call this as "OverloadedMethod_2"
  public void OverloadedMethod(string str) { ... }

  // COM client can call this as "OverloadedMethod_3"
  public void OverloadedMethod(short s) { ... }
}
```

COM clients could call these methods as OverloadedMethod, OverloadedMethod_2, and OverloadedMethod_3, respectively. If the author of C adds an overload in the middle without changing the assembly version number (or ships it with publisher policy claiming that the assembly is compatible with a previous version), then the public APIs have now changed for COM clients only. This could be done as follows with the C class:

```
public class C
{
  // COM client can call this as "OverloadedMethod"
  public void OverloadedMethod() { ... }

  // COM client can call this as "OverloadedMethod_2"
  public void OverloadedMethod(long l) { ... }

  // COM client can call this as "OverloadedMethod_3"
  public void OverloadedMethod(string str) { ... }

  // COM client can call this as "OverloadedMethod_4"
  public void OverloadedMethod(short s) { ... }
}
```

DON'T DO THIS

A COM client that calls OverloadedMethod_3, late-bound or not, is now calling a different method than it used to.

The recommended solution for COM-friendly .NET classes is to use `ClassInterfaceType.None` and implement an interface that contains all the methods of the class. Examples of this can be seen in the `mscorlib` assembly with the following class/interface pairs:

- `AppDomainSetup` and `IAppDomainSetup` in the `System` namespace.
- `AppDomain` and `_AppDomain` in the `System` namespace.
- `RegistrationServices` and `IRegistrationServices` in the `System.Runtime.InteropServices` namespace.
- `TypeLibConverter` and `ITypeLibConverter` in the `System.Runtime.InteropServices` namespace.

(Note that `_AppDomain` is actually a real .NET interface, not a class interface generated for COM clients.) The benefit of this is that developers are likely to be more careful when adding members to the class because adding members to the corresponding interface can't be done in a version-compatible way. And if members were only added to the class and not the interface (to avoid versioning problems) COM clients wouldn't break; they simply wouldn't be able to take advantage of the new functionality.

> **CAUTION**
>
> Using `ClassInterfaceType.None` is the only way to expose your own default interface to COM, although which interface becomes the default can be unreliable for classes that implement multiple interfaces. Usually the order that the interfaces are listed in metadata matches the order in source code, but it ultimately depends on your .NET compiler. For example, a C# class that implements two interfaces that are related via inheritance always lists the base interface first in metadata, regardless of their order in source code.

> **CAUTION**
>
> Auto-dual class interfaces expose all of the methods of base classes, even if the base class has no class interface or an auto-dispatch class interface. Exposing such an auto-dual class interface by an author who doesn't control the base classes is a very bad idea. Because the designer of a base class didn't expose an auto-dual class interface, she may decide to add methods to the class without changing its version number (or applying a policy to make it treated as version-compatible). Any derived auto-dual class interfaces would then be broken because additional methods are inserted in the middle of the interface.

12

COM's View OF .NET COMPONENTS

> Therefore, never ship a class that exposes an auto-dual class interface unless all of its base classes also expose an auto-dual class interface. Even then, use caution if the base class definitions are not under your control.

If a class author chooses to expose an auto-dual class interface (such as for `System.Reflection.Assembly`), this does not mean that she cannot add members in the future in a compatible way. The author can add the members and mark them with a custom attribute that makes them invisible to COM (discussed in the "Making APIs Invisible to COM" section). This way, .NET clients can take advantage of the new methods but the class interface that COM clients rely on doesn't change. Of course, COM clients aren't able to call these new methods, but at least the functionality they already rely on continues to work. If the author wants the new methods to be available to COM, she should give the new assembly an incompatible version number and set the policy so that existing COM clients bind to the older assembly but new ones can choose to bind to the new one.

Using Visual Basic .NET's `ComClassAttribute`

Visual Basic .NET defines its own custom attribute for COM Interoperability with the goal of making the process of exposing a Visual Basic .NET class to COM easier. However, due to poor versioning behavior, it's probably best to avoid using this custom attribute altogether.

This custom attribute is `Microsoft.VisualBasic.ComClassAttribute`, and can be marked only on classes. When you mark a class with `ComClassAttribute`, the VB .NET compiler marks the class with `<ClassInterface(ClassInterfaceType.None)>` and makes the class implement a hidden nested interface called _`ClassName`. By doing this, Visual Basic .NET effectively creates its own kind of class interface that's distinct from auto-dispatch or auto-dual class interfaces. `ComClassAttribute` also causes the VB .NET compiler to do a few extra tasks when the marked class has events. This is the best feature of `ComClassAttribute`, and is described in Chapter 13, "Exposing .NET Events to COM Clients."

`ComClassAttribute` has four constructors:

```
Public Sub New()
Public Sub New(_ClassID As String)
Public Sub New(_ClassID As String, _InterfaceID As String)
Public Sub New(_ClassID As String, _InterfaceID As String, _EventId As String)
```

When adding a new "COM class" in a Visual Basic .NET project (`Project`, `Add New Item…`, `COM Class`), Visual Studio .NET creates the following template:

```
<ComClass(ComClass1.ClassId, ComClass1.InterfaceId, ComClass1.EventsId)> _
Public Class ComClass1

#Region "COM GUIDs"
    ' These  GUIDs provide the COM identity for this class
    ' and its COM interfaces. If you change them, existing
    ' clients will no longer be able to access the class.
    Public Const ClassId As String = "9CC4547F-CE33-46A4-8583-36AC54C93693"
    Public Const InterfaceId As String = "38A6BBD7-6BA6-431E-A94B-B69C50AAFE45"
    Public Const EventsId As String = "49447BA2-37D8-4853-A09F-1C94A07DFDED"
#End Region

    ' A creatable COM class must have a Public Sub New()
    ' with no parameters, otherwise, the class will not be
    ' registered in the COM registry and cannot be created
    ' via CreateObject.
    Public Sub New()
        MyBase.New()
    End Sub

End Class
```

The `ClassId` value is used for the class's CLSID, and the `InterfaceId` value is used for the generated _ComClass1 interface's IID. The `EventsId` value is explained in the following chapter. Having to use fixed GUIDs for the .NET class and its generated interface is not ideal because it places the responsibility of proper versioning on the programmer. If you don't change the CLSID from one version of your assembly to another, it's easy to introduce incompatible types that break existing COM clients. Furthermore, as discussed in the previous chapter, fixed GUIDs negatively impact side-by-side assemblies.

Despite the danger of using explicit GUIDs, using the `ComClassAttribute` overload that expects all three GUIDs is the best one to use, due to the way that the VB .NET compiler automatically chooses any GUIDs that you don't explicitly pass. Unlike the CLR's algorithm for automatically generating GUIDs (covered in the previous chapter), the VB .NET compiler generates different GUIDs each time you recompile (using `Build`, `Rebuild Solution` in Visual Studio .NET), even if nothing about the assembly or class changes! This behavior is very bad because a simple re-compilation can break your compatibility with COM clients.

The nested _ClassName interface generated by the VB .NET compiler is a dual interface containing all the public COM-visible members defined directly on the class. Unlike auto-dual or auto-dispatch class interfaces, it does *not* provide access to members of base classes. Although this attribute internally uses the recommended approach of `ClassInterfaceType.None` with an explicitly defined interface, the problem is that the developer doesn't have enough control over

12

COM's VIEW OF .NET COMPONENTS

this interface generated by the VB .NET compiler. If you add or rearrange members of a class marked with `ComClassAttribute`, its auto-generated interface changes (while keeping the same IID if you passed one to the attribute's constructor) and can easily break COM clients. If you had explicitly defined the interface implemented by a .NET class instead, then you would have had to go out of your way to break compatibility with COM.

Making APIs Invisible to COM

By default, all public types and members are exposed to COM whereas non-public types and members are not. (The two exceptions to this rule are non-public fields of a value type, as discussed in Chapter 9, "An In-Depth Look at Exported Type Libraries," and interfaces marked with `ComImportAttribute`, discussed in Chapter 21, "Manually Defining COM Types in Source Code.") This behavior can be changed with `ComVisibleAttribute`, which takes a boolean parameter. The custom attribute can be placed on assemblies, classes, structs, enums, methods, properties, fields, interfaces, and delegates.

Using `ComVisibleAttribute`, you can't make private types or members appear public, but you can make public types or members appear private. Thus, `ComVisibleAttribute` is used to *restrict* the direct use of a .NET component from COM. Like C#'s `internal` keyword which means "public inside the assembly but private outside," `ComVisibleAttribute` enables you to express "public to .NET clients but private to COM clients." If you mark an assembly with `ComVisible(false)`, you can override the setting on individual types (classes, structs, etc.) to make them visible to COM. This is the only scenario in which the attribute overriding behavior works. For example, you can't mark a class with `ComVisible(false)` and some of its methods with `ComVisible(true)` and expect the marked methods to be visible.

FAQ: Why would someone want to limit the use of APIs to exclude COM clients?

Three reasons typically arise:

1. "My .NET APIs aren't COM-friendly, so rather than exposing hard-to-use pieces to COM, I'm making the whole thing invisible." For example, if your APIs make heavy use of static members and parameterized constructors, this might be an attractive option.

2. "I'm afraid of supporting customers who would use my component from COM because I don't test it." I believe this is a little like worrying about testing a component from every .NET language in existence, which is practically impossible.

3. "I need to add members to a class that already exposes an auto-dual class interface." This use of `ComVisibleAttribute` is really the only crucial need so such classes can be versioned without breaking COM clients. Even if you don't expose an auto-dual class interface, you might be concerned about others authoring classes that derive from yours and expose a class interface. This is a valid concern, because adding members to your base class would break such clients.

As discussed in Chapter 8, a COM-invisible *type* does not appear in an exported type library and is not registered. A COM-invisible *member* is omitted from the COM view of an interface (including the class interface, if one is generated). This, along with behavior enforced internally by the CLR, means that:

- A COM-invisible class cannot be created from COM.
- A COM-invisible interface can never be accessed via IUnknown's `QueryInterface` method (unless it's also marked with `ComImportAttribute`, which overrides `ComVisibleAttribute`).
- A COM-invisible member cannot be called from COM, even when late binding via `IDispatch`.

If a COM-invisible type is used as a parameter in a COM-visible method in a COM-visible type, one of two things can occur:

- If the invisible type is a reference type, the parameter is replaced with an `IUnknown` interface pointer. COM clients could only query for COM-visible interfaces and any standard interfaces implemented by the CCW except for `IDispatch`.
- If the invisible type is a value type, there is no generic replacement for it in the exported method, so the type library exporter skips the entire method. Unless the method appears at the end of an interface, there would be a gap between its surrounding methods that some type library viewers display with a dummy method.

The effects of having invisible types exposed as visible parameters are demonstrated in Listing 12.3.

LISTING 12.3   Exporting an Assembly Containing a COM-Visible Type with Members That Use COM-Invisible Types

C#:

```csharp
using System.Runtime.InteropServices;

// A reference type that's invisible to COM
[ComVisible(false)]
public class ClassForManagedEyesOnly
{
  ...
}

// A value type that's invisible to COM
[ComVisible(false)]
public struct StructForManagedEyesOnly
{
  ...
}

public interface IAmVisibleToAll
{
  void Method1(ClassForManagedEyesOnly x);
  void Method2(StructForManagedEyesOnly x);
}
```

The Only Type in the Exported Type Library:

```
[
  odl,
  uuid(03DD8145-5A1B-310F-9AFA-9132E7244590),
  version(1.0),
  dual,
  oleautomation,
  custom(0F21F359-AB84-41E8-9A78-36D110E6D2F9, IAmVisibleToAll)
]
interface IAmVisibleToAll : IDispatch {
    [id(0x60020000)]
    HRESULT Method1([in] IUnknown* x);
};
```

The exporter reports the method with the invisible value type parameter as a warning, giving the following message:

```
Type library exporter warning processing 'IAmVisibleToAll.Method2(x),
Chapter12'.  Warning: Non COM visible value type IAmVisibleToAll is being
referenced either from the type currently being exported or from
one of its base types.
```

> **TIP**
>
> If you decide to selectively make some types invisible to COM, make sure that the transitive closure is invisible, otherwise you might frustrate clients with unusable visible APIs that rely on invisible types. The least confusing thing to do for your customers is to leave everything visible to COM.

Marking a field of a value type or formatted reference type with `ComVisible(false)` has no effect because it's impossible to hide a structure's field from unmanaged code. Marking a field of a regular reference type with `ComVisible(false)` does have an effect; it hides the property that normally would be exposed for such a field.

Having gone through all the details of hiding types and members from COM, keep in mind that you really can't prevent COM clients from using your APIs. If nothing else, someone could write a COM-visible intermediate .NET layer that hands out all your COM-invisible functionality to COM. But, as demonstrated in Chapter 10, "Advanced Topics for Using .NET Components," by simply deriving from a COM-invisible class, a .NET class exposes these base members automatically—and can even expose them via an auto-dual class interface. If you have versioning concerns about users of your class doing this, you could make your class sealed (`NotInheritable` in VB .NET) or mark every member of the class with `ComVisible` (`false`). COM clients could still use these members as long as the class implements an interface that doesn't mark the members as COM-invisible.

Customizing Registration

Chapter 8 explained what `REGASM.EXE` places in the registry for each .NET class. To recap, for each public, COM-visible, and COM-creatable class in a regular .NET assembly, the built-in registration process places the following entries in the registry:

```
HKEY_CLASSES_ROOT\ProgID\[default]="NamespaceQualifiedClassName"
HKEY_CLASSES_ROOT\ProgID\CLSID\[default]="{CLSID}"
HKEY_CLASSES_ROOT\CLSID\{CLSID}\[default]="NamespaceQualifiedClassName"
HKEY_CLASSES_ROOT\CLSID\{CLSID}\Implemented Categories\
➡ {62C8FE65-4EBB-45E7-B440-6E39B2CDBF29}
HKEY_CLASSES_ROOT\CLSID\{CLSID}\InprocServer32\[default]=
➡ "WindowsSystemDirectory\mscoree.dll"
HKEY_CLASSES_ROOT\CLSID\{CLSID}\InprocServer32\Assembly="FullAssemblyName"
HKEY_CLASSES_ROOT\CLSID\{CLSID}\InprocServer32\Class=
➡ "NamespaceQualifiedClassName"
```

```
HKEY_CLASSES_ROOT\CLSID\{CLSID}\InprocServer32\RuntimeVersion="Version"
HKEY_CLASSES_ROOT\CLSID\{CLSID}\InprocServer32\ThreadingModel="Both"
HKEY_CLASSES_ROOT\CLSID\{CLSID}\ProgID\[default]="ProgID"
```

These entries enable the activation of the component via class identifier (CLSID) or programmatic identifier (ProgID) using the CLR execution engine as the in-process server. To customize these registry entries, COM Interoperability provides two features. One is a simple way to customize ProgIDs, and the other is a more complex but extremely flexible way to add or change arbitrary information at registration time. COM Interoperability also enables you to customize registered GUIDs, but this is covered in the next section because GUIDs have a wider scope than just registration.

Choosing Your Own ProgID

By default, the ProgID registered for a .NET class is simply the fully-qualified name (namespace + class name). Using `ProgIdAttribute`, you can change a class's ProgID to any string you'd like. `ProgIdAttribute` can be placed on classes only, and has one required string parameter that becomes the new ProgID. Why would you want to change the default ProgID? In most cases you won't, because it could cause confusion for COM users. The reason for this custom attribute's existence is that the fully-qualified class name is not always a valid ProgID. The rules of COM dictate that a ProgID must:

- Have 39 characters or less.
- Contain no punctuation besides periods—not even underscores.
- Not start with a digit.
- Be different from the class name of any OLE 1 application.

Thus, if you have a class name that violates any of these conditions, you might consider changing the ProgID. The first condition is pretty easy to break because a namespace alone can often be around 30 characters. That said, none of the classes in the .NET Framework use `ProgIdAttribute`, even for long names such as `System.Runtime.InteropServices.RegistrationServices`. Another reason for changing the default ProgID is to create a .NET class that replaces an existing COM class in a compatible way. This is discussed in Chapter 14, "Implementing COM Interfaces for Binary Compatibility." To suppress the registration of any ProgID for a .NET class, pass an empty string or null to `ProgIdAttribute`.

CAUTION

To the users of case-sensitive languages, be aware that the case of "ProgID" differs between `System.Type.GetTypeFromProgID` and `System.Runtime.InteropServices.ProgIdAttribute` (plus a few more APIs whose case matches `ProgIdAttribute`).

Adding Arbitrary Registration Code

If your COM clients require additional registry entries than those listed in the previous section, you basically have two options to provide these entries:

- Add logic to your installation program to add the necessary registry entries. This can easily be done with one of Visual Studio .NET's "Setup and Deployment Projects."

- Hook into the standard registration process. It's possible to define a registration method and an unregistration method that get invoked by the `RegistrationServices.RegisterAssembly` API in `System.Runtime.InteropServices`, the same method called by `REGASM.EXE` to perform assembly registration.

The first option is pictured in Figure 12.1. To create a setup project with custom registry entries, perform the following steps:

1. In Visual Studio .NET, create a new `Setup Project`, found under the `Setup and Deployment Projects` folder in the `New Project` dialog.

2. Inside the project, select the `View, Editor, Registry` menu to use the Visual Studio .NET Registry Editor.

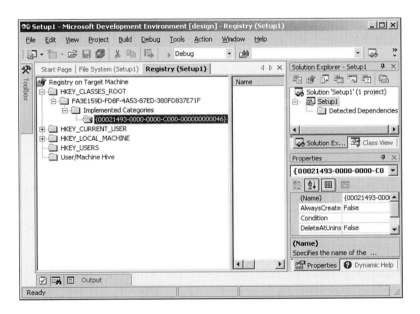

FIGURE 12.1

Adding custom registry entries in a Visual Studio .NET deployment project.

The registry editor is easy to use, although it only works with static information. For example, you most likely need to know the CLSID of your .NET class and hard-code it into the registry keys. The easiest way to know your CLSIDs is to mark your .NET classes with explicit CLSIDs (as shown in the next section). However, using explicit CLSIDs is not preferred because it involves more effort and is error-prone when it comes to versioning.

The second option can be done using two custom attributes—ComRegisterFunctionAttribute and ComUnregisterFunctionAttribute. A method marked with either one of these attributes must be static and return void (a Shared Sub in Visual Basic .NET), and have one by-value System.Type parameter.

When each class is registered by REGASM.EXE (or RegistrationServices.RegisterAssembly) a method marked with ComRegisterFunction is executed if it exists. Similarly, when each class is unregistered using REGASM.EXE with the /unregister option (or RegistrationServices. UnregisterAssembly) a method marked with ComUnregisterFunction is executed if it exists. These methods can do anything you want, but typically they only update the registry using the APIs in the Microsoft.Win32 namespace. If registering an assembly causes a security exception to be thrown, chances are that the assembly has a custom registration function that doesn't have permission to do what it's trying to do. This can often happen when registering assemblies from the intranet zone.

When executed, the System.Type parameter is the type of the class being registered. This is handy for getting information like the class's CLSID, because you don't know the CLR-generated GUID when defining the class. To obtain the CLSID of the class being registered, simply use System. Type's GUID property. An example of a custom registration and unregistration function is demonstrated in the following Visual Basic .NET code:

```
Imports System
Imports System.Runtime.InteropServices

Public Class ClassWithCustomRegistration
  <ComRegisterFunction> _
  Private Shared Sub RegisterFunction(t As Type)
    ' Add a custom key to the registry
    Dim key As Microsoft.Win32.RegistryKey
    key = Microsoft.Win32.Registry.ClassesRoot.CreateSubKey( _
      "CLSID\" & t.GUID.ToString("B") & "\Implemented Categories\" _
      & "{00021493-0000-0000-C000-000000000046}")
    key.Close()
  End Sub

  <ComUnregisterFunction> _
  Private Shared Sub UnregisterFunction(t As Type)
    ' Undo the work from the registration function
```

```
   Microsoft.Win32.Registry.ClassesRoot.DeleteSubKey( _
      "CLSID\" & t.GUID.ToString("B") & "\Implemented Categories\" _
      & "{00021493-0000-0000-C000-000000000046}", False)
   End Sub
End Class
```

The preceding code is an example of how to register a .NET class with an arbitrary COM component category. The extra registry key added by the registration function adds a category indicated with `{00021493-0000-0000-C000-000000000046}` under the `Implemented Categories` registry branch. This GUID (also known as a Category ID, or CATID) belongs to the "Internet Explorer Browser Band" category.

TIP

Custom unregistration functions should be robust enough to handle double unregistration. In other words, if a user runs `REGASM.EXE` with the /u option twice in a row on your assembly, your unregistration function should not throw an exception. When using `RegistryKey.DeleteSubKey` to accomplish key deletion, this is as simple as using the overloaded method with two parameters and passing false for the second `throwOnMissingSubKey` parameter. All custom unregistration functions in this book use this overloaded method in order to be well-behaved.

FAQ: Is there a .NET replacement for COM component categories?

No, there is not in version 1.0 of the .NET Framework. COM component categories can be useful for applications with plug-ins to quickly enumerate the available components it can work with. However, because xcopy deployment is a major theme of .NET applications, there's no central registry-like location that advertises the categories in which .NET components on the computer belong to. Of course, the same COM component category mechanism can be used for .NET components, as demonstrated in this section.

A .NET application could load every assembly in the Global Assembly Cache and use reflection to find the desired components (typically looking for classes that implement a certain interface), but the performance of such an approach is usually unacceptable. Typically .NET applications that wish to enable plug-in functionality instead maintain a private subdirectory that should contain copies of any assemblies it wishes to use for plug-ins. The application can then load and reflect over these private assemblies (usually in a separate application domain), which is faster than using the GAC because all of the assemblies should be relevant to the host application.

> **TIP**
>
> Registration functions should use an overload of `System.Guid.ToString` to ensure that GUIDs written to the registry have their customary curly braces. Passing "B" as a string format specifier parameter can do just that. For a `System.Guid` object g, this:
>
>   g.ToString("B")
>
> is equivalent to:
>
>   "{" + g.ToString() + "}"
>
> The following table shows the handful of GUID format specifiers available:
>
> | Use of Format Specifier | Format of the Returned String |
> | --- | --- |
> | g.ToString() or g.ToString("D") | 051fdbdb-f1a0-41ef-bf21-ddae8bd34546 |
> | g.ToString("B") | {051fdbdb-f1a0-41ef-bf21-ddae8bd34546} |
> | g.ToString("P") | (051fdbdb-f1a0-41ef-bf21-ddae8bd34546) |
> | g.ToString("N") | 051fdbdbf1a041efbf21ddae8bd34546 |

The pair of custom registration methods can have any visibility—public, private, protected, and so on—and still be invoked by the system. In fact, private registration and unregistration functions are recommended because there should be no need to expose them to your users. The class containing the methods, however, must be public and COM-visible. If not, the assembly registration process would skip over the class without checking its methods.

An assembly can have multiple registration and unregistration functions, but one type cannot have more than one of each. Such an error is caught by the `RegistrationServices` API, so `REGASM.EXE`, for example, would print a message like the following:

```
RegAsm error: Type ABC has more than one COM registration function.
```

If any classes derive from a base class with a registration function, the function is called for the base class as well as every class that derives from it. The one exception is that if a derived class defines its own registration function, the base function is not called by the system. Instead, if desired, the derived function is responsible for calling the base function. In short, `RegisterAssembly` invokes the most derived method marked with `ComRegisterFunction` and the most derived method marked with `ComUnregisterFunction`—at most one per class. Furthermore, the `System.Type` parameter is always set to the type of the class currently being registered, so a single registration function in a base class may get invoked several times, each time with a different parameter value. Having generic registration and unregistration functions in a common base class can be useful so derived classes that may require custom registration can get it with no effort and without even realizing that custom registration is occurring. (If a derived class happens to define its own custom registration function, however, it would need to know to call the base function.)

There are four main guidelines for implementing custom registration functions:

1. Define registration and unregistration functions only if absolutely necessary.

2. Although it is possible to define only one or the other, implement both a registration and an unregistration function as a complimentary pair.

3. Be sure that the unregistration function undoes *everything* that was done in the registration function.

4. Although arbitrary code could be written inside such methods, stick to modifying the registry. This is most easily done using the Windows Registry APIs provided by the .NET Framework in the `Microsoft.Win32` namespace (in the `mscorlib` assembly).

Developers are strongly discouraged from using custom registration functions because user-written registration code is error-prone and hard to track. This mechanism is provided solely for backward compatibility with COM clients that expect the extra registration.

12

COM's View
OF .NET
Components

Digging Deeper

A class's custom registration function is invoked *after* the standard registry entries have been added for the class. Thus, you can safely add new entries under `HKEY_CLASSES_ROOT\CLSID\{CLSID}` or `HKEY_CLASSES_ROOT\CLSID\{CLSID}\InprocServer32`, for example, without having to worry about creating the keys. It's even possible to modify the standard values set by `REGASM.EXE`, but there should be no reason to do this. Similarly, a class's custom unregistration function is invoked *before* the standard registry entries have been removed for the class. You only need to worry about removing the keys or values you added. The entire `HKEY_CLASSES_ROOT\CLSID\{CLSID}` branch will be removed by the system as long as you cleaned up any values you may have added underneath.

If `REGASM.EXE` was invoked with its `/tlb` switch, however, the type library registration is done *after* all the custom registration methods have been invoked. Thus, you can't rely on type library-related values being in the registry, nor can you determine whether or not the user used the `/tlb` option inside your custom registration functions.

Windows Media Player is one example of a COM client that looks in a special section of the registry to locate COM objects that implement *visualizations*. More information on this is given in Chapter 24, "Writing .NET Visualizations for Windows Media Player." Listing 12.6 shows what registering such an object for Windows Media Player might look like using the Windows Registry APIs provided by the .NET Framework.

LISTING 12.6   Custom Registration Required for Plugging a Component into Windows Media Player

```
1: public class MyVisualization
2: {
3:   [ComRegisterFunction]
4:   private static void ComRegisterFunction(Type t)
5:   {
6:     Microsoft.Win32.RegistryKey key =
➥ Microsoft.Win32.Registry.LocalMachine;
7:     key = key.CreateSubKey("Software\\Microsoft\\MediaPlayer\\" +
8:       "Objects\\Effects\\Visualization Sample\\Properties");
9:     key.SetValue("classid", t.GUID.ToString("B"));
10:    key.SetValue("name", "Visualization Sample");
11:    key.SetValue("description",
12:      "This collection includes a visualization written in C#.");
13:    key.Close();
14:  }
15:
16:   [ComUnregisterFunction]
17:   private static void ComUnregisterFunction(Type t)
18:   {
19:     Microsoft.Win32.RegistryKey key =
➥ Microsoft.Win32.Registry.LocalMachine;
20:     key.DeleteSubKey("Software\\Microsoft\\MediaPlayer\\" +
21:       "Objects\\Effects\\Visualization Sample\\Properties", false);
22:     key.DeleteSubKey("Software\\Microsoft\\MediaPlayer\\" +
23:       "Objects\\Effects\\Visualization Sample", false);
24:  }
25:
26:   ...
27: }
```

Unfortunately, there are two major drawbacks that make ComRegisterFunctionAttribute and ComUnregisterFunctionAttribute useless in some common deployment scenarios. First, the registry files (.reg files) produced by REGASM.EXE do not contain any information about custom registration because there's no standard mechanism for REGASM.EXE to determine what a custom registration function does; it simply invokes it. The fact that .reg files can be incomplete is not a big deal by itself because users shouldn't directly be using these files anyway. (In version 1.0, the .reg files produced contain the full path of mscoree.dll, which can change on a machine-by-machine basis. Also, the backslashes in this path are not properly escaped, so using them directly won't even work on the same machine without modifications.)

The second drawback is that the built-in Visual Studio .NET support for registering an assembly in a Setup project bases its actions on the .reg file produced by REGASM.EXE. It does this intentionally because of the widely-held belief that user-written registration code should be avoided whenever possible. That way, the uninstallation process is guaranteed to clean up everything that was installed. You can exercise the built-in support using the following steps:

1. Inside a Visual Studio .NET Setup Project, select Project, Add, Assembly... from the menu.
2. Select the assembly that you want added to the Setup project using the Component Selector dialog, which works much like the Add Reference dialog introduced in Chapter 3, "The Essentials for Using COM in Managed Code."
3. Select the assembly in the Solution Explorer then change its Register property in the Properties window to something other than vsdraDoNotRegister, as shown in Figure 12.2.

FIGURE 12.2
Registering an assembly with built-in Visual Studio .NET support.

When building a Setup project with assemblies to be registered upon installation, Visual Studio .NET effectively runs REGASM.EXE with its /regfile option on any appropriate assemblies to figure out what to register when the installation is run. It treats all InProcServer entries specially, however, so they work on any computer.

If you want to run custom registration functions in a Setup project, you must add a custom action to run REGASM.EXE during the installation and possibly uninstallation phases.

Providing Your Own GUIDs

The automatically-generated GUIDs should always be sufficient, but if you'd like to choose your own GUIDs, you can use the GuidAttribute custom attribute to mark a variety of targets with a GUID. Be careful when doing this, however, because it's easy to make mistakes (such as using the same CLSID in multiple versions of a class and limiting its side-by-side capability). The attribute has one required string parameter that must be in a format like "051fdbdb-f1a0-41ef-bf21-ddae8bd34546" (with dashes but no curly braces). The attribute can be placed on the following targets, taking on the following meanings:

Assembly	The LIBID of the exported type library.
Class	The coclass's CLSID.
Interface	The interface's IID.
Delegate	The CLSID of the delegate class.
Struct	The GUID for the exported struct.
Enum	The GUID for the exported enum.

For example, you can use GuidAttribute to choose your own LIBID as follows:

C#:

```
[assembly:Guid("051fdbdb-f1a0-41ef-bf21-ddae8bd34546")]
```

Visual Basic .NET:

```
<Assembly:Guid("051fdbdb-f1a0-41ef-bf21-ddae8bd34546")>
```

C++:

```
[assembly:Guid("051fdbdb-f1a0-41ef-bf21-ddae8bd34546")]
```

Providing Your Own DISPIDs

As covered in earlier chapters, a DISPID is a number assigned to members of an interface derived from IDispatch. By default, DISPIDs are automatically assigned to members of exported interfaces. There's no real compelling reason to choose your own DISPIDs when defining new .NET types, but it can be done with the DispIdAttribute. This attribute can be placed on methods, properties, and fields, and has a required integer parameter set to the DISPID's value.

The special DISPID value `DISPID_NEWENUM` (-4) should normally not be marked directly but rather obtained by implementing `IEnumerable`, as shown in the previous chapter. Of course, when implementing `IEnumerable` "privately," `DispId(-4)` should be added to the strongly-typed public enumeration method named `GetEnumerator`, if it exists.

The special DISPID value `DISPID_VALUE` (0) also does not normally need to be used. When defining a default *property* in managed code (which, at the metadata level, is indicated by the class or interface having the `DefaultMemberAttribute`) the type library exporter automatically marks it with a DISPID equal to zero. When defining a default *method*, however, the type library exporter assigns it a regular DISPID unless you manually mark it with `DispId(0)`. This is asymmetrical to the type library *importer*, which generates `DefaultMemberAttribute` when encountering default methods in a type library.

As described in Chapter 8, auto-generated class interfaces have a default `ToString` property. However, if you define your own default property (using `DefaultMemberAttribute` or `DispIdAttribute`) or default method or field (using `DispIdAttribute`), `ToString` is assigned a regular DISPID because only one member can be the default. This is demonstrated with the C# code in Listing 12.7.

LISTING 12.7   Exposing a Different Default Member Than `ToString` to COM Clients

C#:

```csharp
using System.Runtime.InteropServices;
using System.Reflection;

// Generate dual interfaces so we can see what is exposed to COM
[assembly:ClassInterface(ClassInterfaceType.AutoDual)]

public class C1
{
  // A regular C# indexer
  public int this[int i]
  {
    get { return 0; }
  }
}

[DefaultMember("Item")]
public class C2
{
  // A plain default property
  public int Item
  {
```

LISTING 12.7   Continued

```
    get { return 0; }
  }
}

[DefaultMember("Item")]
public class C3
{
  // A default method
  [DispId(0)]
  public int Item() { return 0; }
}
```

Class Interfaces in Exported Type Library:

```
[
  odl,
  uuid(4E65E783-E8E4-3C8D-A635-A000FC200936),
  hidden,
  dual,
  nonextensible,
  oleautomation,
  custom(0F21F359-AB84-41E8-9A78-36D110E6D2F9, "C1")
]
interface _C1 : IDispatch {
  [id(0x60020000), propget, custom(54FC8F55-38DE-4703-9C4E-250351302B1C, 1)]
  HRESULT ToString([out, retval] BSTR* pRetVal);
  [id(0x60020001)]
  HRESULT Equals([in] VARIANT obj, [out, retval] VARIANT_BOOL* pRetVal);
  [id(0x60020002)]
  HRESULT GetHashCode([out, retval] long* pRetVal);
  [id(0x60020003)]
  HRESULT GetType([out, retval] _Type** pRetVal);
  [id(00000000), propget]
  HRESULT Item([in] long i, [out, retval] long* pRetVal);
};

[
  odl,
  uuid(587F665C-54E3-3EC1-8A45-877BF20334AA),
  hidden,
  dual,
  nonextensible,
  oleautomation,
  custom(0F21F359-AB84-41E8-9A78-36D110E6D2F9, "C2")
]
```

Customizing COM's View of .NET Components

Chapter 12

577

12

COM's VIEW
OF .NET
COMPONENTS

LISTING 12.7   Continued

```
interface _C2 : IDispatch {
  [id(0x60020000), propget, custom(54FC8F55-38DE-4703-9C4E-250351302B1C, 1)]
  HRESULT ToString([out, retval] BSTR* pRetVal);
  [id(0x60020001)]
  HRESULT Equals([in] VARIANT obj, [out, retval] VARIANT_BOOL* pRetVal);
  [id(0x60020002)]
  HRESULT GetHashCode([out, retval] long* pRetVal);
  [id(0x60020003)]
  HRESULT GetType([out, retval] _Type** pRetVal);
  [id(00000000), propget]
  HRESULT Item([out, retval] long* pRetVal);
};

[
  odl,
  uuid(36F2A0CF-7264-3F12-8F17-CEB1EC1F20C3),
  hidden,
  dual,
  nonextensible,
  oleautomation,
  custom(0F21F359-AB84-41E8-9A78-36D110E6D2F9, "C3")
]
interface _C3 : IDispatch {
  [id(0x60020000), propget]
  HRESULT ToString([out, retval] BSTR* pRetVal);
  [id(0x60020001)]
  HRESULT Equals([in] VARIANT obj, [out, retval] VARIANT_BOOL* pRetVal);
  [id(0x60020002)]
  HRESULT GetHashCode([out, retval] long* pRetVal);
  [id(0x60020003)]
  HRESULT GetType([out, retval] _Type** pRetVal);
  [id(00000000), propget, custom(54FC8F55-38DE-4703-9C4E-250351302B1C, 1)]
  HRESULT Item([out, retval] long* pRetVal);
};
```

The C1 class uses a standard C# indexer, which produces similar metadata to the default member in C2. The only difference between these default members is that C2's Item property does not have a parameter (and thus isn't treated by C# as a default member). The C3 class has a default method rather than a property. The DispId(0) is needed to be treated as a default member by COM, and the DefaultMember("Item") is needed to be treated as a default member by .NET. Either one could be used independently, but using both provides a consistent picture to both worlds. Notice that C3.Item is transformed from a method to a property when exposed to COM. This is done for the same reason that ToString is transformed to a property, and is mainly for the benefit of Visual Basic 6 clients.

> **CAUTION**
>
> The results of marking a class's member with `DispId(0)` is a little quirky when inheritance is involved. Every member of an interface must have a unique DISPID, which is why marking a member with `DispId(0)` causes the exporter to give the base `ToString` property a regular DISPID. However, if more than one member (excluding `ToString`) is marked with `DispId(0)` anywhere in the class or its base classes, the custom attributes are ignored and `ToString` is left as the default member for the corresponding class interface.

Controlling Interface Derivation

By default, all .NET interfaces are seen as dual interfaces from COM. This gives COM clients both choices—the flexibility of late binding or the performance of early binding. If you don't want to expose dual interfaces, this behavior can be modified with `InterfaceTypeAttribute`. This custom attribute can be placed on—you guessed it—interfaces. This custom attribute has one required parameter—a value of the `ComInterfaceType` enumeration. This enumeration defines three values:

- `ComInterfaceType.InterfaceIsDual`. This is the default behavior, so this value never needs to be used explicitly.

- `ComInterfaceType.InterfaceIsIUnknown`. Exposes the interface as deriving directly from `IUnknown`, so COM clients cannot late bind to members of the interface.

- `ComInterfaceType.InterfaceIsIDispatch`. Exposes the interfaces as a dispinterface, so late binding is the *only* way for COM clients to call its members.

Usually there's no need to change the default behavior when defining new .NET interfaces. One area in which these attributes are essential is the re-definition of COM interfaces, so the metadata can faithfully represent the original interface definitions (covered in Chapter 21). You could mark an interface with `InterfaceType(ComInterfaceType.InterfaceIsIUnknown)` if you want to disallow late binding to the interface's methods. However, a class implementing such an interface could make the methods available through its class interface if it didn't specify `ClassInterface (ClassInterfaceType.None)`. Also, using `InterfaceType(ComInterfaceType. InterfaceIsIDispatch)` is necessary when exposing event interfaces to Visual Basic 6 clients. This technique is described in Chapter 13.

> **CAUTION**
>
> Beware of the misleading `InterfaceIsIDispatch` name. This does not simply mean an interface deriving from `IDispatch`, because such an interface can be (and usually is) dual. An interface marked with `InterfaceIsIDispatch` can *only* be called using late binding. Think of it as "InterfaceIsDispOnly." Furthermore, as with all the COM Interoperability custom attributes, it is *not* valid to combine the enumeration values with bitwise operators. For example (in Visual Basic .NET terminology), `ComInterfaceType.InterfaceIsIUnknown Or ComInterfaceType.InterfaceIsIDispatch` does not give you a dual interface—that's what `ComInterfaceType.InterfaceIsDual` is for.
>
> A hint that tells you that the enumeration's values are not bit flags is that the enumeration itself is not marked with `System.FlagsAttribute`. This custom attribute should be marked on any enumerations that represent bit flags. Although not all enumerations in the .NET Framework obey this rule (as there are several that represent bit flags yet are not marked with `Flags`), the enumerations in the `System.Runtime.InteropServices` namespace do (plus their names actually end with a `Flags` suffix).

`InterfaceTypeAttribute` cannot be used to affect auto-generated class interfaces. Class interfaces fabricated by the CLR are either dual or disp-only based on the `ClassInterfaceAttribute` custom attribute.

Returning a Specific HRESULT

You can control the failure HRESULTs seen by COM clients by the type of exceptions thrown in error situations. Assuming .NET clients might use your .NET component, you should avoid throwing a `COMException`. Instead, stick to the .NET exception types such as `ApplicationException`, `ArgumentException`, and so on. Refer to the table in Appendix D, ".NET Exception to HRESULT Transformations," to see how each exception is exposed as an HRESULT return value.

If you must return a well-known COM HRESULT that isn't covered by the .NET exceptions (such as `DISP_E_EXCEPTION`), go ahead and throw a `COMException` with that value. You could even throw a `COMException` with a success HRESULT value to make the method return a success HRESULT to COM, but this is strongly discouraged due to the cost of throwing an exception.

The preferred way to expose success HRESULTs to COM is to use the familiar `PreserveSigAttribute`, valid on methods only. As you've seen throughout previous chapters, placing `PreserveSigAttribute` on a method causes whatever return type to remain the return type in the COM signature. Listing 12.8 demonstrates the good and the bad ways of returning a success HRESULT to COM.

LISTING 12.8   Returning the Success HRESULT S_FALSE (a Value of 1) from C# Code

```
 1: using System.Runtime.InteropServices;
 2:
 3: public class C
 4: {
 5:   public void ReturnSFalseBad()
 6:   {
 7:     // Throwing an exception should be reserved for failure due
 8:     // to the overhead of exception handling
 9:     throw new COMException("Success Result", 1);
10:   }
11:
12:   [return:MarshalAs(UnmanagedType.Error)]
13:   [PreserveSig]
14:   public int ReturnSFalseGood()
15:   {
16:     // Returning an integer is much faster than throwing an exception
17:     return 1;
18:   }
19: }
```

When throwing the "success exception" on Line 9, a description is given simply because no constructor for COMException accepts only an HRESULT value. MarshalAsAttribute is used on Line 12 so the exported method looks like it returns an HRESULT in the exported type library rather than simply a long type.

> **TIP**
>
> Both techniques in Listing 12.8 should be done only if absolutely required for backward compatibility. Throwing a success exception is bad for performance, and returning an HRESULT with PreserveSigAttribute is not appropriate for .NET clients. If you're creating new .NET APIs, there should be no reason to create a design involving success HRESULTs (or HRESULTs at all, for that matter).

Disabling Type Library Marshaling of .NET Interfaces

By default, all .NET interfaces are registered with the OLE Automation type library marshaler. When an exported type library is registered (using REGASM.EXE's /tlb option, for instance), the following entries are added to the registry for each interface:

```
HKEY_CLASSES_ROOT\Interface\{IID}\[default]="InterfaceName"
HKEY_CLASSES_ROOT\Interface\{IID}\ProxyStubClsid\(Default)=
  "{00020424-0000-0000-C000-000000000046}"
HKEY_CLASSES_ROOT\Interface\{IID}\ProxyStubClsid32\(Default)=
  "{00020424-0000-0000-C000-000000000046}"
HKEY_CLASSES_ROOT\Interface\{IID}\TypeLib\[default]="{LIBID}"
HKEY_CLASSES_ROOT\Interface\{IID}\TypeLib\Version="Major.Minor"
```

(The GUID {00020424-0000-0000-C000-000000000046} is the LIBID for the OLE Automation type library.) This means that if a .NET interface needs to be marshaled COM-style across context boundaries (apartments, threads, or processes), the interface had better only use OLE Automation-compatible data types and the exported type library had better be registered.

Just as with traditional COM objects, you can register your own proxy/stub marshaler for .NET objects to handle interface marshaling if type library marshaling is not acceptable. Custom proxy/stub marshalers can achieve higher performance, can work with any data types, and usually don't require a type library containing the interface definitions to be registered. There is no extra support in the .NET Framework or Visual Studio .NET for creating such a proxy/stub marshaler, however. You could create one by defining the interfaces that need to be marshaled in IDL and running MIDL.EXE to generate the proxy/stub code, just as you did before .NET existed.

The problem with registering a custom proxy/stub marshaler is that registering an exported type library adds the registry entries shown previously and can overwrite registry entries for a custom proxy/stub marshaler. Furthermore, it's pretty easy to accidentally register a type library, as opening one in OLEVIEW.EXE causes this registration. To prevent this from happening, you can use AutomationProxyAttribute to suppress this registration.

AutomationProxyAttribute has a boolean parameter, and can be marked on classes, interfaces, or assemblies. Just like ComVisibleAttribute, a default behavior can be marked for an entire assembly and overridden on individual types. Because AutomationProxyAttribute only applies to COM interfaces, marking it on a class determines the behavior of the class interface, if it exists.

The default for all interfaces is AutomationProxy(true), but marking an interface with AutomationProxy(false) means that the type library exporter will mark the exported interface with the TYPEFLAG_FPROXY flag. This flag is what suppresses the interface registration. Typically when this flag is set, [oleautomation] is not set (and vice-versa), but the [oleautomation] flag appears for all exported interfaces regardless of AutomationProxyAttribute settings. The TYPELIB_FPROXY flag is not displayed by OLEVIEW.EXE, so the only way to see the difference between interfaces marked with AutomationProxy(false) and interfaces that aren't is to register an exported type library and notice the difference in registration.

If you must define an interface that uses types that are not OLE Automation-compatible, the best approach is to define a COM interface in IDL that gets registered with a proxy/stub marshaler, and then import a type library containing its definition so it can be implemented by a .NET class. Such an interface doesn't need to be marked with AutomationProxyAttribute to affect its proper registration because MIDL already takes care of that when emitting its definition to a type library.

Creating Multi-Cultured Methods

COM methods and properties sometimes have a special parameter containing a locale identifier (LCID) marked in a type library with the lcid IDL attribute. Such a parameter enables the method implementer to take special action based on the user's locale. The parameter is marked with lcid so rich clients can recognize its purpose and automatically pass an appropriate value for it. For example, Visual Basic 6 hides lcid parameters just like it hides HRESULT return values. At run time, the Visual Basic 6 runtime fills in the value of the user's locale, obtained from the operating system. Similarly, COM's ITypeInfo.Invoke method handles the LCID for the user.

.NET methods and properties that wish to expose an lcid parameter to COM can do so using LCIDConversionAttribute. This has an integer parameter that represents a zero-based offset of which parameter should be the lcid parameter. Unlike the zero-based offset used with MarshalAsAttribute's SizeParamIndex named parameter, this offset doesn't refer to an existing parameter, but one that is inserted into the COM definition. For example, marking a method as follows:

```
[LCIDConversion(0)]
void MultiCulturalMethod(int a, int b) { ... }
```

causes a new 0th parameter to be inserted containing the LCID. The view from IDL is:

```
HRESULT MultiCulturalMethod([in, lcid] long p1, [in] long a, [in] long b);
```

and the view from a VB6 user's perspective is the same as if no LCID were listed because the runtime takes care of the extra parameter. LCIDConversionAttribute can be used with any number from 0 to the number of parameters, so you could make the last parameter of the preceding method an LCID parameter by marking it as follows:

```
[LCIDConversion(2)]
void MultiCulturalMethod(int a, int b) { ... }
```

In this case the third parameter contains the LCID (or the second, counting from zero):

```
HRESULT MultiCulturalMethod([in] long a, [in] long b, [in, lcid] long p3);
```

In fact, although an lcid parameter can appear anywhere, the convention is for the last parameter (not counting the retval parameter) to contain the LCID.

Because, from the perspective of the .NET method implementer, the `lcid` parameter does not exist, how can you find its value and take action appropriately? You can find its value from the current thread's culture, obtained from the `CurrentCulture` on the `System.Threading.Thread` class.

`LCIDConversionAttribute` is only allowed on a method. Therefore, to use it with a property you must place it on the get and/or set accessors. For example, in Visual Basic .NET:

```
Public Property MyProperty As String
  <LCIDConversion(0)> _
  Get
    ...
  End Get
  <LCIDConversion(0)> _
  Set
    ...
  End Set
End Property
```

`LCIDConversionAttribute` is not supported on dispinterfaces.

Using Optional Parameters in Any Language

For languages (like C#) that don't support optional parameters, it is still possible to *define* methods with optional parameters, thanks to the `OptionalAttribute` custom attribute. Although C# clients ignore the attribute, COM clients or even .NET clients written in Visual Basic .NET can treat them optionally! For example, the following C# method:

```
using System.Runtime.InteropServices;
using System;

public class UsingOptional
{
  public void HasOptional([Optional] int x, [Optional] object y)
  {
    Console.WriteLine("x = " + x);
    Console.WriteLine("y = " + y);
  }
}
```

can be called from Visual Basic .NET as follows, omitting both parameters:

```
Public Module Client
  Public Sub Main
    Dim x as UsingOptional = new UsingOptional()
    x.HasOptional()
  End Sub
End Module
```

Because C# doesn't know anything about optional parameters, what will it see inside the method at run time? Missing value type parameters appear as zeroed-out structures, and missing reference type parameters appear as `System.Reflection.Missing` types. Thus, running the previous code would produce the following output:

```
x = 0
y = System.Reflection.Missing
```

Unfortunately, there's no way to specify default values for optional parameters unless the language supports it.

When designing .NET APIs, it's a good idea to avoid optional parameters because they aren't always supported. If you're primarily concerned about COM clients, however, optional parameters are a better choice than overloaded methods due to name conflict resolution (_2, _3, ...). `OptionalAttribute` is mainly intended for manually defining COM interfaces that use optional parameters in languages like C#. This technique is shown in Chapter 21.

Exposing .NET Objects As COM+ Objects

Any .NET class that derives from `System.EnterpriseServices.ServicedComponent` (defined in the `System.EnterpriseServices` assembly) can be exposed as a COM+ configured component. An assembly containing at least one serviced component acts as a COM+ application. COM+ attributes that customize component behavior are configurable in managed code as .NET custom attributes in the `System.EnterpriseServices` namespace. These custom attributes include:

- `ApplicationCrmEnabledAttribute`. Can be marked on an assembly to enable the Compensating Resource Manager (CRM). Unlike the others, this custom attribute resides in the `System.EnterpriseServices.CompensatingResourceManager` namespace.

- `ApplicationAccessControlAttribute`. Can be marked on an assembly to control the security of the host application.

- `ApplicationActivationAttribute`. Can be marked on an assembly to control whether the assembly runs as a library application or a server application. By default, assemblies are treated as library applications.

- `ApplicationIDAttribute`. Can be marked on an assembly to specify an application identifier (AppID). This is a GUID in the same string format used with `System.Runtime.InteropServices.GuidAttribute`.

- `ApplicationNameAttribute`. Can be marked on an assembly to control the name of the COM+ application.

- `ApplicationQueuingAttribute`. Can be marked on an assembly to control the queuing support of the host application.

Customizing COM's View of .NET Components

CHAPTER 12

585

12

COM'S VIEW
OF .NET
COMPONENTS

- `AutoCompleteAttribute`. Can be marked on a method to enable automatic object deactivation when the method call returns.

- `ComponentAccessControlAttribute`. Can be marked on a class to enable or disable security checks.

- `COMTIIntrinsicsAttribute`. Can be marked on a class to enable passing context properties from the COM Transaction Integrator (COMTI) into the COM+ context.

- `ConstructionEnabledAttribute`. Can be marked on a class to enable support for a construction string and to provide a default string.

- `DescriptionAttribute`. Can be marked on an assembly, class, interface, or method, to apply descriptions that can be seen in the Component Services (COM+) Explorer.

- `EventClassAttribute`. Can be marked on a class to designate it as an event class in the COM+ loosely-coupled events system.

- `EventTrackingEnabledAttribute`. Can be marked on a class to advertise that it supports events and statistics tracking.

- `ExceptionClassAttribute`. Can be marked on a class to designate it as an exception class for a queued component.

- `IISIntrinsicsAttribute`. Can be marked on a class to enable `ContextUtil.GetNamedProperty` to access ASP intrinsics.

- `InterfaceQueuingAttribute`. Can be marked on a class or interface to enable queuing support.

- `JustInTimeActivationAttribute`. Can be marked on a class to enable or disable just-in-time activation.

- `LoadBalancingSupportedAttribute`. Can be marked on a class to advertise whether it contributes to load balancing.

- `MustRunInClientContextAttribute`. Can be marked on a class to state that it must be activated in its caller's context.

- `ObjectPoolingAttribute`. Can be marked on a class to configure its object pooling characteristics, such as minimum pool size, maximum pool size, and a timeout for object creation.

- `PrivateComponentAttribute`. Can be marked on a class to make it usable only from other components in the same COM+ application.

- `SecureMethodAttribute`. Can be marked on an assembly, class, or method to ensure a certain level of security on method invocations.

- `SecurityRoleAttribute`. Can be marked on an assembly, class, interface, or method to add and configure roles.

- `SynchronizationAttribute`. Can be marked on a class to set its synchronization behavior to one of the `SynchronizationOption` enumeration values: `Disabled`, `NotSupported`, `Required`, `RequiresNew`, or `Supported`.

- `TransactionAttribute`. Can be marked on a class to set its transactional behavior to one of the `TransactionOption` enumeration values: `Disabled`, `NotSupported`, `Required`, `RequiresNew`, or `Supported`.

For more information about .NET Enterprise Services, see the .NET Framework SDK documentation.

Conclusion

You've now seen how to use most of the custom attributes in `System.Runtime.InteropServices` to customize your .NET applications to be COM-conscious. The designers of COM Interoperability intended that in the vast majority of cases, none of these custom attributes would be necessary. You should find this to be true, with `MarshalAsAttribute` being by far the most widely-used custom attribute.

With all the custom attributes used by COM Interoperability, it can often be confusing to know what context they can be used in. After all, a custom attribute is meaningless unless someone looks for it and acts upon it. Some custom attributes are used during import but are ignored by the type library exporter. For example, it is not possible to set flags in the exported type library using `TypeLibFuncAttribute`, `TypeLibTypeAttribute`, or `TypeLibVarAttribute`. Although the type library *importer* marks metadata with these when encountering type library flags such as `hidden`, `restricted`, and so on, the type library *exporter* ignores these custom attributes. On the other hand, some custom attributes are only used during export and never emitted by the type library importer, whereas other custom attributes are used in both directions.

To keep all of the custom attributes straight, Table 12.3 lists, in alphabetical order, the custom attributes in `System.Runtime.InteropServices` and explains which attributes are involved with the four main processes—importing, exporting, registration, and run-time marshaling. The only attribute from this namespace that is not listed is `DllImportAttribute`. This custom attribute is only used for PInvoke, and is covered in depth in Part VI, "Platform Invocation Services."

TABLE 12.3 The COM-Related Custom Attributes in System.Runtime.InteropServices (Minus the "Attribute" Suffix for Brevity), Marked by the Processes That Use Them

Custom Attribute	Emitted by Importer	Honored by Exporter	Used in Registration	Used at Run Time
AutomationProxy		✓	✓	✓
ClassInterface	✓	✓		✓
CoClass	✓			✓
ComAliasName	✓			
ComConversionLoss	✓			✓
ComEventInterface	✓			✓
ComImport	✓	✓	✓	
ComRegisterFunction			✓	
ComSourceInterfaces	✓	✓		✓
ComUnregisterFunction			✓	
ComVisible	✓	✓	✓	✓
DispId	✓	✓		✓
FieldOffset	✓	✓		✓
Guid	✓	✓	✓	✓
IDispatchImpl			✓	✓
ImportedFromTypeLib	✓	✓		✓
In	✓	✓		✓
InterfaceType	✓	✓		✓
LCIDConversion	✓	✓		✓
MarshalAs	✓	✓		✓
Optional	✓	✓		
Out		✓		✓

TABLE 12.3 Continued

Custom Attribute	Emitted by Importer	Honored by Exporter	Used in Registration	Used at Run Time
PreserveSig	✓	✓		✓
PrimaryInteropAssembly	✓		✓	
ProgId			✓	
StructLayout	✓	✓		✓
TypeLibFunc	✓			
TypeLibType	✓			
TypeLibVar	✓			

Some of the attributes emitted by the type library importer might surprise you. The type library importer always marks imported coclasses with a `ClassInterfaceAttribute` value of `ClassInterfaceType.None` because they don't have a class interface from the CLR's perspective. The importer only uses the `ComVisibleAttribute` to make newly-generated event classes invisible to COM. Also, the importer only marks methods of dispinterfaces with `PreserveSigAttribute`.

The exporter honors `ComImportAttribute` by resolving references to such types to the original type library rather than the assembly containing the .NET definition. This attribute is described in Chapter 21. The registration process ensures that registering classes marked with `ComImportAttribute` does not overwrite necessary COM entries. This mechanism enables the registration of Interop Assemblies. The exporter uses `ImportedFromTypeLibAttribute` to know when to export a referenced assembly and when to resolve a reference to an original type library instead. `ImportedFromTypeLibAttribute` is used during registration to determine whether a type library should be unregistered when a user runs `REGASM.EXE` with the `/u` and `/tlb` options.

`IDispatchImplAttribute` is described in Chapter 14. Although it doesn't visibly affect an exported type library, it changes the run-time behavior of the `IDispatch` interface that .NET components expose to COM. One last point worth noting is that `AutomationProxyAttribute` is not used directly by the .NET registration process. Because the exported type library changes when using this attribute, the standard COM type library registration that occurs when using `REGASM.EXE`'s `/tlb` option changes.

Chapter 13 focuses solely on one custom attribute—`ComSourceInterfacesAttribute`. Using this, you can expose events to COM in a natural way rather than forcing COM clients to call the add and remove accessors displayed in Chapter 10.

12

COM's VIEW
OF .NET
COMPONENTS

Exposing .NET Events to COM Clients

IN THIS CHAPTER

- Exposing Events Without Using Extra CLR Support   592

- Exposing Events Using Extra CLR Support   598

- Example: Handling a .NET Windows Form's Events from COM   611

Events are a popular way to expose callback functionality in .NET, and are used extensively in the .NET Framework. That's why it's great that the type library importer exposes COM classes that use COM's connection point protocol as .NET classes with .NET events, as explained in Chapter 5, "Responding to COM Events." Unfortunately, as described in Chapter 10, "Advanced Topics for Using .NET Components," the reverse direction (exposing .NET events via connection points) isn't automatically handled by COM Interoperability. A .NET instance with event members is not exposed to COM as a connectable object. Instead, event members are exposed as a pair of accessor methods—add_*EventName* and remove_*EventName*.

As explained in Chapter 10, COM clients cannot hook and unhook unmanaged event handlers using these accessor methods. Attempting to work around this is especially painful for Visual Basic 6 clients because the language, runtime, and IDE are tailored for connection points, exposing them as easy to use events.

Fortunately, the Common Language Runtime (CLR) does have built-in support for exposing components with .NET events as connectable objects to COM—you just have to do a little work to enable it. This chapter discusses the steps to do this and issues you should be aware of.

The easiest way to expose callback functionality to COM would be to use a callback interface, as discussed in Chapter 5. But if you design your .NET type with events and you want it to be useable to COM clients, you should follow the steps in this chapter to enable connection-point support. Exposing .NET events as connection points involves a small amount of effort for a great gain in COM usability. None of the classes in the .NET Framework take advantage of this support to expose events nicely to COM, but then again most types are marked as COM-invisible anyway.

Exposing Events Without Using Extra CLR Support

Before discussing how to use the built-in support, let's examine the state of affairs without any special support in the CLR to expose .NET events as COM connection points. Imagine that we want to write a simple .NET Phone class that defines two events—Ring and CallerId. This could be defined as follows in C#:

```
// Delegates for the events
public delegate void RingEventHandler();
public delegate void CallerIdEventHandler(string callerName,
  byte [] callerPhoneNumber);

public class Phone
{
  // The two events
  public event RingEventHandler Ring;
  public event CallerIdEventHandler CallerId;
  ...
}
```

Each event is associated with a delegate that defines the signature that any corresponding event handler must have. `Ring` is raised with no parameters, but the `CallerId` event is raised with the caller's name and phone number (represented as a byte array to accommodate ever-growing phone numbers).

Whereas such a class works great in .NET languages, it cannot work from COM without extra effort. If a dual class interface were exposed for `Phone` (using `ClassInterface(ClassInterfaceType.AutoDual)`), we'd see the following four event accessor methods in an exported type library:

```
[id(0x60020004)]
HRESULT add_Ring([in] _RingEventHandler* value);
[id(0x60020005)]
HRESULT remove_Ring([in] _RingEventHandler* value);
[id(0x60020006)]
HRESULT add_CallerId([in] _CallerIdEventHandler* value);
[id(0x60020007)]
HRESULT remove_CallerId([in] _CallerIdEventHandler* value);
```

Theoretically, a COM client could call `add_Ring` to hook up an event handler to the `Ring` event, and `remove_Ring` to unhook an event handler. The problem is that a COM client has no good way to pass an object implementing `_RingEventHandler` or `_CallerIdEventHandler` to any of these methods, as discussed in Chapter 10. The COM client would need to write some managed code that does the job of hooking and unhooking event handlers and exposing that code to COM in a usable way.

DIGGING DEEPER

To expose .NET events in a COM-usable manner, one might try to use C#'s advanced event syntax (introduced in Chapter 5) and mark the event accessors with `MarshalAs (UnmanagedType.FunctionPtr)` so COM clients could pass a function pointer to the exported methods rather than an interface pointer such as `_RingEventHandler`. This would not work, however.

First, the C# compiler incorrectly forbids the placement of `MarshalAsAttribute` on an add accessor; it lets you place it only on a remove accessor. But even if you could do this, it still would not work because version 1.0 of the CLR does not support marshaling an unmanaged function pointer to a .NET delegate—only the reverse action of marshaling a .NET delegate to an unmanaged function pointer. Attempting to call such a method from COM would fail.

Rather than forcing COM clients to come up with a way of exposing .NET events in a usable way, Listing 13.1 updates the Phone class and adds some supporting types to make it COM-friendly without sacrificing the design exposed to .NET clients.

LISTING 13.1   One Way to Expose .NET Events to COM Without Using Built-In Connection Point Support from the CLR

```
 1: using System.Collections;
 2: using System.Runtime.InteropServices;
 3:
 4: // Interface with "event handlers" for COM objects to implement
 5: public interface IPhoneEvents
 6: {
 7:   void Ring();
 8:   void CallerId(string callerName, ref byte [] callerPhoneNumber);
 9: }
10:
11: // Interface providing COM access to usable add/remove methods
12: public interface IPhoneEventHookup
13: {
14:   int Add(IPhoneEvents comObject);
15:   void Remove(int cookie);
16: }
17:
18: // Delegates for the events
19: public delegate void RingEventHandler();
20: public delegate void CallerIdEventHandler(string callerName,
21:   byte [] callerPhoneNumber);
22:
23: // The class with the events
24: [ClassInterface(ClassInterfaceType.None)]
25: public class Phone : IPhoneEventHookup
26: {
27:   // The two events
28:   public event RingEventHandler Ring;
29:   public event CallerIdEventHandler CallerId;
30:
31:   // Collection of COM objects to call when event is raised
32:   Hashtable comObjects;
33:   // Number to uniquely identify COM sinks
34:   int cookie;
35:
36:   // Constructor
37:   public Phone()
38:   {
```

LISTING 13.1   Continued

```
39:      comObjects = new Hashtable();
40:      cookie = 0;
41:
42:      // Hook up the class's private methods to the events
43:      Ring += new RingEventHandler(OnRing);
44:      CallerId += new CallerIdEventHandler(OnCallerId);
45:    }
46:
47:    // Implementation of IPhoneEventHookup.Add
48:    int IPhoneEventHookup.Add(IPhoneEvents comObject)
49:    {
50:      cookie++;
51:      // Add object to the collection
52:      comObjects.Add(cookie, comObject);
53:      return cookie;
54:    }
55:
56:    // Implementation of IPhoneEventHookup.Remove
57:    void IPhoneEventHookup.Remove(int cookie)
58:    {
59:      // Remove the object from the collection
60:      comObjects.Remove(cookie);
61:    }
62:
63:    // Handles the Ring event and calls all COM objects that
64:    // added themselves to the list using IPhoneEventHookup.Add
65:    private void OnRing()
66:    {
67:      foreach (IPhoneEvents comObject in comObjects)
68:        comObject.Ring();
69:    }
70:
71:    // Handles the CallerId event and calls all COM objects that
72:    // added themselves to the list using IPhoneEventHookup.Add
73:    private void OnCallerId(string callerName, byte [] callerPhoneNumber)
74:    {
75:      foreach (IPhoneEvents comObject in comObjects)
76:        comObject.CallerId(callerName, ref callerPhoneNumber);
77:    }
78:
79:    // More methods to communicate with hardware and raise the events...
80: }
```

13

EXPOSING .NET
EVENTS TO COM
CLIENTS

Lines 1 and 2 use the `System.Collections` namespace for `Hashtable` and the `System.Runtime.InteropServices` namespace for `ClassInterfaceAttribute` and `ClassInterfaceType`. Lines 5–9 define a callback interface that COM clients can implement to provide an event handler for each of the two events. This `IPhoneEvents` interface serves as a replacement for both the `_RingEventHandler` and `_CallerIdEventHandler` class interfaces that COM objects can't usefully implement. Note that by using a single interface for both events, a COM object must now provide some sort of implementation (even if it's just an empty implementation) for both event handlers even if it only wants to handle one of the events.

The signature of `IPhoneEvents.CallerId` differs from the signature of `CallerIdEventHandler` in that `callerPhoneNumber` is defined as a *by-reference* array. This is done for the sake of Visual Basic 6 clients who can't consume signatures with by-value `SAFEARRAY` parameters. Changing `CallerIdEventHandler`'s signature to use a by-reference array would be misleading to .NET clients because the array reference should not be modified by event handlers. Therefore, the COM-focused signature and the .NET-focused signatures are left as being different, and the implementation of `OnCallerId` (Lines 73–77) negotiate their differences.

Lines 12–16 define another interface, but this is one for COM clients to *use* rather than implement in order to add and remove event handlers. The `Phone` class implements this interface, which serves as a COM-friendly version of the add and remove event accessors. The `Add` method takes the place of both `add_Ring` and `add_CallerId`, and takes an `IPhoneEvents` interface parameter. Therefore, a COM object that implements `IPhoneEvents` can be passed in so its `Ring` and `CallerId` methods can be invoked when the corresponding events are raised. `Add` returns a "cookie" value that uniquely identifies the event sink from the event source's perspective. This cookie can be passed to the `Remove` method defined in Line 15 to unhook a specific event sink.

Lines 48–61 contain the `Phone` class's implementation of the `IPhoneEventHookup` interface. The `Add` method simply adds the passed in object to the class's private `Hashtable` and returns a unique cookie that is used as the object's key in the `Hashtable`. The `Remove` method removes the object from the `Hashtable` using the passed-in cookie value. Because these `Add` and `Remove` methods are meant for COM clients only, `Phone` attempts to hide them from .NET clients by using explicit interface implementation. .NET clients browsing or using the `Phone` class directly don't see these methods, yet because COM can only communicate with `Phone` via the `IPhoneEventHookup` interface, these methods are quite visible. Note that if `Phone` has other methods that should be exposed to COM (like `Dial`, `HangUp`, and so on) then another interface defining these methods should be implemented or a class interface should be exposed.

The `Phone` class's constructor in Lines 37–45 initializes the `Hashtable` and hooks up two private event handlers to its own events—`OnRing` and `OnCallerId`, defined in Lines 65–77. Both of these methods iterate through the `Hashtable` and invoke the appropriate callback methods on each COM object. This technique transforms a single .NET event handler into a source of a semantically related COM event.

Using the types from Listing 13.1 in a COM client is fairly straightforward, but it's a custom protocol that doesn't provide the same kind of support and widespread understanding as do connection points. Listing 13.2 contains code from a Visual Basic 6 class module that references an exported type library for the assembly containing the Phone class in Listing 13.1 and hooks up its event handlers using the custom protocol. It assumes the existence of a ConvertPhoneNumberToString method that formats a byte array as a suitable phone number string.

LISTING 13.2   A Visual Basic 6 Class That Implements the IPhoneEvents Interface and Hooks Up Event Handlers to the Phone Class

```
 1: Implements IPhoneEvents
 2:
 3: Private myPhone As IPhoneEventHookup
 4: Private cookie As Long
 5:
 6: Private Sub Class_Initialize()
 7:   Set myPhone = New Phone
 8:   cookie = myPhone.Add(Me)
 9: End Sub
10:
11: Private Sub Class_Terminate()
12:   myPhone.Remove cookie
13: End Sub
14:
15: Private Sub IPhoneEvents_Ring()
16:   MsgBox "Ring!"
17: End Sub
18:
19: Private Sub IPhoneEvents_CallerId(ByVal callerName As String, _
20:   callerPhoneNumber() As Byte)
21:   MsgBox "Call from " & callerName & ", " & _
22:     ConvertPhoneNumberToString(callerPhoneNumber)
23: End Sub
```

The communication between the COM client in Listing 13.2 and the .NET component in Listing 13.1 is similar to the connection point protocol. The IPhoneEventHookup interface acts like a customized IConnectionPoint interface, with Add serving the same purpose as an interface-specific Advise method, and Remove functioning as an Unadvise method. (Even the use of a cookie to identify event sinks works the same way.) In addition, the IPhoneEvents interface serves the same role as a source interface. Consult Chapter 5 for a refresher on COM's connection point protocol.

Exposing Events Using Extra CLR Support

Unless possible increased performance of a custom protocol is desired, using the general connection points mechanism is more COM-friendly because many COM clients are designed to use connection points. Visual Basic 6 clients, for example, don't need to worry about calling Advise and Unadvise like Listing 13.2 calls Add and Remove. Instead, when a variable is declared using WithEvents, instantiating the object causes a QueryInterface call to IConnectionPointContainer, followed by a call to IConnectionPointContainer. FindConnectionPoint, then a call to IConnectionPoint.Advise. The Visual Basic 6 runtime even generates a sink object that implements the source interface on-the-fly, which forwards calls to any event handlers you define in your code.

Using ComSourceInterfacesAttribute

A .NET class could manually implement IConnectionPointContainer and IConnectionPoint to expose itself as an official connectable object, but COM Interoperability provides special support that achieves the same thing through the use of a custom attribute. This custom attribute is ComSourceInterfacesAttribute, which is defined in the System.Runtime. InteropServices namespace. This attribute can only be marked on a class, and contains the types of any source interfaces that the class supports. Using this attribute looks like the following:

C#:

```
[ComSourceInterfaces(typeof(IPhoneEvents))]
public class Phone
{
  ...
}
```

Visual Basic .NET:

```
<ComSourceInterfaces(GetType(IPhoneEvents))> _
Public Class Phone
  ...
End Class
```

C++:

```
[ComSourceInterfaces(__typeof(IPhoneEvents))]
public __gc class Phone
{
  ...
};
```

By using this custom attribute, classes can be exposed to COM with source interfaces that can be implemented by COM event sinks to handle .NET events.

The constructor for `ComSourceInterfacesAttribute` has several overloads to accommodate specifying one to four types of source interfaces, for example (in Visual Basic .NET):

```
<ComSourceInterfaces(GetType(IPhoneEvents), GetType(IPhoneEvents2), _
  GetType(IPhoneEvents3), GetType(IPhoneEvents4))> _
Public Class Phone
  ...
End Class
```

As with listing regular interfaces implemented by a class, the first parameter corresponds to the default source interface, whereas the others are just regular additional source interfaces.

In the rare case that you need to specify more than four source interfaces, you could instead use a constructor overload with a string parameter and provide a list of type names delimited with a null character. Here's an example in Visual Basic .NET using just two source interfaces (for brevity):

```
<ComSourceInterfaces("IPhoneEvents" & Chr(0) & "IPhoneEvents2")> _
Public Class Phone
  ...
End Class
```

In C# and C++, the same string would be specified as:

```
"IPhoneEvents\0IPhoneEvents2"
```

The first interface listed represents the default source interface.

> **TIP**
>
> You should design classes that only use one source interface to expose methods for all the class's events. Although unmanaged C++ clients can use multiple source interfaces, Visual Basic 6 only supports `WithEvents` syntax for a single default source interface. Using multiple source interfaces should be restricted to the case of writing a COM-compatible class for COM clients already written to expect multiple source interfaces.

As demonstrated by the example, a string can be used for any number of source interfaces. It may seem odd that a constructor exists to use such a string (rather than an array of `Types`) but regardless of whether an overload with `Type` parameters is used or the overload with a string parameter is used, the information is persisted as one null-delimited string in metadata anyway. Plus, using a string is useful to make a "late bound" type reference—one that doesn't require the interface type's metadata at compilation time.

As is the case with late binding in general, extra care is required because a compiler doesn't check that the string is in the correct format or that it corresponds to a valid interface type. The string used to specify an interface (or a substring when more than one interface is specified) has the same format as a string used in the `System.Type.GetType`. This means that a simple interface name can be used if the type is in the same assembly as the custom attribute; otherwise, a string of the following form must be used:

TypeName, AssemblyName

The *AssemblyName* portion can be a partial name like `MyAssembly` or `MyAssembly, Version=1.0.0.0` if the referenced assembly is not in the Global Assembly Cache; or a complete specification including the simple name, version, culture, and public key token, for example:

```
MyAssembly, Version=1.0.0.0, Culture=neutral, PublicKeyToken=b1bf107f04d50a3a
```

> **CAUTION**
>
> If you must use a string parameter with `ComSourceInterfacesAttribute`, you should always use a full assembly name if the interface is defined in a different assembly. This is the only string that works if the assembly ends up being installed in the Global Assembly Cache. Specifying the version number in the assembly name does not mean that your class won't work with a later version of the referenced assembly; .NET version policy can redirect requests for the original version to a new version if desired.
>
> Using a constructor overload with `Type` parameter(s) is preferred over using a string because the `Type` instances are automatically persisted with complete assembly names for types in different assemblies. Plus, using the type is faster and less error-prone than using lengthy strings.

Defining a Source Interface

Using `ComSourceInterfacesAttribute` requires a definition of at least one source interface that would not be required if COM clients weren't involved. Defining the event members alone is not enough! You could define your own source interface, or import a type library containing the definition of an existing COM source interface for your .NET class to expose. A source interface has no special marking to make it a source interface; any interface can be used as a source interface simply by listing it inside the `ComSourceInterfacesAttribute` custom attribute.

For a source interface to be useful, each of its methods should correspond to an event defined on a .NET class (or on its base classes) marked with `ComSourceInterfacesAttribute`. Each source interface method must have the exact same name as the corresponding event, and must have the exact same signature as the event's delegate type, with two exceptions:

- A parameter defined on a source interface could be replaced with a class that it derives from (a superclass). This fact comes in handy in the "Example: Handling Windows Forms Events from COM" section at the end of this chapter.

- A delegate and the corresponding source interface method could have different custom attributes.

A source interface's methods can be listed in any order. The CLR determines which source interface methods correspond to which events by name and signature only. Failure to follow these rules is unfortunately not caught by any .NET compilers (because they don't have knowledge about source interfaces) and prevents raised events from reaching COM clients.

DIGGING DEEPER

Not every source interface method needs to correspond to a class's event, nor does every event require a source interface method if you don't care about exposing it to COM. Therefore, a source interface can validly expose a subset of a class's events, or a class could provide events for a subset of a source interface's methods. In fact, you could even expose a private event to COM via this source interface! As long as at least one of the methods of a source interface corresponds to one of the events on a class, COM clients can successfully call `FindConnectionPoint` to retrieve a connection point.

Although a source interface definition doesn't require any special custom attributes to work with C++ COM clients, there are two custom attributes you should use to make a source interface usable for Visual Basic 6 and script COM clients:

- `InterfaceTypeAttribute`. Mark the source interface with `InterfaceType(ComInterfaceType.InterfaceIsIDispatch)` to make it exposed to COM as a dispinterface. Visual Basic 6 and scripting languages only support the use of source interfaces that are pure dispinterfaces.

- `DispIdAttribute`. Mark each of the source interface's methods with `DispId(n)`, where n is a unique number greater than zero. This is needed to support Visual Basic 6 clients who provide event handlers for only a subset of the source interface's methods.

Making the source interface a dispinterface is understandable, but the reason for marking each method with a DISPID is subtle. If a COM event sink implementing the source interface is connected to a .NET class with events, the CLR invokes the appropriate source interface methods when its events are raised. When the source interface is a dispinterface, the CLR must call the event sink late bound via IDispatch. If a source interface method is marked with a DISPID in metadata (with DispIdAttribute), the CLR directly calls IDispatch.Invoke. Otherwise, it must call IDispatch.GetIDsOfNames first to get the method's DISPID. However, if a Visual Basic 6 client doesn't provide an event handler corresponding to the event being raised, the VB6 dynamic sink object returns the failure HRESULT value DISP_E_UNKNOWNNAME when calling GetIDsOfNames with that event's name. Yet if Invoke is called with its DISPID, the call succeeds and just does nothing because the VB6 user didn't provide any implementation.

Therefore, if you don't mark your source interface's methods with DISPIDs, an exception like the following occurs if a Visual Basic 6 client doesn't provide event handlers for *every* source interface method:

```
System.Runtime.InteropServices.COMException (0x80020006): Unknown name.
   at System.RuntimeType.InvokeDispMethod(...)
   at System.RuntimeType.InvokeMember(...)
   at System.RuntimeType.ForwardCallToInvokeMember(...)
   at ISourceInterface.MyEvent()
   at ManagedClass.MethodThatRaisesEvent()
```

Future versions of the CLR are likely to solve this problem by always avoiding the call to GetIDsOfNames, because .NET methods without explicit DISPIDs have CLR-assigned DISPIDs that could be used. But since version 1.0 of the CLR does call GetIDsOfNames when no explicit DISPID exists, you should always provide them explicitly.

The Phone Example Revisited

Listing 13.3 updates the Phone class from Listing 13.1 to expose a connection point to COM using ComSourceInterfacesAttribute and a source interface, complete with explicit DISPIDs. Because the source interface signatures used by COM must match the delegate signatures used by .NET, the second parameter of CallerIdEventHandler has been changed from a byte array to a string to avoid the unnatural situation of making the array a by-reference parameter for the sake of VB6.

LISTING 13.3   Defining a Source Interface and Using ComSourceInterfacesAttribute to Expose Connection Points to COM

```
1: using System;
2: using System.Runtime.InteropServices;
3:
```

LISTING 13.3 Continued

```
 4: // Source interface with "event handlers" for COM objects to implement
 5: [InterfaceType(ComInterfaceType.InterfaceIsIDispatch)]
 6: public interface IPhoneEvents
 7: {
 8:   [DispId(1)] void Ring();
 9:   [DispId(2)] void CallerId(string callerName, string callerPhoneNumber);
10: }
11:
12: // Delegates for the events
13: public delegate void RingEventHandler();
14: public delegate void CallerIdEventHandler(string callerName,
15:   string callerPhoneNumber);
16:
17: [ComSourceInterfaces(typeof(IPhoneEvents))]
18: public class Phone
19: {
20:   public event RingEventHandler Ring;
21:   public event CallerIdEventHandler CallerId;
22:
23:   // More methods to communicate with hardware and raise the events...
24: }
```

No code inside the Phone class needs to be concerned with treating the events specially for COM purposes. The custom attribute in Line 17 and source interface in Lines 5–10 enable the CLR to handle it all. A type library exported for an assembly with the code from Listing 13.3 contains the following coclass:

```
[
  uuid(9963B116-B0DC-3AAB-81DF-286170D63E85),
  version(1.0),
  custom({0F21F359-AB84-41E8-9A78-36D110E6D2F9}, "Phone")
]
coclass Phone {
  [default] interface _Phone;
  interface _Object;
  [default, source] dispinterface IPhoneEvents;
};
```

Listing 13.4 shows an update to the Visual Basic 6 code from Listing 13.2 that hooks up event handlers to the Phone class from Listing 13.3. This code is much simpler than Listing 13.4, as Visual Basic 6 code should be. The event handler hookup is handled by the VB6 runtime because the WithEvents keyword is used.

LISTING 13.4 A Visual Basic 6 Class That Uses the `WithEvents` Keyword to Enable Automatic Event Handler Hookup to the `Phone` Class

```
1: Private WithEvents myPhone As Phone
2:
3: Private Sub IPhoneEvents_Ring()
4:    MsgBox "Ring!"
5: End Sub
6:
7: Private Sub IPhoneEvents_CallerId(callerName As String, _
8:    callerPhoneNumber As String)
9:    MsgBox "Call from " & callerName & ", " & callerPhoneNumber
10: End Sub
```

Figure 13.1 shows the list of events that appears in the Visual Basic 6 IDE for a type declared using `WithEvents`.

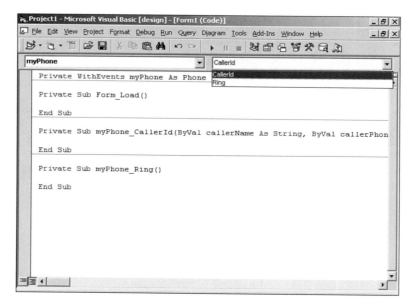

FIGURE 13.1

The Visual Basic 6 IDE provides a drop-down list of events for easy event handler hookup.

> **FAQ: Since defining a source interface in managed code is tedious and error-prone (due to limited compile-time checking), and because all the information needed to construct one exists in metadata, why do I need to define one manually?**
>
> No matter which direction COM Interoperability is being used, the CLR always bases its actions from managed types and managed signatures. One could imagine that the type library exporter could automatically export the appropriate source interfaces for each public .NET class with public events. (In Chapter 22, you'll see that this is fairly easy to do yourself using the type library exporter APIs.) However, having such source interfaces in a type library does no good if the .NET type definitions aren't altered. All source interfaces need to be described somewhere in metadata and the classes need to be marked with the appropriate custom attribute in order for the .NET connection point support to work.
>
> A post-processing tool could be written that scans assemblies and produces the necessary source interfaces and custom attributes. Unfortunately, the reflection and reflection emit technologies do not enable editing and re-saving an existing assembly. However, a tool could use reflection to scan an assembly and use Reflection Emit to generate the necessary source interfaces in a second assembly. The only catch is that the original assembly's classes with events would already need to be marked with `ComSourceInterfacesAttribute`, but by using a string parameter the classes could refer to an interface in an assembly that doesn't exist until the post-processing tool makes it exist.
>
> A tool could also be written that edits the input assembly by simply using the IL Disassembler and IL Assembler to enable the editing and resaving! With such a tool, no COM event-related work would need to be done prior to compilation because the source interface types plus the `ComSourceInterfacesAttribute` custom attributes could all be added afterwards!
>
> The easiest solution is to take advantage of the Visual Basic .NET compiler's support for automatically generating source interfaces. This is discussed in the next section, "Visual Basic .NET's `ComClassAttribute`."

Visual Basic .NET's `ComClassAttribute`

A great feature of VB .NET's `ComClassAttribute` custom attribute, introduced in the previous chapter, is that it prompts the VB .NET compiler to automatically emit a source interface for any class marked with the attribute that has public event members. The generated source interface has an IID equal to the third GUID specified in the `ComClassAttribute` constructor (identified as the `EventsId` constant in the Visual Studio .NET `COM Class` template). The interface contains one method for every public event (excluding events on base classes), is a dispinterface, and is marked with explicit DISPIDs. The compiler also emits the appropriate `ComSourceInterfacesAttribute` on the class so no extra work is required to expose .NET events as connection points using the best practices described in the previous section. Listing 13.5 is a translation of the C# code from Listing 13.3 that takes advantage of `ComClassAttribute`'s event support.

LISTING 13.5   Using `Microsoft.VisualBasic.ComClassAttribute` to Expose Connection Points to COM

```
 1: Imports Microsoft.VisualBasic
 2:
 3: <ComClass(Phone.ClassId, Phone.InterfaceId, Phone.EventsId)> _
 4: Public Class Phone
 5:    ' GUIDs needed for ComClassAttribute
 6:    Public Const ClassId As String = "F7EB2080-18FE-43CE-8FB1-B7CB7DE91C4B"
 7:    Public Const InterfaceId As String = _
 8:       "68146151-1D31-4C75-91D5-7920F8C25798"
 9:    Public Const EventsId As String = "4E4B25B1-7266-41D9-BC09-425394E14D1B"
10:
11:    ' The events
12:    Public Event Ring()
13:    Public Event CallerId(ByVal callerName As String, _
14:       ByVal callerPhoneNumber As String)
15:
16:    ' More methods to communicate with hardware and raise the events...
17: End Class
```

Using the IL Disassembler (`ILDASM.EXE`) to examine the metadata produced by compiling Listing 13.5, you can see the various .NET supporting types emitted by the VB .NET compiler, all of which are nested types of the `Phone` class. Besides the `_Phone` class interface and the `RingEventHandler` and `CallerIdEventHandler` delegates, the compiler generates a source interface called `__Phone`. This interface looks like the `IPhoneEvents` interface in Listing 13.3, just with a different name. The compiler even emits DISPIDs the same way: sequentially starting from one based on the order the events are defined.

You can also see these compiler-generated types when exporting a type library for an assembly containing the code from Listing 13.5. The `Phone` class is exported as follows, in IDL syntax:

```
[
  uuid(F7EB2080-18FE-43CE-8FB1-B7CB7DE91C4B),
  version(1.0),
  custom(0F21F359-AB84-41E8-9A78-36D110E6D2F9, "Phone")
]
```

```
coclass Phone {
  interface _Object;
  [default] interface _Phone;
  [default, source] dispinterface __Phone;
};
```

The __Phone source interface is exported as follows, in IDL syntax:

```
[
  uuid(4E4B25B1-7266-41D9-BC09-425394E14D1B),
  version(1.0),
  custom(0F21F359-AB84-41E8-9A78-36D110E6D2F9, "Phone+__Phone")
]
dispinterface __Phone {
  properties:
  methods:
    [id(0x00000001)]
    void Ring();
    [id(0x00000002)]
    void CallerId([in] BSTR callerName, [in] BSTR callerPhoneNumber);
};
```

CAUTION

The behavior of ComClassAttribute does not version properly when you add new events to your class, because you have little control over the source interface generated for you. First, if you don't list the new events last in your class definition, the DISPIDs for existing source interface methods will change, which would be problematic for any component that cached the DISPIDs from the previous version of your exported type library. (This also means you should never rearrange the order of your class's events in source code when using ComClassAttribute, something that could be done if you controlled the definition of the corresponding source interface.) Second, existing COM clients would no longer be implementing the entire source interface, causing failures whenever the .NET class raised the new events. Adding methods to an interface is never compatible when existing clients implement it!

To solve this problem, you could switch away from using ComClassAttribute if you need to add new events, and instead use ComSourceInterfacesAttribute as in Listing 13.3. When you explicitly define your source interface, you can omit methods corresponding to the new events in order to remain compatible with the previous version of your class. Plus, you could define a second source interface with new methods corresponding to the new events and add this interface as a second type listed in your class's ComSourceInterfacesAttribute custom attribute.

An easier solution would be to continue using `ComClassAttribute` then catching and ignoring `COMExceptions` thrown when raising the new events, because raising a new event would cause the event sink's `IDispatch.Invoke` method to return a failure `HRESULT`. This is not ideal because, besides worse performance, the exception could prevent other clients from receiving the event when multiple event sinks are listening.

Design Guidelines

The `Phone` example from all the previous listings used events and delegates in the simplest possible way so as not to complicate the demonstration of exposing events to COM. However, the .NET Framework SDK lists design guidelines regarding events, and the `Phone` class in Listings 13.3 and 13.5 does not follow these guidelines. Since this chapter is about designing .NET events, it would be a disservice not to discuss these guidelines. They include the following:

- An event's delegate should return `void` (be a `Sub` in VB .NET) and have two parameters. The first one should be a `System.Object` representing the source or sender of the event (the class who raised it), and the second one should be a class derived from `System.EventArgs` containing properties that can be read and/or written by an event sink. (These parameters should be named `sender` and `e`, respectively.) If the event has no associated data to send or receive, the second parameter should just be the `System.EventArgs` type. If you want an event sink to be able to "return" a value, this can simply be done via properties on the `EventArgs`-derived class. Since classes are reference types, any changes to property values within an event handler can be seen by the event source without having to pass the `EventArgs`-derived instance by-reference.

> **CAUTION**
>
> Don't ever use a user-defined value type as a delegate parameter. If a source interface contains a method with the matching signature, and if the source interface is a dispinterface (as it should be), COM clients would be unable to handle the event. This is because the CLR would make a late-bound call to the source interface's method with the value type parameter, which would not work because the Interop Marshaler does not support `VARIANTs` with the `VT_RECORD` type in version 1.0. Fortunately, by sticking to the .NET design guidelines of encapsulating all data in an `EventArgs`-derived class, you avoid any such problems.

- For clarity and consistency, a delegate used by an event should be named
  *EventName*EventHandler and the EventArgs-derived class should be called
  *EventName*EventArgs. If the delegate and EventArgs-derived class are used for multiple
  events, a more generic name should be used that describes the type of events these should
  be applied to.

- The raising of each event should be done in a protected On*EventName* method. This way,
  subclasses can override the event behavior because it's not possible for them to directly
  raise base class events by default.

Listing 13.6 updates Listing 13.5, keeping these design guidelines in mind. Although the delegates
are hidden by Visual Basic .NET, the compiler generates them with names that coincide with
the .NET design guidelines.

LISTING 13.6   An Update to Listing 13.5 That Makes the Phone Class and Its Events
Compliant with .NET Design Guidelines

```
 1: Imports Microsoft.VisualBasic
 2:
 3: <ComClass(Phone.ClassId, Phone.InterfaceId, Phone.EventsId)> _
 4: Public Class Phone
 5:   ' GUIDs needed for ComClassAttribute
 6:   Public Const ClassId As String = "F7EB2080-18FE-43CE-8FB1-B7CB7DE91C4B"
 7:   Public Const InterfaceId As String _
 8:     = "68146151-1D31-4C75-91D5-7920F8C25798"
 9:   Public Const EventsId As String = "4E4B25B1-7266-41D9-BC09-425394E14D1B"
10:
11:   ' The events
12:   Public Event Ring(ByVal sender As Object, ByVal e As EventArgs)
13:   Public Event CallerId(ByVal sender As Object, _
14:     ByVal e As CallerIdEventArgs)
15:
16:   ' On<EventName> methods so subclasses can customize event behavior
17:
18:   Protected Sub OnRing(ByVal e As EventArgs)
19:     RaiseEvent Ring(Me, e)
20:   End Sub
21:
22:   Protected Sub OnCallerId(ByVal e As CallerIdEventArgs)
23:     RaiseEvent CallerId(Me, e)
24:   End Sub
25:
26:   ' More methods to communicate with hardware...
27: End Class
28:
29: ' CallerIdEventArgs
30: Public Class CallerIdEventArgs
```

LISTING 13.6   Continued

```
31:    Inherits EventArgs
32:    Private name As String
33:    Private phoneNumber As String
34:
35:    Public Sub New(ByVal callerName As String, _
36:      ByVal callerPhoneNumber As String)
37:      name = callerName
38:      phoneNumber = callerPhoneNumber
39:    End Sub
40:
41:    Public ReadOnly Property CallerName() As String
42:      Get
43:        Return name
44:      End Get
45:    End Property
46:
47:    Public ReadOnly Property CallerPhoneNumber() As String
48:      Get
49:        Return phoneNumber
50:      End Get
51:    End Property
52: End Class
```

Lines 12–14 contain the new delegate signatures that comply with .NET design guidelines. The methods on the corresponding source interface must match these new signatures, which is taken care of by the VB .NET compiler. Lines 30–52 define the new CallerIdEventArgs class that exposes what used to be parameters of the CallerIdEventHandler delegate as read-only properties.

Lines 18–24 define the two On… methods that encapsulate raising each event. In Listing 13.5, code that raises the two events was omitted because it could've been done in any of the class's methods that were omitted. Here, this code is shown because we're assuming that any other methods implemented by Phone call OnRing and OnCallerId to raise the events rather than doing it directly.

TIP

Before raising an event, you should always check to see if the event member is null first. Visual Basic .NET's RaiseEvent statement does this for you, so an equivalent implementation of OnRing would look as follows in C#:

```
protected virtual void OnRing(EventArgs e)
{
  if (Ring != null)
    Ring(this, e);
}
```

An event is null when no event handlers are hooked up to its underlying delegate, so attempting to raise the event in this situation results in a `NullReferenceException`.

Example: Handling a .NET Windows Form's Events from COM

For a realistic example of exposing events to COM, this section examines what it takes to expose all of a .NET Windows Form's events to COM event sinks. We'll create an application that consists of a Visual Basic 6 COM client functioning as an event sink for a .NET Windows Form it instantiates. Every event raised by the Windows Form is recorded by the COM client by adding it to a `TreeView` control with the time it was raised plus additional data communicated through the event's delegate.

The .NET Event Source

`System.Windows.Forms.Form` raises a whopping 71 events, most of which are inherited from base classes. The event members and delegate types are already defined by the .NET Framework, so all that's needed is a source interface definition containing 71 methods whose names match the event names and whose signatures match the delegate signatures. (These event members can be seen in the Visual Studio .NET object browser marked with lightning bolts, or in the IL Disassembler with red triangles pointing upward. In both cases you need to check all the base classes to see all the inherited events.) Of course, a subset of the methods could be defined if we aren't concerned with exposing *all* of `Form`'s events to COM.

Since the `Form` class isn't marked with the necessary `ComSourceInterfacesAttribute`, we need to define a new class—`ComFriendlyForm`—that has this custom attribute. The easiest way to have `ComFriendlyForm` raise the same events as `Form` appropriately is to derive the class from `Form`. Any instance of `ComFriendlyForm` would then inherit all of the event-raising functionality, yet COM clients could use it as a connectable object thanks to the custom attribute. Such a class would look simply like the following (in Visual Basic .NET):

```
' An empty Windows Form that exposes its
' events to COM using connection points
<ComSourceInterfaces(GetType(IFormEvents))> _
```

```
Public Class ComFriendlyForm
  Inherits Form
End Class
```

This assumes that we've defined an `IFormEvents` source interface containing all of the necessary methods. Doing this with `Form` is not so easy, however, because many of its events' delegate parameters are marked as COM-invisible. This means that many methods of the source interface would be exported with `IUnknown` parameters. For example, `Form` has a `Validating` event that uses the `System.ComponentModel.CancelEventHandler` delegate type defined as follows (in Visual Basic .NET):

```
Public Delegate Sub CancelEventHandler(ByVal sender As Object, _
  ByVal e As CancelEventArgs)
```

`CancelEventHandler` is COM-invisible, but that's actually irrelevant because COM clients interact with source interface methods directly rather than using delegates. What is important, however, is that the `CancelEventHandler` delegate's second parameter—`System.ComponentModel.CancelEventArgs`—is COM-invisible. Therefore, a source interface method corresponding to the `Validating` event, as the following in Visual Basic .NET:

```
<InterfaceTypeAttribute(ComInterfaceType.InterfaceIsIDispatch)> _
Public Interface IFormEvents
  ...
  <DispId(68)> Sub Validating(sender As Object, e As CancelEventArgs)
  ...
End Interface
```

would be exported as follows (in IDL):

```
void Validating([in] VARIANT sender, [in] IUnknown* e);
```

This isn't always a problem for unmanaged C++ clients; they could just ignore the second parameter or attempt to query for COM-visible interfaces. In this case, however, a `CancelEventArgs` instance doesn't implement any useful COM-visible interfaces.

Such a signature is more problematic for Visual Basic 6 clients. Visual Basic 6 doesn't support event handler signatures with `IUnknown` parameters, so handling the `Validating` event isn't an option—even when ignoring the second parameter! Referencing a type library containing the previous `Validating` signature and selecting it in the Visual Basic 6 IDE (for a `windowsForm` variable declared using `WithEvents`) generates the following signature:

```
Private Sub windowsForm_Validating(ByVal sender As Variant, ByVal e As 0)
End Sub
```

Unfortunately, neither changing nor leaving such a signature results in something that can be compiled by VB6. Therefore, we have three options for accommodating Visual Basic 6 clients:

- Option 1—Omit problematic methods from the source interface we define.

- Option 2—Replace COM-invisible parameters in source interface methods with COM-visible superclasses. For example, we could replace `System.ComponentModel.CancelEventArgs` with `System.EventArgs`.

- Option 3—Change the signatures of problematic source interface methods to expose the same data with different COM-visible types. This involves defining new delegates to match these signatures and defining corresponding events that are raised whenever the original events are raised.

The first option is the easiest but doesn't enable the problematic events to be raised to COM clients. The second option is a slick way to enable COM clients to handle all events, but they would not be able to access the COM-invisible data that accompanies the event. The VB .NET compiler performs option 2 when encountering COM-invisible delegate parameters used by a class marked with the `ComClassAttribute` custom attribute.

The third option involves the most work but provides the best experience for COM clients, because they can access all the data that accompanies every event. Listing 13.8 demonstrates this technique. For `System.Windows.Forms.Form`, this involves defining 10 new events that correspond to problematic events, and 8 new delegates for these events (because some events share the same delegate type). You can compile this listing with the C# command-line compiler as follows:

```
csc /t:library Listing13_7.cs /r:System.Windows.Forms.dll
➥ /r:System.Drawing.dll /r:System.dll
```

CAUTION

Version 7.0 of the Visual C# .NET compiler emits ten warnings when compiling Listing 13.7 stating that the ten events in Lines 143–154 require the new keyword, but these events *are* defined with the new keyword. This is a bug in the compiler, but because they're just warnings they can be safely ignored.

DIGGING DEEPER

The example in Listing 13.7 could not have been achieved using `ComClassAttribute`. Besides the fact that it replaces COM-invisible parameters with COM-visible base types (and not doing anything extra to present all the data to COM event sinks), the VB .NET compiler ignores events defined on base classes when producing a source interface. Had `ComClassAttribute` been marked on an empty class deriving from `System.Windows.Forms.Form`, no source interface would even be generated.

LISTING 13.7   A .NET Windows Form with an `IFormEvents` Source Interface Exposing All 71 Events to COM

```
 1: using System;
 2: using System.Globalization;
 3: using System.Windows.Forms;
 4: using System.ComponentModel;
 5: using System.Runtime.InteropServices;
 6:
 7: // The source interface representing all events for Form
 8: [InterfaceType(ComInterfaceType.InterfaceIsIDispatch)]
 9: public interface IFormEvents
10: {
11:    // Component's event
12:    [DispId(1)] void Disposed (object sender, EventArgs e);
13:
14:    // Control's events with COM-visible parameters
15:    [DispId(2)] void BackColorChanged (object sender, EventArgs e);
16:    [DispId(3)] void BackgroundImageChanged (object sender, EventArgs e);
17:    [DispId(4)] void BindingContextChanged (object sender, EventArgs e);
18:    [DispId(5)] void CausesValidationChanged (object sender, EventArgs e);
19:    [DispId(6)] void Click (object sender, EventArgs e);
20:    [DispId(7)] void ContextMenuChanged (object sender, EventArgs e);
21:    [DispId(8)] void CursorChanged (object sender, EventArgs e);
22:    [DispId(9)] void DockChanged (object sender, EventArgs e);
23:    [DispId(10)] void DoubleClick (object sender, EventArgs e);
24:    [DispId(11)] void DragDrop (object sender, DragEventArgs e);
25:    [DispId(12)] void DragEnter (object sender, DragEventArgs e);
26:    [DispId(13)] void DragLeave (object sender, EventArgs e);
27:    [DispId(14)] void DragOver (object sender, DragEventArgs e);
28:    [DispId(15)] void EnabledChanged (object sender, EventArgs e);
29:    [DispId(16)] void Enter (object sender, EventArgs e);
30:    [DispId(17)] void FontChanged (object sender, EventArgs e);
31:    [DispId(18)] void ForeColorChanged (object sender, EventArgs e);
```

LISTING 13.7   Continued

```
32:    [DispId(19)] void GiveFeedback (object sender, GiveFeedbackEventArgs e);
33:    [DispId(20)] void GotFocus (object sender, EventArgs e);
34:    [DispId(21)] void HandleCreated (object sender, EventArgs e);
35:    [DispId(22)] void HandleDestroyed (object sender, EventArgs e);
36:    [DispId(23)] void HelpRequested (object sender, HelpEventArgs e);
37:    [DispId(24)] void ImeModeChanged (object sender, EventArgs e);
38:    [DispId(25)] void KeyDown (object sender, KeyEventArgs e);
39:    [DispId(26)] void KeyPress (object sender, KeyPressEventArgs e);
40:    [DispId(27)] void KeyUp (object sender, KeyEventArgs e);
41:    [DispId(28)] void Leave (object sender, EventArgs e);
42:    [DispId(29)] void LocationChanged (object sender, EventArgs e);
43:    [DispId(30)] void LostFocus (object sender, EventArgs e);
44:    [DispId(31)] void MouseDown (object sender, MouseEventArgs e);
45:    [DispId(32)] void MouseEnter (object sender, EventArgs e);
46:    [DispId(33)] void MouseHover (object sender, EventArgs e);
47:    [DispId(34)] void MouseLeave (object sender, EventArgs e);
48:    [DispId(35)] void MouseMove (object sender, MouseEventArgs e);
49:    [DispId(36)] void MouseUp (object sender, MouseEventArgs e);
50:    [DispId(37)] void MouseWheel (object sender, MouseEventArgs e);
51:    [DispId(38)] void Move (object sender, EventArgs e);
52:    [DispId(39)] void ParentChanged (object sender, EventArgs e);
53:    [DispId(40)] void Resize (object sender, EventArgs e);
54:    [DispId(41)] void RightToLeftChanged (object sender, EventArgs e);
55:    [DispId(42)] void SizeChanged (object sender, EventArgs e);
56:    [DispId(43)] void StyleChanged (object sender, EventArgs e);
57:    [DispId(44)] void SystemColorsChanged (object sender, EventArgs e);
58:    [DispId(45)] void TabIndexChanged (object sender, EventArgs e);
59:    [DispId(46)] void TabStopChanged (object sender, EventArgs e);
60:    [DispId(47)] void TextChanged (object sender, EventArgs e);
61:    [DispId(48)] void Validated (object sender, EventArgs e);
62:    [DispId(49)] void VisibleChanged (object sender, EventArgs e);
63:    [DispId(50)] void QueryAccessibilityHelp (object sender,
64:      QueryAccessibilityHelpEventArgs e);
65:    [DispId(51)] void QueryContinueDrag (object sender,
66:      QueryContinueDragEventArgs e);
67:
68:    // Form's events with COM-visible parameters
69:    [DispId(52)] void Activated (object sender, EventArgs e);
70:    [DispId(53)] void Closed (object sender, EventArgs e);
71:    [DispId(54)] void Deactivate (object sender, EventArgs e);
72:    [DispId(55)] void Load (object sender, EventArgs e);
73:    [DispId(56)] void MaximizedBoundsChanged (object sender, EventArgs e);
74:    [DispId(57)] void MaximumSizeChanged (object sender, EventArgs e);
75:    [DispId(58)] void MdiChildActivate (object sender, EventArgs e);
76:    [DispId(59)] void MenuComplete (object sender, EventArgs e);
```

13

EXPOSING .NET
EVENTS TO COM
CLIENTS

LISTING 13.7   Continued

```
77:     [DispId(60)] void MenuStart (object sender, EventArgs e);
78:     [DispId(61)] void MinimumSizeChanged (object sender, EventArgs e);
79:
80:     // Control's events with COM-invisible parameters
81:     [DispId(62)] void ChangeUICues (object sender, bool changeFocus,
82:       bool changeKeyboard, bool showFocus, bool showKeyboard);
83:     [DispId(63)] void ControlAdded (object sender, IComponent control);
84:     [DispId(64)] void ControlRemoved (object sender, IComponent control);
85:     [DispId(65)] void Invalidated (object sender, int x, int y, int width,
86:       int height);
87:     [DispId(66)] void Layout (object sender, IComponent affectedControl,
88:       string affectedProperty);
89:     [DispId(67)] void Paint (object sender, IntPtr hdc, int x, int y,
90:       int width, int height);
91:     [DispId(68)] void Validating (object sender, ref bool cancel);
92:
93:     // Form's events with COM-invisible parameters
94:     [DispId(69)] void Closing (object sender, ref bool cancel);
95:     [DispId(70)] void InputLanguageChanged (object sender, byte charSet,
96:       CultureInfo culture, IntPtr inputLanguageHandle,
97:       string inputLanguageLayoutName);
98:     [DispId(71)] void InputLanguageChanging (object sender, ref bool cancel,
99:       bool sysCharSet, CultureInfo culture, IntPtr inputLanguageHandle,
100:       string inputLanguageLayoutName);
101: }
102:
103: // A Windows Form that exposes its events to COM using connection points
104: [ComSourceInterfaces(typeof(IFormEvents))]
105: public class ComFriendlyForm : Form
106: {
107:     //----------------------------------------------------------
108:     // Delegates for the COM-friendly event handlers
109:     //----------------------------------------------------------
110:
111:     public delegate void UICuesExpandedEventHandler(object sender,
112:       bool changeFocus, bool changeKeyboard, bool showFocus,
113:       bool showKeyboard);
114:
115:     public delegate void ControlExpandedEventHandler(object sender,
116:       IComponent control);
117:
118:     public delegate void InvalidateExpandedEventHandler(object sender,
119:       int x, int y, int width, int height);
120:
```

LISTING 13.7 Continued

```
121:   public delegate void LayoutExpandedEventHandler(object sender,
122:     IComponent affectedControl, string affectedProperty);
123:
124:   public delegate void PaintExpandedEventHandler(object sender,
125:     IntPtr hdc, int x, int y, int width, int height);
126:
127:   public delegate void CancelExpandedEventHandler(object sender,
128:     ref bool cancel);
129:
130:   public delegate void InputLanguageChangedExpandedEventHandler(
131:     object sender, byte charSet, CultureInfo culture,
132:     IntPtr inputLanguageHandle, string inputLanguageLayoutName);
133:
134:   public delegate void InputLanguageChangingExpandedEventHandler(
135:     object sender, ref bool cancel, bool sysCharSet, CultureInfo culture,
136:     IntPtr inputLanguageHandle, string inputLanguageLayoutName);
137:
138:   //--------------------------------------------------------
139:   // New events using COM-friendly delegates
140:   // (with the same names as the unfriendly events)
141:   //--------------------------------------------------------
142:
143:   public new event UICuesExpandedEventHandler ChangeUICues;
144:   public new event ControlExpandedEventHandler ControlAdded;
145:   public new event ControlExpandedEventHandler ControlRemoved;
146:   public new event InvalidateExpandedEventHandler Invalidated;
147:   public new event LayoutExpandedEventHandler Layout;
148:   public new event PaintExpandedEventHandler Paint;
149:   public new event CancelExpandedEventHandler Validating;
150:   public new event CancelExpandedEventHandler Closing;
151:   public new event InputLanguageChangedExpandedEventHandler
152:     InputLanguageChanged;
153:   public new event InputLanguageChangingExpandedEventHandler
154:     InputLanguageChanging;
155:
156:   //--------------------------------------------------------
157:   // Overridden On<Event> methods that not only call the
158:   // base On<Event> methods but also raise the new COM-friendly
159:   // events in case anyone's listening
160:   //--------------------------------------------------------
161:
162:   protected override void OnChangeUICues(UICuesEventArgs e)
163:   {
164:     base.OnChangeUICues(e);
```

LISTING 13.7   Continued

```
165:      if (ChangeUICues != null)
166:      {
167:        ChangeUICues(this, e.ChangeFocus, e.ChangeKeyboard, e.ShowFocus,
168:          e.ShowKeyboard);
169:      }
170:    }
171:
172:    protected override void OnControlAdded(ControlEventArgs e)
173:    {
174:      base.OnControlAdded(e);
175:      if (ControlAdded != null)
176:        ControlAdded(this, e.Control);
177:    }
178:
179:    protected override void OnControlRemoved(ControlEventArgs e)
180:    {
181:      base.OnControlRemoved(e);
182:      if (ControlRemoved != null)
183:        ControlRemoved(this, e.Control);
184:    }
185:
186:    protected override void OnInvalidated(InvalidateEventArgs e)
187:    {
188:      base.OnInvalidated(e);
189:      if (Invalidated != null)
190:      {
191:        Invalidated(this, e.InvalidRect.X, e.InvalidRect.Y,
192:          e.InvalidRect.Width, e.InvalidRect.Height);
193:      }
194:    }
195:
196:    protected override void OnLayout(LayoutEventArgs e)
197:    {
198:      base.OnLayout(e);
199:      if (Layout != null)
200:        Layout(this, e.AffectedControl, e.AffectedProperty);
201:    }
202:
203:    protected override void OnPaint(PaintEventArgs e)
204:    {
205:      base.OnPaint(e);
206:      if (Paint != null)
207:      {
208:        IntPtr hdc = e.Graphics.GetHdc();
209:        try
```

LISTING 13.7 Continued

```
210:      {
211:        Paint(this, hdc, e.ClipRectangle.X,
212:          e.ClipRectangle.Y, e.ClipRectangle.Width,
213:          e.ClipRectangle.Height);
214:      }
215:      finally { e.Graphics.ReleaseHdc(hdc); }
216:    }
217:  }
218:
219:  protected override void OnInputLanguageChanged(
220:    InputLanguageChangedEventArgs e)
221:  {
222:    base.OnInputLanguageChanged(e);
223:    if (InputLanguageChanged != null)
224:    {
225:      InputLanguageChanged(this, e.CharSet, e.Culture,
226:        e.InputLanguage.Handle, e.InputLanguage.LayoutName);
227:    }
228:  }
229:
230:  //----------------------------------------------------------
231:  // On<Event> methods that handle raised events then raise
232:  // the corresponding COM-friendly events, done this way
233:  // due to the by-reference parameter
234:  //----------------------------------------------------------
235:
236:  private void HandleValidating(object sender, CancelEventArgs e)
237:  {
238:    if (Validating != null)
239:    {
240:      // Pass the CancelEventArgs.Cancel value by-reference
241:      bool cancel = e.Cancel;
242:      Validating(this, ref cancel);
243:      e.Cancel = cancel;
244:    }
245:  }
246:
247:  private void HandleClosing(object sender, CancelEventArgs e)
248:  {
249:    if (Closing != null)
250:    {
251:      // Pass the CancelEventArgs.Cancel value by-reference
252:      bool cancel = e.Cancel;
253:      Closing(this, ref cancel);
254:      e.Cancel = cancel;
```

13

EXPOSING .NET
EVENTS TO COM
CLIENTS

LISTING 13.7   Continued

```
255:     }
256:   }
257:
258:   private void HandleInputLanguageChanging(object sender,
259:     InputLanguageChangingEventArgs e)
260:   {
261:     if (InputLanguageChanging != null)
262:     {
263:       // Pass the CancelEventArgs.Cancel value by-reference
264:       bool cancel = e.Cancel;
265:       InputLanguageChanging(this, ref cancel, e.SysCharSet, e.Culture,
266:         e.InputLanguage.Handle, e.InputLanguage.LayoutName);
267:       e.Cancel = cancel;
268:     }
269:   }
270:
271:   //------------------------------------------------------------
272:   // Constructor
273:   //------------------------------------------------------------
274:   public ComFriendlyForm()
275:   {
276:     base.Validating += new CancelEventHandler(HandleValidating);
277:     base.Closing += new CancelEventHandler(HandleClosing);
278:     base.InputLanguageChanging +=
279:       new InputLanguageChangingEventHandler(HandleInputLanguageChanging);
280:
281:     this.Text = ".NET Windows Form";
282:   }
283: }
```

Lines 1–5 use the System namespace for EventArgs and IntPtr, System.Globalization for CultureInfo, System.Windows.Forms for Form and the various EventArgs-derived classes, System.ComponentModel for CancelEventArgs and IComponent, and System.Runtime. InteropServices for ComSourceInterfacesAttribute, DispIdAttribute, and InterfaceTypeAttribute.

Lines 8–101 define the IFormEvents source interface with all 71 methods. It's defined as a dispinterface and has explicit DISPIDs to provide maximum flexibility to COM clients. Since the order of the source interface's methods doesn't matter, they are arranged by first listing the unaltered event handlers for Form and its two base classes (Control and Component), followed by the altered event handlers. These altered signatures (in Lines 81–100) match the delegate signatures in Lines 111–136.

These delegates are nested inside the `ComFriendlyForm` class, which is a common practice for expressing the relationship between delegates and the class that makes use of them. They could have easily been defined outside of the `ComFriendlyForm` declaration, and would have no effect on COM clients. The new delegate replacing `UICuesEventHandler` is named `UICues`**Expanded**`EventHandler`, the new delegate replacing `ControlEventHandler` is named `Control`**Expanded**`EventHandler`, and so on. These names are chosen because the various COM-invisible `EventArgs`-derived classes are expanded in these delegate signatures; rather than being contained inside a single `EventArgs`-derived parameter, the properties are exposed directly because they are often COM-visible types like strings and integers.

DIGGING DEEPER

Listing 13.7 could have defined new COM-visible `EventArgs`-derived classes such as `ComFriendlyUICuesEventArgs` and used these types instead so the new delegates would still have signatures that match the .NET design guidelines. However, besides cluttering the listing with 8 additional classes, the expanded delegates more closely represent COM expectations. In COM, source interface methods typically don't follow any particular pattern. For example, a Visual Basic 6 form's `MouseMove` event handler has the following form that resembles our expanded delegate:

```
Private Sub Form_MouseMove(Button As Integer, Shift As Integer, _
    X As Single, Y As Single)
```

Looking at `UICuesExpandedEventHandler` in Lines 111–113, notice how the original delegate signature:

```
public delegate void UICuesEventHandler(object sender, UICuesEventArgs e);
```

is "replaced" with:

```
public delegate void UICuesExpandedEventHandler(object sender,
    bool changeFocus, bool changeKeyboard, bool showFocus, bool showKeyboard);
```

because `UICuesEventArgs` has four boolean properties. `ControlEventArgs` has a single `Control` property, but exposing a `Control` parameter in `ControlExpandedEventHandler` doesn't help much because `Control` is also COM-invisible. Therefore, Lines 115 and 116 define `ControlExpandedEventHandler` with an `IComponent` parameter because `Control` implements this COM-visible interface. (Making the parameter a `Control` type would work for unmanaged C++ clients because they could call `QueryInterface` on the exported `IUnknown` type and obtain an `IComponent` interface pointer, but Visual Basic 6 clients would still be stuck due to lack of support for event handler signatures with `IUnknown` parameters.)

For `InvalidateExpandedEventHandler` in Lines 118 and 119, exposing the single `Rectangle` property from `InvalidateEventArgs` is undesirable because `System.Drawing.Rectangle` is COM-invisible. Therefore, `Rectangle`'s integer properties are exposed instead. For `PaintExpandedEventHandler` in Lines 124–125, we expose an HDC (a handle to a Windows Device Context) for the COM-invisible `Graphics` property of `PaintEventArgs` because unmanaged clients are accustomed to using HDCs when handling painting. The `CancelExpandedEventHandler` delegate in Lines 127 and 128 must define the boolean `cancel` parameter by-reference because the client can validly set its value inside the event handler code to indicate whether or not to cancel a raised event that uses this delegate.

The new events that use these delegate types are defined in Lines 143–154. Because they are given the same names as the events in the base classes, the `new` keyword is used (`Shadows` in Visual Basic .NET) with the goal of avoiding compiler warnings about hiding members of the base class. (It doesn't work in this case, however, as mentioned earlier.) These events could have been given different names, for example:

```
public event UICuesExpandedEventHandler ComFriendlyChangeUICues;
```

However, because the methods on the source interface must match the names of the events, keeping the original event names is desirable so our customized method signatures on the source interface can retain the familiar event names.

To make the new delegates and events we've defined useful, these new events must be raised with the appropriate data at the appropriate times. This is accomplished in Lines 162–228 by overriding `Form`'s `On`*`EventName`* methods and firing the new events inside these methods.

For example, the overridden `OnChangeUICues` method in Lines 162–170 first calls the base `OnChangeUICues`, which raises the original `ChangeUICues` event. Then, in Lines 167 and 168, it raises the new `ChangeUICues` event if there are any event handlers hooked up. This is checked by comparing the event member to null. To fill in the parameters of the new `ChangeUICues` delegate, the properties of the passed-in `UICuesEventArgs` instance are used. Most of the remaining methods follow this simple pattern of gluing the two events together.

The `Validating`, `Closing`, and `InputLanguageChanging` events are handled specially because their delegates have a boolean by-reference `cancel` parameter whose value may be changed by the event sink. Rather than overriding `Form`'s `OnValidating`, `OnClosing`, and `OnInputLanguageChanging` methods, `ComFriendlyForm` defines three event handlers (Lines 236–269) that it hooks up to these three events inside its constructor (Lines 274–282). Looking at `HandleValidating` as an example in Lines 236–245, a temporary variable is declared on Line 241 to retrieve and store the boolean value. This is done because C# doesn't allow passing an object's property by-reference directly. After the new event is raised to any COM event sinks that may be listening in Line 242, the `cancel` member of the passed-in `CancelEventArgs` instance is set to value of the by-reference parameter so the original event source can act on it appropriately. This technique of using an event handler to raise a similar event to COM event sinks was used back in Listing 13.1.

> **TIP**
>
> Listing 13.7 takes advantage of the fact that `Form` exposes a virtual `OnEventName` method for every event that needs to be customized. When an event doesn't have such a method, you could simply do what was done for the `Validating`, `Closing`, and `InputLanguageChanging` events—create a managed event handler that handles the COM interaction. An example of an event that doesn't have a corresponding `On...` method is `Form`'s `QueryAccessibilityHelp` event, but fortunately its parameters are COM-visible.

The COM Event Sink

Listing 13.8 lists parts of a Visual Basic 6 event sink that references an exported type library from Listing 13.7 and acts as an event sink for `ComFriendlyForm`. For brevity, portions of the code are omitted, but the full source code is available on this book's Web site. To compile this listing, first register the assembly from Listing 13.7 and export a type library. For example:

```
regasm /tlb Listing13_7.dll /codebase
```

The `/codebase` option can be used for convenience so the COM client can run within the VB6 IDE without having to install the assembly in the GAC or placing it in the directory containing `VB6.EXE`. Once a type library has been exported, ensure that the Visual Basic 6 project references not only `Listing13_7.tlb`, but also `mscorlib.tlb`, `System.Windows.Forms.tlb`, and `System.tlb`. These additional type libraries must be referenced because the `IFormEvents` methods have parameters whose types are defined in these dependent type libraries, such as `IComponent` or `KeyEventArgs`.

LISTING 13.8   A Visual Basic 6 Form that Sinks All the Events Exposed by `ComFriendlyForm` from Listing 13.7

```
1: Private WithEvents windowsForm As ComFriendlyForm
2:
3: Private Sub Form_Load()
4:   Set windowsForm = New ComFriendlyForm
5:   windowsForm.Show
6: End Sub
7:
```

LISTING 13.8   Continued

```
 8: Private Sub Form_Resize()
 9:   TreeView1.width = ScaleWidth
10:   TreeView1.height = ScaleHeight
11: End Sub
12:
13: ' Add an event notification to the TreeView. If this is the first
14: ' time the event has been raised, create a new node for it.
15: Private Sub AddMessage(node As String, message As String)
16:   On Error GoTo CreateNode
17:   TreeView1.Nodes.Add node, tvwChild, , message
18:   Exit Sub
19: CreateNode:
20:   TreeView1.Nodes.Add , , node, node
21:   TreeView1.Nodes.Add node, tvwChild, , message
22: End Sub
23:
24: Private Sub windowsForm_Activated(ByVal sender As Variant, _
25: ByVal e As mscorlib.EventArgs)
26:   AddMessage "Activated", Time
27: End Sub
28: ...
29: Private Sub windowsForm_ChangeUICues(ByVal sender As Variant, _
30: ByVal changeFocus As Boolean, ByVal changeKeyboard As Boolean, _
31: ByVal showFocus As Boolean, ByVal showKeyboard As Boolean)
32:   AddMessage "ChangeUICues", Time & ", ChangeFocus = " & changeFocus & _
33:     ", ChangeKeyboard = " & changeKeyboard & ", ShowFocus = " & showFocus & _
34:     ", ShowKeyboard = " & showKeyboard
35: End Sub
36: ...
37: Private Sub windowsForm_DragDrop(ByVal sender As Variant, _
38: ByVal e As System_Windows_Forms.DragEventArgs)
39:   ' Late bind to members of DragEventArgs
40:   Dim o As Object
41:   Set o = e
42:   AddMessage "DragDrop", Time & ", x = " & o.x & ", y = " & o.y & _
43:     ", KeyState = " & o.KeyState
44: End Sub
45: ...
```

Line 1 declares a ComFriendlyForm variable using WithEvents to enable the automatic event hookup, and Line 4 instantiates the ComFriendlyForm object, triggering the FindConnectionPoint calls behind-the-scenes. Lines 8–11 contain a standard event handler for the Visual Basic 6 Form's resize event, simply resizing the TreeView control named TreeView1 to occupy the entire surface area of the form. The TreeView control is the form's only control.

Lines 15–22 define the `AddMessage` method used by all of the Windows Form event handlers. This method adds a node to the `TreeView` control whose parent is specified by the `node` parameter, containing the text in the `message` parameter. If the tree node specified by the `node` string doesn't already exist, one is created so the child node can be added. With this technique, only the events raised show up in the `TreeView` control, and in the order each was first raised.

The `windowsForm_Activated` method in Lines 24–27 is the event handler for the `Activated` event. It's an example of a handler for a simple event that conveys no extra information besides the sender. For this kind of event, `AddMessage` is called with the event name for the node and the current time (using Visual Basic 6's `Time` method) for the message. The `windowsForm_ChangeUICues` method in Lines 29–35 demonstrates using additional parameters from a customized event handler and appending the information to the string sent to `AddMessage`.

For many of the event handlers whose signatures weren't modified, the `EventArgs`-derived class exposed has properties that need to be invoked via late binding because the class has an auto-dispatch class interface. The `windowsForm_DragDrop` method shown in Lines 37–44 late binds to the `DragEventArgs` parameter by setting it to an `Object` variable before invoking the properties. Some of the `EventArgs`-derived classes not shown in this listing have COM-invisible enum members, but their integral values can still be obtained from COM thanks to the internal `IDispatch` implementation used by .NET objects (described in the next chapter).

Figure 13.2 demonstrates what happens when running the Visual Basic 6 client application from Listing 13.8 and manipulating the Windows Form in order to provoke events.

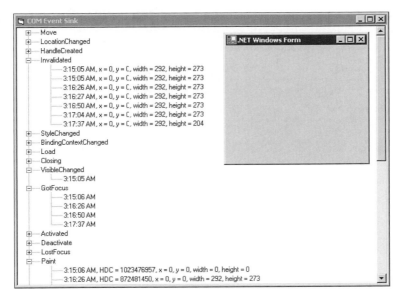

FIGURE 13.2

The Visual Basic 6 Form displays events raised by the foreground .NET Windows Form.

Conclusion

This chapter was mainly about the proper use of a single custom attribute—
ComSourceInterfacesAttribute. It's important to highlight this custom attribute more than
the ones from Chapter 12, "Customizing COM's View of .NET Components," because of its
importance in providing COM clients with a useable programming experience "out of the box."
Exposing .NET events to COM is the most notable area for which the default behavior performed by COM Interoperability is not the behavior that most people want.

Because defining an appropriate source interface, marking it as a dispinterface, and placing
DISPIDs on all of its members is tedious and a bit mysterious to those not familiar with COM
Interoperability or connection points, VB .NET's ComClassAttribute provides a nice mechanism
for shielding developers from this work and enabling a rapid application development (RAD)
experience. There's a price to pay for this easy-to-use mechanism, and that's the inability to
customize the generated source interface (without making use of the IL Disassembler and IL
Assembler, which defeats the RAD motivation behind using ComClassAttribute). The main
drawback of using ComClassAttribute for events support is the negative impact on versioning
when you want to add more events to your class, an action that would have been safe to do
otherwise.

> **TIP**
>
> If you want your .NET class to expose a source interface already defined in a type
> library (say ISourceInterface), you can go one step further than importing the type
> library and marking the class with a ComSourceInterfacesAttribute that lists the
> source interface. You can also have your class implement the type library importer-
> generated interface ISourceInterface_Event, which contains all the event members
> that correspond to the methods of the source interface. These events use the delegate
> types also generated by the importer, so you don't have to go through the hassle of
> defining your own delegates. Plus, by implementing the ISourceInterface_Event
> interface you get compile-time errors rather than run-time errors if your class doesn't
> correctly define all the necessary event members. You might even consider defining a
> brand new source interface in a type library and importing a Primary Interop Assembly
> (rather than starting in managed code) to take advantage of this extra support.

Implementing COM Interfaces for Binary Compatibility

IN THIS CHAPTER

- Getting Interface Definitions   628
- Binary Compatibility with Visual Basic 6 Classes   629
- Example: Implementing Office XP Smart Tag Interfaces   634
- Interface Implementation Shortcuts in Visual Studio .NET   650
- Common Problems When Implementing COM Interfaces   653
- COM Interfaces with Default CCW Implementations   657
- COM Interfaces Bridged to Different .NET Types   678

To conclude our examination of developing .NET components that are exposed to COM, we're going to focus on implementing COM interfaces in managed code. A COM interface is simply an interface originally defined in COM with a unique IID.

A .NET component that implements a COM interface is sometimes said to be a *COM-compatible* component, or one that is *binary-compatible* with an existing COM component. This means that existing COM clients don't need to be re-written or even recompiled in order to take advantage of .NET components because these new components implement the same old interfaces that COM clients expect. This process usually begins by importing a type library containing a COM interface definition, and ends with registering the assembly containing the .NET class implementing the interface (and possibly exporting a type library).

The process of implementing a COM interface is really no different than implementing a .NET interface. The main difference is that the interface's documentation won't exactly match the signatures in the .NET definition of the interface unless it happens to have any .NET-specific documentation. The other issue, discussed in the first section, is that whereas a metadata definition always exists for a .NET interface (otherwise it wouldn't be a .NET interface), a metadata definition of a COM interface often doesn't exist until you create one.

Many COM interfaces are already implemented by the CLR-supplied COM-Callable Wrapper (CCW) for any .NET object, so they don't need to be implemented in managed code. If you look back at Figure 11.5 at the end of Chapter 11, ".NET Design Guidelines for Components Used by COM Clients," you can see a bunch of COM interfaces listed as implemented by the Grid class inside OLEVIEW.EXE, such as IConnectionPointContainer, IMarshal, and ISupportErrorInfo. These extra interfaces make any .NET object a premier COM object with bells and whistles to enhance its interaction with other COM objects. These interfaces can be automatically implemented by CCWs because all .NET objects have rich information available that doesn't come freely in the world of COM.

Because all of these "plumbing interfaces" are already implemented for your .NET classes, you'll typically only need to worry about implementing application-specific COM interfaces to get higher level tasks accomplished. This chapter walks you through the process of implementing two COM interfaces defined by Microsoft Office XP. After that, we'll look at what can be done if you want to provide your own customized implementations of the COM interfaces already implemented by your object's CCW.

Getting Interface Definitions

One of the tricky parts of implementing a COM interface is getting the required metadata definition of it. There are essentially three ways to get a .NET definition of a COM interface:

- Use a COM interface already defined in a Primary Interop Assembly or elsewhere in the .NET Framework.

- Generate an Interop Assembly with the type library importer and use the definition contained inside.
- Write your own interface definition in source code.

The first option is recommended due to the identity issues discussed in Chapter 3, "The Essentials for Using COM in Managed Code." Although implementing a COM interface is usually done for communication with COM components, there may be .NET components that wish to talk to yours using a well-known COM interface, and all .NET components must agree on the official interface definition. This option is also the easiest because you don't have to worry about generating the interface definition. Therefore, this option is no different than implementing any .NET interface.

The second option is easy to do when a type library containing the interface definition already exists. The only caveats to this approach are the same caveats to using your own Interop Assemblies rather than Primary Interop Assemblies. If only COM components communicate with your object via the COM interface, then it doesn't matter where you get the interface definition from. Of course, if no type library exists then you might be forced to create one from an IDL file or via some other mechanism.

The third option is the most difficult, and is the subject of Chapter 21, "Manually Defining COM Types in Source Code."

> **CAUTION**
>
> Don't attempt to define a COM interface in managed code before reading Chapter 21. Omitting the necessary custom attributes can be harmful to the Windows Registry.

Binary Compatibility with Visual Basic 6 Classes

Visual Basic 6 projects have a "binary compatibility" option that enables users to express their desire to be binary-compatible with an existing COM component. This option ensures that the same CLSIDs, IIDs, and LIBIDs are used when recompiling a project by examining the CLSIDs, IIDs, and LIBIDs in an existing type library. Because the CLR's algorithms for generating LIBIDs, CLSIDs, and IIDs (discussed in Chapter 11) keeps them fixed when recompiling as long as you don't make incompatible changes, and also because you can control your GUIDs using custom attributes, there's no need for such an option in Visual Studio .NET when recompiling a .NET project. But if you're rewriting a Visual Basic 6 component in Visual Basic .NET but want the new component to be binary compatible with the old one, you should reference the old component and implement its interfaces to be sure that you're exposing everything in a compatible way.

Assume you have a simple VB6 class module called `Class1` that has some methods and properties in a project called `Project1`. Although the class doesn't appear to implement an interface within the VB6 IDE, the `Class1` coclass actually implements a hidden `_Class1` class interface. If you were to translate the source code for `Class1` to VB .NET syntax, compiling it would not result in a class that's binary compatible because it would have a different CLSID and its class interface would have a different IID. You could mark your class with `GuidAttribute` to give it the appropriate CLSID (which you'd need to obtain by opening your VB6 component's type library in a viewer such as `OLEVIEW.EXE`). Because you can't control the IID for your class interface, you'd need to suppress it using `ClassInterface(ClassInterfaceType.None)`, then define and implement a real .NET interface containing the appropriate IID with the members of `_Class1`. (Or you could use `ComClassAttribute` and give it the appropriate CLSID and IID, which effectively does the same thing.) Still, you manually need to ensure that your new interface is binary-compatible with the old `_Class1` interface, which may not even be possible. For example, there's no way to define a .NET property that gets exposed to COM as a property with all three accessors (`Get`, `Let`, and `Set`).

Therefore, the way to ensure binary compatibility is to reference an imported Interop Assembly for the VB6 project and implement its `_Class1` interface, still suppressing the CLR-generated class interface because it's not binary compatible with the VB6-generated class interface. Alternatively, you could implement the `Class1` coclass interface generated by the type library importer, because it has the same members. This would look like the following in Visual Basic .NET:

```
Imports System.Runtime.InteropServices

Namespace NewProject
  <Guid("0e65a036-beed-465d-b162-8e5561de3c17"), ProgId("Project1.Class1"), _
    ClassInterface(ClassInterfaceType.None)> _
  Public Class Class1
    Implements Project1.Class1
    ...
  End Class
End Namespace
```

The VB .NET `NewProject.Class1` class is binary compatible with the VB6 `Class1` class. The `GuidAttribute` is still needed to give the class the same CLSID as the VB6 class, and `ProgIdAttribute` is used to preserve the old ProgID because we had to change the fully-qualified name of the class to avoid a name conflict with the imported coclass interface.

> **TIP**
>
> It might seem undesirable to reference the old COM component when you're writing a new .NET component that's supposed to replace it. However, once you've obtained the type definitions from the imported Interop Assembly, you can discard the old COM component. Only .NET interface definitions in the Interop Assembly are required to make binary compatibility work.

If the original Visual Basic 6 class defined events, then the coclass would have not only implemented a hidden _Class1 class interface, but also exposed a hidden __Class1 source interface. The benefit of having the VB .NET class implement the coclass interface (Class1) rather than the real interface (_Class1) is that the event members are inherited by the coclass interface so the compiler can enforce that you're implementing all the required events. To accomplish the same thing without implementing the coclass interface, you'd need to implement the two interfaces it would derive from: _Class1 and the importer-generated __Class1_Event interface. Still, in order to be binary compatible with a coclass that exposes a source interface, you'd need to use ComSourceInterfacesAttribute as follows:

```
Imports System.Runtime.InteropServices

Namespace NewProject
  <Guid("0e65a036-beed-465d-b162-8e5561de3c17"), ProgId("Project1.Class1"), _
    ClassInterface(ClassInterfaceType.None), _
    ComSourceInterfaces(GetType(Project1.__Class1))> _
  Public Class Class1
    Implements Project1.Class1

    ...
  End Class
End Namespace
```

This NewProject.Class1 class is now binary compatible with a Class1 class that exposes events. Such a class would be exported as follows (shown in IDL):

```
[
  uuid(0E65A036-BEED-465D-B162-8E5561DE3C17),
  version(1.0),
  custom(0F21F359-AB84-41E8-9A78-36D110E6D2F9, "NewProject.Class1")
]
coclass Class1 {
  interface _Object;
  [default] interface Class1;
  [default, source] dispinterface __Class1;
};
```

If your VB6 class implemented any interfaces besides its class interface, you'd need to obtain .NET definitions for those interfaces and implement them as well.

CAUTION

Be careful with .NET classes that implement coclass interfaces generated by the type library importer (such as Class1 in the previous example). Version 1.0 of the CLR has a bug such that passing a .NET object as a parameter typed as a coclass interface exposes a v-table to COM that contains only the methods of IUnknown and IDispatch (since, after all, the .NET coclass interface has no members directly defined on it). Therefore, attempting to call members of the original coclass's default interface fails due to accessing memory that doesn't belong to the v-table. This does not affect passing COM objects in such a way; only .NET objects passed to unmanaged code.

If a COM client queries for the original default interface (_Class1), it will receive the expected v-table rather than an empty one. Therefore, this problem is usually not noticed when COM marshaling is involved (which performs QueryInterface calls), but can appear when COM marshaling is avoided since the interface pointer is given directly to the client! To fix this, you could undo the coclass interface parameter/field replacement done by the importer in an Interop Assembly (by changing Class1 parameters and fields to _Class1) using the techniques of Chapter 7, "Modifying Interop Assemblies."

DIGGING DEEPER

To be truly binary compatible with a COM component, you should implement all of its interfaces (and source all of its source interfaces, if it has them). Visual Basic 6 classes implement a number of COM interfaces that are hidden from the author, such as IConnectionPoint, IConnectionPointContainer, IExternalConnection, and so on, and these interface would need to be implemented by the .NET component attempting to be binary compatible. Fortunately, as discussed in the "COM Interfaces With Default CCW Implementations" section later in this chapter, all CCWs for .NET classes also implement a number of COM interfaces automatically. However, two interfaces that are implemented by a VB6 ActiveX DLL are *not* automatically implemented by a CCW: IConnectionPoint and IExternalConnection. In the rare case that you had COM clients that depend on a successful QueryInterface call for either of these two interfaces, you'd need to implement them manually in your .NET class.

Unrelated to interfaces, Visual Basic 6 class modules have an Instancing property that determines whether or not external components are allowed to use or create instances of the class, as well as some additional behavior. The `Instancing` property has six valid values, and the type of project you create decides which of the values you can use. The rules for the `Instancing` property are summarized in Table 14.1.

TABLE 14.1 Values of the `Instancing` Property in Visual Basic 6, and the Project Types to Which Each Applies

Instancing	*Project Types*		
`Private`	ActiveX EXE Standard EXE	ActiveX DLL	ActiveX Control
`PublicNotCreatable`	ActiveX EXE	ActiveX DLL	ActiveX Control
`SingleUse`	ActiveX EXE		
`GlobalSingleUse`	ActiveX EXE		
`MultiUse`	ActiveX EXE	ActiveX DLL	
`GlobalMultiUse`	ActiveX EXE	ActiveX DLL	

If you're concerned about replacing Visual Basic 6 components with .NET components that should exhibit the same instancing behavior, here is an explanation of what each of these settings mean, and how to achieve the same results with .NET components:

- `Private`. Other components cannot create instances of the class and the class isn't described in the project's type library. In .NET, making a class non-public achieves the same effect for both .NET and COM clients.

- `PublicNotCreatable`. Other components can use the class but cannot create instances of it. (This is the default setting for classes added to an ActiveX Control project.) In .NET, defining an internal default constructor achieves the same effect. Whereas any classes in the current assembly can instantiate the object and pass it to other components, other assemblies or COM components can only use an instance if one is passed to them.

- `SingleUse`. Allows other applications to create instances of the class, but each time an instance is created, a new instance of the component is started. There's no built-in way to get this behavior in .NET, but you could create a surrogate executable that enforces this behavior.

- `GlobalSingleUse`. Like `SingleUse`, but the class's members can be invoked like global functions. Doing the same thing as for `SingleUse` but defining all the members as static (or using a `Module` in VB .NET) can provide similar behavior for .NET clients. COM clients, however, are out of luck because only instance members are directly exposed.

- `MultiUse`. Allows other applications to create instances of the class. This is a standard public class with a public default constructor in .NET. (There needs to be a public *default* constructor for COM's sake.)

- **GlobalMultiUse**. Like `MultiUse`, except that class members can be invoked like global functions (from other components only). Again, a similar effect can be achieved with static members, but COM clients cannot directly use them.

Example: Implementing Office XP Smart Tag Interfaces

To demonstrate implementing a regular COM interface (not a VB6 class interface), we're going to create a smart tag component for Office XP. Smart Tags is a feature of Microsoft Office XP that enables certain types of data in a Word document or Excel spreadsheet to be recognized and tagged with extra information. A user can then choose customized actions by hovering the mouse over a tagged word or phrase and clicking on an icon that presents a context menu. Tagged text is indicated by a faint, dotted purple line. A canonical example is shown in Figure 14.1, in which a date is recognized by a smart tag. The user is given the choices of scheduling a meeting on this date or showing this date on a calendar.

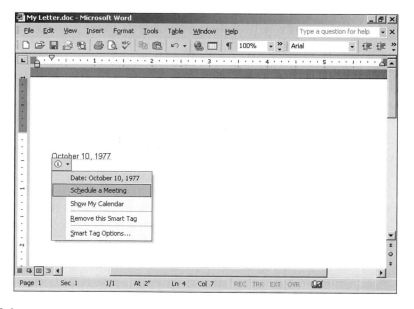

FIGURE 14.1

A smart tag recognizes a date typed in a Word 2002 document.

Smart tags can be created either with an XML file or with a COM DLL. Of course, we're going to look at the COM-based implementation for which smart tags are simply COM objects that need to implement interfaces defined in the Smart Tags type library. The two important interfaces are ISmartTagRecognizer and ISmartTagAction.

An object that implements ISmartTagRecognizer has the task of viewing text and recognizing the data it's looking for. Applications such as Word 2002 or Excel 2002 continually call the ISmartTagRecognizer.Recognize method with strings from the document currently being edited. If the COM object recognizes the special text that it's searching for, it can mark it with a unique label that essentially gives the text a "strong type" such as a date in the previous example.

But recognizing special types of information is only half the story. Acting upon special information is the other half. An object that implements ISmartTagAction enables applications to present the user with one or more actions (such as "Schedule a Meeting" or "Show My Calendar") and implements those actions.

For our smart tag example, we're going to implement a simple "Developer Terminology Smart Tag" (or DevTag for short). The idea is that a .NET component implementing ISmartTagRecognizer searches the active document for programming-related terms. If it finds any, it presents the user with the option to look up the term at MSDN Online (msdn.microsoft.com). While the commercial success of such a smart tag seems unlikely, developers such as yourself should appreciate such an addition to Office.

The recognizer and action objects in this example support two kinds of smart tags for two types of data—interfaces and technologies. The action for either type of information is the same; simply look up the word on MSDN Online. To recognize interfaces typed by the user, the recognizer simply looks for words at least three characters long that begin with a capital "I." To recognize technologies, the recognizer checks for keywords. For simplicity, there are only two possible technologies—".NET" and "COM."

Figure 14.2 shows a .NET and COM representation of the two classes we're going to implement—DevTagRecognizer and DevTagAction. According to the smart tag documentation, recognizers and actions need to implement the IDispatch interface in addition to the smart tag-specific interfaces. Fortunately, we know that this interface implementation is already taken care of by the CLR. In order to plug into Office XP, smart tag components must be registered in a special location of the Windows Registry. Therefore, we'll use custom registration and unregistration functions to perform this extra work.

Listing 14.1 contains an implementation of the DevTag component in Visual Basic .NET. It uses an Interop Assembly imported from the Smart Tags type library.

14

IMPLEMENTING
COM INTERFACES
FOR BINARY
COMPATIBILITY

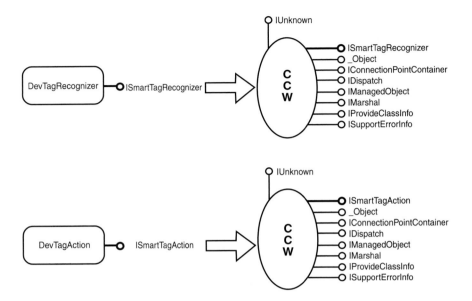

FIGURE 14.2
.NET and COM representations of the two classes implemented in Listing 14.1.

LISTING 14.1   Implementing Two COM Interfaces—`ISmartTagRecognizer` and `ISmartTagAction`—in Visual Basic .NET

```
 1: Imports System
 2: Imports SmartTagLib
 3: Imports Microsoft.VisualBasic
 4: Imports System.Runtime.InteropServices
 5: Imports Microsoft.Win32
 6:
 7: Namespace Sams.SmartTags
 8:
 9:     ' Enumeration of verbs
10:     Public Enum Verbs
11:         LookupInterface = 1
12:         LookupTechnology = 2
13:     End Enum
14:
15:     ' Enumeration of smart tag types
16:     Public Enum TagTypes
17:         IsInterface = 1
18:         IsTechnology = 2
19:     End Enum
```

LISTING 14.1 Continued

```
20:
21:   ' The recognizer class
22:   <ClassInterface(ClassInterfaceType.None)> Public Class DevTagRecognizer
23:     Implements ISmartTagRecognizer
24:
25:     ' Add a custom key to the registry
26:     <ComRegisterFunction()> _
27:     Private Shared Sub RegisterFunction(ByVal t As Type)
28:       Registry.CurrentUser.CreateSubKey( _
29:         "Software\Microsoft\Office\Common\Smart Tag\Recognizers\" _
30:         & t.GUID.ToString("B")).Close()
31:     End Sub
32:
33:     ' Undo the work from the registration function
34:     <ComUnregisterFunction()> _
35:     Private Shared Sub UnregisterFunction(ByVal t As Type)
36:       Registry.CurrentUser.DeleteSubKey( _
37:         "Software\Microsoft\Office\Common\Smart Tag\Recognizers\" _
38:         & t.GUID.ToString("B"), False)
39:     End Sub
40:
41:     ' Return the ProgID for this class
42:     Public ReadOnly Property ProgId() As String _
43:       Implements ISmartTagRecognizer.ProgId
44:       Get
45:         ProgId = "Sams.SmartTags.DevTagRecognizer"
46:       End Get
47:     End Property
48:
49:     ' Return a name to be displayed in the
50:     ' Tools/Autocorrect Options/Smart Tags dialog
51:     Public ReadOnly Property Name(ByVal LocaleID As Integer) As String _
52:       Implements ISmartTagRecognizer.Name
53:       Get
54:         Name = "Developer Terminology Recognizer"
55:       End Get
56:     End Property
57:
58:     ' Return a description
59:     Public ReadOnly Property Desc(ByVal LocaleID As Integer) As String _
60:       Implements ISmartTagRecognizer.Desc
61:       Get
62:         Desc = "The Developer Terminology Recognizer recognizes two " & _
63:           "kinds of programming terms - interfaces and technologies."
```

14

IMPLEMENTING
COM INTERFACES
FOR BINARY
COMPATIBILITY

LISTING 14.1   Continued

```
64:        End Get
65:      End Property
66:
67:      ' Return the number of smart tag types supported
68:      Public ReadOnly Property SmartTagCount() As Integer _
69:        Implements ISmartTagRecognizer.SmartTagCount
70:        Get
71:          SmartTagCount = [Enum].GetValues(GetType(TagTypes)).Length
72:        End Get
73:      End Property
74:
75:      ' Return the name of the smart tag type specified by SmartTagID
76:      Public ReadOnly Property SmartTagName(ByVal SmartTagID As Integer) _
77:        As String Implements ISmartTagRecognizer.SmartTagName
78:        Get
79:          If (SmartTagID = TagTypes.IsInterface) Then
80:            SmartTagName = "schemas-sams-com/DevTag#interface"
81:          ElseIf (SmartTagID = TagTypes.IsTechnology) Then
82:            SmartTagName = "schemas-sams-com/DevTag#technology"
83:          Else
84:            Throw New ArgumentOutOfRangeException("SmartTagID", _
85:              SmartTagID, _
86:              "Expected TagTypes.IsInterface or TagTypes.IsTechnology.")
87:          End If
88:        End Get
89:      End Property
90:
91:      ' Return a URL where actions can be downloaded
92:      Public ReadOnly Property SmartTagDownloadURL( _
93:        ByVal SmartTagID As Integer) As String _
94:        Implements ISmartTagRecognizer.SmartTagDownloadURL
95:        Get
96:          ' We don't have such a URL
97:          SmartTagDownloadURL = ""
98:        End Get
99:      End Property
100:
101:      ' Recognize the programmer terms
102:      Public Sub Recognize(ByVal Text As String, _
103:        ByVal DataType As IF_TYPE, ByVal LocaleID As Integer, _
104:        ByVal RecognizerSite As ISmartTagRecognizerSite) _
105:        Implements ISmartTagRecognizer.Recognize
106:
107:        Dim word As String
```

LISTING 14.1 Continued

```
108:        Dim words() As String = Text.Split()
109:        Dim index As Integer = 1
110:
111:        For Each word In words
112:          If (Char.IsPunctuation(word.Chars(word.Length-1))) Then
113:            word = word.Substring(0, word.Length-1)
114:          End If
115:
116:          If (word.StartsWith("I") And word.Length > 3) Then
117:            RecognizerSite.CommitSmartTag("schemas-sams-com/" & _
118:              "DevTag#interface", index, word.Length, Nothing)
119:          ElseIf (word = ".NET" Or word = "COM") Then
120:            RecognizerSite.CommitSmartTag("schemas-sams-com/" & _
121:              "DevTag#technology", index, word.Length, Nothing)
122:          End If
123:          index = index + word.Length + 1
124:        Next word
125:      End Sub
126:    End Class
127:
128:    ' The action class
129:    <ClassInterface(ClassInterfaceType.None)> Public Class DevTagAction
130:      Implements ISmartTagAction
131:
132:      ' Add a custom key to the registry
133:      <ComRegisterFunction()> _
134:      Private Shared Sub RegisterFunction(ByVal t As Type)
135:        Registry.CurrentUser.CreateSubKey( _
136:          "Software\Microsoft\Office\Common\Smart Tag\Actions\" _
137:          & t.GUID.ToString("B")).Close()
138:      End Sub
139:
140:      ' Undo the work from the registration function
141:      <ComUnregisterFunction()> _
142:      Private Shared Sub UnregisterFunction(ByVal t As Type)
143:        Registry.CurrentUser.DeleteSubKey( _
144:          "Software\Microsoft\Office\Common\Smart Tag\Actions\" _
145:          & t.GUID.ToString("B"), False)
146:      End Sub
147:
148:      ' Return the ProgID for this class
149:      Public ReadOnly Property ProgId() As String _
150:        Implements ISmartTagAction.ProgId
151:        Get
```

14

IMPLEMENTING
COM INTERFACES
FOR BINARY
COMPATIBILITY

LISTING 14.1   Continued

```
152:           ProgId = "Sams.SmartTags.DevTagAction"
153:        End Get
154:     End Property
155:
156:     ' Return a simple name
157:     Public ReadOnly Property Name(ByVal LocaleID As Integer) As String _
158:        Implements ISmartTagAction.Name
159:        Get
160:           Name = "Developer Terminology Actions"
161:        End Get
162:     End Property
163:
164:     ' Return a description
165:     Public ReadOnly Property Desc(ByVal LocaleID As Integer) As String _
166:        Implements ISmartTagAction.Desc
167:        Get
168:           Desc = "Provides actions for programming terms"
169:        End Get
170:     End Property
171:
172:     ' Return the number of smart tag types supported
173:     Public ReadOnly Property SmartTagCount() As Integer _
174:        Implements ISmartTagAction.SmartTagCount
175:        Get
176:           SmartTagCount = [Enum].GetValues(GetType(TagTypes)).Length
177:        End Get
178:     End Property
179:
180:     ' Return the name of the smart tag type specified by SmartTagID
181:     Public ReadOnly Property SmartTagName(ByVal SmartTagID As Integer) _
182:        As String Implements ISmartTagAction.SmartTagName
183:        Get
184:          If (SmartTagID = TagTypes.IsInterface) Then
185:             SmartTagName = "schemas-sams-com/DevTag#interface"
186:          ElseIf (SmartTagID = TagTypes.IsTechnology) Then
187:             SmartTagName = "schemas-sams-com/DevTag#technology"
188:          Else
189:             Throw New ArgumentOutOfRangeException("SmartTagID", _
190:                SmartTagID, _
191:                "Expected TagTypes.IsInterface or TagTypes.IsTechnology.")
192:          End If
193:        End Get
194:     End Property
195:
```

LISTING 14.1 Continued

```
196:    ' Return the caption of the smart tag type specified by SmartTagID
197:    Public ReadOnly Property SmartTagCaption( _
198:      ByVal SmartTagID As Integer, ByVal LocaleID As Integer) As String _
199:      Implements ISmartTagAction.SmartTagCaption
200:      Get
201:        If (SmartTagID = TagTypes.IsInterface) Then
202:          SmartTagCaption = "Developer Term: Interface"
203:        ElseIf (SmartTagID = TagTypes.IsTechnology) Then
204:          SmartTagCaption = "Developer Term: Technology"
205:        Else
206:          Throw New ArgumentOutOfRangeException("SmartTagID", _
207:            SmartTagID, _
208:            "Expected TagTypes.IsInterface or TagTypes.IsTechnology.")
209:        End If
210:      End Get
211:    End Property
212:
213:    ' Return the number of verbs supported for the
214:    ' smart tag type specified by SmartTagName
215:    Public ReadOnly Property VerbCount(ByVal SmartTagName As String) _
216:      As Integer Implements ISmartTagAction.VerbCount
217:      Get
218:        If (SmartTagName = "schemas-sams-com/DevTag#interface" Or _
219:          SmartTagName = "schemas-sams-com/DevTag#technology") Then
220:          VerbCount = 1
221:        Else
222:          Throw New ArgumentException("Only tag names of 'interface'" & _
223:            " or 'technology' are supported.", SmartTagName)
224:        End If
225:      End Get
226:    End Property
227:
228:    ' Return a unique identifier for the verb
229:    ' specified by VerbIndex and the tag specified by SmartTagName
230:    Public ReadOnly Property VerbID(ByVal SmartTagName As String, _
231:      ByVal VerbIndex As Integer) As Integer _
232:      Implements ISmartTagAction.VerbID
233:      Get
234:        If (SmartTagName = "schemas-sams-com/DevTag#interface") Then
235:          VerbID = Verbs.LookupInterface
236:        ElseIf (SmartTagName = "schemas-sams-com/DevTag#technology") Then
237:          VerbID = Verbs.LookupTechnology
238:        Else
239:          Throw New ArgumentException("Only tag names of 'interface'" & _
```

14

Listing 14.1   Continued

```
240:                " or 'technology' are supported.", SmartTagName)
241:          End If
242:       End Get
243:    End Property
244:
245:    ' Return a caption for the verb specified by VerbID
246:    Public ReadOnly Property VerbCaptionFromID( _
247:      ByVal VerbID As Integer, ByVal ApplicationName As String, _
248:      ByVal LocaleID As Integer) As String _
249:      Implements ISmartTagAction.VerbCaptionFromID
250:      Get
251:        If (VerbID = Verbs.LookupInterface) Then
252:          VerbCaptionFromID = _
253:            "Find online documentation for this interface"
254:        ElseIf (VerbID = Verbs.LookupTechnology) Then
255:          VerbCaptionFromID = _
256:            "Find online documentation for this technology"
257:        Else
258:          Throw New ArgumentOutOfRangeException("VerbID", VerbID, _
259:            "Expected Verbs.LookupInterface or Verbs.LookupTechnology.")
260:        End If
261:      End Get
262:    End Property
263:
264:    ' Return a name for the verb specified by VerbID
265:    Public ReadOnly Property VerbNameFromID(ByVal VerbID As Integer) _
266:      As String Implements ISmartTagAction.VerbNameFromID
267:      Get
268:        VerbNameFromID = [Enum].Format(GetType(Verbs), VerbID, "G")
269:      End Get
270:    End Property
271:
272:    ' Act upon a verb
273:    Public Sub InvokeVerb( _
274:      ByVal VerbID As Integer, ByVal ApplicationName As String, _
275:      ByVal Target As Object, ByVal Properties As ISmartTagProperties, _
276:      ByVal Text As String, ByVal XML As String) _
277:      Implements ISmartTagAction.InvokeVerb
278:
279:      Dim explorer As Object
280:
281:      If (VerbID = Verbs.LookupInterface Or _
282:        VerbID = Verbs.LookupTechnology) Then
283:        explorer = CreateObject("InternetExplorer.Application")
```

LISTING 14.1 Continued

```
284:            explorer.Navigate2( _
285:              "http://search.microsoft.com/us/dev/default.asp?qu=" & Text & _
286:              "&boolean=ALL&nq=NEW&so=RECCNT&ig=01&i=00&i=01&i=02&i=03" & _
287:              "&i=04&i=05&i=06&i=07&i=08&i=09&i=10&i=11&i=12&i=13&i=14" & _
288:              "&i=15&i=16&i=17&i=18&ig=02&i=19&i=20&i=21&i=22&i=23&i=24" & _
289:              "&i=25&i=26&i=27&i=28&i=29&i=30&i=31&i=32&i=33&i=34&ig=03" & _
290:              "&i=35&i=36&i=37&i=38&i=39&i=40&i=41&ig=04&i=42&i=43&i=44" & _
291:              "&i=45&i=46&i=47&i=48&i=49&i=50&i=51&i=52&i=53&i=54&i=55" & _
292:              "&i=56&i=57&i=58&ig=05&ig=06&ig=07&p=1&nq=NEW")
293:
294:            explorer.Visible = True
295:          Else
296:            Throw New ArgumentOutOfRangeException("VerbID", VerbID, _
297:              "Expected Verbs.LookupInterface or Verbs.LookupTechnology.")
298:          End If
299:      End Sub
300:    End Class
301: End Namespace
```

Lines 1–6 list several namespaces:

- System for Enum, Type, ArgumentException, and ArgumentOutOfRangeException
- SmartTagLib for the ISmartTagRecognizer and ISmartTagAction interfaces and related types
- Microsoft.VisualBasic for CreateObject
- System.Runtime.InteropServices for ComRegisterFunctionAttribute and ComUnregisterFunctionAttribute
- Microsoft.Win32 for Registry

Line 7 declares a namespace of Sams.SmartTags. The first two types in Lines 10–19 are enumerations that are used by the recognizer and actions. The Verbs enum defines the supported actions (also called "verbs" in some places of the API)—looking up an interface and looking up a technology. Although these two actions are really the same simple lookup, they are split into two because the text displayed to the user is slightly different depending on whether the current word is an interface or technology. The TagTypes enum defines the two tags supported—tags for interfaces and tags for technologies.

Line 22 begins the DevTagRecognizer class that implements ISmartTagRecognizer. Both the DevTagRecognizer and DevTagAction classes are marked with ClassInterfaceType.None to suppress their class interfaces. This isn't necessary but it's good practice, especially because each class already implements an interface exposing its important functionality. This interface

14

IMPLEMENTING
COM INTERFACES
FOR BINARY
COMPATIBILITY

contains five properties plus the important `Recognize` method. But first, the `DevTagRecognizer` class contains a pair of custom registration methods that should look familiar from Chapter 12, "Customizing COM's View of .NET Components."

The `RegisterFunction` method in Lines 26–31 uses the `Microsoft.Win32.Registry` class to add a custom subkey that Microsoft Office needs in order to know about the recognizer. We must add a subkey with the recognizer's CLSID (including curly braces) so using `t.GUID.ToString("B")` does the trick. Because `RegisterFunction` is marked with `ComRegisterFunctionAttribute`, it gets invoked whenever the assembly is registered.

The `UnregisterFunction` method in Lines 34–39 undoes the registration by simply deleting the subkey that was added in `RegisterFunction`. As advised in Chapter 12, the two-parameter `DeleteSubKey` overload is used with `False` as the second parameter so no exception is thrown if the subkey doesn't already exist. Because `UnregisterFunction` is marked with `ComUnregisterFunctionAttribute`, it gets invoked whenever the assembly is unregistered.

The `ProgId` property in Lines 42–47 has the job of returning the ProgID string for the recognizer class. Because the class has no `ProgIdAttribute`, it's simply the fully-qualified class name. The `Name` property in Lines 51-56 returns a short title for the recognizer, and the `Desc` property in Lines 59–65 returns a description. For this simple example, all `LocaleID` parameters are ignored because we're only prepared to deal with English.

The `SmartTagCount` property in Lines 68–73 returns the number of smart tags supported. We could just return 2, but to be more robust in case someone later adds members to the `TagTypes` enum, Line 71 calls `GetValues` on `System.Enum` to obtain an array of the `TagType` values, then calls `Array.Length` to get the desired number. The `Enum` identifier needs to be placed in square brackets on Line 88 because it's a keyword in Visual Basic .NET.

TIP

When using enumerations, check out the handy static methods of the `System.Enum` type in the .NET Framework SDK documentation, such as `Enum.GetValues` and `Enum.Format` used in Listing 14.1.

The `SmartTagName` property in Lines 76–89 returns the official smart tag name for the corresponding integer passed in. The incoming integer is a number from 1 to `SmartTagCount`, which is represented by the `TagTypes` enum. (That's why the values of the `TagTypes` enumeration needed to be explicitly defined as starting with the number 1.) An official smart tag name must be a unique string. The convention for this string is *UniqueResourceIdentifier#TagName*. The unique resource identifier (URI) should be related to your company name or URL. For this example, we use "schemas-sams-com/DevTag" for the URI in Lines 80 and 82. For the tag name, we use "interface" for interface tags and "technology" for technology tags. The `SmartTagDownloadURL` property returns an empty string in Line 97 because this simple smart tag does not support downloadable actions.

Finally, the `Recognize` method in Lines 102–125 does the work of recognizing the developer terms. Because the incoming `Text` string can contain multiple words and we're just interested in recognizing single words, Line 108 calls the string's `Split` method to obtain an array of words (using whitespace as the delimiter). Lines 111–124 enumerate through the collection of words. After removing the ending punctuation if it exists (Lines 112–114), Line 116 checks for an interface-like word and Line 119 checks for a technology word. If such a word has been found, the method calls `CommitSmartTag` on the `RecognizerSite` parameter to embed the smart tag in the active document. `CommitSmartTag` needs the official tag name, the index in the `Text` string where the tag should begin, the length of the tagged portion of text, and sometimes custom information (not used in this example). The `index` variable, which gets updated on Line 123, keeps track of the current index in the `Text` string. That completes the simple recognizer.

The `DevTagAction` class begins on Line 129, implementing `ISmartTagAction`'s ten properties and an important `InvokeVerb` method. As with `DevTagRecognizer`, custom registration methods appear in Lines 133–146 to add a custom subkey to make Microsoft Office aware of the action. The `ProgId`, `Name`, `Desc`, `SmartTagCount`, and `SmartTagName` properties in Lines 149–194 serve the same purpose as in the recognizer.

The `SmartTagCaption` property in Lines 197–211 returns a string caption corresponding to the incoming `SmartTagID` parameter. These captions are displayed in the context menu when a user clicks on the Smart Tag icon. In this implementation, we return "Developer Term: Interface" for the interface lookup action and "Developer Term: Technology" for the technology lookup action. The `VerbCount` property in Lines 215–226 returns the number of verbs for the passed-in smart tag name. Both smart tag types in this example have only one verb, which is the action of looking up a word.

The `VerbID` property in Lines 230–243 returns an integer corresponding to a Smart Tag name and verb index. These IDs can be arbitrary non-zero numbers, and this property uses the values of the `Verbs` enumeration to return either `LookupInterface` or `LookupTechnology` as the verb IDs. These are used by the `InvokeVerb` method and `VerbCaptionFromID` property for distinguishing between different actions.

The `VerbCaptionFromID` property is implemented in Lines 246–262, and returns text that is displayed to the user for each action. We return either "Find online documentation for this interface" or "Find online documentation for this technology" depending on the value of the `VerbID` parameter.

The `VerbNameFromID` property in Lines 265–270 returns a short name corresponding to each verb ID. For this, we use the handy `System.Enum.Format` method to return the name of the `Verbs` member that corresponds to the `VerbID` value. This means that `LookupInterface` is returned for 1 and `LookupTechnology` is returned for 2. The "G" format specifier instructs `Enum.Format` to return the name rather than a number represented as a string.

Finally, the `InvokeVerb` method in Lines 273–299 gets to do some real work! For both `LookupInterface` and `LookupTechnology` verbs, we create an instance of an Internet Explorer `Application` object from its ProgID. Line 283 uses the `Microsoft.VisualBasic.CreateObject` method to instantiate the object, then Line 284 makes a late-bound call to `Navigate2` to browse to the appropriate MSDN Online search page. Notice the string passed to `Navigate2`: a reasonable-looking URL concatenated with the `Text` string (which is the word tagged by the recognizer) concatenated with a huge amount of information. This ugly string currently works when searching for a word on MSDN Online. Of course, because MSDN's search engine is outside of our control, we can't always count on this URL always working. However, for illustration, it works just fine at the time of writing. Line 294 makes Internet Explorer visible so the user is presented with the desired `Search Results` page.

Running the Example Using Visual Studio .NET

To see this example in action, you need to have Office XP installed on your computer. Although the Office XP Smart Tag SDK has helpful documentation and samples, it is not necessary to download it because the Smart Tag type library is installed by Office XP itself.

If you use Visual Studio .NET as your development environment, you can perform the following steps:

1. Create a new Visual Basic .NET class library project and replace the contents of `Class1.vb` with the contents of Listing 14.1 (available on this book's Web site).

2. Right-click on the project in the Solution Explorer and select `Properties`.

3. Under `Configuration Properties, Build`, check the `Register for COM Interop` option.

4. After clicking `OK`, select `Project, Add Reference…` from the menu.

5. On the COM tab, select `Microsoft Smart Tags 1.0 Type Library`. This is the file `MSTAG.TLB` that should be registered if Office XP is installed.

6. Build the project by selecting `Build`, `Build` from the menu.

7. Close all running instances of Office XP applications and Internet Explorer.

8. Open Microsoft Word and try it out. To ensure that your smart tag was found and activated, select `AutoCorrect Options…` from the `Tools` menu and look for the recognizer's name in the list on the `Smart Tags` tab. This is pictured in Figure 14.3.

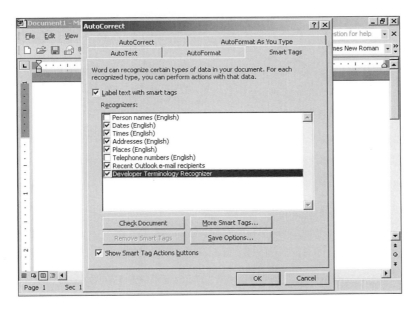

FIGURE 14.3

Viewing the list of recognizers registered and instantiated by Microsoft Office.

Figure 14.4 shows the use of our smart tag in a Word document, and Figure 14.5 shows the Internet Explorer window that appears when an action is executed. You might have to adjust the Office security settings to get this example to work on your computer.

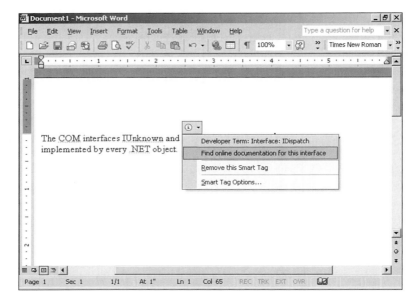

FIGURE 14.4

The DevTag component being used by Microsoft Word 2002.

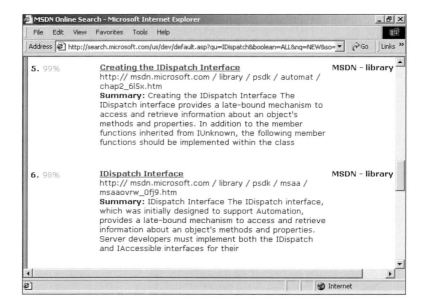

FIGURE 14.5

Selecting "Find online documentation for this interface" for "IDispatch" presents a Web browser window with useful links.

Because the `Register for COM Interop` option registers the assembly created in Listing 14.1 with a codebase, no extra work was needed for the example to work. In practice, you would want to give both assemblies a strong name, and perhaps install them in the Global Assembly Cache (GAC) by doing the following:

1. Generate a key pair using the .NET Framework Strong Name Utility (`SN.EXE`), if you don't already have your own key pair:

   `sn -k MyKey.snk`

   Copy the output `MyKey.snk` file to your Visual Studio .NET project directory.

2. Import a type library for the Smart Tags type library (MSTAG.TLB) by running `TLBIMP.EXE` with the /keyfile option, using the file created in Step 1:

   `TlbImp path\MSTAG.TLB /keyfile:MyKey.snk`

   The *path* should point to the location of `MSTAG.TLB`, which should be the `Common Files\Microsoft Shared\Smart Tag` directory under your `Program Files` folder. This creates an assembly with the filename `SmartTagLib.dll`. If there were a Primary Interop Assembly available for the Smart Tags type library, you could skip this step and use the PIA in Step 4 because it would already have a strong name.

3. Add the following at the top of the source file, after the existing `Imports` statements:

   ```
   Imports System.Reflection
   <Assembly: AssemblyKeyFile("..\..\MyKey.snk")>
   ```

   The `..\..\` is needed because the path for the key file is relative to the output directory.

4. Rather than referencing the Smart Tags type library from Visual Studio .NET (causing a new Interop Assembly to be imported without a strong name), reference the Smart Tags Interop Assembly created in Step 2 as a regular .NET component. This can be done by selecting `Project`, `Add Reference…`, then clicking the `Browse…` button on the `.NET` tab to find the assembly.

> **TIP**
>
> In a Visual C# project, you can reference a type library and give the imported Interop Assembly a strong name all within the IDE, without having to run `TLBIMP.EXE` separately. To do this, go to the project's `Properties` page (by right-clicking on the project in the Solution Explorer) and select `Common Properties`, then `General`. Next to `Wrapper Assembly Key File`, type the name of the key file. Unlike using `AssemblyKeyFileAttribute`, this filename is relative to the project directory. Visual Basic .NET projects don't have this option because it is assumed that any strong-named Interop Assemblies should be Primary Interop Assemblies, and you need to use `TLBIMP.EXE` to create a Primary Interop Assembly anyway (discussed in Chapter 15, "Creating and Deploying Useful Primary Interop Assemblies").

14

IMPLEMENTING COM INTERFACES FOR BINARY COMPATIBILITY

5. Install both assemblies in the GAC using Global Assembly Cache Utility (GACUTIL.EXE):

```
gacutil -i DevTag.dll
gacutil -i SmartTagLib.dll
```

Running the Example Using Only the .NET Framework SDK

Using a computer that only has Office XP and the .NET Framework SDK, you can perform the following steps:

1. Import a type library for the Smart Tags type library (MSTAG.TLB) by running TLBIMP.EXE, as shown in the previous section. The /keyfile option could be omitted if you plan to rely on registering a codebase:

   ```
   TlbImp path\MSTAG.TLB
   ```

   This creates an assembly with the filename SmartTagLib.dll.

2. Create a DevTag.vb text file with the contents of Listing 14.1.

3. Compile the file:

   ```
   vbc /t:library DevTag.vb /r:SmartTagLib.dll
   ```

4. Register the assembly:

   ```
   regasm DevTag.dll /codebase
   ```

   Be sure that the Smart Tag Interop Assembly (SmartTagLib.dll) and DevTag.dll are either in the same directory or in the GAC (if they have strong names).

5. Close all running instances of Office XP applications and Internet Explorer.

6. Open Microsoft Word and try it out. To ensure that your smart tag was found and activated, select AutoCorrect Options… from the Tools menu and look for the recognizer's name in the list on the Smart Tags tab, shown earlier in Figure 14.3.

Interface Implementation Shortcuts in Visual Studio .NET

If you were implementing an interface from scratch rather than copying and pasting this book's source code, you could take advantage of interface implementation shortcuts built into Visual Studio .NET projects. In a Visual Basic .NET project, All you need to do is list your class as implementing an interface, for example:

```
Implements ISmartTagRecognizer
```

Then, you can select the interface name from the left drop-down box above the code, and select each member you want to implement in the right drop-down box. The IDE inserts an empty definition for each member you select, one at a time. This is shown in Figure 14.6.

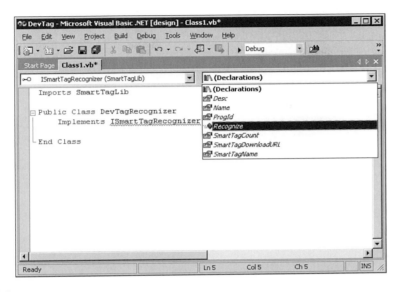

FIGURE 14.6
Selecting members of an interface in a Visual Basic .NET project to avoid typing the signatures.

The same kind of shortcut is available for Visual C# projects, but it's well hidden. Again, all you need to do in source code is mark your class as implementing an interface, for example:

```
public class DevTagRecognizer : ISmartTagRecognizer
```

Once you've done this, open the `Class View` window, expand your class node, then expand the `Bases and Interfaces` node. Right-click on the name of the interface you wish to implement, then select `Add` then `Implement Interface...`. This fills the class with dummy implementations of all the methods all at once. This process is shown in Figure 14.7.

Both of these shortcuts require that you first list the interface in the source code class declaration as one you're planning on implementing. If the interface is defined in a different assembly, you must also reference that assembly before attempting to use either shortcut.

CAUTION

The danger of using these shortcuts for COM interfaces is that the interface members' custom attributes (such as `DispIdAttribute`, `MarshalAsAttribute`, and so on) are not automatically placed on the generated class signatures. If you plan on exposing class members to COM via a class interface, you should manually add the necessary custom attributes. Otherwise, marking the class with

> `ClassInterface(ClassInterfaceType.None)` to suppress the class interface means that you never have to worry about marking the class signatures with the custom attributes that already exist on the interfaces you're implementing.

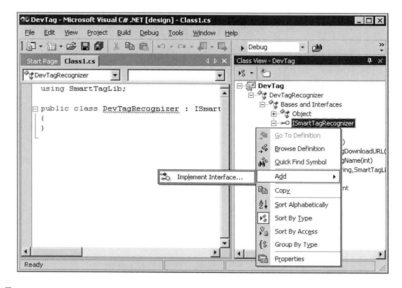

FIGURE 14.7

Selecting `Implement Interface...` *in a Visual C# Project to avoid typing the signatures.*

If you don't have Visual Studio .NET, then you can't take advantage of the IDE's ability to fill in method signatures for an implemented interface. This can make implementing a large interface quite tedious. For a .NET interface such as `System.IConvertible`, the .NET Framework SDK documentation displays every member prototype in Visual Basic .NET, C#, C++, and JScript, so copying and pasting can be done to speed up the process. For COM interfaces such as `ISmartTagRecognizer`, the documentation typically doesn't address the needs of .NET languages. Still, the Visual Basic 6-focused documentation in the Office XP Smart Tag SDK works fine for Visual Basic .NET programming once you remember the various syntax changes.

CAUTION

> When declaring and implementing interface methods using documentation geared toward Visual Basic 6 code, remember that `Long` in VB6 is now `Integer` in Visual Basic .NET, and `Integer` in VB6 is now `Short` in Visual Basic .NET!

As an example of such syntax changes, the following Visual Basic 6 code:

```
Private Property Get ISmartTagRecognizer_Name(ByVal LocaleID As Long) As String
  ISmartTagRecognizer_Name = "Developer Terminology Recognizer"
End Property
```

must be translated to the following Visual Basic .NET code:

```
Public ReadOnly Property Name(ByVal LocaleID As Integer) As String _
  Implements ISmartTagRecognizer.Name
  Get
    Name = "Developer Terminology Recognizer"
  End Get
End Property
```

By default, members of Visual Basic 6 classes that implement an interface member are private, because you typically don't want to expose the member with the mangled *InterfaceName_MemberName* name on your Visual Basic 6 class interface. In Visual Basic .NET, such members are public by default because the member name is preserved and calling members directly on classes is common practice in .NET.

> **TIP**
>
> If you're unsure about signature transformations from a type library to an assembly, you can always run ILDASM.EXE on the Interop Assembly to get the exact .NET interface definition rather than guessing at what the members look like. Of course, this requires the ability to understand IL Assembler syntax in terms of your programming language. IL Assembler syntax is covered in Chapter 7.

Common Problems When Implementing COM Interfaces

Three common problems arise when attempting to implement COM interfaces in a .NET class, dealing with:

- Parameterized properties
- Interface inheritance
- Returning Specific HRESULTs

Parameterized Properties

This book's Web site includes the previous DevTag example in C#. Implementing the two Smart Tag interfaces in C# ends up being confusing, because the language doesn't enable you to define, use, or implement non-default parameterized properties. Because most of the properties in ISmartTagRecognizer and ISmartTagAction are parameterized (with at least a LocaleID parameter), the accessor methods must be implemented instead. For ISmartTagRecognizer, this means implementing get_Name, get_Desc, get_SmartTagName, and get_SmartTagDownloadURL methods instead of Name, Desc, SmartTagName, and SmartTagDownloadURL properties. For ISmartTagAction, this means implementing get_Name, get_Desc, get_SmartTagName, get_SmartTagCaption, get_VerbCount, get_VerbID, get_VerbCaptionFromID, and get_VerbNameFromID instead of the corresponding properties. For example, implementing the accessor method looks like the following for ISmartTagRecognizer.get_Name:

```
// Return a name for the Tools/Autocorrect Options/Smart Tags dialog
public string get_Name(int LocaleID)
{
  return "Developer Terminology Recognizer";
}
```

Fortunately, the interface implementation shortcut in Visual Studio .NET (for Visual C# projects) recognizes when interfaces have unsupported properties and emits accessor method signatures instead.

Another confusing aspect of properties is that although Visual Basic .NET lets you use properties with by-reference parameters, the compiler does not allow you to *define* such a property. What's worse is that unlike C#, which enables you to define accessor methods when encountering an unsupported property, Visual Basic .NET provides no workaround for implementing such an interface. Therefore any COM interfaces with parameterized properties whose parameters are passed by-reference cannot be implemented in Visual Basic .NET.

Interface Inheritance

Implementing a COM interface that derives from an interface other than IUnknown or IDispatch requires special care in Visual Basic .NET. As mentioned in Chapter 4, "An In-Depth Look at Imported Assemblies," .NET definitions of COM interfaces must contain all their base interface members except for IUnknown and IDispatch, despite the fact that their base interfaces also contain definitions for the same members. These duplicated member definitions can cause unexpected compilation errors, described in this section.

Chapter 21 describes how to define a proper definition for the IPersistStream COM interface, which derives from IPersist. The base IPersist interface has a GetClassID method that must be redefined on the derived IPersistStream definition. If you reference this definition and attempt to implement IPersistStream in Visual Basic .NET in the straightforward manner:

```
Public Sub GetClassID(ByRef pClassID As System.Guid) _
  Implements IPersistStream.GetClassID
  pClassID = Me.GetType().GUID
End Sub
```

you'll get a compilation error:

```
'PersistableClass' must implement
➡'Sub GetClassID(ByRef pClassID As System.Guid)' for interface 'IPersist'.
```

Because there are two definitions of GetClassID—one directly on IPersistStream and one on the base IPersist interface—you must state that you're implementing both:

```
' Implementation for both IPersistStream.GetClassID and IPersist.GetClassID
Public Sub GetClassID(ByRef pClassID As System.Guid) _
  Implements IPersistStream.GetClassID, IPersist.GetClassID
  pClassID = Me.GetType().GUID
End Sub
```

Unfortunately, the interface implementation shortcut in Visual Studio .NET projects doesn't provide an easy way to handle this situation. You must manually add the base interface member names to each applicable Implements statement.

You don't usually encounter this problem in C# because interface members are implemented simply by having a member with the same name:

```
// Implementation for both IPersistStream.GetClassID and IPersist.GetClassID
public void GetClassID(out Guid pClassID) { pClassID = this.GetType().GUID; }
```

C#, however, runs into the same problem as VB .NET when using *explicit interface implementation*, requiring both copies of the GetClassID method to be implemented separately:

```
// Implementation for IPersistStream.GetClassID
void IPersistStream.GetClassID(out Guid pClassID)
{
  ((IPersist)this).GetClassID(out pClassID);
}

// Implementation for IPersist.GetClassID
void IPersist.GetClassID(out Guid pClassID)
{
  pClassID = Guid.NewGuid();
}
```

Using explicit interface implementation on a member, indicated by adding the interface name and a period before its name, means that the member can't be called on the class type directly. Instead, an instance of the class must be cast to the interface (such as IPersist or IPersistStream) in order to call it. This capability enables you to implement several

14

IMPLEMENTING
COM INTERFACES
FOR BINARY
COMPATIBILITY

interfaces with a member of the same name and provide separate implementations for each interface's member. Explicit interface implementation is used throughout the .NET Framework as a way of "hiding" members for documentation purposes. For instance, the base types like System.Int32 and System.Boolean explicitly implement System.IConvertible so their class definitions in object browsers aren't cluttered with methods that aren't commonly used.

The exact equivalent of C# explicit interface implementation in Visual Basic .NET is simply marking a class's member (that implements an interface member) Private rather than Public.

> **TIP**
>
> Using explicit interface implementation in conjunction with a COM interface can be useful for making the interface's methods less noticeable to .NET clients used to dealing with the class itself. At the same time, an explicitly implemented COM interface looks no different to COM clients that call methods through the COM interface anyway.
>
> When manually defining a COM interface in source code (covered in Chapter 21), making it private and explicitly implementing it is a handy way to make ".NET-invisible" methods that only COM clients can call directly. Other .NET assemblies cannot use private interface types, and if a class explicitly implements the interface then there is no way other .NET assemblies can call the members.

Returning Specific HRESULTs

If you're implementing a COM interface, it's likely that its members require your implementation to return specific HRESULTs in response to specific error or warning situations. There's no real problem with returning specific HRESULTs to COM clients when implementing a member of a COM interface, but it's often unclear how to go about it.

.NET definitions of COM interfaces don't typically expose HRESULT return values directly, especially if the interface definitions were generated by the type library importer. Therefore, you typically need to throw an exception with a specific HRESULT value in order for your COM clients to see the appropriate return value. This can always be done with System.Runtime.InteropServices.COMException, for example (in C#):

```
// return CO_E_WRONG_SERVER_IDENTITY (0x80004015)
throw new COMException("Wrong Server Identity", unchecked((int)0x80004015));
```

The unchecked syntax is required to cast this unsigned value to a signed integer. See Chapter 11 for more information about throwing other exception types that can be exposed to COM with the desired HRESULT values.

You could even throw an exception with a success HRESULT value if necessary, although your performance will suffer if this needs to be done often. The best way to return a success HRESULT is to change the .NET definition of the interface to use PreserveSigAttribute, as shown in Chapter 7. This could also be done even when returning failure HRESULT values to help performance by never throwing exceptions.

COM Interfaces with Default CCW Implementations

Although implementing a COM interface such as ISmartTagRecognizer or ISmartTagAction may have been straightforward, there are a handful of well-known COM interfaces that require special consideration. From COM's view, the interfaces covered in this section appear to be magically implemented by any .NET object because all CCWs provide default implementations of them based on the metadata for the .NET object being wrapped. For these interfaces, it can be important to understand the behavior of each default implementation and what you can do to alter it.

Having a few standard COM interfaces implemented on your behalf is nothing new for programmers using Visual Basic 6, ATL in Visual C++, or Visual J++. For example, a simple ActiveX DLL authored in Visual Basic 6 automatically implements IUnknown, IDispatch, IConnectionPoint, IConnectionPointContainer, IExternalConnection, IProvideClassInfo, and ISupportErrorInfo. A simple ActiveX Control authored in Visual Basic 6 automatically implements over 20 interfaces!

IUnknown

As discussed in Chapter 2, "Bridging the Two Worlds—Managed and Unmanaged Code," all COM objects must implement the IUnknown interface. The three methods of IUnknown enable clients to use reference counting on COM objects and enable clients to discover other implemented interfaces at run time (like a cast operation). No .NET classes need to implement IUnknown in order to be exposed to COM because every CCW provides an IUnknown implementation on behalf of its .NET object.

Unlike any other COM interface, the CLR does not provide a way to replace the IUnknown implementation provided for .NET objects (besides swapping the object with your own COM object while performing custom marshaling, as explained in Chapter 20, "Custom Marshaling"). If you attempt to obtain a metadata definition of IUnknown by importing a type library containing its definition, you'll find that the imported definition contains no methods. Even if you defined your own managed IUnknown interface with the appropriate methods, implementing such an interface would have no effect because the CCW would ignore it.

A CCW's implementation of AddRef and Release does what you'd expect to manage its reference count. The QueryInterface implementation, which enables the user to ask for an interface pointer, is more interesting. Although you can't provide your own implementation, you *can* control its behavior using the custom attributes explained in Chapter 12.

Of course, the supplied QueryInterface implementation follows the COM rules, namely:

- QueryInterface must preserve an object's identity. Calling QueryInterface with the same IID multiple times on the same object instance must return the same physical pointer value.
- The set of interface pointers returned by QueryInterface on the same instance must be static. If QueryInterface succeeds for a given IID once, it must always succeed in future calls (and vice-versa).
- QueryInterface must be reflexive, symmetric, and transitive. These rules boil down to the fact that no matter what the type of the interface pointer is on which you're calling QueryInterface, you can get back a pointer to any of the interfaces the object instance implements. It doesn't matter if it's the same interface type as the one you already have, or one that you used before.

When a CCW's QueryInterface method is called, it successfully returns an interface pointer corresponding to the IID passed for the riid parameter if its value corresponds to:

- IUnknown
- The other COM interfaces that the CCW provides on behalf of the .NET object: IDispatch (but only if the .NET class is COM-visible), IMarshal, IProvideClassInfo, ISupportErrorInfo, IConnectionPointContainer, and sometimes IObjectSafety.
- IManagedObject, a CLR-specific interface also provided by the CCW that contains a handful of methods used internally by the CLR. Clients could query for this interface to check whether the COM object is a CCW for a .NET object.
- Any class interfaces exposed by the object instance for its class type and any COM-visible base classes (although any class interface contains the COM-visible members of base class interfaces regardless of the COM-visibility of the base classes themselves). Because the definition of System.Object is marked with ClassInterface(ClassInterfaceType.AutoDual), you can always successfully obtain an _Object interface from a CCW's QueryInterface implementation.
- Any COM-visible public interfaces implemented by the object instance. This includes interfaces implemented by the class and its base classes.
- Any COM interfaces implemented by the object instance (indicated with the ComImportAttribute on the interface definition). This also includes interfaces implemented by the class and its base classes. COM interfaces do *not* require a public .NET definition in order to be obtainable by QueryInterface. Interfaces that are marked

COM-invisible are even obtainable via `QueryInterface` if (and only if) they are marked with `ComImportAttribute`. For a COM interface, a COM client would need to obtain its definition from somewhere other than the assembly's exported type library because interfaces marked with `ComImportAttribute` are not re-exported.

DIGGING DEEPER

The rules for which interfaces can be obtained via `QueryInterface` only applies when custom marshaling (discussed in Chapter 20) is not involved. With custom marshaling, a separate object is usually passed to COM that may implement an entirely different set of interfaces.

IDispatch

`IDispatch`, introduced in Chapter 2, is the most common interface other than `IUnknown` that COM objects implement. Although Chapter 12 demonstrated that not every .NET *interface* is exposed to COM as deriving from `IDispatch`, every COM-visible .NET *object* has an `IDispatch` implementation exposed through its CCW. If a class is marked with `ClassInterface(ClassInterfaceType.AutoDual)` or left with the default `ClassInterface(ClassInterfaceType.AutoDispatch)`, then the CCW's `IDispatch` implementation provides access to all public COM-visible members of the class and its base classes. If a class is marked with `ClassInterface(ClassInterfaceType.None)` and it only implements interfaces that derive directly from `IUnknown` when exposed to COM, the methods of `IDispatch` can still be called on any dual interfaces exposed by base classes, such as the ever-present `_Object` class interface. However, calling the `IDispatch` members of an interface such as `_Object` only provides access to methods defined directly on that interface (such as the methods of `System.Object`).

As with `IUnknown`, the CLR does not enable a .NET class to implement `IDispatch` directly and have it used by a CCW. Even if you reference the Interop Assembly for the OLE Automation type library defining `IDispatch` and write a class that implements this interface, it will be completely ignored by the CLR and unusable from COM.

14

TIP

`IUnknown` and `IDispatch` are the only two interfaces special-cased by CCWs such that .NET classes cannot *directly* implement them to expose custom implementations to COM. Any other COM interface can be directly implemented, even ones that otherwise would have been implemented by the CCW.

The CLR's handling of IDispatch differs from its handling of IUnknown in two major ways:

- The CLR provides two different implementations of IDispatch, selected via (what else?) custom attributes on .NET classes.
- Any .NET class can provide its own implementation of IDispatch by implementing a different interface—System.Reflection.IReflect.

Two Built-In Implementations

The two CLR implementations of IDispatch are:

- The internal implementation. This is the default implementation and is based on the CLR's reflection technology.
- The compatible implementation. This implementation simply delegates to the standard OLE Automation implementation of IDispatch.

The two implementations behave almost identically for common uses. After discussing how to choose an implementation for a .NET class, we'll examine the differences between them.

Selecting an Implementation

The desired implementation can be chosen via the IDispatchImplAttribute custom attribute defined in System.Runtime.InteropServices. This attribute has an enum parameter of type IDispatchImplType with the following values:

- InternalImpl. Use the internal implementation.
- CompatibleImpl. Use the OLE Automation implementation.
- SystemDefinedImpl. This is obsolete and should not be used. The CLR treats SystemDefinedImpl the same as InternalImpl.

CAUTION

.NET classes that are exposed to COM with a default dispinterface always use the internal IDispatch implementation. This affects two types of classes:

- Those marked with ClassInterface(ClassInterfaceType.None) whose first implemented interface is a dispinterface (one marked with InterfaceType(ComInterfaceType.InterfaceIsIDispatch)).
- Those with the default class interface behavior, as if they were marked with ClassInterface(ClassInterfaceType.AutoDispatch).

For such classes, the IDispatchImplAttribute custom attribute is simply ignored. This means that IDispatchImplAttribute must be used in conjunction with ClassInterfaceAttribute so either an auto-dual class interface or an explicitly defined dual interface is exposed as the coclass's default interface.

As with other custom attributes that can be placed on classes, `IDispatchImplAttribute` can be marked on an entire assembly to control the implementation for all the classes contained within, and individual classes can override the assembly-level setting. This looks like the following in Visual Basic .NET:

```
Imports System.Runtime.InteropServices
<Assembly: IDispatchImpl(IDispatchImplType.CompatibleImpl)>

<ClassInterface(ClassInterfaceType.AutoDual)> _
Public Class UsingCompatibleIDispatch
  ...
End Class

<IDispatchImpl(IDispatchImplType.InternalImpl)> _
Public Class UsingInternalIDispatch
  ...
End Class
```

Notice that it was necessary to mark the `UsingCompatibleIDispatch` class with an auto-dual class interface so the `CompatibleImpl` setting isn't ignored.

Both implementations are always based on a single interface—the default interface. This means that when a COM client makes a `QueryInterface` call for `IDispatch`, the returned interface pointer can only be used to invoke members of the default interface, not the members of the other interfaces that the class might implement. This "single" default interface, however, is usually the class interface that contains all the public members of the class. Plus, you can still call the `IDispatch` methods on any dual interface implemented by a .NET object to access additional methods that might not be exposed on a default interface. The `IDispatch` implementation chosen affects the `IDispatch` methods for *all* interfaces that the class implements; not just the default interface.

The Compatible `IDispatch`

The compatible implementation uses the standard implementation provided by OLE Automation (in `OLEAUT32.DLL`), which is equivalent to using the `CreateStdDispatch` API. The important drawback to this implementation is that it requires a type library containing definitions of the types being used. If the CLR can find an existing type library for the assembly, it will use it. Otherwise, the CLR generates an in-memory type library on-the-fly, which can cause a significant slow-down in an application. Note that an *entire* type library (and possibly additional type libraries for referenced assemblies) must be generated, even if type information is only required for a single interface. Generated type libraries are never persisted to a file nor registered.

> **Tip**
>
> If you decide to use the compatible IDispatch implementation, you should export, deploy, and register a type library with your assembly to avoid the expense of on-the-fly type library generation every time the application is run.

The following algorithm is used to locate an existing type library:

1. Look for a registered type library with the appropriate Library Identifier (LIBID).

2. If no type library is registered, check if the assembly has its type library embedded as a resource.

3. If no type library is embedded, look for a file in the same directory with the same name as the assembly but with a .tlb extension.

Only when all of these attempts fail will an in-memory type library be generated. Furthermore, this process of searching for a type library and possibly generating one on-the-fly only occurs when and if a client calls the methods of IDispatch on a .NET class that uses the compatible implementation. If not, no type library will be sought after or generated. Therefore, if your .NET object only exposes IUnknown-only interfaces then no type library would ever be generated on-the-fly. (.NET objects always expose a dual _Object interface, but if a COM client called its IDispatch methods then the existing type library for the mscorlib assembly would be loaded and used because it's registered for the _Object interface.)

> **Digging Deeper**
>
> The .NET Framework SDK tools don't provide built-in support for embedding type libraries in assemblies. For an example of how to do this, check the "TlbGen" sample installed with the .NET Framework SDK.

The Internal IDispatch

Because the internal IDispatch implementation is based on reflection, no type library is required for *most* of its functionality. The internal IDispatch implementation is consistent with the IDispatch specification, but what follows is a brief description of the implementation. You might want to refer back to the definition of IDispatch displayed in the "About COM" section of Chapter 2.

The GetIDsOfNames method gives back one or more Dispatch IDs (DISPIDs) via the rgdispid out parameter that correspond to the member name and potentially the parameter names passed in the `rgszNames` parameter. When an array of names is passed, the first element corresponds to the member name. As the `GetIDsOfNames` contract requires, the name lookup is case-insensitive. For consistency with exported type libraries (and therefore the compatible `IDispatch` implementation), the names passed to `GetIDsOfNames` must match COM's view of the .NET member. This means using suffixes such as _2, _3, and so on for overloaded methods, or using *InterfaceName_MemberName* for methods on a class interface when multiple implemented interfaces have the same member name.

For member DISPIDs, the CLR returns the values it internally assigns to each member, unless the definition is marked with `DispIdAttribute` on the interface the implementation is based on. (For class interfaces, the attribute would need to be on the class's member definition.) These same DISPID values can be seen when exporting a type library. The DISPIDs returned for named parameters are simply 0, 1, 2, and so on.

The `Invoke` method invokes the method that corresponds to the DISPID passed as the `dispidMember` parameter. The parameters can be passed as a mixture of positional arguments and named arguments (if `GetIDsOfNames` were called with parameter names as well). Any error information from a .NET exception is accessible via the `pExcepInfo` parameter rather than having to obtain error information via the `GetErrorInfo` API.

`GetTypeInfo` returns an `ITypeInfo` interface pointer for the interface, and `GetTypeInfoCount` returns the number of type information interfaces that an object provides (always one for .NET objects). Both of these methods require a type library to be present to return the expected type information. Therefore, if either of these are called by a COM client, the same type library generation process used for the compatible `IDispatch` implementation is invoked.

Differences Between the Implementations

The compatible implementation gives the most backward-compatibility for existing COM clients, because most COM clients are designed to work with the OLE Automation `IDispatch` implementation. There are only a few noticeable differences between the two implementations, but these differences can be important depending on your class's members.

The internal implementation supports the following which the compatible implementation does not:

- Mixing signed and unsigned parameter types. For example, you can pass a signed integer (`VT_I4`) to a method expecting an unsigned integer (`VT_U4`) and vice-versa. In general, the internal implementation is more flexible with data types. For example, it accepts a `VT_ERROR` type for a parameter defined as an integer. The compatible implementation would give a type mismatch `HRESULT` for all of these situations (0x80020005).

- Invoking methods with COM-invisible enum parameters. The internal implementation treats enum parameters as their underlying type. Because the type library exporter omits methods containing any COM-invisible value types (including enums), the compatible `IDispatch` implementation cannot do this.

The compatible implementation supports the following which the internal implementation does not:

- Invoking members with user-defined value type parameters (`VT_RECORD`). Note that the parameter type itself must be a value type. If it's typed as a `System.Object` and the instance happens to be a user-defined value type, it is not supported.

- Invoking members with parameters that are pointer types. The internal implementation supports by-reference parameters, but not pointers. Public .NET signatures that use pointers should be avoided, however, for the reasons discussed in Chapter 11.

TIP

The fact that the compatible implementation supports `VT_RECORD` to some degree can come in handy for working around the significant limitation of COM clients not being able to late bind to a .NET member with user-defined value type parameters. If you have members with user-defined value type parameters and are concerned about COM's ability to late bind to these members, you should definitely use the compatible `IDispatch` implementation. Also, when a COM component exposes a source dispinterface with UDT parameters, marking the importer-generated event sink helper class with the compatible `IDispatch` implementation (using the techniques of Chapter 7) can make such events get properly raised to .NET sinks. If you aren't affected by either of these scenarios, it's usually best to accept the default behavior of using the internal `IDispatch` implementation.

Besides these differences, there are several discrepancies in HRESULTs that are returned for error conditions. For example, the internal implementation might return an HRESULT meaning "Type Mismatch" rather than "Parameter Not Optional"; or "Catastrophic Failure" rather than "Bad Variable Type." If you have COM clients that are sensitive to the HRESULTs returned by `IDispatch`, then the compatible implementation is better suited for them.

In some cases the internal implementation even conforms to the OLE Automation documentation more than the OLE Automation implementation does! One example of this is the behavior of `IDispatch.GetIDsOfNames` when passing an array of names (the member name plus parameter names). The OLE Automation documentation states that in the returned array of DISPIDs, each element corresponding to an unknown name is given the value -1. Yet the OLE Automation implementation returns -1 for the element corresponding to the first unknown name and every element thereafter, even if it corresponds to a known name. The internal implementation, on the other hand, complies with the documentation.

DIGGING DEEPER

Although the compatible implementation aims to be backwards-compatible with COM objects that use the standard OLE Automation IDispatch implementation, it is not completely backwards-compatible. Part of it is due to the nature of the CLR, and part of strict backwards-compatibility was broken for performance reasons.

For example, if a COM client passes a VARIANT containing a reference to a type (for instance, VT_BOOL | VT_BYREF) but the pointer (pboolVal) is null, a COM component using the OLE Automation IDispatch implementation returns E_INVALIDARG. A .NET component using the compatible IDispatch implementation, however, returns E_POINTER. (And the internal implementation returns a different HRESULT than either of these two—DISP_E_EXCEPTION.)

Writing Your Own IDispatch Implementation

In the rare case that neither IDispatch implementation is appropriate for your needs, you can implement System.Reflection.IReflect to plug in your own custom implementation. Why IReflect? It's the .NET interface that provides the same sort of dynamic invocation as IDispatch. Because the CLR bridges an IReflect implementation to an IDispatch implementation from COM's perspective, .NET classes only need to worry about implementing one common interface when they need to customize their dynamic invocation behavior. Unfortunately, an implementer of IReflect often needs to handle calls routed from IDispatch specially in many ways, so the benefits of a single interface implementation are diminished.

CAUTION

The IReflect implementation you provide is only exposed as an IDispatch implementation when a COM client calls QueryInterface for IDispatch (or IDispatchEx) directly and uses the methods of the returned interface pointer. If a COM client simply uses the IDispatch methods inherited by dual interfaces (including auto-dual class interfaces), the standard internal or compatible implementation is used, based on the IDispatchImplAttribute custom attribute.

Although IReflect is not a well-known interface, its methods certainly are. That's because System.Type implements IReflect to provide much of its reflection services. IReflect has

12 members, shown in the upcoming Listing 14.2, but only four of them are used by the CLR when exposing an implementation as IDispatch—GetProperties, GetFields, GetMethods, and InvokeMember. The GetProperties, GetFields, and GetMethods methods are invoked by the CLR at some unspecified point before the first call to IDispatch.GetIDsOfNames or IDispatch.Invoke. When these calls are made, the CLR is able to retrieve all the information (names and DISPIDs) from the returned PropertyInfo, FieldInfo, and MethodInfo instances. The value passed for the BindingFlags parameter for all three methods is:

BindingFlags.Instance | BindingFlags.Static | BindingFlags.Public

This means that by default, an IReflect implementation exposes static members to COM clients via IDispatch, which neither of the built-in IDispatch implementations do. A custom IReflect implementation could choose to not expose static members or even expose non-public members by using different binding flags inside these members and inside InvokeMember.

CAUTION

Implementing IReflect as a custom IDispatch has a glitch in Version 1.0 of the .NET Framework. The DISPIDs presented to COM (obtained from the calls to GetProperties, GetFields, and GetMethods) do not respect explicit DISPIDs marked on a class's members with DispIdAttribute. Instead, the DISPIDs are the values that the members would have had if they weren't marked with the custom attribute. This problem does not affect the internal or compatible implementations. The implications of this and a workaround are discussed in the analysis of Listing 14.2.

When the CLR calls IReflect.InvokeMember in response to an IDispatch.Invoke call, its parameters have the following values:

- name—The name of the member as defined by its MemberInfo previously obtained from GetFields, GetProperties, or GetMethods. If the COM client called IDispatch.Invoke with an unknown DISPID, the name would appear as "[DISPID=*value*]", where *value* represents the DISPID value.

- invokeAttr—BindingFlags.InvokeMethod | BindingFlags.OptionalParamBinding if the user is invoking a method. If getting or setting a field or property, BindingFlags. InvokeMethod is replaced with BindingFlags.GetField or BindingFlags.SetField; or BindingFlags.GetProperty or BindingFlags.SetProperty, respectively. BindingFlags. SetProperty only appears, however, if the COM client passes DISPATCH_PROPERTYPUT | DISPATCH_PROPERTYPUTREF to IDispatch.Invoke. If the COM client passes just DIS-PATCH_PROPERTYPUT, BindingFlags.PutDispProperty is passed to InvokeMember. If the COM client passes just DISPATCH_PROPERTYPUTREF, BindingFlags.PutRefDispProperty is passed to InvokeMember.

- binder—A System.OleAutBinder instance, a type internal to the mscorlib assembly that's used for performing argument coercion in a similar fashion as OLE Automation. This is the binder used by the *internal* IDispatch implementation, so it doesn't exactly match OLE Automation behavior.

- target—a reference to the current instance (this in C# or C++ or Me in VB .NET).

- args—the array of arguments passed to IDispatch.Invoke, with the leftmost argument in element zero.

- modifiers—a null reference.

- culture—a CultureInfo instance that corresponds to the LCID being used by IDispatch.Invoke.

- namedParameters—Filled with some named parameters if IDispatch.Invoke was called with named parameters.

> **TIP**
>
> Notice that the name given to InvokeMember is not necessarily the same string that the user passed to IDispatch.GetIDsOfNames. This means that you can count on the string being in the correct case assuming that the MemberInfo types returned in GetFields, GetProperties, and GetMethods had the correct case. The CLR handles the case-insensitive request from COM so you don't have to. Case sensitivity is all that is handled automatically, however. If the exported names of any members are different than their .NET names (as with overloaded methods), the implementer of IReflect must do the work of mapping COM member names to .NET member names.

Listing 14.2 shows a sample implementation of IReflect that delegates to System.Type to do most of the work. One reason you might decide to implement IReflect is to handle special DISPIDs that may not be a part of your interface definition. This listing maps any request for a special DISPID called DISPID_EVALUATE (with the value -5) to a member called Evaluate, regardless of its real DISPID. Other differences between this custom implementation and the internal IDispatch implementation are:

- This implementation exposes static members to COM.

- InvokeMember returns an HRESULT that COM expects when attempting to invoke a member that doesn't exist—DISP_E_MEMBERNOTFOUND. Of course, .NET clients using the IReflect implementation wouldn't appreciate a COMException being thrown, but this is just done for illustrative purposes.

- This implementation pays no attention to COM-visibility rules.

- If a COM client tries to set a property passing only one of the DISPATCH_PROPERTYPUT or DISPATCH_PROPERTYPUTREF flags (which is often done implicitly, as with a VBScript client), InvokeMember will fail because attempting to invoke a .NET property setter using BindingFlags.PutDispProperty or BindingFlags.PutRefDispProperty throws an exception.

- This implementation doesn't properly handle GetIDsOfNames calls if the exported member name doesn't match the .NET member name (as with overloaded methods).

To mimic the work of the internal IDispatch implementation, this custom implementation would have to handle the last three items in the list. For the last item, it would have to return PropertyInfo, FieldInfo, and MethodInfo instances from GetProperties, GetFields, and GetMethods with names that match what would be seen in an exported type library.

LISTING 14.2   Implementing System.Reflection.IReflect to Control the Class's Exposed IDispatch Implementation

```
 1: using System;
 2: using System.Reflection;
 3: using System.Globalization;
 4: using System.Collections;
 5: using System.Runtime.InteropServices;
 6:
 7: public class CustomDispatch : IReflect
 8: {
 9:   private Type t;
10:   private Hashtable names;
11:
12:   // Well-known HRESULT returned by IDispatch.Invoke:
13:   private const int DISP_E_MEMBERNOTFOUND = unchecked((int)0x80020003);
14:
15:   // Constructor
16:   public CustomDispatch()
17:   {
18:     t = this.GetType();
19:
20:     // Fill Hashtable with explicit DISPIDs and their member names
21:     names = new Hashtable();
22:     DispIdAttribute [] ids;
23:     foreach (MemberInfo mi in t.GetMembers())
24:     {
25:       ids = (DispIdAttribute []) mi.GetCustomAttributes(
26:         typeof(DispIdAttribute), false);
27:
```

LISTING 14.2   Continued

```
28:          if (ids.Length > 0) names.Add(ids[0].Value, mi.Name);
29:      }
30:    }
31:
32:    // Called by CLR to get DISPIDs and names for properties
33:    PropertyInfo [] IReflect.GetProperties(BindingFlags bindingAttr)
34:    {
35:      return t.GetProperties(bindingAttr);
36:    }
37:
38:    // Called by CLR to get DISPIDs and names for fields
39:    FieldInfo [] IReflect.GetFields(BindingFlags bindingAttr)
40:    {
41:      return t.GetFields(bindingAttr);
42:    }
43:
44:    // Called by CLR to get DISPIDs and names for methods
45:    MethodInfo [] IReflect.GetMethods(BindingFlags bindingAttr)
46:    {
47:      return t.GetMethods(bindingAttr);
48:    }
49:
50:    // Called by CLR to invoke a member
51:    object IReflect.InvokeMember(string name, BindingFlags invokeAttr,
52:      Binder binder, object target, object [] args,
53:      ParameterModifier [] modifiers, CultureInfo culture,
54:      string [] namedParameters)
55:    {
56:      // Special case for any member marked with DispIdAttribute
57:      if (name.StartsWith("[DISPID="))
58:      {
59:        int dispid = Convert.ToInt32(name.Substring(8, name.Length-9), 10);
60:        name = (string)names[dispid];
61:      }
62:      // Special case for DISPID_EVALUATE (-5)
63:      else if (name.Equals("[DISPID=-5]"))
64:      {
65:        name = "Evaluate";
66:      }
67:
68:      try
69:      {
70:        return t.InvokeMember(name, invokeAttr, binder, target,
71:          args, modifiers, culture, namedParameters);
```

14

IMPLEMENTING
COM INTERFACES
FOR BINARY
COMPATIBILITY

LISTING 14.2   Continued

```
72:      }
73:      catch (MissingMemberException ex)
74:      {
75:        throw new COMException(ex.Message, DISP_E_MEMBERNOTFOUND);
76:      }
77:    }
78:
79:    FieldInfo IReflect.GetField(string name, BindingFlags bindingAttr)
80:    {
81:      return t.GetField(name, bindingAttr);
82:    }
83:
84:    MemberInfo [] IReflect.GetMember(string name, BindingFlags bindingAttr)
85:    {
86:      return t.GetMember(name, bindingAttr);
87:    }
88:
89:    MemberInfo [] IReflect.GetMembers(BindingFlags bindingAttr)
90:    {
91:      return t.GetMembers(bindingAttr);
92:    }
93:
94:    MethodInfo IReflect.GetMethod(string name, BindingFlags bindingAttr)
95:    {
96:      return t.GetMethod(name, bindingAttr);
97:    }
98:
99:    MethodInfo IReflect.GetMethod(string name, BindingFlags bindingAttr,
100:      Binder binder, Type [] types, ParameterModifier [] modifiers)
101:    {
102:      return t.GetMethod(name, bindingAttr, binder, types, modifiers);
103:    }
104:
105:    PropertyInfo IReflect.GetProperty(string name, BindingFlags bindingAttr,
106:      Binder binder, Type returnType, Type [] types,
107:      ParameterModifier [] modifiers)
108:    {
109:      return t.GetProperty(name, bindingAttr, binder,
110:        returnType, types, modifiers);
111:    }
112:
113:    PropertyInfo IReflect.GetProperty(string name, BindingFlags bindingAttr)
114:    {
115:      return t.GetProperty(name, bindingAttr);
```

LISTING 14.2   Continued

```
116:    }
117:
118:    Type IReflect.UnderlyingSystemType
119:    {
120:      get { return t.UnderlyingSystemType; }
121:    }
122: }
```

Lines 1–3 list the necessary namespaces for `IReflect` and its parameter types. Line 4 lists `System.Collections` for `Hashtable` and Line 5 lists `System.Runtime.InteropServices` for `DispIdAttribute` and `COMException`. Notice that this `CustomDispatch` uses explicit interface implementation, indicated by the "`IReflect.`" preceding each member name. We'll come back to the constructor in Lines 16–30 in a moment. First, the `GetProperties`, `GetFields`, and `GetMethods` methods in Lines 32–48 simply call the same methods on the `System.Type` member created in the class's constructor on Line 18.

The implementation of `InvokeMember` in Lines 51–77 calls `Type.InvokeMember` in Lines 70–71, but first it does a few things to support incoming names of the form "[DISPID=*value*]". As mentioned earlier, `IReflect.InvokeMember` receives such a string whenever `IDispatch.Invoke` is called with a DISPID that the CLR doesn't recognize from the calls to `GetProperties`, `GetFields`, and `GetMethods`. Ordinarily, receiving such a string would be a rare occurrence. But because the CLR ignores the use of `DispIdAttribute` in this scenario, this happens whenever a COM client directly calls `IDispatch.Invoke` with an explicitly-marked DISPID rather than using the different DISPID that would be returned from `IDispatch.GetIDsOfNames`. For example, a COM client that obtains DISPIDs from an exported type library rather than from `IDispatch.GetIDsOfNames`, which is often done implicitly by Visual Basic 6, would fall into this trap because the two sets of DISPIDs don't match; the type library exporter respects `DispIdAttribute`. (This technique of calling `IDispatch.Invoke` without `IDispatch.GetIDsOfNames` is sometimes called *early binding* to distinguish it from v-table binding or late binding. In this book, however, everything other than v-table binding is labeled as late binding.)

`Type.InvokeMember` doesn't accept strings of the form "[DISPID=*value*]" when invoking members of .NET objects (although it does when invoking members of COM objects), so the implementer of `IReflect.InvokeMember` must map the incoming DISPIDs to the appropriate member names. Therefore, the constructor contains code that examines every member in the current type (Lines 23–29) and adds a DISPID paired with its member name to a `Hashtable` for any members marked with `DispIdAttribute`. That way, `InvokeMember` can check for the special string format (Line 57), extract its DISPID (Line 59), and obtain the desired name from the `Hashtable` (Line 60).

14

IMPLEMENTING
COM INTERFACES
FOR BINARY
COMPATIBILITY

The other special thing done by this implementation is to treat any call for DISPID_EVALUATE as a request to invoke the class's Evaluate method (if it has one) regardless of its real DISPID. Lines 73–76 catch a MissingMemberException and throw an exception with the DISP_E_MEMBERNOTFOUND HRESULT instead. Although the remaining methods are properly implemented in Lines 79–121, they are not used by COM when calling through IDispatch. A worthwhile, yet easy, improvement to this listing's InvokeMember implementation would be to detect when the binding flags passed in contain the PutDispProperty or PutRefDispProperty flag and replace it with the SetProperty flag.

This class doesn't have any members besides a constructor and the methods of IReflect, so it's expected that classes that want the custom IDispatch implementation exposed to COM can simply inherit the CustomDispatch class:

```
// Class that exposes the custom IDispatch implementation
public class MyClass : CustomDispatch
{
  ...
}
```

IMarshal

The IMarshal interface enables COM-style custom marshaling. IMarshal is already implemented by a CCW for any .NET object but, unlike IUnknown and IDispatch, it could be directly implemented to override the default behavior. Because there is no managed definition of IMarshal in the .NET Framework or in a Primary Interop Assembly, implementing it means that you must generate your own definition. Listing 14.3 contains a C# definition of the IMarshal interface. This listing and the next few use the techniques covered in Chapter 21 to create the interface definitions.

LISTING 14.3   A C# Definition of IMarshal

```
using System;
using System.Runtime.InteropServices;

[
  ComImport,
  Guid("00000003-0000-0000-C000-000000000046"),
  InterfaceType(ComInterfaceType.InterfaceIsIUnknown)
]
interface IMarshal
{
  Guid GetUnmarshalClass([In] ref Guid iid,
    [MarshalAs(UnmanagedType.Interface)] Object pvInterface,
    int dwDestContext, IntPtr pvDestContext, int mshlflags);
  uint GetMarshalSizeMax([In] ref Guid iid,
```

LISTING 14.3   Continued

```
    [MarshalAs(UnmanagedType.Interface)] Object pvInterface,
    int dwDestContext, IntPtr pvDestContext, int mshlflags);
  void MarshalInterface(UCOMIStream pstm, [In] ref Guid iid,
    [MarshalAs(UnmanagedType.Interface)] Object pvInterface,
    int dwDestContext, IntPtr pvDestContext, int mshlflags);
  [return:MarshalAs(UnmanagedType.Interface)]
  Object UnmarshalInterface(UCOMIStream pstm, [In] ref Guid iid);
  void ReleaseMarshalData(UCOMIStream pstm);
  void DisconnectObject(int dwReserved);
}
```

The default implementation of IMarshal essentially exposes all .NET objects as free-threaded objects. This behavior should suffice except in rare situations. Providing your own implementation of IMarshal could yield higher performance if you're able to make optimizations for your specific scenario, but you really need to know what you're doing!

IProvideClassInfo

The IProvideClassInfo interface enables a COM object to expose type information about itself. Without IProvideClassInfo, a client of a COM object has no standard way of knowing what the class type of the object is; only what interfaces it may or may not implement. When a COM object implements IProvideClassInfo, its class information can be discovered via its single GetClassInfo method that returns an ITypeInfo pointer. As discussed in Chapter 2, ITypeInfo is the COM equivalent to the .NET Framework's System.Type class.

Because the class type of any .NET component is always exposed at run time, the CLR is always able to expose an IProvideClassInfo implementation for any .NET components exposed to COM. The CCW's default implementation of IProvideClassInfo requires a type library in order to create and return an ITypeInfo instance, and generates one on-the-fly if it can't find one (using the same algorithm discussed in the earlier "The Compatible IDispatch" section). There's no need to provide your own implementation for this interface, but perhaps you'd like to implement it in a way that doesn't rely on a type library. Listing 14.4 contains a definition for IProvideClassInfo written in Visual Basic .NET that could be implemented to override the CCW's implementation.

14

LISTING 14.4   Visual Basic .NET Definition of IProvideClassInfo

```
Imports System.Runtime.InteropServices

< _
  ComImport, _
```

LISTING **14.4**   Continued

```
  Guid("B196B283-BAB4-101A-B69C-00AA00341D07"), _
  InterfaceType(ComInterfaceType.InterfaceIsIUnknown) _
> _
Interface IProvideClassInfo
  Function GetClassInfo() As UCOMITypeInfo
End Interface
```

ISupportErrorInfo

The `ISupportErrorInfo` interface is used by COM objects to indicate whether or not they support rich error information via the `IErrorInfo` interface. The interface's single method—`InterfaceSupportsErrorInfo`—takes an IID as input and returns `S_OK` if the interface with that IID supports rich error information or `S_FALSE` if the interface does not support rich error information.

Because all .NET exception objects expose an `IErrorInfo` interface to COM, the CLR implements this for every .NET object and always returns `S_OK` from `InterfaceSupportsErrorInfo`. It's possible to implement `ISupportErrorInfo` yourself in a .NET class to return `S_FALSE` instead, but this should never be done because it deprives your clients of helpful error information. Nevertheless, Listing 14.5 contains a managed definition of `ISupportErrorInfo` in Visual C++ .NET. Notice that the `PreserveSigAttribute` is used so either `S_OK` or `S_FALSE` can be returned by the implementer.

LISTING **14.5**   A C++ Managed Definition of `ISupportErrorInfo`

```
#using <mscorlib.dll>
using namespace System;
using namespace System::Runtime::InteropServices;

[
  ComImport,
  Guid("DF0B3D60-548F-101B-8E65-08002B2BD119"),
  InterfaceType(ComInterfaceType::InterfaceIsIUnknown)
]
__gc __interface ISupportErrorInfo
{
  [PreserveSig] int InterfaceSupportsErrorInfo(Guid* riid);
};
```

Because the standard CCW implementation of `ISupportErrorInfo`. `InterfaceSupportsErrorInfo` *always* returns `S_OK`—even for interfaces that the object doesn't implement—one potential customization is to return `S_FALSE` for interfaces that the object doesn't implement, in the rare chance that a COM client is adversely affected by the default behavior.

IConnectionPointContainer

As discussed in Chapter 5, "Responding to COM Events," the IConnectionPointContainer interface is implemented by a COM object to make it connectable. As with the other three standard connection point interfaces (IConnectionPoint, IEnumConnectionPoints, and IEnumConnections), IConnectionPointContainer already has an official managed definition in the System.Runtime.InteropServices namespace. The important thing to realize is that the managed interface is called UCOMIConnectionPointContainer.

FAQ: **What are all the UCOM... interfaces in System.Runtime.InteropServices?**

The System.Runtime.InteropServices namespace defines 19 common COM interfaces such as IEnumString, IMoniker, IRunningObjectTable, and so on. The confusing thing about these definitions is that each interface has been renamed with a "UCOM" prefix. The "U" stands for unmanaged and the "COM" indicates that it's an interface originally defined in COM.

Despite the unfamiliar names, there is absolutely no difference between a "UCOM" interface and its corresponding unmanaged definition from COM's perspective. For example, think of System.Runtime.InteropServices.UCOMIStream as the official .NET definition of IStream. Because no separate Primary Interop Assembly exists for these 19 interfaces, mscorlib could be considered the Primary Interop Assembly for them. By sticking with these definitions (rather than getting a managed definition of IStream elsewhere), you'll not only get the correct behavior from COM's perspective but you'll be using the same interface types that other .NET components should be using. In fact, you may have noticed a few "UCOM" interfaces being used in Listings 14.3 and 14.4.

Listing 14.6 displays the definition of UCOMIConnectionPointContainer in C# syntax.

LISTING 14.6   System.Runtime.InteropServices.UCOMIConnectionPointContainer, Shown Here in C# Syntax

```
using System;
namespace System.Runtime.InteropServices
{
  [
    ComImport,
```

LISTING **14.6**   Continued

```
    Guid("B196B284-BAB4-101A-B69C-00AA00341D07"),
    InterfaceType(ComInterfaceType.InterfaceIsIUnknown)
  ]
  public interface UCOMIConnectionPointContainer
  {
    void EnumConnectionPoints(out UCOMIEnumConnectionPoints ppEnum);
    void FindConnectionPoint(ref Guid riid, out UCOMIConnectionPoint ppCP);
  }
}
```

With the standard CCW implementation, COM clients can call EnumConnectionPoints to obtain an enumeration of all the connection points supported by the .NET object—one per interface listed in the ComSourceInterfacesAttribute custom attribute. If the .NET class specifies no source interfaces, then this method returns an empty enumeration.

COM clients can call FindConnectionPoint with a specific IID to ask the object if it supports a connection point for the IID. Again, this implementation is based on the ComSourceInterfacesAttribute that may be marked on the class in question.

If a .NET class implements UCOMIConnectionPointContainer explicitly, then it can plug in its own behavior rather than using the standard implementation. One motivation for doing this would be to use your own scheme of returning connection points that doesn't rely on ComSourceInterfacesAttribute.

IObjectSafety

The IObjectSafety interface is interesting because it's the only standard COM interface that a CCW conditionally implements based on external factors. (IDispatch is also conditionally implemented, but based on the class's COM-visibility.) The purpose of IObjectSafety is to be implemented by trusted COM objects to express that they are safe for initialization or scripting. Internet Explorer uses this interface in its "Safe For Scripting" and "Safe For Initialization" features. Only .NET objects that are believed to be secure should advertise themselves as safe via IObjectSafety, so a CCW only implements the interface if the .NET object resides in an application domain with sufficient security evidence.

When .NET objects are hosted in Internet Explorer, IObjectSafety is automatically implemented by CCWs when created with the new <object> tag syntax that doesn't require assembly registration. This is fine because such controls can run in a semi-trusted state, unlike ActiveX controls. By default, .NET objects created via CLSID do not implement IObjectSafety.

This interface doesn't have an official .NET definition, so Listing 14.7 defines it in Visual Basic .NET.

LISTING 14.7 A Visual Basic .NET Definition of `IObjectSafety`

```
Imports System
Imports System.Runtime.InteropServices

< _
  ComImport, _
  Guid("CB5BDC81-93C1-11CF-8F20-00805F2CD064"), _
  InterfaceType(ComInterfaceType.InterfaceIsIUnknown) _
> _
Interface IProvideClassInfo

  Sub GetInterfaceSafetyOptions(<[In]> ByRef riid As Guid, _
    <Out> ByRef pdwSupportedOptions As Integer, _
    <Out> ByRef pdwEnabledOptions As Integer)

  Sub SetInterfaceSafetyOptions(<[In]> ByRef riid As Guid, _
    dwOptionSetMask As Integer, _
    dwEnabledOptions As Integer)

End Interface
```

When a CCW implements `IObjectSafety`, its `GetInterfaceSafetyOptions` method returns

`INTERFACESAFE_FOR_UNTRUSTED_DATA | INTERFACESAFE_FOR_UNTRUSTED_CALLER`

in both `pdwSupportedOptions` and `pdwEnabledOptions` parameters for every interface implemented by a .NET object. Under this circumstance, all .NET interfaces implemented by the object are considered to be safe for scripting and initialization. The standard values for `IObjectSafety` options are:

```
// Caller of interface may be untrusted
#define INTERFACESAFE_FOR_UNTRUSTED_CALLER 0x00000001
// Data passed into interface may be untrusted
#define INTERFACESAFE_FOR_UNTRUSTED_DATA   0x00000002
// Object knows to use IDispatchEx
#define INTERFACE_USES_DISPEX              0x00000004
// Object knows to use IInternetHostSecurityManager
#define INTERFACE_USES_SECURITY_MANAGER   0x00000008
```

The CLR's implementation of `SetInterfaceSafetyOptions` doesn't allow clients to change these options to anything other than what they already are. If you don't like this default behavior, or if you want `IObjectSafety` to be implemented at all times, you could simply implement it yourself using a definition like the one in Listing 14.7.

> **CAUTION**
>
> Be extremely careful about claiming that a component is safe for scripting or initialization within Internet Explorer. Because ActiveX controls can't run in a semi-trusted state, it's up to you to properly enforce security once you've convinced your clients to trust your control. Authors of objects (.NET or COM) that implement `IObjectSafety` to mark themselves as safe should ensure that no malicious scripts could take advantage of the exposed functionality to do harmful things.

COM Interfaces Bridged to Different .NET Types

In three special cases you should avoid implementing a COM interface because it has a corresponding newer .NET type that the CLR can already expose as the older COM interface. For these cases, the .NET type has the same sort of role in the .NET Framework as the COM interface has in COM. These three interfaces are:

- `IDispatchEx`, which can be exposed to COM by implementing `System.Reflection.IReflect` and/or `System.Runtime.InteropServices.Expando.IExpando`.

- `IEnumVARIANT`, which can be exposed to COM by implementing `IEnumerator` and using the type in the appropriate `GetEnumerator` method.

- `ITypeInfo`, which can be exposed on `System.Type` parameters, fields, and return values using a custom marshaler already defined in the .NET Framework — `System.Runtime.InteropServices.CustomMarshalers.TypeToTypeInfoMarshaler` in the `CustomMarshalers` assembly.

> **TIP**
>
> Besides using built-in custom marshalers, as in the `ITypeInfo` case, you should consider custom marshaling whenever you want to expose a certain interface to COM while at the same time exposing the functionality to .NET with a familiar .NET type. See Chapter 20 for more details.

`ITypeInfo` and `IEnumVARIANT` are mentioned throughout the book, but `IDispatchEx` is a little-known interface that extends `IDispatch`, adding capabilities for dynamic member addition and deletion plus case-sensitive member lookup. Scripting languages like JScript make use of `IDispatchEx`, whose definition can be found in `dispex.idl` in the Windows Platform SDK.

As mentioned at the beginning of this section, the CLR exposes an IDispatchEx implementation for a class that implements IReflect or IExpando (from the System.Runtime.InteropServices.Expando namespace), an interface that derives from IReflect. This means that an IDispatchEx pointer could be successfully obtained from COM for the CustomDispatch class in Listing 14.2. The CLR implementation for IDispatchEx is based on the object's IReflect implementation much like the customized IDispatch implementation is. However, the IDispatchEx implementation exposed from IReflect alone is incomplete because IReflect doesn't have any facilities for member addition and deletion. The main benefit of this half-implementation is case-sensitive member lookup.

To get the most functionality out of the IDispatchEx implementation that the CLR exposes, a class must implement IExpando, a simple interface that adds four methods to IReflect. Because there are limitations to the mapping between IExpando/IReflect and IDispatchEx, you still may wish to generate a managed definition of IDispatchEx and implement it directly.

Conclusion

The two main points discussed in this chapter are

- Implementing regular COM interfaces is no different than implementing a .NET interface once you have the interface definition described in metadata. However, you may occasionally want to implement a COM interface that can't be expressed naturally in your .NET language and thus may require workarounds.
- Certain well-known COM interfaces can't be directly implemented by a .NET class, might not need to be directly implemented by a .NET class (because they already are by its CCW), or shouldn't be directly implemented by a .NET class because the CLR maps them to a new .NET way of exposing the same functionality.

Because many COM interfaces may not have a type library available, manually creating a managed interface definition is often needed. Therefore, Chapter 21 is a must-read for those needing to implement such COM interfaces.

Many COM interfaces were briefly discussed in this chapter. For more information about Smart Tag technology in Office XP, consult the Microsoft Office XP Smart Tag SDK, which can be downloaded at msdn.microsoft.com/office. For more information about the standard COM interfaces covered in this chapter, consult MSDN Online at msdn.microsoft.com.

This concludes Part IV, "Designing Great .NET Components for COM Clients." The next three chapters look at the reverse scenario of designing COM components that work well in managed code.

Designing Great COM Components for .NET Clients

IN THIS PART

15 Creating and Deploying Useful Primary Interop Assemblies   683

16 COM Design Guidelines for Components Used by .NET Clients   715

17 Implementing .NET Interfaces for Type Compatibility   739

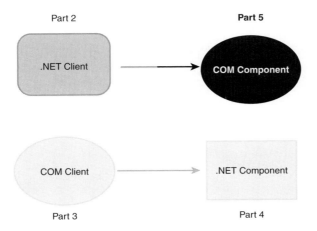

Creating and Deploying Useful Primary Interop Assemblies

IN THIS CHAPTER

- Primary Interop Assembly or Brand New Assembly?   684
- Creating a Primary Interop Assembly   686
- Deploying and Registering a Primary Interop Assembly   694
- Writing IDL That Produces Good Type Libraries   697
- What About ActiveX Controls?   712

As discussed in Chapter 3, "The Essentials for Using COM in Managed Code," a Primary Interop Assembly (PIA) is the official assembly for a corresponding type library, digitally signed and distributed by the author of the type library. The notion of PIAs is simply a convention used by tools such as Visual Studio .NET and TLBIMP.EXE to encourage clients of a COM component to use the same Interop Assembly that others are using. Since the identity of .NET types is based on the assembly in which they reside, it's important that COM types have a single .NET definition. In addition, PIAs are incredibly useful for distributing an assembly with customizations to make using the COM component easier from managed code. Several of the PIAs distributed by Microsoft have customizations that solve incompatibilities or limitations of the type library importer.

Creating and deploying a PIA is not hard to do, but this chapter also focuses on what makes some type libraries produce better PIAs than other type libraries when doing nothing more than using the importer to create PIAs. We'll also discuss how you can tweak your own IDL files to create type libraries that achieve the best results. You may want to refer to Chapter 7, "Modifying Interop Assemblies," which applies to Primary Interop Assemblies just as much as it applies to any other Interop Assemblies. Chapter 7 is extremely important for customizing the PIAs created using the techniques in this chapter in ways that can't be done in a type library.

This chapter focuses on existing COM components that you cannot (or simply don't want to) modify. Chapter 16, "COM Design Guidelines for Components Used by .NET Clients," focuses on ways to either add new functionality to existing COM components, modify existing COM components, or write brand new COM components that naturally work well in .NET, making the task of creating a good Primary Interop Assembly that much easier.

Primary Interop Assembly or Brand New Assembly?

Before looking into the process of creating a Primary Interop Assembly, let's step back and view the motivation for creating one. Many people view the creation of a Primary Interop Assembly as a temporary measure to satisfy .NET clients until the COM component itself is rewritten in managed code as a brand new assembly (which doesn't rely on the original COM component). It might make sense, however, to put off rewriting the COM component indefinitely.

Although the CLR's interoperability services enable incremental migration, these same interoperability services remove the need for migration in the first place! Because the same old COM components can be used in .NET applications, why bother rewriting them? Here are some reasons you might replace old COM components with new .NET components:

- Deployment is easier when a .NET application doesn't rely on COM components. For example, registering COM components makes the goal of xcopy deployment impossible.

- If you plan on improving a COM component and adding features that involve significant development, migration to .NET might be appropriate to take advantage of new features, higher productivity, easier maintainability, and so on.

- You might want to expose XML Web services or replace RPC or DCOM communication with SOAP, which can be done naturally by taking advantage of the .NET Framework.

- Using interoperability services involves some overhead, so an all-.NET application might perform better than one using COM and .NET.

- If you want to provide .NET clients with the most natural experience, sometimes migration is necessary for COM components whose use from managed code would be awkward without major rewriting, due to fundamental differences in programming models.

There can be many good reasons for migration, but you should be absolutely sure that migration makes sense in your application before beginning such an undertaking. For large COM components, the process of redesigning, rewriting, and testing replacement .NET components takes a significant amount of time and resources. It's not as simple as using a wizard to convert Visual Basic 6 code to Visual Basic .NET code, or recompiling unmanaged C++ code with the /CLR switch; it can be a major undertaking to transform code to take advantage of the underlying .NET platform.

If you currently have a Web application with ASP Web pages that use COM objects, it might make sense to convert these ASP pages to ASP.NET pages. This is often easier than migrating COM components to .NET components, although converting ASP pages to take advantage of the new ASP.NET programming model and host of features is non-trivial. You can even do this conversion incrementally, because ASP and ASP.NET can run side-by-side. Be aware, however, that the ASP `Application` and `Session` objects (used to store application and session state) are completely separate from the ASP.NET `Application` and `Session` objects.

If you currently have a standalone Win32 application, migrating it to a .NET Windows Forms application is questionable. Besides adding the requirement that all clients must have the .NET Framework redistributable package (as opposed to requiring it on all Web servers), the features gained by using .NET Windows Forms are usually not nearly as dramatic as the features gained by using ASP.NET. If the existing client application serves as an ActiveX container, however, there's a good case for migration because hosting Windows Forms controls in arbitrary ActiveX containers is not officially supported, as mentioned in Chapter 8, "The Essentials for Using .NET Components from COM."

TIP
Re-using existing Win32 graphical clients with .NET back-end components is one of the most productive uses of COM Interoperability as an alternative to migration.

Creating a Primary Interop Assembly

A Primary Interop Assembly isn't necessarily different from any other Interop Assembly except for a single custom attribute—System.Runtime.InteropServices. PrimaryInteropAssemblyAttribute—marking it as such. There is no support in Visual Studio .NET for *creating* a Primary Interop Assembly, but it can be easily done with the type library importer SDK utility (TLBIMP.EXE). By importing a type library using its /primary option, TLBIMP.EXE marks the output assembly with PrimaryInteropAssemblyAttribute. This custom attribute contains the type library's major and minor version numbers. The type library's LIBID is already captured in an assembly-level GuidAttribute that all Interop Assemblies contain. (Its file-name is also captured in the ImportedFromTypeLibAttribute, but this is just for informational purposes.)

This section examines the following topics that are essential for creating a Primary Interop Assembly:

- Generating a strong name
- Handling references to other type libraries
- Naming the output assembly
- Customizing the metadata

Generating a Strong Name

All Primary Interop Assemblies must have a strong name, so TLBIMP.EXE requires that the /primary option must be used with one of three command-line options to specify a strong name key or key pair:

- /publickey:*FileName*. This option should be used with a binary file containing only your public key. In this case, the resultant strong-named assembly is considered *partially signed*. Only the public key (and not the private key, of course) is used in an assembly's strong name, so it's valid to create a partially signed Primary Interop Assembly and even install it into the Global Assembly Cache. However, partially-signed assemblies don't have the same protection as fully-signed assemblies. For example, anyone who knows your public key could have created the assembly without needing to know your private key. Or, someone with access to your deployed files could tamper with your assembly after you distribute it without being detected by the CLR, since the assembly's original contents were not hashed with your private key and stored in the assembly's manifest. (For these reasons, partially-signed assemblies are typically given less privileges than fully-signed assemblies.) Therefore, partially-signed assemblies should only be created for testing purposes, or as a precursor to fully-signing it using the Assembly Linker SDK utility (`AL.EXE`). The two-step process of creating a partially-signed assembly and fully signing it later, known as *delay signing*, is a common practice since developers often don't have direct access to the company's private key.

- `/keyfile:FileName`. This option should be used with a binary file containing your key pair (both the public and private key). In this case, the resultant strong-named assembly is fully-signed and ready for deployment.

- `/keycontainer:KeyContainerName`. This option should be used with the name of a key container containing your key pair (both the public and private key). This name is used by your computer's cryptographic service provider (CSP) to locate and use the key pair. Depending on the CSP, this option can be considered safer than `/keyfile` since the key data doesn't have to be stored as an unencrypted file in the file system. For example, a CSP may store keys in hardware, minimizing the possibility of them being compromised. A key container can be created using the Windows `CryptAcquireContext` API. See MSDN Online (`msdn.microsoft.com`) for more information. As with using `/keyfile`, the resultant strong-named assembly is fully-signed and ready for deployment.

There's a fourth signing option that can be used at the same time as using `/keyfile` or `/keycontainer`, and that's the `/delaysign` option. Specifying this option means that only the public key will be extracted from the key file or key container, so the output assembly is partially signed. The output is the same as using the `/publickey` option, except that you're in possession of the private key but deliberately ignoring it. This option should only be used for testing purposes.

If you don't already have a key pair of your very own, you can generate one using the Strong Name utility (`SN.EXE`) that is included in the .NET Framework SDK. For example, I can create my own key file at any time by simply executing the following at a command prompt:

```
sn -k "Adam's Top-Secret Key Pair.snk"
```

Then, I can create a Primary Interop Assembly for my type library by executing:

```
TlbImp AdamCo.tlb /keyfile:"Adam's Top-Secret Key Pair.snk" /primary
```

Handling References to Other Type Libraries

Creating a Primary Interop Assembly may not be quite as simple as just using `TLBIMP.EXE`'s `/primary` and `/keyfile` options if your type library references other type libraries. The rules governing Primary Interop Assemblies state that a PIA can only reference other PIAs, because duplicate definitions could be produced otherwise. `TLBIMP.EXE` enforces this rule, and looks for dependent PIAs for any type library you attempt to import.

15

USEFUL PRIMARY
INTEROP
ASSEMBLIES

> **TIP**
>
> To determine if your type library references other type libraries, you can open it with
> OLEVIEW.EXE and look for any importlib statements at the beginning of the library
> block, for example:
>
>   importlib("stdole2.tlb");
>
> Most type libraries reference stdole2.tlb, the type library for OLE Automation,
> which fortunately already has a PIA that ships with Visual Studio .NET.

When attempting to generate a PIA for a type library that depends on other type libraries, you have four possible scenarios:

- If your type library references another type library that has a PIA registered on your computer, TLBIMP.EXE automatically makes your PIA reference the registered PIA.

- If your type library references another type library that has a PIA, but the PIA is not registered on your computer, you can either register the PIA using REGASM.EXE (discussed in the "Deploying and Registering a Primary Interop Assembly" section), or use the /reference option to list the PIA file at the command line. For example:

      tlbimp TalkingComponents.tlb /primary /keyfile:MyKey.snk
      /reference:SpeechEngine.dll

- If your type library references another type library for *your own* COM component that doesn't have a PIA, generate a PIA for the dependent type library. Then follow the instructions for the previous scenario of registering it or using /reference when generating the PIA that depends on it.

- If your type library references another type library for another company's COM component that doesn't have a PIA, you should attempt to obtain a PIA from that company so you can reference it. There may eventually be a standard place to search for and obtain PIAs, but nothing exists at the time of writing.

Creating a PIA for some type libraries may involve a mixture of the previous techniques if they reference multiple type libraries.

FAQ: What can I do if I want to distribute a Primary Interop Assembly for my COM component but it depends on another company's type library for which a Primary Interop Assembly doesn't exist?

The first thing you should do is contact the author of the COM component to beg and plead for a PIA! If the author will not or cannot produce one in a timely manner, you should attempt to remove your dependency from this type library. This doesn't mean that you're removing your run-time dependency from the external COM component; it simply means that your type information is vague enough to not require exposing the component's type definitions publicly. This can be done as follows:

- If your type library contains a class that implements an interface defined in the PIA-less type library, don't list it as being implemented in the type library's `coclass` statement. Because COM clients can still successfully call `QueryInterface` to get the interface pointer, .NET clients can still cast the object to any .NET interface definition they may have, as long as it has the appropriate IID. This is an easy change to make in an IDL file, but for a Visual Basic 6 class this could only be done by modifying its type library. Type library modification could be attempted by disassembling it with `OLEVIEW.EXE` and reassembling it with `MIDL.EXE`, but this is usually not a viable solution.

- If your type library contains members with parameters whose types are interfaces defined in a PIA-less type library, replace each interface type with `IUnknown`. (The same apply for structs with fields of such interface types.) As with the last case, .NET clients can still cast an instance of the generic object type to the desired interface. Again, this is an easy change to make in an IDL file and the corresponding member implementation, which now needs to call `QueryInterface` to obtain the appropriate interface pointer. In Visual Basic 6, you could define the parameter as `stdole.IUnknown`, or use the more natural `Object` type (which means `IDispatch` in VB6) if the interface in question happens to derive from `IDispatch`.

- If your type library contains members with parameters whose types are structs or enums, you could simply redefine those types in your own type library. Duplicate definitions of such types aren't too problematic, compared to duplicate definitions of classes or interfaces. Alternatively, an enum parameter could be replaced with its underlying type if you feel strongly against duplicating an enum definition.

If you're concerned that the first two cases make the use of your PIA too difficult for .NET clients (because where are they going to get an appropriate interface definition from besides writing it themselves?), you could redefine the external interfaces in your own type library and still avoid using them anywhere in your own type definitions. That way, non-official interfaces are available for your clients, but none of your APIs *force* them to use these definitions.

Naming the Output Assembly

The TLBIMP.EXE utility has two important options (/out and /namespace) that enable you to control the output assembly's filename and namespace, respectively. As described in the following sections, the use of either option requires some careful consideration of the needs of your users and your plans for the future of your COM components.

Choosing a Filename

It's imperative that you choose a filename that doesn't conflict with an existing DLL name such as one that's a part of your application or one in the Windows system32 directory. Often, a COM component may have a DLL and a standalone type library with the same name, such as MSHTML.DLL and MSHTML.TLB. If the type library has a library name that matches its file name (minus the extension), then TLBIMP.EXE produces an assembly with a conflicting filename by default—MSHTML.DLL (assuming you saved it to a different directory than the original file).

Conflicting filenames can cause all sorts of confusion. For example, imagine that you need to make a PInvoke call into an entry point in the original MSHTML.DLL. (See Chapter 18, "The Essentials of PInvoke," for more information about PInvoke.) If an Interop Assembly named MSHTML.DLL is encountered first in the current path or if it's already loaded, the CLR will attempt to call the function in the Interop Assembly and fail to find the desired entry point.

Fortunately, when Visual Studio .NET users import a type library in the IDE, the resultant assembly is given the name Interop.*LibraryName*.dll, which is unlikely to have a conflicting name with any existing DLLs. But when creating an Interop Assembly using TLBIMP.EXE, as you must do when creating a Primary Interop Assembly, be aware that its default behavior of producing *LibraryName*.DLL can cause it to be loaded instead of an unmanaged DLL with the same name.

Choosing a Namespace

As with the default filename chosen by TLBIMP.EXE, the default namespace is set to the library's name. When deciding whether to accept the default namespace or choose a new one, consider the following:

- The library name is always a single word, for example MSHTML, SHDocVw, MSXML, SpeechLib, and so on, so using it as a namespace doesn't look very .NET-like. The .NET convention for a namespace is *CompanyName*.*TechnologyName*, using pascal casing and no abbreviations, so you might consider choosing a namespace that matches the conventions.

- If you anticipate that you'll be creating revamped .NET APIs in the future that replace the COM APIs, you might want to reserve the best namespace for later to provide a clear separation between the old types and the new types. In the meantime, your Primary Interop Assembly could use a namespace like *CompanyName.TechnologyName.Compatibility* or *CompanyName.TechnologyName.Interop*. If you plan on migrating functionality from COM to .NET while keeping your public APIs compatible, you might as well use your ideal namespace like *CompanyName.TechnologyName* now.

- Visual C++ and Visual Basic COM clients already use the library name like a namespace, so keeping the library name as the Primary Interop Assembly namespace can make life easier for clients porting existing code to .NET languages. For example, a class like `SpeechLib.SpVoice` remains `SpeechLib.SpVoice` instead of something like `Microsoft.Speech.Interop.SpVoice`, giving clients a degree of source code compatibility. Changing the namespace usually isn't a big deal, however, since most people use it once in C++ or simply omit it in Visual Basic 6.

- Assemblies typically have the same filename as their primary namespace (plus a `.dll` extension), so choosing a namespace that matches the PIA filename might be desirable. Using `TLBIMP.EXE`'s `/out` option automatically changes the default namespace to match the filename (without `.dll`). Be extremely careful when using `/out` without the `/namespace` option, however, because whatever case you use from a command prompt— `mylibrary`, `MyLibrary`, `MYLIBRARY`, and so on—will become the case of the namespace.

There's one more way to choose a namespace besides `TLBIMP.EXE`'s `/namespace` option. It provides some more flexibility, but it involves recompiling your type library. The type library importer recognizes an IDL custom attribute that can be marked on the `library` statement, containing a string with the namespace desired for an imported assembly (whether it's a PIA or not). This custom attribute's name (GUID) is `0F21F359-AB84-41E8-9A78-36D110E6D2F9`, and it can be used as follows:

```
[
  uuid(18343A02-E9B7-40BA-A8F6-AFB47510A0BF),
  version(1.0),
  custom(0F21F359-AB84-41E8-9A78-36D110E6D2F9, "MyCompany.MyTechnology")
]
library MyLibrary
{
  ...
};
```

Importing an assembly for this type library always results in a namespace of `MyCompany`. `MyTechnology`, even if you try to give it a different namespace using `/namespace` or `/out`. The attribute does not affect the output assembly's filename in any way (and if the string in the attribute ends with `.dll` when placed on a `library` statement, the suffix is ignored).

So far, there's been no compelling reason to use this custom attribute instead of `TLBIMP.EXE`'s `/namespace` option. But there is an interesting aspect of this custom attribute—it can be placed on individual types to customize their names and namespaces on a type-by-type basis. This means that you can make the type library importer produce an assembly containing types in multiple namespaces. Listing 15.1 demonstrates this technique.

LISTING 15.1   Using an IDL Custom Attribute Recognized by the Type Library Importer to Choose Namespace-Qualified Names for Types Defined in an IDL File

```
 1: [
 2:   odl,
 3:   uuid(CB073C07-6863-4D52-9332-CF15CA16489E),
 4:   dual,
 5:   oleautomation,
 6:   custom(0F21F359-AB84-41E8-9A78-36D110E6D2F9,
 7:     "MyCompany.MyTechnology.2D.ISquare")
 8: ]
 9: interface ISquare : IDispatch {
10:   ...
11: };
12:
13: ...
14:
15: [
16:   odl,
17:   uuid(B3EA7299-6E27-412C-8F0D-EDD1B64D4218),
18:   dual,
19:   oleautomation,
20:   custom(0F21F359-AB84-41E8-9A78-36D110E6D2F9,
21:     "MyCompany.MyTechnology.3D.ICube")
22: ]
23: interface ICube : IDispatch {
24:   ...
25: };
26:
27: ...
28:
29: [custom(0F21F359-AB84-41E8-9A78-36D110E6D2F9,
30:   "MyCompany.MyTechnology.3D.CubeStyles")]
31: typedef enum {
32:   ...
33: } 3DCubeStyles;
```

The custom attribute, when used in Lines 6–7 and 20–21, simply causes the two interfaces to be given two distinct sub-namespaces of MyCompany.MyTechnology. In Lines 29–30, the custom attribute *renames* the enumeration to get rid of the now-redundant 3D prefix. Renaming types using this custom attribute is a legal thing to do, but it's probably not a good idea to make use of this functionality since clients may have trouble searching for the renamed types.

When using this IDL custom attribute on type definitions, the string must include the namespace *and* type name. These attributes on types always override any namespace specified by the same attribute on the library statement or specified by a user running the type library importer.

Changing the appearance of your APIs via namespace hierarchies or type renaming is probably not worth the trouble if you're eventually planning on overhauling your public APIs with a purely managed implementation. If you don't anticipate changing the APIs in the future, however, using the IDL custom attribute shown in Listing 15.1 can be a handy way of cleaning up and .NET-ifying your APIs.

Customizing the Metadata

It's often necessary to customize the Primary Interop Assembly produced by the type library importer. Chapter 7 covered the process of making modifications plus all the common modifications one usually needs to make. Chapter 21, "Manually Defining COM Types in Source Code," also discusses how to customize metadata describing COM types, but uses a different route that avoids the type library importer altogether. These same techniques apply to Primary Interop Assemblies, so they won't be covered in this chapter.

How do you know if the Primary Interop Assembly needs the customizations shown in Chapters 7 and 21, or if it's ready to be released as-is? One good sign is if TLBIMP.EXE gives no errors or warnings when importing your type library. However, some warnings—such as the importer encountering a pointer to a pointer to a structure that it converts to a System.IntPtr type—are unavoidable without redesigning the COM component and okay to leave alone.

Most importantly, however, is to realize that getting no errors or warnings from TLBIMP.EXE doesn't mean that the PIA is useable! Be sure to "kick the tires" a little and try it out from a .NET perspective before releasing it. It's a good idea to browse your PIA using either the Visual Studio .NET object browser or ILDASM.EXE and, if nothing else, write some small programs that exercise your COM component. Before even invoking the type library importer, it might be worthwhile to view your type library in OLEVIEW.EXE to get a good idea about the type of APIs you'll be exposing to .NET. If you're used to viewing them in IDL files or in Visual Basic 6, you might be surprised by what the type library actually contains. Type libraries for Visual Basic 6 COM components contain hidden interfaces, and type libraries created by MIDL from IDL files can omit important information (such as the size_is attribute), or use different data types (such as long instead of BOOL).

15

> **CAUTION**
>
> Don't use `TLBIMP.EXE`'s lack of errors or warnings as a stamp of approval for your Primary Interop Assembly! Running `TLBIMP.EXE` with no warnings is neither sufficient nor necessary for producing a good Primary Interop Assembly! In most cases, (such as C-style array parameters that look just like pointers to a single instance) the type library doesn't have enough information for the importer to issue a warning. If there were enough information, no warning would be necessary because the importer would be able to do the right thing!

One important decision to make when generating a Primary Interop Assembly with `TLBIMP.EXE` is whether to use the `/sysarray` option to convert `SAFEARRAY` parameters and fields to `System.Array` types. If your type library doesn't use `SAFEARRAY`s, then it makes no difference. If your public APIs use `SAFEARRAY`s but they are always single-dimensional with zero lower bounds, then you should definitely *not* use `/sysarray`, so the imported arrays can be naturally used in .NET languages. If your public APIs use `SAFEARRAY`s that could be multi-dimensional or have non-zero lower bounds, then you should either use the `/sysarray` option or consider some alternatives discussed in Chapter 7.

Deploying and Registering a Primary Interop Assembly

Creating a Primary Interop Assembly doesn't do any good if nobody can find it. Visual Studio .NET, `TLBIMP.EXE`, and `AXIMP.EXE` look for certain registry values to locate PIAs. The tool that can be used for registering a Primary Interop Assembly is none other than the Assembly Registration SDK utility, `REGASM.EXE`. It can be used as follows:

```
regasm MyPIA.dll
```

When registering a Primary Interop Assembly, `REGASM.EXE` adds the following registry value in addition to the usual ones:

```
HKEY_CLASSES_ROOT\TypeLib\{LIBID}\Major.Minor\PrimaryInteropAssemblyName
```

This value has a string containing the assembly's full name, for example:

```
stdole, Version=2.0.0.0, Culture=neutral, PublicKeyToken=b03f5f7f11d50a3a
```

Notice that the value appears under where the type library is registered. This is a natural location because Visual Studio .NET already looks at registered type libraries when presenting the list of COM components in its `Add Reference` dialog.

The rules for locating a PIA from its assembly name are no different than usual. Because the client attempting to locate the assembly in this case is Visual Studio .NET (or sometimes `TLBIMP.EXE` or `AXIMP.EXE`), however, the assembly better be installed into the Global Assembly Cache or it won't be found. If the assembly can't be found, Visual Studio .NET imports a fresh Interop Assembly from the type library without notifying the user.

To avoid the requirement of Global Assembly Cache installation, you can use `REGASM.EXE`'s `/codebase` option. Besides registering the assembly's location under every CLSID entry, it registers the assembly's location under the type library branch with the following value (for PIAs only):

```
HKEY_CLASSES_ROOT\TypeLib\{LIBID}\Major.Minor\PrimaryInteropAssemblyCodeBase
```

This value's string is in "codebase format," for example:

```
file:///C:/Program Files/My Application/MyPIA.dll
```

With such a value registered, Visual Studio .NET, `TLBIMP.EXE`, and `AXIMP.EXE` are able to find and use a Primary Interop Assembly from the directory specified. There is no way to get `REGASM.EXE` to apply `/codebase` *only* to the Primary Interop Assembly entries or *only* to the regular CLSID entries, other than using its `/regfile` option to produce a registration file and manually editing it. Using a `REGASM.EXE`-generated registration file is an acceptable way to register PIAs, unlike the case for regular assemblies, because Interop Assemblies do not contain custom registration functions, and the registration files produced do not contain `InProcServer32` values.

Also, note that `REGASM.EXE` supports Primary Interop Assemblies that have multiple `PrimaryInteropAssemblyAttribute` markings. This can be useful so a single Primary Interop Assembly can represent multiple versions of the same type library (as long as all versions have the same LIBID). When encountering such a PIA, `REGASM.EXE` places the `PrimaryInteropAssemblyName` value and (if applicable) the `PrimaryInteropAssemblyCodeBase` value under each type library version. `TLBIMP.EXE`, however, does not support creating a Primary Interop Assembly corresponding to more than one type library. To do this, you'd need to resort to the techniques in Chapter 7.

Because any dependent PIAs registered on your computer are automatically referenced when creating a PIA, you may not always be aware of the dependencies that your PIA has. It's important to be aware of all dependencies so you know what needs to be shipped and registered along with your PIA. A good way to double-check is to open the PIA using `ILDASM.EXE` and open its manifest. There, besides the ever-present reference to the `mscorlib` assembly, you'll see every other assembly your PIA requires, for example:

```
.assembly extern mscorlib
{
  .publickeytoken = (B7 7A 5C 56 19 34 E0 89 )        // .z\V.4..
  .ver 1:0:3300:0
}
.assembly extern DependentAssemblyOne
{
  .publickeytoken = (54 5E 88 26 7B A4 28 1F )        // T^.&{.(.
  .ver 1:1:0:0
}
.assembly extern DependentAssemblyTwo
{
  .publickeytoken = (54 5E 88 26 7B A4 28 1F )        // T^.&{.(.
  .ver 6:0:0:0
}
```

TIP

Use the /verbose mode when importing a type library with TLBIMP.EXE. Among other output, this will display any assemblies that it automatically references plus any dependent type libraries it automatically generates.

To summarize, all Primary Interop Assemblies and their dependent Primary Interop Assemblies must be registered and installed in the appropriate location on any software developer's computer. The registration is only useful when a Visual Studio .NET user references a type library, or when a TLBIMP.EXE or AXIMP.EXE user imports a type library that references other type libraries with PIAs. A Primary Interop Assembly does not have to be registered in order to work at run time. So when shipping a product to a non-developer end user, registering Primary Interop Assemblies is not necessary.

TIP

Although registering Primary Interop Assemblies on end user computers is not necessary, registering any Interop Assemblies with REGASM.EXE on an end user's computer (primary or not) can be beneficial anyway, as explained in Chapter 6, "Advanced Topics for Using COM Components." Because REGASM.EXE registers .NET class types under their corresponding CLSIDs, the CLR can use this information to minimize the number of times that COM objects are wrapped in the System.__ComObject type.

Writing IDL That Produces Good Type Libraries

It should be obvious that having a type library describing the types in your COM application goes a long way in making it easily accessible from .NET programs. With a type library, you can instantly generate a Primary Interop Assembly using TLBIMP.EXE or a regular Interop Assembly by referencing the type library in Visual Studio .NET.

Fortunately, creating a type library is already a natural part of COM development. COM components written in Visual Basic 6 have a type library automatically generated and embedded in the output DLL or EXE (for project types such as ActiveX EXE, ActiveX DLL, and ActiveX Control, although not Standard EXE). Using the ATL COM AppWizard in Visual C++ 6 or the updated ATL Project Wizard in Visual C++ .NET also generates an embedded type library.

If you ship a Primary Interop Assembly with your COM component, as you should, a type library isn't necessary for .NET components to compile against your types, but shipping a type library is still convenient for any COM clients, such as Visual Basic 6 programs. Note that shipping (and registering) a type library is always necessary if you rely on the OLE Automation marshaler to marshal your interfaces across context boundaries (type library marshaling).

> **TIP**
>
> For maximum usability, make sure any COM types you define reside in a type library. This includes classes, interfaces, structures, unions, and enums. Only defining them in a C++ header file or IDL file isn't enough. You should define them inside a library block in an IDL file so MIDL includes them when compiling a type library.

When creating a type library, there are some guidelines to follow to take advantage of the transformations done by the type library importer. These apply to developers who create IDL files that are compiled to a type library using the MIDL compiler (as is the case with Visual C++ projects). Visual Basic 6 programmers don't have direct control over the kind of issues discussed in this section, but fortunately the automatically-generated type libraries follow these guidelines anyway.

Although you can tweak your Primary Interop Assembly using the techniques from Chapter 7, it's much easier to tweak your type library so it automatically produces the correct results when imported. This is especially true for COM components still under development. The kind of manual modifications to PIAs would have to be automated since APIs could be in a state of flux, perhaps on a daily basis.

Having a type library isn't even necessary for creating a PIA since one can be created manually from any .NET language (as shown in Chapter 21). However, this is a lengthy, error-prone process, and also suffers if your COM types are still under development and constantly changing.

This section covers the following topics for those who deal with IDL files directly, such as C++ programmers:

- Referencing external types
- Defining classes
- Defining structures, enums, and unions
- Using constants appropriately
- Avoiding ignored constructs
- Registering the type library

Although Visual C++ .NET has introduced *attributed programming,* which can remove the need for a separate IDL file, the same concepts apply in making sure that the right information gets into the project's type library.

Referencing External Types

The MIDL compiler has two ways to reference types defined externally to the current IDL file—the import directive and the importlib directive.

The import directive is much like using #include in C++; it dumps definitions of interfaces, typedefs, and constants into the current IDL file as a pre-processing step. Fortunately, using import only brings in definitions that you use in your IDL file (plus any dependent definitions). So the following line, which often appears at the top of standard IDL files:

```
import "oaidl.idl";
```

has no effect unless you make use of one of the types defined inside. This is true regardless of where import is used—inside or outside of the library statement. Be aware, however, that using a single type from an imported file can suck in a whole bunch of definitions. By the single action of using IRecordInfo as a parameter type from oaidl.idl, the type library MIDL generates not only contains the definition of IRecordInfo, but also the ITypeInfo, ITypeComp, and ITypeLib interfaces, 11 structs, seven enums, two unions, and a typedef.

The importlib directive, which must appear inside a library statement, references a *type library* rather than an IDL file. Any definitions in the referenced type library are available for use by your IDL file, but none of them get copied into the output type library as they do in the import case. Because of this, any type libraries listed in importlib statements need to be distributed with your type library. The price of not having duplicated definitions is that your type library, not just your IDL file, has dependencies.

The `importlib` semantics match the .NET mechanism of referencing assemblies. Because .NET type identities are based on the assembly in which they are defined, they are never duplicated in the source code for other assemblies as a pre-processing step. Instead, the types must be referenced via their containing binary files and these dependent files must be available wherever the referencing programs are used.

Therefore, it should come as no surprise that using `importlib` rather than `import` in your type library works better when the type library is imported to an assembly. Any separate type libraries referenced using `importlib` are imported as separate assemblies, whereas any type definitions referenced using `import` are imported to the same assembly since the type library used as input for the type library importer shows no evidence that `import` was used. The difference between using `import` and `importlib` is pictured in Figure 15.1.

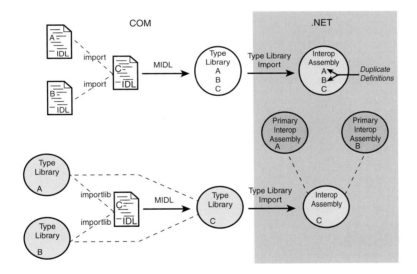

FIGURE 15.1

Using the IDL import *directive "flattens out" type definitions by copying them into the type library, which can cause undesirable duplicate definitions for .NET clients.*

Both cases in the diagram involve defining a type C that uses the externally defined types A and B in its signatures. In the case when `import` is used, the type library produced by MIDL contains the definitions of A, B, and C just as if they were all defined in the same IDL file. Therefore, the type library importer creates an Interop Assembly with all three types. If Primary Interop Assemblies containing the official .NET definitions of A and B exist (as shown in the diagram), the A and B types exposed by C are completely incompatible, causing difficulties for .NET clients.

In the case when `importlib` is used (which requires existing type libraries with the definitions of A and B), the type library produced by MIDL only contains the definition of C, referencing the other two type libraries for the necessary definitions of A and B. Because this dependency information is preserved in the type library, the importer knows to create an Interop Assembly with only the definition of C, then find or create dependent assemblies containing definitions of A and B. In Figure 15.1, the importer automatically references the Primary Interop Assemblies, which results in an optimal experience for .NET clients.

Fortunately, referencing a type library in a Visual Basic 6 project uses `importlib` in the project's type library. Many C++-based COM projects, however, use `import` in their type libraries. In fact, the documentation for MIDL *recommends* `import` instead of `importlib` for three main reasons:

- In COM, duplicate definitions don't cause problems since type identity is based on GUIDs rather than the definition's location.
- Using `import` is easier because you don't have to worry about having dependent type libraries available and registered.
- Many COM types aren't defined in a type library, so using `import` is sometimes the only option. You could create a type library with the definitions of the needed COM types, but (unless you're the author of the types) that would be no better than using `import` and causing those types to be defined in your own type library.

Using `import` rather than `importlib` is fine for a COM-only world but, now that .NET is in the picture, it's no longer desirable.

> **TIP**
>
> Always prefer `importlib` rather than `import` when creating a type library from an IDL file. One of the unenforceable rules of creating a Primary Interop Assembly is that it should not contain any type definitions whose official definition belongs elsewhere. Using `import` can easily violate this rule.

Listing 15.2 demonstrates the discouraged use of `import` to be able to use the `IHTMLControlElement` in the Microsoft HTML Object Library, whereas Listing 15.3 demonstrates the encouraged use of `importlib` for the same scenario. This library has a publicly available IDL file (`MSHTML.IDL`), type library (`MSHTML.TLB`), and even a Primary Interop Assembly (`Microsoft.mshtml.dll`, distributed with Visual Studio .NET). Therefore, importing a type library based on Listing 15.2 incorrectly duplicates type definitions, whereas importing a type library based on Listing 15.3 correctly references the Primary Interop Assembly.

LISTING 15.2   Using the IDL `import` Directive to Reference Types in Other IDL Files Can Cause Type Identity Problems in .NET

```
 1: import "mshtml.idl";
 2:
 3: [
 4:   uuid(F6D98BCB-DE0A-4608-BA1C-D3923351D176),
 5:   version(1.0),
 6:   helpstring("Don't Try This at Home")
 7: ]
 8: library BadLibrary
 9: {
10:   importlib("stdole32.tlb");
11:   importlib("stdole2.tlb");
12:
13:   [
14:     object,
15:     uuid(59E94546-5BBE-4028-A6A0-985B236B0249),
16:     dual,
17:     helpstring("ISampleInterface Interface"),
18:     pointer_default(unique)
19:   ]
20:   interface ISampleInterface : IDispatch
21:   {
22:     [id(1), helpstring("method GetControlElement")]
23:     HRESULT GetControlElement([out, retval] IHTMLControlElement** pRetVal);
24:   };
25: };
```

DON'T DO THIS

LISTING 15.3   Using the IDL `importlib` Directive to Reference Types in Other Type Libraries Is the Best Mechanism When Imported for .NET

```
 1:
 2: [
 3:   uuid(F6D98BCB-DE0A-4608-BA1C-D3923351D176),
 4:   version(1.0),
 5:   helpstring("Do Try This at Home")
 6: ]
 7: library GoodLibrary
 8: {
 9:   importlib("stdole32.tlb");
10:   importlib("stdole2.tlb");
11:   importlib("mshtml.tlb");
12:
```

LISTING 15.3   Continued

```
13:    [
14:       object,
15:       uuid(59E94546-5BBE-4028-A6A0-985B236B0249),
16:       dual,
17:       helpstring("ISampleInterface Interface"),
18:       pointer_default(unique)
19:    ]
20:    interface ISampleInterface : IDispatch
21:    {
22:       [id(1), helpstring("method GetControlElement")]
23:       HRESULT GetControlElement([out, retval] IHTMLControlElement** pRetVal);
24:    };
25: };
```

What should you do if the external type you wish to use is not defined in any type library? You can take the same steps that are recommended for using types defined in someone else's type library for which you don't have a Primary Interop Assembly, mentioned in the FAQ sidebar earlier in the chapter. This includes omitting external interfaces from coclass lists, replacing interface parameters with IUnknown or IDispatch (which requires source code changes), and duplicating struct or enum definitions.

> **TIP**
>
> Don't worry about using parameters with the ITypeInfo, IEnumVARIANT, and IDispatchEx types defined in an IDL file. These interface types are treated specially by the type library importer and custom marshaled to the System.Type, Sytem.Collections.IEnumerator, and System.Runtime.InteropServices.Expando. IExpando types, respectively. This only applies to parameters and fields, however, so a coclass should avoid listing one of these interfaces as being implemented because the .NET class will appear to implement a custom definition of ITypeInfo, IEnumVARIANT, or IDispatchEx.

Defining Classes

Because classes don't play a big role in COM, they are sometimes overlooked when defining a type library. Neither .NET nor COM clients require a class definition since a class can be instantiated using its registered CLSID or ProgID. After instantiation, a class's members can be invoked either by casting to an appropriate interface or by late binding to the object (if it implements IDispatch).

However, .NET clients expect to be able to instantiate an object without using COM-specific mechanisms. In C#, Visual Basic .NET, and C++, this means using the new keyword (New in VB .NET). Defining a class in a type library enables the type library importer to create a .NET class definition that can be used with the new keyword. Although COM-specific mechanisms must be used by the CLR to instantiate the object, the .NET client doesn't need to be aware of this. Even in COM, defining a class in a type library should be done for Visual Basic 6 clients so they can use New instead of calling CreateObject with a ProgID.

There are two separate issues to consider when defining a coclass in an IDL file:

- Listing implemented and source interfaces
- Choosing an appropriate default interface

Listing Implemented and Source Interfaces

A COM class is defined in an IDL file as follows:

```
[uuid(3050f2c4-98b5-11cf-bb82-00aa00bdce0b)]
coclass HTMLInputImage
{
  [default]           dispinterface DispIHTMLInputImage;
  [source, default] dispinterface HTMLInputImageEvents;
                      interface IHTMLInputImage;
                      interface IHTMLControlElement;
                      interface IHTMLElement;
};
```

Although MIDL requires that a coclass lists at least one interface (either an implemented or source interface), you should make sure that any coclass statements you define list all interfaces that you expect to be used from .NET clients (omitting IUnknown and IDispatch, for example). For the identity reasons listed in the last section, any external COM interfaces that are only defined in an IDL file should probably be omitted from the list.

.NET clients can still use interfaces not listed by the coclass statement (since casts result in QueryInterface calls), but listing them has the following advantages:

- It ensures that a .NET definition of the interface gets imported. Otherwise, clients might need to find or create their own interface definition in order to cast the object to the interface type and call its members.
- The CLR can determine that casting the coclass interface to a different interface can succeed based on metadata alone (when the instance's class type isn't System.__ComObject) rather than resorting to a poorer-performing QueryInterface call.

- For clients that may use the class type directly (rather than its imported coclass interface), it can be implicitly coerced to any of the listed interface types rather than requiring an explicit cast.

- The type library importer can only transform source interfaces into .NET events if a coclass lists its source interfaces. Otherwise, .NET clients that wish to hook up event handlers need to do a lot more work by manually setting up connection points as they would in unmanaged C++.

TIP

Although listing both implemented and source interfaces is important when defining a coclass in an IDL file, listing all source interfaces is far more important than listing all implemented interfaces. If a coclass statement omits an implemented interface that already has a .NET definition, a .NET client can still easily cast an instance of the coclass to the interface. If a coclass statement omits a *source* interface, however, a .NET client has to do a lot more work, as demonstrated in Chapter 5, "Responding to COM Events." Fortunately, any VB6-friendly connectable coclass would already list a source interface since failure to do so prevents event handling from Visual Basic 6.

Choosing an Appropriate Default Interface

Every coclass has an interface that's treated as its default interface. This is either the one marked with [default] or the first interface listed. The default interface is important for .NET clients due to two transformations done by the type library importer, described in Chapter 4, "An In-Depth Look at Imported Assemblies":

- A coclass interface is generated with the name of the coclass that derives from the default interface.

- If a coclass is defined in the same type library as its default interface, and if no other coclass in the same type library claims to implement the interface, any parameters or fields of the default interface type are replaced with the coclass interface.

Due to these transformations, a coclass's default interface should accurately represent the entire class. Visual Basic 6 classes use an automatically-generated class interface as the default interface, which contains all the members of the class. This type of default interface works best when imported to an assembly.

The important thing is that you must choose a default interface, otherwise one will be chosen for you! If you don't already have an interface containing all the class's members (and don't want to define one), you should choose an interface that:

- most naturally represents the class's important functionality
- will not be implemented by coclasses in other type libraries

The second point means that you shouldn't choose a famous COM interface as a default interface; rather, it should be one you defined yourself. Here's an example demonstrating why. The following class lists its interfaces in alphabetical order, not paying attention to the implied default designation being assigned to the first interface:

```
[
  uuid(147E9116-9628-4BBE-BA31-9F555C0BDFA6),
  helpstring("MultiPurposeObject Class")
]
coclass MultiPurposeObject
{
  interface IProvideClassInfo;
  interface IReader;
  interface IWriter;
};
```

DON'T DO THIS

Because `IProvideClassInfo` is the default interface, the imported `MultiPurposeObject` coclass interface derives from it, which may seem a little strange since either `IReader` or `IWriter` is probably more appropriate. Furthermore, suppose that the type library defining `MultiPurposeObject` also defines an interface with the following pair of methods, unrelated to `MultiPurposeObject`:

```
HRESULT IsGoodClass([in] IProvideClassInfo* classInfo,
  [out, retval] VARIANT_BOOL bRet);

HRESULT GetInfo([out, retval] IProvideClassInfo** pRetVal);
```

If no other coclass in the type library lists `IProvideClassInfo` as an implemented interface, these methods get imported as follows (in C# syntax):

```
public MultiPurposeObject GetInfo();

public bool IsGoodClass([in] MultiPurposeObject classInfo);
```

The parameters are replaced with the coclass interface! Having `GetInfo` return a `MultiPurposeObject` interface rather than an `IProvideClassInfo` interface seems odd, but everything still works just as if it returns an `IProvideClassInfo` interface since the coclass interface derives from it. So, calling the method can still be done with code like the following (in C#):

15

```
IProvideClassInfo classInfo = obj.GetInfo();
```

But the C# code could also call it like so:

```
MultiPurposeObject mpo = obj.GetInfo();
```

Had the `MultiPurposeObject` coclass listed any source interfaces, the preceding line of code could mislead the .NET client into believing that it can hook up event handlers to the returned object. After all, the `MultiPurposeObject` .NET definition would inherit event members. But the `GetInfo` method could easily return a non-connectable object that implements `IProvideClassInfo`, causing an exception if the client attempted to hook up handlers to any events.

If a client wants to call `IsGoodClass`, it has to pass an object that implements the `MultiPurposeObject` interface. Although this interface has the same IID as `IProvideClassInfo`, you can't substitute one for the other in managed code without a cast:

```
IProvideClassInfo classInfo = obj.GetInfo();
bool b = IsGoodClass((MultiPurposeObject)classInfo);
```

This cast works only if the source object is an RCW, because in this case the cast results in a successful `QueryInterface` call. If you wanted to pass a .NET object that implements the .NET definition of `IProvideClassInfo`, you'd have to change the class's definition or wrap it in a second class that implements the `MultiPurposeObject` interface. Furthermore, as discussed in Chapter 14, "Implementing COM Interfaces for Binary Compatibility," version 1.0 of the CLR doesn't properly expose such .NET objects to COM when the parameter or field is defined as a coclass interface type.

TIP

If your coclass doesn't implement any interfaces that are good candidates for the parameter and field replacement done with coclass interfaces, you should mark `IUnknown` or `IDispatch` as its default interface. Because these interfaces are defined in a different type library than your own, your coclass would no longer qualify for these transformations. Version 1.0 of `TLBIMP.EXE` provides no way to suppress the coclass interface parameter and field replacement that is done for coclasses that qualify.

By now, you should be convinced that you must be really careful about which interface you mark as the default. A rule governing the importer's parameter/field replacement is supposed to prevent such confusion: The replacement is only done if the coclass and its default interface are defined in the same type library. The problem in the `IProvideClassInfo` case is that the definition is obtained via the IDL `import` directive on `ocidl.idl`, so they appear to be defined in the same type library.

TIP

When creating a Primary Interop Assembly, be sure to check all of your default interfaces and determine whether or not the potential parameter/field replacement makes sense for all reasonable situations. It's important because the parameter/field replacement applies to any type libraries that reference your interface definition, even if those dependent type libraries contain coclasses that also implement your interface!

Defining Structures, Enums, and Unions

The most important guideline when defining a structure in an IDL file is to mark it with a GUID. That's because in version 1.0 of the CLR, the Interop Marshaler's support for SAFEARRAYs of user-defined structures (SAFEARRAYs with the VT_RECORD type) only works with structures that have GUIDs. Marking a structure with a GUID has the following IDL syntax:

```
typedef [uuid(3215A2FA-ED29-45AE-97EA-7BABC5E4C18E)]
struct MyStructure
{
  short MyField;
} MyStructure;
```

Fortunately, any UDTs defined in Visual Basic 6 are automatically marked with GUIDs when emitted to a type library. However, many structures defined originally in an IDL file do not have GUIDs. It's certainly an easy thing to forget when writing struct definitions manually.

The other guideline for defining structures, which also applies to enums and unions, deals with choosing names. MIDL generates its own names for structures, enums, and unions that it believes to be nameless. These auto-generated names are always ugly, like __MIDL___MIDL_itf_MyProject_1010_0001, so you want to avoid this from happening wherever possible. The following are two IDL definitions of a structure:

Do use:

```
typedef [uuid(7EC0FB07-3B65-45F6-9F7D-1AB93F53781C)]
struct MyNamedType
{
  short MyField;
} MyNamedType;
```

Don't use:

```
typedef struct
{
  short MyField;
} MyUnnamedType;
```

DON'T DO THIS

The portion in bold is where MIDL picks up the name of the struct. The second struct, while a legal definition, gets an automatically-generated name from MIDL (and isn't marked with a GUID as it should be). Also notice that the first struct uses the same identifier before and after the curly braces. This is legal, and the best way to define a struct in IDL. The common pattern of adding a tag prefix to the first identifier causes the imported structure to begin with the undesirable tag prefix.

Don't use:

```
typedef struct tagMySecondNamedType
{
  short MyField;
} MySecondNamedType;
```

DON'T DO THIS

To make matters more confusing, OLEVIEW.EXE displays structs using the following rule:

```
typedef [...] struct tagStructName
{
      ...
} StructName;
```

So the three previously defined structures would be incorrectly viewed as follows:

```
typedef [uuid(7EC0FB07-3B65-45F6-9F7D-1AB93F53781C)]
struct tagMyNamedType
{
  short MyField;
} MyNamedType;

typedef [public]
   __MIDL___MIDL_itf_myproj_1010_0001 MyUnnamedType;

typedef struct tag__MIDL___MIDL_itf_myproj_0209_0001
{
  short MyField;
} __MIDL___MIDL_itf_myproj_1010_0001;

typedef struct tagtagMySecondNamedType
{
  short MyField;
} tagMySecondNamedType;
```

This unfortunate behavior is one of the aspects of OLEVIEW.EXE that limits its usefulness as a type library disassembler.

Notice that MIDL *does* generate a typedef for the auto-named structure. Since the type library importer imports two copies of a non-primitive typedef (one with the original name and one with the typedef name), any .NET signatures that use the second structure definition as a parameter would fortunately use the .NET value type with the desired name (MyUnnamedType). The metadata would still be cluttered, however, with useless types named by MIDL.

Using Constants Appropriately

Many IDL files make use of two equivalent directives—cpp_quote and midl_echo—in order to inject text directly into C++ header files produced by the MIDL compiler. One problem with using these directives is that there's a tendency to use them too heavily such that only C++ clients can take full advantage of useful items, ignoring the needs of other languages. An example of this is often seen with constant values.

Rather than using cpp_quote or midl_echo to define constants in a header file only, you should define constants inside a module block in order to make the identifiers available to everyone consuming the type library. The following code snippets demonstrate this:

Don't use:

```
cpp_quote("#define MAX_LENGTH    256")
cpp_quote("#define MIN_LENGTH    3")
```

DON'T DO THIS

Don't use:

```
#pragma midl_echo("#define MAX_LENGTH    256")
#pragma midl_echo("#define MIN_LENGTH    3")
```

DON'T DO THIS

Do use:

```
module MyConstants
{
  const unsigned short MaxLength = 256;
  const unsigned short MinLength = 3;
};
```

Make sure that the module block is defined inside the library statement so it gets emitted to the type library produced by MIDL. Defining constants this way not only makes them available for .NET and Visual Basic 6 users, but it still makes them available in the MIDL-generated C++ header file. For example, MIDL generates the following for the preceding MyConstants module:

```
#ifndef __MyConstants_MODULE_DEFINED__
#define __MyConstants_MODULE_DEFINED__
```

15

USEFUL PRIMARY
INTEROP
ASSEMBLIES

```
/* module MyConstants */
const unsigned short MaxLength = 256;
const unsigned short MinLength = 3;
#endif /* __MyConstants_MODULE_DEFINED__ */
```

Avoiding Ignored Constructs

There are two classes of ignored constructs to be aware of—those that appear in an IDL file and are omitted from a type library (simply because they cannot be expressed in a type library's binary format), and those that appear in a type library but are omitted from an Interop Assembly.

For example, the following commonly-used IDL attributes do not exist inside a type library:

- size_is
- length_is
- first_is
- last_is
- max_is
- min_is
- iid_is
- switch_is
- async
- ref
- unique
- ptr

There are three main constructs that are emitted to type libraries but ignored by the type library importer:

- IDL custom attributes (except for the one used to control imported namespaces and type names)
- Methods in a module block
- Typedefs of primitive types

There's no technical reason for the omission of these items, so they could be added to an Interop Assembly manually. But, because the type library importer doesn't handle these for you, it's best to avoid them if at all possible.

Registering the Type Library

As mentioned in Chapter 6, registering a type library can sometimes be necessary for using COM components in .NET. There's nothing inherent in .NET that requires type library registration, but registration might be required for cross-context COM marshaling. Most COM interfaces rely on the OLE Automation marshaler to marshal interfaces pointers across COM contexts. But the OLE Automation marshaler requires a type library to be registered (which places information about the type library under each interface's IID in the registry) in order to get the type information it needs to be able to marshal the interface.

You should ensure that your COM components are registered appropriately to support cross-context marshaling when deployed. Often, type libraries embedded in DLLs are registered at the same time the COM components themselves are registered via REGSVR32.EXE. This is the case for COM DLLs generated by Visual Basic 6 or ATL because their implementation of DllRegisterServer, which is called by REGSVR32.EXE, registers the embedded type library. Standalone type libraries can be registered by calling the LoadTypeLibEx Win32 API with the REGKIND_REGISTER flag (see Chapter 22, "Using APIs Instead of SDK Tools," for an example). The REGASM.EXE SDK utility also registers type libraries, but only for ones that it exports from assemblies.

For COM components that rely on custom proxy/stub marshaling, make sure that the appropriate proxy/stub marshaler is registered for your interfaces instead of the type library. Accidentally registering a type library marshaler can result in incorrect marshaling for types that aren't supported by the OLE Automation marshaler, such as C-style arrays. Recall that type libraries can be accidentally registered by doing something as innocent as opening them with OLEVIEW.EXE, but this won't necessarily affect the registration of interfaces. See Chapter 12, "Customizing COM's View of .NET Components," for more information.

> **Caution**
>
> The default behavior of the Visual C++ 6 ATL COM Wizard does not properly register a proxy/stub DLL when selecting Allow merging of proxy/stub code. See Chapter 6 for steps to fix this problem.

What About ActiveX Controls?

There's no such thing as a "Primary ActiveX Assembly"; one ActiveX Assembly is no more official than another. This is fine, because the only interesting types defined in an ActiveX Assembly are the Ax-prefixed classes, and there's no compelling reason for .NET components to send an instance of one to another .NET component. Any cross-assembly communication should be done with the core classes and interfaces from a Primary Interop Assembly.

What this means, however, is that Visual Studio .NET users selecting your ActiveX control from the Customize Toolbox dialog will not be automatically redirected to your pre-built, potentially customized, ActiveX Assembly. You should still create, customize (using AXIMP.EXE's /source option), sign, and ship an ActiveX Assembly. Users will just need to know to select your new component from the .NET Framework Components tab of the Customize Toolbox dialog rather than the COM Components tab.

You should be sure that any ActiveX Assembly that you create references only Primary Interop Assemblies. If you don't plan on publicly exposing any members that use types from the referenced assemblies, it's not strictly necessary but it's still a good idea because otherwise you'd be shipping your component with assemblies that are potentially duplicates of PIAs already installed on the user's computer. Because AXIMP.EXE only runs on a type library and has no way to reference pre-imported assemblies (as does TLBIMP.EXE's /reference option), you can follow these steps to create an ActiveX Assembly that references PIAs:

1. Create a Primary Interop Assembly for the type library describing the ActiveX control(s) using TLBIMP.EXE. This may involve creating or obtaining PIAs for dependent type libraries.

2. Register the Primary Interop Assembly (plus any dependent PIAs) using REGASM.EXE. If you don't also install it in the Global Assembly Cache, be sure to use the /codebase option.

3. Run AXIMP.EXE on the type library. The ActiveX control importer checks for a registered Primary Interop Assembly before invoking the type library importer, and will use it if it can locate the assembly.

The other option would be to use AXIMP.EXE's /source option, then reference the necessary PIAs when compiling the output C# source code.

> **TIP**
>
> It's a really good idea use AXIMP.EXE's /source option to generate C# source code for the ActiveX assembly and customize its contents. As discussed in Chapter 5, the types generated by the ActiveX importer do not conform to .NET guidelines. In the generated source code, you should rename the ...Event classes to ...EventArgs classes, perhaps

capitalize the public fields of these classes, and make them derive from `System.EventArgs`. Another user-friendly change would be to rename the delegate types from *SourceInterfaceName_MethodName*`EventHandler` to simply *MethodName*`EventHandler`, as long as the name doesn't conflict with others.

Note that when compiling source code generated from `AXIMP.EXE`, you'll need to reference `System.Windows.Forms.dll` and `System.dll` in addition to the corresponding Interop Assembly (and its dependencies).

Conclusion

Although the main purpose of this chapter is to describe how to create and deploy Primary Interop Assemblies, we also discussed IDL tweaks to make a type library for which the importer produces a usable PIA naturally. This can hopefully avoid the need to disassemble, modify, and reassemble the result. It's easy to generate one with `TLBIMP.EXE` and have the urge to ship it as-is (especially if there were no warnings during import), but it may not necessarily be usable from .NET languages depending on what techniques are used in the input type library.

We also discussed issues with migrating existing COM components, something which needs serious evaluation before undertaking. The huge time and effort required by migration often doesn't pay off. Sometimes a good approach is to attempt to use COM Interoperability and see if it meets your needs before planning a large migration.

Although using the type library importer is the easiest and recommended way to create a Primary Interop Assembly, it's sometimes desirable to create a Primary Interop Assembly in source code, especially if you're planning on making additions to the assembly. For example, you could create a brand new assembly in your favorite language and mark it as a Primary Interop Assembly by simply using `PrimaryInteropAssemblyAttribute` and registering it appropriately. Then, this assembly could define new .NET types that encapsulate definitions of COM types in a way that hides any COM complexity, handling things like resource management or custom data type transformations. However, PIAs must at least contain public definitions of all the types in the original type library. An assembly that's radically different should just be considered the next version of a technology and not be tied to an older type library.

COM Interoperability is not the only way to re-use COM components in .NET. Instead, you could use existing COM objects via the other technologies described in Chapter 2, "Bridging the Two Worlds—Managed and Unmanaged Code." For example, by exposing your APIs as simple static entry points, you can use PInvoke to expose unmanaged functionality with higher performance. You could then create a new .NET object model that encapsulates these APIs in a .NET style. This technique is used throughout the .NET Framework—for example, the `System.IO` namespace encapsulates the Windows file system APIs and the `System.Windows.Forms` namespace encapsulates a whole bunch of Windows APIs inside .NET object models.

Mixed mode programming using Visual C++ .NET is the most raw and powerful option. Whereas PInvoke and COM Interoperability make use of the Interop Marshaler for data transformations and Visual J# .NET automatically handles Java/.NET transformations, any data transformations in mixed-mode C++, such as exposing a .NET `String` type for a `char*` or `BSTR` type, need to be done manually by the programmer. To help with this, several helper functions exist in a `vcclr.h` header file that ships with the .NET Framework SDK, or in the `System.Runtime.InteropServices.Marshal` class.

Visual C++ .NET is valuable for gradual migration and fine-grained mixing of managed and unmanaged types. For algorithms that must be ultra-efficient, you can take advantage of optimized unmanaged code that perhaps can't be matched by the .NET just-in-time compiler. There are three main drawbacks to writing managed code using Visual C++ .NET:

- The generated assemblies contain some unmanaged code in addition to IL, so are not instantly portable to other platforms.

- In an environment with multiple .NET application domains, programming in C++ requires great care with unmanaged code interaction. When you call unmanaged code that calls back into managed code, you need to manually ensure that it executes in the proper application domain.

- Assemblies produced by Visual C++ do not pass .NET verification, but this often doesn't matter for assemblies that interoperate with unmanaged code anyway.

COM Design Guidelines for Components Used by .NET Clients

IN THIS CHAPTER

- General Guidelines   716
- Using Array Parameters   717
- Issues with VARIANT Parameters   720
- Reporting Errors   720
- Adjusting Certain COM-Specific Idioms   729
- Managing Limited Resources   731
- Threading and Apartment Guidelines   733
- Providing Self-Describing Type Information   734
- Naming Guidelines   734
- Performance Considerations   735

This chapter focuses on developing new software using COM. With the arrival of .NET, the recommendations for designing COM APIs have changed, assuming you care about .NET clients using your COM components (either now or in the future). Most existing COM components have a disadvantage of being designed before .NET existed, so their authors did not know what COM Interoperability handles well and what it doesn't. Today, however, it would be foolish to design new COM components or add new functionality to existing COM components without considering how this functionality gets exposed to .NET.

Don't worry too much if you must use a technique that conflicts with the guidelines in this chapter. These guidelines point out what works best so you can avoid a suboptimal design when you have no constraints. (Although, if you have no constraints, why are you developing the new object as a COM object rather than a .NET object?) Many of the techniques advised against can still work for .NET clients—it just may involve extra work on your behalf in customizing your Primary Interop Assembly, or extra work for clients attempting to work around the quirks of your APIs.

Many of the IDL and type library guidelines given in the previous chapter apply to new COM applications as well, so you should refer to the previous chapter as well as this one when designing new COM components.

General Guidelines

Before examining a few major areas in detail, here's a laundry list of guidelines that you should follow when designing COM objects that will work well for .NET clients. The effects of not following these guidelines were examined in Part II.

- Don't define a struct with a SAFEARRAY field because the Interop Marshaler doesn't support it.

- Don't define a struct with a VARIANT_BOOL field because the type library importer transforms it into a 16-bit integer, unless you plan on manually modifying the corresponding metadata.

- Don't use struct parameters in a dispinterface method (such as a source interface), because it necessitates late binding and structs passed inside VARIANTs aren't automatically supported.

- Don't use parameter types that lose their meaning in a type library, such as the Win32 BOOL type.

- Don't define properties with both a Let and a Set accessor (propput and propputref) because this doesn't transform naturally into properties supported by .NET languages.

- Avoid typedefs of primitive types, because they don't naturally translate to metadata.

- Avoid optional parameters because C# clients can't treat them as optional. Unfortunately, overloaded methods aren't an alternative in COM.

- Use dual interfaces wherever possible because they match the .NET expectations of being able to early bind or late bind, and because `Type.InvokeMember` doesn't work without an underlying `IDispatch` implementation—even if invoking on a strongly-typed Runtime-Callable Wrapper (RCW).

- Avoid unions, especially if they contain types that become reference types in .NET (such as `BSTR` or `VARIANT`) because the type library importer can't import them naturally.

- As when creating COM components for use by Visual Basic 6, it's best when a coclass lists a single implemented interface and single source interface. Although multiples of either can work without problems for .NET clients, it can cause name collisions when multiple interface members are added to the class type, and it causes .NET clients to cast to the non-intuitive importer-generated event interfaces when hooking up event handlers to non-default source interfaces.

- Expose events in the natural COM way (using connection points) and expose enumerators in the natural COM way (using `DISPID_NEWENUM` and `IEnumVARIANT`) because they are both mapped naturally to .NET events and .NET enumeration functionality.

Using Array Parameters

Arrays are often used as COM parameters, and there are many different options for expressing them. The guidelines for defining array parameters that work well for .NET clients can be summarized in once sentence: Use single-dimensional `SAFEARRAY`s with a lower bound of zero. Let's discuss the three different parts of this recommendation:

- Use `SAFEARRAY`s
- Use Zero Lower Bounds
- Use Single-Dimensional Arrays

Use SAFEARRAYs

When exposing array parameters, you should stick to `SAFEARRAY`s (normal arrays in Visual Basic 6). C-style arrays don't get imported as arrays because they look like simple pointers in a type library without any `size_is` information. So, the following transformation occurs:

IDL:

```
HRESULT SetBytes(
    [in, size_is(dwDataInLen)] byte *pbDataIn, [in] long dwDataInLen);
```

DON'T DO THIS

C# Representation of Imported Method:

```
public void SetBytes([In] ref byte pbDataIn, [In] int dwDataInLen);
```

This is unusable from managed code unless the user wants to pass a single element. As you saw in Chapter 7, "Modifying Interop Assemblies," the .NET signature can be (and should be) hand-tuned to be marshaled as an array instead:

```
public void SetBytes([MarshalAs(UnmanagedType.LPArray, SizeParamIndex=1)]
  byte [] pbDataIn, int dwDataInLen);
```

However, having to pass an array's length as a separate parameter still looks bizarre to .NET clients because .NET arrays are self-describing. The Interop Marshaler doesn't use the dwDataInLen length parameter when marshaling the array from managed code to unmanaged code; it decides how many elements need to be marshaled by checking the array's Length property. The length parameter (and the SizeParamIndex marking) *is* needed when marshaling from unmanaged code to managed code, as is the case if a .NET object implements a COM interface with such a method.

Had the COM method used a SAFEARRAY instead:

```
HRESULT SetBytes([in] SAFEARRAY(byte) bytes);
```

then the .NET signature would look natural in managed code:

```
public void SetBytes(byte [] bytes);
```

SAFEARRAYs can be much more difficult to use in unmanaged C++ code, but it spares you from having to modify the Interop Assembly produced by the type library importer. Having the importer do the right thing automatically saves a lot of effort, especially for an ever-changing type library under development.

For by-reference or out-only array parameters, defining an array as a C-style array makes its use even harder for .NET clients. The Interop Marshaler would need to know the rank and size of the array in order to marshal it to managed code, yet using MarshalAsAttribute's SizeParamIndex and SizeConst values are not supported for anything other than by-value arrays and by-value length parameters. This means that an IDL signature such as:

```
HRESULT GetBytes(
  [out, size_is(dwDataInLen)] byte **ppbDataOut,
➥[out] long* dwDataOutLen);
```

DON'T DO THIS

would be translated by the type library importer into the following .NET signature (shown in C#):

```
public void GetBytes(IntPtr ppbDataOut, out int dwDataOutLen);
```

Then, as shown in Chapter 7, you'd likely want to change the signature to:

```
public void GetBytes(out IntPtr ppbDataOut, out int dwDataOutLen);
```

so that a client can process the array data using methods of the `System.Runtime.InteropServices.Marshal` class. Defining the COM method to return a `SAFEARRAY` instead:

```
HRESULT GetBytes([out, retval] SAFEARRAY(byte)* bytes);
```

would naturally produce a usable .NET signature:

```
public byte [] GetBytes();
```

Use Zero Lower Bounds

If you have a choice, always choose zero-bounded arrays. Choosing a bound other than zero means that the array can only ever be used as a `System.Array` type in managed code. The result is that clients must access its elements using the `Array.GetValue` and `Array.SetValue` methods that are much more awkward than using array indexing syntax. Also, .NET clients can only create instances of arrays with non-zero lower bounds using the `Array.CreateInstance` method. Using `TLBIMP.EXE`'s `/sysarray` option (used by Visual Studio .NET by default) imports all array parameters as `System.Array` types rather than single-dimensional zero-lower-bound arrays, in case you already use non-zero based arrays and it's too difficult to change them.

Use Single-Dimensional Arrays

Prefer single-dimensional arrays over multi-dimensional because the type library importer automatically treats `SAFEARRAY`s as single-dimensional (when not using the `/sysarray` option).

For example, rather than exposing a method that requires a list of paired strings (such as an employee name with his or her social security number):

```
HRESULT GetEmployeeList([out, retval] SAFEARRAY(BSTR)* employees);
```

consider splitting the array into two one-dimensional arrays:

```
HRESULT GetEmployeeList([out] SAFEARRAY(BSTR)* employeeNames,
  [out] SAFEARRAY(BSTR)* employeeNumbers);
```

Of course, this is not feasible for larger arrays or arrays with more dimensions.

If you must expose a multi-dimensional array, you have two options to properly expose it to .NET clients:

- Use TLBIMP.EXE's /sysarray option to expose array parameters as System.Array types. If your array parameter doesn't have a fixed rank (in other words, it's sometimes a two-dimensional array and other times a three-dimensional array), this is the only option.

- Use the techniques discussed in Chapter 7 to change the array parameter in the .NET signature to be multi-dimensional. This only works for array parameters with a fixed rank.

Issues with VARIANT Parameters

Care should be used when exposing VARIANT parameters. Ask yourself why you aren't defining the VARIANT as a more specific type. Exposing VARIANT parameters is fine as long as you don't expect users to pass a type such as CURRENCY or a user-defined structure. For CURRENCY, .NET clients must use the non-intuitive CurrencyWrapper type. For user-defined structures, .NET clients must use a variety of workarounds, as seen in Chapter 6, "Advanced Topics for Using COM Components," since the Interop Marshaler doesn't support them inside VARIANTs.

For Visual Basic 6 COM components, don't use public VARIANT fields because they get exposed as properties with all three accessors. Use a property instead or a more specific data type.

For C++ COM components manually inspecting the vt field of a passed-in VARIANT, you should be as lenient as possible when determining what is a legal value. For example, if you're expecting an interface pointer inside the VARIANT, don't check to see whether the type is VT_UNKNOWN and report an error if it is not. Most .NET objects appear as VT_DISPATCH when passed inside a VARIANT, so your code should be prepared to expect that type as well. In addition, don't require the VT_BYREF flag to be set if it's not necessary, because it can be difficult for .NET callers to set this flag. See Chapter 3, "The Essentials for Using COM in Managed Code," for more details about how .NET types are exposed as VARIANTs to COM.

Reporting Errors

With any software, good error reporting is critical to keeping the frustration level of your consumers (and often yourself) low. Understanding how COM errors are converted to .NET errors is critical so your COM components can take advantage of this transformation.

As described in Chapter 3, when a COM member returns a failure HRESULT value, the CLR throws a .NET exception on the COM component's behalf. The exception type depends on the HRESULT value, according to the table shown in Appendix C, "HRESULT to .NET Exception Transformations." Any HRESULT values not in this list become a user-unfriendly COMException type.

There are three guidelines to keep in mind when reporting errors from COM:

- Reserve Failure HRESULTs for Exceptional Circumstances
- Don't Use Success HRESULTs Other than S_OK
- Set Additional Error Information

All three of these guidelines were already considered good practice for COM components that may be used from Visual Basic 6, so hopefully your existing COM components follow them anyway.

TIP

There are two more guidelines worth mentioning, both of which also apply when .NET isn't in the picture. The first is to document all your HRESULTs clearly in your help files. This includes documenting every HRESULT that every member might return. The second is to never return an HRESULT with the value E_FAIL. This value is too generic to convey meaningful information to the caller.

Reserve Failure HRESULTs for Exceptional Circumstances

In COM, there's no performance penalty inherent to returning a failure HRESULT value; regardless of success or failure, a 32-bit integer is returned to the caller. When .NET clients are involved, however, the transformation from returning a failure HRESULT to throwing a .NET exception incurs a significant performance penalty that *is* inherent to throwing an exception. This is similar to returning a failure HRESULT value to a Visual Basic 6 client; the VB6 runtime does more work to raise an error, therefore making failures slightly slower than successes. The difference in performance between error versus no error is much greater in .NET however. Exception handling is optimized such that .NET clients that are prepared to handle exceptions incur almost no performance penalty for the common case of no exception being thrown.

Therefore, the same .NET design guideline of "reserve exceptions for exceptional situations" applies to failure HRESULTs. Only return failure HRESULTs (or, in Visual Basic 6, only raise an error) in important and sufficiently rare cases. Don't use different failure values to signal different program states that are useful in normal program operation.

Don't Return Success HRESULTs Other than S_OK

This section doesn't apply to COM members implemented in Visual Basic 6, because they cannot return success HRESULT values.

You've seen in Part II how much of a nuisance a COM component can be in .NET if it returns multiple success HRESULTs that need to be seen by the client. Because any success HRESULT values (values for which the most significant bit is not set) are swallowed by the Runtime-Callable Wrapper, the values are unattainable from .NET clients unless the managed signature corresponding to the member returning the HRESULT is marked with the PreserveSigAttribute pseudo-custom attribute.

Technically, it doesn't matter which success HRESULT you return, just so you don't require that the caller needs the ability to distinguish between different success HRESULT values. The S_OK HRESULT (with value 0), however, is the conventional success HRESULT that should always be used for success to avoid potential confusion for any COM clients.

You might now be saying to yourself, "I'm not supposed to use failure HRESULTs in non-exceptional situations, and I'm never supposed to use multiple success HRESULTs, so how can I communicate informational status?" You should use an [out, retval] parameter (or in Visual Basic 6, a return type) that's a boolean value or an enumeration value instead. Save the "real" HRESULT return value for exception transport only.

Set Additional Error Information

There's not much that's more annoying than using a COM object in a .NET program and seeing an exception thrown with the message, "Exception from HRESULT: 0x80090324." To spare your users from this aggravation, you should always set additional error information when returning a failure HRESULT in unmanaged C++ or raising an error in Visual Basic 6. If nothing else, set a descriptive message.

To make exceptions caused by failure HRESULTs more user-friendly, the CLR fills in an exception's properties with data from a COM error object if one exists. An error object implements the IErrorInfo COM interface, and the mechanism for making it available to clients such as the CLR is discussed in the following sections. If no error object has been made available by the COM member, the resultant exception contains less helpful information.

The following text summarizes how the CLR fills in an exception object's properties:

- Message—The string returned from IErrorInfo.GetDescription (Err.Description in VB6). If no error object is available, the CLR attempts to use the FormatMessage Windows API to see if the operating system recognizes the HRESULT and returns a descriptive message. Otherwise, the message is the generic "Exception from HRESULT: *HRESULT displayed in hexadecimal.*"

- ErrorCode—The failure HRESULT value.

- Source—The string returned from IErrorInfo.GetSource (Err.Source in VB6). If no error object is available, then the string is either set to the name of the Interop Assembly defining the RCW that threw the exception, or an empty string if the RCW is System.__ComObject.

- TargetSite—A System.Reflection.MethodBase instance that corresponds to the method (or property accessor) that returned the failure HRESULT. More precisely, it's the top-most member in the call stack with a .NET definition (which could be Type.InvokeMember when late-binding to a COM component with no metadata).

- StackTrace—Because there's no stack information for the COM component, the bottom of the stack trace is the method where the exception is caught, and the top is the call into unmanaged code (the same member corresponding to the TargetSite property). Even if the failure HRESULT returned from the COM object originated as an exception thrown from a .NET object (managed code calling into COM which calls into managed code), the top of the stack trace is still the first transition into unmanaged code.

- InnerException—The IErrorInfo interface doesn't have the notion of an "inner error," so this property is null (Nothing in VB .NET). If the failure HRESULT returned from the COM object originated as an exception thrown from a .NET object, the InnerException property is set to the original exception's InnerException object.

- HelpLink—The string returned from IErrorInfo.GetHelpFile (Err.HelpFile in VB6), or an empty string if no error object is available. If IErrorInfo.GetHelpContext returns a non-zero number, a "#" symbol and this number are appended to the end of the HelpLink string, because in .NET the HelpLink is supposed to represent a URL, and in COM the HelpContext is supposed to represent a section of the HelpFile.

The mechanism for setting this additional error information is different in unmanaged C++ than in Visual Basic 6, and, of course, the Visual Basic mechanism is much easier to use. Each of these mechanisms is discussed in more detail in the following sections.

Setting Additional Error Information in Visual Basic 6

Returning an error without any additional information is done as follows in Visual Basic 6:

```
Err.Raise 5640
```

If a member that raised this error were called by a .NET client, it would receive the following exception:

```
System.Runtime.InteropServices.COMException (0x800A1608):
➡Application-defined or object-defined error
   at Project1.Class1Class.FindUser(String name)
   at client.Main()
```

Notice that the message isn't the default "Exception from HRESULT" message. That's because the Visual Basic 6 runtime always makes a COM error object available and sets "Application-defined or object-defined error" as its default message for any error codes it doesn't recognize.

FAQ: **How does a Visual Basic 6 error code translate into an HRESULT value?**

Under normal circumstances, a user-defined Visual Basic 6 error code can be set to a value from 512 to 65535. This represents the allowable range for the lower 16-bits of an HRESULT value. The HRESULT's facility is set to FACILITY_CONTROL (the hexadecimal number A) by the Visual Basic 6 runtime, and the severity bit is always set. Values below 512 (0x200) are reserved for system use, and still fall into the FACILITY_CONTROL facility.

If you want to return an HRESULT value with a different facility in Visual Basic 6, you can specify an entire 32-bit HRESULT value with Err.Raise. This only works, however, if the severity bit is set because VB6 won't allow you to raise an error with a success HRESULT value. So, you can return an HRESULT like 0x80040016 by doing the following:

```
Err.Raise &H80040016
```

HRESULTs beginning with &H8004 (0x8004) are in the FACILITY_ITF facility, and are the only type of HRESULT values allowed to be defined by someone other than Microsoft. The ITF stands for *interface*, meaning that the interpretation of the lower 16 bits of the HRESULT depends on the specific interface containing the member that returned the value. Because this HRESULT facility is so widely used, Visual Basic 6 defines a vbObjectError constant in one of its standard type libraries set to the hexadecimal value 0x80040000. Users can add this constant to raised error codes in order to easily return an HRESULT with FACILITY_ITF. Therefore, the previous line of code can be rewritten as follows:

```
Err.Raise vbObjectError + &H16
```

Or, without using hexadecimal notation:

```
Err.Raise vbObjectError + 22
```

Adding the additional information is simply a matter of passing values for Err.Raise's optional parameters. These are, in order, Source, Description, HelpFile, HelpContext, and can be set as follows:

```
Err.Raise 5640, "My Component", _
  "The name 'Sue' does not match any existing records.", _
  "http://www.samspublishing.com/help.html", 44444
```

This would result in a .NET exception thrown that looks like the following, which is much more helpful than in the previous case:

```
System.Runtime.InteropServices.COMException (0x800A1608):
➥The name 'Sue' does not match any existing records.
  at Project1.Class1Class.FindUser(String name)
  at Client.Main()
```

Setting Additional Error Information in Unmanaged Visual C++

Setting additional error information in unmanaged Visual C++ is significantly more involved than in Visual Basic 6, and requires dealing with the IErrorInfo interface directly. First, any COM object that wants to return additional error information via IErrorInfo must implement the ISupportErrorInfo interface. This interface is used by the CLR (as well as other COM clients) to determine whether or not to bother attempting to retrieve an error object via the GetLastError Windows API.

As discussed in Chapter 14, "Implementing COM Interfaces for Binary Compatibility," ISupportErrorInfo has a single method—InterfaceSupportsErrorInfo—with a single parameter containing an IID. This method's implementation must return S_OK if the interface identified by the passed-in IID uses IErrorInfo to report additional error information, or S_FALSE otherwise. All COM classes authored in Visual Basic 6 implicitly have an implementation of ISupportErrorInfo that returns S_OK from InterfaceSupportsErrorInfo for any interfaces implemented by the class.

When using the Visual C++ 6 ATL COM Wizard to create a COM object, it does not implement ISupportErrorInfo by default. However, by checking the Support ISupportErrorInfo check box on the Attributes tab, an appropriate implementation is filled in by the wizard. This is pictured in Figure 16.1. Using the Visual C++ .NET ATL Simple Object Wizard, you can check the ISupportErrorInfo check box to enable the same behavior. This is pictured in Figure 16.2.

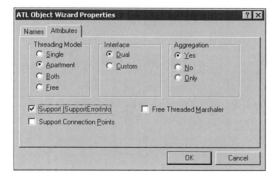

FIGURE 16.1
Telling the Visual C++ 6 ATL COM Wizard to generate an implementation of ISupportErrorInfo.

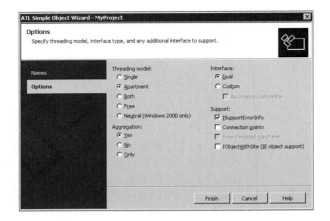

Figure 16.2
Telling the Visual C++ .NET ATL Simple Object Wizard to generate an implementation of ISupportErrorInfo.

The filled-in implementation of ISupportErrorInfo.InterfaceSupportsErrorInfo looks like the following (in Visual C++ 6), returning S_OK for every interface whose IID is listed in the arr array:

```
STDMETHODIMP CMyObject::InterfaceSupportsErrorInfo(REFIID riid)
{
  static const IID* arr[] =
  {
    &IID_IMyObject
    ...other interfaces implemented by the class
  };
  for (int i=0; i < sizeof(arr) / sizeof(arr[0]); i++)
  {
    if (InlineIsEqualGUID(*arr[i],riid))
      return S_OK;
  }
    return S_FALSE;
}
```

> **Caution**
>
> Don't forget to make your COM objects implement ISupportErrorInfo and ensure that all the necessary IIDs are accounted for in the InterfaceSupportsErrorInfo implementation. Otherwise, any effort spent setting rich error information will be ignored by the CLR and not visible to .NET users.

The code in Listing 16.1, when used by a COM object that appropriately implements `ISupportErrorInfo`, has the exact same result as the following Visual Basic 6 code from the previous section:

```
Err.Raise 5640, "My Component", _
  "The name 'Sue' does not match any existing records.", _
  "http://www.samspublishing.com/help.html", 44444
```

LISTING 16.1 Unmanaged C++ Code That Sets Rich Error Information to be Used by the CLR When Constructing a .NET Exception

```
 1: ICreateErrorInfo *pcerrinfo;
 2: IErrorInfo *perrinfo;
 3: HRESULT hr;
 4:
 5: BSTR description = SysAllocString(
 6:   L"The name 'Sue' does not match any existing records.");
 7: BSTR helpfile = SysAllocString(L"http://www.samspublishing.com/help.html");
 8: long helpcontext = 44444;
 9: BSTR source = SysAllocString(L"My Component");
10:
11: hr = CreateErrorInfo(&pcerrinfo);
12: if (SUCCEEDED(hr))
13: {
14:   pcerrinfo->SetDescription(description);
15:   pcerrinfo->SetHelpFile(helpfile);
16:   pcerrinfo->SetHelpContext(helpcontext);
17:   pcerrinfo->SetSource(source);
18:
19:   hr = pcerrinfo->QueryInterface(IID_IErrorInfo, (void**)&perrinfo);
20:   if (SUCCEEDED(hr))
21:   {
22:     SetErrorInfo(0, perrinfo);
23:     perrinfo->Release();
24:   }
25:
26:   pcerrinfo->Release();
27: }
28:
29: return 0x800A1608;
```

Lines 5–9 define the four aspects of the rich error information that we'll be setting. The first step in setting this information is to obtain an object implementing `ICreateErrorInfo`. This is obtained in Line 11 by calling the `CreateErrorInfo` Windows API. `CreateErrorInfo` can return `E_OUTOFMEMORY` if there's not enough memory to allocate an error object, but if the call succeeds, Lines 14–17 call the methods of ICreateErrorInfo to set the information initialized in Lines 5–9.

ICreateErrorInfo has a method that's not used in this code listing: SetGUID. This is skipped because an error object's GUID value is not used by the CLR when constructing a .NET exception; there's no corresponding property in a .NET exception. Because COM clients may use an error object's GUID value to interpret HRESULTs in an interface-specific yet object-independent manner, a proper COM object should call ICreateErrorInfo.SetGUID.

After setting the error information, Line 19 queries for the IErrorInfo interface from the error object. This is the interface type that we must pass to the SetErrorInfo Windows API on Line 22. Its first parameter is reserved and must always be set to zero, and the second parameter is the IErrorInfo type. After releasing the two interface pointers in Lines 23 and 26, the only thing left to do is to return the failure HRESULT. Notice that the code is structured such that if the process of setting rich error information fails, we silently fall back to simply returning the HRESULT. This is desirable so the client can see the original error rather than getting confused by an HRESULT that doesn't directly apply to the original error we're trying to communicate to the user.

DIGGING DEEPER

If you want your COM client to return HRESULTs that are directly transformed into .NET exceptions other than COMException, you'd need to return one of the HRESULTs listed in Appendix C. For example, it might be appropriate for this section's example to use the famous E_INVALIDARG HRESULT rather than a custom one. This would make .NET clients see the following exception:

System.ArgumentException: The name 'Sue' does not match any existing records.

    at Project1.Class1Class.FindUser(String name)

    at Client.Main()

Most of the HRESULTs that get transformed, however, are new .NET HRESULTs (beginning with 0x8013), so returning these values, while natural for .NET clients, might be confusing for existing COM clients you may be interacting with.

See Chapter 17, "Implementing .NET Interfaces for Type Compatibility," for more information and examples of returning .NET HRESULT values.

Adjusting Certain COM-Specific Idioms

Just as defining a method with an array parameter and a length parameter looks unusual in .NET, there are other common idioms used in COM methods that betray their COM heritage when used in managed code. To provide as seamless of an experience as possible, this section outlines some minor changes that can be made to COM members to make them work more seamlessly for .NET clients (and still be reasonable to use from COM).

We'll look at three common patterns:

* Passing a Pointer to Anything
* Passing Type Information
* Passing Error Information

Passing a Pointer to Anything

The following COM method, shown in IDL, uses a common pattern of returning an interface pointer that corresponds to a passed-in IID:

```
HRESULT GetSite(
  [in]                REFIID riid,
  [out, iid_is(riid)] void **ppvObject
);
```

This gets imported as the following .NET signature (shown in C#), which is not very user-friendly:

```
void GetSite([In] ref Guid riid, IntPtr ppvObject);
```

If the item returned via the second parameter is always an interface pointer (as the IDL signature with iid_is implies) then the metadata can be legally changed so the second parameter is a System.Object marked with MarshalAs(UnmanagedType.Interface). However, the IDL source for the type library can also be changed instead, which is more maintainable. For example, GetSite could be changed to the following:

```
HRESULT GetSite(
  [in]                           REFIID riid,
  [out, retval, iid_is(riid)] IUnknown **ppvObject
);
```

Notice both changes—IUnknown** instead of void** and the addition of the retval attribute. Both of these have zero effect on the method's implementation, but make a huge difference in the imported signature. The .NET signature for the updated GetSite would be (in C#):

```
[return:MarshalAs(UnmanagedType.IUnknown)] object GetSite([In] ref Guid riid);
```

The returned object could then be naturally cast to the desired interface.

Passing Type Information

Despite the changes made to GetSite in the previous section, the method still doesn't look very .NET-like, does it? Even with our .NET-ifications to change the [out] to an [out, retval] and the void to IUnknown, the use of the method is still unnatural for .NET clients because of the GUID parameter. The point of this method is to enable clients to request an object implementing a certain interface. Because the interface is identified by a GUID, a .NET client would need code like the following to call this (in VB .NET):

```
Dim g As Guid = GetType(IDesired).GUID
Dim returnedObj As Object = obj.GetSite(g)
```

Ideally, .NET clients could use a Type instance directly, for example:

```
Dim returnedObj As Object = obj.GetSite(GetType(IDesired))
```

Such a method wouldn't betray its COM roots as the existing GetSite definition does.

The GetSite definition could instead require a _Type interface as its first parameter (the class interface for System.Type), but using such a method from COM would be even more unnatural than using a GUID in .NET. Fortunately, the automatic bridging of the COM ITypeInfo interface and the .NET System.Type class provides a way to satisfy both COM and .NET clients simultaneously. The GetSite method can be defined as follows:

```
HRESULT GetSite(
  [in]           ITypeInfo* desiredType,
  [out, retval] IUnknown** ppvObject
);
```

Such a method is imported as follows (shown in VB .NET syntax):

```
Public Function GetSite( _
  <MarshalAs(UnmanagedType.CustomMarshaler, _
  MarshalTypeRef:=GetType(TypeToTypeInfoMarshaler))> _
  desiredType As Type) As <MarshalAs(UnmanagedType.IUnknown)> Object
```

Although the custom attributes clutter the definition almost to the point of unreadability, from a client's perspective this signature is used no differently than a signature like:

```
Public Function GetSite(desiredType As Type) As Object
```

So .NET clients can use this definition of GetSite in a natural way. There's some work to be done by the COM client that implements this method, however. Rather than getting an IID value directly, it now has to extract it from the ITypeInfo interface passed in by calling ITypeInfo.GetTypeAttr and checking the guid field of the returned TYPEATTR structure.

Also, be aware that whereas every COM interface has an IID, not every COM interface necessarily has a corresponding ITypeInfo implementation that describes it. But any interfaces defined in a type library do, so the client would likely want to ensure that all the interface types it expects are defined in a type library.

Passing Error Information

COM components sometimes pass error information as a parameter. For example, the Microsoft Direct Animation type library defines an `IDASite` interface with the following method (in IDL):

```
HRESULT ReportError([in] HRESULT hr, [in] BSTR ErrorText);
```

Such a method can be called fairly naturally from managed code with an exception object by using the `ErrorWrapper` type, for example (in C#):

```
obj.ReportError(new ErrorWrapper(myException), myException.Message);
```

Although passing an error as a parameter is kind of bizarre anyway, it would be more natural if the .NET client could simply pass the exception type rather than wrapping it with `ErrorWrapper` and extracting its message to pass as a separate parameter:

```
obj.ReportError(myException);
```

When a .NET exception object is exposed to COM, clients can successfully query for the `IErrorInfo` interface and get the error information in a way that's natural for COM. However, if the parameter type were changed to `IErrorInfo`, it would be imported as a .NET `IErrorInfo` interface type rather than being transformed to an exception object. Using such a method from .NET would be pretty awkward. The client would have to define a class that implements `IErrorInfo`, instantiate it, then set its various properties with information (perhaps from an `Exception` object), then pass that.

On the other hand, if the parameter were defined as an `IUnknown` pointer, then the .NET client would be able to pass a .NET exception object (circumventing strong type checking because the parameter is just a `System.Object`) and the COM client can call `QueryInterface` to get an `IErrorInfo` pointer from the object. Such a method would look like the following:

```
HRESULT ReportError([in] IUnknown* errorInformation);
```

The `IErrorInfo` interface doesn't contain an `HRESULT` value, however, so using it isn't necessarily a suitable replacement for an `HRESULT` parameter.

Managing Limited Resources

Besides memory, COM objects often use other kinds of limited resources, such as database connections, Windows graphics objects, file handles, and so on. Because these system-wide resources can be scarce, components should ensure that they are released as soon as possible.

In COM, releasing such resources is often done at the same time the object's memory is released during object destruction.

This scheme of releasing resources on an object's destruction works well in COM because objects can be deterministically destroyed when users are finished with them. In .NET, however, tying the use of a limited resource to an object's lifetime does not work well. The .NET garbage collector decides when it's time to free memory, and if there is an abundance of available memory on the computer, it can choose not to waste processor cycles on such a task.

From the standpoint of memory usage alone, it's fine if memory isn't freed immediately if there's no demand for it. But by tying the release of other resources to the release of memory, you're effectively marking some memory as more important than other memory in a way that the garbage collector doesn't understand. That's because garbage collection handles one type of resource for you—memory in a GC heap—but not any other types of resources. (The .NET garbage collector is also aware of the *total* amount of unmanaged memory being consumed on a computer, which can affect when collection occurs, but it cannot attribute the memory to individual COM objects.)

As demonstrated in Chapter 6, COM components that continue the practice of only releasing resources on destruction can cause quite a bit of subtle problems for .NET clients that aren't familiar with garbage collection and its interactions with RCWs. The solution for this is to expose a method with a name like `Close` or `Dispose` that enables clients to dispose resources independently of the object's lifetime. Besides adding such a method, this entails guarding any uses of these resources with a check that they're still "alive" because the resources may have been destroyed while the object is still active. The class's destructor can still release the resources, but only if they haven't been released already (for example, a client forgot to call the `Dispose` method). This is the same design pattern used in .NET with `IDisposable` and a finalizer that releases resources if they haven't been already.

TIP

The best way to expose a method that clients can call to free non-memory resources is to have the COM class implement the .NET `IDisposable` interface. This works well when freeing resources both in the implementation of `IDisposable.Dispose` and also in the object's destructor if `Dispose` is never called, because COM clients that are oblivious to `IDisposable` can still use the object as it always has (releasing it immediately to dispose the resources) whereas .NET clients can naturally use the `IDisposable` interface (such as with the C# `using` construct).

Implementing .NET interfaces in COM is discussed and an example of implementing `IDisposable` is shown in Chapter 17.

If you don't want to change your existing source code to add such an explicit disposing method, at least clearly document which classes encapsulate limited non-memory resources, and warn users if instances of these classes should be destroyed as soon as possible.

Threading and Apartment Guidelines

There are two basic guidelines regarding threading and apartments:

- Favor giving all COM objects the Both threading model, so they can run on either an STA or MTA thread.
- Follow the rules of COM.

Except for Visual Basic .NET programs, .NET programs run in a multithreaded apartment (MTA) by default (although Windows Forms applications are usually marked with the STAThreadAttribute so they run in an STA). COM objects that can't be used from either type of thread can cause performance problems due to COM marshaling, or can impose restrictions for .NET clients if not all interfaces are marshalable. Web services always run in an MTA with no way to change the apartment state (other than manually starting a new thread), so STA COM objects can be particularly troublesome for them. Unfortunately, components authored in Visual Basic 6 don't have a choice and are always STA components.

The second guideline, "follow the rules of COM," should be a no-brainer. However, several COM components exist that don't follow COM rules yet haven't run into problems until being used from .NET applications due to forgiving COM clients. Such problems often arise in COM components authored in unmanaged C++ that are primarily used from Visual Basic 6.

For example, COM clients need to be able to handle the fact that they may be called from a different apartment. The previous chapter discussed the importance of registering an interface marshaler, whether you use type library marshaling or your own proxy/stub DLL. When registering your COM component, make sure that the threading model value accurately represents the COM component's capabilities. COM components have been known to register themselves with the Both threading model value to get increased performance over using the Apartment value, but do not have the necessary logic to cope with multiple threads. This may work from clients running in an STA or clients running in an MTA that don't use the objects in a multi-threaded fashion, but can cause problems when used by .NET clients.

> **CAUTION**
>
> If your COM component is registered with the Both threading model value, you can count on the component being called on multiple threads when used from .NET. The Runtime-Callable Wrapper's finalizer runs on a *finalizer thread* separate from the thread on which the object was created.

Providing Self-Describing Type Information

In some cases, the CLR doesn't know the class type of a COM object when wrapping it in a Runtime-Callable Wrapper, so it must wrap it in the generic `System.__ComObject` type. For example, this can occur when a COM member returns an interface pointer to an anonymous COM object (when the interface type isn't the coclass interface). .NET clients that use `System.__ComObject` instances run into the following difficulties:

- Confusion if examining the object's type in a debugger or when printing the result of calling `GetType`.
- Inability to call members of the COM object using reflection unless using `Type.InvokeMember`. Reflecting on the type provides information about `System.__ComObject` rather than the expected COM type.
- Inability to cast the object to a COM class type.

To prevent these problems from happening, a COM object can implement the `IProvideClassInfo` interface to provide information about its class type. But the CLR can only get the class's CLSID from `IProvideClassInfo`; not the .NET class type that should wrap the COM object. The way to give the CLR this information is to register your (Primary) Interop Assembly with `REGASM.EXE`. When doing this, the .NET class and assembly information is registered under the `CLSID` key in the registry. The CLR can then use this information to map a CLSID to the appropriate .NET class type.

Naming Guidelines

When designing new COM APIs, try to follow the .NET naming conventions discussed in the .NET Framework SDK documentation and touched on in Chapter 11, ".NET Design Guidelines for Components Used by COM Clients." Failure to do so makes the APIs seem antiquated, and COM clients have little reason to complain about the .NET naming conventions. These include suggestions such as:

- Give public type and members pascal casing (`PascalCasing`) and parameters camel casing (`camelCasing`).
- Avoid abbreviations.
- Avoid expressing type information in parameter names. Instead, focus on the meaning (like using `name` instead of `bstrName`).
- Avoid keywords in .NET languages or classes with common namespace or class names (such as `System`, `Form`, and so on).
- Don't give enum names an `Enum` suffix, and choose a sensible name because .NET languages like C# require full qualification of enum members.

In addition, avoid the unmanaged convention of prefixing pointer parameters with p (or pp for pointers to pointers), although the parameter name of an [out, retval] parameter doesn't matter because its name is not preserved in metadata under normal circumstances.

Another thing to avoid is choosing member names that conflict with members of a Runtime-Callable Wrapper's base classes. An RCW either derives from or is a System.__ComObject type, which derives from System.MarshalByRefObject, which derives from System.Object. These classes have the following public members:

- CreateObjRef
- Equals
- GetHashCode
- GetLifetimeService
- GetType
- InitializeLifetimeService
- ReferenceEquals
- ToString

Reusing these names as COM interface members isn't an error; they are emitted as "new slot" members, which translates to new in C# (when specified on a signature) and Shadows in VB .NET. However, this can easily cause confusion for .NET clients that may be expecting different functionality when calling one of these methods.

Performance Considerations

Bridging the world of COM with the world of .NET is not a trivial task. Because of this, every transition from managed code to unmanaged code and vice-versa involves some overhead. Besides marshaling non-blittable parameters from one representation to another (and besides pinning blittable parameters), the CLR needs to do additional tasks. For example, the CLR does the following when transitioning from managed to unmanaged code:

- Ensures that the garbage collector won't block unmanaged threads during the call
- Protects callee-saved registers
- Handles the calling convention appropriately
- Handles unmanaged exceptions
- Converts the RCW being called on into a COM interface pointer appropriate for the current context (COM Interoperability only)

This extra work is done with as little as 8 processor instructions for a PInvoke call that doesn't require marshaling, or 31 instructions if marshaling is required (not including the marshaling itself). For COM Interoperability, the work typically equates to around 65 instructions, not counting marshaling. (These figures don't include security stack walking for unmanaged code permission, which is done unless `SuppressUnmanagedCodeSecurityAttribute` is used.)

When a single unmanaged method does a large amount of work, the overhead involved in calling it from managed code is a small percentage of the total amount of time occupied, and therefore barely noticeable or undetectable. If an unmanaged method does a small amount of work, however, the overhead could occupy a significant percentage of the total amount of time, and could noticeably diminish performance if such a method is called many times.

Therefore, it is recommended that COM objects exposed to .NET have a small number of members that each performs a significant amount of work when called. This is sometimes called a "chunky" interface. The opposite is called a "chatty" interface, which requires numerous transitions between managed and unmanaged code to do small amounts of work. An interface with several property accessors is often a "chatty" interface because it involves separate calls usually just to set the value of a single private field. Figure 16.3 illustrates the difference between a "chatty" COM object being called from .NET versus a "chunky" COM object being called from .NET.

In both cases, this diagram shows the same amount of unmanaged work, the same amount of managed work, and the same amount of marshaling done by the Interop Marshaler. The only difference between the two programs is making three transitions versus one, and that's where the time savings comes from. This concept is nothing new; it also applies to remote objects, for which the overhead of calling across a network encourages the use of chunky calls.

Although the diagram assumes that the same amount of marshaling is involved in both cases, the consolidation of method calls can often result in a savings of marshaling because you don't have to pass the same data to the COM object multiple times. A good example is a COM method that is invoked from .NET inside a loop with a large number of iterations. By creating a larger COM method that does all the work of the loop, a significant savings can be realized, eliminating n-1 transitions and potentially a lot of marshaling for a loop whose body executes n times.

Of course, whether or not you can make a COM interface chunky highly depends on what the COM object is doing, and in many cases it can involve doing more work on the managed side than before, so there's a tradeoff. The goal simply is to minimize the number of unmanaged/managed transitions as much as possible.

Besides minimizing transitions, cutting down on marshaling results in big savings if it's possible to do, because marshaling takes much longer than the standard transition overhead. You should stick to blittable types as much as possible, because they don't require complex marshaling. See Chapter 3 for a list of blittable types.

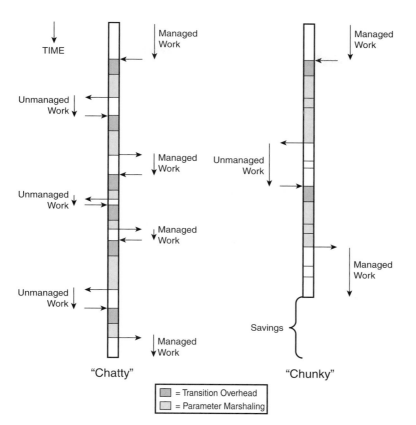

FIGURE 16.3

A chunky COM object can realize a significant performance boost over a chatty COM object doing the same tasks.

Unmanaged ANSI strings should also be avoided at all costs because .NET strings are Unicode internally, and the transformation from Unicode to ANSI and back can take a lot of time.

Therefore, the combination of a chunky API and blittable types shrinks transition overhead and parameter marshaling, the two items specific to managed/unmanaged interoperability that can diminish performance.

Finally, as mentioned in the "Threading and Apartment Guidelines" section, STA COM objects should be avoided because .NET clients may not be aware that they should use STAThreadAttribute (or use AspCompat=true in ASP.NET). If you have no other choice besides single-threaded apartments (because you're developing in Visual Basic 6, for example), clearly document that .NET clients should use STAThreadAttribute to avoid the performance hit of COM apartment marshaling. For the most lightweight transitions, you may even consider exposing unmanaged entry points and using PInvoke (discussed in Chapters 18 and 19) to access them from managed code. You could then wrap these flat APIs in an object model that can provide .NET clients with the same or better usability of COM APIs plus better performance.

Conclusion

We began the chapter by listing many general design guidelines, array guidelines, and VARIANT guidelines that should have been obvious after reading Chapters 3–7 and seeing how .NET clients must use a variety of workarounds when attempting to use COM objects that don't follow these guidelines. We then looked at the details of reporting good error information. The importance of setting an appropriate error message can't be emphasized enough. C++ COM programmers may be used to receiving a failure HRESULT and looking up what the error code means, but .NET programmers have higher expectations!

We looked at a handful of common COM idioms and examined how they might get a facelift to avoid looking outdated to .NET clients while still looking reasonable to COM clients. Finally, after examining a handful of miscellaneous guidelines, we took a look at the performance of .NET's interoperability services and strategies for avoiding unnecessary performance penalties.

If you follow the guidelines in this chapter when designing new COM APIs, you just may succeed in making COM an implementation detail that's not noticeable to users, rather than presenting a design that is clearly meant for unmanaged clients. Plus, the more .NET-like your COM APIs are, the more likely you'll be able to remain compatible if you ever decide to migrate any pieces to managed code.

Implementing .NET Interfaces for Type Compatibility

IN THIS CHAPTER

- Class Interfaces   741

- Interface Inheritance   743

- Considerations for Visual C++ Programmers   747

- Considerations for Visual Basic 6 Programmers   759

To conclude our examination of developing COM components that are exposed to .NET, we're going to focus on implementing .NET interfaces in unmanaged code. A .NET interface is any interface defined in metadata that's not marked with the `ComImportAttribute` pseudo-custom attribute.

Just as a .NET class that implements a COM interface is sometimes said to be a "COM-compatible" class, a COM class that implements a .NET interface could be called a ".NET-compatible" class. This scenario is much rarer than the reverse, however, because programmers writing new code that implements .NET interfaces are likely writing managed code. But having a COM class implement a .NET interface can be a minor but important tweak that can greatly improve the use of an existing COM object from managed code. Because .NET is not a binary standard like COM but a *type standard*, COM objects implementing .NET interfaces can achieve a degree of *type compatibility* with .NET objects.

This process begins by exporting a type library containing an interface definition if one doesn't already exist, and ends with importing a type library for your COM component that references the exported type library. Implementing a .NET interface is really no different than implementing a COM interface, but there are some surprises that you may encounter, as you'll see in this chapter.

Unlike the reverse direction (covered in Chapter 14, "Implementing COM Interfaces for Binary Compatibility") in which a COM-Callable Wrapper (CCW) implements several COM interfaces, a Runtime-Callable Wrapper (RCW) doesn't implement any .NET interfaces by default. This is because none of a Runtime-Callable Wrapper's base classes (`System.__ComObject`, `System.MarshalByRefObject`, and `System.Object`) implement any interfaces. Therefore, it's up to the COM object to implement any .NET interfaces it wishes to expose.

DIGGING DEEPER

There are a handful of .NET interfaces that Runtime-Callable Wrappers sometimes implement automatically: `IReflect`, `IExpando`, `IEnumerator`, and `IEnumerable`. All of them either require that the COM object implement a specific COM interface or have a member with a specific DISPID. For example, `IEnumerable` is implemented by an RCW whenever a coclass implements an interface with a `DISPID_NEWENUM` member of the appropriate form (has no parameters and returns `IEnumVARIANT`). In fact, a COM class should never attempt to implement `IEnumerable` if it already exposes a COM-style enumeration. If it does, version 1.0 of the type library importer creates a class definition that is unverifiable because it is marked as implementing `IEnumerable` twice.

Class Interfaces

Class interfaces exposed for .NET classes require special care. Although they can be *used* by COM clients, they cannot be *implemented* in a way that is meaningful for the .NET world because class interfaces do not exist from the .NET perspective. For example, suppose a Visual Basic 6 application attempts to implement the _Object class interface exposed for System.Object as follows:

```
Implements mscorlib.Object

Private Function Object_Equals(ByVal obj As Variant) As Boolean
  ...
End Function

Private Function Object_GetHashCode() As Long
  ...
End Function

Private Function Object_GetType() As mscorlib.Type
  ...
End Function

Private Property Get Object_ToString() As String
  ...
End Property
```

(Visual Basic 6 hides the underscore for the _Object interface, making it look like we're implementing something called Object.) Although a separate COM component could consume such an object and use its _Object implementation, chances are that the author of the previous code wanted to expose the class to .NET and have its methods override the default implementation of the System.Object methods in its Runtime-Callable Wrapper. Things don't work that way, however. Thanks to the IDL custom attribute on the _Object interface definition linking it to the System.Object type, attempting to import a type library for the previous code results in an error because it appears that the class is trying to implement a *class* rather than an interface:

```
TlbImp error: System.TypeLoadException - Could not load type
➥ Project1.Class1Class from assembly Project1, Version=1.0.0.0 because it
➥ attempts to implement a class as an interface.
```

> **CAUTION**
>
> You cannot *implement* a .NET class interface in COM in a meaningful way for .NET clients. Although COM clients could communicate amongst themselves using a .NET class interface definition, you should never do this.

DON'T DO THIS

You cannot override methods nor can you control the class type of a COM object's Runtime-Callable Wrapper by implementing a class interface. Note that this differs from the class interfaces generated by Visual Basic 6 for any coclass because these are real interfaces that can always be treated as such. Fortunately, users can only run into this confusion for auto-dual class interfaces, which are sufficiently rare. There should be no temptation to implement auto-dispatch class interfaces because their definitions contain no members.

CAUTION

When a .NET class type is used as a parameter of a .NET member (or field of a struct), the parameter that's exported to a type library is always replaced with the corresponding coclass's default interface. When a .NET class implements a real interface and suppresses its class interface with the recommended `ClassInterface(ClassInterfaceType.None)` setting, the result can be confusing when the class type is used as a parameter rather than the interface type. Consider the following C# code:

```
[ClassInterface(ClassInterfaceType.None)]
public class MyClass : IRealInterface
{
   ...
}

public interface IRealInterface
{
   ...
}

public interface IDemo
{
  void GoodMethod(IRealInterface x);
  void BadMethod(MyClass x);
}
```

The `IDemo` interface appears as follows in an exported type library:

```
interface IDemo : IDispatch {
  [id(0x60020000)]
  HRESULT GoodMethod([in] IRealInterface* x);
  [id(0x60020001)]
  HRESULT BadMethod([in] IRealInterface* x);
};
```

> Regardless of whether the `IRealInterface` interface or `MyClass` class is used as the .NET parameter, the exported parameter looks the same! However, a COM object can implement `IRealInterface` and be passed to `GoodMethod`, whereas no COM object can ever be passed to `BadMethod`. That's because an instance of `MyClass` is needed at run time, despite the misleading type library description of `BadMethod`.
>
> Therefore, sometimes COM objects can't even usefully implement *real* interfaces in order to be used with certain .NET APIs! This is why using class types for parameters when defining public .NET methods should be avoided wherever possible.

Often developers are tempted to implement `_Object`, because the ability to override its members' default implementation can be very useful. Although this isn't possible, there are reasonable alternatives for plugging in new functionality related to the members of `System.Object`. The following list contains the public and protected virtual (`Overridable` in VB .NET) instance methods of `System.Object` and what a COM object can do to customize related functionality:

- `Equals`—Can implement `IComparer` instead to use in some scenarios, described in the "Example: Implementing `IHashCodeProvider` and `IComparer` to Use a COM Object as a Hashtable Key" section.

- `Finalize`—A COM object is released during its RCW's finalization, so its destructor (or `Class_Terminate` method in Visual Basic 6) is run at this time if it's ready to be destroyed. Any COM objects that release limited resources upon destruction should also implement `IDisposable`, covered in the "Example: Implementing `IDisposable` to Clean Up Resources" section.

- `GetHashCode`—Can implement `IHashCodeProvider` instead to use in some scenarios, described in the "Example: Implementing `IHashCodeProvider` and `IComparer` to Use a COM Object as a Hashtable Key" section.

- `ToString`—Can implement `IFormattable` instead, shown in the "Example: Implementing `IFormattable` to Customize `ToString`" section.

Notice that none of these alternatives are specific to COM objects. .NET objects can and do use these additional interfaces.

Interface Inheritance

Recall that interface hierarchies are "sliced" when exposed to COM. Listing 17.1 demonstrates how three related interfaces in the `System.Collections` namespace are transformed by the type library exporter when defined in `mscorlib.tlb`.

LISTING 17.1 An Interface Hierarchy Is Exported to COM as Unrelated Interfaces Containing Only their Direct Members

C#:

```csharp
public interface IDictionary : ICollection
{
  object this[object key] { get; set; }
  ICollection Keys { get; }
  ICollection Values { get; }
  bool Contains(object key);
  void Add(object key, object value);
  void Clear();
  bool IsReadOnly { get; }
  bool IsFixedSize { get; }
  new IDictionaryEnumerator GetEnumerator();
  void Remove(Object key);
}

public interface ICollection : IEnumerable
{
  void CopyTo(Array array, int index);
  int Count { get; }
  Object SyncRoot { get; }
  bool IsSynchronized { get; }
}

public interface IEnumerable
{
  IEnumerator GetEnumerator();
}
```

IDL Representation in Exported Type Library:

```
[
  odl,
  uuid(6A6841DF-3287-3D87-8060-CE0B4C77D2A1),
  version(1.0),
  dual,
  oleautomation,
  custom(0F21F359-AB84-41E8-9A78-36D110E6D2F9,
    "System.Collections.IDictionary")
]
interface IDictionary : IDispatch {
  [id(00000000), propget]
  HRESULT Item([in] VARIANT key, [out, retval] VARIANT* pRetVal);
  [id(00000000), propputref]
```

LISTING 17.1 Continued

```
  HRESULT Item([in] VARIANT key, [in] VARIANT pRetVal);
  [id(0x60020002), propget]
  HRESULT Keys([out, retval] ICollection** pRetVal);
  [id(0x60020003), propget]
  HRESULT Values([out, retval] ICollection** pRetVal);
  [id(0x60020004)]
  HRESULT Contains([in] VARIANT key, [out, retval] VARIANT_BOOL* pRetVal);
  [id(0x60020005)]
  HRESULT Add([in] VARIANT key, [in] VARIANT value);
  [id(0x60020006)]
  HRESULT Clear();
  [id(0x60020007), propget]
  HRESULT IsReadOnly([out, retval] VARIANT_BOOL* pRetVal);
  [id(0x60020008), propget]
  HRESULT IsFixedSize([out, retval] VARIANT_BOOL* pRetVal);
  [id(0x60020009)]
  HRESULT GetEnumerator([out, retval] IDictionaryEnumerator** pRetVal);
  [id(0x6002000a)]
  HRESULT Remove([in] VARIANT key);
};

[
  odl,
  uuid(DE8DB6F8-D101-3A92-8D1C-E72E5F10E992),
  version(1.0),
  dual,
  oleautomation,
  custom(0F21F359-AB84-41E8-9A78-36D110E6D2F9,
    "System.Collections.ICollection")
]
interface ICollection : IDispatch {
  [id(0x60020000)]
  HRESULT CopyTo([in] _Array* Array, [in] long index);
  [id(0x60020001), propget]
  HRESULT Count([out, retval] long* pRetVal);
  [id(0x60020002), propget]
  HRESULT SyncRoot([out, retval] VARIANT* pRetVal);
  [id(0x60020003), propget]
  HRESULT IsSynchronized([out, retval] VARIANT_BOOL* pRetVal);
};

[
  odl,
  uuid(496B0ABE-CDEE-11D3-88E8-00902754C43A),
```

17

IMPLEMENTING
.NET INTERFACES

LISTING 17.1   Continued

```
    version(1.0),
    dual,
    oleautomation,
    custom(0F21F359-AB84-41E8-9A78-36D110E6D2F9,
      "System.Collections.IEnumerable")
]
interface IEnumerable : IDispatch {
  [id(0xfffffffc)]
  HRESULT GetEnumerator([out, retval] IEnumVARIANT** pRetVal);
};
```

This slicing of interfaces is significant when writing a COM object implementing a .NET interface that derives from other .NET interfaces. That's because a COM object can implement a derived interface like IDictionary without bothering to implement its base ICollection and IEnumerable interfaces! A COM object implementing only IDictionary and its ten members defined in mscorlib.tlb compiles without errors because compilers consuming the type library are not aware of any relationship IDictionary has with other interfaces. The type library importer even successfully imports an Interop Assembly containing such a class; the metadata description indicates that it implements IDictionary.

But what does this mean for .NET programs that attempt to use such an object that only partially implements the interface? .NET languages enable calling base interface members without even a cast. Suppose you have the following C# code that uses the IDictionary interface:

```
public void PrintDictionaryProperties(IDictionary d)
{
  // Call property defined directly on IDictionary
  Console.WriteLine(d.IsReadOnly);
  // Call property on base ICollection
  Console.WriteLine(d.Count);
}
```

If a COM object implementing IDictionary but not ICollection were passed to this method, the first call to IDictionary.IsReadOnly would succeed, but the second call to ICollection.Count would throw the following exception:

```
System.InvalidCastException: QueryInterface for interface
➥ System.Collections.ICollection failed.
  at System.Collections.ICollection.get_Count()
  at Chapter17.PrintDictionaryProperties(IDictionary d)
  at Chapter17.Main()
```

It just goes to show you that what you see isn't always what you get when dealing with COM objects. Fortunately the exception message is clear enough to determine what happened.

CAUTION

Whenever implementing a .NET interface, be sure to check its .NET definition for any base interfaces and implement them too. Passing an object with an incomplete interface definition to .NET objects is likely to behave incorrectly.

Considerations for Visual C++ Programmers

Implementing a .NET interface in an unmanaged C++ project is just like implementing any other interface defined in an external type library. There are a few things to be careful with, however. Here are the steps for implementing a .NET interface in an ATL COM project in Visual C++ 6:

1. Right-click on your class in the ClassView window and select Implement Interface…, as shown in Figure 17.1. If you haven't compiled your project yet, a dialog will appear warning that your project doesn't have a type library. You can click OK to get past that because we want to implement an interface in an external type library anyway.

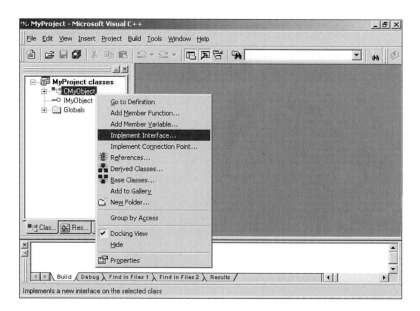

FIGURE 17.1

Implementing a COM interface in Visual C++ 6 using the ATL Wizard.

2. On the `Implement Interface` dialog that appears, click the `Add Typelib...` button. This brings up the dialog shown in Figure 17.2, listing all the type libraries registered on your computer. Select one and click `OK`. As in the Visual Basic 6 `References` dialog and the Visual Studio .NET `Add Reference` dialog, you can click the `Browse...` button to select a type library that isn't registered. In the figure, the user selects `Common Language Runtime Library`, which is the type library exported from the `mscorlib` assembly.

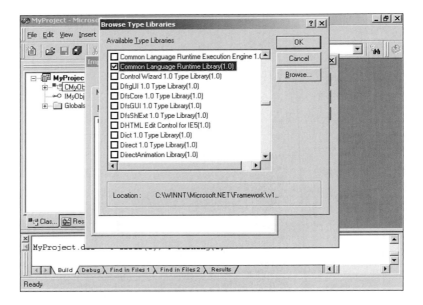

FIGURE 17.2
Selecting a type library containing the desired interface to implement in Visual C++ 6.

3. After selecting a type library, we're now back to the `Implement Interface` dialog. Select the interface you wish to implement and press `OK`. This is shown in Figure 17.3.

These steps are sufficient for implementing an interface, but if you plan to use the object from .NET clients, you should also list the interface as being implemented by your coclass in the project's IDL file (as recommended in Chapter 15, "Creating and Deploying Useful Primary Interop Assemblies"). The wizard does not do this for you. This involves two extra steps:

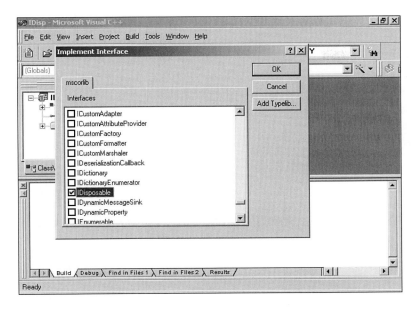

FIGURE 17.3
Selecting the COM interface you wish to implement in Visual C++ 6.

4. Add an `importlib` statement inside your `library` block listing the type library containing the interface definition, for example: `importlib("mscorlib.tlb")`.

5. List the interface inside the coclass statement, for example:

```
[
  uuid(1700FAA2-790D-4D27-AD0E-89AAB1EC39F2)
]
coclass FileWriter
{
  [default] interface IFileWriter;
  interface IDisposable;
};
```

CAUTION

If you're implementing an interface defined in `mscorlib.tlb`, the ATL wizard generates a line like the following in your header file:

```
#import "path\\mscorlib.tlb" raw_interfaces_only, raw_native_types,
   no_namespace, named_guids
```

However, the class interface for `System.Reflection.Module` is exported as a `_Module` interface, and this causes compilation errors in a Visual C++ 6 ATL project because it already defines a `CComModule` instance with the name `_Module`. To fix this, you could remove the `no_namespace` directive or add the `#import` statement's `rename` directive to rename the `_Module` identifier from the type library. For example:

```
#import "path\\mscorlib.tlb" raw_interfaces_only, raw_native_types,
➥ no_namespace, named_guids, rename("_Module", "_ReflectionModule")
```

ATL projects in Visual C++ .NET no longer use `_Module`, so this error does not occur for them.

Example: Implementing `IDisposable` to Clean Up Resources

Now that you've seen how to implement a .NET interface, let's see how to update an existing COM component with an additional implemented interface. Listings 17.2 and 17.3 contain a C++ header file and implementation for the following simple `FileWriter` coclass that implements the `IFileWriter` interface, shown here in IDL:

```
[
  object,
  uuid(379FF39A-2404-4FAE-B928-B53FADF9255B),
  dual,
  pointer_default(unique)
]
interface IFileWriter : IDispatch
{
  [id(1)] HRESULT WriteLine([in] BSTR message);
};


[
  uuid(1700FAA2-790D-4D27-AD0E-89AAB1EC39F2)
]
coclass FileWriter
{
  [default] interface IFileWriter;
};
```

The `CFileWriter` C++ class contains the implementation, which opens a file upon construction and closes it upon destruction. Therefore, this is a good candidate to be updated to implement the .NET `IDisposable` interface, as discussed in Chapter 16, "COM Design Guidelines for Components Used by .NET Clients."

To create such a project in Visual C++ 6, do the following:

1. Create a new ATL COM AppWizard project, and on the two dialogs that follow, click Finish, then OK.

2. Right-click on the topmost node in the ClassView window and select New ATL Object….

3. Select Simple Object from the Objects category, then click the Next button.

4. Type "FileWriter" in the Short Name text box, then click the Attributes tab, check Support ISupportErrorInfo, and click OK.

5. Right-click on IFileWriter in the ClassView window and select Add method….

6. Type "WriteLine" in the Method Name text box and type "[in] BSTR message" in the Parameters text box, then click OK. This creates an IDL file with the class and interface previously shown (but with different GUIDs) and a header file similar to Listing 17.2.

7. Fill in the implementation as in Listing 17.3 and update the header file with the contents of Listing 17.2.

LISTING 17.2   FileWriter.h. The Initial Header File for the CFileWriter Class, Originally Generated by the ATL COM AppWizard

```
 1: // FileWriter.h : Declaration of the CFileWriter class
 2:
 3: #ifndef __FILEWRITER_H_
 4: #define __FILEWRITER_H_
 5:
 6: #include "resource.h"
 7:
 8: /////////////////////////////////////////////////////////////////////////
 9: // CFileWriter
10: class ATL_NO_VTABLE CFileWriter :
11:    public CComObjectRootEx<CComSingleThreadModel>,
12:    public CComCoClass<CFileWriter, &CLSID_FileWriter>,
13:    public ISupportErrorInfo,
14:    public IDispatchImpl<IFileWriter, &IID_IFileWriter, &LIBID_MyLib>
15: {
16: public:
17:    CFileWriter();
18:    ~CFileWriter();
19:
20: DECLARE_REGISTRY_RESOURCEID(IDR_FILEWRITER)
21:
22: DECLARE_PROTECT_FINAL_CONSTRUCT()
23:
24: BEGIN_COM_MAP(CFileWriter)
```

LISTING 17.2   Continued

```
25:    COM_INTERFACE_ENTRY(IFileWriter)
26:    COM_INTERFACE_ENTRY(ISupportErrorInfo)
27:    COM_INTERFACE_ENTRY2(IDispatch, IFileWriter)
28: END_COM_MAP()
29:
30: // ISupportErrorInfo
31:    STDMETHOD(InterfaceSupportsErrorInfo)(REFIID riid);
32: // IFileWriter
33:    STDMETHOD(WriteLine)(/*[in]*/ LPWSTR message);
34:
35: private:
36:    FILE* filePointer;
37: };
38:
39: #endif //__FILEWRITER_H_
```

LISTING 17.3   FileWriter.cpp. Initial Implementation of the `CFileWriter` Class that Keeps a File Open During the Course of the Object's Lifetime

```
 1: // FileWriter.cpp : Implementation of CFileWriter
 2: #include "stdafx.h"
 3: #include "FileComponent.h"
 4: #include "FileWriter.h"
 5:
 6: //////////////////////////////////////////////////////////////////////////
 7: // CFileWriter
 8:
 9: //
10: // ISupportErrorInfo.InterfaceSupportsErrorInfo
11: //
12: STDMETHODIMP CFileWriter::InterfaceSupportsErrorInfo(REFIID riid)
13: {
14:    static const IID* arr[] =
15:    {
16:      &IID_IFileWriter
17:    };
18:    for (int i=0; i < sizeof(arr) / sizeof(arr[0]); i++)
19:    {
20:      if (InlineIsEqualGUID(*arr[i],riid))
21:        return S_OK;
22:    }
23:    return S_FALSE;
24: }
25:
```

LISTING 17.3 Continued

```
26: //
27: // Constructor
28: //
29: CFileWriter::CFileWriter()
30: {
31:   // Open a file that eventually must be closed
32:   filePointer = fopen("tempfile.txt", "a+");
33: }
34:
35: //
36: // Destructor
37: //
38: CFileWriter::~CFileWriter()
39: {
40:   fclose(filePointer);
41: }
42:
43: //
44: // WriteLine
45: //
46: STDMETHODIMP CFileWriter::WriteLine(BSTR message)
47: {
48:   fwprintf(filePointer, message);
49:   fwprintf(filePointer, L"\n");
50:   return S_OK;
51: }
```

Notice that the class implements `ISupportErrorInfo`, so the ATL wizard-generated implementation of `InterfaceSupportsErrorInfo` appears in Lines 12–24. This listing doesn't use `IErrorInfo` because it doesn't return any failure `HRESULT`s, but we'll be making use of it when we update the code in Listing 17.5.

Lines 29–33 contain the class's constructor, which opens a file for reading and appending using the `fopen` C runtime library function. The destructor in Lines 38–41 uses the `fclose` C runtime library function to close the file. The only other method is `WriteLine`, in Lines 46–51, which prints the passed-in message to the file using `fwprintf`, followed by a newline character.

This simple COM component's strategy of opening and closing the file has no problems when COM objects release the component as soon as they are finished (as they usually do). When called from .NET clients, however, the file can remain open a long time longer than it should because of the time difference between being finished and garbage collection.

Listings 17.4 and 17.5 update the two files from Listings 17.2 and 17.3 to make the class implement the .NET IDisposable interface, using the steps outlined previously, at the beginning of the "Considerations for Visual C++ Programmers" section.

LISTING 17.4   FileWriter.h. Updated C++ Header File for the CFileWriter Class That Implements IDisposable

```
 1: // FileWriter.h : Declaration of the CFileWriter class
 2:
 3: #ifndef __FILEWRITER_H_
 4: #define __FILEWRITER_H_
 5:
 6: #include "resource.h"
 7: #import "path\\mscorlib.tlb" raw_interfaces_only, raw_native_types,
 8: ➥ no_namespace, named_guids rename("_Module", "_ReflectionModule")
 9:
10: ///////////////////////////////////////////////////////////////////////
11: // CFileWriter
12: class ATL_NO_VTABLE CFileWriter :
13:    public CComObjectRootEx<CComSingleThreadModel>,
14:    public CComCoClass<CFileWriter, &CLSID_FileWriter>,
15:    public ISupportErrorInfo,
16:    public IDispatchImpl<IFileWriter, &IID_IFileWriter, &LIBID_MyLib>,
17:    public IDispatchImpl<IDisposable, &IID_IDisposable, &LIBID_mscorlib>
18: {
19: public:
20:    CFileWriter();
21:    ~CFileWriter();
22:
23: DECLARE_REGISTRY_RESOURCEID(IDR_FILEWRITER)
24:
25: DECLARE_PROTECT_FINAL_CONSTRUCT()
26:
27: BEGIN_COM_MAP(CFileWriter)
28:    COM_INTERFACE_ENTRY(IFileWriter)
29:    COM_INTERFACE_ENTRY(ISupportErrorInfo)
30:    COM_INTERFACE_ENTRY2(IDispatch, IFileWriter)
31:    COM_INTERFACE_ENTRY(IDisposable)
32: END_COM_MAP()
33:
34: // ISupportErrorInfo
35:    STDMETHOD(InterfaceSupportsErrorInfo)(REFIID riid);
36: // IFileWriter
37:    STDMETHOD(WriteLine)(/*[in]*/ BSTR message);
38: // IDisposable
39:    STDMETHOD(Dispose)();
40:
```

17

LISTING 17.4   Continued

```
41: private:
42:   FILE* filePointer;
43: };
44:
45: #endif //__FILEWRITER_H_
```

The differences between Listings 17.4 and 17.2 appear in bold. All of the additional lines were added by the ATL wizard when choosing to implement IDisposable. The one line that was tweaked is Line 8, to add the rename directive for the _Module type to avoid conflicts with ATL's _Module definition.

LISTING 17.5   FileWriter.cpp. Updated Implementation of the CFileWriter Class That Implements IDisposable

```
 1: // FileWriter.cpp : Implementation of CFileWriter
 2: #include "stdafx.h"
 3: #include "FileComponent.h"
 4: #include "FileWriter.h"
 5: #include <CorError.h>    // Contains definitions of .NET HRESULTs
 6:
 7: /////////////////////////////////////////////////////////////////////////
 8: // CFileWriter
 9:
10: //
11: // ISupportErrorInfo.InterfaceSupportsErrorInfo
12: //
13: STDMETHODIMP CFileWriter::InterfaceSupportsErrorInfo(REFIID riid)
14: {
15:   static const IID* arr[] =
16:   {
17:     &IID_IFileWriter,
18:     &IID_IDisposable
19:   };
20:   for (int i=0; i < sizeof(arr) / sizeof(arr[0]); i++)
21:   {
22:     if (InlineIsEqualGUID(*arr[i],riid))
23:       return S_OK;
24:   }
25:   return S_FALSE;
26: }
27:
28: //
29: // Constructor
```

LISTING 17.5   Continued

```
30: //
31: CFileWriter::CFileWriter()
32: {
33:    // Open a file that eventually must be closed
34:    filePointer = fopen("tempfile.txt", "a+");
35: }
36:
37: //
38: // Destructor
39: //
40: CFileWriter::~CFileWriter()
41: {
42:    // The filePointer is NULL if it has already been disposed
43:    if (NULL != filePointer)
44:      fclose(filePointer);
45: }
46:
47: //
48: // WriteLine
49: //
50: STDMETHODIMP CFileWriter::WriteLine(BSTR message)
51: {
52:    // Check to see if the object has been disposed
53:    if (NULL == filePointer)
54:    {
55:      // We can't throw an ObjectDisposedException from COM since
56:      // it shares an HRESULT with its base InvalidOperationException
57:      // class, but this is close.
58:
59:      ICreateErrorInfo *pcerrinfo;
60:      IErrorInfo *perrinfo;
61:      HRESULT hr;
62:
63:      BSTR description = SysAllocString(
64:        L"Cannot access the disposed FileWriter object.");
65:      BSTR source = SysAllocString(L"File Components");
66:
67:      hr = CreateErrorInfo(&pcerrinfo);
68:      if (SUCCEEDED(hr))
69:      {
70:        pcerrinfo->SetDescription(description);
71:        pcerrinfo->SetSource(source);
72:
73:        hr = pcerrinfo->QueryInterface(IID_IErrorInfo, (void**)&perrinfo);
```

LISTING 17.5 Continued

```
 74:        if (SUCCEEDED(hr))
 75:        {
 76:          SetErrorInfo(0, perrinfo);
 77:          perrinfo->Release();
 78:        }
 79:
 80:        pcerrinfo->Release();
 81:      }
 82:
 83:      return COR_E_INVALIDOPERATION;
 84:    }
 85:    else
 86:    {
 87:      fwprintf(filePointer, message);
 88:      fwprintf(filePointer, L"\n");
 89:      return S_OK;
 90:    }
 91: }
 92:
 93: //
 94: // IDisposable.Dispose
 95: //
 96: STDMETHODIMP CFileWriter::Dispose()
 97: {
 98:    // IDisposable.Dispose is idempotent
 99:    if (NULL != filePointer)
100:    {
101:      // Close the file
102:      fclose(filePointer);
103:      filePointer = NULL;
104:    }
105:    return S_OK;
106: }
```

Again, the differences between Listings 17.5 and 17.3 appear in bold. None of the changes in this listing were done by the ATL wizard, but had to be done manually instead. Line 5 includes CorError.h, the header file defining .NET HRESULTs (with FACILITY_URT), which ships with the .NET Framework SDK. Line 18 adds the IID of IDisposable to the list of interfaces for which InterfaceSupportsErrorInfo returns S_OK. Although this listing's implementation of IDisposable doesn't use IErrorInfo, it's important to remember to update your implementation of InterfaceSupportsErrorInfo whenever you implement a new interface. Otherwise, any IErrorInfo information you set in the members belonging to the interface gets ignored.

The constructor is the same as in Listing 17.3, but the destructor in Lines 40–45 has a new check for NULL before calling `fclose`. This is necessary because the file might have already been closed by a call to `Dispose` (which also sets the `filePointer` variable to NULL). If `Dispose` has already been called, then the destructor simply exits without doing any work. This is analogous to a .NET `Dispose` implementation calling `GC.SuppressFinalize` to suppress any work done by a finalizer during garbage collection. Because the class's destructor is always called, the check must be done to suppress its own behavior.

The implementation of `WriteLine` (Lines 50–91) is now significantly longer than before, but the logic is simple. If the file has already been closed (meaning `filePointer` is NULL), a failure HRESULT is returned, otherwise the message is printed to the file. This extra check is a necessity (in managed or unmanaged code) when the encapsulated resource can be disposed while the object instance is still alive.

Before returning the failure HRESULT, Lines 59–81 set the `IErrorInfo` information so .NET clients see a descriptive exception message when trying to call `WriteLine` after `Dispose` has been called. Objects that implement `IDisposable` are supposed to throw a `System.ObjectDisposedException`, but it's not possible for a COM object to cause that exception type to be thrown because it doesn't have a distinct HRESULT value. Instead, it returns the HRESULT corresponding to `ObjectDisposedException`'s base `InvalidOperationException` class and sets the message to explain that it's related to the object being disposed prematurely.

TIP

When implementing a .NET interface, try to return HRESULT values that correspond to the exceptions .NET clients would expect to be thrown by .NET components implementing the same interface. This isn't always possible, however, because only exception types that are defined in the `mscorlib` assembly *and* have distinct HRESULT values can be thrown by COM clients. When you can't return an HRESULT that corresponds exactly to the desired exception, you can do two things to make up for it:

1. Return the HRESULT value corresponding to the exception's most derived base class that defines a distinct value. This is the same value you'd get by calling `Marshal.GetHRForException` from the `System.Runtime.InteropServices` namespace. If this ends up being a generic HRESULT like E_FAIL that results in a `COMException` when thrown, you might as well define and return your own custom HRESULT value (and document it). See Appendix C, "HRESULT to .NET Exception Transformations," to see which HRESULTs correspond to which .NET exception types.

2. Use `IErrorInfo` to give the exception a message that describes exactly what the problem is. This is often just as critical as returning the appropriate HRESULT value.

Even when you can return the desired HRESULT that corresponds to a .NET exception, COM components have a disadvantage because they can't use a .NET exception's default message (which would be seen when a .NET client throws the exception without setting a message). If a COM method returns a .NET HRESULT without setting a message, it will always be "Exception from HRESULT...," so setting a message is always critical.

Finally, IDisposable's Dispose method appears on Lines 96–106. In this method, the file is closed if it hasn't been already. As the contract for Dispose requires, calling it multiple times has the same effect as calling it once.

A .NET client can now use the FileWriter object and take advantage of its IDisposable implementation to close the file in a timely and familiar fashion. For example, a C# client can use the using construct as follows:

```
using ((IDisposable)FileWriter f = new FileWriter())
{
  foreach(int i in new int[]{1,2,3,4,5,6,7,8,9,10})
    f.WriteLine(i.ToString());
}
```

COM objects implementing .NET interfaces aren't quite as natural to use in managed code as .NET objects implementing .NET interfaces simply because a coclass interface must be explicitly cast to any interface other than the coclass's default interface. To avoid the cast, you could use the actual class type instead (with the Class suffix):

```
using (FileWriterClass f = new FileWriterClass())
{
  foreach(int i in new int[]{1,2,3,4,5,6,7,8,9,10})
    f.WriteLine(i.ToString());
}
```

Considerations for Visual Basic 6 Programmers

Implementing a .NET interface in a Visual Basic 6 project is pretty easy; just reference the appropriate type library, as shown in Chapter 8, "The Essentials for Using .NET Components from COM," then type Implements *InterfaceName* at the top of the class module file.

There's one unfortunate limitation to implementing interfaces in Visual Basic 6—the compiler doesn't allow implementing an interface containing a member whose name contains an underscore. Because of that, any interface with overloaded members cannot be implemented by a

Visual Basic 6 class. Figure 17.4 demonstrates what happens when a Visual Basic 6 user attempts to implement `System.Reflection.ICustomAttributeProvider` from the `mscorlib` assembly. This interface has two `GetCustomAttribute` methods, so cannot be implemented. As shown, the Visual Basic 6 IDE silently omits the interface from the drop-down list that usually lists all implemented interfaces.

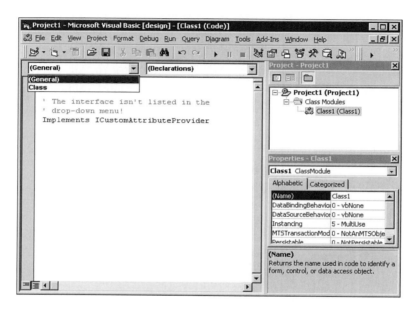

FIGURE 17.4

Attempting to implement a .NET interface with overloaded methods in Visual Basic 6.

When attempting to compile such a project, the error message shown in Figure 17.5 is displayed.

FIGURE 17.5

The error message when attempting to implement a .NET interface with overloaded methods in Visual Basic 6.

There is no good workaround for this problem. If the interface were derived directly from IUnknown rather than IDispatch (so late binding via name is out of the question), you could safely modify the exported method names to something without underscores, using OLEVIEW.EXE to save the IDL representation of mscorlib.tlb and using MIDL.EXE to create a new type library from the altered IDL file. Or, you could create a new type library that contains an updated definition of ICustomAttributeProvider with the new names. But this is not a good idea when the interface in question derives from IDispatch, as ICustomAttributeProvider does, because such modified names would be unrecognized by the object's IDispatch implementation if COM clients attempted to use late binding.

Example: Implementing IFormattable to Customize ToString

As mentioned in the "Class Interfaces" section at the beginning of the chapter, it's impossible for a COM object to override Object.ToString in its Runtime-Callable Wrapper. The functionality for this handy method, however, can be controlled by implementing the .NET System.IFormattable interface.

IFormattable has a single ToString method that returns a string and has two parameters— a string specifying a format and an IFormatProvider instance for customizing the output with locale-specific information. Listing 17.6 contains a Visual Basic 6 class that implements IFormattable in order to control its ToString output.

LISTING 17.6 FormattableClass.cls. A Visual Basic 6 Class That Implements IFormattable to Control its ToString Formatting

```
 1: Option Explicit
 2: Implements IFormattable
 3:
 4: Private list(9) As Integer
 5:
 6: Private Sub Class_Initialize()
 7:   Dim i As Integer
 8:   For i = LBound(list) To UBound(list)
 9:     list(i) = i
10:   Next i
11: End Sub
12:
13: Private Property Get IFormattable_ToString(ByVal format As String, _
14:   ByVal formatProvider As mscorlib.IFormatProvider) As String
15:
16:   ' This formatting is culture-independent, so we ignore the
17:   ' IFormatProvider instance
18:
```

LISTING 17.6 Continued

```
19:    ' Clients can pass a null format to accept the default
20:    If (format = "") Then format = "G"
21:
22:    Select Case format
23:
24:      ' The general formatting code "G" that all IFormattable
25:      ' implementations must support
26:      Case "G"
27:        IFormattable_ToString = "COM Class: MyProject.FormattableClass " & _
28:          "{C2FBA9E3-B523-47C5-AFB6-F6180EEB6CD4}"
29:
30:      ' Matches System.Guid "N" formatting
31:      Case "GN"
32:        IFormattable_ToString = "C2FBA9E3B52347C5AFB6F6180EEB6CD4"
33:
34:      ' Matches System.Guid "D" formatting
35:      Case "GD"
36:        IFormattable_ToString = "C2FBA9E3-B523-47C5-AFB6-F6180EEB6CD4"
37:
38:      ' Matches System.Guid "B" formatting
39:      Case "GB"
40:        IFormattable_ToString = "{C2FBA9E3-B523-47C5-AFB6-F6180EEB6CD4}"
41:
42:      ' Matches System.Guid "P" formatting
43:      Case "GP"
44:        IFormattable_ToString = "(C2FBA9E3-B523-47C5-AFB6-F6180EEB6CD4)"
45:
46:      ' ProgID
47:      Case "P"
48:        IFormattable_ToString = "MyProject.FormattableClass"
49:
50:      ' State of the object
51:      Case "S"
52:        IFormattable_ToString = "FormattableClass with Array { "
53:        Dim i As Integer
54:        For i = LBound(list) To UBound(list)
55:          IFormattable_ToString = IFormattable_ToString & list(i) & " "
56:        Next i
57:        IFormattable_ToString = IFormattable_ToString & "}"
58:
59:      ' Invalid format specifier
60:      Case Else
61:        ' Throw a System.FormatException by returning COR_E_FORMAT
62:        Err.Raise &H80131537, "MyProject", _
```

LISTING 17.6 Continued

```
63:          "Invalid format for MyProject.FormattableClass. " & _
64:          "Expected 'G', 'GN', 'GD', 'GB', 'GP', 'P', or 'S'."
65:    End Select
66: End Property
```

Line 2 contains the critical line that makes the class implement IFormattable, defined in mscorlib.tlb, which must be referenced by the Visual Basic 6 project. The definition of IFormattable.ToString appears in Lines 13–66. Notice that it's defined as a property get accessor rather than a method. That's because of the type library exporter's transformation of any ToString methods into read-only properties, as explained in Chapter 9, "An In-Depth Look at Exported Type Libraries." This doesn't affect the .NET view of the method, so you can just implement the property the same way you'd implement the method.

By default, calling ToString on a COM object returns the fully-qualified type name of the Runtime-Callable Wrapper, which could be MyProject.FormattableClass in this case or System.__ComObject if the class has no metadata available or associated with an instance. The goal of this IFormattable implementation is to enable a variety of different formats to be displayed, including displaying the class's CLSID or even the internal state of the object's private array member.

The IFormatProvider parameter is ignored in this simple implementation, making it culture-neutral. The format string parameter can be one of the following values: "G", "GN", "GD", "GB", "GP", "P", "S", an empty string or a null string. The documentation for IFormattable states that all implementations must support at least the "G" formatting code (which stands for "General"). Every implementation should also be prepared to handle a null string to accept the default formatting. The default formatting doesn't have to match the "G" formatting, although it's a good idea in order to prevent confusion.

Line 20 chooses the "G" formatting if a null string or empty string is passed. Visual Basic 6 strings cannot be null, so if a .NET client passes null (Nothing in VB.NET), the VB6 object simply sees an empty string. Line 22 begins a Select Case statement to return the correct string for each valid formatting specifier. The "G" formatting returns "COM Class: *ProgID* {*CLSID*}", and "GN", "GD", "GB", and "GP" return the CLSID with formatting that matches System.Guid.ToString's "N", "D", "B", and "P" formatting, respectively. The CLSID needs to be hardcoded after compiling once and checking the project's type library, because Visual Basic 6 doesn't provide a way to control CLSIDs.

The "P" formatting returns the class's ProgID, and "S" returns "*ClassName* with Array { *contents of array* }". If an unsupported formatting specifier was given, Lines 62–64 cause a FormatException to be thrown, as specified by the IFormattable contract. A FormatException can be thrown simply by raising an error with the COR_E_FORMAT HRESULT value.

A Visual Basic .NET client can use an instance of `FormattableClass` as follows:

```
Dim c As FormattableClass = new FormattableClass()
Console.WriteLine(c)
Console.WriteLine(c.ToString("GN", Nothing))
Console.WriteLine(c.ToString("GD", Nothing))
Console.WriteLine(c.ToString("GB", Nothing))
Console.WriteLine(c.ToString("GP", Nothing))
Console.WriteLine(c.ToString("P", Nothing))
Console.WriteLine(c.ToString("S", Nothing))
```

Running this would produce the following output:

```
COM Class: MyProject.FormattableClass {C2FBA9E3-B523-47C5-AFB6-F6180EEB6CD4}
C2FBA9E3B52347C5AFB6F6180EEB6CD4
C2FBA9E3-B523-47C5-AFB6-F6180EEB6CD4
{C2FBA9E3-B523-47C5-AFB6-F6180EEB6CD4}
(C2FBA9E3-B523-47C5-AFB6-F6180EEB6CD4)
MyProject.FormattableClass
FormattableClass with Array { 0 1 2 3 4 5 6 7 8 9 }
```

Example: Implementing `IHashCodeProvider` and `IComparer` to Use a COM Object as a Hashtable Key

An object's `GetHashCode` and `Equals` methods are important for objects serving as keys in a hashtable. The default implementation provided by `System.Object` is acceptable if two keys should be compared based on their object references, but developers often want key objects to be compared based on some sort of value that's independent of object references.

For example, imagine that you have instances of a chess board that you want to use as keys in a hashtable. You want to consider two chess boards as equal if they "look" exactly the same—both have the exact same pieces in the exact same places. To get this behavior, a `ChessBoard` class would normally need to override its `Equals` method to choose a behavior other than reference equality and override its `GetHashCode` method to return the same hash code for "equal" instances.

Although COM objects can't override the `System.Object` implementation of `Equals` or `GetHashCode`, they can implement the .NET `IComparer` interface (which has a single `Equals` method) and the .NET `IHashCodeProvider` interface (which has a single `GetHashCode` method) to plug in the same sort of functionality used by certain .NET types. For example, an `IComparer` instance can be passed to `System.Array.BinarySearch`, `System.Array.Sort`, a `System.Collections.Hashtable` constructor, or a `System.Collections.SortedList` constructor, and these types will use its `Equals` method rather than the usual `Object.Equals` method to test equality. Similarly, an `IHashCodeProvider` instance can be passed to a `System.Collections.Hashtable` constructor, and it will use its `GetHashCode` method rather than the usual `Object.GetHashCode` method to retrieve the hash code for any key.

These interfaces exist in order to provide hash codes or equality comparisons on behalf of a separate object that doesn't appropriately override its GetHashCode and Equals methods. Therefore, you could author a new .NET class implementing IHashCodeProvider and IComparer that can be used in conjunction with an existing COM object. However, a COM object could easily implement these two interfaces on behalf of itself. Listing 17.7 does this for a Visual Basic 6 COM class that represents a chess board.

LISTING 17.7 ChessBoard.cls. A Visual Basic 6 Class That Implements IHashCodeProvider and IComparer So the ChessBoard Type Can Be Used as Keys in a Hashtable

```
 1: Implements IHashCodeProvider
 2: Implements IComparer
 3:
 4: Private spaces(7, 7) As Byte
 5:
 6: Public Property Get Space(x As Integer, y As Integer) As Byte
 7:   Space = spaces(x, y)
 8: End Property
 9:
10: ...
11:
12: Private Function IComparer_Compare(ByVal x As Variant, _
13:   ByVal y As Variant) As Long
14:
15:   ' If two boards have the exact same pieces in the exact
16:   ' same squares, then they are equal
17:   For i = 0 To 7
18:     For j = 0 To 7
19:       If (x.Space(i, j) <> y.Space(i, j)) Then
20:         IComparer_Compare = False
21:         Exit Function
22:       End If
23:     Next j
24:   Next i
25:
26:   IComparer_Compare = True
27: End Function
28:
29: Private Function IHashCodeProvider_GetHashCode(ByVal obj As Variant) _
30:   As Long
31:
32:   ' Return a simple hash code that is always the same for a given board,
33:   ' although not all boards will have a unique hash code
34:   IHashCodeProvider_GetHashCode = 0
```

LISTING 17.7 Continued

```
35:   For i = 0 To 7
36:     For j = 0 To 7
37:       IHashCodeProvider_GetHashCode = IHashCodeProvider_GetHashCode + _
38:         i * j * obj.Space(i, j)
39:     Next j
40:   Next i
41: End Function
```

Lines 1 and 2 make the class implement IHashCodeProvider and IComparer, referenced from mscorlib.tlb. Line 4 contains the class's raw representation of the chess board—an 8×8 array of bytes. Each element represents a square on the chess board, and each value represents the contents of the square, such as 0 for empty, 1 for white king, 2 for white queen, and so on. Lines 6–8 contain a public read-only property for accessing the contents of each square. The ellipses in Line 10 represent additional ChessBoard functionality that's not important for this listing.

The implementation of IComparer.Compare in Lines 12–27 returns true if the value of every element of the array belonging to x matches every element of the array belonging to y, or false if a single element doesn't match. The passed-in x and y parameters are assumed to be instances of ChessBoard. The implementation of IHashCodeProvider.GetHashCode in Lines 29–41 does a simple mathematical operation to ensure that a given chess board arrangement always returns the same hash code value, which is the only requirement of a hash code. Coming up with one that's unique for every key gives the best performance, but is not necessary. In this example, the same hash code can correspond to multiple board states, but it still enables appropriate hashing behavior whereas Object.GetHashCode would not. (For example, any two boards that differ only by the value of element (0,0) return the same hash code in our implementation. That's why GetHashCode isn't used by the Equals method.)

A C# client can use ChessBoard instances in a System.Collections.Hashtable instance it constructs as follows:

```
ChessBoard b = new ChessBoard();
Hashtable t = new Hashtable((IHashCodeProvider)b, (IComparer)b);
```

or:

```
ChessBoardClass b = new ChessBoardClass();
Hashtable t = new Hashtable(b, b);
```

The first parameter is used for its IHashCodeProvider implementation, and the second parameter (which could have been a completely different object) is used for its IComparer implementation.

Conclusion

You should now know everything there is to know about writing COM classes that implement .NET interfaces. The four main points are:

- Implementing regular .NET interfaces is no different than implementing a COM interface once you reference an exported type library.
- Do not attempt to implement a .NET class interface.
- Visual Basic 6 classes can't implement .NET interfaces with overloaded methods because of the renaming that includes an underscore.
- Try to return failure HRESULTs that are as close as possible to the .NET exception expected, and always return additional error information that includes a message.

Many interfaces in the .NET Framework are COM-invisible because of their assemblies being marked with ComVisible(false). There's no way for a COM object to implement such an interface without resorting to custom marshaling, discussed in Chapter 20, "Custom Marshaling."

17

IMPLEMENTING
.NET INTERFACES

CAUTION

When using the type library importer to create an Interop Assembly for a COM class that implements a .NET interface, two things must be true:

- The exported type library describing COM's view of the .NET interface must be registered so the importer can resolve the dependency.
- The assembly containing the original .NET interface must be in a location that can be loaded (such as the GAC or the directory in which you're running TLBIMP.EXE). The importer must load this assembly to get the .NET type of the interface being implemented. Failure to have it in a loadable location results in a System.IO.FileNotFoundException.

Platform Invocation Services (PInvoke)

IN THIS PART

18 The Essentials of PInvoke   771

19 Deeper Into PInvoke and Useful Examples   809

The Essentials of PInvoke

IN THIS CHAPTER

- **Using PInvoke in Visual Basic .NET**   773

- **Using PInvoke in Other .NET Languages**   776

- **Choosing the Right Parameter Types**   778

- **Customizing** `Declare` **and** `DllImportAttribute`   **795**

Up until now, this book has focused on one kind of unmanaged code—COM components. There's plenty of unmanaged code, however, that does not expose functionality via COM. Instead, DLLs often expose a list of static *entry points*—functions that can be called directly from other applications. Such functions are not organized in objects or interfaces, but rather are exposed as a simple, flat list. The most common example of static entry points is the thousands of Win32 APIs exposed by system DLLs such as KERNEL32.DLL, GDI32.DLL, USER32.DLL, and more.

> **TIP**
>
> DUMPBIN.EXE is a useful utility for inspecting the contents of DLLs, such as the static entry points they expose. To see a list of functions that any DLL exports, use the following command (shown here for ADVAPI32.DLL):
>
>   dumpbin /exports advapi32.dll
>
> DUMPBIN.EXE is one of the many tools that comes with Visual Studio.

The mechanism that enables calling DLL entry points in a .NET language is called *Platform Invocation Services (PInvoke)*, also known as *Platform Invoke*. Through the use of a simple custom attribute—DllImportAttribute in the System.Runtime.InteropServices namespace—PInvoke enables developers to define functions and mark them with the name of the DLL in which their implementation resides. PInvoke makes use of the same Interop Marshaler used by COM Interoperability (but with different default marshaling rules) to marshal data types across the managed/unmanaged boundary.

PInvoke can be used with any DLLs that expose entry points, but the examples in this chapter and the next use Win32 APIs since such examples can be easily run on any Windows computer. Furthermore, there are enough APIs available to demonstrate all of the important concepts that need to be understood to be a PInvoke expert! Because the .NET Framework provides a rich set of APIs that expose much of the same functionality of the Win32 APIs, it's often not necessary to use the Win32 APIs in managed code. Besides the disadvantage of requiring unmanaged code permission, using PInvoke is not easy, because you have to manually write proper function definitions without much compiler or runtime support to help. But for developers who want to stick with performing a task with familiar APIs, PInvoke can be a great help. Plus, there are many, many areas in which there are simply no APIs in the .NET Framework that expose the same sort of functionality provided by Win32.

> **TIP**
>
> Documentation for Win32 APIs can be found at MSDN Online (msdn.microsoft.com). This Web site houses the Win32 documentation referred to throughout this chapter.

> **TIP**
>
> If you're planning on using PInvoke with functions defined in KERNEL32.DLL, GDI32.DLL, OLE32.DLL, SHELL32.DLL, or USER32.DLL, be sure to check out Appendix E, "PInvoke Definitions for Win32 Functions." This appendix defines just about every API exposed by these DLLs in C# syntax, which should be a big help in getting you started. Even if you're not planning on using any of these functions, looking at them might be helpful for figuring out how to define PInvoke signatures for similar APIs.

Using PInvoke in Visual Basic .NET

The Visual Basic language has had the capability to call DLL entry points for years by using its Declare statement. In Visual Basic .NET, Declare can still be used to accomplish this. Behind the scenes, PInvoke is now used to make the call and marshal the parameters rather than the mechanism used by earlier versions of Visual Basic.

The Declare statement has the following form when used without extra customizations:

```
' For a subroutine (no return value)
Declare Sub FunctionName Lib "DLLName" (Parameter list)

' For a function
Declare Function FunctionName Lib "DLLName" (Parameter list) As ReturnType
```

The customizations that can be made to Declare statements are discussed in the "Customizing Declare and DllImportAttribute" section later in the chapter. Declare statements effectively define static (Shared in VB .NET) methods, so they must be members of a module or class. If an entry point with *FunctionName* cannot be found in the DLL specified by *DLLName*, a System.EntryPointNotFoundException is thrown. The *DLLName* string can contain a full path or a relative path, but often just the filename is given (as when using Win32 DLLs). In this case (which is recommended), the DLL can be found in the current directory or via the PATH environment variable.

> **TIP**
>
> Functions exposed by DLLs have case-sensitive names, so even in Visual Basic .NET you must use the correct case when defining the function.

Listing 18.1 demonstrates the use of `Declare` in Visual Basic .NET with the `QueryPerformanceCounter` and `QueryPerformanceFrequency` functions in `KERNEL32.DLL`. These are defined as follows in `winbase.h`, part of the Windows Platform SDK:

```
BOOL QueryPerformanceCounter(LARGE_INTEGER *lpPerformanceCount);

BOOL QueryPerformanceFrequency(LARGE_INTEGER *lpFrequency);
```

A performance counter is a timer that gives time measurements with the high resolution. `QueryPerformanceCounter` is useful for getting precise time measurements for scientific applications, performance testing, and games (as shown in Chapter 23, "Writing a .NET Arcade Game Using DirectX"). The frequency of the counter depends on the capability of the computer and can be determined by calling `QueryPerformanceFrequency`. These APIs are useful in .NET programs because the .NET Framework does not expose timing functionality as accurate as what these APIs provide.

LISTING 18.1　The `QueryPerformanceCounter` and `QueryPerformanceFrequency` Functions Enable High-Precision Measurement

```
 1: Imports System
 2:
 3: Public Module SimpleTiming
 4:    ' PInvoke signatures:
 5:    Declare Function QueryPerformanceCounter Lib "kernel32.dll" _
 6:      (ByRef lpPerformanceCount As Long) As Boolean
 7:
 8:    Declare Function QueryPerformanceFrequency Lib "kernel32.dll" _
 9:      (ByRef lpFrequency As Long) As Boolean
10:
11:    Sub Main()
12:      Dim timeBefore, timeAfter, frequency As Long
13:      Dim timeDiff As Double
14:      Dim i As Integer
15:
16:      If Not QueryPerformanceFrequency(frequency) Then
17:        Console.WriteLine("Computer doesn't support performance counters")
18:        Exit Sub
```

LISTING 18.1 Continued

```
19:     End If
20:
21:     ' Time how long it takes to calculate 100,000,000 square roots
22:     QueryPerformanceCounter(timeBefore)
23:     For i = 1 to 100000000
24:       Math.Sqrt(100)
25:     Next i
26:     QueryPerformanceCounter(timeAfter)
27:
28:     timeDiff = (timeAfter - timeBefore) / frequency
29:
30:     Console.WriteLine("Time to calculate square root 100,000,000 times: " _
31:        & timeDiff & " seconds")
32:   End Sub
33: End Module
```

Lines 4–9 use the Declare statement to define the two Win32 functions. Notice that the Long data type is used as the parameter for both functions because it needs to be a 64-bit value. A common mistake for developers who have used Declare in Visual Basic 6 is to use Long where Integer is needed or Integer where Short is needed. Don't forget about these language changes because PInvoke provides very few diagnostics when a signature is incorrect!

Once the functions are defined, using them is straightforward. Line 16 calls QueryPerformanceFrequency to determine the capabilities of the computer. Like many Win32 APIs, QueryPerformanceFrequency doesn't simply return the desired value. Instead, it requires you to declare a variable to contain the value and pass it by reference. Because the frequency variable is passed by-reference, it contains the desired value after the call. The boolean return value indicates success or failure.

The remainder of the listing times how long it takes to calculate the square root of 100 one hundred million times, using System.Math.Sqrt. Line 22 calls QueryPerformanceCounter to get the initial time, and Line 26 calls QueryPerformanceCounter again to get the time after the calculations have finished. The values returned by these calls aren't too meaningful by themselves. To get the number of seconds elapsed, Line 28 divides the difference between the two values by the frequency obtained in Line 16. Finally, Line 30 prints the result to the console. This might look like the following:

```
Time to calculate square root 100,000,000 times: 0.621486232838442 seconds
```

18

THE ESSENTIALS OF PINVOKE

Using PInvoke in Other .NET Languages

Currently, no other .NET languages have a built-in keyword equivalent to Visual Basic's `Declare`. Instead, these languages must use the `DllImportAttribute` pseudo-custom attribute directly. C# is the only other language that we'll cover besides Visual Basic .NET in this chapter and the next. You could apply the same concepts in the C# examples to C++ with Managed Extensions, but there's not much point in doing this since you can call the unmanaged functions directly simply by including the appropriate C++ header file.

In C#, the `QueryPerformanceCounter` and `QueryPerformanceFrequency` functions from Listing 18.1 could be defined as follows:

```csharp
[DllImport("kernel32.dll")]
static extern bool QueryPerformanceCounter(out long lpPerformanceCount);

[DllImport("kernel32.dll")]
static extern bool QueryPerformanceFrequency(out long lpFrequency);
```

`DllImportAttribute` has one required parameter, which is the name of the DLL containing the function implementation. As with `Declare`, this can contain a full or relative path, or no path at all. Because you aren't providing an implementation for the method, C# requires that you use the static and extern keywords.

Notice that the parameter to `QueryPerformanceCounter` uses C#'s out keyword. This could have been `ref` (C#'s equivalent to VB .NET's `ByRef` keyword), but C# makes it easy to be a little more specific regarding the method's intent. Because the purpose of the by-reference parameter is only for these functions to send a value out to the caller, the functions don't care what the value is coming in. Whereas C#'s `ref` keyword indicates that the incoming value and outgoing value are both important, out makes it clear that we only care about the outgoing value. Besides resulting in clearer code, using out instead of `ref` when data doesn't need to be passed in is a slight performance optimization (not perceivable here since only three PInvoke calls are made). The equivalent behavior could be enabled in Visual Basic .NET by using a combination of the `ByRef` keyword and `OutAttribute`:

```vbnet
' <Out> ByRef is the same as C#'s out keyword
Declare Function QueryPerformanceCounter Lib "kernel32.dll" _
  (<Out> ByRef lpPerformanceCount As Long) As Boolean

Declare Function QueryPerformanceFrequency Lib "kernel32.dll" _
  (<Out> ByRef lpFrequency As Long) As Boolean
```

Listing 18.2 demonstrates the same code shown in Listing 18.1, but in C# using `DllImportAttribute` rather than in Visual Basic .NET using `Declare`.

LISTING 18.2   Using `QueryPerformanceCounter` and `QueryPerformanceFrequency` in C#

```csharp
1: using System;
2: using System.Runtime.InteropServices;
3:
4: public class SimpleTiming
5: {
6:   // PInvoke signatures:
7:   [DllImport("kernel32.dll")]
8:   static extern bool QueryPerformanceCounter(out long lpPerformanceCount);
9:
10:   [DllImport("kernel32.dll")]
11:   static extern bool QueryPerformanceFrequency(out long lpFrequency);
12:
13:   public static void Main()
14:   {
15:     long timeBefore, timeAfter, frequency;
16:     double timeDiff;
17:     int i;
18:
19:     if (!QueryPerformanceFrequency(out frequency))
20:     {
21:       Console.WriteLine("Computer doesn't support performance counters");
22:       return;
23:     }
24:
25:     QueryPerformanceCounter(out timeBefore);
26:     for (i = 1; i <= 100000000; i++)
27:     {
28:       Math.Sqrt(100);
29:     }
30:     QueryPerformanceCounter(out timeAfter);
31:
32:     timeDiff = (timeAfter - timeBefore) / (double)frequency;
33:
34:     Console.WriteLine("Time to calculate square root 100,000,000 times: "
35:       + timeDiff + " seconds");
36:   }
37: }
```

18

THE ESSENTIALS OF
PINVOKE

TIP

To get maximum performance with the calls to `QueryPerformanceCounter` and `QueryPerformanceFrequency`, which can be especially important when using them to precisely measure elapsed time, you can define them as follows (in C#):

```
[DllImport("kernel32.dll"), SuppressUnmanagedCodeSecurity]
static extern int QueryPerformanceCounter(out long lpPerformanceCount);

[DllImport("kernel32.dll"), SuppressUnmanagedCodeSecurity]
static extern int QueryPerformanceFrequency(out long lpFrequency);
```

Defining the boolean return value as an integer (which is the same size as the Win32 BOOL type) causes the Interop Marshaler to do less work, because integers are blittable whereas booleans are not. The SuppressUnmanagedCodeSecurityAttribute custom attribute from the System.Security namespace, introduced in Chapter 6, "Advanced Topics for Using COM Components," helps performance by disabling the run-time stack walk for unmanaged code permission and causing a link demand to be performed instead. This attribute must be used with great care, only on PInvoke functions that could not be used maliciously (such as these two).

Choosing the Right Parameter Types

The hardest part about PInvoke is defining each signature correctly. Unfortunately, there are no good diagnostics if you get the signature wrong—your program simply won't behave correctly, perhaps it will exhibit random behavior, or it will even crash!

FAQ: Why doesn't PInvoke give better diagnostics when I'm using it incorrectly?

PInvoke has been designed to give high-performance access to unmanaged APIs. As a result, very little validation is done during the process of calling into unmanaged code. Although PInvoke diagnostics could be improved in some areas at the expense of good performance, there are plenty of situations in which the CLR simply doesn't have enough information to catch errors. An example of such an error is using a dangling pointer in unmanaged code.

The first step in defining a signature is to know how to convert Win32 data types into .NET data types. Table 18.1 lists commonly used data types in Win32 functions and the .NET Framework's equivalent types. Keep in mind that many of the .NET types have language-specific aliases, shown in Chapter 1, "Introduction to the .NET Framework." Any data types that require MarshalAsAttribute to customize marshaling behavior are listed with the UnmanagedType enumeration value that should be used. MarshalAsAttribute is discussed in Chapter 12, "Customizing COM's View of .NET Components."

> **TIP**
>
> Pasting `Declare` statements from pre-.NET versions of Visual Basic code into Visual Basic .NET code can be a handy way of getting function definitions. However, most `Declare` statements from earlier versions will need to be updated if used in VB .NET to account for the changes in data types. For example, `Short` is now `Integer`, and `Integer` is now `Long`.

TABLE 18.1 Common Win32 Data Types and Their Equivalent Data Types To Use in a PInvoke Signature

Win32 Data Type	.NET Data Type
BOOL, BOOLEAN	System.Int32 or System.Boolean
BSTR	System.String (UnmanagedType.BStr)
BYTE	System.Byte
CHAR	System.Char (UnmanagedType.U1)
COLORREF	System.UInt32 or System.Int32
DOUBLE	System.Double
DWORD	System.UInt32 or System.Int32
DWORD_PTR	System.UIntPtr or System.IntPtr
DWORD32	System.UInt32 or System.Int32
DWORD64	System.UInt64 or System.Int64
FLOAT	System.Single
HANDLE, HBITMAP, HBRUSH, HCURSOR, HDC, HFONT, HGLOBAL, HICON, HINSTANCE, HKEY, HMENU, HWND, H...	System.UIntPtr, System.IntPtr, or System.Runtime.InteropServices.HandleRef
HRESULT	System.UInt32 or System.Int32
INT	System.Int32
INT_PTR	System.IntPtr
INT32	System.Int32
INT64	System.Int64
LANGID	System.UInt16 or System.Int16
LARGE_INTEGER	System.Int64
LCID	System.UInt32 or System.Int32

TABLE 18.1   Continued

Win32 Data Type	.NET Data Type
LCTYPE	System.UInt32 or System.Int32
LONG	System.Int32
LONG_PTR	System.IntPtr
LONG32	System.Int32
LONG64	System.Int64
LONGLONG	System.Int64
LPARAM	System.UIntPtr, System.IntPtr, or System.Object
LPCSTR	System.String (UnmanagedType.LPStr)
LPCTSTR	System.String
LPCWSTR	System.String (UnmanagedType.LPWStr)
LPSTR	System.String or System.Text.StringBuilder (UnmanagedType.LPStr)
LPTSTR	System.String or System.Text.StringBuilder
LPWSTR	System.String or System.Text.StringBuilder (UnmanagedType.LPWStr)
LPVOID (void*)	System.UIntPtr, System.IntPtr, or System.Object
LRESULT	System.IntPtr
REGSAM	System.UInt32 or System.Int32
SAFEARRAY	.NET array (UnmanagedType.SafeArray)
SHORT	System.Int16
SIZE_T	System.UIntPtr or System.IntPtr
SSIZE_T	System.IntPtr
TBYTE, TCHAR	System.Char
UCHAR	System.SByte
UINT	System.UInt32 or System.Int32
UINT_PTR	System.UIntPtr or System.IntPtr
UINT32	System.UInt32 or System.Int32
UINT64	System.UInt64 or System.Int64
ULARGE_INTEGER	System.UInt64
ULONG	System.UInt32 or System.Int32
ULONG_PTR	System.UIntPtr or System.IntPtr
ULONG32	System.UInt32 or System.Int32

TABLE 18.1   Continued

Win32 Data Type	.NET Data Type
ULONG64	System.UInt64 or System.Int64
ULONGLONG	System.UInt64 or System.Int64
USHORT	System.UInt16 or System.Int16
VARIANT	System.Object (UnmanagedType.Struct)
VARIANT_BOOL	System.Boolean (UnmanagedType.VariantBool)
WCHAR	System.Char (UnmanagedType.U2)
WORD	System.UInt16 or System.Int16
WPARAM	System.UIntPtr, System.IntPtr, or System.Object
C-style array	.NET array
function pointer	delegate
struct	value type or formatted reference type

Either `System.IntPtr` or `System.UIntPtr` is used for any types that are pointer-sized: 32 bits on a 32-bit platform, 64 bits on a 64-bit platform, and so on. Notice in Table 18.1 that some of the Win32 types have two .NET types listed. We have a little bit of flexibility when defining parameter types. For example, although the Win32 `BOOL` type is really a 32-bit integer, it's handy to treat it as a `System.Boolean` type so you can check for `True` or `False` rather than a numeric value. (However, treating a `BOOL` type as a `System.Boolean` type is slightly slower than treating it as an integer due to the transformation done by the CLR.) Similarly, because Visual Basic .NET doesn't support unsigned types, it can be handy to use a signed type even when an unsigned type more accurately represents the original type (assuming that the unsigned value always falls in the range of signed values). The group of types beginning with H represents handles, which are platform-sized integers. This excludes `HRESULT` because, despite the misleading name, it is not a handle; it's always a 32-bit integer. Although `System.IntPtr` or `System.UIntPtr` is commonly used to represent a handle, using the `HandleRef` value type from the `System.Runtime.InteropServices` namespace is recommended. `HandleRef` is discussed in the following chapter.

When a .NET definition of a COM class or interface has a `System.Boolean` parameter, it is marshaled to a `VARIANT_BOOL` type by default. In a PInvoke signature, however, a `System.Boolean` parameter is marshaled to a Win32 `BOOL` type by default. A few .NET data types have different default marshaling behavior depending on whether they are used as parameters of a PInvoke signature or parameters of a COM class or interface. Table 18.2 lists the data types that behave differently in the two situations. With `MarshalAsAttribute`, you could make any of these .NET data types behave like either column in the table regardless of where the type is used.

TABLE 18.2   Default Marshaling for Parameters in PInvoke Signatures Versus COM Interoperability Parameters

.NET Data Type	PInvoke	COM Interoperability
System.Boolean	BOOL	VARIANT_BOOL
System.Object	void*	VARIANT
System.String	LPSTR	BSTR
array	C-style array	SAFEARRAY
delegate	function pointer	default interface

PInvoke's default treatment of System.Object parameters is represented by the UnmanagedType.AsAny enumeration value. This UnmanagedType value means void*, so a pointer to the instance is directly passed to unmanaged code. Such an instance should either be a boxed value type or a formatted reference type. Because there's no protection from unmanaged code illegally overwriting memory beyond the bounds of the passed-in object (and it's easy to forget to check the size of the object passed-in), using the default UnmanagedType.AsAny behavior with System.Object PInvoke parameters is not recommended.

The default marshaling behavior for PInvoke parameters is almost identical to the default marshaling behavior of structure fields, which stays the same regardless of whether the structure is used with COM Interoperability or with PInvoke. The two differences appear with arrays and System.Object:

- Whereas Object is marshaled as void* by default for PInvoke parameters (and VARIANT by default for COM parameters), it is marshaled as an IUnknown interface pointer by default for fields.

- Whereas an array is marshaled as LPArray by default for PInvoke parameters (and SAFEARRAY by default for COM parameters), it is treated as SAFEARRAY by default for fields. The Interop Marshaler does not support SAFEARRAY fields in version 1.0, however, so such fields must be marked with MarshalAsAttribute, as discussed in the next chapter.

There are four kinds of parameters that require special attention: strings, arrays, function pointers, and structures. The first two are covered in this chapter, and the second two are covered in the next chapter.

Strings

The .NET String type is immutable. This means that once a string has been created, it can't be changed. This may not be obvious in C# or Visual Basic .NET code because you may "modify" strings all the time, such as in this example:

```
myString = myString + ".";
```

However, code such as this doesn't actually modify the contents of myString; it creates a new String object with the contents of myString concatenated with "." and assigns the new object to the myString reference. The old string that myString referenced is discarded and eventually collected by the garbage collector.

System.Text.StringBuilder, on the other hand, represents a string buffer whose contents can change. Both String and StringBuilder can be marshaled to unmanaged code as LPSTR or LPWSTR types. Due to their different characteristics, String should only be used as a parameter when the unmanaged function does not modify its contents and StringBuilder should be used when you're expected to pass a buffer that can be modified by the function.

> **TIP**
>
> StringBuilder is useful for more than just PInvoke. If you find yourself performing a lot of string concatenation and manipulation, you can probably boost performance by using StringBuilder types instead of String. This way, you can reuse the same buffer rather than creating many intermediate String objects.

Using System.String

Listing 18.3 defines a Win32 function that can be used with String parameter types since it doesn't attempt to change the contents of the strings: SetVolumeLabel. This function can set the name of your computer's hard drive, and is defined in winbase.h as follows:

```
BOOL SetVolumeLabel(LPCTSTR lpRootPathName, LPCTSTR lpVolumeName);
```

Because both parameters are constant strings, indicated by the C, it's easy to know that the function is not going to change the string contents. Sometimes, however, you can only know by a function's documentation whether it plans to modify string contents.

LISTING 18.3 Using a Win32 Function That Expects Constant String Parameters in C#

```
1: using System;
2: using System.Runtime.InteropServices;
3:
4: public class DriveNamer
5: {
6:   [DllImport("kernel32.dll")]
7:   static extern bool SetVolumeLabel(string lpRootPathName,
8:     string lpVolumeName);
9:
10:   public static void Main()
11:   {
```

LISTING 18.3   Continued

```
12:     if (SetVolumeLabel("C:\\", "My C Drive"))
13:       Console.WriteLine("Success!");
14:     else
15:       Console.WriteLine("Failure!");
16:   }
17: }
```

Lines 6–8 declare the SetVolumeLabel function with two string parameters, and Line 12 changes the name of the computer's C drive to "My C Drive" by passing two string literals. This listing also serves as a reminder why calling a PInvoke method requires unmanaged code permission; you wouldn't want any managed code (potentially running from the Internet zone) changing the name of your computer's hard drive!

Using System.Text.StringBuilder

Listing 18.4 defines a Win32 function that must be used with a StringBuilder parameter type: GetWindowsDirectory. This function retrieves the path of the Windows directory, such as C:\Windows or D:\WINNT. It is defined in winbase.h as follows:

UINT GetWindowsDirectory(LPTSTR lpBuffer, UINT uSize);

The lpBuffer parameter is an out parameter that points to a buffer that receives the string with the user's name. The nSize parameter tells GetWindowsDirectory how many characters are in the buffer. If the buffer isn't large enough to contain the whole string, the function returns the number of characters required for the call to be successful. Otherwise, it returns the number of characters that were copied into the buffer.

LISTING 18.4   Using a Win32 Function that Requires a StringBuilder Parameter in C#

```
 1: using System;
 2: using System.Text;
 3: using System.Runtime.InteropServices;
 4:
 5: public class DisplayWindowsDirectory
 6: {
 7:   [DllImport("kernel32.dll")]
 8:   static extern int GetWindowsDirectory(StringBuilder lpBuffer, int uSize);
 9:
10:   public static void Main()
11:   {
12:     // Pick an arbitrary initial size
13:     StringBuilder buffer = new StringBuilder(20);
14:
15:     int returnedSize = GetWindowsDirectory(buffer, buffer.Capacity);
```

LISTING 18.4   Continued

```
16:
17:     if (returnedSize <= buffer.Capacity)
18:     {
19:       Console.WriteLine("Windows Directory: '" + buffer.ToString() + "'");
20:     }
21:     else
22:     {
23:       // Try again with the required buffer size
24:       buffer.Capacity = returnedSize;
25:
26:       GetWindowsDirectory(buffer, buffer.Capacity);
27:
28:       Console.WriteLine("Windows Directory: '" + buffer.ToString() + "'");
29:     }
30:   }
31: }
```

Lines 7–8 declare the GetWindowsDirectory function with the StringBuilder parameter. When passing a StringBuilder to a PInvoke function, it is critical that it is initialized to a size that's large enough to contain whatever data the function plans to write in it. Line 13 initializes a StringBuilder variable to an arbitrary size of 20, and Line 15 calls the GetWindowsDirectory method, passing the value of the StringBuilder's Capacity property as the length of the passed-in buffer.

If the function call succeeds, then the returned value is less than or equal to the StringBuilder's capacity. In this case, Line 19 prints the contents of the StringBuilder simply by calling ToString. When the Interop Marshaler marshals an unmanaged string to a StringBuilder (as done here when marshaling the parameters back to the caller after the unmanaged function finishes), it stops copying the unmanaged string contents at the first null character it encounters. It does this because there's no mechanism to tell the Interop Marshaler how many characters to copy back. Therefore, printing the entire contents of the StringBuilder in Line 19 is fine even if the original buffer contained existing data because after the call its length is simply the length of the null-terminated string passed back by GetWindowsDirectory.

If the function call fails, Line 24 sets the StringBuilder's capacity to the necessary number of characters and then Line 26 calls the GetWindowsDirectory function again with a buffer that's large enough. Line 28 prints the result when this code path is taken. According to GetWindowsDirectory's documentation, passing a buffer of size MAX_PATH (plus one more character for a null terminator) would guarantee that the buffer is large enough, avoiding the need to have code that attempts to call the method again with a larger buffer size. The MAX_PATH constant is defined as 260 in current versions of Windows.

> **TIP**
>
> Always initialize a StringBuilder with the appropriate capacity before passing it to
> an unmanaged function expecting a buffer. Many Win32 APIs that expect a buffer
> have documentation that specifies a maximum size that should always be sufficient.
> By initializing a StringBuilder to this size, you can avoid having to call the same
> method twice.
>
> StringBuilder types are guaranteed to have a null character immediately following
> its contents (not counted as part of the StringBuilder's capacity) so you don't have
> to worry about making space for a null terminator.

StringBuilder types are the only by-value reference types that marshal with in/out behavior
by default (rather than in-only). Because the StringBuilder used with GetWindowsDirectory
only needs to marshal the string contents in the out direction, we could make a slight optimization by marking the parameter with OutAttribute. This changes the in/out marshaling to just
out marshaling:

```
[DllImport("kernel32.dll")]
static extern int GetWindowsDirectory([Out] StringBuilder lpBuffer, int uSize);
```

Without OutAttribute, the Interop Marshaler would allocate an unmanaged buffer of the
appropriate size and copy the data in the StringBuilder parameter on the way into the
GetWindowsDirectory call. With OutAttribute, the data-copying step is skipped. (In either
case, the behavior after the call is the same: The data is copied from the unmanaged buffer to
the StringBuilder and then the unmanaged buffer is freed.)

> **TIP**
>
> Marking a by-value parameter with OutAttribute can be useful on StringBuilders,
> arrays, and formatted reference types. It does not make sense to mark it on any other
> types of parameters. Because StringBuilder marshals as in/out by default, marking it
> with OutAttribute is an optimization. But because arrays and formatted reference
> types marshal as in-only by default, marking it with OutAttribute (or both
> InAttribute and OutAttribute) is necessary to get out-marshaling behavior (at least
> for non-blittable types).

For backward compatibility with Visual Basic 6, Visual Basic .NET enables you to pass a by-
value String in a Declare statement to represent the same kind of in/out buffer. Listing 18.5
demonstrates this backwards-compatible way of achieving the functionality in Listing 18.4.

LISTING 18.5 Using `String` Rather Than `StringBuilder` to Represent a Buffer in Visual Basic .NET

```
 1: Imports System
 2: Imports System.Text
 3: Imports Microsoft.VisualBasic
 4: Imports System.Runtime.InteropServices
 5:
 6: Public Module DisplayWindowsDirectory
 7:
 8:    Declare Auto Function GetWindowsDirectory Lib "kernel32.dll" _
 9:      (ByVal lpBuffer as String, ByVal uSize As Integer) As Integer
10:
11:    Public Sub Main()
12:      ' Pick an arbitrary initial size
13:      Dim buffer As String = New String(CChar(" "), 20)
14:
15:      Dim returnedSize As Integer
16:      returnedSize = GetWindowsDirectory(buffer, buffer.Length)
17:
18:      If (returnedSize <= buffer.Length)
19:        Console.WriteLine("Windows Directory: '" & _
20:          Left(buffer, returnedSize) & "'")
21:      Else
22:        ' Try again with the required buffer size
23:        buffer = New String(CChar(" "), returnedSize)
24:
25:        GetWindowsDirectory(buffer, buffer.Length)
26:
27:        Console.WriteLine("Windows Directory: '" & _
28:          Left(buffer, returnedSize) + "'")
29:      End If
30:    End Sub
31: End Module
```

This example works just like the previous one, but the definition of the `GetWindowsDirectory` function in Lines 8–9 uses a by-value `String` instead of a `StringBuilder`. Notice that the `Declare` statement has something new—an `Auto` keyword. Ignore this for now; it is explained later in the chapter in the section "Customizing `Declare` and `DllImportAttribute`."

Line 13 initializes the string to be 20 spaces. This is just like setting a `StringBuilder`'s capacity, and is necessary so the buffer passed to unmanaged code is large enough.

Line 16 calls `GetWindowsDirectory` and uses the value of `String`'s `Length` property to pass \as the size of the buffer. If the call fails due to insufficient buffer length, Line 23 creates a new string filled with the returned number of spaces. When the contents of the `buffer` variable is printed in Lines 19–20 or Lines 27–28, we must use the `Microsoft.VisualBasic.Left` function to cut off any part of the buffer not overwritten by `GetWindowsDirectory`. This is necessary, unlike with `StringBuilder`, because the buffer is never resized after the call. Because `GetWindowsDirectory` returns the number of characters written when successful, we can pass that value to the `Left` function to state how many characters to leave in the returned string.

To make `String` work as a buffer, the Visual Basic .NET compiler does something special for all by-value `String` parameters in `Declare` statements. It treats them as by-reference `String` parameters marked with `MarshalAs(UnmanagedType.VBByRefStr)`. This custom attribute value makes use of support in the Interop Marshaler for exactly this scenario of treating a by-reference string as a by-value string buffer. The magic can be seen by viewing the program from Listing 18.5 with the IL Disassembler (`ILDASM.EXE`). It shows the `GetWindowsDirectory` method as follows:

```
.method public static pinvokeimpl("kernel32.dll" autochar lasterr winapi)
        int32  GetWindowsDirectory(string&  marshal( byvalstr) lpBuffer,
                                   int32 uSize) cil managed preservesig
{
}
```

The ampersand following `string` indicates that it's really passed by-reference, and `marshal(byvalstr)` is the IL Assembler syntax for `MarshalAs(UnmanagedType.VBByRefStr)`, believe it or not.

This same metadata could be produced in a language like C# to make use of the same support, for example:

```
[DllImport("kernel32.dll")]
static extern int GetWindowsDirectory(
  [MarshalAs(UnmanagedType.VBByRefStr)] ref string lpBuffer, int uSize);
```

This is not recommended, however. Even in Visual Basic .NET, you should use `StringBuilder` rather than `String` if backwards compatibility with existing source code isn't important.

TIP

You should use `StringBuilder` to represent a buffer in Visual Basic .NET, just like you would in C#. Using `String` types for this case is simply a second option for backward compatibility.

Using `System.IntPtr`

Sometimes it's necessary to define string parameters as `System.IntPtr` rather than `String` or `StringBuilder`. One example of this is when a function fills a buffer with a string containing embedded null characters. The .NET `String` and `StringBuilder` types are both capable of containing embedded nulls (since their length is always known), but the way the Interop Marshaler works prevents strings marshaled from unmanaged code to managed code from containing embedded nulls. As mentioned in the previous section, when the Interop Marshaler marshals an unmanaged string to a `StringBuilder`, it stops copying the unmanaged string contents at the first null character it encounters.

By defining a string parameter as an `IntPtr` type, we have total control over the marshaling process, as discussed in Chapter 6. One such function that often fills a buffer with embedded nulls is the `GetPrivateProfileSectionNames` API, defined as follows in `winbase.h`:

```
DWORD GetPrivateProfileSectionNames(LPTSTR lpszReturnBuffer, DWORD nSize,
  LPCTSTR lpFileName);
```

This function extracts section names from a `.ini` file containing text such as the following:

```
[Section 1]
A=B
C=D

[Section 2]
E=F

[Section 3]
G=H
I=J
K=L

[Section 4]
M=N
```

If you call `GetPrivateProfileNames` with the name of a file containing these contents, it attempts to fill the passed-in buffer with the following (using \0 to indicate null):

```
Section 1\0Section 2\0Section 3\0Section 4\0\0
```

Listing 18.6 demonstrates the use of the `IntPtr` technique with this API.

18

LISTING 18.6   Using `IntPtr` for a Buffer Containing Embedded Nulls

```
1: using System;
2: using System.Runtime.InteropServices;
3:
4: public class UsingIntPtr
5: {
6:    [DllImport("kernel32.dll")]
7:    static extern int GetPrivateProfileSectionNames(IntPtr lpszReturnBuffer,
8:      int nSize, string lpFileName);
9:
10:   public static void Main()
11:   {
12:     IntPtr ptr = IntPtr.Zero;
13:     string s;
14:
15:     try
16:     {
17:       // Allocate a buffer in unmanaged memory
18:       ptr = Marshal.AllocHGlobal(1024);
19:
20:         int numChars = GetPrivateProfileSectionNames(ptr, 1024,
➥"c:\\sample.ini");
21:
22:       // Convert the entire written part of the unmanaged buffer to a string
23:       s = Marshal.PtrToStringAnsi(ptr, numChars-1);
24:     }
25:     finally
26:     {
27:       // Free the original unmanaged buffer
28:       if (ptr != IntPtr.Zero) Marshal.FreeHGlobal(ptr);
29:     }
30:
31:     // Split the string into an array of strings, using null as the delimiter
32:     string [] sections = s.Split('\0');
33:
34:     foreach (string section in sections)
35:     {
36:       Console.WriteLine("Section: " + section);
37:     }
38:   }
39: }
```

Lines 6–8 define `GetPrivateProfileSectionNames` with `System.IntPtr` as the type of the first parameter. Line 18 allocates a large buffer of unmanaged memory using `Marshal.AllocHGlobal`, which returns an `IntPtr` type that effectively points to the memory. Line 20 calls `GetPrivateProfileSectionNames`, passing in this pointer as the buffer. After the call, Line 23 uses `Marshal.PtrToStringAnsi` to convert the buffer (which is now filled with ANSI characters) to a .NET string. If we called the Unicode version of `GetPrivateProfileSectionNames` instead (discussed in the "Customizing `Declare` and `DllImportAttribute`" section), we would need to use `Marshal.PtrToStringUni`.

Because `GetPrivateProfileSectionNames` returns the number of characters written, we can pass that to `PtrToStringAnsi` to tell it exactly how many characters to copy to the .NET string. (We subtract one character from `numChars` because this includes the first of the two terminating null characters, and we don't want or need a null character at the end of the new .NET string.) If the overload of `PtrToStringAnsi` (that does not have a length parameter) were used, the copying would stop at the first null character and would defeat the purpose of using `IntPtr` in the first place!

Once the contents of the unmanaged buffer are copied to the .NET string, Line 28 frees the memory because it's no longer needed. Rather than leaving the data as one long string, Line 32 uses `String.Split` to create an *array* of strings, using a null character as the delimiter. Finally, Lines 34–37 print each array element one-by-one. Had `numChars` been passed as the second parameter to `PtrToStringAnsi` in Line 23 rather than `numChars-1`, the array would end with an empty string due to the null character that would have been at the end of the string.

Another case that requires the use of `IntPtr` occurs when a function allocates memory and expects the caller to free the memory. This is fairly rare in Win32 APIs, because most operate on a caller-allocated buffer (as in the examples that use `StringBuilder`). When a PInvoke signature returns a string (either via a return type or a by-reference parameter), the Interop Marshaler internally copies the contents of the unmanaged string to a .NET string, then calls `CoTaskMemFree` (the unmanaged equivalent of `Marshal.FreeCoTaskMem`) to free the unmanaged string. This is a problem, however, if the unmanaged string was not allocated with `CoTaskMemAlloc`! An example of this problem is shown in the next chapter, but with structures rather than strings.

> **TIP**
>
> Defining a correct PInvoke signature for any DLL entry point is not an automatic process. How you treat certain parameters depends on semantic information that can only be found in documentation. One exception to this rule is C# unsafe code, which can enable automatic translations from unmanaged C++ signatures. Using C# unsafe code with PInvoke is discussed in Chapter 19, "Deeper Into PInvoke and Useful Examples."

Arrays

In most cases, PInvoke signatures that use array parameters work naturally. Most exported signatures use C-style arrays, so the default marshaling of PInvoke array parameters works well. The main issue to be aware of is the requirement of using InAttribute and OutAttribute for functions that expect you to pass an array so it can fill it in with data.

Although we're used to array parameters having in/out behavior (that is, the function may change the data contained in the array's elements), the default behavior in Declare and DllImport signatures is to treat arrays as "in only" unless its elements are simple value types like Short, Integer, or Long. (Such simple value types are called *blittable*, meaning that the managed and unmanaged data representations are identical so complex marshaling is unnecessary.)

Marshaling data only in the "in" direction performs better than marshaling data in both directions, and is acceptable when you don't care about the array contents after the call. If you do care about the contents afterward, however, be sure to mark the array parameter with In and Out! It's good practice to mark types with In and Out even if they are blittable, to be explicit about the desired behavior and in case a future version of the CLR treats blittable and non-blittable types consistently.

Listing 18.7 shows an example in which marking an array parameter with at least OutAttribute is necessary to get the desired behavior. Microsoft Active Accessibility defines a function called AccessibleChildren in OLEACC.DLL with the following signature:

```
STDAPI AccessibleChildren(IAccessible* paccContainer, LONG iChildStart,
  LONG cChildren, VARIANT* rgvarChildren, LONG* pcObtained);
```

The rgVarChildren parameter represents a C-style array of VARIANTs, which the function fills in with information about each of the passed in paccContainer object's children, if it has any. To compile this listing, you must reference Accessibility.dll. This Interop Assembly ships with the .NET Framework, and contains the types defined in the type library embedded in OLEACC.DLL, including the IAccessible interface. Although it's technically not a Primary Interop Assembly, you should treat it as such.

LISTING 18.7   Marking an Array Parameter with InAttribute and OutAttribute in C#

```
1: using System;
2: using System.Text;
3: using System.Runtime.InteropServices;
4: using Accessibility;
5:
6: struct POINT
7: {
```

LISTING 18.7 Continued

```
 8:    public int x;
 9:    public int y;
10: }
11:
12: public class ArrayExample
13: {
14:    [DllImport("oleacc.dll")]
15:    static extern uint AccessibleChildren(IAccessible paccContainer,
16:      int iChildStart, int cChildren, [Out] object [] rgvarChildren,
17:      out int pcObtained);
18:
19:    [DllImport("oleacc.dll")]
20:    static extern uint AccessibleObjectFromPoint(POINT ptScreen,
21:      out IAccessible ppacc,
22:      [MarshalAs(UnmanagedType.Struct)] out object pvarChild);
23:
24:    [DllImport("user32.dll")]
25:    static extern bool GetCursorPos(out POINT lpPoint);
26:
27:    public static void Main()
28:    {
29:      IAccessible acc = null;
30:      POINT p;
31:      Object var;
32:
33:      if (GetCursorPos(out p))
34:      {
35:        // Try to get an accessible object under the cursor
36:        uint hresult = AccessibleObjectFromPoint(p, out acc, out var);
37:
38:        if (hresult >= 0)
39:        {
40:          object [] children = new object[acc.accChildCount];
41:          int obtained;
42:
43:          // Fill in our allocated array with children
44:          hresult = AccessibleChildren(acc, 0, acc.accChildCount, children,
45:            out obtained);
46:
47:          if (hresult >= 0)
48:          {
49:            // Print out the children to prove that this worked
50:            Console.WriteLine("obtained = " + obtained);
51:            foreach (object o in children)
```

Listing 18.7   Continued

```
52:                    Console.WriteLine(o);
53:            }
54:         }
55:      }
56:   }
57: }
```

The three PInvoke signatures are defined in Lines 14–25, and the focus of this listing—
`AccessibleChildren`—is defined in Lines 14–17. Without the `OutAttribute` marking on
Line 16, this listing would not behave as desired.

In order to obtain an `IAccessible` instance, Line 33 calls the `GetCursorPos` API from
`USER32.DLL` to get the current location of the mouse, and Line 36 calls the
`AccessibleObjectFromPoint` API from `OLEACC.DLL` to attempt to extract an accessible object
from whatever is under the mouse. Lines 44–45 call `AccessibleChildren` with the .NET array
initialized to the appropriate length, and Lines 51–52 print out the array contents after the call.
Had `OutAttribute` not been used in the definition of `AccessibleChildren`, the obtained variable would still report the number of array elements that should have data, but the array would
not contain the data because the Interop Marshaler would never have copied it back into its
elements.

CAUTION

Don't ever define a PInvoke function with a by-reference array parameter. Such a
function may pass back a completely new array with any number of elements
(because the array itself was passed by reference), and PInvoke has no way to
discover the size of the outgoing array. `MarshalAsAttribute` does have a
`SizeParamIndex` named parameter that can specify the length of a C-style array, but
this only works for by-value arrays and by-value size parameters. Therefore, only one
element would be copied back to your array after the call; the array would always be
resized to a length of 1.

If you must call a function that uses a by-reference array parameter, you can define
the parameter as a `System.IntPtr` type to expose a raw pointer and use methods of
the `System.Runtime.InteropServices.Marshal` class to manipulate the pointer. If
using C#, you can use unsafe code, introduced in Chapter 6.

Customizing `Declare` and `DllImportAttribute`

Sometimes it's useful to alter an aspect of a PInvoke signature's behavior, depending on what the DLL entry point looks like and how it expects to receive its parameters. The `Declare` statement and `DllImportAttribute` custom attribute both have easy ways to achieve a variety of customizations. You'll see that `DllImportAttribute` has many more ways to be customized than `Declare`. In this section, we're going to look at all of the possible customizations:

- Choosing a different function name
- Customizing the behavior of strings
- Changing the "exact spelling" setting
- Choosing a calling convention
- Customizing error handling

The first two types of customizations listed apply to both `Declare` and `DllImportAttribute`, but the last three are specific to `DllImportAttribute`. Although a `Declare` statement is just an abstraction over the `DllImportAttribute` pseudo-custom attribute, it doesn't expose all of its "knobs," choosing default behaviors that can't be overridden.

> **TIP**
>
> The required DLL name passed to `Declare` or `DllImportAttribute` should always be used in a consistent format. Although loading the DLL on Windows works the same way regardless of the case used or whether you include the `.dll` suffix, the CLR treats each distinct string as a distinct module. Evidence of this can be seen by using the IL Disassembler (`ILDASM.EXE`) to view the manifest of an assembly that uses inconsistent DLL name strings. This can contain the following, for an assembly that uses several different variations of `KERNEL32.DLL`:
>
> ```
> .module extern kernel32.dll
> .module extern Kernel32.dll
> .module extern KERNEL32
> .module extern kernel32.DLL
> ```
>
> Although these inconsistencies don't cause incorrect behavior (only one `KERNEL32.DLL` ends up being loaded in the process), the duplicate entries can hurt the performance of your application. Consider defining string constants with DLL names and using them for all PInvoke signatures to ensure consistency.

Choosing a Different Function Name

Both `Declare` and `DllImportAttribute` enable you to give your function definition a name that's different from the "real" function (a.k.a. entry point) exposed in the DLL. When choosing a different name, you must specify the real name as an alias so the correct entry point can be found. For the first PInvoke examples using `QueryPerformanceCounter`, let's say we want to change the function's name to a more intuitive one like `GetTimerValue`. This is done using the `Alias` keyword as follows in Visual Basic .NET:

```
Declare Function GetTimerValue Lib "kernel32.dll" _
  Alias "QueryPerformanceCounter" (ByRef lpPerformanceCount As Long) As Boolean
```

And here's the same example in C#, which accomplishes the same behavior with an `EntryPoint` named parameter:

```
[DllImport("kernel32.dll", EntryPoint="QueryPerformanceCounter")]
static extern bool GetTimerValue(out long lpPerformanceCount);
```

For clarity, programmers typically keep the original name rather than using an alias. However, changing the function's name can come in handy for resolving name conflicts or if the function's name happens to be a keyword in your programming language.

The string given to `Alias` or `EntryPoint` can even be an *ordinal*—a number that identifies the entry point rather than a name. Using a tool such as DUMPBIN.EXE, you can see that the ordinal for `QueryPerformanceCounter` is 556, so a hard-core programmer could define the previous method as follows:

Visual Basic .NET:

```
Declare Function GetTimerValue Lib "kernel32.dll" Alias "#556" _
  (ByRef lpPerformanceCount As Long) As Boolean
```

C#:

```
[DllImport("kernel32.dll", EntryPoint="#556")]
static extern bool GetTimerValue(out long lpPerformanceCount);
```

Customizing the Behavior of Strings

Win32 functions with string parameters often come in two varieties—one to handle ANSI strings and one to handle Unicode strings (also known as *wide strings*). By convention, these two entry points are named as follows:

- *FunctionName*A. An ANSI version of *FunctionName* (indicated by "A" at the end of the name)
- *FunctionName*W. A Unicode version of *FunctionName* (indicated by "W" at the end of the name)

FunctionName represents the name of the PInvoke method, or the name specified using `EntryPoint` or `Alias` as shown in the previous section.

For example, none of the functions used in the "Strings" section—`SetVolumeLabel`, `GetWindowsDirectory`, and/or `GetPrivateProfileSectionNames`—really exist! Instead, `KERNEL32.DLL` exports the following functions:

- `SetVolumeLabelA`
- `SetVolumeLabelW`
- `GetWindowsDirectoryA`
- `GetWindowsDirectoryW`
- `GetPrivateProfileSectionNamesA`
- `GetPrivateProfileSectionNamesW`

`Declare` and `DllImportAttribute` both have syntax that makes dealing with these multiple method definitions manageable. `DllImportAttribute` enables you to specify a character set of `Ansi`, `Unicode`, or `Auto` as follows:

```
[DllImport("kernel32.dll", CharSet=CharSet.Ansi)]
static extern bool SetVolumeLabel(...);

[DllImport("kernel32.dll", CharSet=CharSet.Unicode)]
static extern bool SetVolumeLabel(...);

[DllImport("kernel32.dll", CharSet=CharSet.Auto)]
static extern bool SetVolumeLabel(...);
```

Here are the ways in which these settings change `DllImportAttribute`'s behavior:

- `Ansi` is the default in C#. This indicates that any string arguments are treated as ANSI strings unless otherwise specified with `MarshalAsAttribute`. In addition, the CLR looks for an entry point called *FunctionName*A and invokes that if the given *FunctionName* entry point doesn't exist. If the specified entry point does exist, it will be invoked regardless of whether there is also one with an "A" suffix.

- `Unicode` means that any string arguments are treated as Unicode strings unless otherwise specified with `MarshalAsAttribute`. It also causes the CLR to look for an entry point called *FunctionName*W, *even if* there is an entry point called *FunctionName*. (If there is no *FunctionName*W function, *FunctionName* will be invoked if it exists.) Notice the subtle ordering difference between the `Ansi` and `Unicode` options: The "W" version is chosen over the given name, but the "A" version is chosen only if the given name doesn't exist.

- `Auto` behaves either like `CharSet.Ansi` or `CharSet.Unicode`, depending on the current operating system.

18

THE ESSENTIALS OF PINVOKE

DIGGING DEEPER

The `CharSet` enumeration also has a `None` value, but this is obsolete and shouldn't be used. It has the same effect as specifying `Ansi`.

`Declare` also enables you to specify `Ansi`, `Unicode`, or `Auto`, as follows:

```
Declare Ansi Function SetVolumeLabelA Lib "kernel32.dll" (...) As Boolean

Declare Unicode Function SetVolumeLabelW Lib "kernel32.dll" (...) As Boolean

Declare Auto Function SetVolumeLabel Lib "kernel32.dll" (...) As Boolean
```

However, the behavior of the `Ansi` and `Unicode` settings are different than with `DllImportAttribute`. Here are the ways in which these keywords change the `Declare` statement's behavior:

- `Ansi` is the default. This indicates that any string arguments are treated as ANSI strings unless otherwise specified with `MarshalAsAttribute`. Unlike when used with `DllImportAttribute`, the CLR doesn't search for an entry point with the "A" suffix. If an entry point with the exact name given does not exist, the call fails.

- `Unicode` means that any string arguments are treated as Unicode strings unless otherwise specified with `MarshalAsAttribute`. Unlike when used with `DllImportAttribute`, the CLR doesn't search for an entry point with the "W" suffix. If an entry point with the exact name given does not exist, the call fails.

- `Auto` behaves just like `CharSet.Auto` with `DllImportAttribute`. Besides treating string parameters as platform-dependent, the CLR looks for the entry point name given plus an ending "A" or "W", depending on the platform. This uses the same algorithm described earlier, in which "W" is chosen over the exact name, but the exact name is chosen over "A".

TIP

The reason that an entry point like `SetVolumeLabelW` is chosen over `SetVolumeLabel` when using the `Auto` setting is that executing the Unicode version of a function is best for performance since .NET strings are internally Unicode. Occasionally Win32 APIs have three exports, one with an "A", one with a "W", and one with no suffix that calls the "A" version. If the "W" version was not given precedence, using the `Auto` setting would choose the ANSI version even on operating systems that supported Unicode!

You should mark your PInvoke signatures with `Auto` whenever possible so they utilize Unicode on the platforms that support it yet fall back to ANSI on the platforms that don't.

Therefore, setting the `CharSet` value with `DllImportAttribute` affects both how string arguments are marshaled and what entry point is called, whereas using the similar-looking setting in `Declare` (with the exception of `Auto`) only affects the string arguments. This is the reason `Auto` is used in Listing 18.5 when calling `GetWindowsDirectory`. Removing `Auto` would cause the following exception:

```
System.EntryPointNotFoundException: Unable to find an entry point named
➥ GetWindowsDirectory in DLL kernel32.dll.
   at DisplayWindowsDirectory.GetWindowsDirectory(String& lpBuffer, Int32
uSize)
   at DisplayWindowsDirectory.Main()
```

Changing the "Exact Spelling" Setting

With `DllImportAttribute` only, you can turn "exact spelling" on or off by setting a named parameter to true or false. Here's an example:

```
[DllImport("kernel32.dll", ExactSpelling=true)]
static extern bool SetVolumeLabel(...);
```

`ExactSpelling` refers to the name of the entry point and specifies whether the system searches for an alternative name ending in "A" or "W". Therefore, setting `ExactSpelling` to true along with setting `CharSet` causes `DllImportAttribute` to behave just like `Declare` when using `Ansi` or `Unicode`. The previous example would not work since there's no entry point called `SetVolumeLabel`, but the following would work since the "A" suffix is added to the method name:

```
' Behave just like Declare's Ansi option
[DllImport("kernel32.dll", CharSet=CharSet.Ansi, ExactSpelling=true)]
static extern bool GetUserNameA(...);
```

`CharSet.Ansi` is specified just for clarity, since it's the default setting in C#. By default, `ExactSpelling` is set to false in C#. Visual Basic .NET's `Declare` statement internally sets `ExactSpelling` to true except for the `Auto` character setting.

Choosing a Calling Convention

The calling convention of an entry point can be specified using another `DllImportAttribute` named parameter, called `CallingConvention`. The choices for this are as follows:

- `CallingConvention.Cdecl`. The caller is responsible for cleaning the stack. Therefore, this calling convention is appropriate for methods that accept a variable number of parameters (like `printf`).

- `CallingConvention.FastCall`. This is not supported by version 1.0 of the .NET Framework.

- `CallingConvention.StdCall`. This is the default convention for PInvoke methods running on Windows. The callee is responsible for cleaning the stack.

- `CallingConvention.ThisCall`. This is used for calling unmanaged methods defined on a class. All but the first parameter is pushed on the stack since the first parameter is the *this* pointer, stored in the ECX register.

- `CallingConvention.Winapi`. This isn't a real calling convention, but rather indicates to use the default calling convention for the current platform. On Windows (but not Windows CE), the default calling convention is `StdCall`.

`Declare` always uses `Winapi`, and the default for `DllImportAttribute` is also `Winapi`. As you might guess, this is the calling convention used by Win32 APIs, so this setting doesn't need to be used in this chapter's examples.

Customizing Error Handling

In the previous listings, we saw a standard error handling technique for Win32 APIs—simply checking whether each method call returned true or false. This method of checking after each method is error-prone and cumbersome, and the true/false return value doesn't provide any detailed information about the cause or type of error that occurred. To enable improved error handling, `DllImportAttribute` has two options that can customize the way errors are handled. One involves getting a Win32 error code, and the other involves transforming the signature to throw exceptions on failure.

Getting a Win32 Error Code

When Win32 functions fail, they often return false. If you'd like to get more information about why a failure occurred, you can often call the Win32 function `GetLastError` to obtain an error code (assuming that the function provides an error code by internally calling the `SetLastError` Win32 API).

`DllImportAttribute` enables you to turn on or off the ability to successfully obtain extra error information with a boolean named parameter called `SetLastError`. Due to the nature of the .NET Framework's interactions with the operating system, if you directly call `GetLastError` (defined in `KERNEL32.DLL`) using PInvoke, the results would be unreliable. Instead, you must call `Marshal.GetLastWin32Error` in the `System.Runtime.InteropServices` namespace or use the `LastDllError` property in VB .NET's global `Err` object. Listing 18.8 demonstrates the use of `DllImportAttribute`'s `SetLastError` named parameter and `Marshal.GetLastWin32Error` by updating the code from Listing 18.3.

LISTING 18.8 An Update to Listing 18.3 Using Extra Error Information

```
 1: using System;
 2: using System.Runtime.InteropServices;
 3:
 4: public class DriveNamer
 5: {
 6:   [DllImport("kernel32.dll", SetLastError=true)]
 7:   static extern bool SetVolumeLabel(string lpRootPathName,
 8:     string lpVolumeName);
 9:
10:   public static void Main()
11:   {
12:     if (SetVolumeLabel("C:\\", "My C Drive"))
13:       Console.WriteLine("Success!");
14:     else
15:       Console.WriteLine("Failure! Error Code: " +
➥ Marshal.GetLastWin32Error());
16:   }
17: }
```

Why would you ever want to set `SetLastError` to false? Turning this functionality off provides a slight performance improvement since the system doesn't need to worry about tracking the last error. In fact, false is the default in C#, so you must explicitly set it to true if you plan to use `Marshal.GetLastWin32Error`. With `Declare`, this functionality is always "on," so checking the `Err.LastDllError` property always works if the function you called returned additional information.

Both `Err.LastDllError` (in the `Microsoft.VisualBasic` assembly) and `Marshal.GetLastWin32Error` do the exact same thing, but `Err.LastDllError` is meant to be VB .NET-specific (and present for backward compatibility with earlier versions of Visual Basic) whereas `Marshal.GetLastWin32Error` is the language-neutral way of getting the same functionality.

> **CAUTION**
>
> Never define and use the `GetLastError` Win32 API directly via PInvoke. Instead, call `Marshal.GetLastWin32Error` in `System.Runtime.InteropServices` or the global `Err.LastDllError` in Visual Basic .NET code.

Getting a numeric error code is nice, but it usually involves manually looking up what the error code actually means—unless you've seen it enough times in the past to memorize its meaning.

Listing 18.9 demonstrates the use of the `FormatMessage` API from `KERNEL32.DLL` to convert an error code into a human-readable message. This is similar to the popular `ERRLOOK.EXE` utility from Visual Studio, and only works if the system recognizes the error code.

LISTING 18.9   Obtaining an Error String from an Error Code

```
 1: using System;
 2: using System.Text;
 3: using System.Runtime.InteropServices;
 4:
 5: public class ErrorHelper
 6: {
 7:   const uint FORMAT_MESSAGE_FROM_SYSTEM = 0x1000;
 8:   const ushort LANG_NEUTRAL = 0x0;
 9:   const ushort SUBLANG_DEFAULT = 0x1;
10:
11:   [DllImport("kernel32.dll", CharSet=CharSet.Auto)]
12:   static extern uint FormatMessage(uint dwFlags, IntPtr lpSource,
13:     int dwMessageId, int dwLanguageId, [Out] StringBuilder lpBuffer,
14:     int nSize, IntPtr Arguments);
15:
16:   static int MakeLangId(ushort p, ushort s) { return (s << 10) | p; }
17:
18:   public static string GetErrorMessage(int errorCode)
19:   {
20:     StringBuilder sb = new StringBuilder(1024);
21:
22:     if (FormatMessage(FORMAT_MESSAGE_FROM_SYSTEM, IntPtr.Zero, errorCode,
23:       MakeLangId(LANG_NEUTRAL, SUBLANG_DEFAULT), sb, sb.Capacity,
24:       IntPtr.Zero) != 0)
25:     {
26:       return sb.ToString();
27:     }
28:     else
29:     {
30:       return "<Unrecognized error>";
31:     }
32:   }
33: }
```

The integer passed to `GetErrorMessage` can be a Win32 error code, as obtained by `Marshal.GetLastWin32Error`, or an `HRESULT`. In the former case, a client can simply call it as follows:

```
string message = ErrorHelper.GetErrorMessage(Marshal.GetLastWin32Error());
```

Causing Exceptions to be Thrown on Failure

Normally the signature of a DLL's function is "preserved" when you define it. If the function returns an HRESULT, however, you can use another named parameter of DllImportAttribute to enable the same kind of HRESULT to .NET exception transformations that occur with COM Interoperability. The named parameter is called PreserveSig, and can be set to false to enable the signature transformation. As with the signature transformation for COM methods, the returned HRESULT is hidden from the signature and an exception is thrown instead if the HRESULT contains a value in a range corresponding to failure.

Note that this PreserveSig named parameter is separate from the PreserveSigAttribute pseudo-custom attribute! The reason PreserveSigAttribute can't be used on PInvoke methods is because PInvoke methods have preserved signatures by default. PreserveSigAttribute doesn't have a boolean parameter to turn the behavior on and off, so DllImportAttribute needed a boolean named parameter that does just that.

Listing 18.10 demonstrates error handling with and without PreserveSig set to true. It defines the following function from OLE32.DLL:

```
HRESULT ProgIDFromCLSID(REFCLSID clsid, LPOLESTR * lplpszProgID);
```

This function returns a string containing a ProgID corresponding to the passed-in CLSID, obtained from the Windows Registry.

LISTING 18.10   Making PInvoke Methods Throw Exceptions Upon Failure Using PreserveSig

```
 1: using System;
 2: using System.Runtime.InteropServices;
 3:
 4: public class ErrorHandling
 5: {
 6:   [DllImport("ole32.dll", CharSet=CharSet.Unicode,
 7:     EntryPoint="ProgIDFromCLSID")]
 8:   static extern int ProgIDFromCLSID1([In] ref Guid clsid,
 9:     out string lplpszProgID);
10:
11:   [DllImport("ole32.dll", CharSet=CharSet.Unicode,
12:     EntryPoint="ProgIDFromCLSID", PreserveSig=false)]
13:   static extern void ProgIDFromCLSID2([In] ref Guid clsid,
14:     out string lplpszProgID);
15:
16:   public static void Main()
17:   {
18:     Guid g = Guid.NewGuid();
```

LISTING 18.10 Continued

```
19:      string progID;
20:
21:      // Check for error by looking for a failure HRESULT value
22:      int hresult = ProgIDFromCLSID1(ref g, out progID);
23:      if (hresult < 0)
24:        Console.WriteLine("The call failed: 0x{0:X}", hresult);
25:
26:      // Check for error by catching an exception
27:      try
28:      {
29:        ProgIDFromCLSID2(ref g, out progID);
30:      }
31:      catch (Exception e)
32:      {
33:        Console.WriteLine("The call failed: " + e.ToString());
34:      }
35:    }
36: }
```

Lines 6–14 define two PInvoke signatures for `ProgIDFromCLSID`—one that keeps the default behavior of `PreserveSig=false`, and one that sets `PreserveSig` to true. Because these two signatures differ only by return type, we gave them different names and used `EntryPoint` so they both use the same `ProgIDFromCLSID` entry point. Had the two methods differed in their parameters, we could have left each with its original name and had overloaded methods! Also notice that `CharSet.Unicode` was specified rather than marking the string parameter with `[MarshalAs(UnmanagedType.LPWStr)]`. Although `ProgIDFromCLSID` returns a string that must be freed by the client, its documentation states that callers must free it with `CoTaskMemFree`. Because this is what the Interop Marshaler does when copying and freeing strings, its safe to use the `System.String` type for this out parameter.

Lines 22–24 call the version of `ProgIDFromCLSID` that returns the raw `HRESULT` value. The call fails if the failure bit is set, meaning the integer is less than zero. Lines 27–34 call the version of `ProgIDFromCLSID` that throws an exception on failure. Therefore, structured exception handling is used and the contents of the exception are printed on Line 33. This listing produces the following output when run:

```
The call failed: 0x80040154
The call failed: System.Runtime.InteropServices.COMException (0x80040154):
➥Class not registered
   at ErrorHandling.ProgIDFromCLSID2(Guid& clsid, String& lplpszProgID)
   at ErrorHandling.Main()
```

Listing 18.7, which used Microsoft Active Accessibility, called two APIs from OLEACC.DLL that returned HRESULTs. Therefore, PreserveSig could be used in that example for improved error handling. Listing 18.11 updates Listing 18.7 to take advantage of setting PreserveSig to true.

LISTING 18.11   Using PreserveSig to Update Listing 18.7

```
 1: using System;
 2: using System.Text;
 3: using System.Runtime.InteropServices;
 4: using Accessibility;
 5:
 6: struct POINT
 7: {
 8:   public int x;
 9:   public int y;
10: }
11:
12: public class ArrayExample
13: {
14:   [DllImport("oleacc.dll", PreserveSig=false)]
15:   static extern void AccessibleChildren(IAccessible paccContainer,
16:   int iChildStart, int cChildren, [Out] object [] rgvarChildren,
17:   out int pcObtained);
18:
19:   [DllImport("oleacc.dll", PreserveSig=false)]
20:   static extern void AccessibleObjectFromPoint(POINT ptScreen,
21:   out IAccessible ppacc,
22:   [MarshalAs(UnmanagedType.Struct)] out object pvarChild);
23:
24:   [DllImport("user32.dll")]
25:   static extern bool GetCursorPos(out POINT lpPoint);
26:
27:   public static void Main()
28:   {
29:     IAccessible acc = null;
30:     POINT p;
31:     Object var;
32:
33:     try
34:     {
35:       if (GetCursorPos(out p))
36:       {
37:         // Try to get an accessible object under the cursor
38:         AccessibleObjectFromPoint(p, out acc, out var);
39:
```

LISTING 18.11   Continued

```
40:            object [] children = new object[acc.accChildCount];
41:            int obtained;
42:
43:            // Fill in our allocated array with children
44:            AccessibleChildren(acc, 0, acc.accChildCount,
45:              children, out obtained);
46:
47:            // Print out the children to prove that this worked
48:            Console.WriteLine("obtained = " + obtained);
49:            foreach (object o in children)
50:              Console.WriteLine(o);
51:          }
52:        }
53:        catch (Exception ex)
54:        {
55:          Console.WriteLine("Error: " + ex.ToString());
56:        }
57:    }
58: }
```

Setting PreserveSig to false cannot be done using Declare.

TIP

We've covered many additional customizations available only to DllImportAttribute. Fortunately, all the additional customizations enabled by DllImportAttribute are also available in Visual Basic .NET because you can use DllImportAttribute in Visual Basic .NET! Simply put the attribute on an empty shared Sub or Function, like the following:

```
<DllImport("ole32.dll")> _
Shared Function ProgIDFromCLSID(<[In]> ByRef clsid As Guid, _
  <Out> ByRef lplpszProgID As String) As Integer
End Function
```

Be aware that because the default behavior implied by the Declare statement is different from the default behavior chosen by the Common Language Runtime for DllImportAttribute (which also differs from C#'s default behavior), the statement

```
<DllImport("ole32.dll", _
  CharSet:=CharSet.Ansi, _
  ExactSpelling:=True, _
  SetLastError:=True)> _
```

```
Shared Function ProgIDFromCLSID(<[In]> ByRef clsid As Guid, _
   <Out> ByRef lplpszProgID As String) As Integer
End Function
```

is the exact equivalent of

```
Declare Function ProgIDFromCLSID Lib "ole32.dll" (<[In]> ByRef clsid As
Guid, _
   <Out> ByRef lplpszProgID As String) As Integer
```

You cannot mark a `Declare` statement with `DllImportAttribute` to customize its behavior; you must use it on a regular `Shared` method.

Conclusion

This chapter introduced PInvoke and covered all the essentials for getting started. Two critical topics are saved for the next chapter: calling unmanaged APIs that expect function pointers, and calling unmanaged APIs that use structures.

Unlike COM Interoperability, PInvoke does not involve a wide area of topics that need to be mastered. It all comes down to two mechanisms:

- The use of `DllImportAttribute` (or a language-specific abstraction such as `Declare` in Visual Basic .NET)
- The rules of the Interop Marshaler

The first area was completely covered in this chapter, as were the areas in which the Interop Marshaler behaves differently for PInvoke signatures compared to signatures on COM interfaces. Understanding all the nuances of the Interop Marshaler, however, is a daunting task that often is accomplished using trial and error. Chapter 4, "An In-Depth Look at Imported Assemblies," and Chapter 9, "An In-Depth Look at Exported Type Libraries," can greatly help your understanding because these type information transformations follow the Interop Marshaler's rules.

Unfortunately, in general there's no mechanical way to look at an unmanaged signature and determine what its corresponding PInvoke signature should look like (without using something like C# unsafe code, discussed in the next chapter). Defining a PInvoke signature correctly sometimes involves understanding the semantics of the function, most notably who is responsible for allocating memory, who is responsible for freeing memory, and how this memory management should be accomplished. In these cases, thorough documentation (as on MSDN Online) is a life-saver. I've already gone through this exercise of understanding the semantics of all the Win32 APIs listed in Appendix E, so these definitions should save you time and frustration if you need to use any of the listed functions.

18

THE ESSENTIALS OF PINVOKE

DIGGING DEEPER

Internally, the CLR calls LoadLibrary and GetProcAddress to make PInvoke work. These calls are made as late as possible. For LoadLibrary, it's the first time an export from a given DLL is called (if the DLL isn't already loaded). For GetProcAddress, it's the first time a PInvoke method is called. In addition, before calling GetProcAddress, the CLR checks the validity of the signature's metadata and ensures that all the parameters and the return type are legal to use with PInvoke.

By using Marshal.Prelink or Marshal.PrelinkAll, you can perform this DLL loading and initialization at any earlier time you desire. This can be helpful when using methods like QueryPerformanceCounter, introduced at the beginning of the chapter, so time measurements are not affected by this extra work. See Appendix A, "System.Runtime.InteropServices Reference," for more details.

Deeper Into PInvoke and Useful Examples

IN THIS CHAPTER

- Callbacks   810

- Passing Structures   821

- Handling Variable-Length Structures and Signatures   847

- Using C# Unsafe Code   849

- Guarding Against Premature Garbage Collection   852

- Choosing the DLL Location or Name Dynamically   863

- Example: Responding Immediately to Console Input   865

- Example: Clearing the Console Screen   868

- Example: Using `CoCreateInstanceEx` to Activate Remote COM Objects   871

In this chapter, we cover a variety of advanced topics, but focus mainly on two essential topics that weren't covered in the previous chapter: callbacks and structure marshaling. In examining these topics, we cover useful examples that you might want to copy and paste into your own applications. You can never have too many PInvoke examples!

Many of the examples in this chapter demonstrate Win32 console APIs, because `System.Console` exposes only a small fraction of everything that Win32 APIs enable you to accomplish. The most useful examples in this chapter show you how to:

- Receive progress notifications while copying a file (Listing 19.1)
- Trap `Ctrl+C`, `Ctrl+Break`, or other Windows termination signals in a console application (Listing 19.2)
- Write colored text to the console (Listing 19.4)
- Respond immediately to console input without waiting for the user to press the `Enter` key (Listing 19.13)
- Clear the console window (Listing 19.14)
- Use `CoCreateInstanceEx` to activate remote COM objects (Listing 19.15)

FAQ: How do I make a sound in a .NET application?

Although not covered in this chapter's examples, PInvoke is usually required for playing sounds in .NET. To play `.wav` sound files, you can call the `PlaySound` API in `WINMM.DLL`, or you could use DirectX via COM Interoperability.

If you just want to make a simple beep sound, you don't have to use PInvoke to call the Win32 `MessageBeep` API. Instead, you could call the `Microsoft.VisualBasic.Interaction.Beep` method in the `Microsoft.VisualBasic` assembly, which makes the same call for you. (In VB .NET code, `Beep` can be called as if it's a global method.) Or, in Windows, you can also cause a beep by calling `Console.WriteLine("\a")`!

For an example of playing sounds in a .NET application, see Chapter 23, "Writing a .NET Arcade Game Using DirectX."

Callbacks

Often, static entry points such as Win32 functions require callback behavior. The most common mechanism for this is function pointers. For example, the `CopyFileEx` API in `KERNEL32.DLL` copies a file, enabling the caller to pass a callback function to receive progress updates. This function, declared in `winbase.h`, is documented with the following signature:

```
BOOL CopyFileEx(
  LPCTSTR lpExistingFileName,         // name of existing file
  LPCTSTR lpNewFileName,              // name of new file
  LPPROGRESS_ROUTINE lpProgressRoutine, // callback function
  LPVOID lpData,                      // callback parameter
  LPBOOL pbCancel,                    // cancel status
  DWORD dwCopyFlags                   // copy options
);
```

The `LPPROGRESS_ROUTINE` type represents a pointer to a function with the following signature:

```
DWORD CALLBACK ProgressRoutine(
  LARGE_INTEGER TotalFileSize,        // file size
  LARGE_INTEGER TotalBytesTransferred, // bytes transferred
  LARGE_INTEGER StreamSize,           // bytes in stream
  LARGE_INTEGER StreamBytesTransferred, // bytes transferred for stream
  DWORD dwStreamNumber,               // current stream
  DWORD dwCallbackReason,             // callback reason
  HANDLE hSourceFile,                 // handle to source file
  HANDLE hDestinationFile,            // handle to destination file
  LPVOID lpData                       // from CopyFileEx
);
```

For .NET applications that wish to define managed callback functions used by unmanaged code, the Interop Marshaler provides support for bridging the unmanaged concept of function pointers with the managed concept of delegates. For the other direction of passing an unmanaged function pointer to a .NET component for callbacks, there is no built-in support. This section examines what can be done in both of these directions.

Using Delegates as Function Pointers

To take advantage of the function pointer callback mechanism in managed code, we can define a delegate with the desired signature. For the `CopyFileEx` example, the delegate would look as follows in C#:

```
delegate uint CopyProgressDelegate(long TotalFileSize,
  long TotalBytesTransferred, long StreamSize,
  long StreamBytesTransferred, uint dwStreamNumber,
  uint dwCallbackReason, IntPtr hSourceFile,
  IntPtr hDestinationFile, IntPtr lpData);
```

This delegate type can be used in a `CopyFileEx` PInvoke signature where a function pointer is expected:

```
[DllImport("kernel32.dll", CharSet=CharSet.Auto, SetLastError=true)]
static extern bool CopyFileEx(string lpExistingFileName,
  string lpNewFileName, CopyProgressDelegate lpProgressRoutine,
  IntPtr lpData, [In] ref bool pbCancel, uint dwCopyFlags);
```

Listing 19.1 demonstrates the use of the `CopyFileEx` function and its `CopyProgressDelegate` delegate. It uses the `ErrorHelper.GetErrorMessage` function we defined in the previous chapter, so it should be compiled with `ErrorHelper.cs` from Listing 18.9.

LISTING 19.1   The `CopyFileEx` Function Calls Back into Managed Code

```
1: using System;
2: using System.Runtime.InteropServices;
3:
4: public class CopyFile
5: {
6:   const uint CALLBACK_CHUNK_FINISHED = 0x0;
7:   const uint CALLBACK_STREAM_SWITCH  = 0x1;
8:   const uint PROGRESS_CONTINUE       = 0x0;
9:
10:   delegate uint CopyProgressDelegate(long TotalFileSize,
11:     long TotalBytesTransferred, long StreamSize,
12:     long StreamBytesTransferred, uint dwStreamNumber,
13:     uint dwCallbackReason, IntPtr hSourceFile,
14:     IntPtr hDestinationFile, IntPtr lpData);
15:
16:   [DllImport("kernel32.dll", CharSet=CharSet.Auto, SetLastError=true)]
17:   static extern bool CopyFileEx(string lpExistingFileName,
18:     string lpNewFileName, CopyProgressDelegate lpProgressRoutine,
19:     IntPtr lpData, [In] ref bool pbCancel, uint dwCopyFlags);
20:
21:   static CopyProgressDelegate d;
22:
23:   public static void Main()
24:   {
25:     bool cancel = false;
26:     d = new CopyProgressDelegate(OnProgress);
27:
28:     Console.WriteLine("Copy file...");
29:     bool result;
30:     result = CopyFileEx("c:\\file1.txt", "c:\\file2.txt",
31:       d, IntPtr.Zero, ref cancel, 0);
32:
33:     if (!result)
34:     {
35:       int errorCode = Marshal.GetLastWin32Error();
36:       string message = ErrorHelper.GetErrorMessage(errorCode);
37:
38:       if (message == "")
39:         Console.WriteLine("Failed with error code " + errorCode);
```

LISTING 19.1 Continued

```
40:      else
41:        Console.WriteLine("Failed: " + message);
42:    }
43:    else
44:    {
45:      Console.WriteLine("...Finished");
46:    }
47:  }
48:
49:  // Callback method
50:  static uint OnProgress(long TotalFileSize, long TotalBytesTransferred,
51:    long StreamSize, long StreamBytesTransferred, uint dwStreamNumber,
52:    uint dwCallbackReason, IntPtr hSourceFile, IntPtr hDestinationFile,
53:    IntPtr lpData)
54:  {
55:    if (dwCallbackReason == CALLBACK_CHUNK_FINISHED)
56:    {
57:      Console.WriteLine("************ Chunk Finished ************");
58:      Console.WriteLine("File Bytes:   " + TotalBytesTransferred +
59:        " of " + TotalFileSize);
60:      Console.WriteLine("Stream Bytes: " + StreamBytesTransferred +
61:        " of " + StreamSize);
62:    }
63:    else if (dwCallbackReason == CALLBACK_STREAM_SWITCH)
64:    {
65:      Console.WriteLine("************** New Stream **************");
66:    }
67:    else
68:    {
69:      Console.WriteLine("*********** Unknown Callback ***********");
70:    }
71:    return PROGRESS_CONTINUE;
72:  }
73: }
```

Lines 6–8 define some Win32 constants to be used inside the callback function, found in winbase.h. Lines 10–14 define the delegate, and Lines 16–19 define the PInvoke signature. CopyFileEx is actually exported as a pair of methods—CopyFileExA and CopyFileExW—so Line 17 sets the function's character set to Auto. SetLastError is set to true because CopyFileEx uses SetLastError to return an error code upon failure. This PInvoke signature would look as follows in Visual Basic .NET:

```
Declare Auto Function CopyFileEx Lib "kernel32.dll" _
  (ByVal lpExistingFileName As String, ByVal lpNewFileName As String, _
  ByVal lpProgressRoutine As CopyProgressDelegate, _
  ByVal lpData As IntPtr, <[In]> ByRef pbCancel As Boolean, _
  ByVal dwCopyFlags As Integer) As Boolean
```

Line 21 defines a static `CopyProgressDelegate` field to store a reference to the delegate we create in Line 26. Storing a static reference isn't necessary for this example, because the callbacks only occur during the `CopyFileEx` function call. However, you generally need to take explicit action to prevent delegates from being garbage collected prematurely when unmanaged code holds onto a corresponding function pointer for later callbacks. The garbage collector has no way of knowing that unmanaged code plans to call back on your delegates, so if no managed code references the object, it is considered eligible for garbage collection.

CAUTION

The *number one* mistake made when using delegates as unmanaged function pointers is to allow them to be garbage collected before unmanaged code is finished using them. Premature collection of delegates can result in several different symptoms, depending on the implementation of the unmanaged code using the function pointers. For example, it could cause an access violation, or it could cause your callback methods to never be called while the rest of the program runs normally. An easy way to prevent collection is to assign the delegate reference to a static field, as done in Listing 19.1.

When the delegate is created in Line 26, we specify the `OnProgress` function defined later in the listing, which has the appropriate signature. Lines 30–31 call the `CopyFileEx` function, passing the names of the source file and destination file, the delegate instance, and a few miscellaneous parameters.

If the call fails (indicated by a false return value), Line 35 calls `Marshal.GetLastWin32Error` and Line 36 uses the `ErrorHelper.GetErrorMessage` method we defined in the previous chapter to retrieve an error message if `errorCode` is recognized by the operating system.

The callback method is defined in Lines 50–72, and prints some of the passed-in information to the console. Line 71 returns the `PROGRESS_CONTINUE` value because the Win32 documentation for the callback method states that it must return this value in order for the file copying to continue.

When this program runs, it prints out information like the following (as long as you have a `c:\file1.txt` file ready to be copied):

```
Copy file...
*************** New Stream ***************
************ Chunk Finished ************
File Bytes:    65536 of 89430
Stream Bytes: 65536 of 89430
************ Chunk Finished ************
File Bytes:    89430 of 89430
Stream Bytes: 89430 of 89430
...Finished
```

For another example of calling a Win32 function that calls back into managed code, Listing 19.2 contains Visual Basic .NET code that uses the `SetConsoleCtrlHandler` function in `KERNEL32.DLL`, which has the following unmanaged definition:

```
BOOL SetConsoleCtrlHandler(PHANDLER_ROUTINE HandlerRoutine, BOOL Add);
```

`PHANDLER_ROUTINE` represents a pointer to a function with the following signature:

```
BOOL WINAPI HandlerRoutine(DWORD dwCtrlType);
```

The `SetConsoleCtrlHandler` function enables a console application to handle *control signals* that ordinarily end the process. These signals are provoked when:

- The user presses `Ctrl+C`
- The user presses `Ctrl+Break`
- The user closes the console window (by selecting either `Close` from its menu or `End Task` from Task Manager)
- The user logs off
- The computer is being shut down (for services only)

An application can be notified of these events to perform cleanup upon closing or to prevent closing, although the user can still force the program to close in the latter three cases.

> **CAUTION**
>
> In Version 1.0 of the .NET Framework, delegates are always marshaled as function pointers with the `StdCall` calling convention (also known as `Winapi`). If you require passing a function pointer with a different calling convention to unmanaged code, you can't use a delegate. Your best bet is to use an unmanaged function pointer via an `IntPtr` type. Fortunately, Win32 APIs use `StdCall` for all callback function pointers.

19

DEEPER INTO
PINVOKE AND
USEFUL EXAMPLES

LISTING 19.2   The `SetConsoleCtrlHandler` Function Enables a Console Application to Trap Control Signals

```
 1: Imports System
 2:
 3: Public Enum ControlSignals
 4:    CTRL_C_EVENT        = 0
 5:    CTRL_BREAK_EVENT    = 1
 6:    CTRL_CLOSE_EVENT    = 2
 7:    CTRL_LOGOFF_EVENT   = 5
 8:    CTRL_SHUTDOWN_EVENT = 6
 9: End Enum
10:
11: Class HandlesControlSignals
12:
13:    Declare Function SetConsoleCtrlHandler Lib "kernel32.dll" _
14:      (ByVal HandlerRoutine As ConsoleCtrlDelegate, ByVal Add As Boolean) _
15:      As Boolean
16:
17:    Delegate Function ConsoleCtrlDelegate( _
18:      ByVal dwControlType As ControlSignals) As Boolean
19:
20:    Shared d As ConsoleCtrlDelegate
21:
22:    Public Shared Sub Main()
23:      ' Required to prevent early collection of delegate
24:      d = AddressOf OnSignal
25:
26:      ' Add our OnSignal method to the list of handlers
27:      SetConsoleCtrlHandler(d, True)
28:
29:      Console.WriteLine("Press 'Q' (followed by Enter) to quit.")
30:      While (Console.ReadLine() <> "Q")
31:      End While
32:
33:      ' Restore normal processing
34:      SetConsoleCtrlHandler(Nothing, False)
35:    End Sub
36:
37:    Public Shared Function OnSignal( _
38:      ByVal dwControlType As ControlSignals) As Boolean
39:      Select Case dwControlType
40:        Case ControlSignals.CTRL_C_EVENT:
41:          Console.WriteLine("[Ctrl+C]  Press 'Q' to quit.")
42:          OnSignal = True
43:        Case ControlSignals.CTRL_BREAK_EVENT:
```

LISTING 19.2 Continued

```
44:            Console.WriteLine("[Ctrl+Break]  Press 'Q' to quit.")
45:            OnSignal = True
46:        Case ControlSignals.CTRL_CLOSE_EVENT:
47:            Console.WriteLine("[Window Close]  Press 'Q' to quit.")
48:            OnSignal = True
49:        Case Else
50:            OnSignal = False
51:    End Select
52:  End Function
53: End Class
```

Lines 3–9 contain an enumeration of all the values that can be passed to the callback function. Lines 13–15 contain the PInvoke signature for `SetConsoleCtrlHandler` and Lines 17–18 contain the delegate definition used for callbacks.

Line 24 creates an instance of the delegate (using VB .NET's shortcut syntax of `AddressOf FunctionName`) and assigns it to the shared (static) field defined on Line 20. This is critical for this example because all the callbacks occur after the call to `SetConsoleCtrlHandler` in Line 27 yet there's no evidence to the garbage collector that unmanaged code is effectively holding onto a reference to the delegate. After calling the method with the delegate instance and true (to indicate that we're adding a handler rather than removing one), Lines 30–31 contain a while loop that keeps the program waiting until the user presses `Q` followed by the `Enter` key to exit the program. Line 34 unhooks our handler to end the program.

The `OnSignal` callback method is defined in Lines 37–52, and handles three of the signal types by printing a message at the console. Returning true indicates that the signal has been handled, so the process does not end as usual.

> **TIP**
>
> When a delegate is marshaled as an unmanaged function pointer, its parameters and return type have PInvoke's default marshaling behavior rather than COM Interoperability's default marshaling behavior. This is true regardless of whether the function pointer is passed to a static entry point or to a COM member. For example, the `Boolean` return value for `ConsoleCtrlDelegate` in Listing 19.2 is correctly marshaled as `BOOL` rather than `VARIANT_BOOL`.

Invoking Unmanaged Function Pointers in Managed Code

Version 1.0 of the .NET Framework has a limitation that function pointer/delegate marshaling is supported only in one direction. Delegates can be marshaled to unmanaged function pointers, but in the reverse direction, unmanaged function pointers *cannot* be marshaled to managed code as delegates (except for function pointers that originated as delegates). This means that unmanaged code can naturally use a managed callback function, but managed code cannot naturally use an unmanaged callback function.

This section demonstrates one way to get around this limitation and still invoke unmanaged functions whose pointer is somehow passed into managed code. The first step is to treat the unmanaged function pointer being passed to managed code as an IntPtr type. This is necessary in order to prevent the Interop Marshaler from recognizing it as a type that it can't marshal. For example, the GetProcAddress API in KERNEL32.DLL returns a function pointer, but can be defined in C# as follows:

```
[DllImport("kernel32.dll")]
static extern IntPtr GetProcAddress(IntPtr hModule, string lpProcName);
```

Had you attempted to define the return type as a delegate, calling this method would cause an ArgumentException with the message, "Function pointer was not created by a Delegate."

Although unmanaged function pointers can't be treated as .NET delegates, they can be directly invoked in managed code using the MSIL calli instruction. Such a call can be emitted by the Visual C++ .NET compiler when casting an IntPtr instance to an unmanaged function pointer and subsequently calling it. Such a call can also be done in IL Assembler syntax, but there is no built-in language construct in C# or Visual Basic .NET to enable such an invocation on an IntPtr type.

If you're programming in C# or VB .NET, you could create a helper assembly using C++ or raw IL Assembler to be used by your .NET components. This helper assembly could contain a method that invokes on an IntPtr instance as a function pointer with the appropriate signature. However, thanks to Reflection Emit technology, any .NET language can *dynamically* create an assembly with a helper method that performs the necessary calli instruction, then simply invoke that. Listing 19.3 demonstrates how this advanced technique can be done in C#.

LISTING 19.3   Invoking an Unmanaged Function Pointer via a Dynamic Method Containing Hand-Crafted MSIL

```
1: using System;
2: using System.Reflection;
3: using System.Reflection.Emit;
4: using System.Runtime.InteropServices;
5:
```

LISTING 19.3 Continued

```
 6: public class InvokeFunctionPointer
 7: {
 8:    [DllImport("kernel32.dll")]
 9:    static extern IntPtr LoadLibrary(string lpFileName);
10:
11:    [DllImport("kernel32.dll")]
12:    static extern IntPtr GetProcAddress(IntPtr hModule, string lpProcName);
13:
14:    public static void Main()
15:    {
16:      // Call any unmanaged method that returns a function pointer.
17:      // GetProcAddress is a canonical example.
18:      IntPtr hModule = LoadLibrary("user32.dll");
19:      IntPtr functionPointer = GetProcAddress(
20:        hModule, "CountClipboardFormats");
21:
22:      // The returned function pointer returns an integer and
23:      // has no parameters, so invoke the function with our helper method
24:      int returnValue = (int)InvokeFunctionWithNoParams(
25:        functionPointer, typeof(int));
26:
27:      // Print the result from calling CountClipboardFormats
28:      // via the function pointer
29:      Console.WriteLine("CountClipboardFormats returned: " + returnValue);
30:    }
31:
32:    // Helper method that generates a dynamic method capable of invoking a
33:    // function pointer (via the calli instruction), then calls the dynamic
34:    // method and returns the result from the unmanaged function.
35:    public static object InvokeFunctionWithNoParams(IntPtr functionPointer,
36:      Type returnType)
37:    {
38:      // Create a dynamic assembly and a dynamic module
39:      AssemblyName asmName = new AssemblyName();
40:      asmName.Name = "tempAssembly";
41:      AssemblyBuilder dynamicAsm =
42:        AppDomain.CurrentDomain.DefineDynamicAssembly(asmName,
43:        AssemblyBuilderAccess.Run);
44:      ModuleBuilder dynamicMod =
45:        dynamicAsm.DefineDynamicModule("tempModule");
46:
47:      // Create a global method capable of invoking the function pointer
48:      MethodBuilder dynamicMethod = dynamicMod.DefineGlobalMethod(
49:        "DoTheDirtyWork", MethodAttributes.Public |
```

LISTING 19.3   Continued

```
50:          MethodAttributes.Static, returnType, null);
51:
52:     // Generate the MSIL for this method
53:     ILGenerator generator = dynamicMethod.GetILGenerator();
54:
55:     if (IntPtr.Size == 4)
56:       generator.Emit(OpCodes.Ldc_I4, functionPointer.ToInt32());
57:     else if (IntPtr.Size == 8)
58:       generator.Emit(OpCodes.Ldc_I8, functionPointer.ToInt64());
59:     else
60:       throw new PlatformNotSupportedException();
61:
62:     // If the method had parameters, we'd push them on the stack first
63:     generator.EmitCalli(OpCodes.Calli, CallingConvention.StdCall,
64:       returnType, new Type[]{});
65:     generator.Emit(OpCodes.Ret);
66:
67:     // This global method is now complete
68:     dynamicMod.CreateGlobalFunctions();
69:
70:     // Call the method we just created and return whatever it returns
71:     MethodInfo mi = dynamicMod.GetMethod("DoTheDirtyWork");
72:     return mi.Invoke(null, null);
73:   }
74: }
```

Reflection Emit is beyond the scope of this book, but we'll examine the highlights of this listing. Lines 19–20 call the PInvoke method that returns a function pointer as an `IntPtr` type. This example calls `GetProcAddress` for `CountClipboardFormats` in `USER32.DLL`, so the function pointer returned matches the signature of the `CountClipboardFormats` API. This function has no parameters and returns a 32-bit integer. Lines 24–25 call our `InvokeFunctionWithNoParams` helper method, which is designed to handle any function with no parameters and a non-void return type. The returned integer, printed at the console in Line 29, is the value returned from the function being pointed to.

`InvokeFunctionWithNoParams` is defined in Lines 35–73. Lines 39–45 perform the standard action of creating a dynamic assembly containing a dynamic module. In this example, we throw away the dynamic assembly after invoking its method, but if we wanted to save it, then Line 43 would need to use `AssemblyBuilderAccess.RunAndSave` rather than `AssemblyBuilderAccess.Run`. Rather than defining a dynamic type to contain our dynamic method, Lines 48–50 define a static method directly on the module called `DoTheDirtyWork`.

This method will call the function pointer and return whatever value it returns. Therefore, the input returntype parameter is passed to DefineGlobalMethod to ensure that the return type of the dynamic method matches the return type that corresponds to the function pointer.

Lines 53–65 generate fill the dynamic method with the necessary MSIL instructions to perform the calli operation. By checking the static IntPtr.Size property, Lines 55–60 ensure that the generated code works on 32-bit and 64-bit platforms. Once the dynamic method is completed (Line 68), Lines 71–72 invoke the method and return the result.

Of course, this listing demonstrates an unrealistic use of invoking on a function pointer. If you want to call the Win32 CountClipboardFormats API in C#, you should use the standard PInvoke mechanism to call it directly rather than calling LoadLibrary and GetProcAddress yourself.

Passing Structures

Signatures of static entry points frequently have structure parameters, so using PInvoke often involves not just defining a function signature, but defining several structs as well. For the first example of using a PInvoke signature with a structure parameter, let's look at the GetConsoleScreenBufferInfo Win32 function, which provides information about the console's current settings (such as its background and foreground colors). It has the following unmanaged signature:

```
BOOL GetConsoleScreenBufferInfo(
  HANDLE hConsoleOutput,                            // screen buffer handle
  PCONSOLE_SCREEN_BUFFER_INFO lpConsoleScreenBufferInfo // screen buffer info
);
```

PCONSOLE_SCREEN_BUFFER_INFO represents a pointer to a CONSOLE_SCREEN_BUFFER_INFO structure, defined as follows:

```
typedef struct _CONSOLE_SCREEN_BUFFER_INFO {
  COORD       dwSize;
  COORD       dwCursorPosition;
  WORD        wAttributes;
  SMALL_RECT  srWindow;
  COORD       dwMaximumWindowSize;
} CONSOLE_SCREEN_BUFFER_INFO;
```

This structure has two fields that are structures themselves—SMALL_RECT:

```
typedef struct _SMALL_RECT {
  SHORT Left;
  SHORT Top;
  SHORT Right;
  SHORT Bottom;
} SMALL_RECT;
```

and COORD:

```
typedef struct _COORD {
  SHORT X;
  SHORT Y;
} COORD;
```

Listing 19.4 defines a PInvoke signature for GetConsoleScreenBufferInfo and value types representing these three structures, as part of my favorite example in the entire book. Using PInvoke, this C# listing defines a class for printing text with different foreground and background colors. Rather than just using Win32 APIs as the previous examples do, this listing defines a reusable class that can be easily used by other .NET applications.

LISTING 19.4   The ColorfulConsole Class Wraps Win32 APIs for Printing in Color

```
 1: using System;
 2: using System.Runtime.InteropServices;
 3:
 4: // Structs used by the PInvoke methods:
 5:
 6: internal struct CONSOLE_SCREEN_BUFFER_INFO
 7: {
 8:   internal COORD dwSize;
 9:   internal COORD dwCursorPosition;
10:   internal ushort wAttributes;
11:   internal SMALL_RECT srWindow;
12:   internal COORD dwMaximumWindowSize;
13: }
14:
15: internal struct COORD
16: {
17:   internal short X;
18:   internal short Y;
19: }
20:
21: internal struct SMALL_RECT
22: {
23:   internal short Left;
24:   internal short Top;
25:   internal short Right;
26:   internal short Bottom;
27: }
28:
29: // Constants used with PInvoke methods
30: internal class Constants
31: {
```

LISTING 19.4   Continued

```
32:    // Control foreground color
33:    internal const ushort FOREGROUND_BLUE      = 0x01;
34:    internal const ushort FOREGROUND_GREEN     = 0x02;
35:    internal const ushort FOREGROUND_RED       = 0x04;
36:    internal const ushort FOREGROUND_INTENSITY = 0x08;
37:
38:    // Control background color
39:    internal const ushort BACKGROUND_BLUE      = 0x10;
40:    internal const ushort BACKGROUND_GREEN     = 0x20;
41:    internal const ushort BACKGROUND_RED       = 0x40;
42:    internal const ushort BACKGROUND_INTENSITY = 0x80;
43:
44:    // Standard input, output, and error
45:    internal const int STD_INPUT_HANDLE  = -10;
46:    internal const int STD_OUTPUT_HANDLE = -11;
47:    internal const int STD_ERROR_HANDLE  = -12;
48:
49:    // Returned by GetStdHandle when an error occurs
50:    internal static readonly IntPtr INVALID_HANDLE_VALUE = new IntPtr(-1);
51: }
52:
53: // The public ColorfulConsole class
54: public class ColorfulConsole
55: {
56:    // Three PInvoke signatures:
57:
58:    [DllImport("kernel32.dll")]
59:    private static extern IntPtr GetStdHandle(int nStdHandle);
60:
61:    [DllImport("kernel32.dll")]
62:    private static extern bool GetConsoleScreenBufferInfo(
63:      IntPtr hConsoleOutput,
64:      out CONSOLE_SCREEN_BUFFER_INFO lpConsoleScreenBufferInfo);
65:
66:    [DllImport("kernel32.dll")]
67:    private static extern bool SetConsoleTextAttribute(
68:      IntPtr hConsoleOutput,
69:      ushort wAttributes);
70:
71:    private static CONSOLE_SCREEN_BUFFER_INFO csbi =
72:      new CONSOLE_SCREEN_BUFFER_INFO();
73:
74:    // Two overloads of WriteLine:
75:
```

LISTING 19.4 Continued

```
76:    // Print text with the given foreground color and background color
77:    public static void WriteLine(string text, ForegroundColors foreColor,
78:      BackgroundColors backColor)
79:    {
80:      IntPtr stdout = GetStdHandle(Constants.STD_OUTPUT_HANDLE);
81:
82:      if (stdout == Constants.INVALID_HANDLE_VALUE)
83:        throw new Exception("Unable to get standard output handle");
84:
85:      // Save existing console settings
86:      if (!GetConsoleScreenBufferInfo(stdout, out csbi))
87:        throw new Exception("Unable to get existing console settings");
88:
89:      // Set the color
90:      if (!SetConsoleTextAttribute(stdout,
91:        (ushort)((ushort)foreColor | (ushort)backColor)))
92:        throw new Exception("Unable to set console colors");
93:
94:      // Write the text using System.Console
95:      Console.WriteLine(text);
96:
97:      // Restore the old console settings
98:      if (!SetConsoleTextAttribute(stdout, csbi.wAttributes))
99:        throw new Exception("Unable to restore normal console colors");
100:   }
101:
102:   // Print text with the given foreground color
103:   // and current console background color
104:   public static void WriteLine(string text, ForegroundColors foreColor)
105:   {
106:     IntPtr stdout = GetStdHandle(Constants.STD_OUTPUT_HANDLE);
107:
108:     if (stdout == Constants.INVALID_HANDLE_VALUE)
109:       throw new Exception("Unable to get standard output handle");
110:
111:     // Retrieve the current background color
112:     if (!GetConsoleScreenBufferInfo(stdout, out csbi))
113:       throw new Exception("Unable to get existing console settings");
114:
115:     BackgroundColors defaultBackground =
116:       (BackgroundColors)(csbi.wAttributes & 0xF0);
117:
118:     WriteLine(text, foreColor, defaultBackground);
119:   }
```

LISTING 19.4   Continued

```
120: }
121:
122: // Enumeration of foreground colors
123: public enum ForegroundColors : ushort
124: {
125:    Black = 0,
126:    Blue = Constants.FOREGROUND_BLUE,
127:    Green = Constants.FOREGROUND_GREEN,
128:    Cyan = Constants.FOREGROUND_BLUE | Constants.FOREGROUND_GREEN,
129:    Red = Constants.FOREGROUND_RED,
130:    Magenta = Constants.FOREGROUND_RED | Constants.FOREGROUND_BLUE,
131:    Brown = Constants.FOREGROUND_RED | Constants.FOREGROUND_GREEN,
132:    Gray = Constants.FOREGROUND_RED | Constants.FOREGROUND_BLUE |
133:       Constants.FOREGROUND_GREEN,
134:    DarkGray = Constants.FOREGROUND_INTENSITY,
135:    LightBlue = Constants.FOREGROUND_BLUE | Constants.FOREGROUND_INTENSITY,
136:    LightGreen = Constants.FOREGROUND_GREEN |
137:       Constants.FOREGROUND_INTENSITY,
138:    LightCyan = Constants.FOREGROUND_BLUE | Constants.FOREGROUND_GREEN |
139:       Constants.FOREGROUND_INTENSITY,
140:    LightRed = Constants.FOREGROUND_RED | Constants.FOREGROUND_INTENSITY,
141:    LightMagenta = Constants.FOREGROUND_RED | Constants.FOREGROUND_BLUE |
142:       Constants.FOREGROUND_INTENSITY,
143:    Yellow = Constants.FOREGROUND_RED | Constants.FOREGROUND_GREEN |
144:       Constants.FOREGROUND_INTENSITY,
145:    White = Constants.FOREGROUND_RED | Constants.FOREGROUND_BLUE |
146:       Constants.FOREGROUND_GREEN | Constants.FOREGROUND_INTENSITY
147: }
148:
149: // Enumeration of background colors
150: public enum BackgroundColors : ushort
151: {
152:    Black = 0,
153:    Blue = Constants.BACKGROUND_BLUE,
154:    Green = Constants.BACKGROUND_GREEN,
155:    Cyan = Constants.BACKGROUND_BLUE | Constants.BACKGROUND_GREEN,
156:    Red = Constants.BACKGROUND_RED,
157:    Magenta = Constants.BACKGROUND_RED | Constants.BACKGROUND_BLUE,
158:    Brown = Constants.BACKGROUND_RED | Constants.BACKGROUND_GREEN,
159:    Gray = Constants.BACKGROUND_RED | Constants.BACKGROUND_BLUE |
160:       Constants.BACKGROUND_GREEN,
161:    DarkGray = Constants.BACKGROUND_INTENSITY,
162:    LightBlue = Constants.BACKGROUND_BLUE | Constants.BACKGROUND_INTENSITY,
163:    LightGreen = Constants.BACKGROUND_GREEN |
```

19

**DEEPER INTO
PINVOKE AND
USEFUL EXAMPLES**

LISTING 19.4   Continued

```
164:        Constants.BACKGROUND_INTENSITY,
165:      LightCyan = Constants.BACKGROUND_BLUE | Constants.BACKGROUND_GREEN |
166:        Constants.BACKGROUND_INTENSITY,
167:      LightRed = Constants.BACKGROUND_RED | Constants.BACKGROUND_INTENSITY,
168:      LightMagenta = Constants.BACKGROUND_RED | Constants.BACKGROUND_BLUE |
169:        Constants.BACKGROUND_INTENSITY,
170:      Yellow = Constants.BACKGROUND_RED | Constants.BACKGROUND_GREEN |
171:        Constants.BACKGROUND_INTENSITY,
172:      White = Constants.BACKGROUND_RED | Constants.BACKGROUND_BLUE |
173:        Constants.BACKGROUND_GREEN | Constants.BACKGROUND_INTENSITY
174: }
```

Lines 6–27 define the CONSOLE_SCREEN_BUFFER_INFO, COORD, and SMALL_RECT value types, which are straightforward translations of their corresponding unmanaged structs. The CONSOLE_SCREEN_BUFFER_INFO type could have been defined without requiring the definitions of additional structs by expanding the fields of the sub-structs; for example:

```
internal struct CONSOLE_SCREEN_BUFFER_INFO
{
  // Fields of COORD:
  internal short dwSizeX;
  internal short dwSizeY;

  // Fields of COORD:
  internal short dwCursorPositionX;
  internal short dwCursorPositionY;

  // A simple unsigned 16-bit integer:
  internal ushort wAttributes;

  // Fields of SMALL_RECT:
  internal short srWindowLeft;
  internal short srWindowTop;
  internal short srWindowRight;
  internal short srWindowBottom;

  // Fields of COORD:
  internal short dwMaximumWindowSizeX;
  internal short dwMaximumWindowSizeY;
}
```

Either way, the memory layout is the same. Furthermore, because wAttributes is the only field of CONSOLE_SCREEN_BUFFER_INFO used by this listing, the struct could be further simplified as follows:

```
internal struct CONSOLE_SCREEN_BUFFER_INFO
{
  internal long fourUnusedShortFields;
  internal ushort wAttributes;
  internal long fourMoreUnusedShortFields;
  internal int twoUnusedShortFields;
}
```

As long as wAttributes is at the same memory offset from the beginning of the structure, using it works the same way in Listing 19.4. Still, it's best to stay as faithful to the unmanaged struct definitions as possible.

Lines 30–51 define a Constants class containing relevant Win32 constants, marked internal so it's not exposed to users. Lines 58–69 define three PInvoke methods: GetConsoleScreenBufferInfo discussed earlier, GetStdHandle to get the standard output handle, and SetConsoleTextAttribute to set the colors of text that we'll output. ColorfulConsole exposes two public static WriteLine methods. The first one can be called with a string, a foreground color and a background color. The second one can be called with a string and a foreground color, and uses the console's current background color for the text's background.

These WriteLine methods use the public ForegroundColors and BackgroundColors enumerations we define in Lines 123–174. The colors in a console can be set to 16 different colors, but Windows defines just four color constants that need to be combined as bit flags in order to get the 16 colors. (There are separate values for foreground colors and background colors because both get bitwise-ORed in a 16-bit value.) Because these are sometimes unintuitive to use, our enumerations expose all the combinations with descriptive names like Cyan, Brown, LightGreen, and so forth. These enumeration values are not meant to be combined, so we don't mark the enums with System.FlagsAttribute.

In Lines 77–87, the first overload of WriteLine calls GetStdHandle to get the standard output handle, then calls GetConsoleScreenBufferInfo to retrieve the existing console settings. Lines 90–99 call SetConsoleTextAttribute to set the console's colors, Console.WriteLine to write the text, then SetConsoleTextAttribute with the structure passed back from GetConsoleScreenBufferInfo to restore the console to its old state. Notice that in Line 91, the two enumeration values are bitwise-ORed to obtain the single 16-bit value required by SetConsoleTextAttribute. This way, all of the bit flags treatment is hidden from the user.

The second overload of WriteLine (Lines 104–120) figures out the current console background color, then calls the first overload of WriteLine using this color. After calling GetConsoleScreenBufferInfo in Line 112, Line 116 extracts the background color from the CONSOLE_SCREEN_BUFFER_INFO structure's wAttributes field by bitwise-ANDing it with a mask of 0xF0, and then casting the value to an instance of the BackgroundColors enumeration.

A .NET application can use this `ColorfulConsole` class as follows:

```
public class Example
{
  public static void Main ()
  {
    ColorfulConsole.WriteLine("Red", ForegroundColors.Red);
    ColorfulConsole.WriteLine("Magenta", ForegroundColors.Magenta);
    ColorfulConsole.WriteLine("LightCyan", ForegroundColors.LightCyan);
    ColorfulConsole.WriteLine("Yellow", ForegroundColors.Yellow);
    ColorfulConsole.WriteLine("BlackOnLightGreen", ForegroundColors.Black,
      BackgroundColors.LightGreen);
    ColorfulConsole.WriteLine("RedOnWhite", ForegroundColors.Red,
      BackgroundColors.White);
  }
}
```

TIP

Listing 19.4 compiles with the following warnings:

```
ColorfulConsole.cs(17,18): warning CS0649: Field 'COORD.X' is never
assigned to,and will always have its default value 0
ColorfulConsole.cs(18,18): warning CS0649: Field 'COORD.Y' is never
assigned to,and will always have its default value 0
ColorfulConsole.cs(23,18): warning CS0649: Field 'SMALL_RECT.Left' is
never assigned to, and will always have its default value 0
ColorfulConsole.cs(24,18): warning CS0649: Field 'SMALL_RECT.Top' is never
assigned to, and will always have its default value 0
ColorfulConsole.cs(25,18): warning CS0649: Field 'SMALL_RECT.Right' is
never assigned to, and will always have its default value 0
ColorfulConsole.cs(26,18): warning CS0649: Field 'SMALL_RECT.Bottom' is
never assigned to, and will always have its default value 0
```

Yet attempting to assign initial values to these struct members to silence the warnings results in compilation *errors* explaining that structs cannot have instance field initializers.

This is a common problem when using PInvoke in C# because it's common to have non-public structs with fields that appear to be unused, but are actually read and written to by unmanaged code. There are a few things you could do to prevent these warnings:

- Use these fields somewhere in the class in a trivial way, simply to silence the warnings.

- Define structs as formatted classes instead, so you can initialize the field values. This can't always be done, however, as discussed in the "Using Formatted Classes" section later in this chapter.

- Change the structs and their fields to be public, if you don't mind exposing them to others.

- Define only the fields you use in managed code, but use `StructLayoutAttribute` and `FieldOffsetAttribute` to align them appropriately, discussed in the "Using `FieldOffsetAttribute`" section later in this chapter.

Do not make a struct's fields static in order to initialize them. Static fields are not part of the instance passed to a PInvoke method. Passing the wrong-sized structure to unmanaged code can cause your application to crash pretty quickly.

Customizing Structures with Custom Attributes

The structures used in Listing 19.4 were simple enough to not require any custom attributes, but often customizations are required to make .NET type definitions match the expected memory layout of the unmanaged structures they need to represent. Struct customization can be done with three pseudo-custom attributes:

- `StructLayoutAttribute`
- `FieldOffsetAttribute`
- `MarshalAsAttribute`

Using `StructLayoutAttribute`

`StructLayoutAttribute` requires that you specify a member of the `LayoutKind` enumeration. This can be one of three values:

- `Auto`—The CLR chooses how to arrange the fields in the structure, and could rearrange them at any time. This should never be used on a type that is marshaled to unmanaged code as a structure.

- `Sequential`—The fields are arranged sequentially, in the order they appear in source code. This is typically the desired setting for types marshaled to unmanaged code as structures.

- `Explicit`—The fields are arranged using byte offsets specified by the user on each field using a second custom attribute: `FieldOffsetAttribute`. This gives you complete control over the layout of a struct, and even makes it possible to define a union (by giving every field an offset of zero).

Although LayoutKind.Auto is the CLR's default for all types not marked with the StructLayoutAttribute pseudo-custom attribute, the Visual C# .NET, Visual Basic .NET, and Visual C++ .NET compilers all mark value types with LayoutKind.Sequential by default. This is why the value types in Listing 19.4 did not require StructLayoutAttribute with the LayoutKind.Sequential attribute; the compiler implicitly marks it as such.

StructLayoutAttribute has the following three optional named parameters:

- CharSet—Controls the default character set for string and character fields. CharSet can be set to a value of the same CharSet enumeration used with DllImportAttribute. With CharSet.Ansi, all string and character fields that don't explicitly choose a character set (with MarshalAsAttribute) are marshaled as ANSI. With CharSet.Unicode, all string and character fields that don't explicitly choose a character set are marshaled as Unicode. With CharSet.Auto, all string and character fields that don't explicitly choose a character set are marshaled as either ANSI or Unicode, depending on the operating system. The Visual C# .NET, Visual Basic .NET, and Visual C++ .NET compilers all use CharSet.Ansi by default.
- Pack—Controls the struct's packing alignment when using LayoutKind.Sequential. Pack can be set to one of the following values (representing a number of bytes): 0, 1, 2, 4, 8, 16, 32, 64, or 128. The default is 8, and 0 indicates that the default packing alignment for the current operating system should be used.
- Size—Controls the total size of a value type. Size can be set to any number of bytes greater than or equal to the size that the value type would be without any Size customization. Therefore, Size can be used to increase the size of a structure.

The packing of a struct is often a source of confusion. Without packing in the equation, fields align on their *natural boundary*. A natural boundary is a byte offset that is a multiple of the field's size. So byte fields can begin anywhere, 2-byte short fields can begin on even byte boundaries, 4-byte integer fields can begin on boundaries that are multiples of 4, and so on. This means that if you had a structure with a byte field followed by an integer field, the byte would begin at offset 0, and the integer would begin at offset 4 (leaving empty space at bytes 1, 2, and 3), so the total size of the structure would be 8 bytes.

With packing in the equation, fields align on either their natural boundary *or* to the pack size— *whichever results in the smaller offset*. This is pictured in Figure 19.1.

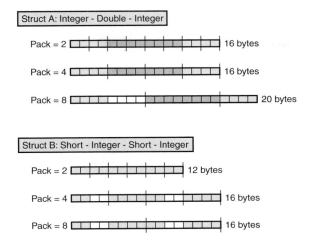

FIGURE 19.1

The memory layout of structures can be controlled with the Pack *named parameter.*

This figure contains two different structures, each set to three different packing alignments. Struct A corresponds to the following (in C#), where *n* could be 2, 4, or 8:

```
[StructLayout(LayoutKind.Sequential, Pack=n)]
public struct A
{
  public int One;
  public double Two;
  public int Three;
}
```

Struct B corresponds to the following (pictured in VB .NET), where *n* could be 2, 4, or 8:

```
<StructLayout(LayoutKind.Sequential, Pack:=n)> _
Public Structure B
  Public One As Short
  Public Two As Integer
  Public Three As Short
  Public Four As Integer
End Structure
```

Whether struct A has a packing alignment of 2 or 4 bytes, the memory layout is the same. In both cases, the end of every field touches a packing boundary (indicated with longer vertical lines), so each field resides immediately after the previous field. When it has a packing alignment of 8 bytes, it creates a 4-byte "hole" between the first and second field. That's because the closest natural boundary for the double field resides at 8 bytes, which happens to coincide with the next packing boundary. Because all three fields reside at their natural boundaries in the 8-byte packing case, increasing the packing size would have no effect on the memory layout.

The memory layout of struct B, on the other hand, changes when the packing alignment changes from 2 bytes to 4 bytes. In the Pack = 4 case, the end of the first field stops short of the natural boundary for the second field, which also coincides with the packing boundary. The same thing occurs for the third and fourth fields. Because all fields reside at their natural boundaries when the packing is 4 bytes, changing the packing to 8 bytes changes nothing.

> **TIP**
>
> Ensure that any value types you define to use with PInvoke signatures have the appropriate memory layout to match the unmanaged structure definitions expected by the unmanaged functions. Fortunately, structs are usually arranged such that fields align to their natural boundaries without any gaps, so changing their packing alignment size has no effect.

The packing alignment affects the unmanaged layout of a value type, not necessarily the managed layout. If the value type is blittable, then StructLayoutAttribute happens to affect the managed layout, but all that StructLayoutAttribute is guaranteed to do is control the unmanaged representation of a type.

Using FieldOffsetAttribute

As mentioned in the previous section, FieldOffsetAttribute can and must be used with LayoutKind.Explicit in order to choose your own memory offsets for each field. It could be applied to the previously defined A and B structs as follows:

C#:

```
[StructLayout(LayoutKind.Explicit)]
public struct A
{
  [FieldOffset(1)] public int One;
  [FieldOffset(7)] public double Two;
  [FieldOffset(15)] public int Three;
}
```

Visual Basic .NET:

```
<StructLayout(LayoutKind.Explicit)> _
Public Structure B
  <FieldOffset(0)> Public One As Short
  <FieldOffset(0)> Public Two As Integer
  <FieldOffset(0)> Public Three As Short
  <FieldOffset(0)> Public Four As Integer
End Structure
```

The memory layout for these two structs is illustrated in Figure 19.2.

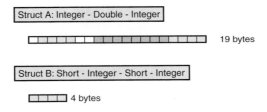

FIGURE 19.2

The memory layout of fields with explicit offsets.

Struct A uses unconventional offsets just for demonstration, and struct B is a more typical scenario: defining a union by overlapping fields at the same memory location. Only blittable fields are allowed to have overlapping offsets. Every field of a struct with explicit layout must be marked with FieldOffsetAttribute. Furthermore, the Pack named parameter should *not* be used with explicit layout because packing alignment doesn't matter when you're specifying exactly where you want each field to appear.

> **TIP**
>
> If you are creating a .NET definition of a structure with an embedded union, you should define the union as a separate structure and define a field of that union type in the original structure. That way, you can mark every union field with FieldOffset(0) and not bother with marking the fields of the main structure (unless it has unconventional memory layout that requires it). If you define it all as one big structure, then you must determine the proper memory offset of every field, which is error prone.

Using MarshalAsAttribute

The use of MarshalAsAttribute was covered in Chapter 12, "Customizing COM's View of .NET Components," including using it on structure fields. Here, we'll summarize the few UnmanagedType values that are commonly used with MarshalAsAttribute on struct fields passed to PInvoke signatures:

- ByValArray—This is the only supported way to pass an array to unmanaged code as a struct field, rather than LPArray or SafeArray. This must be used with MarshalAsAttribute's SizeConst parameter to indicate how many elements are in the array. If the array instance's length is smaller than SizeConst, an exception is thrown. If it is larger, only SizeConst elements are copied.

- ByValTStr—Used on a string field to make it a by-value buffer (such as CHAR[128]). Used with MarshalAsAttribute's SizeConst parameter to indicate how many elements are in the character array. If a .NET string has at least SizeConst characters, only SizeConst-1 characters are copied followed by a null character.

- Interface—Used on an object or class field to make it marshal as an interface. This is often required because the default void* marshaling (UnmanagedType.AsAny) for class types causes an exception to be thrown.

- LPStr, LPTStr, LPWStr—Used to customize the character set of string fields that are not passed as by-value buffers.

- U1, U2—Used to customize the character set of a System.Char field.

DIGGING DEEPER

The Microsoft.VisualBasic assembly contains two custom attributes in the Microsoft.VisualBasic namespace that sound as if they could be used for PInvoke: VBFixedArrayAttribute and VBFixedStringAttribute. These are completely unrelated to PInvoke, however, so they are not a replacement for using MarshalAsAttribute.

By default, strings and characters (System.String and System.Char) inherit their character set from the structure's CharSet marking in StructLayoutAttribute, so the default marshaling is ANSI in C#, VB .NET, and C++. The ByValTStr and LPStr values behave a little differently than you might expect, because these settings do not mean that the character set is determined at run time. Instead, it means that the struct's character set is used for such fields. Therefore, fields marked with ByValTStr or LPStr only have a platform-dependent character set when the struct is marked with CharSet.Auto. Because the UnmanagedType enumeration has no Char or WChar values, U1 can be used for a 1-byte ANSI character, and U2 can be used for a 2-byte Unicode character.

Special attention must be paid to by-value buffers passed as fields. Unlike the case for parameters, the Interop Marshaler does not enable passing `StringBuilder` types as structure fields! Instead, a string buffer field can be defined one of two ways:

- `System.String` with `MarshalAs(UnmanagedType.ByValTStr, SizeConst=`*bufferSize*`+1)`
- A character array with `MarshalAs(UnmanagedType.ByValArray, SizeConst=`*bufferSize*`)`

In both cases, the character set must be controlled by the containing structure. In the `System.String` case, the string instance must be initialized to a large enough string before being passed to unmanaged code (similar to using `System.String` for a buffer in VB .NET, discussed in the previous chapter). Internally, the CLR makes a copy of the string, passes it to unmanaged code, and replaces the original string reference with the new string potentially altered by unmanaged code. Therefore, this does not violate the rule that .NET strings are immutable; the string reference is silently swapped to a new string object.

> **CAUTION**
>
> When the Interop Marshaler passes a `System.String` field as a by-value buffer (`ByValTStr`), it copies the first `SizeConst-1` characters and places a null character at the end. Because of this, you can't pass a 128-character string as a field marked with `SizeConst=128`, but are limited to a 127-character string. If the memory layout of the structure is such that the byte following the string is unused (but still a part of the structure), you could extend the string by defining it with `SizeConst=129`. But if you're constrained by the layout of the unmanaged structure whose definition you're attempting to match, you must instead define the field as a character array marked with `ByValArray` and `SizeConst=128`. For character arrays, you can successfully fill every element with a valid character.

Listing 19.5 demonstrates both techniques of using a character buffer field with the `GetVersionEx` Windows API, with the following unmanaged definition:

```
BOOL GetVersionEx(LPOSVERSIONINFO lpVersionInfo);
```

`LPOSVERSIONINFO` is a pointer to an `OSVERSIONINFO` struct, which looks like the following:

```
typedef struct _OSVERSIONINFO{
  DWORD dwOSVersionInfoSize;
  DWORD dwMajorVersion;
  DWORD dwMinorVersion;
  DWORD dwBuildNumber;
  DWORD dwPlatformId;
  TCHAR szCSDVersion[128];
} OSVERSIONINFO;
```

LISTING 19.5   Using Strings and Character Arrays to Represent Character Buffer Fields of Structures

```
 1: using System;
 2: using System.Runtime.InteropServices;
 3:
 4: [StructLayout(LayoutKind.Sequential, CharSet=CharSet.Auto)]
 5: internal struct OSVERSIONINFO_1
 6: {
 7:    internal int dwOSVersionInfoSize;
 8:    internal int dwMajorVersion;
 9:    internal int dwMinorVersion;
10:    internal int dwBuildNumber;
11:    internal int dwPlatformId;
12:    [MarshalAs(UnmanagedType.ByValTStr, SizeConst=128)]
13:    internal string szCSDVersion;
14: }
15:
16: [StructLayout(LayoutKind.Sequential, CharSet=CharSet.Auto)]
17: public struct OSVERSIONINFO_2
18: {
19:    internal int dwOSVersionInfoSize;
20:    internal int dwMajorVersion;
21:    internal int dwMinorVersion;
22:    internal int dwBuildNumber;
23:    internal int dwPlatformId;
24:    [MarshalAs(UnmanagedType.ByValArray, SizeConst=128)]
25:    internal char [] szCSDVersion;
26: }
27:
28: class GetWindowsVersion
29: {
30:    [DllImport("kernel32.dll", CharSet=CharSet.Auto)]
31:    static extern bool GetVersionEx(ref OSVERSIONINFO_1 lpVersionInfo);
32:
33:    [DllImport("kernel32.dll", CharSet=CharSet.Auto)]
34:    static extern bool GetVersionEx(ref OSVERSIONINFO_2 lpVersionInfo);
35:
36:    public static void Main()
37:    {
38:      OSVERSIONINFO_1 os1 = new OSVERSIONINFO_1();
39:      os1.dwOSVersionInfoSize = Marshal.SizeOf(os1);
40:      os1.szCSDVersion = new String(' ', 128);
41:
42:      if (GetVersionEx(ref os1))
43:      {
```

LISTING 19.5 Continued

```
44:        Console.WriteLine("String returned: '" + os1.szCSDVersion + "'");
45:      }
46:
47:      OSVERSIONINFO_2 os2 = new OSVERSIONINFO_2();
48:      os2.dwOSVersionInfoSize = Marshal.SizeOf(os2);
49:      os2.szCSDVersion = new char[128];
50:
51:      if (GetVersionEx(ref os2))
52:      {
53:        string desiredString = new String(os2.szCSDVersion).Trim('\0');
54:        Console.WriteLine("String returned: '" + desiredString + "'");
55:      }
56:    }
57:  }
```

Lines 4–14 define one version of the OSVERSIONINFO structure, which uses a string marked with UnmanagedType.ByValTStr to represent the buffer. To truly make it a TSTR buffer, the structure is marked with CharSet.Auto. (That's the only reason that StructLayoutAttribute is used because LayoutKind.Sequential is the default for C# structs.) To differentiate between the two OSVERSIONINFO types we're defining, we name this OSVERSIONINFO_1. The name has no effect on the proper operation with unmanaged code; all that matters is the memory layout. Both GetVersionEx methods are marked with CharSet.Auto to match the marking on the structures. A mismatch in the character set between function and structs passed to it can cause errors.

Lines 16–26 define an OSVERSIONINFO_2 structure that's identical to OSVERSIONINFO_1 except that a character array marked with UnmanagedType.ByValArray is used to represent the character buffer. Lines 30–34 define GetVersionEx twice as overloaded methods, with each one accepting a different value type parameter. After the OSVERSIONINFO_1 instance is created in Line 38, Line 39 sets its dwOSVersionInfoSize field to the size of the structure using Marshal.SizeOf. The documentation for GetVersionEx states that this should be done before calling the method, and is typical for Win32 APIs.

19

DEEPER INTO
PINVOKE AND
USEFUL EXAMPLES

TIP

Use Marshal.SizeOf in the System.Runtime.InteropServices namespace to determine the unmanaged size of a struct. This may be different than its managed size due to the marshaling of non-blittable fields, but it's precisely the size required by the unmanaged function. A struct's size often needs to be passed as a parameter to Win32 APIs.

Because value types can contain methods, the call to Marshal.SizeOf can be wrapped inside a simple method, as follows:

```
[StructLayout(LayoutKind.Sequential, CharSet=CharSet.Auto)]
internal struct OSVERSIONINFO
{
  internal void Init()
  {
    dwOSVersionInfoSize = Marshal.SizeOf(this);
  }
  internal int dwOSVersionInfoSize;
  internal int dwMajorVersion;
  internal int dwMinorVersion;
  internal int dwBuildNumber;
  internal int dwPlatformId;
  [MarshalAs(UnmanagedType.ByValTStr, SizeConst=128)]
  internal string szCSDVersion;
}
```

Because the OSVERSIONINFO_1.szCSDVersion string is being used as if it's a character buffer, it must be initialized to the appropriate number of characters (128). This is done in Line 40 with one of System.String's constructors. Remember that only 127 characters are usable due to the trailing null character used by the Interop Marshaler, but in this example we expect the string returned to be much shorter. Line 42 makes the call to GetVersionEx and Line 44 prints the string after the call.

The code in Lines 38–45 is duplicated in Lines 47–55 but uses OSVERSIONINFO_2 instead. Line 49 creates an array of 128 null characters, and Line 51 calls the GetVersionEx overload that works with the OSVERSIONINFO_2 structure. To extract the string after the call, Line 53 uses a System.String constructor that creates a string with the contents of a character array. String.Trim must be called on the new string to trim all the trailing null characters.

GetVersionEx places text in the szCSDVersion buffer only when a Windows service pack is installed. It returns a string such as "Service Pack 1." If you run this listing on a computer without a service pack, you'll see an empty string returned from both method calls.

Although defining a by-value `System.String` type to represent a character buffer can be done successfully for struct fields, it should *never* be done for a parameter (with the exception of signatures defined in VB .NET, due to the implicit transformation done with `UnmanagedType.VBByRefStr`). Defining such parameters can provide random results caused by string interning or strings being allocated in read-only memory. .NET strings are immutable and the CLR takes advantage of this fact, so you should never use the power of unmanaged code to overwrite a string's memory.

TIP

Calling `Marshal.SizeOf` is a quick way to see if a value type you defined has an unmarshalable definition. For example, attempting to call it with a struct that has a `StringBuilder` field or a struct that uses `ByValArray` without setting the corresponding `SizeConst` value causes an `ArgumentException` with the message, "Type *TypeName* can not be marshaled as an unmanaged structure; no meaningful size or offset can be computed."

Using Formatted Classes

`StructLayoutAttribute` can be marked on a class with `LayoutKind.Sequential` or `LayoutKind.Explicit` to enable marshaling to unmanaged code as a struct rather than a reference type. Using `OSVERSIONINFO` as an example, it could be defined as follows in C#:

```
[StructLayout(LayoutKind.Sequential, CharSet=CharSet.Auto)]
internal class OSVERSIONINFO
{
  internal int dwOSVersionInfoSize;
  internal int dwMajorVersion;
  internal int dwMinorVersion;
  internal int dwBuildNumber;
  internal int dwPlatformId;
  [MarshalAs(UnmanagedType.ByValTStr, SizeConst=128)]
  internal string szCSDVersion;
}
```

Or, in Visual Basic .NET:

```
<StructLayout(LayoutKind.Sequential, CharSet:=CharSet.Auto)> _
Friend Class OSVERSIONINFO
  Friend dwOSVersionInfoSize As Integer
  Friend dwMajorVersion As Integer
  Friend dwMinorVersion As Integer
  Friend dwBuildNumber As Integer
  Friend dwPlatformId As Integer
  <MarshalAs(UnmanagedType.ByValTStr, SizeConst:=128)> _
  Friend szCSDVersion As String
End Class
```

TIP

When defining a structure as a formatted class, you can define a default constructor to initialize its size field. For example, OSVERSIONINFO could be defined as follows:

```
[StructLayout(LayoutKind.Sequential, CharSet=CharSet.Auto)]
internal struct OSVERSIONINFO
{
  internal OSVERSIONINFO()
  {
    dwOSVersionInfoSize = Marshal.SizeOf(this);
  }
  internal int dwOSVersionInfoSize;
  internal int dwMajorVersion;
  internal int dwMinorVersion;
  internal int dwBuildNumber;
  internal int dwPlatformId;
  [MarshalAs(UnmanagedType.ByValTStr, SizeConst=128)]
  internal string szCSDVersion;
}
```

This is similar to the OSVERSIONINFO value type's Init method from the previous section, but the client doesn't need to remember to call it. Defining a separate method was done simply because value types cannot be defined with explicit default constructors.

The marshaling rules are the same as with a value type marshaled as a structure. Any methods, properties, or events are ignored by the Interop Marshaler; the instance fields (regardless of visibility) comprise the structure. The single difference between marshaling a value type as an unmanaged structure and marshaling a reference type as an unmanaged structure is that reference types have an implicit level of indirection that value types do not have. Table 19.1 summarizes how marshaling a type called MyStruct differs depending on whether it is defined as a value type or formatted reference type.

TABLE 19.1   Differing Levels of Indirection with Value Types Versus Formatted Classes

Unmanaged Parameter	MyStruct as Value Type	MyStruct as Reference Type
MyStruct	by-value MyStruct	not possible
MyStruct*	by-reference MyStruct	by-value MyStruct
MyStruct**	IntPtr or C# unsafe code	by-reference MyStruct

A formatted reference type passed by value should typically be marked with `InAttribute` and `OutAttribute` to ensure that data is copied back and forth.

Listing 19.6 is an update to Listing 19.5, using formatted classes instead of reference types. Notice that the PInvoke signatures pass the `OSVERSIONINFO_1` and `OSVERSIONINFO_2` instances by-value instead of by-reference. It's crucial that these by-value parameters are marked as `InAttribute` and `OutAttribute` because reference types other than `StringBuilder` marshal as in-only parameters by default. This in-only behavior would not be noticed had the `OSVERSIONINFO_1` and `OSVERSIONINFO_2` types only had integer fields, but the string and character array fields make them non-blittable, forcing the copy to occur.

LISTING 19.6   Using Formatted Classes To Represent Pointers to Structures

```
 1: using System;
 2: using System.Runtime.InteropServices;
 3:
 4: [StructLayout(LayoutKind.Sequential, CharSet=CharSet.Auto)]
 5: internal class OSVERSIONINFO_1
 6: {
 7:   internal int dwOSVersionInfoSize;
 8:   internal int dwMajorVersion;
 9:   internal int dwMinorVersion;
10:   internal int dwBuildNumber;
11:   internal int dwPlatformId;
12:   [MarshalAs(UnmanagedType.ByValTStr, SizeConst=128)]
13:   internal string szCSDVersion;
14: }
15:
16: [StructLayout(LayoutKind.Sequential, CharSet=CharSet.Auto)]
17: public class OSVERSIONINFO_2
18: {
19:   internal int dwOSVersionInfoSize;
20:   internal int dwMajorVersion;
21:   internal int dwMinorVersion;
22:   internal int dwBuildNumber;
23:   internal int dwPlatformId;
```

19

DEEPER INTO PINVOKE AND USEFUL EXAMPLES

LISTING 19.6   Continued

```
24:   [MarshalAs(UnmanagedType.ByValArray, SizeConst=128)]
25:   internal char [] szCSDVersion;
26: }
27:
28: class GetWindowsVersion
29: {
30:   [DllImport("kernel32.dll", CharSet=CharSet.Auto)]
31:   static extern bool GetVersionEx([In, Out] OSVERSIONINFO_1 lpVersionInfo);
32:
33:   [DllImport("kernel32.dll", CharSet=CharSet.Auto)]
34:   static extern bool GetVersionEx([In, Out] OSVERSIONINFO_2 lpVersionInfo);
35:
36:   public static void Main()
37:   {
38:     OSVERSIONINFO_1 os1 = new OSVERSIONINFO_1();
39:     os1.dwOSVersionInfoSize = Marshal.SizeOf(os1);
40:     os1.szCSDVersion = new String(' ', 128);
41:
42:     if (GetVersionEx(os1))
43:     {
44:       Console.WriteLine("String returned: '" + os1.szCSDVersion + "'");
45:     }
46:
47:     OSVERSIONINFO_2 os2 = new OSVERSIONINFO_2();
48:     os2.dwOSVersionInfoSize = Marshal.SizeOf(os2);
49:     os2.szCSDVersion = new char[128];
50:
51:     if (GetVersionEx(os2))
52:     {
53:       string desiredString = new String(os2.szCSDVersion).Trim('\0');
54:       Console.WriteLine("String returned: '" + desiredString + "'");
55:     }
56:   }
57: }
```

The main advantage of using formatted classes is that they give you the ability to pass null for what would otherwise be a by-reference value type parameter. You could even use a formatted class in place of a by-reference primitive type that could be null. For example, the GetWindowThreadProcessId function in USER32.DLL has the following unmanaged signature:

```
DWORD GetWindowThreadProcessId(HWND hWnd, LPDWORD lpdwProcessId);
```

This function returns the thread identifier for the thread that created the specified window, but also returns the window's process identifier if a valid pointer is passed as the second parameter. A caller can pass null for the second parameter if it doesn't care about the process identifier.

If we wanted to define a PInvoke signature such that a managed client could either pass a valid reference or null, we'd likely define the signature as either:

```
[DllImport("user32.dll")]
static extern uint GetWindowThreadProcessId(IntPtr hWnd, IntPtr lpdwProcessId);
```

or:

```
[DllImport("user32.dll")]
static extern uint GetWindowThreadProcessId(IntPtr hWnd, int [] lpdwProcessId);
```

This technique was discussed in Chapter 6, "Advanced Topics for Using COM Components." The first technique is the most typical, and used throughout Appendix E, "PInvoke Definitions for Win32 Functions." A third option would be to define a formatted class like the following:

```
[StructLayout(LayoutKind.Sequential)]
class RefInt32
{
  public int Value;
}
```

Then you could define the signature for `GetWindowThreadProcessId` as follows:

```
[DllImport("user32.dll")]
static extern uint GetWindowThreadProcessId(
  IntPtr hWnd, [In, Out] RefInt32 lpdwProcessId);
```

Using such a signature, you could pass null when you don't want to pass a valid instance. The `InAttribute` and `OutAttribute` markings aren't strictly necessary because the type is blittable and the Interop Marshaler doesn't copy the instance during the call. It's a good idea to include these attributes anyway, because the lack of copying for blittable types is really just an implementation detail of the Interop Marshaler.

Another option would be to define two overloads of the same PInvoke method—one that enables passing null as `IntPtr.Zero` and one that expects a valid instance:

```
// Call with IntPtr.Zero to pass null
[DllImport("user32.dll")]
static extern uint GetWindowThreadProcessId(IntPtr hWnd, IntPtr lpdwProcessId);

// Call with a valid integer value
[DllImport("user32.dll")]
static extern uint GetWindowThreadProcessId(
  IntPtr hWnd, ref int lpdwProcessId);
```

It's not always possible to use formatted classes with PInvoke, however. For example, consider the `localtime` API from `MSVCRT.DLL`:

```
tm* localtime(const time_t* timer);
```

The `tm` type is a struct that could be defined in C# as follows:

```
public struct tm
{
  public int tm_sec;   // seconds after the minute
  public int tm_min;   // minutes after the hour
  public int tm_hour;  // hours since midnight
  public int tm_mday;  // day of the month
  public int tm_mon;   // months since January
  public int tm_year;  // years since 1900
  public int tm_wday;  // days since Sunday
  public int tm_yday;  // days since January 1
  public int tm_isdst; // daylight savings time flag
}
```

Because the `localtime` function returns a *pointer* to a struct, and because you can't add a level of indirection to a managed return type, the PInvoke signature for `localtime` must be defined as follows:

```
[DllImport("msvcrt.dll")]
static extern IntPtr localtime(ref int timer);
```

To avoid using `IntPtr`, you might be tempted to define `tm` as a formatted class so you can simply return a `tm` instance from `localtime`. This does not work, however. The reason is that when a pointer to a struct is returned, the Interop Marshaler copies the data to the managed object then frees the unmanaged struct using the `CoTaskMemFree` API. But according to `localtime`'s documentation, it returns a pointer to a statically allocated `tm` structure that should *not* be freed by the user. Therefore, attempting to define and use `tm` as a formatted class causes heap corruption.

> **Tip**
>
> Whenever an unmanaged API allocates memory that it doesn't want the user to free using `CoTaskMemFree`, either the `IntPtr` type or C# unsafe code must be used.

The Structure Inspector

When defining a value type or formatted class to be marshaled as an unmanaged structure, it's often handy to view the type's unmanaged memory representation. By doing so, you can ensure that all the fields reside where they should be and that they contain the data you expect.

> **CAUTION**
>
> Structures are not deep-marshaled by the Interop Marshaler, so fields of formatted classes, by-reference arrays, or pointers to structures are not supported. Instead, such fields must be defined as `IntPtr` for do-it-yourself marshaling. In addition, structure fields that are by-value arrays of other structures are not supported in version 1.0 of the .NET Framework.

Listing 19.7 defines a C# class with a single static method that can be used to print out the unmanaged memory representation of any value type or formatted class. By using methods of the `System.Runtime.InteropServices.Marshal` class (most notably, `StructureToPtr`), it prints out the structure's contents in the following format:

```
Total Bytes = 16
01 00 00 00    _...
01 00 44 00    _.D.
01 00 64 00    _.d.
64 00 00 00    d...
```

After printing the total number of bytes in the marshaled unmanaged structure, it displays the hexadecimal values on the left and each byte's character representation on the right. This class can be used as a simple debugging aid, without having to write unmanaged code in order to inspect the contents and layout of a struct after marshaling occurs.

LISTING 19.7 `MarshaledStructInspector.DisplayStruct` Can Display the Unmanaged Memory Representation of Any Value Type or Formatted Class

```
 1: using System;
 2: using System.Runtime.InteropServices;
 3:
 4: public class MarshaledStructInspector
 5: {
 6:   public static void DisplayStruct(object o)
 7:   {
 8:     int totalBytes = Marshal.SizeOf(o);
 9:     Console.WriteLine("Total Bytes = " + totalBytes);
10:
11:     IntPtr ptr = IntPtr.Zero;
12:     try
13:     {
14:       // Allocate unmanaged memory
15:       ptr = Marshal.AllocCoTaskMem(totalBytes);
16:       // Marshal the type to its unmanaged representation
```

LISTING 19.7   Continued

```
17:        Marshal.StructureToPtr(o, ptr, false);
18:
19:        byte [] bytes = new byte[4];
20:
21:        for (int i = 0; i < totalBytes; i += 4)
22:        {
23:          // Print each byte in hexadecimal format
24:          for (int j = 0; j < 4; j++)
25:          {
26:            if (i + j < totalBytes)
27:            {
28:              bytes[j] = Marshal.ReadByte(ptr, i+j);
29:              Console.Write("{0:X2} ", bytes[j]);
30:            }
31:            else
32:            {
33:              Console.Write("   ");
34:            }
35:          }
36:          Console.Write("  ");
37:
38:          // Print each byte as if it's a character
39:          for (int j = 0; j < 4 && i + j < totalBytes; j++)
40:          {
41:            if (bytes[j] == 0)
42:              Console.Write(".");
43:            else
44:              Console.Write(Convert.ToChar(bytes[j]));
45:          }
46:          Console.WriteLine("");
47:        }
48:      }
49:      finally
50:      {
51:        // Free the unmanaged memory
52:        if (ptr != IntPtr.Zero) Marshal.FreeCoTaskMem(ptr);
53:      }
54:    }
55: }
```

> **TIP**
>
> A great way to debug any PInvoke failure is to define your own method in unmanaged C++ code with the same signature as the one you're trying to call. Then temporarily switch your managed code to call your custom function instead, and inspect exactly how all data is presented to the unmanaged function.

Handling Variable-Length Structures and Signatures

Signatures used with PInvoke are static in nature. Any information in custom attributes, the parameters used in methods, and the fields used in structures, must be determined at compile time. Sometimes, however, unmanaged functions are dynamic in nature and require a variable number of parameters or variable-length structures. Fortunately, there are ways to achieve this behavior with PInvoke.

A Win32 security identifier (SID) is one example of a variable-length structure that must sometimes be passed to unmanaged functions. It is defined as follows in `winnt.h`:

```
typedef struct _SID {
  BYTE Revision;
  BYTE SubAuthorityCount;
  SID_IDENTIFIER_AUTHORITY IdentifierAuthority;
  [size_is(SubAuthorityCount)] DWORD SubAuthority[*];
} SID, *PISID;
```

The array field is problematic because there is no way to express such an array in a .NET structure. `MarshalAsAttribute`'s `SizeParamIndex` named parameter only works for *parameters*, not fields.

Listing 19.8 demonstrates one way to handle this variable-length structure when defining `ConvertStringSidToSid`, which is defined as follows in `sddl.h`:

```
BOOL ConvertStringSidToSid(LPCTSTR StringSid, PSID *Sid);
```

LISTING 19.8   Handling Variable-Length Structures Using Multiple Definitions

```
1: using System;
2: using System.Runtime.InteropServices;
3:
4: internal struct SID1
5: {
```

LISTING 19.8 Continued

```
 6:    internal byte Revision;
 7:    internal byte SubAuthorityCount;
 8:    [MarshalAs(UnmanagedType.ByValArray, SizeConst=6)]
 9:    internal byte [] Value;
10:    [MarshalAs(UnmanagedType.ByValArray, SizeConst=1)]
11:    internal uint [] SubAuthority;
12: }
13:
14: internal struct SID16
15: {
16:    internal byte Revision;
17:    internal byte SubAuthorityCount;
18:    [MarshalAs(UnmanagedType.ByValArray, SizeConst=6)]
19:    internal byte [] Value;
20:    [MarshalAs(UnmanagedType.ByValArray, SizeConst=16)]
21:    internal uint [] SubAuthority;
22: }
23:
24: internal struct SID256
25: {
26:    internal byte Revision;
27:    internal byte SubAuthorityCount;
28:    [MarshalAs(UnmanagedType.ByValArray, SizeConst=6)]
29:    internal byte [] Value;
30:    [MarshalAs(UnmanagedType.ByValArray, SizeConst=256)]
31:    internal uint [] SubAuthority;
32: }
33:
34: public class UsingVariableStructs
35: {
36:    [DllImport("advapi32.dll", CharSet=CharSet.Auto)]
37:    static extern bool ConvertStringSidToSid(string StringSid,
38:      out IntPtr Sid);
39:
40:    ...
41: }
```

In this listing, the SID structure is defined three times—as SID1, SID16, SID256, depending on the length chosen for the SubAuthority array. (The Value field is also defined as an array because SID_IDENTIFIER_AUTHORITY is simply a six-element byte array.) Because ConvertStringSidToSid defines its SID parameter as IntPtr, the caller of the method can choose which version of the SID structure to use to ensure that it has enough elements in the array. Before the call, Marshal.StructureToPtr can be used to convert either SID1, SID16, or SID256 to an IntPtr. After the call, Marshal.PtrToStructure can be used to convert it back.

It turns out that defining the SID parameter as IntPtr is a requirement anyway (even if the structure were a fixed size) because it represents a pointer to a pointer to a SID structure that must be freed with the LocalFree API.

> **TIP**
>
> If you don't want to define multiple copies of a structure to simulate a variable-sized array, you could define a pointer-to-structure parameter as a byte array instead. Then, the .NET caller could dynamically allocate an array of the exact size desired, fill its elements appropriately with the structure's raw data, and pass it to unmanaged code. As long as the unmanaged function sees the expected memory contents, it doesn't matter how you represent it on the .NET side.

That covers variable-sized structures, but what about methods that accept a variable number of arguments? You can define several overloaded methods that cover all possible ways in which you want to call the method. Using wsprintf from USER32.DLL as an example, you could define four overloads as follows:

```
[DllImport("user32.dll", CallingConvention=CallingConvention.Cdecl)]
static extern int wsprintf([Out] StringBuilder lpOut, string lpFmt);

[DllImport("user32.dll", CallingConvention=CallingConvention.Cdecl)]
static extern int wsprintf([Out] StringBuilder lpOut, string lpFmt, object o1);

[DllImport("user32.dll", CallingConvention=CallingConvention.Cdecl)]
static extern int wsprintf([Out] StringBuilder lpOut, string lpFmt, object o1,
  object o2);

[DllImport("user32.dll", CallingConvention=CallingConvention.Cdecl)]
static extern int wsprintf([Out] StringBuilder lpOut, string lpFmt, object o1,
  object o2, object o3);
```

With these four signatures, a user could call wsprintf with two, three, four, or five parameters. Make sure that the calling convention for any such methods is set to CallingConvention. Cdecl, because the caller must pop off the appropriate number of parameters in every case.

Using C# Unsafe Code

Using C# unsafe code, introduced in Chapter 6, in combination with PInvoke enables you to avoid complex Interop Marshaling while, at the same time, using data types more descriptive than IntPtr. Although avoiding complicated marshaling can improve performance, a big benefit of using C#

unsafe code in PInvoke signatures is that you don't have to figure out the rules of the Interop Marshaler when defining methods! Instead, the PInvoke signature can be a direct translation of the unmanaged signature (once you figure out what any C++ typedefs used as parameters really represent).

To demonstrate this technique, let's look at the GetPrivateProfileSectionNames API used in the previous chapter. The unmanaged signature looks like the following:

```
DWORD GetPrivateProfileSectionNames(LPTSTR lpszReturnBuffer, DWORD nSize,
  LPCTSTR lpFileName);
```

When we defined a PInvoke signature for this function in the previous chapter, we needed to understand how both string parameters are used to determine whether to define them as String, StringBuilder, or IntPtr types. If we use C# unsafe code instead, the unmanaged signature gives us all the information we need to define it in C#. We could define it as:

```
[DllImport("kernel32.dll")]
static unsafe extern int GetPrivateProfileSectionNamesA(
  sbyte* lpszReturnBuffer, int nSize, sbyte* lpFileName);
```

or:

```
[DllImport("kernel32.dll")]
static unsafe extern int GetPrivateProfileSectionNamesW(
  char* lpszReturnBuffer, int nSize, char* lpFileName);
```

With these signatures, the Interop Marshaler simply passes the pointer values for the first and third parameters, so any additional work is left for the users of these methods. No InAttribute, OutAttribute, or MarshalAsAttribute needs to be (or can be) applied to pointer parameters because the Interop Marshaler effectively treats them as by-value IntPtr parameters. Notice that we must choose either the ANSI or Unicode version of GetPrivateProfileSectionNames because the Interop Marshaler can only transform the character set of string parameters when they are defined as String or StringBuilder. In the ANSI version, sbyte is used to represent a one-byte character, and in the Unicode version, char is used to represent a two-byte Unicode character.

Caution

Although using C# unsafe code when defining a PInvoke method can look like a direct translation, don't forget about differences between ANSI and Unicode. In C++, char* represents an ANSI string, but in C#, char* represents an unsafe Unicode string!

C# unsafe code makes it easy to *define* PInvoke methods without understanding their semantics, but *calling* them still requires such understanding, of course! In addition, callers of PInvoke signatures with unsafe data types have the burden of doing work that would ordinarily be done by the Interop Marshaler. However, this technique gives developers full control. It also opens the possibility of writing an application that can automatically produce correct PInvoke signatures by simply scanning unmanaged signatures (in a header file, for example). That's because, unlike the case when you're relying on Interop marshaling for non-blittable types, each unmanaged data type can be mechanically transformed into a compatible managed data type with no exceptions. Remember that C# unsafe code inherently is no more unsafe than using standard PInvoke; it's just a convention enforced by the C# compiler because it's easy for programmers to make mistakes when directly manipulating pointers.

Listing 19.9 updates Listing 18.6 from the previous chapter, using C# unsafe code instead.

LISTING 19.9   Using C# Unsafe Code with PInvoke

```
 1: using System;
 2: using System.Runtime.InteropServices;
 3:
 4: public unsafe class UsingUnsafeCode
 5: {
 6:   [DllImport("kernel32.dll")]
 7:   static extern int GetPrivateProfileSectionNamesW(char* lpszReturnBuffer,
 8:     int nSize, char* lpFileName);
 9:
10:   public static void Main()
11:   {
12:     char* ptr = null;
13:     int numChars = 0;
14:     string s;
15:
16:     try
17:     {
18:       // Allocate a buffer in unmanaged memory
19:       ptr = (char*)Marshal.AllocHGlobal(1024);
20:
21:       fixed (char* iniFile = "c:\\sample.ini")
22:       {
23:         numChars = GetPrivateProfileSectionNamesW(ptr, 1024, iniFile);
24:       }
25:       // Convert the relevant part of the unmanaged buffer to a string
26:       s = new String(ptr, 0, numChars-1);
27:     }
28:     finally
```

LISTING 19.9 Continued

```
29:    {
30:      // Free the original unmanaged buffer
31:      if (ptr != null) Marshal.FreeHGlobal((IntPtr)ptr);
32:    }
33:
34:    // Split the string into an array of strings,
35:    // using null as the delimiter
36:    string [] sections = s.Split('\0');
37:
38:    foreach (string section in sections)
39:    {
40:      Console.WriteLine("Section: " + section);
41:    }
42:  }
43: }
```

Lines 6–8 define the unsafe Unicode version of GetPrivateProfileSectionNames. The ptr variable declared in Line 12 is treated like it was in Listing 18.6, except that it's given the more specific char* type rather than IntPtr. The main difference between this listing and Listing 18.6 is in Line 21. Because the third parameter of GetPrivateProfileSectionNames is defined as char*, Line 21 pins a string and assigns it to a char* variable using C#'s fixed statement.

Because the first string parameter was allocated in unmanaged memory (Line 19), Line 26 creates a new .NET string with its contents (embedded nulls included) using an overloaded String constructor that accepts a char* parameter. Alternatively, Line 26 could have been the following to achieve the same result:

```
s = Marshal.PtrToStringUni((IntPtr)ptr, numChars-1);
```

Guarding Against Premature Garbage Collection

Great care is required when using PInvoke to ensure that garbage collection doesn't interfere with the proper operation of your application. As described in the "Using Delegates as Function Pointers" section, unmanaged code is invisible to the .NET garbage collector, so it has no way to know when entities such as delegates might still be in use by unmanaged clients. Once a delegate is not being referenced by any managed code, it can be collected at any time.

Premature garbage collection mostly affects PInvoke rather than COM Interoperability because the CLR can take advantage of the standard reference counting used by COM components to manage object lifetime. When passing a .NET object to unmanaged code, the CLR increments its CCW reference count and ensures that it does not get collected until this reference count reaches zero (resulting from IUnknown.Release calls from unmanaged clients).

When passing a delegate to unmanaged code as a function pointer, however, the CLR does not keep it alive by default because there's no standard way for unmanaged code to notify the CLR that it's finished with the pointer. The CLR would have to keep delegates alive forever once they are passed to unmanaged code, and this is clearly not acceptable. Therefore, programmers must take explicit action to guard against premature collection when passing entities other than regular objects across the Interop boundary. (Using COM Interoperability often has the opposite problem of keeping objects alive too long!)

Premature garbage collection can affect more than just delegates, however. Using .NET classes that wrap Windows handles can suffer from the same problem, although in a more subtle way. Handles are another example of a communication mechanism that does not use reference counting on the objects they represent. Listing 19.10 demonstrates the problem by defining three classes:

- RegistryKey—A class that wraps an HKEY (a handle to a registry key)
- RegistryKeyEnumerator—A class that uses RegistryKey and enumerates subkeys for any registry key
- Client—A class that uses RegistryKeyEnumerator

See if you can identify the problem in this listing. The RegistryKey and related classes are just meant to demonstrate how premature garbage collection problems can manifest; if you were really interacting with the Windows Registry, you would use the Microsoft.Win32. RegistryKey class in the mscorlib assembly. This listing uses the ErrorHelper. GetErrorMessage function we defined in the previous chapter, so it should be compiled with ErrorHelper.cs from Listing 18.9.

LISTING 19.10   A Demonstration of Incorrect Windows Handle Wrapping

```
 1: using System;
 2: using System.Text;
 3: using System.Collections;
 4: using System.Runtime.InteropServices;
 5:
 6: public class RegistryKey
 7: {
 8:   IntPtr hKey;
 9:
10:   [DllImport("advapi32.dll", CharSet=CharSet.Auto)]
11:   static extern int RegOpenKey(IntPtr hKey, string lpSubKey,
12:     out IntPtr phkResult);
13:
14:   [DllImport("advapi32.dll")]
15:   static extern int RegCloseKey(IntPtr hKey);
```

LISTING 19.10   Continued

```
16:
17:    // Constructor
18:    public RegistryKey(IntPtr rootKey, string subKey)
19:    {
20:      // Open the key
21:      int result = RegOpenKey(rootKey, subKey, out hKey);
22:      if (result != 0)
23:        throw new ApplicationException("Could not open registry key: " +
24:          ErrorHelper.GetErrorMessage(result));
25:    }
26:
27:    // Read-only property
28:    public IntPtr Handle
29:    {
30:      get { return hKey; }
31:    }
32:
33:    // Finalizer
34:    ~RegistryKey()
35:    {
36:      // Close the key
37:      RegCloseKey(hKey);
38:    }
39: }
40:
41: public class RegistryKeyEnumerator : IEnumerator
42: {
43:    const int ERROR_NO_MORE_ITEMS = 259;
44:
45:    IntPtr hKey;
46:    int currentSubKeyIndex;
47:    StringBuilder currentSubKeyText;
48:
49:    [DllImport("advapi32.dll", CharSet=CharSet.Auto)]
50:    static extern int RegEnumKey(IntPtr hKey, int dwIndex,
51:      [Out] StringBuilder lpName, int cchName);
52:
53:    // Create a new enumerator based on the passed-in information
54:    public RegistryKeyEnumerator(IntPtr hKeyRoot, string subKey)
55:    {
56:      RegistryKey key = new RegistryKey(hKeyRoot, subKey);
57:      hKey = key.Handle;
58:      currentSubKeyText = new StringBuilder(256);
59:      Reset();
```

LISTING 19.10 Continued

```
60:    }
61:
62:    public void Reset()
63:    {
64:      currentSubKeyIndex = -1;
65:    }
66:
67:    public bool MoveNext()
68:    {
69:      currentSubKeyIndex++;
70:      int result = RegEnumKey(hKey, currentSubKeyIndex, currentSubKeyText,
71:        currentSubKeyText.Capacity);
72:      if (result == 0)
73:        return true;
74:      else if (result == ERROR_NO_MORE_ITEMS)
75:        return false;
76:      else
77:        throw new ApplicationException(ErrorHelper.GetErrorMessage(result));
78:    }
79:
80:    public object Current
81:    {
82:      get { return currentSubKeyText.ToString(); }
83:    }
84: }
85:
86: public class Client
87: {
88:    static readonly IntPtr HKEY_LOCAL_MACHINE =
89:      new IntPtr(unchecked((int)0x80000002));
90:
91:    public static void Main()
92:    {
93:      RegistryKeyEnumerator enumerator =
94:        new RegistryKeyEnumerator(HKEY_LOCAL_MACHINE, "SOFTWARE");
95:
96:      // Force a garbage collection for demonstration
97:      GC.Collect();
98:      GC.WaitForPendingFinalizers();
99:
100:     enumerator.Reset();
101:     while (enumerator.MoveNext())
102:       Console.WriteLine(enumerator.Current);
103:   }
104: }
```

The RegistryKey class, defined in Lines 6–39, contains a constructor that opens a registry key using the RegOpenKey API. It also contains a property that exposes the wrapped HKEY finalizer that closes the registry key using the RegCloseKey API.

The RegistryKeyEnumerator class, defined in Lines 41–84, is a simple enumerator that uses the RegEnumKey API to provide its data. Rather than defining and using RegOpenKey and RegCloseKey APIs to open and close a registry key directly, Line 56 creates a RegistryKey instance. For the HKEY that it needs to pass to RegEnumKey (represented as IntPtr), it extracts the value from the RegistryKey.Handle property in Line 57.

Finally, the Client class, in Lines 86–104, uses the RegistryKeyEnumerator class, and forces garbage collection and finalization of collected objects in Lines 97–98. This is done in order to make the program consistently fail. Without this determinism, failure could occur at seemingly random times depending on when and if garbage collection ever occurs before the program logic finishes.

So what's the problem with this listing? Calling RegistryKeyEnumerator.MoveNext in Line 101 causes an ApplicationException with the message "The handle is invalid." This exception is thrown in Line 77. That's because the RegistryKey instance created in Line 56 is eligible for collection immediately after Line 57. At this point, there are no more references to the RegistryKey object, only to its handle. From the garbage collector's perspective, there is no relationship between the value returned by the RegistryKey.Handle property. Therefore, when garbage collection occurs in Line 97, the RegistryKey instance is collected and finalized. The RegistryKey finalizer, defined in Lines 34–38, closes the registry key and therefore makes the handle stored in RegistryKeyEnumerator's hKey field invalid before its enumeration functionality is used in Lines 100–102. The call to Reset in Line 100 isn't affected because its implementation does a simple variable assignment, but the call to MoveNext causes the error as soon as it calls into unmanaged code. The RegEnumKey method detects that the handle no longer corresponds to an open registry key and returns an error code, which causes the exception to be thrown in Line 77.

To ensure that the RegistryKey instance is never collected until the program finishes using RegistryKeyEnumerator, a few simple modifications could be made. These are shown in Listing 19.11.

LISTING 19.11 An Update to Listing 19.10 That Prevents Premature Garbage Collection

```
1: using System;
2: using System.Text;
3: using System.Collections;
4: using System.Runtime.InteropServices;
5:
```

LISTING 19.11 Continued

```
 6: public class RegistryKey : IDisposable
 7: {
 8:   IntPtr hKey;
 9:
10:   [DllImport("advapi32.dll", CharSet=CharSet.Auto)]
11:   static extern int RegOpenKey(IntPtr hKey, string lpSubKey,
12:     out IntPtr phkResult);
13:
14:   [DllImport("advapi32.dll")]
15:   static extern int RegCloseKey(IntPtr hKey);
16:
17:   // Constructor
18:   public RegistryKey(IntPtr rootKey, string subKey)
19:   {
20:     // Open the key
21:     int result = RegOpenKey(rootKey, subKey, out hKey);
22:     if (result != 0)
23:       throw new ApplicationException("Could not open registry key: " +
24:         ErrorHelper.GetErrorMessage(result));
25:   }
26:
27:   // Read-only property
28:   public IntPtr Handle
29:   {
30:     get { return hKey; }
31:   }
32:
33:   // Finalizer
34:   ~RegistryKey()
35:   {
36:     // Close the key
37:     RegCloseKey(hKey);
38:   }
39:
40:   public void Dispose()
41:   {
42:     // Close the key
43:     RegCloseKey(hKey);
44:     GC.SuppressFinalize(this);
45:   }
46: }
47:
48: public class RegistryKeyEnumerator : IEnumerator, IDisposable
49: {
```

19

**DEEPER INTO
PINVOKE AND
USEFUL EXAMPLES**

LISTING 19.11   Continued

```
50:    const int ERROR_NO_MORE_ITEMS = 259;
51:
52:    IntPtr hKey;
53:    int currentSubKeyIndex;
54:    StringBuilder currentSubKeyText;
55:    RegistryKey key;
56:
57:    [DllImport("advapi32.dll", CharSet=CharSet.Auto)]
58:    static extern int RegEnumKey(IntPtr hKey, int dwIndex,
59:      [Out] StringBuilder lpName, int cchName);
60:
61:    // Finalizer
62:    ~RegistryKeyEnumerator()
63:    {
64:      if (key != null) key.Dispose();
65:    }
66:
67:    public void Dispose()
68:    {
69:      if (key != null) key.Dispose();
70:      GC.SuppressFinalize(this);
71:    }
72:
73:    // Create a new enumerator based on the passed-in information
74:    public RegistryKeyEnumerator(IntPtr hKeyRoot, string subKey)
75:    {
76:      key = new RegistryKey(hKeyRoot, subKey);
77:      hKey = key.Handle;
78:      currentSubKeyText = new StringBuilder(256);
79:      Reset();
80:    }
81:
82:    public void Reset()
83:    {
84:      currentSubKeyIndex = -1;
85:    }
86:
87:    public bool MoveNext()
88:    {
89:      currentSubKeyIndex++;
90:      int result = RegEnumKey(hKey, currentSubKeyIndex, currentSubKeyText,
91:        currentSubKeyText.Capacity);
92:
93:      if (result == 0)
```

LISTING 19.11 Continued

```
 94:        return true;
 95:      else if (result == ERROR_NO_MORE_ITEMS)
 96:        return false;
 97:      else
 98:        throw new ApplicationException(ErrorHelper.GetErrorMessage(result));
 99:    }
100:
101:    public object Current
102:    {
103:      get { return currentSubKeyText.ToString(); }
104:    }
105: }
106:
107: public class Client
108: {
109:    static readonly IntPtr HKEY_LOCAL_MACHINE =
110:      new IntPtr(unchecked((int)0x80000002));
111:
112:    public static void Main()
113:    {
114:      using (RegistryKeyEnumerator enumerator =
115:              new RegistryKeyEnumerator(HKEY_LOCAL_MACHINE, "SOFTWARE"))
116:      {
117:        // Force a garbage collection for demonstration
118:        GC.Collect();
119:        GC.WaitForPendingFinalizers();
120:
121:        enumerator.Reset();
122:        while (enumerator.MoveNext())
123:          Console.WriteLine(enumerator.Current);
124:      }
125:    }
126: }
```

In this listing, the RegistryKey class has been changed to implement IDisposable. This is recommended to provide clients with a means of closing the HKEY without having to wait for garbage collection. Because RegistryKeyEnumerator now has a RegistryKey member (declared in Line 55), it also implements IDisposable and disposes the RegistryKey member when appropriate. Finally, the Client class now uses C#'s using construct so that RegistryKeyEnumerator.Dispose is implicitly called at the end of the listing. The listing now works as desired because the RegistryKey instance used by RegistryKeyEnumerator is a class member that won't be eligible for garbage collection until RegistryKey itself is.

Although Listing 19.10 demonstrates premature garbage collection with the use of two classes, clients of a single handle-wrapping class can run into this problem, too. For example, imagine that we added a `DeleteSubKey` method to the `RegistryKey` class that calls the `RegDeleteKey` API:

```
public class RegistryKey : IDisposable
{
  ...

  [DllImport("advapi32.dll", CharSet=CharSet.Auto)]
  static extern int RegDeleteKey(IntPtr hKey, string lpSubKey);

  public void Delete(string subKey)
  {
    // Delete the subkey
    int result = RegDeleteKey(hKey, subKey);
    if (result != 0)
      throw new ApplicationException("Could not delete registry key: " +
        ErrorHelper.GetErrorMessage(result));
  }
}
```

A C# client might use this as follows:

```
public class Client
{
  static readonly IntPtr HKEY_LOCAL_MACHINE =
    new IntPtr(unchecked((int)0x80000002));

  public static void Main()
  {
    RegistryKey key =
      new RegistryKey(HKEY_LOCAL_MACHINE, "SOFTWARE\\.NET and COM");
    key.DeleteSubKey("TemporaryKey");
    // The client forgets to call key.Dispose
  }
}
```

DON'T DO THIS

The call to `DeleteSubKey` is the last time the `RegistryKey` instance is used, and the implementation of `DeleteSubKey` calls a PInvoke method with parameter types that don't keep the object alive (a simple by-value `IntPtr` and string). Therefore, there's a rare chance that the call to `DeleteSubKey` will cause an exception to be thrown. Right before the PInvoke call to `RegDeleteKey`, the garbage collector could free the `RegistryKey` instance because there's no further use of it anywhere in the program. (Had `this` been passed to a PInvoke method, the instance would not be eligible for collection.) If this happens, and if the object's finalizer runs before `RegDeleteKey` uses the `HKEY` passed to it, an `ApplicationException` would be thrown with the message, "The handle is invalid," due to the finalizer's call to `RegCloseKey`.

If the client had remembered to call `Dispose` after `DeleteSubKey`, this problem could not occur because the garbage collector would see that the instance is still being used after the call.

> **TIP**
>
> The pattern of implementing and using `IDisposable` for classes that wrap unmanaged resources (in other words, Windows handles) goes a long way in preventing premature garbage collection. The presence of a call to `Dispose` keeps an object alive at least until `Dispose` is called.

Although proper use of `IDisposable` can help prevent premature garbage collection, two simple mechanisms exist specifically to prevent premature garbage collection:

- The `System.GC.KeepAlive` method
- The `System.Runtime.InteropServices.HandleRef` value type

The `System.GC.KeepAlive` Method

The static `KeepAlive` method can be passed an instance that you don't want to be collected prematurely. The passed-in instance is guaranteed to be ineligible for collection starting at the beginning of the method that contains the call to `KeepAlive`, and ending immediately after the call to `KeepAlive`. Therefore, this method is called *after* relevant PInvoke invocations, for example:

```
ObjectWrappingHandle obj = new ObjectWrappingHandle();
PInvokeMethod(obj.Handle);
GC.KeepAlive(obj); // Keep the object alive during the call to PInvokeMethod
```

Passing an object to *any* virtual method has the same characteristics as passing it to `GC.KeepAlive`, so using this method is simply a convention (and a convenience).

The `System.Runtime.InteropServices.HandleRef` Value Type

Remembering to use `GC.KeepAlive` in the appropriate places can be a difficult task, so the `System.Runtime.InteropServices` namespace defines a value type that can be used with PInvoke methods to prevent premature garbage collection in an easier fashion. This value type is called `HandleRef`, which has a constructor that takes two parameters—a `System.Object` representing the wrapper object that must be kept alive, and a `System.IntPtr` that represents the unmanaged handle.

19

DEEPER INTO
PINVOKE AND
USEFUL EXAMPLES

When a `HandleRef` instance is passed to unmanaged code, the Interop Marshaler extracts the handle and passes only that to unmanaged code. At the same time, however, the marshaler guarantees that the object passed as the first parameter to `HandleRef`'s constructor is not collected for the duration of the call.

When defining a PInvoke signature that expects a handle, you should make the argument type a `HandleRef` rather than an `IntPtr`. This way, callers are forced to pass `HandleRef` and automatically avoid premature garbage collection without understanding this subtle issue. For the `RegistryKey` example, the PInvoke signatures could be defined as follows:

```
[DllImport("advapi32.dll", CharSet=CharSet.Auto)]
static extern int RegOpenKey(HandleRef hKey, string lpSubKey,
  out IntPtr phkResult);

[DllImport("advapi32.dll")]
static extern int RegCloseKey(HandleRef hKey);

[DllImport("advapi32.dll", CharSet=CharSet.Auto)]
static extern int RegDeleteKey(HandleRef hKey, string lpKeyName);
```

Whenever these are called inside the `RegistryKey` class, the caller can simply pass `this` plus the handle that should be passed to unmanaged code, for example:

```
public void DeleteSubKey(string subKey)
{
  // Delete the subkey
  int result = RegDeleteKey(new HandleRef(this, hKey), subKey);
  if (result != 0)
    throw new ApplicationException("Could not delete registry key: " +
      ErrorHelper.GetErrorMessage(result));
}
```

Although the PInvoke signatures listed in Appendix E use `IntPtr` to represent handle parameters, you should seriously consider using `HandleRef` instead. Although using `HandleRef` is slightly slower, the gain in productivity by avoiding subtle bugs is well worth it.

DIGGING DEEPER

Besides `HandleRef`, there's one more type that can be used with PInvoke signatures that is flagged specially by the Interop Marshaler—`System.Runtime.InteropServices.ArrayWithOffset`. See Appendix A, "`System.Runtime.InteropServices` Reference," for information about using this type.

Choosing the DLL Location or Name Dynamically

The PInvoke mechanism requires a static DLL name stored inside the `DllImportAttribute` pseudo-custom attribute. Because there's no way to control the attribute's contents at run time, this can be problematic for developers who wish to dynamically choose the location of a DLL.

Usually, the DLL name used with `DllImportAttribute` (or used with VB .NET's `Declare`, which ends up emitting `DllImportAttribute` in metadata) does not include any path information. Such a DLL is located using the standard search strategy of `LoadLibrary`, such as in the current directory, the Windows `system32` directory, or somewhere listed in the `PATH` environment variable. But what can you do if you want to specify the DLL at run time via a registry key, an environment variable other than `PATH`, or some other custom way? As long as you know the DLL name at compile time (in other words, only the location is dynamic), you can simply do the following:

1. Define your PInvoke signatures using the name of the desired DLL without a path. For example:

   ```
   [DllImport("MyFunctions.dll")]
   ```

2. Before you call any of the PInvoke signatures for a given DLL, manually call the Win32 `LoadLibrary` API in `KERNEL32.DLL` using your dynamic path information:

   ```
   // Get desired path from a custom location, such as the registry
   string path = ...
   // Call LoadLibrary with the desired path
   LoadLibrary(path + "\\MyFunctions.dll");
   ```

   `LoadLibrary` can be called once you've defined a PInvoke signature for it, as done in Listing 19.3.

This works because once a DLL is loaded, the CLR uses it for all remaining PInvoke calls. Had `LoadLibrary` not been manually called in managed code, the CLR would call it with the exact string inside `DllImportAttribute` the first time a function in the DLL is called.

If you want everything about the loaded DLL to be dynamic, including its name, then your best choice (other than using C++) is to use Reflection Emit to dynamically define an entire PInvoke signature. This is similar to the use of Reflection Emit in Listing 19.3, and is demonstrated in Listing 19.12.

LISTING 19.12   Dynamic PInvoke for When the DLL Name Is Not Known at Compile Time

```
1: using System;
2: using System.Reflection;
3: using System.Reflection.Emit;
4: using System.Runtime.InteropServices;
```

LISTING 19.12   Continued

```
 5:
 6: public class DynamicBeeper
 7: {
 8:   public static void Main()
 9:   {
10:     DynamicPInvoke("user32.dll", "MessageBeep", typeof(bool),
11:       new Type[]{ typeof(uint) }, new Object[]{ (uint)0 });
12:   }
13:
14:   public static object DynamicPInvoke(string dll, string entryPoint,
15:     Type returnType, Type [] parameterTypes, object [] parameterValues)
16:   {
17:     // Create a dynamic assembly and a dynamic module
18:     AssemblyName asmName = new AssemblyName();
19:     asmName.Name = "tempAssembly";
20:     AssemblyBuilder dynamicAsm =
21:       AppDomain.CurrentDomain.DefineDynamicAssembly(asmName,
22:       AssemblyBuilderAccess.Run);
23:     ModuleBuilder dynamicMod =
24:       dynamicAsm.DefineDynamicModule("tempModule");
25:
26:     // Dynamically construct a global PInvoke signature
27:     // using the input information
28:     MethodBuilder dynamicMethod = dynamicMod.DefinePInvokeMethod(
29:       entryPoint, dll, MethodAttributes.Static | MethodAttributes.Public
30:       | MethodAttributes.PinvokeImpl, CallingConventions.Standard,
31:       returnType, parameterTypes, CallingConvention.Winapi,
32:       CharSet.Ansi);
33:
34:     // This global method is now complete
35:     dynamicMod.CreateGlobalFunctions();
36:
37:     // Get a MethodInfo for the PInvoke method
38:     MethodInfo mi = dynamicMod.GetMethod(entryPoint);
39:
40:     // Invoke the static method and return whatever it returns
41:     return mi.Invoke(null, parameterValues);
42:   }
43: }
```

Lines 10–11 show an example use of the DynamicPInvoke method defined in Lines 14–42—calling the MessageBeep API in USER32.DLL. The DynamicPInvoke method uses reflection emit much like Listing 19.3, creating a dynamic assembly with a dynamic module in Lines 18–24.

Lines 28–32 call `ModuleBuilder.DefinePInvokeMethod` with all the information necessary to dynamically emit a PInvoke signature. Once `CreateGlobalFunctions` is called in Line 35, the global PInvoke signature is ready to be called. Line 38 obtains the `MethodInfo` instance for the method, and Line 41 invokes the method.

This `DynamicPInvoke` method is able to handle any number and types of parameters and any type of return value. It is a bit too simplistic to handle many PInvoke signatures, however, because it needs to provide a way of specifying by-reference parameters and attributes such as `MarshalAsAttribute`, `InAttribute`, and `OutAttribute`. All of this is possible with reflection emit; see the .NET Framework SDK documentation if you're interested.

Example: Responding Immediately to Console Input

In managed code, a console program can call `Console.Read` or `Console.ReadLine` to respond to user input, but both calls wait for the user to hit the `Enter` key before giving control back to the user! An example of this behavior was seen in Listing 19.2. Developers often don't want to wait for the `Enter` key but rather want to respond to key presses immediately. No methods in the .NET Framework provide this behavior, but Listing 19.13 accomplishes this task using PInvoke calls to the `ReadConsoleInput` API in `KERNEL32.DLL`.

Listing 19.13   Responding Immediately to Console Input Using `ReadConsoleInput`

```
 1: using System;
 2: using System.Runtime.InteropServices;
 3:
 4: internal struct COORD
 5: {
 6:   internal short X;
 7:   internal short Y;
 8: }
 9:
10: [StructLayout(LayoutKind.Sequential, CharSet=CharSet.Unicode)]
11: internal struct KEY_EVENT_RECORD
12: {
13:   internal bool bKeyDown;
14:   internal ushort wRepeatCount;
15:   internal ushort wVirtualKeyCode;
16:   internal ushort wVirtualScanCode;
17:   internal char UnicodeChar;
18:   internal uint dwControlKeyState;
19: }
20:
```

LISTING 19.13   Continued

```
21: internal struct MOUSE_EVENT_RECORD
22: {
23:   internal COORD dwMousePosition;
24:   internal uint dwButtonState;
25:   internal uint dwControlKeyState;
26:   internal uint dwEventFlags;
27: }
28:
29: internal struct WINDOW_BUFFER_SIZE_RECORD
30: {
31:   internal COORD dwSize;
32: }
33:
34: internal struct MENU_EVENT_RECORD
35: {
36:   internal uint dwCommandId;
37: }
38:
39: internal struct FOCUS_EVENT_RECORD
40: {
41:   internal bool bSetFocus;
42: }
43:
44: internal struct INPUT_RECORD
45: {
46:   internal EventTypes EventType;
47:   internal KEY_EVENT_RECORD KeyEvent;
48:   internal MOUSE_EVENT_RECORD MouseEvent;
49:   internal WINDOW_BUFFER_SIZE_RECORD WindowBufferSizeEvent;
50:   internal MENU_EVENT_RECORD MenuEvent;
51:   internal FOCUS_EVENT_RECORD FocusEvent;
52: }
53:
54: internal enum EventTypes : ushort
55: {
56:   KEY_EVENT               = 0x01,
57:   MOUSE_EVENT             = 0x02,
58:   WINDOW_BUFFER_SIZE_EVENT = 0x04,
59:   MENU_EVENT              = 0x08,
60:   FOCUS_EVENT             = 0x10
61: }
62:
63: // Constants used with PInvoke methods
64: internal class Constants
65: {
```

LISTING 19.13   Continued

```
66:    // Standard input, output, and error
67:    internal const int STD_INPUT_HANDLE  = -10;
68:    internal const int STD_OUTPUT_HANDLE = -11;
69:    internal const int STD_ERROR_HANDLE  = -12;
70:
71:    // Returned by GetStdHandle when an error occurs
72:    internal static readonly IntPtr INVALID_HANDLE_VALUE = new IntPtr(-1);
73: }
74:
75: public class Echo
76: {
77:    [DllImport("kernel32.dll", SetLastError=true)]
78:    private static extern IntPtr GetStdHandle(int nStdHandle);
79:
80:    [DllImport("kernel32.dll", SetLastError=true)]
81:    static extern bool ReadConsoleInput(IntPtr hConsoleInput,
82:      [Out] INPUT_RECORD [] lpBuffer, uint nLength,
83:      out uint lpNumberOfEventsRead);
84:
85:    public static void Main()
86:    {
87:      IntPtr stdin = GetStdHandle(Constants.STD_INPUT_HANDLE);
88:
89:      if (stdin == Constants.INVALID_HANDLE_VALUE)
90:        throw new Exception("Unable to get standard input handle");
91:
92:      INPUT_RECORD [] records = new INPUT_RECORD[1];
93:      uint eventsRead = 0;
94:
95:      // Loop forever
96:      while (true)
97:      {
98:        if (ReadConsoleInput(stdin, records, (uint)records.Length,
99:          out eventsRead))
100:       {
101:         if (records[0].EventType == EventTypes.KEY_EVENT &&
102:           records[0].KeyEvent.bKeyDown)
103:         {
104:           Console.WriteLine("You pressed '" +
105:             records[0].KeyEvent.UnicodeChar + "' (" +
106:             records[0].KeyEvent.wVirtualKeyCode + ")!");
107:         }
108:       }
109:     }
110:   }
111: }
```

Lines 4–52 define several structures that are used with the ReadConsoleInput method. For this example, it was only necessary to define INPUT_RECORD and KEY_EVENT_RECORD, but the remaining structs are defined as well so INPUT_RECORD can be defined completely.

Because ReadConsoleInput requires a handle to console input, Line 87 begins the Main method by making a PInvoke call to GetStdHandle. If that succeeds, Lines 96–109 continually call ReadConsoleInput and prints the character and corresponding virtual key code if it detects that a key was pressed.

Running this program produces output such as the following after pressing some keys:

```
You pressed '.' (190)!
You pressed 'n' (78)!
You pressed 'e' (69)!
You pressed 't' (84)!
You pressed ' ' (32)!
You pressed 'a' (65)!
You pressed 'n' (78)!
You pressed 'd' (68)!
You pressed ' ' (32)!
You pressed 'c' (67)!
You pressed 'o' (79)!
You pressed 'm' (77)!
```

Example: Clearing the Console Screen

Listing 19.14 demonstrates how to clear a console screen just like the CLS command in DOS. The System.Console class does not expose a way to do this.

LISTING 19.14   Clearing the Console Screen Like the CLS DOS Command

```
 1: using System;
 2: using System.Runtime.InteropServices;
 3:
 4: internal struct CONSOLE_SCREEN_BUFFER_INFO
 5: {
 6:   internal COORD dwSize;
 7:   internal COORD dwCursorPosition;
 8:   internal ushort wAttributes;
 9:   internal SMALL_RECT srWindow;
10:   internal COORD dwMaximumWindowSize;
11: }
12:
13: internal struct COORD
14: {
```

LISTING 19.14 Continued

```
15:   internal short X;
16:   internal short Y;
17: }
18:
19: internal struct SMALL_RECT
20: {
21:   internal short Left;
22:   internal short Top;
23:   internal short Right;
24:   internal short Bottom;
25: }
26:
27: // Constants used with PInvoke methods
28: internal class Constants
29: {
30:   // Standard input, output, and error
31:   internal const int STD_INPUT_HANDLE  = -10;
32:   internal const int STD_OUTPUT_HANDLE = -11;
33:   internal const int STD_ERROR_HANDLE  = -12;
34:
35:   // Returned by GetStdHandle when an error occurs
36:   internal static readonly IntPtr INVALID_HANDLE_VALUE = new IntPtr(-1);
37: }
38:
39: public class Cls
40: {
41:   [DllImport("kernel32.dll", SetLastError=true)]
42:   static extern IntPtr GetStdHandle(int nStdHandle);
43:
44:   [DllImport("kernel32.dll", SetLastError=true)]
45:   static extern bool GetConsoleScreenBufferInfo(IntPtr hConsoleOutput,
46:     out CONSOLE_SCREEN_BUFFER_INFO lpConsoleScreenBufferInfo);
47:
48:   [DllImport("kernel32.dll", SetLastError=true)]
49:   static extern bool FillConsoleOutputCharacter(IntPtr hConsoleOutput,
50:     char cCharacter, uint nLength, COORD dwWriteCoord, out uint
51:     lpNumberOfCharsWritten);
52:
53:   [DllImport("kernel32.dll", SetLastError=true)]
54:   static extern bool FillConsoleOutputAttribute(IntPtr hConsoleOutput,
55:     ushort wAttribute, uint nLength, COORD dwWriteCoord, out uint
56:     lpNumberOfAttrsWritten);
57:
58:   [DllImport("kernel32.dll", SetLastError=true)]
59:   static extern bool SetConsoleCursorPosition(IntPtr hConsoleOutput,
```

LISTING 19.14 Continued

```
60:       COORD dwCursorPosition);
61:
62:    public static void Main()
63:    {
64:      IntPtr stdout = GetStdHandle(Constants.STD_OUTPUT_HANDLE);
65:      uint length;
66:
67:      if (stdout == Constants.INVALID_HANDLE_VALUE)
68:        throw new Exception("Unable to get standard output handle");
69:
70:      // Place the cursor at the beginning of the window (0,0)
71:      COORD coord = new COORD();
72:
73:      // Get number of character cells in the buffer
74:      CONSOLE_SCREEN_BUFFER_INFO csbi = new CONSOLE_SCREEN_BUFFER_INFO();
75:      if (!GetConsoleScreenBufferInfo(stdout, out csbi))
76:        throw new Exception("Unable to get existing console settings");
77:
78:      uint size = (uint)(csbi.dwSize.X * csbi.dwSize.Y);
79:
80:      // Fill the entire screen with spaces
81:      if (!FillConsoleOutputCharacter(stdout, ' ', size, coord, out length))
82:        throw new Exception("Unable to fill console with spaces");
83:
84:      // Set the buffer's attributes
85:      if (!FillConsoleOutputAttribute(stdout, csbi.wAttributes, size,
86:        coord, out length))
87:        throw new Exception("Unable to set console attributes");
88:
89:      // Set the cursor's position to (0,0)
90:      if (!SetConsoleCursorPosition(stdout, coord))
91:        throw new Exception("Unable to set cursor position");
92:    }
93: }
```

Lines 4–25 define the necessary structures, and Lines 28–37 contain a Constants class with a few values used by the PInvoke methods. The five PInvoke methods used by this listing are defined in Lines 41–60.

Whereas the previous listing required an input handle, this listing requires an output handle, obtained in Line 64. Line 74 extracts the existing console settings, so Line 81 can fill the screen with spaces. Lines 85–86 ensure that the buffer's attributes are the same as before, and finally Line 90 sets the cursor position to the (0,0) coordinate. This takes advantage of the fact that when the COORD instance was created in Line 71, its memory is automatically zeroed. Therefore, neither field needs to be explicitly set to zero.

Example: Using `CoCreateInstanceEx` to Activate Remote COM Objects

As promised in Chapter 6, the next example uses `CoCreateInstanceEx` to activate a COM object on a remote computer. `CoCreateInstanceEx` is defined as follows in `objbase.h`:

```
HRESULT CoCreateInstanceEx(
    REFCLSID rclsid,            // CLSID of the object to be created
    IUnknown *punkOuter,        // Controlling IUnknown, if part of an aggregate
    DWORD dwClsCtx,             // CLSCTX values
    COSERVERINFO *pServerInfo,  // Machine on which the object is to be created
    ULONG cmq,                  // Number of MULTI_QI structures in pResults
    MULTI_QI *pResults          // C-style array of MULTI_QI structures
);
```

Listing 19.15 wraps a call to `CoCreateInstanceEx` inside a method called `CreateRemoteInstance`. This method exhibits similar behavior as calling `Type.GetTypeFromProgID` with the server name overload followed by `Activator.CreateInstance`, so this listing simply demonstrates how to accomplish the same task in PInvoke. The only compelling reason to use this method rather than `Type.GetTypeFromProgID` and `Activator.CreateInstance` is that the CLR calls `CoGetClassObject` instead of `CoCreateInstanceEx`, which does not behave appropriately on older versions of Windows, as described in Chapter 6. However, one could imagine defining a `CreateRemoteInstance` method that exposes more of `CoCreateInstanceEx`'s functionality in a user-friendly way, such as customizing authentication settings for the remote activation request.

LISTING 19.15   Instantiating a Remote COM Object Using `CoCreateInstanceEx`

```
 1: using System;
 2: using System.Runtime.InteropServices;
 3:
 4: internal struct MULTI_QI
 5: {
 6:    internal IntPtr pIID;
 7:    [MarshalAs(UnmanagedType.IUnknown)] internal object pItf;
 8:    internal int hr;
 9: }
10:
11: [StructLayout(LayoutKind.Sequential, CharSet=CharSet.Unicode)]
12: internal struct COSERVERINFO
13: {
14:    internal uint dwReserved1;
15:    internal string pwszName;
```

LISTING 19.15 Continued

```
16:    internal IntPtr pAuthInfo;
17:    internal uint dwReserved2;
18: }
19:
20: public class ComHelpers
21: {
22:    const uint CLSCTX_REMOTE_SERVER = 0x10;
23:    static readonly Guid IID_IUnknown =
24:      new Guid("00000000-0000-0000-C000-000000000046");
25:
26:    [DllImport("ole32.dll", CharSet=CharSet.Unicode, PreserveSig=false)]
27:    static extern void CLSIDFromProgIDEx(string lpszProgID, out Guid pclsid);
28:
29:    [DllImport("ole32.dll", PreserveSig=false)]
30:    static extern void CoCreateInstanceEx(
31:      [MarshalAs(UnmanagedType.LPStruct)] Guid rclsid,
32:      [MarshalAs(UnmanagedType.IUnknown)] object punkOuter,
33:      uint dwClsCtx,
34:      [In] ref COSERVERINFO pServerInfo,
35:      uint cmq,
36:      [In, Out] MULTI_QI [] pResults);
37:
38:    public static object CreateRemoteInstance(
39:      string progId, string serverName)
40:    {
41:      // Specify just the server name in the COSERVERINFO structure
42:      COSERVERINFO csi = new COSERVERINFO();
43:      csi.pwszName = serverName;
44:      csi.pAuthInfo = IntPtr.Zero;
45:      csi.dwReserved1 = 0;
46:      csi.dwReserved2 = 0;
47:
48:      // Find the CLSID for the input ProgID
49:      Guid clsid;
50:      CLSIDFromProgIDEx(progId, out clsid);
51:
52:      // Query for only one interface (IUnknown)
53:      MULTI_QI [] mqi = new MULTI_QI[1];
54:      mqi[0] = new MULTI_QI();
55:
56:      GCHandle handle = new GCHandle();
57:      try
58:      {
59:        // Pin the Guid representing IID_IUnknown
```

LISTING 19.15   Continued

```
60:         handle = GCHandle.Alloc(IID_IUnknown, GCHandleType.Pinned);
61:
62:         // Set the field to the address of the Guid instance
63:         mqi[0].pIID = handle.AddrOfPinnedObject();
64:
65:         // Make the PInvoke call
66:         CoCreateInstanceEx(clsid, null,
67:           CLSCTX_REMOTE_SERVER, ref csi, 1, mqi);
68:       }
69:     finally
70:     {
71:       if (handle.IsAllocated) handle.Free();
72:     }
73:
74:     // Return the RCW
75:     return mqi[0].pItf;
76:   }
77: }
```

Lines 4–9 define the MULTI_QI structure. The pIID field must be defined as an IntPtr type
because there's no way to express a reference to a Guid value type as a structure field. Lines
11–18 define the COSERVERINFO structure, giving it a Unicode character set rather than marking
the pwszName field with MarshalAs(UnmanagedType.LPWStr). The pAuthInfo field represents
a pointer to a COAUTHINFO structure, which can be used to override the default activation security. Because we accept the default security in this listing, we don't bother defining the
COAUTHINFO structure. Even if we did define it, the pAuthInfo field would still require being
defined as an IntPtr because it represents a *pointer* to a structure rather than an embedded
structure.

In case you wanted to use COAUTHINFO in your application, here's how it could be defined in C#:

```
[StructLayout(LayoutKind.Sequential, CharSet=CharSet.Unicode)]
internal struct COAUTHINFO
{
  internal uint dwAuthnSvc;
  internal uint dwAuthzSvc;
  internal string pwszServerPrincName;
  internal uint dwAuthnLevel;
  internal uint dwImpersonationLevel;
  internal IntPtr pAuthIdentityData;
  internal uint dwCapabilities;
}
```

Line 22 defines the CLSCTX_REMOTE_SERVER used for the CoCreateInstanceEx call, and Lines 23–24 define a Guid instance representing the IID for IUnknown, which is needed to query the remote object for the IUnknown interface. Lines 26–36 define the two PInvoke signatures used for this listing. The definitions of both methods are straightforward except for the first parameter of CoCreateInstanceEx. The straightforward way of defining this parameter would be:

```
[In] ref Guid rclsid
```

However, UnmanagedType.LPStruct can be used in this specific case to convert a by-value Guid to [in] GUID* on the unmanaged side.

TIP

Other places in this book, including the back cover, state that UnmanagedType. LPStruct is not used in version 1.0 of the .NET Framework. As Listing 19.15 demonstrates, this is not quite true. In version 1.0, the one and only place it can be used is on a by-value Guid parameter in a PInvoke signature to add an implicit level of indirection. It can't be used with other data types, and it can't even be used on Guid fields; otherwise we could have avoided defining the pIID field of MULTI_QI as an IntPtr type.

Because UnmanagedType.LPStruct is often misused (due to its limited support and confusing name), it's best to avoid using it altogether unless support is added in future versions of the CLR to make it useful on more than just Guid parameters.

The CreateRemoteInstance method is defined in Lines 38–76. The first thing it does is fill in a COSERVERINFO instance with the passed-in server name. The pAuthInfo field is set to null (IntPtr.Zero) in order to accept the default activation security. Line 50 calls CLSIDFromProgIDEx to extract the needed CLSID for the passed in ProgID from the local computer's registry. Alternatively, the code could have called System.Type.GetTypeFromProgID and then extracted the CLSID from the returned type's GUID property.

Line 53 creates a single-element MULTI_QI array that will hold the IID for IUnknown. MULTI_QI can be used to query for multiple interfaces in the same round-trip to the server, to optimize network performance. Because we need to pass a pointer to IID_IUnknown that is defined as an IntPtr, Line 60 pins the Guid instance using GCHandle and Line 63 calls AddrOfPinnedObject to set the pIID field to the appropriate address in memory. Lines 66–67 call CoCreateInstanceEx, and Line 75 extracts the returned interface pointer from the MULTI_QI structure. Because the pItf field was defined as a System.Object type, the Interop Marshaler automatically wraps the interface pointer in an RCW. Had pItf been defined as IntPtr instead, Line 75 would need to be changed to the following:

```
return Marshal.GetObjectForIUnknown(mqi[0].pItf);
```

Conclusion

PInvoke can be a tricky technology that takes lots of practice to get right. Hopefully this chapter, the previous one, and Appendix E give you all the information you need to dive into some "PInvoke challenges" with confidence.

Although certain types of failure during a PInvoke call do not occur in a predictable or easily-debuggable manner, there are several cases in which a descriptive exception is thrown. These cases mainly consist of limitations of the Interop Marshaler. For example, if you attempt to use `UnmanagedType.AsAny` to marshal a return type or by-reference parameter as `void*`, or if you attempt to return a `System.Guid` or `System.Drawing.Color` instance, you'll get an exception (in version 1.0 of the CLR) that such a signature is not PInvoke compatible.

> **Tip**
>
> Don't forget to consider security when writing .NET class libraries or other .NET applications that use PInvoke. Calling any function via PInvoke requires unmanaged code permission, so it's safe by default. However, it's often useful to carefully reduce security requirements to provide your functionality to clients that aren't fully trusted. (In addition, reducing security with techniques such as using `SuppressUnmanagedCodeSecurityAttribute` can significantly boost performance.)
>
> For example, the `ColorfulConsole.WriteLine` methods in Listing 19.4 could assert unmanaged code permission so partially trusted code (running from the Intranet zone, for instance) could still write to the console in multiple colors. Had the standard `System.Console.WriteLine` method required some sort of console-writing permission, we would want to demand this permission before asserting unmanaged code permission to be consistent with the .NET Framework and avoid exposing a potential security hole. See the discussion on security in Chapter 6 for more information.
>
> One easy rule to follow is that you should never expose public PInvoke methods. Making them private to a class or internal to an assembly is a good defensive tactic to prevent the possibility of abuse by malicious code. The PInvoke signatures listed in Appendix E all omit the `public` keyword to make them private, which is the preferred visibility.

FAQ: How do I call functions from a static library (.lib) from managed code, rather than functions from a dynamic link library?

You can't directly call static library methods in managed code, with the exception of using mixed mode programming with Visual C++ .NET. The easiest workaround for using them in other languages is to wrap calls to these library functions in a dynamic link library.

Advanced Topics

PART
VII

IN THIS PART

20 Custom Marshaling   879

21 Manually Defining COM Types in Source
Code   957

22 Using APIs Instead of SDK Tools   1039

Custom Marshaling

IN THIS CHAPTER

- Transforming Types Without Custom Marshaling   882
- Custom Marshaling Architecture   895
- Marshalers, Marshalers, Marshalers!   913
- Limitations   952

Custom marshaling is the extensibility mechanism for the Interop Marshaler. The term *custom marshaling* can mean different things in different situations, but this chapter refers to customizing Interop marshaling across managed/unmanaged boundaries. COM-style custom marshaling across contexts (performed by implementing IMarshal) is completely independent of Interop custom marshaling, and both can coexist peacefully.

The work done by the Interop Marshaler without custom marshaling is summarized in Figure 20.1. These are the same diagrams that were presented in Chapter 2, "Bridging the Two Worlds—Managed and Unmanaged Code."

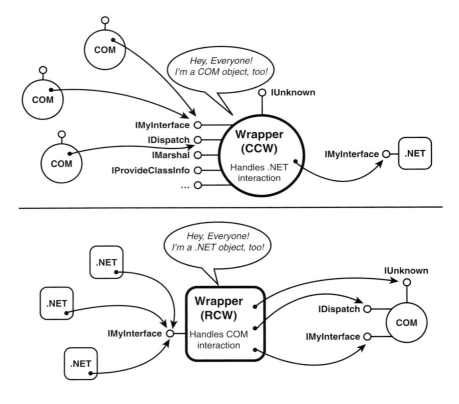

FIGURE 20.1

COM and .NET interaction when no custom marshaling is involved.

The CLR's custom marshaling infrastructure enables you to replace the system-supplied COM-Callable Wrappers (CCWs) and Runtime-Callable Wrappers (RCWs) on a call-by-call basis. This capability is illustrated in Figure 20.2.

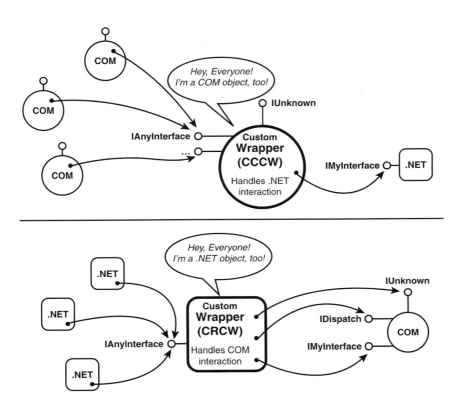

Figure 20.2

COM and .NET interaction with custom marshaling.

Notice how an object implementing `IMyInterface` is exposed via a wrapper implementing `IAnyInterface` instead. When you control the wrappers, you can transform objects however you'd like (within some limitations discussed in the "Limitations" section at the end of the chapter).

Transforming one data type to a completely different type may sound like a crazy thing to do, but it's actually the Number One application of custom marshaling. This occurs because the arrival of .NET has introduced several brand-new data types that, at some logical level, serve the same purpose as existing COM types. For example, although the .NET `System.IO.Stream` is unrelated to COM's `IStream` interface (from the perspective of any runtimes or compilers), they are extremely similar abstractions that enable reading, writing, and seeking over a buffer.

Likewise, the .NET `System.Drawing.Font` class and the COM `IFont` interface are just different ways of exposing the same operating system font objects. The same goes for `System.Drawing.Color` and `OLE_COLOR`, `System.Collections.IEnumerator` and `IEnumVARIANT`, and so forth. Such transformations are really no different than the data type transformations done by the standard Interop Marshaler, which bridges the "unrelated" `System.String` and `BSTR` types, .NET arrays and `SAFEARRAY`s, `System.Guid` and `GUID` types, and so on.

Custom marshaling provides the glue between objects that use different but semantically similar data types. It can also be used to customize standard marshaling in more subtle ways (shown in the last example in the "Marshalers, Marshalers, Marshalers!" section) but this isn't as common.

In this chapter, we begin by examining how one could convert one data type to another without any custom marshaling support from the CLR. Then we examine the custom marshaling infrastructure that standardizes such conversions. Finally, we end the chapter with lots of examples and a discussion of custom marshaling limitations.

Transforming Types Without Custom Marshaling

Imagine that you're using a COM object in managed code that returns a stream to you in the form of an object implementing COM's `IStream` interface. You want to use some .NET APIs that operate on `System.IO.Stream` objects, such as constructing a `System.IO.StreamReader` with this `IStream` instance. The following C# code would not compile because you must pass a `Stream` instance to the `StreamReader` constructor:

```
IStream s = comObject.GetXml();
StreamReader sr = new StreamReader(s); // This line doesn't compile because
                                       // IStream isn't a Stream

Console.SetIn(sr);
...
sr.Close();
```

🚫

DON'T DO THIS

To make this work, you could define an *adapter class* that wraps an object implementing `IStream` inside a class that derives from `Stream`. An instance of such a class is called an *adapter object*, which could be used as follows:

```
IStream origStream = comObject.GetXml();
Stream s = new ComStream(origStream); // Convert IStream to Stream
StreamReader sr = new StreamReader(s);
Console.SetIn(sr);
...
sr.Close();
```

Just like System.IO.FileStream or System.IO.MemoryStream, the ComStream class can be used anywhere Stream is required thanks to the polymorphism provided by inheritance. The ComStream class is responsible for wrapping IStream appropriately so Stream.Read calls IStream.Read, Stream.Write calls IStream.Write, and so on. All of IStream's methods are displayed in Listing 20.1, which contains the definition for System.Runtime. InteropServices.UCOMIStream—the official .NET definition of the COM IStream interface.

LISTING 20.1 The .NET Definition of UCOMIStream Shown in C# Syntax

```
[
  ComImport,
  Guid("0000000C-0000-0000-C000-000000000046"),
  InterfaceTypeAttribute(ComInterfaceType.InterfaceIsIUnknown)
]
public interface UCOMIStream
{
  void Read([MarshalAs(UnmanagedType.LPArray, SizeParamIndex=1), Out]
    byte [] pv, int cb, IntPtr pcbRead);
  void Write([MarshalAs(UnmanagedType.LPArray, SizeParamIndex=1)]
    byte [] pv, int cb, IntPtr pcbWritten);
  void Seek(long dlibMove, int dwOrigin, IntPtr plibNewPosition);
  void SetSize(long libNewSize);
  void CopyTo(UCOMIStream pstm, long cb, IntPtr pcbRead, IntPtr pcbWritten);
  void Commit(int grfCommitFlags);
  void Revert();
  void LockRegion(long libOffset, long cb, int dwLockType);
  void UnlockRegion(long libOffset, long cb, int dwLockType);
  void Stat(out STATSTG pstatstg, int grfStatFlag);
  void Clone(out UCOMIStream ppstm);
}
```

Representing streams in .NET, the System.IO.Stream abstract class has abstract Read, Write, Seek, SetLength, and Flush methods, a handful of abstract properties, and many more public members. Although the mapping of core functionality (read/write/seek) might be straightforward, other areas might require some thought. Listing 20.2 defines a ComStream adapter class in C# that exposes UCOMIStream functionality as a .NET Stream.

LISTING 20.2 ComStream.cs. An Adapter Class That Exposes an IStream Implementation as a .NET Stream

```
1: using System;
2: using System.IO;
```

LISTING 20.2   Continued

```
 3: using System.Runtime.InteropServices;
 4:
 5: public class ComStream : Stream
 6: {
 7:   // The managed stream being wrapped
 8:   UCOMIStream originalStream;
 9:
10:   // Constructor
11:   public ComStream(UCOMIStream stream)
12:   {
13:     if (stream != null)
14:     {
15:       originalStream = stream;
16:     }
17:     else
18:     {
19:       throw new ArgumentNullException("stream");
20:     }
21:   }
22:
23:   // Finalizer
24:   ~ComStream()
25:   {
26:     Close();
27:   }
28:
29:   // Property to get original stream object
30:   public UCOMIStream UnderlyingStream
31:   {
32:     get { return originalStream; }
33:   }
34:
35:   // Reads a sequence of bytes from the current stream and advances the
36:   // current position within the stream by the number of bytes read
37:   public unsafe override int Read(byte [] buffer, int offset, int count)
38:   {
39:     if (originalStream == null)
40:       throw new ObjectDisposedException("originalStream");
41:
42:     if (offset != 0)
43:       throw new NotSupportedException("Only a zero offset is supported.");
44:
45:     int bytesRead;
46:
```

LISTING 20.2   Continued

```
47:     // Use unsafe code to easily get the address of a value type
48:     IntPtr address = new IntPtr(&bytesRead);
49:
50:     originalStream.Read(buffer, count, address);
51:
52:     return bytesRead;
53:   }
54:
55:   // Writes a sequence of bytes to the current stream and advances the
56:   // current position within this stream by the number of bytes written
57:   public override void Write(byte [] buffer, int offset, int count)
58:   {
59:     if (originalStream == null)
60:       throw new ObjectDisposedException("originalStream");
61:
62:     if (offset != 0)
63:       throw new NotSupportedException("Only a zero offset is supported.");
64:
65:     // Pass "null" for the last parameter since we don't use the value
66:     originalStream.Write(buffer, count, IntPtr.Zero);
67:   }
68:
69:   // Sets the position within the current stream
70:   public unsafe override long Seek(long offset, SeekOrigin origin)
71:   {
72:     if (originalStream == null)
73:       throw new ObjectDisposedException("originalStream");
74:
75:     long position = 0;
76:
77:     // Use unsafe code to easily get the address of a value type
78:     IntPtr address = new IntPtr(&position);
79:
80:     // The enum values of SeekOrigin match the enum values of
81:     // STREAM_SEEK, so we can just cast the origin to an integer.
82:     originalStream.Seek(offset, (int)origin, address);
83:
84:     return position;
85:   }
86:
87:   // Returns the length, in bytes, of the stream
88:   public override long Length
89:   {
90:     get
```

Listing 20.2   Continued

```
 91:        {
 92:          if (originalStream == null)
 93:            throw new ObjectDisposedException("originalStream");
 94:
 95:          // Call IStream.Stat to retrieve info about the stream,
 96:          // which includes the length. STATFLAG_NONAME means that we don't
 97:          // care about the name (STATSTG.pwcsName), so there is no need for
 98:          // the method to allocate memory for the string.
 99:
100:          STATSTG statstg;
101:          originalStream.Stat(out statstg, 1 /*STATFLAG_NONAME*/);
102:          return statstg.cbSize;
103:        }
104:      }
105:
106:      // Determines the position within the current stream
107:      public override long Position
108:      {
109:        get { return Seek(0, SeekOrigin.Current); }
110:        set { Seek(value, SeekOrigin.Begin); }
111:      }
112:
113:      // Sets the length of the current stream
114:      public override void SetLength(long value)
115:      {
116:        if (originalStream == null)
117:          throw new ObjectDisposedException("originalStream");
118:
119:        originalStream.SetSize(value);
120:      }
121:
122:      // Closes (disposes) the stream
123:      public override void Close()
124:      {
125:        if (originalStream != null)
126:        {
127:          originalStream.Commit(0); // STGC_DEFAULT
128:          Marshal.ReleaseComObject(originalStream);
129:          originalStream = null;
130:          GC.SuppressFinalize(this);
131:        }
132:      }
133:
134:      // Updates the underlying data source or repository with the current
135:      // state of the buffer and then clears the buffer
```

LISTING 20.2 Continued

```
136:    public override void Flush()
137:    {
138:      originalStream.Commit(0);
139:    }
140:
141:    // Determines whether the current stream supports reading
142:    public override bool CanRead
143:    {
144:      get { return true; }
145:    }
146:
147:    // Determines whether the current stream supports writing
148:    public override bool CanWrite
149:    {
150:      get { return true; }
151:    }
152:
153:    // Determines whether the current stream supports seeking
154:    public override bool CanSeek
155:    {
156:      get { return true; }
157:    }
158: }
```

Lines 1–3 use the System namespace for IntPtr and a handful of exception types, the System.IO namespace for Stream, and the System.Runtime.InteropServices namespace for UCOMIStream and Marshal. The constructor in Lines 11–21 sets the private UCOMIStream field to the passed-in instance if it's not null. The class's finalizer in Lines 24–27 calls the Close method, which is Stream's equivalent to IDisposable.Dispose. (The base Stream class explicitly implements IDisposable, and its Dispose implementation simply calls Close.) Lines 30–33 define an UnderlyingStream property that publicly exposes the raw COM stream object. This property can be useful in cases where the COM object implements other interfaces for a client to make use of.

Line 37 begins the implementation of Stream's members, which forward calls to the UCOMIStream interface. The first two lines of the Read method (39 and 40) perform a common task for a class that operates on a disposable instance—checking to see if the object has been disposed already and throwing an ObjectDisposedException if it has. Notice that this implementation of Read only accepts an offset value of zero. This is done for simplicity and performance, because the only way to pass UCOMIStream.Read an appropriate array when a non-zero offset is given would be to instantiate a new array and copy the source array's elements beginning at the offset.

The tricky part of the `Read` implementation is that it needs to obtain the address of an integer variable, represented as an `IntPtr` type, to pass as the third parameter to `UCOMIStream.Read`. Line 48 uses C# unsafe code to cleanly accomplish this. Because of this, the method must be marked with the `unsafe` keyword and the class must be compiled with the `/unsafe` option from the command line. (Or, `Allow unsafe code blocks` must be set to `True` within Visual Studio .NET.) See Chapter 6, "Advanced Topics for Using COM Components," for another way to get a value type's address that works for any .NET language.

`ComStream.Write` in Lines 57–67 works just like `ComStream.Read`, but because it doesn't return how many bytes were written, Line 66 can simply pass a "null pointer" (`IntPtr.Zero`) as the third parameter to `UCOMIStream.Write`. `ComStream.Seek` (Lines 70–85) also has a similar implementation, and uses unsafe code just like `ComStream.Read` to pass an address of a 64-bit variable. Fortunately, the `STREAM_SEEK` enumeration used by `UCOMIStream` and the `SeekOrigin` enumeration used by `Stream` have the exact same values with the exact same meanings, so the input `origin` variable can simply be cast to the integer type (which represents a `STREAM_SEEK` value) expected by `UCOMIStream.Seek` in Line 82.

The remaining methods and properties in Lines 88–157 do what they can to bridge the functionality from `UCOMIStream` to the functionality of `Stream`, but the mapping isn't always obvious. For example, `ComStream.Length` uses `UCOMIStream.Stat` to obtain the stream's length, and `ComStream.Flush` calls `UCOMIStream.Commit` with the value 0 to represent `STGC_DEFAULT` (an enumeration value used with COM's `IStream` interface).

This `ComStream` class doesn't bother overriding members of `Stream` that already have a suitable implementation, such as `ReadByte`, `WriteByte`, `BeginRead`, `BeginWrite`, `EndRead`, and `EndWrite`. The class also lets any exceptions thrown be exposed directly. To be more user-friendly, it could have caught some exceptions and rethrown them with different exception types that a user of `Stream` would expect from its methods. This can be especially helpful when the inner object throws lots of `COMExceptions`.

The problem with the adapter class approach used in Listing 20.1 is that it uses `System.Runtime.InteropServices.UCOMIStream` for the .NET definition of `IStream`, but no Interop Assemblies generated by the type library importer use this type unless they were manually altered as in Chapter 7, "Modifying Interop Assemblies." Most likely, any APIs that use `IStream` exposed by an Interop Assembly end up using a .NET `IStream` interface definition contained in the same assembly (due to the `#import` effect described in Chapter 15, "Creating and Deploying Useful Primary Interop Assemblies"). This isn't a huge setback when the object implementing `IStream` is a COM object. You can explicitly cast a COM object to any .NET definition of `IStream` you'd like and it will always succeed as long as its `QueryInterface` implementation responds positively to the IID of `IStream`. Therefore, the `ComStream` adapter class defined in Listing 20.2 could be used as follows if an object returns a non-standard `IStream` interface:

```
IStream origStream = comObject.GetXml();
Stream s = new ComStream((UCOMIStream)origStream);
StreamReader sr = new StreamReader(s);
Console.SetIn(sr);
...
sr.Close();
```

An adapter class may be desired in the other direction as well. Suppose you're using a .NET class that returns a `Stream` instance, and you need to pass the stream to a COM object. Again, doing this directly isn't possible:

```
Stream s = System.Console.OpenStandardOutput();
comObject.WriteContentsToStream(s); // This line doesn't compile because
                                    // Stream doesn't implement IStream
s.Close();
```

Instead, you could define an adapter class that wraps an object derived from `Stream` inside a class that implements `IStream`. This could then be used as follows:

```
Stream s = System.Console.OpenStandardOutput();
UCOMIStream istream = new ManagedIStream(s); // Convert Stream to IStream
comObject.WriteContentsToStream(istream);
s.Close();
```

Listing 20.3 contains a definition of the `ManagedIStream` adapter class that internally acts upon a `Stream` class.

LISTING 20.3 `ManagedIStream.cs`. An Adapter Class That Exposes a `Stream` Object Through an `IStream` Implementation

```
 1: using System;
 2: using System.IO;
 3: using System.Runtime.InteropServices;
 4:
 5: [ClassInterface(ClassInterfaceType.None)]
 6: public class ManagedIStream : UCOMIStream, IDisposable
 7: {
 8:   // The managed stream being wrapped
 9:   Stream originalStream;
10:
11:   // Constructor
12:   public ManagedIStream(Stream stream)
13:   {
14:     if (stream != null)
15:     {
16:       originalStream = stream;
17:     }
```

20

LISTING 20.3   Continued

```
18:     else
19:     {
20:       throw new ArgumentNullException("stream");
21:     }
22:   }
23:
24:   // Finalizer
25:   ~ManagedIStream()
26:   {
27:     Close();
28:   }
29:
30:   // Property to get original stream object
31:   public Stream UnderlyingStream
32:   {
33:     get
34:     {
35:       if (originalStream == null)
36:         throw new ObjectDisposedException("originalStream");
37:
38:       return originalStream;
39:     }
40:   }
41:
42:   // Reads a specified number of bytes from the stream object
43:   // into memory starting at the current seek pointer
44:   public void Read(byte [] pv, int cb, IntPtr pcbRead)
45:   {
46:     if (originalStream == null)
47:       throw new ObjectDisposedException("originalStream");
48:
49:     if (pcbRead == IntPtr.Zero)
50:     {
51:       // User isn't interested in how many bytes were read
52:       originalStream.Read(pv, 0, cb);
53:     }
54:     else
55:     {
56:       Marshal.WriteInt32(pcbRead, originalStream.Read(pv, 0, cb));
57:     }
58:   }
59:
60:   // Writes a specified number of bytes into the stream object
61:   // starting at the current seek pointer
```

LISTING 20.3   Continued

```
62:  public void Write(byte [] pv, int cb, IntPtr pcbWritten)
63:  {
64:    if (originalStream == null)
65:      throw new ObjectDisposedException("originalStream");
66:
67:    if (pcbWritten == IntPtr.Zero)
68:    {
69:      // User isn't interested in how many bytes were written
70:      originalStream.Write(pv, 0, cb);
71:    }
72:    else
73:    {
74:      long originalPosition = originalStream.Position;
75:      originalStream.Write(pv, 0, cb);
76:      Marshal.WriteInt32(pcbWritten,
77:        (int)(originalStream.Position - originalPosition));
78:    }
79:  }
80:
81:  // Changes the seek pointer to a new location relative to the beginning
82:  // of the stream, the end of the stream, or the current seek pointer
83:  public void Seek(long dlibMove, int dwOrigin, IntPtr plibNewPosition)
84:  {
85:    if (originalStream == null)
86:      throw new ObjectDisposedException("originalStream");
87:
88:    // The enum values of SeekOrigin match the enum values of
89:    // STREAM_SEEK, so we can just cast the dwOrigin to a SeekOrigin
90:
91:    if (plibNewPosition == IntPtr.Zero)
92:    {
93:      // User isn't interested in new position
94:      originalStream.Seek(dlibMove, (SeekOrigin)dwOrigin);
95:    }
96:    else
97:    {
98:      Marshal.WriteInt64(plibNewPosition,
99:        originalStream.Seek(dlibMove, (SeekOrigin)dwOrigin));
100:   }
101: }
102:
103: // Changes the size of the stream object
104: public void SetSize(long libNewSize)
105: {
```

LISTING 20.3   Continued

```
106:     if (originalStream == null)
107:       throw new ObjectDisposedException("originalStream");
108:
109:     originalStream.SetLength(libNewSize);
110:   }
111:
112:   // Copies a specified number of bytes from the current seek pointer
113:   // in the stream to the current seek pointer in another stream
114:   public void CopyTo(UCOMIStream pstm, long cb,
115:     IntPtr pcbRead, IntPtr pcbWritten)
116:   {
117:     if (originalStream == null)
118:       throw new ObjectDisposedException("originalStream");
119:
120:     byte [] sourceBytes = new byte[cb];
121:     int currentBytesRead = 0;
122:     int bytesWritten = 0;
123:
124:     while (bytesWritten < cb)
125:     {
126:       currentBytesRead =
127:         originalStream.Read(sourceBytes, 0, (int)(cb - bytesWritten));
128:
129:       // Has the end of the stream been reached?
130:       if (currentBytesRead == 0) break;
131:
132:       // Stream.Write throws an exception if all bytes can't be written
133:       originalStream.Write(sourceBytes, 0, currentBytesRead);
134:       bytesWritten += currentBytesRead;
135:     }
136:
137:     if (pcbRead != IntPtr.Zero) Marshal.WriteInt64(pcbRead, bytesWritten);
138:     if (pcbWritten != IntPtr.Zero)
139:       Marshal.WriteInt64(pcbWritten, bytesWritten);
140:   }
141:
142:   // Ensures that any changes made to a stream object open in
143:   // transacted mode are reflected in the parent storage object
144:   public void Commit(int grfCommitFlags)
145:   {
146:     if (originalStream == null)
147:       throw new ObjectDisposedException("originalStream");
148:
149:     originalStream.Flush();
```

LISTING 20.3 Continued

```
150:     }
151:
152:     // Discards all changes that have been made to a transacted
153:     // stream since the last IStream.Commit call
154:     public void Revert()
155:     {
156:       throw new NotImplementedException(
157:         "This stream does not support reverting.");
158:     }
159:
160:     // Restricts access to a specified range of bytes in the stream
161:     public void LockRegion(long libOffset, long cb, int dwLockType)
162:     {
163:       throw new COMException("This stream does not support locking.",
164:         unchecked((int)0x80030001));
165:     }
166:
167:     // Removes the access restriction on a range of bytes
168:     public void UnlockRegion(long libOffset, long cb, int dwLockType)
169:     {
170:       throw new COMException("This stream does not support unlocking.",
171:         unchecked((int)0x80030001));
172:     }
173:
174:     // Retrieves the STATSTG structure for this stream
175:     public void Stat(out STATSTG pstatstg, int grfStatFlag)
176:     {
177:       if (originalStream == null)
178:         throw new ObjectDisposedException("originalStream");
179:
180:       pstatstg = new STATSTG();
181:       pstatstg.type = 2; // STGTY_STREAM
182:       pstatstg.cbSize = originalStream.Length;
183:       pstatstg.grfMode = 2; // STGM_READWRITE;
184:       pstatstg.grfLocksSupported = 2; // LOCK_EXCLUSIVE
185:     }
186:
187:     // Creates a new stream object that references the same bytes as the
188:     // original stream but provides a separate seek pointer to those bytes
189:     public void Clone(out UCOMIStream ppstm)
190:     {
191:       throw new NotImplementedException("This stream cannot be cloned.");
192:     }
193:
```

LISTING 20.3   Continued

```
194:    // Closes (disposes) the stream
195:    public void Close()
196:    {
197:      if (originalStream != null)
198:      {
199:        originalStream.Close();
200:        originalStream = null;
201:        GC.SuppressFinalize(this);
202:      }
203:    }
204:
205:    // IDisposable.Dispose
206:    void IDisposable.Dispose()
207:    {
208:      Close();
209:    }
210: }
```

Lines 1–3 use the System namespace for IntPtr and a handful of exception types, the System.IO namespace for Stream, and the System.Runtime.InteropServices namespace for UCOMIStream and Marshal. The class is marked with ClassInterfaceType.None because any COM access should be done through the UCOMIStream interface. This also removes the need to mark the class's members with the necessary attributes that make them work correctly when called from unmanaged code. These attributes can be seen in Listing 20.1 on the UCOMIStream interface definition, such as [MarshalAs(UnmanagedType.LPArray, SizeParamIndex=1), Out] on the first parameter of UCOMIStream.Read.

The constructor, finalizer, and UnderlyingStream property in Lines 12–40 work just like they do in Listing 20.2. The ManagedIStream.Read, ManagedIStream.Write, and ManagedIStream.Seek methods (Lines 44–101) all have an IntPtr third parameter that can either be "null" (IntPtr.Zero) or have a value if the caller wants to know how many bytes were read, written, or moved past. Therefore, Lines 49, 67, and 91 check the value of the third parameter to determine whether to do the extra work. Writing to the "dereferenced pointer" is done with Marshal.WriteInt32 in Lines 56 and 76–77 and Marshal.WriteInt64 in Lines 98–99. The cast to an integer in Line 77 could fail if more than 0x7FFFFFFF bytes were written, so a robust adapter class may wish to check for this case.

The Revert and Clone methods (Lines 154–158 and 189–192, respectively) throw a NotImplementedException because there's no corresponding functionality in the Stream class. For an implementation of ManagedIStream.Clone, you might be tempted to try casting the originalStream instance to ICloneable and using its cloning functionality, if it exists.

However, this does not give the same semantics as UCOMIStream's Clone method, which is supposed to clone just the seek pointer so that the new seek pointer operates on the same underlying bytes. This functionality is not available from System.IO.Stream.

Rather than throwing a NotImplementedException, LockRegion and UnlockRegion (Lines 161–165 and 168–172, respectively) throw a COMException with the HRESULT STG_E_ INVALIDFUNCTION because the documentation for these functions states that this is the HRESULT that should be returned when a stream does not support locking. In the upcoming "Example: Marshaling Between System.IO.Stream and IStream" section, we'll see how to support locking when the .NET stream is an instance of System.IO.FileStream.

By defining a pair of adapter classes like ComStream in Listing 20.2 and ManagedIStream in Listing 20.3, you can transform one type to another without using any custom marshaling support from the CLR. At this point, you might be asking why we spent so much time looking at this approach because this chapter is supposed to be about custom marshaling. The answer is that this same approach is exactly what is done when you use the built-in custom marshaling support—it's just encapsulated. The next section describes how custom marshaling works and how adapter classes like the ones in the previous two listings fit in.

Custom Marshaling Architecture

There are usually three components involved in custom marshaling:

- The custom marshaler
- The consumers
- The adapter objects

The custom marshaler is an object that the CLR calls into when data transformations need to occur. The consumers of a custom marshaler are signatures marked with the MarshalAsAttribute pseudo-custom attribute and the value UnmanagedType. CustomMarshaler, specifying that a given parameter, return type, or field should not use the standard marshaling support. When a member marked with a custom marshaler (via MarshalAsAttribute) is invoked, the CLR instructs the custom marshaler to do the marshaling and return an object representing the marshaled result. These objects are typically adapter objects but, as discussed in the "The Adapter Objects" section later in this chapter, they may not be.

Just as CCWs and RCWs are largely transparent to their users, so are adapter objects when they are used with the custom marshaling infrastructure. This transparency is the only reason for bothering with custom marshaling because everything can be accomplished by directly using adapter classes the same way they were used in the previous section.

> **TIP**
>
> Use custom marshaling to save your users the extra step of directly instantiating adapter classes to convert between two different data types.

The Custom Marshaler

There are two requirements for a custom marshaler. It must:

- Implement the System.Runtime.InteropServices.ICustomMarshaler interface
- Implement a static GetInstance method

The reason there are two requirements rather than just one (such as only implementing the ICustomMarshaler interface) is that interfaces cannot have static members. (Well, they can in IL Assembler but not with the semantics needed here.)

The ICustomMarshaler Interface

System.Runtime.InteropServices.ICustomMarshaler is a relatively simple interface, shown as follows in C# syntax:

```
public interface ICustomMarshaler
{
  object MarshalNativeToManaged(IntPtr pNativeData);
  IntPtr MarshalManagedToNative(object ManagedObj);
  void CleanUpNativeData(IntPtr pNativeData);
  void CleanUpManagedData(object ManagedObj);
  int GetNativeDataSize();
}
```

In these methods, *native* is used as another term for *unmanaged*. Here are descriptions of the five methods:

- MarshalNativeToManaged. This method is called by the CLR whenever an object must be marshaled from unmanaged code to managed code. It's called with a pointer to the unmanaged object, represented as a System.IntPtr type. The implementer must return an appropriate .NET object representing the "managed view" of the unmanaged object. This can be an instance of an adapter class like ComStream in the previous section.

- MarshalManagedToNative. This method is called by the CLR whenever an object must be marshaled from managed code to unmanaged code. It's called with the managed object instance. The implementer must return a pointer to an appropriate unmanaged object (as a System.IntPtr type) representing the "unmanaged view" of the .NET object. This object can be an instance of an adapter class like ManagedIStream in the previous section. If a COM interface pointer is returned, its reference count must be incremented.

- `CleanUpNativeData`. This method is called by the CLR when it's appropriate to clean up the unmanaged object allocated in the `MarshalManagedToNative` method. This can include decrementing the reference count for a COM object that was incremented in `MarshalManagedToNative`, freeing memory that was allocated, unpinning memory that was pinned, and so on. The passed-in `System.IntPtr` parameter is a pointer to whatever needs to be cleaned up.

- `CleanUpManagedData`. This method is called by the CLR when it's appropriate to clean up the managed object allocated in the `MarshalNativeToManaged` method. Of course, because managed objects are garbage-collected, typically nothing needs to be done in this method. Even if the object implements `IDisposable`, you should not call its `Dispose` method unless you're performing custom marshaling by value. This is discussed in the upcoming "An Alternative to Adapter Objects" section. The passed-in object parameter is the instance that could potentially require clean-up.

- `GetNativeDataSize`. This method is supposed to return the size, in bytes, of the unmanaged type being marshaled if it's a value type, or –1 to indicate that you're not marshaling a value type. Because custom marshaling of value types is not supported in version 1.0 of the .NET Framework, this method is never called by the CLR. See the "Limitations" section in this chapter for more information. This method's implementation should always return –1.

The `GetInstance` Method

Besides implementing `ICustomMarshaler`, a custom marshaler must implement a static (`Shared` in VB .NET) method named `GetInstance` with the following signature (shown in C#):

```
static ICustomMarshaler GetInstance(string cookie)
```

Because this method is not part of the `ICustomMarshaler` interface definition, you can't rely on the compiler to remind you to implement this method.

TIP	

Remember to implement `GetInstance` when writing a custom marshaler (and be sure to make it static), because your compiler can't enforce this requirement. Failure to do so causes an exception at run time when the CLR attempts to use your custom marshaler.

`GetInstance` is called by the CLR in order to get an instance of the custom marshaler. The string parameter is a "cookie" value that can be specified by the custom marshaler consumer and used by the custom marshaler however it wishes. The following is a proper implementation of `GetInstance` in C# that ignores the cookie value and assumes the presence of a private class member called `marshaler`:

```
public static ICustomMarshaler GetInstance(string cookie)
{
  if (marshaler == null)
    marshaler = new MyMarshaler();

  return marshaler;
}
```

This instantiation pattern makes the custom marshaler a singleton object, which is appropriate because custom marshalers must not maintain any state. This is the case because the CLR calls GetInstance only once per application domain per parameter, field, or return type that uses the custom marshaler, regardless of how many times the marshaler is used.

Similar to the custom registration functions presented in Chapter 12, "Customizing COM's View of .NET Components," the GetInstance method doesn't have to be public because the CLR can invoke it regardless of its visibility, but it must be static.

The Consumers

The consumers of a custom marshaler were described earlier as any member signatures with a parameter, return type, or field marked with MarshalAsAttribute and the value UnmanagedType.CustomMarshaler. This works on any parameters and return values, regardless of whether they belong to a PInvoke signature or a member of a COM object, and works on any fields, regardless of whether they are exposed as fields of a structure or properties of a class. Recall that to use MarshalAsAttribute with a property, you must mark the parameter and return type of its accessor methods.

MarshalAsAttribute has the following named parameters relevant to custom marshaling:

- MarshalTypeRef. This can be set to the type of a custom marshaler class, using typeof in C#, GetType in VB .NET, or __typeof in C++. Either this named parameter or MarshalType must be used with UnmanagedType.CustomMarshaler, but MarshalTypeRef is recommended.

- MarshalType. This can be set to a string specifying the custom marshaler type. This can be simply the namespace-qualified type name if it resides in the same assembly, but it must be qualified with a full assembly name if it's in a different assembly. This is useful for a "late bound" reference to a custom marshaler type, which does not require its metadata at compile time.

- MarshalCookie. This can be set to a string that will be passed to the custom marshaler's GetInstance method. If MarshalCookie is not set, an empty string is passed.

Either MarshalTypeRef or MarshalType must be used to specify the custom marshaler type, but MarshalCookie is optional. If both MarshalTypeRef and MarshalType are specified (which you should never do), `MarshalTypeRef` is ignored. If the custom marshaler type specified by `MarshalTypeRef` or `MarshalType` cannot be loaded when a marked member is called, a `TypeLoadException` is thrown.

The use of `MarshalAsAttribute` for custom marshaling is demonstrated in the following C# signatures:

```
[return: MarshalAs(UnmanagedType.CustomMarshaler,
  MarshalTypeRef=typeof(StreamMarshaler))]
Stream GetStream();

void WriteToStream(
  [MarshalAs(UnmanagedType.CustomMarshaler, MarshalType="StreamMarshaler,
➥ StreamMarshaler, Version=1.0.0.0, Culture=neutral,
➥ PublicKeyToken=b26ada3712d5a923")] Stream s);

bool GetStreamViaOutParameter([MarshalAs(UnmanagedType.CustomMarshaler,
  MarshalTypeRef=typeof(StreamMarshaler))] out Stream s);

bool GetStreamViaByRefParameter([MarshalAs(UnmanagedType.CustomMarshaler,
  MarshalTypeRef=typeof(StreamMarshaler))] ref Stream s);

void PrintString([MarshalAs(UnmanagedType.CustomMarshaler,
  MarshalTypeRef=typeof(StringMarshaler), MarshalCookie="XYZ")] string s);

void SetData([MarshalAs(UnmanagedType.CustomMarshaler,
  MarshalTypeRef=typeof(ArrayMarshaler),
  MarshalCookie="first_is(10), last_is(20)")] int [] data);
```

TIP

The choice of using `MarshalTypeRef` with a `Type` object versus `MarshalType` with a string is just like the choice encountered with `ComSourceInterfacesAttribute`, discussed in Chapter 13, "Exposing .NET Events to COM Clients." You should use `MarshalTypeRef` whenever possible, because the compiler emits a string with the full assembly name, as can be seen using `ILDASM.EXE`:

```
.method public instance class [mscorlib]System.IO.Stream
  marshal( custom ("StreamMarshaler,
➥StreamMarshaler, Version=1.0.0.0, Culture=neutral,
➥PublicKeyToken=b26ada3712d5a923","")) GetStream() cil managed
```

Or, if the custom marshaler type happens to be in the same assembly as the attribute using `MarshalTypeRef`, only the type name is emitted.

Although using a partial assembly name with `MarshalType`, such as `"StreamMarshaler, StreamMarshaler"` works for assemblies not in the Global Assembly Cache, you should not use this if there's a chance that the custom marshaler will ever be installed in the GAC at a later date.

By-reference or out parameters are automatically supported without any extra work
needed by the custom marshaler. For example, both MarshalManagedToNative and
MarshalNativeToManaged are called when marshaling a by-reference parameter, but only one
of them is called when marshaling a by-value parameter. Which one is called depends on the
direction of the call. To get both MarshalManagedToNative and MarshalNativeToManaged to
be invoked when marshaling a by-value reference type, a consumer would need to mark the
parameter with both InAttribute and OutAttribute, a requirement that matches the behavior
of standard marshaling. This is often not necessary, however, because the use of adapter classes
means that changes to the reference type's state (such as the bits in a stream) are seen after the
call anyway because the callee is indirectly using the same object instance.

The previously shown C# signatures are exported to a type library as follows:

```
HRESULT GetStream([out, retval] IUnknown** pRetVal);

HRESULT WriteToStream([in] IUnknown* s);

HRESULT GetStreamViaOutParameter([out] IUnknown** s,
  [out, retval] VARIANT_BOOL* pRetVal);

HRESULT GetStreamViaByRefParameter([in, out] IUnknown** s,
  [out, retval] VARIANT_BOOL* pRetVal);

HRESULT PrintString([in] long s);

HRESULT SetData([in] long data);
```

Notice that the unmanaged type to which each managed type is being custom-marshaled does
not show up in an exported type library. That's because the MarshalAsAttribute contains no
information about what *unmanaged* type a custom marshaler marshals; it's hidden as an implementation detail. Users of a custom-marshaled object must call QueryInterface to get a
pointer to the desired interface. Visual Basic 6 users don't have to do anything because the
VB6 runtime does the QueryInterface call, although the type will appear as Unknown in the
object browser and IntelliSense.

Also, notice that custom-marshaled string and array parameters are exported as long. This
really represents a pointer value; in other words, void*. Such a type library works fine on a
32-bit platform, but is not a portable way to express a pointer.

TIP

To work around limitations of what the type library exporter produces for custom-
marshaled parameters, you could change the type library (using OLEVIEW.EXE to get
an IDL representation then using MIDL.EXE to compile a new type library) or create a

new one yourself. It's valid to change a custom-marshaled IUnknown* to a specific interface like IStream* *if and only if* the custom marshaler always produces a pointer to IStream or a derived interface. This depends on the implementation of the custom marshaler, because it may validly produce a plain IUnknown pointer instead of a more specific interface. It's also a good idea to change the long type exported to void* for custom-marshaled strings and arrays.

The Adapter Objects

Adapter objects are typically what a custom marshaler returns from ICustomMarshaler. MarshalNativeToManaged and ICustomMarshaler.MarshalManagedToNative. To demonstrate, Listing 20.4 (when combined with the previous two listings) contains a complete custom marshaler to transform a .NET Stream to a COM IStream and vice-versa. This can be compiled from a command prompt as follows:

```
csc StreamMarshaler.cs ComStream.cs ManagedIStream.cs /unsafe
```

LISTING 20.4   StreamMarshaler.cs. A C# Custom Marshaler That Converts Stream to IStream and Vice-Versa

```
 1: using System;
 2: using System.IO;
 3: using System.Runtime.InteropServices;
 4:
 5: public class StreamMarshaler : ICustomMarshaler
 6: {
 7:   static StreamMarshaler marshaler;
 8:
 9:   public object MarshalNativeToManaged(IntPtr pNativeData)
10:   {
11:     if (pNativeData == IntPtr.Zero) return null;
12:
13:     Object rcw = Marshal.GetObjectForIUnknown(pNativeData);
14:     if (!(rcw is UCOMIStream))
15:       throw new ArgumentException("The object must implement IStream.");
16:
17:     return new ComStream((UCOMIStream)rcw);
18:   }
19:
20:   public IntPtr MarshalManagedToNative(object ManagedObj)
21:   {
```

20

LISTING 20.4   Continued

```
22:        if (ManagedObj == null) return IntPtr.Zero;
23:
24:        if (!(ManagedObj is Stream))
25:        {
26:          throw new MarshalDirectiveException(
27:            "This custom marshaler must be used on Stream or a derived type.");
28:        }
29:
30:        ManagedIStream customObject = new ManagedIStream((Stream)ManagedObj);
31:        return Marshal.GetComInterfaceForObject(customObject,
32:          typeof(UCOMIStream));
33:      }
34:
35:      public void CleanUpNativeData(IntPtr pNativeData)
36:      {
37:        Marshal.Release(pNativeData);
38:      }
39:
40:      public void CleanUpManagedData(object ManagedObj)
41:      {
42:        // Nothing to do
43:      }
44:
45:      public int GetNativeDataSize()
46:      {
47:        return -1;
48:      }
49:
50:      public static ICustomMarshaler GetInstance(string cookie)
51:      {
52:        // Always return the same instance
53:        if (marshaler != null) marshaler = new StreamMarshaler();
54:        return marshaler;
55:      }
56: }
```

MarshalNativeToManaged returns null on Line 11 if the incoming pointer value represents null, or returns a new ComStream instance from the object implementing UCOMIStream on Line 17. This object is the standard RCW obtained from the incoming IntPtr value using Marshal.GetObjectForIUnknown on Line 13.

In the reverse direction, `MarshalManagedToNative` constructs a new `ManagedIStream` instance from the incoming object on Line 30 and uses `Marshal.GetComInterfaceForObject` to create a standard CCW for the object. The pointer to the CCW is returned in Lines 31–32. `Marshal.GetComInterfaceForObject` increments the reference count for the CCW, so `CleanUpNativeData` calls `Release` on the same object in Line 37 to avoid a reference count leak.

`Marshal.GetIUnknownForObject` could have been called instead of `Marshal. GetComInterfaceForObject`, but it's better to return an `IStream` pointer rather than an `IUnknown` pointer in case consumers of the custom marshaler are tempted to modify a type library to change an exported `IUnknown*` corresponding to a custom marshaled `Stream` parameter to `IStream*`.

TIP

Using members of the `Marshal` class in custom marshalers is a great way to leverage bits and pieces of standard marshaling functionality inside your custom transformations. Several of its methods, such as the `GetHRForException` and `ThrowExceptionForHR` methods used in the upcoming "Marshalers, Marshalers, Marshalers!" section, were designed to be used inside custom marshalers. Appendix A, "`System.Runtime.InteropServices` Reference," covers every method of the `Marshal` class.

Because C# code cannot interact with COM objects directly, it can't truly provide a custom CCW and custom RCW as explained at the beginning of the chapter. Instead, the custom marshaler in Listing 20.4 uses the *standard* CCW for the adapter object to act as a custom CCW for the original .NET `Stream` object when marshaling from .NET to COM. In the reverse direction, the marshaler wraps a standard RCW with the `ComStream` wrapper rather than actually replacing the RCW that directly wraps the COM object. These two situations are pictured in Figures 20.3 and 20.4, using the example of `Stream` on the .NET side and `IStream` on the COM side.

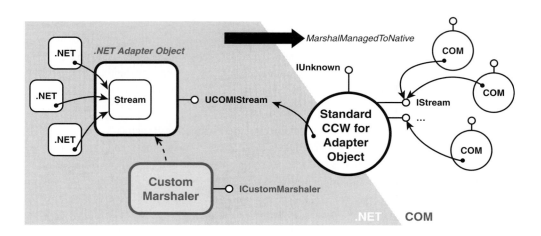

FIGURE 20.3

Using the standard CCW for an adapter object when marshaling from .NET to COM.

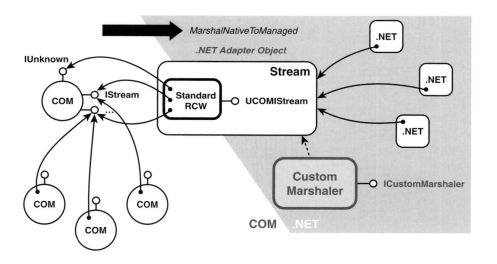

FIGURE 20.4

Using the standard RCW with an adapter object when marshaling from COM to .NET.

This approach is valid, and is pretty straightforward to implement because everything primarily stays in the managed realm. Using Visual C++ .NET with Managed Extensions, however, you can make one adapter object *the* RCW and the other one *the* CCW. This means using the C++ capabilities of mixing managed and unmanaged code to handle most or all of the interactions normally done by the CLR-supplied wrappers. The custom CCW is a full-fledged COM class (even with an explicit implementation of IUnknown) that happens to interact with managed objects. The custom RCW is still a .NET class, but one that does not need to rely on COM Interoperability to interact with unmanaged objects.

Figures 20.5 and 20.6 illustrate this approach in both directions, using the example of Stream on the .NET side and IStream on the COM side. Although these diagrams show no use of standard RCWs, in practice a standard RCW is often used by the custom RCW as an easy way to ensure context-safe calls on the wrapped COM interface. This will be demonstrated in Listing 20.9 later in the chapter. Listings 20.9 and 20.10 will re-implement the two adapter classes from Listings 20.2 and 20.3 in C++ to demonstrate how to implement this custom marshaling technique.

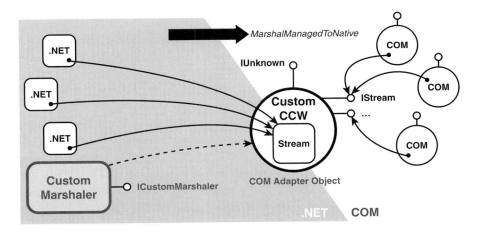

FIGURE 20.5
Using an unmanaged adapter object that is a custom CCW when marshaling from .NET to COM.

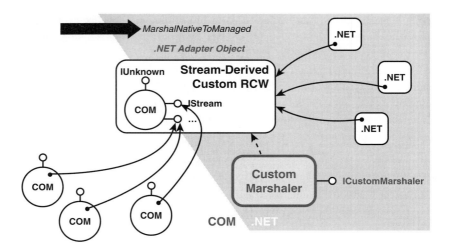

FIGURE 20.6

Using a managed adapter object that is a custom RCW when marshaling from COM to .NET.

Although the diagrams for this case are simpler, implementing the adapter objects may be more complicated. Here are the pros and cons of using C++ to implement adapter objects that work directly with managed and unmanaged code:

PROS:

- Better performance. Besides the fact that you can eliminate a wrapper in each direction, the other approach sometimes involves extra data transformations. For example, supporting non-zero offsets in `ComStream.Read` and `ComStream.Write` in Listing 20.2 would've involved copying one .NET array to another before exposing it to COM. When the adapter class is rewritten in Listing 20.9, you'll see that a pointer to the correct element in the array can be exposed directly without performing any copying.

- No limitations. Because the COM adapter object uses its .NET object directly and the .NET adapter object uses its COM object directly, you aren't limited by the support given by the standard RCW and CCW objects. For example, you could support `VARIANT`s with the `VT_RECORD` type.

CONS:

- Less built-in support. The price of total freedom is the fact that you have to do more yourself. For example, you're responsible for *all* data transformations between COM and .NET—manually converting between .NET strings and `BSTR`s, .NET arrays and `SAFEARRAY`s, .NET objects and `VARIANT`s, and so on. (The `System.Runtime.InteropServices.Marshal` class helps a great deal, however, by providing small chunks of standard marshaling functionality that can be used by your custom wrappers.)

Also, whereas a standard CCW implements many standard interfaces (like IProvideClassInfo, ISupportErrorInfo, IConnectionPointContainer, and so on), a custom CCW COM object doesn't magically implement any interfaces that you don't explicitly implement in your source code.

- Difficulty integrating with .NET code in other languages. If you don't mind having your custom marshaler in a separate assembly or are doing your development in C++ anyway, this doesn't apply. People often have the urge to contain all their functionality in a single file, but if your primary development language is C# or VB .NET, you can't merge your custom marshaling code with your other code without ILDASM.EXE and ILASM.EXE trickery. You could also opt to produce a C++ module and a C# module and link them into a multi-file assembly.

Listing 20.5 contains the code for a typical custom marshaler written in C++, assuming the existence of two adapter classes: CustomCCW—an unmanaged COM class, and CustomRCW—a .NET class. This custom marshaler will be used with the C++ adapter classes implemented in the "Marshalers, Marshalers, Marshalers!" section later in this chapter, replacing *UnmanagedType* and *ManagedType* with the types being custom-marshaled.

LISTING 20.5   A Typical Custom Marshaler Written in C++ That Uses Adapter Classes Serving Directly as Custom CCWs and RCWs

```
 1: public __gc class TypicalCustomMarshaler : public ICustomMarshaler
 2: {
 3: private:
 4:   static TypicalCustomMarshaler *marshaler = NULL;
 5:
 6: public:
 7:   Object* MarshalNativeToManaged(IntPtr pNativeData)
 8:   {
 9:     if (pNativeData == IntPtr::Zero) return NULL;
10:     return new CustomRCW(
11:       static_cast<UnmanagedType*>(pNativeData.ToPointer()));
12:   };
13:
14:   IntPtr MarshalManagedToNative(Object* ManagedObj)
15:   {
16:     if (ManagedObj == NULL) return IntPtr::Zero;
17:     CustomCCW *ccw = new CustomCCW(static_cast<ManagedType*>(ManagedObj));
18:     UnmanagedType* intf = NULL;
19:     ccw->QueryInterface(IID_UnmanagedType, (void**)&intf);
20:     return (IntPtr)intf;
21:   };
22:
23:   void CleanUpNativeData(IntPtr pNativeData)
```

20

LISTING 20.5 Continued

```
24:    {
25:      Marshal::Release(pNativeData);
26:    };
27:
28:    void CleanUpManagedData(Object* ManagedObj)
29:    {
30:      // Nothing to do
31:    };
32:
33:    int GetNativeDataSize()
34:    {
35:      return -1;
36:    };
37:
38:    static ICustomMarshaler* GetInstance(String* cookie)
39:    {
40:      // Always return the same instance
41:      if (marshaler != NULL) marshaler = new TypicalCustomMarshaler();
42:      return marshaler;
43:    };
44: };
```

In the C#-authored custom marshaler, `Marshal.GetObjectForIUnknown` was used to convert an `IntPtr` to an object inside `MarshalNativeToManaged`. Here, in Line 11, `IntPtr`'s `ToPointer` method is called, which returns `void*`. This `void*` can then be cast to the desired .NET type. This type is passed to the .NET `CustomRCW` adapter object.

> **TIP**
>
> In C++, use `IntPtr.ToPointer` as an intermediate step when converting an `IntPtr` value to a class or interface type. This is necessary because you cannot cast an `IntPtr` value to a reference type directly.

In `MarshalManagedToNative`, Line 19 calls `QueryInterface` directly on the `CustomCCW` object and Line 20 casts the returned interface pointer to return directly to an `IntPtr` value. This can only be done when `CustomCCW` is an unmanaged COM class. If `CustomCCW` is a .NET class instead, it wouldn't *really* be a CCW, so `Marshal.GetComInterfaceForObject` could be used to obtain an `IntPtr` value representing an interface pointer for the CLR-supplied CCW for the `CustomCCW` .NET class.

The rest of the listing is essentially the same as the C# version. The "Marshalers, Marshalers, Marshalers!" section later in this chapter shows examples demonstrating how to write `CustomCCW` and `CustomRCW` classes that can be used by such a custom marshaler.

DIGGING DEEPER

In this chapter, all custom marshalers are implemented as .NET classes because a custom marshaler cannot directly be a COM object. A COM class could implement the exported definition of `ICustomMarshaler` defined in `mscorlib.tlb`, but the requirement of having a static `GetInstance` method can't be fulfilled because COM classes don't have a notion of static members. You could write a .NET class that inherits a COM class implementing `ICustomMarshaler` and add a `GetInstance` method, but there's no compelling reason to do so. As Listings 20.4 and 20.5 demonstrate, there's not much code involved in custom marshalers that use adapter objects.

Implementing ICustomAdapter

Both adapter classes in Listings 20.2 and 20.3 had an `UnderlyingStream` property that provided users of the adapter object the ability to retrieve the original object. This is helpful if the original object contains other functionality that is not made available by the adapter object that only knows about the stream functionality. Such a mechanism is important for adapter objects used by a custom marshaler because users of the custom marshaler don't have access to the original objects from the other side of the managed/unmanaged transition.

For an illustration of why this can be important, consider the Visual Basic 6 error object (`ErrObject`). The VB6 runtime wraps an incoming object that implements `IErrorInfo`, presenting the information in the way expected by Visual Basic 6 programs. However, because there's no way to access the original object implementing `IErrorInfo` from a Visual Basic 6 error object, you can't get a hold of `_Exception` or any other interfaces implemented by error objects created from .NET exceptions. Had `ErrObject` been defined with a method like `GetErrorInfoObject`, .NET-aware Visual Basic 6 programs could have taken advantage of this extra functionality.

The `System.Runtime.InteropServices` namespace defines an interface that formalizes the practice of exposing the wrapped object. This interface is called `ICustomAdapter` and has a single parameter-less method—`GetUnderlyingObject`. As you might expect, `GetUnderlyingObject` returns a `System.Object` instance that should be the original object. All adapter objects should implement this interface, so those clients that know to look for it can take advantage of it. Unlike COM aggregation, the outer object can't dynamically support arbitrary interfaces of the inner object directly, so providing access to the inner object is the next best thing.

An Alternative to Adapter Objects

Using adapter objects can be considered custom marshaling *by reference*. The term *marshal by reference* is used elsewhere in the .NET Framework when discussing objects marshaled across application domain boundaries. When an object is marshaled by reference across an application domain, a proxy handles communication with the original object. Similarly, when an object is custom marshaled by reference across the managed/unmanaged boundary, the adapter object acts like a proxy.

But adapter objects aren't the only means of implementing custom marshalers, and sometimes aren't even an option. Adapter objects can always be used when transforming from one *interface* to another. Consider a class such as System.Drawing.Font, however, which we want to custom marshal with IFont, the interface representing a font in COM. The issue here is that Font is sealed (NotInheritable in VB .NET), so it's impossible to create a derived class that acts like a Font and forwards its implementation to an object implementing IFont.

Instead, when marshaling IFont (a "COM font") to Font (a ".NET font"), a custom marshaler could simply create an instance of the Font class, initialize it with the state of an IFont object, and pass this new "detached" object as the custom-marshaled IFont. In the reverse direction, an adapter object could still be used to provide an IFont implementation that forwards calls to a Font object. Or, the copying approach could be used here as well: instantiate a StdFont class (a standard OLE Automation class that implements IFont), initialize it with the state of a Font object, and pass this new object as the custom-marshaled Font.

This approach that doesn't use adapter objects can be considered custom marshaling *by value*. When an object is marshaled by value across an application domain boundary, it is copied from one domain to another. Similarly, when an object is custom marshaled by value across the managed/unmanaged boundary, the original object's state is copied to an object of a different but related type.

Figures 20.7 and 20.8 illustrate custom marshaling by value in both directions. They assume that a language like C# or Visual Basic .NET is being used. If custom marshaling by value is performed in Visual C++ .NET, the standard RCW can be eliminated because the COM object (in this case, StdFont) can be used directly by the custom marshaler.

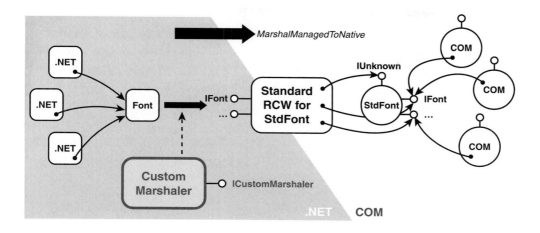

FIGURE 20.7
Custom marshaling by value from .NET to COM.

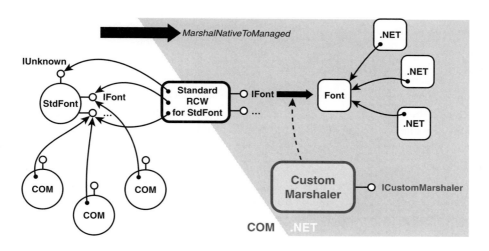

FIGURE 20.8
Custom marshaling by value from COM to .NET.

Custom marshaling by value works naturally for fonts, as it's easy to imagine initializing a COM font object with the state of a .NET font object, and vice-versa. As long as two font objects have the same name, size, and settings for bold, italic, and so on, the new object should represent the old one just fine. In addition, the System.Drawing.Font class already has methods that facilitate such a transformation, so you don't have to get and set properties one-by-one to perform the copying. This will be demonstrated in Listing 20.6.

Although the sealed nature of Font requires custom marshaling by value (at least in one direction), it's sometimes a more attractive approach than custom marshaling by reference anyway. Here's a list of pros and cons to custom marshaling by value:

PROS:

- Ease in custom marshaler implementation. For a pair of objects that provide a public means for getting/setting their state (or for immutable objects that provide a public means of getting their state), custom marshaling by value can be much easier than writing adapter classes that implement all of an object's public members and forward the calls appropriately. In addition, existing objects that you instantiate often implement several other interfaces that clients might find handy. For example, the StdFont class implements IFontDisp in addition to IFont.

CONS:

- Poorer performance. The overhead of copying an object's state at every managed/unmanaged transition can substantially hurt performance. For font objects the copying may not be noticeable, but for streams with large buffers the extra copying can be unacceptable. When marshaling needs to occur in both directions for a single call (as with a by-reference parameter), the copying needs to occur twice.

- Subtlety for consumers. When types are custom marshaled by value, any changes made by the callee to the state of an object do not get reflected to the caller after the call by default. This behavior is often non-intuitive for reference types because they exhibit marshal-by-reference behavior in pure managed code. (The marshal-by-value behavior *does* match the default behavior for non-blittable reference types when called across the managed/unmanaged boundary, however.) To get changes to an object's state propagated back to the caller, a signature either must use the custom marshaler on a by-reference parameter or mark a by-value parameter with InAttribute and OutAttribute.

- Limiting. Custom marshaling by value means that providing functionality like ICustomAdapter.GetUnderlyingObject isn't possible. For example, once an object implementing IFont has been returned by a custom marshaler, the original Font object cannot be accessed (just like the IErrorInfo/ErrObject example).

> **DIGGING DEEPER**
>
> Custom marshaling by value would work naturally for value types, because they are typically small (so not much copying would be involved) and users know that a value type's state won't change when passed to a method as a by-value parameter. Unfortunately, custom marshaling of value types is not supported in version 1.0 of the .NET Framework.

Regardless of whether you choose custom marshaling by reference or custom marshaling by value, you should document the behavior for consumers of your custom marshaler so they know what behavior to expect in terms of seeing changes to a parameter's state after a method call (and whether to use `InAttribute` and `OutAttribute`).

FAQ: When do I call `IDisposable.Dispose` inside `ICustomMarshaler.CleanUpManagedData`?

When custom marshaling a .NET object that implements `IDisposable`, you should always call `IDisposable.Dispose` if the object is custom marshaled *by value* inside `ICustomMarshaler.MarshalNativeToManaged`. Instead, if the object is custom marshaled *by reference*, you almost certainly don't want to call `Dispose`, but this ultimately depends on the implementation of the adapter object. Typically, an adapter object's `Dispose` implementation releases the original object, so in this case calling `Dispose` inside `CleanUpManagedData` would be a very bad thing to do. The original object would be disposed during the marshaling process despite the fact that clients may still be using it.

Marshalers, Marshalers, Marshalers!

Now that we've covered all the background information about custom marshaling, it's time for some examples. First we'll look at three examples of converting between related COM and .NET types:

- `System.Drawing.Font` and `IFont`
- `System.IO.Stream` and `IStream`
- `System.String` and `SAFEARRAY`

The first example uses custom marshaling by value, as pictured in Figures 20.7 and 20.8. The second example is similar to the custom marshaler already covered in Listings 20.2, 20.3, and 20.4, but uses C++ to demonstrate more direct custom marshaling by reference, as pictured in Figures 20.5 and 20.6. Plus, the second example adds a few more features that the C# StreamMarshaler does not have. The third example isn't practical like the first two, but demonstrates custom marshaling with something other than an interface on the COM side—a SAFEARRAY.

In addition to these three examples of transforming one type to another, we'll cover a fourth example that modifies a type while preserving its interface identity. In this example, we'll see how to use a custom RCW to provide deterministic release of resources held by any .NET object exposed to COM.

Example: Marshaling Between .NET and COM Fonts

Here's the first example of a custom marshaler that marshals its objects by value. As you'll see in these listings, custom marshaling by value often involves much less code than custom marshaling by reference because no adapter objects are involved. This example is broken up into two parts:

- The custom marshaler
- A sample consumer and its client

The remaining examples only show custom marshalers, because the consumers of any custom marshalers should be self-explanatory once you see an example of one.

The Custom Marshaler

Listing 20.6 contains FontMarshaler, a complete custom marshaler class that marshals System.Drawing.Font to IFont and vice-versa. This class requires .NET type definitions for the IFont interface and FONTDESC and LOGFONT structures. FONTDESC and LOGFONT are defined in the listing, but the definition of IFont is available on this book's Web site in the IFont.cs file. This definition is written in C# due to a Visual Basic .NET limitation described in the next chapter, "Manually Defining COM Types in Source Code." Therefore, you must perform the following command-line steps to compile Listing 20.6:

1. `csc /t:library IFont.cs`
2. `vbc /t:library FontMarshaler.vb /r:IFont.dll /r:System.Drawing.dll`

LISTING 20.6   FontMarshaler.vb—A Custom Marshaler That Marshals Between .NET Fonts and COM Fonts

```
1: Imports System
2: Imports System.Drawing
```

LISTING 20.6 Continued

```
 3: Imports System.Runtime.InteropServices
 4:
 5: ' The Font Custom Marshaler
 6: Public Class FontMarshaler
 7:   Implements ICustomMarshaler
 8:
 9:   Private Shared marshaler As ICustomMarshaler
10:
11:   Public Function MarshalNativeToManaged(pNativeData As IntPtr) _
12:     As Object Implements ICustomMarshaler.MarshalNativeToManaged
13:     If (pNativeData.Equals(IntPtr.Zero)) Then
14:       MarshalNativeToManaged = Nothing
15:     End If
16:
17:     ' Extract the IFont interface
18:     Dim unmanagedFont As IFont = _
19:       CType(Marshal.GetObjectForIUnknown(pNativeData), IFont)
20:
21:     ' Create a .NET Font from IFont's hFont property.  This throws
22:     ' an ArgumentException if the unmanaged font isn't TrueType
23:     MarshalNativeToManaged = Font.FromHFont(unmanagedFont.hFont)
24:   End Function
25:
26:   Public Function MarshalManagedToNative(ManagedObj As Object) _
27:     As IntPtr Implements ICustomMarshaler.MarshalManagedToNative
28:     If (ManagedObj Is Nothing) Then
29:       MarshalManagedToNative = IntPtr.Zero
30:     End If
31:
32:     Dim managedFont As Font = ManagedObj
33:     Dim log As New LOGFONT
34:     managedFont.ToLogFont(log)
35:
36:     ' Extract information about the .NET font
37:     Dim desc As FONTDESC
38:     desc.cbSizeofstruct = Marshal.SizeOf(desc)
39:     desc.lpstrName = managedFont.Name
40:     desc.cySize = managedFont.SizeInPoints * 10000
41:     desc.sWeight = log.lfWeight
42:     desc.sCharset = log.lfCharSet
43:     desc.fItalic = managedFont.Italic
44:     desc.fUnderline = managedFont.Underline
45:     desc.fStrikethrough = managedFont.Strikeout
46:
```

LISTING 20.6   Continued

```
47:      ' Create a StdFont object using the FONTDESC
48:      Dim unmanagedFont As IFont
49:      Dim hresult As Integer = _
50:        OleCreateFontIndirect(desc, GetType(IFont).GUID, unmanagedFont)
51:      If (hresult < 0) Then Marshal.ThrowExceptionForHR(hresult)
52:
53:      MarshalManagedToNative = _
54:        Marshal.GetComInterfaceForObject(unmanagedFont, GetType(IFont))
55:    End Function
56:
57:    Public Sub CleanUpNativeData(pNativeData As IntPtr) _
58:      Implements ICustomMarshaler.CleanUpNativeData
59:      ' Call release twice due to two AddRefs in MarshalManagedToNative
60:      Marshal.Release(pNativeData)
61:      Marshal.Release(pNativeData)
62:    End Sub
63:
64:    Public Sub CleanUpManagedData(ManagedObj As Object) _
65:      Implements ICustomMarshaler.CleanUpManagedData
66:      ' Font implements IDisposable
67:      CType(ManagedObj, IDisposable).Dispose()
68:    End Sub
69:
70:    Public Function GetNativeDataSize() As Integer _
71:      Implements ICustomMarshaler.GetNativeDataSize
72:      GetNativeDataSize = -1
73:    End Function
74:
75:    Public Shared Function GetInstance(cookie As String) As ICustomMarshaler
76:      If (marshaler Is Nothing) Then
77:        marshaler = New FontMarshaler()
78:      End If
79:      GetInstance = marshaler
80:    End Function
81:
82:    ' Used to create a StdFont object that implements IFont
83:    Declare Function OleCreateFontIndirect Lib "oleaut32.dll" _
84:      (<[In]> ByRef fontdesc As FONTDESC, <[In]> ByRef refiid As Guid, _
85:      <Out, MarshalAs(UnmanagedType.Interface)> ByRef ppvObj As Object) _
86:      As Integer
87: End Class
88:
89: Public Structure FONTDESC
90:    Public cbSizeofstruct As Integer
```

LISTING 20.6   Continued

```
 91:     <MarshalAs(UnmanagedType.LPWStr)> Public lpstrName As String
 92:     Public cySize As Long
 93:     Public sWeight As Short
 94:     Public sCharset As Short
 95:     Public fItalic As Boolean
 96:     Public fUnderline As Boolean
 97:     Public fStrikethrough As Boolean
 98: End Structure
 99:
100: <StructLayout(LayoutKind.Sequential, CharSet:=CharSet.Auto)> _
101: Public Class LOGFONT
102:     Public lfHeight As Integer
103:     Public lfWidth As Integer
104:     Public lfEscapement As Integer
105:     Public lfOrientation As Integer
106:     Public lfWeight As Integer
107:     Public lfItalic As Byte
108:     Public lfUnderline As Byte
109:     Public lfStrikeOut As Byte
110:     Public lfCharSet As Byte
111:     Public lfOutPrecision As Byte
112:     Public lfClipPrecision As Byte
113:     Public lfQuality As Byte
114:     Public lfPitchAndFamily As Byte
115:     <MarshalAs(UnmanagedType.ByValTStr, SizeConst:=32)> _
116:     Public lfFaceName As String
117: End Class
```

To perform the custom marshaling, we need a way to convert a .NET font to a COM font, and vice-versa. System.Drawing.Font doesn't have a method to construct an instance of itself from an IFont interface, but it does have a method to construct one from a Windows font handle (an HFONT)—Font.FromHFont. Fortunately, IFont has a property called hFont that retrieves a Windows handle to the font object. Therefore, the MarshalNativeToManaged implementation creates a .NET font from the incoming pointer to a COM font by calling Font.FromHFont on Line 23. An interesting point about Font.FromHFont is that it throws an exception if the input font isn't a TrueType font, because GDI+ doesn't support fonts that aren't. A more accommodating custom marshaler could use a heuristic to find a best match TrueType font for any incoming non-TrueType font. In this simple example, we let the exception get exposed to the user.

In the reverse direction, MarshalManagedToNative calls the Windows API OleCreateFontIndirect in Line 50 to create a StdFont object that implements IFont.

20

CUSTOM MARSHALING

Creating such an object requires a FONTDESC structure filled with information explaining what kind of font is desired. Lines 39–45 fill in this information with data obtained from the incoming .NET Font instance. Font.ToLongFont is called in Line 34 so we can get information about the font's weight and character set because this information isn't available directly from the Font class itself. A font's size is stored differently in COM fonts than in .NET fonts, so the .NET font size is multiplied by 10,000 in Line 40 to account for the different representation. OleCreateFontIndirect returns an HRESULT, so Line 51 checks for a failure value then, if necessary, throws the appropriate exception using Marshal.ThrowExceptionForHR. By defining the OleCreateFontIndirect PInvoke signature with DllImportAttribute and setting PreserveSig to false, the HRESULT to exception transformation could've been handled by the CLR instead. But for the simplicity of this example, Declare is used to define the PInvoke method in Lines 83–86.

The call to OleCreateFontIndirect increments the StdFont object's reference count, *and* the call to Marshal.GetComInterfaceForObject increments the object's reference count again, so CleanUpNativeData calls Marshal.Release *twice* in Lines 60–61 to properly restore its reference count. Because Font implements IDisposable, and because we're marshaling it by value, CleanUpManagedData calls IDisposable.Dispose in Line 67.

Lines 89–117 contain the .NET definitions of the FONTDESC and LOGFONT structures. Although FONTDESC is defined as a value type, LOGFONT is defined as a formatted reference type for an extremely subtle reason. The System.Drawing.Font.ToLogFont method called in Line 34 has a System.Object parameter that must be a LONGFONT instance to be filled in with information. Had LOGFONT been defined as a value type, it would be boxed for the call to ToLogFont and any changes to the boxed object's fields would be lost after the call. If you want the state of a by-value parameter to be changed after the call, it must be a reference type. The use of StructLayoutAttribute in Line 100 not only formats the LOGFONT reference type with sequential layout, but it also sets the character set of the lfFaceName field appropriately.

A Sample Consumer and Its Client

Listing 20.7 contains a .NET Windows Form that uses the FontMarshaler custom marshaler from Listing 20.6 on a property that gets/sets the font of its TextBox control. This form is the consumer of the custom marshaler, and can be built from a command prompt as follows:

```
vbc /t:library ManagedForm.vb /r:System.Windows.Forms.dll /r:System.Drawing.dll
➥/r:System.dll /r:FontMarshaler.dll
```

LISTING 20.7 ManagedForm.vb — A Windows Forms Control That Uses the FontMarshaler Custom Marshaler

```
1: Imports System
2: Imports System.Drawing
3: Imports System.Windows.Forms
```

LISTING 20.7 Continued

```vb
4:  Imports System.Runtime.InteropServices
5:
6:  Public Class ManagedForm
7:    Inherits Form
8:
9:    Friend WithEvents TextBox1 As TextBox
10:   Friend WithEvents Button1 As Button
11:   Friend WithEvents FontDialog1 As FontDialog
12:   'Required by the Windows Form Designer
13:   Private components As System.ComponentModel.IContainer
14:
15:   Public Sub New()
16:     MyBase.New()
17:     ' This call is required by the Windows Form Designer
18:     InitializeComponent()
19:   End Sub
20:
21:   ' Form overrides Dispose to clean up the component list
22:   Protected Overloads Overrides Sub Dispose(ByVal disposing As Boolean)
23:     If disposing Then
24:       If Not (components Is Nothing) Then
25:         components.Dispose()
26:       End If
27:     End If
28:     MyBase.Dispose(disposing)
29:   End Sub
30:
31:   ' Property that uses the custom marshaler
32:   Public Property TextBoxFont() As _
33:     <MarshalAs(UnmanagedType.CustomMarshaler, _
34:     MarshalTypeRef:=GetType(FontMarshaler))> Font
35:     Get
36:       TextBoxFont = TextBox1.Font
37:     End Get
38:     Set(<MarshalAs(UnmanagedType.CustomMarshaler, _
39:       MarshalTypeRef:=GetType(FontMarshaler))> ByVal Value As Font)
40:       TextBox1.Font = Value
41:     End Set
42:   End Property
43:
44:   Private Sub Button1_Click(ByVal sender As System.Object, _
45:     ByVal e As System.EventArgs) Handles Button1.Click
46:     FontDialog1.Font = TextBox1.Font
47:     FontDialog1.ShowDialog()
```

20

CUSTOM
MARSHALING

LISTING 20.7   Continued

```
48:      TextBox1.Font = FontDialog1.Font
49:    End Sub
50:
51:    ' The following procedure is required by the Windows Form Designer
52:    Private Sub InitializeComponent()
53:      Me.TextBox1 = New System.Windows.Forms.TextBox()
54:      Me.Button1 = New System.Windows.Forms.Button()
55:      Me.FontDialog1 = New System.Windows.Forms.FontDialog()
56:      Me.SuspendLayout()
57:
58:      Me.TextBox1.Anchor = (((System.Windows.Forms.AnchorStyles.Top _
59:        Or System.Windows.Forms.AnchorStyles.Bottom) _
60:        Or System.Windows.Forms.AnchorStyles.Left) _
61:        Or System.Windows.Forms.AnchorStyles.Right)
62:      Me.TextBox1.Multiline = True
63:      Me.TextBox1.Name = "TextBox1"
64:      Me.TextBox1.Size = New System.Drawing.Size(392, 144)
65:      Me.TextBox1.Text = ""
66:
67:      Me.Button1.Anchor = ((System.Windows.Forms.AnchorStyles.Bottom _
68:        Or System.Windows.Forms.AnchorStyles.Left) _
69:        Or System.Windows.Forms.AnchorStyles.Right)
70:      Me.Button1.Location = New System.Drawing.Point(8, 152)
71:      Me.Button1.Name = "Button1"
72:      Me.Button1.Size = New System.Drawing.Size(376, 24)
73:      Me.Button1.Text = "Change Font"
74:
75:      Me.AutoScaleBaseSize = New System.Drawing.Size(5, 13)
76:      Me.ClientSize = New System.Drawing.Size(388, 181)
77:      Me.Controls.AddRange(New System.Windows.Forms.Control() _
78:        {Me.Button1, Me.TextBox1})
79:      Me.Name = "ManagedForm"
80:      Me.Text = "Visual Basic .NET Form"
81:      Me.ResumeLayout(False)
82:    End Sub
83: End Class
```

This is a standard Windows Form with a TextBox, a Button for changing the font, and a FontDialog. The important part is emphasized in Lines 31–42—a TextBoxFont property of type Font, marked with the FontMarshaler custom marshaler on both accessors. This property gets and sets the font of the form's TextBox control.

If .NET clients were to use the `ManagedForm` class and get/set its `TextBoxFont` property, custom marshaling would not be involved because there would be no managed/unmanaged transition. The `MarshalAsAttribute` marking would be ignored and `Font` instances could be passed back and forth as usual. If COM clients use the `ManagedForm` class, however, they view the property as enabling them to get/set the font using an `IFont` instance.

Listing 20.8 contains such a Visual Basic 6 client that instantiates the Windows Forms component and enables a user to invoke the .NET property's get and set accessors. The combination of these two forms is a testing application that enables you to see the successful custom marshaling of fonts right before your eyes. The application is pictured Figure 20.9.

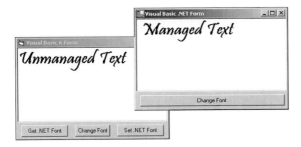

FIGURE 20.9
Using `FontMarshaler` *to achieve font interoperability.*

LISTING 20.8   `VB6Form.frm`—A Visual Basic 6 Form That Uses the Visual Basic .NET Form

```
 1: Private windowsForm As ManagedForm.ManagedForm
 2:
 3: Private Sub Form_Load()
 4:    ' Initialize the text box to a TrueType font
 5:    Text1.FontName = "Arial"
 6:
 7:    ' Instantiate the Windows Form
 8:    Set windowsForm = New ManagedForm.ManagedForm
 9:    windowsForm.Show
10: End Sub
11:
12: ' Set the COM font to a custom-marshaled .NET font
13: Private Sub GetFontButton_Click()
14:    Dim f As Object
15:    Set f = windowsForm.TextBoxFont
16:    Text1.Font.Name = f.Name
17:    Text1.Font.Size = f.Size
```

LISTING 20.8   Continued

```
18:    Text1.Font.Bold = f.Bold
19:    Text1.Font.Italic = f.Italic
20:    Text1.Font.Underline = f.Underline
21:    Text1.Font.Strikethrough = f.Strikethrough
22: End Sub
23:
24: ' Set the .NET font to a custom-marshaled COM font
25: Private Sub SetFontButton_Click()
26:    windowsForm.TextBoxFont = Text1.Font
27: End Sub
28:
29: Private Sub ChangeFontButton_Click()
30:    CommonDialog1.CancelError = True
31:    On Error GoTo ErrHandler
32:    ' Show only TrueType fonts
33:    CommonDialog1.Flags = cdlCFEffects Or cdlCFBoth Or cdlCFTTOnly
34:    ' Show the current font in the dialog
35:    CommonDialog1.FontName = Text1.Font.Name
36:    CommonDialog1.FontSize = Text1.Font.Size
37:    CommonDialog1.FontBold = Text1.Font.Bold
38:    CommonDialog1.FontItalic = Text1.Font.Italic
39:    CommonDialog1.FontUnderline = Text1.Font.Underline
40:    CommonDialog1.FontStrikethru = Text1.Font.Strikethrough
41:    CommonDialog1.Color = &H0&
42:    ' Display the Font dialog box
43:    CommonDialog1.ShowFont
44:    Text1.Font.Name = CommonDialog1.FontName
45:    Text1.Font.Size = CommonDialog1.FontSize
46:    Text1.Font.Bold = CommonDialog1.FontBold
47:    Text1.Font.Italic = CommonDialog1.FontItalic
48:    Text1.Font.Underline = CommonDialog1.FontUnderline
49:    Text1.Font.Strikethrough = CommonDialog1.FontStrikethru
50:    If (CommonDialog1.Color <> &H0&) Then
51:      MsgBox "Ignoring color choice since it is not part of the font.", _
52:        vbOKOnly, "Color Not Changed"
53:    End If
54:    Exit Sub
55: ErrHandler:
56:    ' User pressed the Cancel button
57: End Sub
```

This form is a standard Visual Basic 6 form with a TextBox, three Buttons, and a CommonDialog control used for selecting a font. Line 5 initializes the TextBox to a TrueType font because those are the only fonts supported by the .NET Font type. Line 8 instantiates the Windows Form, and Line 9 makes it visible by calling Show through its class interface.

Lines 12–27 contain the two methods that invoke the .NET property's accessors. Line 15 calls the custom-marshaled `TextBoxFont` property get accessor when the user clicks Get .NET Font, and Line 26 calls the custom-marshaled `TextBoxFont` property set accessor when the user clicks Set .NET Font. Notice how the fact that the property is of type `IUnknown` doesn't affect the Visual Basic 6 client code one bit.

The `ChangeFontButton_Click` method in Lines 29–57 handles the font dialog displayed to the user. Although the dialog presents the user with a choice of font color, color information is not part of the information stored with `IFont`.

To build this application, you should register the `ManagedForm` assembly and generate a type library. For example:

```
regasm ManagedForm.dll /tlb
```

Then create a new Visual Basic 6 Standard EXE project, reference the exported type library, and paste the code from Listing 20.8. Add the controls pictured in Figure 20.9 to the form and rename them appropriately. Don't forget that if you plan to run the application within the Visual Basic 6 IDE, you should either add the `ManagedForm` assembly (and its dependent `FontMarshaler` and `IFont` assemblies) to the GAC, or simply use `REGASM.EXE`'s /codebase option when performing the registration.

Example: Marshaling Between `System.IO.Stream` and `IStream`

This example contains two listings—one with the contents of `CustomRCW` and one with the contents of `CustomCCW`. The `CustomRCW` class serves the same purpose as `ComStream` in Listing 20.2 except that it uses the power of mixed-mode C++ programming to wrap a COM object directly rather than wrapping its RCW. The `CustomCCW` class serves the same purpose as `ManagedIStream` in Listing 20.3 but is actually a COM class wrapping a .NET `Stream` object.

These two classes can be used with a custom marshaler just like `TypicalCustomMarshaler` in Listing 20.5, replacing *UnmanagedType* with `IStream` and *ManagedType* with `Stream`. So the two important `ICustomMarshaler` methods would look like the following:

```
Object* MarshalNativeToManaged(IntPtr pNativeData)
{
  if (pNativeData == IntPtr::Zero) return NULL;
    return new CustomRCW(
      static_cast<IStream*>(pNativeData.ToPointer()));
};

IntPtr MarshalManagedToNative(Object* ManagedObj)
{
```

```
if (ManagedObj == NULL) return IntPtr::Zero;
CustomCCW *ccw = new CustomCCW(static_cast<Stream*>(ManagedObj));
IStream* intf = NULL;
ccw->QueryInterface(IID_IStream, (void**)&intf);
return (IntPtr)intf;
}
```

The resultant custom marshaler can be found on this book's Web site in the file
StreamMarshaler.cpp.

Listing 20.9 contains the definition of CustomRCW, which wraps an IStream implementation in
a Stream-derived object.

LISTING 20.9   The CustomRCW Adapter Class That Exposes IStream as Stream

```
 1: #using <mscorlib.dll> // Contains definition of Stream
 2: #include "objidl.h"   // Contains definition of IStream
 3:
 4: using namespace System;
 5: using namespace System::IO;
 6: using namespace System::Runtime::InteropServices;
 7:
 8: // CustomRCW - A Custom Runtime-Callable Wrapper
 9: public __gc class CustomRCW : public Stream, public ICustomAdapter
10: {
11: public:
12:   // Constructor
13:   CustomRCW(IStream* stream)
14:   {
15:     if (stream != NULL)
16:     {
17:       standardRCW = Marshal::GetObjectForIUnknown(stream);
18:     }
19:     else
20:     {
21:       throw new ArgumentNullException(S"stream");
22:     }
23:   };
24:
25:   // Finalizer
26:   ~CustomRCW()
27:   {
28:     Close();
29:   };
30:
31:   // Method to get original stream object
```

LISTING 20.9 Continued

```
32:  Object* GetUnderlyingObject()
33:  {
34:    return standardRCW;
35:  };
36:
37:  // Reads a sequence of bytes from the current stream and advances the
38:  // current position within the stream by the number of bytes read
39:  int Read(unsigned char buffer __gc[], int offset, int count)
40:  {
41:    if (standardRCW == NULL)
42:      throw new ObjectDisposedException(S"standardRCW");
43:    if (offset >= buffer->Length)
44:    {
45:      throw new ArgumentException(
46:        S"The offset must be less than the length of the buffer");
47:    }
48:
49:    ULONG bytesRead;  // Number of bytes actually read
50:    GCHandle gcHandle;
51:    IStream* originalStream = NULL;
52:
53:    try
54:    {
55:      // Pin the managed array
56:      gcHandle = GCHandle::Alloc(buffer, GCHandleType::Pinned);
57:
58:      // Extract the interface pointer in the correct context
59:      originalStream = (IStream*)Marshal::GetComInterfaceForObject(
60:        standardRCW, __typeof(UCOMIStream)).ToPointer();
61:
62:      // Call ISequentialStream.Read
63:      HRESULT hresult = originalStream->Read(
64:        (byte*)gcHandle.AddrOfPinnedObject().ToPointer() + offset,
65:        count, &bytesRead);
66:      if (FAILED(hresult))
67:        Marshal::ThrowExceptionForHR(hresult);
68:    }
69:    __finally
70:    {
71:      if (gcHandle.IsAllocated) gcHandle.Free();
72:      if (originalStream != NULL) originalStream->Release();
73:    }
74:
75:    return bytesRead;
```

20

CUSTOM
MARSHALING

LISTING 20.9   Continued

```cpp
 76:   };
 77:
 78:   // Writes a sequence of bytes to the current stream and advances the
 79:   // current position within this stream by the number of bytes written
 80:   void Write(unsigned char buffer __gc[], int offset, int count)
 81:   {
 82:     if (standardRCW == NULL)
 83:       throw new ObjectDisposedException(S"standardRCW");
 84:
 85:     if (offset >= buffer->Length)
 86:     {
 87:       throw new ArgumentException(
 88:         S"The offset must be less than the length of the buffer");
 89:     }
 90:
 91:     ULONG cbWritten;    // Number of bytes actually written
 92:     GCHandle gcHandle;
 93:     IStream* originalStream = NULL;
 94:
 95:     try
 96:     {
 97:       // Pin the managed array
 98:       GCHandle gcHandle = GCHandle::Alloc(buffer, GCHandleType::Pinned);
 99:
100:       // Extract the interface pointer in the correct context
101:       originalStream = (IStream*)Marshal::GetComInterfaceForObject(
102:         standardRCW, __typeof(UCOMIStream)).ToPointer();
103:
104:       // Call ISequentialStream.Write
105:       HRESULT hresult = originalStream->Write(
106:         (byte*)gcHandle.AddrOfPinnedObject().ToPointer() + offset,
107:         count, &cbWritten);
108:       if (FAILED(hresult))
109:         Marshal::ThrowExceptionForHR(hresult);
110:     }
111:     __finally
112:     {
113:       if (gcHandle.IsAllocated) gcHandle.Free();
114:       if (originalStream != NULL) originalStream->Release();
115:     }
116:   };
117:
118:   // Sets the position within the current stream
119:   __int64 Seek(__int64 offset, SeekOrigin origin)
```

LISTING 20.9   Continued

```
120:    {
121:      if (standardRCW == NULL)
122:        throw new ObjectDisposedException(S"standardRCW");
123:
124:      ULARGE_INTEGER plibNewPosition;  // Position after Seek
125:      LARGE_INTEGER off;
126:      off.QuadPart = offset;
127:      IStream* originalStream = NULL;
128:
129:      try
130:      {
131:        // Extract the interface pointer in the correct context
132:        originalStream = (IStream*)Marshal::GetComInterfaceForObject(
133:          standardRCW, __typeof(UCOMIStream)).ToPointer();
134:
135:        // The enum values of SeekOrigin match the enum values of
136:        // STREAM_SEEK, so we can just cast the origin to a DWORD
137:        HRESULT hresult = originalStream->Seek(off, (DWORD)origin,
138:          &plibNewPosition);
139:        if (FAILED(hresult))
140:          Marshal::ThrowExceptionForHR(hresult);
141:      }
142:      __finally
143:      {
144:        if (originalStream != NULL) originalStream->Release();
145:      }
146:
147:      return plibNewPosition.QuadPart;
148:    };
149:
150:    // Returns the length, in bytes, of the stream
151:    __property __int64 get_Length()
152:    {
153:      if (standardRCW == NULL)
154:        throw new ObjectDisposedException(S"standardRCW");
155:
156:      tagSTATSTG statstg;
157:      IStream* originalStream = NULL;
158:
159:      try
160:      {
161:        // Extract the interface pointer in the correct context
162:        originalStream = (IStream*)Marshal::GetComInterfaceForObject(
163:          standardRCW, __typeof(UCOMIStream)).ToPointer();
```

LISTING 20.9   Continued

```
164:
165:          // Call Stat to retrieve info about the stream, such as the length
166:          HRESULT hresult = originalStream->Stat(&statstg, STATFLAG_NONAME);
167:          if (FAILED(hresult))
168:            Marshal::ThrowExceptionForHR(hresult);
169:        }
170:      __finally
171:      {
172:        if (originalStream != NULL) originalStream->Release();
173:      }
174:
175:      return statstg.cbSize.QuadPart;
176:    };
177:
178:    // Determines the position within the current stream
179:    __property __int64 get_Position()
180:    {
181:      return Seek(0, SeekOrigin::Current);
182:    };
183:    __property void set_Position(__int64 value)
184:    {
185:      Seek(value, SeekOrigin::Begin);
186:    };
187:
188:    // Sets the length of the current stream
189:    void SetLength(__int64 value)
190:    {
191:      if (standardRCW == NULL)
192:        throw new ObjectDisposedException(S"standardRCW");
193:
194:      ULARGE_INTEGER val;
195:      val.QuadPart = value;
196:      IStream* originalStream = NULL;
197:
198:      try
199:      {
200:        // Extract the interface pointer in the correct context
201:        originalStream = (IStream*)Marshal::GetComInterfaceForObject(
202:          standardRCW, __typeof(UCOMIStream)).ToPointer();
203:
204:        HRESULT hresult = originalStream->SetSize(val);
205:        if (FAILED(hresult))
206:          Marshal::ThrowExceptionForHR(hresult);
207:      }
```

LISTING 20.9 Continued

```
208:     __finally
209:     {
210:       if (originalStream != NULL) originalStream->Release();
211:     }
212:   };
213:
214:   // Closes the current stream and releases any resources (such as
215:   // sockets and file handles) associated with the current stream
216:   void Close()
217:   {
218:     if (standardRCW != NULL)
219:     {
220:       IStream* originalStream = NULL;
221:       try
222:       {
223:         // Extract the interface pointer in the correct context
224:         originalStream = (IStream*)Marshal::GetComInterfaceForObject(
225:           standardRCW, __typeof(UCOMIStream)).ToPointer();
226:         originalStream->Commit(STGC_DEFAULT);
227:       }
228:       __finally
229:       {
230:         if (originalStream != NULL) originalStream->Release();
231:       }
232:
233:       Marshal::ReleaseComObject(standardRCW);
234:       standardRCW = NULL;
235:       GC::SuppressFinalize(this);
236:     }
237:   };
238:
239:   // Updates the underlying data source or repository with the current
240:   // state of the buffer and then clears the buffer
241:   void Flush()
242:   {
243:     IStream* originalStream = NULL;
244:     try
245:     {
246:       // Extract the interface pointer in the correct context
247:       originalStream = (IStream*)Marshal::GetComInterfaceForObject(
248:         standardRCW, __typeof(UCOMIStream)).ToPointer();
249:       originalStream->Commit(STGC_DEFAULT);
250:     }
251:     __finally
```

LISTING 20.9 Continued

```
252:    {
253:       if (originalStream != NULL) originalStream->Release();
254:    }
255:  };
256:
257:  // Determines whether the current stream supports reading
258:  __property bool get_CanRead() { return true; };
259:
260:  // Determines whether the current stream supports seeking
261:  __property bool get_CanSeek() { return true; };
262:
263:  // Determines whether the current stream supports writing
264:  __property bool get_CanWrite() { return true; };
265:
266: private:
267:    Object* standardRCW;
268: };
```

Line 2 includes the `objidl.h` header file, part of the Windows Platform SDK, because it contains an unmanaged definition of the `IStream` interface. The class is defined as a managed class with the `__gc` in Line 9. Besides deriving from `Stream`, it implements `ICustomAdapter`, as all adapter classes should.

The `CustomRCW` constructor in Lines 13–23 is passed an unmanaged COM `IStream` interface pointer. Notice, however, that rather than storing the `IStream` pointer as a class member to be used directly by `CustomRCW`'s other methods, it calls `GetObjectForIUnknown` in Line 17 to construct a *standard* RCW for the COM object. This RCW is used by the other methods, which call `GetComInterfaceForObject` to extract the original `IStream` interface pointer wrapped by this RCW. Why does `CustomRCW` do this extra wrapping and unwrapping instead of storing and using the `IStream` pointer directly? The answer is that storing and using a COM interface pointer directly is not context-safe. For example, if managed code uses `CustomRCW` from a different apartment than the one it was created in, calling a cached COM interface pointer directly would violate COM rules. The easiest way to ensure context safety is to let the CLR handle cross-context COM marshaling automatically. When you use a standard RCW, calls to the COM object always occur in the correct context. Of course, you could alternatively use your own mechanism to ensure context-safety that doesn't involve standard RCWs, such as COM's global interface table (GIT).

The Read method in Lines 39–76 is noticeably different from the C# ComStream.Read method in Listing 20.2. In Line 56, the incoming .NET array is pinned so the address of the object can be passed directly to IStream.Read in Line 64. The call to GCHandle.Alloc is placed inside a try...finally block so the allocated GC handle always gets freed. Also inside the try...finally block, Lines 59–60 extract the IStream COM interface pointer from the standard RCW created in the constructor using GetComInterfaceForObject (which increments the reference count), and Line 72 releases the pointer. This same pattern is used in every method that needs to call a member of IStream.

Because a pointer to the pinned array is directly accessible, we can support non-zero offsets without having to perform any copying, unlike in Listing 20.2. (Listing 20.2 could have achieved the same effect as this listing by using a custom .NET definition of IStream that uses the ArrayWithOffset value type. See Appendix A, "System.Runtime.InteropServices Reference," for more information about this type.) Line 64 simply adds the offset to the pointer value. Lines 66–67 check the HRESULT returned from the call to IStream.Read and use the handy Marshal.ThrowExceptionForHR method to throw an exception just like the standard Interop marshaler would if it were throwing an exception for a failure HRESULT. If the IStream.Read implementation sets rich error info via IErrorInfo, the thrown exception gets automatically populated with this information.

The Write method in Lines 80–116 is structured just like the Read method. The get_Length property accessor in Lines 151–176 has an interesting detail that's worth pointing out. The unmanaged STATSTG struct is used by its other name of tagSTATSTG because using STATSTG would be ambiguous between the unmanaged struct defined in objidl.h and the .NET definition of the same struct in System.Runtime.InteropServices. The only other way around this problem would be to omit the using namespace System::Runtime::InteropServices directive from Line 6, but doing so would make the code practically unreadable due to the abundance of System::Runtime::InteropServices qualifications that would litter the code. Doing mixed-mode programming in Visual C++ .NET is filled with little nuances such as this to appease both managed and unmanaged worlds simultaneously.

Listing 20.10 contains the definition of CustomCCW, which wraps a Stream implementation in a COM object that implements IStream. It has a few special cases to provide more functionality if the object being wrapped is an instance of FileStream.

LISTING 20.10   The CustomCCW Adapter Class That Exposes Stream as IStream, with Extra Support for FileStream

```
 1: #using <mscorlib.dll> // Contains definition of Stream
 2: #include "objidl.h"   // Contains definition of IStream
 3: #include <vcclr.h>    // Contains the gcroot template
 4:
 5: using namespace System;
 6: using namespace System::IO;
 7: using namespace System::Runtime::InteropServices;
 8:
 9: // CustomCCW - A Custom COM-Callable Wrapper
10: class CustomCCW : public IStream
11: {
12: public:
13:   // Constructor
14:   CustomCCW(Stream *stream)
15:   {
16:     if (stream != NULL)
17:     {
18:       originalStream = stream;
19:       referenceCount = 0;
20:
21:       // If the Stream is a FileStream, give a better mapping to IStream
22:       if (stream->GetType() == __typeof(FileStream))
23:         isFileStream = true;
24:       else
25:         isFileStream = false;
26:     }
```

LISTING 20.10   Continued

```
27:    else
28:    {
29:      throw new ArgumentNullException(S"stream");
30:    }
31:  };
32:
33:  // IUnknown.QueryInterface
34:  HRESULT STDMETHODCALLTYPE QueryInterface(const IID& iid, void** ppv)
35:  {
36:    if (iid == IID_IUnknown)
37:    {
38:      *ppv = static_cast<IStream*>(this);
39:    }
40:    else if (iid == IID_IStream)
41:    {
42:      *ppv = static_cast<IStream*>(this);
43:    }
44:    else
45:    {
46:      *ppv = NULL;
47:      return E_NOINTERFACE;
48:    }
49:    static_cast<IUnknown*>(*ppv)->AddRef();
50:    return S_OK;
51:  };
52:
53:  // IUnknown.AddRef
54:  ULONG STDMETHODCALLTYPE AddRef()
55:  {
56:    InterlockedIncrement(&referenceCount);
57:    return referenceCount;
58:  };
59:
60:  // IUnknown.Release
61:  ULONG STDMETHODCALLTYPE Release()
62:  {
63:    InterlockedDecrement(&referenceCount);
64:    if (referenceCount == 0)
65:    {
66:      Close();
67:      delete this;
68:      return 0;
69:    }
70:    return referenceCount;
```

20

CUSTOM MARSHALING

LISTING 20.10 Continued

```
 71:   };
 72:
 73:   // Method to get original stream object
 74:   Object* GetUnderlyingObject()
 75:   {
 76:     return originalStream;
 77:   };
 78:
 79:   // Reads a specified number of bytes from the stream object
 80:   // into memory starting at the current seek pointer.
 81:   HRESULT STDMETHODCALLTYPE Read(void *pv, ULONG cb, ULONG* pcbRead)
 82:   {
 83:     if (originalStream == NULL)
 84:     {
 85:       return Marshal::GetHRForException(
 86:         new ObjectDisposedException(S"originalStream"));
 87:     }
 88:     try
 89:     {
 90:       // Allocate managed array to get the data from Stream.Read
 91:       unsigned char array __gc[] = new unsigned char __gc[cb];
 92:
 93:       if (pcbRead == NULL)
 94:       {
 95:         // User isn't interested in how many bytes were read
 96:         *pcbRead = originalStream->Read(array, 0, cb);
 97:       }
 98:       else
 99:       {
100:         originalStream->Read(array, 0, cb);
101:       }
102:
103:       // Copy the contents of the managed array to the unmanaged buffer
104:       Marshal::Copy(array, 0, __nogc new IntPtr(pv), cb);
105:     }
106:     catch (Exception* e)
107:     {
108:       return Marshal::GetHRForException(e);
109:     }
110:     return S_OK;
111:   };
112:
113:   // Writes a specified number of bytes into the stream object
114:   // starting at the current seek pointer
```

LISTING 20.10 Continued

```
115: HRESULT STDMETHODCALLTYPE Write(const void *pv, ULONG cb,
116:   ULONG* pcbWritten)
117: {
118:   if (originalStream == NULL)
119:   {
120:     return Marshal::GetHRForException(
121:       new ObjectDisposedException(S"originalStream"));
122:   }
123:   try
124:   {
125:     // Allocate managed array to hold the data for Stream.Write
126:     unsigned char array __gc[] = new unsigned char __gc[cb];
127:
128:     if (pcbWritten == NULL)
129:     {
130:       // User isn't interested in how many bytes were written
131:       originalStream->Write(array, 0, cb);
132:     }
133:     else
134:     {
135:       __int64 originalPosition = originalStream->Position;
136:       originalStream->Write(array, 0, cb);
137:       *pcbWritten = (ULONG)
138:         (originalStream->Position - originalPosition);
139:     }
140:
141:     // Copy the contents of the unmanaged buffer to the managed array
142:     Marshal::Copy(__nogc new IntPtr((void*)pv), array, 0, cb);
143:   }
144:   catch (Exception* e)
145:   {
146:     return Marshal::GetHRForException(e);
147:   }
148:   return S_OK;
149: };
150:
151: // Changes the seek pointer to a new location relative to the beginning
152: // of the stream, the end of the stream, or the current seek pointer
153: HRESULT STDMETHODCALLTYPE Seek(LARGE_INTEGER dlibMove, DWORD dwOrigin,
154:   ULARGE_INTEGER* plibNewPosition)
155: {
156:   if (originalStream == NULL)
157:   {
158:     return Marshal::GetHRForException(
```

Listing 20.10 Continued

```
159:              new ObjectDisposedException(S"originalStream"));
160:      }
161:    try
162:    {
163:      // The enum values of SeekOrigin match the enum values of
164:      // STREAM_SEEK, so we can just cast the dwOrigin to a SeekOrigin
165:
166:      if (plibNewPosition == NULL)
167:      {
168:        // User isn't interested in new position
169:        originalStream->Seek(dlibMove.QuadPart, (SeekOrigin)dwOrigin);
170:      }
171:      else
172:      {
173:        plibNewPosition->QuadPart = originalStream->Seek(
174:          dlibMove.QuadPart, (SeekOrigin)dwOrigin);
175:      }
176:    }
177:    catch (Exception* e)
178:    {
179:      return Marshal::GetHRForException(e);
180:    }
181:    return S_OK;
182:  };
183:
184:  // Changes the size of the stream object.
185:  HRESULT STDMETHODCALLTYPE SetSize(ULARGE_INTEGER libNewSize)
186:  {
187:    if (originalStream == NULL)
188:    {
189:      return Marshal::GetHRForException(new ObjectDisposedException(
190:        S"originalStream"));
191:    }
192:    try
193:    {
194:      originalStream->SetLength(libNewSize.QuadPart);
195:    }
196:    catch (Exception* e)
197:    {
198:      return Marshal::GetHRForException(e);
199:    }
200:    return S_OK;
201:  };
202:
```

LISTING 20.10   Continued

```
203:  // Copies a specified number of bytes from the current seek pointer
204:  // in the stream to the current seek pointer in another stream
205:  HRESULT STDMETHODCALLTYPE CopyTo(IStream* pstm, ULARGE_INTEGER cb,
206:    ULARGE_INTEGER* pcbRead, ULARGE_INTEGER* pcbWritten)
207:  {
208:    if (originalStream == NULL)
209:    {
210:      return Marshal::GetHRForException(new ObjectDisposedException(
211:        S"originalStream"));
212:    }
213:    IntPtr sourceBytes;
214:    ULONG currentBytesRead = 0;
215:    int bytesWritten = 0;
216:    HRESULT hresult;
217:
218:    try
219:    {
220:      // AllocHGlobal throws an OutOfMemoryException if it fails,
221:      // so we don't have to check the returned value
222:      sourceBytes = Marshal::AllocHGlobal((int)cb.QuadPart);
223:
224:      while (bytesWritten < cb.QuadPart)
225:      {
226:        // Call CustomCCW's Read method
227:        hresult = Read(sourceBytes.ToPointer(),
228:          cb.QuadPart - bytesWritten, &currentBytesRead);
229:        if (FAILED(hresult))
230:          return hresult;
231:
232:        // Has the end of the stream been reached?
233:        if (currentBytesRead == 0) break;
234:
235:        // Call CustomCCW's Write method
236:        hresult = Write(sourceBytes.ToPointer(), currentBytesRead, NULL);
237:        if (FAILED(hresult))
238:          return hresult;
239:
240:        bytesWritten += currentBytesRead;
241:      }
242:    }
243:    catch (Exception* e)
244:    {
245:      return Marshal::GetHRForException(e);
246:    }
```

20

LISTING 20.10   Continued

```
247:      __finally
248:      {
249:        Marshal::FreeHGlobal(sourceBytes);
250:      }
251:
252:      if (pcbRead != NULL)    pcbRead->QuadPart = bytesWritten;
253:      if (pcbWritten != NULL) pcbWritten->QuadPart = bytesWritten;
254:      return S_OK;
255:    };
256:
257:    // Ensures that any changes made to a stream object open in
258:    // transacted mode are reflected in the parent storage object
259:    HRESULT STDMETHODCALLTYPE Commit(DWORD grfCommitFlags)
260:    {
261:      if (originalStream == NULL)
262:      {
263:        return Marshal::GetHRForException(new ObjectDisposedException(
264:          S"originalStream"));
265:      }
266:      try
267:      {
268:        originalStream->Flush();
269:      }
270:      catch (Exception* e)
271:      {
272:        return Marshal::GetHRForException(e);
273:      }
274:      return S_OK;
275:    };
276:
277:    // Discards all changes that have been made to a transacted
278:    // stream since the last IStream::Commit call
279:    HRESULT STDMETHODCALLTYPE Revert()
280:    {
281:      return E_NOTIMPL;
282:    };
283:
284:    // Restricts access to a specified range of bytes in the stream
285:    HRESULT STDMETHODCALLTYPE LockRegion(ULARGE_INTEGER libOffset,
286:      ULARGE_INTEGER cb, DWORD dwLockType)
287:    {
288:      if (originalStream == NULL)
289:      {
290:        return Marshal::GetHRForException(new ObjectDisposedException(
```

LISTING 20.10 Continued

```
291:          S"originalStream"));
292:        }
293:      // We only provide an implementation if the Stream is a FileStream
294:      if (!isFileStream) return E_NOTIMPL;
295:
296:      // We only support LOCK_EXCLUSIVE
297:      if (dwLockType != LOCK_EXCLUSIVE) return STG_E_INVALIDFUNCTION;
298:
299:      try
300:      {
301:        // Call FileStream.Lock
302:        static_cast<FileStream*>((Stream*)originalStream)->
303:          Lock(libOffset.QuadPart, cb.QuadPart);
304:      }
305:      catch (Exception* e)
306:      {
307:        return Marshal::GetHRForException(e);
308:      }
309:      return S_OK;
310:    };
311:
312:    // Removes the access restriction on a range of bytes
313:    HRESULT STDMETHODCALLTYPE UnlockRegion(ULARGE_INTEGER libOffset,
314:      ULARGE_INTEGER cb, DWORD dwLockType)
315:    {
316:      if (originalStream == NULL)
317:      {
318:        return Marshal::GetHRForException(new ObjectDisposedException(
319:          S"originalStream"));
320:      }
321:      // We only provide an implementation if the Stream is a FileStream
322:      if (!isFileStream) return E_NOTIMPL;
323:
324:      // We only support LOCK_EXCLUSIVE
325:      if (dwLockType != LOCK_EXCLUSIVE) return STG_E_INVALIDFUNCTION;
326:
327:      try
328:      {
329:        // Call FileStream.Unlock
330:        static_cast<FileStream*>((Stream*)originalStream)->
331:          Unlock(libOffset.QuadPart, cb.QuadPart);
332:      }
333:      catch (Exception* e)
334:      {
```

LISTING 20.10   Continued

```
335:          return Marshal::GetHRForException(e);
336:        }
337:      return S_OK;
338:    };
339:
340:    // Retrieves the STATSTG structure for this stream.
341:    // If this is a FileStream, the mtime, ctime, atime, and pwcsName
342:    // fields will contain information.
343:    HRESULT STDMETHODCALLTYPE Stat(tagSTATSTG* pstatstg, DWORD grfStatFlag)
344:    {
345:      if (originalStream == NULL)
346:      {
347:        return Marshal::GetHRForException(new ObjectDisposedException(
348:          S"originalStream"));
349:      }
350:      try
351:      {
352:        pstatstg->type = STGTY_STREAM;
353:        pstatstg->cbSize.QuadPart = originalStream->Length;
354:        pstatstg->grfMode = STGM_READWRITE;
355:        pstatstg->grfLocksSupported = LOCK_EXCLUSIVE;
356:
357:        if (isFileStream)
358:        {
359:          _FILETIME creationTime;
360:          _FILETIME lastAccessTime;
361:          _FILETIME lastWriteTime;
362:          IntPtr hFile = static_cast<FileStream*>((Stream*)originalStream)->
363:            Handle;
364:          BOOL b = GetFileTime((HANDLE)hFile.ToPointer(), &creationTime,
365:            &lastAccessTime, &lastWriteTime);
366:
367:          pstatstg->mtime = lastWriteTime;
368:          pstatstg->ctime = creationTime;
369:          pstatstg->atime = lastAccessTime;
370:
371:          // Only give the name if the user passed STATFLAG_DEFAULT
372:          if (grfStatFlag == STATFLAG_DEFAULT)
373:          {
374:            pstatstg->pwcsName = (LPWSTR)Marshal::StringToCoTaskMemUni(
375:              static_cast<FileStream*>((Stream*)originalStream)->
376:              Name).ToPointer();
377:          }
378:        }
```

LISTING 20.10   Continued

```
379:     }
380:     catch (Exception* e)
381:     {
382:       return Marshal::GetHRForException(e);
383:     }
384:
385:     return S_OK;
386:   };
387:
388:   // Creates a new stream object that references the same bytes as the
389:   // original stream but provides a separate seek pointer to those bytes
390:   HRESULT STDMETHODCALLTYPE Clone(IStream** ppstm)
391:   {
392:     return E_NOTIMPL;
393:   };
394:
395:   // Closes (disposes) the stream
396:   HRESULT Close()
397:   {
398:     try
399:     {
400:       if (originalStream != NULL)
401:       {
402:         originalStream->Close();
403:         originalStream = NULL;
404:       }
405:     }
406:     catch (Exception* e)
407:     {
408:       return Marshal::GetHRForException(e);
409:     }
410:     return S_OK;
411:   }
412:
413: private:
414:   gcroot<Stream*> originalStream;
415:   LONG referenceCount;
416:   bool isFileStream;
417: };
```

Line 10 begins the definition of the CustomCCW class that implements IStream. It can't implement IDisposable or ICustomAdapter like the CustomRCW class does in Listing 20.9 because COM classes can't directly implement .NET interfaces using mixed-mode C++ programming.

Still, it implements a custom `GetUnderlyingObject` method (Lines 74–77) for the benefit of COM clients. (Alternatively, it could implement the exported `ICustomAdapter` interface defined in `MSCORLIB.TLB`, which would involve returning the `IStream` interface pointer inside a `VARIANT`.)

An important aspect of this listing is the use of the `gcroot` template on Line 414. Visual C++ .NET does not allow an unmanaged class to contain a managed member (a `__gc` pointer type), so defining the `originalStream` field of type `Stream` would cause a compilation error. Fortunately, the `vcclr.h` header file referenced in Line 3, which contains helper functions specifically for C++ managed extensions, defines a `gcroot` type-safe wrapper template to use specifically for this purpose. This template provides the illusion of having a managed member of an unmanaged class, but in reality an integer representing a `GCHandle` is being stored inside the unmanaged object. The template has a destructor that frees the `GCHandle`.

> **TIP**
>
> In Visual C++ .NET, use the `gcroot` template defined in `vcclr.h` whenever you require a managed member of an unmanaged class. Through clever wrapping of a `GCHandle`, you can use a `gcroot<Type*>` variable just as if it were defined as `Type*`. This is sometimes called a *virtual __gc pointer*.

The constructor in Lines 14–31 differs from the `ManagedIStream` constructor in Listing 20.3 in two ways. First, because `CustomCCW` is a COM class, it must maintain a reference count, so Line 19 initializes it to zero. Second, Line 22 checks to see if the `Stream` object being wrapped is also a `FileStream`. The boolean `isFileStream` variable is used later in the listing to provide more functionality specific to file streams. Lines 34–71 contain a standard implementation of `IUnknown`'s methods. The `InterlockedIncrement` and `InterlockedDecrement` Windows APIs are used to provide thread-safe reference counting.

The `IStream` methods follow the opposite pattern as in the previous listing—each method implementation is contained inside a `try...catch` block and `Marshal.GetHRForException` is used to return the failure `HRESULT` corresponding to any .NET exception that may be thrown. The `CopyTo` implementation in Lines 205–255 differs from the `CopyTo` implementation from Listing 20.3 because it calls `CustomCCW.Read` and `CustomCCW.Write` rather than calling the underlying stream's `Read` and `Write` methods directly. This works more naturally in this case because calling `Stream.Read` and `Stream.Write` would require more lines of code. `Marshal.AllocHGlobal` is used in Line 222 to allocate memory for the temporary buffer and `Marshal.FreeHGlobal` frees it in Line 249.

The `LockRegion`, `UnlockRegion`, and `Stat` methods are the ones that do extra work if the wrapped `Stream` object is a `FileStream` instance. Although generic `Stream` objects don't support any locking or unlocking functionality, `FileStream` objects do. `FileStream` has a `Lock` method called by `LockRegion` in Lines 285–310, and an `Unlock` method called by `UnlockRegion` in Lines 313–338. In `Stat` (Lines 343–386), more information in the structure can be filled in that applies to file streams only—the stream's creation time, last access time, last write time, and possibly its name. The `Stat` method uses `_FILETIME` in Lines 359–361, rather than `FILETIME`, for the same reason the previous listing used `tagSTATSTG`—to avoid a name collision with `System.Runtime.InteropServices.FILETIME`.

Example: Marshaling With Arrays

So far all the examples have custom marshaled .NET types to COM interfaces. This example demonstrates custom marshaling a .NET string to a `SAFEARRAY` instead. This isn't a practical custom marshaler like the others, but it's an easy-to-follow example of custom marshaling to something other than an interface pointer on the COM side. The marshaling is accomplished by value, so Listing 20.11 contains the complete custom marshaler in the `StringMarshaler` class, written in C++. This listing can be compiled from a command prompt as follows:

```
cl /CLR /LD StringMarshaler.cpp /link oleaut32.lib
```

LISTING 20.11 The `StringMarshaler` Custom Marshaler Marshals .NET Strings to COM SAFEARRAYs and Vice-Versa

```
 1: #using <mscorlib.dll>
 2: #include <wtypes.h>
 3: #include <oleauto.h>  // Contains SAFEARRAY functions
 4:
 5: using namespace System;
 6: using namespace System::Text;
 7: using namespace System::Runtime::InteropServices;
 8:
 9: public __gc class StringMarshaler : public ICustomMarshaler
10: {
11: private:
12:
13:    SAFEARRAY* safeArray;
14:    UnicodeEncoding* encoding;
15:    static StringMarshaler* marshaler = NULL;
16:
17:    StringMarshaler()
18:    {
19:      encoding = new UnicodeEncoding(!BitConverter::IsLittleEndian, false);
```

LISTING 20.11   Continued

```
20:    };
21:
22: public:
23:
24:    Object* MarshalNativeToManaged(IntPtr pNativeData)
25:    {
26:      if (pNativeData == NULL)
27:        throw new ArgumentNullException(L"pNativeData");
28:
29:      HRESULT hresult;
30:      long lowerBound;
31:      long upperBound;
32:      SAFEARRAY* psa = (SAFEARRAY*)pNativeData.ToPointer();
33:
34:      // Check that the incoming array is one-dimensional
35:      if (SafeArrayGetDim(psa) != 1)
36:        throw new ArgumentException(S"Array must be one-dimensional");
37:
38:      // Check that each element is one byte in size
39:      if (SafeArrayGetElemsize(psa) != 1)
40:        throw new ArgumentException(S"Array must contain byte elements");
41:
42:      // Get the upper and lower bounds
43:      hresult = SafeArrayGetLBound(psa, 1, &lowerBound);
44:      if (FAILED(hresult))
45:        Marshal::ThrowExceptionForHR(hresult);
46:
47:      hresult = SafeArrayGetUBound(psa, 1, &upperBound);
48:      if (FAILED(hresult))
49:        Marshal::ThrowExceptionForHR(hresult);
50:
51:      // Create a new .NET array
52:      unsigned char array __gc[] =
53:        new unsigned char __gc[upperBound - lowerBound + 1];
54:
55:      // Copy data from the SAFEARRAY to the .NET array
56:      for (long i = lowerBound; i <= upperBound; i++)
57:      {
58:        SafeArrayGetElement(safeArray, &i, (void*)array[i]);
59:      }
60:
61:      return BitConverter::ToString(array);
62:    };
63:
```

LISTING 20.11 Continued

```
64:    IntPtr MarshalManagedToNative(Object* ManagedObj)
65:    {
66:      if (ManagedObj == NULL)
67:        throw new ArgumentNullException(L"ManagedObj");
68:
69:      String* s;
70:
71:      try
72:      {
73:        s = __try_cast<String*>(ManagedObj);
74:      }
75:      catch (InvalidCastException*)
76:      {
77:        throw new ArgumentException(
78:          S"This custom marshaler must be used on String types only.");
79:      }
80:
81:      unsigned char array __gc[] = encoding->GetBytes(s);
82:
83:      try
84:      {
85:        // Create a new SAFEARRAY
86:        safeArray = SafeArrayCreateVectorEx(
87:        VT_UI1, 0, array->Length, NULL);
88:
89:        // Copy data from the .NET array to the SAFEARRAY
90:        for (long i = 0; i < array->Length; i++)
91:        {
92:          SafeArrayPutElement(safeArray, &i, (void*)array[i]);
93:        }
94:      }
95:      __finally
96:      {
97:        CleanUpNativeData(safeArray);
98:      }
99:      return __nogc new IntPtr(safeArray);
100:   };
101:
102:   void CleanUpNativeData(IntPtr pNativeData)
103:   {
104:     // Free the allocated SAFEARRAY
105:     SafeArrayDestroy(safeArray);
106:   };
107:
```

LISTING 20.11   Continued

```
108:    void CleanUpManagedData(Object* ManagedObj)
109:    {
110:      // Nothing to do
111:    };
112:
113:    static ICustomMarshaler* GetInstance(String* cookie)
114:    {
115:      // Always return the same instance
116:      if (marshaler != NULL) marshaler = new StringMarshaler();
117:      return marshaler;
118:    };
119:
120:    int GetNativeDataSize()
121:    {
122:      return -1;
123:    };
124: };
```

Line 3 includes `oleauto.h`, a header file containing the definitions of several `SAFEARRAY`-related functions. The `System.Text` namespace is used in Line 6 for the `UnicodeEncoding` class. The `StringMarshaler` constructor initializes its `encoding` member on Line 19, used by `MarshalManagedToNative` to convert a .NET string to an array of bytes. The first parameter passed to the `UnicodeEncoding` constructor chooses big-endian or little-endian ordering based on the current operating system. Passing false for the second parameter turns off the byte order mark (BOM), which we don't want to include as part of the string data.

Lines 24–62 contain the implementation of `MarshalNativeToManaged`. After obtaining a pointer to the `SAFEARRAY` by calling `ToPointer` on the input `IntPtr` value, several `SAFEARRAY` APIs defined in `oleauto.h` are called using the `IntPtr` value. Lines 35–40 ensure that the incoming array has only a single dimension and contains byte elements. The `SafeArrayGetVartype` API only works reliably on `SAFEARRAY`s created using `SafeArrayCreateEx` or `SafeArrayCreateVectorEx`, so checking for an element size of 1 byte instead is a sure-fire way to check the type of elements.

Lines 43–49 get the array's upper and lower bounds, so the contents of the array can be copied regardless of the bounds. Lines 52–53 create a new .NET array with the correct number of elements, then the loop in Lines 56–59 fill the new array with the `SAFEARRAY`'s data. This is done simply so it can be passed to the static `BitConverter.ToString` method in Line 61.

`MarshalManagedToNative` is defined in Lines 64–100. Line 81 obtains a .NET array for the string by calling the `UnicodeEncoding.GetBytes` method. Then a new `SAFEARRAY` is created using `SafeArrayCreateVectorEx` in Lines 86–87, and the data from the .NET array is copied to the SAFEARRAY in Lines 90–93. Line 99 returns an `IntPtr` value representing the pointer to the SAFEARRAY. The implementation of `CleanUpNativeData` in Lines 102–106 frees the SAFEARRAY allocated in Lines 86–87 with a call to `SafeArrayDestroy`.

Example: Providing Deterministic Release of Resources

The standard CCW does not provide a means for deterministic release of resources other than having COM clients call `IDisposable.Dispose` explicitly (if the .NET object implements `IDisposable`). This can be problematic when .NET objects implementing COM interfaces are exposed to pre-.NET COM clients that can't be modified. Such clients may rely on the fact that resources must be released in a timely manner, and calling an additional method is not an option. When defining a custom CCW, however, you can insert a call to `IDisposable.Dispose` that executes when the CCW's reference count reaches zero.

CAUTION

Disposing a .NET object when its CCW's reference count reaches zero should not be done for objects that can potentially be used simultaneously by COM clients and .NET clients. Any .NET clients using the object are invisible to the object's CCW, so the object could get disposed prematurely while others are still using it.

Another problematic situation occurs if the same .NET instance is passed to COM using custom marshaling with some signatures and standard marshaling with other signatures (due to a consumer not using the appropriate `MarshalAsAttribute` everywhere the type is exposed). In this case, COM clients using an interface pointer for the standard CCW can become victims of premature disposal because the custom CCW cannot track this usage.

Therefore, the approach demonstrated by this custom marshaler should only be used in controlled situations.

Writing a custom marshaler to add dispose functionality must be done on an interface-by-interface basis, because custom marshalers must statically implement interfaces exposed to COM users. In this example, the custom marshaler is written for the `IPersistFile` COM interface.

The custom marshaler class looks just like the `TypicalCustomMarshaler` class in Listing 20.5, but with the following implementation of `MarshalNativeToManaged` and `MarshalManagedToNative`:

```
Object* MarshalNativeToManaged(IntPtr pNativeData)
{
  if (pNativeData == IntPtr::Zero) return NULL;
```

```
  // Just use the standard RCW
  return Marshal::GetObjectForIUnknown(pNativeData);
};

IntPtr MarshalManagedToNative(Object* ManagedObj)
{
  if (ManagedObj == NULL) return IntPtr::Zero;
  CustomCCW *ccw = new CustomCCW(static_cast<UCOMIPersistFile*>(ManagedObj));
  IPersistFile* intf = NULL;
  ccw->QueryInterface(IID_IPersistFile, (void**)&intf);
  return (IntPtr)intf;
};
```

The complete source code is available on this book's Web site. No special marshaling is required in the native-to-managed direction because all we care about is customizing the exposure of a .NET object to COM. Therefore, calling `Marshal.GetObjectForIUnknown` inside `MarshalNativeToManaged` acquires the standard RCW for the COM object.

DIGGING DEEPER

If a custom marshaler were interested only in customizing the RCW (the opposite of this section's example), then the implementation of `MarshalManagedToNative` would look as follows:

```
IntPtr MarshalManagedToNative(Object* ManagedObj)
{
  if (ManagedObj == NULL) return IntPtr::Zero;

  // Just use the standard CCW
  return Marshal::GetIUnknownForObject(ManagedObj);
};
```

The C++ `CustomCCW` adapter class used by the custom marshaler in `MarshalManagedToNative` is implemented in Listing 20.12. This is unique from the other custom marshalers because the source and target types appear to be the same to their users—`System.Runtime.InteropServices.UCOMIPersistFile` on the .NET side and `IPersistFile` on the COM side.

LISTING 20.12   Disposing an Object on Its Last Release Inside a Custom CCW

```
1: #using <mscorlib.dll> // Contains managed definition of UCOMIPersistFile
2: #include <objidl.h>    // Contains unmanaged definition of IPersistFile
3: #include <vcclr.h>     // Contains the gcroot template
```

LISTING 20.12   Continued

```cpp
4:
5: using namespace System;
6: using namespace System::Runtime::InteropServices;
7:
8: // CustomCCW - A Custom COM-Callable Wrapper
9: class CustomCCW : public IPersistFile
10: {
11: public:
12:
13:    // Constructor
14:    CustomCCW (UCOMIPersistFile *obj)
15:    {
16:      originalObject = obj;
17:      referenceCount = 0;
18:    };
19:
20:    // IUnknown.QueryInterface
21:    HRESULT STDMETHODCALLTYPE QueryInterface(const IID& iid, void** ppv)
22:    {
23:      if (iid == IID_IUnknown)
24:      {
25:        *ppv = static_cast<IPersistFile*>(this);
26:      }
27:      else if (iid == IID_IPersistFile)
28:      {
29:        *ppv = static_cast<IPersistFile*>(this);
30:      }
31:      else
32:      {
33:        *ppv = NULL;
34:        return E_NOINTERFACE;
35:      }
36:      static_cast<IUnknown*>(*ppv)->AddRef();
37:      return S_OK;
38:    };
39:
40:    // IUnknown.AddRef
41:    ULONG STDMETHODCALLTYPE AddRef()
42:    {
43:      InterlockedIncrement(&referenceCount);
44:      return referenceCount;
45:    };
46:
47:    // IUnknown.Release
```

LISTING 20.12 Continued

```
48:    ULONG STDMETHODCALLTYPE Release()
49:    {
50:      InterlockedDecrement(&referenceCount);
51:      if (referenceCount == 0)
52:      {
53:        // Dispose the .NET object when the reference count reaches zero
54:        try
55:        {
56:          IDisposable *d = __try_cast<IDisposable*>
57:            ((UCOMIPersistFile*)originalObject);
58:          d->Dispose();
59:        }
60:        catch (InvalidCastException*) {}
61:
62:        delete this;
63:        return 0;
64:      }
65:      return referenceCount;
66:    };
67:
68:    // Implementation of the unmanaged IPersistFile methods, which do the
69:    // appropriate marshaling then call the corresponding managed methods
70:
71:    HRESULT STDMETHODCALLTYPE GetClassID(CLSID *pClassID)
72:    {
73:      try
74:      {
75:        Guid* g = __nogc new Guid(pClassID->Data1, pClassID->Data2,
76:          pClassID->Data3, pClassID->Data4[0], pClassID->Data4[1],
77:          pClassID->Data4[2], pClassID->Data4[3], pClassID->Data4[4],
78:          pClassID->Data4[5], pClassID->Data4[6], pClassID->Data4[7]);
79:
80:        originalObject->GetClassID(g);
81:      }
82:      catch (Exception* ex)
83:      {
84:        return Marshal::GetHRForException(ex);
85:      }
86:    };
87:
88:    HRESULT STDMETHODCALLTYPE IsDirty()
89:    {
90:      return originalObject->IsDirty();
91:    };
```

LISTING 20.12 Continued

```
 92:
 93:   HRESULT STDMETHODCALLTYPE Load(LPCOLESTR pszFileName, DWORD dwMode)
 94:   {
 95:     try
 96:     {
 97:       String* s = Marshal::PtrToStringUni((IntPtr)(int)pszFileName);
 98:       originalObject->Load(s, dwMode);
 99:     }
100:     catch (Exception* ex)
101:     {
102:       return Marshal::GetHRForException(ex);
103:     }
104:   };
105:
106:   HRESULT STDMETHODCALLTYPE Save(LPCOLESTR pszFileName, BOOL fRemember)
107:   {
108:     try
109:     {
110:       String* s = Marshal::PtrToStringUni(
111:         __nogc new IntPtr((void*)pszFileName));
112:       originalObject->Save(s, fRemember);
113:     }
114:     catch (Exception* ex)
115:     {
116:       return Marshal::GetHRForException(ex);
117:     }
118:   };
119:
120:   HRESULT STDMETHODCALLTYPE SaveCompleted(LPCOLESTR pszFileName)
121:   {
122:     try
123:     {
124:       String* s = Marshal::PtrToStringUni(
125:         __nogc new IntPtr((void*)pszFileName));
126:       originalObject->SaveCompleted(pszFileName);
127:     }
128:     catch (Exception* ex)
129:     {
130:       return Marshal::GetHRForException(ex);
131:     }
132:   };
133:
134:   HRESULT STDMETHODCALLTYPE GetCurFile(LPOLESTR *ppszFileName)
135:   {
```

20

CUSTOM MARSHALING

LISTING 20.12   Continued

```
136:      try
137:      {
138:        String* s = Marshal::PtrToStringUni(
139:          __nogc new IntPtr(*ppszFileName));
140:        originalObject->GetCurFile(&s);
141:      }
142:      catch (Exception* ex)
143:      {
144:        return Marshal::GetHRForException(ex);
145:      }
146:    };
147:
148: private:
149:    gcroot<UCOMIPersistFile*> originalObject;
150:    LONG referenceCount;
151: };
```

This listing is straightforward because the IPersistFile methods simply call their corresponding UCOMIPersistFile methods in Lines 71–146. The implementation mimics the work that would normally be done by the standard Interop Marshaler. The unique part of the listing occurs inside the implementation of IUnknown.Release (Lines 53–60). If the wrapped object implementing UCOMIPersistFile also implements IDisposable, the object will be disposed when the CCW reference count equals zero. Otherwise, object release is performed the standard way.

The adapter class doesn't bother exposing a GetUnderlyingObject method because this custom CCW is meant for COM clients that aren't .NET-aware. If they could be modified to call GetUnderlyingObject, then they could be modified to call IDisposable.Dispose and avoid the need for the custom marshaler in the first place.

Limitations

Even when implementing a custom marshaler (and possibly adapter objects) using Visual C++ .NET, the custom marshaling infrastructure has some limitations. Some of these limitations were mentioned earlier in the chapter, but here's a summary:

- Value types can't be custom marshaled. Only reference types are supported in version 1.0 of the .NET Framework. This applies to both the .NET and COM sides of marshaling so, as an example, custom marshaling a System.Decimal type to anything unmanaged or custom marshaling anything managed to a by-value VARIANT type cannot be done.

Note that you can custom marshal a *boxed* value type defined as an Object type, or a formatted reference type. The formal type of the unmanaged parameter does not matter as long as it's pointer-sized, so you could custom marshal a managed type to a pointer to an unmanaged structure (similar to the SAFEARRAY example). Attempting to use a custom marshaler on a parameter, return type, or field defined as a value type causes a MarshalDirectiveException to be thrown at run time.

- The type library exporter can't faithfully represent the unmanaged view of a custom marshaled type in an exported type library. This isn't a big limitation for classes or interfaces being exported as IUnknown*, but the behavior of exporting strings or arrays as long can be problematic.

- The type library importer can't be taught to use additional custom marshalers. The importer makes use of a handful of built-in custom marshalers shipped with the .NET Framework, but there's no way to plug in additional custom marshalers. Adding custom marshaling to an Interop Assembly would have to be done using the techniques in Chapter 7 instead.

- Only uses of a type can be marked as custom marshaled rather than a type itself. Because there's no way to force a data type to always be custom marshaled when used, MarshalAsAttribute must be applied to every parameter, return type, and field that desires custom marshaling. A side effect of this is that if you export a class called MyStream derived from Stream, there's no way to get the exporter to transform it into a MyStream coclass that implements IStream. Instead, any uses of MyStream as a parameter, return type, or field would need to be marked with the custom marshaler. The same applies to import as well: a coclass implementing IEnumVARIANT is imported as a class implementing IEnumVARIANT, even though any IEnumVARIANT parameters, return types, or fields in a type library are changed to a custom-marshaled IEnumerator.

You can usually work around these limitations by expanding the scope of the custom marshaler. For example, because you can't directly custom marshal a .NET parameter type to a VARIANT with type VT_RECORD, you can instead custom marshal the entire interface containing the method with the parameter you need to custom marshal.

Conclusion

Custom marshaling is useful for working around limitations of the built-in COM Interoperability support. The .NET Framework ships with a CustomMarshalers assembly containing a handful of custom marshalers used by the CLR. These custom marshalers marshal between ITypeInfo and System.Type, IEnumVARIANT and IEnumerator, IDispatchEx and System.Runtime.InteropServices.Expando.IExpando or System.Reflection.IReflect (based on a cookie value), and finally IDispatch and IEnumerable. The ITypeInfo/System.Type custom marshaler marshals by value, but the others all marshal by reference, using the adapter object approach covered throughout this chapter.

20

CUSTOM MARSHALING

> **TIP**
>
> All the adapter objects used by the .NET Framework's custom marshalers implement `ICustomAdapter`. For an example of how this can be useful, consider a COM enumerator object (implementing `IEnumVARIANT`) that holds onto limited resources until it's destroyed. Suppose you want to use this object in managed code (which, thanks to a custom marshaler, now appears to implement `IEnumerator`), but you also want to release it as soon as you're finished. For example, in C#:
>
> ```
> IEnumerator enumerator = comObj.GetEnumerator();
> try
> {
>   while (enumerator.MoveNext())
>   {
>     ...
>   }
> }
> finally
> {
>   // How do I release the COM enumerator object here?
> }
> ```
>
> Calling `Marshal.ReleaseComObject` on the enumerator object returned by `GetEnumerator` doesn't work because it's not the original COM object. It's not even a COM object at all; it's a .NET adapter object returned by the built-in `IEnumVARIANT`/`IEnumerator` custom marshaler! To release the original COM object, you must cast the object implementing `IEnumerator` to `ICustomAdapter`. Then you can call `Marshal.ReleaseComObject` on the object returned by `GetUnderlyingObject`:
>
> ```
> finally
> {
>   // Here's how I release the COM enumerator object
>   ICustomAdapter adapter = (ICustomAdapter)enumerator;
>   Marshal.ReleaseComObject(adapter.GetUnderlyingObject());
> }
> ```
>
> Using C#'s `foreach` statement or VB .NET's `For Each` statement should not be used with such COM enumerators, because the object implementing `IEnumerator` is never directly exposed to you.

The IStream/Stream custom marshaler covered in this chapter fulfills a common need when using COM Interoperability, but there are numerous other custom marshalers you could create for common scenarios. For example, you could write a "visibility marshaler" that transforms COM-invisible .NET classes into visible COM classes. Of course, such an approach would have to be done on a type-by-type basis, because a generic custom marshaler can't be written unless you expose an IDispatch implementation that internally uses reflection on the wrapped .NET type. As another example, you could support marshaling a .NET array to a varying con-formant array, using the cookie string to enable users to specify first_is and last_is infor-mation. Or, you could create a custom RCW that stores the most recently returned HRESULT in thread local storage (TLS) and expose it to managed code as a LastHResult property (similar to Marshal.GetLastWin32Error). With such a property, success HRESULTs could be obtained without resorting to PreserveSig to change the look of the .NET signature.

Another useful custom marshaler would be one that transforms an ADO.NET DataSet into an ADO Recordset and vice-versa. In one direction, you can use System.Data.OleDb.OleDbDataAdapter.Fill to convert a Recordset to a DataSet. In the other direction, you could use DataSet.GetXml to obtain an XML representation of the DataSet, use an XSLT transform to convert it into the XML format usable by ADO, then load it into an ADO Recordset. The possibilities are endless!

Manually Defining COM Types in Source Code

IN THIS CHAPTER

- Using SDK Tools for Support   960
- Manually Defining COM Interfaces   962
- Manually Defining Coclass Interfaces and Event Types   1003
- Manually Defining COM Structures   1019
- Manually Defining COM Enums   1022
- Manually Defining COM Classes   1022
- Avoiding the Balloon Effect   1033

In an ideal world, a .NET definition of every COM interface, class, enum, and so on, would exist somewhere in a Primary Interop Assembly that's readily available. Furthermore, every definition would be completely usable in every .NET language, no matter how non-standard it may be. Of course, this is not the world we live in, but there are a variety of things we can do when a desired Primary Interop Assembly does not exist.

We could easily create an Interop Assembly from an existing type library containing the desired type definitions using the type library importer (or even create a Primary Interop Assembly if we're the author of the COM component). Sometimes the produced assembly still needs some tweaks to be fully usable from managed code (such as returning success HRESULT values or using C-style array parameters), so the IL Disassembler and IL Assembler can be used to alter the Interop Assembly's metadata. This is the subject of Chapter 7, "Modifying Interop Assemblies."

If a type library doesn't exist for a COM component, perhaps because it was only designed for C++ clients, one could be created from an IDL file using existing tools like MIDL.EXE or MKTYPLIB.EXE, then this type library could be imported to an assembly. If only a C++ header describes an interface, then the task of creating .NET type information using this process is even tougher because there's no automatic way to create an IDL file from a C++ header file.

Another approach for creating .NET type information that describes COM types, the subject of this chapter, is to manually write definitions of COM types in your favorite high-level .NET language. After all, .NET compilers can produce metadata and IL, which is what the type library importer produces. There's nothing magical about the metadata inside Interop Assemblies—they're just marked with the appropriate custom attributes to make the CLR treat them as COM types. Because the type library importer makes an effort to generate metadata that complies with the Common Language Specification (whenever it doesn't restrict functionality), most COM type definitions can be written in any compliant .NET language, although with some huge caveats discussed in this chapter.

If you need to use COM types that aren't defined in a type library or IDL file, the usefulness of this technique should be obvious. But why would you want to write COM type definitions manually, if using the support of the type library importer is also an option? Here are pros and cons to manually defining COM types in source code:

PROS:

- Writing your own COM type definitions can be much more lightweight than referencing a large Interop Assembly. You can define only the types (and sometimes only the methods) that you need. For example, instead of using the Primary Interop Assembly for the Microsoft HTML Object Library (MSHTML.TLB) that's over seven megabytes in size, perhaps you might define only a handful of interfaces that you want to use or implement. In addition, you no longer need a separate DLL containing the COM types. You could simply compile your source definitions into your own assembly.

Manually Defining COM Types in Source Code

CHAPTER 21

959

21

DEFINING COM
TYPES IN SOURCE
CODE

- It's pretty easy to make modifications to the signatures to make them usable or simply more user-friendly. Because most people are more comfortable with a higher-level language like C#, Visual Basic .NET, or C++ rather than IL Assembler, it's a lot easier to make the same kind of necessary tweaks explained in Chapter 7.

- COM types that you don't wish to expose can remain private or internal to your assembly. Because the type library importer only generates assemblies, all COM types inside must be public to be usable by other assemblies. But if you ship an Interop Assembly with your product, you're now exposing public COM types that you might rather not expose to your users. By placing the types in your own assembly, you can restrict their .NET visibility (besides only shipping one DLL). Using this technique, you can publicly expose a new .NET object model that is a thin wrapper over private COM types.

CONS:

- Writing your own COM type definitions from scratch is hard to do. It's a process much like writing PInvoke signatures. You have to get every detail just right, including data types and custom attributes, (plus more requirements specific to COM Interoperability like the order you define the members) or your code may fail in completely unpredictable ways. In general, there is very little (but some) diagnostic information provided by the CLR if you don't define the types correctly.

- Writing your own COM type definitions is undesirable for the same reasons that using Primary Interop Assemblies is encouraged, as described in Chapter 3, "The Essentials for Using COM in Managed Code." If you expose a public COM type in your own assembly, such as the ISmartTagAction interface (used in Chapter 14, "Implementing COM Interfaces for Binary Compatibility"), its .NET identity becomes tied to your assembly. Therefore, source code COM definitions should be kept non-public as much as possible.

This chapter first looks at some .NET Framework SDK utilities that can be useful when writing your own type information. Then, the subject of manually defining COM type information is broken down into the following tasks:

- Manually defining COM interfaces (the most important task), including powerful customizations that are easy to do in high-level source code

- Manually defining coclass interfaces and event-related types, just like what the type library importer would produce

- Manually defining COM structures and enums

- Manually defining COM classes (the most difficult topic, and one with plenty of limitations)

Finally, we end the chapter with some tricks that helps to avoid defining the entire transitive closure of the types you wish to use.

> **Tip**
>
> When defining a COM type in managed code, *do not* base it solely on the original type's definition found in documentation. Documentation often has errors, or the format isn't appropriate for discovering the order of members. Instead, find a "real" definition somewhere in a C++ header file, IDL file, or type library, and base your definition on that instead.

Using SDK Tools for Support

If you're manually defining COM types that are already defined in a type library or IDL file, using the type library importer and then comparing its generated definitions to your manual type definitions is a great sanity check, because you should trust that the importer generates "correct" metadata (excluding limitations discussed in Chapter 7). It's important to realize, however, that producing identical metadata is not necessary because there can be minor differences that don't affect the CLR's interoperability behavior, not to mention all sorts of allowable customizations described in the upcoming "Handy Customizations" section. Depending on the types being defined, creating types whose definitions exactly match those generated by the importer can be difficult or impossible without using the IL Assembler. The process of comparing type definitions is summarized in Figure 21.1.

If you don't like the idea of scrounging through IL Assembler syntax, the Windows Forms Class Viewer (WINCV.EXE) that ships with the .NET Framework SDK might come in handy. This graphical tool displays searchable C#-ish syntax for types in any assembly. It only displays metadata—no source code. Therefore, you could take an Interop Assembly produced by the type library importer and run WINCV.EXE on it as follows:

```
wincv /r:InteropAssembly.dll /nostdlib
```

Once the window appears, you can type in names of types (or partial names of types) to search the list. This is shown in Figure 21.2.

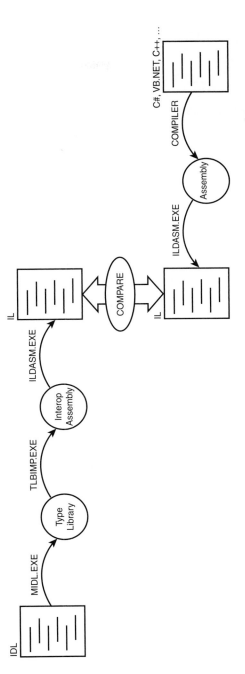

FIGURE 21.1

Comparing metadata produced by the type library importer with metadata produced by compiling high-level source code.

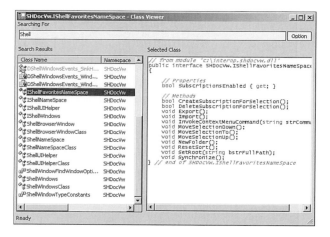

FIGURE 21.2

Using the Windows Forms Class Viewer (WINCV.EXE) to browse metadata in a C#-like source representation.

However, the definitions produced by this tool can be misleading. Its two greatest limitations are:

- Because the tool uses reflection to browse metadata, methods are not guaranteed to be displayed in their original order (which is necessary for interfaces).
- No custom attributes are displayed.

Other than these limitations, non-C#isms are easy to spot, like listing System.Object as an explicit base class, showing all base class methods in a derived class, or showing event accessors as separate methods.

Manually Defining COM Interfaces

As interfaces are the most important types in COM, often interface definitions are all one needs to worry about defining manually. For example, a .NET definition of a COM interface is often unavailable (yet needed) when one wants to implement it in a .NET class in order to plug into an existing architecture (the topic of Chapter 14). Another common case in which such definitions are needed but not available is when a COM interface returns a generic IUnknown or IDispatch interface and one wants to cast the resultant System.Object to a specific COM interface so members can be invoked in an early-bound fashion.

In this section, we examine the following:

- Custom attributes that turn an otherwise purely-managed interface definition to one that's associated with a COM interface
- Defining all three types of COM interfaces
- Interface inheritance details that are easy to get wrong
- Limitations of the high-level language you might be using to define COM interfaces
- Interesting customizations that can make COM interfaces more .NET-like

Important Custom Attributes

A COM interface must always be marked with two custom attributes defined in `System.Runtime.InteropServices`:

- `ComImportAttribute`. This is the single attribute that means "this is a COM type." The name is a little confusing because it sounds like it's only meant for types imported by the type library importer, but it must be placed on every COM type regardless of whether it was imported or manually defined. `ComImport`-marked types (also referred to as `ComImport` types or simply COM types) are never exported by the type library exporter and are only partially registered by the assembly registration process so critical registry entries aren't overwritten. At run time, the attribute on a class instructs the CLR to call `CoCreateInstance` for instantiation and to call `QueryInterface` when casting to an interface.
- `GuidAttribute`. This is needed to give the interface its identity from COM's perspective. The GUID contained in the attribute is used by the CLR in `QueryInterface` calls.

> **CAUTION**
>
> It is critical that every COM interface and class definition is marked with `ComImportAttribute`. Registering an assembly with COM types that aren't marked with `ComImportAttribute` or exporting its type library and registering the type library (or even viewing the type library in `OLEVIEW.EXE`, which registers it) can overwrite important registry entries and wreak havoc on your computer. For example, a coclass's `InprocServer32` key's default value could be changed from the file containing the correct class factory to `MSCOREE.DLL` instead!

Besides these two custom attributes, a third custom attribute is often needed (and should probably always be used for clarity):

- `InterfaceTypeAttribute`. This attribute describes which type of COM interface you're defining—a dual interface, a dispinterface, or an `IUnknown`-only interface (one that does not derive from `IDispatch`). Although this attribute does not effect how the interface is used in managed code, it is essential for proper operation when the interface is passed to unmanaged code. The CLR uses this attribute to determine how to present a v-table to COM, so not setting the attribute's value correctly can cause clients to call different members than they thought they were calling, with the end result being subtle incorrect behavior or hopefully a crash to alert you that something is wrong.

As mentioned in Chapter 12, "Customizing COM's View of .NET Components," `InterfaceTypeAttribute` is used with a `ComInterfaceType` enumeration value that can be set to one (and only one) of its three values—`InterfaceIsDual`, `InterfaceIsIDispatch`, or `InterfaceIsIUnknown`. `InterfaceIsDual` is the default that's assumed if no `InterfaceTypeAttribute` exists, because most COM interfaces are dual. Remember to never use `InterfaceIsIDispatch` unless the interface is a pure dispinterface.

IUnknown-Only Interfaces

In addition to the three custom attributes just introduced, the COM and .NET data type conversions are just about all you need to know when defining simple interfaces that derive directly from `IUnknown`. Refer to Chapter 4, "An In-Depth Look at Imported Assemblies," for more details about these conversions.

So, now it's time for an example. Listing 21.1 contains an IDL definition of the `IWMPEffects` interface defined by the Windows Media Player SDK. This file gets generated when you use the Windows Media Visualization Wizard in a Visual C++ ATL COM project (available after downloading and installing the SDK from MSDN Online). The IDL file is also available on this book's Web site. We'll be discussing and using this interface in Chapter 24, "Writing .NET Visualizations for Windows Media Player," so, for now, we'll just focus on creating an appropriate .NET definition.

LISTING 21.1   The `IWMPEffects` Interface in IDL

```
1: [
2:    object,
3:    uuid(D3984C13-C3CB-48e2-8BE5-5168340B4F35),
4:    helpstring("IWMPEffects Interface"),
5:    pointer_default(unique)
6: ]
7: interface IWMPEffects : IUnknown
8: {
```

LISTING 21.1   Continued

```
 9:    [helpstring("method Render")]
10:    HRESULT Render([in] TimedLevel *pLevels, [in] HDC hdc, [in] RECT *prc);
11:
12:    [helpstring("method MediaInfo")]
13:    HRESULT MediaInfo([in] LONG lChannelCount, [in] LONG lSampleRate,
14:      [in] BSTR bstrTitle);
15:
16:    [helpstring("method GetCapabilities")]
17:    HRESULT GetCapabilities([out] DWORD * pdwCapabilities);
18:
19:    [helpstring("method GetTitle")]
20:    HRESULT GetTitle([out] BSTR *bstrTitle);
21:
22:    [helpstring("method GetPresetTitle")]
23:    HRESULT GetPresetTitle([in] LONG nPreset, [out] BSTR *bstrPresetTitle);
24:
25:    [helpstring("method GetPresetCount")]
26:    HRESULT GetPresetCount([out] LONG * pnPresetCount);
27:
28:    [helpstring("method SetPreset")]
29:    HRESULT SetCurrentPreset([in] LONG nPreset);
30:    [helpstring("method GetPreset")]
31:    HRESULT GetCurrentPreset([out] LONG * pnPreset);
32:
33:    [helpstring("method DisplayPropertyPage")]
34:    HRESULT DisplayPropertyPage([in] HWND hwndOwner);
35:
36:    [helpstring("method GoFullscreen")]
37:    HRESULT GoFullscreen([in] BOOL fFullScreen);
38:
39:    [helpstring("method RenderFullScreen")]
40:    HRESULT RenderFullScreen([in] TimedLevel *pLevels);
41: };
```

Listing 21.2 contains a translation of IWMPEffects to C# based on the rules we've seen so far
in this chapter plus knowledge of data type conversions discussed in Chapter 4.

LISTING 21.2   A Straightforward Definition of the IWMPEffects Interface in C#

```
1: using System;
2: using System.Runtime.InteropServices;
3:
```

LISTING 21.2   Continued

```
 4: [
 5:   ComImport,
 6:   Guid("D3984C13-C3CB-48E2-8BE5-5168340B4F35"),
 7:   InterfaceType(ComInterfaceType.InterfaceIsIUnknown)
 8: ]
 9: interface IWMPEffects
10: {
11:   void Render([In] ref TimedLevel pLevels, IntPtr hdc, [In] ref RECT prc);
12:   void MediaInfo(int lChannelCount, int lSampleRate, string bstrTitle);
13:   void GetCapabilities(out VisualizationCapabilities pdwCapabilities);
14:   void GetTitle(out string bstrTitle);
15:   void GetPresetTitle(int nPreset, out string bstrPresetTitle);
16:   void GetPresetCount(out int pnPresetCount);
17:   void SetCurrentPreset(int nPreset);
18:   void GetCurrentPreset(out int pnPreset);
19:   void DisplayPropertyPage(IntPtr hwndOwner);
20:   void GoFullscreen([MarshalAs(UnmanagedType.Bool)] bool fFullScreen);
21:   void RenderFullScreen([In] ref TimedLevel pLevels);
22: }
```

> **TIP**
>
> Make sure that you define the interface's methods in the exact same order that they appear in the COM definition. Although the order of methods isn't important in the pure .NET world, order is critical to COM due to dependence on v-table layout.

This listing assumes that the `TimedLevel`, `RECT`, and `VisualizationCapabilities` types also have an available .NET definition. `TimedLevel` and `RECT` are defined later in the "Manually Defining COM Structures" section. Because they are blittable, the marshaler pins them when transitioning to unmanaged code so the `InAttribute` markings in Lines 11 and 21 don't have any effect at run time. Still, from a documentation perspective they faithfully represent the intention that the values of these parameters should not change after the method calls.

The definition of `VisualizationCapabilities`, an enum representing the original `DWORD` parameter, is deferred to Chapter 24 because it's not relevant at this time. Notice that by not being marked with the `public` keyword, the interface is private, so it can be used and implemented by .NET types without being exposed to .NET types in other assemblies.

Manually Defining COM Types in Source Code

CHAPTER 21

967

21

DEFINING COM
TYPES IN SOURCE
CODE

> **TIP**
>
> Non-public interfaces marked with `ComImportAttribute`, such as the `IWMPEffects` interface in Listing 21.2, are still "public" to COM, in that a COM client can successfully call `QueryInterface` on a COM-Callable Wrapper for a .NET class implementing the interface and obtain an interface pointer to such an interface. This is why implementing a non-public COM interface works when interacting with COM clients that use the interface. Marking a non-public type with `ComImport` works like the inverse of marking a public type `ComVisible(false)`. Because a definition of a `ComImport` interface is not exported, it's assumed that COM clients obtain a definition of the interface elsewhere. If it truly is a COM interface, it should already be defined in a type library, IDL file, or header file.

Although this should seem like a straightforward transformation of the IDL signatures to C# code, the definition in Listing 21.2 actually has three customizations that make it easier to use than the definition of `IWMPEffects` that would have been generated by the type library importer:

- Listing 21.2 defines `Render`'s `hdc` parameter (originally an `HDC` type) and `DisplayPropertyPage`'s `hwndOwner` parameter (originally an `HWND` type) as `System.IntPtr` types, because we know they'll be platform-sized integers. However, due to aliasing, the importer generates something different, as you will see in Listing 21.3.

- Although the `GetCapabilities` method is defined in IDL with a `DWORD` parameter (which would look like a `long` type in a type library), the interface's documentation states that it's really an enumeration. Therefore, we can define a `VisualizationCapabilities` enumeration with the documented values and make the `GetCapabilities` method more strongly typed by using this parameter type instead.

- Listing 21.2 defines the `BOOL` parameter used in `GoFullScreen` as a `System.Boolean` (`bool`) type. And because boolean parameters map to `VARIANT_BOOL` COM types by default, we had to mark it with `UnmanagedType.Bool`. However, recall that a `BOOL` type in IDL becomes just a 32-bit integer in a type library, so the importer could only generate a `System.Int32` type for this parameter which is definitely not as user-friendly.

Speaking of the `IWMPEffects` definition that would have been generated by the type library importer, let's see what that would look like. Listing 21.3 shows this metadata in IL Assembler syntax by following these steps:

1. Run `MIDL.EXE` on an IDL file containing the original `IWMPEffects` definition *inside a library statement* in order to create a type library. You must use `MIDL`'s `/tlb` option, for example:

```
midl IWMPEffects.idl /tlb IWMPEffects.tlb
```

2. Run `TLBIMP.EXE` on the type library created in step 1 to create a temporary assembly:

   ```
   tlbimp IWMPEffects.tlb /out=TempAssembly.dll
   ```

3. Run `ILDASM.EXE` using its `/out` option on the assembly created in step 2 and view the output text file in your favorite editor:

   ```
   ildasm TempAssembly.dll /out=TempAssembly.il
   notepad TempAssembly.il
   ```

CAUTION

If using the IL Disassembler to view metadata produced by the type library importer, producing an IL text file with the `/out` option is the most accurate way to get the information. If you're working with the graphical mode instead, be sure to turn off the alphabetical sorting of names, otherwise you might attempt to define interface members in that order instead of the order required. This can be turned off by opening the View menu and unchecking `Sort by name`.

LISTING 21.3   Metadata for the `IWMPEffects` Interface Produced by the Type Library Importer in IL Assembler Syntax

```
 1: .class interface public abstract auto ansi import IWMPEffects
 2: {
 3:   .custom instance void [mscorlib]
 4:   System.Runtime.InteropServices.InterfaceTypeAttribute::.ctor(int16) =
 5:   ( 01 00 01 00 00 00 )
 6:
 7:   .custom instance void [mscorlib]
 8:   System.Runtime.InteropServices.GuidAttribute::.ctor(string) =
 9:   ( 01 00 24 44 33 39 38 34 43 31 33 2D 43 33 43 42   // ..$D3984C13-C3CB
10:     2D 34 38 45 32 2D 38 42 45 35 2D 35 31 36 38 33   // -48E2-8BE5-51683
11:     34 30 42 34 46 33 35 00 00 )                      // 40B4F35..
12:
13:   .method public hidebysig newslot virtual abstract
14:   instance void  Render([in] valuetype TempAssembly.tagTimedLevel& pLevels,
15:     [in] valuetype TempAssembly._RemotableHandle& hdc,
16:     [in] valuetype TempAssembly.tagRECT& prc) runtime managed internalcall
17:   {
18:     .param [2]
19:     .custom instance void [mscorlib]
20:     System.Runtime.InteropServices.ComAliasNameAttribute::.ctor(string) =
21:     ( 01 00 14 54 65 6D 70 41 73 73 65 6D 62 6C 79 2E   // ...TempAssembly.
22:       77 69 72 65 48 44 43 00 00 )                      // wireHDC..
23:   } // end of method IWMPEffects::Render
24:
```

Manually Defining COM Types in Source Code

CHAPTER 21

969

21

DEFINING COM
TYPES IN SOURCE
CODE

LISTING 21.3   Continued

```
25:     .method public hidebysig newslot virtual abstract
26:       instance void  MediaInfo([in] int32 lChannelCount,
27:         [in] int32 lSampleRate,
28:         [in] string  marshal( bstr) bstrTitle) runtime managed internalcall
29:     {
30:     } // end of method IWMPEffects::MediaInfo
31:
32:     .method public hidebysig newslot virtual abstract
33:       instance void  GetCapabilities([out] unsigned int32& pdwCapabilities)
34:       runtime managed internalcall
35:     {
36:     } // end of method IWMPEffects::GetCapabilities
37:
38:     .method public hidebysig newslot virtual abstract
39:       instance void  GetTitle([out] string&  marshal( bstr) bstrTitle)
40:       runtime managed internalcall
41:     {
42:     } // end of method IWMPEffects::GetTitle
43:
44:     .method public hidebysig newslot virtual abstract
45:       instance void  GetPresetTitle([in] int32 nPreset,
46:       [out] string&  marshal( bstr) bstrPresetTitle)
47:       runtime managed internalcall
48:     {
49:     } // end of method IWMPEffects::GetPresetTitle
50:
51:     .method public hidebysig newslot virtual abstract
52:       instance void  GetPresetCount([out] int32& pnPresetCount)
53:       runtime managed internalcall
54:     {
55:     } // end of method IWMPEffects::GetPresetCount
56:
57:     .method public hidebysig newslot virtual abstract
58:       instance void  SetCurrentPreset([in] int32 nPreset)
59:       runtime managed internalcall
60:     {
61:     } // end of method IWMPEffects::SetCurrentPreset
62:
63:     .method public hidebysig newslot virtual abstract
64:       instance void  GetCurrentPreset([out] int32& pnPreset)
65:       runtime managed internalcall
66:     {
67:     } // end of method IWMPEffects::GetCurrentPreset
68:
```

LISTING 21.3   Continued

```
69:    .method public hidebysig newslot virtual abstract
70:      instance void  DisplayPropertyPage([in] valuetype
71:      TempAssembly._RemotableHandle& hwndOwner) runtime managed internalcall
72:    {
73:      .param [1]
74:      .custom instance void [mscorlib]
75:      System.Runtime.InteropServices.ComAliasNameAttribute::.ctor(string) =
76:      ( 01 00 15 54 65 6D 70 41 73 73 65 6D 62 6C 79 2E   // ...TempAssembly.
77:        77 69 72 65 48 57 4E 44 00 00 )                   // wireHWND..
78:    } // end of method IWMPEffects::DisplayPropertyPage
79:
80:    .method public hidebysig newslot virtual abstract
81:      instance void  GoFullscreen([in] int32 fFullScreen)
82:      runtime managed internalcall
83:    {
84:    } // end of method IWMPEffects::GoFullscreen
85:
86:    .method public hidebysig newslot virtual abstract
87:      instance void  RenderFullScreen([in] valuetype
88:      TempAssembly.tagTimedLevel& pLevels) runtime managed internalcall
89:    {
90:    } // end of method IWMPEffects::RenderFullScreen
91: } // end of class IWMPEffects
```

For the specifics about IL Assembler syntax, consult Chapter 7. As you can see in Lines 3–11, the type library importer has marked the interface with InterfaceTypeAttribute and GuidAttribute. Where's ComImportAttribute? It's a pseudo-custom attribute, so it appears as import before the interface name in Line 1. In Lines 15 and 71, you can see that the HDC and HWND parameters are imported as by-reference _RemotableHandle types. Furthermore, Lines 18–22 mark the HDC type with ComAliasAttribute ("TempAssembly.wireHDC") and 73–77 mark the HWND type with ComAliasAttribute ("TempAssembly.wireHWND"). They are imported like this because although the IDL definition used HDC and HWND types, the types emitted into the type library are wireHDC and wireHWND due to directives in the included wtypes.idl. Furthermore, these types are both typedefs for the same _RemotableHandle type, so _RemotableHandle is the type seen in the typedef-less world of .NET. HDC and HWND are system handles that are partially remoted, meaning that they are remoted only as an integral type for both local and remote cases. Therefore, it's safe (and much more user-friendly) to change these types to a simple IntPtr.

Manually Defining COM Types in Source Code

CHAPTER 21

971

21

DEFINING COM
TYPES IN SOURCE
CODE

As previously shown in Figure 21.1, a good way to double-check your manual type definition is to compile your assembly containing the definition, view the definition in IL Assembler syntax (using ILDASM.EXE just like you did with the Interop Assembly) and compare it to the IL Assembler output from the Interop Assembly.

How does Listing 21.2 compare to Listing 21.3? Besides three parameters with different types and the interface being private instead of public, there are four major differences that can be seen by viewing the raw metadata for our C# definition:

- All of the methods defined in Listing 21.2 are marked with cil managed whereas the imported methods in Listing 21.3 are marked with runtime managed internalcall.

- The imported parameters all have explicit in/out markings with the InAttribute and OutAttribute pseudo-custom attributes, but the parameters in Listing 21.2 only have OutAttribute markings where C#'s out keyword is used and InAttribute markings where the by-reference parameters were explicitly marked in the C# source code.

- The imported string parameters are all marked with MarshalAs(UnmanagedType.BStr) but the string parameters in Listing 21.2 omit this marking.

- The methods in Listing 21.3 are all marked hidebysig, but the methods in Listing 21.2 do not get this marking.

The only other difference is that Listing 21.2 uses InterfaceTypeAttribute with an enumeration parameter whereas the type library importer uses the overload that takes a 16-bit integer. However, using the enumeration is preferred for its clarity.

Despite these differences that appear when viewing both interface definitions in IL Assembler syntax, there is no functional difference between the definitions in Listing 21.2 and Listing 21.3. The cil managed versus runtime managed internalcall markings have no effect on COM interfaces; the import designation ensures that the CLR handles these members correctly. The additional InAttribute, OutAttribute, and MarshalAs(UnmanagedType.BStr) markings all simply indicate the default behavior explicitly. The hidebysig designations, which indicate that the methods can be overridden by derived class methods with the same name *and the same signature*, make no difference for COM interface methods.

It is possible, however, to generate metadata that more closely resembles what is produced by the type library importer. Listing 21.4 updates Listing 21.2 with custom attributes that eliminate the first three of these four major differences. The hidebysig difference could be eliminated by adding the new keyword to each method (or Shadows in Visual Basic .NET), but then the C# compiler gives a bunch of warnings about the keyword not being required because the members aren't hiding inherited members. Therefore, eliminating this difference is not worth the annoyance.

LISTING 21.4   A Definition of the `IWMPEffects` Interface in C# That, from a Metadata Perspective, Closely Represents What the Type Library Importer Generates

```
 1: using System;
 2: using System.Runtime.InteropServices;
 3: using System.Runtime.CompilerServices;
 4:
 5: [
 6:   ComImport,
 7:   Guid("D3984C13-C3CB-48E2-8BE5-5168340B4F35"),
 8:   InterfaceType(ComInterfaceType.InterfaceIsIUnknown)
 9: ]
10: interface IWMPEffects
11: {
12:   [MethodImpl(MethodImplOptions.InternalCall,
13:    MethodCodeType=MethodCodeType.Runtime)]
14:   void Render([In] ref TimedLevel pLevels, [In] IntPtr hdc,
15:     [In] ref RECT prc);
16:
17:   [MethodImpl(MethodImplOptions.InternalCall,
18:    MethodCodeType=MethodCodeType.Runtime)]
19:   void MediaInfo([In] int lChannelCount, [In] int lSampleRate,
20:     [In, MarshalAs(UnmanagedType.BStr)] string bstrTitle);
21:
22:   [MethodImpl(MethodImplOptions.InternalCall,
23:    MethodCodeType=MethodCodeType.Runtime)]
24:   void GetCapabilities(out VisualizationCapabilities pdwCapabilities);
25:
26:   [MethodImpl(MethodImplOptions.InternalCall,
27:    MethodCodeType=MethodCodeType.Runtime)]
28:   void GetTitle([MarshalAs(UnmanagedType.BStr)] out string bstrTitle);
29:
30:   [MethodImpl(MethodImplOptions.InternalCall,
31:    MethodCodeType=MethodCodeType.Runtime)]
32:   void GetPresetTitle([In] int nPreset, [MarshalAs(UnmanagedType.BStr)]
33:     out string bstrPresetTitle);
34:
35:   [MethodImpl(MethodImplOptions.InternalCall,
36:    MethodCodeType=MethodCodeType.Runtime)]
37:   void GetPresetCount(out int pnPresetCount);
38:
39:   [MethodImpl(MethodImplOptions.InternalCall,
40:    MethodCodeType=MethodCodeType.Runtime)]
41:   void SetCurrentPreset([In] int nPreset);
42:
```

Manually Defining COM Types in Source Code

CHAPTER 21

973

21

DEFINING COM
TYPES IN SOURCE
CODE

LISTING 21.4 Continued

```
43:    [MethodImpl(MethodImplOptions.InternalCall,
44:     MethodCodeType=MethodCodeType.Runtime)]
45:    void GetCurrentPreset(out int pnPreset);
46:
47:    [MethodImpl(MethodImplOptions.InternalCall,
48:     MethodCodeType=MethodCodeType.Runtime)]
49:    void DisplayPropertyPage([In] IntPtr hwndOwner);
50:
51:    [MethodImpl(MethodImplOptions.InternalCall,
52:     MethodCodeType=MethodCodeType.Runtime)]
53:    void GoFullScreen([In, MarshalAs(UnmanagedType.Bool)] bool fFullScreen);
54:
55:    [MethodImpl(MethodImplOptions.InternalCall,
56:     MethodCodeType=MethodCodeType.Runtime)]
57:    void RenderFullScreen([In] ref TimedLevel pLevels);
58: }
```

The way to get the methods marked as `runtime managed internalcall` instead of
`cil managed` is to use the `MethodImplAttribute` pseudo-custom attribute defined in the
`System.Runtime.CompilerServices` namespace with a value set to `InternalCall` and its
`MethodCodeType` named parameter set to `Runtime`, as shown in the listing.

Although this listing is much more cluttered with custom attributes, this definition is no better
than the one in Listing 21.2. The moral of the story is to not bother with `MethodImplAttributes`
on interface members, but some use of `InAttribute` and `OutAttribute` custom attributes
might be a good idea for clarity (or to gain optimizations for non-blittable types) by more
faithfully representing the data flow of parameters.

DIGGING DEEPER

Occasionally, the type library importer produces metadata that is technically illegal,
so it may be impossible to generate the exact same metadata in anything other
than IL Assembler syntax. These illegal items are harmless, such as putting informational
custom attributes on a target type not listed in the custom attribute's
`AttributeUsageAttribute`. An example of this is that the importer places the
`SuppressUnmanagedCodeSecurityAttribute` on enums (when using the option to
generate unsafe interfaces) although this attribute is not valid on enums. How can
the importer do this? It creates metadata using reflection emit technology (in the
`System.Reflection.Emit` namespace) and unmanaged metadata APIs, which are
lenient enough to allow all kinds of constructs that can't be written in high-level
languages.

Listing 21.5 shows how to produce the same metadata as running the C# compiler on Listing 21.4, but using the Visual Basic .NET compiler. Notice that the combination of OutAttribute and ByRef is needed to produce the same effect as C#'s out keyword.

LISTING 21.5   A Definition of the IWMPEffects Interface in VB .NET That, from a Metadata Perspective, Closely Represents What the Type Library Importer Generates

```vb
 1: Imports System
 2: Imports System.Runtime.InteropServices
 3: Imports System.Runtime.CompilerServices
 4:
 5: < _
 6:   ComImport, _
 7:   Guid("D3984C13-C3CB-48E2-8BE5-5168340B4F35"), _
 8:   InterfaceType(ComInterfaceType.InterfaceIsIUnknown) _
 9: > _
10: Interface IWMPEffects
11:
12:   <MethodImpl(MethodImplOptions.InternalCall, _
13:     MethodCodeType:=MethodCodeType.Runtime)> _
14:   Sub Render(<[In]> ByRef pLevels As TimedLevel, <[In]> hdc As IntPtr, _
15:     <[In]> ByRef prc As RECT)
16:
17:   <MethodImpl(MethodImplOptions.InternalCall, _
18:     MethodCodeType:=MethodCodeType.Runtime)> _
19:   Sub MediaInfo(<[In]> lChannelCount As Integer, <[In]> lSampleRate As _
20:     Integer, <[In], MarshalAs(UnmanagedType.BStr)> bstrTitle As String)
21:
22:   <MethodImpl(MethodImplOptions.InternalCall, _
23:     MethodCodeType:=MethodCodeType.Runtime)> _
24:   Sub GetCapabilities(<Out> ByRef pdwCapabilities _
25:     As VisualizationCapabilities)
26:
27:   <MethodImpl(MethodImplOptions.InternalCall, _
28:     MethodCodeType:=MethodCodeType.Runtime)> _
29:   Sub GetTitle(<Out, MarshalAs(UnmanagedType.BStr)> _
30:     ByRef bstrTitle As String)
31:
32:   <MethodImpl(MethodImplOptions.InternalCall, _
33:     MethodCodeType:=MethodCodeType.Runtime)> _
34:   Sub GetPresetTitle(<[In]> nPreset As Integer, _
35:     <Out, MarshalAs(UnmanagedType.BStr)> bstrPresetTitle As String)
36:
37:   <MethodImpl(MethodImplOptions.InternalCall, _
38:     MethodCodeType:=MethodCodeType.Runtime)> _
39:   Sub GetPresetCount(<Out> ByRef pnPresetCount As Integer)
40:
```

Manually Defining COM Types in Source Code

CHAPTER 21

975

21

DEFINING COM
TYPES IN SOURCE
CODE

LISTING 21.5 Continued

```
41:    <MethodImpl(MethodImplOptions.InternalCall, _
42:      MethodCodeType:=MethodCodeType.Runtime)> _
43:    Sub SetCurrentPreset(<[In]> nPreset As Integer)
44:
45:    <MethodImpl(MethodImplOptions.InternalCall, _
46:      MethodCodeType:=MethodCodeType.Runtime)> _
47:    Sub GetCurrentPreset(<Out> ByRef pnPreset As Integer)
48:
49:    <MethodImpl(MethodImplOptions.InternalCall, _
50:      MethodCodeType:=MethodCodeType.Runtime)> _
51:    Sub DisplayPropertyPage(<[In]> hwndOwner As IntPtr)
52:
53:    <MethodImpl(MethodImplOptions.InternalCall, _
54:      MethodCodeType:=MethodCodeType.Runtime)> _
55:    Sub GoFullScreen(<[In], MarshalAs(UnmanagedType.Bool)> _
56:      fFullScreen As Boolean)
57:
58:    <MethodImpl(MethodImplOptions.InternalCall, _
59:      MethodCodeType:=MethodCodeType.Runtime)> _
60:    Sub RenderFullScreen(<[In]> ByRef pLevels As TimedLevel)
61:
62: End Interface
```

Dual Interfaces

The only difference about defining a dual interface instead of an IUnknown-only interface, besides changing the value of InterfaceTypeAttribute, is that methods on a dual interface have DISPIDs. These DISPIDs must be marked on the members you define using the DispIdAttribute, so a .NET class that implements the interface can respond properly to IDispatch.Invoke calls from COM clients that don't obtain DISPIDs from IDispatch. GetIDsFromNames. The DISPIDs are never used when a .NET component invokes dual interface methods on a COM object because the CLR always calls through the v-table.

Listing 21.6 contains an IDL definition of IRunningAppCollection, a dual COM interface found in ComAdmin.idl, which ships with the Windows Platform SDK.

LISTING 21.6 The Dual IRunningAppCollection Interface in IDL

```
1: [
2:    object,
3:    uuid(ab9d3261-d6ea-4fbd-80f6-cf7bad0732f3),
4:    dual,
5:    helpstring("IRunningAppCollection interface"),
```

LISTING 21.6   Continued

```
 6:    pointer_default(unique)
 7:]
 8: interface IRunningAppCollection : IDispatch
 9: {
10:    import "oaidl.idl";
11:    [ propget, restricted, id(DISPID_NEWENUM) ]
12:    HRESULT _NewEnum( [out, retval] IUnknown** ppEnumVariant );
13:
14:    [ propget, id(1), helpstring("Gets count of apps in collection") ]
15:    HRESULT Count([out,retval]long* pCount);
16:
17:    [ propget, id(2), helpstring("Returns an app instance by index") ]
18:    HRESULT Item([in]long lIndex, [out,retval]IDispatch** ppAppObject);
19: };
```

The three methods—_NewEnum, Count, and Item in Lines 11–18—have the DISPIDs DISPID_NEWENUM (-4), 1, and 2, respectively. Listing 21.7 contains a relatively simple translation to C#, making use of DispIdAttribute.

LISTING 21.7   A Straightforward Definition of the IRunningAppCollection Interface in C#

```
 1: using System.Runtime.InteropServices;
 2:
 3: [
 4:    ComImport,
 5:    Guid("ab9d3261-d6ea-4fbd-80f6-cf7bad0732f3"),
 6:    InterfaceType(ComInterfaceType.InterfaceIsDual)
 7: ]
 8: interface IRunningAppCollection
 9: {
10:    [DispId(-4)]
11:    object _NewEnum
12:    {
13:      [return: MarshalAs(UnmanagedType.IUnknown)] get;
14:    }
15:
16:    [DispId(1)]
17:    int Count { get; }
18:
19:    [DispId(2)]
20:    [return: MarshalAs(UnmanagedType.IDispatch)]
21:    object get_Item(int lIndex);
22: }
```

Manually Defining COM Types in Source Code

CHAPTER 21

977

21

DEFINING COM
TYPES IN SOURCE
CODE

In Listing 21.7, Line 6 marks the interface as dual, and Lines 10, 16, and 19 apply the appropriate DISPIDs. The first two property definitions are straightforward, once you recall that marshaling directives for a property's type must be applied to accessors, as in Line 13. Item is a non-default parameterized property, which C# doesn't support, so Line 21 defines a get_Item accessor method instead.

> **CAUTION**
>
> COM interfaces with parameterized properties or properties with by-reference parameters cannot be appropriately defined in C# due to language restrictions. Although such a property's accessor methods can be defined directly, clients become forced to use the accessor methods rather than a property regardless of their language.

As we've seen in previous chapters, a DISPID equal to –4 (DISPID_NEW_ENUM) is not any ordinary DISPID. It represents a member that returns an enumerator interface such as IEnumVARIANT in COM. The type library exporter does some special transformations and uses custom marshaling to convert an appropriate member with DISPID -4 to IEnumerable's GetEnumerator method.

Using metadata produced by the type library importer as a guide, Listing 21.8 contains an updated definition of IRunningAppCollection that matches what the importer would produce much more closely.

LISTING 21.8 A Definition of the IRunningAppCollection Interface in C# That Produces the Almost Identical Metadata as the Type Library Importer

```
 1: using System.Collections;
 2: using System.Runtime.CompilerServices;
 3: using System.Runtime.InteropServices;
 4: using System.Runtime.InteropServices.CustomMarshalers;
 5:
 6: [
 7:   ComImport,
 8:   Guid("ab9d3261-d6ea-4fbd-80f6-cf7bad0732f3"),
 9:   TypeLibType(TypeLibTypeFlags.FDual | TypeLibTypeFlags.FDispatchable)
10: ]
11: interface IRunningAppCollection : IEnumerable
12: {
13:   [
14:     DispId(-4),
15:     TypeLibFuncAttribute(TypeLibFuncFlags.FRestricted),
```

LISTING 21.8   Continued

```
16:      MethodImpl(MethodImplOptions.InternalCall,
17:      MethodCodeType=MethodCodeType.Runtime)
18:    ]
19:    [return: MarshalAs(UnmanagedType.CustomMarshaler,
20:     MarshalTypeRef=typeof(EnumeratorToEnumVariantMarshaler))]
21:    new IEnumerator GetEnumerator();
22:
23:    [DispId(1)]
24:    int Count
25:    {
26:      [MethodImpl(MethodImplOptions.InternalCall,
27:       MethodCodeType=MethodCodeType.Runtime)]
28:      get;
29:    }
30:
31:    [DispId(2)]
32:    object this[int lIndex]
33:    {
34:      [MethodImpl(MethodImplOptions.InternalCall,
35:       MethodCodeType=MethodCodeType.Runtime)]
36:      [return: MarshalAs(UnmanagedType.IDispatch)] get;
37:    }
38: }
```

In addition to System.Runtime.InteropServices, this listing uses the System.Collections namespace for IEnumerable and IEnumerator, the System.Runtime.CompilerServices namespace for MethodImplAttribute, and the System.Runtime.InteropServices.CustomMarshalers namespace for EnumeratorToEnumVariantMarshaler. In addition, compiling the listing requires referencing CustomMarshalers.dll for the definition of EnumeratorToEnumVariantMarshaler.

Although the type library importer tends to be slightly more explicit with pseudo-custom attributes than it needs to be, it omits regular custom attributes that specify default behavior because emitting them can significantly add to the size of the Interop Assembly. This is why IRunningAppCollection is not marked with InterfaceType(ComInterfaceType.InterfaceIsDual). Instead, the TypeLibTypeAttribute is placed on the interface with the flags FDual and FDispatchable. This custom attribute is completely ignored by the CLR; it simply preserves miscellaneous type library flags found in IDL attributes for informational purposes only and therefore can safely be omitted.

To match the importer's transformation for DISPID –4, IRunningAppCollection now derives from IEnumerable and its first member in Lines 13–21 is now GetEnumerator marked with the appropriate custom attributes. TypeLibFuncAttribute captures the fact that the original _NewEnum property was marked restricted. The new keyword not only makes the resultant metadata contain the hidebysig attribute, but eliminates a compiler warning because IRunningAppcollection.GetEnumerator hides the inherited IEnumerable.GetEnumerator.

The Count property in Lines 23–29 hasn't changed from the previous listing except for the addition of MethodImplAttribute. Notice that the attribute belongs on accessor methods, not on properties.

The last member in Lines 31–37 uses a bizarre trick to work around the C# parameterized property limitation. C# types can have one parameterized property—the indexer. Because IRunningAppCollection has only one parameterized property and because its semantics are appropriate for an indexer, we simply make it an indexer. This has the advantage of making it a full-fledged property with an associated accessor method rather than simply a method. The remaining issue is that default properties are emitted with DISPID 0 because that DISPID represents a default property to COM, but the Item property must have a DISPID equal to 2. Fortunately, the DISPID can be overridden with the DispIdAttribute, which is done in Line 31. Because C# generates a property called Item for an indexer, its metadata ends up matching that produced by the type library importer. The result is a non-default property (from COM's perspective) that happens to be treated like a default property in .NET.

> **TIP**
>
> Most of the time, an Item property on a COM interface is naturally suited to be a default property (indexer). If it's not marked with DISPID 0, it could simply be an oversight by the interface's designer.

The only differences between Listing 21.8 and what the importer would generate for IRunningAppCollection are as follows. In Listing 21.8:

- The interface is private
- Custom attributes that accept either enums or plain integers are used with the enum values
- The second and third properties are not marked with hidebysig
- The interface has a DefaultMemberAttribute custom attribute listing the Item property (emitted automatically by the C# compiler).

All occurrences of MethodImplAttribute, TypeLibTypeAttribute, and TypeLibFuncAttribute could be removed for a much more readable yet functionally equivalent definition.

Listing 21.9 shows a VB .NET definition of IRunningAppCollection equivalent to the definition in Listing 21.8, but omitting the unnecessary MethodImplAttribute for readability and leaving the Item property as non-default because VB .NET can handle this kind of property. Of course, the Item property could still be made into a default property if desirable, but here it's left alone to more accurately represent the original interface.

LISTING 21.9 A Definition of the IRunningAppCollection Interface in Visual Basic .NET

```
 1: Imports System.Collections
 2: Imports System.Runtime.InteropServices
 3: Imports System.Runtime.InteropServices.CustomMarshalers
 4:
 5: < _
 6:   ComImport, _
 7:   Guid("ab9d3261-d6ea-4fbd-80f6-cf7bad0732f3"), _
 8:   TypeLibType(TypeLibTypeFlags.FDual Or TypeLibTypeFlags.FDispatchable) _
 9: > _
10: Interface IRunningAppCollection
11:   Inherits IEnumerable
12:
13:   < _
14:     DispId(-4), _
15:     TypeLibFuncAttribute(TypeLibFuncFlags.FRestricted) _
16:   > _
17:   Shadows Function GetEnumerator() As _
18:     <MarshalAs(UnmanagedType.CustomMarshaler, _
19:     MarshalTypeRef:=GetType(EnumeratorToEnumVariantMarshaler))> IEnumerator
20:
21:   <DispId(1)> _
22:   ReadOnly Property Count As Integer
23:
24:   <DispId(2)> _
25:   ReadOnly Property Item(lIndex As Integer) As _
26:     <MarshalAs(UnmanagedType.IDispatch)> Object
27:
28: End Interface
```

Manually Defining COM Types in Source Code

CHAPTER 21

981

21

DEFINING COM
TYPES IN SOURCE
CODE

> **CAUTION**
>
> Version 7.0 of the Visual Basic .NET compiler does not provide a way to mark a property setter's parameter with `MarshalAsAttribute` when that property is defined on an interface. Notice how Line 26 in Listing 21.9 places `MarshalAsAttribute` directly on the property's return type since Visual Basic .NET doesn't allow explicitly declaring get and set accessors on an interface's property. In this example, the compiler does the right thing and places the attribute on the get accessor method's return type. Had the property not been read-only, there would be no VB .NET syntax for defining it correctly.

Just as with a DISPID value of -4, DISPIDs equal to 0 (`DISPID_VALUE`) should be treated specially to ensure that an interface's semantics are preserved in .NET. Besides preserving its DISPID of 0, this means marking such a member as a .NET default member. In C#, this can be accomplished by creating an indexer, as we did for the `IRunningAppCollection.Item` property. Marking the indexer with `DispId(0)` is not strictly necessary because the C# compiler gives an indexer this DISPID by default.

> **TIP**
>
> If you want to define a C# indexer that gets emitted with a name other than `Item`, you can use `IndexerNameAttribute` defined in the `System.Runtime.CompilerServices.CSharp` namespace to choose a different name.

In Visual Basic .NET, you can define a default property with the `Default` keyword as follows:

```
Public Interface IHaveADefaultProperty
  Default Property Item(ByVal i As Integer) As Integer
End Interface
```

C++ doesn't have built-in syntax for creating a default member, so the only way to define a default property is the "raw" approach of marking the class with `DefaultMemberAttribute`. This might look like the following:

```
#using <mscorlib.dll>
using namespace System::Reflection;
using namespace System::Runtime::InteropServices;
```

```
[DefaultMember("Item")]
public __gc __interface IHaveADefaultProperty
{
  [DispId(0)] __property int get_Item(int i);
};
```

Dispinterfaces

As with dual interfaces, the definition of a dispinterface (a.k.a. dispatch-only interfaces) must contain the DispIdAttribute on every member. When managed code calls members on a dispinterface implemented by a COM object, the CLR can avoid a call to GetIDsOfNames by obtaining the necessary DISPIDs directly from metadata.

Unlike other interfaces, the ordering of dispinterface members doesn't matter because all method invocations are done via IDispatch. Listing 21.10 contains an IDL representation of the AddressLists dispinterface defined by the Microsoft CDO 1.21 Library (CDO.DLL).

LISTING 21.10 The AddressLists Dispinterface in IDL

```
 1: [
 2:   uuid(3FA7DEB2-6438-101B-ACC1-00AA00423326),
 3:   helpstring("AddrLists collection")
 4: ]
 5: dispinterface AddressLists {
 6:   properties:
 7:     [id(0x00000014), readonly]
 8:     VARIANT Application;
 9:     [id(0x00000019)]
10:     VARIANT Parent;
11:     [id(0x00000022)]
12:     VARIANT Session;
13:     [id(0x00000006), readonly]
14:     VARIANT Class;
15:     [id(0x00000009), readonly]
16:     VARIANT Count;
17:   methods:
18:     [id(0x00000015), propget]
19:     VARIANT Item(VARIANT Index);
20: };
```

Listing 21.11 contains a suitable definition of this interface in C++ with Managed Extensions.

LISTING 21.11   A .NET Definition of AddressLists in Visual C++ .NET

```
 1: #using <mscorlib.dll>
 2:
 3: using namespace System;
 4: using namespace System::Runtime::InteropServices;
 5:
 6: [
 7:   ComImport,
 8:   Guid("3FA7DEB2-6438-101B-ACC1-00AA00423326"),
 9:   InterfaceType(ComInterfaceType::InterfaceIsIDispatch)
10: ]
11: __gc __interface AddressLists
12: {
13:   [DispId(14)] __property Object* get_Application();
14:   [DispId(19)] __property Object* get_Parent();
15:                __property void set_Parent(Object* parent);
16:   [DispId(22)] __property Object* get_Session();
17:                __property void set_Session(Object* session);
18:   [DispId(6)]  __property Object* get_Class();
19:   [DispId(9)]  __property Object* get_Count();
20:   [DispId(15)] __property Object* get_Item(Object* Index);
21: };
```

Line 9 contains the necessary `InterfaceIsIDispatch` marking that all dispinterfaces must have.

CAUTION

Never mark an interface with `InterfaceIsIDispatch` unless it's a pure dispinterface. Although using `InterfaceIsIDispatch` on a dual interface is the only misuse of `InterfaceTypeAttribute` that works without errors, making this mistake always forces late binding. Because the CLR enables you to call methods of a dispinterface just like any other interface (hiding the late binding as in Visual Basic .NET), there are no warning indicators for making this mistake except for poor performance.

At first it might catch you by surprise that the listing defines a `get_Item` property accessor in Line 20 rather than an `Item` method. However, although the definition of `Item` in Listing 21.10 is listed under the methods section, notice the `propget` attribute on the method that makes it a property.

Each DISPID in Listing 21.11 is only marked on one of each property's accessor methods. This is done because the C++ compiler knows to place the attribute on the property instead of the accessor for custom attributes that can be placed on a property. If the listing placed a `DispIdAttribute` on both of a property's accessors, the property would end up with two `DispIdAttributes` in metadata. This is harmless, but it's better to not cause the duplicate definitions.

As in C# and Visual Basic .NET, the C++ method definitions don't have `hidebysig` set by default. Besides slightly different property metadata produced by the C++ compiler that doesn't affect the use of the COM interface, there are no surprises in the metadata generated for this definition.

> **CAUTION**
>
> The Visual C++ .NET compiler doesn't emit metadata for a private interface such as the one in Listing 21.11 unless it is used somewhere, such as implemented by a public class. Therefore, to check the metadata of Listing 21.11, you should make it public or add a type that uses the interface.

Interface Inheritance

The COM interfaces we've examined so far inherit directly from `IUnknown` or `IDispatch`. Special care is needed when defining a COM interface that directly inherits from an interface other than these famous two.

When constructing a v-table to expose to COM, the CLR uses only the methods of `IUnknown`, the methods of `IDispatch` (unless `InterfaceTypeAttribute` marks it as an `IUnknown`-only interface), plus the methods defined directly on the interface type. No methods of base interfaces with a .NET definition are considered. Because of this, all base interface methods must be duplicated on the definition of a derived interface. As mentioned in Chapter 4, the type library importer does exactly that when defining interfaces. (One could imagine a `ComInterfaceType.Derived` value that could be used on interfaces to direct the CLR to include base interface methods in the v-table rather than having to redefine the methods. Unfortunately, no such value exists.)

> **CAUTION**
>
> It's easy to forget to redefine base interface members on a derived interface because simply expressing the inheritance relationship, such as the following in C#, exhibits the expected *compile-time* behavior:

Manually Defining COM Types in Source Code

CHAPTER 21

985

21

DEFINING COM
TYPES IN SOURCE
CODE

> ```
> interface IProvideClassInfo2 : IProvideClassInfo
> ```
> At run time, however, such an omission can cause catastrophic failures for such COM interfaces.

Listing 21.12 contains the definitions of two well-known COM persistence interfaces defined in objidl.idl that are related via inheritance—IPersist and IPersistStream.

LISTING 21.12 The IPersist and IPersistStream Interfaces in IDL

```
 1: [
 2:   object,
 3:   uuid(0000010c-0000-0000-C000-000000000046)
 4: ]
 5: interface IPersist : IUnknown
 6: {
 7:   typedef [unique] IPersist *LPPERSIST;
 8:   HRESULT GetClassID([out] CLSID *pClassID);
 9: }
10:
11: [
12:   object,
13:   uuid(00000109-0000-0000-C000-000000000046),
14:   pointer_default(unique)
15: ]
16: interface IPersistStream : IPersist
17: {
18:   typedef [unique] IPersistStream *LPPERSISTSTREAM;
19:   HRESULT IsDirty(void);
20:   HRESULT Load([in, unique] IStream *pStm);
21:   HRESULT Save(
22:     [in, unique] IStream *pStm,
23:     [in] BOOL fClearDirty
24:   );
25:   HRESULT GetSizeMax([out] ULARGE_INTEGER *pcbSize);
26: }
```

Listing 21.13 demonstrates how to properly provide .NET definitions of these two interfaces in C#.

LISTING 21.13   C# Definitions of `IPersist` and the Derived `IPersistStream` Interfaces

```
 1: using System;
 2: using System.Runtime.InteropServices;
 3:
 4: [
 5:   ComImport,
 6:   Guid("0000010c-0000-0000-C000-000000000046"),
 7:   InterfaceType(ComInterfaceType.InterfaceIsIUnknown)
 8: ]
 9: interface IPersist
10: {
11:   void GetClassID(out Guid pClassID);
12: }
13:
14: [
15:   ComImport,
16:   Guid("00000109-0000-0000-C000-000000000046"),
17:   InterfaceType(ComInterfaceType.InterfaceIsIUnknown)
18: ]
19: interface IPersistStream : IPersist
20: {
21:   // IPersist Method
22:   new void GetClassID(out Guid pClassID);
23:
24:   // IPersistStream Methods
25:   [PreserveSig]
26:   int IsDirty();
27:   void Load([In] UCOMIStream pStm);
28:   void Save([In] UCOMIStream pStm,
29:     [In, MarshalAs(UnmanagedType.Bool)] bool fClearDirty);
30:   void GetSizeMax(out long pcbSize);
31: }
```

This listing contains four important customizations that the type library importer could not have done. One is in Line 29—preserving the boolean-ness of the `fClearDirty` parameter just like what was done with the `IWMPEffects` interface in Listing 21.2. A second customization is done in Line 30, making the parameter type of `pcbSize` a simple `long` rather than `ULARGE_INTEGER`. The `ULARGE_INTEGER` type is also a 64-bit type, but is a union of a 64-bit integer and two 32-bit integers (to accommodate compilers that can't handle 64-bit types):

```
typedef union _ULARGE_INTEGER {
  struct {
      DWORD LowPart;
      DWORD HighPart;
```

Manually Defining COM Types in Source Code

CHAPTER 21

987

21

DEFINING COM
TYPES IN SOURCE
CODE

```
        };
        ULONGLONG QuadPart;
    } ULARGE_INTEGER, *PULARGE_INTEGER;
```

Unions don't natively exist in .NET (and would have to be treated like a regular structure with distinct fields), so replacing the type with a simple 64-bit integer is not only much more convenient, but safe for all .NET languages because 64-bit signed integers are included in the Common Language Specification (CLS).

Another customization is the use of the UCOMIStream type in Lines 27 and 28. This is used for convenience because the .NET Framework already provides a .NET definition of the IStream COM interface, but it's also important because it's the "Primary Interop Definition" of IStream so it's *the* type that people should use to represent IStream. The type library importer would have used a different definition of IStream originating from wherever the input type library obtained its definition.

The most vital customization is the use of PreserveSigAttribute in Line 25. IPersistStream.IsDirty only returns either S_OK or S_FALSE HRESULT values, so making this change is the only way the method can be useful in managed code. Technically, the integer return value should be marked with MarshalAs(UnmanagedType.Error), but omitting it is safe.

Line 22 contains the base GetClassID method redefined in the derived interface. Notice that the new keyword is required (or Shadows in Visual Basic .NET) to prevent a compilation warning about hiding an inherited member. If you define a COM interface that derives from IPersistStream, the members of both IPersistStream and IPersist would have to be redefined on that interface, and so on.

TIP

You might be inclined to omit the inheritance relationship when defining a COM interface (for example, having IPersistStream derive directly from IUnknown) because the base methods are copied anyway and you don't have to deal with the mess of multiply defined members. However, don't omit the relationship because it's still important for proper operation on both .NET and COM sides. Not only does it provide the expected behavior in .NET clients using such interfaces (such as implicitly converting an IPersistStream type to an IPersist type, but for COM as well because a CCW makes QueryInterface calls on the derived interface succeed for any of its base interfaces. If the definition of IPersistStream didn't show it deriving from IPersist, the only way for a .NET class to respond successfully to COM QueryInterface calls for both interfaces would be to implement both interfaces, and the class would still have to deal with duplicate members.

Working With Language Limitations

Because most COM interfaces were designed without regard to the yet-to-be invented Common Language Specification for the CLR, not every interface can be accurately represented in your language of choice. Many were designed to be OLE Automation-compatible, a similar notion, but these two subsets of functionality have some areas where they don't overlap. Most notably, optional parameters and parameterized properties are OLE Automation-compatible yet the CLS doesn't require languages like C# to support defining them.

For an example of a troubling interface, look at the IHTMLStyleSheet interface defined in the Microsoft HTML Object Library (MSHTML.TLB). This interface is shown in Listing 21.14 as it's defined in the IDL file MSHTML.IDL.

LISTING 21.14   The IHTMLStyleSheet Interface Defined in IDL

```
 1: [
 2:    odl,
 3:    oleautomation,
 4:    dual,
 5:    uuid(3050f2e3-98b5-11cf-bb82-00aa00bdce0b)
 6: ]
 7: interface IHTMLStyleSheet : IDispatch
 8: {
 9:    [propput, id(DISPID_IHTMLSTYLESHEET_TITLE)]
10:    HRESULT title([in] BSTR v);
11:    [propget, id(DISPID_IHTMLSTYLESHEET_TITLE)]
12:    HRESULT title([retval, out] BSTR * p);
13:
14:    [propget, id(DISPID_IHTMLSTYLESHEET_PARENTSTYLESHEET)]
15:    HRESULT parentStyleSheet([retval, out] IHTMLStyleSheet* * p);
16:
17:    [propget, id(DISPID_IHTMLSTYLESHEET_OWNINGELEMENT)]
18:    HRESULT owningElement([retval, out] IHTMLElement* * p);
19:
20:    [propput, id(DISPID_IHTMLSTYLESHEET_DISABLED)]
21:    HRESULT disabled([in] VARIANT_BOOL v);
22:    [propget, id(DISPID_IHTMLSTYLESHEET_DISABLED)]
23:    HRESULT disabled([retval, out] VARIANT_BOOL * p);
24:
25:    [propget, id(DISPID_IHTMLSTYLESHEET_READONLY)]
26:    HRESULT readOnly([retval, out] VARIANT_BOOL * p);
27:
28:    [propget, id(DISPID_IHTMLSTYLESHEET_IMPORTS)]
29:    HRESULT imports([retval, out] IHTMLStyleSheetsCollection* * p);
30:
```

LISTING 21.14 Continued

```
31:    [propput, id(DISPID_IHTMLSTYLESHEET_HREF)]
32:    HRESULT href([in] BSTR v);
33:    [propget, id(DISPID_IHTMLSTYLESHEET_HREF)]
34:    HRESULT href([retval, out] BSTR * p);
35:
36:    [propget, id(DISPID_IHTMLSTYLESHEET_TYPE)]
37:    HRESULT type([retval, out] BSTR * p);
38:
39:    [propget, id(DISPID_IHTMLSTYLESHEET_ID)]
40:    HRESULT id([retval, out] BSTR * p);
41:
42:    [id(DISPID_IHTMLSTYLESHEET_ADDIMPORT)]
43:    HRESULT addImport([in] BSTR bstrURL, [defaultvalue(-1), in] long lIndex,
44:      [retval, out] long* plIndex);
45:
46:    [id(DISPID_IHTMLSTYLESHEET_ADDRULE)] HRESULT addRule(
47:      [in] BSTR bstrSelector, [in] BSTR bstrStyle,
48:      [defaultvalue(-1), in] long lIndex, [retval, out] long* plNewIndex);
49:
50:    [id(DISPID_IHTMLSTYLESHEET_REMOVEIMPORT)]
51:    HRESULT removeImport([in] long lIndex);
52:
53:    [id(DISPID_IHTMLSTYLESHEET_REMOVERULE)]
54:    HRESULT removeRule([in] long lIndex);
55:
56:    [propput, id(DISPID_IHTMLSTYLESHEET_MEDIA)]
57:    HRESULT media([in] BSTR v);
58:    [propget, id(DISPID_IHTMLSTYLESHEET_MEDIA)]
59:    HRESULT media([retval, out] BSTR * p);
60:
61:    [propput, id(DISPID_IHTMLSTYLESHEET_CSSTEXT)]
62:    HRESULT cssText([in] BSTR v);
63:    [propget, id(DISPID_IHTMLSTYLESHEET_CSSTEXT)]
64:    HRESULT cssText([retval, out] BSTR * p);
65:
66:    [propget, id(DISPID_IHTMLSTYLESHEET_RULES)]
67:    HRESULT rules([retval, out] IHTMLStyleSheetRulesCollection* * p);
68: };
```

Because Listing 21.14 shows the contents directly from an IDL file, there are some non-standard markings that would show up differently when viewed inside a type library. For example, this interface has two optional parameters—lIndex in the addImport and addRule methods. But rather than being marked [optional, defaultvalue(-1), in] they are only marked [defaultvalue(-1), in]. Both are treated as equivalent by MIDL, which can be seen by viewing this interface's definition by running OLEVIEW.EXE on the MSHTML.TLB type library.

Every DISPID is marked with a constant value defined in an included header file, such as DISPID_IHTMLSTYLESHEET_RULES. (If you're defining a .NET interface based on an IDL definition, you'll sometimes need to search through header files to get all the necessary information.) The non-standard practice of listing the IDL in and out attributes last rather than first (such as retval, out) does not make a difference. However, the non-standard practice of listing a property's set accessor (propput) before its get accessor (propget) does give us a problem, which is discussed in the following section.

Most language limitations encountered when defining COM interfaces revolve around properties. For example, although Visual Basic .NET permits *calling* properties with by-reference parameters (as sometimes used in COM interfaces), it does not permit *defining* such a property. Also, when placing a custom attribute such as MarshalAsAttribute on a VB .NET interface property, the compiler only applies it to the get accessor and not the set accessor. This is why the previous chapter manually defined the IFont COM interface in C# for the font custom marshaler (whose source is available on this book's Web site); some boolean properties required MarshalAs(UnmanagedType.Bool) on their set accessors. (An alternative definition could have been written in Visual Basic .NET using plain integers instead, but it would not be as user-friendly.)

The next two sections examine the following frequently-encountered limitations that are both demonstrated by IHTMLStyleSheet in Listing 21.14:

- Location and ordering of property accessors
- Optional parameters and default values

Location and Ordering of Property Accessors

It's natural to want to define a property like IHTMLStyleSheet.title as follows inside a Visual Basic .NET interface definition:

```
' Incorrect property definition
<DispId(DispIds.IHTMLSTYLESHEET_TITLE)> _
Property title As String
```

DON'T DO THIS

(This assumes the existence of a DispIds class defining the appropriate constants.) This code is not correct, however, because properties defined in VB .NET interfaces always get emitted into metadata with the get accessor method before the set accessor method, as can be seen using the IL Disassembler. The metadata for the preceding property looks like the following after being compiled then viewed in ILDASM.EXE:

```
.method public newslot specialname virtual abstract
        instance string  get_title() cil managed
{
} // end of method IHTMLStyleSheet::get_title

.method public newslot specialname virtual abstract
        instance void  set_title(string Value) cil managed
{
} // end of method IHTMLStyleSheet::set_title

.property string title()
{
  .custom instance void [mscorlib]
    System.Runtime.InteropServices.DispIdAttribute::.ctor(int32) =
    ( 01 00 E9 03 00 00 00 00 )
  .get instance string IHTMLStyleSheet::get_title()
  .set instance void IHTMLStyleSheet::set_title(string)
} // end of property IHTMLStyleSheet::title
```

The definition of this property contains three parts—a get accessor, followed by set accessor, followed by the property itself. The location of the property is not important for the layout of the COM interface because COM only sees the accessors. But the location and ordering of the get and set accessors on an interface are critical, unless it's a dispinterface. Therefore, the two options for defining the IHTMLStyleSheet interface in Visual Basic .NET are:

- After compilation, use the IL Disassembler to generate an IL file, switch the order of get_title and set_title, then reassemble the file into an assembly.

- Make the definition less convenient for .NET clients by changing the title property into two methods, as follows:

```
<DispId(DispIds.IHTMLSTYLESHEET_TITLE)> _
Sub SetTitle(title As String)

<DispId(DispIds.IHTMLSTYLESHEET_TITLE)> _
Function GetTitle()As String
```

This way the accessors can be defined in the correct order for the interface's v-table—set before get. This is only compatible with the original COM interface when v-table binding, however, because IDispatch and Type.InvokeMember require different flags to be passed when invoking a method versus invoking a property accessor.

C# and C++, on the other hand, enable you to control the ordering of the accessors for an interface's property as follows:

C#:

```
[DispId(DispIds.IHTMLSTYLESHEET_TITLE)]
string title { set; get; }
```

C++:

```
[DispId(DispIds.IHTMLSTYLESHEET_TITLE)]
__property void set_title(String* title);
__property String* get_title();
```

Both of these properties have their set accessors emitted to metadata before their set accessors. The implementer of an interface containing properties doesn't need to worry about the order of the get and set accessors in the class definition. As long as the interface through which COM communication is done exactly matches the COM definition, it works.

If a COM interface defines property accessors that are not listed consecutively (in other words, there's an unrelated method between two accessors) then you'd have to resort to the two workarounds listed earlier or use C++ with Managed Extensions because no .NET language besides C++ lets you define a property with accessors in arbitrary locations.

Non-contiguous property accessors occur more often than you might imagine due to the transformation done when three property accessors exist (Get, Let, and Set, also known as propget, propput, and propputref). In the ActiveX Data Objects (ADO) type library, the _Recordset interface has the following property:

```
[id(0x000003e9), propputref]
HRESULT ActiveConnection([in] IDispatch* pvar);
[id(0x000003e9), propput]
HRESULT ActiveConnection([in] VARIANT pvar);
[id(0x000003e9), propget]
HRESULT ActiveConnection([out, retval] VARIANT* pvar);
```

In IL Assembler syntax, the type library importer generates the metadata shown in Listing 21.15.

LISTING 21.15   Metadata Generated by the Type Library Importer for the _Recordset.ActiveConnection Property, Shown in IL Assembler Syntax

```
 1: .method public hidebysig newslot specialname virtual abstract
 2:   instance void  set_ActiveConnection([in] object  marshal( idispatch)
 3:   pvar) runtime managed internalcall
 4: {
 5:   .custom instance void [mscorlib]
 6:     System.Runtime.InteropServices.DispIdAttribute::.ctor(int32) =
 7:     ( 01 00 E9 03 00 00 00 00 )
 8: } // end of method _Recordset::set_ActiveConnection
 9:
10: .method public hidebysig newslot specialname virtual abstract
11:   instance void  let_ActiveConnection([in] object  marshal( struct) pvar)
12:   runtime managed internalcall
13: {
```

Manually Defining COM Types in Source Code

CHAPTER 21

993

21

DEFINING COM
TYPES IN SOURCE
CODE

LISTING 21.15   Continued

```
14:   .custom instance void [mscorlib]
15:      System.Runtime.InteropServices.DispIdAttribute::.ctor(int32) =
16:      ( 01 00 E9 03 00 00 00 00 )
17: } // end of method _Recordset::let_ActiveConnection
18:
19: .method public hidebysig newslot specialname virtual abstract
20:    instance object marshal( struct)
21:    get_ActiveConnection() runtime managed internalcall
22: {
23:   .custom instance void [mscorlib]
24:      System.Runtime.InteropServices.DispIdAttribute::.ctor(int32) =
25:      ( 01 00 E9 03 00 00 00 00 )
26: } // end of method _Recordset::get_ActiveConnection
27:
28: ...
29:
30: .property object ActiveConnection()
31: {
32:   .custom instance void [mscorlib]
33:      System.Runtime.InteropServices.DispIdAttribute::.ctor(int32) =
34:      ( 01 00 E9 03 00 00 00 00 )
35:   .get instance object ADODB._Recordset::get_ActiveConnection()
36:   .set instance void ADODB._Recordset::set_ActiveConnection(object)
37:   .other instance void ADODB._Recordset::let_ActiveConnection(object)
38: } // end of property _Recordset::ActiveConnection
```

The importer necessarily generates the three property accessors in the same order as defined in the type library. (It generates the property itself at the end of the interface because its location doesn't matter.) No .NET language, however, enables you to specify an *other accessor* as the type library importer does. Had the Let accessor (propput) been defined as the last of the three accessors, you could simply define a let_ActiveConnection method immediately after the property with the set and get accessors (but again, only if clients of the interface use v-table binding, and not if the interface is defined in VB .NET because the set accessor must come first). In C#, this would look like:

```
// This would have been correct if the unmanaged Let accessor were defined last
[DispId(1001)]
object ActiveConnection
{
  [MarshalAs(UnmanagedType.IDispatch)] set;
  get;
}
[DispId(1001)]
void let_ActiveConnection(object pvar);
```

DON'T DO THIS

But this does not work for the `ActiveConnection` property because the `Let` accessor is in the middle. The previous C# code could be compiled and then corrected using the IL Disassembler and IL Assembler and switching the order around as a post-processing step. Or, the COM property could be defined as three methods in your language of choice (here again in C#):

```
[DispId(1001)]
void set_ActiveConnection([MarshalAs(UnmanagedType.IDispatch)] object pvar);
[DispId(1001)]
void let_ActiveConnection(object pvar);
[DispId(1001)]
object get_ActiveConnection();
```

This .NET version of `ActiveConnection` is easily definable in any .NET language, but only appropriate for v-table binding (so the fact that the methods are marked with DISPIDs is misleading). In addition, the user experience suffers by having to call all three accessors explicitly.

Optional Parameters and Default Values

Going back to the `IHTMLStyleSheet` interface from Listing 21.14, it contains two methods with optional parameters—`addImport` and `addRule`. These could be defined in Visual Basic .NET as follows:

```
<DispId(DispIds.IHTMLSTYLESHEET_ADDIMPORT)> _
Function addImport(bstrURL As String, Optional lIndex As Integer = -1) _
  As Integer

<DispId(DispIds.IHTMLSTYLESHEET_ADDRULE)> _
Function addRule(bstrSelector As String, bstrStyle As String, _
  Optional lIndex As Integer = -1) As Integer
```

There's no problem with this, but due to the previously discussed problems with defining `IHTMLStyleSheet`'s properties in VB .NET, you might opt to define the interface in C# instead.

Ah, but C# doesn't support optional parameters. No problem—`System.Runtime.InteropServices` defines the `OptionalAttribute` pseudo-custom attribute that can be used in languages like C#. This attribute sets the exact same metadata bit as VB .NET does with its `Optional` keyword. C# clients still couldn't call the method while omitting the optional parameter, but VB .NET clients could. Using `OptionalAttribute` gives the following two definitions in C#:

```
// Incorrect definitions because they don't account for default values
[DispId(DispIds.IHTMLSTYLESHEET_ADDIMPORT)]
int addImport(string bstrURL, [Optional] int lIndex);

[DispId(DispIds.IHTMLSTYLESHEET_ADDRULE)]
int addRule(string bstrSelector, string bstrStyle,
➥[Optional] int lIndex);
```

DON'T DO THIS

But there's still a problem—there's no way to place the default value of –1 in the signature in C#. The same goes for signatures defined in C++. This could, again, be "fixed up" by using the IL Disassembler to produce an IL file from the C#-generated assembly, by changing this:

```
.method public hidebysig newslot virtual abstract
  instance int32  addImport(string bstrURL, [opt] int32 lIndex) cil managed
{
  .custom instance void [mscorlib]
    System.Runtime.InteropServices.DispIdAttribute::.ctor(int32) =
  ( 01 00 F1 03 00 00 00 00 )
} // end of method IHTMLStyleSheet::addImport

.method public hidebysig newslot virtual abstract
  instance int32  addRule(string bstrSelector, string bstrStyle,
  [opt] int32 lIndex) cil managed
{
  .custom instance void [mscorlib]
    System.Runtime.InteropServices.DispIdAttribute::.ctor(int32) =
  ( 01 00 F2 03 00 00 00 00 )
} // end of method IHTMLStyleSheet::addRule
```

to this:

```
.method public hidebysig newslot virtual abstract
  instance int32  addImport(string bstrURL, [opt] int32 lIndex) cil managed
{
  .custom instance void [mscorlib]
    System.Runtime.InteropServices.DispIdAttribute::.ctor(int32) =
  ( 01 00 F1 03 00 00 00 00 )
  .param [2] = int32(0xFFFFFFFF)
} // end of method IHTMLStyleSheet::addImport

.method public hidebysig newslot virtual abstract
  instance int32  addRule(string bstrSelector, string bstrStyle,
  [opt] int32 lIndex) cil managed
{
  .custom instance void [mscorlib]
    System.Runtime.InteropServices.DispIdAttribute::.ctor(int32) =
  ( 01 00 F2 03 00 00 00 00 )
  .param [3] = int32(0xFFFFFFFF)
} // end of method IHTMLStyleSheet::addRule
```

and then using the IL Assembler to reassemble the DLL. This process adds the same default value information that the type library importer would add.

> **TIP**
>
> Using `OptionalAttribute` without specifying a default value can only be done safely on `System.Object` types that were `VARIANT`s in the COM definition. In this case, compilers like VB .NET fill in a `Type.Missing` type for the parameters omitted by the client code and COM Interoperability maps the value appropriately. For other types, the value passed depends on the implementation of the client's compiler, so you can't count on it being the desired default value.

Finally, Listing 21.16 defines the complete `IHTMLStyleSheet` in C#. Because the optional parameters' default values can't be given directly in the C# definition, `OptionalAttribute` is omitted altogether. Using it alone can cause subtle incorrect behavior, so either both the optional marking and default value could later be added in a custom disassemble/assemble step or both can be safely omitted (although less convenient for VB .NET clients).

LISTING 21.16   The `IHTMLStyleSheet` Interface Defined in C#

```
 1: using System.Runtime.InteropServices;
 2:
 3: [
 4:   ComImport,
 5:   Guid("3050f2e3-98b5-11cf-bb82-00aa00bdce0b"),
 6:   InterfaceType(ComInterfaceType.InterfaceIsDual),
 7:   TypeLibType(TypeLibTypeFlags.FDual | TypeLibTypeFlags.FDispatchable)
 8: ]
 9: interface IHTMLStyleSheet
10: {
11:   [DispId(DispIds.IHTMLSTYLESHEET_TITLE)]
12:   string title { set; get; }
13:   [DispId(DispIds.IHTMLSTYLESHEET_PARENTSTYLESHEET)]
14:   IHTMLStyleSheet parentStyleSheet { get; }
15:   [DispId(DispIds.IHTMLSTYLESHEET_OWNINGELEMENT)]
16:   IHTMLElement owningElement { get; }
17:   [DispId(DispIds.IHTMLSTYLESHEET_DISABLED)]
18:   bool disabled { set; get; }
19:   [DispId(DispIds.IHTMLSTYLESHEET_READONLY)]
20:   bool readOnly { get; }
21:   [DispId(DispIds.IHTMLSTYLESHEET_IMPORTS)]
22:   IHTMLStyleSheetsCollection imports { get; }
23:   [DispId(DispIds.IHTMLSTYLESHEET_HREF)]
24:   string href { set; get; }
25:   [DispId(DispIds.IHTMLSTYLESHEET_TYPE)]
```

Manually Defining COM Types in Source Code

CHAPTER 21

997

21

DEFINING COM
TYPES IN SOURCE
CODE

LISTING 21.16 Continued

```
26:    string type { get; }
27:    [DispId(DispIds.IHTMLSTYLESHEET_ID)]
28:    string id { get; }
29:    [DispId(DispIds.IHTMLSTYLESHEET_ADDIMPORT)]
30:    int addImport(string bstrURL, /*defaultvalue(-1)*/ int lIndex);
31:    [DispId(DispIds.IHTMLSTYLESHEET_ADDRULE)]
32:    int addRule(string bstrSelector, string bstrStyle,
33:      /*defaultvalue(-1)*/ int lIndex);
34:    [DispId(DispIds.IHTMLSTYLESHEET_REMOVEIMPORT)]
35:    void removeImport(int lIndex);
36:    [DispId(DispIds.IHTMLSTYLESHEET_REMOVERULE)]
37:    void removeRule(int lIndex);
38:    [DispId(DispIds.IHTMLSTYLESHEET_MEDIA)]
39:    string media { set; get; }
40:    [DispId(DispIds.IHTMLSTYLESHEET_CSSTEXT)]
41:    string cssText { set; get; }
42:    [DispId(DispIds.IHTMLSTYLESHEET_RULES)]
43:    IHTMLStyleSheetRulesCollection rules { get; }
44: }
45:
46: class DispIds
47: {
48:    public const int IHTMLSTYLESHEET_TITLE = 1001;
49:    public const int IHTMLSTYLESHEET_PARENTSTYLESHEET = 1002;
50:    public const int IHTMLSTYLESHEET_OWNINGELEMENT = 1003;
51:    public const int IHTMLSTYLESHEET_DISABLED = unchecked((int)2147549260);
52:    public const int IHTMLSTYLESHEET_READONLY = 1004;
53:    public const int IHTMLSTYLESHEET_IMPORTS = 1005;
54:    public const int IHTMLSTYLESHEET_HREF = 1006;
55:    public const int IHTMLSTYLESHEET_TYPE = 1007;
56:    public const int IHTMLSTYLESHEET_ID = 1008;
57:    public const int IHTMLSTYLESHEET_ADDIMPORT = 1009;
58:    public const int IHTMLSTYLESHEET_ADDRULE = 1010;
59:    public const int IHTMLSTYLESHEET_REMOVEIMPORT = 1011;
60:    public const int IHTMLSTYLESHEET_REMOVERULE = 1012;
61:    public const int IHTMLSTYLESHEET_MEDIA = 1013;
62:    public const int IHTMLSTYLESHEET_CSSTEXT = 1014;
63:    public const int IHTMLSTYLESHEET_RULES = 1015;
64:    public const int IHTMLSTYLESHEET2_PAGES = 1016;
65:    public const int IHTMLSTYLESHEET2_ADDPAGERULE = 1017;
66: }
```

This listing assumes that the COM interfaces `IHTMLElement`, `IHTMLStyleSheetsCollection`, `IHTMLStyleSheetRulesCollection`, and `IHTMLStyleSheetPagesCollection` have also been given a suitable .NET definition.

Handy Customizations

The .NET definitions created so far have some useful customizations regarding parameter types, exposing `HRESULT` values, and omitting custom attributes that aren't strictly necessary. However, many more customizations can be made to give COM interfaces more of a ".NET feel" by morphing them to follow .NET design guidelines, all the while staying within the rules that produce correct run time behavior.

> **TIP**
>
> Any customizations made in this chapter can also be made when customizing an Interop Assembly using the techniques in Chapter 7 and vice-versa. Some different ones are mentioned here simply because making changes to higher-level source code is much easier and less error-prone for most people. Also, the customizations in Chapter 7 focused on necessary changes, whereas the customizations made in this section border on being frivolous.

One interesting customization is that names of types, members, and parameters can be changed. Because the real "name" of a COM class or interface is its GUID, the corresponding .NET type name can be changed without consequence. A great example of this is all the `UCOM...` types in the `System.Runtime.InteropServices` namespace. The price to pay of changing COM type names is potential confusion by making the connection to the original COM type less obvious. (Many people don't realize at first that the `UCOMIStream` interface and the familiar `IStream` interface are one and the same.)

As for changing member and parameter names, this can only be done safely for `IUnknown`-only interfaces because late binding clients rely on invoking by member names and sometimes even specifying parameter names (when users invoke members using named parameters). Furthermore, because type information is never exposed for a managed type marked with `ComImport`-Attribute, any new COM clients written will never use your new definition of a COM interface, so they won't see your changed names.

Manually Defining COM Types in Source Code

CHAPTER 21

999

21

DEFINING COM
TYPES IN SOURCE
CODE

CAUTION

Even changing member and parameter names on `IUnknown`-only interfaces can produce undesirable results. For example, suppose that a COM client late binds to a .NET class that implements a .NET `IPersistStream` interface with renamed methods. Although the `IPersistStream` interface doesn't support late binding, the same methods appear on the class interface (if they weren't privately implemented). If a COM client expects to dynamically invoke the members of `IPersistStream` through the class interface, this would fail if, for example, the `GetSizeMax` method were renamed to `GetMaxSize`. Of course, because the class interface has no contractual relationship with `IPersistStream`, this behavior might be acceptable to you. If not, then only do such renaming on non-public `IUnknown`-only COM interfaces that are always privately implemented. This ensures that no COM clients would be able to late bind to such members.

So let's take a look at how we can legally ".NET-ize" the members of `IPersistStream`. By staying faithful to their original definitions, the methods look like the following in C#:

```
void GetClassID(out Guid pClassID);

[PreserveSig] int IsDirty();

void Load([In] UCOMIStream pStm);

void Save([In] UCOMIStream pStm,
  [In, MarshalAs(UnmanagedType.Bool)] bool fClearDirty);

void GetSizeMax(out long pcbSize);
```

The parameter names certainly don't follow .NET design guidelines, so we can easily change those. In addition, there's a neat trick we can do to make `GetClassID` and `GetSizeMax` more user-friendly. The IDL definitions of these methods were:

```
HRESULT GetClassID([out] CLSID *pClassID);

HRESULT GetSizeMax([out] ULARGE_INTEGER *pcbSize);
```

Had they been defined as:

```
HRESULT GetClassID([out, retval] CLSID *pClassID);

HRESULT GetSizeMax([out, retval] ULARGE_INTEGER *pcbSize);
```

then we would have initially written their .NET definitions as:

```
Guid GetClassID();

long GetSizeMax();
```

which is much cleaner to use in managed code. Fortunately, there's no functional difference between the two sets of IDL signatures just shown (when v-table binding). In IDL, marking the final parameter with retval (assuming it's already marked out and is a pointer) is simply a convention to convey the intention that the parameter represents a return value. The type library importer follows the rules and only changes the last parameter to a return value when it is marked with retval. For cases in which the retval marking is omitted but could be validly used, however, you can decide for yourself whether or not to treat the parameter as a return value. If you look back at the manual COM interface definitions shown in Chapter 14, this trick is used a few times.

Also, consider what would happen if the GetClassID method were originally defined as follows in IDL:

```
[propget]
HRESULT GetClassID([out, retval] CLSID *pClassID);
```

Although this definition changes the method to a property get accessor, which looks much different (and perhaps more appealing) in managed code, there is no difference between this definition and the original one from COM's perspective when only calling it via v-table binding.

TIP

Out parameters can be transformed into return values if they are the method's last parameter, making the method easier to use in .NET. Methods can even be turned into properties so long as the accessor methods have the same signatures and occupy the same v-table slots as the original COM methods.

Just as with changing the names of members or parameters, any of these changes should not be done when late binding is possible. These changes break the interface's contract via late binding because IDispatch treats return values and member types (method versus property) specially.

Using all these transformations, Listing 21.17 contains an update to the IPersist and IPersistStream interfaces defined in Listing 21.13.

LISTING 21.17   .NET-Friendly C# Definitions of the IPersist and IPersistStream Interfaces

```
1: using System;
2: using System.Runtime.InteropServices;
3:
4: [
5:   ComImport,
```

LISTING 21.17 Continued

```
 6:    Guid("0000010c-0000-0000-C000-000000000046"),
 7:    InterfaceType(ComInterfaceType.InterfaceIsIUnknown)
 8:  ]
 9: interface IPersist
10: {
11:   Guid Clsid { get; }
12: }
13:
14: [
15:   ComImport,
16:   Guid("00000109-0000-0000-C000-000000000046"),
17:   InterfaceType(ComInterfaceType.InterfaceIsIUnknown)
18:  ]
19: interface IPersistStream : IPersist
20: {
21:   // IPersist Property
22:   new Guid Clsid { get; }
23:
24:   // IPersistStream Members
25:   int IsDirty { [PreserveSig] get; }
26:   void Load([In] UCOMIStream stream);
27:   void Save([In] UCOMIStream stream,
28:     [In, MarshalAs(UnmanagedType.Bool)] bool clearDirty);
29:   long MaxSize { get; }
30: }
```

Lines 11 and 22 change the GetClassID method to a Clsid property using both the retval and method-to-property trick. Line 25 changes the IsDirty method to an IsDirty property, and Line 29 changes the GetSizeMax method to a MaxSize property using both tricks used for GetClassID. The parameters for the Load and Save methods were also updated to better match .NET design guidelines.

The one member that is still not ideal is the IsDirty property because it returns a 32-bit integer (0 for S_OK or 1 for S_FALSE) instead of a boolean type that a .NET client might expect. We could change the type to [MarshalAs(UnmanagedType.Bool)] bool, but the values returned would be represented incorrectly. Non-zero (S_FALSE) would mean true whereas zero (S_OK) would mean false, but the IsDirty method returns S_FALSE if the object is *not* dirty and S_OK if the object *is* dirty—the exact opposite meaning. To get around this, we could change the property name to IsClean or IsNotDirty and have it successfully return a boolean type! Of course, such a change may be considered straying too far from the original COM interface.

Listing 21.18 updates the IWMPEffects interface defined at the beginning of the chapter. Compared to Listing 21.2, this new definition contains several customizations that make it more .NET–friendly.

LISTING 21.18   A .NET-Friendly Update to the IWMPEffects Interface Defined in Listing 21.2

```
 1: using System;
 2: using System.Runtime.InteropServices;
 3:
 4: [
 5:   ComImport,
 6:   Guid("D3984C13-C3CB-48E2-8BE5-5168340B4F35"),
 7:   InterfaceType(ComInterfaceType.InterfaceIsIUnknown)
 8: ]
 9: interface IWMPEffects
10: {
11:   void Render(ref TimedLevel levels, IntPtr hdc, ref RECT r);
12:   void MediaInfo(int channelCount, int sampleRate, string title);
13:   VisualizationCapabilities Capabilities { get; }
14:   string Title { get; }
15:   string GetPresetTitle(int preset);
16:   int PresetCount { get; }
17:   int CurrentPreset { set; get; }
18:   void DisplayPropertyPage(IntPtr hwndOwner);
19:   void GoFullScreen(
20:     [MarshalAs(UnmanagedType.Bool)] bool startFullScreen);
21:   void RenderFullScreen(ref TimedLevel levels);
22: }
```

Just about every parameter is renamed from the original names seen in Listing 21.2. Besides this, the GetTitle, GetPresetCount, SetCurrentPreset, and GetCurrentPreset methods are all transformed into properties without the Get/Set prefix. The unique aspect to these transformations is that a pair of methods—SetCurrentPreset and GetCurrentPreset—is transformed into a single property with two accessor methods. The original definition of IWMPEffects has the SetCurrentPreset method occurring first in the interface, so it's crucial that the order of the .NET property accessors match in metadata. Fortunately, by listing set before the get (Line 17), the C# compiler emits the accessors in that order.

The only other difference from Listing 21.2 is that GoFullscreen has been renamed to GoFullScreen and GetPresetTitle method's second parameter is now a return value. GetPresetTitle could have been made into a parameterized property but because C# only supports this for a single indexer and GetPresetTitle is not appropriate for an indexer, it's left as a method.

Manually Defining COM Types in Source Code

CHAPTER 21

1003

21

DEFINING COM
TYPES IN SOURCE
CODE

> **TIP**
>
> If you want to manually create a Primary Interop Assembly in source code, simply add `GuidAttribute` and `PrimaryInteropAssemblyAttribute` to your assembly with the appropriate values. For example (in C#):
>
> ```
> // Specify the LIBID of the corresponding type library
> [assembly:Guid("29527e1e-689a-45f8-a035-7878b75d98cd")]
>
> // Specify which version of the type library this applies to
> // (Major, Minor)
> [assembly:PrimaryInteropAssembly(1, 0)]
> ```
>
> When registering an assembly with these custom attributes, the extra PIA-specific values are added to the registry. Although `REGASM.EXE` can recognize multiple `PrimaryInteropAssemblyAttribute` custom attributes on the same assembly in order to register a PIA for multiple versions of a type library, you cannot use multiple `PrimaryInteropAssemblyAttribute` attributes in a high-level language because the attribute is not marked with `AllowMultiple` set to true. You can only do this in a low-level language like IL Assembler.

Manually Defining Coclass Interfaces and Event Types

If your goal is to write source code that produces metadata as close as possible to what the type library importer would produce, you might want to create a coclass interface. For simple coclasses, a coclass interface is essentially nothing more than a renamed default interface. But for a coclass that lists source interfaces, the coclass interface is the most intuitive means through which a client can hook and unhook event handlers, demonstrated in Chapter 5, "Responding to COM Events." In this section, we'll first look at how to define a coclass interface for a coclass without a source interface, then we'll look at defining a coclass interface that inherits all the importer-style event-related types for a coclass with a source interface.

For the first example, we'll use the Microsoft HTML Object Library, which defines the following `HTMLStyleSheet` class:

```
[
  uuid(3050f2e4-98b5-11cf-bb82-00aa00bdce0b)
]
coclass HTMLStyleSheet
{
```

```
[default]  dispinterface DispHTMLStyleSheet;
                interface IHTMLStyleSheet;
                interface IHTMLStyleSheet2;
};
```

For classes like this without source interfaces, defining a coclass interface is straightforward. After defining the default interface, all that is required is defining an interface with the coclass name that derives from the default interface. This interface must be marked with three custom attributes—ComImportAttribute, GuidAttribute, and CoClassAttribute. GuidAttribute, in this case, contains the same IID as the default interface (if no interface is marked default, it's the first one listed). CoClassAttribute, recognized by C# and VB .NET, links the coclass interface to the .NET class definition. Unlike other interfaces, marking a coclass interface with InterfaceTypeAttribute is unnecessary because it has no members.

DIGGING DEEPER

What about marking a coclass interface with TypeLibTypeAttribute to capture whatever type library flags (like hidden) exist on the original coclass? You could do this if you want, but the type library importer does not. Instead, it captures these flags with the TypeLibTypeAttribute on the .NET class type (with the Class suffix).

Listing 21.19 defines the default DispHTMLStyleSheet interface and the HTMLStyleSheet coclass interface in Visual Basic .NET. DispHTMLStyleSheet is a dispinterface that contains all the same members as IHTMLStyleSheet plus two more (that are also defined on IHTMLStyleSheet2). Because the troubling property layout (setter before getter) doesn't matter for dispinterfaces, this interface can be defined correctly in VB .NET. It can't be correctly defined in C# or C++, however, because some members have optional parameters with default values.

LISTING 21.19   The HTMLStyleSheet Coclass Interface and the Default Interface It Derives from, Both Defined in Visual Basic .NET

```
1: Imports System.Runtime.InteropServices
2:
3: ' The coclass interface
4: < _
5:   ComImport, _
6:   Guid("3050f58d-98b5-11cf-bb82-00aa00bdce0b"), _
7:   CoClass(GetType(HTMLStyleSheetClass)) _
8: > _
9: Interface HTMLStyleSheet
10:    Inherits DispHTMLStyleSheet
11: End Interface
12:
```

LISTING 21.19 Continued

```vb
13: ' The default interface
14: '
15: ' Since this is a dispinterface, we don't have
16: ' to worry about member layout.
17: < _
18:   ComImport, _
19:   Guid("3050f58d-98b5-11cf-bb82-00aa00bdce0b"), _
20:   InterfaceType(ComInterfaceType.InterfaceIsIDispatch), _
21:   TypeLibType(TypeLibTypeFlags.FHidden Or TypeLibTypeFlags.FDispatchable) _
22: > _
23: Interface DispHTMLStyleSheet
24:   <DispId(DispIds.IHTMLSTYLESHEET_TITLE)> _
25:   Property title As String
26:
27:   <DispId(DispIds.IHTMLSTYLESHEET_PARENTSTYLESHEET)> _
28:   ReadOnly Property parentStyleSheet As IHTMLStyleSheet
29:
30:   <DispId(DispIds.IHTMLSTYLESHEET_OWNINGELEMENT)> _
31:   ReadOnly Property owningElement As IHTMLElement
32:
33:   <DispId(DispIds.IHTMLSTYLESHEET_DISABLED)> _
34:   Property disabled As Boolean
35:
36:   <DispId(DispIds.IHTMLSTYLESHEET_READONLY)> _
37:   ReadOnly Property [readOnly] As Boolean
38:
39:   <DispId(DispIds.IHTMLSTYLESHEET_IMPORTS)> _
40:   ReadOnly Property [imports] As IHTMLStyleSheetsCollection
41:
42:   <DispId(DispIds.IHTMLSTYLESHEET_HREF)> _
43:   Property href As String
44:
45:   <DispId(DispIds.IHTMLSTYLESHEET_TYPE)> _
46:   ReadOnly Property type As String
47:
48:   <DispId(DispIds.IHTMLSTYLESHEET_ID)> _
49:   ReadOnly Property id As String
50:
51:   <DispId(DispIds.IHTMLSTYLESHEET_ADDIMPORT)> _
52:   Function addImport(bstrURL As String, Optional lIndex As Integer = -1) _
53:     As Integer
54:
55:   <DispId(DispIds.IHTMLSTYLESHEET_ADDRULE)> _
56:   Function addRule(bstrSelector As String, bstrStyle As String, _
57:     Optional lIndex As Integer = -1) As Integer
58:
```

Listing 21.19   Continued

```
59:    <DispId(DispIds.IHTMLSTYLESHEET_REMOVEIMPORT)> _
60:    Sub removeImport(lIndex As Integer)
61:
62:    <DispId(DispIds.IHTMLSTYLESHEET_REMOVERULE)> _
63:    Sub removeRule(lIndex As Integer)
64:
65:    <DispId(DispIds.IHTMLSTYLESHEET_MEDIA)> _
66:    Property media As String
67:
68:    <DispId(DispIds.IHTMLSTYLESHEET_CSSTEXT)> _
69:    Property cssText As String
70:
71:    <DispId(DispIds.IHTMLSTYLESHEET_RULES)> _
72:    ReadOnly Property rules As IHTMLStyleSheetRulesCollection
73:
74:    <DispId(DispIds.IHTMLSTYLESHEET2_PAGES)> _
75:    ReadOnly Property pages As IHTMLStyleSheetPagesCollection
76:
77:    <DispId(DispIds.IHTMLSTYLESHEET2_ADDPAGERULE)> _
78:    Function addPageRule(bstrSelector As String, bstrStyle As String, _
79:       Optional lIndex As Integer = -1) As Integer
80: End Interface
```

This listing, like Listing 21.16, requires .NET definitions of IHTMLElement,
IHTMLStyleSheetsCollection, IHTMLStyleSheetRulesCollection, and
IHTMLStyleSheetPagesCollection. It also requires the definitions of IHTMLStyleSheet and
DispIds from Listing 21.16, plus the definition of HTMLStyleSheetClass—the .NET class as
generated by the type library importer. Creating such a class is discussed in the "Manually
Defining COM Classes" section.

Caution

The Visual C# .NET compiler (version 7.0) has a limitation regarding coclass interfaces
defined in source code. If you instantiate a class using its coclass interface, and if the
coclass interface is defined in a different file of the same project, you must make sure
that the file *defining* the coclass interface is compiled before the file *using* the coclass
interface. From a command prompt, this means doing the following:

```
csc DefinesCoclassInterface.cs UsesCoclassInterface.cs
```

rather than:

```
csc UsesCoclassInterface.cs DefinesCoclassInterface.cs
```

Manually Defining COM Types in Source Code

CHAPTER 21

1007

21

DEFINING COM
TYPES IN SOURCE
CODE

The latter would cause an error as if the coclass interface is just a regular interface, with the message:

```
Cannot create an instance of the abstract class or interface 'InterfaceName'.
```

For an example of a coclass that lists a source interface, let's look at the `NetMeeting` coclass defined by the Microsoft Windows NetMeeting 3 SDK in `netmeeting.idl`:

```
[
  uuid(3E9BAF2D-7A79-11D2-9334-0000F875AE17),
  helpstring("NetMeeting Application")
]
coclass NetMeeting
{
  [default] interface INetMeeting;
  [default, source] dispinterface _INetMeetingEvents;
};
```

Listing 21.20 contains the IDL definitions of the two short interfaces listed by the `NetMeeting` coclass: the `INetMeeting` default interface and the `INetMeetingEvents` source interface (a dispinterface).

LISTING 21.20 The `_INetMeetingEvents` Dispinterface and `INetMeeting` Interface

```
 1: [
 2:   uuid(3E9BAF2C-7A79-11D2-9334-0000F875AE17),
 3:   helpstring("NetMeeting Events Interface")
 4: ]
 5: dispinterface _INetMeetingEvents {
 6:   properties:
 7:   methods:
 8:     [id(0x000000ca), helpstring("Event triggered when a call is accepted")]
 9:     void ConferenceStarted();
10:     [id(0x000000cb),
11:       helpstring("Event triggered when the current call is over")]
12:     void ConferenceEnded();
13: };
14:
15: [
16:   odl,
17:   uuid(5572984E-7A76-11D2-9334-0000F875AE17),
18:   helpstring("NetMeeting Application Interface"),
19:   hidden,
20:   dual,
```

LISTING 21.20   Continued

```
21:    nonextensible,
22:    oleautomation
23:  ]
24: interface INetMeeting : IDispatch {
25:    [id(0x00000064),
26:      helpstring("Get the build number for NetMeeting on the local machine")]
27:    HRESULT Version([out, retval] long* pdwBuildNumber);
28:    [id(0x00000065), helpstring("Undock a copy of the UI")]
29:    HRESULT UnDock();
30:    [id(0x00000066), helpstring("Is the local user in a conference")]
31:    HRESULT IsInConference([out, retval] BOOL* pbInConference);
32:    [id(0x00000067),
33:      helpstring("Place a NetMeeting call using CallTo addressing")]
34:    HRESULT CallTo([in] BSTR strCallToString);
35:    [id(0x00000068), helpstring("Leave the current conference")]
36:    HRESULT LeaveConference();
37: };
```

Because these types are meant for scripting, they are also defined in the NetMeeting 1.1 type library, embedded in CONF.EXE in your Program Files\NetMeeting directory.

Besides defining the _INetMeetingEvents and INetMeeting interfaces, the NetMeeting coclass interface, and the NetMeetingClass class, the type library importer would also define the following .NET types if importing the NetMeeting coclass (described in Chapter 5).

- __INetMeetingEvents_Event—An interface just like _INetMeetingEvents but with event members rather than plain methods.

- __INetMeetingEvents_ConferenceStartedEventHandler and __INetMeetingEvents_ConferenceEndedEventHandler—The delegate types, one for each member originally defined in _NetMeetingEvents.

- __INetMeetingEvents_EventProvider—A private class that implements each event's add and remove accessors and handles the interaction with COM connection point interfaces.

- __INetMeetingEvents_SinkHelper—A private sink class that implements the source interface and raises the events when its methods are called.

The interesting detail about the last two classes is that these are the only kind of types generated by the type library importer that contain IL instructions. So when re-creating these types in source code, we need to write some implementation besides just type definitions. Because

Chapter 5 discusses the details of what these types do, how they work, and how to use them, we'll focus here mainly on defining these types in source code so the coclass interface can be fully defined. Listing 21.21 defines 8 of the 9 types that would result from importing the NetMeeting coclass and the two interfaces from Listing 21.20. The only type omitted is the NetMeetingClass class.

The type and member names used in Listing 21.21 match those that would be produced by the type library importer. The importer chooses names that can be predictably generated with little chance of name conflicts. However, because these names are fairly lengthy (and at times don't coincide with .NET design guidelines), it's certainly appropriate to rename these types (and members inside the sink helper and event provider classes) to be more user-friendly.

LISTING 21.21   C# Definitions of the NetMeeting Coclass Interface, Both Interfaces Listed by the NetMeeting Coclass, and Event-Related Types

```
 1: using System;
 2: using System.Collections;
 3: using System.Runtime.InteropServices;
 4:
 5: // Coclass Interface
 6: [
 7:   ComImport,
 8:   Guid("5572984E-7A76-11D2-9334-0000F875AE17"),
 9:   CoClass(typeof(NetMeetingClass))
10: ]
11: public interface NetMeeting : INetMeeting, _INetMeetingEvents_Event {}
12:
13: // Raw Source Interface
14: [
15:   ComImport,
16:   Guid("3E9BAF2C-7A79-11D2-9334-0000F875AE17"),
17:   InterfaceType(ComInterfaceType.InterfaceIsIDispatch)
18: ]
19: public interface _INetMeetingEvents
20: {
21:   [DispId(202)]
22:   void ConferenceStarted();
23:   [DispId(203)]
24:   void ConferenceEnded();
25: }
26:
27: // Default Interface
28: [
29:   ComImport,
```

LISTING 21.21   Continued

```
30:    Guid("5572984E-7A76-11D2-9334-0000F875AE17"),
31:    TypeLibType(TypeLibTypeFlags.FDual | TypeLibTypeFlags.FHidden |
32:      TypeLibTypeFlags.FNonExtensible)
33: ]
34: public interface INetMeeting
35: {
36:    [DispId(100)]
37:    int Version();
38:    [DispId(101)]
39:    void UnDock();
40:    [DispId(102)]
41:    [return: MarshalAs(UnmanagedType.Bool)] bool IsInConference();
42:    [DispId(103)]
43:    void CallTo(string strCallToString);
44:    [DispId(104)]
45:    void LeaveConference();
46: }
47:
48: // Event Interface
49: [
50:    ComVisible(false),
51:    ComEventInterfaceAttribute(typeof(_INetMeetingEvents),
52:      typeof(_INetMeetingEvents_EventProvider))
53: ]
54: public interface _INetMeetingEvents_Event
55: {
56:    event _INetMeetingEvents_ConferenceEndedEventHandler ConferenceEnded;
57:    event _INetMeetingEvents_ConferenceStartedEventHandler
58:      ConferenceStarted;
59: }
60:
61: // Delegates, one for each event
62: [ComVisible(false)]
63: public delegate void _INetMeetingEvents_ConferenceEndedEventHandler();
64:
65: [ComVisible(false)]
66: public delegate void _INetMeetingEvents_ConferenceStartedEventHandler();
67:
68: // Sink Helper Class
69: [ClassInterface(ClassInterfaceType.None)]
70: sealed class _INetMeetingEvents_SinkHelper : _INetMeetingEvents
71: {
72:    // Delegates, one per method
73:    public _INetMeetingEvents_ConferenceEndedEventHandler
```

LISTING 21.21   Continued

```
74:      m_ConferenceEndedDelegate;
75:   public _INetMeetingEvents_ConferenceStartedEventHandler
76:     m_ConferenceStartedDelegate;
77:
78:   // The connection point cookie from Advise, saved for Unadvise
79:   public int m_dwCookie;
80:
81:   // Constructor
82:   internal _INetMeetingEvents_SinkHelper()
83:   {
84:     m_dwCookie = 0;
85:     m_ConferenceEndedDelegate = null;
86:     m_ConferenceStartedDelegate = null;
87:   }
88:
89:   public void ConferenceEnded()
90:   {
91:     // Invoke the corresponding delegate
92:     if (m_ConferenceEndedDelegate != null)
93:       m_ConferenceEndedDelegate();
94:   }
95:
96:   public void ConferenceStarted()
97:   {
98:     // Invoke the corresponding delegate
99:     if (m_ConferenceStartedDelegate != null)
100:       m_ConferenceStartedDelegate();
101:   }
102: }
103:
104: // Event Provider Class
105: sealed class _INetMeetingEvents_EventProvider : _INetMeetingEvents_Event,
106:   IDisposable
107: {
108:   private UCOMIConnectionPointContainer m_ConnectionPointContainer;
109:   private UCOMIConnectionPoint m_ConnectionPoint;
110:   private ArrayList m_aEventSinkHelpers;
111:
112:   // Constructor
113:   public _INetMeetingEvents_EventProvider(object container)
114:   {
115:     m_ConnectionPointContainer = (UCOMIConnectionPointContainer)container;
116:   }
117:
```

LISTING 21.21   Continued

```
118:    // Enables lazy initialization of connection point.
119:    // Called the first time someone hooks up to an event.
120:    private void Init()
121:    {
122:      Guid iid = typeof(_INetMeetingEvents).GUID;
123:      m_ConnectionPointContainer.FindConnectionPoint(ref iid,
124:        out m_ConnectionPoint);
125:      m_aEventSinkHelpers = new ArrayList();
126:    }
127:
128:    // Implementation of IDisposable.Dispose
129:    public void Dispose()
130:    {
131:      Cleanup();
132:      // It's no longer necessary for the garbage collector
133:      // to call the finalizer
134:      GC.SuppressFinalize(this);
135:    }
136:
137:    // Finalizer
138:    ~_INetMeetingEvents_EventProvider()
139:    {
140:      Cleanup();
141:    }
142:
143:    // Called by Dispose and Finalizer to unhook all events
144:    private void Cleanup()
145:    {
146:     _INetMeetingEvents_SinkHelper sinkHelper;
147:
148:      if (m_ConnectionPoint != null)
149:      {
150:        lock (this)
151:        {
152:          try
153:          {
154:            // Go through all sink helpers and "unhook" them
155:            for (int i = 0; i < m_aEventSinkHelpers.Count; i++)
156:            {
157:              // Remove the sink helper from the list and call Unadvise
158:              sinkHelper = (_INetMeetingEvents_SinkHelper)
159:                m_aEventSinkHelpers[i];
160:              m_ConnectionPoint.Unadvise(sinkHelper.m_dwCookie);
161:            }
```

Manually Defining COM Types in Source Code

CHAPTER 21

1013

21

DEFINING COM
TYPES IN SOURCE
CODE

LISTING 21.21   Continued

```
162:            } catch (Exception)
163:            {
164:                // Swallow exceptions
165:            }
166:        }
167:    }
168: }
169:
170: // Event #1: ConferenceEnded
171: public event _INetMeetingEvents_ConferenceEndedEventHandler
172: ConferenceEnded
173: {
174:   add
175:   {
176:     _INetMeetingEvents_SinkHelper sinkHelper;
177:
178:     lock (this)
179:     {
180:       if (m_ConnectionPoint == null)
181:         Init();
182:
183:       // Call Advise on a new sink helper, initializing its cookie
184:       sinkHelper = new _INetMeetingEvents_SinkHelper();
185:       m_ConnectionPoint.Advise(sinkHelper, out sinkHelper.m_dwCookie);
186:
187:       // Initialize the sink helper's delegate to the passed-in value
188:       sinkHelper.m_ConferenceEndedDelegate = value;
189:
190:       // Add the sink helper to the list
191:       m_aEventSinkHelpers.Add(sinkHelper);
192:     }
193:   }
194:   remove
195:   {
196:     _INetMeetingEvents_SinkHelper sinkHelper;
197:
198:     lock (this)
199:     {
200:       // Go through all sink helpers until we find the right one
201:       for (int i = 0; i < m_aEventSinkHelpers.Count; i++)
202:       {
203:         sinkHelper = (_INetMeetingEvents_SinkHelper)
204:           m_aEventSinkHelpers[i];
205:
```

LISTING 21.21   Continued

```
206:               // Check if this is the correct sink helper
207:               if (sinkHelper.m_ConferenceEndedDelegate != null &&
208:                   sinkHelper.m_ConferenceEndedDelegate.Equals(value))
209:               {
210:                 // Remove the sink helper from the list
211:                 m_aEventSinkHelpers.RemoveAt(i);
212:
213:                 // Call Unadvise using the cookie saved from Advise
214:                 m_ConnectionPoint.Unadvise(sinkHelper.m_dwCookie);
215:
216:                 // If this is the last sink helper in the list, set the
217:                 // connection point and array list to null
218:                 if (m_aEventSinkHelpers.Count == 0)
219:                 {
220:                   m_ConnectionPoint = null;
221:                   m_aEventSinkHelpers = null;
222:                 }
223:                 break;
224:               }
225:             } // end for
226:           } // end lock
227:         } // end remove
228:   }
229:
230:   // Event #2: ConferenceStarted
231:   public event _INetMeetingEvents_ConferenceStartedEventHandler
232:   ConferenceStarted
233:   {
234:     add
235:     {
236:       _INetMeetingEvents_SinkHelper sinkHelper;
237:
238:       lock (this)
239:       {
240:         if (m_ConnectionPoint == null)
241:           Init();
242:
243:         // Call Advise on a new sink helper, initializing its cookie
244:         sinkHelper = new _INetMeetingEvents_SinkHelper();
245:         m_ConnectionPoint.Advise(sinkHelper, out sinkHelper.m_dwCookie);
246:
247:         // Initialize the sink helper's delegate to the passed-in value
248:         sinkHelper.m_ConferenceStartedDelegate = value;
249:
```

Manually Defining COM Types in Source Code

CHAPTER 21

1015

21

DEFINING COM
TYPES IN SOURCE
CODE

LISTING 21.21   Continued

```
250:            // Add the sink helper to the list
251:            m_aEventSinkHelpers.Add(sinkHelper);
252:          }
253:        }
254:      remove
255:      {
256:        _INetMeetingEvents_SinkHelper sinkHelper;
257:
258:        lock (this)
259:        {
260:          // Go through all sink helpers until we find the right one
261:          for (int i = 0; i < m_aEventSinkHelpers.Count; i++)
262:          {
263:            sinkHelper = (_INetMeetingEvents_SinkHelper)
264:              m_aEventSinkHelpers[i];
265:
266:            // Check if this is the correct sink helper
267:            if (sinkHelper.m_ConferenceStartedDelegate != null &&
268:                sinkHelper.m_ConferenceStartedDelegate.Equals(value))
269:            {
270:              // Remove the sink helper from the list
271:              m_aEventSinkHelpers.RemoveAt(i);
272:
273:              // Call Unadvise using the cookie saved from Advise
274:              m_ConnectionPoint.Unadvise(sinkHelper.m_dwCookie);
275:
276:              // If this is the last sink helper in the list, set the
277:              // connection point and array list to null
278:              if (m_aEventSinkHelpers.Count == 0)
279:              {
280:                m_ConnectionPoint = null;
281:                m_aEventSinkHelpers = null;
282:              }
283:              break;
284:            }
285:          } // end for
286:        } // end lock
287:      } // end remove
288:    }
289: }
```

Listing 21.21 assumes that the NetMeetingClass class type is defined. We'll be defining this in the upcoming "Manually Defining COM Classes" section. In addition to the System and System.Runtime.InteropServices namespaces, Line 2 lists the System.Collections namespace because the event provider class uses an ArrayList to manage the list of event sinks.

Lines 6–11 define the NetMeeting coclass interface. This is just like the HTMLStyleSheet defined previously, except that it also derives from the _INetMeetingEvents_Event event interface. Lines 13–25 define the raw source interface, which is a straightforward translation. Lines 28–46 define the INetMeeting default interface. This, too, is straightforward but with one customization—the return type of IsInConference is defined as a boolean type in Line 41, preserving the original method's intent. This is the only place in the listing that is noticeably different from what would be generated by the type library importer, and fortunately it's an improvement.

Lines 49–59 define the event interface, with an event for each of the two methods of the _INetMeetingEvents source interface. This interface is marked COM-invisible simply because there's no need to expose it to COM. This is the type that must be marked with ComEventInterfaceAttribute. This attribute must be given the type of the raw source interface followed by the type of the event provider class. The CLR uses this to magically associate the event implementation to these event members because the COM objects to which clients appear to be hooking and unhooking event handlers certainly does not implement them. (Note that this does not refute the statement at the beginning of the chapter that "There's nothing magical about the metadata inside Interop Assemblies." The metadata just contains a regular custom attribute; the magic is inside the CLR!)

Lines 62–66 define the two delegate types for the two source interface methods. If a source interface method has parameters or a return type other than void, the corresponding delegate type must have matching parameters and return type.

Lines 69–102 contain the sink helper class—the first (and simpler) of the two private classes containing implementation. The sink helper class implements the raw source interface and converts the method calls into invocations on its delegate fields; in essence, the sink helper raises the events. On Line 79, the class defines a public cookie field. This is used by the event provider class to store the cookie returned by a call to IConnectionPoint.Advise, and used again when calling IConnectionPoint.Unadvise. The constructor simply sets the three fields to initial values, and the implementation of each source interface's method simply invokes the corresponding delegate if it is a valid instance. All three fields are public, set by the event provider. Inside the sink helper is the other place that would change if any of the source interface methods had parameters. These parameters would simply be passed to the delegate invocation.

The _INetMeetingEvents_EventProvider class begins on Line 105 and occupies the rest of the listing. Whereas the sink helper class implements the raw source interface, the event provider class implements the event interface (plus System.IDisposable). Fortunately, we can use the pre-defined UCOMIConnectionPointContainer and UCOMIConnectionPoint types when defining the fields in Lines 108 and 109.

The constructor, called when instantiated by the CLR, initializes its connection point container field to the passed-in object. The connection point field isn't initialized until the Init method (Lines 120–126) is called. This occurs the first time a .NET client attempts to hook up to an event member (rather than when the COM class is instantiated).

Lines 129–135 define the implementation of IDisposable.Dispose, and Lines 138–141 define the implementation of the class's finalizer. Both methods make the same call to Cleanup, but Dispose also calls System.GC.SuppressFinalize in Line 134. This is the standard pattern of disabling finalization if the client remembered to call Dispose to eagerly clean up the object's state. The code that would be generated by the type library importer doesn't define a Cleanup method. Instead, it simply calls Finalize directly from Dispose. However, C# doesn't allow calling the class's finalizer, hence the use of a separate method containing the common code.

The job of Cleanup (Lines 144–168) is to remove each sink helper from the class's ArrayList and call Unadvise on each one to "unhook" the event handler. The lock(this) statement is equivalent to:

```
System.Threading.Monitor.Enter(this);
try { ... }
finally { System.Threading.Monitor.Exit(this); }
```

All exceptions are silently ignored in this cleanup phase because failure to release everything is not considered fatal.

Lines 171–228 contain the implementation for the ConferenceEnded event defined by the event interface. The implementation of the ConferenceStarted event in Lines 231–288 is almost identical, as is the event implementation corresponding to any kind of source interface's method.

The code makes use of C#'s advanced event syntax to implement custom actions inside the add and remove accessors, much like implementing get and set property accessors. The add accessor begins by calling Init if the class's connection point member is still null (Line 181). It then creates a new sink helper object and passes it to the call to UCOMIConnectionPoint.Advise. The call ends up setting the sink helper's cookie field through the out parameter. After this, there are only two things left to do—set the sink helper's corresponding delegate field to the passed-in delegate reference (Line 188), and add the sink helper to the ArrayList (Line 191).

DIGGING DEEPER

Because customizing an event's add and remove accessors is required for defining event types just as the type library importer does, Listing 21.21 could not be rewritten in a language that does not support such advanced event syntax, such as Visual Basic .NET.

The remove accessor is similar to Cleanup, but only removes and unhooks the passed-in delegate rather than all of them. The for loop in Lines 201–225 scans each element in the ArrayList, and when the right one is found, it is removed (Line 211). UCOMIConnectionPoint.Unadvise is called in Line 214 with the current sink helper's cookie. Finally, if the ArrayList is empty, the connection point and ArrayList members are set to null.

DIGGING DEEPER

Notice that the event implementations in Listing 21.21 call Advise every time an event handler is hooked up (even to events on the same source interface) and Unadvise is called every time an event handler is unhooked. Each event handler, therefore, has a corresponding sink object, rather than sharing the same sink object (one per source interface) as you might expect. Each sink object (an instance of _INetMeetingEvents_SinkHelper) receives callbacks from COM on all methods of the source interface it implements, but only raises the single appropriate event to .NET clients since only one delegate member per sink object is non-null.

This behavior matches the types generated by version 1.0 of the type library importer, but it could clearly be optimized by creating only one sink object per source interface. This reduces the number of managed/unmanaged transitions made when a .NET client hooks up event handlers to more than one event per source interface.

If you compare the metadata generated by the C# compiler for Listing 21.21 to metadata that would be generated by the type library importer, you'll notice slight differences in delegate definitions. For example, C# delegates automatically define BeginInvoke and EndInvoke for asynchronous communication, but the importer-generated delegates do not.

Manually Defining COM Types in Source Code

CHAPTER 21

1019

21

DEFINING COM
TYPES IN SOURCE
CODE

> **TIP**
>
> If you want to manually define the minimum number of types possible while still maintaining the ability to hook up to events in the .NET style, you can skip defining a coclass interface and the corresponding class type. Because a coclass interface has the same IID as the coclass's default interface, you can simply add the event interface (the one named *SourceInterfaceName*_Event) to the list of interfaces that the default interface derives from (if any). Clients would then be able to directly hook and unhook event handlers using the event members inherited by the default interface. This is risky, however, if the default interface is public because nothing prevents other COM components from having the same default interface but not sourcing the same events.

Manually Defining COM Structures

Chapter 19, "Deeper Into PInvoke and Useful Examples," already described how to define unmanaged structures in .NET source code. Unmanaged structures are dealt with no differently in the context of COM Interoperability as in the context of PInvoke. There is no difference in default marshaling behavior regardless of whether the structure is used in a PInvoke signature or a COM interface's signature. For example, string fields in a struct are always marshaled as LPSTR types by default. Evidence that there's no such thing as a COM-specific structure is that the ComImportAttribute can't be applied to structures—only classes and interfaces.

There is one detail to be concerned about that is important for structures used with COM APIs related to packing alignment (introduced in Chapter 19). The default packing alignment for structures in a type library is 4 bytes. The default packing alignment for .NET structures, however, is 8 bytes. This means that you may need to set an explicit packing alignment using the Pack property of StructLayoutAttribute to create a correct definition of a COM structure, depending on the order and types of its fields. In cases where the packing alignment of 4 bytes versus 8 bytes makes a difference, failure to mark the packing alignment correctly can cause potentially subtle failure (just like making any other kind of improper definition of unmanaged entities). For example, the layout of the following structure (shown in IDL) is different depending on whether it uses a packing alignment of 4 bytes or 8 bytes:

```
typedef struct UnalignedStruct
{
  long one;
  double two;
  long three;
} UnalignedStruct;
```

Remember that the `IWMPEffects` interface from Listing 21.2 requires the definition of two structures—`TimedLevel` and `RECT`. Now it's time to define these in managed code. First, Listing 21.22 displays the structure definitions that would be created by the type library importer in IL Assembler syntax.

LISTING 21.22   Definitions of the `RECT` and `TimedLevel` Structures Generated by the Type Library Importer, Shown in IL Assembler Syntax

```
 1: .class public sequential ansi sealed beforefieldinit tagRECT
 2:        extends [mscorlib]System.ValueType
 3: {
 4:   .pack 4
 5:   .size 0
 6:   .field public int32 left
 7:   .field public int32 top
 8:   .field public int32 right
 9:   .field public int32 bottom
10: } // end of class tagRECT
11:
12: .class public sequential ansi sealed beforefieldinit tagTimedLevel
13:        extends [mscorlib]System.ValueType
14: {
15:   .pack 8
16:   .size 0
17:   .field public  marshal( fixed array [2048]) unsigned int8[] frequency
18:   .field public  marshal( fixed array [2048]) unsigned int8[] waveform
19:   .field public int32 state
20:   .field public int64 timeStamp
21: } // end of class tagTimedLevel
```

Notice that the types are defined as `tagRECT` and `tagTimedLevel` instead of `RECT` and `TimedLevel`. This is because, as commonly seen in IDL, the structs are defined in the following manner:

```
typedef struct tagTimedLevel
{
  ...
} TimedLevel;

instead of:
typedef struct TimedLevel
{
  ...
} TimedLevel;
```

The important thing to notice is that tagRECT has a packing alignment of 4 bytes (specified in Line 4) and tagTimedLevel has a packing alignment of 8 bytes (specified in Line 15). The type library importer always sets a struct's packing to whatever value is set in the input type library. Unfortunately, tools such as OLEVIEW.EXE do not display the packing alignment of structures. (IDL can't express this information.) You can obtain this information programmatically using ITypeLib and its related COM interfaces, or hopefully from the documentation of the structures you're attempting to define.

The .size 0 in Lines 5 and 16 simply indicate that StructLayoutAttribute's Size property isn't set. This is no different than when the .size directive is omitted altogether; the IL Disassembler only omits the .size directive when neither Pack nor Size are explicitly set by the metadata producer.

Listing 21.23 shows how to define these same two structures in Visual Basic .NET.

LISTING 21.23 .NET definitions of the RECT and TimedLevel Structures Written in Visual Basic .NET

```
 1: Imports System.Runtime.InteropServices
 2:
 3: <StructLayout(LayoutKind.Sequential, Pack:=4)> _
 4: Structure RECT
 5:   Public Left As Integer
 6:   Public Top As Integer
 7:   Public Right As Integer
 8:   Public Bottom As Integer
 9: End Structure
10:
11: <StructLayout(LayoutKind.Sequential)> _
12: Structure TimedLevel
13:   <MarshalAs(UnmanagedType.ByValArray, SizeConst:=2048)> _
14:     Public Frequency() As Byte
15:   <MarshalAs(UnmanagedType.ByValArray, SizeConst:=2048)> _
16:     Public Waveform() As Byte
17:   Public State As Integer
18:   Public TimeStamp As Long
19: End Structure
```

Both structures are renamed to remove their tag prefix, because this is undesirable in a .NET type's name. Just like renaming classes and interfaces, renaming a structure is always safe in that it doesn't affect the proper operation of COM clients using the structure. The fields of both structs are also capitalized to match .NET conventions because they are public.

The RECT structure is marked with a packing alignment of 4 bytes in Line 3, and the TimedLevel structure is left with its default packing alignment of 8 bytes to match the COM definitions. Although the setting the packing alignment to 4 bytes doesn't affect the layout of the simple RECT structure, it's good practice to mark it anyway. Ensuring that the TimedLevel structure has a packing alignment of 8 bytes is critical, because its layout would change if it were marked with a packing alignment of 4 bytes instead.

Manually Defining COM Enums

Defining a COM enumeration is straightforward, and is just like defining a .NET enumeration. No special custom attributes are required, although it's good practice to always explicitly list the value of each member because the definition must exactly match the unmanaged definition and you may not be aware of how the compiler assigns values by default (for example, zero-based or one-based). If the COM enumeration's values are sequential and start with zero, then this is not strictly necessary because .NET enumeration values begin at zero by default in C#, Visual Basic .NET, and C++. Also, be sure to give the enumeration the correct underlying type. Most enumerations have a 32-bit underlying type, and this is the default underlying type when defining enumerations in C#, Visual Basic .NET, and C++.

> **Tip**
>
> For enumerations with values that can be combined like bit flags, it's helpful to mark the enumeration with System.FlagsAttribute. This strictly informational custom attribute lets clients know that combining the enumeration values with bitwise operators is a valid thing to do. In the future, development environments could make use of this attribute, perhaps to display the marked enumerations differently.

Manually Defining COM Classes

COM interfaces and their parameter types (such as structures or other COM interfaces) are really all you need to define in order to fully interact with COM. The various event-related classes are nice for exposing COM connection points as .NET events, but these aren't necessary because you could always use the connection point interfaces directly as you would in unmanaged C++. Enums aren't necessary because their underlying type could always be used as a replacement. Class types and coclass interfaces aren't necessary, either. For example, to write a new COM-compatible class in managed code, you only need to implement COM interfaces. If you need to instantiate and use an *existing* coclass, you can do this with only interface definitions, Activator.CreateInstance, and Type.GetTypeFromCLSID.

Manually Defining COM Types in Source Code

CHAPTER 21

1023

21

DEFINING COM
TYPES IN SOURCE
CODE

For example, let's instantiate instances of the two coclasses from earlier in the chapter, HTMLStyleSheet:

```
[
  uuid(3050f2e4-98b5-11cf-bb82-00aa00bdce0b)
]
coclass HTMLStyleSheet
{
  [default] dispinterface DispHTMLStyleSheet;
  interface IHTMLStyleSheet;
  interface IHTMLStyleSheet2;
};
```

and NetMeeting:

```
[
  uuid(3E9BAF2D-7A79-11D2-9334-0000F875AE17),
  helpstring("NetMeeting Application")
]
coclass NetMeeting
{
  [default] interface INetMeeting;
  [default, source] dispinterface _INetMeetingEvents;
};
```

Without a .NET definition of these classes, instances can still be created as follows:

C#:

```
DispHTMLStyleSheet sheet = (DispHTMLStyleSheet)Activator.CreateInstance(
    Type.GetTypeFromCLSID(new Guid("3050f2e4-98b5-11cf-bb82-00aa00bdce0b")));

INetMeeting meeting = (INetMeeting)Activator.CreateInstance(
    Type.GetTypeFromCLSID(new Guid("3E9BAF2D-7A79-11D2-9334-0000F875AE17")));
```

Visual Basic .NET:

```
Dim sheet As DispHTMLStyleSheet = CType(Activator.CreateInstance( _
    Type.GetTypeFromCLSID( _
    New Guid("3050f2e4-98b5-11cf-bb82-00aa00bdce0b"))), DispHTMLStyleSheet)

Dim meeting As INetMeeting = CType(Activator.CreateInstance( _
    Type.GetTypeFromCLSID( _
    New Guid("3E9BAF2D-7A79-11D2-9334-0000F875AE17"))), INetMeeting)
```

C++:

```
DispHTMLStyleSheet* sheet = (DispHTMLStyleSheet*)Activator::CreateInstance(
    Type::GetTypeFromCLSID(new Guid("3050f2e4-98b5-11cf-bb82-00aa00bdce0b")));

INetMeeting* meeting = (INetMeeting*)Activator::CreateInstance(
    Type::GetTypeFromCLSID(new Guid("3E9BAF2D-7A79-11D2-9334-0000F875AE17")));
```

After the object is created, members can be called on the `DispHTMLStyleSheet` and `INetMeeting` interfaces, or the objects could be cast to any other interfaces that the coclasses implement.

Besides lengthier source code, there's nothing wrong with having to use `Activator.CreateInstance`; because the returned object is cast to a COM interface, we're still using the COM object in an early-bound fashion (except when calling through a dispinterface like `DispHTMLStyleSheet`). If you don't like using CLSIDs in source code, using `GetTypeFromProgID` instead of `GetTypeFromCLSID` would look a little nicer and be less error-prone for coclasses registered with a ProgID. Still, defining a COM class that can be instantiated by simply using the `new` keyword is sometimes desirable to make coclasses appear more like .NET classes (like what the type library importer does).

Therefore, the following sections describe two ways to create type information for coclasses that enable instantiation just like a .NET class.

Defining Classes the Simple Way

Defining a .NET class type that is able to represent a coclass is surprisingly simple. Furthermore, such a class stands on its own—no additional type definitions are needed to define it. That's because all that is needed is an empty class marked with `ComImportAttribute` and `GuidAttribute` containing the CLSID. This looks like the following for the `HTMLStyleSheetClass` and `NetMeetingClass` classes (in C#):

```
using System.Runtime.InteropServices;

[
  ComImport,
  Guid("3050f2e4-98b5-11cf-bb82-00aa00bdce0b")
]
public class HTMLStyleSheetClass {}

[
  ComImport,
  Guid("3E9BAF2D-7A79-11D2-9334-0000F875AE17")
]
public class NetMeetingClass {}
```

Because the C# compiler emits a public default constructor by default, each class can be instantiated properly. The CLR knows to call `CoCreateInstance` with the CLSID contained in the `GuidAttribute` because each class is marked with `ComImportAttribute`. Because casting the class to an interface results in a `QueryInterface` call that succeeds or fails based purely on the COM object's implementation, it's not necessary to list the interfaces it implements. In

Manually Defining COM Types in Source Code

CHAPTER 21

1025

21

DEFINING COM
TYPES IN SOURCE
CODE

fact, listing them is discouraged because you'd then be forced to implement each interface and that can get you into trouble if it's not done right (explained in the next section). Therefore, these class types can be used in conjunction with the coclass interfaces defined earlier or just used on their own and provide the proper behavior.

The rules to follow when defining a COM class the simple way are:

- Mark the class with ComImportAttribute and GuidAttribute containing the CLSID.
- Make the class derive directly from System.Object (which is implicit in C#, Visual Basic .NET, and C++).
- Don't list any interfaces that it implements, and leave the class completely empty.

The first rule is important for obvious reasons. Without ComImportAttribute, you've just got an empty class that does nothing. An incorrect CLSID means that the CoCreateInstance call made by the CLR during the object's instantiation cannot succeed.

DIGGING DEEPER

Although it doesn't check for COM interfaces, the C# compiler does not allow you to define a COM class without specifying a CLSID. Using ComImportAttribute on a class without the Guid attribute results in the following error:

```
error CS0596: The Guid attribute must be specified with the ComImport
attribute
```

No other languages enforce this rule.

The second and third rules, if not followed, result in a TypeLoadException at run time. Excluding one case described in the next section, a ComImport-marked class must not have any members besides those of System.Object and a public default constructor. Furthermore, this constructor *must* be marked with runtime managed internal (in IL Assembler syntax), unlike COM interface members for which cil managed is acceptable, and must have a Runtime Virtual Address (RVA) of zero.

Every member emitted into metadata has an RVA, which specifies the location of the member's body relative to the start of the file in which it is defined. The CLR enforces a rule that all members in a ComImport-marked class must have an RVA equal to zero. Not all compilers, however, enforce this rule.

When defining a `ComImport`-marked class in C#, the public default constructor automatically generated by the compiler is marked with `runtime managed internal` and has an RVA of zero. Attempting to manually define a `ComImport`-marked class (such as the previously defined `HTMLStyleSheetClass`) in Visual Basic .NET or C++ fails for two reasons:

- Neither compiler marks the automatically-generated constructor with the necessary attributes to make it appear as `runtime managed internal`.

- Neither compiler gives the automatically-generated constructor an RVA of zero.

The first problem could be solved by explicitly defining a public default constructor and marking it with `MethodImplAttribute` as we've done earlier in the chapter. However, the second problem can't be solved in a high-level language because there's no mechanism for customizing a member's RVA.

For example, the C++ compiler emits a public default constructor with a non-zero RVA for the following definition:

```
#using <mscorlib.dll>
using namespace System::Runtime::InteropServices;

[
  ComImport,
  Guid("3050f2e4-98b5-11cf-bb82-00aa00bdce0b")
]
public __gc class HTMLStyleSheetClass {};
```

Running a program that attempted to use this class would throw a `TypeLoadException` with a non-descriptive message, for example:

```
Could not load type HTMLStyleSheetClass from assembly Chapter21,
Version=1.0.0.0, Culture=neutral, PublicKeyToken=null.
```

Running the `PEVERIFY.EXE` SDK tool on the assembly containing the C++ `HTMLStyleSheetClass` definition gives a more informative error message:

```
Error: Method marked Abstract/Runtime/InternalCall/Imported must have zero RVA,
and vice versa.
```

To see members' RVA values, you have to dig a little deeper into the IL Disassembler (`ILDASM.EXE`) and press `Crtl+M` once you have an assembly open in graphical mode. You can then see RVA values as follows:

```
TypeDef #1
-------------------------------------------------------
  TypDefName: HTMLStyleSheetClass  (02000002)
    Flags     : [Public] [AutoLayout] [Class] [Import] [AnsiClass]  (00001001)
```

```
    Extends   : 01000004 [TypeRef] System.Object
  Method #1
  - - - - - - - - - - - - - - - - - - - - - - - - - - - - - - - - - - - - - -
    MethodName: .ctor (06000002)
    Flags     : [Public] [ReuseSlot] [SpecialName] [RTSpecialName] [.ctor]
  (00001806)
    RVA        : 0x00001000
    ImplFlags : [IL] [Managed]   (00000000)
    CallCnvntn: [DEFAULT]
    hasThis
    ReturnType: Void
    No arguments.
```

> **DIGGING DEEPER**
>
> You can also get this detailed metadata information at a command prompt by issuing the following "advanced" command:
>
> ```
> ildasm /noil /adv /meta FileName /text
> ```

Note that when producing an IL file with `ILDASM.EXE`'s `/out` option, no RVA information is included. The IL Assembler, just like any other compiler, chooses its own RVA values when assembling the IL. Furthermore, the IL Assembler always chooses an RVA equal to zero on any member marked `runtime managed internal`! Therefore, the following steps can be a suitable workaround for defining COM classes in languages other than C#:

1. Explicitly define a public default constructor, or a private default constructor if the class is not creatable, and mark it with `[MethodImpl(MethodImplOptions::InternalCall, MethodCodeType=MethodCodeType::Runtime)]` in C++ or `<MethodImpl(MethodImplOptions.InternalCall, MethodCodeType:=MethodCodeType.Runtime)>` in Visual Basic .NET (the syntax varies with the language).

2. Use the IL Disassembler to produce an IL file from your compiled assembly, for example:

   ```
   ildasm MyAssembly.dll /out:MyAssembly.il
   ```

3. Use the IL Assembler to reassemble the assembly from the *exact same* IL file, for example:

   ```
   ilasm /dll MyAssembly.il
   ```

The simple process of disassembling then assembling changes the necessary RVA values to zero without modifying the IL file. See Chapter 7 for more details about the process of disassembling and assembling, because the commands used differ if the assembly has strong name or embedded resources.

This process works for Visual Basic .NET assemblies, but may fail for C++ assemblies, however, if they contain embedded native code. The IL Disassembler cannot properly disassemble such code, so the re-assembled file would not be correct. Fortunately, ILDASM.EXE warns you when attempting to disassemble embedded native code.

> ## TIP
>
> As in Chapter 7, running PEVERIFY.EXE on assemblies with manually-defined types is a good idea to make sure you aren't breaking any CLR rules that aren't enforced by the compiler. In addition, any errors caught are likely to give you more information than the exception thrown at run time. Fortunately, the compilers for high-level languages like C# and Visual Basic .NET catch most problems that would cause bogus type definitions to be emitted (unlike the much less strict IL Assembler).

With correct .NET HTMLStyleSheetClass and NetMeetingClass class definitions (such as the C# definitions given earlier), the classes can now be instantiated as follows:

C#:

```
DispHTMLStyleSheet sheet = (DispHTMLStyleSheet)new HTMLStyleSheetClass();
INetMeeting meeting = (INetMeeting)new NetMeetingClass();
```

Visual Basic .NET:

```
Dim sheet As DispHTMLStyleSheet = CType(new HTMLStyleSheetClass(),
DispHTMLStyleSheet)
Dim meeting As INetMeeting = CType(new NetMeetingClass(), INetMeeting)
```

C++:

```
DispHTMLStyleSheet* sheet = (DispHTMLStyleSheet*)new HTMLStyleSheetClass();
INetMeeting* meeting = (INetMeeting*)new NetMeetingClass();
```

After the objects are created, members still must be called by casting sheet and meeting to the appropriate interfaces first. If you defined a coclass interface for HTMLStyleSheet and NetMeeting, as we did in the "Manually Defining Coclass Interfaces and Event Types" section, then the C# and Visual Basic .NET code can use them instead of the Class-suffixed class names. If you don't want to bother with defining a coclass interface, you can omit the Class suffix from the .NET class to make its use more natural to clients.

Manually Defining COM Types in Source Code

CHAPTER 21

1029

21

DEFINING COM
TYPES IN SOURCE
CODE

There's one difference between the instantiation code just shown and the code using `Activator.CreateInstance` in the previous section—the class types in the previous section are both `System.__ComObject` whereas the class types in this section are specifically `HTMLStyleSheetClass` and `NetMeetingClass`. However, because both of these class types are empty and all we're doing in all cases is calling through interfaces, there's no perceivable difference between the two methods of instantiation.

Defining Classes the Hard Way

Besides being simple to do, defining .NET classes representing coclasses as done in the previous section is probably sufficient. Still, you might wish to create a full "importer-style" .NET class that not only lists the interfaces it implements, but contains the methods (as you'd expect for a .NET class) so casting to interfaces is unnecessary. This is the hard way of defining a .NET class (although the result is easier for clients).

The bad news is that producing .NET classes that match those produced by the type library importer cannot be done directly by any other compiler but the IL Assembler. (The same metadata can be emitted, however, in any *language* by using the reflection emit APIs to generate and persist a dynamic assembly.) The metadata required is strange enough that no high-level language has syntax to support it, although C# and Visual Basic .NET come close.

C# supports defining non-static `extern` members in a class specifically for COM Interoperability. For this to work, the method (or property/event accessors) must be marked with `MethodImplAttribute` as done in previous listings, plus explicit interface implementation must be used in order to tell the CLR which COM interface method should be called if somebody were to call the class's method. This technique is demonstrated in Listing 21.24 with the `NetMeetingClass` class, which uses the types defined in Listing 21.21.

LISTING 21.24 The `NetMeetingClass` Type Uses the C# Feature of Non-Static `extern` Members to Produce a Class Definition Closer to What the Type Library Importer Would Generate

```
1: using System.Runtime.InteropServices;
2: using System.Runtime.CompilerServices;
3:
4: [
5:   ComImport,
6:   Guid("3E9BAF2D-7A79-11D2-9334-0000F875AE17"),
7:   TypeLibType(TypeLibTypeFlags.FCanCreate),
```

Listing 21.24   Continued

```
 8:    ComSourceInterfaces(typeof(_INetMeetingEvents)),
 9:    ClassInterface(ClassInterfaceType.None)
10: ]
11: public class NetMeetingClass : NetMeeting, INetMeeting,
12:   _INetMeetingEvents_Event
13: {
14:   [DispId(100), MethodImpl(MethodImplOptions.InternalCall,
15:     MethodCodeType=MethodCodeType.Runtime)]
16:   extern int INetMeeting.Version();
17:
18:   [DispId(101), MethodImpl(MethodImplOptions.InternalCall,
19:     MethodCodeType=MethodCodeType.Runtime)]
20:   extern void INetMeeting.UnDock();
21:
22:   [DispId(102), MethodImpl(MethodImplOptions.InternalCall,
23:     MethodCodeType=MethodCodeType.Runtime)]
24:   [return: MarshalAs(UnmanagedType.Bool)]
25:   extern bool INetMeeting.IsInConference();
26:
27:   [DispId(103), MethodImpl(MethodImplOptions.InternalCall,
28:     MethodCodeType=MethodCodeType.Runtime)]
29:   extern void INetMeeting.CallTo(string strCallToString);
30:
31:   [DispId(104), MethodImpl(MethodImplOptions.InternalCall,
32:     MethodCodeType=MethodCodeType.Runtime)]
33:   extern void INetMeeting.LeaveConference();
34:
35:   extern event _INetMeetingEvents_ConferenceEndedEventHandler
36:     _INetMeetingEvents_Event.ConferenceEnded
37:   {
38:     [MethodImpl(MethodImplOptions.InternalCall,
39:       MethodCodeType=MethodCodeType.Runtime)]
40:     add {}
41:
42:     [MethodImpl(MethodImplOptions.InternalCall,
43:       MethodCodeType=MethodCodeType.Runtime)]
44:     remove {}
45:   }
46:
47:   extern event _INetMeetingEvents_ConferenceStartedEventHandler
48:     _INetMeetingEvents_Event.ConferenceStarted
49:   {
50:     [MethodImpl(MethodImplOptions.InternalCall,
51:       MethodCodeType=MethodCodeType.Runtime)]
52:     add {}
53:
```

Manually Defining COM Types in Source Code

CHAPTER 21

1031

21

DEFINING COM
TYPES IN SOURCE
CODE

LISTING 21.24   Continued

```
54:        [MethodImpl(MethodImplOptions.InternalCall,
55:          MethodCodeType=MethodCodeType.Runtime)]
56:        remove {}
57:    }
58: }
```

Lines 5–9 mark the class with the same custom attributes that the type library importer would. The ComSourceInterfacesAttribute captures the fact that this class is an event source, and can be useful if a .NET class derives from NetMeetingClass.

NetMeetingClass implements every interface that the type library importer would make it implement—its coclass interface, all the interfaces it listed as implementing (in this case, only INetMeeting), and an event interface corresponding to each source interface listed in the original coclass statement (here, only the event interface corresponding to _INetMeetingEvents).

To compile without errors, the class must explicitly implement every member from each of its implemented interfaces. As required, each member is marked extern, and each method and accessor must is marked with MethodImplAttribute to give it the runtime managed internal marking in IL Assembler syntax. Because the NetMeeting coclass interface has no members, the listing only needs to implement the five methods of INetMeeting and the two events of _INetMeetingEvents_Event. The DispIdAttributes on the class's members match what the type library importer does, but is not strictly required because they only apply to the class interface exposed to COM, and this class interface is disabled in Line 9. It's still a good idea to use them, however, in case a derived .NET class wants to expose a class interface with these same DISPIDs on the base members. Unlike interfaces, the order in which members are listed doesn't matter.

This listing encounters two bugs with the Visual C# .NET compiler (version 7.0). First, the event accessors must have {} rather than a semicolon in order to avoid errors that say, "An add or remove accessor must have a body." In later versions of the C# compiler, this will likely need to change to use semicolons instead. Second, the listing compiles with several warnings from these same event accessors, stating that the accessors are marked external yet have no custom attributes. The compiler produces the correct metadata, however, so these warnings can be safely ignored.

There's one important limitation to this C# support. Methods using explicit interface implementation must be private. Because they're private, nobody can call them directly on the class—users have to cast to the interface anyway. So what's the point of using this feature? There's really only one reason: It's useful to be able to mark the class as implementing the various interfaces so clients can *implicitly* convert the class type to one of the interface types. A cast is no longer required.

If you wanted to start with C# code like the previous listing and tweak it using the usual steps of disassembling, editing, assembling, this can work fairly well for some examples. For Listing 21.24, you could disassemble the compiled assembly to an IL file then change every method (like `Version`) from private:

```
.method private hidebysig newslot final virtual
  instance int32  INetMeeting.Version() runtime managed internalcall
{
  .custom instance void [mscorlib]
    System.Runtime.InteropServices.DispIdAttribute::.ctor(int32) =
    ( 01 00 64 00 00 00 00 00 )                        // ..d.....
  .override INetMeeting::Version
} // end of method NetMeetingClass::INetMeeting.Version
```

to public, and also renaming the member to remove the "*IntefaceName.*" prefix:

```
.method public hidebysig newslot final virtual
  instance int32  Version() runtime managed internalcall
{
  .custom instance void [mscorlib]
    System.Runtime.InteropServices.DispIdAttribute::.ctor(int32) =
    ( 01 00 64 00 00 00 00 00 )                        // ..d.....
  .override INetMeeting::Version
} // end of method NetMeetingClass::Version
```

and then reassembling the new IL file. But unfortunately, that's not enough for properties or events. When explicitly implementing a property or event, the C# compiler only emits the accessor methods in the class definition and not the property or event itself. Therefore, to make the class's metadata work like the metadata produced by the importer, adding these missing members is necessary.

There's often another complication, however, and that's when the class implements interfaces that share the same method name. A great example is the `HTMLSytleSheet` coclass. Due to the strong relationship between `IHTMLStyleSheet`, `IHTMLStyleSheet2`, and `DispHTMLStyleSheet`, all three interfaces share 16 members with the same name. The type library importer decorates these as *InterfaceName_MemberName* when adding them to the class definition. Because explicitly implemented members are named *InterfaceName.MemberName*, this is a simple change to turn dots into underscores when editing the IL file. This needs to be done because most languages can't consume a public member name with a dot in it.

Unlike C#, Visual Basic .NET makes it easy to explicitly *and publicly* implement interface members, and even rename the class's members. Unfortunately, there's still one missing piece—the ability to specify an external method with a keyword like C#'s `extern`. Therefore, any class definition written in VB .NET similar to Listing 21.24 would still require modifications using the IL Disassembler and IL Assembler.

Manually Defining COM Types in Source Code

CHAPTER 21

1033

21

DEFINING COM
TYPES IN SOURCE
CODE

> **CAUTION**
>
> Attempting to place implementation directly in a `ComImport`-marked class or failure
> to mark a method or accessor with the appropriate `MethodImplAttribute` causes a
> `TypeLoadException`, as described in the "Defining Classes the Simple Way" section,
> because such an assembly fails CLR verification.

Avoiding the Balloon Effect

One of the benefits for manually defining your own COM types listed at the beginning of the
chapter is that it can be more lightweight than using an entire Interop Assembly because you
only need to define the types you use. Taking a closer look at the `IHTMLStyleSheet` example,
however, you'll notice that defining this interface alone also requires the definitions of
`IHTMLElement`, `IHTMLStyleSheetRulesCollection`, `IHTMLStyleSheetPagesCollection`, and
`IHTMLStyleSheetsCollection`, because these types are used as parameters in `IHTMLStyleSheet`.
If you go ahead and start defining the `IHTMLElement` interface, you'll quickly discover that this
interface requires the definitions of `IHTMLStyle` and `IHTMLFiltersCollection`. Meanwhile,
`IHTMLStyleSheetRulesCollection` requires the definition of `IHTMLStyleSheetRule` which
requires the definition of `IHTMLRuleStyle`, and so on. Before you know it, you're redefining an
entire type library's contents! This is the *balloon effect*.

Fortunately, there are ways to combat this. For example, if you don't think you're ever going to
need to call `IHTMLStyleSheet`'s `imports` property, you could change its definition from (in
C#):

```
[DispId(DispIds.IHTMLSTYLESHEET_IMPORTS)]
IHTMLStyleSheetsCollection imports { get; }
```

to:

```
[DispId(DispIds.IHTMLSTYLESHEET_IMPORTS)]
[return: MarshalAs(UnmanagedType.IUnknown)] object imports { get; }
```

or:

```
[DispId(DispIds.IHTMLSTYLESHEET_IMPORTS)]
[return: MarshalAs(UnmanagedType.IDispatch)] object imports { get; }
```

In essence, you're changing the COM definition from the following (in IDL):

```
[propget, id(DISPID_IHTMLSTYLESHEET_IMPORTS)]
HRESULT imports([retval, out] IHTMLStyleSheetsCollection** p);
```

to:

```
[propget, id(DISPID_IHTMLSTYLESHEET_IMPORTS)]
HRESULT imports([retval, out] IUnknown** p);
```

or:

```
[propget, id(DISPID_IHTMLSTYLESHEET_IMPORTS)]
HRESULT imports([retval, out] IDispatch** p);
```

This is a valid change to make because `IHTMLStyleSheetsCollection` derives from both `IDispatch` and `IUnknown`. Not only is it valid, but it removes the need to define the `IHTMLStyleSheetsCollection` in managed code. If you end up wanting to use this property in the future but don't want to change its signature, you could always define the `IHTMLStyleSheetsCollection` interface at that time then cast the returned object to that interface. (Or you could even late bind to the returned object if you didn't want to define the interface.)

This transformation is only valid for reference types (COM interfaces). For value types that you don't want to define, changing a parameter to the `System.IntPtr` type works instead as long as the value type parameter has at least one level of indirection. Using another example from the Microsoft HTML Object Library, the `IElementBehaviorRender` interface defines the following method:

```
HRESULT HitTestPoint([in] tagPOINT* pPoint,
    [in] IUnknown* pReserved, [out, retval] long* pbHit);
```

This can be correctly defined as follows in Visual Basic .NET:

```
Function HitTestPoint(ByRef pPoint As tagPOINT, _
    <MarshalAs(UnmanagedType.IUnknown)> pReserved As Object) As Integer
```

or defined the short-cut way as follows:

```
Function HitTestPoint(pPoint As IntPtr, _
    <MarshalAs(UnmanagedType.IUnknown)> pReserved As Object) As Integer
```

This technique was shown in Chapter 6, "Advanced Topics for Using COM Components," when encountering pointers to structures for which passing `Nothing` (null) is desired. A caller can pass a value like `IntPtr.Zero` or pass a valid structure by calling `Marshal.StructureToPtr` (or `Marshal.PtrToStructure` if the `IntPtr` value is being returned).

Using the `IntPtr` type works for COM interface parameters as well. A caller can get an `IntPtr` type that represents a COM interface by calling either `Marshal.GetIUnknownForObject`, `Marshal.GetIDispatchForObject`, or the general `Marhsal.GetComInterfaceForObject`. The returned `IntPtr` value can then be passed to a method that expects an interface pointer in a parameter changed to be the `IntPtr` type. For an `IntPtr` value returned, a caller can call `Marshal.GetObjectForIUnknown` to convert an `IntPtr` value to an object that can be cast to

COM interfaces that it implements. These methods are covered in more detail in Appendix A, "System.Runtime.InteropServices Reference."

The kinds of modifications discussed so far should be done on private type definitions because they aren't as convenient to use as "the real thing." There's one more major shortcut that should definitely be restricted to non-public types in well-controlled situations. That shortcut is to replace a member that you're not going to use with a dummy method to fill the slot in the v-table. For example, if you know that your program will be passed an object that implements IHTMLStyleSheet and all you need to do is cast it to the IHTMLStyleSheet type and call its addImport and addRule methods, you could define the interface as shown in Listing 21.25.

LISTING 21.25 A Bare-Bones C# Definition of the IHTMLStyleSheet Interface That Defines Only Two Methods, Using Placeholders for the Other Members

```
 1: using System.Runtime.InteropServices;
 2:
 3: [
 4:   ComImport,
 5:   Guid("3050f2e3-98b5-11cf-bb82-00aa00bdce0b"),
 6:   InterfaceType(ComInterfaceType.InterfaceIsDual)
 7: ]
 8: interface IHTMLStyleSheet_AbridgedVersion
 9: {
10:   void slot1();
11:   void slot2();
12:   void slot3();
13:   void slot4();
14:   void slot5();
15:   void slot6();
16:   void slot7();
17:   void slot8();
18:   void slot9();
19:   int addImport(string bstrURL, /*defaultvalue(-1)*/ int lIndex);
20:   int addRule(string bstrSelector, string bstrStyle,
21:     /*defaultvalue(-1)*/ int lIndex);
22:   void slot12();
23:   void slot13();
24:   void slot14();
25:   void slot15();
26:   void slot16();
27: }
```

This listing omits the `TypeLibTypeAttribute` because we're the only client and we don't care about this information. It also doesn't bother to mark the members with DISPIDs because we aren't going to implement this interface. Renaming the interface is good practice because it draws attention to the fact that this isn't the full COM interface by the same name.

If you have the time, it's probably better to use the original member names for the placeholders rather than `slotn`, because it makes it easier to plug in remaining members if desired.

This quick and dirty approach is useful when attempting to write a quick prototype application that requires several COM interface definitions. Because defining signatures correctly and dealing with the balloon effect can be quite time consuming, this placeholder technique enables you to define the most important members first and then fill in the remaining members when (and if) time permits.

Conclusion

This chapter highlighted all the major steps and roadblocks when manually defining type information for COM interfaces, classes, structures, and enumerations. Each .NET language has strengths and weaknesses. Whereas C# has the most comprehensive support for defining COM classes, Visual Basic .NET is usually best for defining COM interfaces because, for example, parameterized properties and optional parameters are more common than properties that define set accessors before get accessors. On the other hand, not being able to place `MarshalAsAttribute` on a VB .NET interface's property setter can be a big problem.

Unfortunately, defining types correctly can be a time-consuming and frustrating process much like defining PInvoke signatures. When checking the correctness of your type definitions, an easier-sounding approach than the one pictured in Figure 21.1 would be to temporarily remove `ComImportAttribute` from interface definitions, export a type library, and view it in OLEVIEW.EXE to compare the exported IDL syntax to the syntax in the original IDL file or original type library. Don't do this! Because OLEVIEW.EXE registers the input type library, you could overwrite important registry entries. If you have a type library viewer that doesn't touch the registry, however, then this approach can work well (as long as you export the type library using TLBEXP.EXE instead of REGASM.EXE, which also registers the type library).

FAQ: Why isn't there a tool that uses reflection on an Interop Assembly to produce the appropriate source code definitions?

Reflection has two main drawbacks that prevents such a tool from working (one that uses only reflection, anyway):

- When discovering a type's members, reflection returns them in no particular order. This won't work when defining COM interfaces, of course, because the order of members matters.

- Not all pseudo-custom attributes and their data can be obtained through reflection. A great example of this is `MarshalAsAttribute`, which is mostly invisible to reflection.

Another problem is that IL can't be obtained through reflection, but this isn't a big setback because the IL generated in the event-related classes is boilerplate code (shown in Listing 21.21) that can be generated by just knowing the types that are defined.

Instead of or in addition to using reflection, a tool could use the unmanaged .NET metadata APIs, or even use COM type description APIs to produce the correct source code based on a type library (although you might end up effectively re-implementing the type library importer).

Even if you were able to produce source code, what language would you produce? If generating C# code, optional parameters would have to be ignored if they have default values or parameterized properties would sometimes need to be transformed into methods (which doesn't work in late binding scenarios); if generating VB .NET code, some properties would have to be transformed into methods or unsigned types would need to be transformed into signed types; class types are troublesome regardless of the destination language; and so on.

As IL Assembler is the only .NET language with the expressiveness to handle everything generated by the type library importer, a tool already exists that creates the only source code that truly represents an Interop Assembly's contents—`ILDASM.EXE`!

Using APIs Instead of SDK Tools

IN THIS CHAPTER

- Generating an Assembly from a Type Library   1040

- Generating a Type Library from an Assembly   1050

- Registering and Unregistering Assemblies   1056

- Installing and Uninstalling Serviced Components   1059

- Example: Using the APIs in an Interactive Application   1061

The .NET Framework SDK provides tools for the common tasks essential for COM and COM+ Interoperability. These tools are:

- Type Library Importer (TLBIMP.EXE)
- Type Library Exporter (TLBEXP.EXE)
- Assembly Registration Tool (REGASM.EXE)
- .NET Services Installation Tool (REGSVCS.EXE)

All of these tools are based on .NET Framework APIs that are available for anyone to use. This chapter describes the use of these APIs as an alternative to using the tools. In other words, this chapter demonstrates how to programmatically do the work of TLBIMP.EXE, TLBEXP.EXE, REGASM.EXE, and REGSVCS.EXE, and perhaps even customize the process for your particular needs.

First, each of the four sets of "tool APIs" is discussed in detail. While reading this, you'll see how much of each of the tool's functionality is available in the corresponding APIs and how much is provided by the tool itself. Then, we'll examine a large application that uses all of these APIs to form a single "mega tool" with a graphical user interface.

Tip

Another .NET Framework SDK tool whose functionality can be used programmatically is the .NET Global Assembly Cache Utility (GACUTIL.EXE). By defining the IAssemblyCache COM interface manually in source code and using PInvoke to call the CreateAssemblyCache function exported by FUSION.DLL, you can install assemblies, uninstall assemblies, and list the contents of the cache. See the .NET Framework SDK for a sample called "ComReg" that demonstrates how to do this.

Generating an Assembly from a Type Library

The process of generating an assembly from a type library (also known as type library import) can be done using the TypeLibConverter class in the System.Runtime.InteropServices namespace. This class has the following three methods relevant to import, shown here in C#, Visual Basic .NET, and C++ syntax:

C#:

```
public virtual AssemblyBuilder ConvertTypeLibToAssembly(object typeLib,
  string asmFileName, TypeLibImporterFlags flags,
  ITypeLibImporterNotifySink notifySink, byte [] publicKey,
  StrongNameKeyPair keyPair, string asmNamespace, Version asmVersion);
```

```
public virtual AssemblyBuilder ConvertTypeLibToAssembly(object typeLib,
    string asmFileName, int flags, ITypeLibImporterNotifySink notifySink,
    byte [] publicKey, StrongNameKeyPair keyPair, bool unsafeInterfaces);

public virtual bool GetPrimaryInteropAssembly(Guid g, int major, int minor,
    int lcid, ref string asmName, ref string asmCodeBase);
```

Visual Basic .NET:

```
Overloads Public Function ConvertTypeLibToAssembly(ByVal typeLib As Object, _
    ByVal asmFileName As String, ByVal flags As TypeLibImporterFlags, _
    ByVal notifySink As ITypeLibImporterNotifySink, ByVal publicKey() As Byte, _
    ByVal keyPair As StrongNameKeyPair, ByVal asmNamespace As String, _
    ByVal asmVersion As Version) As AssemblyBuilder

Overloads Public Function ConvertTypeLibToAssembly(ByVal typeLib As Object, _
    ByVal asmFileName As String, ByVal flags As Integer, _
    ByVal notifySink As ITypeLibImporterNotifySink, ByVal publicKey() As Byte, _
    ByVal keyPair As StrongNameKeyPair, ByVal unsafeInterfaces As Boolean _
    ) As AssemblyBuilder

Public Function GetPrimaryInteropAssembly(ByVal g As Guid, _
    ByVal major As Integer, ByVal minor As Integer, ByVal lcid As Integer, _
    ByRef asmName As String, ByRef asmCodeBase As String) As Boolean
```

C++:

```
public: __sealed virtual AssemblyBuilder* ConvertTypeLibToAssembly(
    Object* typeLib, String* asmFileName, TypeLibImporterFlags flags,
    ITypeLibImporterNotifySink* notifySink, unsigned char publicKey __gc[],
    StrongNameKeyPair* keyPair, String* asmNamespace, Version* asmVersion);

public: __sealed virtual AssemblyBuilder* ConvertTypeLibToAssembly(
    Object* typeLib, String* asmFileName, int flags,
    ITypeLibImporterNotifySink* notifySink, unsigned char publicKey __gc[],
    StrongNameKeyPair* keyPair, bool unsafeInterfaces);

public: __sealed virtual bool GetPrimaryInteropAssembly(Guid g, int major,
    int minor, int lcid, String** asmName, String** asmCodeBase);
```

TLBIMP.EXE and Visual Studio .NET use these methods to import a type library.
ConvertTypeLibToAssembly takes an in-memory type library as input and produces an in-memory assembly as output. This method converts an entire type library (and any dependent type libraries) to an assembly (and any dependent assemblies). No APIs exist for more fine-grained conversions, such as converting one type at a time.

> **TIP**
>
> Although there are two versions of the `ConvertTypeLibToAssembly` method, you should always use the first one shown (with the `asmNamespace` and `asmVersion` parameters). The other overload gives less flexibility and exists primarily for backwards compatibility with the beta versions of the .NET Framework.

> **DIGGING DEEPER**
>
> The `TypeLibConverter` class implements an interface called `ITypeLibConverter`. This is mainly done so the class can be used easily from COM. Of course, nothing would prevent someone from providing his own implementation of `ITypeLibConverter`. All the necessary APIs for reading type libraries, emitting type libraries, reading metadata, and emitting metadata are publicly available and documented. Getting all the transformations right is extremely difficult, however, and such an implementation could not be plugged into the SDK tools `TLBIMP.EXE` and `TLBEXP.EXE` or into the equivalent processes in Visual Studio .NET. These applications use the built-in `TypeLibConverter` class.

Creating a Dynamic Assembly

Let's take a look at the first `ConvertTypeLibToAssembly` overload, and examine what is needed for each parameter when making the method call. The input `typeLib` object must be an object that implements the COM interface `ITypeLib` (`UCOMITypeLib` in `System.Runtime.InteropServices`). Typically, when you want to convert a type library, you're starting with a filename rather than an `ITypeLib` interface. To get such an interface, you can use the OLE Automation `LoadTypeLibEx` method. This can be defined as follows using PInvoke, shown here in C# syntax:

```
[DllImport("oleaut32.dll", CharSet=CharSet.Unicode, PreserveSig=false)]
static extern UCOMITypeLib LoadTypeLibEx(string szFile, REGKIND regkind);
```

This can then be used as follows in C#:

```
// Load the type library without registering it
UCOMITypeLib typeLib = LoadTypeLibEx(filename, REGKIND.REGKIND_NONE);
```

The `REGKIND` enumeration is defined in the "Example: Using the APIs in an Interactive Application" section.

CAUTION

If you just want to load a type library, you must call LoadTypeLibEx with the REGKIND_NONE value to indicate that you don't want the type library to be registered at the same time. LoadTypeLibEx should always be used rather than the older LoadTypeLib method because LoadTypeLib registers the type library that gets loaded (if the filename doesn't contain a path). It's good practice not to interfere with the Windows Registry unless absolutely necessary.

The asmFileName parameter must be set to a string representing the filename of the output assembly. This string must not contain any drive or path information. Furthermore, this string must end with a .dll suffix, otherwise an ArgumentException is thrown. It might seem strange to require specifying a filename up-front for a dynamic assembly, but this is a limitation of the reflection emit API used by the TypeLibConverter class.

The flags parameter is a TypeLibImporterFlags enumeration type, which has the following values that are used as bit flags:

- PrimaryInteropAssembly. This flag should be set when you want to create a Primary Interop Assembly. TLBIMP.EXE exposes this as its /primary option.
- SafeArrayAsSystemArray. This flag should be set when you want to import all SAFEARRAY types as System.Array types instead of one-dimensional arrays. This is handy when a type library contains SAFEARRAY parameters that are multi-dimensional or have non-zero lower bounds, because it makes their managed signatures usable. TLBIMP.EXE exposes this as its /sysarray option.
- UnsafeInterfaces. This flag should be set when you want every imported class and interface to be marked with System.Security.SuppressUnmanagedCodeSecurityAttribute. "UnsafeInterfaces" is a bit of a misnomer because it applies to classes as well. This attribute tells the .NET security system to not do a run-time security check for UnmanagedCode permission (which involves a stack walk) when calling into unmanaged code. Instead, the check for UnmanagedCode is only done at "link time"—during just-in-time compilation. TLBIMP.EXE exposes this as its /unsafe option.

CAUTION

Although the use of the UnsafeInterfaces option can boost performance significantly, the callers of such types must take on the responsibility of using them in a secure fashion and not exposing functionality that can be abused by their callers.

> Misuse of `SuppressUnmanagedCodeSecurityAttribute` can jeopardize the security of your code, so this option should only be used when the gain in performance is absolutely essential. Also, as mentioned in Chapter 6, "Advanced Topics for Using COM Components," code that calls members on an interface marked with `SuppressUnmanagedCodeSecurityAttribute` must always have unmanaged code permission, even if the interface is implemented by a .NET class.

The `notifySink` parameter is an `ITypeLibImporterNotifySink` interface, which has the following two methods:

C#:

```
public void ReportEvent(ImporterEventKind eventKind, int eventCode,
    string eventMsg);
```

```
public Assembly ResolveRef(object typeLib);
```

Visual Basic .NET:

```
Public Sub ReportEvent(ByVal eventKind As ImporterEventKind, _
    ByVal eventCode As Integer, ByVal eventMsg As String)
```

```
Public Function ResolveRef(ByVal typeLib As Object) As Assembly
```

C++:

```
public: void ReportEvent(ImporterEventKind eventKind, int eventCode,
    String* eventMsg);
```

```
public: Assembly* ResolveRef(Object* typeLib);
```

This interface is used as a callback mechanism so the type library importer can report progress and ask you to make decisions about dependent type libraries. The `TypeLibConverter` class actually *requires* you to pass a valid instance that implements `ITypeLibImporterNotifySink`—you cannot pass null for the `notifySink` parameter.

The `ReportEvent` method is called for three different kinds of events, specified by its first `eventKind` parameter. This is an `ImporterEventKind` enumeration with the following values:

- `ERROR_REFTOINVALIDTYPELIB`. This reports the fatal error of the input type library (or one of its dependent type libraries) referencing an "invalid" type library. This event is never reported by `TypeLibConverter` in version 1.0 of the CLR.

- `NOTIF_CONVERTWARNING`. This reports any warnings, such as pointing out parameters that are not automatically marshaled as one might expect. `TLBIMP.EXE` suppresses these warnings when the `/silent` option is used.

- NOTIF_TYPECONVERTED. This event is reported every time a type is imported into metadata. TLBIMP.EXE only displays these messages when the /verbose option is used.

ReportEvent's eventCode parameter is an HRESULT value that corresponds to the type of event. These are success HRESULT values for the latter two types of events, and the value sent with NOTIF_CONVERTWARNING differs based on the type of warning. This enables you to programmatically act on different types of events in a more fine-grained manner. All of these values are defined in CorError.h that ships with the .NET Framework SDK. The eventMsg parameter is a string that contains a message describing the event that is suitable for printing.

22

USING APIS INSTEAD OF SDK TOOLS

> **TIP**
>
> The NOTIF_TYPECONVERTED events can be used to create progress bar functionality. The one missing piece is the total number of types to use as the progress bar's maximum value. Fortunately, this can easily be obtained by calling UCOMITypeLib's GetTypeInfoCount method. This method takes no parameters and simply returns the total number of types in a type library.

Although the ReportEvent method only exists for informational purposes, the ResolveRef method is vital for proper operation of the type library importer when a type library references other type libraries. This method is called with a typeLib parameter and is responsible for returning an Assembly instance to satisfy the reference for the type library. Although typeLib is a generic Object type, you can count on the fact that the object passed in from the TypeLibConverter callback implements UCOMITypeLib.

The simplest implementation of ResolveRef could call ConvertTypeLibToAssembly using the typeLib object as input, and return the freshly-imported assembly. However, a more sophisticated implementation could enable a user to specify a pre-imported Interop Assembly—perhaps with special customizations—to satisfy the reference instead. TLBIMP.EXE enables a user to do this with its /reference option. Or, it could search for a registered Primary Interop Assembly to satisfy a reference, which TLBIMP.EXE does.

> **CAUTION**
>
> An implementer of ResolveRef must keep track of all dependent assemblies that have been imported during the process of importing the input type library. The TypeLibConverter class may call ResolveRef multiple times requesting an assembly for the same type library, so it's important that the same assembly returned the first time is also returned for subsequent requests.

CAUTION

Be aware that the `ResolveRef` mechanism is not completely flexible. For example, before getting the chance to plug in your own assembly to satisfy a reference, the type library importer must locate the dependent type library. If it cannot find it, `ResolveRef` is not called. This happens because the importer must obtain a valid `ITypeLib` reference before calling `ResolveRef`. So, you cannot choose an arbitrary *type library* to satisfy a reference; just an arbitrary *assembly* to satisfy a reference for a located type library. There is no way in `ResolveRef` to help the type library importer locate a type library.

The `publicKey` and `keyPair` parameters are used for creating an Interop Assembly with a strong name. Both may be set to null (`Nothing` in VB .NET) if you want to generate an assembly that doesn't have a strong name. If you do, then `publicKey` can be set to a byte array containing the key data, or `keyPair` can be set to an instance of `System.Reflection.StrongNameKeyPair`. A `StrongNameKeyPair` instance can be created from a `FileStream` representing a file containing the key pair, from a byte array containing the key pair data, or from a string with the name of a key container.

Only one of the two key-related parameters should be set to something non-null for any single call. If you pass data in both parameters simultaneously, `ConvertTypeLibToAssembly` doesn't throw an exception but the resulting behavior is unspecified.

The `asmNamespace` parameter can be set to a string that represents the namespace in the output assembly. If `asmNamespace` is set to null, the default namespace is used, which is the library name of the input type library.

DIGGING DEEPER

If a .NET-aware type library contains an IDL custom attribute for specifying a namespace when imported, this namespace is always used regardless of whether or not one is passed in for the `asmNamespace` parameter. An example of this is the Microsoft Office XP `MSO.DLL` type library, which always gets imported with the `Microsoft.Office.Core` namespace. This IDL custom attribute is discussed in Chapter 15, "Creating and Deploying Useful Primary Interop Assemblies."

Finally, the `asmVersion` parameter can be set to the version of the output assembly. If set to null, the default version (*TlbMajor.TlbMinor*.0.0) is used.

Getting a Primary Interop Assembly

The ConvertTypeLibToAssembly method is the only one that's strictly necessary for type library import. The GetPrimaryInteropAssembly method, however, is useful for checking if a Primary Interop Assembly is already registered for the input type library (and warning the user, as TLBIMP.EXE does), and for locating PIAs for dependent type libraries. You could discover whether or not a Primary Interop Assembly is registered by simply using Windows Registry APIs and looking in the appropriate place under the TypeLib branch, but using this built-in method is much easier (and safer in case registry details change in the future).

The GetPrimaryInteropAssembly method expects four by-value parameters describing the type library—its LIBID, major version number, minor version number, and LCID. How can you get this information if all you have is an UCOMITypeLib variable? With a simple method call to UCOMITypeLib.GetLibAttr—but there are two complications:

- The definition of UCOMITypeLib.GetLibAttr has an IntPtr out parameter to represent a pointer to a TYPELIBATTR structure, so Marshal.PtrToStructure must be used to extract the structure from the returned value.

- As documented for ITypeLib, UCOMITypeLib.ReleaseTLibAttr should be called after UCOMITypeLib.GetLibAttr to release the attributes.

Listing 22.1 contains Visual Basic .NET code that demonstrates extracting these four values needed in order to call GetPrimaryInteropAssembly.

LISTING 22.1 Extracting Type Library Attributes from UCOMITypeLib.GetLibAttr in Order to Call TypeLibConverter.GetPrimaryInteropAssembly

```
 1: Dim typeLib As UCOMITypeLib = LoadTypeLibEx(filename, REGKIND.REGKIND_NONE)
 2: Dim converter As New TypeLibConverter
 3: Dim name As String
 4: Dim codebase As String
 5: Dim attributes As TYPELIBATTR
 6: Dim attributesPtr As IntPtr = IntPtr.Zero
 7:
 8: Try
 9:   typeLib.GetLibAttr(attributesPtr)
10:   ' Copy the data from the unmanaged structure to a new value type
11:   attributes = Marshal.PtrToStructure(attributesPtr, _
12:     GetType(TYPELIBATTR))
13: Finally
14:   ' We must release the structure as documented by ITypeLib
15:   If (Not attributesPtr.Equals(IntPtr.Zero)) Then
16:     typeLib.ReleaseTLibAttr(attributesPtr)
17:   End If
```

LISTING 22.1   Continued

```
18: End Try
19:
20: ' Now that we have all the type library information, we can
21: ' call TypeLibConverter.GetPrimaryInteropAssembly
22: converter.GetPrimaryInteropAssembly(attributes.guid, _
23:    attributes.wMajorVerNum, attributes.wMinorVerNum, attributes.lcid, _
24:    name, codebase)
```

The Marshal class in System.Runtime.InteropServices has handy methods that can extract the LIBID and LCID from a UCOMITypeLib instance (GetTypeLibGuid and GetTypeLibLcid, respectively), but unfortunately there are no methods to get the version number. This is why calling UCOMITypeLib.GetLibAttr is necessary.

Saving the Dynamic Assembly

The type returned by ConvertTypeLibToAssembly is an AssemblyBuilder — a dynamic assembly. Although we had to choose a filename when calling ConvertTypeLibToAssembly, it is not persisted to disk until AssemblyBuilder.Save is called. The surprising aspect of the AssemblyBuilder.Save method is that it requires a filename string. This should be the same string passed into ConvertTypeLibToAssembly for the asmName parameter. As with ConvertTypeLibToAssembly, this string must not contain any drive or path information. The assembly is always saved in the same directory as the input type library.

If you give a different filename than the one passed to ConvertTypeLibToAssembly, then a multi-file assembly will be produced. In this case, the filename given to ConvertTypeLibToAssembly becomes a module containing all of the type definitions, and the filename given to AssemblyBuilder.Save would contain only the assembly manifest.

> **CAUTION**
>
> An AssemblyBuilder can only be saved once. Any attempts to call Save a second time after a successful first time results in an InvalidOperationException.

Any imported assemblies remain loaded for the life of the process unless you create them inside separate application domains that you unload. An application domain is a lightweight logical process, providing the same benefits of isolation as operating system processes. However, multiple application domains may exist in the same operating system process. By default, a .NET program runs in a single process-wide application domain.

If you're planning on importing lots of assemblies and don't need them to remain loaded, using the single default application domain wastes memory. Instead, if you created a new application domain each time you import an assembly then unload the domain afterward, the assemblies all get unloaded in a timely fashion. To unload an application domain, simply call the static `System.AppDomain.Unload` method that takes an `AppDomain` parameter. This technique of using a separate application domain applies to all the "tool APIs" examined in this chapter because they all involve loading assemblies.

Suppose that you define a class called `MyImporter` with an `Import` method that calls `ConvertTypeLibToAssembly` then `AssemblyBuilder.Save`. If you called `Import` normally, the assembly would remain in memory for the lifetime of the application:

```
MyImporter importer = new MyImporter();
Importer.Import(...);
```

However, by creating a new application domain (`System.AppDomain`) that runs the `Import` method, you can unload it when you're finished. This is demonstrated in the C# code in Listing 22.2.

LISTING 22.2   Importing a Type Library in a Separate Application Domain

```
 1: MyImporter importer = null;
 2:
 3: // Create a new AppDomain
 4: AppDomain domain = AppDomain.CreateDomain("MyImporterDomain");
 5:
 6: if (domain != null)
 7: {
 8:   string asmFullName = typeof(MyImporter).Assembly.FullName;
 9:   string typeFullName = typeof(MyImporter).FullName;
10:
11:   // Create an instance of MyImporter in the separate AppDomain.
12:   // This is done instead of using "new MyImporter()" which would create
13:   // the type in the current AppDomain.
14:   ObjectHandle handle = domain.CreateInstance(asmFullName, typeFullName);
15:
16:   if (handle != null)
17:   {
18:     // Unwrap the ObjectHandle so we can use the importer object
19:     importer = (MyImporter)handle.Unwrap();
20:
21:     // Now call the method
22:     importer.Import(...);
23:   }
24:
```

LISTING 22.2   Continued

```
25:    // Unload the application domain
26:    AppDomain.Unload(domain);
27: }
```

For more information about application domains, consult the .NET Framework documentation.

Generating a Type Library from an Assembly

The process of generating a type library from an assembly (also known as type library export) can be done using one more method on the `TypeLibConverter` class—`ConvertAssemblyToTypeLib`—shown here in C#, Visual Basic .NET, and C++ syntax:

C#:

```
public virtual object ConvertAssemblyToTypeLib(Assembly assembly,
   string strTypeLibName, TypeLibExporterFlags flags,
   ITypeLibExporterNotifySink notifySink);
```

Visual Basic .NET:

```
Public Function ConvertAssemblyToTypeLib(ByVal assembly As Assembly, _
   ByVal strTypeLibName As String, ByVal flags As TypeLibExporterFlags, _
   ByVal notifySink As ITypeLibExporterNotifySink) As Object
```

C++:

```
public: __sealed virtual Object* ConvertAssemblyToTypeLib(
   Assembly* assembly, String* strTypeLibName, TypeLibExporterFlags flags,
   ITypeLibExporterNotifySink* notifySink);
```

TLBEXP.EXE, REGASM.EXE, and Visual Studio .NET's `Register for COM Interop` option use this method to export a type library. `ConvertAssemblyToTypeLib` works much like `ConvertTypeLibToAssembly`. It takes an in-memory assembly as input and produces an in-memory type library as output.

Creating a Dynamic Type Library

The assembly parameter is a `System.Reflection.Assembly` type. When starting with a filename, the static `Assembly.LoadFrom` method can be used to obtain the `Assembly` instance. (For multi-file assemblies, the file must be the one containing the manifest.) When starting with an assembly reference, such as "System.Runtime.Remoting, Version=1.0.3300.0, Culture=neutral, PublicKeyToken=b77a5c561934e089", the static `Assembly.Load` method can be used.

The `strTypeLibName` parameter is the desired filename for the exported type library. Unlike `ConvertTypeLibToAssembly`'s `asmFileName` parameter, this can include drive and path information, and therefore can be chosen in any desired directory. Still, however, the destination file must be chosen before beginning export. This is the only parameter that may be left null to accept the default type library filename equal to the assembly name plus .tlb.

FAQ: How can I use the import and export APIs in my application to generate dynamic type libraries and assemblies, while enabling the user to choose the filenames and paths in a saving process *after* importing/exporting finishes?

You could settle for the default filenames and paths when performing import/export and later move and/or rename the files based on the user's choice, but this can get really messy when worrying about overwriting existing files and any dependent files generated by the process.

You could delay or repeat the import/export process in a separate application domain (so a new path could be chosen) after the user chooses to save file(s), but this may be undesirable for large type libraries or assemblies.

You could even do a sort of in-memory copy from the existing dynamic type library or assembly to a new dynamic type library or assembly that will be saved with the desired name and location, because all the APIs for reading and writing both type libraries and assemblies are publicly available. Again, this can yield unacceptable performance.

The bottom line is that these APIs were designed to choose the destination file(s) before beginning the import or export process. By the time a dynamic assembly or type library is created, the would-be-saved filename is already determined.

The flags parameter is a TypeLibExporterFlags enumeration type, which has a single value that may be set as a bit flag—OnlyReferenceRegistered. This flag should be set when you want the exporter to only look for dependent type libraries in the registry rather than also looking in the same directory as the input assembly. TLBEXP.EXE and REGASM.EXE do not expose this option. The exporter searches for dependencies itself, unlike the importer.

The notifySink parameter is an ITypeLibExporterNotifySink interface, which is extremely similar to the ITypeLibImporterNotifySink interface introduced in the "Generating an Assembly from a Type Library" section. This interface has the following two methods:

C#:

```
public void ReportEvent(ExporterEventKind eventKind, int eventCode,
  string eventMsg);

public object ResolveRef(Assembly assembly);
```

Visual Basic .NET:

```
Public Sub ReportEvent(ByVal eventKind As ExporterEventKind, _
  ByVal eventCode As Integer, ByVal eventMsg As String)
```

```
Public Function ResolveRef(ByVal assembly As Assembly) As Object
```

C++:

```
public: void ReportEvent(ExporterEventKind eventKind, int eventCode,
  String* eventMsg);
```

```
public: Object* ResolveRef(Assembly* assembly);
```

As with `ITypeLibImporterNotifySink`, this interface is used as a callback mechanism so the type library exporter can report progress and ask you to make decisions about dependent assemblies. The `TypeLibConverter` class requires you to pass a valid instance that implements `ITypeLibExporterNotifySink`—you cannot pass null for the `notifySink` parameter.

The `ITypeLibExporterNotifySink.ReportEvent` method works just like `ITypeLibImporterNotifySink.ReportEvent`, except that the `eventKind` parameter is an `ExporterEventKind` enumeration with the following almost identical values:

- `ERROR_REFTOINVALIDASSEMBLY`. This theoretically reports the same kind of fatal error as `ImporterEventKind.ERROR_REFTOINVALIDTYPELIB` does. However, this event is never reported by `TypeLibConverter` in version 1.0 of the CLR.

- `NOTIF_CONVERTWARNING`. This is the same as `ImporterEventKind.NOTIF_CONVERTWARNING`.

- `NOTIF_TYPECONVERTED`. This is the same as `ImporterEventKind.NOTIF_TYPECONVERTED`.

TIP

As with import, `NOTIF_TYPECONVERTED` events can be used to create progress bar functionality during export. However, in this case, getting the total number of types that will be exported is more tricky. For type library import it was easy because every type in a type library gets converted. For type library export, only public types that are not marked with `ComImport` and are not marked with `ComVisible(false)` (either directly or indirectly via the assembly) are exported.

The `Assembly.GetExportedTypes` method sounds promising but it simply returns all public types in an assembly. Instead, you might have tried the following incorrect code:

```
int totalTypes = 0;
foreach (Type t in assembly.GetTypes())
{                                                    DON'T DO THIS
    // ComImportAttribute is a pseudo-custom attribute so it can't be
    // found via reflection in this manner
    if (Marshal.IsTypeVisibleFromCom(t) &&
        t.GetCustomAttributes(typeof(ComImportAttribute), false).Length == 0)
        totalTypes++;
}
```

Calling `Marshal.IsTypeVisibleFromCom` is useful because it returns true if the type is COM-visible, so it excludes any non-public types (from the .NET perspective) as well as any types that are marked with `ComVisible(false)` either directly or indirectly. However, remember that `ComImportAttribute` is a pseudo-custom attribute, so reflection will never find any in metadata as regular custom attributes. The second half of the previous `if` statement will always evaluate to be true.

Not all pseudo-custom attribute data is attainable via reflection, but fortunately there's a way to find out whether a type is marked with `ComImportAttribute`, which is to use the `System.Type`'s `IsImport` property. Therefore, the previous code would need to be replaced with:

```
int totalTypes = 0;
foreach (Type t in assembly.GetTypes())
{
    if (Marshal.IsTypeVisibleFromCom(t) && !t.IsImport)
        totalTypes++;
}
```

This `ResolveRef` method is called with an `Assembly` instance as input and expects an `Object` as output. Although not enforced by the return type in the signature, this returned object must implement `UCOMITypeLib`.

The simplest implementation of `ResolveRef` could call `ConvertAssemblyToTypeLib` using the `assembly` object as input, and return the freshly-exported type library. However, a more sophisticated implementation could enable a user to specify a pre-exported type library—perhaps with special customizations—to satisfy the reference instead. `TLBEXP.EXE` does not enable a user to make such a customization.

> **CAUTION**
>
> Despite having the same name, ITypeLibExporterNotifySink's ResolveRef method works differently than ITypeLibImporterNotifySink's ResolveRef method. There are two asymmetries:
>
> - Before calling ResolveRef, the exporter loads a dependent assembly, attempts to find its corresponding type library via the Windows registry, and then attempts to find it in the current directory (if OnlyReferenceRegistered is not set). It only calls ResolveRef if the type library cannot be found from these steps. The importer, on the other hand, always calls ResolveRef after loading a dependent type library.
> - The exporter maintains a list of type libraries used to satisfy references, so it never calls ResolveRef more than once with the same assembly. The importer does not do this, so it may call ResolveRef multiple times with the same type library.
>
> This means that a custom exporter application has even less flexibility for satisfying references than a custom importer application. The benefit is that the implementer of ITypeLibExporterNotifySink.ResolveRef does not need to maintain a list of dependent type libraries, as the implementer of ITypeLibImporterNotifySink.ResolveRef must do.

There is one extra twist to exporting a type library, and that lies in the ability to control the capitalization of exported names. As described in Chapter 10, "Advanced Topics for Using .NET Components," type library identifiers can sometimes have an unexpected case based on the order in which identifiers are exported. The TypeLibConverter class enables its client to supply a list of identifiers, thereby picking the case with which the identifiers in the list will be exported.

To enable this, the notifySink object passed to ConvertAssemblyToTypeLib can implement a second interface besides ITypeLibExporterNotifySink. That interface is System.Runtime.InteropServices.ITypeLibExporterNameProvider, and has a single method that returns an array of strings:

C#:

```
public string GetNames();
```

Visual Basic .NET:

```
Public Function GetNames() As String()
```

C++:

```
public: String* GetNames() __gc[];
```

Using APIs Instead of SDK Tools

CHAPTER 22

1055

22

USING APIs
INSTEAD OF SDK
TOOLS

If the callback object implements this interface, then its `GetNames` method gets called before export begins. The callback object can then return an array of identifiers whose case determines how every occurrence of each identifier will appear in the output type library. If an implementation of `GetNames` has no names to return, it must return an empty array rather than null. Returning null causes `ConvertAssemblyToTypeLib` to throw a `COMException` with the `TLBX_E_BAD_NAMES` HRESULT defined in `CorError.h` as 0x8013117B.

Each identifier should have no spaces. If the same identifier appears in the returned array multiple times, all but the first occurrence is ignored. If an identifier in the array is not used by any of the types and members exported, it is still added to the type library's string table but has no noticeable effect.

`TLBEXP.EXE` exposes this functionality with its `/names` option, used with a file containing identifiers. For the rules about such *names files*, see Appendix B, "SDK Tools Reference."

Saving the Dynamic Type Library

The object returned by `ConvertAssemblyToTypeLib` not only implements the type description interfaces `ITypeLib` (a.k.a. `UCOMITypeLib`) and `ITypeLib2`, but also the type building interfaces `ICreateTypeLib` and `ICreateTypeLib2`. This is analogous to the assembly returned by `ConvertTypeLibToAssembly` being an `Assembly` and an `AssemblyBuilder`.

Because the object implements `ICreateTypeLib`, the object can be cast to this interface and `ICreateTypeLib.SaveAllChanges` can be called to persist the type library to disk. This method has no parameters, and it saves the type library as whatever filename was passed into `ConvertAssemblyToTypeLib`. Note that unlike `AssemblyBuilder.Save`, you can save a type library multiple times without error.

One catch is that the .NET Framework doesn't provide a .NET definition of `ICreateTypeLib` like it does for `ITypeLib`. Therefore, you need to write your own definition, which is done in Listing 22.2 in the "Example: Using the APIs in an Interactive Application" section.

TIP

Before calling `SaveAllChanges`, you could call other methods of `ICreateTypeLib` or `ICreateTypeLib2` to make additional modifications to the type library. For example, you could call `ICreateTypeLib.SetName` to choose a different library name—something that `ConvertAssemblyToTypeLib` alone does not let you do. This technique is demonstrated in the "Example: Using the APIs in an Interactive Application" section. Similarly, during type library import, you could add new types to the `AssemblyBuilder` instance before calling `Save` (although you can't change the existing types).

Registering and Unregistering Assemblies

The methods used to register and unregister assemblies for use by COM belong to the RegistrationServices class in the System.Runtime.InteropServices namespace. Similar to TypeLibConverter, RegistrationServices implements the IRegistrationServices interface, which contains all of its methods for ease in calling these methods from COM. This class has two important methods:

C#:

```
public virtual bool RegisterAssembly(Assembly assembly,
  AssemblyRegistrationFlags flags);
```

```
public virtual bool UnregisterAssembly(Assembly assembly);
```

Visual Basic .NET:

```
Public Function RegisterAssembly(ByVal assembly As Assembly, _
  ByVal flags As AssemblyRegistrationFlags) As Boolean
```

```
Public Function UnregisterAssembly(ByVal assembly As Assembly) As Boolean
```

C++:

```
public: virtual bool RegisterAssembly(Assembly* assembly,
  AssemblyRegistrationFlags flags);
```

```
public: virtual bool UnregisterAssembly(Assembly* assembly);
```

These methods are used by REGASM.EXE and Visual Studio .NET to add or remove COM-enabling registry entries for .NET components. Also, remember that besides adding to the registry, these methods invoke custom registration or unregistration functions for any types that define them, as explained in Chapter 12, "Customizing COM's View of .NET Components."

Both RegisterAssembly and UnregisterAssembly take an Assembly instance as input and return true if types were (un)registered successfully, or false if the assembly has no types that are appropriate to be registered by COM. This would include non-public types or classes without public default constructors.

RegisterAssembly has a second parameter that is an AssemblyRegistrationFlags enumeration. This enumeration has the following values that can be set like bit flags:

- None. Setting this value is the same as setting no values.
- SetCodeBase. Setting this value means that a codebase entry will be added to every registered class that the CLR can use to locate the assembly. REGASM.EXE exposes this as its /codebase option.

Although dynamic assemblies (`AssemblyBuilder` instances) derive from the `Assembly` class, they cannot be registered or unregistered with these methods.

And that's all there is to know about these APIs. They are much simpler than the previous ones presented because they don't produce any output files, don't report any progress, and don't involve dependencies with other files.

Notice that the ability to export and register a type library, exposed by `REGASM.EXE`'s `/tlb` option, is not part of these APIs. In addition, the ability to generate a registry file (`.reg` file), exposed by `REGASM.EXE`'s `/regfile` option, is not part of these registration methods. There are, however, several methods on the `RegistrationServices` class that facilitate the process of generating a registry file. These methods are (shown only in C# syntax for brevity):

```
public virtual Guid GetManagedCategoryGuid();

public virtual string GetProgIdForType(Type type);

public virtual Type [] GetRegistrableTypesInAssembly(Assembly assembly);

public virtual bool TypeRepresentsComType(Type type);
```

- The `GetManagedCategoryGuid` method returns the CATID for the ".NET Category" listed as an implemented category by every registered .NET type. This CATID is `62C8FE65-4EBB-45E7-B440-6E39B2CDBF29`.

- The `GetProgIdForType` method returns a string that represents what the ProgID would be for the input type if it were registered. This string is either a string specified in a `ProgIdAttribute` marked on the type or the fully-qualified type name if no such attribute exists.

- The `GetRegistrableTypesInAssembly` method returns an array of every type that would be registered. This means every public class with a public default constructor that isn't COM-invisible due to `ComVisibleAttribute` markings on the class or assembly.

- The `TypeRepresentsComType` method returns true if the input type is marked as `ComImport` (or if it derives from the `ComImport` type and has the same GUID), false otherwise. This is useful for creating registry files because the registry entries differ based on whether the type is marked with `ComImport`. For `ComImport` types, the only keys added are `Class`, `Assembly`, `RuntimeVersion`, and possibly `CodeBase` under the `InprocServer32` key.

> ### DIGGING DEEPER
>
> The .NET Framework has four similar ways to ask if a type represents a COM object, and the differences between them are subtle. To set the record straight, here's exactly what each one does:
>
> - `System.Type.IsImport` — returns true if the type is marked with the `ComImportAttribute` pseudo-custom attribute, false otherwise.
> - `System.Type.IsCOMObject` — returns true if the type represents a *class* either marked with `ComImport` or derived from a class that is marked with `ComImport`, false otherwise.
> - `System.Runtime.InteropServices.Marshal.IsComObject` — works the same way as `System.Type.IsCOMObject` but on an instance rather than a type.
> - `System.Runtime.InteropServices.RegistrationServices.` `TypeRepresentsComType` — returns true if the type is marked with `ComImport` or derives from the `ComImport` type *with the same GUID*, false otherwise.

With these methods, you could create a registry file by:

1. Getting all the appropriate types in the assembly using `GetRegistrableTypesInAssembly`.
2. Check for `PrimaryInteropAssemblyAttribute`(s) and add the necessary PIA-specific entries. The type library information (such as major and minor version numbers) can be obtained from the attribute's properties.
3. For each type returned by `GetRegistrableTypesInAssembly`, check which kind of entries it requires by calling `TypeRepresentsComType` and add the appropriate entries.

Of course, remember that no entries added or removed by custom registration functions would be taken into account.

There are two more methods provided by `RegistrationServices` (shown in C#):

```
public virtual void RegisterTypeForComClients(Type type, ref Guid g);

public virtual bool TypeRequiresRegistration(Type type);
```

`RegisterTypeForComClients` is equivalent to calling the `CoRegisterClassObject` COM API, which registers the class factory for the specified type using the GUID passed as the second parameter. You should avoid this method because of subtle threading behavior—if the current thread's state has not already been initialized, calling this method causes it to be set to MTA. `TypeRequiresRegistration` simply returns true if the input type would be registered by a call to `RegisterAssembly`, false otherwise.

Installing and Uninstalling Serviced Components

.NET serviced components (classes deriving from `System.EnterpriseServices.ServicedComponent`) can either be dynamically registered at run time, or manually registered at install time. Although dynamic registration enables xcopy deployment, manual registration is desirable because it can alert you to problems during the registration process.

The `RegistrationHelper` class in the `System.EnterpriseServices` namespace provides the necessary APIs for performing this manual registration, which includes installation and uninstallation into the Component Services Catalog (a.k.a. COM+ Catalog). This class contains the following methods:

C#:

```
public virtual void InstallAssembly(string assembly, ref string application,
  string partition, ref string tlb, InstallationFlags installFlags);

public void InstallAssembly(string assembly, ref string application,
  ref string tlb, InstallationFlags installFlags);

public virtual void UninstallAssembly(string assembly, string application,
  string partition);

public void UninstallAssembly(string assembly, string application);
```

Visual Basic .NET:

```
Overloads Public Sub InstallAssembly(ByVal assembly As String, _
  ByRef application As String, ByVal partition As String, _
  ByRef tlb As String, ByVal installFlags As InstallationFlags)

Overloads NotOverridable Public Sub InstallAssembly( _
  ByVal assembly As String, ByRef application As String, ByRef tlb As String, _
  ByVal installFlags As InstallationFlags)

Overloads Public Sub UninstallAssembly(ByVal assembly As String, _
  ByVal application As String, ByVal partition As String)

Overloads NotOverridable Public Sub UninstallAssembly( _
  ByVal assembly As String, ByVal application As String)
```

C++:

```
public: __sealed virtual void InstallAssembly(String* assembly, String**
application,
  String* partition, String** tlb, InstallationFlags installFlags);

public: __sealed void InstallAssembly(String* assembly,
  String** application, String** tlb, InstallationFlags installFlags);
```

```
public: __sealed virtual void UninstallAssembly(String* assembly, String*
application,
  String* partition);
```

```
public: __sealed void UninstallAssembly(String* assembly,
  String* application);
```

These methods are used by REGSVCS.EXE when manually installing or uninstalling an assembly as a COM+ application, and are also used during automatic registration when a serviced component is first activated.

TIP

Although there are two versions of the InstallAssembly and UninstallAssembly methods, the first one listed is preferred because it includes the ability to specify a partition name. If the partition parameter doesn't apply, you can simply leave it null. Notice, however, that RegistrationHelper implements an IRegistrationHelper interface that only includes the partition-less versions of both methods. This is for backwards compatibility with beta versions of these types.

The InstallAssembly method does everything required to install assemblies into the Component Services (COM+) catalog. This includes registering the assembly, exporting a type library, registering the type library, installing the type library for the specified application, and configuring any serviced component types in the assembly.

The assembly parameter is a string containing the filename containing the assembly's manifest. This filename can include a full or relative path. Notice how this differs from the previous APIs because it doesn't use in-memory assemblies but rather loads them itself. If this parameter does not contain a valid filename, or if the corresponding assembly does not have a strong name, a System.EnterpriseServices.RegistrationException is thrown.

The application and partition strings can be used to specify the appropriate application and partition names. Both of these can be set to null to accept the default behavior—no partition name and an application name equal to either the string contained in a System.EnterpriseServices.ApplicationNameAttribute marking or the assembly name if no such attribute exists.

The tlb parameter is a by-reference string that can be set to the desired filename of the output type library. This can be a null reference, in which case the default name and location is used. On return from the call, the tlb string contains the filename used by RegistrationHelper.

The installFlags parameter is an InstallationFlags enumeration type, which has the following values that can be used as bit flags:

- `Configure`. This is obsolete and should not be used.

- `ConfigureComponentsOnly`. With this set, no configuration is done for methods or interfaces. REGSVCS.EXE exposes this as its `/componly` option.

- `CreateTargetApplication`. Creates a new target application. If an application with the same name already exists, an error occurs. REGSVCS.EXE exposes this as its `/c` option.

- `Default`. Setting this is the same as setting nothing at all. This instructs `RegistrationHelper` to perform the default configuration, installation, and registration and assumes that the application already exists. This is the default behavior for REGSVCS.EXE, but it can also be specified explicitly using the `/fc` and `/reconfig` options.

- `ExpectExistingTypeLib`. With this set, no type library will be exported. Instead, the type library filename given as the `tlb` parameter (or the default type library filename that is used if null is passed) must exist. REGSVCS.EXE exposes this as its `/extlb` option.

- `FindOrCreateTargetApplication`. This instructs `RegistrationHelper` to use an existing application with the given name (or default name if none is given) if it exists, or simply create a new application with that name if one doesn't already exist. REGSVCS.EXE exposes this as its `/fc` option.

- `Install`. This is obsolete and should not be used.

- `ReconfigureExistingApplication`. This option can be used with an existing application, and it makes the application's properties match the assembly's properties if it doesn't already. REGSVCS.EXE exposes this as its `/reconfig` option (and it exposes a `/noreconfig` option for turning this setting off).

- `Register`. This is obsolete and should not be used.

- `ReportWarningsToConsole`. This causes warnings to be printed to the console. REGSVCS.EXE sets this by default, but enables you to turn it off using its `/quiet` option.

The `UninstallAssembly` method has only three parameters. These `assembly`, `application`, and `partition` string parameters work just like they do for `InstallAssembly`.

Example: Using the APIs in an Interactive Application

Now that you've been introduced to the relevant tool APIs, it's time to put them to use in a realistic C# application to demonstrate subtleties in their use. In this section we'll put together an application called the *Interactive Interop Tool*. This is an interactive graphical application that enables the user to import type libraries, export type libraries, register assemblies and type libraries, and install and uninstall serviced components as COM+ applications. This application is pictured in Figure 22.1, which has a tab for each SDK tool.

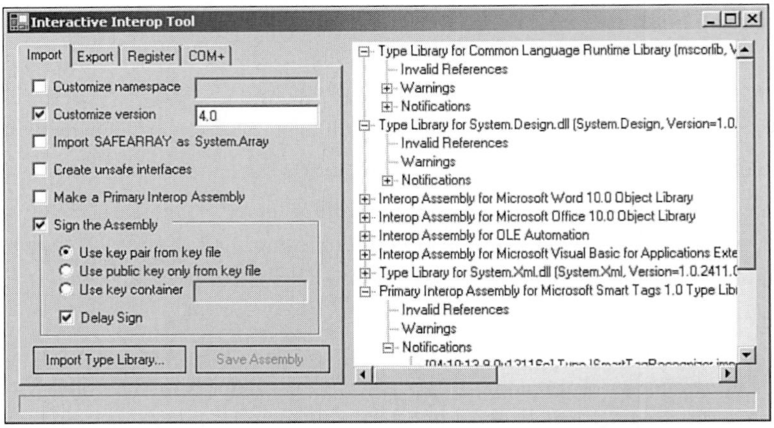

FIGURE 22.1
The Interactive Interop Tool combines all of the tool APIs into one program.

This application attempts to provide much of the same functionality as the corresponding SDK tools and at the same time provide additional benefits. This tool offers the following additional features compared to the standard SDK tools:

- This example shows progress information for type library import and export and tells the user the total number of types to be imported/exported, whereas TLBIMP.EXE and TLBEXP.EXE do not.

- Every type library and assembly loaded is displayed and can be left in memory without persisting it to disk.

- TLBEXP.EXE doesn't allow you to specify existing type libraries to satisfy references, but this tool does (if the dependent type libraries can't be found by the TypeLibConverter implementation).

- TLBEXP.EXE doesn't allow you to customize the output library name or specify a help file, but this tool does.

- For multi-file assemblies, TLBEXP.EXE and REGASM.EXE (when using its /tlb option) only check the file containing the manifest for an embedded type library. (If one is found, TLBEXP.EXE warns the user but exports a new type library, and REGASM.EXE registers the embedded type library rather than a new type library.) In this tool, we check every file for an embedded type library.

For simplicity, this application does not provide certain features that the SDK tools provide. For example:

- TLBIMP.EXE enables specifying an input type library filename with a resource ID for files containing multiple type libraries embedded as resources. For example, you could specify "msvbvm60.dll\3".

- TLBIMP.EXE allows you to list dependent Primary Interop Assemblies to satisfy references with its /reference option when generating a Primary Interop Assembly. In contrast, when generating a Primary Interop Assembly with this tool, any dependent type libraries must have a Primary Interop Assembly registered.

- Unlike REGASM.EXE, there is no mechanism for creating a registration file.

The application is structured as shown in Figure 22.2.

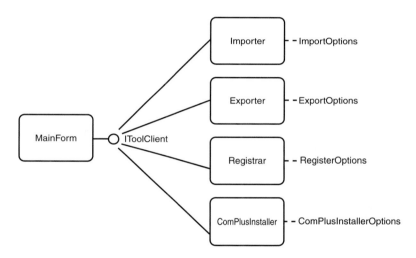

FIGURE 22.2
The structure of the Interactive Interop Tool application.

Each of the four SDK tools is represented by a class—Importer for TLBIMP.EXE, Exporter for TLBEXP.EXE, Registrar for REGASM.EXE, and ComPlusInstaller for REGSVCS.EXE. Each of these classes have behavior that can be customized by using an associated structure containing options, shown to the right of each class in the diagram. Communication with MainForm, the Windows Forms client, is done via an IToolClient interface. All of these types are shown in the upcoming code listings.

The full source code for this application is available on this book's Web site. To compile it from a command prompt, you can place all six source files in the same directory then run:

```
csc /out:Interop.exe *.cs /r:System.Windows.Forms.dll
➥/r:System.EnterpriseServices.dll /r:System.dll /r:System.Drawing.dll
```

Then, you can run `Interop.exe` to try it out. To compile it inside Visual Studio .NET, add all six files to an empty Visual C# Windows Application project, and make sure it references the `System.Windows.Forms`, `System.EnterpriseServices`, `System.Drawing`, and `System` assemblies.

Listing 22.3 contains `MiscTypes.cs`, the file that defines `IToolClient` as well as some other types used throughout the application.

LISTING 22.3   `MiscTypes.cs`. Definitions of a Handful of Interfaces, Enumerations, and a Class Used Throughout the Application

```
 1: using System;
 2: using System.Reflection;
 3: using System.Runtime.InteropServices;
 4:
 5: // Contains common functions used by the other classes
 6: internal class Util
 7: {
 8:   // Load a type library from a filename
 9:   [DllImport("oleaut32.dll", CharSet=CharSet.Unicode, PreserveSig=false)]
10:   internal static extern UCOMITypeLib LoadTypeLibEx(string szFile,
11:     REGKIND regkind);
12:
13:   // Unregister a type library
14:   [DllImport("oleaut32.dll", PreserveSig=false)]
15:   internal static extern void UnRegisterTypeLib(ref Guid libID,
16:     short wVerMajor, short wVerMinor, int lcid, SYSKIND syskind);
17:
18:   // Return a nice-looking "display name" for the input assembly
19:   internal static string GetDisplayNameForAssembly(Assembly assembly)
20:   {
21:     if (assembly.GetCustomAttributes(
22:       typeof(AssemblyTitleAttribute), false).Length > 0)
23:     {
24:       AssemblyTitleAttribute attribute =
25:         (AssemblyTitleAttribute)(assembly.GetCustomAttributes(
26:         typeof(AssemblyTitleAttribute), false)[0]);
27:
28:       return attribute.Title + " (" + assembly.FullName + ")";
29:     }
30:     else if (assembly.GetCustomAttributes(
31:       typeof(AssemblyDescriptionAttribute), false).Length > 0)
32:     {
33:       AssemblyDescriptionAttribute attribute =
34:         (AssemblyDescriptionAttribute)(assembly.GetCustomAttributes(
```

LISTING 22.3   Continued

```
35:            typeof(AssemblyDescriptionAttribute), false)[0]);
36:
37:        return attribute.Description + " (" + assembly.FullName + ")";
38:      }
39:      else
40:      {
41:        return assembly.FullName;
42:      }
43:    }
44:
45:    // Return a nice-looking "display name" for the input type library
46:    internal static string GetDisplayNameForTypeLib(UCOMITypeLib typeLib)
47:    {
48:      string typeLibName;
49:      string typeLibDocString;
50:      string typeLibHelpFile;
51:      int typeLibHelpContext;
52:
53:      // Calling GetDocumentation with an index of -1 gets documentation
54:      // for the library itself.
55:      typeLib.GetDocumentation(-1, out typeLibName, out typeLibDocString,
56:        out typeLibHelpContext, out typeLibHelpFile);
57:
58:      if (typeLibDocString != null)
59:        return typeLibDocString;
60:      else
61:        return typeLibName;
62:    }
63:  }
64:
65: // Implemented by users of the Importer, Exporter, Registrar, and/or
66: // ComPlusInstaller classes to receive notifications
67: public interface IToolClient
68: {
69:   void SendMessage(MessageTypes type, string message, object data);
70:   string GetTypeLibReference(Guid typeLibGuid, string typeLibDisplayName);
71:   string GetAssemblyReference(string assemblyDisplayName);
72:   bool AskYesNoQuestion(string question, bool defaultIsYes);
73:   int ProgressMaximum { get; set; }
74:   int Progress { get; set; }
75: }
76:
77: // Message types sent via IToolClient.SendMessage
78: public enum MessageTypes
79: {
```

LISTING 22.3   Continued

```
 80:    InvalidRef,
 81:    Warning,
 82:    Notification,
 83:    BeginFile,
 84:    EndFile
 85: }
 86:
 87: // REGKIND enumeration used by LoadTypeLibEx
 88: internal enum REGKIND
 89: {
 90:   REGKIND_DEFAULT = 0,
 91:   REGKIND_REGISTER = 1,
 92:   REGKIND_NONE = 2
 93: }
 94:
 95: // An almost-complete definition of ICreateTypeLib that returns
 96: // an IntPtr from CreateTypeInfo rather than an ICreateTypeInfo
 97: // interface, to avoid having to define ICreateTypeInfo.
 98: [
 99:   ComImport,
100:   Guid("00020406-0000-0000-C000-000000000046"),
101:   InterfaceType(ComInterfaceType.InterfaceIsIUnknown)
102: ]
103: internal interface ICreateTypeLib
104: {
105:   IntPtr CreateTypeInfo(string szName, TYPEKIND tkind);
106:   void SetName(string szName);
107:   void SetVersion(short wMajorVerNum, short wMinorVerNum);
108:   void SetGuid(ref Guid guid);
109:   void SetDocString(string szDoc);
110:   void SetHelpFileName(string szHelpFileName);
111:   void SetHelpContext(int dwHelpContext);
112:   void SetLcid(int lcid);
113:   void SetLibFlags(uint uLibFlags);
114:   void SaveAllChanges();
115: }
```

Lines 1–3 list the System namespace for Guid and IntPtr, the System.Reflection namespace for Assembly and several related custom attributes, and System.Runtime.InteropServices for a handful of custom attributes plus the UCOMITypeLib, SYSKIND, and TYPEKIND types. Lines 6–63 contain the internal Util class, which has four methods used by other classes in the application. Two of them—LoadTypeLibEx and UnRegisterTypeLib—are PInvoke signatures for unmanaged methods defined in OLEAUT32.DLL. LoadTypeLibEx (the COM equivalent of

`Assembly.LoadFrom`) loads a type library from a filename and registers it depending on the `REGKIND` value. `UnRegisterTypeLib` unregisters a type library based on information like its GUID and version number. The other two methods—`GetDisplayNameForAssembly` and `GetDisplayNameForTypeLibrary`—are implemented in Lines 19–62.

`GetDisplayNameForAssembly` takes an assembly as input and outputs a string that is supposed to represent a readable yet informative name that the client can display in a list of assemblies. For lists of type libraries (such as in Visual Studio .NET's Add Reference dialog), "doc strings" are usually displayed if they exist, otherwise library names with version numbers are displayed. For lists of assemblies, however, the best way to display them is unclear at the time of writing. There are so many custom attributes defined in the .NET Framework that can be placed on an assembly, it makes it hard to choose (and at this early stage, hard to anticipate if and how developers will use them).

For our *display names*, Lines 21–29 first look for a title string inside `System.Reflection.AssemblyTitleAttribute`. If the input assembly isn't marked with this custom attribute, Lines 30–38 look for a description string inside `System.Reflection.AssemblyDescriptionAttribute`. If the assembly isn't marked with this custom attribute either, Line 41 falls back to using the assembly's full name by calling its `FullName` property. Even if a title or description is found, we append the assembly's full name anyway (in Lines 28 and 37) because it might help to reduce ambiguities if any assemblies have poorly chosen titles or descriptions.

As described earlier, picking a display name for a type library is much easier due to a lesser amount of built-in attributes and a history of using type library doc strings. Therefore, Lines 55–56 call `GetDocumentation` on the input `UCOMITypeLib` interface to obtain all the needed information about the type library. Although `GetDocumentation` can obtain information on any type in the type library, passing –1 for the first parameter gives us information for the library itself. If the `typeLibDocString` is still null after the call, then no doc string exists and we return the library name (which always exists) in Line 61. Otherwise, the doc string is returned in Line 59.

TIP	

The `Marshal` class in the `System.Runtime.InteropServices` namespace has a few handy methods for extracting type library information—`GetTypeLibGuid`, `GetTypeLibLcid`, and `GetTypeLibName`. However, it doesn't have a method for extracting a doc string, which is why calling `UCOMITypeLib.GetDocumentation` is necessary in Listing 22.3.

22

USING APIs INSTEAD OF SDK TOOLS

Lines 67–75 define the `IToolClient` interface, which is implemented by the graphical client in order to enable communication during the processes such as type library import and type library export. The `Importer`, `Exporter`, `Registrar`, and `ComPlusInstaller` classes all need a reference to an `IToolClient` implementation when constructed. Think of `IToolClient` as a consolidation of `ITypeLibImporterNotifySink` and `ITypeLibExporterNotifySink` with more explicit support for a progress bar. `SendMessage` is much like the `ReportEvent` method on both `ITypeLibImporterNotifySink` and `ITypeLibExporterNotifySink` interfaces. `GetTypeLibReference` functions much like `ITypeLibImporterNotifySink.ResolveRef`, and `GetAssemblyReference` functions much like `ITypeLibExporterNotifySink.ResolveRef`. Because the various tool classes defined in the upcoming listing rely on ongoing interaction with the user, the `AskYesNoQuestion` method facilitates this interaction. The `ProgressMaximum` and `Progress` properties enable the getting and setting of a client's progress information.

The `MessageTypes` enumeration in Lines 78–85 defines the messages that can be sent using `IToolClient.SendMessage`. The first three message types correspond to the three message types in both the `ImporterEventKind` and `ExporterEventKind` enumerations defined in `System.Runtime.InteropServices`. The last two message types are new. A `BeginFile` message is sent whenever a type library or assembly has been successfully loaded. When sending such a message, `SendMessage`'s `message` argument contains a display name for the type library or assembly, and its `data` argument is either null if the file is an assembly or a string containing the would-be filename when saved if the file is a type library. The `EndFile` message is sent when whatever was being done to the loaded assembly or type library is finished. With an `EndFile` message, `SendMessage`'s `message` argument contains the same display name that was sent with the corresponding `BeginFile` message and its `data` argument, if appropriate, contains a reference to the loaded assembly or type library (an `Assembly` or `UCOMITypeLib` type, or possibly an `AssemblyBuilder` or `ICreateTypeLib` type if it's a dynamic assembly/type library).

Lines 88–93 define the `REGKIND` enumeration that's needed by `Util.LoadTypeLibEx`. Although `System.Runtime.InteropServices` defines a handful of widely-used structures and enumerations (like `SYSKIND`), `REGKIND` is not one of them.

Because `ICreateTypeLib` is the interface that represents a dynamic type library that can be modified and saved, we need a definition of it. A definition is not provided in `System.Runtime.InteropServices`, so Lines 98–115 contain a "good enough" definition of the interface. It's fully functional, however the `CreateTypeInfo` method simply returns an `IntPtr` rather than an `ICreateTypeInfo` interface as it should. This way, we don't have to bother with defining the `ICreateTypeInfo` interface that we don't need to use. The interface is marked `internal` so we don't have to worry about other applications attempting to use this interface definition.

The Importer

The Import tab is shown in Figure 22.3, and the progress bar functionality when performing type library import is shown in Figure 22.4.

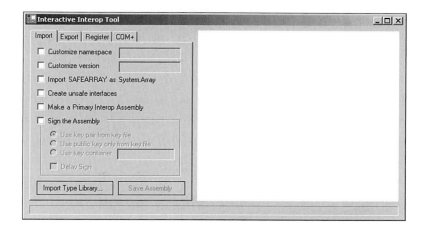

FIGURE 22.3

The Import tab can be used to import type libraries and save the Interop Assemblies.

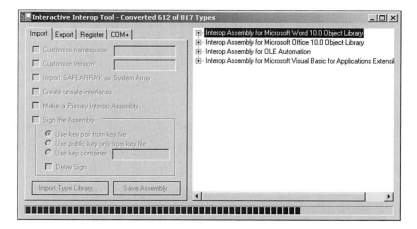

FIGURE 22.4

The progress bar and caption show progress during type library import.

The Importer class is shown in Listing 22.4.

LISTING 22.4 Importer.cs. Using the System.Runtime.InteropServices. TypeLibConverter Class to Import Assemblies from Type Libraries

```csharp
 1: using System;
 2: using System.IO;
 3: using System.Reflection;
 4: using System.Collections;
 5: using System.Runtime.InteropServices;
 6:
 7: // Import Options
 8: public struct ImportOptions
 9: {
10:   public TypeLibImporterFlags Flags;
11:   public bool UseKeyPairFromFile;
12:   public bool DelaySign;
13:   public string KeyFile;
14:   public string KeyContainer;
15: }
16:
17: // Creates an assembly from a type library
18: public class Importer : ITypeLibImporterNotifySink
19: {
20:   private ImportOptions options;
21:   private TypeLibConverter converter;
22:   private IToolClient client;
23:   private Hashtable loadedAssemblies;
24:   private string outputDirectory;
25:
26:   // Constructor
27:   public Importer(IToolClient client, Hashtable loadedAssemblies)
28:   {
29:     this.client = client;
30:     this.loadedAssemblies = loadedAssemblies;
31:     this.converter = new TypeLibConverter();
32:   }
33:
34:   // Property to get/set options
35:   public ImportOptions Options
36:   {
37:     get { return options; }
38:     set { options = value; }
39:   }
40:
41:   // Output directory where type libraries will be saved
42:   public string OutputDirectory
```

LISTING 22.4   Continued

```
43:    {
44:      set { outputDirectory = value; }
45:    }
46:
47:    // Creates an assembly with the given assembly name, namespace,
48:    // and version from the type library specified by typeLibFilename
49:    public Assembly Import(string typeLibFilename, string asmName,
50:      string @namespace, Version version)
51:    {
52:      UCOMITypeLib typeLib;
53:
54:      try
55:      {
56:        // Load the type library without registering it
57:        typeLib = Util.LoadTypeLibEx(typeLibFilename, REGKIND.REGKIND_NONE);
58:      }
59:      catch
60:      {
61:        throw new ApplicationException("Unable to load the type library '" +
62:          typeLibFilename + "'.");
63:      }
64:
65:      return Import(typeLib, asmName, @namespace, version);
66:    }
67:
68:    // Creates a type library with the given assembly name, namespace,
69:    // and version from the loaded input type library
70:    public Assembly Import(UCOMITypeLib typeLib, string asmName,
71:      string @namespace, Version version)
72:    {
73:      string typeLibDisplayName;
74:      string piaName;
75:      string piaCodebase;
76:      Assembly returnAssembly;
77:      StrongNameKeyPair keyPair = null;
78:      byte [] keyData = null;
79:
80:      // Before beginning import, check if a Primary Interop Assembly for
81:      // this type library is already registered
82:      if (GetPrimaryInteropAssembly(typeLib, out piaName, out piaCodebase))
83:      {
84:        if (client.AskYesNoQuestion("A Primary Interop Assembly is " +
85:          "already registered for the type library '" +
86:          Util.GetDisplayNameForTypeLib(typeLib) + "' with full name '" +
```

LISTING 22.4   Continued

```
87:             piaName + "' and codebase '" + piaCodebase + "'. Do you want " +
88:             "to load this assembly instead of importing a new one?", true))
89:         {
90:           returnAssembly = LoadPrimaryInteropAssembly(piaName, piaCodebase);
91:
92:           client.SendMessage(MessageTypes.BeginFile,
93:             "Primary Interop Assembly for " +
94:             Util.GetDisplayNameForTypeLib(typeLib), null);
95:           client.SendMessage(MessageTypes.EndFile,
96:             "Primary Interop Assembly for " +
97:             Util.GetDisplayNameForTypeLib(typeLib), returnAssembly);
98:
99:           loadedAssemblies[Marshal.GetTypeLibGuidForAssembly(
100:            returnAssembly).ToString() +
101:            returnAssembly.GetName().Version.ToString(2)] = returnAssembly;
102:          return returnAssembly;
103:        }
104:      }
105:
106:      // Construct a nice looking "display name" for the assembly
107:      if ((options.Flags &
108:        TypeLibImporterFlags.PrimaryInteropAssembly) != 0)
109:      {
110:        typeLibDisplayName = "Primary ";
111:      }
112:      else
113:      {
114:        typeLibDisplayName = "";
115:      }
116:
117:      typeLibDisplayName += "Interop Assembly for " +
118:        Util.GetDisplayNameForTypeLib(typeLib);
119:
120:      // Choose a default assembly filename if none was chosen
121:      if (asmName == null)
122:        asmName = Marshal.GetTypeLibName(typeLib);
123:
124:      asmName += ".dll";
125:
126:      client.SendMessage(MessageTypes.BeginFile, typeLibDisplayName,
127:        outputDirectory + Path.DirectorySeparatorChar + asmName);
128:
129:      // Get the total number of types for the progress bar
130:      // by getting the number of types in the type library
```

LISTING 22.4   Continued

```
131:     client.ProgressMaximum += typeLib.GetTypeInfoCount();
132:
133:     // Extract key data if a key file is used
134:     if (options.KeyFile != null)
135:     {
136:       FileStream stream = null;
137:       try
138:       {
139:         stream = new FileStream(options.KeyFile, FileMode.Open,
140:           FileAccess.Read);
141:         keyData = new byte[stream.Length];
142:         stream.Read(keyData, 0, (int)stream.Length);
143:       }
144:       catch
145:       {
146:         throw new ApplicationException("Unable to read key data from '" +
147:           options.KeyFile + "'.");
148:       }
149:       finally
150:       {
151:         if (stream != null) stream.Close();
152:       }
153:
154:       // Construct a SrongNameKeyPair if desired
155:       if (options.UseKeyPairFromFile)
156:       {
157:         keyPair = new StrongNameKeyPair(keyData);
158:         keyData = null;
159:       }
160:     }
161:     else if (options.KeyContainer != null)
162:     {
163:       // Construct a StrongNamePair from a key container
164:       keyPair = new StrongNameKeyPair(options.KeyContainer);
165:     }
166:
167:     // If the user chose delay signing, extract only the public key
168:     // from the key pair
169:     if (options.DelaySign && keyPair != null)
170:     {
171:       keyData = keyPair.PublicKey;
172:       keyPair = null;
173:     }
174:
```

22

LISTING 22.4   Continued

```
175:      // Create an assembly from the type library
176:      returnAssembly = converter.ConvertTypeLibToAssembly(typeLib, asmName,
177:        options.Flags, this, keyData, keyPair, @namespace, version);
178:
179:      client.SendMessage(MessageTypes.EndFile, typeLibDisplayName,
180:        returnAssembly);
181:      loadedAssemblies[Marshal.GetTypeLibGuidForAssembly(
182:        returnAssembly).ToString() +
183:        returnAssembly.GetName().Version.ToString(2)] = returnAssembly;
184:      return returnAssembly;
185:    }
186:
187:    // For the input type library, find out if a Primary Interop Assembly
188:    // exists. If so, return its name and codebase via two out parameters
189:    private bool GetPrimaryInteropAssembly(UCOMITypeLib typeLib,
190:      out string name, out string codebase)
191:    {
192:      TYPELIBATTR attributes;
193:      IntPtr attributesPtr = IntPtr.Zero;
194:
195:      try
196:      {
197:        typeLib.GetLibAttr(out attributesPtr);
198:        attributes = (TYPELIBATTR)Marshal.PtrToStructure(attributesPtr,
199:          typeof(TYPELIBATTR));
200:      }
201:      finally
202:      {
203:        // As documented by ITypeLib, we must release the attributes
204:        if (attributesPtr != IntPtr.Zero)
205:          typeLib.ReleaseTLibAttr(attributesPtr);
206:      }
207:
208:      // Now that we have all the type library information, we can
209:      // call TypeLibConverter.GetPrimaryInteropAssembly
210:      return converter.GetPrimaryInteropAssembly(attributes.guid,
211:        attributes.wMajorVerNum, attributes.wMinorVerNum, attributes.lcid,
212:        out name, out codebase);
213:    }
214:
215:    // Return the version of a type library as a "Major.Minor" string
216:    private string GetTypeLibVersion(UCOMITypeLib typeLib)
217:    {
218:      TYPELIBATTR attributes;
```

LISTING 22.4   Continued

```
219:      IntPtr attributesPtr = IntPtr.Zero;
220:
221:      try
222:      {
223:        typeLib.GetLibAttr(out attributesPtr);
224:        attributes = (TYPELIBATTR)Marshal.PtrToStructure(attributesPtr,
225:          typeof(TYPELIBATTR));
226:      }
227:      finally
228:      {
229:        // As documented by ITypeLib, we must release the attributes
230:        if (attributesPtr != IntPtr.Zero)
231:          typeLib.ReleaseTLibAttr(attributesPtr);
232:      }
233:
234:      // Now that we have all the type library information, we can
235:      // call TypeLibConverter.GetPrimaryInteropAssembly
236:      return attributes.wMajorVerNum + "." + attributes.wMinorVerNum;
237:    }
238:
239:    // Load a Primary Interop Assembly from the given name and codebase.
240:    // The codebase may be null if none exists
241:    private Assembly LoadPrimaryInteropAssembly(string name,
242:      string codebase)
243:    {
244:      Assembly returnAssembly;
245:
246:      try
247:      {
248:        // First attempt to load from its assembly name alone
249:        returnAssembly = Assembly.Load(name);
250:      }
251:      catch (FileNotFoundException)
252:      {
253:        // If the load failed, there better be a codebase so we can load
254:        // it from that location
255:        if (codebase != null)
256:          returnAssembly = Assembly.LoadFrom(codebase);
257:        else
258:          throw;
259:      }
260:
261:      // Check that the loaded assembly is in fact a Primary
262:      // Interop Assembly
```

LISTING 22.4   Continued

```
263:       if (returnAssembly.GetCustomAttributes(
264:         typeof(PrimaryInteropAssemblyAttribute), false).Length == 0)
265:       {
266:         throw new ApplicationException("The assembly '" + name +
267:           "' is registered as a Primary Interop Assembly, but is not " +
268:           "marked with the PrimaryInteropAssembly custom attribute. " +
269:           "Please check your registration settings.");
270:       }
271:
272:       return returnAssembly;
273:     }
274:
275:     // Implementation of ITypeLibImporterNotifySink.ReportEvent
276:     public void ReportEvent(ImporterEventKind eventKind, int eventCode,
277:       string eventMsg)
278:     {
279:       MessageTypes messageType;
280:
281:       // Get the MessageType for the corresponding ImporterEventKind
282:       switch (eventKind)
283:       {
284:         case ImporterEventKind.ERROR_REFTOINVALIDTYPELIB:
285:           messageType = MessageTypes.InvalidRef;
286:           break;
287:         case ImporterEventKind.NOTIF_CONVERTWARNING:
288:           messageType = MessageTypes.Warning;
289:           break;
290:         case ImporterEventKind.NOTIF_TYPECONVERTED:
291:           messageType = MessageTypes.Notification;
292:           // Update the progress for type conversions
293:           client.Progress++;
294:           break;
295:         default:
296:           throw new ApplicationException(
297:             "Encountered unknown ImporterEventKind value.");
298:       }
299:
300:       client.SendMessage(messageType, "[" +
301:         DateTime.Now.ToString("hh:mm:ss.f") + " 0x" +
302:         eventCode.ToString("x") + "] " + eventMsg, null);
303:     }
304:
305:     // Implementation of ITypeLibImporterNotifySink.ReportEvent
306:     public Assembly ResolveRef(object typeLib)
```

LISTING 22.4 Continued

```
307:    {
308:      string piaName;
309:      string piaCodebase;
310:      UCOMITypeLib pTypeLib = (UCOMITypeLib)typeLib;
311:
312:      // If we've already loaded the necessary assembly, return it
313:      Assembly returnAssembly = (Assembly)
314:        loadedAssemblies[Marshal.GetTypeLibGuid(pTypeLib).ToString() +
315:        GetTypeLibVersion(pTypeLib)];
316:
317:      // If we're generating a Primary Interop Assembly and this dependent
318:      // assembly is not a Primary Interop Assembly, don't use it
319:      if (returnAssembly != null)
320:      {
321:        if ((options.Flags &
322:          TypeLibImporterFlags.PrimaryInteropAssembly) != 0 &&
323:          returnAssembly.GetCustomAttributes(
324:          typeof(PrimaryInteropAssemblyAttribute), false).Length == 0)
325:        {
326:          // Erase the fact that we found an assembly
327:          returnAssembly = null;
328:        }
329:      }
330:
331:      if (returnAssembly != null)
332:        return returnAssembly;
333:
334:      // Before asking for a reference, attempt to find a Primary Interop
335:      // Assembly for the referenced type library
336:      if (GetPrimaryInteropAssembly(pTypeLib, out piaName, out piaCodebase))
337:      {
338:        // We found one, so load it
339:        returnAssembly = LoadPrimaryInteropAssembly(piaName, piaCodebase);
340:
341:        client.SendMessage(MessageTypes.Notification, "[" +
342:          DateTime.Now.ToString("hh:mm:ss.f") +
343:          "] Successfully referenced PIA for " +
344:          Marshal.GetTypeLibName(pTypeLib), null);
345:
346:        return returnAssembly;
347:      }
348:
349:      // If we're creating a Primary Interop Assembly but no
350:      // Primary Interop Assembly exists for the referenced type library,
351:      // this is a fatal error
```

22

LISTING 22.4   Continued

```
352:        if ((options.Flags & TypeLibImporterFlags.PrimaryInteropAssembly)
353:          != 0)
354:          throw new ApplicationException("No registered Primary Interop " +
355:            "Assembly was found for the dependent type library '" +
356:            Marshal.GetTypeLibName(pTypeLib) + "' with LIBID " +
357:            Marshal.GetTypeLibGuid(pTypeLib) + ". Either locate or create " +
358:            "one first, or choose not to create a Primary Interop Assembly " +
359:            "for the current type library.");
360:
361:        // Ask the client for a filename to satisfy the reference
362:        string filename = client.GetTypeLibReference(
363:          Marshal.GetTypeLibGuid(pTypeLib),
364:          Util.GetDisplayNameForTypeLib(pTypeLib));
365:
366:        if (filename != null)
367:        {
368:          // First treat the file as an assembly
369:          try
370:          {
371:            returnAssembly = Assembly.LoadFrom(filename);
372:            client.SendMessage(MessageTypes.BeginFile,
373:              Util.GetDisplayNameForAssembly(returnAssembly), null);
374:            client.SendMessage(MessageTypes.EndFile,
375:              Util.GetDisplayNameForAssembly(returnAssembly), returnAssembly);
376:            return returnAssembly;
377:          }
378:          catch
379:          {
380:              // Since LoadFrom didn't work, this must be a type library
381:          }
382:        }
383:
384:        // Accept default assembly name, namespace, and version number
385:        if (filename != null)
386:          return Import(filename, null, null, null);
387:        else
388:          return Import(pTypeLib, null, null, null);
389:    }
390: }
```

Lines 1–5 list the System namespace for Version, the System.IO namespace for FileStream and FileNotFoundException, the System.Reflection namespace for Assembly and StrongNameKeyPair, the System.Collections namespace for Hashtable, and System.Runtime.InteropServices for UCOMITypeLib, TypeLibConverter, and its associated types. Lines 8–15 contain the ImportOptions structure which contains several fields that encapsulate the various importing options provided by the application. The first field is a TypeLibImporterFlags type, so it can contain all of the options enabled by the enumeration. The additional four fields support strong naming—two boolean values indicating whether to use a key pair from a file and whether to delay sign the output assembly or assemblies, and two string fields representing the name of the key file or key container if one is specified.

These options don't include setting the assembly name, namespace, or version number because they represent options that apply not only to the type library that's currently being imported but also any dependent type libraries that must be imported to satisfy references. No matter how many dependent type libraries end up getting imported, they will all have the same settings described in the ImportOptions structure. It would not be desirable to have the same assembly name, namespace, or version number applied to multiple type libraries.

Line 18 begins the Importer class, which implements ITypeLibImporterNotifySink. Importer has five private fields containing an ImportOptions structure, a TypeLibConverter instance, the client represented by IToolClient, a hashtable of loaded assemblies, and a string to remember the directory containing an assembly loaded from a filename. The constructor in Lines 27–32 initializes the last three fields, and the Options property in Lines 35–39 gets and sets the options field. The OutputDirectory property in Lines 42–45 enables the client to set the directory where the output assembly and any dependent assemblies can be saved. Although assemblies are saved in a separate step done by the client program, the directory needs to be chosen ahead of time.

The user of the Importer class must pass a valid IToolClient reference for callback purposes, as well as a Hashtable reference that is used to remember all the assemblies that have been loaded. The reason that Import doesn't maintain its own hashtable internally is that another class (Registrar in Listing 22.6) also loads assemblies. Therefore, all the "tool classes" in the upcoming listings follow the pattern of expecting a Hashtable type when constructed.

The Importer class has two Import methods. Both accept parameters for customizing the output assembly's name, namespace, and version on an assembly-by-assembly basis, but the difference is how the input assembly is given. The first version expects a filename containing the type library, and the second version expects a type library loaded in memory (a UCOMITypeLib interface).

The first version of Import in Lines 49–66 attempts to load the type library from its filename by calling Util.LoadTypeLibEx. If that succeeds, it calls the Import overload using the returned UCOMITypeLib reference in Line 65.

The second version of `Import` in Lines 70–185 has a lot of work to do. If we want to provide similar behavior to `TLBIMP.EXE`, there's a lot of extra details to take care of that the `TypeLibConverter` API does not. First, before attempting import, Line 82 checks for the presence of a Primary Interop Assembly for the current type library by calling `Importer.GetPrimaryInteropAssembly`. If one can be found, Lines 84–88 ask the user if he'd like to load the existing Primary Interop Assembly rather than creating a new assembly. This is done using the `IToolClient.AskYesNoQuestion` method, which returns true if the answer is yes and false if the answer is no. If the user decides to load the existing assembly, Line 90 loads it using `Importer.LoadPrimaryInteropAssembly`. After that, a `BeginFile` message and an `EndFile` message are sent to the client immediately because all the work is done. Lines 99–101 add the Primary Interop Assembly to the list of loaded assemblies, and Line 102 returns it. Loading the existing Primary Interop Assembly can be useful in case the user wants to register it, because the application allows the user to register any of the loaded assemblies. The key to this hashtable is a string that consists of the LIBID and version of the would-be-exported type library. Using the LIBID alone would not be enough in case multiple versions of a type library share the same LIBID.

> **CAUTION**
>
> Version 1.0 of `TLBIMP.EXE` does not properly handle a type library that references other type libraries differing by version number only. Once it encounters the first dependent type library with a given LIBID, it incorrectly uses it to satisfy all subsequent references with that LIBID, even if a different version is required. Inside Visual Studio .NET, however, type library import handles this case correctly.

If there is no Primary Interop Assembly already or if the user decides to go ahead with import anyway, Line 107 starts constructing a readable display name for the assembly. The display name either becomes "Interop Assembly for *result of* `Util.GetDisplayNameForTypeLib`" or "Primary Interop Assembly for *result of* `Util.GetDisplayNameForTypeLib`", depending on whether the user elected to generate a Primary Interop Assembly. Line 122 chooses the library name as the default assembly name if none is given, and Line 124 appends the necessary ".dll" because this should be omitted by the string given by the user.

Lines 126–127 send the `BeginFile` message with the type library's display name to indicate that the import process is beginning. Here `outputDirectory` is concatenated with the output assembly filename so the application can remember the fully-qualified filename that an assembly must be saved as. This isn't necessary to be able to save the assembly, but used so the application can first check if a file with the same name already exists and warn the user before saving the assembly. Because the import process always begins with a type library filename and the first overload of Import, the value of outputDirectory will be valid each time the second overload of Import is called for any dependent type libraries because all dependent assemblies must also be saved in the same directory as the original type library.

Line 131 obtains the total number of types in the type library by calling UCOMITypeLib. GetTypeInfoCount and adding that to the IToolClient.ProgressMaximum property so the application's progress bar is scaled appropriately as it receives notifications for each type conversion.

> **TIP**
>
> The progress bar's maximum value is *increased* by the total number of types in the current type library rather than simply set to this value. This needs to be done because Import may be called multiple times for the same assembly if the input type library references other type libraries that need an assembly imported for them. Each time a dependent type library must be imported, the progress bar's capacity needs to be increased to account for a higher number of total types.

Before calling TypeLibConverter.ConvertTypeLibToAssembly, we need to present the strong name data and assembly filename. Import's namespace and version parameters can be left untouched because ConvertTypeLibToAssembly accepts null values to indicate default behavior.

The strong name data is processed in Lines 134–173. Lines 134–160 handle the case for which the user wants to use a key file. Because all we have is a filename (stored in the ImportOptions.KeyFile field), Lines 137–152 attempt to extract the binary data from the file. This involves creating a new FileStream from the file with read access, giving the keyData array of bytes the same length as the number of bytes in the stream, then reading all of those bytes into the array. The try...catch...finally block is used to make sure the FileStream gets closed even if an exception is thrown. If the user chose Use key pair from key file, Lines 157–158 construct a new StrongNameKeyPair from the keyData array and set the array to null. If the user had instead selected Use public key only from key file, then the keyData array is left alone and keyPair is left as null. For the Use key container case, Line 164 constructs a new StrongNameKeyPair directly from the key container name. If the user selected Delay Sign and the key pair is non-null, keyData is set to only the public key bits from the key pair and keyPair is reset to null. Therefore, the combination of Use key pair from key file plus Delay Sign is equivalent to just Use public key only from key file except that in the latter case the key file must *only* contain the public key data, whereas in the first case the key file must contain both the public and private key data.

Finally, Lines 176 and 177 make the call to `TypeLibConverter.ConvertTypeLibToAssembly`. Lines 179–180 send an `EndFile` message with the returned assembly and Lines 181–183 add the assembly to the list of ones loaded.

Lines 189–213 define the `GetPrimaryInteropAssembly` method used earlier in `Import` and used again in `ResolveRef`. The issue with `TypeLibConverter.GetPrimaryInteropAssembly`, as discussed in the "Getting a Primary Interop Assembly" section, is that it requires you to pass in a type library's GUID, version number, and LCID. The means of getting this information from `UCOMITypeLib` is lengthy enough to warrant encapsulating it in a separate function. Therefore, `Importer.GetPrimaryInteropAssembly` takes a `UCOMITypeLib` reference as input and does the work of extracting the information required by `TypeLibConverter`. The resultant Boolean return value and `name` and `codebase` out parameters get propagated back to the caller of `Import.GetPrimaryInteropAssembly`.

Lines 216–237 contain the definition of `GetTypeLibVersion`, which extracts a type library version from a `UCOMITypeLib` instance. This method is used by `Import` for part of the key in the `loadedAssemblies` hashtable.

Lines 241–273 contain the implementation of `LoadPrimaryInteropAssembly`, another method used both by `Import` and `ResolveRef`. This method first attempts to load the Primary Interop Assembly without the help of the codebase (which may or may not exist). Line 249 accomplishes this by calling `Assembly.Load` on the assembly name. If this call fails with a `FileNotFoundException`, then Line 256 attempts to use the codebase if it exists by calling `Assembly.LoadFrom`. If an assembly is successfully loaded, either by `Assembly.Load` or `Assembly.LoadFrom`, Lines 263–264 check to see if the loaded assembly is in fact a Primary Interop Assembly. We do this simply by checking for the presence of at least one `PrimaryInteropAssemblyAttribute` on the assembly.

Line 276 begins the implementation of `ITypeLibImporterNotifySink`'s two methods. `ReportEvent`, in Lines 276–303, simply converts the `ImporterEventKind` message type to our own `MessageTypes` type. In addition, Line 293 updates the progress of type conversions when a `NOTIF_TYPECONVERTED` notification is received. When sending the message in Lines 300–302, we include the current time and the passed-in `HRESULT` value.

`ResolveRef`, in Lines 306–389, begins by checking if we've already loaded the assembly needed to satisfy the reference. Such an assembly gets returned on Line 332 unless the user decided to generate a Primary Interop Assembly and the assembly loaded for the dependent type library is not a Primary Interop Assembly itself. In this case, the `returnAssembly` variable is reset to null in Line 327, because Primary Interop Assemblies may not reference non-Primary Interop Assemblies.

> **CAUTION**
>
> The `TypeLibConverter` implementation does not enforce the rule that Primary Interop Assemblies can only reference other Primary Interop Assemblies, so it is the responsibility of the `ResolveRef` implementer to follow this rule.

If no matching assembly has already been loaded (or if we're generating a Primary Interop Assembly and the matching assembly is not one), Line 336 attempts to find a Primary Interop Assembly for the dependent type library. Regardless of whether the user is generating a Primary Interop Assembly, it's always preferable that the output assembly references Primary Interop Assemblies as much as possible. If a Primary Interop Assembly is found, Line 339 loads it, then Lines 341–344 send a custom `Notification` message before returning it.

If no Primary Interop Assembly could be found for the referenced type library, we continue with the import unless the user is generating a Primary Interop Assembly. Again, this enforces the restriction that Primary Interop Assemblies must not reference non-Primary Interop Assemblies. The next step is to ask the client if she'd like to supply a filename to satisfy the reference. Therefore, `IToolClient.GetTypeLibReference` is called in Lines 362–364. If a filename is returned, it could either correspond to a type library or an assembly. Line 371 attempts to treat it as an assembly's filename by calling `Assembly.LoadFrom`. If this succeeds, we can simply send the appropriate `BeginFile` and `EndFile` messages then return it. If it fails, then the filename must correspond to a type library. Line 386 calls the first overload of `Import` using the filename, and Line 388 calls the second overload of `Import` using the default `UCOMITypeLib` reference if the user chose to accept the default behavior.

The Exporter

The `Export` tab is shown in Figure 22.5, and the progress bar functionality when performing type library export is shown in Figure 22.6.

The `Exporter` class is shown in Listing 22.5.

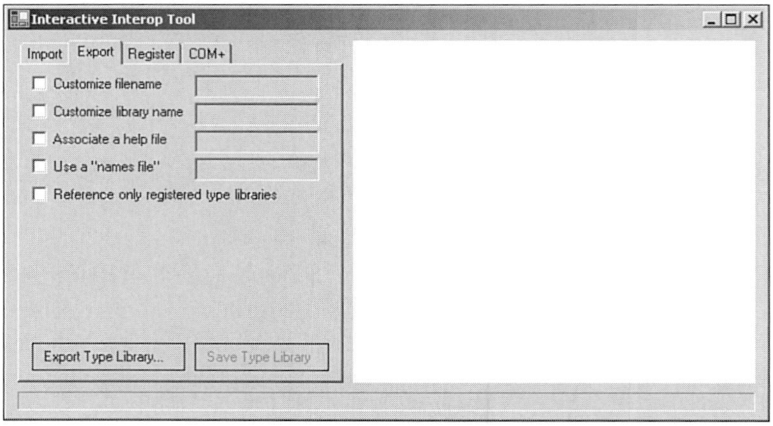

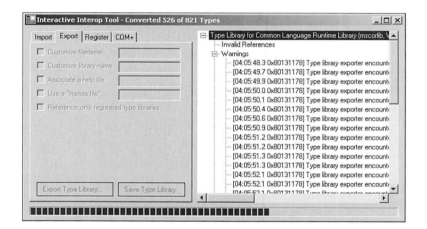

FIGURE 22.5

The Export *tab can be used to export type libraries and save them.*

FIGURE 22.6

The progress bar and caption show progress during type library export.

LISTING 22.5   Exporter.cs. Using the System.Runtime.InteropServices.
TypeLibConverter Class to Export Type Libraries from Assemblies

```
1: using System;
2: using System.IO;
```

LISTING 22.5   Continued

```
 3: using System.Reflection;
 4: using System.Collections;
 5: using System.Runtime.InteropServices;
 6:
 7: // Export Options
 8: public struct ExportOptions
 9: {
10:    public string [] Names;
11:    public TypeLibExporterFlags Flags;
12: }
13:
14: // Creates a type library from an assembly
15: public class Exporter : ITypeLibExporterNotifySink,
16:    ITypeLibExporterNameProvider
17: {
18:    private ExportOptions options;
19:    private TypeLibConverter converter;
20:    private IToolClient client;
21:    private Hashtable loadedTypeLibs;
22:    private string outputDirectory;
23:
24:    // Constructor
25:    public Exporter(IToolClient client, Hashtable loadedTypeLibs)
26:    {
27:      this.client = client;
28:      this.loadedTypeLibs = loadedTypeLibs;
29:      this.converter = new TypeLibConverter();
30:    }
31:
32:    // Property to get/set options
33:    public ExportOptions Options
34:    {
35:      get { return options; }
36:      set { options = value; }
37:    }
38:
39:    // Output directory where type libraries will be saved
40:    public string OutputDirectory
41:    {
42:      set { outputDirectory = value; }
43:    }
44:
45:    // Creates a type library with the given filename, library name,
46:    // and help file from the assembly specified by assemblyFilename
```

LISTING 22.5   Continued

```
47:   public UCOMITypeLib Export(string assemblyFilename, string tlbFilename,
48:     string libraryName, string helpFile)
49:   {
50:     Assembly assembly;
51:
52:     try
53:     {
54:       // Load the assembly
55:       assembly = Assembly.LoadFrom(assemblyFilename);
56:     }
57:     catch
58:     {
59:       throw new ApplicationException("Unable to load the assembly '" +
60:         assemblyFilename + "'.");
61:     }
62:
63:     outputDirectory = Path.GetDirectoryName(assemblyFilename);
64:     return Export(assembly, tlbFilename, libraryName, helpFile);
65:   }
66:
67:   // Creates a type library with the given filename, library name,
68:   // and help file from the loaded input assembly
69:   public UCOMITypeLib Export(Assembly assembly, string tlbFilename,
70:     string libraryName, string helpFile)
71:   {
72:     UCOMITypeLib returnTypeLib;
73:     int numTypes = 0;
74:
75:     // Before beginning export, check if the assembly has a type library
76:     // already embedded as a resource
77:     foreach (FileStream file in assembly.GetFiles())
78:     {
79:       try
80:       {
81:         // Attempt to load a type library
82:         returnTypeLib = Util.LoadTypeLibEx(file.Name,
83:           REGKIND.REGKIND_NONE);
84:
85:         // It worked!
86:         if (client.AskYesNoQuestion("The assembly '" + assembly.FullName +
87:           " contains an embedded type library inside the file '" +
88:           file.Name + "'. Would you like to load this type library " +
89:           "instead of exporting a new one?", true))
90:         {
```

LISTING 22.5   Continued

```
 91:            client.SendMessage(MessageTypes.BeginFile,
 92:              "Embedded Type Library in " + file.Name, null);
 93:            client.SendMessage(MessageTypes.EndFile,
 94:              "Embedded Type Library in " + file.Name, returnTypeLib);
 95:            loadedTypeLibs[Marshal.GetTypeLibGuid(returnTypeLib)]
 96:              = returnTypeLib;
 97:            return returnTypeLib;
 98:          }
 99:        }
100:      catch
101:      {
102:        // There must not be a type library embedded in this file
103:      }
104:    }
105:
106:    // At this point, either none of the assembly's files contain a type
107:    // library or the user selected not to use any of them.
108:
109:    string assemblyDisplayName = "Type Library for " +
110:      Util.GetDisplayNameForAssembly(assembly);
111:
112:    if (tlbFilename == null)
113:      tlbFilename = assembly.GetName().Name + ".tlb";
114:
115:    client.SendMessage(MessageTypes.BeginFile, assemblyDisplayName,
116:      outputDirectory + Path.DirectorySeparatorChar + tlbFilename);
117:
118:    // Get the total number of types for the progress bar
119:    // by tallying the number of types that will be exported
120:    foreach (Type t in assembly.GetTypes())
121:    {
122:      if (Marshal.IsTypeVisibleFromCom(t) && !t.IsImport)
123:        numTypes++;
124:    }
125:
126:    client.ProgressMaximum += numTypes;
127:
128:    // Create a type library from the assembly
129:    returnTypeLib = (UCOMITypeLib)converter.ConvertAssemblyToTypeLib(
130:      assembly,
131:      tlbFilename,
132:      options.Flags,
133:      this);
134:
```

LISTING 22.5   Continued

```
135:      // Change the library name if one is given
136:      if (libraryName != null)
137:        ((ICreateTypeLib)returnTypeLib).SetName(libraryName);
138:
139:      // Add a help file name if one is given
140:      if (helpFile != null)
141:        ((ICreateTypeLib)returnTypeLib).SetHelpFileName(helpFile);
142:
143:      client.SendMessage(MessageTypes.EndFile, assemblyDisplayName,
144:        returnTypeLib);
145:      loadedTypeLibs[Marshal.GetTypeLibGuid(returnTypeLib)] = returnTypeLib;
146:
147:      return returnTypeLib;
148:    }
149:
150:    // Implementation of ITypeLibExporterNotifySink.ReportEvent
151:    public void ReportEvent(ExporterEventKind eventKind, int eventCode,
152:      string eventMsg)
153:    {
154:      MessageTypes messageType;
155:
156:      // Get the MessageType for the corresponding ExporterEventKind
157:      switch (eventKind)
158:      {
159:        case ExporterEventKind.ERROR_REFTOINVALIDASSEMBLY:
160:          messageType = MessageTypes.InvalidRef;
161:          break;
162:        case ExporterEventKind.NOTIF_CONVERTWARNING:
163:          messageType = MessageTypes.Warning;
164:          break;
165:        case ExporterEventKind.NOTIF_TYPECONVERTED:
166:          messageType = MessageTypes.Notification;
167:          // Update the progress for type conversions
168:          client.Progress++;
169:          break;
170:        default:
171:          throw new ApplicationException(
172:            "Encountered unknown ExporterEventKind value.");
173:      }
174:
175:      client.SendMessage(messageType, "[" +
176:        DateTime.Now.ToString("hh:mm:ss.f") + " 0x" +
177:        eventCode.ToString("x") + "] " + eventMsg, null);
178:    }
179:
```

LISTING 22.5   Continued

```
180:    // Implementation of ITypeLibExporterNotifySink.ResolveRef
181:    public object ResolveRef(Assembly assembly)
182:    {
183:      // If we've already loaded the necessary type library, return it
184:      UCOMITypeLib returnTypeLib = (UCOMITypeLib)
185:        loadedTypeLibs[Marshal.GetTypeLibGuidForAssembly(assembly)];
186:
187:      if (returnTypeLib != null)
188:        return returnTypeLib;
189:
190:      // Ask the user for either an assembly or type library to satisfy
191:      // the reference
192:      string filename = client.GetAssemblyReference(
193:        Util.GetDisplayNameForAssembly(assembly));
194:
195:      if (filename != null)
196:      {
197:        try
198:        {
199:          // Load the type library without registering it
200:          returnTypeLib =
201:            Util.LoadTypeLibEx(filename, REGKIND.REGKIND_NONE);
202:        }
203:        catch
204:        {
205:          // Since LoadTypeLibEx didn't work, this must be an assembly.
206:          // Export it with its default filename, library name, and
207:          // help file
208:          returnTypeLib = Export(filename, null, null, null);
209:        }
210:      }
211:      else
212:      {
213:        // Export the assembly passed into ResolveRef with its
214:        // default filename, library name, and help file
215:        returnTypeLib = Export(assembly, null, null, null);
216:      }
217:
218:      return returnTypeLib;
219:    }
220:
221:    // Implementation of ITypeLibExporterNameProvider.GetNames
222:    public string [] GetNames()
223:    {
```

LISTING 22.5   Continued

```
224:     if (options.Names == null)
225:        return new string[]{};
226:     else
227:        return options.Names;
228:   }
229: }
```

Lines 1–5 list the System namespace for Type, DateTime, and ApplicationException, the System.IO namespace for FileStream, the System.Reflection namespace for Assembly, the System.Collections namespace for Hashtable, and System.Runtime.InteropServices for UCOMITypeLib, TypeLibConverter, and its associated types. Lines 8–12 contain the ExportOptions structure which has one additional field besides the TypeLibExporterFlags enumeration—a string array representing identifiers with their desired casing. As with ImportOptions, these represent the options applied to the current assembly as well as any dependent assemblies.

Line 15 begins the Exporter class, which implements ITypeLibExporterNotifySink. It has four private fields—its options structure, the TypeLibConverter instance, the client, and an outputDirectory string. The constructor in Lines 24–29 initialize the middle three fields, the Options property in Lines 31–35 gets and sets the options field, and OutputDirectory property in Lines 38–41 sets the outputDirectory field.

Besides the implementation of the two ITypeLibExporterNotifySink methods, Exporter has two public Export methods—one that operates on a filename containing an assembly's manifest and another that operates on an assembly loaded in memory. Both of these methods also accept three strings to potentially customize the output type library's filename, library name, and help file. (The help file is just chosen arbitrarily as an example of an additional customization that can be made using the ICreateTypeLib interface.)

The first Export method in Lines 45–62 loads the assembly from the filename using Assembly.LoadFrom. If this succeeds, it calls the Export overload with the returned Assembly instance in Line 61. The second Export method in Lines 66–138 does the bulk of the work. Before attempting to export a type library, Export checks if the assembly contains a type library embedded as a resource. Type libraries are often embedded in COM DLLs, and there's no reason why one can't be embedded in a managed DLL. Currently, however, there are no Microsoft tools that do this automatically.

DIGGING DEEPER

Check out the .NET Framework SDK for a sample called "TlbGen" that demonstrates how to embed a type library in an assembly's file.

Using APIs Instead of SDK Tools

CHAPTER 22

1091

22

USING APIs
INSTEAD OF SDK
TOOLS

If the author of an assembly went to the trouble of embedding a type library, she probably wants it to be used by COM rather than a user exporting a fresh one. (After all, it may be customized in some way such as having IDL custom attributes.) To give the user full control, however, we call IToolClient.AskYesNoQuestion in Lines 83–86 to alert the user that an embedded type library exists and enable him to choose whether to load that type library or export a new one based on the assembly's metadata. Why bother even loading the type library if we're not going to export a new one? The user may want to register the embedded type library (as if using REGASM.EXE's /tlb option) and, due to this application's structure, loading the embedded type library and adding it to the TreeView control is the only way to support this.

Remember, however, that an assembly may consist of multiple files and any one of them may contain a type library (although its likely that a developer would place it in the file containing the manifest). Therefore, Lines 74–99 iterate through each file in the assembly by calling Assembly.GetFiles, which returns an array of FileStream objects. On each FileStream object, Lines 79–80 call LoadTypeLibEx using FileStream's Name property to get the filename.

If LoadTypeLibEx fails (because the file doesn't contain a type library), it throws an exception thanks to the PreserveSig=false in its DllImport attribute. In this case, the catch statement in Lines 95–98 does nothing, so the foreach statement simply moves on to the next file if one exists. If LoadTypeLibEx succeeds, then it returns a valid UCOMITypeLib reference. If the client answers "Yes" to the question asked in Lines 83–86, Lines 88–91 send the client a BeginFile message immediately followed by an EndFile message, because no exporting needs to be performed.

Unlike our importer, our exporter does not need to maintain a list of loaded type libraries because the TypeLibConverter object never calls ResolveRef for the same dependent assembly twice during a single type library export. It could have maintained a list anyway, so loaded type libraries can potentially be reused from subsequent runs of the type library exporter. But because ResolveRef is almost never called in export scenarios, this listing doesn't bother.

> **CAUTION**
>
> Type libraries returned by LoadTypeLibEx cannot be modified and saved. In other words, the object returned does not implement ICreateTypeLib.

If we've reached Line 104, then either the assembly had no embedded type library or the user elected not to load any of them. Therefore, it's time to prepare for exporting the type library. Lines 104–105 construct a display name for the type library, and Line 108 chooses a name for the type library if one wasn't chosen by the user. The choice of assembly name plus ".tlb" is the same default chosen by TLBEXP.EXE. Because ConvertAssemblyToTypeLib requires a type library name, choosing a default name is the responsibility of its caller.

Lines 110–111 send the client a BeginFile message, then Lines 115–119 calculate the total number of types that will be exported so the progress bar's capacity can be set appropriately in Line 121.

Finally, Lines 124–125 call the ConvertAssemblyToTypeLib method with the input assembly, the chosen type library filename, the Flags filed of the ExportOptions structure, and a reference to the current instance because it implements ITypeLibExporterNotifySink. If the call succeeds, Lines 135–136 send the client an EndFile message, and Line 137 returns the type library.

To showcase the ability to make modifications above and beyond what TLBEXP.EXE can do, Lines 128–133 call ICreateTypeLib methods on the returned type library because we know that the object returned by ConvertAssemblyToTypeLib implements this interface. Line 129 calls SetName if the user chose a name for the library, and Line 133 calls SetHelpFileName if the user chose a name for the help file.

Line 141 begins the implementation of ITypeLibExporterNotifySink's two methods. The implementation of ReportEvent is identical to the implementation of it from the Importer class in the previous listing. ResolveRef, in Lines 171–204, begins by asking the client for a reference to the needed assembly in Lines 177–178. If the client returns a filename, we first attempt to load it as a type library in Lines 185–186 and use it as the type library to return. If LoadTypeLibEx fails, then the filename must correspond to an assembly, so we call Export with that filename on Line 193. By passing null for the filename, library name, and help file parameters, we accept the default behavior. If the client did not choose a file to satisfy the reference, then we call the Export overload with the assembly instance passed to ResolveRef in Line 200. Line 203 returns the type library no matter which of the three ways it was obtained. Unfortunately, type library references satisfied by TypeLibConverter cannot be communicated to the client because ResolveRef is never called.

Lines 207–213 contain the implementation of ITypeLibExporterNameProvider's GetNames method. This simply returns the array field of the options structure. If it happens to be null, however, it instead returns an empty array to prevent causing an exception.

The Registrar

The Register tab is shown in Figure 22.7.

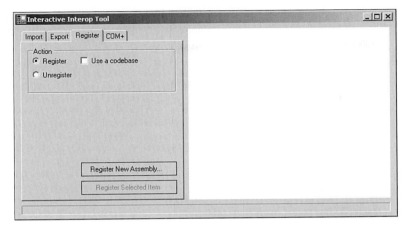

FIGURE 22.7
The Register *tab can be used to register and unregister assemblies and type libraries.*

The Registrar class is shown in Listing 22.6.

LISTING 22.6   Registrar.cs. Using the System.Runtime.InteropServices.
RegistrationServices Class to Register and Unregister Assemblies as COM Components

```
 1: using System;
 2: using System.Reflection;
 3: using System.Collections;
 4: using System.Runtime.InteropServices;
 5:
 6: // Registration Options
 7: public struct RegisterOptions
 8: {
 9:    public AssemblyRegistrationFlags Flags;
10: }
11:
12: // Registers and unregisters assemblies for COM
13: public class Registrar
14: {
15:    private RegisterOptions options;
16:    private RegistrationServices registration;
17:    private IToolClient client;
18:    private Hashtable loadedAssemblies;
19:
20:    // Constructor
21:    public Registrar(IToolClient client, Hashtable loadedAssemblies)
```

LISTING 22.6   Continued

```
22:    {
23:      this.client = client;
24:      this.loadedAssemblies = loadedAssemblies;
25:      this.registration = new RegistrationServices();
26:    }
27:
28:    // Property to get/set options
29:    public RegisterOptions Options
30:    {
31:      get { return options; }
32:      set { options = value; }
33:    }
34:
35:    // Registers the assembly given by the filename
36:    public string Register(string assemblyName)
37:    {
38:      return Register(LoadAndDisplayAssembly(assemblyName));
39:    }
40:
41:    // Unregisters the assembly given by the filename
42:    public string Unregister(string assemblyName)
43:    {
44:      return Unregister(LoadAndDisplayAssembly(assemblyName));
45:    }
46:
47:    // Registers the loaded assembly
48:    public string Register(Assembly assembly)
49:    {
50:      try
51:      {
52:        // Register the assembly
53:        if (registration.RegisterAssembly(assembly, options.Flags))
54:          return "Types registered successfully.";
55:        else
56:          return "There were no types to register.";
57:      }
58:      catch (TargetInvocationException ex)
59:      {
60:        // Construct a better message for registration function error
61:        throw new Exception("Error from custom registration function: " +
62:          ex.InnerException.Message, ex.InnerException);
63:      }
64:    }
65:
66:    // Unregisters the loaded assembly
```

Using APIs Instead of SDK Tools

CHAPTER 22

1095

22

USING APIS
INSTEAD OF SDK
TOOLS

LISTING 22.6   Continued

```
67:    public string Unregister(Assembly assembly)
68:    {
69:      try
70:      {
71:        // Unregister the assembly
72:        if (registration.UnregisterAssembly(assembly))
73:          return "Types unregistered successfully.";
74:        else
75:          return "There were no types to unregister.";
76:      }
77:      catch (TargetInvocationException ex)
78:      {
79:        // Construct a better message for unregistration function error
80:        throw new Exception("Error from custom unregistration function: " +
81:          ex.InnerException.Message, ex.InnerException);
82:      }
83:    }
84:
85:    // Loads an assembly from the input filename and notifies
86:    // the client so it can display it.
87:    private Assembly LoadAndDisplayAssembly(string assemblyName)
88:    {
89:      Assembly returnAssembly;
90:
91:      try
92:      {
93:        // Load the assembly
94:        returnAssembly = Assembly.LoadFrom(assemblyName);
95:      }
96:      catch
97:      {
98:        throw new ApplicationException("Unable to load the assembly '" +
99:          assemblyName + "'.");
100:     }
101:
102:     // Construct a nice "display name" for the assembly
103:     string assemblyDisplayName = "Assembly: " +
104:       Util.GetDisplayNameForAssembly(returnAssembly);
105:
106:     // Notify the client that the assembly has been loaded.
107:     // Give both beginning and ending notifications since there's no
108:     // progress to report.
109:     client.SendMessage(MessageTypes.BeginFile, assemblyDisplayName, null);
110:     client.SendMessage(MessageTypes.EndFile, assemblyDisplayName, null);
```

LISTING 22.6   Continued

```
111:        loadedAssemblies[Marshal.GetTypeLibGuidForAssembly(returnAssembly)]
112:          = returnAssembly;
113:
114:        return returnAssembly;
115:    }
116: }
```

Lines 1–4 list the System namespace for ApplicationException and Exception, the System.Reflection namespace for Assembly, the System.Collections namespace for Hashtable, and System.Runtime.InteropServices for RegistrationServices and AssemblyRegistrationFlags. The RegisterOptions structure in Lines 7–10 only contains a single field of the AssemblyRegistrationFlags enumeration type because there are no other options used by the Registrar class.

Line 13 begins the Registrar class, which begins with the usual pattern of members, constructor, and Options property. Besides these, Registrar has four public methods—two versions of Register and two versions of Unregister. The first version of Register and Unregister in Lines 36–45 take a filename as input and calls the private LoadAndDisplayAssembly method defined further in the listing in order to obtain an Assembly instance to pass to the respective Register/Unregister overload.

The Register overload in Lines 48–64 calls RegistrationServices.RegisterAssembly with the input Assembly instance and the AssemblyRegistrationFlags enumeration value contained in the options type. If RegisterAssembly returns true, Register returns a simple success message. Otherwise, it explains that there were no types to register.

The catch statement in Line 58 catches a TargetInvocationException and re-throws it with a more helpful message. Why? Because RegisterAssembly throws a TargetInvocationException when an exception is thrown from a class's custom registration function. For clients that only display an exception's message (such as the graphical client in this example), the user would only see "Exception has been thrown by the target of an invocation." which is not very helpful. With the code in Lines 61–62, the user can now see the original exception message. Just so the original exception and its other information isn't lost (such as a stack trace), the new exception's inner exception is set to the TargetInvocationException's inner exception.

The Unregister overload in Lines 67–83 calls RegistrationServices.UnregisterAssembly with the input Assembly instance and returns the same sort of messages that Register returns. This method also handles TargetInvocationExceptions the same way.

The `LoadAndDisplayAssembly` method in Lines 87–115 first loads the assembly from the input filename using `Assembly.LoadFrom`, then notifies the client that it has been loaded. In Lines 103–104 it uses `Util.GetDisplayNameForAssembly` to show an appropriate name, then in Lines 109–110 it sends `BeginFile` and `EndFile` messages all at once. This is done because there's no way to report progress during registration. Finally, the loaded assembly is returned on Line 114.

> **CAUTION**
>
> The `RegistrationServices` class does not support registering dynamic assemblies, even after they have been saved to disk! This is caused by `AssemblyBuilder's` `GetExportedTypes` method throwing a `System.NotSupportedException` despite the fact that this method is supported by the base `Assembly` class. Therefore, to register a dynamic assembly you must save it then reload it from disk before calling `RegistrationServices.RegisterAssembly`.

The COM+ Installer

The COM+ tab is shown in Figure 22.8.

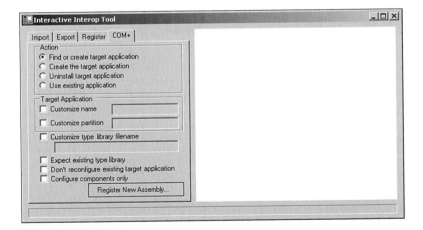

FIGURE 22.8
The COM+ tab can be used to install and uninstall assemblies as COM+ applications.

The `ComPlusInstaller` class has the easiest implementation of all the tool classes. Listing 22.7 contains the code.

LISTING 22.7   ComPlusInstaller.cs. Using the System.EnterpriseServices.
RegistrationHelper Class to Install and Uninstall Assemblies as COM+ Applications

```
 1: using System.EnterpriseServices;
 2:
 3: // COM+ Installation Options
 4: public struct ComPlusInstallerOptions
 5: {
 6:   public string ApplicationName;
 7:   public string PartitionName;
 8:   public string TypeLibName;
 9:   public InstallationFlags Flags;
10: }
11:
12: // Installs and uninstalls assemblies for COM+
13: public class ComPlusInstaller
14: {
15:   private ComPlusInstallerOptions options;
16:   private RegistrationHelper registration;
17:   private IToolClient client;
18:
19:   // Constructor
20:   public ComPlusInstaller(IToolClient client)
21:   {
22:     this.client = client;
23:     this.registration = new RegistrationHelper();
24:   }
25:
26:   // Property to get/set options
27:   public ComPlusInstallerOptions Options
28:   {
29:     get { return options; }
30:     set { options = value; }
31:   }
32:
33:   // Installs the assembly
34:   public string Install(string assemblyName)
35:   {
36:     registration.InstallAssembly(assemblyName,
37:       ref options.ApplicationName, options.PartitionName,
38:       ref options.TypeLibName, options.Flags);
39:
40:     if (options.ApplicationName == null)
41:     {
42:       return "The assembly contains no ServicedComponent " +
43:         "types to register.";
```

LISTING 22.7 Continued

```
44:      }
45:
46:      if (options.PartitionName == null)
47:      {
48:        return "Successfully registered '" + assemblyName +
49:          "' as the application '" + options.ApplicationName +
50:          "' with type library '" + options.TypeLibName + "'.";
51:      }
52:      else
53:      {
54:        return "Successfully registered '" + assemblyName +
55:          "' as the application '" + options.ApplicationName +
56:          "' with partition '" + options.PartitionName +
57:          "' and type library '" + options.TypeLibName + "'.";
58:      }
59:    }
60:
61:    // Uninstalls the assembly
62:    public string Uninstall(string assemblyName)
63:    {
64:      registration.UninstallAssembly(assemblyName,
65:        options.ApplicationName, options.PartitionName);
66:      return "Successfully unregistered '" + assemblyName + "'.";
67:    }
68: }
```

Line 1 lists the System.EnterpriseServices namespace used for RegistrationHelper and InstallationFlags. Lines 4–10 contain the structure of options, which contains strings for customizing the application name, partition name and type library name in addition to the options exposed by the InstallationFlags enumeration.

Line 13 begins the ComPlusInstaller class, which begins with the usual pattern of members, constructor, and Options property. This time, however, the client member type won't be used. Besides these members, ComPlusInstaller has two methods—Install and Uninstall—which simply call the respective InstallAssembly and UninstallAssembly methods on the RegistrationHelper class.

The Install method, beginning on Line 34, spends most of its work formatting a message to return. If InstallAssembly doesn't throw an exception, then it returns one of three possible messages. One explains that there was nothing to register (if the application name is null after the call), one omits the partition name if it's null after the call, and one shows all the information. The `Uninstall` method in Lines 62–67 simply calls `UninstallAssembly` and returns a standard message if no exception is thrown.

Unfortunately, an assembly is loaded when calling `InstallAssembly` or `UninstallAssembly`, but we're not notifying the client because we never get to touch the `Assembly` instance itself. Therefore, the list displayed by the client application is not representative off all the assemblies that are loaded and sitting around in our application domain.

The Windows Forms Client

The remaining piece of the application is contained in `MainForm.cs`, which contains the `MainForm` class that displays the graphical user interface. This class implements `IToolClient` and uses the `Importer`, `Exporter`, `Registrar`, and `ComPlusInstaller` classes. This listing is too long to include in this chapter, but in this section we'll discuss a few interesting points.

`MainForm` executes type library import and export on a background thread so the user interface can be updated appropriately during the process. The implementation of `IToolClient.SendMessage`, which gets called by `Importer` and `Exporter` on the separate thread, calls the base `System.Windows.Forms.Control.Invoke` method to marshal the call back to the original thread before doing its work. This is necessary because it updates part of the user interface.

DIGGING DEEPER

Windows Forms controls are apartment threaded due to their ties to Win32. This is why the `STAThreadAttribute` is needed for Windows Forms applications in languages that don't set the attribute by default like Visual Basic .NET. This means that a control's members may only be invoked on the same thread the control was created on. Because multithreading is practically a must in labor-intensive graphical applications, `System.Windows.Forms.Control` has three methods that allow you to marshal a call originating in a different thread back to the thread that the control was created on. These three methods are `Invoke` (used in `MainForm.cs`) for synchronous calls, and `BeginInvoke` and `EndInvoke` for asynchronous calls. These methods (in addition to `CreateGraphics`) are `Control`'s only members that may be called from any thread.

Below is the `exportOpenButton_Click` method, which is called when the user clicks Export Type Library... on the Export tab. This method creates and starts a new background thread:

```
// Called when user clicks "Export Type Library..." on Export tab
private void exportOpenButton_Click(object sender, System.EventArgs e)
{
```

```
    // Do the exporting on the background thread
    backgroundThread = new Thread(new ThreadStart(Export));
    backgroundThread.IsBackground = true;
    backgroundThread.ApartmentState = ApartmentState.MTA;
    backgroundThread.Start();
    tabControl1.Enabled = false;
}
```

It's important that the thread's apartment state is set to MTA, because it would otherwise be set to STA as a result of interactions with Windows Forms. Once the background thread terminates, the STA would be destroyed without properly notifying the CLR, so any subsequent use of the in-memory type library on the main thread would throw an `InvalidComObjectException` with the message, "COM object that has been separated from its underlying RCW cannot be used." Forcing the background thread to be an MTA thread avoids this problem. Another approach would be to keep the background STA thread alive for as long as we need to use the objects created on it.

Conclusion

This chapter presented the APIs that enable the same actions as the commonly used SDK tools, and presented a basic but realistic example of using this functionality in a way that may be more appealing than the way in which the available tools work.

DIGGING DEEPER

Another tool related to COM Interoperability that has corresponding APIs exposed in the .NET Framework is the ActiveX Control Importer (`AXIMP.EXE`). By using the `System.Windows.Forms.Design.AxImporter` class in the `System.Windows.Forms` assembly, you can programmatically perform the work of `AXIMP.EXE`. This isn't too compelling, however, because `AXIMP.EXE` already generates source code that is fully and easily customizable.

One could imagine going even further with such an application. For example, reflection could be used to browse and display type information for the loaded assemblies, or OLE Automation type description interfaces could be used to browse and display type information for loaded type libraries. A tool could then allow the user to selectively tweak types or members to provide customizations in an easier fashion than the methods that exist today. Settings in the various options structures could even be chosen based on the contents of the assembly or type library. For example, the `Importer` class could check if the input type library contained any `SAFEARRAY` parameters and then ask the user whether she wants them imported as single-dimensional arrays or `System.Array` types.

Comprehensive Examples

IN THIS PART

23 Writing a .NET Arcade Game Using DirectX   1105

24 Writing .NET Visualizations for Windows Media
    Player   1195

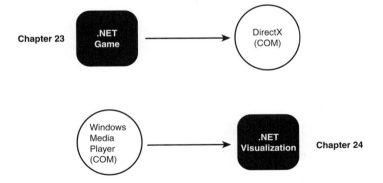

Writing a .NET Arcade Game Using DirectX

IN THIS CHAPTER

- The User's Perspective   1106
- The Programmer's Perspective   1108
- DirectX Interaction   1112
- The Game Class   1119
- Sounds and Pictures   1133
- Layers   1150
- Screens   1155
- The Actors   1157
- Using the Game Class   1166
- E-mail Attack—The Advanced Version   1171

In this chapter, we have some fun and write an arcade game in C# using Microsoft DirectX. DirectX is a technology consisting of low-level APIs for graphics, sound, music, and much more. Because DirectX exposes its functionality through COM objects, we can use it naturally in managed code. Although previous chapters have discussed DirectX, this chapter uses it in the context of a real application.

> **TIP**
>
> At the time of writing, .NET DirectX components have been announced in beta form that provide APIs designed for .NET languages. After these components are released, they will be the preferred way to take advantage of DirectX in managed code. In the meantime, COM Interoperability provides access to the same COM APIs that you use from unmanaged code today.

The DirectX SDK has two versions of type information—header files for C/C++ clients and a type library for Visual Basic 6 clients. The type library contains types with more VB-friendly features that wrap the raw C++ types. (For example, GUID parameters are replaced with String parameters.) Thus, the type library and associated extra functionality is called *DirectX for VB*. The application in this chapter uses the type library meant for Visual Basic 6, because it's the easiest way to take advantage of DirectX's functionality. At the end of the chapter, we'll generate the type information manually to demonstrate removing the dependency on the DirectX for VB Interop Assembly.

Running the application in this chapter requires DirectX 7 or later, which can be downloaded from msdn.microsoft.com/directx/. The full source code and supporting files can be downloaded from this book's Web site.

We begin by describing the game in "The User's Perspective," then giving an overview of how the code is organized in "The Programmer's Perspective." The remaining sections examine each part of the application in depth.

The User's Perspective

The game in this chapter is called *E-mail Attack*. In it, the player takes on the role of a virus that tries to infect as many e-mail messages as possible. The messages (represented as envelopes) appear in various places on the screen and only last for a short time, constantly shrinking until they disappear. When envelopes become close to disappearing, they flash to alert the player. The virus (represented as a bug) can move up, down, left, and right, stepping from one envelope to another. Stepping on an envelope infects it, turning it to a sickly green color. If the player moves to a location without an envelope or stands on an envelope that disappears, the player loses a life. To make things harder, the screen scrolls forward, and if the player doesn't keep up, the player loses a life when the bug goes off the left edge of the screen. Figure 23.1 shows a screen shot of the game being played. The screen consists of several layers that scroll at different speeds to provide the illusion of depth.

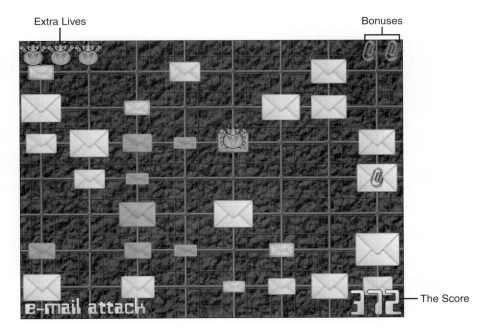

FIGURE 23.1

In the E-mail Attack game, you try to infect e-mail messages by stepping on them.

The e-mail messages sometimes contain attachments, represented as rotating paper clips. When stepping on an envelope with an attachment, the player gets a bonus that can be used later. Having a bonus means that the player can move to a location without an envelope, and an envelope will appear instantly underneath the player's feet. Bonuses are stored in the top right corner of the screen, as shown in Figure 23.1. You can have at most 10 bonuses. When you get the 11th bonus, an extra life is awarded and the bonuses are reset to zero. Extra lives are stored in the top left corner of the screen.

One point is awarded for each envelope infected, 100 points for each bonus obtained, and 1000 points for each extra life obtained. The highest score obtained on the current computer is persisted in the Windows Registry. The player can never conquer the game; it continues until the player loses every life. The player starts each game with three extra lives and one bonus.

The Programmer's Perspective

The game uses several pictures (saved as Windows bitmaps) and .wav sound files that can be found at the book's Web site (in addition to the complete source code). For example, the layered game screen comprises the four individual bitmaps shown in Figure 23.2.

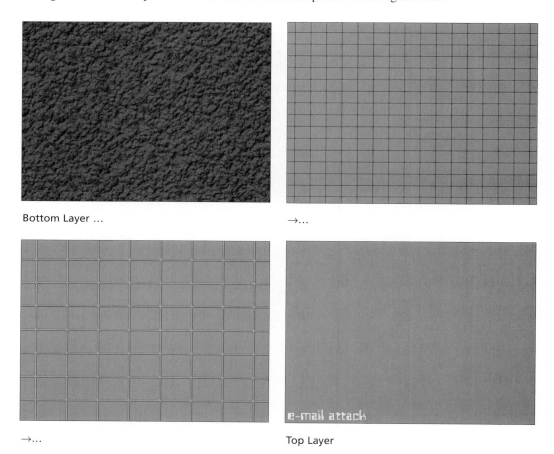

Bottom Layer ...   →...

→...   Top Layer

FIGURE 23.2
The four layers comprising the game's main screen.

These layers scroll at different speeds, giving an illusion of depth known as *parallax*. The bitmaps shown in Figure 23.2, like many of the other bitmaps used for the game, need transparent areas so pictures underneath can be seen. (Otherwise, we'd only ever see the top layer.)

Transparent areas are indicated with red, which is treated specially by the application. In graphics terms, the bitmaps use a red *color key* to mark transparent areas. The picture for the bottom layer has no transparent areas, whereas the picture for the top layer is almost completely transparent.

The game also uses a handful of bitmaps for screens shown at times other than normal game play. These screens, whose bitmaps are shown in Figure 23.3, are used when the application is first started, when the game is paused, and after the player loses a life.

FIGURE 23.3
The Title screen, Paused screen, and "Press Any Key" screen use full-screen bitmaps.

The application consists of 17 source files, listed below in Table 23.1. It is designed with simplicity in mind, so it could be changed to be more general or more efficient, if desired.

TABLE 23.1   E-mail Attack's 17 Source Files, Grouped into Seven Areas

Area	Files
DirectX Interaction	**LISTING 23.1** Util.cs contains the Util class, which contains a higher-level abstraction for DirectX.
The Game	**LISTING 23.2** Enums.cs contains enumerations used throughout the application.
	LISTING 23.3 Game.cs contains the Game class that represents the game, containing all the pictures, sounds, and basic logic.
Sounds and Pictures	**LISTING 23.4** Sound.cs contains the Sound class that represents a playable sound.
	LISTING 23.5 Picture.cs contains the Picture class that represents a simple picture.
	LISTING 23.6 AnimatedPicture.cs contains the AnimatedPicture class that represents a picture that changes over time.
	LISTING 23.7 AnimatedEnvelopePicture.cs contains the AnimatedEnvelopePicture class that represents the animated picture used for each envelope.
	LISTING 23.8 NumberPicture.cs contains the NumberPicture class, which displays a picture capable of displaying any number.
Layers	**LISTING 23.9** Layer.cs contains the Layer class that represents a scrolling layer.
	LISTING 23.10 GroundLayer.cs contains the GroundLayer class that represents the scrolling layer on which the player and envelopes reside.
	LISTING 23.11 FrontLayer.cs contains the FrontLayer class that represents the front-most stationary layer with the extra lives, bonuses, and score.
Screens	**LISTING 23.12** Screen.cs contains the Screen class that represents a stationary screen.
	LISTING 23.13 IntroScreen.cs contains the IntroScreen class which represents the first game screen containing the current score and high score.
The Actors	**LISTING 23.14** Character.cs contains the Character class that represents the virus moved by the user.
	LISTING 23.15 Envelope.cs contains the Envelope class that represents each e-mail message

TABLE 23.1 Continued

Area	Files
Using the Game Class	**LISTING 23.16** Win32.cs contains classes in the Win32 namespace. The classes contains PInvoke methods used by the EmailAttack class.
	LISTING 23.17 EmailAttack.cs contains the EmailAttack class with the Main entry point.

The pictures are all managed by the Game class and shared by the other classes because each one holds onto a system resource. For example, rather than each Envelope object containing its own AnimatedEnvelopePicture instance, the Game class has a static AnimatedEnvelopePicture instance shared by each Envelope object.

To compile the program, first run the type library importer on the DirectX 7 for VB type library, contained in DX7VB.DLL in your Windows system directory (such as C:\Windows\system32) once you have DirectX 7 or 8 installed. In the example, we give the output Interop Assembly the name and namespace DirectX:

```
TlbImp dx7vb.dll /out:DirectX.dll
```

When you have the Interop Assembly, place all the source files for this chapter from this book's Web site in the same directory, excluding the files in the Advanced folder. (These are the 17 files listed in Table 23.1.) Then you can compile all the source files as follows:

```
csc /out:Game.exe /t:winexe *.cs /r:DirectX.dll
➥/r:System.Windows.Forms.dll /r:System.dll
```

If compiling from within the Visual Studio .NET IDE, create a new C# Windows Application, add all the source files, and reference the DirectX for VB Interop Assembly using the *Add Reference* dialog.

After successfully compiling the application, make sure that all 11 bitmap files (.bmp) and all seven sound files (.wav) from the Web site are in the same directory as the output Game.exe executable.

> **CAUTION**
>
> If you fail to place all the picture and sound files in the same directory as the game executable, an unhandled exception will occur when the application starts.

DirectX Interaction

To begin examining the source code, let's look at a portion of the code that directly uses the DirectX COM objects. As mentioned in Table 23.1, the Util class handles the interaction with DirectX, providing higher-level methods that can be used throughout the application. These methods are:

- Initialize. Initializes DirectX and the DirectX objects that we use. This must be called before using any of the other methods.

- CreateSoundBufferFromFile. Returns a DirectX sound buffer with the contents of a .wav sound file.

- CreateSurfaceFromFile. Returns a DirectX surface with the contents of a bitmap.

- DrawSurface. Draws the specified portion of the input surface on the back buffer. This must eventually be followed by a call to RenderComplete to display the contents on the screen.

- ResizeAndDrawSurface. Draws the specified portion of the input surface stretched or shrunken to the specified size on the back buffer. This must eventually be followed by a call to RenderComplete in order to display the contents on the screen.

- RenderComplete. Swaps the image on the back buffer onto the front buffer so it can be displayed on the screen.

- IsTimeToMove. This doesn't involve DirectX, but encapsulates the commonly used functionality that signals when it's time to move an object with a given frequency.

The Util class also has two public fields unrelated to DirectX but useful throughout the application:

- Counter. A number that is updated with every frame, used for timing animations.

- RandomNumber. A field of type System.Random, enabling the generation of pseudo-random numbers.

LISTING 23.1   Util.cs. The Util Class Handles Interaction with DirectX So the Rest of the Application Doesn't Have To

```
1: using DirectX;
2: using System;
3: using System.Runtime.InteropServices;
4:
5: public class Util
6: {
7:    // A counter that is updated with every frame
8:    public static int Counter;
```

LISTING 23.1 Continued

```
 9:    // A pseudo-random number
10:    public static Random RandomNumber;
11:
12:    // Main DirectX objects
13:    private static DirectX7 directX;
14:    private static DirectDraw7 directDraw;
15:    private static DirectSound directSound;
16:
17:    // Two surfaces used for double-buffered animation
18:    private static DirectDrawSurface7 frontBuffer;
19:    private static DirectDrawSurface7 backBuffer;
20:
21:    // This must be called before using any of the other Util methods
22:    public static void Initialize(IntPtr hWnd)
23:    {
24:      // Create the main DirectX objects
25:      directX = new DirectX7();
26:      directDraw = directX.DirectDrawCreate("");
27:      directSound = directX.DirectSoundCreate("");
28:
29:      // Set our cooperative level for drawing and sound
30:      directDraw.SetCooperativeLevel(hWnd.ToInt32(),
31:        CONST_DDSCLFLAGS.DDSCL_EXCLUSIVE |
32:        CONST_DDSCLFLAGS.DDSCL_FULLSCREEN);
33:      directSound.SetCooperativeLevel(hWnd.ToInt32(),
34:        CONST_DSSCLFLAGS.DSSCL_NORMAL);
35:
36:      // Set the display mode
37:      directDraw.SetDisplayMode(Screen.Width, Screen.Height, 16, 0, 0);
38:      // Create the primary surface with one back buffer
39:      DDSURFACEDESC2 description = new DDSURFACEDESC2();
40:      DDSCAPS2 capabilities = new DDSCAPS2();
41:
42:      description.lSize = Marshal.SizeOf(description);
43:      description.lFlags = CONST_DDSURFACEDESCFLAGS.DDSD_CAPS |
44:                            CONST_DDSURFACEDESCFLAGS.DDSD_BACKBUFFERCOUNT;
45:      description.ddsCaps.lCaps =
46:        CONST_DDSURFACECAPSFLAGS.DDSCAPS_PRIMARYSURFACE |
47:        CONST_DDSURFACECAPSFLAGS.DDSCAPS_FLIP |
48:        CONST_DDSURFACECAPSFLAGS.DDSCAPS_COMPLEX;
49:      description.lBackBufferCount = 1;
50:
51:      frontBuffer = directDraw.CreateSurface(ref description);
52:      // Get the single back buffer.
```

23

WRITING A .NET
ARCADE GAME
USING DIRECTX

LISTING 23.1   Continued

```
53:       capabilities.lCaps = CONST_DDSURFACECAPSFLAGS.DDSCAPS_BACKBUFFER;
54:       capabilities.lCaps2 = 0;
55:       capabilities.lCaps3 = 0;
56:       capabilities.lCaps4 = 0;
57:       backBuffer = frontBuffer.GetAttachedSurface(ref capabilities);
58:
59:       // Initialize the pseudo-random number generator.
60:       RandomNumber = new Random();
61:   }
62:
63:   // Creates a surface from the input bitmap
64:   public static DirectDrawSurface7 CreateSurfaceFromFile(
65:       string bitmapFile, bool hasTransparentColor, ref RECT size)
66:   {
67:       DirectDrawSurface7 dxSurface = null;
68:
69:       try
70:       {
71:         // Create the DirectDraw surface
72:         DDSURFACEDESC2 description = new DDSURFACEDESC2();
73:         description.lSize = Marshal.SizeOf(description);
74:         description.lFlags = CONST_DDSURFACEDESCFLAGS.DDSD_CAPS |
75:           CONST_DDSURFACEDESCFLAGS.DDSD_WIDTH |
76:           CONST_DDSURFACEDESCFLAGS.DDSD_HEIGHT;
77:         description.ddsCaps.lCaps =
78:           CONST_DDSURFACECAPSFLAGS.DDSCAPS_OFFSCREENPLAIN;
79:         dxSurface = directDraw.CreateSurfaceFromFile(
80:           bitmapFile, ref description);
81:
82:         // Save the picture's dimensions
83:         size.Left = 0;
84:         size.Top = 0;
85:         size.Right = description.lWidth;
86:         size.Bottom = description.lHeight;
87:
88:         if (hasTransparentColor)
89:         {
90:           // Get the pixel format
91:           DDPIXELFORMAT format = new DDPIXELFORMAT();
92:           format.lSize=Marshal.SizeOf(format);
93:           dxSurface.GetPixelFormat(ref format);
94:
95:           // Set the color key to Red
```

LISTING 23.1 Continued

```
 96:            int KeyColor = format.lRBitMask;
 97:            DDCOLORKEY key = new DDCOLORKEY();
 98:            key.low = KeyColor;
 99:            key.high = KeyColor;
100:            dxSurface.SetColorKey(CONST_DDCKEYFLAGS.DDCKEY_SRCBLT, ref key);
101:          }
102:        }
103:      catch (Exception e)
104:      {
105:        throw new ApplicationException("Failed to create surface for " +
106:          bitmapFile + ".", e);
107:      }
108:      return dxSurface;
109:    }
110:
111:    // Returns true if it's time to move, based on the
112:    // global counter and input frequency.
113:    public static bool IsTimeToMove(int frequency)
114:    {
115:      if (Counter % frequency == 0)
116:        return true;
117:      else
118:        return false;
119:    }
120:
121:    // After drawing to the back buffer with DrawSurface or
122:    // ResizeAndDrawSurface, this must be called to show the
123:    // result on the front buffer.
124:    public static void RenderComplete()
125:    {
126:      try
127:      {
128:        frontBuffer.Flip(null, CONST_DDFLIPFLAGS.DDFLIP_WAIT);
129:      }
130:      catch
131:      {
132:          try { directDraw.RestoreAllSurfaces(); }
133:          catch { // Attempt to continue
134:          }
135:      }
136:    }
137:
```

LISTING 23.1   Continued

```
138:   // Draw the portion of the surface specified with r at location (x,y).
139:   // This must eventually be followed by a call to RenderComplete.
140:   public static void DrawSurface(DirectDrawSurface7 surface, int x,
141:     int y, RECT r, bool hasTransparentColor)
142:   {
143:     CONST_DDBLTFASTFLAGS transparentFlagFast;
144:
145:     if (hasTransparentColor)
146:       transparentFlagFast = CONST_DDBLTFASTFLAGS.DDBLTFAST_SRCCOLORKEY;
147:     else
148:       transparentFlagFast = 0;
149:
150:     try
151:     {
152:       backBuffer.BltFast(x, y, surface, ref r,
153:         CONST_DDBLTFASTFLAGS.DDBLTFAST_WAIT | transparentFlagFast);
154:     }
155:     catch
156:     {
157:         try { directDraw.RestoreAllSurfaces(); }
158:         catch { // Attempt to continue
159:         }
160:     }
161:   }
162:
163:   // Draw the portion of the surface specified with the RECT dest using
164:   // the location and size specified in the RECT source.
165:   // This must eventually be followed by a call to RenderComplete.
166:   public static void ResizeAndDrawSurface(DirectDrawSurface7 surface,
167:     RECT source, RECT dest, bool hasTransparentColor)
168:   {
169:     CONST_DDBLTFLAGS transparentFlag;
170:
171:     if (hasTransparentColor)
172:       transparentFlag = CONST_DDBLTFLAGS.DDBLT_KEYSRC;
173:     else
174:       transparentFlag = 0;
175:
176:     try
177:     {
178:       backBuffer.Blt(ref dest, surface, ref source,
179:         CONST_DDBLTFLAGS.DDBLT_WAIT | transparentFlag);
180:     }
181:     catch
```

LISTING 23.1   Continued

```
182:    {
183:        try { directDraw.RestoreAllSurfaces(); }
184:        catch { // Attempt to continue
185:        }
186:    }
187:  }
188:
189:  // Create a sound buffer from the input .WAV file.
190:  public static DirectSoundBuffer
191:    CreateSoundBufferFromFile(string waveFile)
192:  {
193:    try
194:    {
195:      WAVEFORMATEX format = new WAVEFORMATEX();
196:
197:      DSBUFFERDESC description = new DSBUFFERDESC();
198:      description.lSize = Marshal.SizeOf(description);
199:      description.lFlags = CONST_DSBCAPSFLAGS.DSBCAPS_CTRLFREQUENCY |
200:        CONST_DSBCAPSFLAGS.DSBCAPS_CTRLPAN |
201:        CONST_DSBCAPSFLAGS.DSBCAPS_CTRLVOLUME |
202:        CONST_DSBCAPSFLAGS.DSBCAPS_STATIC;
203:      return directSound.CreateSoundBufferFromFile(waveFile,
204:        ref description, out format);
205:    }
206:    catch (Exception e)
207:    {
208:      throw new ApplicationException("Failed to create buffer for "
209:        + waveFile + ".", e);
210:    }
211:  }
212:
213:  // Play a sound buffer
214:  public static void PlayBuffer(DirectSoundBuffer buffer)
215:  {
216:    CONST_DSBSTATUSFLAGS dwStatus = buffer.GetStatus();
217:
218:    // Ensure that the buffer isn't lost
219:    if ((dwStatus & CONST_DSBSTATUSFLAGS.DSBSTATUS_BUFFERLOST) != 0)
220:      buffer.restore();
221:
222:    buffer.Play(CONST_DSBPLAYFLAGS.DSBPLAY_DEFAULT);
223:  }
224: }
```

23

WRITING A .NET ARCADE GAME USING DIRECTX

Lines 1–3 use three namespaces—DirectX for a variety of objects, System for IntPtr and Random, and System.Runtime.InteropServices for Marshal. Lines 13–15 declare the three main DirectX objects used. DirectX7 is the parent object from which we create the others. This object's methods are also implemented as static entry points, and these are what are typically used from an unmanaged C++ application. DirectDraw7 is an interface used for graphics, and DirectSound is an interface used for sound, both obtained from methods of DirectX7.

Lines 18 and 19 define two *surfaces* known as a front buffer (also called the primary surface) and a back buffer. The front buffer is the area in memory containing the image displayed on the screen. The back buffer is the area in memory on which the game is rendered. This enables us to perform drawing in a temporary area that doesn't affect the contents of the screen. When we're finished drawing on the back buffer, the two buffers are swapped so the contents of the back buffer now reside on the front buffer, and on the screen. This process is known as *page flipping*, and is the key to smooth animation. DirectX supports many different page flipping schemes that can have many back buffers. In this application, we use the simplest double-buffered approach.

The Initialize method on Lines 22–61 creates the necessary objects, initializes the screen, and sets up the buffers. Lines 30–37 set the *cooperative level* and display mode, indicating that we're taking over the entire screen and setting its resolution to Screen.Width by Screen.Height (defined as 640 by 480 in Listing 23.12). Lines 39–57 creates the front buffer and single back buffer, and Line 60 initializes the pseudo-random number generator.

The CreateSurfaceFromFile method is implemented in Lines 64–109. This method creates a new surface from the input bitmap file in Lines 72–80. If successful, it saves the dimensions of the surface in the by-reference RECT parameter in Lines 83–86. As in Windows programming, DirectX heavily relies on bounding rectangles when drawing objects. Because not everything we want to draw is rectangular, many of the bitmaps used in the application use a red color key to indicate transparent areas. Lines 91–100 tell DirectX to treat red as a color key if the caller of the method passed true for hasTransparentColor. This is done by getting the format of the surface, setting the color key to red using the 1RBitMask bit mask, then calling SetColorKey on the surface object.

The IsTimeToMove method on Lines 113–119 returns true every time the Counter variable increases by the number of steps indicated by frequency. This is achieved with the modulo operator, because the result of Counter % frequency will equal zero at the appropriate intervals. This method is used throughout the game to assist with timing the animations. The Counter variable is updated on a regular basis by the EmailAttackForm class in Listing 23.17.

The RenderComplete method on Lines 124–136 implements the page flipping by swapping the front and back buffers when called. The DrawSurface method on Lines 140–161 draws on the back buffer. This is done using the BltFast method, performing a "fast bit block transfer"—

copying of pixels from one surface to another. It's fast because no resizing of images is done. The ResizeAndDrawSurface method in Lines 166–187, on the other hand, calls the Blt method which resizes the input surface if necessary. The CreateSoundBufferFromFile method in Lines 190–211 is analogous to the CreateSurfaceFromFile method, creating a DirectSoundBuffer object from the input .wav file. Finally, the PlayBuffer method in Lines 214–223 plays whatever DirectSoundBuffer instance is passed in.

This is all the interaction we need with DirectX to implement the E-mail Attack arcade game. If we wanted to update the application to use APIs specific to DirectX 8 or the new .NET APIs, this file is where almost all of the changes would go. For more information about DirectX and its multitude of APIs, consult the online reference at msdn.microsoft.com/directx.

The Game Class

The Game class is the largest portion of the application. The never-ending field of envelopes is managed by the Game class as a wrap-around array of Envelope objects. The width of the array is just enough so that once a column of envelopes disappears off the left side, they reappear as if they are new envelopes when coming into view on the right side. This is pictured in Figure 23.4.

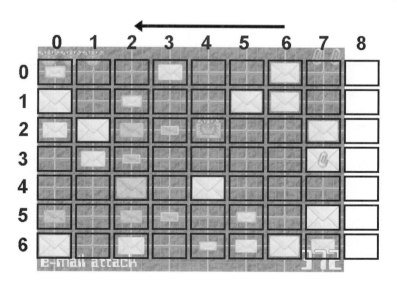

FIGURE 23.4
The wrap-around envelope grid provides the illusion of a never-ending field of envelopes.

Whereas the user sees envelopes as being present or not, the code sees each envelope as always being present but either visible or invisible. Understanding this minor difference should make the rest of the code clearer. Before examining the Game class, let's view Enums.cs in Listing 23.2, a file that contains two important enumerations.

LISTING 23.2   Enums.cs. The GameStates and Moves Enumerations Used Throughout the Application

```
1: // The 4 different states during game execution
2: public enum GameStates
3: {
4:   Paused,      // The paused screen is displayed
5:   Running,     // The game is being played
6:   NotStarted,  // The title screen is displayed
7:   TryAgain     // The screen shown in-between lives is displayed
8: }
9:
10: // The 4 valid player moves
11: public enum Moves
12: {
13:   Up,
14:   Down,
15:   Left,
16:   Right
17: }
```

The game is always in one of four states, listed in the GameStates enumeration. It begins in the NotStarted state, then enters the Running state after the user presses any key (but Esc) to begin. The TryAgain state occurs after the loss of a life and before the user presses a key to begin the next life. Finally, when all lives are lost, the game once again enters the NotStarted state. As the name implies, the Paused state is entered whenever the user presses the Pause key during the Running state.

The player can move one of four ways—up, down, left, and right—and this is captured by the Moves enumeration.

Now we're ready to see the Game class in Listing 23.3. All of Game's members are static except for the constructor, finalizer, and Dispose method. Game has the following public fields:

- Player. The virus character that the player controls.
- EnvelopeGrid. The matrix of envelopes.
- BonusPicture. The rotating paperclip picture used for bonuses.
- EnvelopePicture. The animated picture used for each envelope.

- `PlayerPicture`. The animated picture used for the player.
- `ScorePicture`. The picture used to display the score.

`Game` also has the following public properties:

- `State`. The current state of game execution; one of the values of the `GameStates` enumeration.
- `NumLives`. The number of lives remaining.
- `NumBonuses`. The number of bonuses remaining.
- `Score`. The current score.
- `HighScore`. The highest score achieved on the current computer.

The class has the following methods:

- `Game`. The constructor which initializes the game and the objects it contains.
- `MovePlayer`. Moves the player and determines what to do afterwards, such as adjusting the score or killing the player if it was moved into a spot without a visible envelope.
- `CheckForDeath`. Check to see if the player died in a scenario that doesn't involve moving—going off the left edge of the screen or staying on an envelope that disappears.
- `Render`. Draw the contents of the current frame.
- `Dispose`. The implementation of `IDisposable.Dispose`, which causes all resources to be released.
- `KillPlayer`. A private method that ends the current life, beginning a dying animation.

The `Game` class also has a bunch of private fields:

- `titleScreen`, `pauseScreen`, and `tryAgainScreen`. The screens shown in Figure 23.3.
- `layers`. An array of independently scrolling layers.
- `state`, `highScore`, `numLives`, `numBonuses`, and `score`. Fields that correspond to the public properties listed earlier.
- `moveSound`, `infectSound`, `getBonusSound`, `useBonusSound`, `invalidMoveSound`, `lostLifeSound`, and `extraLifeSound`. Sounds played when different activities occur.

LISTING 23.3   `Game.cs`. The `Game` Class is the Glue That Holds Everything Together

```
1: using System;
2: using Microsoft.Win32;
3:
4: public class Game : IDisposable
5: {
```

23

WRITING A .NET
ARCADE GAME
USING DIRECTX

LISTING 23.3   Continued

```
 6:    // Number of envelopes in the grid horizontally
 7:    public const int GridWidth = 9;
 8:    // Number of envelopes in the grid vertically
 9:    public const int GridHeight = 7;
10:    // Space between envelopes
11:    public const int EnvelopePadding = 6;
12:    // Space between the top of the screen and the topmost row of envelopes
13:    public const int TopSpace = 26;
14:    // Space between the left edge of the screen and
15:    // the leftmost column of envelopes
16:    public const int LeftSpace = 3;
17:    // Number of frames between each movement of the scrolling ground
18:    public const int ScrollFrequency = 2;
19:    // Space between digits in the ScorePicture
20:    public const int DigitPadding = 4;
21:    // Height of digits in the ScorePicture
22:    public const int DigitHeight = 44;
23:    // Maximum width of the digits in the ScorePicture
24:    public const int MaxDigitWidth = 30;
25:    // Width of each digit in the ScorePicture, 0 to 9
26:    public readonly int [] DigitWidths =
27:      new int[]{27, 13, 28, 24, 30, 26, 27, 26, 27, 28};
28:
29:    // The player
30:    public static Character Player;
31:    // The grid of envelopes
32:    public static Envelope [,] EnvelopeGrid;
33:    // The picture for each bonus
34:    public static AnimatedPicture BonusPicture;
35:    // The picture for each envelope
36:    public static AnimatedEnvelopePicture EnvelopePicture;
37:    // The picture for the player
38:    public static AnimatedPicture PlayerPicture;
39:    // The picture for the score
40:    public static NumberPicture ScorePicture;
41:
42:    // The first screen shown
43:    private static IntroScreen titleScreen;
44:    // The pause screen
45:    private static Screen pauseScreen;
46:    // The screen shown after each life lost
47:    private static Screen tryAgainScreen;
48:
49:    // The scrolling layers
```

LISTING 23.3 Continued

```
50:    private static Layer [] layers;
51:    // The current state of the game
52:    private static GameStates state;
53:    // Number of lives remaining
54:    private static int numLives;
55:    // Number of bonuses remaining
56:    private static int numBonuses;
57:    // The current score
58:    private static int score;
59:    // The high score, stored in the Windows Registry
60:    private static int highScore;
61:
62:    // Sound made when the player moves
63:    private static Sound moveSound;
64:    // Sound made when the player infects an envelope
65:    private static Sound infectSound;
66:    // Sound made when the player gets a bonus
67:    private static Sound getBonusSound;
68:    // Sound made when the player uses a bonus
69:    private static Sound useBonusSound;
70:    // Sound made when the player makes an invalid move
71:    private static Sound invalidMoveSound;
72:    // Sound made when the player loses a life
73:    private static Sound lostLifeSound;
74:    // Sound made when the player gains an extra life
75:    private static Sound extraLifeSound;
76:
77:    // Initializes the pictures and sounds, and displays the first screen
78:    public Game(IntPtr hWnd)
79:    {
80:      // Initialize the Util helper class.
81:      Util.Initialize(hWnd);
82:
83:      // Create the screens.
84:      titleScreen = new IntroScreen("title.bmp");
85:      pauseScreen = new Screen("paused.bmp");
86:      tryAgainScreen = new Screen("tryagain.bmp");
87:
88:      // Create the pictures.
89:      EnvelopePicture = new AnimatedEnvelopePicture("envelope.bmp");
90:      BonusPicture = new AnimatedPicture("bonus.bmp", true, 21, 3, 2);
91:      PlayerPicture = new AnimatedPicture("character.bmp", true, 2, 1, 2);
92:      ScorePicture = new NumberPicture("digits.bmp", true, DigitWidths,
93:        MaxDigitWidth, DigitPadding);
```

Listing 23.3 Continued

```
 94:
 95:      // Create the layers.
 96:      layers = new Layer[4];
 97:      layers[0] = new Layer("layer1.bmp", false, ScrollFrequency * 4);
 98:      layers[1] = new Layer("layer2.bmp", true, ScrollFrequency * 2);
 99:      layers[2] = new GroundLayer("layer3.bmp", true, ScrollFrequency);
100:      layers[3] = new FrontLayer("layer4.bmp");
101:
102:      // Fill the grid with envelopes.
103:      EnvelopeGrid = new Envelope[GridWidth, GridHeight];
104:      for (int i = 0; i < GridWidth; i++)
105:        for (int j = 0; j < GridHeight; j++)
106:          EnvelopeGrid[i,j] = new Envelope(
107:            LeftSpace + i * (EnvelopePicture.Width + EnvelopePadding),
108:            TopSpace + j * (EnvelopePicture.Height + EnvelopePadding),
109:            layers[2].Frequency);
110:
111:      // Create the sounds.
112:      moveSound = new Sound("move.wav");
113:      infectSound = new Sound("infect.wav");
114:      getBonusSound = new Sound("getbonus.wav");
115:      useBonusSound = new Sound("usebonus.wav");
116:      invalidMoveSound = new Sound("invalidmove.wav");
117:      lostLifeSound = new Sound("lostlife.wav");
118:      extraLifeSound = new Sound("extralife.wav");
119:
120:      // Create the player.
121:      Player = new Character();
122:
123:      highScore = -1;
124:      score = 0;
125:      State = GameStates.NotStarted;
126:    }
127:
128:    // Disposes the game
129:    ~Game()
130:    {
131:      Dispose();
132:    }
133:
134:    // Disposes the game
135:    public void Dispose()
136:    {
137:      // Since we're cleaning up now, suppress finalization
```

LISTING 23.3 Continued

```
138:      GC.SuppressFinalize(this);
139:
140:      foreach (Layer l in layers)
141:        l.Dispose();
142:
143:      BonusPicture.Dispose();
144:      EnvelopePicture.Dispose();
145:      PlayerPicture.Dispose();
146:      ScorePicture.Dispose();
147:
148:      titleScreen.Dispose();
149:      pauseScreen.Dispose();
150:      tryAgainScreen.Dispose();
151:
152:      moveSound.Dispose();
153:      infectSound.Dispose();
154:      getBonusSound.Dispose();
155:      useBonusSound.Dispose();
156:      invalidMoveSound.Dispose();
157:      lostLifeSound.Dispose();
158:      extraLifeSound.Dispose();
159:    }
160:
161:    // Returns the current state
162:    public static GameStates State
163:    {
164:      get { return state; }
165:      set
166:      {
167:        if (value == GameStates.NotStarted)
168:        {
169:          if (Score > HighScore) HighScore = Score;
170:        }
171:        else if (value == GameStates.TryAgain)
172:        {
173:          numLives--;
174:
175:          // Check for game over
176:          if (numLives < 0)
177:          {
178:            // Call the property setter again
179:            State = GameStates.NotStarted;
180:            return;
181:          }
```

LISTING 23.3   Continued

```
182:        }
183:        else if (value == GameStates.Running)
184:        {
185:          if (state != GameStates.Paused)
186:          {
187:            // Re-initialize the layers,
188:            // envelopes, and player
189:            foreach (Layer l in layers)
190:              l.Reset();
191:
192:            foreach (Envelope m in EnvelopeGrid)
193:              m.Reset();
194:
195:            Player.Reset();
196:          }
197:
198:          if (state == GameStates.NotStarted)
199:          {
200:            score = 0;
201:            numLives = 3;
202:            numBonuses = 1;
203:            ScorePicture.SetPosition(Screen.Width,
204:              Screen.Height - DigitPadding - DigitHeight, false);
205:          }
206:        }
207:        state = value;
208:      }
209:    }
210:
211:    // Returns the number of lives remaining
212:    public static int NumLives
213:    {
214:      get { return numLives; }
215:    }
216:
217:    // Returns the number of bonuses remaining
218:    public static int NumBonuses
219:    {
220:      get { return numBonuses; }
221:    }
222:
223:    // Returns the current score
224:    public static int Score
225:    {
```

LISTING 23.3   Continued

```
226:      get { return score; }
227:    }
228:
229:    // Gets/sets the highest score achieved on the machine
230:    public static int HighScore
231:    {
232:      get
233:      {
234:        if (highScore >= 0)
235:        {
236:          // We don't need to check the registry since
237:          // we must have obtained the value previously
238:          return highScore;
239:        }
240:        else
241:        {
242:          // Get the value from the registry.  If the value doesn't
243:          // already exist, set it to zero.
244:          RegistryKey key = null;
245:          object registryValue = null;
246:
247:          try
248:          {
249:            key = Registry.LocalMachine.OpenSubKey(
250:              "SOFTWARE\\.NET and COM", true);
251:
252:            if (key == null)
253:              key = Microsoft.Win32.Registry.LocalMachine.CreateSubKey(
254:                "SOFTWARE\\.NET and COM");
255:
256:            registryValue = key.GetValue("HighScore");
257:            if (registryValue == null)
258:            {
259:              key.SetValue("HighScore", 0);
260:              registryValue = 0;
261:              highScore = 0;
262:            }
263:          }
264:          catch { highScore = 0;  return 0; }
265:          finally { if (key != null) key.Close(); }
266:
267:          return (int)registryValue;
268:        }
269:      }
```

LISTING 23.3   Continued

```
270:        set
271:        {
272:          // Save the high score
273:          highScore = value;
274:
275:          // Place the high score in the registry.
276:          RegistryKey key = null;
277:
278:          try
279:          {
280:            key = Registry.LocalMachine.OpenSubKey(
281:              "SOFTWARE\\.NET and COM", true);
282:
283:            if (key == null)
284:              key = Microsoft.Win32.Registry.LocalMachine.CreateSubKey(
285:                "SOFTWARE\\.NET and COM");
286:
287:            key.SetValue("HighScore", highScore);
288:          }
289:          catch { }
290:          finally { if (key != null) key.Close(); }
291:        }
292:      }
293:
294:      // Moves the player and determines what to do afterwards
295:      public static void MovePlayer(Moves move)
296:      {
297:        if (!Player.IsDying && Player.Move(move))
298:        {
299:          // The player has moved, so check for the presence
300:          // of a visible envelope underneath.
301:
302:          Envelope currentEnvelope = Player.EnvelopeUnderneath;
303:
304:          if (currentEnvelope.IsVisible)
305:          {
306:            if (currentEnvelope.HasAttachment)
307:            {
308:              // Remove the attachment from the envelope and add it
309:              // to the player's list of bonuses
310:
311:              currentEnvelope.HasAttachment = false;
312:              currentEnvelope.IsInfected = true;
313:              numBonuses++;
```

LISTING 23.3   Continued

```
314:
315:            // On the 11th bonus, remove all of them and add
316:            // an extra life
317:            if (numBonuses == 11)
318:            {
319:              numBonuses = 0;
320:              numLives++;
321:              score += 1000;
322:              extraLifeSound.Play();
323:            }
324:            else
325:            {
326:              score += 100;
327:              getBonusSound.Play();
328:            }
329:          }
330:          else if (!currentEnvelope.IsInfected)
331:          {
332:            currentEnvelope.IsInfected = true;
333:            score++;
334:            infectSound.Play();
335:          }
336:          else
337:          {
338:            // No points are given for stepping on an
339:            // already-infected envelope
340:            moveSound.Play();
341:          }
342:        }
343:        else
344:        {
345:          // If the envelope is invisible, the player is still alive
346:          // if there are any bonuses stored
347:          if (numBonuses > 0)
348:          {
349:            // Make a visible envelope right under the player
350:            currentEnvelope.MakeVisibleAndInfected();
351:            numBonuses--;
352:            useBonusSound.Play();
353:          }
354:          else
355:          {
356:            // The player dies
357:            KillPlayer();
```

LISTING 23.3   Continued

```
358:            }
359:          }
360:        }
361:      else
362:      {
363:        invalidMoveSound.Play();
364:      }
365:    }
366:
367:    // Check to see if the player died in the scenarios in which a key press
368:    // doesn't cause it: going off the left edge of the screen, and staying
369:    // on an envelope that disappears.
370:    public static void CheckForDeath()
371:    {
372:      if ((Player.LocationX + PlayerPicture.Width < 0) ||
373:          !Player.EnvelopeUnderneath.IsVisible)
374:      {
375:        KillPlayer();
376:      }
377:    }
378:
379:    // Kill the player
380:    private static void KillPlayer()
381:    {
382:      lostLifeSound.Play();
383:      Player.Kill();
384:    }
385:
386:    // Draw the contents of the current frame
387:    public static void Render()
388:    {
389:      if (state == GameStates.Running)
390:      {
391:        foreach (Layer l in layers)
392:          l.Render();
393:
394:        Util.RenderComplete();
395:      }
396:      else if (state == GameStates.TryAgain)
397:      {
398:        tryAgainScreen.Render();
399:      }
400:      else if (state == GameStates.NotStarted)
401:      {
```

LISTING 23.3   Continued

```
402:          titleScreen.Render();
403:       }
404:       else if (state == GameStates.Paused)
405:       {
406:          pauseScreen.Render();
407:       }
408:    }
409: }
```

Lines 1 and 2 list two namespaces—System for IDisposable and IntPtr, and Microsoft.Win32 for RegistryKey. Lines 7–24 define many public constants used by this class and others. These constants specify the characteristics of the envelope grid, the ground's scrolling speed, and characteristics of the digits used for the score display. The DigitWidths readonly field in Line 26 functions much like a constant; the const keyword couldn't be used because an array is a complex type. Lines 30–75 define the many fields described earlier.

Lines 78–126 contain the constructor for Game, which must be called before using any of its static members. The constructor requires a Windows handle to the current window. This handle tells Windows which window to draw the game's frames on. The constructor begins by calling Util.Initialize, the helper method that handles the details of setting up DirectX. Lines 84–86 create the full-screen Screen objects, Lines 89–93 create the pictures shared by the layers, grid, and player, and Lines 96–100 create the layers. The screens and pictures are initialized with bitmap files in the local directory. The last layer is a stationary FrontLayer, the next layer is a GroundLayer which scrolls at the speed given by the ScrollFrequency constant, and the first two are regular Layers that scroll twice as fast as the layer in front of it. This gives the parallax effect described earlier. Lines 103–109 create the grid of Envelope objects and initialize each one with its location. Lines 112–118 initialize Sound objects with .wav files in the local directory, and Line 121 initializes the player's Character object. Finally, Lines 123–125 initialize highScore to a dummy value, set the current score to zero, and set the games state as NotStarted.

Lines 129–159 contain the class's finalizer and the implementation of IDisposable.Dispose. These two methods do the same thing—release any resources. In this case, we call the Dispose method for each object belonging to Game that implements IDisposable.

Lines 162–209 contain the implementation of the State property. The get accessor is simple, returning the value of the private state field. The set accessor sets the value of the state field in Line 207, but it also modifies the values of private members depending on which state we're entering and which state we're leaving. If the game is entering the NotStarted state, we check to see if the current score is better than the high score and update the high score if necessary.

The update never happens when the game first starts because the current score is initialized to zero and the high score is initialized to –1, but this check is important for when this state is entered after the game has been played at least once. If the game is entering the TryAgain state (Lines 171–182), this means that the player has just died. Thus, the number of lives remaining is decremented and we check to see if the game is over. If it's over, we set the State property to NotStarted which causes the setter to be invoked again. If the game is entering the Running state (Lines 183–205), we take a different action depending on the current state. If we're leaving any state but Paused, the layers, envelopes, and player are reset to initial values that correspond to the beginning of a turn. If we're in the NotStarted state, we do additional initialization of the current score, lives remaining, and bonuses remaining. The position of the ScorePicture is also set to the bottom right corner. If we're leaving the Paused state, nothing special needs to be done; the fact that the private field is set to Paused is enough.

Lines 212–227 contain the NumLives, NumBonuses, and Score properties which simply return the value of the corresponding private field in a get accessor. This is done so other classes can view but can't modify these values.

> **TIP**
>
> Use public read-only properties (properties with only get accessors) in conjunction with private fields when other classes shouldn't be able to modify the values of the fields.

The HighScore property in Lines 230–292 gets and sets the value of the private highScore field and uses the Windows Registry to persist the high score value. The get accessor only checks the registry the first time it's called and only if the set accessor hasn't been called, because this is the only time the highScore field is less than zero. If highScore is greater than or equal to zero we return it, otherwise we get the value from the registry in Lines 244–267. This uses the Microsoft.Win32.RegistryKey class to open a key and get/set a HighScore value. If the HighScore value doesn't already exist in the registry (as in the first time the game is run on a computer), the value is added and initialized to zero. If something goes wrong when trying to access the registry (such as insufficient user permissions), we swallow the exception and simply return a high score of zero. The set accessor works in a similar way, saving the high score in the private highScore field (so the get accessor always returns the up-to-date value) and persisting the value in the registry. If an error occurs with registry access, the score won't be persisted. The result of doing this in the getter and setter is that a user without sufficient registry permissions can still play the game without errors, and the high score will simply apply to the currently running game instance only.

Lines 295–365 contain the first method—MovePlayer. In the if statement on Line 297, we first check to make sure that the player isn't dying. If the player is currently dying, this means that a special animation is occurring and we don't want the user to be able to move around. Thus, the second portion of the if statement moves the player only if the first part evaluated to true. The call to Player.Move returns true if the move was valid. If the player is dying or if the move is invalid, we play the sound corresponding to an invalid move in Line 363. Otherwise, we check the envelope that is now underneath the player in Line 302 to figure out how to proceed. If the envelope is visible, then the player hasn't died. If the envelope has an attachment, we remove it from the envelope, mark it as infected, and increment the number of the bonuses. If the player already collected 10 bonuses, we clear them all and add an extra life. This causes the score to increment by 1000 and play a special sound (Lines 320 and 321). If the player doesn't have that many bonuses, we increment the score by 100 and we play a different sound (Lines 326 and 327). Finally, if the envelope was already infected, we don't add any points to the score and play the normal sound for movement. Lines 343–359 handle the case in which the player moved to an invisible envelope. If there are any bonuses remaining, an envelope is made visible under the player's feet and the number of bonuses remaining is decremented. If there are no bonuses remaining, the player is killed.

Lines 370–377 contain the CheckForDeath method, which simply kills the player if one of two conditions are met—either the player has scrolled off the left edge of the screen or the envelope has vanished underneath the player. Both of these situations can occur without the player moving. Lines 380–384 contain the KillPlayer method, used by CheckForDeath and MovePlayer. This method simply plays the appropriate sound then calls the Kill method on the Character class which will take care of the rest.

The final method—Render—is on Lines 387–408. This method delegates to other Render methods depending on the current state. If the game is in the Running state, we render each layer in Lines 391 and 392, followed by a call to Util.RenderComplete. In any other state, we call the Render method on the appropriate Screen object. No call to RenderComplete is necessary because this is handled by each Screen's Render method.

Sounds and Pictures

Let's now look at the classes that represent sounds and pictures, represented in Figure 23.5. There's only one kind of sound, but four kinds of pictures. The Picture base class represents a simple static picture, and is used by the Layer and Screen classes. The three classes deriving from Picture—AnimatedPicture, AnimatedEnvelopePicture, and NumberPicture each specialize the picture in a slightly different way, as you'll see in the following listings. These five classes are dependent on DirectX because the pictures contain protected DirectDrawSurface7 and RECT types and Sound contains a private DirectSoundBuffer type.

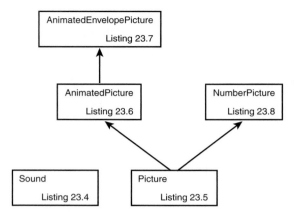

FIGURE 23.5

Five classes used for sounds and pictures.

Listing 23.4 contains the Sound class. This is a simple class with three public methods:

- Sound. The constructor, which creates the object from a .wav sound file.
- Play. Plays the sound.
- Dispose. The implementation of IDisposable.Dispose, which releases the DirectSoundBuffer COM object.

LISTING 23.4   Sound.cs. The Sound Class Encapsulates a Sound File

```
 1: using DirectX;
 2: using System;
 3: using System.Runtime.InteropServices;
 4:
 5: public class Sound : IDisposable
 6: {
 7:   private DirectSoundBuffer buffer;  // The DirectX sound buffer
 8:
 9:   // Creates the sound from the .WAV file
10:   public Sound(string waveFile)
11:   {
12:     try
13:     {
14:       buffer = Util.CreateSoundBufferFromFile(waveFile);
15:     }
16:     catch { // If we can't create the sound, silently fail
17:     }
18:   }
19:
```

LISTING 23.4   Continued

```
20:   // Disposes the sound
21:   public void Dispose()
22:   {
23:      Marshal.ReleaseComObject(buffer);
24:   }
25:
26:   // Plays the sound
27:   public void Play()
28:   {
29:      if (buffer != null)
30:         Util.PlayBuffer(buffer);
31:   }
32: }
```

Lines 1–3 list three namespaces—DirectX for DirectSoundBuffer, System for IDisposable and GC, and System.Runtime.InteropServices for Marshal. Line 7 declares the private buffer that is passed to the Util class from Listing 23.1.

The constructor in Lines 10–18 attempts to initialize buffer by calling Util.CreateSoundBufferFromFile. This method could throw an exception, but we silently fail because the inability to create a sound should not be a fatal error. Instead, the game can continue and emit no sound when it normally should be occurring. (A debug assertion would be a nice thing to add here, however.) Lines 21–24 contain the Dispose method, which has a raw resource to dispose, held by the COM object represented by buffer. To release the resource immediately we need to release the COM object using Marshal.ReleaseComObject.

DIGGING DEEPER

Notice that Listing 23.4 and later listings don't follow the typical .NET pattern of implementing a finalizer that does the same thing as the IDisposable.Dispose method, with the implementation of Dispose also calling GC.SuppressFinalize. This pattern doesn't have much value when the only thing that needs to be released is a COM object. That's because the purpose of the pattern is to avoid leaking resources when clients forget to call Dispose when finished with an object; rather than releasing resources immediately, they get released at some later point.

But COM objects wrapped by RCWs *do* get released eventually anyway, so there's no leak that needs to be avoided. If users really need instant release of a COM object, then they would have to call Dispose anyway. Otherwise, there's not much difference between waiting for an RCW to be garbage collected versus waiting for its container class to be garbage collected. Plus, finalizers should be avoided when they are not necessary, because they have a negative impact on the performance of garbage collection.

Lines 27–31 contain the Play method, which either plays the sound or silently exits if buffer isn't initialized. Util.PlayBuffer does the dirty work of making the sound play.

Listing 23.5 contains the Picture class. Picture has the following protected fields:

- dxSurface. The "raw" surface used by DirectX.
- size. The size of the picture, stored as the RECT type used by DirectX.
- hasTransparentColor. True if the picture uses red for a color key, false otherwise.

Picture has the following public properties:

- Width. The width of the picture, in pixels.
- Height. The height of the picture, in pixels.

The class also contains the following methods:

- Picture. The constructor, which creates the object from a bitmap file.
- DrawAt. Draws the picture at the given location.
- ResizeAndDrawAt. Draws the picture at the given location, stretched or shrunken to the given size.
- Dispose. The implementation of IDisposable.Dispose, which releases the DirectX surface.
- ClippedRectangle. A protected method that chops off the necessary portion of the picture if part of it is off the left or right side of the screen.

LISTING 23.5   Picture.cs. The Picture Class Represents a Simple Picture, and Is Also Used as a Base Class for More Complex Pictures

```
1: using DirectX;
2: using System;
3: using System.Runtime.InteropServices;
4:
5: public class Picture : IDisposable
6: {
7:   protected DirectDrawSurface7 dxSurface;  // The DirectX surface
8:   protected RECT size;                     // Contains the dimensions
9:   protected bool hasTransparentColor;      // True if the input bitmap
10:                                            // uses a transparent color
11:
12:   // Creates the picture from the bitmap
13:   public Picture(string bitmapFile, bool hasTransparentColor)
14:   {
15:     this.hasTransparentColor = hasTransparentColor;
16:     size = new RECT();
```

LISTING 23.5 Continued

```
17:       dxSurface = Util.CreateSurfaceFromFile(
18:         bitmapFile, hasTransparentColor, ref size);
19:     }
20:
21:     // Disposes the picture
22:     public void Dispose()
23:     {
24:       Marshal.ReleaseComObject(dxSurface);
25:     }
26:
27:     // Returns the width of the picture
28:     public virtual int Width
29:     {
30:       get { return size.Right - size.Left; }
31:     }
32:
33:     // Returns the height the picture
34:     public virtual int Height
35:     {
36:       get { return size.Bottom - size.Top; }
37:     }
38:
39:     // Returns the input rectangle, but "clipped" if part of it
40:     // is located outside the range of the screen.
41:     // The coordinates are changed to zero if they are negative.
42:     protected RECT ClippedRectangle(ref int x, ref int y, RECT size)
43:     {
44:       RECT r = size;
45:
46:       // Check if the picture would be off the left edge of the screen
47:       if (x < 0)
48:       {
49:         r.Left -= x;
50:         x = 0;
51:       }
52:       // Check if the picture would be off the right edge of the screen
53:       else if (x + (r.Right - r.Left) >= Screen.Width)
54:       {
55:         r.Right = r.Left + Screen.Width - x;
56:       }
57:
58:       // Check if the picture would be off the top edge of the screen
59:       if (y < 0)
60:       {
```

LISTING 23.5   Continued

```
61:          r.Top -= y;
62:          y = 0;
63:        }
64:        // Check if the picture would be off the bottom edge of the screen
65:        else if (y + (r.Bottom - r.Top) >= Screen.Height)
66:        {
67:          r.Bottom = r.Top + Screen.Height - y;
68:        }
69:
70:      return r;
71:    }
72:
73:    // Draw the picture with the top left corner at the
74:    // (x,y) coordinate.  The picture is clipped if part
75:    // of the picture is off the screen.
76:    public virtual void DrawAt(int x, int y)
77:    {
78:      RECT r = ClippedRectangle(ref x, ref y, size);
79:      Util.DrawSurface(dxSurface, x, y, r, hasTransparentColor);
80:    }
81:
82:    // Draw the picture with the top left corner at the
83:    // (x,y) coordinate, resized to the width and height given.
84:    // The picture is clipped if part of the picture is off
85:    // the screen.
86:    public virtual void ResizeAndDrawAt(int x, int y, int width, int height)
87:    {
88:      RECT r = ClippedRectangle(ref x, ref y, size);
89:
90:      RECT dest = new RECT();
91:      dest.Left = x;
92:      dest.Top = y;
93:      dest.Right = x + width;
94:      dest.Bottom = y + height;
95:
96:      Util.ResizeAndDrawSurface(dxSurface, r, dest, hasTransparentColor);
97:    }
98: }
```

Lines 1–3 list three namespaces—DirectX for DirectDrawSurface7 and RECT, System for IDisposable and GC, and System.Runtime.InteropServices for Marshal. Line 7 declares the protected dxSurface that is passed to the Util class, Line 8 defines the RECT structure that contains the size of the surface (and thus the size of the picture), and Line 15 defines the hasTransparentColor flag that indicates if the picture uses a red color key.

The constructor in Lines 13–19 attempts to initialize the surface by calling
Util.CreateSurfaceFromFile. If creating the surface fails, we let the exception be thrown
because this is a fatal error that would affect game play. Lines 22–25 contain Dispose method
that works just like in the previous listing. The Width and Height properties in Lines 28–37
calculate the returned values using the values of the stored RECT.

The ClippedRectangle method in Lines 42–71 is used by the remaining two methods to check
that we don't try to draw outside the boundaries of the screen, which would cause an exception
originating from DirectX. If the area is off the left or top edge of the screen, we not only need
to adjust the size of the rectangle but also its location, thus the x and y parameters are passed
by-reference.

The DrawAt method in Lines 76–80 simply calls ClippedRectangle then the Util class's
DrawSurface method. The ResizeAndDrawAt method in Lines 86–97 calls ClippedRectangle
and Util.ResizeAndDrawSurface. This requires a little more work because
Util.ResizeAndDrawSurface requires a RECT for both the input picture and the buffer
we're drawing on.

The AnimatedPicture class adds the element of animation to a picture. Rather than a bitmap
representing the entire picture, the input bitmap for AnimatedPicture contains several frames
of animation that are used when appropriate. This class is used for the picture of the virus
character and the picture of the bonus item, both shown in Figure 23.6.

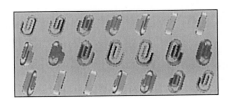

FIGURE 23.6

Animations for the character and bonus items.

The bitmap is "sliced" into smaller frames based on its dimensions and additional information
given in the AnimatedPicture constructor. Only one frame is displayed at a time, chosen based
on the time that has elapsed. Figure 23.7 demonstrates how the bitmap containing the bonus
item is sliced into individual frames numbered from zero. Each time the picture is rendered,
the calculations for the left and top edges are performed as shown in the figure.

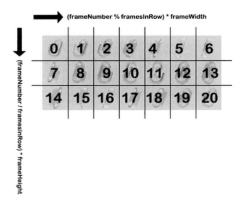

FIGURE 23.7

Slicing an input bitmap into animated frames.

AnimatedPicture, shown in Listing 23.6, adds the following protected fields to the ones inherited from the base class:

- frames. Number of frames in the animation.
- framesInRow. Number of frames in one row of the input bitmap.
- frameWidth. The width of each frame, in pixels.
- frameHeight. The height of each frame, in pixels.
- frequency. Number of times the picture is drawn before switching to the next frame. The higher this number, the slower the animation.

AnimatedPicture overrides both of Picture's properties:

- Width. The width of one frame, in pixels.
- Height. The height of one frame, in pixels.

The class also contains the following methods:

- AnimatedPicture. The constructor, which creates the object from a bitmap file and figures out the frame information from additional parameters.
- DrawAt. Overrides the base method and draws the current frame at the given location.
- ResizeAndDrawAt. Overrides the base method and draws the current frame at the given location, stretched or shrunken to the given size.

LISTING 23.6   AnimatedPicture.cs. The AnimatedPicture Class Represents a Picture That Changes at a Regular Interval

```
 1: using DirectX;
 2:
 3: public class AnimatedPicture : Picture
 4: {
 5:   // Number of frames in the animation
 6:   protected int frames;
 7:   // Number of frames in one row of the input bitmap
 8:   protected int framesInRow;
 9:   // Width of each frame
10:   protected int frameWidth;
11:   // Height of each frame
12:   protected int frameHeight;
13:   // Number of times drawn before changing the frame.
14:   // Thus, this controls the speed of the animation.
15:   protected int frequency;
16:
17:   // Creates the picture from the bitmap.
18:   // The bitmap contains each frame of the animation.
19:   public AnimatedPicture(string bitmapFile, bool hasTransparentColor,
20:     int numFrames, int rows, int frequency)
21:     : base(bitmapFile, hasTransparentColor)
22:   {
23:     frames = numFrames;
24:     framesInRow = numFrames / rows;
25:     frameWidth = (size.Right - size.Left) / framesInRow;
26:     frameHeight = (size.Bottom - size.Top) / (numFrames / framesInRow);
27:     this.frequency = frequency;
28:   }
29:
30:   // Returns the width of the picture
31:   public override int Width
32:   {
33:     // Return the width of just one frame, not the entire input bitmap
34:     get { return frameWidth; }
35:   }
36:
37:   // Returns the height the picture
38:   public override int Height
39:   {
40:     // Return the height of just one frame, not the entire input bitmap
41:     get { return frameHeight; }
42:   }
43:
```

23

LISTING 23.6   Continued

```
44:   // Draw the picture with the top left corner at the
45:   // (x,y) coordinate.  The picture is clipped if part
46:   // of the picture is off the screen.
47:   public override void DrawAt(int x, int y)
48:   {
49:     RECT frame = new RECT();
50:
51:     // Get the correct "slice" of the input bitmap based
52:     // on the current frame number.
53:     int frameNumber = (Util.Counter / frequency) % frames;
54:     frame.Left = (frameNumber % framesInRow) * frameWidth;
55:     frame.Top = (frameNumber / framesInRow) * frameHeight;
56:     frame.Right = frame.Left + frameWidth;
57:     frame.Bottom = frame.Top + frameHeight;
58:
59:     RECT r = ClippedRectangle(ref x, ref y, frame);
60:
61:     Util.DrawSurface(dxSurface, x, y, r, hasTransparentColor);
62:   }
63:
64:   // Draw the picture with the top left corner at the
65:   // (x,y) coordinate, resized to the width and height given.
66:   // The picture is clipped if part of the picture is off
67:   // the screen (horizontally only).
68:   public override void ResizeAndDrawAt(
69:     int x, int y, int width, int height)
70:   {
71:     RECT frame = new RECT();
72:
73:     // Get the correct "slice" of the input bitmap based
74:     // on the current frame number.
75:     int frameNumber = (Util.Counter / frequency) % frames;
76:     frame.Left = (frameNumber % framesInRow) * frameWidth;
77:     frame.Top = (frameNumber / framesInRow) * frameHeight;
78:     frame.Right = frame.Left + frameWidth;
79:     frame.Bottom = frame.Top + frameHeight;
80:
81:     RECT r = ClippedRectangle(ref x, ref y, frame);
82:
83:     RECT dest = new RECT();
84:     dest.Left = x;
85:     dest.Top = y;
86:     dest.Right = x + width;
87:     dest.Bottom = y + height;
```

LISTING 23.6 Continued

```
88:
89:     Util.ResizeAndDrawSurface(dxSurface, r, dest, hasTransparentColor);
90:   }
91: }
```

Line 1 lists the DirectX namespace, used for RECT. Inside the constructor in Lines 19–28, the protected fields are calculated and set. Lines 31–42 contain the overriding Width and Height properties which simply return frameWidth and frameHeight, respectively.

> **CAUTION**
>
> The implementation of AnimatedPicture requires that the number of frames is always a multiple of the number of rows in the input bitmap. If you plan on using this with different pictures, be aware of this limitation or update the code to not require it.

The DrawAt method on Lines 47–62 calls ClippedRectangle and Util.DrawSurface just like the base method, but first figures out the current frame and selects the appropriate slice of the picture to draw. This is the implementation of the calculation shown in Figure 23.7. The ResizeAndDrawAt method does the exact same thing except for the call to Util.ResizeAndDrawSurface.

The AnimatedEnvelopePicture class is another class that expects a bitmap containing several frames of animation. Unlike the more general AnimatedPicture, however, AnimatedEnvelopePicture is tailored specifically to the envelope picture shown in Figure 23.8.

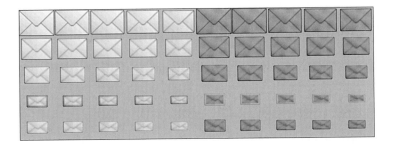

FIGURE 23.8
The envelope picture, containing all possible frames of animation.

The reason a different class is required is that the smaller pictures in Figure 23.8 don't represent a single sequence of animation. Instead, there are two separate sets of animations—one for a regular envelope and one for an infected envelope. Furthermore, each smaller size of envelope pictures has two versions—one with a colored border and one without. These sub-pictures are used to provide the blinking effect when the envelopes are small.

The `AnimatedEnvelopePicture`, shown in Listing 23.7, has a public `NumFrames` constant set to 20. This value serves the same function as the protected `frames` field inherited from `AnimatedPicture`, but made public so the `Envelope` class can use it. The class contains the following methods:

- `AnimatedEnvelopePicture`. The constructor, which creates the object from a bitmap file and sets the frame information.

- `DrawAt`. There are two versions of this method. The one that overrides the base method throws a `NotSupportedException` because it doesn't apply. The overload of this method has additional parameters needed to display the picture.

- `ResizeAndDrawAt`. Overrides the base method and throws a `NotSupportedException` because it doesn't apply.

LISTING 23.7   `AnimatedEnvelopePicture.cs`. The `AnimatedEnvelopePicture` Class Represents an Animated Envelope Picture, Which Is More Complex Than a Typical Animated Picture

```
 1: using System;
 2: using DirectX;
 3:
 4: public class AnimatedEnvelopePicture : AnimatedPicture
 5: {
 6:   // Number of frames in the animation
 7:   public const int NumFrames = 20;
 8:   // Frequency of the blinking of small envelopes
 9:   private int blinkFrequency;
10:
11:   // Creates the picture from the bitmap.
12:   // The bitmap contains each frame of the animation.
13:   public AnimatedEnvelopePicture(string bitmapFile)
14:     : base(bitmapFile, true, NumFrames, 4, 0)
15:   {
16:     frameWidth = (size.Right - size.Left) / (framesInRow * 2);
17:     frameHeight = (size.Bottom - size.Top) / 5;
18:     blinkFrequency = 4;
19:   }
20:
21:   // Draw the specified frame of the picture with the top left
```

LISTING 23.7   Continued

```
22:    // corner at the (x,y) coordinate.  If infected is true, an
23:    // infected envelope is displayed.  The picture is clipped if part
24:    // of the picture is off the screen.
25:    public void DrawAt(int x, int y, int frameNumber, bool infected)
26:    {
27:      RECT frame = new RECT();
28:
29:      // Choose the left edge of the "slice" of the input bitmap
30:      // based on whether or not we display an infected envelope.
31:      if (infected)
32:        frame.Left = ((frameNumber % framesInRow) * frameWidth) +
33:          frameWidth * framesInRow;
34:      else
35:        frame.Left = (frameNumber % framesInRow) * frameWidth;
36:
37:      // Make the envelope flash when it's small.
38:      // This effects the top edge of the "slice".
39:      if (frameNumber >= 15 && ((Util.Counter / blinkFrequency) % 2 == 0))
40:        frame.Top = ((frameNumber / framesInRow) * frameHeight)
41:          + frameHeight;
42:      else
43:        frame.Top = (frameNumber / framesInRow) * frameHeight;
44:
45:      // The right and bottom edges are always
46:      // a simple offset from the left and top
47:      frame.Right = frame.Left + frameWidth;
48:      frame.Bottom = frame.Top + frameHeight;
49:
50:      RECT r = ClippedRectangle(ref x, ref y, frame);
51:
52:      Util.DrawSurface(dxSurface, x, y, r, hasTransparentColor);
53:    }
54:
55:    // This overload isn't supported on an AnimatedEnvelopePicture
56:    public override void DrawAt(int x, int y)
57:    {
58:      throw new NotSupportedException(
59:        "This action is not supported on an AnimatedEnvelopePicture.");
60:    }
61:
62:    // This method isn't supported on an AnimatedEnvelopePicture
63:    public override void ResizeAndDrawAt(
64:      int x, int y, int width, int height)
65:    {
```

LISTING 23.7   Continued

```
66:       throw new NotSupportedException(
67:         "This action is not supported on an AnimatedEnvelopePicture.");
68:    }
69: }
```

Lines 1 and 2 list two namespaces—System for NotSupportedException, and DirectX for RECT. Inside the constructor in Lines 13–19, the frameWidth and frameHeight fields are set to custom values specific to the layout of the envelope bitmap. Line 18 sets the value of a private blinkFrequency to 4, a number chosen arbitrarily for the speed of the envelope blinking effect.

Notice that the overriding DrawAt and ResizeAndDrawAt methods in Lines 56–68 throw a NotSupportedException. This is done because the AnimatedEnvelopePicture has its own DrawAt overload with special requirements, so calling either of these virtual methods would be an error.

This special DrawAt method is contained in Lines 25–53, and has two additional parameters: the frame number and a boolean value indicating whether the envelope is infected or not. Unlike the AnimatedPicture, which manages its own animation, the AnimatedEnvelopePicture class lets its client decide what frame to draw and in what state the envelope is in. We'll see in Listing 23.15 that the controlling client is each Envelope object. This enables each envelope to be drawn in a different state simultaneously, unlike the bonus items or bugs which all move in sync.

To interpret the contents of the overloaded DrawAt method, refer back to the picture of envelopes in Figure 23.8. In Lines 31–35, the left edge of the slice is determined based on whether we're told to draw an infected envelope, because all the infected envelopes are further to the right than the normal ones. In Lines 39–43, the top edge is chosen based on the blinking frequency if the frame corresponds to one of the smaller sub-pictures that can blink. Once these two points are chosen, the right and bottom edges of the slice are always at the same offset, so the code in Lines 47–52 is straightforward.

The NumberPicture class, shown in Listing 23.8, can display any number once initialized with a bitmap containing each digit. We use this class to display the score and high score. The input bitmap used in the game is shown in Figure 23.9.

FIGURE 23.9

Numbers used for the game's score display.

When describing this class, the "input picture" refers to the bitmap shown in Figure 23.9 and the "output picture" refers to the number picture displayed on the screen. NumberPicture contains the following private fields:

- sideEdge. The position on the screen (in pixels) of either the left edge or the right edge of the output picture, depending on the value of leftAligned.
- topEdge. The position on the screen (in pixels) of the top edge of the output picture.
- leftAligned. True if sideEdge marks the left side of the output picture, or false otherwise.
- digitWidths. An array containing the width (in pixels) for each digit. Element 0 contains the width of 0, element 1 contains the width of 1, and so on.
- digitSpacing. The amount of space between the left edges of each digit in the input picture. Although each digit may have a different width, they must be spaced apart such that a multiple of digitSpacing points to the beginning of a digit.
- padding. Space between digits in the output picture.

The class also contains the following public methods:

- NumberPicture. The constructor, which creates the object from a bitmap file and sets the frame information.
- SetPosition. Sets the location of the output picture.
- Draw. Draws the number passed as an argument at the location set by the last call to SetPosition.

LISTING 23.8   NumberPicture.cs. The NumberPicture Class Can Transform Any Number Into a Picture

```
1: using System;
2: using DirectX;
3:
4: public class NumberPicture : Picture
5: {
6:     // The left or right edge of the picture on the screen
7:     private int sideEdge;
8:     // The top edge of the picture on the screen
9:     private int topEdge;
10:     // If true, sideEdge is the left edge. Otherwise, it is the right edge.
11:     private bool leftAligned;
12:     // Width of each digit in the input bitmap, 0 to 9
13:     private int [] digitWidths;
14:     // Amount of space between left edges of each digit in the input bitmap
15:     private int digitSpacing;
16:     // Space between digits in the output picture
17:     private int padding;
```

LISTING 23.8   Continued

```
18:
19:    // Creates the picture from the bitmap
20:    public NumberPicture(string bitmapFile, bool hasTransparentColor,
21:      int [] digitWidths, int digitSpacing, int padding)
22:      : base(bitmapFile, hasTransparentColor)
23:    {
24:      this.digitWidths = digitWidths;
25:      this.digitSpacing = digitSpacing;
26:      this.padding = padding;
27:      this.sideEdge = 0;
28:      this.topEdge = 0;
29:      this.leftAligned = true;
30:    }
31:
32:    // Sets the edges and alignment for the picture
33:    public void SetPosition(int sideEdge, int topEdge, bool leftAligned)
34:    {
35:      this.sideEdge = sideEdge;
36:      this.topEdge = topEdge;
37:      this.leftAligned = leftAligned;
38:    }
39:
40:    // Draws the picture of the number passed in
41:    public void Draw(int number)
42:    {
43:      try
44:      {
45:        string stringNumber = number.ToString();
46:        int currentEdge = sideEdge;
47:
48:        RECT r = new RECT();
49:
50:        if (leftAligned)
51:        {
52:          for (int i = 0; i <= stringNumber.Length - 1; i++)
53:          {
54:            int digit = (int)Char.GetNumericValue(stringNumber[i]);
55:
56:            r.Top = size.Top;
57:            r.Left = digitSpacing * digit;
58:            r.Bottom = size.Bottom;
59:            r.Right = r.Left + digitWidths[digit];
60:
61:            Util.DrawSurface(dxSurface, currentEdge, topEdge, r,
62:              hasTransparentColor);
```

LISTING 23.8   Continued

```
63:
64:                currentEdge = currentEdge + digitWidths[digit] + padding;
65:            }
66:        }
67:        else
68:        {
69:          for (int i = stringNumber.Length - 1; i >= 0; i--)
70:          {
71:            int digit = (int)Char.GetNumericValue(stringNumber[i]);
72:
73:            currentEdge = currentEdge - digitWidths[digit] - padding;
74:
75:            r.Top = size.Top;
76:            r.Left = digitSpacing * digit;
77:            r.Bottom = size.Bottom;
78:            r.Right = r.Left + digitWidths[digit];
79:
80:            Util.DrawSurface(dxSurface, currentEdge, topEdge, r,
81:              hasTransparentColor);
82:          }
83:        }
84:      }
85:      catch
86:      {
87:        // If there's an error, just don't render a number.
88:      }
89:    }
90: }
```

Lines 1 and 2 list two namespaces—System for Char and DirectX for RECT. The constructor in Lines 20–26 initializes its private fields, and the SetPosition method in Lines 35–37 sets the score location, used to display the score in the lower right corner during game play and the lower left corner during the title screen.

Lines 41–89 contain the Draw method, which begins by converting the input number into a string. We then go through one of the two for loops, depending on whether the number should be rendered along the left edge or right edge. If we're rendering along the left edge, each character is examined from left to right in the loop on Lines 52–65. The current digit is obtained from the current character by calling the static Char.GetNumericValue. The slice of the input bitmap is then selected based on the digit. Because the digits appear in order from 0 to 9 (as seen in Figure 23.9) and are spaced apart evenly, finding the appropriate left edge can be done by multiplying the digit's value by digitSpacing. Every digit reaches from top to bottom of the input bitmap, so size.Top and size.Bottom are used for the upper and lower edges.

Finally, because each digit has its own width, the corresponding value of the `digitWidths` array is added to the left edge to set the right edge. The selected slice is then drawn on the background in Lines 61–62 at the left edge indicated by `currentEdge`. On Line 64, `currentEdge` is updated to place the next digit to the right of the current one, plus the value of `padding` so the digits aren't touching. The `for` loop in Lines 69–82 functions much like the previous one, except the digits are processed from right to left. If some sort of error occurs, we swallow it because failure to render the number is not considered a fatal error.

Layers

The classes that represent the main screen's layers are represented in Figure 23.10. The base `Layer` class contains a background `Picture` that scrolls repeatedly across the screen. The background is tiled horizontally to give the appearance of one never-ending surface. The two derived classes add some objects that are drawn on top of the background.

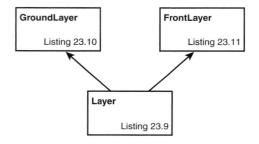

FIGURE 23.10

Three Classes are used for the game's layers.

Listing 23.9 contains the `Layer` class. It contains the following fields:

- `Frequency`. A public `readonly` field that specifies how many frames occur before the layer scrolls left by one pixel.
- `pixelsOffscreen`. A protected field that specifies how many pixels have been scrolled off the screen. This value resets to zero each time the entire background has left the screen.
- `background`. A private field that is the background `Picture` object.

The class also contains the following public methods:

- `Layer`. The constructor, which creates the layer with the input bitmap and sets its scrolling frequency.

- Reset. Reinitializes the layer to the state when it was constructed. This is used by the Game class whenever a new turn begins so we don't have to create new objects each time. Instead, the existing objects are reset to be as good as new.

- Render. Draws the layer. In the game's multilayered screen, each layer contributes to the rendering. Thus, the call to Util.RenderComplete is done by the Game class after calling each of its layers' Render method.

- Dispose. The implementation of IDisposable.Dispose, which calls Dispose on the class's Picture object.

LISTING 23.9   Layer.cs. The Layer Class Represents a Simple Scrolling Layer, and Is Also Used as a Base Class for More Complex Layers

```
 1: using System;
 2:
 3: public class Layer : IDisposable
 4: {
 5:   // Number of frames between each movement of one pixel
 6:   public readonly int Frequency;
 7:   // Number of pixels that have been "scrolled" off the screen.
 8:   // Resets to zero once an entire screen width has been scrolled.
 9:   protected int pixelsOffscreen;
10:   // The background image
11:   private Picture background;
12:
13:   // Creates the layer with the background picture
14:   // and initializes its characteristics
15:   public Layer(string bitmapFile, bool hasTransparentColor, int frequency)
16:   {
17:     background = new Picture(bitmapFile, hasTransparentColor);
18:     this.Frequency = frequency;
19:     pixelsOffscreen = 0;
20:   }
21:
22:   // Disposes the picture
23:   public void Dispose()
24:   {
25:     background.Dispose();
26:   }
27:
28:   // Re-initializes the layer to the state when constructed
29:   public virtual void Reset()
30:   {
31:     // In the base implementation, simply reset the # of pixels scrolled
32:     pixelsOffscreen = 0;
```

Listing 23.9   Continued

```
33:    }
34:
35:    // Draw the contents of the layer.
36:    // This must be followed by a call to Util.RenderComplete().
37:    public virtual void Render()
38:    {
39:      if (Frequency == 0)
40:      {
41:        // Always draw the background in the top left corner
42:        background.DrawAt(0, 0);
43:      }
44:      else
45:      {
46:        // Check if it's time to update the # of pixels scrolled
47:        if (Util.IsTimeToMove(Frequency))
48:          pixelsOffscreen = (pixelsOffscreen + 1) % Screen.Width;
49:
50:        // Draw the background picture consecutively until the screen is
51:        // filled horizontally
52:        for (int i = -pixelsOffscreen; i < Screen.Width; i +=
background.Width)
53:        {
54:          // Draw the background at the current offset
55:          background.DrawAt(i, 0);
56:        }
57:      }
58:    }
59: }
```

Line 1 lists the System namespace, used for IDisposable. The constructor initializes the three fields in Lines 15–20, including the creation of the background picture. The Dispose method in Lines 23–26 should look familiar, calling dispose on the Picture object. The Reset method in Lines 29–33 only needs to reset pixelsOffscreen to zero to reinitialize the object because frequency and background are never changed.

The Render method in Lines 37–58 either draws the background with the top left corner at (0,0) if its stationary, or handles the scrolling and tiling of the picture if Frequency is set to a non-zero value. Line 47 uses Util.IsTimeToMove to determine when to update pixelsOffscreen, causing the image to shift to the left by one pixel. The loop in Lines 52–56 handles the tiling of the image, repeatedly drawing the background picture until hitting the right edge of the screen.

The `GroundLayer` class in Listing 23.10 simply overrides `Layer`'s `Render` method. This is done to draw the envelopes and character in addition to the background.

LISTING 23.10 `GroundLayer.cs`. The `GroundLayer` Class Represents the Layer on Which the Character and Envelopes Move

```
 1: public class GroundLayer : Layer
 2: {
 3:   // Creates the layer with the background picture
 4:   // and initializes its characteristics.
 5:   public GroundLayer(string bitmapFile, bool hasTransparentColor,
 6:     int frequency) : base(bitmapFile, hasTransparentColor, frequency) {}
 7:
 8:   // Draw the contents of the layer.
 9:   // This must be followed by a call to Util.RenderComplete().
10:   public override void Render()
11:   {
12:     // Call the base method to draw the background picture
13:     base.Render();
14:
15:     // If the background has moved, move the player along with it
16:     if (Util.IsTimeToMove(Frequency))
17:       Game.Player.LocationX--;
18:
19:     // Render each envelope
20:     for (int i = 0; i < Game.GridWidth; i++)
21:     {
22:       for (int j = 0; j < Game.GridHeight; j++)
23:       {
24:         Game.EnvelopeGrid[i,j].Render();
25:       }
26:     }
27:
28:     // Render the player
29:     Game.Player.Render();
30:   }
31: }
```

The `Render` method in Lines 10–30 begins by calling the base `Render` method to draw the background picture. After this, it must draw each envelope and the bug character. The `for` loop in Lines 20–26 calls each of the envelope's `Render` method. Line 29 renders the bug by simply calling another `Render` method. The implementation of these `Render` methods is shown in Listings 23.14 and 23.15.

The `FrontLayer` class in Listing 23.11, like `GroundLayer`, simply overrides `Layer`'s `Render` method. This is done in order to draw the lives remaining, bonuses remaining, and score (in addition to the background).

LISTING 23.11   `FrontLayer.cs`. The `FrontLayer` Class Represents the Stationary Top-Most Layer Containing the Lives Remaining, Bonuses Remaining, and the Score

```
 1: public class FrontLayer : Layer
 2: {
 3:   // Create a FrontLayer with the background in bitmapFile.
 4:   // It will always have a transparent color and be stationary.
 5:   public FrontLayer(string bitmapFile) : base(bitmapFile, true, 0) {}
 6:
 7:   // Draw the contents the layer, including
 8:   // bonuses, lives remaining, and the score.
 9:   // This must be followed by a call to Util.RenderComplete().
10:   //
11:   public override void Render()
12:   {
13:     // Call the base method to draw the background picture
14:     base.Render();
15:
16:     // Draw each bonus, starting at the top right corner of the screen
17:     for (int i = 1; i <= Game.NumBonuses; i++)
18:     {
19:       Game.BonusPicture.DrawAt(
20:         Screen.Width - (i * Game.BonusPicture.Width), 0);
21:     }
22:
23:     // Draw each life remaining,
24:     // starting at the top left corner of the screen
25:     for (int i = 1; i <= Game.NumLives; i++)
26:     {
27:       Game.PlayerPicture.DrawAt((i - 1) * Game.PlayerPicture.Width, 0);
28:     }
29:
30:     // Draw the ScorePicture object.
31:     Game.ScorePicture.Draw(Game.Score);
32:   }
33: }
```

The `Render` method in Lines 11–32 also begins by calling the base `Render` method to draw the background picture. After this, it uses three pictures exposed by the `Game` class—`BonusPicture`, `PlayerPicture`, and `ScorePicture` to draw the bonuses remaining, lives remaining, and score.

Screens

Two classes represent screens besides the layers: Screen and IntroScreen. The Screen class is very similar to the Layer class, but nothing can be drawn on top of a Screen without it being done inside its Render method. IntroScreen is a derived class used to show the current score and high score.

Listing 23.12 contains the Screen class. This class defines two public constants—Width and Height—that define the size of the screen in pixels. These are set to 640 and 480, respectively, and control the screen's resolution when the game is running.

Like Layer, Screen has a protected Picture object that represents the background, and the following public methods:

- Screen. The constructor, which creates the background picture from the input bitmap.
- Render. Draws the contents of the screen. It calls Util.RenderComplete, so no additional rendering can be done outside of this method.
- Dispose. The implementation of IDisposable.Dispose, which calls Dispose on the class's Picture object.

LISTING 23.12   Screen.cs. The Screen Class Represents a Static Image That Is Displayed Without Additional Items Drawn on Top of It

```
 1: using System;
 2:
 3: public class Screen : IDisposable
 4: {
 5:    public const int Width = 640;  // Width of the screen in pixels
 6:    public const int Height = 480; // Height of the screen in pixels
 7:    protected Picture background;  // The background image
 8:
 9:    // Creates the screen with the background picture
10:    public Screen(string bitmapFile)
11:    {
12:      background = new Picture(bitmapFile, false);
13:    }
14:
15:    // Disposes the picture
16:    public void Dispose()
17:    {
18:      background.Dispose();
19:    }
20:
21:    // Draws the contents of the screen.
```

LISTING 23.12   Continued

```
22:    // Overridding methods should not call the base implementation
23:    // since it calls Util.RenderComplete().
24:    public virtual void Render()
25:    {
26:      // In the base implementation, just draw the background
27:      // starting in the top left corner
28:      background.DrawAt(0, 0);
29:
30:      // We're done rendering
31:      Util.RenderComplete();
32:    }
33: }
```

Line 1 lists the System namespace, used for IDisposable. The constructor in Lines 21–24 simply initializes the screen's picture. The Dispose method in Lines 16–19 is no different from the one in the Layer class. Finally, the Render method in Lines 24–32 simply draws the background picture starting from the top left corner of the screen, and calls Util.RenderComplete to flip the back buffer to the screen. The call to Util.RenderComplete means that nothing can be rendered on top of a Screen.

The IntroScreen class in Listing 23.13 overrides Screen's Render method. This is done to draw the current score and high score on top of the background.

LISTING 23.13   IntroScreen.cs. The IntroScreen Class Represents a Stationary Screen with a Background Picture, Current Score, and High Score

```
1: public class IntroScreen : Screen
2: {
3:   // Creates the screen with the background picture
4:   public IntroScreen(string bitmapFile) : base(bitmapFile) {}
5:
6:   // Draws the contents of the screen
7:   public override void Render()
8:   {
9:     // Draw the background at the top left corner.
10:     // Don't call the base Render method since it calls
11:     // Util.RenderComplete().
12:     background.DrawAt(0, 0);
13:
14:     // Draw the high score at the bottom of the screen
15:     Game.ScorePicture.SetPosition(190,
16:       Screen.Height - Game.DigitPadding - Game.DigitHeight, true);
17:     Game.ScorePicture.Draw(Game.HighScore);
```

LISTING 23.13 Continued

```
18:
19:     // Draw the current score above the high score
20:     Game.ScorePicture.SetPosition(190,
21:       Screen.Height - (Game.DigitPadding + Game.DigitHeight) * 2, true);
22:     Game.ScorePicture.Draw(Game.Score);
23:
24:     // We're done rendering
25:     Util.RenderComplete();
26:   }
27: }
```

This listing is just like the previous one except for Lines 14–22, between the calls to DrawAt and RenderComplete. These lines draw the two scores—the current score and high score.

The screen that results from Listing 23.13 is displayed in Figure 23.11.

FIGURE 23.11
The first screen of the game, with the current score and high score drawn on top of the background.

The Actors

The *actors* in the game are the character and the envelopes. These are represented by the Character and Envelope classes. The Character class, shown in Listing 23.14, has the following public fields:

- `LocationX`. The current horizontal location of the character, in pixels.

- `LocationY`. The current vertical location of the character, in pixels.

- `IsDying`. True if the character is currently dying (and shrinking); false otherwise.

The class has the following private fields:

- `framesSinceDeath`. The number of frames passed because the character died, used to control the shrinking animation.

- `envelopeX`. The horizontal index of the envelope currently under the character.

- `envelopeY`. The vertical index of the envelope currently under the character.

`Character` has the following public methods:

- `Character`. The constructor, which initializes the character and its position.

- `Reset`. Reinitializes the character to the state when it was constructed. This is used by the `Game` class whenever a new turn begins so we don't have to create a new object each time.

- `Render`. Draws the character at its current location. If the character is dying, it shrinks and then ends the current turn.

- `Move`. Moves the character and returns true if the move is valid. Examples of invalid moves are trying to move above or below the edges of the screen.

- `Kill`. Puts the character in a dying state, kicking off the shrinking animation.

`Character` also has one public property, `EnvelopeUnderneath`, which returns the envelope currently underneath the character.

LISTING 23.14   `Character.cs`. The `Character` Class Represents the Creature Controlled by the User

```
 1: public class Character
 2: {
 3:    // # of pixels character moves horizontally
 4:    public const int HorizontalJump = 80;
 5:    // # of pixels character moves vertically
 6:    public const int VerticalJump = 62;
 7:
 8:    // horizontal index of the starting envelope
 9:    private const int InitialEnvelopeX = 7;
10:    // vertical index of the starting envelope
11:    private const int InitialEnvelopeY = 4;
12:
13:    // Current horizontal location in pixels
```

LISTING 23.14 Continued

```
14:    public int LocationX;
15:    // Current vertical location in pixels
16:    public int LocationY;
17:    // true if the character is dying, false otherwise
18:    public bool IsDying;
19:
20:    // Number of frames since the character died
21:    private int framesSinceDeath;
22:    // Horizontal index of the envelope under the character
23:    private int envelopeX;
24:    // Vertical index of the envelope under the character
25:    private int envelopeY;
26:
27:    // Create the character and initialize its position
28:    public Character()
29:    {
30:      Reset();
31:    }
32:
33:    // Re-initializes the character to the state when constructed
34:    public void Reset()
35:    {
36:      envelopeX = InitialEnvelopeX;
37:      envelopeY = InitialEnvelopeY;
38:      LocationX = Game.LeftSpace + InitialEnvelopeX *
39:        (Game.EnvelopePicture.Width + Game.EnvelopePadding) +
40:        ((Game.EnvelopePicture.Width - Game.PlayerPicture.Width) / 2);
41:      LocationY = Game.TopSpace + (InitialEnvelopeY *
42:        (Game.EnvelopePicture.Height + Game.EnvelopePadding)) -
43:        ((Game.EnvelopePicture.Height - Game.PlayerPicture.Height) / 2)
44:        + (Game.EnvelopePadding / 2);
45:      IsDying = false;
46:      EnvelopeUnderneath.MakeVisibleAndInfected();
47:    }
48:
49:    // Returns the envelope currently underneath the character
50:    public Envelope EnvelopeUnderneath
51:    {
52:      get { return Game.EnvelopeGrid[envelopeX, envelopeY]; }
53:    }
54:
55:    // Moves the character.  Returns true if the move is valid,
56:    // false otherwise.
57:    public bool Move(Moves move)
```

LISTING 23.14   Continued

```
58:   {
59:     switch (move)
60:     {
61:       case Moves.Down:
62:         if (LocationY + VerticalJump + Game.PlayerPicture.Height
63:           < Screen.Height)
64:         {
65:           LocationY += VerticalJump;
66:           envelopeY++;
67:           return true;
68:         }
69:         break;
70:       case Moves.Up:
71:         if (LocationY - HorizontalJump > 0)
72:         {
73:           LocationY -= VerticalJump;
74:           envelopeY--;
75:           return true;
76:         }
77:         break;
78:       case Moves.Left:
79:         if (LocationX - HorizontalJump + Game.PlayerPicture.Width > 0)
80:         {
81:           LocationX -= HorizontalJump;
82:           envelopeX--;
83:           if (envelopeX < 0) envelopeX = Game.GridWidth - 1;
84:           return true;
85:         }
86:         break;
87:       case Moves.Right:
88:         if (LocationX + HorizontalJump < Screen.Width)
89:         {
90:           LocationX += HorizontalJump;
91:           envelopeX = (envelopeX + 1) % Game.GridWidth;
92:           return true;
93:         }
94:         break;
95:       default:
96:         break;
97:     }
98:     return false;
99:   }
100:
```

LISTING 23.14 Continued

```
101:   // Draws the character at the current location.  If the character is
102:   // dying, draws a shrinking character and ends the current life
103:   public void Render()
104:   {
105:     if (IsDying)
106:     {
107:       framesSinceDeath++;
108:
109:       // Make the character's image shrink
110:       Game.PlayerPicture.ResizeAndDrawAt(
111:         LocationX + framesSinceDeath,
112:         LocationY + (int)(framesSinceDeath * 1.5),
113:         Game.PlayerPicture.Width - (framesSinceDeath * 2),
114:         Game.PlayerPicture.Height - (framesSinceDeath * 2)
115:       );
116:
117:       // If the character is finished dying, change the game's state
118:       if (Game.PlayerPicture.Width - (framesSinceDeath * 2) < 2 ||
119:         LocationX + Game.PlayerPicture.Width < 0)
120:         Game.State = GameStates.TryAgain;
121:     }
122:     else
123:     {
124:       Game.PlayerPicture.DrawAt(LocationX, LocationY);
125:     }
126:   }
127:
128:   // Kills the character
129:   public void Kill()
130:   {
131:     IsDying = true;
132:     framesSinceDeath = 0;
133:   }
134: }
```

The constructor for Character simply calls Reset, because the same actions are done at initialization and reinitialization. Reset, in Lines 34–47, initializes the character's position to a certain location dictated by the InitialEnvelopeX and InitialEnvelopeY constants. The location of the character in terms of indices in the envelope grid is mathematically related to its position in pixels, and this relationship is used in Lines 38–44 to initialize LocationX and LocationY. The last work that Reset does is make the character alive and ensure that there's an envelope under its feet.

The `EnvelopeUnderneath` property is defined in Lines 50–53, and simply returns the appropriate element of `Game.EnvelopeGrid`. This can be done in one simple step because we keep track of the current envelope indices at all times. The `Move` method in Lines 57–99 updates the location of the character appropriately. Whereas the `envelopeX` and `envelopeY` variables are incremented and decremented by one (except at the edges of the wrap-around grid), the `LocationX` and `LocationY` variables are incremented by the `HorizontalJump` and `VerticalJump` constant values because they are measured in terms of pixels.

The `Render` method in Lines 103–126 has a simple task if the character isn't dying—draw the picture at (`LocationX`, `LocationY`). If it is dying, it increments the counter that stores how many times the character has been rendered since death, then draws a shrunken picture. The higher `framesSinceDeath` gets, the smaller the picture becomes. Finally, once the shrunken picture gets small enough, the state of the game is changed to `TryAgain` in Line 120. The `Kill` method is defined in Lines 129–133, kicking off the dying process by setting `IsDying` to true.

The `Envelope` class, shown in Listing 23.15, contains many private fields to keep track of its internal state. Most important are its three Boolean public fields:

- `IsVisible`. True if the envelope is visible.
- `IsInfected`. True if the envelope has been stepped on because it has last become visible.
- `HasAttachment`. True if the envelope contains an attachment.

`Envelope` also contains the following public methods:

- `Envelope`. The constructor, which initializes the envelope at the given position.
- `Reset`. Reinitializes the envelope to the state when it was constructed. This is used by the `Game` class whenever so we don't have to continually create new objects.
- `MakeVisibleAndInfected`. Ensures that the envelope is visible, infected, slow-shrinking, and has no attachment. This is used at the beginning of each turn because the character must start on top of an envelope. It's also used whenever the player uses a bonus to create an envelope underneath the character's feet.
- `Render`. Draws the envelope in the appropriate state and at the appropriate location. This method handles the screen wrap-around for each envelope.

`Envelope` also has a private method, `ChooseNewCharacteristics`, which is used whenever an envelope needs to be reborn with different properties.

LISTING 23.15   `Envelope.cs`. The `Envelope` Class Represents an Envelope That Appears, Shrinks, Then Disappears on the Ground Layer

```
1: public class Envelope
2: {
```

LISTING 23.15   Continued

```
 3:    // Number of different speeds that envelopes may have
 4:    private const int numSpeeds = 3;
 5:    // Frequency of the fastest envelopes.
 6:    // The next fastest are 2 * frequencyUnit, then 3 * frequencyUnit, ...
 7:    private const int frequencyUnit = 15;
 8:    // True if the envelope is visible
 9:    public bool IsVisible;
10:    // True if the character has stepped on the envelope
11:    public bool IsInfected;
12:    // True if the envelope has an attachment
13:    public bool HasAttachment;
14:
15:    // Size of the envelope, corresponding to the frame in
16:    // the EnvelopePicture.  0 is the largest size.
17:    private int size;
18:    // Number of frames between size changes
19:    private int shrinkFrequency;
20:    // "ticks" since envelope became visible
21:    private int timeVisible;
22:    // Current horizontal location of the envelope (in pixels)
23:    private int locationX;
24:    // Current vertical location of the envelope (in pixels)
25:    private int locationY;
26:    // Initial horizontal location of the envelope (in pixels)
27:    private int initialX;
28:    // Frequency of the layer containing the envelopes
29:    private int layerFrequency;
30:
31:    // Creates the envelope at the initial location given
32:    public Envelope(int initialX, int initialY, int layerFrequency)
33:    {
34:      locationX = initialX;
35:      locationY = initialY;
36:      this.initialX = initialX;
37:      this.layerFrequency = layerFrequency;
38:      ChooseNewCharacteristics();
39:    }
40:
41:    // Re-initializes the envelopes to the state when constructed
42:    public void Reset()
43:    {
44:      locationX = initialX;
45:      ChooseNewCharacteristics();
46:    }
```

LISTING 23.15 Continued

```
47:
48:    // Sets new characteristics for the envelope.  The values for
49:    // IsVisible, HasAttachment, and shrinkFrequency are chosen randomly.
50:    private void ChooseNewCharacteristics()
51:    {
52:      timeVisible = 0;
53:      size = 0;
54:      IsInfected = false;
55:      IsVisible = (Util.RandomNumber.Next(4) == 0);
56:      HasAttachment = (Util.RandomNumber.Next(20) == 0);
57:      shrinkFrequency =
58:        (Util.RandomNumber.Next(numSpeeds) + 1) * frequencyUnit;
59:    }
60:
61:    // Ensures that the envelope is visible and infected with no attachment.
62:    // The envelope also shrinks at the slowest speed.
63:    public void MakeVisibleAndInfected()
64:    {
65:      ChooseNewCharacteristics();
66:      shrinkFrequency = numSpeeds * frequencyUnit;
67:      IsInfected = true;
68:      IsVisible = true;
69:      HasAttachment = false;
70:    }
71:
72:    // Draw the envelope in its current state.
73:    // This must be followed by a call to Util.RenderComplete().
74:    public void Render()
75:    {
76:      timeVisible++;
77:
78:      // Move the envelope along with the scrolling layer it's on.
79:      if (Util.IsTimeToMove(layerFrequency))
80:        locationX--;
81:
82:      // Make the envelope wrap around the screen.  When it reappears
83:      // on the right, it's a "new" envelope with new characteristics.
84:      if (locationX + Game.EnvelopePicture.Width < 0)
85:      {
86:        ChooseNewCharacteristics();
87:        locationX = Screen.Width + Game.EnvelopePadding - 1;
88:        return;
89:      }
90:
91:      if (IsVisible)
```

LISTING 23.15 Continued

```
 92:      {
 93:        // Make it the correct size
 94:        if (timeVisible % (shrinkFrequency) == 0)
 95:        {
 96:          size++;
 97:          if (size == AnimatedEnvelopePicture.NumFrames)
 98:          {
 99:            // The envelope is past its smallest size,
100:            // so make it invisible.
101:            IsVisible = false;
102:            return;
103:          }
104:        }
105:
106:        Game.EnvelopePicture.DrawAt(locationX, locationY, size, IsInfected);
107:
108:        // Draw an attachment, if it exists
109:        if (HasAttachment)
110:        {
111:          Game.BonusPicture.DrawAt(
112:            locationX + (Game.EnvelopePicture.Width/2) -
113:              (Game.BonusPicture.Width / 2),
114:            locationY + (Game.EnvelopePicture.Height/2) -
115:              (Game.BonusPicture.Height / 2)
116:          );
117:        }
118:      }
119:      else if (!Game.Player.IsDying)
120:      {
121:        // Choose new characteristics with a low chance of visibility,
122:        // since this is done every frame when its invisible.
123:        // This is only done when the player isn't in the process
124:        // of dying so it's not possible for an envelope to appear
125:        // under the falling character.
126:        ChooseNewCharacteristics();
127:        IsVisible = (Util.RandomNumber.Next(600) == 0);
128:      }
129:    }
130: }
```

The Envelope class's constructor in Lines 32–39 sets the location of the envelope and the frequency of the ground layer it sits on. This is needed so the envelope scrolls in sync with its background. The initial horizontal location is saved, but the vertical location doesn't need to be saved in a separate variable because its value never changes. The constructor also calls ChooseNewCharacteristics to give its additional fields initial values.

Reset, in Lines 42–46, simply resets the horizontal position stored during construction and calls ChooseNewCharacteristics, containing the common resetting code. ChooseNewCharacteristics is defined in Lines 50–59. In it, the pseudo-random attributes are initialized: visibility, shrinking speed, and presence of an attachment. The remaining three attributes are always reset the same way. The number of frames because becoming visible is set to zero, the size is set to the largest (represented by zero), and it is not infected.

The MakeVisibleAndInfected method in Lines 63–70 calls ChooseNewCharacteristics, but sets some fields afterward to guarantee that the envelope has the slowest shrinking speed, is infected and visible, and does not contain an attachment.

Finally, the Render method in Lines 74–129 is the most complicated Render method in the application. It begins by incrementing the timeVisible counter and scrolling the envelope along with the ground layer if it's time to do so (Lines 76–80). Next, we check to see if the envelope is completely off the left side of the screen. If so, we turn it into a new envelope by calling ChooseNewCharacteristics and update its location to now appear just past the right edge of the screen. Because it's still offscreen, there's nothing to draw and we return in Line 88.

If the envelope is visible, it is drawn on Line 106. Before doing this, however, we must check to see if it's time for it to shrink. If so, we increment the size variable in Line 96, because zero represents the largest size. If the envelope was already the smallest size (AnimatedEnvelopePicture.NumFrames-1), we make it invisible and return in Line 102.

After drawing the envelope, Lines 109–117 check if an attachment needs to be drawn on top of it. If so, it is centered on the envelope. If the envelope isn't visible and the player isn't dying, Line 126 chooses new characteristics for the envelope. Otherwise, invisible envelopes would never become visible again. Because this action occurs every frame for each invisible envelope, Line 127 decreases the likelihood that the envelope becomes visible (to a 1 in 600 chance). If this were not done, the playing field would almost always be completely filled with envelopes and the game wouldn't be challenging.

Using the Game Class

Now that we've seen the Game class and all the supporting classes, it's time to view the part of the application that drives the entire process. This is handled with the EmailAttackForm class, a Windows Form that serves as the canvas on which the game is drawn. EmailAttackForm uses PInvoke to call a few Win32 APIs, and these are defined in the Win32 namespace shown in Listing 23.16.

LISTING 23.16   Win32.cs. The Win32 Namespace Contains Two Classes That Represent Win32 DLLs

```
 1: using System.Runtime.InteropServices;
 2:
 3: namespace Win32
 4: {
 5:   internal class WinMM
 6:   {
 7:     [DllImport("WinMM.dll")]
 8:     internal static extern int timeGetTime();
 9:   }
10:
11:   internal class Kernel32
12:   {
13:     [DllImport("kernel32.dll")]
14:     internal static extern bool QueryPerformanceCounter(out long
15:       lpPerformanceCount);
16:
17:     [DllImport("kernel32.dll")]
18:     internal static extern bool QueryPerformanceFrequency(out long
19:       lpFrequency);
20:   }
21: }
```

The methods in Listing 23.16 have been grouped into classes based on the DLLs exposing them. The Kernel32 class contains two methods used for high-performance timing: QueryPerformanceCounter and QueryPerformanceFrequency. These functions should look familiar from Chapter 18, "The Essentials of PInvoke."

Because not all computer systems may contain hardware that supports performance counters, we also define timeGetTime from WINMM.DLL. Although this function exposes a less-precise timer, we can count on it being useable on any PC.

Listing 23.17 contains the EmailAttackForm class, as well as the GameStates and Moves enumerations seen earlier. The EmailAttackForm class has the following public methods:

- EmailAttackForm. Initializes the game and runs it indefinitely (until the user hits the Esc key).
- OnKeyDown. Overrides the base method to handle key presses.
- Dispose. Overrides the base method to dispose the Game when finished.
- Main. The game's entry point.

23

WRITING A .NET
ARCADE GAME
USING DIRECTX

LISTING 23.17   `EmailAttack.cs`. The `EmailAttackForm` Class Contains the Game Loop Which Renders the Game at a Regular Interval

```
 1: using System;
 2: using System.Windows.Forms;
 3: using Win32;
 4:
 5: public class EmailAttackForm : Form
 6: {
 7:   private Game game;   // The game to play
 8:
 9:   // Initializes and runs the game
10:   public EmailAttackForm()
11:   {
12:     long currentTime;        // Current time
13:     int timeBetweenFrames;   // Number of milliseconds between frames
14:     bool useBetterTimer;     // True if system has a performance counter
15:     long timeForNextFrame;   // Time to render the next frame
16:
17:     Cursor.Hide();
18:
19:     // Use a performance counter for higher precision timing, if available
20:     long frequency;
21:     if (Kernel32.QueryPerformanceFrequency(out frequency))
22:     {
23:       Kernel32.QueryPerformanceCounter(out timeForNextFrame);
24:       // Make the time between frames approx. 16 milliseconds
25:       timeBetweenFrames = (int)(frequency / 60);
26:       useBetterTimer = true;
27:     }
28:     else
29:     {
30:       timeForNextFrame = WinMM.timeGetTime();
31:       timeBetweenFrames = 16;
32:       useBetterTimer = false;
33:     }
34:
35:     game = new Game(this.Handle);
36:
37:     while (true)
38:     {
39:       if (useBetterTimer)
40:         Kernel32.QueryPerformanceCounter(out currentTime);
41:       else
42:         currentTime = WinMM.timeGetTime();
43:
```

LISTING 23.17   Continued

```
44:         if (currentTime > timeForNextFrame)
45:         {
46:           // Update the global counter.
47:           Util.Counter = (Util.Counter + 1) % 30000;
48:
49:           Game.Render();
50:
51:           // Check to see if the player died by
52:           // going off the left edge of the screen
53:           // or staying on an envelope that disappeared
54:           if (Game.State == GameStates.Running && !Game.Player.IsDying)
55:             Game.CheckForDeath();
56:
57:           // Set the time for the next frame
58:           timeForNextFrame = currentTime + timeBetweenFrames;
59:         }
60:         Application.DoEvents();
61:       }
62:     }
63:
64:     // Disposes the game
65:     protected override void Dispose(bool disposing)
66:     {
67:       if (disposing)
68:       {
69:         game.Dispose();
70:       }
71:       base.Dispose(disposing);
72:     }
73:
74:     // Handles key presses by the user
75:     protected override void OnKeyDown(KeyEventArgs e)
76:     {
77:       if (Game.State == GameStates.Running)
78:       {
79:         // Pressing escape exits the game, pressing pause
80:         // pauses it, and pressing one of the arrow keys
81:         // moves the player
82:         switch (e.KeyCode)
83:         {
84:           case Keys.Down:
85:             Game.MovePlayer(Moves.Down);
86:             break;
```

LISTING 23.17 Continued

```
 87:          case Keys.Up:
 88:            Game.MovePlayer(Moves.Up);
 89:            break;
 90:          case Keys.Left:
 91:            Game.MovePlayer(Moves.Left);
 92:            break;
 93:          case Keys.Right:
 94:            Game.MovePlayer(Moves.Right);
 95:            break;
 96:          case Keys.Escape:
 97:            Environment.Exit(0);
 98:            return;
 99:          case Keys.Pause:
100:            Game.State = GameStates.Paused;
101:            break;
102:          default:
103:            break;
104:        }
105:      }
106:      else
107:      {
108:        // Pressing escape exits the game, and pressing
109:        // any other key starts it
110:        switch (e.KeyCode)
111:        {
112:          case Keys.Escape:
113:            Environment.Exit(0);
114:            return;
115:          default:
116:            Game.State = GameStates.Running;
117:            break;
118:        }
119:      }
120:      base.OnKeyDown(e);
121:    }
122:
123:    // The entry point
124:    public static void Main()
125:    {
126:      EmailAttackForm eaf = new EmailAttackForm();
127:    }
128: }
```

Lines 1–3 list three namespaces—`System` for the `Environment` class, `System.Windows.Forms` for the `Form` class, and `Win32` for the methods defined in Listing 23.16. The form's constructor in Lines 10–62 contain the *game loop*—a loop that continually renders the game at a regular interval. It begins by hiding the cursor in Line 17, because we don't want the mouse pointer floating around the screen. Lines 20–33 set up our timing mechanism. If the system supports performance counters, we set `useBetterTimer` to true and set the desired rendering frequency to approximately 16 milliseconds. If it doesn't support them (indicated by `QueryPerformanceFrequency` returning false), we set `useBetterTimer` to false and set the desired rendering frequency to exactly 16 milliseconds.

Line 35 creates the `Game` object, initializing it with the form's `Handle` property. The loop in Lines 37–61 continues indefinitely, so only the user pressing the Esc key will end the application. Inside the loop, we get the current value of whichever timer we're using (Lines 39–42) then determine if it's time to render the frame. If it is, `Util.Counter` is incremented and the `Game.Render` method is called. The value of the counter resets to zero after 29,999 just so the number doesn't overflow. After the current scene has been rendered, the code checks to see if the player has died by calling `CheckForDeath` in Line 55. Line 58 updates the time that the next frame should be rendered, and Line 60 calls `Application.DoEvents` so the window can process any messages (such as key presses).

`Form`'s virtual `Dispose` method, which has a Boolean parameter, is overridden in Lines 65–71 in order to dispose of the game object. The `OnKeyDown` method in Lines 75–121 overrides the base implementation in order to handle the player's key presses. If the game is in the `Running` state, pressing the down, up, left, or right arrow keys calls `Game.MovePlayer` with the corresponding value from the `Moves` enumeration. Pressing the Esc key ends the game, and pressing Pause pauses it. All of this is handled in Lines 77–105. In any other state, however, pressing the Esc ends the game and pressing any other key puts the game in the `Running` state. This is handled in Lines 106–119. Last but not least, the `Main` method in Lines 152–155 creates the `EmailAttackForm` object.

This completes the walk-through of the E-mail Attack application. The next section looks at an alternative way to provide some of the exact same functionality without using any additional assembly except for `mscorlib`.

E-mail Attack—The Advanced Version

The advanced version of E-mail Attack removes dependencies on all assemblies except for `mscorlib`. Rather than relying on `System.Windows.Forms`, it uses PInvoke to achieve the same results with classic Win32 programming. To eliminate the dependency on the DirectX for VB Interop Assembly, the advanced version defines its own DirectX type information in C# source code, following the techniques of Chapter 21, "Manually Defining COM Types in Source Code."

The advanced version offers no additional functionality and is not the recommended way of writing new programs in managed code, but it's a useful exercise to see how it's done. If you're porting a Win32 application to C# or Visual Basic .NET, it can be handy to use the techniques shown here to quickly get your program running "as is." This version of the application does use less memory, but most people find that the significant amount of extra work involved usually doesn't justify the difference.

The advanced version uses the same code listings examined throughout the chapter, but replaces Listings 23.16 and 23.17 with 23.18 and 23.19, respectively. There is also a new file—DirectX.cs— (Listing 23.20) that replaces the assembly imported from the DX7VB.DLL type library.

To compile the advanced version, place all the necessary files in the same directory and invoke the C# compiler as follows:

```
csc /out:Game.exe /t:winexe *.cs
```

The new Win32.cs file is shown in Listing 23.18. It has the three methods of Listing 23.16, but adds significantly more methods as well as structs and enums used as parameters in the new methods. Also notice the delegate defined in Lines 13 and 14. The use of a delegate enables us to define a window procedure that receives callbacks.

LISTING 23.18   Win32.cs. The Win32 Namespace Contains Several Classes, Structs, enums, and a Delegate Used by the Advanced Version of the Game

```
 1: using System;
 2: using System.Runtime.InteropServices;
 3:
 4: namespace Win32
 5: {
 6:   internal delegate int WndProcDelegate(IntPtr hWnd, Messages msg,
 7:     int wParam, int lParam);
 8:
 9:   internal class WinMM
10:   {
11:     [DllImport("WinMM.dll")]
12:     internal static extern int timeGetTime();
13:   }
14:
15:   internal class Kernel32
16:   {
17:     [DllImport("Kernel32.dll")]
18:     internal static extern bool QueryPerformanceCounter(
19:       out long lpPerformanceCount);
20:
```

LISTING 23.18 Continued

```
21:     [DllImport("Kernel32.dll")]
22:     internal static extern bool QueryPerformanceFrequency(
23:       out long lpFrequency);
24:
25:     [DllImport("Kernel32.dll")]
26:     internal static extern IntPtr GetModuleHandle(String lpModuleName);
27:   }
28:
29:   internal class User32
30:   {
31:     // Constants used with GetSystemMetrics
32:     internal const int SM_CXSCREEN = 0;
33:     internal const int SM_CYSCREEN = 1;
34:
35:     // Constant used with LoadCursor
36:     internal const int IDC_ARROW = 32512;
37:
38:     [DllImport("User32.dll")]
39:     internal static extern IntPtr RegisterClassEx(
40:       [In] ref WndClassEx rWndClassEx);
41:
42:     [DllImport("User32.dll")]
43:     internal static extern IntPtr CreateWindowEx(int dwExStyle,
44:       String lpClassName, String lpWindowName, WindowStyles dwStyle,
45:       int x, int y, int nWidth, int nHeight, IntPtr hWndParent,
46:       IntPtr hMenu, IntPtr hInstance, IntPtr lpParam);
47:
48:     [DllImport("User32.dll")]
49:     internal static extern bool ShowWindow(
50:       IntPtr hWnd, WindowState nCmdShow);
51:
52:     [DllImport("User32.dll")]
53:     internal static extern bool UpdateWindow(IntPtr hWnd);
54:
55:     [DllImport("User32.dll")]
56:     internal static extern bool DestroyWindow(IntPtr hWnd);
57:
58:     [DllImport("User32.dll")]
59:     internal static extern bool PeekMessage(out Msg lpMsg, IntPtr hWnd,
60:       int wMsgFilterMin, int wMsgFilterMax, PeekMessages wRemoveMsg);
61:
62:     [DllImport("User32.dll")]
63:     internal static extern int GetMessage(out Msg lpMsg, IntPtr hWnd,
64:       int wMsgFilterMin, int wMsgFilterMax);
```

LISTING 23.18   Continued

```
65:
66:        [DllImport("User32.dll")]
67:        internal static extern bool TranslateMessage(ref Msg lpMsg);
68:
69:        [DllImport("User32.dll")]
70:        internal static extern int DispatchMessage(ref Msg lpMsg);
71:
72:        [DllImport("User32.dll")]
73:        internal static extern void PostQuitMessage(int nExitCode);
74:
75:        [DllImport("User32.dll")]
76:        internal static extern IntPtr LoadCursor(
77:          IntPtr hInstance, int lpCursorName);
78:
79:        [DllImport("User32.dll")]
80:        internal static extern int ShowCursor(bool bShow);
81:
82:        [DllImport("User32.dll")]
83:        internal static extern int GetSystemMetrics(int nIndex);
84:
85:        [DllImport("User32.dll")]
86:        internal static extern int DefWindowProc(IntPtr hWnd, Messages msg,
87:          int wParam, int lParam);
88:    }
89:
90:    internal class Gdi32
91:    {
92:      // Contant used with GetStockObject
93:      internal const int BLACK_BRUSH = 4;
94:
95:        [DllImport("Gdi32.dll")]
96:        internal static extern IntPtr GetStockObject(int fnObject);
97:    }
98:
99:    // Structs
100:
101:    internal struct WndClassEx
102:    {
103:      internal int cbSize;
104:      internal ClassStyles style;
105:      internal WndProcDelegate lpfnWndProc;
106:      internal int cbClsExtra;
107:      internal int cbWndExtra;
108:      internal IntPtr hInstance;
```

LISTING 23.18 Continued

```
109:       internal IntPtr hIcon;
110:       internal IntPtr hCursor;
111:       internal IntPtr hbrBackground;
112:       internal String lpszMenuName;
113:       internal String lpszClassName;
114:       internal IntPtr hIconSm;
115:    }
116:
117:    internal struct Point
118:    {
119:      internal short x;
120:      internal short y;
121:    }
122:
123:    internal struct Msg
124:    {
125:      internal IntPtr hwnd;
126:      internal Messages message;
127:      internal IntPtr wParam;
128:      internal IntPtr lParam;
129:      internal int time;
130:      internal Point pt;
131:    }
132:
133:    // Enums
134:
135:    internal enum ClassStyles : uint
136:    {
137:      CS_VREDRAW         = 0x0001,
138:      CS_HREDRAW         = 0x0002,
139:      CS_DBLCLKS         = 0x0008,
140:      CS_OWNDC           = 0x0020,
141:      CS_CLASSDC         = 0x0040,
142:      CS_PARENTDC        = 0x0080,
143:      CS_NOCLOSE         = 0x0200,
144:      CS_SAVEBITS        = 0x0800,
145:      CS_BYTEALIGNCLIENT = 0x1000,
146:      CS_BYTEALIGNWINDOW = 0x2000,
147:      CS_GLOBALCLASS     = 0x4000
148:    }
149:
150:    internal enum WindowStyles : uint
151:    {
152:      WS_OVERLAPPED      = 0x00000000,
```

23

WRITING A .NET
ARCADE GAME
USING DIRECTX

LISTING 23.18 Continued

```
153:        WS_POPUP            = 0x80000000,
154:        WS_CHILD            = 0x40000000,
155:        WS_MINIMIZE         = 0x20000000,
156:        WS_VISIBLE          = 0x10000000,
157:        WS_DISABLED         = 0x08000000,
158:        WS_CLIPSIBLINGS     = 0x04000000,
159:        WS_CLIPCHILDREN     = 0x02000000,
160:        WS_MAXIMIZE         = 0x01000000,
161:        WS_CAPTION          = 0x00C00000,
162:        WS_BORDER           = 0x00800000,
163:        WS_DLGFRAME         = 0x00400000,
164:        WS_VSCROLL          = 0x00200000,
165:        WS_HSCROLL          = 0x00100000,
166:        WS_SYSMENU          = 0x00080000,
167:        WS_THICKFRAME       = 0x00040000,
168:        WS_GROUP            = 0x00020000,
169:        WS_TABSTOP          = 0x00010000,
170:        WS_MINIMIZEBOX      = 0x00020000,
171:        WS_MAXIMIZEBOX      = 0x00010000,
172:        WS_TILED            = WS_OVERLAPPED,
173:        WS_ICONIC           = WS_MINIMIZE,
174:        WS_SIZEBOX          = WS_THICKFRAME,
175:        WS_TILEDWINDOW      = WS_OVERLAPPEDWINDOW,
176:        WS_OVERLAPPEDWINDOW = WS_OVERLAPPED   |
177:                              WS_CAPTION      |
178:                              WS_SYSMENU      |
179:                              WS_THICKFRAME   |
180:                              WS_MINIMIZEBOX  |
181:                              WS_MAXIMIZEBOX,
182:        WS_POPUPWINDOW      = WS_POPUP        |
183:                              WS_BORDER       |
184:                              WS_SYSMENU,
185:        WS_CHILDWINDOW      = WS_CHILD
186:    }
187:
188:    internal enum WindowState
189:    {
190:      SW_HIDE            = 0,
191:      SW_SHOWNORMAL      = 1,
192:      SW_NORMAL          = 1,
193:      SW_SHOWMINIMIZED   = 2,
194:      SW_SHOWMAXIMIZED   = 3,
195:      SW_MAXIMIZE        = 3,
196:      SW_SHOWNOACTIVATE  = 4,
```

LISTING 23.18   Continued

```
197:      SW_SHOW              = 5,
198:      SW_MINIMIZE          = 6,
199:      SW_SHOWMINNOACTIVE   = 7,
200:      SW_SHOWNA            = 8,
201:      SW_RESTORE           = 9,
202:      SW_SHOWDEFAULT       = 10,
203:      SW_FORCEMINIMIZE     = 11
204:  }
205:
206:  internal enum Messages : uint
207:  {
208:      WM_NULL              = 0x0000,
209:      WM_CREATE            = 0x0001,
210:      WM_DESTROY           = 0x0002,
211:      WM_MOVE              = 0x0003,
212:      WM_SIZE              = 0x0005,
213:      WM_ACTIVATE          = 0x0006,
214:      WM_SETFOCUS          = 0x0007,
215:      WM_KILLFOCUS         = 0x0008,
216:      WM_ENABLE            = 0x000A,
217:      WM_SETREDRAW         = 0x000B,
218:      WM_SETTEXT           = 0x000C,
219:      WM_GETTEXT           = 0x000D,
220:      WM_GETTEXTLENGTH     = 0x000E,
221:      WM_PAINT             = 0x000F,
222:      WM_CLOSE             = 0x0010,
223:      WM_QUIT              = 0x0012,
224:      WM_ERASEBKGND        = 0x0014,
225:      WM_SYSCOLORCHANGE    = 0x0015,
226:      WM_SHOWWINDOW        = 0x0018,
227:      WM_WININICHANGE      = 0x001A,
228:      WM_SETTINGCHANGE     = WM_WININICHANGE,
229:      WM_DEVMODECHANGE     = 0x001B,
230:      WM_ACTIVATEAPP       = 0x001C,
231:      WM_FONTCHANGE        = 0x001D,
232:      WM_TIMECHANGE        = 0x001E,
233:      WM_CANCELMODE        = 0x001F,
234:      WM_SETCURSOR         = 0x0020,
235:      WM_MOUSEACTIVATE     = 0x0021,
236:      WM_CHILDACTIVATE     = 0x0022,
237:      WM_QUEUESYNC         = 0x0023,
238:      WM_GETMINMAXINFO     = 0x0024,
239:      WM_KEYFIRST          = 0x0100,
240:      WM_KEYDOWN           = 0x0100,
```

23

WRITING A .NET
ARCADE GAME
USING DIRECTX

LISTING 23.18   Continued

```
241:       WM_KEYUP          = 0x0101,
242:       WM_CHAR           = 0x0102,
243:       WM_DEADCHAR       = 0x0103,
244:       WM_SYSKEYDOWN     = 0x0104,
245:       WM_SYSKEYUP       = 0x0105,
246:       WM_SYSCHAR        = 0x0106,
247:       WM_SYSDEADCHAR    = 0x0107
248:     }
249:
250:     internal enum PeekMessages : uint
251:     {
252:       PM_NOREMOVE = 0x0000,
253:       PM_REMOVE   = 0x0001,
254:       PM_NOYIELD  = 0x0002
255:     }
256:
257:     // For brevity, this enumeration contains
258:     // only the key codes used in this application.
259:     internal enum Keys : uint
260:     {
261:       VK_PAUSE  = 0x13,
262:       VK_ESCAPE = 0x1B,
263:       VK_LEFT   = 0x25,
264:       VK_UP     = 0x26,
265:       VK_RIGHT  = 0x27,
266:       VK_DOWN   = 0x28
267:     }
268: }
```

Listing 23.19 contains the updated EmailAttack.cs that should look familiar to Win32 programmers. The EmailAttack class is the replacement for the EmailAttackForm class that uses the convenience of .NET Windows Forms. The code does essentially the same thing as Listing 23.17, only the raw platform-specific details are exposed directly.

LISTING 23.19   EmailAttack.cs. The EmailAttack Class Is the Advanced Version of the EmailAttackForm Class from Listing 23.17

```
1: using System;
2: using System.Runtime.InteropServices;
3: using Win32;
4:
5: public class EmailAttack
6: {
```

LISTING 23.19 Continued

```
 7:   static WndProcDelegate d;
 8:
 9:   // The entry point.  Initializes and runs the game.
10:   public static void Main()
11:   {
12:     Msg msg;                 // Windows message
13:     long currentTime;        // Current time
14:     int timeBetweenFrames;   // Number of milliseconds between frames
15:     bool useBetterTimer;     // True if system has a performance counter
16:     long timeForNextFrame;   // Time to render the next frame
17:
18:     // Create and register a window class
19:     WndClassEx wc = new WndClassEx();
20:     d = new WndProcDelegate(WndProc);
21:
22:     wc.cbSize = Marshal.SizeOf(typeof(WndClassEx));
23:     wc.style = ClassStyles.CS_HREDRAW | ClassStyles.CS_VREDRAW;
24:     wc.lpfnWndProc = d;
25:     wc.cbClsExtra = 0;
26:     wc.hInstance = Kernel32.GetModuleHandle(null);
27:     wc.hIcon = IntPtr.Zero;
28:     wc.hCursor = User32.LoadCursor(IntPtr.Zero, User32.IDC_ARROW);
29:     wc.hbrBackground = Gdi32.GetStockObject(Gdi32.BLACK_BRUSH);
30:     wc.lpszMenuName = null;
31:     wc.lpszClassName = "E-mail Attack";
32:
33:     if (User32.RegisterClassEx(ref wc) == IntPtr.Zero)
34:     {
35:       throw new ApplicationException(
36:         "Fatal error.  Unable to register the window class.");
37:     }
38:
39:     // Create the window and display it
40:     IntPtr hWnd = User32.CreateWindowEx(0,               // extra style
41:         "E-mail Attack",                                 // class name
42:         "E-mail Attack",                                 // window name
43:         WindowStyles.WS_VISIBLE | WindowStyles.WS_POPUP, // style
44:         0,                                               // left
45:         0,                                               // top
46:         User32.GetSystemMetrics(User32.SM_CXSCREEN),     // width
47:         User32.GetSystemMetrics(User32.SM_CYSCREEN),     // height
48:         IntPtr.Zero,                                     // parent window
49:         IntPtr.Zero,                                     // menu
50:         wc.hInstance,                                    // instance
```

23

WRITING A .NET
ARCADE GAME
USING DIRECTX

LISTING 23.19   Continued

```
51:            IntPtr.Zero);                                    // param
52:
53:     if (hWnd == IntPtr.Zero)
54:       throw new ApplicationException(
55:         "Fatal error.  Unable to create the window.");
56:
57:     User32.ShowWindow(hWnd, WindowState.SW_SHOWDEFAULT);
58:     User32.UpdateWindow(hWnd);
59:     User32.ShowCursor(false);
60:
61:     // Use a performance counter for higher precision timing, if available
62:     long frequency;
63:     if (Kernel32.QueryPerformanceFrequency(out frequency))
64:     {
65:       Kernel32.QueryPerformanceCounter(out timeForNextFrame);
66:       // Make the time between frames approx. 16 milliseconds.
67:       timeBetweenFrames = (int)(frequency / 60);
68:       useBetterTimer = true;
69:     }
70:     else
71:     {
72:       timeForNextFrame = WinMM.timeGetTime();
73:       timeBetweenFrames = 16;
74:       useBetterTimer = false;
75:     }
76:
77:     using (Game game = new Game(hWnd))
78:     {
79:       // Windows message loop
80:       msg = new Msg();
81:       while(msg.message != Messages.WM_QUIT)
82:       {
83:         if (User32.PeekMessage(
84:           out msg, IntPtr.Zero, 0, 0, PeekMessages.PM_REMOVE))
85:         {
86:           User32.TranslateMessage(ref msg);
87:           User32.DispatchMessage(ref msg);
88:         }
89:         else
90:         {
91:           if (useBetterTimer)
92:             Kernel32.QueryPerformanceCounter(out currentTime);
93:           else
94:             currentTime = WinMM.timeGetTime();
```

LISTING 23.19 Continued

```
 95:
 96:               if (currentTime > timeForNextFrame)
 97:               {
 98:                  // Update the global counter.
 99:                  Util.Counter = (Util.Counter + 1) % 30000;
100:
101:                  Game.Render();
102:
103:                  // Check to see if the player died by
104:                  // going off the left edge of the screen
105:                  // or staying on an envelope that disappeared.
106:                  if (Game.State == GameStates.Running)
107:                  {
108:                     Game.CheckForDeath();
109:                  }
110:
111:                  // Set the time for the next frame
112:                  timeForNextFrame = currentTime + timeBetweenFrames;
113:               }
114:            }
115:         }
116:      }
117: }
118:
119: // Handles the Windows messages
120: private static int WndProc(
121:    IntPtr hWnd, Messages msg, int wParam, int lParam)
122: {
123:    switch (msg)
124:    {
125:      case Messages.WM_DESTROY:
126:        User32.PostQuitMessage(0);
127:        return 0;
128:      case Messages.WM_KEYDOWN:
129:        if (Game.State == GameStates.Running)
130:        {
131:           // Pressing escape exits the game, pressing pause
132:           // pauses it, and pressing one of the arrow keys
133:           // moves the player
134:           switch ((Keys)wParam)
135:           {
136:             case Keys.VK_DOWN:
137:               Game.MovePlayer(Moves.Down);
138:               break;
```

LISTING 23.19   Continued

```
139:              case Keys.VK_UP:
140:                Game.MovePlayer(Moves.Up);
141:                break;
142:              case Keys.VK_LEFT:
143:                Game.MovePlayer(Moves.Left);
144:                break;
145:              case Keys.VK_RIGHT:
146:                Game.MovePlayer(Moves.Right);
147:                break;
148:              case Keys.VK_ESCAPE:
149:                User32.DestroyWindow(hWnd);
150:                return 0;
151:              case Keys.VK_PAUSE:
152:                Game.State = GameStates.Paused;
153:                break;
154:            default:
155:                break;
156:          }
157:        }
158:        else
159:        {
160:          // Pressing escape exits the game, and pressing
161:          // any other key starts it
162:          switch ((Keys)wParam)
163:          {
164:            case Keys.VK_ESCAPE:
165:                User32.DestroyWindow(hWnd);
166:                return 0;
167:            default:
168:                Game.State = GameStates.Running;
169:                break;
170:          }
171:        }
172:        break;
173:      default:
174:        break;
175:    }
176:    return User32.DefWindowProc(hWnd, msg, wParam, lParam);
177:  }
178: }
```

The final listing contains the manually defined type information for the DirectX types used in the application. For consistency with the previous version, Listing 23.20 defines the same types as in the DirectX for VB type library. The C++ versions of the types could be defined in the same manner, however.

LISTING 23.20   DirectX.cs. The DirectX Namespace Defines a Minimal Amount of Type Information—Just Enough for the E-mail Attack Application to Work

```
 1: using System.Runtime.InteropServices;
 2:
 3: namespace DirectX
 4: {
 5:   // The DirectX7 class
 6:   [ComImport, Guid("E1211353-8E94-11D1-8808-00C04FC2C602")]
 7:   public class DirectX7 {}
 8:
 9:   // Interfaces
10:
11:   [
12:     ComImport,
13:     Guid("FAFA3599-8B72-11D2-90B2-00C04FC2C602"),
14:     InterfaceType(ComInterfaceType.InterfaceIsIUnknown)
15:   ]
16:   public interface IDirectX7
17:   {
18:     void slot1();
19:     DirectDraw7 DirectDrawCreate(string guid);
20:     void slot3();
21:     DirectSound DirectSoundCreate(string guid);
22:   }
23:
24:   [
25:     ComImport,
26:     Guid("9F76FB00-8E92-11D1-8808-00C04FC2C602"),
27:     InterfaceType(ComInterfaceType.InterfaceIsIUnknown)
28:   ]
29:   public interface DirectSound
30:   {
31:     void slot1();
32:     void slot2();
33:     void slot3();
34:     DirectSoundBuffer CreateSoundBufferFromFile(string filename,
35:       ref DSBUFFERDESC bufferDesc, out WAVEFORMATEX format);
36:     void slot5();
37:     void slot6();
38:     void slot7();
39:     void SetCooperativeLevel(int hwnd, CONST_DSSCLFLAGS level);
40:   }
41:
42:   [
43:     ComImport,
```

23

WRITING A .NET
ARCADE GAME
USING DIRECTX

LISTING 23.20 Continued

```
44:        Guid("9F76FB01-8E92-11D1-8808-00C04FC2C602"),
45:        InterfaceType(ComInterfaceType.InterfaceIsIUnknown)
46:    ]
47:    public interface DirectSoundBuffer
48:    {
49:      void slot1();
50:      void slot2();
51:      void slot3();
52:      void slot4();
53:      void slot5();
54:      void slot6();
55:      void slot7();
56:      void slot8();
57:      void slot9();
58:      void slot10();
59:      CONST_DSBSTATUSFLAGS GetStatus();
60:      void slot12();
61:      void slot13();
62:      void slot14();
63:      void Play(CONST_DSBPLAYFLAGS flags);
64:      void slot16();
65:      void slot17();
66:      void slot18();
67:      void slot19();
68:      void slot20();
69:      void slot21();
70:      void restore();
71:    }
72:
73:    [
74:      ComImport,
75:      Guid("9F76FDE8-8E92-11D1-8808-00C04FC2C602"),
76:      InterfaceType(ComInterfaceType.InterfaceIsIUnknown)
77:    ]
78:    public interface DirectDrawSurface7
79:    {
80:      void slot1();
81:      void slot2();
82:      void slot3();
83:      int Blt(ref RECT destRect, DirectDrawSurface7 ddS,
84:        ref RECT srcRect, CONST_DDBLTFLAGS flags);
85:      void slot5();
86:      int BltFast(int dx, int dy, DirectDrawSurface7 ddS,
87:        ref RECT srcRect, CONST_DDBLTFASTFLAGS trans);
```

LISTING 23.20 Continued

```
 88:      void slot7();
 89:      void slot8();
 90:      void slot9();
 91:      void slot10();
 92:      void slot11();
 93:      void slot12();
 94:      void slot13();
 95:      void slot14();
 96:      void slot15();
 97:      void slot16();
 98:      void Flip(DirectDrawSurface7 ddS, CONST_DDFLIPFLAGS flags);
 99:      DirectDrawSurface7 GetAttachedSurface(ref DDSCAPS2 caps);
100:      void slot19();
101:      void slot20();
102:      void GetCaps(ref DDSCAPS2 caps);
103:      void slot22();
104:      void GetColorKey( int flags, ref DDCOLORKEY val);
105:      void slot24();
106:      void slot25();
107:      void slot26();
108:      void slot27();
109:      void slot28();
110:      void slot29();
111:      void slot30();
112:      void slot31();
113:      void slot32();
114:      void slot33();
115:      void slot34();
116:      void slot35();
117:      void slot36();
118:      void GetPixelFormat(ref DDPIXELFORMAT pf);
119:      void slot38();
120:      void slot39();
121:      void slot40();
122:      void slot41();
123:      void slot42();
124:      void slot43();
125:      void slot44();
126:      void SetColorKey(CONST_DDCKEYFLAGS flags, ref DDCOLORKEY val);
127:  }
128:
129:  [
130:    ComImport,
131:    Guid("9F76FDE7-8E92-11D1-8808-00C04FC2C602"),
```

LISTING 23.20 Continued

```
132:      InterfaceType(ComInterfaceType.InterfaceIsIUnknown)
133:      ]
134:     public interface DirectDraw7
135:     {
136:       void slot1();
137:       void slot2();
138:       void slot3();
139:       void slot4();
140:       DirectDrawSurface7 CreateSurface(ref DDSURFACEDESC2 dd);
141:       DirectDrawSurface7 CreateSurfaceFromFile(
142:         string file, ref DDSURFACEDESC2 dd);
143:       void slot7();
144:       void slot8();
145:       void slot9();
146:       void slot10();
147:       void slot11();
148:       void slot12();
149:       void slot13();
150:       void slot14();
151:       void slot15();
152:       void slot16();
153:       void slot17();
154:       void slot18();
155:       void slot19();
156:       void slot20();
157:       void slot21();
158:       void slot22();
159:       void slot23();
160:       void slot24();
161:       void RestoreAllSurfaces();
162:       void slot26();
163:       void SetCooperativeLevel(int hdl, CONST_DDSCLFLAGS flags);
164:       void SetDisplayMode(int w, int h, int bpp, int iref, CONST_DDSDMFLAGS
➥ mode);
165:     }
166:
167:     // Structs
168:
169:     public struct RECT
170:     {
171:       public int Left;
172:       public int Top;
173:       public int Right;
174:       public int Bottom;
```

LISTING 23.20   Continued

```
175:
176:     public override string ToString()
177:     {
178:       return
179:         "[" + Left + ", " + Top + "] - [" + Right + ", " + Bottom + "]";
180:     }
181:   }
182:
183:   [StructLayout(LayoutKind.Sequential, Pack=4)]
184:   public struct DSBUFFERDESC
185:   {
186:     public int lSize;
187:     public CONST_DSBCAPSFLAGS lFlags;
188:     public int lBufferBytes;
189:     public int lReserved;
190:     public int lpwfxFormat;
191:   }
192:
193:   [StructLayout(LayoutKind.Sequential, Pack=4)]
194:   public struct WAVEFORMATEX
195:   {
196:     public short nFormatTag;
197:     public short nChannels;
198:     public int lSamplesPerSec;
199:     public int lAvgBytesPerSec;
200:     public short nBlockAlign;
201:     public short nBitsPerSample;
202:     public short nSize;
203:     public int lExtra;
204:   }
205:
206:   [StructLayout(LayoutKind.Sequential, Pack=4)]
207:   public struct DDSCAPS2
208:   {
209:     public CONST_DDSURFACECAPSFLAGS lCaps;
210:     public int lCaps2;
211:     public int lCaps3;
212:     public int lCaps4;
213:   }
214:
215:   [StructLayout(LayoutKind.Sequential, Pack=4)]
216:   public struct DDSURFACEDESC2
217:   {
218:     public int lSize;
```

LISTING 23.20 Continued

```
219:        public CONST_DDSURFACEDESCFLAGS lFlags;
220:        public int lHeight;
221:        public int lWidth;
222:        public int lPitch;
223:        public int lBackBufferCount;
224:        public int lZBufferBitDepth;
225:        public int lAlphaBitDepth;
226:        public int lReserved;
227:        public int lpSurface;
228:        public DDCOLORKEY ddckCKDestOverlay;
229:        public DDCOLORKEY ddckCKDestBlt;
230:        public DDCOLORKEY ddckCKSrcOverlay;
231:        public DDCOLORKEY ddckCKSrcBlt;
232:        public DDPIXELFORMAT ddpfPixelFormat;
233:        public DDSCAPS2 ddsCaps;
234:        public int lTextureStage;
235:        public int lLinearSize;
236:        public int lMipMapCount;
237:        public int lRefreshRate;
238:    }
239:
240:    [StructLayout(LayoutKind.Sequential, Pack=4)]
241:    public struct DDCOLORKEY
242:    {
243:      public int low;
244:      public int high;
245:    }
246:
247:    [StructLayout(LayoutKind.Sequential, Pack=4)]
248:    public struct DDPIXELFORMAT
249:    {
250:      public int lSize;
251:      public int lFlags;
252:      public int lFourCC;
253:      public int internalVal1;
254:      public int internalVal2;
255:      public int internalVal3;
256:      public int internalVal4;
257:      public int internalVal5;
258:      public int lRGBBitCount;
259:      public int lYUVBitCount;
260:      public int lZBufferBitDepth;
261:      public int lAlphaBitDepth;
262:      public int lLuminanceBitCount;
```

LISTING 23.20 Continued

```
263:        public int lBumpBitCount;
264:        public int lRBitMask;
265:        public int lYBitMask;
266:        public int lStencilBitDepth;
267:        public int lLuminanceBitMask;
268:        public int lBumpDuBitMask;
269:        public int lGBitMask;
270:        public int lUBitMask;
271:        public int lZBitMask;
272:        public int lBumpDvBitMask;
273:        public int lBBitMask;
274:        public int lVBitMask;
275:        public int lStencilBitMask;
276:        public int lBumpLuminanceBitMask;
277:        public int lRGBAlphaBitMask;
278:        public int lYUVAlphaBitMask;
279:        public int lLuminanceAlphaBitMask;
280:        public int lRGBZBitMask;
281:        public int lYUVZBitMask;
282:    }
283:
284:    // Enums
285:
286:    public enum CONST_DDSDMFLAGS
287:    {
288:      DDSDM_DEFAULT        = 0,
289:      DDSDM_STANDARDVGAMODE = 1
290:    }
291:
292:    public enum CONST_DDSCLFLAGS : uint
293:    {
294:      DDSCL_FULLSCREEN         = 0x1,
295:      DDSCL_ALLOWREBOOT        = 0x2,
296:      DDSCL_NOWINDOWCHANGES    = 0x4,
297:      DDSCL_NORMAL             = 0x8,
298:      DDSCL_EXCLUSIVE          = 0x10,
299:      DDSCL_ALLOWMODEX         = 0x40,
300:      DDSCL_SETFOCUSWINDOW     = 0x80,
301:      DDSCL_SETDEVICEWINDOW    = 0x100,
302:      DDSCL_CREATEDEVICEWINDOW = 0x200,
303:      DDSCL_MULTITHREADED      = 0x400
304:    }
305:
306:    public enum CONST_DDSURFACEDESCFLAGS : uint
```

23

WRITING A .NET
ARCADE GAME
USING DIRECTX

LISTING 23.20 Continued

```
307:    {
308:       DDSD_CAPS            = 0x1,
309:       DDSD_HEIGHT          = 0x2,
310:       DDSD_WIDTH           = 0x4,
311:       DDSD_PITCH           = 0x8,
312:       DDSD_BACKBUFFERCOUNT = 0x20,
313:       DDSD_ZBUFFERBITDEPTH = 0x40,
314:       DDSD_ALPHABITDEPTH   = 0x80,
315:       DDSD_TEXTURESTAGE    = 0x100000,
316:       DDSD_LPSURFACE       = 0x800,
317:       DDSD_PIXELFORMAT     = 0x1000,
318:       DDSD_CKDESTOVERLAY   = 0x2000,
319:       DDSD_CKDESTBLT       = 0x4000,
320:       DDSD_CKSRCOVERLAY    = 0x8000,
321:       DDSD_CKSRCBLT        = 0x10000,
322:       DDSD_MIPMAPCOUNT     = 0x20000,
323:       DDSD_REFRESHRATE     = 0x40000,
324:       DDSD_LINEARSIZE      = 0x80000,
325:       DDSD_ALL             = 0xFF9EE
326:    }
327:
328:    public enum CONST_DDSURFACECAPSFLAGS : uint
329:    {
330:       DDSCAPS_ALPHA             = 0x2,
331:       DDSCAPS_BACKBUFFER        = 0x4,
332:       DDSCAPS_COMPLEX           = 0x8,
333:       DDSCAPS_FLIP              = 0x10,
334:       DDSCAPS_FRONTBUFFER       = 0x20,
335:       DDSCAPS_OFFSCREENPLAIN    = 0x40,
336:       DDSCAPS_OVERLAY           = 0x80,
337:       DDSCAPS_PALETTE           = 0x100,
338:       DDSCAPS_PRIMARYSURFACE    = 0x200,
339:       DDSCAPS_PRIMARYSURFACELEFT = 0x400,
340:       DDSCAPS_SYSTEMMEMORY      = 0x800,
341:       DDSCAPS_TEXTURE           = 0x1000,
342:       DDSCAPS_3DDEVICE          = 0x2000,
343:       DDSCAPS_VIDEOMEMORY       = 0x4000,
344:       DDSCAPS_VISIBLE           = 0x8000,
345:       DDSCAPS_WRITEONLY         = 0x10000,
346:       DDSCAPS_ZBUFFER           = 0x20000,
347:       DDSCAPS_OWNDC             = 0x40000,
348:       DDSCAPS_LIVEVIDEO         = 0x80000,
349:       DDSCAPS_HWCODEC           = 0x100000,
350:       DDSCAPS_MODEX             = 0x200000,
```

LISTING 23.20 Continued

```
351:      DDSCAPS_MIPMAP              = 0x400000,
352:      DDSCAPS_RESERVED2           = 0x800000,
353:      DDSCAPS_ALLOCONLOAD         = 0x4000000,
354:      DDSCAPS_VIDEOPORT           = 0x8000000,
355:      DDSCAPS_LOCALVIDMEM         = 0x10000000,
356:      DDSCAPS_NONLOCALVIDMEM      = 0x20000000,
357:      DDSCAPS_STANDARDVGAMODE     = 0x40000000,
358:      DDSCAPS_OPTIMIZED           = 0x80000000
359:    }
360:
361:    public enum CONST_DDCKEYFLAGS : uint
362:    {
363:      DDCKEY_COLORSPACE  = 0x1,
364:      DDCKEY_DESTBLT     = 0x2,
365:      DDCKEY_DESTOVERLAY = 0x4,
366:      DDCKEY_SRCBLT      = 0x8,
367:      DDCKEY_SRCOVERLAY  = 0x10
368:    }
369:
370:    public enum CONST_DDFLIPFLAGS : uint
371:    {
372:      DDFLIP_WAIT        = 0x1,
373:      DDFLIP_EVEN        = 0x2,
374:      DDFLIP_ODD         = 0x4,
375:      DDFLIP_NOVSYNC     = 0x8,
376:      DDFLIP_STEREO      = 0x10,
377:      DDFLIP_DONOTWAIT   = 0x20,
378:      DDFLIP_INTERFVAL2  = 0x20000000,
379:      DDFLIP_INTERFVAL3  = 0x30000000,
380:      DDFLIP_INTERFVAL4  = 0x40000000
381:    }
382:
383:    public enum CONST_DDBLTFLAGS : uint
384:    {
385:      DDBLT_ASYNC           = 0x200,
386:      DDBLT_COLORFILL       = 0x400,
387:      DDBLT_DDFX            = 0x800,
388:      DDBLT_DDROPS         = 0x1000,
389:      DDBLT_KEYDEST         = 0x2000,
390:      DDBLT_KEYDESTOVERRIDE = 0x4000,
391:      DDBLT_KEYSRC          = 0x8000,
392:      DDBLT_KEYSRCOVERRIDE = 0x10000,
393:      DDBLT_ROP            = 0x20000,
394:      DDBLT_ROTATIONANGLE  = 0x40000,
```

23

WRITING A .NET ARCADE GAME USING DIRECTX

LISTING 23.20   Continued

```
395:        DDBLT_WAIT            = 0x1000000,
396:        DDBLT_DEPTHFILL       = 0x2000000,
397:        DDBLT_DONOTWAIT       = 0x8000000,
398:    }
399:
400:    public enum CONST_DDBLTFASTFLAGS : uint
401:    {
402:      DDBLTFAST_NOCOLORKEY   = 0x0,
403:      DDBLTFAST_SRCCOLORKEY  = 0x1,
404:      DDBLTFAST_DESTCOLORKEY = 0x2,
405:      DDBLTFAST_WAIT         = 0x10,
406:      DDBLTFAST_DONOTWAIT    = 0x20
407:    }
408:
409:    public enum CONST_DSBCAPSFLAGS : uint
410:    {
411:      DSBCAPS_PRIMARYBUFFER       = 0x1,
412:      DSBCAPS_STATIC             = 0x2,
413:      DSBCAPS_LOCHARDWARE        = 0x4,
414:      DSBCAPS_LOCSOFTWARE        = 0x8,
415:      DSBCAPS_CTRL3D             = 0x10,
416:      DSBCAPS_CTRLFREQUENCY      = 0x20,
417:      DSBCAPS_CTRLPAN            = 0x40,
418:      DSBCAPS_CTRLVOLUME         = 0x80,
419:      DSBCAPS_CTRLPOSITIONNOTIFY = 0x100,
420:      DSBCAPS_STICKYFOCUS        = 0x4000,
421:      DSBCAPS_GLOBALFOCUS        = 0x8000,
422:      DSBCAPS_GETCURRENTPOSITION2 = 0x10000,
423:      DSBCAPS_MUTE3DATMAXDISTANCE = 0x20000
424:    }
425:
426:    public enum CONST_DSBPLAYFLAGS
427:    {
428:      DSBPLAY_DEFAULT = 0,
429:      DSBPLAY_LOOPING = 1
430:    }
431:
432:    public enum CONST_DSBSTATUSFLAGS
433:    {
434:      DSBSTATUS_PLAYING    = 1,
435:      DSBSTATUS_BUFFERLOST = 2,
436:      DSBSTATUS_LOOPING    = 4
437:    }
438:
```

LISTING 23.20 Continued

```
439:    public enum CONST_DSSCLFLAGS
440:    {
441:      DSSCL_NORMAL       = 1,
442:      DSSCL_PRIORITY     = 2,
443:      DSSCL_EXCLUSIVE    = 3,
444:      DSSCL_WRITEPRIMARY = 4
445:    }
446: }
```

There are a few things to note about the previous listing. Only the methods used in the application are defined in the various DirectX interfaces; the rest are filled with placeholders or omitted altogether if occurring at the end of an interface. Also, in a couple of places the underlying type of an enumeration is used for a struct field instead of the enum type. All of this cuts down the amount of type information that needs to be supplied. If these shortcuts weren't performed, the entire DirectX type library would need to be defined manually. This "balloon effect" was discussed in Chapter 21.

> **TIP**
>
> In the definition of RECT in Lines 174–185, a ToString overload has been added to return a nicely formatted string with the RECT's contents. Adding a ToString overload to structs can be a handy debugging technique that can be added harmlessly; COM still sees the "original" struct without methods.

Because the DirectX type information is manually defined in C#, we need to make two minor changes to the beginning of Util.cs to get the advanced version to compile, highlighted here in a code snippet from Listing 23.1:

```
...
12:    // Main DirectX objects
13:    private static IDirectX7 directX;
14:    private static DirectDraw7 directDraw;
15:    private static DirectSound directSound;
16:
17:    // Two surfaces used for double-buffered animation
18:    private static DirectDrawSurface7 frontBuffer;
19:    private static DirectDrawSurface7 backBuffer;
20:
21:    // This must be called before using any of the other Util methods
22:    public static void Initialize(IntPtr hWnd)
```

```
23:    {
24:      // Create the main DirectX objects
25:      directX = (IDirectX)new DirectX7();
...
```

The members of the `IDirectX` interface must be called on the interface instead of the class directly, resulting in the changes in Lines 13 and 25. See Chapter 21 for details about how you could define methods on the `DirectX7` class directly using the `extern` keyword.

Conclusion

Something that should strike you about this chapter is that the bulk of it has nothing to do with COM Interoperability or PInvoke. Once a handful of calls to unmanaged code are tucked away inside a .NET class, .NET application development involving unmanaged code may not seem any different from .NET application development that doesn't rely on unmanaged code (besides the unmanaged code used internally by the .NET Framework). The advanced version of the game demonstrates that whether you write a graphics-intensive application in a .NET style or in a COM style (using plenty of PInvoke), the resulting applications can barely be differentiated from the user's perspective.

If you're interested in improving this sample game, there are plenty of improvements to be made. For example, you could make it properly recover when a user switches to another application and back (using Alt+Tab, for instance). Another good change would be to store high scores in a more secure fashion, and in a way that doesn't involve the Windows Registry. Have fun enhancing this application to learn more about .NET, COM interoperability, and PInvoke.

Writing .NET Visualizations For Windows Media Player

IN THIS CHAPTER

- The COM Visualization API   1197
- Creating a .NET Visualization API   1201
- Using the .NET Visualization API   1224

In this chapter, we have some fun using Windows Media Player, a popular application for playing music files and much more. Windows Media Player has a variety of interesting areas for software developers, and the area this chapter focuses on is visualizations.

A *visualization* is an animated picture that changes with the music (or any audio) being played by Windows Media Player. Visualizations usually change shape or color based on the characteristics of the music, giving the user something to watch while listening. Windows Media Player 7 comes with over 25 visualizations, such as "Water" shown in Figure 24.1 (bearing a similar resemblance to this book's cover), and Windows Media Player 8 comes with even more visualizations. The fun part for programmers is that any number of visualizations can be created and added to the list shown by the player's menus.

FIGURE 24.1
Windows Media Player, showing a visualization while music plays.

The look of the player itself is known as its *skin* and, in the case of Figure 24.1, looks like a human head. The skin, which can be customized, is completely independent of the visualization, which displays itself inside the dedicated area that often looks like a little television screen.

Unlike skins, each visualization is implemented as a COM object that gets called upon to turn sound into a picture. This works as follows:

1. Windows Media Player records a "snapshot" of the current audio at regular intervals. This snapshot contains frequency and waveform data.

2. As soon as the snapshot is taken, Windows Media Player calls a function implemented by the currently selected visualization COM object, passing the audio data.

3. The COM object's implementation uses the data to output a static picture.

4. Windows Media Player displays the output picture. The way in which it is displayed can depend upon the player's current skin.

This process repeats continuously, so the series of pictures can look like an animation.

Whereas the arcade game in the previous chapter demonstrated using COM Interoperability with a .NET client, this chapter's example demonstrates using COM Interoperability with a *COM* client. Although the direction of interaction is opposite, we're still going to be writing the .NET side of the application. With Windows Media Player as a COM client, you can write .NET objects that plug seamlessly into an architecture designed for COM.

In addition to just writing visualizations that are compatible with Windows Media Player's requirements, this chapter puts together a .NET class library that exposes visualization functionality with a .NET style, complete with events and its own custom attribute. After this new .NET API is introduced, we'll show a few sample visualizations built on top of it.

The code in this chapter uses Windows Media Player 7, which can be downloaded from `www.microsoft.com/windows/windowsmedia/`. It can also be used with Windows Media Player for Windows XP (Version 8). As with the previous chapter, all of the source code can be downloaded from this book's Web site.

The COM Visualization API

Before creating the .NET Visualization API, we'll begin with an overview of the current COM Visualization API. For a COM object to be a visualization, it must:

- Be registered specially as a visualization under the registry key `HKEY_LOCAL_MACHINE\Software\Microsoft\MediaPlayer\Objects\Effects`.

- Implement a single COM interface known as `IWMPEffects`.

As these two steps indicate, visualizations are also known as *effects*. The special registration is needed so Windows Media Player can quickly provide the user with a list of the visualizations installed on the machine. Figure 24.2 displays the contents of this area of the registry, and Figure 24.3 displays the `View`, `Visualizations` menu in Windows Media Player that corresponds to these registry contents. Each visualization is represented by a registry key with a `Properties` subkey containing a name, description, and CLSID of the COM object that implements `IWMPEffects` for the visualization.

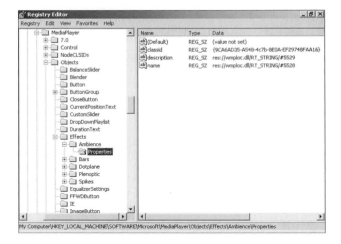

FIGURE 24.2

The Windows Registry branch containing visualization data.

FIGURE 24.3

The list of visualizations, as displayed by Windows Media Player for the registry contents shown in Figure 24.2.

The Windows Media Player SDK comes with a Windows Media Visualization Wizard specifically for unmanaged Visual C++ that helps with the custom registration, and even provides a default implementation of IWMPEffects. We don't make much use of this wizard in this chapter, because our visualizations are written in managed code. This wizard, however, generates an effects.idl file that contains the definition of IWMPEffects, as shown in Listing 21.1 in Chapter 21, "Manually Defining COM Types in Source Code." You should refer to this listing and its instructions for creating the IDL file if you're interested in viewing the original IWMPEffects definition.

The most important method of IWMPEffects is the first one—Render. This is the one method that gets called repetitively to handle the drawing. First we'll look in detail at how to implement Render, then we'll look briefly at the other ten methods.

The Render Method

The Render method has three parameters—a pointer to a TimedLevel structure, an HDC, and a pointer to a RECT structure. The TimedLevel structure contains all the information about the currently playing audio. It is defined as follows in IDL:

```
typedef struct tagTimedLevel
{
  unsigned char frequency[2][SA_BUFFER_SIZE];
  unsigned char waveform[2][SA_BUFFER_SIZE];
  int state;
  hyper timestamp;
} TimedLevel;
```

The two-dimensional frequency array contains a snapshot of the audio's frequency spectrum. The first leftmost dimension corresponds to the left audio channel, and the second leftmost dimension corresponds to the right audio channel. If the audio is not stereo, the data in the second half of the array is undefined. The rightmost dimension has an element for frequency values ranging from 20 Hz in the first slot to 22,050 Hz in the last. Because the array contains unsigned characters (bytes), each data value is a number ranging from 0 to 255. SA_BUFFER_SIZE, the size of the second dimension, is a constant set to 1,024. This data can be used for graphics equalizer effects.

The two-dimensional waveform array is structured just like the frequency array, however each element contains an independent snapshot of the audio's power. Therefore, each time Render is called, the waveform array data consists of 1024 mini-snapshots taken at an extremely short time interval. Although each data value ranges from 0 to 255, the real value falls between –128 and 127, so 128 is sometimes subtracted from the array's elements when visualizations use these values. This data can be used for oscilloscope effects.

The state field has one of the values of the following enumeration:

```
typedef enum PlayerState
{
  stop_state = 0,
```

```
    pause_state = 1,
    play_state = 2
};
```

With this information, a visualization can alter its effects based on whether the audio is currently stopped, paused, or playing.

Finally, the `timestamp` field, a 64-bit integer, gives a relative time for when the data snapshot occurred. This value can be used for timing animations.

`Render`'s `HDC` parameter is a handle to a Windows device context. This is a standard drawing surface in Windows programming, and can be passed directly to many GDI functions. Using this `HDC`, all you have to worry about is drawing on it with Windows pens, brushes, and so on.

The `RECT` structure, just as in the previous chapter, is a standard Windows rectangle that defines the size and position for the usable area of the device context. Because there's no way to know in advance the size of the visualization window (because it can be changed by the user or the skin settings), you should always use the rectangle when drawing on the device context.

Other Methods

Although the `Render` method is the most important one to implement, there are several other methods in the `IWMPEffects` interface. Some of these are necessary (but trivial to implement) whereas others are completely optional.

Before looking at these other methods, you need to understand some of the Windows Media Player visualization terminology. From a programmer's perspective, a visualization is a class that implements `IWMPEffects` and is registered specially. From a user's perspective, however, a visualization is a *group* of effects known as *presets*. Any visualization could have just one preset or hundreds of presets. A common use of presets is to provide variations of the same basic effect. For example, a visualization that displays twinkling stars could have a handful of presets that each use a different background color for the sky. On the other hand, these sorts of options could also be provided to the user using a single preset and a property page with customizable features. The choice is yours, but no matter how many presets you have, you'll need to implement a few methods to tell Windows Media Player about them.

The following list describes the remaining functions in `IWMPEffects`:

- `RenderFullScreen`. Called repeatedly instead of `Render` only if and when the visualization is in full-screen mode.

- `GetCapabilities`. Informs Windows Media Player of the visualization's capabilities. The `DWORD` out parameter must be set to one or more of the following flags bitwise-ORed together:

- EFFECT_CANGOFULLSCREEN (0x1)—The visualization is capable of full-screen rendering.

- EFFECT_HASPROPERTYPAGE (0x2)—The visualization has a property page.

- EFFECT_VARIABLEFREQSTEP (0x4)—The visualization uses frequency data with variable size steps. See Windows Media Player documentation for more information about this setting.

- DisplayPropertyPage. Called when the user requests to see the properties of the visualization, but only if GetCapabilities returns a value that indicates that the visualization has a property page. Has an HWND parameter that should be used as the owner window for the displayed property page.

- GoFullscreen. Called when the visualization is switching into or out of full-screen mode. A boolean parameter is set to true if entering full-screen mode; false if leaving. This is only called if GetCapabilities returns a value that indicates that the visualization supports full-screen rendering.

- GetPresetCount. Called when Windows Media Player wants to know how many presets the visualization supports.

- GetCurrentPreset. Called when Windows Media Player needs to know the index of the current preset.

- SetCurrentPreset. Called when Windows Media Player wants to set the current preset.

- GetPresetTitle. Called when Windows Media Player wants the title for a given preset index.

- GetTitle. Called when Windows Media Player wants the title of the visualization.

- MediaInfo. Supplies the visualization with data about the currently playing audio: title, number of audio channels (1 for mono, 2 for stereo), and the sample rate in Hertz.

Creating a .NET Visualization API

The goal of this chapter is to create and use a .NET Visualization API that, although based on COM, doesn't appear to have anything to do with COM to users of the API. This means using no attributes defined in System.Runtime.InteropServices, no awareness of COM or Win32 data types, and so on. Unfortunately, "hiding the COM" is not entirely possible because any visualizations must be registered, but having to run REGASM.EXE at installation time is something we'll have to live with.

The next four code listings comprise the BookExamples.WindowsMediaPlayer assembly that contains the .NET Visualization API. Because there's no official Windows Media Player type library, this assembly contains the managed definition of the IWMPEffects interface and its supporting types, as well as a `Visualization` class that .NET components will derive from to become visualizations rather than implementing an interface. All of the types in this assembly are placed in the namespace `BookExamples.WindowsMediaPlayer`.

The `IWMPEffects` Interface

Let's begin by looking at the managed definition of `IWMPEffects`. Listing 24.1 contains the same definition created in Chapter 21 with all of its user-friendly modifications above and beyond what the type library importer could do.

LISTING 24.1   `IWMPEffects.cs`. The Manually Written Definition for the `IWMPEffects` COM Interface

```
 1: using System;
 2: using System.Runtime.InteropServices;
 3:
 4: namespace BookExamples.WindowsMediaPlayer
 5: {
 6:   [
 7:     ComImport,
 8:     Guid("D3984C13-C3CB-48E2-8BE5-5168340B4F35"),
 9:     InterfaceType(ComInterfaceType.InterfaceIsIUnknown)
10:   ]
11:   interface IWMPEffects
12:   {
13:     // Render using the rectangle on the normalized device context
14:     void Render(ref TimedLevel levels, IntPtr hdc, ref RECT r);
15:
16:     // Provides the # of channels, sample rate and title of current audio
17:     void MediaInfo(int channelCount, int sampleRate, string title);
18:
19:     // Provides the capabilities of the visualization
20:     VisualizationCapabilities Capabilities { get; }
21:
22:     // Provides the display title of the visualization
23:     string Title { get; }
24:
25:     // Provides the title for a preset
26:     string GetPresetTitle(int preset);
27:
28:     // Provides the # of presets supported
29:     int PresetCount { get; }
30:
31:     // Set/Get the current preset
32:     int CurrentPreset { set; get; }
33:
```

LISTING 24.1   Continued

```
34:        // Display the property page of the effect (if there is one)
35:        void DisplayPropertyPage(IntPtr hwndOwner);
36:
37:        // Called when full screen rendering should start or stop
38:        void GoFullScreen(
39:          [MarshalAs(UnmanagedType.Bool)] bool startFullScreen);
40:
41:        // This is called after a successful a call to GoFullScreen(true).
42:        // Return failure from this method to signal loss of full screen.
43:        void RenderFullScreen(ref TimedLevel levels);
44:    }
45: }
```

Notice that the public keyword is omitted in the definition of IWMPEffects, so it is a private interface. The .NET Visualization API is going to expose a public abstract class instead, so authors of .NET visualizations can derive from the class and implement as little as two members rather than implementing the entire interface.

Despite all the user-friendly customizations to our .NET IWMPEffects definition, it would have been nice if we could have changed Render's third parameter to be a System.Drawing.Rectangle type rather than a simple RECT. Making such a transformation would seamlessly provide .NET components with their native rectangle type instead of a struct that will almost certainly be transformed into a System.Drawing.Rectangle in the method's implementation. In some limited scenarios, making such a modification in a managed signature would be legal—but not here. The System.Drawing.Rectangle value type looks like the following from COM's perspective (in IDL):

```
[
    typedef [uuid(...), version(1.0),
    custom(0F21F359-AB84-41E8-9A78-36D110E6D2F9, "System.Drawing.Rectangle")
]
struct tagRectangle
{
  long x;
  long y;
  long width;
  long height;
} Rectangle;
```

Whereas the third and fourth 32-bit fields of RECT correspond to the rectangle's right edge and bottom edge, respectively, the third and fourth 32-bit fields of Rectangle correspond to the rectangle's *width* and *height*. So, if we were guaranteed that Render is always called with a rectangle whose top and left coordinates are both zero (which is not true), we could have performed this trick. That's okay, though, because you'll see that Listing 24.3 (a little later in the chapter) does the next best thing to avoid having visualizations use the RECT type.

Supporting Structs and Enums

The .NET definition of IWMPEffects used some value types and enumerations that also need .NET definitions. Listing 24.2 contains the definitions for these supporting types.

LISTING 24.2 SupportingTypes.cs. The Manually Written Definitions of Structs and Enums Used by the IWMPEffects Interface

```
 1: using System;
 2: using System.Runtime.InteropServices;
 3:
 4: namespace BookExamples.WindowsMediaPlayer
 5: {
 6:   // A standard Windows rectangle
 7:   [ComVisible(false), StructLayout(LayoutKind.Sequential, Pack=4)]
 8:   public struct RECT
 9:   {
10:     public int Left;
11:     public int Top;
12:     public int Right;
13:     public int Bottom;
14:     public override string ToString()
15:     {
16:       return "[" + Left + ", " + Top + "] - ["
17:         + Right + ", " + Bottom + "]";
18:     }
19:   }
20:
21:   // A visualization's capabilities
22:   [ComVisible(false), Flags]
23:   public enum VisualizationCapabilities : uint
24:   {
25:     None = 0,
26:     CanGoFullScreen = 1,
27:     HasPropertyPage = 2,
28:     VariableFrequencyStep = 4,
29:   }
30:
31:   // The state of the audio
32:   [ComVisible(false)]
33:   public enum AudioState
```

LISTING 24.2   Continued

```
34:    {
35:       Stopped = 0,
36:       Paused  = 1,
37:       Playing = 2
38:    }
39:
40:    // The audio channels
41:    [ComVisible(false)]
42:    public enum AudioChannel
43:    {
44:      Left = 0,
45:      Right = 1
46:    }
47:
48:    // The structure holding the frequency, waveform and
49:    // state data crucial for rendering
50:    [ComVisible(false), StructLayout(LayoutKind.Sequential, Pack=4)]
51:    public struct TimedLevel
52:    {
53:      public const int MaxSamples = 1024;
54:
55:      // Beginning of the unmanaged definition
56:
57:      [MarshalAs(UnmanagedType.ByValArray, SizeConst = 2*MaxSamples)]
58:      private byte [] frequency;
59:
60:      [MarshalAs(UnmanagedType.ByValArray, SizeConst = 2*MaxSamples)]
61:      private byte [] waveform;
62:
63:      public AudioState State;
64:      public long TimeStamp;
65:
66:      // End of the unmanaged definition
67:
68:      // Returns the frequency (0-255) at the specified channel and index
69:      public byte GetFrequency(AudioChannel channel, int index)
70:      {
71:        if (index < 0) index = 0;
72:        return frequency[(int)channel * MaxSamples + index];
73:      }
74:
75:      // Returns the frequency at the specified channel and index,
76:      // scaled between 0 and maxValue
77:      public int GetScaledFrequency(
```

Listing 24.2   Continued

```
78:        AudioChannel channel, int index, int maxValue)
79:      {
80:        return (int)(GetFrequency(channel, index) * (maxValue / 256f));
81:      }
82:
83:      // Returns the waveform value (0-255)
84:      // at the specified channel and index
85:      public byte GetWaveform(AudioChannel channel, int index)
86:      {
87:        if (index < 0) index = 0;
88:        return waveform[(int)channel * MaxSamples + index];
89:      }
90:
91:      // Returns the waveform value at the specified channel and index,
92:      // scaled between 0 and maxValue
93:      public int GetScaledWaveform(
94:        AudioChannel channel, int index, int maxValue)
95:      {
96:        return (int)(GetWaveform(channel, index) * (maxValue / 256f));
97:      }
98:    }
99: }
```

Lines 1 and 2 list two namespaces—System for FlagsAttribute and System.Runtime. InteropServices for ComVisibleAttribute, StructLayoutAttribute, and MarshalAsAttrbiute (and their associated enum types). One thing might strike you about the five types defined in this listing—why are they all marked as COM-invisible? Don't we want to interact with COM? Yes, we do want to interact with COM, but having these value type definitions exposed is not necessary for this to occur. For classes and interfaces originally defined in the COM world (such as IWMPEffects), we can use ComImportAttribute as a way of saying "don't expose my definition to COM because I'm already defined elsewhere." Because ComImportAttribute doesn't apply to structs, this listing uses ComVisible(false) for the same purpose. These types need to be public so .NET components can use them when implementing visualizations, but there's no need to expose them to COM because we can assume, for example, that a COM client would get the definition of TimedLevel from the same place it gets the definition of IWMPEffects (such as effects.idl).

Unlike COM classes and interfaces, for which it is harmful to omit ComImportAttribute from the .NET definition, it is often fine to expose duplicate definitions of a value type. In this case, it's a little nicer to make them COM-invisible so new COM clients that may be written to host visualizations don't have to deal with name ambiguity if using the definitions of RECT and

`TimedLevel` from an IDL file while importing a type library exported from one of our .NET visualizations.

> **CAUTION**
>
> Avoid marking value types with `ComVisible(false)` if they're used in important types that are not marked with `ComImportAttribute`, because this limits what COM clients can directly do with members using such value types as parameters. In the case of `RECT` and `TimedLevel` in Listing 24.2 shown previously, it's okay to make the .NET definitions COM-invisible, because all COM interaction should be done through the single `IWMPEffects` interface (which is marked with `ComImportAttribute`).

The definition of `RECT` in Lines 7–19 should look familiar. It's just like the definition from Listing 23.20 in the previous chapter. Both this struct and `TimedLevel` are marked with sequential layout and a packing size of four just for clarity. The `VisualizationCapabilities`, `AudioState`, and `AudioChannel` enumerations encapsulate information from Windows Media Player documentation. Whereas `VisualizationCapabilities` is used as a parameter inside `IWMPEffects`, the other two enumerations are used by the `TimedLevel` structure. The `System.FlagsAttribute` custom attribute is used on `VisualizationCapabilities` to indicate that the values can be combined together with a bitwise `OR` operator.

The definition of `TimedLevel`, on Lines 50–98, begins by defining a `MaxSamples` constant set to the maximum number of data samples. It then has the four fields that the unmanaged structure also defines—an array containing frequency data, an array containing waveform data, the current state of the player, and a time stamp. Notice that the arrays are defined as one-dimensional despite the fact that they are really two-dimensional. This has to be done because the marshaler doesn't support multidimensional C-style arrays as fields of a structure. Therefore, we have no choice but to define them as one-dimensional and mark the size as the sum of the dimensions from each of the elements (2 * `MaxSamples`). Each array is now "flattened," with the first 1,024 elements containing the samples corresponding to the left audio channel (the 0th leftmost array dimension) and the last 1,024 elements containing the right audio channel's samples (the last leftmost array dimension).

Because dealing directly with these one-dimensional arrays in our visualizations would be cumbersome and error prone, they are defined as private. Instead of allowing .NET components to access these elements directly, public methods are added to the structure to expose the data in an intuitive way. All of these changes are legal because private fields of a value type are equivalent to public fields from COM's point of view, and additional methods don't affect COM's view of a value type. Although COM clients can't see these definitions due to the

24

VISUALIZATIONS FOR WINDOWS MEDIA PLAYER

ComVisible(false) marking, it's still crucial that the definition match the data of the original definition so the marshaler can construct the types appropriately when data is passed in from COM.

DIGGING DEEPER

Although it sounds strange to have a struct with private fields, many value types in the System.Drawing assembly have them to expose a simple structure to COM and user-friendly methods to .NET. These value types include Rectangle, Size, Point, SizeF, and PointF.

The GetFrequency and GetWaveform methods return the raw byte value contained in the respective array corresponding to the passed-in audio channel (left or right) and index. Rather than throwing an exception because of a negative index, these methods simply return zero. This is helpful for visualizations because the Render method sometimes receives rectangles with negative bounds, so this cuts down on the rectangle validation that Render implementations would have to do. Both of these methods have a scaled version, which returns an integer between zero and the passed in maxValue rather than a byte between 0 and 255. These methods are helpful for visualizations because scaling the data to the size of the rectangle is a common task. Had there been one main set of data in TimedLevel rather than two, implementing an indexer (default parameterized property) would be a natural choice to provide users with two-dimensional array syntax rather than having to call a method like GetFrequency. An indexer still could have been defined with three "dimensions"—audio channel, index, data type (frequency or waveform)—but that doesn't seem any easier to use or more readable than the current scheme.

The Visualization Class

As explained earlier, the managed definition of the IWMPEffects interface is private because our .NET visualizations will solely use implementation inheritance. The class they will all extend is Visualization, the only class that implements the IWMPEffects interface. Visualization is an abstract class (MustInherit in VB .NET), requiring derived classes to implement its Render method and Title property. This is done because, from the end user's point of view, it doesn't make sense to have an empty visualization showing up in Windows Media Player's list. By being abstract, subclass authors can derive from it and install their own visualization without worrying about a base visualization appearing in the list. Recall that abstract classes are not registered by the RegistrationServices API because it's impossible to instantiate them.

The Visualization class, shown in Listing 24.3, exposes an API that's slightly different than even the managed definition of IWMPEffects. Although the goal is to provide a .NET-like API, it's important to remain somewhat faithful to the original COM APIs so programmers experienced with the COM APIs can jump right in. In addition, the closer the APIs represent the COM APIs, the more useful existing documentation can be.

LISTING 24.3 Visualization.cs. The Abstract Visualization Class That Exposes the .NET Visualization API

```
 1: using System;
 2: using System.Runtime.InteropServices;
 3: using System.Drawing;
 4: using System.Windows.Forms;
 5: using System.Reflection;
 6: using Microsoft.Win32;
 7:
 8: namespace BookExamples.WindowsMediaPlayer
 9: {
10:   public abstract class Visualization : IWMPEffects
11:   {
12:     private int channelCount;
13:     private int sampleRate;
14:     private string audioTitle;
15:     private int currentPreset;
16:
17:     // Used for double buffering in full-screen mode
18:     Graphics offScreenGraphics;
19:     Graphics onScreenGraphics;
20:     Bitmap offScreenBitmap;
21:     Rectangle fullScreenRect;
22:
23:     [DllImport("user32.dll", ExactSpelling=true)]
24:     private static extern IntPtr GetForegroundWindow();
25:
26:     [DllImport("user32.dll", ExactSpelling=true)]
27:     private static extern bool GetWindowRect(IntPtr hwnd, out RECT r);
28:
29:     // Custom registration
30:     [ComRegisterFunction]
31:     private static void ComRegisterFunction(Type t)
32:     {
33:       Visualization v = (Visualization)Activator.CreateInstance(t);
34:       RegistryKey key = Registry.LocalMachine;
35:       key = key.CreateSubKey(
36:         "Software\\Microsoft\\MediaPlayer\\Objects\\Effects\\"
```

24

VISUALIZATIONS FOR WINDOWS MEDIA PLAYER

LISTING 24.3   Continued

```
37:          + v.Title + "\\Properties");
38:        key.SetValue("classid", t.GUID.ToString("B"));
39:        key.SetValue("name", v.Title);
40:        key.SetValue("description", v.Description);
41:        key.Close();
42:      }
43:
44:      // Custom unregistration
45:      [ComUnregisterFunction]
46:      private static void ComUnregisterFunction(Type t)
47:      {
48:        Visualization v = (Visualization)Activator.CreateInstance(t);
49:        RegistryKey key = Registry.LocalMachine;
50:        key.DeleteSubKey(
51:          "Software\\Microsoft\\MediaPlayer\\Objects\\Effects\\"
52:          + v.Title + "\\Properties");
53:        key.DeleteSubKey(
54:          "Software\\Microsoft\\MediaPlayer\\Objects\\Effects\\"
55:          + v.Title);
56:        key.Close();
57:      }
58:
59:      // The current number of audio channels
60:      public int CurrentChannelCount
61:      {
62:        get { return channelCount; }
63:      }
64:
65:      // The current sample rate of the audio
66:      public int CurrentSampleRate
67:      {
68:        get { return sampleRate; }
69:      }
70:
71:      // The title of the currently playing audio
72:      public string CurrentAudioTitle
73:      {
74:        get { return audioTitle; }
75:      }
76:
77:      // The number of the current preset
78:      public virtual int CurrentPreset
79:      {
80:        get { return currentPreset; }
```

LISTING 24.3 Continued

```
 81:          set { currentPreset = value; }
 82:        }
 83:
 84:        // A description of the visualization
 85:        public virtual string Description
 86:        {
 87:          get { return "A .NET visualization."; }
 88:        }
 89:
 90:        // The title of visualization
 91:        public abstract string Title { get; }
 92:
 93:        // Event raised when the current media changes.
 94:        // Information about the media can be accessed through
 95:        // the CurrentChannelCount, CurrentSampleRate, and
 96:        // CurrentAudioTitle properties.
 97:        public event EventHandler MediaChange;
 98:
 99:        // Event raised when the visualization enters full-screen mode
100:        public event EventHandler EnterFullScreen;
101:
102:        // Event raised when the visualization exits full-screen mode
103:        public event EventHandler ExitFullScreen;
104:
105:        // The original Render method
106:        void IWMPEffects.Render(
107:          ref TimedLevel levels, IntPtr hdc, ref RECT r)
108:        {
109:          using (Graphics g = Graphics.FromHdc(hdc))
110:          {
111:            Render(levels, g, Rectangle.FromLTRB(
112:              r.Left, r.Top, r.Right, r.Bottom));
113:
114:        }
115:
116:        // The public Render method
117:        public abstract void Render(
118:          TimedLevel levels, Graphics g, Rectangle r);
119:
120:        // The original MediaInfo method
121:        void IWMPEffects.MediaInfo(
122:          int channelCount, int sampleRate, string title)
123:        {
124:          this.channelCount = channelCount;
```

LISTING 24.3   Continued

```
125:        this.sampleRate = sampleRate;
126:        this.audioTitle = title;
127:
128:        OnMediaChange(new EventArgs());
129:    }
130:
131:    // Raises the MediaChange event
132:    protected virtual void OnMediaChange(EventArgs e)
133:    {
134:      if (MediaChange != null) MediaChange(this, e);
135:    }
136:
137:    // Returns CanGoFullScreen or CanGoFullScreen | HasPropertyPage
138:    // if the current instance overrides DisplayPropertyPage
139:    public virtual VisualizationCapabilities Capabilities
140:    {
141:      get
142:      {
143:        if (this.GetType().GetMethod("DisplayPropertyPage",
144:          BindingFlags.Public |
145:          BindingFlags.Instance |
146:          BindingFlags.DeclaredOnly) == null)
147:        {
148:          return VisualizationCapabilities.CanGoFullScreen;
149:        }
150:        else
151:        {
152:          return VisualizationCapabilities.CanGoFullScreen |
153:                VisualizationCapabilities.HasPropertyPage;
154:        }
155:      }
156:    }
157:
158:    // Returns the title of the visualization unless the current
159:    // instance uses PresetEnumAttribute to define its presets
160:    public virtual string GetPresetTitle(int preset)
161:    {
162:      // Check for the PresetEnumAttribute
163:      PresetEnumAttribute [] attributes = (PresetEnumAttribute [])
164:        this.GetType().GetCustomAttributes(
165:        typeof(PresetEnumAttribute), true);
166:
167:      if (attributes.Length == 0)
168:      {
```

LISTING 24.3 Continued

```
169:            // By default, return the title as the name of the preset.
170:            return Title;
171:        }
172:        else
173:        {
174:          if (!Enum.IsDefined(attributes[0].EnumType, preset))
175:            throw new ArgumentOutOfRangeException("preset");
176:
177:          return Enum.Format(attributes[0].EnumType, preset, "G");
178:        }
179:    }
180:
181:    // Returns 1 unless the current instance uses
182:    // PresetEnumAttribute to define its presets
183:    public virtual int PresetCount
184:    {
185:      get
186:      {
187:        // Check for the PresetEnumAttribute
188:        PresetEnumAttribute [] attributes = (PresetEnumAttribute [])
189:          this.GetType().GetCustomAttributes(
190:          typeof(PresetEnumAttribute), true);
191:
192:        if (attributes.Length == 0)
193:        {
194:          // By default, return only one preset.
195:          return 1;
196:        }
197:        else
198:        {
199:          return Enum.GetValues(attributes[0].EnumType).Length;
200:        }
201:      }
202:    }
203:
204:    // The original DisplayPropertyPage method
205:    void IWMPEffects.DisplayPropertyPage(IntPtr hwndOwner)
206:    {
207:      OwnerWindow owner = new OwnerWindow();
208:      owner.Handle = hwndOwner;
209:      DisplayPropertyPage(owner);
210:    }
211:
212:    // The public DisplayPropertyPage method
```

LISTING 24.3 Continued

```
213:      public virtual void DisplayPropertyPage(IWin32Window owner)
214:      {
215:          throw new NotImplementedException();
216:      }
217:
218:      // Called when switching between regular and full screen modes
219:      void IWMPEffects.GoFullScreen(bool startFullScreen)
220:      {
221:        if (startFullScreen)
222:        {
223:          IntPtr handle = GetForegroundWindow();
224:          RECT r;
225:          GetWindowRect(handle, out r);
226:
227:          fullScreenRect = Rectangle.FromLTRB(
228:            r.Left, r.Top, r.Right, r.Bottom);
229:
230:          // Create an off-screen bitmap and a Graphics object for it
231:          offScreenBitmap = new Bitmap(r.Right-r.Left, r.Bottom-r.Top);
232:          offScreenGraphics = Graphics.FromImage(offScreenBitmap);
233:
234:          // Construct a Graphics object from the HWND
235:          onScreenGraphics = Graphics.FromHwnd(handle);
236:
237:          OnEnterFullScreen(new EventArgs());
238:        }
239:        else
240:        {
241:          // Dispose the off-screen bitmap and Graphics objects
242:          offScreenBitmap.Dispose();
243:          offScreenGraphics.Dispose();
244:          onScreenGraphics.Dispose();
245:
246:          OnExitFullScreen(new EventArgs());
247:        }
248:      }
249:
250:      // Raises the EnterFullScreen event
251:      protected virtual void OnEnterFullScreen(EventArgs e)
252:      {
253:        if (EnterFullScreen != null) EnterFullScreen(this, e);
254:      }
255:
256:      // Raises the ExitFullScreen event
```

LISTING 24.3   Continued

```
257:      protected virtual void OnExitFullScreen(EventArgs e)
258:      {
259:        if (ExitFullScreen != null) ExitFullScreen(this, e);
260:      }
261:
262:      // Called during full-screen rendering
263:      void IWMPEffects.RenderFullScreen(ref TimedLevel levels)
264:      {
265:        Render(levels, offScreenGraphics, fullScreenRect);
266:
267:        // Draw the entire off-screen bitmap on the screen
268:        onScreenGraphics.DrawImage(offScreenBitmap, 0, 0);
269:      }
270:    }
271:
272:    // Used by Visualization's DisplayPropertyPage to construct
273:    // the managed view of a window with a certain HWND.
274:    class OwnerWindow : IWin32Window
275:    {
276:      private IntPtr handle;
277:
278:      public IntPtr Handle
279:      {
280:        get { return handle; }
281:        set { handle = value; }
282:      }
283:    }
284: }
```

Lines 1–6 list several namespaces—System for IntPtr, Type, Enum, and more; System.Runtime.InteropServices for DllImportAttribute, ComRegisterFunctionAttribute, and ComUnregisterFunctionAttribute; System.Drawing for Graphics, Bitmap, and Rectangle; System.Windows.Forms for IWin32Window; System.Reflection for BindingFlags; and Microsoft.Win32 for Registry and RegistryKey. Lines 12–15 define four private fields that can be accessed with public properties defined later in the listing, and Lines 18–21 define four private fields that are used for double buffering when rendering in full screen mode. The two PInvoke functions in Lines 23–27 are also used later in the listing for full-screen rendering.

Lines 30–42 contain the custom registration function, and Lines 45–57 contain the custom unregistration function. The first thing the registration function does in Line 33 is to use the Type parameter to create an instance of the current type being registered. Although the object created is statically typed as `Visualization`, the instance at run-time is some non-abstract subclass. We can always be sure that the `Type` object corresponds to a non-abstract class with a public default constructor because registration does not occur (and thus no custom registration function is called) for anything else. Lines 34–41 use the .NET Framework's registry APIs in `Microsoft.Win32` to create a subkey in the registry spot where Windows Media Player looks for visualizations. The visualization's `Title` property is used for the subkey containing the other information.

TIP

Although using a short title for the subkey name (Line 37 in Listing 24.3) matches the conventions used by other visualizations, you might want to consider using the type's CLSID instead to prevent name collisions. Windows Media Player displays the contents of the subkey's name value rather than extracting the title from the subkey itself, so a human-readable subkey is not necessary.

The `Title` property is used again for the `name` value, and the `Description` property is used for the `description` value. To obtain the CLSID for the visualization type, Line 38 uses the `GUID` property of `Type` and the "B" string format (just as we saw in Chapter 12, "Customizing COM's View of .NET Components"). In the custom unregistration function, the added subkey and values are removed. On Line 48, we need to create an instance of the class again to determine the title of the visualization we're unregistering. These custom registration functions aren't exposed to subclasses, yet they'll handle all the registration so derived classes don't need to know or care about them.

TIP

Ideally, custom registration functions should avoid instantiating the type being registered. Running the object's constructor could be a slow operation if it contains a lot of code, it could cause unwanted side effects, or even cause failure if the class author didn't expect the object to be created in the context of registration.

For this example, one way to avoid the need to create an instance would be to require subclasses to implement static (`Shared` in VB .NET) `Title` and `Description` properties that can be invoked inside the registration functions without needing an instance of the type. Such a requirement, however, might seem awkward to subclass authors, and compilers won't be able to help in enforcing this rule. (This is the same scheme used with `ICustomMarshaler` and the requirement to also implement a static `GetInstance` method, described in Chapter 20, "Custom Marshaling.") Contrast this to having an abstract `Title` property, for which subclasses that don't implement this can't even compile.

For this example, the documentation of the Visualization class should simply warn subclass authors that an instance is created during registration/unregistration, and thus they can avoid doing work in the class's default constructor.

Lines 60–75 define three simple read-only properties that provide access to the channelCount, sampleRate, and audioTitle fields. The contents of these fields are filled in by the MediaInfo method later in the listing. Lines 78–82 define the CurrentPreset property from the IWMPEffects interface. The property is marked virtual (Overridable in VB .NET) in case derived classes want to change the implementation. Notice that although the definition of CurrentPreset in the IWMPEffects interface carefully listed the set accessor before the get accessor, the ordering doesn't matter here. Although the ordering would affect the class interface if the class were marked with ClassInterface(ClassInterfaceType.AutoDual), COM clients would have no prior expectation about the method ordering of such new interfaces.

Lines 85–91 contain the two properties used by the custom registration functions— Description and Title. The Title property is abstract, forcing a derived class to return a string through this property. The Description property, however, is simply virtual because it's not crucial that every visualization has a unique description (although it would be nice). The default description in Line 87 is appropriate, although not very helpful to end users.

Lines 97–103 define three events raised by the Visualization class—MediaChange, EnterFullScreen, and ExitFullScreen. The code that raises these events appears a little later in the listing. All three events use the standard System.EventHandler delegate because they have no additional information to communicate when they are raised.

Lines 106–114 contain the implementation of IWMPEffects.Render using explicit interface implementation. This means that the method is not accessible from the class type. Instead, users can only call such a method by casting an instance of the class to the interface type the method is defined on. Because the IWMPEffects interface is private to the BookExample. WindowsMediaPlayer assembly, this Render method is essentially private to .NET components but COM clients can still call the method through the IWMPEffects interface. Recall that in Visual Basic .NET, the same effect can be achieved by marking the class's method with Private. For example:

```
Private Sub Render _
  (ByRef levels As TimedLevel, hdc As IntPtr, ByRef r As RECT) _
  Implements IWMPEffects.Render
```

So, why do we bother hiding Render from .NET components? Because we added a public overloaded Render method with parameter types that are more natural to work with in managed code. This overloaded Render, defined on Lines 117 and 118, is an abstract method that must be implemented by subclasses. The `TimedLevel` parameter is by-value instead of by-reference (because there's no need to modify the contents of the structure inside `Render`), the `HDC` parameter is now the type `System.Drawing.Graphics`, and the `RECT` parameter is now a `System.Drawing.Rectangle`. To make this work, COM calls the original `Visualization.Render` method and, in Lines 109–113, the `Render` overload implemented by the subclass is called. This code uses `Graphics.FromHdc` to transform the `HDC` into a `Graphics` object, and `Rectangle.FromLTRB` (that's LeftTopRightBottom) to transform the values of `RECT` to a `Rectangle`.

Line 109 uses C#'s `using` construct to dispose the `Graphics` object deterministically. Recall that this is equivalent to the lengthier code:

```
Graphics g = Graphics.FromHdc(hdc);
try
{
  Render(levels, g, Rectangle.FromLTRB(
    r.Left, r.Top, r.Right, r.Bottom));
}
finally
{
  ((System.IDisposable)g).Dispose();
}
```

The cast to `IDisposable` is sometimes necessary, for cases in which the object hides the `Dispose` method through explicit interface implementation. Therefore, in languages without this construct (such as VB .NET), the lengthier try/finally pattern should be used.

DIGGING DEEPER

C#'s `using` construct, like `lock` and `foreach`, are language shortcuts for common tasks. You've already seen the equivalent code for a `using` block, but let's look at `lock` and `foreach`. The following `lock` block:

```
lock(obj)
{
  ...
}
```

is equivalent to:

```
System.Threading.Monitor.Enter(obj);
try
{
  ...
}
finally
```

```
{
    System.Threading.Monitor.Exit(obj);
}
```

The situation with `foreach` is a little more complicated because extra work is done if the enumerator implements `IDisposable`. The following `foreach` block:

```
foreach (String s in obj)
{
    ...
}
```

translates into the following *if* `GetEnumerator` returns the standard `IEnumerator` type:

```
IEnumerator enumerator = obj.GetEnumerator();
try
{
    while (enumerator.MoveNext())
    {
        String s = (String)enumerator.Current;
        ...
    }
}
finally
{
    IDisposable temp = enumerator as IDisposable;
    if (temp != null) temp.Dispose();
}
```

If the enumeration is strongly-typed, (such as returning a `StringEnumerator`) then the code translates into either:

```
StringEnumerator enumerator = obj.GetEnumerator();
while (enumerator.MoveNext())
{
    String s = enumerator.Current;
    ...
}
```

or:

```
StringEnumerator enumerator = obj.GetEnumerator();
try
{
    while (enumerator.MoveNext())
    {
        String s = enumerator.Current;
        ...
    }
}
```

```
finally
{
  ((IDisposable)enumerator).Dispose();
}
```

depending on whether or not the StringEnumerator type implements IDisposable.

Lines 121–129 also use explicit interface implementation for the MediaInfo method. The method simply updates the class's private fields with the data and calls OnMediaChange. OnMediaChange is a protected virtual method defined in Lines 132–135 that raised the MediaChange event so a subclass can find out when a media change occurs. If the subclass is interested in the characteristics of the current media, it can use the CurrentChannelCount, CurrentSampleRate, and CurrentAudioTitle properties.

Lines 139–156 use the power of reflection to give a sensible default implementation of the Capabilities property. Because all visualizations deriving from this class support full-screen rendering (as you'll see later in the listing), this method returns VisualizationCapabilities. CanGoFullScreen by default. However, we'd like the method to return this value bitwise-ORed with VisualizationCapabilities.HasPropertyPage if the current instance overrides the DisplayPropertyPage method. Therefore, we check if the current type has a public instance called DisplayPropertyPage using the binding flag DeclaredOnly. This means that the method has to be defined on the most derived type to be found. If the method is not found, Type.GetMethod returns a null instance. This implementation saves the subclass author from having to override the Capabilities property when overriding HasPropertyPage, which is error prone and easy to forget. Of course, the Capabilities property can always be overridden to provide different behavior if you don't like what it does. Note that the current implementation doesn't work if a subclass overrides HasPropertyPage and then a subclass of the subclass wants to inherit this functionality. To accommodate this, Capabilities would have to use reflection to traverse the inheritance hierarchy, looking for the most-derived HasPropertyPage (and stopping once it reaches the base Visualization type).

The next two methods do some magic with a custom attribute to save subclass authors from additional work. GetPresetTitle, in Lines 160–179, must return a string corresponding to the preset number given. Rather than forcing each subclass with multiple presets to re-implement this method, this base method checks for a custom attribute on the current instance that contains an enumeration of all the supported presets. This custom attribute— PresetEnumAttribute—will be defined in Listing 24.4. We check for the attribute in Lines 163–165 by calling GetCustomAttributes on the current type instance, passing the type of

PresetEnumAttribute. Because we pass true for the inherited parameter (and because the definition of the attribute allows inheritance), the attribute will be found even if the most derived class isn't marked with it. If the attribute isn't found, the length of the returned array is zero and the title is returned as the name of the one and only preset in Line 170. This is a reasonable default since many skins display only the preset name of the currently running visualization. If the custom attribute is found, Line 174 checks to see if the passed-in value is one of the enum's members using Enum.IsDefined. If the number is in the valid range, Enum.Format is used to return the string representation of the enumeration value.

The PresetCount property, implemented in Lines 183–202, uses the same manner of checking for the PresetEnumAttribute. If found, the number of enum members is returned (obtained using Enum.GetValues in Line 199). If not, one is returned because the default behavior is having a single preset. The way in which PresetEnumAttribute is used assumes that the members of the enumeration have contiguous values starting at zero. Also, the preset names can only be as expressive as an enum member (in other words, no spaces). Still, using the attribute can be much more convenient and maintainable than implementing CurrentPreset, GetPresetTitle, and PresetCount. If you want multi-word presets, you can always override these methods instead.

The DisplayPropertyPage method, just like Render, is explicitly implemented so an overloaded method with a .NET-friendly parameter is exposed to others. In this case, the pair of methods is used to transform the HWND parameter into an IWin32Window interface. IWin32Window is defined in the System.Windows.Forms assembly, and has a single read-only Handle property of type System.IntPtr. The System.Windows.Forms.Form class implements this interface. The goal of this method is to display a dialog with the owner window specified by the passed-in HWND. The Form class has a ShowDialog method, but its owner parameter is the IWin32Window type, hence the need for the transformation. The implementation of DisplayPropertyPage in Lines 205–210 needs to construct some object implementing IWin32Window that it can pass to the public DisplayPropertyPage overload. Unfortunately, we can't construct a Form object because there's no way to *set* its handle; only a way to *get* it. Therefore, Line 207 creates an instance of an OwnerWindow object that supports getting and setting its handle. OwnerWindow is a simple class defined in Lines 274–283 that implements IWin32Window but also adds a set accessor to the Handle property. Because it implements the required interface, it can be passed to the DisplayPropertyPage overload, after its Handle property is set to the passed in HWND on Line 208. The base implementation of the DisplayPropertyPage overload (Lines 213–216) simply throws a NotImplementedException.

The base implemenation of GoFullScreen on Lines 219–248 does a few transformations to accommodate rendering in full-screen mode without any additional work needed by derived classes. The transformations done when entering full-screen mode (Lines 223–237) are similar to the implementation of `Render`, except that an `HWND` and `RECT` need to be obtained for the foreground window using the Win32 APIs `GetForegroundWindow` and `GetWindowRect`. To avoid too much flickering, `GoFullScreen`'s implementation sets up double buffering during the render process. It does this by creating an off-screen `Graphics` object as well as an on-screen `Graphics` object. After the objects are initialized, `OnEnterFullScreen` is called in Line 237 to raise the `EnterFullScreen` event. When exiting full-screen mode (Lines 242–246) the necessary objects are disposed, and the `ExitFullScreen` event is raised by a call to `OnExitFullScreen`.

DIGGING DEEPER

Double buffering reduces flickering, but the `Visualization` class only uses double buffering in full-screen mode because it slows down rendering, such that screen updates don't occur as frequently. If the visualizations didn't have to repaint the entire surface area each time, the rendering time could be shortened so that double buffering in all cases would be viable. With the examples in this chapter, flickering is only noticeable when running Windows Media Player in *full mode* (different from full-screen mode) rather than in *skin mode*.

Notice that `GoFullScreen`'s boolean parameter is not marked with `MarshalAs(UnmanagedType.Bool)` as in the interface. This doesn't really matter because Windows Media Player only knows about and uses the `IWMPEffects` interface, which has the correct marking. If other COM clients attempted to use class interfaces for any derived classes, the `GoFullScreen` method would simply have a `VARIANT_BOOL` parameter instead of `BOOL` unless each class used `MarshalAsAttribute` on it. Because the goal is to hide the COM from derived visualization classes, there's no need to do this.

Lines 251–260 contain the `OnEnterFullScreen` and `OnExitFullScreen` methods, which raise the two corresponding events. In Lines 263–269, `RenderFullScreen` is explicitly implemented. It calls the same abstract `Render` method in Line 265 as called by our implementation of `IWMPEffects.Render`, but passes the off-screen `Graphics` object and full-screen `Rectangle` object created inside `GoFullScreen`. After the call, it draws the contents of the off-screen bitmap to the on-screen display because we're using double buffering.

Listing 24.4 contains the code for the `PresetEnumAttribute` that can be used by classes derived from `Visualization`.

LISTING 24.4   `PresetEnumAttribute.cs`. The Custom Attribute Used by Visualization Classes to be Associated with a List of Presets

```
1: using System;
2:
3: [AttributeUsage(AttributeTargets.Class)]
4: public class PresetEnumAttribute : Attribute
5: {
6:   private Type enumType;
7:
8:   // Constructor - called when the attribute is applied
9:   public PresetEnumAttribute(Type zeroBasedEnumType)
10:  {
11:    enumType = zeroBasedEnumType;
12:  }
13:
14:  // Read-only property to get the enum type
15:  public virtual Type EnumType
16:  {
17:    get { return enumType; }
18:  }
19: }
```

The custom attribute is just about as simple as it can get. The `AttributeUsageAttribute` indicates that it's valid only on classes, and the private field on Line 6 stores the enum type. Lines 9–12 contain the constructor with a `Type` parameter, and Lines 15–18 contain a read-only property that returns the type instance.

That completes the source files for the `BookExamples.WindowsMediaPlayer` assembly. To compile it, you can run the following at a command prompt:

```
csc /t:library /out:BookExamples.WindowsMediaPlayer.dll IWMPEffects.cs
➥SupportingTypes.cs Visualization.cs PresetEnumAttribute.cs
➥/r:System.Drawing.dll /r:System.Windows.Forms.dll /r:System.dll
```

For COM components that implement visualizations, Microsoft recommends that they be installed in the `Visualizations` subfolder where Windows Media Player is installed. For .NET components, the Global Assembly Cache is a great place to install the assembly, but you could also place it in the `Visualizations` directory instead. If you decide to put the visualizations created in this chapter in this directory, you should place the `BookExamples.WindowsMediaPlayer` assembly either in this same directory or in the GAC. If you choose the latter you'll need to give the assembly a strong name, but it's a great idea to do this anyway. By installing it in the GAC, you don't need to worry about a different publisher overwriting your assembly with a file that has the same name.

24

VISUALIZATIONS
FOR WINDOWS
MEDIA PLAYER

Using the .NET Visualization API

Now that the BookExamples.WindowsMediaPlayer assembly is available, let's use it to create some visualizations. In this section, we look at four different visualizations. All of these derive directly from Visualization, as shown in Figure 24.4.

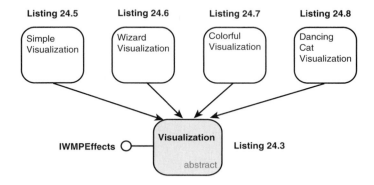

FIGURE 24.4

Four visualizations based on the BookExamples.WindowsMediaPlayer *assembly.*

A Simple Visualization

Listing 24.5 contains the simplest possible visualization (written with Visual Basic .NET), yet the resulting effect is still interesting to watch.

LISTING 24.5   SimpleVisualization.vb. The SimpleVisualization Class Demonstrates a Basic Use of the .NET Visualization API in Visual Basic .NET

```vb
1: Imports System.Drawing
2: Imports BookExamples.WindowsMediaPlayer
3:
4: Public Class SimpleVisualization
5:    Inherits Visualization
6:
7:    Public Overrides ReadOnly Property Title As String
8:       Get
9:          Title = "Simple"
10:       End Get
11:    End Property
12:
13:    Public Overrides Sub Render(levels As TimedLevel, _
14:       g As Graphics, r As Rectangle)
```

LISTING 24.5   Continued

```
15:
16:      ' Fill background with dark blue
17:      g.FillRectangle(Brushes.DarkBlue, r)
18:
19:      ' Walk through the frequencies until we run
20:      ' out of samples or drawing surface
21:      Dim x As Integer = r.Left
22:      While (x < r.Right AndAlso x < TimedLevel.MaxSamples)
23:         If (levels.GetFrequency(AudioChannel.Left, x) >= 128)
24:            g.DrawLine(Pens.Red, x, r.Top, x, r.Bottom)
25:         End If
26:         x = x + 1
27:      End While
28:   End Sub
29: End Class
```

Lines 1–2 import two namespaces: `System.Drawing` for `Render`'s `Graphics` and `Rectangle` parameters and `BookExamples.WindowsMediaPlayer` for the `Visualization` base class. (Notice how `System.Runtime.InteropServices` isn't on the list.) The `SimpleVisualization` class does the minimum amount of work necessary to be a visualization by only implementing the abstract `Render` and `Title` members. The `Title` property is implemented in Lines 7–11, and returns "Simple" as the title. Because it doesn't override the `GetPresetTitle` method, "Simple" is also used for the name of the one and only preset.

Lines 13–28 contain the implementation of `Render`. Because this is the ".NET-ized" `Render`, the implementation can directly use the `System.Drawing.Graphics` and `System.Drawing.Rectangle` parameters seamlessly. Line 17 fills the entire rectangle with a dark blue color, and Lines 21–27 draw a vertical red line in places where a corresponding frequency is greater than a certain threshold.

Each pixel on the rectangle's X-coordinate represents a data point in the array of frequencies. Because the number of samples (`TimedLevel.MaxSamples`) could be less or greater than the width of the rectangle in pixels, the `While` loop stops when hitting either the right edge of the rectangle or the maximum number of samples—whichever comes first. Line 23 checks the frequency for each data point by calling the handy `GetFrequency` method we defined previously in Listing 24.2. For simplicity, the visualization only uses the frequencies in the left audio channel. A threshold of 128 is chosen because it falls in the middle of the range of frequency values returned (0–255). If the frequency is in the upper half, a vertical red line is drawn using `Graphics.DrawLine`.

That's all there is to it. To compile this visualization, run the following:

```
vbc /t:library SimpleVisualization.vb /r:System.Drawing.dll
➥ /r:BookExamples.WindowsMediaPlayer.dll
```

If you're placing it in the same `Visualizations` directory as the `BookExamples.WindowsMediaPlayer.dll`, you should register it with a codebase as follows (after moving it to its final location):

```
regasm SimpleVisualization.dll /codebase
```

If you give it a strong name and install it in the GAC, you'll need the dependent `BookExamples.WindowsMediaPlayer` assembly there, too. It's not necessary to register `BookExamples.WindowsMediaPlayer.dll` because the abstract `Visualization` class doesn't get registered.

To see this simple visualization in action, open Windows Media Player and choose `View`, `Visualizations`, `Simple`, `Simple` from the menu. Figure 24.5 displays the result of using `SimpleVisualization` while music is playing.

FIGURE 24.5

The Simple visualization, as shown in Windows Media Player.

TIP

When running visualizations, be aware that Windows Media Player does not support them when playing MIDI files. To see your visualizations run, be sure you're playing music in a supported format.

The Wizard Visualization

The next visualization we'll create is called WizardVisualization, not because it contains an animated wizard, but because it is based on the visualization generated by the unmanaged C++ Windows Media Visualization Wizard. This visualization makes use of two presets—one called "scope" that looks like an oscilloscope, and another called "bars" that looks like a graphic equalizer. Listing 24.6 contains the C# source code for this visualization.

LISTING 24.6 WizardVisualization.cs. The WizardVisualization Class Is Based on the Sample Visualization Generated by the Windows Media Visualization Wizard

```
 1: using System.Drawing;
 2: using BookExamples.WindowsMediaPlayer;
 3:
 4: // The presets supported by this visualization
 5: enum Presets
 6: {
 7:   Bars,
 8:   Scope
 9: }
10:
11: [PresetEnum(typeof(Presets))]
12: public class WizardVisualization : Visualization
13: {
14:   public override string Title
15:   {
16:     get { return "Wizard"; }
17:   }
18:
19:   public override string Description
20:   {
21:     get { return "A .NET visualization based on the one " +
22:       "generated by the Windows Media Visualization Wizard."; }
23:   }
24:
25:   public override void Render(TimedLevel levels,
26:     Graphics g, Rectangle r)
27:   {
28:     int y;      // The current Y-coordinate
29:     int lastY;  // Stores the previous Y-coordinate for the scope preset
30:
31:     // Fill background with black
32:     g.FillRectangle(Brushes.Black, r);
33:
```

LISTING 24.6   Continued

```
34:       // Draw based on the current preset
35:       switch ((Presets)CurrentPreset)
36:       {
37:         case Presets.Bars:
38:         {
39:           // Walk through the frequencies until we run
40:           // out of samples or drawing surface.
41:           for (int x = r.Left;
42:             x < r.Right && x < TimedLevel.MaxSamples; x++)
43:           {
44:             y = levels.GetScaledFrequency(AudioChannel.Left, x, r.Height);
45:             g.DrawLine(Pens.MintCream, x, r.Bottom,
46:               x, r.Bottom - y);
47:           }
48:         }
49:         break;
50:
51:         case Presets.Scope:
52:         {
53:           y = levels.GetScaledWaveform(AudioChannel.Left, r.Left,
54:             r.Height);
55:           lastY = y;
56:
57:           // Walk through the waveform data until we run
58:           // out of samples or drawing surface.
59:           for (int x = r.Left;
60:             x < r.Right && x < TimedLevel.MaxSamples; x++)
61:           {
62:             g.DrawLine(Pens.Tomato, x - 1, lastY, x, y);
63:             y = levels.GetScaledWaveform(AudioChannel.Left, x, r.Height);
64:             lastY = y;
65:           }
66:         }
67:         break;
68:       }
69:     }
70: }
```

Lines 1–2 use the same two namespaces for the same reasons as the previous listing. Lines 5–9 define the `Presets` enumeration which contains two members, one for each preset. The `WizardVisualization` class begins on Line 11 with the application of the `PresetEnumAttribute` custom attribute to associate the `Presets` type with the `WizardVisualization` class. Lines 14–23 contain the definitions of the overridden `Title` and `Description` properties that return strings to uniquely identify this visualization.

Finally, the Render method is contained in Lines 25–69. We begin again by filling the background with a solid color (Line 32), and this time the background color is black. Line 35 begins a switch statement that chooses which drawing logic is executed, based on the current preset. Notice that thanks to the work done in the base Visualization class, all the code needs to do is check the value of the CurrentPreset property, casting the integer to the appropriate enumeration.

For the bars preset, each X-coordinate has a vertical line extending from the bottom of the rectangle to a point representative of the frequency at that point. Like the previous visualization, the for loop scans the area from left to right, stopping as soon as it runs out of samples or reaches the end of the rectangle. Line 44 calls GetScaledFrequency with the rectangle's height as the final parameter to get a value that ranges from the top to the bottom of the rectangle. Lines 45–46 draw the line using a "mint cream" pen.

The scope preset differs from the bars preset in two major ways:

- The audio's waveform data is used instead of frequency data.
- Each data point is connected with a single line to the previous one, rather than each point connecting to the bottom of the rectangle.

Therefore, the drawing code in Lines 59–65 keeps track of the previous waveform value in each iteration of the loop using the lastY variable that was declared in Line 29. The line is drawn in Line 62 with a tomato-colored pen.

Compared to the unmanaged C++ generated by the Windows Media Player Visualization Wizard, it took very little code to get a visualization with the same functionality. Most of the savings in code can be attributed to using PresetEnumAttribute so the base class can handle the management of presets, and using the helper methods defined on the TimedLevel value type. Visualizations written this way can focus on the important part—drawing the pictures. Compiling and installing this visualization requires the same steps as the simple visualization (although with a different compiler). First, run the following:

```
csc /t:library WizardVisualization.cs /r:System.Drawing.dll
➥/r:BookExamples.WindowsMediaPlayer.dll
```

Copy it to the Visualizations directory with the other assemblies, then register the assembly:

```
regasm WizardVisualization.dll /codebase
```

After this visualization has been installed, open Windows Media Player and select View, Visualizations, Wizard, Bars from the menu, or View, Visualizations, Wizard, Scope.

24

VISUALIZATIONS
FOR WINDOWS
MEDIA PLAYER

Figure 24.6 displays the result of using `WizardVisualization` with the Bars preset, and Figure 24.7 displays the result of using it with the Scope preset.

FIGURE 24.6
The Wizard visualization with the Bars preset, as shown in Windows Media Player.

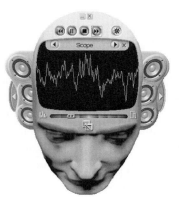

FIGURE 24.7
The Wizard visualization with the Scope preset, as shown in Windows Media Player.

The Colorful Visualization

For this visualization, we'll make use of the ability to display a property page so the user can customize the output. We'll also display some of the media information provided by the base class properties. Listing 24.7 contains the C# source code for this visualization.

LISTING 24.7 ColorfulVisualization.cs. The ColorVisualization Class Enables the User to Select a Background Color for the Visualization

```
 1: using System.Drawing;
 2: using System.Windows.Forms;
 3: using BookExamples.WindowsMediaPlayer;
 4:
 5: public class ColorfulVisualization : Visualization
 6: {
 7:   private static Color backgroundColor = Color.LemonChiffon;
 8:
 9:   public override string Title
10:   {
11:     get { return "Colorful"; }
12:   }
13:
14:   public override string Description
15:   {
16:     get { return "A visualization whose background " +
17:                  "color can be configured."; }
18:   }
19:   }
20:
21:   public override void DisplayPropertyPage(IWin32Window owner)
22:   {
23:     ColorDialog d = new ColorDialog();
24:
25:     // We don't even use the owner window
26:     if (d.ShowDialog() == DialogResult.OK)
27:     {
28:       backgroundColor = d.Color;
29:     }
30:   }
31:
32:   public override void Render(TimedLevel levels,
33:     Graphics g, Rectangle r)
34:   {
35:     int y;        // The current Y-coordinate
```

LISTING 24.7   Continued

```
36:     Pen pen;      // The pen used to draw on the background color
37:     Brush brush;  // The brush used to draw on the background color
38:
39:     using (Brush b = new SolidBrush(backgroundColor))
40:     {
41:       // Fill background with the chosen color
42:       g.FillRectangle(b, r);
43:     }
44:
45:     if (backgroundColor.GetBrightness() > 0.5)
46:     {
47:       pen = Pens.Black;
48:       brush = Brushes.Black;
49:     }
50:     else
51:     {
52:       pen = Pens.White;
53:       brush = Brushes.White;
54:     }
55:
56:     using (Font f = new Font("Arial", 14))
57:     {
58:       // Write the audio title at the top left corner (with some padding)
59:       g.DrawString(CurrentAudioTitle, f, brush, 10, 10);
60:     }
61:
62:     // Walk through the frequencies until we run
63:     // out of samples or drawing surface
64:     for (int x = r.Left;
65:       x < r.Right && x < TimedLevel.MaxSamples; x++)
66:     {
67:       y = levels.GetScaledFrequency(AudioChannel.Left, x, r.Height);
68:       g.DrawLine(pen, x, r.Bottom, x, r.Bottom - y);
69:     }
70:   }
71: }
```

Line 2 lists one more additional namespace than the previous visualizations—
System.Windows.Forms. This is needed because the class overrides the HasPropertyPage
method with an IWin32Window parameter. Line 7 defines a private field of type
System.Drawing.Color that stores the background color chosen by the user. The initial color is
set to lemon chiffon. Notice that the field is static. This is done because every time the user
configures the visualization through its property page, Windows Media Player creates a new
instance of the object.

Lines 9–19 contain the usual Title and Description properties. In the implementation of DisplayPropertyPage (Lines 21–30), the common dialog for choosing colors is used for the user interface. Because these common dialogs (which derive from System.Windows. Forms.CommonDialog) are a different sort of control than a Form, we don't need to use the owner parameter to tie the window to the caller's window. The method simply creates a new ColorDialog instance, calls ShowDialog, and updates the background color if the user hit the OK button. The ColorDialog class has a Color property that makes retrieving the selected color easy (used in Line 28). Displaying a color dialog directly is taking the easy way out. You'd most likely want to create your own form and display that when the user requests it. In this case, simply create an instance of your form class and call ShowDialog, passing owner as the IWin32Window parameter.

The implementation of Render has a few more interesting things going on than in the previous visualizations. Unlike the others, which used only predefined pens and brushes, we need to create a new SolidBrush instance to paint the background with the color chosen by the user. Because brushes are scarce Windows resources, it's important for them to be released as soon as the client is done with them. Hence, Brush implements IDisposable, and Lines 29–43 use C#'s using construct to dispose the brush deterministically. The code in Lines 39–43 is equivalent to:

```
Brush b = new SolidBrush(backgroundColor);
try
{
  // Fill background with the chosen color
  g.FillRectangle(b, r);
}
finally
{
  ((System.IDisposable)b).Dispose();
}
```

After the background has been painted, we're ready to do some drawing. It's important that the foreground drawing is done in a color that shows up nicely against the background. Because the user is only given the option to change the background color and not the foreground color, Lines 45–54 select an appropriate color. The heuristic used in Line 45 is to check the brightness of the color. If the brightness value (a floating point number from 0 to 1) is in the higher half, we'll draw with black. Otherwise, we'll draw with white. This simple check does a fine job at producing nice-looking results. Notice that the code sets both a brush and a pen to the chosen color. This is needed because the method draws text with a brush and draws lines with a pen. Also, notice that the predefined black and white pens and brushes are used, so we don't need to create additional instances.

TIP	
When using pens and brushes, try to use the built-in brushes and pens defined by `System.Drawing.Brushes` and `System.Drawing.Pens` with predefined colors. This eliminates the need to worry about disposing them.	

Lines 56–60 draw a string inside the rectangle, at a location 10 pixels down and ten pixels to the right of the top-left corner. The string used is `CurrentAudioTitle`, the property defined by the base `Visualization` class. Again, C#'s using construct is used because fonts are scarce resources and implement `IDisposable`. Lines 64–69 draw bars in an identical fashion as the bars preset in `WizardVisualization`.

To run this visualization, compile the listing as follows:

```
csc /t:library ColorfulVisualization.cs /r:System.Drawing.dll
➥/r:System.Windows.Forms.dll /r:System.dll
➥/r:BookExamples.WindowsMediaPlayer.dll
```

Copy it into the `Visualizations` directory, then run:

```
regasm ColorfulVisualization.dll /codebase
```

After this visualization has been installed, open Windows Media Player and select `View`, `Visualizations`, `Colorful`, `Colorful` from the menu. Figure 24.8 displays the result of using this visualization. To exercise the `DisplayPropertyPage` functionality, choose `Tools`, `Options…` from the menu, then select the `Visualizations` tab. Select `Colorful` from the list and click the `Properties` button. Here is where `DisplayPropertyPage` is called, the results of which are shown in Figure 24.9.

FIGURE 24.8
The Colorful visualization, as shown in Windows Media Player.

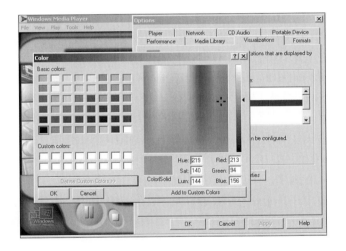

FIGURE 24.9
Configuring the Colorful visualization with ColorDialog *used as a property page.*

The Dancing Cat Visualization

For the final visualization of this chapter, we'll create a cat that dances to the music. This visualization uses bitmaps as a demonstration of .NET resources. Although the game in the previous chapter stored sounds and pictures as individual files, it's doubtful that a professional application would do this. Instead, non-code materials like pictures, sounds, and even strings (for localization purposes) are typically stored as resources.

In the Windows world, there are now two distinct kinds of resources—managed and unmanaged. Both serve the same purpose, so the difference simply comes down to the internal format of the data and the APIs used to read and write them. Unmanaged resources (also called Win32 resources) would have been appropriate for the bitmaps and sounds used in the previous chapter because the DirectX for Visual Basic APIs have methods that work directly with unmanaged resources. Because there's no compelling reason to use unmanaged resources in a visualization, the upcoming code uses managed resources.

FAQ: Why does .NET re-invent resources?

The .NET platform's support for resources is meant to be simpler than the Win32 model, well-suited for multicultural applications, and platform neutral. The .NET Framework provides extensive APIs for creating, reading, and writing resources. It's extremely flexible, because persisting any serializable .NET object is a snap. .NET tools support using an XML file to describe resources, so viewing and maintaining them is fairly easy. There's definitely a learning curve for understanding the .NET resource model (especially because tool support could be improved), but once understood the benefits of using it are clear.

To create the dancing cat animation, the visualization uses the four bitmaps shown in Figure 24.10.

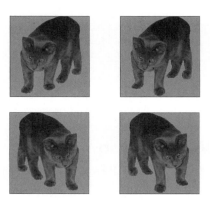

Figure 24.10

Four bitmaps that make up the cat animation.

Two pictures show the cat facing left, and two show the cat facing right. Each pair differs by the location of the cat's paws, so the cat can appear to walk. The red background will be treated as transparent in the visualization source code.

To embed these bitmaps as pictures in the visualization's assembly, we must create a `.resources` file from the four pictures. There are many tools for doing this, and the one I chose was the `ResEditor` sample that is installed with the .NET Framework SDK. With this sample application, I selected the four bitmaps, named them "Left1", "Left2", "Right1", "Right2", then saved the file as `DancingCatVisualization.resources`. Later, the compilation steps show how to use this `.resources` file. This book's Web site contains the `.resources` and corresponding `.resx` file containing these bitmaps. (The `.resx` file is an XML text file that can be converted to a binary `.resources` file using the .NET Resource Generator—RESGEN.EXE— that comes with the .NET Framework SDK.) Listing 24.8 contains the code for the visualization.

LISTING 24.8   `DancingCatVisualization.cs`. The `DancingCatVisualization` Class Displays a Cat That Dances to the Music

```
 1: using System;
 2: using System.Resources;
 3: using System.Drawing;
 4: using System.Drawing.Drawing2D;
 5: using BookExamples.WindowsMediaPlayer;
 6:
 7: public class DancingCatVisualization : Visualization, IDisposable
 8: {
 9:   private Bitmap [,] catPictures;
10:
11:   public DancingCatVisualization()
12:   {
13:     ResourceManager resources =
14:       new ResourceManager(typeof(DancingCatVisualization));
15:     catPictures = new Bitmap[2,2];
16:     catPictures[0,0] = (Bitmap)resources.GetObject("Left1");
17:     catPictures[0,1] = (Bitmap)resources.GetObject("Left2");
18:     catPictures[1,0] = (Bitmap)resources.GetObject("Right1");
19:     catPictures[1,1] = (Bitmap)resources.GetObject("Right2");
20:
21:     foreach (Bitmap b in catPictures)
22:       b.MakeTransparent(Color.Red);
23:   }
24:
25:   ~DancingCatVisualization()
26:   {
```

LISTING 24.8 Continued

```
27:      foreach (Bitmap b in catPictures)
28:        b.Dispose();
29:    }
30:
31:    public void Dispose()
32:    {
33:      // Since we're cleaning up now, suppress finalization.
34:      GC.SuppressFinalize(this);
35:
36:      foreach (Bitmap b in catPictures)
37:        b.Dispose();
38:    }
39:
40:    public override string Title
41:    {
42:      get { return "Dancing Cat"; }
43:    }
44:
45:    public override string Description
46:    {
47:      get { return "A visualization with a cat that dances to the music."; }
48:    }
49:
50:    public override void Render(TimedLevel levels, Graphics g, Rectangle r)
51:    {
52:      Bitmap cat;
53:
54:      switch (levels.State)
55:      {
56:        case AudioState.Stopped:
57:        {
58:          using (Brush b = new LinearGradientBrush(r,
59:            Color.White, Color.DarkGray, LinearGradientMode.Vertical))
60:          {
61:            // Fill background with a gradient
62:            g.FillRectangle(b, r);
63:          }
64:
65:          cat = catPictures[0,0];
66:          g.DrawImage(cat, (r.Width - cat.Width) / 2,
67:            (r.Height - cat.Height) / 2);
68:        }
69:        break;
70:
```

LISTING 24.8   Continued

```
 71:        case AudioState.Paused:
 72:        {
 73:          using (Brush b = new LinearGradientBrush(r,
 74:            Color.Olive, Color.LightYellow, LinearGradientMode.Vertical))
 75:          {
 76:            // Fill background with a gradient
 77:            g.FillRectangle(b, r);
 78:          }
 79:
 80:          cat = catPictures[0,0];
 81:          g.DrawImage(cat,
 82:            (r.Width - cat.Width) / 2, (r.Height - cat.Height) / 2);
 83:        }
 84:        break;
 85:
 86:        case AudioState.Playing:
 87:        {
 88:          using (LinearGradientBrush b = new LinearGradientBrush(r,
 89:            Color.LightYellow, Color.Olive, LinearGradientMode.Vertical))
 90:          {
 91:            // Fill background with a gradient
 92:            g.FillRectangle(b, r);
 93:          }
 94:
 95:          // Alternate orientation and stance at regular intervals
 96:          int orientation = (int)((levels.TimeStamp / 10000000) % 2);
 97:          int stance = (int)((levels.TimeStamp / 1000000) % 2);
 98:
 99:          cat = catPictures[orientation,stance];
100:          g.DrawImage(cat,
101:            (r.Width - cat.Width) / 2
102:            + (levels.GetFrequency(AudioChannel.Left, 0) - 128) / 2,
103:            (r.Height - cat.Height) / 2
104:            + (levels.GetWaveform(AudioChannel.Left, 0) - 128) / 2);
105:        }
106:        break;
107:      }
108:    }
109: }
```

The namespaces listed in Lines 1–5 contain three that the other visualizations don't: System.Resources to read the bitmaps, System.Drawing.Drawing2D for a fancy paintbrush that enables the painting of a *gradient* background (one that smoothly flows from one color to another), and `System` for the `IDisposable` interface and the `GC` class. Line 9 contains the decla-ration of a two-dimensional array that contains the four cat bitmaps.

The constructor in Lines 11–23 does three things: creates a `ResourceManager` that enables us to extract the bitmaps, fills the 2-D array with the bitmaps, and sets a color key of red so the red parts of the bitmaps will appear transparent. When creating the `ResourceManager` in Lines 13 and 14, the type of the current class is passed as a parameter, which enables the embedded resources to be found in the current assembly.

Remember that because of the way the `Visualization` custom registration functions are implemented, the code in this constructor is going to get run during registration and unregistra-tion of the assembly. This isn't ideal, but workable as long as the code doesn't cause an excep-tion to be thrown. (If you didn't embed the assembly's resources correctly, you'll see the error when running `REGASM.EXE` on it.)

Lines 16–19 fill the array so that the first dimension corresponds to the cat's orientation (0 for left and 1 for right) and the second dimension corresponds to the two different stances. Whereas the previous chapter used DirectX APIs to set a red color key on the input bitmaps, Line 22 calls the managed API for "managed bitmaps":
`System.Drawing.Bitmap.MakeTransparent.`

Lines 25–29 contain standard finalizer and `Dispose` methods for disposing the bitmaps. Although the Windows Media Player client isn't going to take advantage of calling `Dispose`, it's good practice do this anyway because the class holds onto bitmaps that should be disposed of as soon as possible. And, when a .NET-aware media player comes along that plans on call-ing `IDisposable.Dispose`, these visualizations will be ready (of course, only if we communi-cate with the player through a COM object that uses the exact same COM interface). To dispose the bitmaps, we simply call `Bitmap.Dispose` on each one in Lines 27–28 and 36–37.

Lines 40–48 contain the standard `Title` and `Description` properties, and Lines 50–108 con-tain the `Render` method. `Render` begins by choosing a different course of action depending upon whether the audio is currently stopped, paused, or playing. This is done simply by check-ing the value of the `TimedLevel` parameter's `State` field that we defined as an `AudioState` enumeration.

Lines 58–67, which contain the drawing code for the stopped state, fills the background using a `LinearGradientBrush` so the top is white, the bottom is dark gray, and points in between are mixtures of the two colors. The `LinearGradientBrush` has many ways to customize its paint-ing, but the simple use here is enough to create a nice effect. In Line 65, we select a static image of the cat to display, and in Lines 66–67 we draw it in the center of the rectangle. The code for drawing in the paused state, in Lines 73–82, is identical to the code for the stopped state except for the color of the gradient (olive on top and light yellow on the bottom).

In Lines 88–105, the code for the playing state, we get to the dancing part. Lines 88–93 fill the background with a gradient that's the exact opposite of the colors in the paused state (light yellow on top and olive on the bottom). Lines 96 and 97 choose an orientation and a stance for the cat. In other words, they determine which of the four bitmaps to display at the current point in time. The code switches these values in a regularly-timed manner using the `TimedLevel` parameter's `TimeStamp` field. Because the `TimeStamp` value is in 100-nanosecond ticks (just like the `Ticks` property of `System.DateTime`), the number is divided so that the orientation reverses every second and the stance changes every tenth of a second.

After the values for `orientation` and `stance` are selected (either 0 or 1, thanks to the `%` 2) the picture is selected in Line 99. Notice that the audio does not affect this aspect of the cat's dancing one bit. What the audio does effect is the placement of the cat bitmap.

Lines 100–104 contain the single lengthy call to `DrawImage` with the calculations for the placement of the cat. To determine the width, we begin by centering the cat (using `(r.Width - cat.Width) / 2`) then add an offset based on a representative frequency. `GetFrequency` is called to get the value for the first data point in the left audio channel. Because this is a value between 0 and 255, Line 111 subtracts 128 to get a value between –128 and 127. Finally, this value is divided by two to get a range of –64 to 63 (so the cat's position doesn't stray too far from the center). The result is that lower frequencies cause the cat to move to the left of the center, and higher frequencies cause the cat to move to the right of the center (assuming that the first frequency data point is good enough as a representative sample). The exact same calculation is done for the height of the cat, but using the waveform data instead.

Again, the code for this visualization is pretty simple but the result is fun to watch. Compiling the assembly can be done as follows, with the `DancingCatVisualization.resources` file in the same directory as `DancingCatVisualization.cs`:

```
csc /t:library DancingCatVisualization.cs /r:System.Drawing.dll
➥/r:BookExamples.WindowsMediaPlayer.dll /res:DancingCatVisualization.resources
```

The `/res` option embeds the resources in the assembly. Copy `DancingCatVisualization.dll` to the `Visualizations` directory, then register it:

```
regasm DancingCatVisualization.dll /codebase
```

After this visualization has been installed, open Windows Media Player and select `View`, `Visualizations`, `Dancing Cat`, `Dancing Cat` from the menu. Figure 24.11 displays the result of using this visualization.

24

VISUALIZATIONS
FOR WINDOWS
MEDIA PLAYER

FIGURE 24.11

The Dancing Cat visualization, as shown in Windows Media Player.

If you feel like getting your hands dirty, you could play around with several improvements to make the dancing cat more lifelike. For example, perhaps the regularly timed picture changing should be replaced with an algorithm based on the audio, or maybe looking at just the first frequency/waveform data point is not good enough.

Looking at the previous listing, you might also be displeased with the handling of the multi-dimensional array. Code in the Render function needs to know what the zeros and ones in each dimension mean. A more readable solution would be to access the array by keys, for example:

```
cat = catPictures["left", "primary"];
```

rather than:

```
cat = catPictures[0, 0];
```

Such an array is often called an *associative array*. Of course, this behavior can be obtained using a default parameterized property, and for C# code this means creating an indexer.

If we wanted to use enumeration types rather than strings for both array indices, then the raw array could be used without having to implement an indexer. However, the result is not very pretty because of necessary casting:

```
cat = catPictures[(int)Orientation.Left, (int)Stance.Primary];
```

> **TIP**
>
> For parameters with a limited set of valid values, favor designing APIs that use enums rather than integers, strings, or even boolean types. Enumerations can be more intuitive than integers because the names of the members convey meaning.
>
> Enumerations are preferable to strings because they are essentially the strongly-typed version of a string. Enums:
>
> - are just as readable to humans
> - are less error-prone because typos are caught at compile time (and the method implementer doesn't need to worry about case-sensitivity issues)
> - clearly show what the valid values are
>
> Enums with only two values are sometimes even preferable to boolean types, because the meaning is clearer in the caller's code. Compare, for example, the following call:
>
> ```
> urlBuilder.BuildUrl(UrlBuilderOptions.NoAbsolute);
> ```
>
> versus
>
> ```
> urlBuilder.BuildUrl(false);
> ```
>
> To someone maintaining the code, `UrlBuilderOptions.NoAbsolute` conveys much more meaning than false.

Conclusion

This chapter demonstrated a real-world application that takes advantage of the way in which inheritance gets exposed to COM. Because every class appears to implement all the interfaces of its base classes, the visualizations were able to expose an `IWMPEffects` interface without necessarily being aware of it. Registration aside, the .NET visualizations written in this chapter don't appear to have anything to do with COM.

When creating and running your own visualizations, any minor mistake could cause a hard-to-diagnose failure inside Windows Media Player. Here are some tips if you're running into troubles:

- If the visualization doesn't show up on the Windows Media Player menu, your class must not have been registered. Even if you've run `REGASM.EXE`, this could occur if your class is accidentally non-public, marked with `ComVisible(false)`, or if it doesn't have a public default constructor.

24

VISUALIZATIONS FOR WINDOWS MEDIA PLAYER

- If the visualization shows up in the menu but no presets appear, registration was successful but instantiating the component fails. Make sure the correct assembly is in the same directory as the `BookExamples.WindowsMediaPlayer` assembly and registered with a codebase that points to it, or make sure that both assemblies are installed in the Global Assembly Cache.

- If the visualization appears as all black, the `Render` method is probably throwing an exception. Consider using a debugger or adding diagnostic code to track down the problem.

- If you're really stuck, you could write a small COM program that hosts your visualization object and attempts to use it the same way Windows Media Player does.

Figure 24.12 illustrates which portion of Windows Media Player's menu gets its data from the registry and which portion gets its data from the instantiated component.

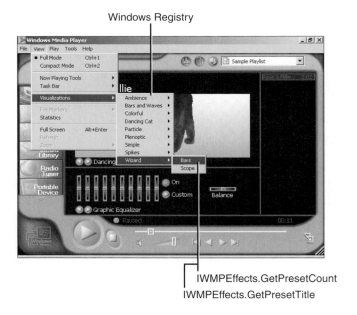

FIGURE 24.12

Windows Media Player menus and the source of their data.

The rendering code in this chapter used some simple APIs from the `System.Drawing` assembly. For more information about these classes and their members, see the .NET Framework documentation for the `System.Drawing` namespace installed with the SDK or online at `msdn.microsoft.com`.

This completes the comprehensive examples section of the book. Hopefully you can have some fun playing with these examples that exercise both directions of COM Interoperability and PInvoke. Even if you have more business-oriented applications in mind when using the .NET platform, these examples should still cover what you need to know when leveraging unmanaged code becomes a necessity.

Appendices

PART

IX

IN THIS PART

A System.Runtime.InteropServices **Reference**   1249

B SDK Tools Reference   1375

C HRESULT **to .NET Exception Transformations**   1399

D .NET Exception to HRESULT **Transformations**   1415

E PInvoke Definitions for Win32 Functions   1431

F Glossary   1487

System.Runtime.
InteropServices Reference

IN THIS APPENDIX

- **The** `System.Runtime.InteropServices` **Namespace** **1250**

- **The** `System.Runtime.InteropServices.` `CustomMarshalers` **Namespace** **1370**

- **The** `System.Runtime.InteropServices.` `Expando` **Namespace** **1372**

The core APIs used for COM Interoperability and Platform Invocation Services reside in the `System.Runtime.InteropServices` namespace. This appendix is an alphabetical reference for types in this namespace, plus its two sub-namespaces:

- `System.Runtime.InteropServices.CustomMarshalers`
- `System.Runtime.InteropServices.Expando`

Entries are cross-referenced with relevant chapters where appropriate. For .NET definitions of famous COM types, the description refers you to their original documentation at MSDN Online rather than describing them in detail. This reference site resides at `msdn.microsoft.com`.

The `System.Runtime.InteropServices` Namespace

The `System.Runtime.InteropServices` namespace contains types used for both COM Interoperability and PInvoke. This is a large namespace, but its types fall into eight broad categories:

- Custom attributes and associated enumerations
- Helper classes and associated enumerations
- `VARIANT` type wrappers
- Custom marshaling
- Custom instantiation
- Exceptions
- Tool APIs
- .NET definitions of famous COM types

To help you navigate through these categories and their types, Figure A.1, which also appears on the inside front cover, displays the entire contents of the `System.Runtime.InteropServices` namespace according to the previous groups. Italicized custom attributes are pseudo-custom attributes.

Custom attributes dominate the namespace, because there are so many ways to customize .NET exposure to unmanaged code and vice versa. The `Marshal` helper class is the centerpiece of `System.Runtime.InteropServices`, providing static methods (`Shared` in VB .NET) that facilitate a wide range of scenarios. The other helper classes are much smaller and serve specific functions. The `VARIANT` type wrappers, discussed in Chapter 3, "The Essentials for Using COM in Managed Code," control the type of a `VARIANT` instance corresponding to a .NET object when the object has more than one possible unmanaged representation.

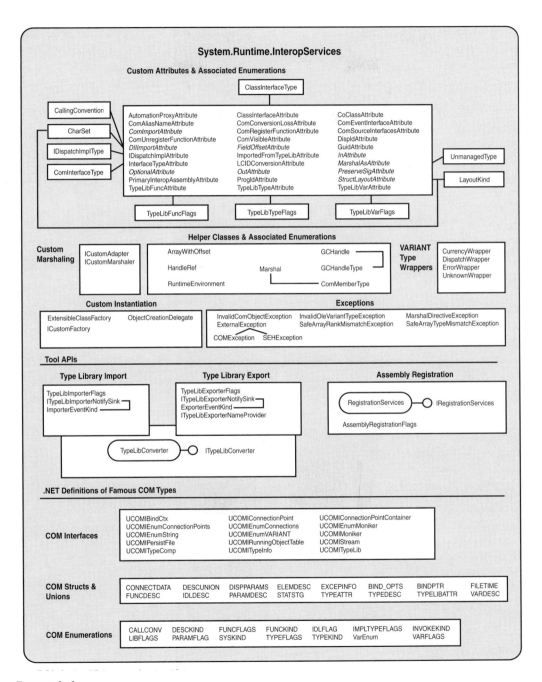

FIGURE A.1

The contents of the System.Runtime.InteropServices *namespace.*

The two custom marshaling interfaces are discussed in Chapter 20, "Custom Marshaling," and the custom instantiation types are discussed in Chapter 6, "Advanced Topics for Using COM Components." The `System.Runtime.InteropServices` namespace defines a handful of exceptions that can be thrown by the CLR when encountering problems related to interoperability services.

The Tool APIs provide the functionality for type library import, type library export, and assembly registration used by the `TLBIMP.EXE`, `TLBEXP.EXE`, and `REGASM.EXE` SDK tools and Visual Studio .NET. These APIs are covered in Chapter 22, "Using APIs Instead of SDK Tools."

> ### DIGGING DEEPER
>
> Two additional SDK tools used in many COM Interoperability scenarios have APIs in other namespaces. The .NET Services Installation Utility (`REGSVCS.EXE`) functionality is exposed through the `RegistrationHelper` class in `System.EnterpriseServices`, and the ActiveX Control Importer (`AXIMP.EXE`) functionality is exposed through the `AxImporter` class in `System.Windows.Forms.Design`.

Finally, a large portion of the types defined in `System.Runtime.InteropServices` are not new .NET-specific types, but rather metadata definitions of some widely used COM interfaces, structures, unions, and enums. Some of these types are used by members of the `Marshal` class, some are used by custom marshalers and the type library importer, and others are simply common types that don't have a definition in a type library. You should treat these as Primary Interop Definitions of the COM types and use them instead of defining the types yourself.

That's the high-level overview of the contents of `System.Runtime.InteropServices`. For the remainder of this section, every type—listed in alphabetical order—is described in further detail.

The `ArrayWithOffset` Value Type

You can use this simple value type when you want to pass a subset of a .NET array to a PInvoke method expecting a C-style array. Similar to the `HandleRef` value type (also in the `System.Runtime.InteropServices` namespace), the PInvoke signature must be modified to use the `ArrayWithOffset` type rather than the usual array.

`ArrayWithOffset` has a constructor with two parameters—a `System.Object` that represents the array, and an integer that specifies the offset where the subset begins. Rather than having to create a new .NET array and copy elements, you can use this type, flagged specially by the Interop Marshaler, as a performance optimization. The marshaler adds the offset multiplied by the array element size to the pointer value passed to unmanaged code, rather than passing a pointer to the first element.

The following code demonstrates the use of this type when calling a PInvoke method with the following unmanaged C++ signature:

```
void UnmanagedMethod(int* someArray);
```

An overload that doesn't use ArrayWithOffset is also used to demonstrate the difference.

C#:

```
[DllImport("...")]
static extern void UnmanagedMethod(int [] someArray);
[DllImport("...")]
static extern void UnmanagedMethod(ArrayWithOffset someArray);
...
int [] largeArray = ...;
// Pass entire array to PInvoke method (using first overload)
UnmanagedMethod(largeArray);
// Pass the array beginning with the 10th element (using second overload)
UnmanagedMethod(new ArrayWithOffset(largeArray, 10));
```

Visual Basic .NET:

```
Declare Sub UnmanagedMethod Lib "..." (someArray As Integer())
Declare Sub UnmanagedMethod Lib "..." (someArray As ArrayWithOffset)
...
Dim largeArray As Integer() = ...
' Pass entire array to PInvoke method (using first overload)
UnmanagedMethod(largeArray)
' Pass the array beginning with the 10th element (using second overload)
UnmanagedMethod(New ArrayWithOffset(largeArray, 10))
```

C++:

```
[DllImport(S"...")]
extern void UnmanagedMethod(int someArray __gc[]);
[DllImport(S"...")]
extern void UnmanagedMethod(ArrayWithOffset someArray);
...
int largeArray __gc[] = ...;
// Pass entire array to PInvoke method (using first overload)
UnmanagedMethod(largeArray);
// Pass the array beginning with the 10th element (using second overload)
UnmanagedMethod(ArrayWithOffset(largeArray, 10));
```

> **CAUTION**
>
> The array passed to `ArrayWithOffset` must have blittable elements, such as primitive types or user-defined value types with primitive fields. If an array with non-blittable elements (or a non-array) is passed to `ArrayWithOffset`'s constructor, an `ArgumentException` is thrown.

`ArrayWithOffset` can be used on COM methods, too, but the signatures would need to be customized to use `ArrayWithOffset` using either the techniques in Chapter 7, "Modifying Interop Assemblies," or Chapter 21, "Manually Defining COM Types in Source Code." Nothing prevents you from creating an `ArrayWithOffset` instance from a multi-dimensional array (or with an offset greater than the array's length), but this is not a correct use of the type.

The `AssemblyRegistrationFlags` Enumeration

The `AssemblyRegistrationFlags` enumeration is used by `RegistrationServices.RegisterAssembly` and `IRegistrationServices.RegisterAssembly` to indicate how an assembly should be registered. It has two values:

- `None`. The default registration should occur.
- `SetCodeBase`. The assembly should be registered with a `CodeBase` value that provides the CLR with a hint as to where the assembly physically resides.

For more information, consult Chapter 22 or the `RegistrationServices` class listed later in this section.

The `AutomationProxyAttribute` Custom Attribute

This custom attribute can be placed on assemblies, classes, or interfaces to affect the behavior of type library export. The custom attribute has a single constructor with a boolean parameter. When set to true (the default), the marked type should be marshaled with the OLE Automation Marshaler (a process known as *type library marshaling*). When set to false, the marked type should be marshaled with a custom proxy/stub marshaler. It is up to the developer to supply and register such a marshaler.

From COM's perspective, this attribute only affects interfaces. Therefore, marking this on an assembly applies to any interfaces contained within (unless individual interfaces override the assembly-level setting with their own `AutomationProxyAttribute`) and marking this on a class applies to its class interface if one is exported.

For more information, consult Chapter 12, "Customizing COM's View of .NET Components."

The `BIND_OPTS` Value Type

This is a .NET definition of the unmanaged `BIND_OPTS` structure used by the `IBindCtx` COM interface. In the .NET Framework, this definition is used by `UCOMIBindCtx.GetBindOptions` and `UCOMIBindCtx.GetBindOptions`.

For more information see the `UCOMIBindCtx` interface listed later in this section or consult MSDN Online for information about the original `BIND_OPTS` structure.

The `BINDPTR` Value Type

This is a .NET definition of the unmanaged `BINDPTR` union used by the `ITypeComp` COM interface. In the .NET Framework, this definition is used by `UCOMITypeComp.Bind`.

For more information see the `UCOMITypeComp` interface listed later in this section or consult MSDN Online for information about the original `BINDPTR` union.

The `CALLCONV` Enumeration

This is a .NET definition of the unmanaged `CALLCONV` enumeration used by the `FUNCDESC` value type.

For more information see the `FUNCDESC` value type listed later in this section or consult MSDN Online for information about the original `CALLCONV` enumeration.

The `CallingConvention` Enumeration

Unlike `CALLCONV`, which is defined only for the sake of existing COM type definitions, the `CallingConvention` enumeration is the official means of specifying a calling convention in managed code. The `DllImportAttribute` pseudo-custom attribute has a property that accepts one of its values. (A few methods in `System.Reflection.Emit` also use the `CallingConvention` enumeration for dynamically emitting PInvoke signatures.) The enumeration has the following values:

- `Cdecl`. The caller is responsible for cleaning the stack. Therefore, this calling convention is appropriate for methods that accept a variable number of parameters (like `printf`).
- `FastCall`. This is not supported by version 1.0 of the .NET Framework.
- `StdCall`. This is the default convention for PInvoke methods running on Windows. The callee is responsible for cleaning the stack.
- `ThisCall`. This is used for calling unmanaged methods defined on a class. All but the first parameter is pushed on the stack because the first parameter is the *this* pointer, stored in the ECX register.

- `Winapi`. This isn't a real calling convention, but instead indicates to use the default calling convention for the current platform. On Windows (but not Windows CE), the default calling convention is `StdCall`.

For more information, consult Chapter 18, "The Essentials of PInvoke," or the `DllImportAttribute` pseudo-custom attribute listed later in this section.

The `CharSet` Enumeration

The `CharSet` enumeration is used to specify how .NET strings should be marshaled to unmanaged code. This is necessary because although there's only one managed string type, there are several unmanaged string types. Both the `DllImportAttribute` and `StructLayoutAttribute` pseudo-custom attributes have a property that accepts one of its values. These values are:

- `Ansi`. With this setting, every character is a one-byte ANSI character. When used with `DllImportAttribute`, the CLR attempts to invoke an entry point with an appended "A" if the entry point specified by the signature doesn't exist.

- `Auto`. The `Ansi` or `Unicode` setting is chosen based on the current operating system. `Ansi` is used on Windows 98 and ME, whereas `Unicode` is used on Windows NT, 2000, XP, and .NET Server.

- `None`. This setting is obsolete and should not be used; it means the same thing as `Ansi`.

- `Unicode`. With this setting, every character is a two-byte Unicode character. When used with `DllImportAttribute`, the CLR attempts to invoke an entry point with an appended "W" *before* attempting to invoke the entry point specified by the signature.

The C#, VB .NET, and C++ compilers default to `Ansi` behavior both in the context of `DllImportAttribute` and `StructLayoutAttribute`. (C++ actually defaults to `None`, but it means the same thing.)

For more information, consult Chapter 18 or the `DllImportAttribute` and `StructLayoutAttribute` pseudo-custom attributes listed later in this section.

The `ClassInterfaceAttribute` Custom Attribute

This custom attribute controls (or suppresses) the class interface exposed to COM for a .NET class. It can be marked on classes and assemblies to affect the behavior of type library export (and also run-time behavior to match what is exported). When marked on an assembly, it applies to all classes within the assembly unless individual classes override the setting with their own `ClassInterfaceAttribute`.

The attribute has two constructors—one that takes a 16-bit integer, and one that takes a `ClassInterfaceType` enumeration. The latter constructor should always be used. The type library importer always marks imported classes with this attribute and the `ClassInterfaceType.None` setting because existing COM classes never expose CLR-generated class interfaces.

For more information, consult Chapter 12 or the `ClassInterfaceType` enumeration listed next.

The `ClassInterfaceType` Enumeration

This enumeration is used by the `ClassInterfaceAttribute` custom attribute to control the behavior of class interfaces. It has the following values:

- `AutoDispatch`. An empty-looking class interface is exposed, whose members can be invoked only through `IDispatch`. Although you can't see them, the class interface with this setting contains all the members of the class interface under the `AutoDual` setting. This is the default setting for `ClassInterfaceAttribute` because COM clients typically can't rely on method order or DISPIDs remaining constant from one version of a .NET class to the next.

- `AutoDual`. A dual class interface is exposed, containing all of the class's public non-static members (including base class members) except for methods directly marked as COM-invisible. This is handy because you get the benefits of early binding without having to bother defining interfaces in managed code, but it's dangerous due to class versioning changing the interface's definition. You should avoid shipping classes marked with this setting.

- `None`. No class interface is exposed. The first public COM-visible interface listed as implemented is exposed as the coclass's default interface. If no interface is listed as being implemented, the first public COM-visible interface implemented by a base class (starting from most-derived and working downward) becomes the default interface. If the class and none of its base classes implement any such interfaces, the exported default interface is `_Object` with this setting.

Using `ClassInterfaceType.None` is the only way to expose your own default interface to COM, although which interface becomes the default can be unreliable for classes that implement multiple interfaces. Usually the order that the interfaces are listed in metadata matches the order in source code, but it ultimately depends on your .NET compiler. For example, a C# class that implements two interfaces that are related via inheritance always lists the base interface first in metadata.

For more information, consult Chapter 12 and the `ClassInterfaceAttribute` custom attribute listed previously.

The `CoClassAttribute` Custom Attribute

This custom attribute is used by the type library importer when creating a coclass interface—an interface with the name of a coclass that derives from the coclass's default interface and possibly an event interface if the coclass exposes any source interfaces. Its constructor takes a `Type` parameter that is the type of the .NET class with the name *CoClassName*`Class`. This attribute is used by the C# and VB .NET compliers to enable you to instantiate the coclass interface in source code but actually be instantiating the .NET class type given in the `CoClassAttribute`.

For more information, consult Chapter 4, "An In-Depth Look at Imported Assemblies," and Chapter 21, "Manually Defining COM Types in Source Code."

The `ComAliasNameAttribute` Custom Attribute

This custom attribute is used by the type library importer when importing a parameter whose type is an alias (typedef) for a different type. The .NET parameter is the underlying type, but the custom attribute, whose only constructor takes a string parameter, gives the name of the original type in the type library. This custom attribute exists for informational purposes only, to show the author's intent that the marked type has more meaning than what the underlying type conveys.

For more information, consult Chapter 4.

The `ComConversionLossAttribute` Custom Attribute

This custom attribute is used by the type library importer when the .NET data type chosen for the COM type loses information. For example, because a parameter that's a pointer to a pointer to a structure cannot be accurately represented in managed code (unless using non-CLS-compliant pointers), the type library importer converts such a type to a `System.IntPtr` and marks its containing interface or class with `ComConversionLossAttribute`. This attribute exists for informational purposes only.

For more information, consult Chapter 4.

The `ComEventInterfaceAttribute` Custom Attribute

This custom attribute is used by the type library importer to mark the event interfaces it generates for a coclass that exposes at least one source interface. Such an event interface has the name *SourceInterfaceName*`_Event`, and contains an event member for each method of the source interface.

The custom attribute's constructor takes two Type parameters. The first one must be set to the type of the source interface defined in metadata, and the second one must be set to the type of the event provider class generated by the type library importer (which has the name *SourceInterfaceName*_EventProvider). The CLR uses this custom attribute at run time to associate events on the interface to their implementation on the event provider class and to link them to the original COM source interface.

For more information, consult Chapters 4 and 21.

The COMException Exception

This is the generic exception type thrown whenever a COM object returns an unfamiliar HRESULT that gets mapped into a .NET exception. (An "unfamiliar HRESULT" is one that's not listed in Table C.2 in Appendix C, "HRESULT to .NET Exception Transformations.") The COMException type has the same members as any exception type plus a public ErrorCode property that contains the HRESULT value returned by the COM object.

If the COM object doesn't set an error message using the IErrorInfo interface (or the Err object in Visual Basic 6), and if the CLR can't obtain an error message from the operating system, the message of a COMException is:

```
Exception from HRESULT: 0xnnnnnnnn
```

where *nnnnnnnn* is the eight-digit hexadecimal HRESULT value.

A COMException could be thrown in managed code in order to return a specific HRESULT value to COM. COMException has several constructor overloads, and if an HRESULT value isn't given, it defaults to the generic E_FAIL value (0x80004005). Throwing a COMException in managed code is never recommended, however, because it's not a nice exception for .NET clients to encounter. Instead, you could define a new exception type and set its protected HResult property to the desired value if no existing exception already corresponds to that HRESULT.

FAQ: Why isn't COMException written like ComException instead, to match the other COM-related types and .NET naming guidelines?

The .NET Framework is in the unique position that it was developed at the same time as .NET design guidelines were being shaped. Because of this, not all types and members are compliant with the final version of these guidelines. Although many such discrepancies were fixed before the .NET Framework was released, several were left alone because it was decided that changing certain types and members would be too disruptive during the beta and product development cycle. So COMException is a common example of such a discrepancy.

COMException derives from ExternalException, which derives from System.SystemException. Be aware, however, that a COMException is usually thrown in response to an application error, not a system error.

For more information, consult Chapter 3, "The Essentials for Using COM in Managed Code," Appendix C, "HRESULT to .NET Exception Transformations," and Appendix D, ".NET Exception to HRESULT Transformations."

The ComImportAttribute Pseudo-Custom Attribute

This parameter-less, pseudo-custom attribute is used by the type library importer to mark every class as a "COM class" and every interface as a "COM interface." The metadata bit set by using this pseudo-custom attribute tells the CLR to call CoCreateInstance when instantiating a COM class and QueryInterface when casting it to an interface. It also indicates to the type library exporter that such types should not be exported to a type library.

Because this is a pseudo-custom attribute, reflection cannot detect that types are marked with ComImportAttribute through the normal means. Instead, the Type.IsImport property can be used to programmatically determine if a class or interface is marked with the attribute.

For more information, consult Chapters 4 and 21.

The ComInterfaceType Enumeration

This enumeration is used by the InterfaceTypeAttribute custom attribute to control how a .NET interface is exposed to COM. It has the following values:

- InterfaceIsDual. The interface derives from IDispatch, supporting both v-table access and late binding. This is the default setting for InterfaceTypeAttribute.
- InterfaceIsIDispatch. The interface is a dispinterface, meaning its methods can only be called by late binding via IDispatch. Defining a new .NET interface as a dispinterface is only desirable if it will serve as a source interface, as discussed in Chapter 13, "Exposing .NET Events to COM Clients."
- InterfaceIsIUnknown. The interface derives directly from IUnknown. Early bound access through the v-table is supported, but late binding is not because the interface doesn't derive from IDispatch.

These values cannot be combined with bitwise operators; only one can be used at a time.

For more information, see Chapters 4, 12, and 21 and the InterfaceTypeAttribute custom attribute listed later in this section.

The `ComMemberType` Enumeration

This enumeration is used by the `Marshal.GetMethodInfoForComSlot` method. It has the following values:

- `Method`. The `MethodInfo` corresponds to a regular method.
- `PropGet`. The `MethodInfo` corresponds to a property's get accessor method.
- `PropSet`. The `MethodInfo` corresponds to a property's set accessor method.

For more information, see the `GetMethodInfoForComSlot` method listed later in this section under "The `Marshal` Class" section.

The `ComRegisterFunctionAttribute` Custom Attribute

This parameter-less custom attribute can be marked on a method of a .NET class. If and when the class gets registered via `RegistrationServices.RegisterAssembly` (either directly or through inheritance), the method is invoked. `RegistrationServices.RegisterAssembly` is the standard assembly registration mechanism used by `REGASM.EXE` and Visual Studio .NET (when using the `Register for COM Interop` option).

The purpose of this custom attribute is to provide class authors the opportunity to run specialized code during the registration process. Whenever defining such a method, a corresponding unregistration method marked with `ComUnregisterFunctionAttribute` should be defined to reverse the custom registration work.

A method marked with `ComRegisterFunctionAttribute` can have any visibility (public, private, and so on) but must be static (`Shared` in VB .NET), and must contain one `Type` parameter. There can be at most one custom registration function per class. When invoked, its `Type` parameter contains an instance of the current type being registered (which may be a subclass of the class defining the registration method).

For more information, consult Chapter 12 and the `ComUnregisterFunctionAttribute` custom attribute listed later in this section.

The `ComSourceInterfacesAttribute` Custom Attribute

This custom attribute can be placed on a .NET class to make the type library exporter expose a coclass with source interfaces. This is necessary in order to expose .NET class with events to COM as a class with "COM events." The custom attribute has several overloaded constructors to list one to four `Type` objects representing one to four source interfaces, and also has an overload that expects a string of null-delimited, assembly-qualified interface names.

A

The interfaces listed in this custom attribute must have .NET definitions, and each of its methods should have the same name as an event defined on the marked class with the same signature as the event's delegate. The type library importer uses this custom attribute to map methods on imported source interfaces into .NET events.

For more information, consult Chapter 13.

The `ComUnregisterFunctionAttribute` Custom Attribute

This parameter-less custom attribute can be marked on a method of a .NET class. If and when the class gets unregistered via `RegistrationServices.UnregisterAssembly` (either directly or through inheritance), the method is invoked. `RegistrationServices.UnregisterAssembly` is the standard assembly registration mechanism used by `REGASM.EXE`'s `/unregister` option. It's also called every time a Visual Studio .NET project using the `Register for COM Interop` option is rebuilt.

The purpose of this custom attribute is to provide class authors the opportunity to run specialized code during the unregistration process. Such a method doesn't need to be defined unless a corresponding registration method marked with `ComRegisterFunctionAttribute` exists. The unregistration method should undo all the work from the custom registration function.

A method marked with `ComUnregisterFunctionAttribute` can have any visibility (public, private, and so on) but must be static (`Shared` in VB .NET), and must contain one `Type` parameter. There can be at most one custom unregistration function per class. When invoked, its `Type` parameter contains an instance of the current type being unregistered (which may be a subclass of the class defining the unregistration method).

For more information, consult Chapter 12 or the `ComRegisterFunctionAttribute` listed previously in this section.

The `ComVisibleAttribute` Custom Attribute

This custom attribute can be used to restrict a .NET type or member's visibility from COM. It can be marked on an assembly, a type (a class, interface, struct, delegate, or enum) or on a member (method, property, or field). Although it can hide public .NET types and members from COM, it can never be used to expose non-public .NET types to COM.

Its constructor takes a single boolean parameter that can be set to true to make something COM-visible (the default behavior), or false to make it COM-invisible. When marked on an assembly, it applies to all the types contained within. When marked on a type, it's never exported to a type library. When marked on a class, it's never registered, and when marked on an interface, it's never attainable from a `QueryInterface` call. When marked on a member, it is excluded from interfaces (including class interfaces) exposed to COM. Marking a type with ComVisibleAttribute overrides the assembly-level setting. Marking members as COM-invisible selectively hides them on a COM-visible type, but marking members as COM-visible on a COM-invisible type has no effect.

Many types and assemblies in the .NET Framework are marked with ComVisibleAttribute to prohibit their direct use from COM.

For more information, consult Chapter 8, "The Essentials for Using .NET Components from COM," and Chapter 12.

The CONNECTDATA Value Type

This is a .NET definition of the unmanaged CONNECTDATA structure used by the IEnumConnections COM interface. In the .NET Framework, this definition is used by UCOMIEnumConnections.Next.

For more information see the UCOMIEnumConnections interface listed later in this section or consult MSDN Online for information about the original BINDPTR union.

The CurrencyWrapper Class

The CurrencyWrapper class can be used to pass a .NET Decimal type inside a VARIANT and have COM see it as VT_CY (a COM CURRENCY type) rather than VT_DECIMAL (a COM DECIMAL type). Although Decimal types are automatically transformed to COM CURRENCY types when passed early-bound to COM signatures expecting CURRENCY, the CLR can't know to do this transformation when late binding or passing a type inside a VARIANT because the COM component's expectations aren't captured in the type information.

The CurrencyWrapper class has two constructors—one that takes a Decimal type and one that takes an Object type. (If the Object passed isn't a Decimal, however, an ArgumentException is thrown.) When passing a System.Object type to a COM method (because Object corresponds to COM's VARIANT), a CurrencyWrapper instance is flagged by the Interop Marshaler so the conversion can be done.

The following code demonstrates the use of this type when calling the following COM method:

```
HRESULT UnmanagedMethod(VARIANT v);
```

Its imported managed signature has a generic System.Object parameter.

C#:

```
Decimal d = ...;
// Pass a VARIANT containing a decimal (VT_DECIMAL)
```

```
obj.UnmanagedMethod(d);
// Pass a VARIANT containing a currency (VT_CY)
obj.UnmanagedMethod(new CurrencyWrapper(d));
```

Visual Basic .NET:

```
Dim d As Decimal = ...
' Pass a VARIANT containing a decimal (VT_DECIMAL)
obj.UnmanagedMethod(d)
' Pass a VARIANT containing a currency (VT_CY)
obj.UnmanagedMethod(New CurrencyWrapper(d))
```

C++:

```
Decimal d = ...;
// Pass a VARIANT containing a decimal (VT_DECIMAL)
obj->UnmanagedMethod(__box(d));
// Pass a VARIANT containing a currency (VT_CY)
obj->UnmanagedMethod(new CurrencyWrapper(d));
```

For more information, consult Chapter 3.

The DESCKIND Enumeration

This is a .NET definition of the unmanaged DESCKIND enumeration used by the ITypeComp COM interface. In the .NET Framework, this definition is used by UCOMITypeComp.Bind.

For more information see the UCOMITypeComp interface listed later in this section or consult MSDN Online for information about the original DESCKIND enumeration.

The DESCUNION Value Type

This is a .NET definition of the unmanaged DESCUNION union used as a field in the unmanaged ELEMDESC and VARDESC structures. In the .NET Framework, this definition is used by .NET definitions of ELEMDESC and VARDESC.

For more information consult MSDN Online for information about the original DESCUNION union.

The DispatchWrapper Class

The DispatchWrapper class can be used to pass a .NET Object type, a derived type, or an interface type inside a VARIANT and have COM see it as VT_DISPATCH (a COM object that implements IDispatch). Such objects are exposed as VT_DISPATCH VARIANTs by default anyway, so of what use is DispatchWrapper? It has one use—passing a VT_DISPATCH VARIANT containing a null pointer. Without the DispatchWrapper, a null instance (Nothing in VB .NET) as an Object parameter is marshaled as a VT_EMPTY VARIANT.

The `DispatchWrapper` class has one constructor that takes an `Object` type. The instance passed must not be a value type or an array, otherwise an `ArgumentException` is thrown. If the object's CCW doesn't implement `IDispatch`, an `InvalidCastException` is thrown. A CCW doesn't implement `IDispatch` if the .NET class is COM-invisible (including being non-public), or if it is marked with `ClassInterface(ClassInterfaceType.None)` and the interface chosen as the default interface is marked with `InterfaceType(ComInterfaceType.InterfaceIsIUnknown)`.

The following code demonstrates the use of this type when calling the following COM method:

```
HRESULT UnmanagedMethod(VARIANT v);
```

Its imported managed signature has a generic `System.Object` parameter.

C#:

```
// Pass a VT_EMPTY VARIANT
obj.UnmanagedMethod(null);
// Pass a VT_DISPATCH VARIANT with a null pdispVal pointer
obj.UnmanagedMethod(new DispatchWrapper(null));
```

Visual Basic .NET:

```
' Pass a VT_EMPTY VARIANT
obj.UnmanagedMethod(Nothing)
' Pass a VT_DISPATCH VARIANT with a null pdispVal pointer
obj.UnmanagedMethod(New DispatchWrapper(Nothing))
```

C++:

```
// Pass a VT_EMPTY VARIANT
obj->UnmanagedMethod(NULL);
// Pass a VT_DISPATCH VARIANT with a null pdispVal pointer
obj->UnmanagedMethod(new DispatchWrapper(NULL));
```

For more information, consult Chapter 3.

The `DispIdAttribute` Custom Attribute

This custom attribute marks class or interface members with DISPIDs. With its single constructor that takes an integer, it can be used to control the DISPIDs used by the type library exporter. The important DISPIDs—`DISPID_VALUE` (0) and `DISPID_NEWENUM` (-4)—are automatically handled by the CLR when you define a default member or a .NET enumerator. Specifying other DISPIDs might be desirable if you expose an auto-dual class interface and add members in a later version that may change the auto-generated DISPIDs of the existing members.

The type library importer marks members with DispIdAttribute in order to preserve the DISPIDs from their definitions in the type library.

For more information, consult Chapter 12.

The DISPPARAMS Value Type

This is a .NET definition of the unmanaged DISPPARAMS structure used by the ITypeInfo COM interface. In the .NET Framework, this definition is used by .NET definition of UCOMITypeInfo.Invoke.

For more information see the UCOMITypeInfo interface listed later in this section or consult MSDN Online for information about the original DISPPARAMS structure.

The DllImportAttribute Pseudo-Custom Attribute

The DllImportAttribute pseudo-custom attribute turns a .NET method definition into a PInvoke method—one that's exposed by an unmanaged DLL as a static entry point. Whereas C# and C++ require that you use this attribute directly, the Visual Basic .NET compiler emits this pseudo-custom attribute when the Declare statement is used. This attribute has one required string parameter that is the name of the DLL containing the entry point with the .NET method's signature. If no path is given, the DLL must be in the path at run time unless it's already loaded by some other means. Otherwise, a full or relative path can be given. Fully qualified paths are not recommended due to their brittleness.

Besides the one required parameter, DllImportAttribute has 6 optional named parameters:

- CallingConvention. This parameter is used with a member of the CallingConvention enumeration to specify the entry point's calling convention. The default value is CallingConvention.Winapi.

- CharSet. This parameter is used with a member of the CharSet enumeration to specify how string parameters should be marshaled and what entry point name should be invoked (the exact name given or one ending with an "A" or "W"). CharSet.Ansi is the default value chosen by C# and VB .NET (when using Declare). The CLR's (and the C++ compiler's) default is CharSet.None, which means the same thing.

- EntryPoint. This parameter is used with a string to specify the entry point name (or ordinal number as "#*ordinal*"). If omitted, the name of the method marked with DllImportAttribute is used.

- ExactSpelling. This boolean parameter controls whether or not the CharSet setting causes the CLR to look for entry point names other than the one specified (ending in "A" or "W"). If true, CharSet only affects the behavior of string parameters. The default value chosen by the CLR, C#, and C++ is false, but VB .NET chooses true by default (when using Declare).

- PreserveSig. This boolean parameter, similar to PreserveSigAttribute, controls whether or not the signature is a direct translation of the unmanaged entry point. If true (the default in all languages), the .NET signature "preserves" the unmanaged signature. If false, then the return type in the .NET signature is assumed to be an [out, retval] parameter, and it's assumed that the unmanaged signature returns an HRESULT value that will be transformed into an exception by the CLR when appropriate.

- SetLastError. This boolean parameter should be set to true if the entry point provides additional error information retrievable via the Win32 GetLastError method, and false otherwise. False is the default value except when using Declare in VB .NET. If this parameter is set to true and if the function internally uses the SetLastError API, then this additional information can be retrieved from managed code by calling Marshal.GetLastWin32Error (or the VB .NET-specific Err.LastDllError).

For more information, consult Part VI, "Platform Invocation Services," and the CallingConvention and CharSet enumerations listed earlier in this section.

The ELEMDESC Value Type

This is a .NET definition of the unmanaged ELEMDESC structure used by the unmanaged FUNCDESC and VARDESC structures. In the .NET Framework, this definition is used by .NET definitions of FUNCDESC and VARDESC.

For more information consult MSDN Online for information about the original ELEMDESC structure.

The ErrorWrapper Class

The ErrorWrapper class can be used to pass a .NET integer or Exception type inside a VARIANT and have COM see either type as VT_ERROR—a 32-bit integer that represents an error code. By default, an integer would be exposed as VT_I4 and an Exception object would be exposed as VT_DISPATCH or VT_UNKNOWN (if the object doesn't implement IDispatch). When creating an ErrorWrapper from an integer, the error code has the exact same value as the integer. When creating an ErrorWrapper from an Exception object, the error code has the value of its protected HResult property.

The ErrorWrapper class has three constructors—one that takes a 32-bit integer, one that takes an Exception object, and one that takes a System.Object type. The object passed to the third overload must be an integer (not an Exception), otherwise an ArgumentException is thrown.

The following code demonstrates the use of this type when calling the following COM method:

```
HRESULT UnmanagedMethod(VARIANT v);
```

Its imported managed signature has a generic `System.Object` parameter.

C#:

```csharp
int errorCode = ...;
// Pass a VARIANT containing an error code (VT_ERROR) from an integer
obj.UnmanagedMethod(new ErrorWrapper(errorCode));
// Pass a VARIANT containing an error code (VT_ERROR) from an Exception
obj.UnmanagedMethod(new ErrorWrapper(new MyException()));
```

Visual Basic .NET:

```vbnet
Dim errorCode As Integer = ...
' Pass a VARIANT containing an error code (VT_ERROR) from an integer
obj.UnmanagedMethod(New ErrorWrapper(errorCode))
' Pass a VARIANT containing an error code (VT_ERROR) from an Exception
obj.UnmanagedMethod(New ErrorWrapper(New MyException()))
```

C++:

```cpp
int errorCode = ...;
// Pass a VARIANT containing an error code (VT_ERROR) from an integer
obj->UnmanagedMethod(new ErrorWrapper(errorCode));
// Pass a VARIANT containing an error code (VT_ERROR) from an Exception
obj->UnmanagedMethod(new ErrorWrapper(new MyException()));
```

For more information, consult Chapter 3.

The EXCEPINFO Value Type

This is a .NET definition of the unmanaged `EXCEPINFO` structure used by the `ITypeInfo` COM interface. In the .NET Framework, this definition is used by .NET definition of `UCOMITypeInfo.Invoke`.

For more information see the `UCOMITypeInfo` interface listed later in this section or consult MSDN Online for information about the original `EXCEPINFO` structure.

The ExporterEventKind Enumeration

This enumeration is used by the `ITypeLibExporterNotifySink` interface's `ReportEvent` method. An implementer of `ITypeLibExporterNotifySink` has its `ReportEvent` method called by the CLR repeatedly during the process of type library export. The `ExporterEventKind` enumeration tells the `ReportEvent` implementer what type of event has just occurred. This enumeration has the following values:

- `ERROR_REFTOINVALIDASSEMBLY`. This value is the one that represents a fatal error. This event is never reported in version 1.0 of the .NET Framework.

- NOTIF_CONVERTWARNING. This value represents a warning during the export process. A common example of such a warning is the exposure of COM-invisible value types in a public signature. Warning notifications are fairly common, but ideally there would be none during export.

- NOTIF_TYPECONVERTED. This value is simply a notification of normal events. Every time a type is exported, this event occurs.

For more information, consult Chapter 22 and the ITypeLibExporterNotifySink interface listed later in this section.

The ExtensibleClassFactory Class

The ExtensibleClassFactory class has a single static method (Shared in VB .NET) that enables .NET classes that derive from a COM class to customize their creation process. This static method is called RegisterObjectCreationCallback, and has a delegate parameter to enable such classes to plug in any implementation into the creation process.

Normally when a Runtime-Callable Wrapper (RCW) is created, the wrapper calls CoCreate-Instance if the COM object being wrapped needs to be instantiated. However, by registering an appropriate delegate, the RCW will invoke this custom method instead of calling CoCreateInstance.

Therefore, calling ExtensibleClassFactory.RegisterObjectCreationCallback is the way to write a customized class factory for .NET objects extending COM objects. (From COM's perspective, the .NET subclass is aggregating the COM class.) The object can be instantiated however you like—as a singleton object, with a COM moniker, and so on. There are two important guidelines for calling this method:

- RegisterObjectCreationCallback must be called inside a class's *class constructor*, also known as a *static initializer*. This is a constructor marked static in C# and C++ or Shared in VB .NET that gets executed the first time an object of the class type is loaded.

- RegisterObjectCreationCallback may only be called once per class type.

RegisterObjectCreationCallback's parameter is a delegate type defined in System.Runtime.InteropServices named ObjectCreationDelegate. The delegate signature has a System.IntPtr parameter called aggregator and returns a System.IntPtr type. The aggregator parameter is never null and represents the pUnkOuter parameter that would be passed to CoCreateInstance. The returned IntPtr should be a pointer to an IUnknown interface, just like what CoCreateInstance would return.

The following code demonstrates the use of ExtensibleClassFactory. RegisterObjectCreationCallback to plug in a CustomCreateInstance method that replaces CoCreateInstance.

C#:

```csharp
public class MyDerivedClass : MyCoClass
{
  // Class constructor
  public static MyDerivedClass()
  {
    MyDerivedClass c = new MyDerivedClass();
    ExtensibleClassFactory.RegisterObjectCreationCallback(
      new ObjectCreationDelegate(c.CustomCreateInstance));
  }

  public IntPtr CustomCreateInstance(IntPtr aggregator)
  {
    ...
  }
}
```

Visual Basic .NET:

```vb
Public Class MyDerivedClass
  Inherits MyCoClass

  ' Class constructor
  Public Shared Sub New()
    Dim c As MyDerivedClass = New MyDerivedClass()
    ExtensibleClassFactory.RegisterObjectCreationCallback( _
      New ObjectCreationDelegate(AddressOf c.CustomCreateInstance))
  End Sub

  Public IntPtr CustomCreateInstance(aggregator As IntPtr)
    ...
  End Sub
End Class
```

C++:

```cpp
public __gc class MyDerivedClass : public MyCoClass
{
  // Class constructor
  public: static MyDerivedClass()
  {
    MyDerivedClass* c = new MyDerivedClass();
    ExtensibleClassFactory::RegisterObjectCreationCallback(
      new ObjectCreationDelegate(c, &MyDerivedClass::CustomCreateInstance));
  }
```

```
public: IntPtr CustomCreateInstance(IntPtr aggregator)
{
  ...
}
};
```

For more information, consult Chapter 6.

The `ExternalException` Exception

This exception type represents an error that occurred external to the CLR. It defines a public `ErrorCode` property that contains an integer identifying the external error. `ExternalException` is the base class for both `COMException` and `SEHException`.

When inherited by `COMException`, the `ErrorCode` property represents an `HRESULT` value. On the other hand, when inherited by `SEHException`, the `ErrorCode` property represents a Structured Exception Handling (SEH) error code.

`ExternalException` derives from `System.SystemException`, and should never be thrown by an application. In fact, the CLR never throws it directly, but rather uses the derived `COMException` or `SEHException` types. Like `COMException`, its default `ErrorCode` value is the `E_FAIL HRESULT` (0x80004005).

For more information see the `COMException` exception and `SEHException` exception listed in this section.

The `FieldOffsetAttribute` Pseudo-Custom Attribute

This pseudo-custom attribute must be used in conjunction with the `StructLayoutAttribute` pseudo-custom attribute and its `LayoutKind.Explicit` setting to specify custom memory offsets for a value type's fields. When using this attribute, all fields in the struct must be marked.

The attribute's constructor takes an integer parameter that specifies the offset of a field in bytes. A union can be defined by setting every field's offset to zero.

The following code demonstrates the use of `FieldOffsetAttribute` to define a union:

C#:

```
[StructLayout(LayoutKind.Explicit)]
struct BINDPTR
{
  [FieldOffset(0)] public IntPtr lpfuncdesc;
  [FieldOffset(0)] public IntPtr lpvardesc;
  [FieldOffset(0)] public IntPtr lptcomp;
}
```

Visual Basic .NET:

```
<StructLayout(LayoutKind.Explicit)> _
Structure BINDPTR
  <FieldOffset(0)> Public lpfuncdesc As IntPtr
  <FieldOffset(0)> Public lpvardesc As IntPtr
  <FieldOffset(0)> Public lptcomp As IntPtr
End Structure
```

C++:

```
[StructLayout(LayoutKind::Explicit)]
public __value struct BINDPTR
{
  [FieldOffset(0)] IntPtr lpfuncdesc;
  [FieldOffset(0)] IntPtr lpvardesc;
  [FieldOffset(0)] IntPtr lptcomp;
};
```

For more information, consult Chapter 19, "Deeper Into PInvoke and Useful Examples."

The FILETIME Value Type

This is a .NET definition of the unmanaged FILETIME structure used by COM interfaces such as IMoniker and IRunningObjectTable. In the .NET Framework, this definition is used by the UCOMIMoniker and UCOMIRunningObjectTable interfaces and the STATSTG value type.

For more information, consult MSDN Online for information about the original FILETIME structure.

The FUNCDESC Value Type

This is a .NET definition of the unmanaged FUNCDESC structure used by the ITypeInfo COM interface. In the .NET Framework, this definition is not directly used by UCOMITypeInfo, because the methods that would use the type (GetFuncDesc and ReleaseFuncDesc) are defined to use the System.IntPtr type instead. However, when using these methods of UCOMITypeInfo, you'll want to use the FUNCDESC type in conjunction with Marshal.PtrToStructure or Marshal.StructureToPtr to convert it to and from System.IntPtr.

For more information, consult MSDN Online for information about the original FUNCDESC structure.

The FUNCFLAGS Enumeration

This is a .NET definition of the unmanaged FUNCFLAGS enumeration used by the FUNCFLAGS COM structure. In the .NET Framework, this definition is not directly used by the .NET

FUNCDESC structure because its underlying type is used in its place. This enumeration defines the same values as the TypeLibFuncFlags enumeration, but with slightly different names (the original names). The one difference is that FUNCFLAGS is a 16-bit enumeration, whereas TypeLibFuncFlags has a 32-bit underlying type.

For more information, consult MSDN Online for information about the original FUNCFLAGS enumeration.

The FUNCKIND Enumeration

This is a .NET definition of the unmanaged FUNCKIND enumeration used by the FUNCDESC COM structure. In the .NET Framework, this definition is used by the .NET FUNCDESC definition.

For more information, consult MSDN Online for information about the original FUNCKIND union.

The GCHandle Value Type

The GCHandle value type, which stands for *Garbage Collector Handle*, is sometimes needed when exposing .NET objects to unmanaged code. Its most important member is the static Alloc method, which enables you to create a handle corresponding to any .NET object. This handle can be one of four types, described by the GCHandleType enumeration.

The two types of handles useful when interacting with unmanaged code are *normal* and *pinned*. A normal handle prevents a .NET object from being garbage collected even when an unmanaged object is the only entity holding a reference to the object. A pinned handle enables you to obtain the memory address of the .NET object, preventing the garbage collector from moving the object in memory.

Unmanaged code permission (SecurityPermission with SecurityPermissionFlag. UnmanagedCode set) is required to be able to use members of the GCHandle type (except for the IsAllocated property).

The following code demonstrates the use of some of GCHandle's members to pass a pointer to a .NET object directly to an unmanaged method. This is almost always how GCHandle is used when it's needed for unmanaged code interaction:

C#:

```
GCHandle handle = new GCHandle();
try
{
  // Allocate a pinned handle for the myManagedObject instance
  handle = GCHandle.Alloc(myManagedObject, GCHandleType.Pinned);
```

```
    // Obtain the memory address value
    IntPtr rawPointer = handle.AddrOfPinnedObject();

    // Call the unmanaged method expecting a pointer to myManagedObject
    obj.UnmanagedMethod(rawPointer);
}
finally
{
    // Free the handle since it's causing myManagedObject to remain pinned
    if (handle.IsAllocated) handle.Free();
}
```

Visual Basic .NET:

```
Dim handle As GCHandle
Try
    ' Allocate a pinned handle for the myManagedObject instance
    handle = GCHandle.Alloc(myManagedObject, GCHandleType.Pinned)

    ' Obtain the memory address value
    Dim rawPointer As IntPtr = handle.AddrOfPinnedObject()

    ' Call the unmanaged method expecting a pointer to myManagedObject
    obj.UnmanagedMethod(rawPointer)
Finally
    ' Free the handle since it's causing myManagedObject to remain pinned
    If (handle.IsAllocated) Then handle.Free()
End Try
```

C++:

```
GCHandle handle;
try
{
    // Allocate a pinned handle for the myManagedObject instance
    handle = GCHandle::Alloc(myManagedObject, GCHandleType::Pinned);

    // Obtain the memory address value
    IntPtr rawPointer = handle.AddrOfPinnedObject();

    // Call the unmanaged method expecting a pointer to myManagedObject
    obj->UnmanagedMethod(rawPointer);
}
__finally
{
    // Free the handle since it's causing myManagedObject to remain pinned
    if (handle.IsAllocated) handle.Free();
}
```

More details about `Alloc`, `Free`, and `AddrOfPinnedObject` conversion appear in the following sections.

For more information about the `GCHandle` value type, consult Chapter 6 and the `GCHandleType` enumeration listed next.

The `Alloc` Method

This static method has two signatures—one that takes a .NET object for which we want a handle, and one that takes a .NET object plus a `GCHandleType` enumeration value that specifies what kind of handle we want to obtain. Both methods return a `GCHandle` instance. The first method always returns a normal handle (`GCHandleType.Normal`). A null object (`Nothing` in VB .NET) can even be passed to `Alloc`, because the handle's corresponding object can be changed at any time using `GCHandle`'s `Target` property.

A pinned handle is required when passing an address of a .NET object out to unmanaged code using the `AddrOfPinnedObject` method. The `GCHandle` instance returned must be freed by calling its `Free` method as soon as it's no longer needed.

The `Free` Method

This instance method must be called on an allocated `GCHandle` instance to release the handle as soon as it's no longer needed. Forgetting to free a normal handle is bad because it prevents the corresponding object (also known as the handle's *referent*) from being garbage collected. Forgetting to free a pinned handle is bad for the same reason, plus it keeps the corresponding object in a fixed memory location, which can cause the .NET garbage collector to perform poorly.

This method throws an `InvalidOperationException` if the handle has not been allocated or if it has already been freed. Therefore, callers must be sure to never call `Free` more than once for a given handle.

The `AddrOfPinnedObject` Method

This instance method takes no parameters and returns an `IntPtr` value that represents the memory address of a pinned object. `AddrOfPinnedObject` throws an `InvalidOperation-Exception` if the handle instance is not a pinned handle.

The `IsAllocated` Property

This read-only boolean property returns true if the `GCHandle` instance is currently allocated (its `Alloc` method has been called and its `Free` method has not been called), and false otherwise. Because calling `Free` on an unallocated handle is an error, this property is useful for checking the handle's state before attempting to call `Free`.

The `Target` Property

This read-write `Object` property enables you to get or set the handle's referent (the .NET object to which the handle applies). Use of the property's set accessor enables you to reuse a single `GCHandle` instance for multiple .NET objects.

The `GCHandle/IntPtr` Explicit Conversion Operator

Every `GCHandle` instance is internally represented as a size-agnostic integer (`System.IntPtr`). Therefore, `GCHandle` defines two explicit conversion operators—one that converts a `GCHandle` instance to an `IntPtr` value, and vice versa.

> **CAUTION**
>
> Converting a `GCHandle` instance to an `IntPtr` value using the explicit conversion operator is *not* the same thing as calling `GCHandle.AddrOfPinnedObject`. The handle's `IntPtr` representation is not the same value as the corresponding object's memory location.

In C#, an explicit conversion operator is invoked when performing an explicit cast. Because Visual Basic .NET doesn't support operator overloads, the "raw" static `GCHandle.op_Explicit` method must be called instead. The following code demonstrates the use of these explicit conversion operators:

C#:

```csharp
GCHandle handle = GCHandle.Alloc(myManagedObject);

// Convert the GCHandle instance to an IntPtr
IntPtr internalValue = (IntPtr)handle;

// Convert the IntPtr to a GCHandle instance
GCHandle handle2 = (GCHandle)internalValue;

// Don't free handle2 because it's really the same handle
handle.Free();
```

Visual Basic .NET:

```vbnet
Dim handle As GCHandle = GCHandle.Alloc(myManagedObject)

' Convert the GCHandle instance to an IntPtr
Dim internalValue As IntPtr = GCHandle.op_Explicit(handle)
```

```
' Convert the IntPtr to a GCHandle instance
Dim handle2 As GCHandle = GCHandle.op_Explicit(internalValue)

' Don't free handle2 because it's really the same handle
handle.Free()
```

It is fine to have multiple GCHandles with the same value as long as you only call Free once.

The GCHandleType Enumeration

This enumeration is used by GCHandle.Alloc to describe the type of garbage collector handle to allocate for a .NET object. This enumeration has the following values:

- Normal. A simple handle that uniquely identifies an object and prevents it from being garbage collected. Such a handle is often called an *opaque handle*. This is useful for keeping a .NET object alive when unmanaged code (which is undetectable from the .NET garbage collector) is the only entity holding a reference to the object.

- Pinned. A Normal handle with the addition that you're allowed to obtain the memory address of the object. Therefore, the garbage collector pins the corresponding object in place so its location doesn't change. When calling unmanaged code, this type of handle is needed when directly exposing pointers to .NET objects that must keep a fixed memory location for the duration of the call.

> **CAUTION**
>
> Using GCHandleType.Pinned interferes with the normal operation of the garbage collector, potentially reducing its efficiency. Therefore, it should be used as infrequently as possible, and any pinned handles should be freed (using GCHandle.Free) as quickly after allocation as possible.

- Weak. This type of handle does not prevent the object's garbage collection. When the object is ready for collection, the handle value is simply set to zero. Because this occurs before finalization, it's possible that a finalizer could resurrect the object. If this happens, however, the handle's value is still zero.

- WeakTrackResurrection. A Weak handle with the addition that a resurrected object does not have a handle value of zero. The CLR waits until the object is actually finalized to set it to zero.

The `GuidAttribute` Custom Attribute

This custom attribute can be used to explicitly choose a GUID for a class, interface, and so on, instead of letting the CLR choose a GUID for you. This can be useful to keep GUIDs stable during the development process of ever-evolving types. The custom attribute has a constructor that takes a single string parameter that must contain a GUID in the following representation (with dashes but without curly braces—case doesn't matter):

```
a08d8c8a-e1a0-40de-b2d9-6e78cd288a5b
```

The custom attribute can be placed on the following targets, taking on the following meanings:

- Assembly—The LIBID of the exported type library.
- Class—The coclass's CLSID.
- Interface—The interface's IID.
- Delegate—The CLSID of the delegate class.
- Struct—The GUID for the exported struct.
- Enum—The GUID for the exported enum.

The type library importer marks types with `GuidAttribute` to preserve the GUIDs from the original type definitions.

For more information, consult Chapter 12.

The `HandleRef` Value Type

The `HandleRef` value type is a special type recognized by the Interop Marshaler that provides a convenient way to prevent a .NET object that wraps an unmanaged resource from being garbage collected while the unmanaged member is being used from unmanaged code. This is needed when the .NET object destroys its unmanaged objects in its finalizer (which is necessary to avoid memory leaks), and only applies when the unmanaged item is not reference counted (such as a handle).

Because the .NET garbage collector cannot "manage" unmanaged code, you can easily run into subtle object lifetime issues when passing a managed object that wraps an unmanaged resource to unmanaged code. The following C# code demonstrates this scenario:

```csharp
public class ManagedObjectThatWrapsUnmanagedObject
{
  Object someComObject;
  IntPtr someUnmanagedResource;

  public static void Main()
  {
    ...
```

```
  ManagedObjectThatWrapsUnmanagedObject managedObject =
    new ManagedObjectThatWrapsUnmanagedObject();

  managedObject.CallUnmanagedCode();

  ... more code that does not use managedObject
}

public void CallUnmanagedCode()
{
  someComObject.UnmanagedMethod(someUnmanagedResource);
}
}
```

The garbage collector might run at the exact moment that the code inside `CallUnmanagedCode` is being executed. Because there is no code on the stack that uses the `managedObject` instance, it could be collected. Assuming that the finalizer for `ManagedObjectThatWrapsUnmanagedObject` destroys `someUnmanagedResource`, the implementation of `UnmanagedMethod` would fail.

To prevent this from happening, the `System.GC.KeepAlive` method could be used after the call to unmanaged code to prevent the object from being collected prematurely. For example:

```
public void CallUnmanagedCode()
{
  someComObject.UnmanagedMethod(someUnmanagedResource);
  GC.KeepAlive(this);
}
```

In fact, any dummy method after the call that uses the object could keep it alive throughout the `UnmanagedMethod` call as long as it's not optimized away by a compiler or the CLR just-in-time compiler. (For example, an empty virtual method would do the trick.)

> **TIP**
>
> Another solution for keeping an unmanaged resource alive would be to use the `GCHandle` type to allocate a normal (not pinned!) handle for its containing object. Using `HandleRef`, however, yields better performance.

The `HandleRef` value type can solve this problem as follows. It has a constructor that takes two parameters, a `System.Object` representing the wrapper object that must be kept alive, and a `System.IntPtr` that represents the unmanaged handle. When a `HandleRef` is passed to unmanaged code, the Interop Marshaler extracts the handle (passed as the second parameter to the constructor) and passes only that to unmanaged code. At the same time, however, the marshaler guarantees that the object passed as the first parameter to HandleRef's constructor is not collected for the duration of the call. This can be used as follows:

```
public void CallUnmanagedCode()
{
  someComObject.UnmanagedMethod(new HandleRef(this, someUnmanagedResource));
}
```

When defining a PInvoke signature that expects such a pointer or platform-sized integer representing some sort of handle, you should make the argument type a HandleRef rather than an IntPtr. This way, callers will automatically avoid premature garbage collection without understanding this subtle issue. If you can't control the signature, you're out of luck. The parameter must be declared as HandleRef for the support to work; you can't pass it as an Object parameter and have it work the desired way.

Rather than instantiating a new HandleRef on each call, the object that exposes a method such as the UnmanagedMethod example could expose a single HandleRef instance that can be used by clients. However, because HandleRef is a value type, instantiating one every time does not significantly hurt performance.

> **TIP**
>
> Had the .NET object implemented IDisposable for disposing its unmanaged resources, and had the client remembered to call Dispose when finished with ManagedObjectThatWrapsUnmanagedObject, this premature collection problem would not occur. That's because the presence of a call to Dispose would keep the object alive up until Dispose is called!

HandleRef can be used on COM methods, too, but the signatures would need to be customized to use HandleRef using either the techniques in Chapter 7 or Chapter 21. You never need to use HandleRef for passing COM objects to unmanaged code, because they are reference counted.

The ICustomAdapter Interface

The ICustomAdapter interface should be implemented by any adapter object returned by a custom marshaler to provide its client with a means of obtaining the original object that's being hidden by the custom marshaler.

The interface has a single method—GetUnderlyingObject—that takes no parameters but returns a System.Object that represents the object originally passed into the custom marshaler. Because a client of a custom marshaled object receives a new adapter object that maps specific functionality to the original object, the original object may provide additional functionality not reachable from the adapter object. If the adapter object implements ICustomAdapter, clients can call GetUnderlyingObject to get the original object and have access to whatever additional functionality it may provide.

For more information, consult Chapter 20.

The `ICustomFactory` Interface

The ICustomFactory interface, although defined in System.Runtime.InteropServices, is used with .NET Remoting rather than COM Interoperability. By implementing the ICustomFactory interface, a .NET proxy class that derives from System.MarshalByRefObject and marked with ProxyAttribute (defined in the System.Runtime.Remoting.Proxies namespace) can plug in custom activation code.

The interface has a single CreateInstance method that has a System.Type parameter and returns a System.MarshalByRefObject instance. The CLR calls CreateInstance when a new instance of the Type parameter is required. The CreateInstance implementer can then return the MarshalByRefObject instance via whatever means desired. Therefore, this is a means of writing a customized class factory, even when no unmanaged code is involved.

For more information, consult the .NET Framework SDK documentation for details about the .NET Remoting infrastructure.

The `ICustomMarshaler` Interface

The ICustomMarshaler interface is implemented by custom marshaler objects that customize interaction between managed and unmanaged code. This interface has five methods:

- MarshalManagedToNative. This method does the transformation of a .NET object to an unmanaged object. It has a single System.Object parameter representing the original object and returns a System.IntPtr representing a pointer to the new unmanaged object.

- MarshalNativeToManaged. This method does the transformation of an unmanaged object to a managed object. It has a single System.IntPtr parameter representing the original object and returns a System.Object that is the new managed object.

- CleanUpNativeData. This method is responsible for freeing any unmanaged memory allocated in MarshalManagedToNative or MarshalNativeToManaged, and decrementing the reference count of any COM interfaces whose reference counts were incremented (via direct calls to QueryInterface or AddRef). It has a single System.IntPtr parameter representing a pointer to the type on which the cleanup action needs to be done.

- CleanUpManagedData. This method is responsible for performing any cleanup of managed objects used in MarshalManagedToNative or MarshalNativeToManaged. It has a single System.Object parameter representing the object whose state should be cleaned up. This method usually has an empty implementation when custom marshaling by reference. When custom marshaling by value, calling IDisposable.Dispose is appropriate if the .NET object implements IDisposable.

- GetNativeDataSize. This method is not used by the CLR in the first version of the .NET Framework, because custom marshaling of value types is not supported. Therefore, this method's implementation should always return -1.

Besides implementing ICustomMarshaler, a custom marshaler must implement a static (Shared in VB .NET) method named GetInstance that has a string parameter and returns an ICustomMarshaler instance. This is called when the CLR requires an instance of the custom marshaler. The string parameter is the "cookie" value that the user of the custom marshaler specifies with MarshalAsAttribute.

The objects handed out by a custom marshaler should implement the ICustomAdapter interface to enable clients to obtain the original object.

For more information, see Chapter 20.

The IDispatchImplAttribute Custom Attribute

This custom attribute controls which of the two built-in IDispatch implementations the CLR provides on behalf of a .NET object. It can be marked on classes or assemblies. When marked on an assembly, it applies to all classes within the assembly unless individual classes override the setting with their own IDispatchImplAttribute.

The attribute has two constructors—one that takes a 16-bit integer and one that takes an IDispatchImplType enumeration. The latter constructor should always be used.

When a .NET object implements System.Reflection.IReflect, its custom implementation is always exposed when a COM client queries for IDispatch or IDispatchEx, but IDispatchImplAttribute still affects the implementation used when a client calls the IDispatch methods of any dual interfaces.

For more information, consult Chapter 14, "Implementing COM Interfaces for Binary Compatibility," or the IDispatchImplType enumeration listed next.

The `IDispatchImplType` Enumeration

The `IDispatchImplType` enumeration is used by the `IDispatchImplAttribute` custom attribute to choose what kind of `IDispatch` implementation is exposed to COM for a .NET class. It has three values:

- `CompatibleImpl`. Use the standard OLE Automation `IDispatch` implementation. This means that the CLR forwards calls to `ITypeInfo.Invoke` with type information from an exported type library. If no exported type library can be found, the CLR generates one in memory. For this setting to work, the interface exposed as the default interface must be dual.
- `InternalImpl`. This is the default implementation, based on reflection technology.
- `SystemDefinedImpl`. This setting is the same as `InternalImpl`, and should not be used.

For more information, consult Chapter 14 or the `IDispatchImplAttribute` custom attribute listed previously.

The `IDLDESC` Value Type

This is a .NET definition of the unmanaged `IDLDESC` structure used by the `DESCUNION` and `TYPEATTR` COM types. In the .NET Framework, this definition is used by .NET definitions of `DESCUNION` and `TYPEATTR`, which can be used with `UCOMITypeInfo`.

For more information, consult MSDN Online for information about the original `IDLDESC` structure.

The `IDLFLAG` Enumeration

This is a .NET definition of the unmanaged `IDLFLAG` enumeration used by the `IDLDESC` COM structure. In the .NET Framework, this definition is used by the .NET definition of `IDLDESC` just listed.

For more information, consult MSDN Online for information about the original `IDLFLAG` enumeration.

The `IMPLTYPEFLAGS` Enumeration

This is a .NET definition of the unmanaged `IMPLTYPEFLAGS` enumeration used by the `ITypeInfo` COM interface's `GetImplTypeFlags` method. In the .NET Framework, this definition is not used directly by .NET definition of `UCOMITypeInfo.GetImplTypeFlags`, but can be handy to use with the method. `UCOMITypeInfo.GetImplTypeFlags` has an out parameter that's an integer type, but this integer represents a value of `IMPLTYPEFLAGS`. Therefore, to interpret the value of this integer, simply convert it to an `IMPLTYPEFLAGS` enumeration first.

For more information, consult MSDN Online for information about the original `IMPLTYPEFLAGS` enumeration.

The `ImportedFromTypeLibAttribute` Custom Attribute

The type library importer places this custom attribute on an assembly to indicate that it was imported from a type library. This custom attribute is what identifies an assembly as an Interop Assembly. For example, the type library exporter checks for this custom attribute and doesn't export a type library for the assembly if it exists.

Unless attempting to manually create an assembly just like what the type library importer produces, you should not mark an assembly with this custom attribute.

For more information, consult Chapter 4.

The `ImporterEventKind` Enumeration

This enumeration is used by the `ITypeLibImporterNotifySink` interface's `ReportEvent` method. An implementer of `ITypeLibImporterNotifySink` has its `ReportEvent` method called by the CLR repeatedly during the process of type library import. The `ImporterEventKind` enumeration tells the `ReportEvent` implementer what type of event has just occurred. This enumeration has the following values:

- `ERROR_REFTOINVALIDTYPELIB`. This value is the one that represents a fatal error. In version 1.0 of the .NET Framework, this event is never reported.

- `NOTIF_CONVERTWARNING`. This value represents a warning during the import process. A common example of such a warning is when a pointer to a pointer to a structure is imported as a `System.IntPtr` type.

- `NOTIF_TYPECONVERTED`. This value is simply a notification of normal events. Every time a type is imported, this event occurs.

For more information, consult Chapter 22 and the `ITypeLibImporterNotifySink` interface listed later in this section.

The `InAttribute` Pseudo-Custom Attribute

The `InAttribute` pseudo-custom attribute can be marked on a member's parameters to affect their data flow when the member is implemented in managed code and called from unmanaged code, or vice versa. The `In` marking means that data flows from the caller to the callee.

In pure managed code, value types have "in" behavior and reference types have behavior like "in/out" because references are passed such that callees can change the object's state (except for the immutable System.String, which has "in" behavior). All by-reference types have "in/out" behavior, and C#-style out parameters have "out" behavior. The Interop Marshaler, however, treats all reference type parameters except StringBuilder with "in" behavior, which is often a source of confusion. When types are blittable, they appear to have "in/out" behavior, because the Interop Marshaler pins them, but this behavior is no longer seen when COM marshaling is involved across contexts.

Marking a C#-style out parameter with InAttribute is disallowed, but it can by marked on a by-reference behavior to suppress the "out" part of marshaling. Marking a formatted reference type parameter with both InAttribute and OutAttribute is often recommended to preserve the "in/out" semantics expected for reference types. This is important not only when crossing the managed/unmanaged boundary, but for any COM clients that may use an exported type library's definitions across context boundaries. If you expect "in/out" behavior, you better mark the parameter as such!

The type library importer marks any parameters with InAttribute when the corresponding parameter has an IDL [in] marking in the input type library. In Visual Basic .NET, square brackets must be used when using the short form of InAttribute (i.e. <[In]>) because In is a keyword.

For more information, see Chapter 12.

The InterfaceTypeAttribute Custom Attribute

This custom attribute can be marked on an interface definition to describe what kind of interface it looks like to COM—dual, IUnknown-only, or disp-only. If no InterfaceTypeAttribute exists, the interface is treated as a dual interface.

The attribute has two constructors—one that takes a 16-bit integer and one that takes a ComInterfaceType enumeration. The latter constructor should always be used. The type library importer always marks non-dual imported interfaces with the custom attribute and the appropriate value.

For more information, see Chapters 4, 12, and 21 and the ComInterfaceType enumeration listed earlier.

The `InvalidComObjectException` Exception

`InvalidComObjectException` is thrown by the CLR when one of the following two situations occur:

- A COM object becomes separated from its RCW.

- Someone attempts to create an instance of a COM object using a `System.__ComObject` type that hasn't been obtained from `Type.GetTypeFromProgID` or `Type.GetTypeFromCLSID`. Such an object doesn't have a class factory associated with it, so instantiation cannot succeed.

The first situation can occur in the graphical application developed in Chapter 22, if you change the background thread to be an STA thread then click on nodes of exported type libraries. In this case, the STA thread on which a COM object was created terminates and leaves the RCW detached.

The following illegal code demonstrates the second situation in C#:

```
// The type returned must be System.__ComObject, meaning that the
// CLR could not locate a metadata definition for the class type.
Object o = comObject.ReturnSomeInterface();

// Attempting to create an instance using this __ComObject type
// causes the InvalidComObjectException to be thrown.
Object o2 = Activator.CreateInstance(o.GetType());
```

`InvalidComObjectException` derives from `System.SystemException`, and should never be thrown by an application. Its protected `HResult` property (which can be exposed to COM when the exception is thrown) has the value `COR_E_INVALIDCOMOBJECT`, defined by the .NET Framework SDK as 0x80131527.

The `InvalidOleVariantTypeException` Exception

The Interop Marshaler throws an `InvalidOleVariantTypeException` when encountering a `VARIANT` instance whose type (specified in its `vt` field) is not valid. The valid types for a `VARIANT` are a subset of the values of the `VARENUM` enumeration, such as `VT_I2`, `VT_BOOL`, and so on. If a COM client attempts to pass a `VARIANT` with an illegal `vt` value such as `VT_VOID` or `VT_BLOB` (or even a number not defined by the `VARENUM` enumeration), the exception is thrown.

This exception only applies when marshaling a COM `VARIANT` to a .NET `Object`. In the reverse direction, it's possible that marshaling a .NET `Object` to a COM `VARIANT` causes a similar error if the object implements `System.IConvertible`. Because the marshaler figures out what type to make the exposed `VARIANT` by calling `IConvertible.GetTypeCode`, an object that returns a `TypeCode` value that doesn't correspond to a valid value from the `VARENUM` subset causes an exception. The exception for this direction, however, is `System.NotSupportedException` rather than `InvalidOleVariantTypeException`.

InvalidOleVariantTypeException derives from System.SystemException, and should never be thrown by an application. Its protected HResult property (which can be exposed to COM when the exception is thrown) has the value COR_E_INVALIDOLEVARIANTTYPE, defined by the .NET Framework SDK as 0x80131531.

The INVOKEKIND Enumeration

This is a .NET definition of the unmanaged INVOKEKIND enumeration used by the ITypeInfo COM interface. In the .NET Framework, this definition is used by UCOMITypeInfo. AddressOfMember, UCOMITypeInfo.GetDllEntry, and also as a field of the FUNCDESC value type.

For more information, consult MSDN Online for information about the original INVOKEKIND enumeration.

The IRegistrationServices Interface

This interface, implemented by the RegistrationServices class, defines methods used for registering and unregistering assemblies for use by COM. It also contains several methods that can be helpful in discovering the entries that would be placed in the registry, so you could create a .reg registry file, for example. The interface defines the following methods:

- GetManagedCategoryGuid
- GetProgIdForType
- GetRegistrableTypesInAssembly
- RegisterAssembly
- RegisterTypeForComClients
- TypeRepresentsComType
- TypeRequiresRegistration
- UnregisterAssembly

For more information, see the RegistrationServices class listed later in this section, as well as Chapter 22.

The ITypeLibConverter Interface

This interface, implemented by the TypeLibConverter class, defines methods used for importing and exporting type libraries. The interface defines the following methods:

- ConvertAssemblyToTypeLib
- ConvertTypeLibToAssembly (two overloads)
- GetPrimaryInteropAssembly

For more information, see the `TypeLibConverter` class listed later in this section, as well as Chapter 22.

The `ITypeLibExporterNameProvider` Interface

An object can implement `ITypeLibExporterNameProvider` to choose the casing of identifiers in an exported type library. Type libraries are case-insensitive, and the first case of any identifier emitted into an exported type library "wins." The result of this is that a parameter name such as name can cause a member name such as `Name` to appear as name in the exported type library, and vice versa. Therefore, adding any exportable types or members to an assembly can change (from COM's perspective only) untouched APIs emitted later in metadata if they use the same identifiers with a different case.

Furthermore, the order in which types are emitted to metadata by a .NET compiler can change based on subtle changes to source code or even the order in which input source files are processed, potentially causing the case of exported names to oscillate on a daily basis! In such a situation, recompiling a case-sensitive COM client (such as one written in unmanaged C++) can cause compilation errors, requiring you to update the case of identifiers on a regular basis.

Implementing the `ITypeLibExporterNameProvider` can solve this problem. The interface has a single method—`GetNames`—that returns an array of strings. Each string is treated as an identifier with the "correct" case. If an exported type library contains one of the identifiers in the array, it will always appear in the casing returned by `GetNames`. (If the returned array contains the same identifier in different cases, the first one is used.)

Of course, an object implementing `ITypeLibExporterNameProvider` needs to be recognized and used by the type library exporter to have any effect. An object implementing the interface can be passed to `ITypeLibConverter.ConvertAssemblyToTypeLib` (as the `notifySink` parameter), which is implemented by the `TypeLibConverter` class. Any object that implements `ITypeLibExporterNameProvider` must also implement `ITypeLibExporterNotifySink` because that's the type of the `notifySink` parameter that the `ConvertAssemblyToTypeLib` implementation requires.

It is the responsibility of the `ITypeLibExporterNameProvider` to determine an array of identifiers that can solve any potential case problems. For example, you could use reflection on the input assembly to find identifiers that appear in multiple cases and would be exported to a type library. For each such identifier, a "correct" version must be chosen.

The `TLBEXP.EXE` SDK tool uses an `ITypeLibExporterNameProvider` implementation if the user specifies the `/names` option with a filename of a *names file*. This file can contain a list of names in the correct case (one per line) that populates the string array returned by `GetNames`.

For more information, see Chapter 22, Appendix B, and the `ITypeLibExporterNotifySink` interface listed next.

The `ITypeLibExporterNotifySink` Interface

An object implementing `ITypeLibExporterNotifySink` must be passed to `TypeLibConverter.` `ConvertAssemblyToTypeLib` as its `notifySink` parameter to handle callbacks during the type library export process. This interface has two methods:

- `ReportEvent`. This method has three parameters—an `ExporterEventKind` enumeration value, an integer, and a string. When called by `TypeLibConverter`, the enumeration value describes the type of event, the integer represents an `HRESULT` value that describes the event more specifically, and the string contains a method describing the event. The "event" is not a .NET event, but a simple callback.

- `ResolveRef`. This method has an `Assembly` parameter and returns an `Object` type. `TypeLibConverter` passes an in-memory dependent assembly, and it's the job of the `ResolveRef` implementation to return an object implementing `UCOMITypeLib` that represents a type library that should be used for this dependent assembly. A typical `ResolveRef` implementation attempts to use an existing type library, and exports a new one from the input assembly if one can't be found.

For more information, see Chapter 22 the `ExporterEventKind` enumeration listed previously, and the `TypeLibConverter` class listed later in this section.

The `ITypeLibImporterNotifySink` Interface

An object implementing `ITypeLibImporterNotifySink` must be passed to `TypeLibConverter.` `ConvertTypeLibToAssembly` as its `notifySink` parameter to handle callbacks during the type library import process. This interface has two methods:

- `ReportEvent`. This method has three parameters—an `ImporterEventKind` enumeration value, an integer, and a string. When called by `TypeLibConverter`, the enumeration value describes the type of event, the integer represents an `HRESULT` value that describes the event more specifically, and the string contains a method describing the event. The "event" is not a .NET event, but a simple callback.

- `ResolveRef`. This method has an `Object` parameter and returns an `Assembly` type. `TypeLibConverter` passes an in-memory dependent type library (an object implementing `UCOMITypeLib`), and it's the job of the `ResolveRef` implementation to return an `Assembly` instance that should be used for this dependent type library. A typical `ResolveRef` implementation attempts to use an existing assembly, and imports a new one from the input type library if one can't be found.

For more information, see Chapter 22 the `ImporterEventKind` enumeration listed previously, and the `TypeLibConverter` class listed later in this section.

The `LayoutKind` Enumeration

This enumeration is used by the `StructLayoutAttribute` pseudo-custom attribute to control the layout of a type when exposed to COM as a structure. It has three values:

- `Auto`. The CLR decides how to arrange a type's fields. This is the best choice for purely .NET applications, because the CLR may be able to make optimizations based on how the type is used. However, this setting cannot be used on types exposed to unmanaged code as structures because memory layout must be known and stable.

- `Explicit`. Every field is marked with an explicit location in memory, as a byte offset from the beginning of the type. This setting must be used in conjunction with the `FieldOffsetAttribute` marked on every field.

- `Sequential`. The type's fields are arranged in memory sequentially, in the order they appear in the value type's definition. The fields are not necessarily contiguous, because value types may have packing behavior (specified with `StructLayoutAttribute`'s `Pack` property) that aligns fields on certain byte boundaries.

Although `Auto` is the default layout chosen by the CLR, the C#, VB .NET, and C++ compilers all specify `Sequential` on value types by default, due to the non-intuitive problems that may arise by passing `Auto` value types to unmanaged code.

.NET clients attempting to manipulate a value type in "unsafe ways" (such as C# unsafe code or mixed mode C++) cannot assume anything about the type's layout if it contains non-blittable fields. In such cases, the layout is only applied to the marshaled structure exposed to unmanaged code via the Interop Marshaler.

For more information, consult Chapter 12, Part VI, and the `StructLayoutAttribute` pseudo-custom attribute listed later in this section.

The `LCIDConversionAttribute` Custom Attribute

This custom attribute can be marked on a .NET method (or property accessor) to indicate that the corresponding unmanaged signature has an LCID parameter that's hidden from the .NET view.

An LCID parameter is a special parameter (marked in a type library with the `lcid` IDL attribute) that contains a locale identifier (LCID). Such a parameter enables the method implementer to take special action based on the user's locale. The parameter is marked with `lcid` so rich clients like Visual Basic 6 can hide it from the user and fill in a value corresponding to the user's locale obtained from the operating system.

The custom attribute's constructor has an integer parameter that represents a zero-based offset of which parameter should be the `lcid` parameter. Note that this offset doesn't refer to an existing parameter, but one that is inserted into the COM method definition. Here is an example of method definitions using `LCIDConversionAttribute` and their exported representation:

C#:

```
[LCIDConversion(0)]
void MultiCulturalMethod1(int a, int b);
[LCIDConversion(2)]
void MultiCulturalMethod2(int a, int b);
```

Visual Basic .NET:

```
<LCIDConversion(0)> _
Sub MultiCulturalMethod1(a As Integer, b As Integer)
<LCIDConversion(2)> _
Sub MultiCulturalMethod2(a As Integer, b As Integer)
```

C++:

```
[LCIDConversion(0)]
void MultiCulturalMethod1(int a, int b);
[LCIDConversion(2)]
void MultiCulturalMethod2(int a, int b);
```

Exported IDL signatures:

```
HRESULT MultiCulturalMethod1([in, lcid] long p1, [in] long a, [in] long b);
HRESULT MultiCulturalMethod2([in] long a, [in] long b, [in, lcid] long p3);
```

The Interop Marshaler takes care of filling in the appropriate value when a .NET client calls such a method (and vice versa), based on the current thread's locale information. .NET clients can determine the LCID parameter value passed by a COM client by checking `System.Threading.Thread.CurrentThread.CurrentCulture`. The raw LCID value can even be obtained by checking `CurrentCulture`'s `LCID` property!

The type library importer marks all methods with an LCID parameter with `LCIDConversionAttribute` in order to hide it from the imported signature.

For more information, consult Chapter 12.

The LIBFLAGS Enumeration

This is a .NET definition of the unmanaged LIBFLAGS enumeration used by the TYPELIBATTR COM structure. In the .NET Framework, this definition is used by the .NET definition of TYPELIBATTR.

For more information, consult MSDN Online for information about the original LIBFLAGS structure.

A

System.Runtime.
InteropServices
REFERENCE

The `Marshal` Class

The `Marshal` class is by far the largest member of the `System.Runtime.InteropServices` namespace. It's your one-stop shopping place for language-neutral interoperability functionality. It provides .NET clients with raw and powerful APIs available to unmanaged clients, exposes pieces of the Interop Marshaler's functionality (useful for high-performance custom marshaling), and much more.

A handful of `Marshal`'s methods are widely used, such as the familiar `BindToMoniker`, `GetLastWin32Error`, `ReleaseComObject`, `SizeOf`, and `StructureToPtr` methods. Most of its members, however, are considered for advanced use only, to work around the areas in which COM Interoperability and PInvoke don't naturally bridge the managed and unmanaged worlds. Most members are useful for custom marshaling (shown in Chapter 20), or when mixing unmanaged and managed code in C++. Members of the `Marshal` class even enable the same kind of manipulations you'd do with pointers in CLS-compliant APIs that are usable from any .NET language!

> **TIP**
>
> Just because Visual Basic .NET doesn't have pointer *syntax*, don't be fooled into believing that you can't do the same kind of high performance pointer manipulations as you could in C++ or C# unsafe code. As described in Chapter 6, using methods of the `Marshal` class, any .NET language can do the same kind of memory manipulations as in C# unsafe code! In some cases, functionality enabled by the `Marshal` class is more powerful than what can be done in C# unsafe code (such as converting an integer to an interface pointer)!

The class is enormous, but its members fall into 12 broad categories:

- Data Transformations
- Memory Management
- Direct Reading & Writing
- Structure Inspection
- COM Library Functions
- IUnknown Methods
- Error Handling
- Type Information

- COM Interop Utilities
- PInvoke Utilities
- Hosting Utilities
- Advanced Marshaling

To help you navigate through these categories and their members, Figure A.2 displays the entire contents of the Marshal class according to the previous groups. This illustration also appears on this book's inside back cover.

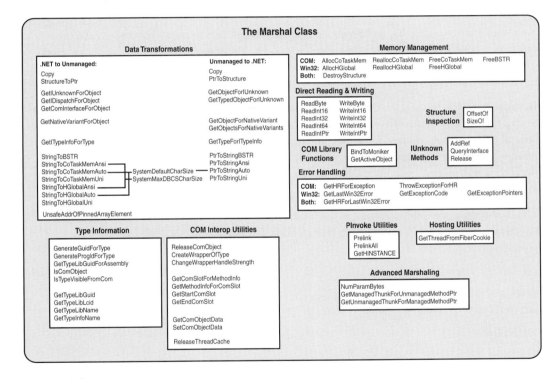

FIGURE A.2

The contents of the System.Runtime.InteropServices.Marshal *class.*

Every member of the Marshal class is static (Shared in VB .NET). Therefore, the class doesn't have or need a public constructor. Unmanaged code permission (SecurityPermission with SecurityPermissionFlag.UnmanagedCode set) is required to be able to use methods of the Marshal class. However, this is required via a link demand, so it's important that users of its methods are careful not to expose functionality to untrusted code that could be exploited maliciously.

For the remainder of this section, every member—listed in alphabetical order—is described in detail.

The `AddRef` Method

All three `IUnknown` methods—`QueryInterface`, `AddRef`, and `Release`—are exposed through the `Marshal` class and can be called on any COM object. `Marshal.AddRef` exposes a COM object's `IUnknown.AddRef` method, which increments the object's reference count. It takes a `System.IntPtr` parameter that represents the `IUnknown` pointer for a COM object, and returns the 32-bit integer returned by the COM object's `AddRef` implementation. This return value roughly represents the object's reference count, and should be used only for testing purposes.

To get an `IntPtr` value that represents an object, you can call `GetComInterfaceForObject`, `GetIDispatchForObject`, or `GetIUnknownForObject`. These methods, plus the `Marshal.AddRef` method, can even be used on purely .NET objects! In this case, the COM interfaces represent the ones implemented by the .NET object's COM-Callable Wrapper.

Because the CLR manages a COM object's reference count for you, it's almost never necessary to call `Marshal.AddRef`. In some advanced cases, however, like custom marshaling or working around COM object oddities, it can become necessary. In these cases, you are given an interface pointer as an `IntPtr` value and want to manipulate its lifetime. As in COM, don't forget to decrement the object's reference count (using a method like `Marshal.Release`) at some point after calling `Marshal.AddRef`.

The following code demonstrates the use of `Marshal.AddRef`, using `Marshal.GetIUnknown-ForObject` to obtain an `IntPtr` value representing the COM object's `IUnknown` interface pointer:

C#:

```
IntPtr pUnk = Marshal.GetIUnknownForObject(myComObject);
int refCount = Marshal.AddRef(pUnk);
```

Visual Basic .NET:

```
Dim pUnk As IntPtr = Marshal.GetIUnknownForObject(myComObject)
Dim refCount As Integer = Marshal.AddRef(pUnk)
```

C++:

```
IntPtr pUnk = Marshal::GetIUnknownForObject(myComObject);
int refCount = Marshal::AddRef(pUnk);
```

For more information, see `Marshal.QueryInterface` and `Marshal.Release` listed later in this section.

The `AllocCoTaskMem` Method

This method is one of the two memory allocation APIs in the `Marshal` class (the other being `AllocHGlobal`). `AllocCoTaskMem` exposes the similarly-named `CoTaskMemAlloc` COM API, the COM task memory allocator. It has a single integer parameter that represents the number of bytes to allocate, and returns a `System.IntPtr` type representing a pointer to the allocated block of memory.

As with using `CoTaskMemAlloc` in COM, any memory allocated with this method must be freed with `CoTaskMemFree`. In the .NET Framework, this method is exposed as `Marshal.FreeCoTaskMem`.

The initial memory content returned is undefined, and the memory allocated might be larger than the requested number of bytes. Whereas `CoTaskMemAlloc` returns null on failure, `Marshal.AllocCoTaskMem` throws an `OutOfMemoryException` on failure.

For more information, see MSDN Online for a description of `CoTaskMemAlloc`, and the `FreeCoTaskMem` and `ReAllocCoTaskMem` methods listed later in this section.

The `AllocHGlobal` Method

This method is one of the two memory allocation APIs in the `Marshal` class (the other being `AllocCoTaskMem`). `AllocHGlobal` allocates fixed memory from the "global heap." Win32 does not provide a separate global heap and local heap, so this method exposes the Win32 `GlobalAlloc` API from `KERNEL32.DLL`, which does the same thing as the `LocalAlloc` API from the same DLL.

This method has two overloads. One has a 32-bit integer parameter specifying the number of bytes to allocate, and one has a `System.IntPtr` parameter specifying the number of bytes to allocate. Both do the same thing, and both return a `System.IntPtr` value representing a pointer to the allocated block of memory.

As with using `LocalAlloc` in Win32 programming, any memory allocated with this method must be freed with `LocalFree`. In the .NET Framework, this method is exposed as `Marshal.FreeHGlobal`. `Marshal.AllocHGlobal` calls `LocalAlloc` with the `LMEM_FIXED` flag to specify that fixed memory is desired.

The initial memory content returned is undefined, and the memory allocated might be larger than the requested number of bytes. (Any extra amounts may be used, and the Win32 `LocalSize` method can be called to determine how much was returned.) Whereas `LocalAlloc` returns null on failure, `Marshal.AllocHGlobal` throws an `OutOfMemoryException` on failure.

For more information, see MSDN Online for a description of `LocalAlloc`, and the `FreeHGlobal` and `ReAllocHGlobal` methods listed later in this section.

The `BindToMoniker` Method

This method enables the location and creation of an object from a COM moniker. It has a single string parameter that contains the moniker name, and returns a `System.Object` instance created by the moniker.

`BindToMoniker` first calls the `CreateBindCtx` COM API to obtain a bind context object, then calls the `MkParseDisplayName` COM API with the bind context object and the user-supplied moniker name to get an `IMoniker` instance. Finally, the `BindMoniker` COM API is called, requesting an `IUnknown` interface pointer that gets marshaled to the returned `System.Object` type. `BindMoniker` locates the COM object and activates it if it isn't already active. The returned object can be cast to whatever COM interface is desired.

This method provides the same functionality as the `GetObject` method in Visual Basic 6 and Visual Basic .NET. The VB .NET `GetObject` method (defined in the global `Microsoft.VisualBasic.Interaction` module) calls either `Marshal.BindToMoniker`, `Marshal.GetActiveObject`, or `Activator.CreateInstance(Type.GetTypeFromProgID("…"))` depending on the strings passed to it.

If `BindToMoniker` fails, a `COMException` is thrown with the `HRESULT` value returned by the COM API that failed, for example `MK_E_SYNTAX` (0x800401E4) from `MkParseDisplayName` or `MK_E_NOOBJECT` (0x800401E5) from `BindMoniker`.

The following code demonstrates using this method to take advantage of the SOAP (Simple Object Access Protocol) moniker provided by Windows XP, to seamlessly use an XML Web service from managed code via COM Interoperability:

C#:

```
object translator = Marshal.BindToMoniker(
  "SOAP:wsdl=http://www.xmethods.net/sd/2001/BabelFishService.wsdl");
```

Visual Basic .NET:

```
Dim translator As Object = Marshal.BindToMoniker( _
  "SOAP:wsdl=http://www.xmethods.net/sd/2001/BabelFishService.wsdl")
```

C++:

```
Object* translator = Marshal::BindToMoniker(
  S"SOAP:wsdl=http://www.xmethods.net/sd/2001/BabelFishService.wsdl");
```

The `ChangeWrapperHandleStrength` Method

This method can change a COM-Callable Wrapper's (CCW's) strength from strong to weak and vice versa. This is used for object pooling functionality, but should never need to be called directly by user code.

ChangeWrapperHandleStrength has two parameters—a System.Object instance whose COM-Callable Wrapper is being changed, and a boolean value. This value can be set to true to make the wrapper always weak, or false to make its strength depend on its reference count.

The Copy Method

The Copy method is useful for copying a subset of a one-dimensional .NET array to an unmanaged C-style array, and vice versa. There are 14 overloads of Copy, covering seven different data types with both directions of copying.

In the managed-to-unmanaged direction, the seven Copy overloads have the following form, where *XXX* represents one of the seven data types covered—System.Byte, System.Char, System.Int16, System.Int32, System.Int64, System.Single, and System.Double:

C#:

```
public static void Copy(XXX [] source, int startIndex,
  IntPtr destination, int length);
```

Visual Basic .NET:

```
Public Overloads Shared Sub Copy(source As XXX(), startIndex As Integer, _
  destination As IntPtr, length As Integer)
```

C++:

```
public: static void Copy(XXX source __gc[], int startIndex,
  IntPtr destination, int length);
```

These methods are useful for copying data into pre-allocated unmanaged memory. For these methods, a one-dimensional .NET array is passed in as the source parameter, a zero-based index where the copying should begin is passed as the startIndex integer, an IntPtr type representing the pointer to the unmanaged C-style array is passed as the destination parameter, and the number of elements to copy is passed as the length integer.

If the startIndex and length values are not valid for the .NET array (for example, extending past the end of it), an ArgumentOutOfRangeException is thrown.

In the unmanaged-to-managed direction, the seven Copy overloads have the following form, where *XXX* represents one of the same seven data types covered—System.Byte, System.Char, System.Int16, System.Int32, System.Int64, System.Single, and System.Double:

C#:

```
public static void Copy(IntPtr source, XXX [] destination,
  int startIndex, int length);
```

Visual Basic .NET:

```
Public Overloads Shared Sub Copy(source As IntPtr, destination As XXX(), _
  startIndex As Integer, length As Integer)
```

C++:

```
public: static void Copy(IntPtr source, XXX destination __gc[],
  int startIndex, int length);
```

For these methods, an `IntPtr` type representing the pointer to the unmanaged C-style array is passed as the `source` parameter, a zero-based index where the copying should begin is passed as the `startIndex` integer, a one-dimensional .NET array is passed in as the `destination` parameter, and the number of elements to copy is passed as the `length` integer.

Unlike with the reverse direction, no validation of the `startIndex` and `length` values can be done because C-style arrays do not carry bounds information with them. Be careful, because whatever data the `IntPtr` value points to will simply get sucked into a .NET array whether it makes sense or not. The .NET destination array must be initialized with the appropriate size before calling `Copy`.

For more information, see Chapter 6.

The `CreateWrapperOfType` Method

The `CreateWrapperOfType` method provides a way to convert one COM class type to another COM class type. The "Wrapper" refers to the fact that these COM objects are Runtime-Callable Wrappers. This method is usually used to convert a COM object whose class type is unknown (and therefore a generic `System.__ComObject` type) to a specific class type. It takes two parameters—a `System.Object` that is the source COM object and a `System.Type` instance of the type of object you want to convert the source object to. The method returns a `System.Object` destination COM object that's an instance of the desired type.

The `Type` instance must represent a `ComImport`-marked class, and the `Object` instance's type must be a `ComImport`-marked class, otherwise an `ArgumentException` is thrown.

This method won't let you convert one wrapper to another arbitrarily. To determine whether one class type can be converted to another class type, this method takes every COM interface that the destination type claims to implement and calls `QueryInterface` for each interface on the source object. If the source object implements *every* COM interface listed by the destination type, the new wrapper is successfully created. Otherwise, an `InvalidCastException` is thrown with the message:

```
Source object cannot be converted to the destination type since it does not
support all the required interfaces.
```

This check does not include any interfaces implemented by the class that aren't marked with `ComImportAttribute`, such as `IEnumerable` if the RCW supports enumeration.

Remember that the type used as the second parameter must be a *class* and not an interface. When using types generated by the type library importer, this means using the `CoClassNameClass` type because the type with the name of the coclass is an interface.

An important aspect of using `CreateWrapperOfType` is that you lose the identity of the input COM object because a new RCW instance ends up wrapping the same `IUnknown` interface pointer. For more information, see Chapter 6.

The `DestroyStructure` Method

The `DestroyStructure` method is used to free reference type fields (such as strings) of an unmanaged structure, using the same deallocation API that would be used by the Interop Marshaler (`CoTaskMemFree`). This method does not free the memory of the structure itself.

The method has two parameters—a `System.IntPtr` type representing the pointer to the unmanaged structure, and a `System.Type` instance representing the type of the structure whose reference type fields are being freed.

The .NET type can be a value type or reference type, but if it is marked with automatic layout (rather than sequential or explicit), an `ArgumentException` is thrown. If the entire structure is blittable, `DestroyStructure` does no work because there are no references whose memory needs to be freed. This method is used by `Marshal.StructureToPtr` to avoid memory leaks when reusing memory occupied by a structure.

For more information, see the `Marshal.StructureToPtr` method and Chapter 6.

The `FreeBSTR` Method

This method is one of the three memory-deallocation APIs in the `Marshal` class (the others being `FreeCoTaskMem` and `FreeHGlobal`). This method calls the `SysFreeString` COM API, which frees a string allocated by any of the following methods:

- `SysAllocString`
- `SysAllocStringByteLen`
- `SysAllocStringLen`
- `SysReAllocString`
- `SysReAllocStringLen`

> **TIP**
>
> None of these string allocation methods are defined in the `Marshal` class because
> `Marshal.StringToBSTR` is defined instead. You could, however, define these signatures
> using PInvoke. See Appendix E for such definitions in C#.

For more information, see MSDN Online for a description of `SysFreeString`.

The `FreeCoTaskMem` Method

This method is one of the three memory-deallocation APIs in the `Marshal` class (the others
being `FreeBSTR` and `FreeHGlobal`). This should be called to free any memory allocated by
`Marshal.AllocCoTaskMem` and `Marshal.ReAllocCoTaskMem` (or an equivalent unmanaged API).
It exposes the similarly named `CoTaskMemFree` COM API, which frees memory allocated by
`CoTaskMemAlloc` or `CoTaskMemRealloc`. `FreeCoTaskMem` has a single `System.IntPtr` parameter
that represents a pointer to the block of memory to free. If `IntPtr.Zero` (a null value) is passed,
the method does nothing.

As with using `CoTaskMemFree` in COM, all the bytes are freed, and the memory pointed to by
the input parameter can no longer be used after the call.

For more information, see MSDN Online for a description of `CoTaskMemFree`, and the
`AllocCoTaskMem` and `ReAllocCoTaskMem` methods listed in this section.

The `FreeHGlobal` Method

This method is one of the three memory-deallocation APIs in the `Marshal` class (the others
being `FreeBSTR` and `FreeCoTaskMem`). This should be called to free any memory allocated on
the "global heap" by `Marshal.AllocHGlobal` and `Marshal.ReAllocHGlobal` (or an equivalent
unmanaged API). Win32 does not provide a separate global heap and local heap, so this
method exposes the Win32 `GlobalFree` API from `KERNEL32.DLL`, which does the same thing
as the `LocalFree` API from the same DLL.

This method has a single `System.IntPtr` parameter representing a pointer to the memory.
Therefore, the `IntPtr` value returned by `AllocHGlobal` or `ReAllocHGlobal` should be passed
as this parameter. If `IntPtr.Zero` (a null value) is passed, the method does nothing.

As with using `LocalFree` in Win32, all the bytes are freed, and the memory pointed to by the
input parameter can no longer be used after the call.

For more information, see MSDN Online for a description of `LocalFree`, and the
`AllocHGlobal` and `ReAllocHGlobal` methods listed in this section.

The `GenerateGuidForType` Method

This method returns a GUID for any .NET type. It has a single `System.Type` parameter and returns a `System.Guid` instance. If the type is marked with the `GuidAttribute` custom attribute, its GUID value is returned. If not, the GUID that is automatically generated for a .NET type by the type library exporter is returned.

Therefore, this method can be used to figure out the GUID that would be used for COM for any .NET types, even COM-invisible ones! The only exported types whose GUIDs cannot be determined programmatically are class interfaces, because they don't directly correspond to any .NET type. This method is redundant with `System.Type`'s `GUID` property; calling this method returns the exact same GUID that the property returns.

For more information about the algorithms used to generate GUIDs for .NET types, see Chapter 11.

The `GenerateProgIdForType` Method

This method returns a ProgID for a .NET class. It has a single `System.Type` parameter and returns a string that's the ProgID. If the type is marked with the `ProgIdAttribute` custom attribute, its string value is returned. If not, the default ProgID that is automatically generated for a .NET class is returned—the namespace-qualified class name.

Unlike `GenerateGuidForType`, this method only works on classes that would be registered. Attempting to use a type that's COM-invisible, not a class, a class that doesn't have a public default constructor, and so on, causes an `ArgumentException` to be thrown.

For more information about ProgIDs of .NET classes, see Chapter 12.

The `GetActiveObject` Method

The `Marshal.GetActiveObject` exposes COM's `GetActiveObject` API, which returns an instance of a currently running COM object. The running object is retrieved from the OLE object table, also known as the *running object table*.

Unlike the unmanaged API, which expects a CLSID of the running object, `Marshal.GetActiveObject` expects a ProgID of the running object. It has a single string parameter (the ProgID) and returns a `System.Object`. This returned object can be cast to the desired COM interface in order to use its members in an early-bound fashion.

If you need to get an instance of a running COM object that is not registered with a ProgID, you'll have to resort to using PInvoke to define the original `GetActiveObject` method from `OLEAUT32.DLL`. There are no methods in the `Marshal` class for *putting* an object in the running object table, so you'll need to use PInvoke for that as well.

For more information, see Chapter 6.

A

System.Runtime.
InteropServices
REFERENCE

The `GetComInterfaceForObject` Method

The `GetComInterfaceForObject` method retrieves a pointer to a COM interface implemented by any object and returns it as a `System.IntPtr` value. In this case, the term "COM interface" means any interface that is visible to COM, not just interfaces marked with `ComImportAttribute`.

The returned interface pointer's reference count is incremented before being returned, so you must decrement it with `Marshal.Release` once you're finished with it. When dealing with "raw" COM interfaces pointers, all the old COM rules apply because you're no longer communicating with an RCW that handles these details for you.

> **TIP**
>
> As the rules of COM dictate, the reference count of a returned interface pointer gets incremented and the caller is responsible to eventually decrement it. Therefore, you must remember to call `Marshal.Release` when you're finished with the interface! This applies to *all* `Marshal` methods that return interface pointers as `IntPtr` types.

Like `Marshal.GetIUnknownForObject` and `Marshal.GetIDispatchForObject`, this method has a `System.Object` parameter and returns a `System.IntPtr`. This method has a second parameter, however—a `System.Type` instance that specifies the desired interface type. This means that the interface being retrieved must have a .NET definition. If the type passed is not an interface, or if it is not visible from COM, an `ArgumentException` is thrown.

This method can even be used on a purely .NET object! In this case, the interface pointer corresponds to the .NET object's COM-Callable Wrapper (so you could get an interface pointer for `UCOMIConnectionPointContainer` on any .NET object). If the object passed in does not support the desired interface, an `InvalidCastException` is thrown.

This method can be useful when calling a method that exposes a COM object parameter as an `IntPtr` type, or with custom marshaling.

It's not possible to directly obtain a .NET object's class interface using this method because there's no corresponding .NET interface type to pass as the second parameter. However, using `Marshal.GetIDispatchForObject` on a .NET object gives you the ability to invoke members on the COM-Callable Wrapper's default interface, which is usually an auto-dispatch class interface.

To get an object's `IUnknown` or `IDispatch` interface pointer, you can call `Marshal.GetIUnknownForObject` or `Marshal.GetIDispatchForObject`.

For more information, see Chapters 6 and 20.

The `GetComObjectData` Method

Every COM object wrapped in a Runtime-Callable Wrapper has a hashtable associated with it. This method is a means of retrieving this data, and `SetComObjectData` is a means of setting the data. User code should have no reason to call this method.

The `GetComSlotForMethodInfo` Method

This method enables you to retrieve an integer for a `System.Reflection.MemberInfo` instance that represents its zero-based slot value in a v-table that would be exposed to COM. It has a single `MemberInfo` parameter and returns a 32-bit integer. Note that although the name uses "MethodInfo," it accepts a `MemberInfo`.

The returned slot number accounts for the presence of three `IUnknown` methods and possibly four `IDispatch` methods. Therefore, the first method on a .NET type will have a slot value of either 3 or 7.

You can even get slot numbers for members of a COM-invisible or private interface. In this case, they simply correspond to the v-table that would be exposed to COM had the interface been exposed to COM. You can also get slot numbers for COM-invisible members because they still occupy a slot in an exposed v-table (although COM clients can't use the slot).

The type must be an interface type or an `ArgumentException` is thrown. This method cannot be used on class interfaces by passing a `MemberInfo` from a class.

This method does the reverse action of `Marshal.GetMethodInfoForComSlot`.

The `GetEndComSlot` Method

This method retrieves the last zero-based slot in a .NET type's v-table. `GetEndComSlot` has a single `System.Type` parameter whose v-table is being inspected, and returns a 32-bit integer containing the last slot number. `GetEndComSlot` throws an `ArgumentException` if the type passed in is COM-invisible. The type can be an interface or a class. The slot numbers given for a class type refer to its class interface. If the class has an auto-dispatch class interface, -1 is always returned because this is a true disp-only interface that doesn't have a v-table exposed to .NET clients, unlike a dispinterface that has a metadata definition.

This method, along with `GetStartComSlot`, can be used with `GetMethodInfoForComSlot` to only pass slots in the valid range.

The `GetExceptionCode` Method

This method exists for compiler support of Structured Exception Handling (SEH). It has no parameters, but returns a 32-bit integer representing the SEH error code of the last exception thrown.

DIGGING DEEPER

Who says that COM is dead? The SEH error code for all .NET exceptions is
0xE0434F4D, which happens to equal 0xE0000000 | 'COM'!

If GetExceptionCode is called before any exception is thrown, this method simply returns
0xCCCCCCCC.

The GetExceptionPointers Method

This method exists for compiler support of Structured Exception Handling (SEH). It has no
parameters, but returns a System.IntPtr representing a pointer to an EXCEPTION_POINTERS
struct. This struct is defined in winnt.h from the Windows Platform SDK as follows:

```
typedef struct _EXCEPTION_POINTERS {
  PEXCEPTION_RECORD ExceptionRecord;
  PCONTEXT ContextRecord;
} EXCEPTION_POINTERS, *PEXCEPTION_POINTERS;
```

The GetHINSTANCE Method

This method returns an instance handle (HINSTANCE) for any .NET module. It has a single
System.Reflection.Module parameter and returns a System.IntPtr value containing the
HINSTANCE value.

This method is useful when calling unmanaged functions that expect an HISNTANCE, such as the
Win32 RegisterClass API. To get the module that any type is contained within, you can use
the System.Type.Module property. For example, to get the module from which an object o was
instantiated, use o.GetType().Module.

CAUTION

Dynamic modules generated by Reflection Emit do not have a corresponding instance
handle. Calling GetHINSTANCE on such a module returns -1.

The GetHRForException Method

The GetHRForException method retrieves the HRESULT value for any kind of .NET exception
and also calls the Windows SetErrorInfo API with the CCW for exception (which implements IErrorInfo appropriately). This is exactly what the Interop Marshaler does when a

COM client calls a .NET member that throws an exception. This method is useful for custom marshaling scenarios because you can determine the HRESULT value COM clients see for any kind of exception thrown. The method has a single Exception parameter and returns an integer representing the exception's corresponding HRESULT.

Most exceptions' HRESULT values are captured in the protected HResult property with no way for clients to check the value directly. This is done because checking error codes is supposed to be a thing of the past; the .NET thing to do is check exception types. Because interoperability scenarios still require error codes at times, GetHRForException enables you to check these values.

An example of a time to use GetHRForException is in a .NET class's implementation of a COM interface with a method marked with the PreserveSigAttribute pseudo-custom attribute. If the method needs to return an HRESULT value, letting an exception propagate outside the method would not give correct behavior. (If a COM client calls such a method through a v-table, a thrown exception would be swallowed by the CLR.) Instead, the method can catch any exception that may be thrown and return the appropriate HRESULT value.

For more information, see Chapter 20 and Appendix D.

The GetHRForLastWin32Error Method
It's a common mistake to treat a Win32 error code as an HRESULT value. Because it's only a portion of an HRESULT however, treating it as an HRESULT would make it look like a *success* value rather than failure! To help users avoid this mistake, Marshal.GetHRForLastWin32Error works just like Marshal.GetLastWin32Error (taking no parameters and returning an integer) but transforms the returned error code into an appropriate HRESULT value. This transformation performs a bitwise-OR operation with the severity bit, Win32 *facility* (a category of HRESULT values), and the error code:

```
SEVERITY_ERROR | FACILITY_WIN32 | ErrorCode
```

In other words, if the Win32 error code were 0x*nnnn*, this method transforms the value to 0x8007*nnnn*.

As with GetLastWin32Error, this method can only be used to obtain error codes set by PInvoke methods if the signature's DllImportAttribute pseudo-custom attribute has its SetLastError named parameter set to true. This is false by default in C# and C++, but true by default when using the Declare statement in Visual Basic .NET.

For more information, see the GetLastWin32Error method listed later in this section.

The GetIDispatchForObject Method
The GetIDispatchForObject method retrieves a pointer to any object's IDispatch interface and returns it as a System.IntPtr value. The method has a single System.Object parameter

and returns a `System.IntPtr`. The returned interface pointer's reference count is incremented before being returned, so you must call `Marshal.Release` when you're finished using it.

In managed code, you rarely need to deal with the `IDispatch` interface directly. This method, however, can be useful when calling a method that exposes a COM object parameter as an `IntPtr` type, or with custom marshaling.

This method can even be used on a purely .NET object! In this case, the `IDispatch` pointer corresponds to the .NET object's COM-Callable Wrapper. If the object passed in does not support the `IDispatch` interface, an `InvalidCastException` is thrown.

To get a COM interface pointer other than `IDispatch`, you can call `Marshal.GetIUnknownForObject` or the generic `Marshal.GetComInterfaceForObject`.

The `GetITypeInfoForType` Method

The `GetITypeInfoForType` method takes a `System.Type` parameter and returns an `IntPtr` value representing a pointer to an `ITypeInfo` implementation based on the original type. This method, together with the `Marshal.GetTypeForITypeInfo` method, exposes the same functionality as the `TypeToTypeInfoMarshaler` custom marshaler from the `System.Runtime.InteropServices.CustomMarshalers` namespace. The returned interface pointer's reference count is incremented before being returned, so you must call `Marshal.Release` when you're finished using it.

To expose a .NET type as an `ITypeInfo` interface to COM, you could therefore use `MarshalAsAttribute` to plug in the `TypeToTypeInfoMarshaler` custom marshaler, or manually call `GetITypeInfoForType` and return the interface pointer directly. To use the returned `IntPtr` value in managed code, you could convert it to a `UCOMITypeInfo` interface using `Marshal.GetObjectForIUnknown`.

The `GetIUnknownForObject` Method

The `GetIUnknownForObject` method retrieves a pointer to any object's `IUnknown` interface and returns it as a `System.IntPtr` value. The method has a single `System.Object` parameter and returns a `System.IntPtr`. The returned interface pointer's reference count is incremented before being returned, so you must call `Marshal.Release` when you're finished using it.

This method does the reverse action of `Marshal.GetObjectForIUnknown`. In managed code, you rarely need to deal with the `IUnknown` interface directly. This method, however, can be useful when calling a method that exposes a COM object parameter as an `IntPtr` type, or with custom marshaling.

This method can even be used on a purely .NET object! In this case, the `IUnknown` pointer corresponds to the .NET object's COM-Callable Wrapper.

To get a COM interface pointer other than `IUnknown`, you can call `Marshal.GetIDispatchForObject` or the generic `Marshal.GetComInterfaceForObject`.

For more information, see Chapters 6 and 20.

The `GetLastWin32Error` Method

This method exposes the Win32 `GetLastError` API from `KERNEL32.DLL`. The method, which takes no parameters and returns an integer, gives the last error code set by a call to the Win32 `SetLastError` API. If you want such an error code while using PInvoke from managed code, you must call `Marshal.GetLastWin32Error` rather than defining your own PInvoke definition of `GetLastError` and calling it. The reason for this is that the CLR may have made calls to operating system APIs between the failure and the call to `GetLastError`, overwriting the error code value.

This method can only be used to obtain error codes set by PInvoke methods if the signature's `DllImportAttribute` pseudo-custom attribute has its `SetLastError` named parameter set to true. This is false by default in C# and C++, but true by default when using the `Declare` statement in Visual Basic .NET.

For more information, see Chapter 18 and `GetHRForLastWin32Error` listed earlier in this section.

The `GetManagedThunkForUnmanagedMethodPtr` Method

This advanced method enables you to directly get a callable signature in managed code from a pointer to an unmanaged method. It is intended for use by compilers rather than regular applications. `GetManagedThunkForUnmanagedMethodPtr` has the following signature:

C#:

```
public static IntPtr GetManagedThunkForUnmanagedMethodPtr(
  IntPtr pfnMethodToWrap, IntPtr pbSignature, int cbSignature);
```

Visual Basic .NET:

```
Public Shared Function GetManagedThunkForUnmanagedMethodPtr( _
  pfnMethodToWrap As IntPtr, pbSignature As IntPtr, cbSignature As Integer _
) As IntPtr
```

C++:

```
public: static IntPtr GetManagedThunkForUnmanagedMethodPtr(
  IntPtr pfnMethodToWrap, IntPtr pbSignature, int cbSignature);
```

This method does the opposite action of `GetUnmanagedThunkForManagedMethodPtr`.

The `GetMethodInfoForComSlot` Method

This method enables you to retrieve a `System.Reflection.MemberInfo` instance corresponding to any type, using a number that represents a slot in the v-table that would be exposed to COM for the .NET type. Note that although the name uses "MethodInfo," it's a `MemberInfo` that gets returned. The method has the following signature:

C#:

```
public static MemberInfo GetMethodInfoForComSlot(
   Type t, int slot, ref ComMemberType memberType);
```

Visual Basic .NET:

```
Public Shared Function GetMethodInfoForComSlot( _
    t As Type, slot As Integer, ByRef memberType As ComMemberType _
) As MemberInfo
```

C++:

```
public: static MemberInfo* GetMethodInfoForComSlot(
    Type* t, int slot, ComMemberType& memberType);
```

The first parameter is the type whose `MemberInfo` will be retrieved. An `ArgumentException` is thrown if the type is COM-invisible. The type can be an interface or a class. Using a class type means that the slot corresponds to its class interface.

The second parameter is the zero-based slot number of the method. This number must correctly account for the presence of `IUnknown` and possibly `IDispatch` methods. The `Marshal.GetStartComSlot` and `Marshal.GetEndComSlot` can be used to get the valid range of values that can be used with this method.

The third by-reference parameter is a `ComMemberType` enumeration defined in `System.Runtime.InteropServices`. Its value passed in doesn't matter, but on return it contains the type of the COM member that corresponds to the returned `MemberInfo`—a regular method, a property accessor (get, set, or other), or an event accessor (add or remove).

This method does the reverse action of `Marshal.GetComSlotForMethodInfo`.

The `GetNativeVariantForObject` Method

The `GetNativeVariantForObject` method enables you to obtain the unmanaged `VARIANT` representation of any object. This involves the same transformation done by the Interop Marshaler when exposing a `System.Object` type to unmanaged code. The method has two parameters, a `System.Object` whose `VARIANT` representation we wish to obtain, and an `IntPtr` value that should contain the address of pre-allocated memory that will hold the `VARIANT`.

This method does the reverse action of `Marshal.GetObjectForNativeVariant`. Although the Interop Marshaler doesn't support the VT_RECORD VARIANT type (a user-defined structure), `GetNativeVariantForObject` returns a VT_DISPATCH or VT_UNKNOWN VARIANT if you pass in a boxed value type.

In order to easily manipulate the VARIANT pointed to by the IntPtr value after the call, a .NET definition of a VARIANT structure is desirable. Chapter 6 defines such a structure and shows some uses of it.

The `GetObjectForIUnknown` Method

The `GetObjectForIUnknown` method creates a .NET object (an RCW) for any COM interface pointer represented as a `System.IntPtr` type. The method has a single `System.IntPtr` parameter and returns a `System.Object`. The IntPtr parameter represents an IUnknown interface pointer, but because all COM interfaces ultimately derive from IUnknown, a pointer value for any COM interface can be passed to this method.

The returned object that wraps the IUnknown pointer is often a `System.__ComObject` type. To invoke members on this object, you could use late binding (if the COM object also implements IDispatch) or cast the object to an appropriate COM interface, which makes the CLR call `QueryInterface` to determine whether the object supports the desired interface.

If the COM object implements IProvideClassInfo and an Interop Assembly containing a corresponding .NET class definition is registered with REGASM.EXE, it can be wrapped in the specific .NET class type. If you want the returned object to have a specific class type other than `System.__ComObject` without these requirements, call `Marshal.GetTypedObjectForIUnknown` instead.

For more information, see Chapter 20.

The `GetObjectForNativeVariant` Method

The `GetObjectForNativeVariant` method enables you to obtain a .NET object corresponding to a raw pointer to an unmanaged VARIANT type. This involves the same transformation done by the Interop Marshaler when exposing a VARIANT type to managed code. The method has a single IntPtr parameter that should contain the address of a VARIANT instance. It returns a `System.Object` which is the .NET view of the VARIANT type.

This method does the reverse action of `Marshal.GetNativeVariantForObject`. If the input VARIANT does not have a valid VARIANT type, an InvalidOleVariantTypeException is thrown. If the input VARIANT has an unsupported type (such as VT_RECORD), a NotSupportedException is thrown, just as if the Interop Marshaler attempted the conversion.

For more information, see Chapter 6.

A

The `GetObjectsForNativeVariants` Method

The `GetObjectsForNativeVariants` method enables you to obtain an array of .NET objects corresponding to a raw pointer to a C-style array of unmanaged `VARIANT` types. This involves the same transformation done by the Interop Marshaler when exposing `VARIANT` types to managed code. This method has the following signature:

C#:

```
public static object [] GetObjectsForNativeVariants(
  IntPtr aSrcNativeVariant, int cVars);
```

Visual Basic .NET:

```
Public Overloads Shared Function GetObjectsForNativeVariants( _
  aSrcNativeVariant As IntPtr, cVars As Integer) As Object()
```

C++:

```
public: static Object* GetObjectsForNativeVariants(
  IntPtr aSrcNativeVariant, int cVars) __gc[];
```

The `IntPtr` parameter should contain the address of the first element of the `VARIANT` array, and the integer parameter should contain the number of `VARIANT`s in the array. It returns an array of `System.Object` types, with each element corresponding to each of the input `VARIANT` types. If 0 is passed for the `cVars` parameter, an empty array is returned. If a negative number is passed, an `ArgumentOutOfRangeException` is thrown.

If any of the input `VARIANT`s in the array does not have a valid `VARIANT` type or an unsupported type (`VT_RECORD`), the same exception is thrown as would be thrown by the Interop Marshaler in such a situation.

For more information, see Chapter 6.

The `GetStartComSlot` Method

This method retrieves the first zero-based slot in a .NET type's v-table that corresponds to a .NET method definition. Because all v-tables begin with the three methods of `IUnknown`, this starting slot is always 3 or greater. Furthermore, because the only other v-table methods that would not correspond to .NET methods are the four `IDispatch` methods, the starting slot can only be 3 or 7.

`GetStartComSlot` has a single `System.Type` parameter whose v-table is being inspected, and returns a 32-bit integer containing the beginning slot number. `GetStartComSlot` throws an `ArgumentException` if the type passed in is COM-invisible. The type can be an interface or a class. The slot numbers given for a class type refer to its class interface. If the class has an auto-dispatch class interface, -1 is always returned because this is a true disp-only interface that doesn't have a v-table exposed to .NET clients, unlike a dispinterface that has a metadata definition.

GetStartComSlot returns 3 for IUnknown-only interfaces and 7 for dual interfaces and dispinterfaces. Although dispinterfaces don't have a v-table from COM's perspective, they do from the .NET perspective so they can be treated just like dual interfaces.

This method, along with GetEndComSlot, can be used with GetMethodInfoForComSlot to only pass slots in the valid range.

The `GetThreadFromFiberCookie` Method

The CLR's hosting APIs enable advanced hosts to schedule *fibers*, lightweight objects consisting of a stack and register context, onto operating system threads. The GetThreadFromFiberCookie returns a System.Threading.Thread instance for a passed-in integer representing a "cookie" value that uniquely identifies the thread on which the fiber is scheduled.

The `GetTypedObjectForIUnknown` Method

The GetTypedObjectForIUnknown method creates a .NET object (an RCW) for any COM interface pointer represented as a System.IntPtr type. The difference between this method and Marshal.GetObjectForIUnknown is that you can get a "strongly-typed" object back rather than a generic System.__ComObject. This method has the following signature:

C#:

```
public static object GetTypedObjectForIUnknown(IntPtr pUnk, Type t);
```

Visual Basic .NET:

```
Public Shared Function GetTypedObjectForIUnknown(pUnk As IntPtr, t As Type) _
  As Object
```

C++:

```
public: static Object* GetTypedObjectForIUnknown(IntPtr pUnk, Type* t);
```

The first parameter represents an IUnknown interface pointer, but because all COM interfaces ultimately derive from IUnknown, a pointer value for any COM interface can be passed to this method. The second parameter is the type of the object you want to be returned. This *must* be a ComImport-marked class type and not an interface type (meaning a coclass interface type won't work), or an ArgumentException is thrown. For types generated by the type library importer, this would be a type named *CoClassName*Class.

The `GetTypeForITypeInfo` Method

The GetTypeForITypeInfo method takes a System.IntPtr parameter that represents a pointer to an ITypeInfo interface and returns a System.Type instance based on the original interface. This method, together with the Marshal.GetITypeInfoForType method, exposes the same functionality as the TypeToTypeInfoMarshaler custom marshaler from the System.Runtime.InteropServices.CustomMarshalers namespace.

The type library importer automatically uses the custom marshaler to convert `ITypeInfo` parameters to `System.Type` parameters. However, if you obtain an `ITypeInfo` interface through some other means (such as an imported signature with an `IUnknown` parameter representing an object that also implements `ITypeInfo`), you can use `GetTypeForITypeInfo` to manually do the same transformation. You can convert a `UCOMITypeInfo` interface to the `IntPtr` value needed to call this method using `Marshal.GetComInterfaceForObject` or `Marshal.GetIUnknownForObject`.

The `GetTypeInfoName` Method

This method tells you the name of the type description passed in as a `UCOMITypeInfo` instance. It has a single `UCOMITypeInfo` parameter and returns a string with the desired name.

You can get this same name by calling `UCOMITypeInfo.GetDocumentation` and passing -1 for its first parameter. This is less convenient, however, because this method has four out parameters that need to be handled.

The `GetTypeLibGuid` Method

This method tells you the LIBID of a type library if you pass it a `UCOMITypeLib` instance. This differs from `GetTypeLibGuidForAssembly` because it extracts the LIBID directly from an existing type library rather than calculating what a LIBID would be that corresponds to an assembly.

`GetTypeLibGuid` has a single `UCOMITypeLib` parameter and returns a `System.Guid` instance with the LIBID value. You can get this same information by calling `UCOMITypeLib.GetLibAttr` and checking the `guid` field of the returned structure. This requires significantly more code, however, to deal with converting an `IntPtr` type to a `TYPELIBATTR` structure and releasing the structure with `UCOMITypeLib.ReleaseTLibAttr`.

Other information about a type library can be obtained from `Marshal.GetTypeLibLcid` and `Marshal.GetTypeLibName`.

The `GetTypeLibGuidForAssembly` Method

This method returns a LIBID for a .NET assembly. This LIBID is the same as the LIBID that an exported type library for the assembly would have, which is based on the assembly's identity. The method has a single `System.Reflection.Assembly` parameter and returns a `System.Guid` representing the LIBID.

If the assembly is marked with the `GuidAttribute` custom attribute, its value is returned. If not, the default LIBID that is automatically generated for a .NET assembly is returned. This method works for any assemblies, even ones marked as COM-invisible, because it's still possible to generate a type library for such assemblies (even if they end up being empty).

For more information about the automatic LIBID generation for assemblies, see Chapter 11.

The `GetTypeLibLcid` Method

This method tells you the locale identifier (LCID) of a type library if you pass it a `UCOMITypeLib` instance. `GetTypeLibLcid` has a single `UCOMITypeLib` parameter and returns a 32-bit integer that contains the LCID value. Using this LCID, you could create a `System.Globalization.CultureInfo` instance by using its constructor that accepts an integer.

You can get this same LCID by calling `UCOMITypeLib.GetLibAttr` and checking the `lcid` field of the returned structure. This requires significantly more code, however, to deal with converting an `IntPtr` type to a `TYPELIBATTR` structure and releasing the structure with `UCOMITypeLib.ReleaseTLibAttr`.

Other information about a type library can be obtained from `Marshal.GetTypeLibGuid` and `Marshal.GetTypeLibName`.

The `GetTypeLibName` Method

This method tells you the name of a type library if you pass it a `UCOMITypeLib` instance. It has a single `UCOMITypeLib` parameter and returns a string with the type library's name. This name is not a filename, but the identifier used with the library statement, such as `ADODB` for the Microsoft ADO type library.

You can get this same name by calling `UCOMITypeLib.GetDocumentation` and passing -1 for its first parameter to get information about the type library itself. This is less convenient, however, because this method has four out parameters that need to be handled.

To get other information about a type library, see `Marshal.GetTypeLibGuid` and `Marshal.GetTypeLibLcid`.

The `GetUnmanagedThunkForManagedMethodPtr` Method

This advanced method enables you to directly get a callable signature to unmanaged code from a pointer to a managed method. It is intended for use by compilers rather than regular applications. `GetUnmanagedThunkForManagedMethodPtr` has the following signature:

C#:

```
public static IntPtr GetUnmanagedThunkForManagedMethodPtr(
  IntPtr pfnMethodToWrap, IntPtr pbSignature, int cbSignature);
```

Visual Basic .NET:

```
Public Shared Function GetUnmanagedThunkForManagedMethodPtr( _
   pfnMethodToWrap As IntPtr, pbSignature As IntPtr, cbSignature As Integer _
) As IntPtr
```

C++:

```
public: static IntPtr GetUnmanagedThunkForManagedMethodPtr(
    IntPtr pfnMethodToWrap, IntPtr pbSignature, int cbSignature);
```

This method does the opposite action of `GetManagedThunkForUnmanagedMethodPtr`.

The `IsComObject` Method

This method can be used to determine whether or not any object is a COM object. Specifically, it returns true if the class type of the instance is marked with `ComImport` or derives from a class marked `ComImport`, and false otherwise.

It has a single `System.Object` parameter and a boolean return type. Calling `IsComObject(o)` is the same as calling `o.GetType().IsCOMObject` because this property of `System.Type` has the same semantics.

This method differs from `System.Type.IsImport`, because this property returns true only if the exact type (class or interface) is marked with `ComImport`. It also differs from the `System.Runtime.InteropServices.RegistrationServices.TypeRepresentsComType` method, which returns true if the type is marked with `ComImport` or derives from the `ComImport` type *with the same GUID*, and false otherwise.

The `IsTypeVisibleFromCom` Method

This method tells you whether or not a .NET type is invisible to COM. It takes a single `System.Type` parameter and returns true if it's COM-visible, false if it's COM-invisible.

This method comes in handy because without it, checking for COM-invisibility is not a one-step process. A type is COM-invisible if it's non-public, or if it's marked with `ComVisibleAttribute` with the value of false, or if its containing assembly is marked with `ComVisibleAttribute` with the value of false, *unless* the type is marked with the `ComImportAttribute` pseudo-custom attribute, which makes it COM-visible regardless of everything else!

For more information about COM-visibility, see Chapter 12.

The `NumParamBytes` Method

`NumParamBytes` returns the number of bytes that is required to hold all of a method's parameters. It has a single `System.Reflection.MethodInfo` parameter and returns a 32-bit integer. This method is intended for use by compilers rather than regular applications.

The `OffsetOf` Method

This method tells you the memory location of a .NET structure's field, as an offset in bytes from the beginning of the structure. This offset applies to the unmanaged view of the structure, which may not correspond to the offset in the managed structure because marshaling can transform a .NET structure into an unmanaged structure with different offsets.

OffsetOf takes two parameters, a System.Type instance for the structure to inspect, and a string parameter called fieldName that contains the case-sensitive name of the field whose offset is desired. It returns a System.IntPtr that contains the offset value.

The type passed to OffsetOf can be a value type or a formatted reference type (which has sequential or explicit layout). If not, or if the type has a field that can't be marshaled to unmanaged code (such as a class type not marked with UnmanagedType.Interface), an ArgumentException is thrown with the message, "Type *typeName* cannot be marshaled as an unmanaged structure; no meaningful size or offset can be computed." If the fieldName parameter doesn't contain a name of a field in the passed-in type, an ArgumentException is thrown with the message, "Field passed in is not a marshaled member of the type *typeName*."

To obtain the size of an entire structure, see the Marshal.SizeOf method.

The Prelink Method

This method, which has a single System.Reflection.MethodInfo parameter and returns nothing, can be used to perform early initialization of a PInvoke method. Without using this method, the first time a PInvoke method is invoked, the CLR performs initialization that does the following:

- Checks the validity of the signature's metadata
- Checks that all the method's parameters are legal to use in a PInvoke signature
- Finds and loads the DLL specified by the DllImportAttribute (or the Declare statement in Visual Basic .NET), if it hasn't been loaded already
- Finds the specified entry point in the DLL

If any of these tasks fail, then an exception is thrown. If you want to catch any such errors without waiting for the first method invocation or if you want to eagerly load the DLL, calling Prelink using a MethodInfo instance representing the PInvoke method causes all these steps to be performed immediately.

The following code demonstrates using Prelink on an instance with a private static PInvoke signature for MessageBox from USER32.DLL.

C#:

```
// Get a MethodInfo for the private static method
MethodInfo mi = obj.GetType().GetMethod("MessageBox",
  BindingFlags.Static | BindingFlags.NonPublic);

// Call Prelink using the MethodInfo instance
Marshal.Prelink(mi);
```

Visual Basic .NET:

```
' Get a MethodInfo for the Private Shared Sub
Dim mi As MethodInfo = obj.GetType().GetMethod("MessageBox", _
  BindingFlags.Static Or BindingFlags.NonPublic)

' Call Prelink using the MethodInfo instance
Marshal.Prelink(mi)
```

C++:

```
// Get a MethodInfo for the private static method
MethodInfo* mi = obj->GetType()->GetMethod(S"MessageBox",
  (BindingFlags)(BindingFlags::Static | BindingFlags::NonPublic));

// Call Prelink using the MethodInfo instance
Marshal::Prelink(mi);
```

Calling `Prelink` on a non-PInvoke method has no effect. To perform this action on all PInvoke methods in a type, use `Marshal.PrelinkAll`.

The `PrelinkAll` Method

The `PrelinkAll` method invokes `Marshal.Prelink` on every method for a given type, which only has an effect on PInvoke methods. This method has a single `System.Type` parameter and returns nothing. It can be used as follows:

C#:

```
Marshal.PrelinkAll(obj.GetType());
```

Visual Basic .NET:

```
Marshal.PrelinkAll(obj.GetType())
```

C++:

```
Marshal::PrelinkAll(obj->GetType());
```

For information about the actions of `Marshal.Prelink`, see the previous section.

The `PtrToStringAnsi` Method

This method copies the contents of an unmanaged ANSI string to a new .NET string. Although the name may lead you to believe the method *produces* an ANSI string, you should think of it as "pointer-to-String: the ANSI version," or "pointer-to-ANSI to String." The method has the following two overloads:

C#:

```
public static string PtrToStringAnsi(IntPtr ptr, int len);

public static string PtrToStringAnsi(IntPtr ptr);
```

Visual Basic .NET:

```
Public Overloads Shared Function PtrToStringAnsi(ptr As IntPtr, _
  len As Integer) As String

Public Overloads Shared Function PtrToStringAnsi(ptr As IntPtr) As String
```

C++:

```
public: static String* PtrToStringAnsi(IntPtr ptr, int len);

public: static String* PtrToStringAnsi(IntPtr ptr);
```

The `System.IntPtr` parameter represents a pointer to the original unmanaged string, and the integer `len` parameter represents the length of the string, in characters. Therefore, `len` characters get copied to the returned string. If you use the overload that doesn't specify a length, all characters up to the first null character get copied.

This method does the opposite of `Marshal.StringToCoTaskMemAnsi` and `Marshal.StringToHGlobalAnsi`, which create an ANSI string from the contents of a `System.String`. Because this method makes a copy of the original unmanaged string's contents, you are still responsible for freeing the original string when appropriate.

You normally don't need to interact with pointers to unmanaged strings in managed code. This method, however, can be useful in custom marshaling scenarios or when mixing managed and unmanaged code in C++. To create a .NET string from an unmanaged Unicode string or a BSTR, see `PtrToStringAuto`, `PtrToStringBSTR`, and `PtrToStringUni`.

The `PtrToStringAuto` Method

This method copies the contents of a platform-dependent unmanaged string to a new .NET string. Although the name may lead you to believe the method *produces* an "auto string," you should think of it as "pointer-to-String: the Auto version," or "pointer-to-Auto to String." The method has the following two overloads:

C#:

```
public static string PtrToStringAuto(IntPtr ptr, int len);

public static string PtrToStringAuto(IntPtr ptr);
```

Visual Basic .NET:

```
Public Overloads Shared Function PtrToStringAuto(ptr As IntPtr, _
  len As Integer) As String

Public Overloads Shared Function PtrToStringAuto(ptr As IntPtr) As String
```

C++:

```
public: static String* PtrToStringAuto(IntPtr ptr, int len);

public: static String* PtrToStringAuto(IntPtr ptr);
```

The System.IntPtr parameter represents a pointer to the original unmanaged string; the integer len parameter represents the length of the string, in characters. Therefore, len characters get copied to the returned string. If you use the overload that doesn't specify a length, all characters up to the first null character get copied.

This method does the opposite of Marshal.StringToCoTaskMemAuto and Marshal.StringToHGlobalAuto, which create a platform-dependent string from the contents of a System.String. Because this method makes a copy of the original unmanaged string's contents, you are still responsible for freeing the original string when appropriate.

You normally don't need to interact with pointers to unmanaged strings in managed code. This method, however, can be useful in custom marshaling scenarios or when mixing managed and unmanaged code in C++. To create a .NET string from a BSTR or a string that's always either ANSI or Unicode, see PtrToStringAnsi, PtrToStringBSTR, and PtrToStringUni.

The PtrToStringBSTR Method

This method copies the contents of a BSTR to a new .NET string. Although the name may lead you to believe the method *produces* a BSTR, you should think of it as "pointer-to-String: the BSTR version," or "pointer-to-BSTR to String." The method has a single System.IntPtr parameter that represents a pointer to a BSTR, and returns a System.String instance with the desired contents.

This method does the opposite of Marshal.StringToBSTR, which creates a BSTR from the contents of a System.String. Because this method makes a copy of the original BSTR's contents, you are still responsible for freeing the original BSTR when appropriate.

You normally don't need to interact with BSTR types in managed code. This method, however, can be useful in custom marshaling scenarios or when mixing managed and unmanaged code in C++. To create a .NET string from an unmanaged ANSI or Unicode string, see PtrToStringAnsi, PtrToStringAuto, and PtrToStringUni.

The `PtrToStringUni` Method

This method copies the contents of an unmanaged Unicode string to a new .NET string. Although the name may lead you to believe the method *produces* an unmanaged Unicode string, you should think of it as "pointer-to-String: the Unicode version," or "pointer-to-Unicode to String." The method has the following two overloads:

C#:

```
public static string PtrToStringUni(IntPtr ptr, int len);

public static string PtrToStringUni(IntPtr ptr);
```

Visual Basic .NET:

```
Public Overloads Shared Function PtrToStringUni(ptr As IntPtr, _
  len As Integer) As String

Public Overloads Shared Function PtrToStringUni(ptr As IntPtr) As String
```

C++:

```
public: static String* PtrToStringUni(IntPtr ptr, int len);

public: static String* PtrToStringUni(IntPtr ptr);
```

The `System.IntPtr` parameter represents a pointer to the original unmanaged string, and the integer `len` parameter represents the length of the string, in characters. Therefore, `len` characters get copied to the returned string. If you use the overload that doesn't specify a length, all characters up to the first null character get copied.

This method does the opposite of `Marshal.StringToCoTaskMemUni` and `Marshal.StringToHGlobalUni`, which create a Unicode string from the contents of a `System.String`. Because this method makes a copy of the original unmanaged string's contents, you are still responsible for freeing the original string when appropriate.

You normally don't need to interact with pointers to unmanaged strings in managed code. This method, however, can be useful in custom marshaling scenarios or when mixing managed and unmanaged code in C++. To create a .NET string from an unmanaged ANSI string or a `BSTR`, see `PtrToStringAnsi`, `PtrToStringAuto`, and `PtrToStringBSTR`.

The `PtrToStructure` Method

The `PtrToStructure` method can be used to obtain a .NET type with sequential or explicit layout from a raw pointer value. (The `Marshal.StructureToPtr` method does the reverse of this.) This is often necessary in COM Interoperability and PInvoke when structure parameters are represented as an `IntPtr` value. This method has two overloads:

C#:

```
public static object PtrToStructure(IntPtr ptr, Type structureType);

public static void PtrToStructure(IntPtr ptr, object structure);
```

Visual Basic .NET:

```
Public Overloads Shared Function PtrToStructure(ptr As IntPtr, _
  structureType As Type) As Object

Public Overloads Shared Sub PtrToStructure(ptr As IntPtr, _
  structure As Object)
```

C++:

```
public: static Object* PtrToStructure(IntPtr ptr, Type* structureType);

public: static void PtrToStructure(IntPtr ptr, Object* structure);
```

The first signature is more commonly used, and expects an `IntPtr` value representing the raw pointer, and a `Type` instance representing the type of structure desired. An instance of this type is returned if successful (and is boxed if it's a value type).

The second signature can be used to convert the pointer to a pre-allocated object (the second parameter). In this case, the object parameter must be a formatted reference type (one with sequential or explicit layout). Passing a boxed value type causes an `ArgumentException` to be thrown.

For either overload, attempting to convert a pointer to an object without sequential or explicit layout results in an `ArgumentException`.

The following code demonstrates using `PtrToStructure` after calling `UCOMITypeInfo`. `GetTypeAttr` to obtain the desired `TYPEATTR` structure. `GetTypeAttr` is defined with a by-reference `IntPtr` parameter because the unmanaged signature's `TYPEATTR**` parameter is not supported by the Interop Marshaler.

C#:

```
UCOMITypeInfo typeInfo = ...;
IntPtr ptr = IntPtr.Zero;
typeInfo.GetTypeAttr(ref ptr);
TYPEATTR attr = (TYPEATTR)Marshal.PtrToStructure(ptr, typeof(TYPEATTR));
```

Visual Basic .NET:

```
Dim typeInfo As UCOMITypeInfo = ...
Dim ptr As IntPtr = IntPtr.Zero
typeInfo.GetTypeAttr(ptr)
Dim attr As TYPEATTR = _
  CType(Marshal.PtrToStructure(ptr, GetType(TYPEATTR)), TYPEATTR)
```

For more information, see the `Marshal.StructureToPtr` method listed later in this section, and Chapter 6.

The `QueryInterface` Method

All three `IUnknown` methods—`QueryInterface`, `AddRef`, and `Release`—are exposed through the `Marshal` class and can be called on any COM object. `Marshal.QueryInterface` exposes a COM object's `IUnknown.QueryInterface` method, which attempts to obtain a specific interface pointer from a COM object.

This method takes three parameters—a `System.IntPtr` parameter representing the `IUnknown` pointer for the COM object whose `QueryInterface` implementation will be called, a by-reference `System.Guid` parameter containing the requested IID, and an out-only `System.IntPtr` parameter representing the returned interface pointer that corresponds to the requested IID if the call succeeds. It returns an integer, which is the `HRESULT` value returned by `IUnknown.QueryInterface`. The `Guid` parameter is passed by-reference simply because the definition of `IUnknown.QueryInterface` expects a pointer to a `GUID` structure, not because the value may be changed by the callee.

To get an `IntPtr` value that represents an object passed as the first parameter, you can call `GetComInterfaceForObject`, `GetIDispatchForObject`, or `GetIUnknownForObject`. These methods, plus the `Marshal.QueryInterface` method, can even be used on purely .NET objects! In this case, the COM interfaces represent the ones implemented by the .NET object's COM-Callable Wrapper. To make use of the third parameter's `IntPtr` value after the call, you can call `GetObjectForIUnknown` to convert it to an interface type. If the call fails, an `InvalidCastException` is thrown because the `E_NOINTERFACE HRESULT` returned by `IUnknown.QueryInterface` always gets mapped to that exception.

`Marshal.QueryInterface` increments the reference count of the returned interface pointer, so you must call `Marshal.Release` when you're finished using it.

For COM objects, the action of using `Marshal.QueryInterface` is the same as doing a casting operation in managed code. Casting is preferred for its brevity and clarity. One interesting behavior that you get from `Marshal.QueryInterface` is with .NET objects; because this acts on the object's COM-Callable Wrapper (CCW), you can successfully obtain interface pointers for interfaces implemented by the CCW, such as `IMarshal` or `IConnectionPointContainer`! A regular cast operation could not do this because casting a .NET object looks solely at its metadata, which knows nothing about these COM interfaces unless implemented directly in managed code. Furthermore, using `Marshal.QueryInterface` can be convenient if you have an `IntPtr` representing a COM interface and you don't want to wrap it in an RCW.

The following code demonstrates the use of `Marshal.QueryInterface`. It uses `Marshal.GetIUnknownForObject` to obtain an `IntPtr` value representing the COM object's `IUnknown` interface pointer. It assumes that the interface we want to "cast" to, `IComInterface`, has a .NET definition. After the call, it uses `Marshal.GetObjectForIUnknown` to convert the returned `IntPtr` value to the `IComInterface` interface type. At some time later, `Marshal.Release` is called on the returned interface pointer. In this contrived scenario, the code is equivalent to the casting operations shown in the beginning comment.

C#:

```csharp
// The following code does the same thing as:
// IComInterface i = (IComInterface)myComObject;

// Prepare the parameters
IntPtr pUnk = Marshal.GetIUnknownForObject(myComObject);
Guid g = typeof(IComInterface).GUID;
IntPtr ppv;

// Make the QueryInterface call
int hresult = Marshal.QueryInterface(pUnk, ref g, out ppv);

// Check for failure HRESULT value
if (hresult < 0)
  Marshal.ThrowExceptionForHR(hresult);

// Convert the raw pointer to a useable instance
IComInterface i = (IComInterface)Marshal.GetObjectForIUnknown(ppv);

...

Marshal.Release(ppv);
Marshal.Release(pUnk);
```

Visual Basic .NET:

```vbnet
' The following code does the same thing as:
' Dim i As IComInterface = CType(myComObject, IComInterface)

' Prepare the parameters
Dim pUnk As IntPtr = Marshal.GetIUnknownForObject(myComObject)
Dim g As Guid = GetType(IComInterface).GUID
Dim ppv As IntPtr

' Make the QueryInterface call
Dim hresult As Integer = _
  Marshal.QueryInterface(pUnk, g, ppv)
```

```
' Check for failure HRESULT value
If (hresult < 0) Then _
  Marshal.ThrowExceptionForHR(hresult)

' Convert the raw pointer to a useable instance
Dim i As IComInterface = _
  CType(Marshal.GetObjectForIUnknown(ppv), IComInterface)


...

Marshal.Release(ppv)
Marshal.Release(pUnk)
```

C++:

```
// The following code does the same thing as:
// IComInterface* i = dynamic_cast<IComInterface*>(myComObject);

// Prepare the parameters
IntPtr pUnk = Marshal::GetIUnknownForObject(myComObject);
Guid g = __typeof(IComInterface)->GUID;
IntPtr ppv;

// Make the QueryInterface call
int hresult = Marshal::QueryInterface(pUnk, &g, &ppv);

// Check for failure HRESULT value
if (hresult < 0)
  Marshal::ThrowExceptionForHR(hresult);

// Convert the raw pointer to a useable instance
IComInterface* i =
  dynamic_cast<IComInterface*>(Marshal::GetObjectForIUnknown(ppv));


...

Marshal::Release(ppv);
Marshal::Release(pUnk);
```

For more information, see `Marshal.Release` and `Marshal.AddRef` listed in this section.

The ReadByte Method

The `ReadByte` method is useful for extracting a single byte value at a given offset from a pointer to an unmanaged object. It has three overloads:

C#:

```
public static byte ReadByte([MarshalAs(UnmanagedType.AsAny)] object ptr,
  int ofs);

public static byte ReadByte(IntPtr ptr, int ofs);

public static byte ReadByte(IntPtr ptr);
```

Visual Basic .NET:

```
Public Overloads Shared Function ReadByte(<MarshalAs(UnmanagedType.AsAny)> _
  ptr As Object, ofs As Integer) As Byte

Public Overloads Shared Function ReadByte(ptr As IntPtr, ofs As Integer) _
  As Byte

Public Overloads Shared Function ReadByte(ptr As IntPtr) As Byte
```

C++:

```
public: static unsigned char ReadByte(
  [MarshalAs(UnmanagedType::AsAny)] Object* ptr, int ofs);

public: static unsigned char ReadByte(IntPtr ptr, int ofs);

public: static unsigned char ReadByte(IntPtr ptr);
```

The first overload takes an object representing the unmanaged entity (marshaled as a `void*`), and an integer offset. The object passed as the first parameter could even be a .NET object with the appropriate format (such as an array), but there would be no reason to pass such an object to this method. Any object passed that can't be treated appropriately causes an `ArgumentException` to be thrown with the message, "No PInvoke conversion exists for value passed to Object-typed parameter."

The second overload works the same way as the first, but expects the pointer to the unmanaged object to be passed via an `IntPtr` type. The third overload works just like the second one, but with an implied offset of zero. For all overloads, it is the responsibility of the caller to ensure that the memory being read is within the range of the input object.

This method enables direct interaction with an unmanaged C-style byte array so you don't need to incur the expense of copying an entire unmanaged array (using `Marshal.Copy`) to a separate .NET array before reading its element values. This is demonstrated in the following code:

C#:

```
IntPtr unmanagedArray = ...;
```

```
// One way to print the 10 elements of the C-style unmanagedArray
byte [] newArray = new byte[10];
Marshal.Copy(unmanagedArray, newArray, 0, 10);
for (int i = 0; i < newArray.Length; i++)
  Console.WriteLine(newArray[i]);

// Another way to print the 10 elements of the C-style unmanagedArray
for (int i = 0; i < 10; i++)
  Console.WriteLine(Marshal.ReadByte(unmanagedArray, i));
```

Visual Basic .NET:

```
Dim unmanagedArray As IntPtr = ...
Dim i As Integer

' One way to print the 10 elements of the C-style unmanagedArray
Dim newArray As Byte(9)
Marshal.Copy(unmanagedArray, newArray, 0, 10)
For i = 0 To newArray.Length
  Console.WriteLine(newArray(i))
Next i

' Another way to print the 10 elements of the C-style unmanagedArray
For i = 0 To 10
  Console.WriteLine(Marshal.ReadByte(unmanagedArray, i))
Next i
```

C++:

```
IntPtr unmanagedArray = ...;

// One way to print the 10 elements of the C-style unmanagedArray
unsigned char newArray __gc[] = new unsigned char __gc[10];
Marshal::Copy(unmanagedArray, newArray, 0, 10);
for (int i = 0; i < newArray.Length; i++)
  Console::WriteLine(newArray[i]);

// Another way to print the 10 elements of the C-style unmanagedArray
for (int i = 0; i < 10; i++)
  Console::WriteLine(Marshal::ReadByte(unmanagedArray, i));
```

To read other data types directly from an unmanaged pointer, see Marshal.ReadInt16, Marshal.ReadInt32, Marshal.ReadInt64, and Marshal.ReadIntPtr. To write data directly to an unmanaged pointer, see Marshal.WriteByte, Marshal.WriteInt16, Marshal.WriteInt32, Marshal.WriteInt64, and Marshal.WriteIntPtr.

The `ReadInt16` Method

The `ReadInt16` method is useful for extracting a single 16-bit integer value at a given offset from a pointer to an unmanaged object. It has three overloads just like `Marshal.ReadByte`, but with an `Int16` return type.

The first overload takes an object representing the unmanaged entity (marshaled as a `void*`), and an integer offset. Any object passed that can't be treated appropriately causes an `ArgumentException` to be thrown with the message, "No PInvoke conversion exists for value passed to Object-typed parameter."

The second overload works the same way as the first, but expects the pointer to the unmanaged object to be passed via an `IntPtr` type. The third overload works just like the second one, but with an implied offset of zero. For all overloads, it is the responsibility of the caller to ensure that the memory being read is within the range of the input object.

This method enables direct interaction with an unmanaged C-style array so you don't need to incur the expense of copying an entire unmanaged array (using `Marshal.Copy`) to a separate .NET array before reading its element values. It is used just like the examples shown in the `Marshal.ReadByte` section, but with a different array element type.

To read other data types directly from an unmanaged pointer, see `Marshal.ReadByte`, `Marshal.ReadInt32`, `Marshal.ReadInt64`, and `Marshal.ReadIntPtr`. To write data directly to an unmanaged pointer, see `Marshal.WriteByte`, `Marshal.WriteInt16`, `Marshal.WriteInt32`, `Marshal.WriteInt64`, and `Marshal.WriteIntPtr`.

The `ReadInt32` Method

The `ReadInt32` method is useful for extracting a single 32-bit integer value at a given offset from a pointer to an unmanaged object. It has three overloads just like `Marshal.ReadByte`, but with an `Int32` return type.

The first overload takes an object representing the unmanaged entity (marshaled as a `void*`), and an integer offset. Any object passed that can't be treated appropriately causes an `ArgumentException` to be thrown with the message, "No PInvoke conversion exists for value passed to Object-typed parameter."

The second overload works the same way as the first, but expects the pointer to the unmanaged object to be passed via an `IntPtr` type. The third overload works just like the second one, but with an implied offset of zero. For all overloads, it is the responsibility of the caller to ensure that the memory being read is within the range of the input object.

This method enables direct interaction with an unmanaged C-style array so you don't need to incur the expense of copying an entire unmanaged array (using `Marshal.Copy`) to a separate .NET array before reading its element values. It is used just like the examples shown in the `Marshal.ReadByte` section, but with a different array element type.

To read other data types directly from an unmanaged pointer, see `Marshal.ReadByte`, `Marshal.ReadInt16`, `Marshal.ReadInt64`, and `Marshal.ReadIntPtr`. To write data directly to an unmanaged pointer, see `Marshal.WriteByte`, `Marshal.WriteInt16`, `Marshal.WriteInt32`, `Marshal.WriteInt64`, and `Marshal.WriteIntPtr`.

The `ReadInt64` Method

The `ReadInt64` method is useful for extracting a single 64-bit integer value at a given offset from a pointer to an unmanaged object. It has three overloads just like `Marshal.ReadByte`, but with an `Int64` return type.

The first overload takes an object representing the unmanaged entity (marshaled as a `void*`), and an integer offset. Any object passed that can't be treated appropriately causes an `ArgumentException` to be thrown with the message, "No PInvoke conversion exists for value passed to Object-typed parameter."

The second overload works the same way as the first, but expects the pointer to the unmanaged object to be passed via an `IntPtr` type. The third overload works just like the second one, but with an implied offset of zero. For all overloads, it is the responsibility of the caller to ensure that the memory being read is within the range of the input object.

This method enables direct interaction with an unmanaged C-style array so you don't need to incur the expense of copying an entire unmanaged array (using `Marshal.Copy`) to a separate .NET array before reading its element values. It is used just like the examples shown in the `Marshal.ReadByte` section, but with a different array element type.

To read other data types directly from an unmanaged pointer, see `Marshal.ReadByte`, `Marshal.ReadInt16`, `Marshal.ReadInt32`, and `Marshal.ReadIntPtr`. To write data directly to an unmanaged pointer, see `Marshal.WriteByte`, `Marshal.WriteInt16`, `Marshal.WriteInt32`, `Marshal.WriteInt64`, and `Marshal.WriteIntPtr`.

The `ReadIntPtr` Method

The `ReadIntPtr` method is useful for extracting a single platform-sized integer value at a given offset from a pointer to an unmanaged object. It has three overloads just like `Marshal.ReadByte`, but with an `IntPtr` return type.

The first overload takes an object representing the unmanaged entity (marshaled as a `void*`), and an integer offset. Any object passed that can't be treated appropriately causes an `ArgumentException` to be thrown with the message, "No PInvoke conversion exists for value passed to Object-typed parameter."

The second overload works the same way as the first, but expects the pointer to the unmanaged object to be passed via an `IntPtr` type. The third overload works just like the second one, but with an implied offset of zero. For all overloads, it is the responsibility of the caller to ensure that the memory being read is within the range of the input object.

This method enables direct interaction with an unmanaged C-style array so you don't need to incur the expense of copying an entire unmanaged array (using `Marshal.Copy`) to a separate .NET array before reading its element values. It is used just like the examples shown in the `Marshal.ReadByte` section, but with a different array element type.

To read other data types directly from an unmanaged pointer, see `Marshal.ReadByte`, `Marshal.ReadInt16`, `Marshal.ReadInt32`, and `Marshal.Read64`. To write data directly to an unmanaged pointer, see `Marshal.WriteByte`, `Marshal.WriteInt16`, `Marshal.WriteInt32`, `Marshal.WriteInt64`, and `Marshal.WriteIntPtr`.

The `ReAllocCoTaskMem` Method

This method is one of the two memory re-allocation APIs in the `Marshal` class (the other being `ReAllocHGlobal`). `ReAllocCoTaskMem` exposes the similarly-named `CoTaskMemRealloc` COM API, which re-allocates COM task memory. It has two parameters—a `System.IntPtr` type representing the pointer to the memory to be reallocated (which must have been previously allocated by `Marshal.AllocCoTaskMem` or the equivalent unmanaged API), and an integer containing the new size, in bytes, of the memory block. The method returns a `System.IntPtr` value representing a pointer to the re-allocated block of memory. If `IntPtr.Zero` (representing a null value) is passed as the first parameter, new memory is allocated just as `AllocCoTaskMem` would do.

As with using `CoTaskMemRealloc` in COM, any memory allocated with this method must be freed with `CoTaskMemFree`. In the .NET Framework, this method is exposed as `Marshal.FreeCoTaskMem`.

The beginning of the reallocated memory content is the same as the original memory, although the entire memory block may be in a different location. Whereas `CoTaskMemRealloc` returns null on failure, `Marshal.ReAllocCoTaskMem` throws an `OutOfMemoryException` on failure.

For more information, see MSDN Online for a description of `CoTaskMemRealloc`, and the `FreeCoTaskMem` and `ReAllocCoTaskMem` methods listed later in this section.

The `ReAllocHGlobal` Method

This method is one of the two memory re-allocation APIs in the `Marshal` class (the other being `ReAllocCoTaskMem`). `ReAllocHGlobal` re-allocates fixed memory from the "global heap." Win32 does not provide a separate global heap and local heap, so this method exposes the Win32 `GlobalRealloc` API from `KERNEL32.DLL`, which does the same thing as the `LocalRealloc` API from the same DLL.

This method has two parameters—a `System.IntPtr` type representing the pointer to the memory to be reallocated (which must have been previously allocated by `Marshal.AllocHGlobal` or the equivalent unmanaged APIs), and a `System.IntPtr` type containing the new size, in bytes, of the memory block. The method returns a `System.IntPtr` value representing a pointer to the re-allocated block of memory.

As with using `LocalRealloc` in Win32 programming, any memory allocated with this method must be freed with `LocalFree`. In the .NET Framework, this method is exposed as `Marshal.FreeHGlobal`. `Marshal.ReAllocHGlobal` calls `LocalRealloc` with the LMEM_MOVEABLE flag.

Whereas `LocalRealloc` returns null on failure, `Marshal.ReAllocHGlobal` throws an `OutOfMemoryException` on failure. If this occurs, the memory that was previously allocated with `Marshal.AllocHGlobal` has not been freed, so calling `Marshal.FreeHGlobal` (or an equivalent unmanaged API) is still necessary.

For more information, see MSDN Online for a description of `LocalRealloc`, and the `FreeHGlobal` and `AllocHGlobal` methods listed in this section.

The `Release` Method

All three `IUnknown` methods—`QueryInterface`, `AddRef`, and `Release`—are exposed through the `Marshal` class and can be called on any COM object. `Marshal.Release` exposes a COM object's `IUnknown.Release` method, which decrements the object's reference count. It takes a `System.IntPtr` parameter that represents the `IUnknown` pointer for a COM object, and returns the 32-bit integer returned by the COM object's `Release` implementation. This return value roughly represents the object's reference count, and should be used only for testing purposes.

To get an `IntPtr` value that represents an object, you can call `GetComInterfaceForObject`, `GetIDispatchForObject`, or `GetIUnknownForObject`. These methods, plus the `Marshal.Release` method, can even be used on purely .NET objects! In this case, the COM interfaces represent the ones implemented by the .NET object's COM-Callable Wrapper. Be sure not to call `Release` unless you were responsible for a corresponding `AddRef` call. Calling `Release` after the reference count has reached zero causes undefined behavior.

Because the CLR manages a COM object's reference count for you, it's almost never necessary to call `Marshal.Release`. In some advanced cases, however, like custom marshaling or working around COM object oddities, it can become necessary. For example, this method should be called after calling any of the other `Marshal` methods that return an `IntPtr` representing a COM interface pointer.

The following code demonstrates the use of `Marshal.Release`, using `Marshal.GetIUnknownForObject` to obtain an `IntPtr` value representing the COM object's `IUnknown` interface pointer:

C#:

```
IntPtr pUnk = Marshal.GetIUnknownForObject(myComObject);
int refCount = Marshal.Release(pUnk);
```

A

System.Runtime.
InteropServices
REFERENCE

Visual Basic .NET:

```
Dim pUnk As IntPtr = Marshal.GetIUnknownForObject(myComObject)
Dim refCount As Integer = Marshal.Release(pUnk)
```

C++:

```
IntPtr pUnk = Marshal::GetIUnknownForObject(myComObject);
int refCount = Marshal::Release(pUnk);
```

For more information, see `Marshal.QueryInterface` and `Marshal.AddRef` listed earlier in this section.

The `ReleaseComObject` Method

`ReleaseComObject` provides a means to instantly release a COM object rather than waiting for its Runtime-Callable Wrapper to be garbage collected. It's often necessary to use this method with COM objects that hold onto limited resources (such as a database connection or Windows graphics objects) and don't release them until the object is destroyed.

The method takes a `System.Object` parameter and returns a 32-bit integer representing the RCW's reference count on the COM object. Note that `ReleaseComObject` only decrements the wrapper's reference count—the original COM object won't be destroyed until its own reference count reaches zero.

DIGGING DEEPER

Usually calling `ReleaseComObject` once does the trick for releasing the wrapped COM object because an RCW's reference count is typically set to 1. However, an RCW's reference count gets incremented every time the same COM interface pointer is passed from unmanaged to managed code. It's rare that this occurs more than once, but to be absolutely sure that calling `ReleaseComObject` releases the underlying COM object, you'd need to call `ReleaseComObject` in a loop until the returned reference count reaches zero.

Unlike typical reference count values returned by `IUnknown.AddRef` and `IUnknown.Release`, you *can* count on the value returned by `ReleaseComObject` to be reliable. Once the count reaches zero, the CLR is guaranteed to release all of the COM object's interface pointers that the CCW holds onto.

For more information, see Chapter 6.

The `ReleaseThreadCache` Method

This method is obsolete, and should never be called.

The `SetComObjectData` Method

Every COM object wrapped in a Runtime-Callable Wrapper has a hashtable associated with it. This method is a means of setting this data, and `GetComObjectData` is a means of retrieving the data. User code should have no reason to call this method.

The `SizeOf` Method

This method can be used to discover the size, in bytes, of the unmanaged view of a structure that has a managed definition. This size might not correspond to the managed size because marshaling can transform a .NET structure into something with a different size.

`SizeOf` has two overloads—both return a 32-bit integer containing the structure's size and both have a single parameter. The first overload takes a `System.Object` parameter whereas the second overload takes a `System.Type` parameter. The overload with a `System.Object` parameter can be used on an instance of the structure. This can be a reference type or a boxed value type, but must have sequential or explicit layout. The overload with a `System.Type` parameter can be used when you don't have an instance of the structure. The same layout restrictions apply to this overload as well. Attempting to call `SizeOf` with an illegal type or instance results in an `ArgumentException` with the message, "Type *typeName* cannot be marshaled as an unmanaged structure; no meaningful size or offset can be computed."

> **TIP**
>
> C# has a built-in `sizeof` operator that works on a type instance, but this is *not* the same thing as `Marshal.SizeOf`! It reports the managed size of a structure rather than the unmanaged size of the marshaled structure. See Chapter 6 for more information.

To obtain the offset of a single field in a structure, see the `Marshal.OffsetOf` method.

The `StringToBSTR` Method

This method creates a COM `BSTR` type with contents copied from a .NET string. It has a single `System.String` parameter and returns a `System.IntPtr` value that represents the pointer to the allocated `BSTR`. This method does the opposite of `Marshal.PtrToStringBSTR`, which creates a `System.String` from the contents of a `BSTR`.

If you pass a null string, this method returns `IntPtr.Zero`. Otherwise, it allocates a `BSTR` with the contents of the input string. This method throws an `OutOfMemoryException` if the string to return could not be allocated. You must always free this `BSTR` when finished with it using `Marshal.FreeBSTR` or one of its corresponding unmanaged APIs.

You normally don't need to interact with BSTR types in managed code. This method, however, can be useful in custom marshaling scenarios or when mixing managed and unmanaged code in C++.

The `StringToCoTaskMemAnsi` Method

This method creates an unmanaged ANSI string, allocated with `CoTaskMemAlloc`, and copies the contents of a .NET string into it. It has a single `System.String` parameter and returns a `System.IntPtr` value that represents the pointer to the allocated string. This method does the opposite of `Marshal.PtrToStringAnsi`, which creates a `System.String` from the contents of an ANSI string.

If you pass a null string, this method returns `IntPtr.Zero`. Otherwise, it allocates an ANSI string with the contents of the input string. This method throws an `OutOfMemoryException` if the string to return could not be allocated. You must always free this string when finished with it using `Marshal.FreeCoTaskMem` or its corresponding unmanaged API.

You normally don't need to interact with unmanaged string types in managed code. This method, however, can be useful in custom marshaling scenarios or when mixing managed and unmanaged code in C++.

If you want the returned string to be allocated on the global heap instead, call `Marshal.StringToHGlobalAnsi`.

The `StringToCoTaskMemAuto` Method

This method creates an unmanaged string, allocated with `CoTaskMemAlloc`, and copies the contents of a .NET string into it. This string is either ANSI or Unicode based on the current operating system. It has a single `System.String` parameter and returns a `System.IntPtr` value that represents the pointer to the allocated string. This method does the opposite of `Marshal.PtrToStringAuto`, which creates a `System.String` from the contents of a platform-dependent string.

If you pass a null string, this method returns `IntPtr.Zero`. Otherwise, it allocates a platform-dependent string with the contents of the input string. This method throws an `OutOfMemoryException` if the string to return could not be allocated. You must always free this string when finished with it using `Marshal.FreeCoTaskMem` or its corresponding unmanaged API.

You normally don't need to interact with unmanaged string types in managed code. This method, however, can be useful in custom marshaling scenarios or when mixing managed and unmanaged code in C++.

If you want the returned string to be allocated on the global heap instead, call `Marshal.StringToHGlobalAuto`.

The `StringToCoTaskMemUni` Method

This method creates an unmanaged Unicode string, allocated with `CoTaskMemAlloc`, and copies the contents of a .NET string into it. It has a single `System.String` parameter and returns a `System.IntPtr` value that represents the pointer to the allocated string. This method does the opposite of `Marshal.PtrToStringUni`, which creates a `System.String` from the contents of a Unicode string.

If you pass a null string, this method returns `IntPtr.Zero`. Otherwise, it allocates a Unicode string with the contents of the input string. This method throws an `OutOfMemoryException` if the string to return could not be allocated. You must always free this string when finished with it using `Marshal.FreeCoTaskMem` or its corresponding unmanaged API. (The original string is always copied despite the fact that .NET strings are Unicode internally.)

You normally don't need to interact with unmanaged string types in managed code. This method, however, can be useful in custom marshaling scenarios or when mixing managed and unmanaged code in C++.

If you want the returned string to be allocated on the global heap instead, call `Marshal.StringToHGlobalUni`.

The `StringToHGlobalAnsi` Method

This method creates an unmanaged ANSI string, allocated with the same memory allocator used by `AllocHGlobal`, and copies the contents of a .NET string into it. It has a single `System.String` parameter and returns a `System.IntPtr` value that represents the pointer to the allocated string. This method does the opposite of `Marshal.PtrToStringAnsi`, which creates a `System.String` from the contents of an ANSI string.

If you pass a null string, this method returns `IntPtr.Zero`. Otherwise, it allocates an ANSI string with the contents of the input string. This method throws an `OutOfMemoryException` if the string to return could not be allocated. You must always free this string when finished with it using `Marshal.FreeHGlobal` or an equivalent unmanaged API.

You normally don't need to interact with unmanaged string types in managed code. This method, however, can be useful in custom marshaling scenarios or when mixing managed and unmanaged code in C++.

If you want the returned string to be allocated using the COM task memory allocator instead, call `Marshal.StringToCoTaskMemAnsi`.

The `StringToHGlobalAuto` Method

This method creates an unmanaged string, allocated with the same memory allocator used by `AllocHGlobal`, and copies the contents of a .NET string into it. This string is either ANSI or

A

System.Runtime.
InteropServices
REFERENCE

Unicode based on the current operating system. It has a single `System.String` parameter and returns a `System.IntPtr` value that represents the pointer to the allocated string. This method does the opposite of `Marshal.PtrToStringAuto`, which creates a `System.String` from the contents of a platform-dependent string.

If you pass a null string, this method returns `IntPtr.Zero`. Otherwise, it allocates a platform-dependent string with the contents of the input string. This method throws an `OutOfMemoryException` if the string to return could not be allocated. You must always free this string when finished with it using `Marshal.FreeHGlobal` or an equivalent unmanaged API.

You normally don't need to interact with unmanaged string types in managed code. This method, however, can be useful in custom marshaling scenarios or when mixing managed and unmanaged code in C++.

If you want the returned string to be allocated using the COM task memory allocator instead, call `Marshal.StringToCoTaskMemAuto`.

The `StringToHGlobalUni` Method

This method creates an unmanaged Unicode string, allocated with the same memory allocator used by `AllocHGlobal`, and copies the contents of a .NET string into it. It has a single `System.String` parameter and returns a `System.IntPtr` value that represents the pointer to the allocated string. This method does the opposite of `Marshal.PtrToStringUni`, which creates a `System.String` from the contents of a Unicode string.

If you pass a null string, this method returns `IntPtr.Zero`. Otherwise, it allocates a Unicode string with the contents of the input string. This method throws an `OutOfMemoryException` if the string to return could not be allocated. You must always free this string when finished with it using `Marshal.FreeHGlobal` or an equivalent unmanaged API. (The original string is always copied despite the fact that .NET strings are Unicode internally.)

You normally don't need to interact with unmanaged string types in managed code. This method, however, can be useful in custom marshaling scenarios or when mixing managed and unmanaged code in C++.

If you want the returned string to be allocated using the COM task memory allocator instead, call `Marshal.StringToCoTaskMemUni`.

The `StructureToPtr` Method

The `StructureToPtr` method can be used to obtain a raw pointer to the memory address of a .NET type with sequential or explicit layout. (The `Marshal.PtrToStructure` method does the reverse of this.) This is often necessary in COM Interoperability and PInvoke when structure parameters are represented as an `IntPtr` value. This method has the following signature:

C#:

```
public static void StructureToPtr(object structure, IntPtr ptr, bool
fDeleteOld);
```

Visual Basic .NET:

```
Public Shared Sub StructureToPtr(structure As Object, ptr As IntPtr, _
  fDeleteOld As Boolean)
```

C++:

```
public: static void StructureToPtr(Object* structure, IntPtr ptr,
  bool fDeleteOld);
```

The first parameter is the object for which the pointer is desired. This can be a reference type or a boxed value type, but if the object does not have sequential or explicit layout, an ArgumentException is thrown.

The second parameter is a pointer value *that must point to memory that has already been allocated.* Therefore, the IntPtr is passed by-value. The .NET object will be copied to the specified location in memory. It's up to the user to free the memory appropriately after the StructureToPtr call, depending on how the memory was allocated.

The last parameter, if true, assumes that the IntPtr parameter points to an existing structure of the same type as the first parameter and destroys any fields that are reference types (but does not free the memory required for the new structure). Passing false suppresses this behavior. If StructureToPtr simply overwrote memory containing a structure with, for example, an unmanaged string field, the string would never get freed and would result in a memory leak. To free the appropriate fields when passing true for fDeleteOld, StructureToPtr calls the Marshal.DestroyStructure method.

> **TIP**
>
> If you don't want to copy a structure but simply want to pin an existing structure and get its address as an IntPtr value, use the GCHandle type in System.Runtime. InteropServices to create a pinned handle for the structure. This is more efficient because it avoids copying.

Although using the GCHandle type is the best language-neutral way to get a pointer from a structure, StructureToPtr is useful for swapping one structure with another in the same memory location. The following code demonstrates this.

C#:

```
IntPtr addressOfStructure1 = ...;
TYPEATTR structure2 = ...;
Marshal.StructureToPtr(structure2, addressOfStructure1, true);
```

Visual Basic .NET:

```
Dim IntPtr addressOfStructure1 As IntPtr = ...
Dim structure2 As TYPEATTR = ...
Marshal.StructureToPtr(structure2, addressOfStructure1, True)
```

C++:

```
IntPtr addressOfStructure1 = ...;
TYPEATTR structure2 = ...;
Marshal::StructureToPtr(__box(structure2), addressOfStructure1, true);
```

For more information, see the `Marshal.PtrToStructure` and `Marshal.DestroyStructure` methods listed earlier in this section, and Chapter 6.

The `SystemDefaultCharSize` Property

This integer read-only property returns the default character size, in bytes, for the current operating system. This value is used by the `PtrToStringAuto`, `StringToHGlobalAuto`, and `StringToCoTaskMemAuto` methods to make the appropriate string transformations from managed to unmanaged and vice versa.

On Unicode platforms, this value is 2. On ANSI platforms, this value is 1.

The `SystemMaxDBCSCharSize` Property

This integer read-only property returns the maximum double-byte character set (DBCS) size, in bytes, for the current operating system. This value is used by the `StringToHGlobalAnsi` and `StringToCoTaskMemAnsi` methods to make the appropriate string transformations.

On English Windows platforms, this value is 1. On some international platforms, such as Japanese, this value is 2.

The `ThrowExceptionForHR` Method

The `ThrowExceptionForHR` method, the opposite of `GetHRForException`, throws a .NET exception type that corresponds to an `HRESULT` value. The nice thing about this method is that it doesn't simply throw a `COMException` with the `ErrorCode` property set to the passed-in `HRESULT`. (Otherwise, there wouldn't be much point in having this method.) Instead, it makes use of the `HRESULT`-to-exception conversions listed in Appendix C. So whereas a custom `HRESULT` is simply mapped to a `COMException`, an `HRESULT` like `E_OUTOFMEMORY` is mapped to an `OutOfMemoryException`.

The method has two overloads—one that takes a 32-bit integer representing the HRESULT, and one that takes the same 32-bit integer plus a System.IntPtr type that represents a pointer to an IErrorInfo interface. This can be used to give the .NET exception a customized error message, source, and so on. If -1 is passed for this IntPtr value, no extra error information is used. If IntPtr.Zero is passed (the same as calling the single-parameter overload), the Windows GetErrorInfo API is called to attempt to retrieve an error object available on the current thread. Otherwise, a valid pointer to an IErrorInfo interface could be passed to directly set this extra information.

Notice that the exception is thrown directly from the method so you can't check the type before throwing it without catching it first then rethrowing the exception. This method is useful for custom marshaling because throwing a reasonable exception for a returned HRESULT can be done without extra work. However, you might wish to further customize the exceptions thrown to reduce the number of situations in which COMException is thrown.

If you want to throw an exception with a success HRESULT value (rather than changing your signature to return an HRESULT directly using PreserveSigAttribute), ThrowExceptionForHR does not enable this. Calling it with a success HRESULT value does nothing. Instead, you could throw a COMException with an ErrorCode set to the success HRESULT value.

For more information, see Chapter 20 and Appendix C.

The UnsafeAddrOfPinnedArrayElement Method

The UnsafeAddrOfPinnedArrayElement method can give you the memory address of any element of a pinned .NET array. It takes two parameters—a System.Array type representing the .NET array, and an integer index of the element whose address is desired. It returns a System.IntPtr value representing the memory address.

> **CAUTION**
>
> The reason the UnsafeAddrOfPinnedArrayElement method begins with the word "Unsafe" is to alert you to the fact that, for maximum performance, it does no validation on the array passed in. This means that you can pass an unpinned array and not cause an exception to be thrown. Use caution, because passing an unpinned array can cause unexpected results.

The WriteByte Method

The WriteByte method is useful for writing a single byte value at a given offset directly to a pointer to an unmanaged object. It has three overloads:

C#:

```
public static void WriteByte([MarshalAs(UnmanagedType.AsAny)] object ptr,
  int ofs, byte val);

public static void WriteByte(IntPtr ptr, int ofs, byte val);

public static void WriteByte(IntPtr ptr, byte val);
```

Visual Basic .NET:

```
Public Overloads Shared Sub WriteByte(<MarshalAs(UnmanagedType.AsAny)> _
  ptr As Object, ofs As Integer, val As Byte)

Public Overloads Shared Sub WriteByte(ptr As IntPtr, ofs As Integer, _
  val As Byte)

Public Overloads Shared Sub WriteByte(ptr As IntPtr, val As Byte)
```

C++:

```
public: static void WriteByte([MarshalAs(UnmanagedType::AsAny)] Object* ptr,
  int ofs, unsigned char val);

public: static void WriteByte(IntPtr ptr, int ofs, unsigned char val);

public: static void WriteByte(IntPtr ptr, unsigned char val);
```

The first overload takes an object representing the unmanaged entity (marshaled as a void*), an integer offset, and the value to write. The object passed as the first parameter could even be a .NET object with the appropriate format (such as an array), but there would be no reason to pass such an object to this method. Any object passed that can't be treated appropriately causes an ArgumentException to be thrown with the message, "No PInvoke conversion exists for value passed to Object-typed parameter."

The second overload works the same way as the first, but expects the pointer to the unmanaged object to be passed via an IntPtr type. The third overload works just like the second one, but with an implied offset of zero. For all overloads, it is the responsibility of the caller to ensure that the memory being written to is within the range of the input object.

This method enables direct interaction with an unmanaged C-style byte array so you don't need to incur the expense of copying an entire unmanaged array (using Marshal.Copy) to a separate .NET array, setting its element values, then copying it back. This is demonstrated in the following code, which sets an unmanaged array's ten elements to the values 1 through 10:

C#:

```
IntPtr unmanagedArray = ...;
```

```csharp
// One way to set the 10 elements of the C-style unmanagedArray
byte [] newArray = new byte[10];
Marshal.Copy(unmanagedArray, newArray, 0, 10);
for (int i = 0; i < newArray.Length; i++)
  newArray[i] = i+1;
Marshal.Copy(newArray, 0, unmanagedArray, 10);

// Another way to set the 10 elements of the C-style unmanagedArray
for (int i = 0; i < 10; i++)
  Marshal.WriteByte(unmanagedArray, i, i+1);
```

Visual Basic .NET:

```vbnet
Dim unmanagedArray As IntPtr = ...
Dim i As Integer

' One way to set the 10 elements of the C-style unmanagedArray
Dim newArray As Byte(9)
Marshal.Copy(unmanagedArray, newArray, 0, 10)
For i = 0 To newArray.Length
  newArray(i) = i+1
Next i
Marshal.Copy(newArray, 0, unmanagedArray, 10)

' Another way to set the 10 elements of the C-style unmanagedArray
For i = 0 To 10
  Marshal.WriteByte(unmanagedArray, i, i+1)
Next i
```

C++:

```cpp
IntPtr unmanagedArray = ...;

// One way to set the 10 elements of the C-style unmanagedArray
unsigned char newArray __gc[] = new unsigned char __gc[10];
Marshal::Copy(unmanagedArray, newArray, 0, 10);
for (int i = 0; i < newArray.Length; i++)
  newArray[i] = i+1;
Marshal::Copy(newArray, 0, unmanagedArray, 10);

// Another way to set the 10 elements of the C-style unmanagedArray
for (int i = 0; i < 10; i++)
  Marshal::WriteByte(unmanagedArray, i, i+1);
```

To write other data types directly to an unmanaged pointer, see Marshal.WriteInt16, Marshal.WriteInt32, Marshal.WriteInt64, and Marshal.WriteIntPtr. To read data directly from an unmanaged pointer, see Marshal.ReadByte, Marshal.ReadInt16, Marshal.ReadInt32, Marshal.ReadInt64, and Marshal.ReadIntPtr.

The `WriteInt16` Method

The `WriteInt16` method is useful for writing a single 16-bit integer value *or a character value* at a given offset directly to a pointer to an unmanaged object. Unlike the other `Write...` methods, it has six overloads—three for writing a plain 16-bit integer, and three for writing a character value.

CAUTION

In version 1.0 of the .NET Framework, the overloads of `Marshal.WriteInt16` that write a character rather than a plain 16-bit value should not be used. This is because they incorrectly write only one byte of the character rather than two; treating it as an ANSI character rather than Unicode! To work around this, you can first convert a `System.Char` type to a 16-bit integer by calling `System.Convert.ToInt16`, and then call `Marshal.WriteInt16` with this value.

Two overloads take an object representing the unmanaged entity (marshaled as a `void*`), an integer offset, and the value to write. Any object passed that can't be treated appropriately causes an `ArgumentException` to be thrown with the message, "No PInvoke conversion exists for value passed to Object-typed parameter."

Two more overloads work the same way as the previous two, but expect the pointer to the unmanaged object to be passed via an `IntPtr` type. The two remaining overloads use an implied offset of zero. For all overloads, it is the responsibility of the caller to ensure that the memory being written to is within the range of the input object.

This method enables direct interaction with an unmanaged C-style array so you don't need to incur the expense of copying an entire unmanaged array (using `Marshal.Copy`) to a separate .NET array, setting its element values, and then copying it back. It is used just like the examples shown in the `Marshal.WriteByte` section, but with a different array element type.

To write other data types directly to an unmanaged pointer, see `Marshal.WriteByte`, `Marshal.WriteInt32`, `Marshal.WriteInt64`, and `Marshal.WriteIntPtr`. To read data directly from an unmanaged pointer, see `Marshal.ReadByte`, `Marshal.ReadInt16`, `Marshal.ReadInt32`, `Marshal.ReadInt64`, and `Marshal.ReadIntPtr`.

The `WriteInt32` Method

The `WriteInt32` method is useful for writing a single 32-bit integer value at a given offset directly to a pointer to an unmanaged object. It has three overloads just like `Marshal.WriteByte`, but with an `Int32` return type.

The first overload takes an object representing the unmanaged entity (marshaled as a void*), an integer offset, and the value to write. Any object passed that can't be treated appropriately causes an ArgumentException to be thrown with the message, "No PInvoke conversion exists for value passed to Object-typed parameter."

The second overload works the same way as the first, but expects the pointer to the unmanaged object to be passed via an IntPtr type. The third overload works just like the second one, but with an implied offset of zero. For all overloads, it is the responsibility of the caller to ensure that the memory being written to is within the range of the input object.

This method enables direct interaction with an unmanaged C-style array so you don't need to incur the expense of copying an entire unmanaged array (using Marshal.Copy) to a separate .NET array, setting its element values, and then copying it back. It is used just like the examples shown in the Marshal.WriteByte section, but with a different array element type.

To write other data types directly to an unmanaged pointer, see Marshal.WriteByte, Marshal.WriteInt16, Marshal.WriteInt64, and Marshal.WriteIntPtr. To read data directly from an unmanaged pointer, see Marshal.ReadByte, Marshal.ReadInt16, Marshal.ReadInt32, Marshal.ReadInt64, and Marshal.ReadIntPtr.

The WriteInt64 Method

The WriteInt64 method is useful for writing a single 64-bit integer value at a given offset directly to a pointer to an unmanaged object. It has three overloads just like Marshal.WriteByte, but with an Int64 return type.

The first overload takes an object representing the unmanaged entity (marshaled as a void*), an integer offset, and the value to write. Any object passed that can't be treated appropriately causes an ArgumentException to be thrown with the message, "No PInvoke conversion exists for value passed to Object-typed parameter."

The second overload works the same way as the first, but expects the pointer to the unmanaged object to be passed via an IntPtr type. The third overload works just like the second one, but with an implied offset of zero. For all overloads, it is the responsibility of the caller to ensure that the memory being written to is within the range of the input object.

This method enables direct interaction with an unmanaged C-style array so you don't need to incur the expense of copying an entire unmanaged array (using Marshal.Copy) to a separate .NET array, setting its element values, and then copying it back. It is used just like the examples shown in the Marshal.WriteByte section, but with a different array element type.

To write other data types directly to an unmanaged pointer, see Marshal.WriteByte, Marshal.WriteInt16, Marshal.WriteInt32, and Marshal.WriteIntPtr. To read data directly from an unmanaged pointer, see Marshal.ReadByte, Marshal.ReadInt16, Marshal.ReadInt32, Marshal.ReadInt64, and Marshal.ReadIntPtr.

The `WriteIntPtr` Method

The `WriteIntPtr` method is useful for writing a single platform-sized integer value at a given offset directly to a pointer to an unmanaged object. It has three overloads just like `Marshal.WriteByte`, but with an `IntPtr` return type.

The first overload takes an object representing the unmanaged entity (marshaled as a `void*`), an integer offset, and the value to write. Any object passed that can't be treated appropriately causes an `ArgumentException` to be thrown with the message, "No PInvoke conversion exists for value passed to Object-typed parameter."

The second overload works the same way as the first, but expects the pointer to the unmanaged object to be passed via an `IntPtr` type. The third overload works just like the second one, but with an implied offset of zero. For all overloads, it is the responsibility of the caller to ensure that the memory being written to is within the range of the input object.

This method enables direct interaction with an unmanaged C-style array so you don't need to incur the expense of copying an entire unmanaged array (using `Marshal.Copy`) to a separate .NET array, setting its element values, and then copying it back. It is used just like the examples shown in the `Marshal.WriteByte` section, but with a different array element type.

To write other data types directly to an unmanaged pointer, see `Marshal.WriteByte`, `Marshal.WriteInt16`, `Marshal.WriteInt32`, and `Marshal.WriteInt64`. To read data directly from an unmanaged pointer, see `Marshal.ReadByte`, `Marshal.ReadInt16`, `Marshal.ReadInt32`, `Marshal.ReadInt64`, and `Marshal.ReadIntPtr`.

The `MarshalAsAttribute` Pseudo-Custom Attribute

`MarshalAsAttribute` is a widely–used, pseudo-custom attribute that controls which .NET data types (when used as parameters, fields, or return values) correspond to which unmanaged data types. Every .NET data type has a corresponding unmanaged type to which they are marshaled by default. Several data types (such as blittable ones) only have a single unmanaged representation that can't be changed. Others have a few corresponding unmanaged types, such as `System.String`, which can be marshaled to a `BSTR`, `LPSTR`, `LPWSTR`, and so on.

The default marshaling behavior of some data types depends on how they are used. For parameters and return types, some types have different default marshaling behavior if used with a COM member or with a PInvoke method. The default marshaling behavior for fields of structures mostly matches the PInvoke behavior regardless of whether the structure is used with COM Interoperability or with PInvoke. For example:

- `String` parameters in COM methods marshal as `BSTR` by default, but `String` parameters in PInvoke methods and `String` fields in value types marshal as `LPSTR` by default.

- `Boolean` parameters in COM methods marshal as `VARIANT_BOOL` by default, but `Boolean` parameters in PInvoke methods and `Boolean` fields in value types marshal as `BOOL` (a 32-bit integer) by default.

- `Object` parameters in COM methods marshal as `VARIANT` by default, but `Object` parameters in PInvoke methods and `Object` fields in value types marshal as an `IUnknown` interface pointer by default.

`MarshalAsAttribute` has two constructors—one that takes a 16-bit integer and one that takes an `UnmanagedType` enumeration. The latter constructor should always be used. It also has several named parameters that can be used with certain `UnmanagedType` values. (In the case of `UnmanagedType.CustomMarshaler` and `UnmanagedType.ByValArray`, an additional named parameter *must* be used.) These parameters are:

- `ArraySubType`. Valid with `UnmanagedType.LPArray` or `UnmanagedType.ByValArray`. This parameter can be set to an `UnmanagedType` value specifying the unmanaged type of the array's elements. The rules are the same for this element type as for applying `MarshalAsAttribute` to a simple parameter. If no value is specified, the default unmanaged type corresponding to the managed array's element type is used.

- `MarshalCookie`. Valid with `UnmanagedType.CustomMarshaler`. This parameter can be set to a string that supplies a custom marshaler with additional information. The `ExpandoToDispatchExMarshaler` that ships with the .NET Framework uses this string set to either "IReflect" or "IExpando."

- `MarshalType`. Valid with `UnmanagedType.CustomMarshaler`. Either `MarshalType` or `MarshalTypeRef` must be used with `UnmanagedType.CustomMarshaler` to specify the custom marshaler type for the marked parameter, return type, or field. `MarshalType` can be set to a string representing the assembly-qualified type name of the custom marshaler. Although this can be useful for late-bound references, using `MarshalTypeRef` is preferred.

- `MarshalTypeRef`. Valid with `UnmanagedType.CustomMarshaler`. Either `MarshalType` or `MarshalTypeRef` must be used with `UnmanagedType.CustomMarshaler` to specify the custom marshaler type for the marked parameter, return type, or field. `MarshalTypeRef` can be set to a `Type` object using `typeof` in C#, `GetType` in VB .NET, or `__typeof` in C++. This is the preferred means of specifying a custom marshaler.

- `SafeArraySubType`. Valid with `UnmanagedType.SafeArray`. This can be set to a value from the `VarEnum` enumeration to specify the type of the `SAFEARRAY`'s elements, such as `VarEnum.VT_R8` or `VarEnum.VT_UNKNOWN`. If none is specified, the managed element type's default type that would be used when passed in a `VARIANT` is chosen.

- `SafeArrayUserDefinedSubType`. Valid with `UnmanagedType.SafeArray` only when `SafeArraySubType` is set to `VarEnum.VT_RECORD`, `VarEnum.VT_DISPATCH`, or

VarEnum.VT_UNKNOWN. This can be set to a `Type` object for the user-defined value type representing the array's element type. This is only useful when the marked data type is the generic `System.Array`, to be able to expose a `SAFEARRAY` of type `VT_RECORD` to COM with an arbitrary rank or non-zero lower bounds.

- `SizeConst`. Valid with `UnmanagedType.ByValArray` or `UnmanagedType.ByValTStr`. This parameter can be set to an integer to specify the number of elements in the array, or to specify the number of *characters* (not bytes) in the string. `UnmanagedType.ByValArray` and `UnmanagedType.ByValTStr` are not valid without the use of `SizeConst`.

- `SizeParamIndex`. Valid with `UnmanagedType.LPArray` or `UnmanagedType.ByValArray`. This parameter can be set to a 16-bit integer to specify the zero-based index of a parameter containing the size of the array. The parameter containing the size must be a by-value integer type. (If both `SizeConst` and `SizeParamIndex` are used with `UnmanagedType.LPArray`, their values are simply added together to get the total size.)

The type library importer marks imported parameters, return types, and fields with this attribute when the data type in the input type library is not the default unmanaged data type for the corresponding managed data type. For clarity, the importer always marks `String` and `Object` types with the attribute even when it exhibits default behavior.

For a complete list of which `UnmanagedType` values can be used on which .NET data types, consult Chapter 12. For `MarshalAsAttribute` information that's helpful for PInvoke, consult Chapter 19. For the special IL Assembler syntax of `MarshalAsAttribute` and its corresponding values, see Chapter 7. For information about the named parameters specific to custom marshaling, see Chapter 20.

The `MarshalDirectiveException` Exception

The Interop Marshaler sometimes throws a `MarshalDirectiveException` when it encounters a signature with an improperly used `MarshalAsAttribute` pseudo-custom attribute. In many cases, unfortunately, the marshaler silently ignores incorrect markings when the correct course of action is obvious.

Because many invalid uses of `MarshalAsAttribute` are caught at compile-time (thanks to being a pseudo-custom attribute), many invalid uses are never emitted into metadata in the first place. However, it's still fairly easy to come up with an example that causes the exception to be thrown. For example, the following C# signature:

```
// Error: Cannot marshal a string as an interface
void InvalidMarshaling([MarshalAs(UnmanagedType.Interface)] string s);
```

DON'T DO THIS

causes MarshalDirectiveException to be thrown with the following message:

```
Cannot marshal parameter #1: Invalid managed/unmanaged type combination
➡ (Strings must be paired with LPStr, LPWStr, LPTStr, BStr, TBStr, or AnsiBStr).
```

However, the exception only occurs when the Interop Marshaler is involved, so either when unmanaged code calls InvalidMarshaling implemented by a .NET class, or vice versa.

An Interop Assembly produced from the type library importer should almost never cause a MarshalDirectiveException to be thrown, assuming it hasn't been modified as in Chapter 7.

MarshalDirectiveException derives from System.SystemException, and should never be thrown by an application. Its protected HResult property (which can be exposed to COM when the exception is thrown) has the value COR_E_MARSHALDIRECTIVE, defined by the .NET Framework SDK as 0x80131535.

The `ObjectCreationDelegate` Delegate

ObjectCreationDelegate is the delegate used by ExtensibleClassFactory.RegisterObjectCreationCallback. The delegate's signature has one aggregator parameter of type System.IntPtr, and returns a System.IntPtr type. When this delegate is passed to RegisterObjectCreationCallback, the method implementation is invoked instead of CoCreateInstance when a .NET object needs to instantiate the COM object it derives from. The input IntPtr parameter represents the IUnknown pointer of the .NET object. The delegate is responsible for returning an IntPtr representing the IUnknown pointer of the COM object. For version 1.0 of the .NET Framework, this delegate must always be constructed with an instance method rather than a static method.

For more information, consult Chapter 6 and the ExtensibleClassFactory class listed earlier in this section.

The `OptionalAttribute` Pseudo-Custom Attribute

The parameter-less OptionalAttribute pseudo-custom attribute can be marked on a parameter in order to turn it into an optional parameter. This pseudo-custom attribute sets the same metadata bit set by VB .NET's Optional keyword. This means that despite popular opinion, members with optional parameters *can* be defined in C#! This doesn't change the important fact, however, that optional parameters can't be *used* like optional parameters in C#.

This pseudo-custom attribute is useful when manually defining type information for COM members that use optional parameters in languages other than Visual Basic .NET. You can define a C# interface with optional parameters, and a VB .NET client can omit the optional arguments when calling its members.

An important restriction of using `OptionalAttribute`, however, is that there's no direct way to set a default value unless the language supports such a concept (as in VB .NET). Therefore, `OptionalAttribute` should only be used on `System.Object` parameters, because such parameters have an implicit default value of `System.Reflection.Missing` (the type of the `Type.Missing` field).

The type library importer marks any optional parameters from the input type library with `OptionalAttribute`.

For more information, consult Chapter 21.

The `OutAttribute` Pseudo-Custom Attribute

The `OutAttribute` pseudo-custom attribute can be marked on a member's parameters to affect their data flow when the member is implemented in managed code and called from unmanaged code, or vice versa. The `Out` marking means that data flows from the callee to the caller.

In pure managed code, value types have "in" behavior and reference types have behavior like "in/out" because references are passed such that callees can change the object's state (except for the immutable `System.String`, which has "in" behavior). All by-reference types have "in/out" behavior, and C#-style out parameters have "out" behavior. The Interop Marshaler, however, treats all reference type parameters except `StringBuilder` with "in" behavior, which is often a source of confusion. When types are blittable, they appear to have "in/out" behavior, because the Interop Marshaler pins them, but this behavior is no longer seen when COM marshaling is involved across contexts.

The following are three valid ways to use `OutAttribute`:

- Marking a by-reference parameter with `OutAttribute` and not `InAttribute` makes it equivalent to a C#-style out parameter. C#, however, forbids this combination because you can use the `out` keyword instead.

- Marking a by-value formatted reference type parameter or array parameter with `OutAttribute` and not `InAttribute` gives it "out"-only behavior rather than "in"-only. Still, the change in behavior isn't noticed when crossing the managed/unmanaged boundary in the same apartment when the type has all blittable fields or elements because the Interop Marshaler pins such instances.

- Marking a by-value formatted reference type parameter or array parameter with both `OutAttribute` and `InAttribute` is often recommended to preserve the "in/out" semantics expected for reference types. For example, unless you mark an array of non-blittable `Object` types with `InAttribute` and `OutAttribute`, callers don't see any changes to the array's elements made by the callee.

Marking a value type parameter that is passed by-value with OutAttribute has no effect, because there's no way for the object's data to be passed out to the caller.

Because the first two actions cancel the default "in" part of the data flow behavior by omitting InAttribute, using OutAttribute can provide better performance for non-blittable types when you don't care about passing data into the callee.

For the third action, OutAttribute is used in conjunction with InAttribute to provide the same .NET semantics to reference type parameters such as arrays when calling into unmanaged code as one would expect when calling into managed code. This is important not only when crossing the managed/unmanaged boundary, but for any COM clients that may use an exported type library's definitions across context boundaries. If you expect "in/out" behavior, you had better mark the parameter as such!

The type library importer marks any parameters with OutAttribute if the corresponding parameter has an IDL [out] marking in the input type library (although it omits it on return values because OutAttribute can only be applied on parameters).

For more information, see Chapter 12.

The PARAMDESC Value Type

This is a .NET definition of the unmanaged PARAMDESC structure used by the DESCUNION COM union. In the .NET Framework, this definition is used by the DESCUNION value type that redefines the unmanaged union for managed clients.

For more information, consult MSDN Online for information about the original PARAMDESC structure.

The PARAMFLAG Enumeration

This is a .NET definition of the unmanaged PARAMFLAG enumeration used by the PARAMDESC value type.

For more information, consult MSDN Online for information about the original PARAMFLAG enumeration.

The PreserveSigAttribute Pseudo-Custom Attribute

The PreserveSigAttribute pseudo-custom attribute can be marked on methods (or property accessors) to indicate that a .NET signature "preserves" its corresponding COM signature. The CLR does not do any HRESULT-to-exception transformation for such signatures. Because most COM members return an HRESULT, most managed signatures marked with PreserveSigAttribute return an integer representing the HRESULT, whether it's a success value or a failure value. Any out, retval parameters are left as out parameters in the managed signature.

Marking a COM signature with PreserveSigAttribute is necessary if the member returns more than one success HRESULT value (such as S_OK and S_FALSE) and you want to detect the different values. Members that aren't marked with PreserveSigAttribute have failure HRESULT return values translated into exceptions, but success HRESULTs for such members are discarded.

The type library importer only marks members of dispinterfaces with PreserveSigAttribute.

For more information, see Chapters 7 and 12.

The PrimaryInteropAssemblyAttribute Custom Attribute

The PrimaryInteropAssemblyAttribute can be marked on an assembly to identify it as a Primary Interop Assembly. The custom attribute's constructor has two integer parameters—major and minor—that identify the version of the type library represented by the assembly. Nothing else about the original type library is contained in the custom attribute because other custom attributes that are marked on any Interop Assembly already contain this information: the assembly's GuidAttribute contains the type library's LIBID, and the assembly's ImportedFromTypeLibAttribute contains the type library's filename.

A Primary Interop Assembly can be created using the TypeLibConverter class or with the TLBIMP.EXE SDK tool and its /primary option. Visual Studio .NET looks for Primary Interop Assemblies registered under HKEY_CLASSES_ROOT\TypeLib\{LIBID} in the Windows Registry. The RegistrationServices class and the REGASM.EXE SDK tool place the necessary Primary Interop Assembly registry entries when encountering an assembly marked with PrimaryInteropAssemblyAttribute.

The registration process can register a single Primary Interop Assembly for multiple versions of the same input type library, simply by having the assembly marked with multiple PrimaryInteropAssemblyAttribute custom attributes. However, the type library importer does not provide a means to create a Primary Interop Assembly with more than one PrimaryInteropAssemblyAttribute custom attribute, so doing this requires the techniques of Chapter 7.

For more information about the process of creating a Primary Interop Assembly, see Chapter 15, "Creating and Deploying Useful Primary Interop Assemblies."

The `ProgIdAttribute` Custom Attribute

The `ProgIdAttribute` custom attribute can be marked on .NET classes to choose a ProgID that gets registered for the class. The attribute has a single constructor that takes a string parameter containing the ProgID. If no `ProgIdAttribute` is used, the class's name is used, qualified with its namespace.

For simplicity, you should refrain from using `ProgIdAttribute`. However, the rules of COM dictate that a ProgID must:

- have 39 characters or fewer
- contain no punctuation besides periods—not even underscores
- not start with a digit
- be different from the class name of any OLE 1 application

It's a good idea to choose a different ProgID if the namespace-qualified class name breaks any of these rules. Many existing COM components don't obey these rules, however.

Another purpose for using `ProgIdAttribute` is to match an existing COM object's ProgID with a new .NET class.

The `RegistrationServices` Class

This class, which implements `IRegistrationServices`, contains methods used to register and unregister assemblies for use by COM. The `REGASM.EXE` SDK tool and Visual Studio .NET use `RegistrationServices` to add or remove COM-enabling registry entries for .NET components. The methods that add and remove registry entries also invoke custom registration or unregistration functions for any types that define them. The action of generating a registry file (exposed by `REGASM.EXE`'s `/regfile` option) is not provided by `RegistrationServices`, but the class contains several methods that can be helpful in discovering the entries that would be placed in such a file.

The `RegistrationServices` methods are described in the following sections. For more information about any them, see Chapter 22. For more information about custom registration functions, see Chapter 12 and the `ComRegisterFunction` and `ComUnregisterFunction` custom attributes listed previously in this section.

The `GetManagedCategoryGuid` Method

The `GetManagedCategoryGuid` method takes no parameters and returns a `Guid` instance representing the CATID for the ".NET Category" that's listed as an implemented category by every registered .NET type. This CATID is: `62C8FE65-4EBB-45e7-B440-6E39B2CDBF29`.

The `GetProgIdForType` Method

The `GetProgIdForType` method takes a `System.Type` parameter and returns a string containing what the ProgID would be for the input type if it were registered. This string is either a string specified in a `ProgIdAttribute` marked on the type or the fully qualified type name if no such attribute exists.

The `GetRegistrableTypesInAssembly` Method

The `GetRegistrableTypesInAssembly` method takes an `Assembly` parameter and returns an array of `Type` instances representing every type inside the assembly that would be registered by the `RegisterAssembly` method. This means that the returned array has a `Type` object for every public and COM-visible class with a public default constructor.

The `RegisterAssembly` Method

`RegisterAssembly`, as you might have guessed, registers an assembly. It takes two parameters—an `Assembly` instance for the assembly to register, and an `AssemblyRegistrationFlags` enumeration value to customize the registration process. It returns true if types were registered successfully, or false if the assembly has no types that are appropriate to be registered by COM. For example, this would occur if every type was non-public, COM-invisible, or a class without a public default constructor.

Besides entering the standard registry entries, `RegisterAssembly` invokes any custom registration functions defined by types using the `ComRegisterFunctionAttribute` custom attribute.

The `RegisterTypeForComClients` Method

`RegisterTypeForComClients` is equivalent to calling the `CoRegisterClassObject` COM API. It takes two parameters, a `System.Type` instance and a `System.Guid` instance. Calling this method registers the class factory for the specified type using the GUID passed as the second parameter.

You should avoid this method due to subtle threading behavior. If the current thread's state has not already been initialized, calling this method causes it to be set to MTA!

The `TypeRepresentsComType` Method

The `TypeRepresentsComType` method returns true if the input type is marked as `ComImport` (or if it derives from the `ComImport` type and has the same GUID), and false otherwise. It takes a single `System.Type` instance as input. See Chapter 22 for a comparison of all the .NET Framework methods for checking whether an object is a COM object.

This method is useful for creating registry files because the registry entries differ based on whether the type is marked with `ComImport`. For `ComImport` types, the only keys added are `Class`, `Assembly`, `RuntimeVersion`, and possibly `CodeBase`, under the `InprocServer32` key.

The `TypeRequiresRegistration` Method

`TypeRequiresRegistration` simply returns true if the input type would be registered by a call to `RegisterAssembly`, and false otherwise. It takes a single `System.Type` instance as input.

The `UnregisterAssembly` Method

`UnregisterAssembly` is the method that unregisters an assembly. It takes only one parameter— an `Assembly` instance for the assembly to unregister. It returns true if types were unregistered successfully, or false if the assembly has no types that were registered.

Besides removing the standard registry entries, `UnregisterAssembly` invokes any custom unregistration functions defined by types using the `ComUnregisterFunctionAttribute` custom attribute.

The `RuntimeEnvironment` Class

This class has four static (`Shared` in VB .NET) members that provide information about the Common Language Runtime that's running in the current process. (Although multiple CLRs can run simultaneously on the same computer, only one can be running in a given process.) These members aren't directly related to COM Interoperability and PInvoke and have nothing to do with unmanaged code, but they can be helpful nonetheless in scenarios requiring knowledge of the CLR's whereabouts. The members are:

- The `SystemConfigurationFile` property. This is a read-only string property that returns the fully qualified name of the currently-running CLR's configuration file. For example, it might return a string that looks like the following:

  `C:\Windows\Microsoft.NET\Framework\v1.2.3456\config\machine.config`

  Using this property requires `FileIOPermission` with the `PathDiscovery` flag.

- The `FromGlobalAccessCache` method. This method takes a single `System.Reflection.Assembly` parameter and returns true if the assembly was loaded from the Global *Assembly* Cache, or false otherwise. (The "Global Access Cache" name is just a historical artifact.)

- The `GetRuntimeDirectory` method. This parameter-less method returns a string containing the directory in which the currently-running CLR resides. Because multiple CLRs can run on the same computer side-by-side, the directory contains the CLR's version number, for example:

  `C:\Windows\Microsoft.NET\Framework\v1.2.3456\`

  Using this method requires `FileIOPermission` with the `PathDiscovery` flag.

A

System.Runtime.
InteropServices
REFERENCE

- The `GetSystemVersion` method. This parameter-less method returns a string containing the version of the currently running CLR. This string has the format *"vVersionNumber"* to match how the version is used in the path returned by `GetRuntimeDirectory`. For example, `GetSystemVersion` might return a string like the following:

```
v1.2.3456
```

The `SafeArrayRankMismatchException` Exception

This exception is thrown by the CLR when an unmanaged component attempts to pass a `SAFEARRAY` parameter or field with a different number of dimensions than the .NET array parameter or field is defined with. For example, a simple, one-dimensional array as a .NET parameter or field is exposed to COM as a `SAFEARRAY` by default, which has no static rank encoded in its type information. If a COM client attempted to pass a multi-dimensional array, this exception would be thrown.

There's a second scenario in which this exception is thrown. If a COM client instead passed a `SAFEARRAY` with the right number of dimensions but the wrong bounds (for instance, a 1-based `SAFEARRAY` passed to managed code expecting a standard 0-based array), `SafeArrayRankMismatchException` is thrown. Therefore, this applies to bounds in addition to rank.

The message that always accompanies `SafeArrayRankMismatchException` is, "SafeArray cannot be marshaled to this array type because it has either nonzero lower bounds or multiple dimensions."

`SafeArrayRankMismatchException` derives from `System.SystemException`, and should never be thrown by an application. Its protected `HResult` property (which can be exposed to COM when the exception is thrown) has the value `COR_E_SAFEARRAYRANKMISMATCH`, defined by the .NET Framework SDK as 0x80131538.

The `SafeArrayTypeMismatchException` Exception

This exception is thrown by the CLR when an unmanaged component attempts to pass a `SAFEARRAY` parameter or field with a different element type than what the .NET array parameter or field is defined with. For example, a COM client attempting to pass a `SAFEARRAY` with type `VT_BSTR` (an array of strings) to managed code expecting an array of integers causes this exception to be thrown.

> **CAUTION**
>
> In version 1.0 of the .NET Framework, this exception is always thrown when attempting to marshal a `SAFEARRAY` of `CURRENCY` types between unmanaged code and managed code. To work around this, you can use do-it-yourself marshaling, as shown in Chapter 6.

SAFEARRAYs created using the `SafeArrayCreateEx` or `SafeArrayCreateVectorEx` COM methods describe their element type. SAFEARRAYs created using the earlier `SafeArrayCreate` or `SafeArrayCreateVector` COM methods do not, so the CLR checks the element size of such arrays to determine whether the element type matches. For this reason, certain SAFEARRAY instances can be passed as .NET arrays with a little more flexibility than others, depending on how they were originally created.

The message that always accompanies `SafeArrayTypeMismatchException` is, "Specified array was not of the expected type."

`SafeArrayTypeMismatchException` derives from `System.SystemException`, and should never be thrown by an application. Its protected `HResult` property (which can be exposed to COM when the exception is thrown) has the value `COR_E_SAFEARRAYTYPEMISMATCH`, defined by the .NET Framework SDK as 0x80131533.

The `SEHException` Exception

Whereas a `COMException` is thrown when a COM object returns a failure `HRESULT`, an `SEHException` is thrown when an unmanaged component throws a C++-style Structured Exception Handling (SEH) exception. It has an `ErrorCode` property that represents the exception's error code. This is not necessarily an `HRESULT` value.

This exception type has a `CanResume` method that returns true if the exception is recoverable (if execution can continue without problems), and false otherwise. It only returns true when a filtered exception handler has corrected the problem that caused the exception in the first place.

CAUTION

In version 1.0 of the .NET Framework, the functionality of recovering from an `SEHException` is not yet implemented. Therefore, `CanResume` always returns false.

`SEHException` derives from `ExternalException` (which derives from `System.SystemException`), and should never be thrown by an application. Its protected `HResult` property (which can be exposed to COM when the exception is thrown) has the generic value `E_FAIL` (0x80004005).

The `STATSTG` Value Type

This is a .NET definition of the unmanaged `STATSTG` structure used by the `IStream` COM interface. In the .NET Framework, this definition is used by the `UCOMIStream.Stat` method.

For more information, consult MSDN Online for information about the original `STATSTG` structure.

The `StructLayoutAttribute` Pseudo-Custom Attribute

This pseudo-custom attribute can be marked on a value type or reference type to control how its members are laid out from the perspective of unmanaged clients.

The attribute has two constructors—one that takes a 16-bit integer and one that takes a `LayoutKind` enumeration. The latter constructor should always be used. The type library importer always marks imported value types with this attribute and the `LayoutKind.Sequential` setting because this accurately describes structures from a type library. The C#, VB .NET, and C++ compilers all mark value types with sequential layout by default unless the user overrides the setting with `StructLayoutAttribute`.

Besides the `LayoutKind` enumeration value, `StructLayoutAttribute` has three named parameters:

- `CharSet`. This can be set to a value from the `System.Runtime.InteropServices.CharSet` enumeration. This affects whether string fields are marshaled as `LPSTR` or `LPWSTR` by default. Any string fields explicitly marked with `MarshalAsAttribute` are not affected by this setting. The C#, VB .NET, and C++ compilers set this to `CharSet.Ansi` by default.

- `Pack`. This must be set to 0, 1, 2, 4, 8, 16, 32, 64, or 128. It affects how a structure's fields are aligned along byte boundaries. The default packing size for value types defined in managed code is 8, although the packing size of unmanaged structures is often 4. A packing size of zero tells the CLR to use a packing size specific to the current operating system.

- `Size`. This can be set to an integer value that specifies the total size of the structure, in bytes. This must be set to a number greater than or equal to the default structure size (the sum of its fields sizes taking into account how fields are packed). This can be useful for extending the memory occupied by a structure for direct unmanaged access, such as dealing with unions that can't be directly represented in metadata.

For more information, see the `LayoutKind` enumeration listed earlier in this section, and Chapter 19.

The `SYSKIND` Enumeration

This is a .NET definition of the unmanaged `SYSKIND` enumeration used by such COM APIs as `LoadTypeLibEx`. In the .NET Framework, this definition is used by the `TYPELIBATTR` structure.

For more information, consult MSDN Online for information about the original `SYSKIND` enumeration.

The TYPEATTR Value Type

This is a .NET definition of the unmanaged TYPEATTR structure used by the ITypeInfo COM interface. In the .NET Framework, this definition is not directly used by UCOMITypeInfo, because the methods that would use the type (GetTypeAttr and ReleaseTypeAttr) are defined to use the System.IntPtr type instead. However, if using these methods of UCOMITypeInfo, you'll want to use the TYPEATTR type in conjunction with Marshal.PtrToStructure or Marshal.StructureToPtr to convert it to and from System.IntPtr.

For more information, consult MSDN Online for information about the original TYPEATTR structure.

The TYPEDESC Value Type

This is a .NET definition of the unmanaged TYPEDESC structure used by the ELEMDESC and TYPEATTR COM structures. In the .NET Framework, this definition is used by .NET definitions of ELEMDESC and TYPEATTR.

For more information, consult MSDN Online for information about the original TYPEDESC structure.

The TYPEFLAGS Enumeration

This is a .NET definition of the unmanaged TYPEFLAGS enumeration used by the TYPEATTR COM structure. In the .NET Framework, this definition is used by the .NET definition of TYPEATTR. This enumeration defines the same values as the TypeLibTypeFlags enumeration, but with slightly different names (the original names). The one difference is that TYPEFLAGS is a 16-bit enumeration, whereas TypeLibTypeFlags has a 32-bit underlying type.

For more information, consult MSDN Online for information about the original TYPEFLAGS enumeration.

The TYPEKIND Enumeration

This is a .NET definition of the unmanaged TYPEKIND enumeration used by the ITypeInfo COM interface. In the .NET Framework, this definition is used by the TYPEATTR value type and the UCOMITypeInfo.GetTypeInfoType method.

For more information, consult MSDN Online for information about the original TYPEKIND structure.

The TYPELIBATTR Value Type

This is a .NET definition of the unmanaged TLIBATTR structure (notice the name change!) used by the ITypeLib COM interface. In the .NET Framework, this definition is not directly used by UCOMITypeLib, because the methods that would use the type (GetLibAttr and ReleaseTLibAttr) are defined to use the System.IntPtr type instead. However, if using these methods of UCOMITypeLib, you'll want to use the TYPELIBATTR type in conjunction with Marshal.PtrToStructure or Marshal.StructureToPtr to convert it to and from System.IntPtr.

This value type is also used by the AxImporter class in the System.Windows.Forms.Design namespace, as the type of its GeneratedTypeLibAttributes property and a parameter of its GetFileOfTypeLib method.

For more information, consult MSDN Online for information about the original TLIBATTR (not TYPELIBATTR!) structure.

The TypeLibConverter Class

This class, which implements ITypeLibConverter, contains methods used to convert a type library to an assembly and vice versa. These actions are commonly referred to as importing and exporting a type library. The TLBIMP.EXE, TLBEXP.EXE, and REGASM.EXE SDK tools and Visual Studio .NET use TypeLibConverter to import and export type libraries.

The TypeLibConverter methods are described in the following sections. For more information about any them, see Chapter 22.

The ConvertAssemblyToTypeLib Method

This method takes a System.Reflection.Assembly instance as input and returns a System.Object that represents an in-memory type library (an object that implements the ITypeLib COM interface). Besides the input Assembly parameter, this method also expects a string with the output type library filename—which can be null (Nothing in VB .NET) to accept the default, a TypeLibExporterFlags enumeration value to customize the process, and an object that implements the ITypeLibExporterNotifySink interface.

Managed clients can save the returned object as a type library file by casting it to UCOMITypeLib and calling its SaveAllChanges method.

The ConvertTypeLibToAssembly Method

This method takes an in-memory type library (an object that implements the ITypeLib COM interface), and returns a System.Reflection.Emit.AssemblyBuilder instance. An AssemblyBuilder is a dynamic assembly, and can be saved by calling its Save method.

Besides the input `System.Object` parameter for the in-memory type library, `ConvertTypeLibToAssembly` expects several additional parameters. Two overloads of this method exist, but the one that should always be used has the following additional parameters:

- `asmFileName`. This is a string that can be set to the desired filename of the output assembly, or null (`Nothing` in VB .NET) to accept the default filename.

- `flags`. This is a `TypeLibImporterFlags` enumeration value that customizes the importing process.

- `notifySink`. This is an object that implements the `ITypeLibImporterNotifySink` interface that is used for callbacks during import.

- `publicKey`. This is an array of bytes that can contain a public key used for producing a strong named assembly with a public key only, or null for producing a simply named assembly (or if `keyPair` is non-null).

- `keyPair`. This is a `StrongNameKeyPair` instance that can be used to produce a strong named assembly, or null for producing a simply named assembly (or if `publicKey` is non-null).

- `asmNamespace`. This is a string that can be set to the desired namespace of the output assembly, or null to accept the default.

- `asmVersion`. This is a `System.Version` instance that can be used to control the output assembly's version, or null to accept the default.

The `GetPrimaryInteropAssembly` Method

The `GetPrimaryInteropAssembly` method is the official means of determining whether a Primary Interop Assembly is registered on the current computer. This method returns true if one exists, and false otherwise. It requires you to pass a `System.Guid` representing the corresponding type library's LIBID, plus the major and minor version numbers and locale identifier (LCID) of the corresponding type library. Via two string by-reference parameters, it returns the assembly name and, if it exists, a codebase value if the method returned true.

The `TypeLibExporterFlags` Enumeration

This enumeration is passed to `ITypeLibConverter.ConvertAssemblyToTypeLib` to control the process of type library export. It has a single value that may be set as a bit flag—`OnlyReferenceRegistered`. This flag should be set when you want the exporter to only look for dependent type libraries in the registry rather than also looking in the same directory as the input assembly.

For more information, see Chapter 22.

The `TypeLibFuncAttribute` Custom Attribute

This custom attribute is used by the type library importer to mark imported members with their original flags from the type library definition. Any flags that have meaning in the .NET world already present themselves in a different way in metadata. However, this attribute is useful for discovering information about imported members that would have been lost in metadata if it weren't for this custom attribute.

The attribute has two constructors—one that takes a 16-bit integer and one that takes a `TypeLibFuncFlags` enumeration. The latter constructor should always be used. Be aware that the type library exporter ignores this custom attribute when exporting member definitions.

For more information, see the `TypeLibFuncFlags` enumeration listed next, and Chapter 21.

The `TypeLibFuncFlags` Enumeration

This enumeration is used by `TypeLibFuncAttribute` to describe various attributes of an imported member definition. It has all the same values as the `FUNCFLAGS` enumeration, but has a 32-bit underlying type rather than 16-bit and fields with slightly different names.

For more information about this enumeration's values, consult MSDN Online for information about the original `FUNCFLAGS` enumeration.

The `TypeLibImporterFlags` Enumeration

This enumeration is passed to `ITypeLibConverter.ConvertTypeLibToAssembly` to control the process of type library import. It has the following values that are used as bit flags:

- `PrimaryInteropAssembly`. This flag should be set when you want to create a Primary Interop Assembly. `TLBIMP.EXE` exposes this as its `/primary` option.
- `SafeArrayAsSystemArray`. This flag should be set when you want to import all `SAFEARRAY` types as `System.Array` types instead of one-dimensional arrays. This is handy when a type library contains `SAFEARRAY` parameters that are multi-dimensional or have non-zero lower bounds, because it makes their managed signatures usable. `TLBIMP.EXE` exposes this as its `/sysarray` option.
- `UnsafeInterfaces`. This flag should be set when you want every imported class and interface to be marked with `System.Security.SuppressUnmanagedCodeSecurityAttribute`. "UnsafeInterfaces" is a bit of a misnomer because it applies to classes as well. This attribute tells the .NET security system to not do a run-time security check for `UnmanagedCode` permission (which involves a stack walk) when calling into unmanaged code. Instead, the check for `UnmanagedCode` is only done at "link time"—during just-in-time compilation, regardless of whether the class implementing an unsafe interface is managed or unmanaged. `TLBIMP.EXE` exposes this as its `/unsafe` option.

For more information, see Chapter 22.

The `TypeLibTypeAttribute` Custom Attribute

This custom attribute is used by the type library importer to mark imported types with their original flags from the type library definition. Any flags that have meaning in the .NET world already present themselves in a different way in metadata. However, this attribute is useful for discovering information about imported types that would have been lost in metadata if it weren't for this custom attribute.

The attribute has two constructors—one that takes a 16-bit integer and one that takes a `TypeLibTypeFlags` enumeration. The latter constructor should always be used. Be aware that the type library exporter ignores this custom attribute when exporting type definitions.

For more information, see the `TypeLibTypeFlags` enumeration listed next, and Chapter 21.

The `TypeLibTypeFlags` Enumeration

This enumeration is used by `TypeLibTypeAttribute` to describe various attributes of an imported member definition. It has all the same values as the `TYPEFLAGS` enumeration, but has a 32-bit underlying type rather than 16-bit and fields with slightly different names.

For more information about this enumeration's values, consult MSDN Online for information about the original `TYPEFLAGS` enumeration.

The `TypeLibVarAttribute` Custom Attribute

This custom attribute is used by the type library importer to mark imported structure fields with their original flags from the type library definition. Any flags that have meaning in the .NET world already present themselves in a different way in metadata. However, this attribute is useful for discovering information about imported fields that would have been lost in metadata if it weren't for this custom attribute.

The attribute has two constructors—one that takes a 16-bit integer and one that takes a `TypeLibVarFlags` enumeration. The latter constructor should always be used. Be aware that the type library exporter ignores this custom attribute when exporting field definitions.

For more information, see the `TypeLibVarFlags` enumeration listed next, and Chapter 21.

The `TypeLibVarFlags` Enumeration

This enumeration is used by `TypeLibVarAttribute` to describe various attributes of an imported member definition. It has all the same values as the `VARFLAGS` enumeration, but has a 32-bit underlying type rather than 16-bit and fields with slightly different names.

For more information about this enumeration's values, consult MSDN Online for information about the original `VARFLAGS` enumeration.

The `UCOMIBindCtx` Interface

This is a .NET definition of the `IBindCtx` COM interface. In the .NET Framework, this interface is used by several methods of the `UCOMIMoniker` interface. This is a "complete" interface definition that requires no workarounds when using it (such as handling `System.IntPtr` types). All of its COM parameter types, such as `IEnumString`, `BIND_OPTS`, and `IRunningObjectTable`, have corresponding .NET definitions.

For more information, consult MSDN Online for information about the original `IBindCtx` interface.

The `UCOMIConnectionPoint` Interface

This is a .NET definition of the `IConnectionPoint` COM interface. In the .NET Framework, this interface is used by the `UCOMIConnectionPointContainer` and `UCOMIEnumConnectionPoints` interfaces. This is a "complete" interface definition that requires no workarounds when using it (such as handling `System.IntPtr` types). All of its COM parameter types, such as `IEnumConnections` and `IConnectionPointContainer`, have corresponding .NET definitions.

For more information, consult MSDN Online for information about the original `IConnectionPoint` interface.

The `UCOMIConnectionPointContainer` Interface

This is a .NET definition of the `IConnectionPointContainer` COM interface. In the .NET Framework, this interface is used by the `UCOMIConnectionPoint.GetConnectionPointContainer` method. This is a "complete" interface definition that requires no workarounds when using it (such as handling `System.IntPtr` types). All of its COM parameter types, such as `IEnumConnectionPoints` and `IConnectionPoint`, have corresponding .NET definitions.

For more information, consult MSDN Online for information about the original `IConnectionPointContainer` interface.

The `UCOMIEnumConnectionPoints` Interface

This is a .NET definition of the `IEnumConnectionPoints` COM interface. In the .NET Framework, this interface is used by the `UCOMIConnectionPointContainer.EnumConnectionPoints` method. This is a "complete" interface definition that requires no workarounds when using it (such as handling `System.IntPtr` types). All of its COM parameter types, such as `IEnumConnectionPoints` and `IConnectionPoint`, have corresponding .NET definitions.

For more information, consult MSDN Online for information about the original `IEnumConnectionPoints` interface.

The `UCOMIEnumConnections` Interface

This is a .NET definition of the `IEnumConnections` COM interface. In the .NET Framework, this interface is used by the `UCOMIConnectionPoint.EnumConnections` method. This is a "complete" interface definition that requires no workarounds when using it (such as handling `System.IntPtr` types). All of its COM parameter types, such as `CONNECTDATA`, have corresponding .NET definitions.

For more information, consult MSDN Online for information about the original `IEnumConnections` interface.

The `UCOMIEnumMoniker` Interface

This is a .NET definition of the `IEnumMoniker` COM interface. In the .NET Framework, this interface is used by the `UCOMIMoniker` and `UCOMIRunningObjectTable` interfaces. This is a "complete" interface definition that requires no workarounds when using it (such as handling `System.IntPtr` types). All of its COM parameter types, such as `IMoniker`, have corresponding .NET definitions.

For more information, consult MSDN Online for information about the original `IEnumMoniker` interface.

The `UCOMIEnumString` Interface

This is a .NET definition of the `IEnumString` COM interface. In the .NET Framework, this interface is used by the `UCOMIBindCtx.EnumObjectParam` method. This is a "complete" interface definition that requires no workarounds when using it (such as handling `System.IntPtr` types).

For more information, consult MSDN Online for information about the original `IEnumString` interface.

The `UCOMIEnumVARIANT` Interface

This is a .NET definition of the `IEnumVARIANT` COM interface. In the .NET Framework, this interface is implemented by `EnumVariantViewOfEnumerator` in the `System.Runtime.InteropServices.CustomMarshalers` namespace, an adapter object used by the custom marshaler that bridges `IEnumVARIANT` with the .NET `IEnumerator` interface.

A

System.Runtime.
InteropServices
REFERENCE

CAUTION

Two methods of UCOMIEnumVARIANT have incorrect definitions in version 1.0 of the .NET Framework. Its Clone method has a 32-bit integer parameter instead of a UCOMIEnumVARIANT parameter. Also, its Next method has three 32-bit integer parameters rather than an integer, a System.Object (representing a VARIANT), and an integer. On 32-bit platforms, you could construct a System.IntPtr from the 32-bit value and use the standard workarounds (such as Marshal.GetObjectForNativeVariant), but this definition won't work on 64-bit platforms. If you require the functionality from Next or Clone, or plan on writing a .NET class that implements the IEnumVARIANT COM interface, you should consider writing your own private .NET definition of IEnumVARIANT.

For more information, consult MSDN Online for information about the original IEnumVARIANT interface.

The UCOMIMoniker Interface

This is a .NET definition of the IMoniker COM interface. In the .NET Framework, this interface is used by the UCOMIEnumMoniker and UCOMIRunningObjectTable interfaces. This is a "complete" interface definition that requires no workarounds when using it (such as handling System.IntPtr types). All of its COM parameter types, such as IBindCtx, IEnumMoniker, FILETIME, and IStream, have corresponding .NET definitions. Some parameters that have an unmanaged type of void** are represented as a by-reference System.Object (marked with MarshalAs(UnmanagedType.Interface)) rather than a System.IntPtr type, which works fine because the value should always point to a COM interface pointer.

CAUTION

The COM IMoniker definition derives from the IPersistStream COM interface, which derives from the IPersist COM interface. Because IPersistStream and IPersist do not have a .NET definition in System.Runtime.InteropServices, UCOMIMoniker does not claim to derive from any interfaces (although it contains the methods of IPersistStream and IPersist). Therefore, a .NET object that implements UCOMIMoniker does not successfully respond to COM QueryInterface calls for the IPersistStream or IPersist interfaces unless the class author has done some additional work. See Chapter 14 for more details.

For more information, consult MSDN Online for information about the original `IMoniker` interface.

The `UCOMIPersistFile` Interface

This is a .NET definition of the `IPersistFile` COM interface. This is a "complete" interface definition that requires no workarounds when using it (such as handling `System.IntPtr` types).

> **CAUTION**
>
> The COM `IPersistFile` definition derives from the `IPersist` COM interface. Because `IPersist` does not have a .NET definition in `System.Runtime.InteropServices`, `UCOMIPersistFile` does not claim to derive from any interfaces (although it contains the methods of `IPersist`). Therefore, a .NET object that implements `UCOMIPersistFile` does not successfully respond to COM `QueryInterface` calls for the `IPersist` interface unless the class author has done some additional work. See Chapter 14 for more details.

For more information, consult MSDN Online for information about the original `IPersistFile` interface.

The `UCOMIRunningObjectTable` Interface

This is a .NET definition of the `IRunningObjectTable` COM interface. In the .NET Framework, this interface is used by the `UCOMIBindCtx.GetRunningObjectTable` method. This is a "complete" interface definition that requires no workarounds when using it (such as handling `System.IntPtr` types). All of its COM parameter types, such as `IEnumMoniker`, `IMoniker`, and `FILETIME`, have corresponding .NET definitions.

One aspect of the interface definition that could be more user-friendly is the fact that the first parameter of `UCOMIRunningObjectTable.Register` is a plain 32-bit integer rather than an enumeration defining its two possible values: `ROTFLAGS_REGISTRATIONKEEPSALIVE` (1) and `ROTFLAGS_ALLOWANYCLIENT` (2). However, the original COM definition of `IRunningObjectTable.Register` defines its first parameter as a plain `DWORD`, so the .NET definition is faithful to the original.

For more information, consult MSDN Online for information about the original `IRunningObjectTable` interface.

The `UCOMIStream` Interface

This is a .NET definition of the `IStream` COM interface. In the .NET Framework, this interface is used by the `UCOMIMoniker` interface. This is a "complete" interface definition that requires no workarounds when using it (such as handling `System.IntPtr` types). All of its COM parameter types, such as `IMoniker`, have corresponding .NET definitions.

One aspect of the interface definition that could be more user-friendly is the fact that `UCOMIStream.Commit`'s parameter, the last parameter of `UCOMIStream.LockRegion` and `UCOMIStream.UnlockRegion`, the second parameter of `UCOMIStream.Seek`, and the last parameter of `UCOMIStream.Stat` are all plain 32-bit integers rather than enumerations defining their possible values. These enumerations are defined in the unmanaged world as `STGC`, `LOCKTYPE`, `STREAM_SEEK`, and `STATFLAG`, respectively. However, the original COM definition of these methods on the `IStream` interface defines all of these parameters as plain `DWORD` types, so the .NET definition is faithful to the original.

> **CAUTION**
>
> The COM `IStream` definition derives from the `ISequentialStream` COM interface. Because `ISequentialStream` does not have a .NET definition in `System.Runtime.InteropServices`, `UCOMIStream` does not claim to derive from any interfaces (although it contains the methods of `ISequentialStream`). Therefore, a .NET object that implements `UCOMIStream` does not successfully respond to COM `QueryInterface` calls for the `ISequentialStream` interface unless the class author has done some additional work. See Chapter 14 for more details.

For more information, consult MSDN Online for information about the original `IStream` interface.

The `UCOMITypeComp` Interface

This is a .NET definition of the `ITypeComp` COM interface. In the .NET Framework, this interface is used by the `UCOMITypeInfo.GetTypeComp` and `UCOMITypeLib.GetTypeComp` methods. This is a "complete" interface definition that requires no workarounds when using it (such as handling `System.IntPtr` types). All of its COM parameter types, such as `ITypeInfo`, `DESCKIND`, and `BINDPTR`, have corresponding .NET definitions.

One aspect of the interface definition that could be more user-friendly is the fact that the third parameter of UCOMITypeComp.Bind is a plain 16-bit integer rather than an INVOKEKIND enumeration defining its possible values. However, the original COM definition of ITypeComp.Bind defines its first parameter as a plain unsigned short, so the .NET definition is faithful to the original signature (except for changing the unsigned type to a CLS-compliant signed type).

For more information, consult MSDN Online for information about the original ITypeComp interface.

The UCOMITypeInfo Interface

This is a .NET definition of the ITypeInfo COM interface. In the .NET Framework, this interface is used by the UCOMITypeComp and UCOMITypeLib interfaces, plus the Marshal.GetTypeInfoName method. This interface can also be used with the Marshal.GetITypeInfoForType and Marshal.GetTypeForITypeInfo methods, although those signatures use a System.IntPtr type to represent the interface. Therefore, using Marshal.GetIUnknownForObject and Marshal.GetObjectForIUnknown need to be used to use these methods with a UCOMITypeInfo instance.

The UCOMITypeInfo has a handful of members using System.IntPtr types, requiring do-it-yourself marshaling using the Marshal class. For example, the AddressOfMember uses a by-reference IntPtr parameter to represent the unmanaged signature's void** parameter. This is necessary because the parameter doesn't point to a COM interface. The CreateInstance method, on the other hand, has an unmanaged void** parameter represented as a by-reference System.Object (marked with MarshalAs(UnmanagedType.IUnknown)) because the value should always point to an IUnknown interface pointer.

The second parameter of GetFuncDesc, GetTypeAttr, and GetVarDesc is an IntPtr type instead of FUNCDESC, TYPEATTR, and VARDESC, respectively. ReleaseFuncDesc, ReleaseTypeAttr, and ReleaseVarDesc also use an IntPtr parameter rather than FUNCDESC, TYPEATTR, and VARDESC, respectively. This is necessary because these unmanaged types use a custom memory allocation scheme, so the standard Interop Marshaling treatment would not work.

An aspect of the interface definition that could be more user-friendly is the fact that the second parameter of GetImplTypeFlags is a 32-bit integer rather than an IMPLTYPEFLAGS enumeration, but the unmanaged definition also defines the parameter as a plain integer, so the .NET definition is faithful to the original signature.

For more information, consult MSDN Online for information about the original ITypeInfo interface.

The `UCOMITypeLib` Interface

This is a .NET definition of the `ITypeLib` COM interface. In the .NET Framework, this interface is used by the `UCOMITypeInfo` interface, a few methods of the `Marshal` class, and a few methods of the `AxImporter` class from the `System.Windows.Forms.Design` namespace. It's also useful with methods of the `TypeLibConverter` class, although the relevant parameters are typed as `System.Object` rather than `UCOMITypeLib`.

`GetLibAttr` and `ReleaseTLibAttr` have an `IntPtr` parameter instead of the .NET `TYPELIBATTR` structure (which represents the unmanaged `TLIBATTR` structure) because the unmanaged type uses a custom memory allocation scheme, so the standard Interop Marshaling treatment would not work.

> **CAUTION**
>
> The definition of `UCOMITypeLib.FindName` is incorrect in version 1.0 of the .NET Framework. Its second-to-last parameter (`rgMemId`) is supposed to be an array of MEMBERIDs (32-bit integers), but instead is defined to be a single 32-bit integer. You can work around this on 32-bit platforms by converting an `IntPtr` that represents a pointer to an array into a 32-bit integer to pass to the `FindName` method, but this will not work on 64-bit platforms. If you want to call `FindName`, or if you plan on writing a .NET class that implements the `ITypeLib` COM interface, you should consider writing your own private .NET definition of `ITypeLib`.

For more information, consult MSDN Online for information about the original `ITypeLib` interface.

The `UnknownWrapper` Class

The `UnknownWrapper` class can be used to pass a .NET `Object` type inside a `VARIANT` and have COM see it as `VT_UNKNOWN` (any COM object) rather than `VT_DISPATCH` (a COM object implementing `IDispatch`). Although `Object` types are automatically transformed to COM `IUnknown` types when passed early-bound to COM signatures expecting `IUnknown`, the CLR can't know to do this transformation when late binding or passing a type inside a `VARIANT` because the COM component's expectations aren't captured in the type information.

By default, a .NET object passed in a `VARIANT` appears with the `VT_DISPATCH` type unless the object doesn't implement `IDispatch`. This occurs when the class is COM-invisible (including being non-public), or if it's marked with `ClassInterface(ClassInterfaceType.None)` and the interface chosen as the default interface is marked with `InterfaceType`

(`ComInterfaceType.InterfaceIsIUnknown`). Most COM clients shouldn't care if they expect a `VT_UNKNOWN VARIANT` and receive a `VT_DISPATCH VARIANT`, but using this wrapper can satisfy those that do.

The `UnknownWrapper` class has one constructor that takes an `Object` type. The `Object` passed must not be a value type or an array, otherwise an `ArgumentException` is thrown.

The following code demonstrates the use of this type when calling a COM method whose managed signature has a generic `System.Object` parameter:

C#:

```
MyClass c = ...;
// Pass a VARIANT containing an IDispatch pointer (VT_DISPATCH)
obj.Method(c);
// Pass a VARIANT containing an IUnknown pointer (VT_UNKNOWN)
obj.Method(new UnknownWrapper(c));
```

Visual Basic .NET:

```
Dim c As MyClass = ...
' Pass a VARIANT containing an IDispatch pointer (VT_DISPATCH)
obj.Method(c)
' Pass a VARIANT containing an IUnknown pointer (VT_UNKNOWN)
obj.Method(New UnknownWrapper(c))
```

C++:

```
MyClass* c = ...;
// Pass a VARIANT containing an IDispatch pointer (VT_DISPATCH)
obj->Method(c);
// Pass a VARIANT containing an IUnknown pointer (VT_UNKNOWN)
obj->Method(new UnknownWrapper(c));
```

For more information, consult Chapter 3.

The `UnmanagedType` Enumeration

The `UnmanagedType` enumeration is used by the `MarshalAsAttribute` pseudo-custom attribute to specify how a .NET data type should be marshaled to unmanaged code. These enumeration values can be categorized as follows:

Strings

AnsiBStr	BStr	ByValTStr
LPStr	LPWStr	TBStr
LPTStr (PInvoke only)	VBByRefStr	

Arrays

ByValArray	LPArray	SafeArray

Types that Don't Exist in .NET

Currency	Error	IDispatch	IUnknown

Simple Blittable Types

I1	I2	I4	I8	R4
R8	U1	U2	U4	U8

Booleans

Bool	VariantBool

Miscellaneous

CustomMarshaler	FunctionPtr	Interface
Struct (for VARIANT)	AsAny (PInvoke only)	

Unused

LPStruct	SysInt	SysUInt

I list LPStruct under "unused" because its name is misleading, but it can be used in one scenario. It can be placed on a by-value Guid parameter in a PInvoke signature to marshal it as an in-only pointer to the Guid. An example of this is shown in Chapter 19.

For a complete description of the meaning of these UnmanagedType values, including which can be used on which .NET data types, consult Chapter 12. For the special IL Assembler syntax of the UnmanagedType enumeration values, see Chapter 7.

The VARDESC Value Type

This is a .NET definition of the unmanaged VARDESC structure used by the ITypeInfo COM interface. In the .NET Framework, this definition is not directly used by UCOMITypeInfo, because the methods that would use the type (GetVarDesc and ReleaseVarDesc) are defined to use the System.IntPtr type instead. However, if using these methods of UCOMITypeInfo, you'll want to use the VARDESC type in conjunction with Marshal.PtrToStructure or Marshal.StructureToPtr to convert it to and from System.IntPtr.

In version 1.0 of the .NET Framework, the definition of `System.Runtime.`
`InteropServices.VARDESC` doesn't correctly match the unmanaged definition, so it
should not be used in managed code. Instead, you could use your own definition like
the following (in C#):

```csharp
internal struct VARDESC
{
    public int memid;
    public IntPtr lpstrSchema;
    public DESCUNION descUnion;
    public ELEMDESC elemdescVar;
    public short wVarFlags;
    public VARKIND varkind;
}
```

where `DESCUNION` and `VARKIND` are defined as follows:

```csharp
[StructLayout(LayoutKind.Explicit)]
internal struct DESCUNION
{
    [FieldOffset(0)] public int oInst;
    [FieldOffset(0)] public IntPtr lpvarValue;
}

internal enum VARKIND
{
    VAR_PERINSTANCE,
    VAR_STATIC,
    VAR_CONST,
    VAR_DISPATCH
}
```

For more information, consult MSDN Online for information about the original `VARDESC` structure.

The `VarEnum` Enumeration

This is a .NET definition of the unmanaged `VARENUM` structure (notice the change in case).
This enumeration is used in OLE Automation to describe the type of a `VARIANT`, `SAFEARRAY`,
`TYPEDESC`, or OLE property set. In the .NET Framework, this definition is used by the
`MarshalAsAttribute` pseudo-custom attribute's `SafeArraySubType` named parameter to
describe the unmanaged element type of an array's elements.

Although VarEnum has 44 values, about half of them are valid for a SAFEARRAY's element type. The following ten values are the ones commonly used to change the default marshaling behavior of SAFEARRAYs:

VT_BOOL	VT_CY	VT_DISPATCH	VT_ERROR	VT_I1
VT_INT	VT_UI1	VT_UINT	VT_UNKNOWN	VT_VARIANT

This is the only use of VarEnum by the Interop Marshaler. If you're performing do-it-yourself marshaling with hand-written VARIANT or SAFEARRAY structures, as shown in Chapter 6, this enumeration may come in handy.

The VARFLAGS Enumeration

This is a .NET definition of the unmanaged VARFLAGS enumeration. This enumeration defines the same values as the TypeLibVarFlags enumeration, but with slightly different names (the original names). The one difference is that VARFLAGS is a 16-bit enumeration, whereas TypeLibVarFlags has a 32-bit underlying type.

For more information, consult MSDN Online for information about the original VARFLAGS enumeration.

The System.Runtime.InteropServices. CustomMarshalers Namespace

This namespace contains a handful of custom marshalers that are included with the .NET Framework. These classes reside in the CustomMarshalers assembly (CustomMarshalers.dll).

The EnumerableToDispatchMarshaler Class

This custom marshaler marshals the COM IDispatch interface to the .NET System. Collections.IEnumerable interface and vice versa (when a member with a DISPID of -4 exists). It's used automatically by the CLR (without the use of MarshalAsAttribute) to enable the bridging of COM enumerators to .NET enumerators. When the type library importer creates a class that implements IEnumerable, it's the EnumerableToDispatchMarshaler custom marshaler that makes it work. When this custom marshaler is used, calling IEnumerable. GetEnumerator results in IDispatch.Invoke being called with DISPID -4, and vice versa.

The `EnumeratorToEnumVariantMarshaler` Class

This custom marshaler marshals the COM `IEnumVARIANT` interface to the .NET `System.Collections.IEnumerator` interface and vice versa. It's used automatically by the CLR (without the use of `MarshalAsAttribute`) to enable the bridging of COM enumerators to .NET enumerators. The `IEnumerator` type returned by an imported COM class's `GetEnumerator` method uses `EnumeratorToEnumVariantMarshaler` to map the calls to the `IEnumVARIANT` interface pointer returned by the COM object's member with DISPID -4.

The `IEnumerator.MoveNext` implementation exposed by the custom marshaler naturally maps to `IEnumVARIANT.Next`. The `IEnumerator.Reset` implementation calls `IEnumVARIANT.Reset`. The `IEnumerator.Current` implementation is handled entirely by the custom marshaler's adapter object because `IEnumVARIANT` doesn't have an analogous property.

In the reverse direction, the `IEnumVARIANT.Next` implementation exposed by the custom marshaler naturally maps to `IEnumerator.MoveNext`, and the `IEnumVARIANT.Skip` implementation also uses `IEnumerator.MoveNext` to provide its functionality. In this direction, `IEnumVARIANT.Reset` is not supported, so it always returns `S_FALSE` as the `IEnumVARIANT` contract requires. `IEnumVARIANT.Clone` is supported if the .NET object that implements `IEnumerator` also implements `ICloneable`. Otherwise, `E_FAIL` is returned.

The type library importer marks `IEnumerable.GetEnumerator` signatures with the appropriate `MarshalAsAttribute` with `UnmanagedType.CustomMarshaler`, but this isn't strictly necessary because the CLR always uses the custom marshaler with `GetEnumerator` methods anyway. This enables type library export to do the desired transformation without the .NET class author having to worry about using the custom marshaler explicitly.

The `ExpandoToDispatchExMarshaler` Class

This custom marshaler marshals the COM `IDispatchEx` interface to either the .NET `System.Runtime.InteropServices.Expando.IExpando` interface or `System.Reflection.IReflect` interface, and vice versa. This bridges the COM means of providing dynamic member addition and deletion with the .NET means. This custom marshaler is not used automatically by the CLR, so it must be used as follows:

C#:

```
void UseCustomMarshaler([MarshalAs(UnmanagedType.CustomMarshaler,
  MarshalTypeRef=typeof(ExpandoToDispatchExMarshaler))] IExpando expando);
```

Visual Basic .NET:

```
Sub UseCustomMarshaler(<MarshalAs(UnmanagedType.CustomMarshaler, _
  MarshalTypeRef:=GetType(ExpandoToDispatchExMarshaler))> expando As IExpando)
```

C++:

```
void UseCustomMarshaler([MarshalAs(UnmanagedType::CustomMarshaler,
  MarshalTypeRef=__typeof(ExpandoToDispatchExMarshaler))] IExpando* expando);
```

For the `IExpando` implementation exposed from `IDispatchEx`, calling `AddField` always throws a `NotSupportedException` because `IDispatchEx` only deals with properties and methods. Calling `AddMethod` also throws a `NotSupportedException`. Only properties can be added via the `AddProperty` method.

The `IExpando.RemoveMember` implementation that's exposed supports removing properties and methods, but not fields.

The `TypeToTypeInfoMarshaler` Class

This custom marshaler marshals the COM `ITypeInfo` interface to the .NET `System.Type` class and vice versa. The `ITypeInfo` interface exposed for a .NET type is based on the information that would appear in an exported type library. Likewise, the `Type` instance exposed for an `ITypeInfo` interface is based on the information that would appear in an imported assembly.

The type library importer marks `ITypeInfo` parameters with the appropriate `MarshalAsAttribute` with `UnmanagedType.CustomMarshaler` when converting signatures that use `ITypeInfo` parameters to signatures that use `Type` parameters.

This same conversion functionality can be accomplished without the custom marshaler, by calling `Marshal.GetITypeInfoForType` and `Marshal.GetTypeForITypeInfo`.

The `System.Runtime.InteropServices.Expando` Namespace

This namespace only contains a single type—the `IExpando` interface. This interface derives from `System.Reflection.IReflect`, adding the capabilities of dynamic member addition and deletion. There are no available classes in the .NET Framework that implement this interface, but the `ExpandoToDispatchExMarshaler` custom marshaler from the previous section provides an implementation of this interface for COM objects that implement `IDispatchEx`, a COM interface that also provides dynamic member addition and deletion.

This interface has four methods:

- `AddField`. This takes a string parameter with a field's name and returns a `FieldInfo` instance that represents the newly added field.

- `AddMethod`. This takes a string parameter with a method's name and a `Delegate` instance with the desired method's signature, and returns a `MethodInfo` instance that represents the newly added method.

- `AddProperty`. This takes a string parameter with a property's name and returns a `PropertyInfo` instance that represents the newly added property.
- `RemoveMember`. This takes a `MemberInfo` instance representing the field, method, or property that should be removed. Usually, only a member that was dynamically added can be removed, but this is ultimately implementation-specific.

This interface is used by JScript .NET to provide the same kind of dynamic behavior available in JScript.

SDK Tools Reference

IN THIS APPENDIX

- TLBIMP.EXE **1376**
- TLBEXP.EXE **1382**
- REGASM.EXE **1385**
- AXIMP.EXE **1390**
- REGSVCS.EXE **1394**

This reference covers five command-line tools that ship with the .NET Framework SDK:

Core COM Interoperability Tools:

- TLBIMP.EXE
- TLBEXP.EXE
- REGASM.EXE

Extended Tools Based on COM Interoperability:

- AXIMP.EXE
- REGSVCS.EXE

TLBIMP.EXE

The .NET Framework Type Library to Assembly Converter (TLBIMP.EXE) imports a type library to create an Interop Assembly describing its types. Visual Studio .NET exposes the functionality of TLBIMP.EXE when you add a reference to a type library that doesn't already have a registered Primary Interop Assembly (PIA). You can also programmatically import type libraries using the System.Runtime.InteropServices.TypeLibConverter class, as covered in Chapter 22, "Using APIs Instead of SDK Tools."

The syntax of TLBIMP.EXE is:

```
tlbimp TypeLibFileName [Options]
```

The *TypeLibFileName* should specify the filename (and the path, if applicable) of the type library or file containing a type library that you want to import. For a filename given without a path, TLBIMP.EXE searches the command window's path if it can't find the file in the current directory. By default, the output assembly is named *LibraryName*.dll and placed in the current directory, not necessarily the same directory as the assembly. *LibraryName* is an identifier internal to the type library that can be viewed using tools like OLEVIEW.EXE. If the input type library uses types defined in other type libraries without registered PIAs, Interop Assemblies for the dependent type libraries are generated alongside the main Interop Assembly and referenced by it.

For files with multiple embedded type libraries, the filename given can end with a \n suffix, where n is the value of a resource ID specifying which type library you want to import. For example:

```
tlbimp MSVBVM60.dll\3
```

You cannot generate an Interop Assembly from an exported type library, but there should be no need to because the assembly from which the type library was exported already exists.

When using any of TLBIMP.EXE's options, you can shorten the names as long as the choice is unambiguous—for example, /pr instead of /primary. You can also use them in any order. All options can be used with a dash prefix (-) or a slash prefix (/). TLBIMP.EXE's options are described in the following sections.

To mimic the behavior of Visual Studio. NET when referencing a type library that doesn't have a registered Primary Interop Assembly using TLBIMP.EXE, you can invoke:

```
tlbimp FullPath\TypeLibFileName /sysarray
➥ /out:Interop.LibraryName.dll /namespace:LibraryName
```

/asmversion

This option can be used to customize the version number of the output Interop Assembly. Without this option, the version number matches the major and minor version numbers specified in the input type library, such as *Major.Minor*.0.0. With this option, you must specify a valid version string with 2, 3, or 4 parts. For example:

```
/asmversion:9.23
```

```
/asmversion=9.23.6
```

```
/asmversion:9.23.6.30
```

/delaysign

This option can be used with either the /keyfile or /keycontainer option to extract just the public key from a cryptographic key pair. The public key is used to give the Interop Assembly a strong name, but the assembly is only partially signed because the private key is ignored. This is similar to using the /publickey option, but used when both the public and private keys are available in the specified file or container.

/keycontainer

This option can be used to digitally sign the Interop Assembly and give it a strong name using a cryptographic key pair contained in a key container. This option is used with a container name that is used by your computer's cryptographic service provider (CSP) to locate and use the key pair. For example:

```
/keycontainer:MyContainer
```

or

```
/keycontainer=MyContainer
```

Depending on the CSP, this option can be safer than the /keyfile option because the key data doesn't have to be stored as an unencrypted file in the file system. For example, a CSP may store keys in hardware, minimizing the possibility of them being compromised. A key container can be created using the Windows CryptAcquireContext API. See MSDN Online (msdn.microsoft.com) for more information. When using the /keycontainer option, the resultant strong-named assembly is fully-signed and ready for deployment. This option cannot be used at the same time as /keyfile or /publickey.

/keyfile

This option can be used to digitally sign the Interop Assembly and give it a strong name using a cryptographic key pair contained in a binary file. This option is used with the filename of the key file, for example:

```
/keyfile:KeyFile.snk
```

or

```
/keyfile=KeyFile.snk
```

As with the /keycontainer option, the resultant strong-named assembly is fully-signed and ready for deployment. This option cannot be used at the same time as /keycontainer or /publickey.

/out

This option can be used to choose the name and location of the output Interop Assembly. For example:

```
/out:MyAssembly.dll
```

or

```
/out=MyAssembly.dll
```

The filename can be specified with a partial or complete path if you want it placed in a directory other than the current directory. Changing the name of the output assembly also changes the name of the output namespace to match the filename (minus the .dll extension), unless you also use the /namespace option.

Giving the output assembly a different name than the default is recommended, especially if the output filename might conflict with an existing unmanaged DLL.

/namespace

This option can be used to choose a namespace containing all the types in the Interop Assembly. For example:

```
/namespace:MyCompany.MyTechnology
```

or

```
/namespace=MyCompany.MyTechnology
```

This overrides the string that would be chosen for the output namespace from either the library name or the filename used with the /out option. .NET-aware type libraries can contain a special IDL custom attribute, however, to choose a namespace that cannot be overridden with the /namespace option. See Chapter 15, "Creating and Deploying Useful Primary Interop Assemblies," for more information.

/primary

This option can be used to create a *Primary Interop Assembly* (PIA). A PIA must have a strong name, so this option must be used with the /publickey, /keyfile, or /keycontainer option. Any dependent type libraries must have registered PIAs or be referenced with the /reference option when using /primary. See Chapter 15 for more information about creating a PIA.

/publickey

This option can be used to give the Interop Assembly a strong name using a binary file that contains only a public key. This option is used with the filename of the public key file, for example:

```
/publickey:PublicKeyFile.snk
```

or

```
/publickey=PublicKeyFile.snk
```

The resulting strong-named assembly is considered *partially signed*. Partially-signed assemblies don't have the same protection as fully-signed assemblies. For example, someone could tamper with your assembly after you distribute it without being detected by the CLR, since the assembly's original contents were not hashed with your private key and stored in the assembly's manifest. Therefore, partially-signed assemblies should only be used for testing purposes, unless they are fully-signed later by using the Assembly Linker SDK utility (AL.EXE) or the Strong Name Utility (SN.EXE). The two-step process of creating a partially-signed assembly and fully signing it later is a common practice since developers often don't have direct access to the company's private key.

This option cannot be used at the same time as /keycontainer or /keyfile.

/reference

This option can be used to list existing Interop Assemblies that can be used to satisfy references for the current Interop Assembly being imported. For a type library C.TLB that references type libraries A.TLB and B.TLB, the following can be done if Interop Assemblies for A.TLB and B.TLB already exist:

```
tlbimp C.tlb /reference:Interop.A.dll /reference:Interop.B.dll
```

or

```
tlbimp C.tlb /reference=Interop.A.dll /reference=Interop.B.dll
```

If you don't specify any references, TLBIMP.EXE attempts to locate PIAs. If no PIA for a dependent type library is registered, TLBIMP.EXE attempts to locate the dependent type library via the Windows Registry and imports a new Interop Assembly to be referenced by the main Interop Assembly. An Interop Assembly listed with /reference is only used if the type library being processed references another type library whose LIBID matches the one found in its assembly-level GuidAttribute custom attribute.

/strictref

This option turns off the automatic import of dependent type libraries. This means that any dependent type libraries must either:

- have a Primary Interop Assembly registered
- have an Interop Assembly listed with the /reference option

If TLBIMP.EXE requires an assembly for a dependent type library that isn't available through one of these two mechanisms, it gives the following error:

```
System.ApplicationException - Type library '...' is not in the list of
references
```

/sysarray

Using this option causes any SAFEARRAY parameters to be imported as generic System.Array types rather than single-dimensional zero-lower bound arrays. Visual Studio .NET always uses the /sysarray option when importing a referenced type library.

/unsafe

Using this option marks all imported types with System.Security. SuppressUnmanagedCodeSecurityAttribute. This suppresses the full stack walk for unmanaged code permission whenever members on these types are called, which improves performance but opens up the possibility of a luring attack. When types or members are marked with this custom attribute, the CLR requires that the immediate caller has unmanaged code permission (via a link demand) but it does not check who has called the immediate caller.

Therefore, as the name implies, this option is not safe to use. Any trusted users of such an Interop Assembly must be careful to use it in such a way that it can't enable untrusted code to run unmanaged code and cause damage. Another side affect of using an interface marked with `SuppressUnmanagedCodeSecurityAttribute` is that if a .NET class implements the interface, a link demand for unmanaged code permission is still required, even if no unmanaged code is involved.

/nologo

This option suppresses the two lines of copyright information printed every time the utility is run.

/silent

This option hides the two lines of copyright information just like `/nologo`, but also suppresses any success messages and warnings. If an error occurs, then the copyright information and error information are printed to the console.

/verbose

This option provides more details about the actions performed by the utility. This includes a message for every type that gets imported, plus notifications when dependent assemblies are imported and/or referenced.

If `/silent` and `/verbose` are used simultaneously, only verbose messages and errors are printed to the console.

/help and /?

These options list a summary of the options, as follows:

```
/out:FileName              File name of assembly to be produced
/namespace:Namespace       Namespace of the assembly to be produced
/asmversion:Version        Version number of the assembly to be produced
/reference:FileName        File name of assembly to use to resolve references
/publickey:FileName        File containing strong name public key
/keyfile:FileName          File containing strong name key pair
/keycontainer:FileName     Key container holding strong name key pair
/delaysign                 Force strong name delay signing
/unsafe                    Produce interfaces without runtime security checks
```

```
/nologo                 Prevents TlbImp from displaying logo
/silent                 Suppresses all output except for errors
/verbose                Displays extra information
/primary                Produce a primary interop assembly
/sysarray               Import SAFEARRAY as System.Array
/strictref              Only use assemblies specified using /reference
/? or /help             Display this usage message
```

TLBEXP.EXE

The .NET Framework Assembly to Type Library Converter (TLBEXP.EXE) exports a type library with type definitions from an assembly. Visual Studio .NET exposes the exporting functionality in its Register for COM Interop option in the settings for a Visual C# or Visual Basic project. Type library exporting can also be done programmatically using the System.Runtime.InteropServices.TypeLibConverter class, as covered in Chapter 22.

The syntax of TLBEXP.EXE is:

```
tlbexp AssemblyFileName [Options]
```

The *AssemblyFileName* should specify the filename (and possibly the path) of the assembly for which you want to export a type library. For multi-file assemblies, the filename must be the one containing the assembly's manifest. (For such an assembly, a single type library containing the types in all the .NET modules is produced.) For a filename given without a path, TLBEXP.EXE searches the command window's path if it can't find the file in the current directory. By default, the output type library is named *AssemblyName*.tlb (where *AssemblyName* is the assembly's simple name found in its manifest) and placed in the current directory, not necessarily the same directory as the assembly. If the input assembly exposes public signatures that use types defined in other assemblies, type libraries for the dependent assemblies are generated alongside the main type library and referenced by it.

Although it's not a common occurrence (due to lack of tool support), assemblies can contain type libraries embedded as resources just like any other file. If TLBEXP.EXE encounters an assembly with an embedded type library, a warning is shown but a new type library is generated based on the assembly's metadata rather than extracting the embedded type library. (For any dependent assemblies with embedded type libraries, however, the exported type library references the embedded type libraries.) You cannot generate a type library for an Interop Assembly, but there should be no need to since Interop Assemblies are normally created from type libraries.

When using any of TLBEXP.EXE's options, you can shorten the names as long as the choice is unambiguous—for example, /v instead of /verbose. You can also use them in any order. All options can be used with a dash prefix (-) or a slash prefix (/). TLBEXP.EXE's options are described in the following sections.

/names

This option can be used to choose a capitalization for any identifiers exported to the type library. Type libraries store identifiers in a case-insensitive table, so identifiers that have multiple cases in an assembly end up with a single case in the exported type library. This can cause undesirable results, such as a .NET member named `Target` being exported as a COM member named `target` due to some other member's parameter named `target` being exported first. Even worse, the behavior can change each time you re-compile your assembly and re-export a type library due to subtle changes in the order that a .NET compiler may emit types into metadata.

With the /names option, you can choose the "correct" case for any identifiers appearing in conflicting cases to avoid these problems. It must be used with a filename, for example:

```
/names:MyNamesFile.txt
```

or

```
/names=MyNamesFile.txt
```

The filename can be specified with a partial or complete path if it isn't in the current directory.

The referenced file (a *names file*) is a simple text file containing one identifier per line, for example:

```
Source
Target
Value
Zone
```

This file can be encoded as ANSI, UTF-8, Unicode, or even Unicode big-endian. Invalid files are simply ignored without reporting an error. Any identifiers listed that aren't used by the input assembly have no effect, and if one appears multiple times in the names file, all but the first instance are ignored. In addition, spaces are ignored and # can be used like a comment character, for example:

```
#
# Names File for MyAssembly.dll
#
Source    # Appears as an uppercase property and lowercase parameter name
Target    # Appears as an uppercase class name and lowercase parameter name
Value     # ...
Zone      # ...
```

/out

This option can be used to choose the name and location of the output type library. For example:

/out:MyAssembly.tlb

or

/out=MyAssembly.tlb

The filename can be specified with a partial or complete path if you want it placed in a directory other than the current directory. Unlike with TLBIMP.EXE, the chosen filename has no effect on the contents of the output type library (such as its library name).

/nologo

This option suppresses the two lines of copyright information printed every time the utility is run.

/silent

This option hides the two lines of copyright information just like /nologo, but also suppresses any success messages and warnings. Only errors are printed to the console when /silent is used.

/verbose

This option provides more details about the actions performed by the utility. This includes a message for every type that gets exported, plus notifications when dependent type libraries are exported and/or referenced.

If /silent and /verbose are used simultaneously, only verbose messages and errors are printed to the console.

/help and /?

These options list a summary of the options, as follows:

```
/out:FileName          File name of type library to be produced
/nologo                Prevents TlbExp from displaying logo
/silent                Prevents TlbExp from displaying success message
/verbose               Displays extra information
/names:FileName        A file in which each line specifies the
                       capitalization of a name in the type library.
/? or /help            Display this usage message
```

REGASM.EXE

The .NET Framework Assembly Registration Utility (REGASM.EXE) registers and unregisters assemblies in the Windows Registry for use by COM. It optionally exports and registers a type library for the input assembly. Usually assemblies authored in a .NET language are registered for COM clients, but Interop Assemblies can also be registered for .NET clients to enable certain features. For example, REGASM.EXE detects when it's used with a Primary Interop Assembly and registers additional entries used by Visual Studio .NET when referencing type libraries.

Visual Studio .NET exposes the registration functionality in its `Register for COM Interop` option in the settings for a Visual C# or Visual Basic project. This functionality can also be used programmatically via the `System.Runtime.InteropServices.RegistrationServices` class, as covered in Chapter 22.

The syntax of REGASM.EXE is:

```
regasm AssemblyFileName [Options]
```

The *AssemblyFileName* should specify the filename (and the path, if applicable) of the assembly you want to (un)register. For multi-file assemblies, the filename must be the one containing the assembly's manifest. For a filename given without a path, REGASM.EXE searches the command window's path if it can't find the file in the current directory.

When used with no options, REGASM.EXE adds the following registry entries for each coclass:

```
HKEY_CLASSES_ROOT\ProgID\[default]="NamespaceQualifiedClassName"
HKEY_CLASSES_ROOT\ProgID\CLSID\[default]="{CLSID}"
HKEY_CLASSES_ROOT\CLSID\{CLSID}\[default]="NamespaceQualifiedClassName"
HKEY_CLASSES_ROOT\CLSID\{CLSID}\Implemented Categories\
➡ {62C8FE65-4EBB-45E7-B440-6E39B2CDBF29}
HKEY_CLASSES_ROOT\CLSID\{CLSID}\InprocServer32\[default]=
➡ "WindowsSystemDirectory\mscoree.dll"
HKEY_CLASSES_ROOT\CLSID\{CLSID}\InprocServer32\Assembly="FullAssemblyName"
HKEY_CLASSES_ROOT\CLSID\{CLSID}\InprocServer32\Class=
➡ "NamespaceQualifiedClassName"
HKEY_CLASSES_ROOT\CLSID\{CLSID}\InprocServer32\RuntimeVersion="Version"
HKEY_CLASSES_ROOT\CLSID\{CLSID}\InprocServer32\ThreadingModel="Both"
HKEY_CLASSES_ROOT\CLSID\{CLSID}\ProgId\[default]="ProgID"
```

When run on an Interop Assembly, only the bold entries are added and the rest are left to whatever their original settings are. When run on a Primary Interop Assembly, one additional entry is registered by default:

```
HKEY_CLASSES_ROOT\TypeLib\{LIBID}\MajorVersion.MinorVersion\
➡ PrimaryInteropAssemblyName="FullAssemblyName"
```

When using any of REGASM.EXE's options, you can shorten the names as long as the choice is unambiguous—for example, /regf instead of /regfile. You can also use them in any order. All options can be used with a dash prefix (-) or a slash prefix (/). REGASM.EXE's options are described in the following sections.

To mimic the behavior of Visual Studio .NET's Register for COM Interop setting using REGASM.EXE, you can invoke:

```
regasm FullPath\AssemblyFileName /codebase /tlb
```

/codebase

This option registers the location of the assembly file under every CLSID with a CodeBase value, for example:

```
HKEY_CLASSES_ROOT\CLSID\{CLSID}\InprocServer32\CodeBase=
➥ file:///C:/.../MyAssembly.dll
```

With this value registered, the CLR can locate assemblies anywhere in the file system, even if they aren't in the Global Assembly Cache or in the application directory. This is a fallback mechanism, so if the registered assembly is found in the GAC or in the local directory, the CodeBase value is not used.

This option should only be used with strong-named assemblies, because simply-named assemblies that rely on a codebase can be negatively impacted by other simply-named assemblies that rely on a codebase. REGASM.EXE doesn't prevent you from registering simply-named assemblies with /codebase, but issues the following warning:

```
RegAsm warning: Registering an unsigned assembly with /codebase can cause
your assembly to interfere with other applications that may be installed on
the same computer. The /codebase switch is intended to be used only with
signed assemblies. Please give your assembly a strong name and re-register it.
```

When using the /codebase option with a Primary Interop Assembly, REGASM.EXE also adds the following registry entry, enabling Visual Studio .NET to use it without being installed in the Global Assembly Cache:

```
HKEY_CLASSES_ROOT\TypeLib\{LIBID}\MajorVersion.MinorVersion\
➥ PrimaryInteropAssemblyCodeBase=file:///C:/.../MyAssembly.dll
```

/regfile

This option creates a registry file instead of performing the registration. This registry file is a simple text file that lists the keys and values in a format recognized by programs such as REGEDIT.EXE for registration at a later time.

This option is meant for strictly informational purposes, as a way to see for yourself what registration entries REGASM.EXE would have placed in the registry. The information placed in the output registration file is not necessarily complete, since it doesn't include any registration that's done by custom registration functions (marked with the ComRegisterFunctionAttribute custom attribute). Additionally, in version 1.0 of REGASM.EXE, the InProcServer32 entries in any generated registry file do not properly escape the backslashes in the path to MSCOREE.DLL. If you attempted to register these entries as-is, none of the .NET classes would be able to be instantiated via CoCreateInstance. Using a REGASM.EXE-generated registration file is an acceptable way to register PIAs, however, because Interop Assemblies do not contain custom registration functions, and the registration files produced do not contain InProcServer32 entries.

This option can be used with the desired filename of the output registration file. For example,

/regfile:MyAssembly.reg

or

/regfile=MyAssembly.reg

If no filename is specified, the input filename is used but with the .reg extension instead of .dll or .exe. By default, the file is placed *in the same directory as the assembly*, not necessarily the current directory. The filename can be specified with a partial or complete path if you want it placed in a different directory.

The /regfile option cannot be used at the same time that the /unregister or /tlb options are used.

/registered

This option tells REGASM.EXE to only reference dependent type libraries that are registered when exporting a type library. Without this option, type libraries in the current directory are used to satisfy references if the desired type libraries are not registered.

This option only makes sense when used with /tlb, since it only applies to exporting a type library. If used without /tlb, it is ignored.

/tlb

The /tlb option causes a type library to be exported and registered. The type library produced is the same that would be produced by TLBEXP.EXE, but it's also registered. Registering a type library adds the following registry entries:

```
HKEY_CLASSES_ROOT\TypeLib\{LIBID}\Major.Minor\[default]="LibraryName"
HKEY_CLASSES_ROOT\TypeLib\{LIBID}\Major.Minor\LCID\win32\[default]=
```

➥ "*TypeLibPathAndFileName*"
```
HKEY_CLASSES_ROOT\TypeLib\{LIBID}\Major.Minor\FLAGS\[default]="Flags"
HKEY_CLASSES_ROOT\TypeLib\{LIBID}\Major.Minor\HELPDIR\[default]="TypeLibPath"
```

For exported type libraries, the *Flags* value, representing binary-ORed values from the LIBFLAGS enumeration, is always 0.

In addition, any exported interfaces are registered with the OLE Automation type library marshaler unless the corresponding .NET interface is marked with AutomationProxyAttribute with its value set to false. These registry entries look like the following:

```
HKEY_CLASSES_ROOT\Interface\{IID}\[default]="InterfaceName"
HKEY_CLASSES_ROOT\Interface\{IID}\ProxyStubClsid="{ProxyStubCLSID}"
HKEY_CLASSES_ROOT\Interface\{IID}\ProxyStubClsid32="{ProxyStubCLSID}"
HKEY_CLASSES_ROOT\Interface\{IID}\TypeLib\[default]="{LIBID}"
HKEY_CLASSES_ROOT\Interface\{IID}\TypeLib\Version="Major.Minor"
```

ProxyStubCLSID represents the OLE Automation marshaler class that handles the COM marshaling of the interface. The type library information enables the marshaler to obtain the type information for the interface.

Type library registration is not specific to .NET components; all COM type libraries are registered the same way, and there are a variety of tools that register type libraries (such as OLEVIEW.EXE). The registry entries are necessary for COM marshaling across context boundaries. The entries under the TypeLib branch can also be useful for Visual Basic 6 clients expecting to find the type library in the list of available references without having to browse for the file.

This option can be used with the desired filename of the output type library. For example:

```
/tlb:MyAssembly.tlb
```

or

```
/tlb=MyAssembly.tlb
```

If no filename is specified, the input assembly name is used with a .tlb extension. By default, the file is placed *in the same directory as the assembly*, not necessarily the current directory. The filename can be specified with a partial or complete path if you want it placed in a different directory. All the exported type libraries (including any dependent ones) are registered. As with TLBEXP.EXE, type libraries for the dependent assemblies are generated alongside the main type library.

A little known fact about the /tlb option is that it supports registering the input assembly *as* the type library file if it contains one embedded as a resource. In fact, using /tlb with a filename raises an error if the input assembly contains an embedded type library. If you really want to export a new type library from such an assembly, you'd have to use TLBEXP.EXE.

Just as running `TLBEXP.EXE` on an Interop Assembly is illegal, using the `/tlb` option with an Interop Assembly causes the following error to be reported:

```
CLR assembly C:\...\ABC.dll was imported from a type library and can not be
➡ re-exported to a type library. Make sure the type library from which the
➡ assembly was imported is registered.
```

The second sentence only applies when exporting non-Interop assemblies that publicly reference types in an Interop Assembly. If the Interop Assembly's corresponding type library isn't registered, automatic export of the Interop Assembly is attempted, causing the failure since this is not allowed.

The `/tlb` option cannot be used at the same time that the `/regfile` option is used.

/unregister

This option unregisters the assembly rather than the default action of registering it. Besides removing any registry entries it would have added, it invokes any custom unregistration functions in the input assembly (marked with `ComUnregisterFunctionAttribute`).

In addition to unregistering the assembly, the corresponding type library can be unregistered, too, when `/unregister` is used with the `/tlb` option. If no filename is given with `/tlb`, then the appropriately-named type library (`AssemblyName.tlb`) must exist in the current directory. Otherwise, the path and filename of the type library to unregister can be specified with the `/tlb` option.

If you attempt to use `/unregister` with `/tlb` on an Interop Assembly, the `/tlb` option is ignored and the following warning is issued:

```
Type library not unregistered since the assembly was imported from COM.
```

Since `REGASM.EXE` only unregisters the entries it adds for an Interop Assembly and not any original registration done by the installer of the COM component, it would not be appropriate for `REGASM.EXE` to unregister the COM component's type library.

The `/unregister` option cannot be used at the same time that the `/regfile` option is used.

/nologo

This option suppresses the two lines of copyright information printed every time the utility is run.

/silent

This option hides the two lines of copyright information just like `/nologo`, but also suppresses any success messages and warnings. Only errors are printed to the console when `/silent` is used.

/verbose

This option provides more details about the actions performed by the utility. This only makes a difference when /tlb is used, because the actions of assembly registration and unregistration don't report anything additional in verbose mode. The messages displayed when using /verbose and /tlb are the same ones displayed when using /verbose with TLBEXP.EXE— for example, listing every type that gets exported.

Unlike TLBEXP.EXE, if /silent and /verbose are used simultaneously, /verbose is ignored.

/help and /?

These options list a summary of the options, as follows:

```
/unregister          Unregister types
/tlb[:FileName]      Export the assembly to the specified type library
                     and register it
/regfile[:FileName]  Generate a reg file with the specified name
                     instead of registering the types. This option
                     cannot be used with the /u or /tlb options
/codebase            Set the code base in the registry
/registered          Only refer to already registered type libraries
/nologo              Prevents RegAsm from displaying logo
/silent              Silent mode. Prevents displaying of success messages
/verbose             Displays extra information
/? or /help          Display this usage message
```

AXIMP.EXE

The .NET ActiveX Control to Windows Forms Assembly Generator (AXIMP.EXE) takes a type library containing at least one registered ActiveX control as input, and usually creates at least two assemblies—an Interop Assembly (and any dependent Interop Assemblies) just like TLBIMP.EXE does, and an ActiveX Assembly with the types needed to host ActiveX controls on Windows Forms as if they are Windows Forms controls. If a Primary Interop Assembly for the input type library is registered on the current computer, AXIMP.EXE references that assembly rather than generating a new one. AXIMP.EXE optionally produces C# source code for easy customization of the ActiveX Assembly.

Visual Studio .NET exposes the functionality of AXIMP.EXE in the Customize Toolbox dialog when selecting a COM component to drag onto a Windows Form. You can programmatically do the same thing using the System.Windows.Forms.Design.AxImporter class, as covered in Chapter 22.

The syntax of AXIMP.EXE is:

```
aximp TypeLibFileName [Options]
```

The *TypeLibFileName* should specify the filename (and the path, if applicable) of the type library or file containing a type library that you want to import. Unlike TLBIMP.EXE, AXIMP.EXE does *not* search the path for the input file. If no path is given at the command line, the file must be in the current directory. By default, the output assembly is named Ax*LibraryName*.dll and placed in the current directory, not necessarily the same directory as the assembly. The dependent assemblies are generated alongside the ActiveX Assembly and referenced by it.

Be aware that any coclasses representing ActiveX controls must be registered on the current computer with the following registry value in order for AXIMP.EXE to recognize it as an ActiveX control:

HKEY_CLASSES_ROOT\CLSID\{*CLSID*}\Control

Being marked in the type library with the [control] attribute is irrelevant.

When using any of AXIMP.EXE's options, you can shorten the names as long as the choice is unambiguous—for example, /keyf instead of /keyfile. You can also use them in any order. All options can be used with a dash prefix (-) or a slash prefix (/). AXIMP.EXE's options are described in the following sections.

/delaysign

This option works just like TLBIMP.EXE's /delaysign option. It only works with either the /keyfile or /keycontainer option to extract just the public key from a cryptographic key pair. The key data is used for the ActiveX Assembly plus the Interop Assembly if AXIMP.EXE generates one.

/keycontainer

This option works just like TLBIMP.EXE's /keycontainer option. It expects a filename containing a cryptographic key container name. For example:

/keycontainer:MyContainer

or

/keycontainer=MyContainer

The key data is used for the ActiveX Assembly plus the Interop Assembly if AXIMP.EXE generates one.

/keyfile

This option works just like `TLBIMP.EXE`'s `/keyfile` option. It expects a filename containing a cryptographic key pair. For example:

```
/keyfile:KeyFile.snk
```

or

```
/keyfile=KeyFile.snk
```

The key data is used for the ActiveX Assembly plus the Interop Assembly if `AXIMP.EXE` generates one.

/out

This option can be used to choose the name and location of the output ActiveX Assembly. For example,

```
/out:AxComponent.dll
```

or

```
/out=AxComponent.dll
```

The filename can be specified with a partial or complete path if you want it placed in a directory other than the current directory. There's no way to choose the name of the referenced Interop Assembly, but if one is generated it will always be placed in whatever directory you choose for the ActiveX Assembly.

Unlike `TLBIMP.EXE`, using this option does not affect the namespace in the output ActiveX Assembly.

/publickey

This option works just like `TLBIMP.EXE`'s `/publickey` option. It expects a filename containing just a public key. For example:

```
/publickey:PublicKeyFile.snk
```

or

```
/publickey=PublicKeyFile.snk
```

The key data is used for the ActiveX Assembly plus the Interop Assembly if `AXIMP.EXE` generates one.

/source

This option can be used to generate C# source code for the ActiveX Assembly. This makes the assembly much easier to customize than an Interop Assembly. Also, this option can be used to make up for AXIMP.EXE's lack of a /reference option. By generating source code then compiling it, you can reference whichever Interop Assembly you'd like.

The C# source file generated has the same name as the output assembly, but with a .cs extension rather than a .dll extension. It is always generated in the same location as the output ActiveX Assembly.

/nologo

This option suppresses the three lines of copyright information that are sometimes printed when the utility is run.

/silent

This option hides the three lines of copyright information just like /nologo, but also suppresses any success messages and warnings. If an error occurs, then the copyright information and error information are printed to the console.

/verbose

This option is meant to provide more details about the actions performed by the utility. However, in version 1.0 of this utility, this option makes no difference in AXIMP.EXE's output.

/help and /?

These options list a summary of the options, as follows:

```
/out:FileName          File name of assembly to be produced
/publickey:FileName    File containing strong name public key
/keyfile:FileName      File containing strong name key pair
/keycontainer:FileName Key container holding strong name key pair
/delaysign             Force strong name delay signing
                       Used with /keyfile or /keycontainer
/source                Generate C# source code for Windows Forms wrapper
/nologo                Prevents AxImp from displaying logo
/silent                Prevents AxImp from displaying success message
/verbose               Displays extra information
/? or /help            Display this usage message
```

REGSVCS.EXE

.NET Framework Services Installation Utility (REGSVCS.EXE) installs and uninstalls assemblies with serviced components into the Component Services (COM+) catalog. This can also involve registering the assembly, exporting a type library, registering the type library, installing the type library for the specified application, and configuration of any serviced component types in the assembly. This same work can be done with dynamic registration, but manually using REGSVCS.EXE gives you the benefit of detailed error reporting.

This functionality can also be used programmatically via the System.EnterpriseServices. RegistrationHelper class, as covered in Chapter 22.

The syntax of REGSVCS.EXE is:

```
regsvcs [options] AssemblyFileName
```

The `AssemblyFileName` should specify the filename (and path, if applicable) of the assembly you want to (un)install. For multi-file assemblies, the filename must be the one containing the assembly's manifest. For a filename given without a path, REGSVCS.EXE searches the command window's path if it can't find the file in the current directory.

The input assembly must have a strong name and must contain at least one serviced component (a class that derives from System.EnterpriseServices.ServicedComponent).

Unlike the previous tools, REGSVCS.EXE's options cannot be shortened but must be fully specified (such as /quiet instead of /q). You can use them in any order, but they must be used before the filename. All options can be used with a dash prefix (-) or a slash prefix (/). Options with values, however, can only be specified with a colon and not with an equals sign. REGSVCS.EXE's options are described in the following sections.

> **WARNING**
>
> Unlike the previous tools, all options must precede the assembly's filename when using REGSVCS.EXE. Any options listed after the name are silently ignored!

/appname

This option can be used to customize the installed application name. An application with this name will either be created or searched for, depending on the other options. The /appname option enables you to customize the name as follows:

```
/appname:MyApplication
```

If no application name is specified, the string contained in the serviced component's
`System.EnterpriseServices.ApplicationNameAttribute` custom attribute is used. If it isn't
marked with the custom attribute, the assembly name is used.

/c

This option, short for "create," forces the creation of a new application rather than attempting
to find an existing one. If an application with the same name is already installed, an error is
reported.

Only one of the /c, /fc, and /u options can be used at a time.

/componly

This option, short for "components only," configures only components, and not any interfaces
or methods.

/exapp

This option, short for "existing application," tells the utility to use an existing application
rather than creating a new one.

/extlb

This option, short for "existing type library," tells the utility to use an existing type library
rather than exporting a new one.

/fc

This option, short for "find or create," is implied when neither /c nor /u options are used. This
means that an existing application should be used if found, otherwise a new application should
be created.

Only one of the /c, /fc, and /u options can be used at a time.

/noreconfig

This option, the opposite of /reconfig, instructs the utility not to reconfigure an existing target application. This option doesn't apply when a new application is being created.

/parname

On a version of Windows that supports COM+ application partitions (such as Windows XP),
this option can be used to choose the partition name or ID to use or create. For example:

```
/parname:MyPartition
```

COM+ application partitions enable multiple versions of the same application to run on the same computer, with each one individually configurable.

/reconfig

This option, the opposite of /noreconfig, is implied when neither /c nor /u options are used. This instructs the tool to reconfigure an existing target application when appropriate. This option doesn't apply when a new application is being created.

/tlb

This option works like REGASM.EXE's /tlb option, enabling the user to choose a name and location for the exported type library. For example:

```
/tlb:MyAssembly.tlb
```

When this option isn't used, REGSVCS.EXE produces a type library in the same directory as the assembly (not necessarily the current directory) and names it with the assembly name plus a .tlb extension.

/u

This option, short for "uninstall," is used to uninstall the target application.

Only one of the /c, /fc, and /u options can be used at a time.

/nologo

This option suppresses the two lines of copyright information printed every time the utility is run.

/quiet

This option hides the two lines of copyright information just like /nologo, but also suppresses any success messages and warnings. Only errors are printed to the console when /quiet is used.

/help and /?

These options list a summary of the options, as follows:

```
/? or /help     Display this usage message.
/fc             Find or create target application (default).
/c              Create target application, error if it already exists.
/exapp          Expect an existing application.
/tlb:<tlbfile>  Filename for the exported type library.
```

```
/appname:<name>  Use the specified name for the target application.
/parname:<name>  Use the specified name or id for the target partition.
/extlb           Use an existing type library.
/reconfig        Reconfigure existing target application (default).
/noreconfig      Don't reconfigure existing target application.
/u               Uninstall target application.
/nologo          Suppress logo output.
/quiet           Suppress logo output and success output.
/componly        Configure components only, no methods or interfaces.
```

HRESULT to .NET Exception Transformations

When a COM member (or PInvoke signature marked with `PreserveSig=false`) returns a failure `HRESULT`, a .NET exception is thrown. The type of the exception depends on the `HRESULT` value, according to the tables in this appendix. The exceptions listed are the only ones that can be directly thrown by the CLR in response to a COM object returning a failure `HRESULT`, and are a subset of the exceptions defined in the `mscorlib` assembly. The only reason that the list doesn't include all exceptions defined in `mscorlib` is that a handful of exceptions share the same `HRESULT` values, so one exception type must be chosen when the shared value is returned from COM.

Table C.1 lists exception types alphabetically (excluding the namespace), to answer the question, "What `HRESULT` caused this exception to be thrown?" for an author of a .NET component using COM. This information can be obtained programmatically by calling `System.Runtime.InteropServices.Marshal.GetHRForException`, although for exceptions that can be caused by multiple `HRESULT`s, only one `HRESULT` (the one listed in bold in the table) is returned.

Table C.2 contains the same information as Table C.1, but lists the `HRESULT`s numerically, to answer a COM component author's question, "If I return this `HRESULT`, what exception will a .NET client see thrown?" This information can be obtained by calling the `System.Runtime.InteropServices.Marshal.ThrowExceptionForHR` method, but this involves catching the thrown exception to discover its type.

Here are a few notes about the tables:

- For some exceptions, multiple `HRESULT` values cause the same exception to be thrown. The bold `HRESULT`s in Table C.1 represent the default values that correspond to the exception when it's thrown from .NET to COM (shown in Appendix D).

- Any listed names beginning with `ERROR` are Win32 error codes that must be added to 0x80070000 to get the listed `HRESULT` values with `FACILITY_WIN32`.

- A few `HRESULT`s have multiple names, because some .NET `HRESULT`s (beginning with `COR`) are defined with the same value as classic COM `HRESULT`s. A list of named .NET `HRESULT`s can be found in `CorError.h`.

- Any returned `HRESULT`s not listed in these tables result in a `System.Runtime.InteropServices.COMException` being thrown.

TABLE C.1   Exception Types Listed Alphabetically

Exception Name	HRESULT *Value*	HRESULT *Name*
System.Reflection. AmbiguousMatchException	0x8000211D	COR_E_AMBIGUOUSMATCH
System.AppDomainUnloadedException	0x80131014	COR_E_APPDOMAINUNLOADED
System.ApplicationException	0x80131600	COR_E_APPLICATION

TABLE C.1 Continued

Exception Name	HRESULT *Value*	HRESULT *Name*
System.ArgumentException	**0x80070057**	**E_INVALIDARG** **(COR_E_ARGUMENT)**
	0x800A01C1	VB6: Argument not optional (449)
	0x800A01C2	VB6: Wrong number of arguments (450)
System. ArgumentOutOfRangeException	0x80131502	COR_E_ARGUMENTOUTOFRANGE
System.ArithmeticException	0x80070216	ERROR_ARITHMETIC_OVERFLOW (COR_E_ARITHMETIC)
System.ArrayTypeMismatchException	0x80131503	COR_E_ARRAYTYPEMISMATCH
System.BadImageFormatException	**0x8007000B**	**ERROR_BAD_FORMAT** **(COR_E_BADIMAGEFORMAT)**
	0x800700C0	ERROR_EXE_MARKED_INVALID
	0x800700C1	ERROR_BAD_EXE_FORMAT
	0x80131107	CLDB_E_FILE_OLDVER
	0x8013110E	CLDB_E_FILE_CORRUPT
	0x8013141D	CORSEC_E_INVALID_IMAGE_FORMAT
System.CannotUnloadAppDomain Exception	0x80131015	COR_E_CANNOTUNLOADAPPDOMAIN
System.Runtime.InteropServices.COM Exception	**0x80004005**	**E_FAIL**
	0x********	*Any HRESULTs not in this list*
System.ContextMarshalException	0x80131504	COR_E_CONTEXTMARSHAL
System.Security.Cryptography. CryptographicException	0x80131430	CORSEC_E_CRYPTO
System.Security.Cryptography. CryptographicUnexpectedOperation Exception	0x80131431	CORSEC_E_CRYPTO_UNEX_OPER
System.Reflection. CustomAttributeFormatException	0x80131605	COR_E_CUSTOMATTRIBUTEFORMAT
System.IO. DirectoryNotFoundException	0x80030003	STG_E_PATHNOTFOUND
	0x80070003	**ERROR_PATH_NOT_FOUND** **(COR_E_DIRECTORYNOTFOUND)**

C

HRESULT TO .NET
EXCEPTION
TRANSFORMATIONS

TABLE C.1   Continued

Exception Name	HRESULT Value	HRESULT Name
	0x800A004C	CTL_E_PATHNOTFOUND
System.DivideByZeroException	**0x80020012**	**DISP_E_DIVBYZERO** **(COR_E_DIVIDEBYZERO)**
	0x800A000B	CTL_E_DIVISIONBYZERO
System.DllNotFoundException	0x80131524	COR_E_DLLNOTFOUND
System.DuplicateWaitObject Exception	0x80131529	COR_E_DUPLICATEWAITOBJECT
System.IO.EndOfStreamException	**0x80070026**	**ERROR_HANDLE_EOF** **(COR_E_ENDOFSTREAM)**
	0x800A003E	VB6: Input past end of file (62)
System.EntryPointNotFoundException	0x80131523	COR_E_ENTRYPOINTNOTFOUND
System.Exception	0x80131500	COR_E_EXCEPTION
System.ExecutionEngineException	0x80131506	COR_E_EXECUTIONENGINE
System.FieldAccessException	0x80131507	COR_E_FIELDACCESS
System.IO.FileLoadException	0x80070004	ERROR_TOO_MANY_OPEN_FILES
	0x80070020	ERROR_SHARING_VIOLATION
	0x80070021	ERROR_LOCK_VIOLATION
	0x8007006E	ERROR_OPEN_FAILED
	0x800703ED	ERROR_UNRECOGNIZED_VOLUME
	0x800703EE	ERROR_FILE_INVALID
	0x8007045A	ERROR_DLL_INIT_FAILED
	0x80070570	ERROR_FILE_CORRUPT
	0x80070571	ERROR_DISK_CORRUPT
	0x80131401	SECURITY_E_INCOMPATIBLE_ SHARE
	0x80131402	SECURITY_E_UNVERIFIABLE
	0x80131403	SECURITY_E_INCOMPATIBLE_ EVIDENCE
	0x80131018	COR_E_ASSEMBLYEXPECTED
	0x80131019	COR_E_FIXUPSINEXE
	0x80131621	**COR_E_FILELOAD**

TABLE C.1 Continued

Exception Name	HRESULT *Value*	HRESULT *Name*
	0x80131039	COR_E_MODULE_HASH_CHECK_FAILED
	0x80131040	FUSION_E_REF_DEF_MISMATCH
	0x80131041	FUSION_E_INVALID_PRIVATE_ASM_LOCATION
	0x80131042	FUSION_E_ASM_MODULE_MISSING
	0x80131045	FUSION_E_SIGNATURE_CHECK_FAILED
	0x80131047	FUSION_E_INVALID_NAME
System.IO.FileNotFoundException	**0x80070002**	**ERROR_FILE_NOT_FOUND (COR_E_FILENOTFOUND)**
	0x80070015	ERROR_NOT_READY
	0x80070035	ERROR_BAD_NETPATH
	0x80070043	ERROR_BAD_NET_NAME
	0x80070574	ERROR_WRONG_TARGET_NAME
	0x8007007B	ERROR_INVALID_NAME
	0x8007007E	ERROR_MOD_NOT_FOUND
	0x800A0035	CTL_E_FILENOTFOUND
System.FormatException	0x80131537	COR_E_FORMAT
System.IndexOutOfRangeException	0x800A0009	VB6: Subscript out of range (9)
	0x80131508	**COR_E_INDEXOUTOFRANGE**
System.InvalidCastException	0x80004002	COR_E_INVALIDCAST (E_NOINTERFACE)
System.Runtime.InteropServices.InvalidComObjectException	0x80131527	COR_E_INVALIDCOMOBJECT
System.Reflection.InvalidFilterCriteriaException	0x80131601	COR_E_INVALIDFILTERCRITERIA
System.Runtime.InteropServices.InvalidOleVariantTypeException	0x80131531	COR_E_INVALIDOLEVARIANTTYPE
System.InvalidOperationException	0x80131509	COR_E_INVALIDOPERATION
System.InvalidProgramException	0x8013153A	COR_E_INVALIDPROGRAM
System.IO.IOException	0x800A0039	CTL_E_DEVICEIOERROR

TABLE C.1   Continued

Exception Name	HRESULT Value	HRESULT Name
	0x800A793C	VB6: Error saving to file (31036)
	0x800A793D	VB6: Error loading from file (31037)
	0x80131620	**COR_E_IO**
System.IO.IsolatedStorage. IsolatedStorageException	0x80131450	ISS_E_ISOSTORE
System.Runtime.InteropServices. MarshalDirectiveException	0x80131535	COR_E_MARSHALDIRECTIVE
System.MemberAccessException	0x8013151A	COR_E_MEMBERACCESS
System.MethodAccessException	0x80131510	COR_E_METHODACCESS
System.MissingFieldException	0x80131511	COR_E_MISSINGFIELD
System.Resources. MissingManifestResourceException	0x80131532	COR_E_ MISSINGMANIFESTRESOURCE
System.MissingMemberException	0x800A01CD	VB6: Method or data member not found (461)
	0x80131512	**COR_E_MISSINGMEMBER**
System.MissingMethodException	0x80131513	COR_E_MISSINGMETHOD
System.MulticastNotSupported Exception	0x80131514	COR_E_MULTICASTNOTSUPPORTED
System.NotFiniteNumberException	0x80131528	COR_E_NOTFINITENUMBER
System.NotImplementedException	0x80004001	E_NOTIMPL
System.NotSupportedException	0x800A01B6	VB6: Object doesn't support this property or method (438)
	0x800A01BD	VB6: Object doesn't support this action (445)
	0x800A01CA	VB6: Variable uses a type not supported in Visual Basic (458)
	0x800A01CB	VB6: This component doesn't support the set of events (459)
	0x80131515	**COR_E_NOTSUPPORTED**

TABLE C.1 Continued

Exception Name	HRESULT Value	HRESULT Name
System.NullReferenceException	0x80004003	E_POINTER (COR_E_NULLREFERENCE)
System.OutOfMemoryException	**0x8007000E**	**E_OUTOFMEMORY (COR_E_OUTOFMEMORY)**
	0x800A0007	CTL_E_OUTOFMEMORY
	0x800A7919	VB6: Out of memory (31001)
System.OverflowException	0x800A0006	CTL_E_OVERFLOW
	0x80131516	**COR_E_OVERFLOW**
System.IO.PathTooLongException	0x800700CE	ERROR_FILENAME_EXCED_RANGE (COR_E_PATHTOOLONG)
System.PlatformNotSupported Exception	0x80131539	COR_E_PLATFORMNOTSUPPORTED
System.Security.Policy. PolicyException	0x80131416	CORSEC_E_POLICY_EXCEPTION
System.RankException	0x80131517	COR_E_RANK
System.Reflection. ReflectionTypeLoadException	0x80131602	COR_E_REFLECTIONTYPELOAD
System.Runtime.Remoting. RemotingException	0x8013150B	COR_E_REMOTING
System.Runtime.InteropServices. SafeArrayRankMismatchException	0x80131538	COR_E_SAFEARRAYRANKMISMATCH
System.Runtime.InteropServices. SafeArrayTypeMismatchException	0x80131533	COR_E_SAFEARRAYTYPEMISMATCH
System.Security.SecurityException	0x800A0046	CTL_E_PERMISSIONDENIED
	0x800A01A3	VB6: Permission to use object denied (419)
	0x80131415	**CORSEC_E_INVALID_STRONGNAME**
	0x8013150A	COR_E_SECURITY
System.Runtime.Serialization. SerializationException	0x8013150C	COR_E_SERIALIZATION
System.Runtime.Remoting. ServerException	0x8013150E	COR_E_SERVER
System.StackOverflowException	**0x800703E9**	**ERROR_STACK_OVERFLOW (COR_E_STACKOVERFLOW)**
	0x800A001C	CTL_E_OUTOFSTACKSPACE

C

HRESULT TO .NET
EXCEPTION
TRANSFORMATIONS

Table C.1   Continued

Exception Name	HRESULT Value	HRESULT Name
System.Threading.SynchronizationLockException	0x80131518	COR_E_SYNCHRONIZATIONLOCK
System.SystemException	0x80131501	COR_E_SYSTEM
System.Reflection.TargetException	0x80131603	COR_E_TARGET
System.Reflection.TargetInvocationException	0x80131604	COR_E_TARGETINVOCATION
System.Reflection.TargetParameterCountException	0x8002000E	DISP_E_BADPARAMCOUNT (COR_E_TARGETPARAMCOUNT)
System.Threading.ThreadAbortException	0x80131530	COR_E_THREADABORTED
System.Threading.ThreadInterruptedException	0x80131519	COR_E_THREADINTERRUPTED
System.Threading.ThreadStateException	0x80131520	COR_E_THREADSTATE
System.Threading.ThreadStopException	0x80131521	COR_E_THREADSTOP
System.TypeInitializationException	0x80131534	COR_E_TYPEINITIALIZATION
System.TypeLoadException	0x80131522	COR_E_TYPELOAD
System.TypeUnloadedException	0x80131013	COR_E_TYPEUNLOADED
System.UnauthorizedAccessException	**0x80070005**	**E_ACCESSDENIED (COR_E_UNAUTHORIZEDACCESS)**
	0x800A004B	CTL_E_PATHFILEACCESSERROR
	0x800A014F	VB6: Could not access system registry (335)
System.Security.VerificationException	0x8013150D	COR_E_VERIFICATION
System.Security.XmlSyntaxException	0x80131419	CORSEC_E_XMLSYNTAX

TABLE C.2   Exception Types Listed Numerically by HRESULT Value

HRESULT *Value*	HRESULT *Name*	*Exception Name*
FACILITY_NULL:		
0x8000211D	COR_E_AMBIGUOUSMATCH	System.Reflection.AmbiguousMatchException
0x80004001	E_NOTIMPL	System.NotImplementedException
0x80004002	E_NOINTERFACE (COR_E_INVALIDCAST)	System.InvalidCastException
0x80004003	E_POINTER (COR_E_NULLREFERENCE)	System.NullReferenceException
0x80004005	E_FAIL	System.Runtime.InteropServices.COMException
FACILITY_DISPATCH:		
0x8002000E	DISP_E_BADPARAMCOUNT COR_E_TARGETPARAMCOUNT)	System.Reflection.TargetParameterCountException
0x80020012	DISP_E_DIVBYZERO (COR_E_DIVIDEBYZERO)	System.DivideByZeroException
FACILITY_STORAGE:		
0x80030003	STG_E_PATHNOTFOUND	System.IO.DirectoryNotFoundException
FACILITY_WIN32:		
0x80070002	ERROR_FILE_NOT_FOUND (COR_E_FILENOTFOUND)	System.IO.FileNotFoundException
0x80070003	ERROR_PATH_NOT_FOUND (COR_E_DIRECTORYNOTFOUND)	System.IO.DirectoryNotFoundException
0x80070004	ERROR_TOO_MANY_OPEN_FILES	System.IO.FileLoadException
0x80070005	E_ACCESSDENIED (COR_E_UNAUTHORIZEDACCESS)	System.UnauthorizedAccessException
0x8007000B	ERROR_BAD_FORMAT (COR_E_BADIMAGEFORMAT)	System.BadImageFormatException
0x8007000E	E_OUTOFMEMORY (COR_E_OUTOFMEMORY)	System.OutOfMemoryException
0x80070015	ERROR_NOT_READY	System.IO.FileNotFoundException
0x80070020	ERROR_SHARING_VIOLATION	System.IO.FileLoadException
0x80070021	ERROR_LOCK_VIOLATION	System.IO.FileLoadException
0x80070026	ERROR_HANDLE_EOF (COR_E_ENDOFSTREAM)	System.IO.EndOfStreamException

C

HRESULT TO .NET
EXCEPTION
TRANSFORMATIONS

Table C.2   Continued

HRESULT *Value*	HRESULT *Name*	*Exception Name*
0x80070035	ERROR_BAD_NETPATH	System.IO.FileNotFoundException
0x80070043	ERROR_BAD_NET_NAME	System.IO.FileNotFoundException
0x80070057	E_INVALIDARG (COR_E_ARGUMENT)	System.ArgumentException
0x8007006E	ERROR_OPEN_FAILED	System.IO.FileLoadException
0x8007007B	ERROR_INVALID_NAME	System.IO.FileNotFoundException
0x8007007E	ERROR_MOD_NOT_FOUND	System.IO.FileNotFoundException
0x800700C0	ERROR_EXE_MARKED_INVALID	System.BadImageFormatException
0x800700C1	ERROR_BAD_EXE_FORMAT	System.BadImageFormatException
0x800700CE	ERROR_FILENAME_EXCED_RANGE (COR_E_PATHTOOLONG)	System.IO.PathTooLongException
0x80070216	ERROR_ARITHMETIC_OVERFLOW (COR_E_ARITHMETIC)	System.ArithmeticException
0x800703E9	ERROR_STACK_OVERFLOW (COR_E_STACKOVERFLOW)	System.StackOverflowException
0x800703ED	ERROR_UNRECOGNIZED_VOLUME	System.IO.FileLoadException
0x800703EE	ERROR_FILE_INVALID	System.IO.FileLoadException
0x8007045A	ERROR_DLL_INIT_FAILED	System.IO.FileLoadException
0x80070570	ERROR_FILE_CORRUPT	System.IO.FileLoadException
0x80070571	ERROR_DISK_CORRUPT	System.IO.FileLoadException
0x80070574	ERROR_WRONG_TARGET_NAME	System.IO.FileNotFoundException
FACILITY_CONTROL:		
0x800A0006	CTL_E_OVERFLOW	System.OverflowException
0x800A0007	CTL_E_OUTOFMEMORY	System.OutOfMemoryException
0x800A0009	VB6: Subscript out of range (9)	System.IndexOutOfRangeException
0x800A000B	CTL_E_DIVISIONBYZERO	System.DivideByZeroException
0x800A001C	CTL_E_OUTOFSTACKSPACE	System.StackOverflowException
0x800A0035	CTL_E_FILENOTFOUND	System.IO.FileNotFoundException
0x800A0039	CTL_E_DEVICEIOERROR	System.IO.IOException
0x800A003E	VB6: Input past end of file (62)	System.IO.EndOfStreamException
0x800A0046	CTL_E_PERMISSIONDENIED	System.Security.SecurityException

TABLE C.2   Continued

HRESULT *Value*	HRESULT *Name*	*Exception Name*
0x800A004B	CTL_E_PATHFILEACCESSERROR	System.UnauthorizedAccessException
0x800A004C	CTL_E_PATHNOTFOUND	System.IO.DirectoryNotFoundException
0x800A014F	VB6: Could not access system registry (335)	System.UnauthorizedAccessException
0x800A01A3	VB6: Permission to use object denied (419)	System.Security.SecurityException
0x800A01B6	VB6: Object doesn't support this property or method (438)	System.NotSupportedException
0x800A01BD	VB6: Object doesn't support this action (445)	System.NotSupportedException
0x800A01C1	VB6: Argument not optional (449)	System.ArgumentException
0x800A01C2	VB6: Wrong number of arguments (450)	System.ArgumentException
0x800A01CA	VB6: Variable uses a type not supported in Visual Basic (458)	System.NotSupportedException
0x800A01CB	VB6: This component doesn't support the set of events (459)	System.NotSupportedException
0x800A01CD	VB6: Method or data member not found (461)	System.MissingMemberException
0x800A7919	VB6: Out of memory (31001)	System.OutOfMemoryException
0x800A793C	VB6: Error saving to file (31036)	System.IO.IOException
0x800A793D	VB6: Error loading from file (31037)	System.IO.IOException
	FACILITY_URT (.NET-Specific HRESULTs):	
	Execution Engine Errors:	
0x80131013	COR_E_TYPEUNLOADED	System.TypeUnloadedException
0x80131014	COR_E_APPDOMAINUNLOADED	System.AppDomainUnloadedException

TABLE C.2   Continued

HRESULT *Value*	HRESULT *Name*	*Exception Name*
0x80131015	COR_E_CANNOTUNLOADAPPDOMAIN	System.CannotUnloadAppDomainException
0x80131018	COR_E_ASSEMBLYEXPECTED	System.IO.FileLoadException
0x80131019	COR_E_FIXUPSINEXE	System.IO.FileLoadException
0x80131039	COR_E_MODULE_HASH_CHECK_FAILED	System.IO.FileLoadException
0x80131040	FUSION_E_REF_DEF_MISMATCH	System.IO.FileLoadException
0x80131041	FUSION_E_INVALID_PRIVATE_ASM_LOCATION	System.IO.FileLoadException
0x80131042	FUSION_E_ASM_MODULE_MISSING	System.IO.FileLoadException
0x80131045	FUSION_E_SIGNATURE_CHECK_FAILED	System.IO.FileLoadException
0x80131047	FUSION_E_INVALID_NAME	System.IO.FileLoadException
Metadata Errors:		
0x80131107	CLDB_E_FILE_OLDVER	System.BadImageFormatException
0x8013110E	CLDB_E_FILE_CORRUPT	System.BadImageFormatException
Security Errors:		
0x80131401	SECURITY_E_INCOMPATIBLE_SHARE	System.IO.FileLoadException
0x80131402	SECURITY_E_UNVERIFIABLE	System.IO.FileLoadException
0x80131403	SECURITY_E_INCOMPATIBLE_EVIDENCE	System.IO.FileLoadException
0x80131415	CORSEC_E_INVALID_STRONGNAME	System.Security.SecurityException
0x80131416	CORSEC_E_POLICY_EXCEPTION	System.Security.Policy.PolicyException
0x80131419	CORSEC_E_XMLSYNTAX	System.Security.XmlSyntaxException
0x8013141D	CORSEC_E_INVALID_IMAGE_FORMAT	System.BadImageFormatException
0x80131430	CORSEC_E_CRYPTO	System.Security.Cryptography.CryptographicException
0x80131431	CORSEC_E_CRYPTO_UNEX_OPER	System.Security.Cryptography.CryptographicUnexpectedOperationException

TABLE C.2 Continued

HRESULT *Value*	HRESULT *Name*	*Exception Name*
0x80131450	ISS_E_ISOSTORE	System.IO.IsolatedStorage. IsolatedStorageException
	Class Library Errors:	
0x80131500	COR_E_EXCEPTION	System.Exception
0x80131501	COR_E_SYSTEM	System.SystemException
0x80131502	COR_E_ARGUMENTOUTOFRANGE	System.ArgumentOutOfRange Exception
0x80131503	COR_E_ARRAYTYPEMISMATCH	System.ArrayTypeMismatch Exception
0x80131504	COR_E_CONTEXTMARSHAL	System.ContextMarshalException
0x80131506	COR_E_EXECUTIONENGINE	System.ExecutionEngineException
0x80131507	COR_E_FIELDACCESS	System.FieldAccessException
0x80131508	COR_E_INDEXOUTOFRANGE	System.IndexOutOfRangeException
0x80131509	COR_E_INVALIDOPERATION	System.InvalidOperationException
0x8013150A	COR_E_SECURITY	System.Security.Security Exception
0x8013150B	COR_E_REMOTING	System.Runtime.Remoting. RemotingException
0x8013150C	COR_E_SERIALIZATION	System.Runtime.Serialization. SerializationException
0x8013150D	COR_E_VERIFICATION	System.Security.Verification- Exception
0x8013150E	COR_E_SERVER	System.Runtime.Remoting. ServerException
0x80131510	COR_E_METHODACCESS	System.MethodAccessException
0x80131511	COR_E_MISSINGFIELD	System.MissingFieldException
0x80131512	COR_E_MISSINGMEMBER	System.MissingMemberException
0x80131513	COR_E_MISSINGMETHOD	System.MissingMethodException
0x80131514	COR_E_MULTICASTNOTSUPPORTED	System.MulticastNotSupported Exception
0x80131515	COR_E_NOTSUPPORTED	System.NotSupportedException
0x80131516	COR_E_OVERFLOW	System.OverflowException
0x80131517	COR_E_RANK	System.RankException

C

HRESULT TO .NET
EXCEPTION
TRANSFORMATIONS

TABLE C.2   Continued

HRESULT *Value*	HRESULT *Name*	*Exception Name*
0x80131518	COR_E_SYNCHRONIZATIONLOCK	System.Threading. SynchronizationLockException
0x80131519	COR_E_THREADINTERRUPTED	System.Threading. ThreadInterruptedException
0x8013151A	COR_E_MEMBERACCESS	System.MemberAccessException
0x80131520	COR_E_THREADSTATE	System.Threading. ThreadStateException
0x80131521	COR_E_THREADSTOP	System.Threading. ThreadStopException
0x80131522	COR_E_TYPELOAD	System.TypeLoadException
0x80131523	COR_E_ENTRYPOINTNOTFOUND	System. EntryPointNotFoundException
0x80131524	COR_E_DLLNOTFOUND	System.DllNotFoundException
0x80131527	COR_E_INVALIDCOMOBJECT	System.Runtime.InteropServices. InvalidComObjectException
0x80131528	COR_E_NOTFINITENUMBER	System.NotFiniteNumberException
0x80131529	COR_E_DUPLICATEWAITOBJECT	System. DuplicateWaitObjectException
0x80131530	COR_E_THREADABORTED	System.Threading. ThreadAbortException
0x80131531	COR_E_INVALIDOLEVARIANTTYPE	System.Runtime.InteropServices. InvalidOleVariantTypeException
0x80131532	COR_E_ MISSINGMANIFESTRESOURCE	System.Resources. MissingManifestResourceException
0x80131533	COR_E_SAFEARRAYTYPE MISMATCH	System.Runtime.InteropServices. SafeArrayTypeMismatchException
0x80131534	COR_E_TYPEINITIALIZATION	System. TypeInitializationException
0x80131535	COR_E_MARSHALDIRECTIVE	System.Runtime.InteropServices. MarshalDirectiveException
0x80131537	COR_E_FORMAT	System.FormatException
0x80131538	COR_E_SAFEARRAYRANK MISMATCH	System.Runtime.InteropServices. SafeArrayRankMismatchException
0x80131539	COR_E_PLATFORMNOTSUPPORTED	System. PlatformNotSupportedException

TABLE C.2 Continued

HRESULT *Value*	HRESULT *Name*	*Exception Name*
0x8013153A	COR_E_INVALIDPROGRAM	System.InvalidProgramException
0x80131600	COR_E_APPLICATION	System.ApplicationException
0x80131601	COR_E_INVALIDFILTERCRITERIA	System.Reflection.InvalidFilterCriteriaException
0x80131602	COR_E_REFLECTIONTYPELOAD	System.Reflection.ReflectionTypeLoadException
0x80131603	COR_E_TARGET	System.Reflection.TargetException
0x80131604	COR_E_TARGETINVOCATION	System.Reflection.TargetInvocationException
0x80131605	COR_E_CUSTOMATTRIBUTEFORMAT	System.Reflection.CustomAttributeFormatException
0x80131620	COR_E_IO	System.IO.IOException
0x80131621	COR_E_FILELOAD	System.IO.FileLoadException

.NET Exception to HRESULT
Transformations

Every .NET exception type has a protected HResult field that is exposed to COM as an HRESULT when the exception is thrown. This appendix lists the HRESULT value for every .NET exception defined in the .NET Framework—more than just the mscorlib assembly.

Table D.1 lists the HRESULTs numerically, answering a COM programmer's question, "What .NET exception was likely thrown to cause this failure HRESULT?" Some of this information can be obtained programmatically by calling the System.Runtime.InteropServices.Marshal.ThrowExceptionForHR method, but only for a subset of the HRESULTs. The word "likely" is used because, in general, it's impossible to know what .NET exception was thrown from an HRESULT value alone. This is true because:

- Many .NET Framework exception types reuse the same HRESULT value.
- Future user-defined exceptions could reuse HRESULT values.
- Any exceptions deriving from System.Runtime.InteropServices.ExternalException have a public ErrorCode property that enables anyone to change the HRESULT value at any time.

Table D.2 contains the same information as Table D.1 but lists the exception types alphabetically, to answer a .NET component author's question, "If I throw this exception, what HRESULT will a COM client see returned?" This information can always be obtained for any .NET exception by calling System.Runtime.InteropServices.Marshal.GetHRForException (which simply returns the value in the exception's protected HResult field).

Here are a few notes about the tables:

- For exception types that share the same HRESULT values, the bold types in Table D.1 correspond to the ones thrown when the HRESULT is returned from COM and exposed to .NET as an exception (shown in Appendix C).
- The italicized exception types derive from (or are) System.Runtime.InteropServices.ExternalException, indicating that their HRESULT values could be easily set to any value—not just the values listed.
- Some exception types listed in Table D.2 have no default HRESULT value; they are always constructed with a value specific to an error-causing situation. These six exception types are not listed in Table D.1.
- Any listed names beginning with ERROR are Win32 error codes that must be added to 0x80070000 to get the listed HRESULT value with FACILITY_WIN32.
- A few HRESULTs have multiple names, because some .NET HRESULTs (beginning with COR) are defined with the same value as classic COM HRESULTs. A list of named .NET HRESULTs can be found in CorError.h.

TABLE D.1 HRESULTs Listed Numerically

HRESULT *Value*	HRESULT *Name*	*Exception Name*
	FACILITY_NULL:	
0x8000211D	COR_E_AMBIGUOUSMATCH	System.Reflection.AmbiguousMatchException
0x80004001	E_NOTIMPL	System.NotImplementedException
0x80004002	E_NOINTERFACE (COR_E_INVALIDCAST)	System.InvalidCastException
0x80004003	E_POINTER (COR_E_NULLREFERENCE)	System.ArgumentNullException
		System.NullReferenceException
0x80004005	E_FAIL	*System.ComponentModel.Design.CheckoutException*
		System.Runtime.InteropServices.COMException
		System.Runtime.InteropServices.ExternalException
		System.Web.HttpCompileException
		System.Web.HttpException
		System.Web.HttpParseException
		System.Web.HttpUnhandledException
		System.Runtime.InteropServices.SEHException
	FACILITY_DISPATCH:	
0x8002000E	DISP_E_BADPARAMCOUNT (COR_E_TARGETPARAMCOUNT)	System.Reflection.TargetParameterCountException
0x80020012	DISP_E_DIVBYZERO (COR_E_DIVIDEBYZERO)	System.DivideByZeroException
	FACILITY_WIN32:	
0x80070002	ERROR_FILE_NOT_FOUND (COR_E_FILENOTFOUND)	System.IO.FileNotFoundException
0x80070003	ERROR_PATH_NOT_FOUND (COR_E_DIRECTORYNOTFOUND)	System.IO.DirectoryNotFoundException
0x80070005	E_ACCESSDENIED (COR_E_UNAUTHORIZEDACCESS)	System.UnauthorizedAccessException
0x8007000B	ERROR_BAD_FORMAT (COR_E_BADIMAGEFORMAT)	System.BadImageFormatException

D

.NET EXCEPTION TO HRESULT TRANSFORMATIONS

Table D.1   Continued

HRESULT *Value*	HRESULT *Name*	*Exception Name*
0x8007000E	E_OUTOFMEMORY (COR_E_OUTOFMEMORY)	System.OutOfMemoryException
0x80070026	ERROR_HANDLE_EOF (COR_E_ENDOFSTREAM)	System.IO.EndOfStreamException
0x80070057	E_INVALIDARG (COR_E_ARGUMENT)	**System.ArgumentException** System.ComponentModel. InvalidEnumArgumentException
0x800700CE	ERROR_FILENAME_EXCED_ RANGE (COR_E_PATHTOOLONG)	System.IO.PathTooLongException
0x80070216	ERROR_ARITHMETIC_OVERFLOW (COR_E_ARITHMETIC)	System.ArithmeticException
0x800703E9	ERROR_STACK_OVERFLOW (COR_E_STACKOVERFLOW)	System.StackOverflowException
FACILITY_URT (.NET-Specific HRESULTs):		
Execution Engine Errors:		
0x80131013	COR_E_TYPEUNLOADED	System.TypeUnloadedException
0x80131014	COR_E_APPDOMAINUNLOADED	System.AppDomainUnloadedException
0x80131015	COR_E_ CANNOTUNLOADAPPDOMAIN	System. CannotUnloadAppDomainException
Security Errors:		
0x80131416	CORSEC_E_POLICY_EXCEPTION	System.Security.Policy. PolicyException
0x80131419	CORSEC_E_XMLSYNTAX	System.Security.XmlSyntaxException
0x80131430	CORSEC_E_CRYPTO	System.Security.Cryptography. CryptographicException
0x80131431	CORSEC_E_CRYPTO_UNEX_ OPER	System.Security.Cryptography. CryptographicUnexpectedOperation Exception
0x80131450	ISS_E_ISOSTORE	System.IO.IsolatedStorage. IsolatedStorageException
Class Library Errors:		
0x80131500	COR_E_EXCEPTION	**System.Exception** System.Windows.Forms. InvalidActiveXStateException

TABLE D.1   Continued

HRESULT *Value*	HRESULT *Name*	*Exception Name*
		System.Runtime.Remoting. MetadataServices. SUDSGeneratorException
		System.Runtime.Remoting. MetadataServices. SUDSParserException
0x80131501	COR_E_SYSTEM	System.ComponentModel.Design. Serialization. CodeDomSerializerException
		System.Data.DBConcurrencyException
		System.Drawing.Printing. InvalidPrinterException
		System.EnterpriseServices. RegistrationException
		System.Web.Services.Protocols. SoapException
		System.Web.Services.Protocols. SoapHeaderException
		System.Data.SqlTypes. SqlNullValueException
		System.Data.SqlTypes. SqlTruncateException
		System.Data.SqlTypes. SqlTypeException
		System.SystemException
		System.ComponentModel. WarningException
0x80131502	COR_E_ARGUMENTOUTOFRANGE	System.ArgumentOutOfRangeException
0x80131503	COR_E_ARRAYTYPEMISMATCH	System.ArrayTypeMismatchException
0x80131504	COR_E_CONTEXTMARSHAL	System.ContextMarshalException
0x80131506	COR_E_EXECUTIONENGINE	System.ExecutionEngineException
0x80131507	COR_E_FIELDACCESS	System.FieldAccessException
0x80131508	COR_E_INDEXOUTOFRANGE	System.IndexOutOfRangeException

TABLE D.1   Continued

HRESULT *Value*	HRESULT *Name*	*Exception Name*
0x80131509	COR_E_INVALIDOPERATION	**System.InvalidOperationException**
		System.ObjectDisposedException
		System.Net.ProtocolViolationException
		System.Net.WebException
0x8013150A	COR_E_SECURITY	System.Security.SecurityException
0x8013150B	COR_E_REMOTING	**System.Runtime.Remoting.RemotingException**
		System.Runtime.Remoting.RemotingTimeoutException
0x8013150C	COR_E_SERIALIZATION	System.Runtime.Serialization.SerializationException
0x8013150D	COR_E_VERIFICATION	System.Security.VerificationException
0x8013150E	COR_E_SERVER	System.Runtime.Remoting.ServerException
0x8013150F	COR_E_SERVICEDCOMPONENT	System.EnterpriseServices.ServicedComponentException
0x80131510	COR_E_METHODACCESS	System.MethodAccessException
0x80131511	COR_E_MISSINGFIELD	System.MissingFieldException
0x80131512	COR_E_MISSINGMEMBER	System.MissingMemberException
0x80131513	COR_E_MISSINGMETHOD	System.MissingMethodException
0x80131514	COR_E_MULTICASTNOTSUPPORTED	System.MulticastNotSupported-Exception
0x80131515	COR_E_NOTSUPPORTED	System.NotSupportedException
0x80131516	COR_E_OVERFLOW	System.OverflowException
0x80131517	COR_E_RANK	System.RankException
0x80131518	COR_E_SYNCHRONIZATIONLOCK	System.Threading.SynchronizationLockException
0x80131519	COR_E_THREADINTERRUPTED	System.Threading.ThreadInterruptedException
0x8013151A	COR_E_MEMBERACCESS	System.MemberAccessException
0x80131520	COR_E_THREADSTATE	System.Threading.ThreadStateException

TABLE D.1   Continued

HRESULT *Value*	HRESULT *Name*	*Exception Name*
0x80131521	COR_E_THREADSTOP	System.Threading.ThreadStopException
0x80131522	COR_E_TYPELOAD	System.TypeLoadException
0x80131523	COR_E_ENTRYPOINTNOTFOUND	System.EntryPointNotFoundException
0x80131524	COR_E_DLLNOTFOUND	System.DllNotFoundException
0x80131527	COR_E_INVALIDCOMOBJECT	System.Runtime.InteropServices.InvalidComObjectException
0x80131528	COR_E_NOTFINITENUMBER	System.NotFiniteNumberException
0x80131529	COR_E_DUPLICATEWAITOBJECT	System.DuplicateWaitObjectException
0x80131530	COR_E_THREADABORTED	System.Threading.ThreadAbortException
0x80131531	COR_E_INVALIDOLEVARIANTTYPE	InvalidOleVariantTypeException System.Runtime.InteropServices.
0x80131532	COR_E_MISSINGMANIFESTRESOURCE	System.Resources.MissingManifestResourceException
0x80131533	COR_E_SAFEARRAYTYPEMISMATCH	System.Runtime.InteropServices.SafeArrayTypeMismatchException
0x80131534	COR_E_TYPEINITIALIZATION	System.TypeInitializationException
0x80131535	COR_E_MARSHALDIRECTIVE	System.Runtime.InteropServices.MarshalDirectiveException
0x80131537	COR_E_FORMAT	System.Net.CookieException
		System.FormatException
		System.UriFormatException
0x80131538	COR_E_SAFEARRAYRANKMISMATCH	System.Runtime.InteropServices.SafeArrayRankMismatchException
0x80131539	COR_E_PLATFORMNOTSUPPORTED	System.PlatformNotSupportedException
0x8013153A	COR_E_INVALIDPROGRAM	System.InvalidProgramException
0x80131600	COR_E_APPLICATION	System.ApplicationException
0x80131601	COR_E_INVALIDFILTERCRITERIA	System.Reflection.InvalidFilterCriteriaException
0x80131602	COR_E_REFLECTIONTYPELOAD	System.Reflection.ReflectionTypeLoadException
0x80131603	COR_E_TARGET	System.Reflection.TargetException

D

.NET EXCEPTION TO HRESULT TRANSFORMATIONS

TABLE D.1   Continued

HRESULT *Value*	HRESULT *Name*	*Exception Name*
0x80131604	COR_E_TARGETINVOCATION	System.Reflection.TargetInvocationException
0x80131605	COR_E_CUSTOMATTRIBUTE-FORMAT	System.Reflection.CustomAttributeFormatException
0x80131620	COR_E_IO	System.IO.IOException
0x80131621	COR_E_FILELOAD	System.IO.FileLoadException
Additional Errors from Exceptions Defined in Assemblies Other Than mscorlib:		
0x80131901	N/A	System.ComponentModel.LicenseException
0x80131902	N/A	System.Configuration.ConfigurationException
0x80131904	N/A	System.Data.SqlClient.SqlException
0x80131905	N/A	System.IO.InternalBufferOverflowException
0x80131906	N/A	System.ServiceProcess.TimeoutException
0x80131907	N/A	System.Configuration.Install.InstallException
0x80131920	N/A	System.Data.DataException
		System.Data.EvaluateException
		System.Data.InvalidExpressionException
		System.Data.SyntaxErrorException
0x80131921	N/A	System.Data.DeletedRowInaccessibleException
0x80131922	N/A	System.Data.DuplicateNameException
0x80131923	N/A	System.Data.InRowChangingEventException
0x80131924	N/A	System.Data.InvalidConstraintException
0x80131925	N/A	System.Data.MissingPrimaryKeyException
0x80131926	N/A	System.Data.NoNullAllowedException
0x80131927	N/A	System.Data.ReadOnlyException

TABLE D.1   Continued

HRESULT *Value*	HRESULT *Name*	*Exception Name*
0x80131928	N/A	System.Data.RowNotInTableException
0x80131929	N/A	System.Data. VersionNotFoundException
0x8013192A	N/A	System.Data.ConstraintException
0x8013192B	N/A	System.Data.StrongTypingException
		System.Data. TypedDataSetGeneratorException
0x80131940	N/A	System.Xml.XmlException
0x80131941	N/A	System.Xml.Schema. XmlSchemaException
0x80131942	N/A	System.Xml.Xsl. XsltCompileException
		System.Xml.Xsl.XsltException
0x80131943	N/A	System.Xml.XPath.XPathException

> **DIGGING DEEPER**
>
> Although the HRESULT values in the 0x801319*nn* range are only used by exception types defined in non-mscorlib .NET Framework assemblies, there are plenty of such exception types that *do* use HRESULT values in the other FACILITY_URT ranges. Also, the 0x801319*nn* values listed in Table D.1 are not defined in a public header file and therefore have no official names.

TABLE D.2   HRESULTs Listed Alphabetically by Exception Type

Exception Name	HRESULT *Value*	HRESULT *Name*
System.Reflection. AmbiguousMatchException	0x8000211D	COR_E_AMBIGUOUSMATCH
System.AppDomainUnloadedException	0x80131014	COR_E_APPDOMAINUN LOADED
System.ApplicationException	0x80131600	COR_E_APPLICATION
System.ArgumentException	0x80070057	E_INVALIDARG (COR_E_ARGUMENT)
System.ArgumentNullException	0x80004003	E_POINTER (COR_E_NULL REFERENCE)

TABLE D.2 Continued

Exception Name	HRESULT Value	HRESULT Name
System.ArgumentOutOfRangeException	0x80131502	COR_E_ ARGUMENTOUTOFRANGE
System.ArithmeticException	0x80070216	ERROR_ARITHMETIC_ OVERFLOW (COR_E_ ARITHMETIC)
System.ArrayTypeMismatchException	0x80131503	COR_E_ ARRAYTYPEMISMATCH
System.BadImageFormatException	0x8007000B	ERROR_BAD_FORMAT (COR_E_BADIMAGEFORMAT)
System. CannotUnloadAppDomainException	0x80131015	COR_E_ CANNOTUNLOADAPPDOMAIN
System.ComponentModel.Design. CheckoutException	0x80004005	E_FAIL
System.ComponentModel.Design. Serialization. CodeDomSerializerException	0x80131501	COR_E_SYSTEM
System.Runtime.InteropServices. COMException	0x80004005	E_FAIL
System.Configuration. ConfigurationException	0x80131902	N/A
System.Data.ConstraintException	0x8013192A	N/A
System.ContextMarshalException	0x80131504	COR_E_CONTEXTMARSHAL
System.Net.CookieException	0x80131537	COR_E_FORMAT
System.Security.Cryptography. CryptographicException	0x80131430	CORSEC_E_CRYPTO
System.Security.Cryptography. CryptographicUnexpected OperatioException	0x80131431	CORSEC_E_CRYPTO_UNEX_ OPER
System.Reflection. CustomAttributeFormatException	0x80131605	COR_E_ CUSTOMATTRIBUTEFORMAT
System.Data.DataException	0x80131920	N/A
System.Data.DBConcurrencyException	0x80131501	COR_E_SYSTEM
System.Data. DeletedRowInaccessibleException	0x80131921	N/A
System.IO.DirectoryNotFoundException	0x80070003	ERROR_PATH_NOT_FOUND (COR_E_ DIRECTORYNOTFOUND)

TABLE D.2 Continued

Exception Name	HRESULT Value	HRESULT Name
System.DivideByZeroException	0x80020012	DISP_E_DIVBYZERO (COR_E_DIVIDEBYZERO)
System.DllNotFoundException	0x80131524	COR_E_DLLNOTFOUND
System.Data.DuplicateNameException	0x80131922	N/A
System.DuplicateWaitObjectException	0x80131529	COR_E_ DUPLICATEWAITOBJECT
System.IO.EndOfStreamException	0x80070026	ERROR_HANDLE_EOF (COR_E_ENDOFSTREAM)
System.EntryPointNotFoundException	0x80131523	COR_E_ ENTRYPOINTNOTFOUND
System.Data.EvaluateException	0x80131920	N/A
System.Exception	0x80131500	COR_E_EXCEPTION
System.ExecutionEngineException	0x80131506	COR_E_EXECUTIONENGINE
System.Runtime.InteropServices. ExternalException	0x80004005	E_FAIL
System.FieldAccessException	0x80131507	COR_E_FIELDACCESS
System.IO.FileLoadException	0x80131621	COR_E_FILELOAD
System.IO.FileNotFoundException (COR_E_FILENOTFOUND)	0x80070002	ERROR_FILE_NOT_FOUND
System.FormatException	0x80131537	COR_E_FORMAT
System.Web.HttpCompileException	0x80004005	E_FAIL
System.Web.HttpException	0x80004005	E_FAIL
System.Web.HttpParseException	0x80004005	E_FAIL
System.Web.HttpUnhandledException	0x80004005	E_FAIL
System.IndexOutOfRangeException	0x80131508	COR_E_INDEXOUTOFRANGE
System.Data. InRowChangingEventException	0x80131923	N/A
System.Configuration.Install. InstallException	0x80131907	N/A
System.IO. InternalBufferOverflowException	0x80131905	N/A
System.Windows.Forms. InvalidActiveXStateException	0x80131500	COR_E_EXCEPTION
System.InvalidCastException	0x80004002	COR_E_INVALIDCAST (E_NOINTERFACE)

TABLE D.2 Continued

Exception Name	HRESULT Value	HRESULT Name
System.Runtime.InteropServices.InvalidComObjectException	0x80131527	COR_E_INVALIDCOMOBJECT
System.Data.InvalidConstraintException	0x80131924	N/A
System.ComponentModel.InvalidEnum-ArgumentException	0x80070057	E_INVALIDARG (COR_E_ARGUMENT)
System.Data.InvalidExpressionException	0x80131920	N/A
System.Reflection.InvalidFilterCriteriaException	0x80131601	COR_E_INVALIDFILTER CRITERIA
System.Runtime.InteropServices.InvalidOleVariantTypeException	0x80131531	COR_E_INVALIDOLEVARIANTTYPE
System.InvalidOperationException	0x80131509	COR_E_INVALIDOPERATION
System.Drawing.Printing.InvalidPrinterException	0x80131501	COR_E_SYSTEM
System.InvalidProgramException	0x8013153A	COR_E_INVALIDPROGRAM
System.IO.IOException	0x80131620	COR_E_IO
System.IO.IsolatedStorage.IsolatedStorageException	0x80131450	ISS_E_ISOSTORE
System.ComponentModel.LicenseException	0x80131901	N/A
System.Management.ManagementException	No default	N/A
System.Runtime.InteropServices.MarshalDirectiveException	0x80131535	COR_E_MARSHALDIRECTIVE
System.MemberAccessException	0x8013151A	COR_E_MEMBERACCESS
System.Messaging.MessageQueueException	No default	N/A
System.MethodAccessException	0x80131510	COR_E_METHODACCESS
System.MissingFieldException	0x80131511	COR_E_MISSINGFIELD
System.Resources.MissingManifestResourceException	0x80131532	COR_E_MISSINGMANIFESTRESOURCE
System.MissingMemberException	0x80131512	COR_E_MISSINGMEMBER
System.MissingMethodException	0x80131513	COR_E_MISSINGMETHOD
System.Data.MissingPrimaryKeyException	0x80131925	N/A

TABLE D.2 Continued

Exception Name	HRESULT Value	HRESULT Name
System.MulticastNotSupported-Exception	0x80131514	COR_E_MULTICASTNOTSUPPORTED
System.Data.NoNullAllowedException	0x80131926	N/A
System.NotFiniteNumberException	0x80131528	COR_E_NOTFINITENUMBER
System.NotImplementedException	0x80004001	E_NOTIMPL
System.NotSupportedException	0x80131515	COR_E_NOTSUPPORTED
System.NullReferenceException	0x80004003	E_POINTER (COR_E_NULLREFERENCE)
System.ObjectDisposedException	0x80131509	COR_E_INVALIDOPERATION
System.Data.OleDb.OleDbException	*No default*	N/A
System.OutOfMemoryException	0x8007000E	E_OUTOFMEMORY (COR_E_OUTOFMEMORY)
System.OverflowException	0x80131516	COR_E_OVERFLOW
System.IO.PathTooLongException	0x800700CE	ERROR_FILENAME_EXCED_RANGE (COR_E_PATHTOOLONG)
System.PlatformNotSupportedException	0x80131539	COR_E_PLATFORMNOTSUPPORTED
System.Security.Policy.Policy-Exception	0x80131416	CORSEC_E_POLICY_EXCEPTION
System.Net.ProtocolViolataionException	0x80131509	COR_E_INVALIDOPERATION
System.RankException	0x80131517	COR_E_RANK
System.Data.ReadOnlyException	0x80131927	N/A
System.Reflection.ReflectionTypeLoadException	0x80131602	COR_E_REFLECTIONTYPELOAD
System.EnterpriseServices.RegistrationException	0x80131501	COR_E_SYSTEM
System.Runtime.Remoting.RemotingException	0x8013150B	COR_E_REMOTING
System.Runtime.Remoting.RemotingTimeoutException	0x8013150B	COR_E_REMOTING
System.Data.RowNotInTableException	0x80131928	N/A
System.Runtime.InteropServices.SafeArrayRankMismatchException	0x80131538	COR_E_SAFEARRAYRANKMISMATCH

TABLE D.2 Continued

Exception Name	HRESULT *Value*	HRESULT *Name*
System.Runtime.InteropServices. SafeArrayTypeMismatchException	0x80131533	COR_E_SAFEARRAYTYPE MISMATCH
System.Security.SecurityException	0x8013150A	COR_E_SECURITY
System.Runtime.InteropServices. SEHException	0x80004005	E_FAIL
System.Runtime.Serialization. SerializationException	0x8013150C	COR_E_SERIALIZATION
System.Runtime.Remoting. ServerException	0x8013150E	COR_E_SERVER
System.EnterpriseServices. ServicedComponentException	0x8013150F	COR_E_SERVICEDCOMPONENT
System.Web.Services.Protocols. SoapException	0x80131501	COR_E_SYSTEM
System.Web.Services.Protocols. SoapHeaderException	0x80131501	COR_E_SYSTEM
System.Net.Sockets.SocketException	*No default*	N/A
System.Data.SqlClient.SqlException	0x80131904	N/A
System.Data.SqlTypes. SqlNullValueException	0x80131501	COR_E_SYSTEM
System.Data.SqlTypes. SqlTruncateException	0x80131501	COR_E_SYSTEM
System.Data.SqlTypes.SqlTypeException	0x80131501	COR_E_SYSTEM
System.StackOverflowException	0x800703E9	ERROR_STACK_OVERFLOW (COR_E_STACKOVERFLOW)
System.Data.StrongTypingException	0x8013192B	N/A
System.Runtime.Remoting. MetadataServices. SUDSGeneratorException	0x80131500	COR_E_EXCEPTION
System.Runtime.Remoting. MetadataServices. SUDSParserException	0x80131500	COR_E_EXCEPTION
System.Threading. SynchronizationLockException	0x80131518	COR_E_SYNCHRONIZATION LOCK
System.Data.SyntaxErrorException	0x80131920	N/A
System.SystemException	0x80131501	COR_E_SYSTEM
System.Reflection.TargetException	0x80131603	COR_E_TARGET

TABLE D.2   Continued

Exception Name	HRESULT *Value*	HRESULT *Name*
System.Reflection.TargetInvocationException	0x80131604	COR_E_TARGETINVOCATION
System.Reflection.TargetParameterCountException	0x8002000E	DISP_E_BADPARAMCOUNT (COR_E_TARGETPARAMCOUNT)
System.Threading.ThreadAbortException	0x80131530	COR_E_THREADABORTED
System.Threading.ThreadInterruptedException	0x80131519	COR_E_THREADINTERRUPTED
System.Threading.ThreadStateException	0x80131520	COR_E_THREADSTATE
System.Threading.ThreadStopException	0x80131521	COR_E_THREADSTOP
System.ServiceProcess.TimeoutException	0x80131906	N/A
System.Data.TypedDataSetGeneratorException	0x8013192B	N/A
System.TypeInitializationException	0x80131534	COR_E_TYPEINITIALIZATION
System.TypeLoadException	0x80131522	COR_E_TYPELOAD
System.TypeUnloadedException	0x80131013	COR_E_TYPEUNLOADED
System.UnauthorizedAccessException	0x80070005	E_ACCESSDENIED (COR_E_UNAUTHORIZEDACCESS)
System.UriFormatException	0x80131537	COR_E_FORMAT
System.Security.VerificationException	0x8013150D	COR_E_VERIFICATION
System.Data.VersionNotFoundException	0x80131929	N/A
Microsoft.Vsa.VsaException	*No default*	N/A
System.ComponentModel.WarningException	0x80131501	COR_E_SYSTEM
System.Net.WebException	0x80131509	COR_E_INVALIDOPERATION
System.ComponentModel.Win32Exception	*No default*	N/A
System.Xml.XmlException	0x80131940	N/A
System.Xml.Schema.XmlSchemaException	0x80131941	N/A
System.Security.XmlSyntaxException	0x80131419	CORSEC_E_XMLSYNTAX
System.Xml.XPath.XPathException	0x80131943	N/A
System.Xml.Xsl.XsltCompileException	0x80131942	N/A
System.Xml.Xsl.XsltException	0x80131942	N/A

D

**.NET EXCEPTION
TO HRESULT
TRANSFORMATIONS**

PInvoke Definitions for Win32 Functions

IN THIS APPENDIX

- GD132.DLL **1433**
- KERNEL32.DLL **1442**
- OLE32.DLL **1461**
- SHELL32.DLL **1470**
- USER32.DLL **1472**

The biggest hassle of using Platform Invocation Services (PInvoke) is correctly defining the signatures of functions you wish to call. This appendix provides a PInvoke signature for just about every function exposed by five Windows DLLs so you don't have to come up with these definitions yourself. The function definitions are listed alphabetically with respect to other functions in the same DLL. The five DLLs covered are:

- GDI32.DLL
- KERNEL32.DLL
- OLE32.DLL
- SHELL32.DLL
- USER32.DLL

To get a better understanding of how to use these signatures, tweak them, or translate them to other .NET languages, consult Part VI, "Platform Invocation Services (PInvoke)." Here are a few notes about the following lists of signatures:

- The definitions are given in C# syntax, but in a way that can easily be translated to other .NET languages. If you rewrite any of these signatures in VB .NET syntax, you'll want to change unsigned types to signed types (such as changing ushort, uint, and UIntPtr to Short, Integer, and IntPtr, respectively). Also, the signatures assume that DllImportAttribute is used with no named parameters set (unless shown otherwise). Therefore, the C# default of CharSet.Ansi is assumed. The easiest way to reproduce the same behavior in VB .NET is to use DllImportAttribute with CharSet.Ansi rather than Declare, because Declare turns on the ExactSpelling setting. ExactSpelling doesn't work for many of these definitions as-is, because they depend on an "A" or "W" suffix being appended to their names.

- The definitions use types in the System namespace (IntPtr and UIntPtr), the System.Text namespace (StringBuilder), and custom attributes in the System.Runtime.InteropServices namespace (DllImportAttribute, MarshalAsAttribute, InAttribute, and OutAttribute).

- Several signatures use structures, interfaces, or delegates (ending with a Delegate suffix) that need to be defined in order to compile and use them. For the sake of space, these additional type definitions are not given.

- All structures are assumed to be defined as value types rather than formatted classes. If a function expects a pointer to a structure that could be null, the parameter is defined with the IntPtr type.

- Several of the signatures have customizations to make them more user-friendly than straightforward definitions, but you may have to tweak the signatures for usability and/or performance, depending on your specific scenario.
- Most of these signatures have not been tested, so it's possible that some have errors. Check this book's Web site for any corrections.

GDI32.DLL

All of these functions should be preceded with the following line when used in source code:

```
[DllImport("gdi32.dll")]
```

Here are signatures from GDI32.DLL:

```
static extern int AbortDoc(IntPtr hdc);
static extern bool AbortPath(IntPtr hdc);
static extern IntPtr AddFontMemResourceEx(IntPtr pbFont, uint cbFont,
   IntPtr pdv, [In] ref uint pcFonts);
static extern int AddFontResource(string lpszFilename);
static extern int AddFontResourceEx(string lpszFilename, uint fl, IntPtr pdv);
static extern bool AngleArc(IntPtr hdc, int X, int Y, uint dwRadius,
   float eStartAngle, float eSweepAngle);
static extern bool AnimatePalette(IntPtr hpal, uint iStartIndex,
   uint cEntries, PALETTEENTRY [] ppe);
static extern bool Arc(IntPtr hdc, int nLeftRect, int nTopRect, int nRightRect,
   int nBottomRect, int nXStartArc, int nYStartArc, int nXEndArc, int nYEndArc);
static extern bool ArcTo(IntPtr hdc, int nLeftRect, int nTopRect,
   int nRightRect, int nBottomRect, int nXRadial1, int nYRadial1,
   int nXRadial2, int nYRadial2);
static extern bool BeginPath(IntPtr hdc);
static extern bool BitBlt(IntPtr hdc, int nXDest, int nYDest, int nWidth,
   int nHeight, IntPtr hdcSrc, int nXSrc, int nYSrc, uint dwRop);
static extern bool CancelDC(IntPtr hdc);
static extern bool CheckColorsInGamut(IntPtr hDC, IntPtr lpRGBTriples,
   IntPtr lpBuffer, uint nCount);
static extern int ChoosePixelFormat(IntPtr hdc,
   [In] ref PIXELFORMATDESCRIPTOR ppfd);
static extern bool Chord(IntPtr hdc, int nLeftRect, int nTopRect,
   int nRightRect, int nBottomRect, int nXRadial1, int nYRadial1,
   int nXRadial2, int nYRadial2);
static extern IntPtr CloseEnhMetaFile(IntPtr hdc);
static extern bool CloseFigure(IntPtr hdc);
static extern IntPtr CloseMetaFile(IntPtr hdc);
static extern bool ColorCorrectPalette(IntPtr hDC, IntPtr hPalette,
   uint dwFirstEntry, uint dwNumOfEntries);
```

```
static extern bool ColorMatchToTarget(IntPtr hDC, IntPtr hdcTarget,
  uint uiAction);
static extern int CombineRgn(IntPtr hrgnDest, IntPtr hrgnSrc1,
  IntPtr hrgnSrc2, int fnCombineMode);
static extern bool CombineTransform(out XFORM lpxformResult,
  [In] ref XFORM lpxform1, [In] ref XFORM lpxform2);
static extern IntPtr CopyEnhMetaFile(IntPtr hemfSrc, string lpszFile);
static extern IntPtr CopyMetaFile(IntPtr hmfSrc, string lpszFile);
static extern IntPtr CreateBitmap(int nWidth, int nHeight, uint cPlanes,
  uint cBitsPerPel, IntPtr lpvBits);
static extern IntPtr CreateBitmapIndirect([In] ref BITMAP lpbm);
static extern IntPtr CreateBrushIndirect([In] ref LOGBRUSH lplb);
static extern IntPtr CreateColorSpace([In] ref LOGCOLORSPACE lpLogColorSpace);
static extern IntPtr CreateCompatibleBitmap(IntPtr hdc, int nWidth,
  int nHeight);
static extern IntPtr CreateCompatibleDC(IntPtr hdc);
static extern IntPtr CreateDC(string lpszDriver, string lpszDevice,
  string lpszOutput, IntPtr lpInitData);
static extern IntPtr CreateDIBitmap(IntPtr hdc, [In] ref BITMAPINFOHEADER
  lpbmih, uint fdwInit, byte [] lpbInit, [In] ref BITMAPINFO lpbmi,
  uint fuUsage);
static extern IntPtr CreateDIBPatternBrush(IntPtr hglbDIBPacked,
  uint fuColorSpec);
static extern IntPtr CreateDIBPatternBrushPt(IntPtr lpPackedDIB, uint iUsage);
static extern IntPtr CreateDIBSection(IntPtr hdc, [In] ref BITMAPINFO pbmi,
  uint iUsage, out IntPtr ppvBits, IntPtr hSection, uint dwOffset);
static extern IntPtr CreateDiscardableBitmap(IntPtr hdc, int nWidth,
  int nHeight);
static extern IntPtr CreateEllipticRgn(int nLeftRect, int nTopRect,
  int nRightRect, int nBottomRect);
static extern IntPtr CreateEllipticRgnIndirect([In] ref RECT lprc);
static extern IntPtr CreateEnhMetaFile(IntPtr hdcRef, string lpFilename,
  [In] ref RECT lpRect, string lpDescription);
static extern IntPtr CreateFont(int nHeight, int nWidth, int nEscapement,
  int nOrientation, int fnWeight, uint fdwItalic, uint fdwUnderline, uint
  fdwStrikeOut, uint fdwCharSet, uint fdwOutputPrecision, uint
  fdwClipPrecision, uint fdwQuality, uint fdwPitchAndFamily, string lpszFace);
static extern IntPtr CreateFontIndirect([In] ref LOGFONT lplf);
static extern IntPtr CreateFontIndirectEx([In] ref ENUMLOGFONTEXDV penumlfex);
static extern IntPtr CreateHalftonePalette(IntPtr hdc);
static extern IntPtr CreateHatchBrush(int fnStyle, uint clrref);
static extern IntPtr CreateIC(string lpszDriver, string lpszDevice,
  string lpszOutput, IntPtr lpdvmInit);
static extern IntPtr CreateMetaFile(string lpszFile);
static extern IntPtr CreatePalette([In] ref LOGPALETTE lplgpl);
static extern IntPtr CreatePatternBrush(IntPtr hbmp);
```

```
static extern IntPtr CreatePen(int fnPenStyle, int nWidth, uint crColor);
static extern IntPtr CreatePenIndirect([In] ref LOGPEN lplgpn);
static extern IntPtr CreatePolygonRgn(POINT [] lppt, int cPoints,
  int fnPolyFillMode);
static extern IntPtr CreatePolyPolygonRgn(POINT [] lppt, int [] lpPolyCounts,
  int nCount, int fnPolyFillMode);
static extern IntPtr CreateRectRgn(int nLeftRect, int nTopRect, int nRightRect,
  int nBottomRect);
static extern IntPtr CreateRectRgnIndirect([In] ref RECT lprc);
static extern IntPtr CreateRoundRectRgn(int x1, int y1, int x2, int y2,
  int cx, int cy);
static extern bool CreateScalableFontResource(uint fdwHidden, string
  lpszFontRes, string lpszFontFile, string lpszCurrentPath);
static extern IntPtr CreateSolidBrush(uint crColor);
static extern bool DeleteColorSpace(IntPtr hColorSpace);
static extern bool DeleteDC(IntPtr hdc);
static extern bool DeleteEnhMetaFile(IntPtr hemf);
static extern bool DeleteMetaFile(IntPtr hmf);
static extern bool DeleteObject(IntPtr hObject);
static extern int DescribePixelFormat(IntPtr hdc, int iPixelFormat,
  uint nBytes, IntPtr ppfd);
static extern bool DPtoLP(IntPtr hdc, [In, Out] POINT [] lpPoints, int nCount);
static extern int DrawEscape(IntPtr hdc, int nEscape, int cbInput,
  string lpszInData);
static extern bool Ellipse(IntPtr hdc, int nLeftRect, int nTopRect,
  int nRightRect, int nBottomRect);
static extern int EndDoc(IntPtr hdc);
static extern int EndPage(IntPtr hdc);
static extern bool EndPath(IntPtr hdc);
static extern bool EnumEnhMetaFile(IntPtr hdc, IntPtr hemf,
  EnhMetaFileDelegate lpEnhMetaFunc, IntPtr lpData, [In] ref RECT lpRect);
static extern int EnumFontFamilies(IntPtr hdc, string lpszFamily,
  EnumFontDelegate lpEnumFontFamProc, IntPtr lParam);
static extern int EnumFontFamiliesEx(IntPtr hdc, [In] ref LOGFONT lpLogfont,
  EnumFontExDelegate lpEnumFontFamExProc, IntPtr lParam, uint dwFlags);
static extern int EnumFonts(IntPtr hdc, string lpFaceName, EnumFontsDelegate
  lpFontFunc, IntPtr lParam);
static extern int EnumICMProfiles(IntPtr hDC, EnumICMProfilesDelegate
  lpEnumICMProfilesFunc, IntPtr lParam);
static extern bool EnumMetaFile(IntPtr hdc, IntPtr hmf, EnumMetaFileDelegate
  lpMetaFunc, IntPtr lParam);
static extern int EnumObjects(IntPtr hdc, int nObjectType, EnumObjectsDelegate
  lpObjectFunc, IntPtr lParam);
static extern bool EqualRgn(IntPtr hSrcRgn1, IntPtr hSrcRgn2);
static extern int Escape(IntPtr hdc, int nEscape, int cbInput,
  string lpvInData, IntPtr lpvOutData);
```

```
static extern int ExcludeClipRect(IntPtr hdc, int nLeftRect, int nTopRect,
  int nRightRect, int nBottomRect);
static extern IntPtr ExtCreatePen(uint dwPenStyle, uint dwWidth,
  [In] ref LOGBRUSH lplb, uint dwStyleCount, uint [] lpStyle);
static extern IntPtr ExtCreateRegion(IntPtr lpXform, uint nCount,
  [In] ref RGNDATA lpRgnData);
static extern int ExtEscape(IntPtr hdc, int nEscape, int cbInput,
  string lpszInData, int cbOutput, IntPtr lpszOutData);
static extern bool ExtFloodFill(IntPtr hdc, int nXStart, int nYStart,
  uint crColor, uint fuFillType);
static extern int ExtSelectClipRgn(IntPtr hdc, IntPtr hrgn, int fnMode);
static extern bool ExtTextOut(IntPtr hdc, int X, int Y, uint fuOptions,
  [In] ref RECT lprc, string lpString, uint cbCount, int [] lpDx);
static extern bool FillPath(IntPtr hdc);
static extern bool FillRgn(IntPtr hdc, IntPtr hrgn, IntPtr hbr);
static extern bool FlattenPath(IntPtr hdc);
static extern bool FloodFill(IntPtr hdc, int nXStart, int nYStart,
  uint crFill);
static extern bool FrameRgn(IntPtr hdc, IntPtr hrgn, IntPtr hbr, int nWidth,
  int nHeight);
static extern bool GdiComment(IntPtr hdc, uint cbSize, [Out] byte [] lpData);
static extern bool GdiFlush();
static extern uint GdiGetBatchLimit();
static extern uint GdiSetBatchLimit(uint dwLimit);
static extern int GetArcDirection(IntPtr hdc);
static extern bool GetAspectRatioFilterEx(IntPtr hdc, out SIZE lpAspectRatio);
static extern int GetBitmapBits(IntPtr hbmp, int cbBuffer,
  [Out] byte [] lpvBits);
static extern bool GetBitmapDimensionEx(IntPtr hBitmap, out SIZE lpDimension);
static extern uint GetBkColor(IntPtr hdc);
static extern int GetBkMode(IntPtr hdc);
static extern uint GetBoundsRect(IntPtr hdc, out RECT lprcBounds, uint flags);
static extern bool GetBrushOrgEx(IntPtr hdc, out POINT lppt);
static extern bool GetCharABCWidths(IntPtr hdc, uint uFirstChar,
  uint uLastChar, [Out] ABC [] lpabc);
static extern bool GetCharABCWidthsFloat(IntPtr hdc, uint iFirstChar,
  uint iLastChar, [Out] ABCFLOAT [] lpABCF);
static extern bool GetCharABCWidthsI(IntPtr hdc, uint giFirst, uint cgi,
  ushort [] pgi, [Out] ABC [] lpabc);
static extern uint GetCharacterPlacement(IntPtr hdc, string lpString,
  int nCount, int nMaxExtent, ref GCP_RESULTS lpResults, uint dwFlags);
static extern bool GetCharWidth(IntPtr hdc, uint iFirstChar, uint iLastChar,
  [Out] int [] lpBuffer);
static extern bool GetCharWidth32(IntPtr hdc, uint iFirstChar, uint iLastChar,
  [Out] int [] lpBuffer);
```

```
static extern bool GetCharWidthFloat(IntPtr hdc, uint iFirstChar,
    uint iLastChar, [Out] float [] pxBuffer);
static extern bool GetCharWidthI(IntPtr hdc, uint giFirst, uint cgi,
    ushort [] pgi, [Out] int [] lpBuffer);
static extern int GetClipBox(IntPtr hdc, out RECT lprc);
static extern int GetClipRgn(IntPtr hdc, IntPtr hrgn);
static extern bool GetColorAdjustment(IntPtr hdc, out COLORADJUSTMENT lpca);
static extern IntPtr GetColorSpace(IntPtr hDC);
static extern IntPtr GetCurrentObject(IntPtr hdc, uint uObjectType);
static extern bool GetCurrentPositionEx(IntPtr hdc, out POINT lpPoint);
static extern uint GetDCBrushColor(IntPtr hdc);
static extern bool GetDCOrgEx(IntPtr hdc, out POINT lpPoint);
static extern uint GetDCPenColor(IntPtr hdc);
static extern int GetDeviceCaps(IntPtr hdc, int nIndex);
static extern bool GetDeviceGammaRamp(IntPtr hdc, IntPtr lpRamp);
static extern uint GetDIBColorTable(IntPtr hdc, uint uStartIndex,
    uint cEntries, [Out] RGBQUAD [] pColors);
static extern int GetDIBits(IntPtr hdc, IntPtr hbmp, uint uStartScan,
    uint cScanLines, [Out] byte [] lpvBits, ref BITMAPINFO lpbmi, uint uUsage);
static extern IntPtr GetEnhMetaFile(string lpszMetaFile);
static extern uint GetEnhMetaFileBits(IntPtr hemf, uint cbBuffer,
    [Out] byte [] lpbBuffer);
static extern uint GetEnhMetaFileDescription(IntPtr hemf, uint cchBuffer,
    [Out] StringBuilder lpszDescription);
static extern uint GetEnhMetaFileHeader(IntPtr hemf, uint cbBuffer,
    IntPtr lpemh);
static extern uint GetEnhMetaFilePaletteEntries(IntPtr hemf, uint cEntries,
    [Out] PALETTEENTRY [] lppe);
static extern uint GetEnhMetaFilePixelFormat(IntPtr hemf, uint cbBuffer,
    ref PIXELFORMATDESCRIPTOR ppfd);
static extern uint GetFontData(IntPtr hdc, uint dwTable, uint dwOffset,
    [Out] byte [] lpvBuffer, uint cbData);
static extern uint GetFontLanguageInfo(IntPtr hdc);
static extern uint GetFontUnicodeRanges(IntPtr hdc, IntPtr lpgs);
static extern uint GetGlyphIndices(IntPtr hdc, string lpsz, int c,
    [Out] ushort [] pgi, uint fl);
static extern uint GetGlyphOutline(IntPtr hdc, uint uChar, uint uFormat,
    out GLYPHMETRICS lpgm, uint cbBuffer, IntPtr lpvBuffer, ref MAT2 lpmat2);
static extern int GetGraphicsMode(IntPtr hdc);
static extern bool GetICMProfile(IntPtr hDC, ref uint lpcbName,
    [Out] StringBuilder lpszFilename);
static extern uint GetKerningPairs(IntPtr hdc, uint nNumPairs,
    [Out] KERNINGPAIR [] lpkrnpair);
static extern uint GetLayout(IntPtr hdc);
static extern bool GetLogColorSpace(IntPtr hColorSpace,
    out LOGCOLORSPACE lpBuffer, uint nSize);
```

```
static extern int GetMapMode(IntPtr hdc);
static extern uint GetMetaFileBitsEx(IntPtr hmf, uint nSize,
  [Out] byte [] lpvData);
static extern int GetMetaRgn(IntPtr hdc, IntPtr hrgn);
static extern bool GetMiterLimit(IntPtr hdc, out float peLimit);
static extern uint GetNearestColor(IntPtr hdc, uint crColor);
static extern uint GetNearestPaletteIndex(IntPtr hpal, uint crColor);
static extern int GetObject(IntPtr hgdiobj, int cbBuffer, IntPtr lpvObject);
static extern uint GetObjectType(IntPtr h);
static extern uint GetOutlineTextMetrics(IntPtr hdc, uint cbData,
  [Out] OUTLINETEXTMETRIC [] lpOTM);
static extern uint GetPaletteEntries(IntPtr hpal, uint iStartIndex,
  uint nEntries, [Out] PALETTEENTRY [] lppe);
static extern int GetPath(IntPtr hdc, [Out] POINT [] lpPoints,
  [Out] byte [] lpTypes, int nSize);
static extern uint GetPixel(IntPtr hdc, int nXPos, int nYPos);
static extern int GetPixelFormat(IntPtr hdc);
static extern int GetPolyFillMode(IntPtr hdc);
static extern int GetRandomRgn(IntPtr hdc, IntPtr hrgn, int iNum);
static extern bool GetRasterizerCaps(out RASTERIZER_STATUS lprs, uint cb);
static extern uint GetRegionData(IntPtr hRgn, uint dwCount,
  out RGNDATA lpRgnData);
static extern int GetRgnBox(IntPtr hrgn, out RECT lprc);
static extern int GetROP2(IntPtr hdc);
static extern IntPtr GetStockObject(int fnObject);
static extern int GetStretchBltMode(IntPtr hdc);
static extern uint GetSystemPaletteEntries(IntPtr hdc, uint iStartIndex,
  uint nEntries, [Out] PALETTEENTRY [] lppe);
static extern uint GetSystemPaletteUse(IntPtr hdc);
static extern uint GetTextAlign(IntPtr hdc);
static extern int GetTextCharacterExtra(IntPtr hdc);
static extern int GetTextCharset(IntPtr hdc);
static extern int GetTextCharsetInfo(IntPtr hdc, IntPtr lpSig, uint dwFlags);
static extern uint GetTextColor(IntPtr hdc);
static extern bool GetTextExtentExPoint(IntPtr hdc, string lpszStr,
  int cchString, int nMaxExtent, IntPtr lpnFit, IntPtr alpDx, out SIZE lpSize);
static extern bool GetTextExtentExPointI(IntPtr hdc, ushort [] pgiIn,
  int cgi, int nMaxExtent, IntPtr lpnFit, IntPtr alpDx, out SIZE lpSize);
static extern bool GetTextExtentPoint(IntPtr hdc, string lpString,
  int cbString, out SIZE lpSize);
static extern bool GetTextExtentPoint32(IntPtr hdc, string lpString,
  int cbString, out SIZE lpSize);
static extern bool GetTextExtentPointI(IntPtr hdc, ushort [] pgiIn, int cgi,
  out SIZE lpSize);
static extern int GetTextFace(IntPtr hdc, int nCount,
  [Out] StringBuilder lpFaceName);
```

```
static extern bool GetTextMetrics(IntPtr hdc, out TEXTMETRIC lptm);
static extern bool GetViewportExtEx(IntPtr hdc, out SIZE lpSize);
static extern bool GetViewportOrgEx(IntPtr hdc, out POINT lpPoint);
static extern bool GetWindowExtEx(IntPtr hdc, out SIZE lpSize);
static extern bool GetWindowOrgEx(IntPtr hdc, out POINT lpPoint);
static extern uint GetWinMetaFileBits(IntPtr hemf, uint cbBuffer,
  [Out] byte [] lpbBuffer, int fnMapMode, IntPtr hdcRef);
static extern bool GetWorldTransform(IntPtr hdc, out XFORM lpXform);
static extern int IntersectClipRect(IntPtr hdc, int nLeftRect, int nTopRect,
  int nRightRect, int nBottomRect);
static extern bool InvertRgn(IntPtr hdc, IntPtr hrgn);
static extern bool LineDDA(int nXStart, int nYStart, int nXEnd, int nYEnd,
  LineDDADelegate lpLineFunc, IntPtr lpData);
static extern bool LineTo(IntPtr hdc, int nXEnd, int nYEnd);
static extern bool LPtoDP(IntPtr hdc, [In, Out] POINT [] lpPoints, int nCount);
static extern bool MaskBlt(IntPtr hdcDest, int nXDest, int nYDest, int nWidth,
  int nHeight, IntPtr hdcSrc, int nXSrc, int nYSrc, IntPtr hbmMask, int xMask,
  int yMask, uint dwRop);
static extern bool ModifyWorldTransform(IntPtr hdc, [In] ref XFORM lpXform,
  uint iMode);
static extern bool MoveToEx(IntPtr hdc, int X, int Y, IntPtr lpPoint);
static extern int OffsetClipRgn(IntPtr hdc, int nXOffset, int nYOffset);
static extern int OffsetRgn(IntPtr hrgn, int nXOffset, int nYOffset);
static extern bool OffsetViewportOrgEx(IntPtr hdc, int nXOffset, int nYOffset,
  IntPtr lpPoint);
static extern bool OffsetWindowOrgEx(IntPtr hdc, int nXOffset, int nYOffset,
  IntPtr lpPoint);
static extern bool PaintRgn(IntPtr hdc, IntPtr hrgn);
static extern bool PatBlt(IntPtr hdc, int nXLeft, int nYLeft, int nWidth,
  int nHeight, uint dwRop);
static extern IntPtr PathToRegion(IntPtr hdc);
static extern bool Pie(IntPtr hdc, int nLeftRect, int nTopRect, int nRightRect,
  int nBottomRect, int nXRadial1, int nYRadial1, int nXRadial2, int nYRadial2);
static extern bool PlayEnhMetaFile(IntPtr hdc, IntPtr hemf, out RECT lpRect);
static extern bool PlayEnhMetaFileRecord(IntPtr hdc, [In] ref HANDLETABLE
  lpHandletable, [In] ref ENHMETARECORD lpEnhMetaRecord, uint nHandles);
static extern bool PlayMetaFile(IntPtr hdc, IntPtr hmf);
static extern bool PlayMetaFileRecord(IntPtr hdc, [In] ref HANDLETABLE
  lpHandletable, [In] ref METARECORD lpMetaRecord, uint nHandles);
static extern bool PlgBlt(IntPtr hdcDest, POINT [] lpPoint, IntPtr hdcSrc,
  int nXSrc, int nYSrc, int nWidth, int nHeight, IntPtr hbmMask, int xMask,
  int yMask);
static extern bool PolyBezier(IntPtr hdc, POINT [] lppt, uint cPoints);
static extern bool PolyBezierTo(IntPtr hdc, POINT [] lppt, uint cCount);
static extern bool PolyDraw(IntPtr hdc, POINT [] lppt, byte [] lpbTypes,
  int cCount);
```

```
static extern bool Polygon(IntPtr hdc, POINT [] lpPoints, int nCount);
static extern bool Polyline(IntPtr hdc, POINT [] lppt, int cPoints);
static extern bool PolylineTo(IntPtr hdc, POINT [] lppt, uint cCount);
static extern bool PolyPolygon(IntPtr hdc, POINT [] lpPoints,
  int [] lpPolyCounts, int nCount);
static extern bool PolyPolyline(IntPtr hdc, POINT [] lppt,
  uint [] lpdwPolyPoints, uint cCount);
static extern bool PolyTextOut(IntPtr hdc, POLYTEXT [] pptxt, int cStrings);
static extern bool PtInRegion(IntPtr hrgn, int X, int Y);
static extern bool PtVisible(IntPtr hdc, int X, int Y);
static extern uint RealizePalette(IntPtr hdc);
static extern bool Rectangle(IntPtr hdc, int nLeftRect, int nTopRect,
  int nRightRect, int nBottomRect);
static extern bool RectInRegion(IntPtr hrgn, RECT [] lprc);
static extern bool RectVisible(IntPtr hdc, [In] ref RECT lprc);
static extern bool RemoveFontMemResourceEx(IntPtr fh);
static extern bool RemoveFontResource(string lpFileName);
static extern bool RemoveFontResourceEx(string lpFileName, uint fl,
  IntPtr pdv);
static extern IntPtr ResetDC(IntPtr hdc, [In] ref DEVMODE lpInitData);
static extern bool ResizePalette(IntPtr hpal, uint nEntries);
static extern bool RestoreDC(IntPtr hdc, int nSavedDC);
static extern bool RoundRect(IntPtr hdc, int nLeftRect, int nTopRect,
  int nRightRect, int nBottomRect, int nWidth, int nHeight);
static extern int SaveDC(IntPtr hdc);
static extern bool ScaleViewportExtEx(IntPtr hdc, int Xnum, int Xdenom,
  int Ynum, int Ydenom, IntPtr lpSize);
static extern bool ScaleWindowExtEx(IntPtr hdc, int Xnum, int Xdenom,
  int Ynum, int Ydenom, IntPtr lpSize);
static extern bool SelectClipPath(IntPtr hdc, int iMode);
static extern int SelectClipRgn(IntPtr hdc, IntPtr hrgn);
static extern IntPtr SelectObject(IntPtr hdc, IntPtr hgdiobj);
static extern IntPtr SelectPalette(IntPtr hdc, IntPtr hpal,
  bool bForceBackground);
static extern int SetAbortProc(IntPtr hdc, AbortDelegate lpAbortProc);
static extern int SetArcDirection(IntPtr hdc, int ArcDirection);
static extern int SetBitmapBits(IntPtr hbmp, uint cBytes, byte [] lpBits);
static extern bool SetBitmapDimensionEx(IntPtr hBitmap, int nWidth,
  int nHeight, IntPtr lpSize);
static extern uint SetBkColor(IntPtr hdc, uint crColor);
static extern int SetBkMode(IntPtr hdc, int iBkMode);
static extern uint SetBoundsRect(IntPtr hdc, IntPtr lprcBounds, uint flags);
static extern bool SetBrushOrgEx(IntPtr hdc, int nXOrg, int nYOrg,
  IntPtr lppt);
static extern bool SetColorAdjustment(IntPtr hdc,
  [In] ref COLORADJUSTMENT lpca);
```

```
static extern IntPtr SetColorSpace(IntPtr hDC, IntPtr hColorSpace);
static extern uint SetDCBrushColor(IntPtr hdc, uint crColor);
static extern uint SetDCPenColor(IntPtr hdc, uint crColor);
static extern bool SetDeviceGammaRamp(IntPtr hDC, IntPtr lpRamp);
static extern uint SetDIBColorTable(IntPtr hdc, uint uStartIndex,
  uint cEntries, RGBQUAD [] pColors);
static extern int SetDIBits(IntPtr hdc, IntPtr hbmp, uint uStartScan, uint
  cScanLines, byte [] lpvBits, [In] ref BITMAPINFO lpbmi, uint fuColorUse);
static extern int SetDIBitsToDevice(IntPtr hdc, int XDest, int YDest, uint
  dwWidth, uint dwHeight, int XSrc, int YSrc, uint uStartScan, uint cScanLines,
  byte [] lpvBits, [In] ref BITMAPINFO lpbmi, uint fuColorUse);
static extern IntPtr SetEnhMetaFileBits(uint cbBuffer, byte [] lpData);
static extern int SetGraphicsMode(IntPtr hdc, int iMode);
static extern int SetICMMode(IntPtr hDC, int iEnableICM);
static extern bool SetICMProfile(IntPtr hDC, string lpFileName);
static extern uint SetLayout(IntPtr hdc, uint dwLayout);
static extern int SetMapMode(IntPtr hdc, int fnMapMode);
static extern uint SetMapperFlags(IntPtr hdc, uint dwFlag);
static extern IntPtr SetMetaFileBitsEx(uint nSize, byte [] lpData);
static extern int SetMetaRgn(IntPtr hdc);
static extern bool SetMiterLimit(IntPtr hdc, float eNewLimit,
  IntPtr peOldLimit);
static extern uint SetPaletteEntries(IntPtr hpal, uint iStart, uint cEntries,
  PALETTEENTRY [] lppe);
static extern uint SetPixel(IntPtr hdc, int X, int Y, uint crColor);
static extern bool SetPixelFormat(IntPtr hdc, int iPixelFormat,
  ref PIXELFORMATDESCRIPTOR ppfd);
static extern bool SetPixelV(IntPtr hdc, int X, int Y, uint crColor);
static extern int SetPolyFillMode(IntPtr hdc, int iPolyFillMode);
static extern bool SetRectRgn(IntPtr hrgn, int nLeftRect, int nTopRect,
  int nRightRect, int nBottomRect);
static extern int SetROP2(IntPtr hdc, int fnDrawMode);
static extern int SetStretchBltMode(IntPtr hdc, int iStretchMode);
static extern uint SetSystemPaletteUse(IntPtr hdc, uint uUsage);
static extern uint SetTextAlign(IntPtr hdc, uint fMode);
static extern int SetTextCharacterExtra(IntPtr hdc, int nCharExtra);
static extern uint SetTextColor(IntPtr hdc, uint crColor);
static extern bool SetTextJustification(IntPtr hdc, int nBreakExtra,
  int nBreakCount);
static extern bool SetViewportExtEx(IntPtr hdc, int nXExtent, int nYExtent,
  IntPtr lpSize);
static extern bool SetViewportOrgEx(IntPtr hdc, int X, int Y, IntPtr lpPoint);
static extern bool SetWindowExtEx(IntPtr hdc, int nXExtent, int nYExtent,
  IntPtr lpSize);
static extern bool SetWindowOrgEx(IntPtr hdc, int X, int Y, IntPtr lpPoint);
```

```
static extern IntPtr SetWinMetaFileBits(uint cbBuffer, IntPtr lpbBuffer,
  IntPtr hdcRef, [In] ref METAFILEPICT lpmfp);
static extern bool SetWorldTransform(IntPtr hdc, [In] ref XFORM lpXform);
static extern int StartDoc(IntPtr hdc, [In] ref DOCINFO lpdi);
static extern int StartPage(IntPtr hDC);
static extern bool StretchBlt(IntPtr hdcDest, int nXOriginDest,
  int nYOriginDest, int nWidthDest, int nHeightDest, IntPtr hdcSrc,
  int nXOriginSrc, int nYOriginSrc, int nWidthSrc, int nHeightSrc, uint dwRop);
static extern int StretchDIBits(IntPtr hdc, int XDest, int YDest,
  int nDestWidth, int nDestHeight, int XSrc, int YSrc, int nSrcWidth,
  int nSrcHeight, byte [] lpBits, [In] ref BITMAPINFO lpBitsInfo, uint iUsage,
  uint dwRop);
static extern bool StrokeAndFillPath(IntPtr hdc);
static extern bool StrokePath(IntPtr hdc);
static extern bool SwapBuffers(IntPtr hdc);
static extern bool TextOut(IntPtr hdc, int nXStart, int nYStart,
  string lpString, int cbString);
static extern bool TranslateCharsetInfo(ref uint pSrc, out CHARSETINFO lpCs,
  uint dwFlags);
static extern bool UnrealizeObject(IntPtr hgdiobj);
static extern bool UpdateColors(IntPtr hdc);
static extern bool UpdateICMRegKey(uint dwReserved, string lpszCMID,
  IntPtr lpszFileName, uint nCommand);
static extern bool WidenPath(IntPtr hdc);
```

KERNEL32.DLL

All of these functions should be preceded with the following line when used in source code:

```
[DllImport("kernel32.dll")]
```

Here are signatures from KERNEL32.DLL:

```
static extern ushort AddAtom(string lpString);
static extern bool AllocateUserPhysicalPages(IntPtr hProcess,
  ref UIntPtr NumberOfPages, out UIntPtr PageArray);
static extern bool AllocConsole();
static extern bool AreFileApisANSI();
static extern bool AssignProcessToJobObject(IntPtr hJob, IntPtr hProcess);
static extern bool BackupRead(IntPtr hFile, [Out] byte [] lpBuffer,
  uint nNumberOfBytesToRead, out uint lpNumberOfBytesRead, bool bAbort,
  bool bProcessSecurity, out IntPtr lpContext);
static extern bool BackupSeek(IntPtr hFile, uint dwLowBytesToSeek,
  uint dwHighBytesToSeek, out uint lpdwLowBytesSeeked, out uint
  lpdwHighBytesSeeked, [In] ref IntPtr lpContext);
```

```
static extern bool BackupWrite(IntPtr hFile, byte [] lpBuffer,
  uint nNumberOfBytesToWrite, out uint lpNumberOfBytesWritten, bool bAbort,
  bool bProcessSecurity, out IntPtr lpContext);
static extern bool Beep(uint dwFreq, uint dwDuration);
static extern IntPtr BeginUpdateResource(string pFileName,
  bool bDeleteExistingResources);
static extern bool BindIoCompletionCallback(IntPtr FileHandle,
  BindIoCompletionDelegate Function, uint Flags);
static extern bool BuildCommDCB(string lpDef, out DCB lpDCB);
static extern bool BuildCommDCBAndTimeouts(string lpDef, out DCB lpDCB,
  [In] ref COMMTIMEOUTS lpCommTimeouts);
static extern bool CallNamedPipe(string lpNamedPipeName, byte [] lpInBuffer,
  uint nInBufferSize, [Out] byte [] lpOutBuffer, uint nOutBufferSize,
  out uint lpBytesRead, uint nTimeOut);
static extern bool CancelIo(IntPtr hFile);
static extern bool CancelWaitableTimer(IntPtr hTimer);
static extern bool ChangeTimerQueueTimer(IntPtr TimerQueue, IntPtr Timer,
  uint DueTime, uint Period);
static extern bool ClearCommBreak(IntPtr hFile);
static extern bool ClearCommError(IntPtr hFile, out uint lpErrors,
  IntPtr lpStat);
static extern bool CloseHandle(IntPtr hObject);
static extern bool CommConfigDialog(string lpszName, IntPtr hWnd,
  ref COMMCONFIG lpCC);
static extern int CompareFileTime([In] ref FILETIME lpFileTime1,
  [In] ref FILETIME lpFileTime2);
static extern int CompareString(uint Locale, uint dwCmpFlags, string lpString1,
  int cchCount1, string lpString2, int cchCount2);
static extern bool ConnectNamedPipe(IntPtr hNamedPipe,
  [In] ref OVERLAPPED lpOverlapped);
static extern bool ContinueDebugEvent(uint dwProcessId, uint dwThreadId,
  uint dwContinueStatus);
static extern uint ConvertDefaultLocale(uint Locale);
static extern IntPtr ConvertThreadToFiber(IntPtr lpParameter);
static extern bool CopyFile(string lpExistingFileName, string lpNewFileName,
  bool bFailIfExists);
static extern bool CopyFileEx(string lpExistingFileName, string lpNewFileName,
  CopyProgressDelegate lpProgressRoutine, IntPtr lpData,
  [In] ref bool pbCancel, uint dwCopyFlags);
static extern IntPtr CreateConsoleScreenBuffer(uint dwDesiredAccess,
  uint dwShareMode, IntPtr lpSecurityAttributes, uint dwFlags,
  IntPtr lpScreenBufferData);
static extern bool CreateDirectory(string lpPathName,
  IntPtr lpSecurityAttributes);
```

```
static extern bool CreateDirectoryEx(string lpTemplateDirectory,
  string lpNewDirectory, IntPtr lpSecurityAttributes);
static extern IntPtr CreateEvent(IntPtr lpEventAttributes, bool bManualReset,
  bool bInitialState, string lpName);
static extern IntPtr CreateFiber(uint dwStackSize,
  CreateFiberDelegate lpStartAddress, IntPtr lpParameter);
static extern IntPtr CreateFile(string lpFileName, uint dwDesiredAccess,
  uint dwShareMode, IntPtr lpSecurityAttributes, uint dwCreationDisposition,
  uint dwFlagsAndAttributes, IntPtr hTemplateFile);
static extern IntPtr CreateFileMapping(IntPtr hFile,
  IntPtr lpFileMappingAttributes, uint flProtect, uint dwMaximumSizeHigh,
  uint dwMaximumSizeLow, string lpName);
static extern bool CreateHardLink(string lpFileName, string lpExistingFileName,
  IntPtr lpSecurityAttributes);
static extern IntPtr CreateIoCompletionPort(IntPtr FileHandle,
  IntPtr ExistingCompletionPort, UIntPtr CompletionKey,
  uint NumberOfConcurrentThreads);
static extern IntPtr CreateJobObject([In] ref SECURITY_ATTRIBUTES
  lpJobAttributes, string lpName);
static extern IntPtr CreateMailslot(string lpName, uint nMaxMessageSize,
  uint lReadTimeout, IntPtr lpSecurityAttributes);
static extern IntPtr CreateMutex(IntPtr lpMutexAttributes, bool bInitialOwner,
  string lpName);
static extern IntPtr CreateNamedPipe(string lpName, uint dwOpenMode,
  uint dwPipeMode, uint nMaxInstances, uint nOutBufferSize, uint nInBufferSize,
  uint nDefaultTimeOut, IntPtr lpSecurityAttributes);
static extern bool CreatePipe(out IntPtr hReadPipe, out IntPtr hWritePipe,
  IntPtr lpPipeAttributes, uint nSize);
static extern bool CreateProcess(string lpApplicationName,
  string lpCommandLine, IntPtr lpProcessAttributes, IntPtr lpThreadAttributes,
  bool bInheritHandles, uint dwCreationFlags, IntPtr lpEnvironment,
  string lpCurrentDirectory, [In] ref STARTUPINFO lpStartupInfo,
  out PROCESS_INFORMATION lpProcessInformation);
static extern IntPtr CreateRemoteThread(IntPtr hProcess,
  IntPtr lpThreadAttributes, uint dwStackSize, ThreadStartDelegate
  lpStartAddress, IntPtr lpParameter, uint dwCreationFlags, IntPtr lpThreadId);
static extern IntPtr CreateSemaphore(IntPtr lpSemaphoreAttributes,
  int lInitialCount, int lMaximumCount, string lpName);
static extern uint CreateTapePartition(IntPtr hDevice, uint dwPartitionMethod,
  uint dwCount, uint dwSize);
static extern IntPtr CreateThread([In] ref SECURITY_ATTRIBUTES
  SecurityAttributes, uint StackSize, ThreadStartDelegate StartFunction,
  IntPtr ThreadParameter, uint CreationFlags, out uint ThreadId);
static extern IntPtr CreateTimerQueue();
static extern bool CreateTimerQueueTimer(ref IntPtr phNewTimer,
  IntPtr TimerQueue, WaitOrTimerDelegate Callback, IntPtr Parameter,
  uint DueTime, uint Period, uint Flags);
```

```
static extern IntPtr CreateToolhelp32Snapshot(uint dwFlags,
  uint th32ProcessID);
static extern IntPtr CreateWaitableTimer(IntPtr lpTimerAttributes,
  bool bManualReset, string lpTimerName);
static extern bool DebugActiveProcess(uint dwProcessId);
static extern void DebugBreak();
static extern bool DefineDosDevice(uint dwFlags, string lpDeviceName,
  string lpTargetPath);
static extern ushort DeleteAtom(ushort nAtom);
static extern void DeleteCriticalSection(ref CRITICAL_SECTION
  lpCriticalSection);
static extern void DeleteFiber(IntPtr lpFiber);
static extern bool DeleteFile(string lpFileName);
static extern bool DeleteTimerQueue(IntPtr TimerQueue);
static extern bool DeleteTimerQueueEx(IntPtr TimerQueue,
  IntPtr CompletionEvent);
static extern bool DeleteTimerQueueTimer(IntPtr TimerQueue, IntPtr Timer,
  IntPtr CompletionEvent);
static extern bool DeleteVolumeMountPoint(string lpszVolumeMountPoint);
static extern bool DeviceIoControl(IntPtr hDevice, uint dwIoControlCode,
  byte [] lpInBuffer, uint nInBufferSize, [Out] byte [] lpOutBuffer,
  uint nOutBufferSize, IntPtr lpBytesReturned, IntPtr lpOverlapped);
static extern bool DisableThreadLibraryCalls(IntPtr hModule);
static extern bool DisconnectNamedPipe(IntPtr hNamedPipe);
static extern bool DnsHostnameToComputerName(string Hostname,
  [Out] StringBuilder ComputerName, ref uint nSize);
static extern bool DosDateTimeToFileTime(ushort wFatDate, ushort wFatTime,
  out FILETIME lpFileTime);
static extern IntPtr DuplicateConsoleHandle(IntPtr hSourceHandle,
  uint dwDesiredAccess, int bInheritHandle, uint dwOptions);
static extern bool DuplicateHandle(IntPtr hSourceProcessHandle,
  IntPtr hSourceHandle, IntPtr hTargetProcessHandle, out IntPtr lpTargetHandle,
  uint dwDesiredAccess, bool bInheritHandle, uint dwOptions);
static extern bool EndUpdateResource(IntPtr hUpdate, bool fDiscard);
static extern void EnterCriticalSection(ref CRITICAL_SECTION
  lpCriticalSection);
static extern bool EnumCalendarInfo(CalInfoDelegate pCalInfoEnumProc,
  uint Locale, uint Calendar, uint CalType);
static extern bool EnumCalendarInfoEx(CalInfoExDelegate pCalInfoEnumProcEx,
  uint Locale, uint Calendar, uint CalType);
static extern bool EnumDateFormats(DateFormatDelegate lpDateFmtEnumProc,
  uint Locale, uint dwFlags);
static extern bool EnumDateFormatsEx(DateFormatExDelegate lpDateFmtEnumProcEx,
  uint Locale, uint dwFlags);
static extern bool EnumLanguageGroupLocales(LangGroupDelegate
  pLangGroupLocaleEnumProc, uint LanguageGroup, uint dwFlags, IntPtr lParam);
```

```
static extern bool EnumResourceLanguages(IntPtr hModule, string lpszType,
  string lpName, ResLangDelegate lpEnumFunc, IntPtr lParam);
static extern bool EnumResourceNames(IntPtr hModule, string lpszType,
  ResNameDelegate lpEnumFunc, IntPtr lParam);
static extern bool EnumResourceTypes(IntPtr hModule, ResTypeDelegate
  lpEnumFunc, IntPtr lParam);
static extern bool EnumSystemCodePages(CodePageDelegate lpCodePageEnumProc,
  uint dwFlags);
static extern bool EnumSystemLanguageGroups(LangGroupsDelegate
  pLangGroupEnumProc, uint dwFlags, IntPtr lParam);
static extern bool EnumSystemLocales(SystemLocalesDelegate lpLocaleEnumProc,
  uint dwFlags);
static extern bool EnumTimeFormats(TimeFormatsDelegate lpTimeFmtEnumProc,
  uint Locale, uint dwFlags);
static extern bool EnumUILanguages(UILanguagesDelegate pUILanguageEnumProc,
  uint dwFlags, IntPtr lParam);
static extern uint EraseTape(IntPtr hDevice, uint dwEraseType,
  bool bImmediate);
static extern bool EscapeCommFunction(IntPtr hFile, uint dwFunc);
static extern void ExitProcess(uint uExitCode);
static extern void ExitThread(uint dwExitCode);
static extern void FatalAppExit(uint uAction, string lpMessageText);
static extern void FatalExit(int ExitCode);
static extern bool FileTimeToDosDateTime([In] ref FILETIME lpFileTime,
  out ushort lpFatDate, out ushort lpFatTime);
static extern bool FileTimeToLocalFileTime([In] ref FILETIME lpFileTime,
  out FILETIME lpLocalFileTime);
static extern bool FileTimeToSystemTime([In] ref FILETIME lpFileTime,
  out SYSTEMTIME lpSystemTime);
static extern bool FillConsoleOutputAttribute(IntPtr hConsoleOutput,
  ushort wAttribute, uint nLength, COORD dwWriteCoord, out uint
  lpNumberOfAttrsWritten);
static extern bool FillConsoleOutputCharacter(IntPtr hConsoleOutput,
  char cCharacter, uint nLength, COORD dwWriteCoord, out uint
  lpNumberOfCharsWritten);
static extern ushort FindAtom(string lpString);
static extern bool FindClose(IntPtr hFindFile);
static extern bool FindCloseChangeNotification(IntPtr hChangeHandle);
static extern IntPtr FindFirstChangeNotification(string lpPathName,
  bool bWatchSubtree, uint dwNotifyFilter);
static extern IntPtr FindFirstFile(string lpFileName, out WIN32_FIND_DATA
  lpFindFileData);
static extern IntPtr FindFirstFileEx(string lpFileName, FINDEX_INFO_LEVELS
  fInfoLevelId, IntPtr lpFindFileData, FINDEX_SEARCH_OPS fSearchOp,
  IntPtr lpSearchFilter, uint dwAdditionalFlags);
```

```
static extern IntPtr FindFirstVolume(string lpszVolumeName,
  uint cchBufferLength);
static extern IntPtr FindFirstVolumeMountPoint(string lpszRootPathName,
  [Out] StringBuilder lpszVolumeMountPoint, uint cchBufferLength);
static extern bool FindNextChangeNotification(IntPtr hChangeHandle);
static extern bool FindNextFile(IntPtr hFindFile, out WIN32_FIND_DATA
  lpFindFileData);
static extern bool FindNextVolume(IntPtr hFindVolume, [Out] StringBuilder
  lpszVolumeName, uint cchBufferLength);
static extern bool FindNextVolumeMountPoint(IntPtr hFindVolumeMountPoint,
  [Out] StringBuilder lpszVolumeMountPoint, uint cchBufferLength);
static extern IntPtr FindResource(IntPtr hModule, IntPtr lpName,
  IntPtr lpType);
static extern IntPtr FindResourceEx(IntPtr hModule, IntPtr lpType,
  IntPtr lpName, ushort wLanguage);
static extern bool FindVolumeClose(IntPtr hFindVolume);
static extern bool FindVolumeMountPointClose(IntPtr hFindVolumeMountPoint);
static extern bool FlushConsoleInputBuffer(IntPtr hConsoleInput);
static extern bool FlushFileBuffers(IntPtr hFile);
static extern bool FlushInstructionCache(IntPtr hProcess, IntPtr lpBaseAddress,
  UIntPtr dwSize);
static extern bool FlushViewOfFile(IntPtr lpBaseAddress,
  UIntPtr dwNumberOfBytesToFlush);
static extern bool FoldString(uint dwMapFlags, string lpSrcStr, int cchSrc,
  [Out] StringBuilder lpDestStr, int cchDest);
static extern uint FormatMessage(uint dwFlags, IntPtr lpSource,
  uint dwMessageId, uint dwLanguageId, StringBuilder lpBuffer,
  uint nSize, IntPtr Arguments);
static extern bool FreeConsole();
static extern bool FreeEnvironmentStrings(string lpszEnvironmentBlock);
static extern bool FreeLibrary(IntPtr hModule);
static extern void FreeLibraryAndExitThread(IntPtr hModule, uint dwExitCode);
static extern bool FreeUserPhysicalPages(IntPtr hProcess, ref UIntPtr
  NumberOfPages, [In] ref UIntPtr UserPfnArray);
static extern bool GenerateConsoleCtrlEvent(uint dwCtrlEvent,
  uint dwProcessGroupId);
static extern uint GetACP();
static extern uint GetAtomName(ushort nAtom, [Out] StringBuilder lpBuffer,
  int nSize);
static extern bool GetBinaryType(string lpApplicationName,
  out uint lpBinaryType);
static extern int GetCalendarInfo(uint Locale, uint Calendar, uint CalType,
  [Out] StringBuilder lpCalData, int cchData, IntPtr lpValue);
static extern IntPtr GetCommandLine();
static extern bool GetCommConfig(IntPtr hCommDev, out COMMCONFIG lpCC,
  ref uint lpdwSize);
```

```
static extern bool GetCommMask(IntPtr hFile, out uint lpEvtMask);
static extern bool GetCommModemStatus(IntPtr hFile, out uint lpModemStat);
static extern bool GetCommProperties(IntPtr hFile, out COMMPROP lpCommProp);
static extern bool GetCommState(IntPtr hFile, ou DCB lpDCB);
static extern bool GetCommTimeouts(IntPtr hFile,
  out COMMTIMEOUTS lpCommTimeouts);
static extern uint GetCompressedFileSize(string lpFileName,
  IntPtr lpFileSizeHigh);
static extern bool GetComputerName([Out] StringBuilder lpBuffer,
  ref uint lpnSize);
static extern bool GetComputerNameEx(COMPUTER_NAME_FORMAT NameType,
  [Out] StringBuilder lpBuffer, ref uint lpnSize);
static extern uint GetConsoleCP();
static extern bool GetConsoleCursorInfo(IntPtr hConsoleOutput,
  out CONSOLE_CURSOR_INFO lpConsoleCursorInfo);
static extern bool GetConsoleMode(IntPtr hConsoleHandle, out uint lpMode);
static extern uint GetConsoleOutputCP();
static extern bool GetConsoleScreenBufferInfo(IntPtr hConsoleOutput,
  out CONSOLE_SCREEN_BUFFER_INFO lpConsoleScreenBufferInfo);
static extern uint GetConsoleTitle([Out] StringBuilder lpConsoleTitle,
  uint nSize);
static extern IntPtr GetConsoleWindow();
static extern bool GetCPInfo(uint CodePage, out CPINFO lpCPInfo);
static extern bool GetCPInfoEx(uint CodePage, uint dwFlags,
  out CPINFOEX lpCPInfoEx);
static extern int GetCurrencyFormat(uint Locale, uint dwFlags, string lpValue,
  IntPtr lpFormat, [Out] StringBuilder lpCurrencyStr, int cchCurrency);
static extern uint GetCurrentDirectory(uint nBufferLength,
  [Out] StringBuilder lpBuffer);
static extern IntPtr GetCurrentProcess();
static extern uint GetCurrentProcessId();
static extern IntPtr GetCurrentThread();
static extern uint GetCurrentThreadId();
static extern int GetDateFormat(uint Locale, uint dwFlags, IntPtr lpDate,
  string lpFormat, [Out] StringBuilder lpDateStr, int cchDate);
static extern bool GetDefaultCommConfig(string lpszName, out COMMCONFIG lpCC,
  ref uint lpdwSize);
static extern bool GetDevicePowerState(IntPtr hDevice, out bool pfOn);
static extern bool GetDiskFreeSpace(string lpRootPathName, out uint
  lpSectorsPerCluster, out uint lpBytesPerSector, out uint
  lpNumberOfFreeClusters, out uint lpTotalNumberOfClusters);
static extern bool GetDiskFreeSpaceEx(string lpDirectoryName, out long
  lpFreeBytesAvailable, out long lpTotalNumberOfBytes, out long
  lpTotalNumberOfFreeBytes);
static extern uint GetDriveType(string lpRootPathName);
static extern IntPtr GetEnvironmentStrings();
```

```
static extern uint GetEnvironmentVariable(string lpName,
  [Out] StringBuilder lpBuffer, uint nSize);
static extern bool GetExitCodeProcess(IntPtr hProcess, out uint lpExitCode);
static extern bool GetExitCodeThread(IntPtr hThread, out uint lpExitCode);
static extern uint GetFileAttributes(string lpFileName);
static extern bool GetFileAttributesEx(string lpFileName,
  GET_FILEEX_INFO_LEVELS fInfoLevelId, IntPtr lpFileInformation);
static extern bool GetFileInformationByHandle(IntPtr hFile,
  out BY_HANDLE_FILE_INFORMATION lpFileInformation);
static extern uint GetFileSize(IntPtr hFile, IntPtr lpFileSizeHigh);
static extern bool GetFileSizeEx(IntPtr hFile, out long lpFileSize);
static extern bool GetFileTime(IntPtr hFile, IntPtr lpCreationTime,
  IntPtr lpLastAccessTime, IntPtr lpLastWriteTime);
static extern uint GetFileType(IntPtr hFile);
static extern uint GetFullPathName(string lpFileName, uint nBufferLength,
  [Out] StringBuilder lpBuffer, out StringBuilder lpFilePart);
static extern bool GetHandleInformation(IntPtr hObject, out uint lpdwFlags);
static extern COORD GetLargestConsoleWindowSize(IntPtr hConsoleOutput);
static extern int GetLocaleInfo(uint Locale, uint LCType,
  [Out] StringBuilder lpLCData, int cchData);
static extern void GetLocalTime(out SYSTEMTIME lpSystemTime);
static extern uint GetLogicalDrives();
static extern uint GetLogicalDriveStrings(uint nBufferLength,
  [Out] StringBuilder lpBuffer);
static extern uint GetLongPathName(string lpszShortPath,
  [Out] StringBuilder lpszLongPath, uint cchBuffer);
static extern bool GetMailslotInfo(IntPtr hMailslot, IntPtr lpMaxMessageSize,
  IntPtr lpNextSize, IntPtr lpMessageCount, IntPtr lpReadTimeout);
static extern uint GetModuleFileName(IntPtr hModule,
  [Out] StringBuilder lpFilename, uint nSize);
static extern IntPtr GetModuleHandle(string lpModuleName);
static extern bool GetNamedPipeHandleState(IntPtr hNamedPipe, IntPtr lpState,
  IntPtr lpCurInstances, IntPtr lpMaxCollectionCount, IntPtr
  lpCollectDataTimeout, [Out] StringBuilder lpUserName, uint nMaxUserNameSize);
static extern bool GetNamedPipeInfo(IntPtr hNamedPipe, IntPtr lpFlags,
  IntPtr lpOutBufferSize, IntPtr lpInBufferSize, IntPtr lpMaxInstances);
static extern int GetNumberFormat(uint Locale, uint dwFlags, string lpValue,
  IntPtr lpFormat, [Out] StringBuilder lpNumberStr, int cchNumber);
static extern bool GetNumberOfConsoleInputEvents(IntPtr hConsoleInput,
  out uint lpcNumberOfEvents);
static extern bool GetNumberOfConsoleMouseButtons(ref lpNumberOfMouseButtons);
static extern uint GetOEMCP();
static extern bool GetOverlappedResult(IntPtr hFile, [In] ref OVERLAPPED
  lpOverlapped, out uint lpNumberOfBytesTransferred, bool bWait);
static extern uint GetPriorityClass(IntPtr hProcess);
static extern uint GetPrivateProfileInt(string lpAppName, string lpKeyName,
  int nDefault, string lpFileName);
```

```csharp
static extern uint GetPrivateProfileSection(string lpAppName,
  IntPtr lpReturnedString, uint nSize, string lpFileName);
static extern uint GetPrivateProfileSectionNames(IntPtr lpszReturnBuffer,
  uint nSize, string lpFileName);
static extern uint GetPrivateProfileString(string lpAppName, string lpKeyName,
  string lpDefault, [Out] StringBuilder lpReturnedString, uint nSize,
  string lpFileName);
static extern bool GetPrivateProfileStruct(string lpszSection, string lpszKey,
  IntPtr lpStruct, uint uSizeStruct, string szFile);
static extern UIntPtr GetProcAddress(IntPtr hModule, string lpProcName);
static extern bool GetProcessAffinityMask(IntPtr hProcess,
  out UIntPtr lpProcessAffinityMask, UIntPtr lpSystemAffinityMask);
static extern IntPtr GetProcessHeap();
static extern uint GetProcessHeaps(uint NumberOfHeaps,
  out IntPtr ProcessHeaps);
static extern bool GetProcessIoCounters(IntPtr hProcess,
  out IO_COUNTERS lpIoCounters);
static extern bool GetProcessPriorityBoost(IntPtr hProcess,
  out bool pDisablePriorityBoost);
static extern bool GetProcessShutdownParameters(out uint lpdwLevel,
  out uint lpdwFlags);
static extern bool GetProcessTimes(IntPtr hProcess, out FILETIME
  lpCreationTime, out FILETIME lpExitTime, out FILETIME lpKernelTime,
  out FILETIME lpUserTime);
static extern uint GetProcessVersion(uint ProcessId);
static extern bool GetProcessWorkingSetSize(IntPtr hProcess,
  out UIntPtr lpMinimumWorkingSetSize, out UIntPtr lpMaximumWorkingSetSize);
static extern uint GetProfileInt(string lpAppName, string lpKeyName,
  int nDefault);
static extern uint GetProfileSection(string lpAppName, IntPtr lpReturnedString,
  uint nSize);
static extern uint GetProfileString(string lpAppName, string lpKeyName,
  string lpDefault, [Out] StringBuilder lpReturnedString, uint nSize);
static extern bool GetQueuedCompletionStatus(IntPtr CompletionPort, out uint
  lpNumberOfBytes, out UIntPtr lpCompletionKey, IntPtr lpOverlapped,
  uint dwMilliseconds);
static extern uint GetShortPathName(string lpszLongPath,
  [Out] StringBuilder lpszShortPath, uint cchBuffer);
static extern void GetStartupInfo(out STARTUPINFO lpStartupInfo);
static extern IntPtr GetStdHandle(int nStdHandle);
static extern bool GetStringType(uint Locale, uint dwInfoType, string lpSrcStr,
  int cchSrc, [Out] ushort [] lpCharType);
static extern bool GetStringTypeEx(uint Locale, uint dwInfoType,
  string lpSrcStr, int cchSrc, [Out] ushort [] lpCharType);
static extern ushort GetSystemDefaultLangID();
static extern uint GetSystemDefaultLCID();
```

```
static extern ushort GetSystemDefaultUILanguage();
static extern uint GetSystemDirectory([Out] StringBuilder lpBuffer,
  uint uSize);
static extern void GetSystemInfo(out SYSTEM_INFO lpSystemInfo);
static extern bool GetSystemPowerStatus(out SYSTEM_POWER_STATUS
  lpSystemPowerStatus);
static extern void GetSystemTime(out SYSTEMTIME lpSystemTime);
static extern bool GetSystemTimeAdjustment(out uint lpTimeAdjustment,
  out uint lpTimeIncrement, out bool lpTimeAdjustmentDisabled);
static extern void GetSystemTimeAsFileTime(out FILETIME
  lpSystemTimeAsFileTime);
static extern uint GetSystemWindowsDirectory([Out] StringBuilder lpBuffer,
  uint uSize);
static extern uint GetTapeParameters(IntPtr hDevice, uint dwOperation,
  out uint lpdwSize, IntPtr lpTapeInformation);
static extern uint GetTapePosition(IntPtr hDevice, uint dwPositionType,
  out uint lpdwPartition, out uint lpdwOffsetLow, IntPtr lpdwOffsetHigh);
static extern uint GetTapeStatus(IntPtr hDevice);
static extern uint GetTempFileName(string lpPathName, string lpPrefixString,
  uint uUnique, [Out] StringBuilder lpTempFileName);
static extern uint GetTempPath(uint nBufferLength,
  [Out] StringBuilder lpBuffer);
static extern bool GetThreadContext(IntPtr hThread, ref CONTEXT lpContext);
static extern uint GetThreadLocale();
static extern int GetThreadPriority(IntPtr hThread);
static extern bool GetThreadPriorityBoost(IntPtr hThread, out bool
  spDisablePriorityBoost);
static extern bool GetThreadSelectorEntry(IntPtr hThread, uint dwSelector,
  out LDT_ENTRY lpSelectorEntry);
static extern bool GetThreadTimes(IntPtr hThread, out FILETIME lpCreationTime,
  out FILETIME lpExitTime, out FILETIME lpKernelTime, out FILETIME lpUserTime);
static extern uint GetTickCount();
static extern int GetTimeFormat(uint Locale, uint dwFlags, IntPtr lpTime,
  string lpFormat, [Out] StringBuilder lpTimeStr, int cchTime);
static extern uint GetTimeZoneInformation(out TIME_ZONE_INFORMATION
  lpTimeZoneInformation);
static extern ushort GetUserDefaultLangID();
static extern uint GetUserDefaultLCID();
static extern ushort GetUserDefaultUILanguage();
static extern uint GetVersion();
static extern bool GetVersionEx(ref OSVERSIONINFO lpVersionInfo);
static extern bool GetVolumeInformation(string lpRootPathName,
  [Out] StringBuilder lpVolumeNameBuffer, uint nVolumeNameSize,
  IntPtr lpVolumeSerialNumber, out uint lpMaximumComponentLength,
  out uint lpFileSystemFlags, [Out] StringBuilder lpFileSystemNameBuffer,
  uint nFileSystemNameSize);
```

```
static extern bool GetVolumeNameForVolumeMountPoint(string
  lpszVolumeMountPoint, [Out] StringBuilder lpszVolumeName,
  uint cchBufferLength);
static extern bool GetVolumePathName(string lpszFileName,
  [Out] StringBuilder lpszVolumePathName, uint cchBufferLength);
static extern uint GetWindowsDirectory([Out] StringBuilder lpBuffer,
  uint uSize);
static extern uint GetWriteWatch(uint dwFlags, IntPtr lpBaseAddress,
  UIntPtr dwRegionSize, out IntPtr lpAddresses, ref UIntPtr lpdwCount,
  out uint lpdwGranularity);
static extern ushort GlobalAddAtom(string lpString);
static extern IntPtr GlobalAlloc(uint uFlags, UIntPtr dwBytes);
static extern ushort GlobalDeleteAtom(ushort nAtom);
static extern ushort GlobalFindAtom(string lpString);
static extern uint GlobalFlags(IntPtr hMem);
static extern IntPtr GlobalFree(IntPtr hMem);
static extern uint GlobalGetAtomName(ushort nAtom,
  [Out] StringBuilder lpBuffer, int nSize);
static extern IntPtr GlobalHandle(IntPtr pMem);
static extern IntPtr GlobalLock(IntPtr hMem);
static extern void GlobalMemoryStatus(out MEMORYSTATUS lpBuffer);
static extern bool GlobalMemoryStatusEx(ref MEMORYSTATUSEX lpBuffer);
static extern IntPtr GlobalReAlloc(IntPtr hMem, UIntPtr dwBytes, uint uFlags);
static extern UIntPtr GlobalSize(IntPtr hMem);
static extern bool GlobalUnlock(IntPtr hMem);
static extern bool Heap32First(ref HEAPENTRY32 lphe, uint th32ProcessID,
  UIntPtr th32HeapID);
static extern bool Heap32ListFirst(IntPtr hSnapshot, ref HEAPLIST32 lphl);
static extern bool eap32ListNext(IntPtr hSnapshot, out HEAPLIST32 lphl);
static extern bool Heap32Next(out HEAPENTRY32 lphe);
static extern IntPtr HeapAlloc(IntPtr hHeap, uint dwFlags, UIntPtr dwBytes);
static extern uint HeapCompact(IntPtr hHeap, uint dwFlags);
static extern IntPtr HeapCreate(uint flOptions, UIntPtr dwInitialSize,
  UIntPtr dwMaximumSize);
static extern bool HeapDestroy(IntPtr hHeap);
static extern bool HeapFree(IntPtr hHeap, uint dwFlags, IntPtr lpMem);
static extern bool HeapLock(IntPtr hHeap);
static extern IntPtr HeapReAlloc(IntPtr hHeap, uint dwFlags, IntPtr lpMem,
  UIntPtr dwBytes);
static extern uint HeapSize(IntPtr hHeap, uint dwFlags, IntPtr lpMem);
static extern bool HeapUnlock(IntPtr hHeap);
static extern bool HeapValidate(IntPtr hHeap, uint dwFlags, IntPtr lpMem);
static extern bool HeapWalk(IntPtr hHeap, ref PROCESS_HEAP_ENTRY lpEntry);
static extern bool InitAtomTable(uint nSize);
static extern void InitializeCriticalSection(out CRITICAL_SECTION
  lpCriticalSection);
```

```
static extern bool InitializeCriticalSectionAndSpinCount(ref CRITICAL_SECTION
  lpCriticalSection, uint dwSpinCount);
static extern int InterlockedCompareExchange(ref int Destination, int Exchange,
  int Comperand);
static extern int InterlockedDecrement(ref int lpAddend);
static extern int InterlockedExchange(ref int Target, int Value);
static extern int InterlockedExchangeAdd(ref int Addend, int Value);
static extern int InterlockedIncrement(ref int lpAddend);
static extern bool IsBadCodePtr(IntPtr lpfn);
static extern bool IsBadReadPtr(IntPtr lp, uint ucb);
static extern bool IsBadStringPtr(string lpsz, uint ucchMax);
static extern bool IsBadWritePtr(IntPtr lp, uint ucb);
static extern bool IsDBCSLeadByte(byte TestChar);
static extern bool IsDBCSLeadByteEx(uint CodePage, byte TestChar);
static extern bool IsDebuggerPresent();
static extern bool IsProcessorFeaturePresent(uint ProcessorFeature);
static extern bool IsSystemResumeAutomatic();
static extern bool IsValidCodePage(uint CodePage);
static extern bool IsValidLanguageGroup(uint LanguageGroup, uint dwFlags);
static extern bool IsValidLocale(uint Locale, uint dwFlags);
static extern int LCMapString(uint Locale, uint dwMapFlags, string lpSrcStr,
  int cchSrc, [Out] StringBuilder lpDestStr, int cchDest);
static extern void LeaveCriticalSection(ref CRITICAL_SECTION
  lpCriticalSection);
static extern IntPtr LoadLibrary(string lpFileName);
static extern IntPtr LoadLibraryEx(string lpFileName, IntPtr hFile,
  uint dwFlags);
static extern uint LoadModule(string lpModuleName, IntPtr lpParameterBlock);
static extern IntPtr LoadResource(IntPtr hModule, IntPtr hResInfo);
static extern IntPtr LocalAlloc(uint uFlags, UIntPtr uBytes);
static extern bool LocalFileTimeToFileTime([In] ref FILETIME lpLocalFileTime,
  out FILETIME lpFileTime);
static extern uint LocalFlags(IntPtr hMem);
static extern IntPtr LocalFree(IntPtr hMem);
static extern IntPtr LocalHandle(IntPtr pMem);
static extern IntPtr LocalLock(IntPtr hMem);
static extern IntPtr LocalReAlloc(IntPtr hMem, UIntPtr uBytes, uint uFlags);
static extern uint LocalSize(IntPtr hMem);
static extern bool LocalUnlock(IntPtr hMem);
static extern bool LockFile(IntPtr hFile, uint dwFileOffsetLow, uint
  dwFileOffsetHigh, uint nNumberOfBytesToLockLow, uint
  nNumberOfBytesToLockHigh);
static extern bool LockFileEx(IntPtr hFile, uint dwFlags, uint dwReserved,
  uint nNumberOfBytesToLockLow, uint nNumberOfBytesToLockHigh,
  [In] ref OVERLAPPED lpOverlapped);
static extern IntPtr LockResource(IntPtr hResData);
```

```
static extern IntPtr lstrcat(StringBuilder lpString1, string lpString2);
static extern int lstrcmp(string lpString1, string lpString2);
static extern int lstrcmpi(string lpString1, string lpString2);
static extern IntPtr lstrcpy([Out] StringBuilder lpString1, string lpString2);
static extern IntPtr lstrcpyn([Out] StringBuilder lpString1, string lpString2,
  int iMaxLength);
static extern int lstrlen(string lpString);
static extern bool MapUserPhysicalPages(IntPtr lpAddress, UIntPtr
  NumberOfPages, IntPtr UserPfnArray);
static extern bool MapUserPhysicalPagesScatter(ref IntPtr VirtualAddresses,
  UIntPtr NumberOfPages, IntPtr PageArray);
static extern IntPtr MapViewOfFile(IntPtr hFileMappingObject, uint
  dwDesiredAccess, uint dwFileOffsetHigh, uint dwFileOffsetLow,
  UIntPtr dwNumberOfBytesToMap);
static extern IntPtr MapViewOfFileEx(IntPtr hFileMappingObject,
  uint dwDesiredAccess, uint dwFileOffsetHigh, uint dwFileOffsetLow,
  UIntPtr dwNumberOfBytesToMap, IntPtr lpBaseAddress);
static extern bool Module32First(IntPtr hSnapshot, ref MODULEENTRY32 lpme);
static extern bool Module32Next(IntPtr hSnapshot, out MODULEENTRY32 lpme);
static extern bool MoveFile(string lpExistingFileName, string lpNewFileName);
static extern bool MoveFileEx(string lpExistingFileName, string lpNewFileName,
  uint dwFlags);
static extern bool MoveFileWithProgress(string lpExistingFileName,
  string lpNewFileName, MoveFileProgressDelegate lpProgressRoutine,
  IntPtr lpData, uint dwFlags);
static extern int MulDiv(int nNumber, int nNumerator, int nDenominator);
static extern bool MultiByteToWideChar(uint CodePage, uint dwFlags, string
  lpMultiByteStr, int cbMultiByte, [Out, MarshalAs(UnmanagedType.LPWStr)]
  StringBuilder lpWideCharStr, int cchWideChar);
static extern IntPtr OpenEvent(uint dwDesiredAccess, bool bInheritHandle,
  string lpName);
static extern IntPtr OpenFile(string lpFileName, out OFSTRUCT lpReOpenBuff,
  uint uStyle);
static extern IntPtr OpenFileMapping(uint dwDesiredAccess, bool bInheritHandle,
  string lpName);
static extern IntPtr OpenJobObject(uint dwDesiredAccess, bool bInheritHandle,
  string lpName);
static extern IntPtr OpenMutex(uint dwDesiredAccess, bool bInheritHandle,
  string lpName);
static extern IntPtr OpenProcess(uint dwDesiredAccess, bool bInheritHandle,
  uint dwProcessId);
static extern IntPtr OpenSemaphore(uint dwDesiredAccess, bool bInheritHandle,
  string lpName);
static extern IntPtr OpenThread(uint dwDesiredAccess, bool bInheritHandle,
  uint dwThreadId);
static extern IntPtr OpenWaitableTimer(uint dwDesiredAccess,
  bool bInheritHandle, string lpTimerName);
```

```
static extern void OutputDebugString(string lpOutputString);
static extern bool PeekConsoleInput(IntPtr hConsoleInput,
    [Out] INPUT_RECORD [] lpBuffer, uint nLength, out uint lpNumberOfEventsRead);
static extern bool PeekNamedPipe(IntPtr hNamedPipe, IntPtr lpBuffer,
    uint nBufferSize, IntPtr lpBytesRead, IntPtr lpTotalBytesAvail,
    IntPtr lpBytesLeftThisMessage);
static extern bool PostQueuedCompletionStatus(IntPtr CompletionPort,
    uint dwNumberOfBytesTransferred, UIntPtr dwCompletionKey,
    [In] ref OVERLAPPED lpOverlapped);
static extern uint PrepareTape(IntPtr hDevice, uint dwOperation,
    bool bImmediate);
static extern bool Process32First(IntPtr hSnapshot, ref PROCESSENTRY32 lppe);
static extern bool Process32Next(IntPtr hSnapshot, out PROCESSENTRY32 lppe);
static extern bool ProcessIdToSessionId(uint dwProcessId, out uint pSessionId);
static extern bool PulseEvent(IntPtr hEvent);
static extern bool PurgeComm(IntPtr hFile, uint dwFlags);
static extern uint QueryDosDevice(string lpDeviceName, IntPtr lpTargetPath,
    uint ucchMax);
static extern bool QueryInformationJobObject(IntPtr hJob, JOBOBJECTINFOCLASS
    JobObjectInformationClass, IntPtr lpJobObjectInfo,
    uint cbJobObjectInfoLength, IntPtr lpReturnLength);
static extern bool QueryPerformanceCounter(out long lpPerformanceCount);
static extern bool QueryPerformanceFrequency(out long lpFrequency);
static extern uint QueueUserAPC(ApcDelegate pfnAPC, IntPtr hThread,
    UIntPtr dwData);
static extern bool QueueUserWorkItem(ThreadStartDelegate Function,
    IntPtr Context, uint Flags);
static extern void RaiseException(uint dwExceptionCode, uint dwExceptionFlags,
    uint nNumberOfArguments, IntPtr lpArguments);
static extern bool ReadConsole(IntPtr hConsoleInput, [Out] StringBuilder
    lpBuffer, uint nNumberOfCharsToRead, out uint lpNumberOfCharsRead,
    IntPtr lpReserved);
static extern bool ReadConsoleInput(IntPtr hConsoleInput, [Out] INPUT_RECORD []
    lpBuffer, uint nLength, out uint lpNumberOfEventsRead);
static extern bool ReadConsoleOutput(IntPtr hConsoleOutput, [Out] CHAR_INFO []
    lpBuffer, COORD dwBufferSize, COORD dwBufferCoord,
    ref SMALL_RECT lpReadRegion);
static extern bool ReadConsoleOutputAttribute(IntPtr hConsoleOutput,
    [Out] ushort [] lpAttribute, uint nLength, COORD dwReadCoord,
    out uint lpNumberOfAttrsRead);
static extern bool ReadConsoleOutputCharacter(IntPtr hConsoleOutput,
    [Out] StringBuilder lpCharacter, uint nLength, COORD dwReadCoord,
    out uint lpNumberOfCharsRead);
static extern bool ReadDirectoryChangesW(IntPtr hDirectory, IntPtr lpBuffer,
    uint nBufferLength, bool bWatchSubtree, uint dwNotifyFilter, out uint
    lpBytesReturned, IntPtr lpOverlapped,
    ReadDirectoryChangesDelegate lpCompletionRoutine);
```

```
static extern bool ReadFile(IntPtr hFile, [Out] byte [] lpBuffer,
  uint nNumberOfBytesToRead, IntPtr lpNumberOfBytesRead, IntPtr lpOverlapped);
static extern bool ReadFileEx(IntPtr hFile, [Out] byte [] lpBuffer,
  uint nNumberOfBytesToRead, [In] ref OVERLAPPED lpOverlapped,
  ReadFileCompletionDelegate lpCompletionRoutine);
static extern bool ReadFileScatter(IntPtr hFile, FILE_SEGMENT_ELEMENT []
  aSegementArray, uint nNumberOfBytesToRead, IntPtr lpReserved,
  [In] ref OVERLAPPED lpOverlapped);
static extern bool ReadProcessMemory(IntPtr hProcess, IntPtr lpBaseAddress,
  [Out] byte [] lpBuffer, UIntPtr nSize, IntPtr lpNumberOfBytesRead);
static extern bool RegisterWaitForSingleObject(out IntPtr phNewWaitObject,
  IntPtr hObject, WaitOrTimerDelegate Callback, IntPtr Context,
  uint dwMilliseconds, uint dwFlags);
static extern bool ReleaseMutex(IntPtr hMutex);
static extern bool ReleaseSemaphore(IntPtr hSemaphore, int lReleaseCount,
  IntPtr lpPreviousCount);
static extern bool RemoveDirectory(string lpPathName);
static extern bool ReplaceFile(string lpReplacedFileName,
  string lpReplacementFileName, string lpBackupFileName, uint dwReplaceFlags,
  IntPtr lpExclude, IntPtr lpReserved);
static extern bool RequestWakeupLatency(LATENCY_TIME latency);
static extern bool ResetEvent(IntPtr hEvent);
static extern uint ResetWriteWatch(IntPtr lpBaseAddress, UIntPtr dwRegionSize);
static extern uint ResumeThread(IntPtr hThread);
static extern bool ScrollConsoleScreenBuffer(IntPtr hConsoleOutput,
  [In] ref SMALL_RECT lpScrollRectangle, IntPtr lpClipRectangle,
  COORD dwDestinationOrigin, [In] ref CHAR_INFO lpFill);
static extern uint SearchPath(string lpPath, string lpFileName,
  string lpExtension, uint nBufferLength, [Out] StringBuilder lpBuffer,
  out StringBuilder lpFilePart);
static extern int SetCalendarInfo(uint Locale, uint Calendar, uint CalType,
  string lpCalData);
static extern bool SetCommBreak(IntPtr hFile);
static extern bool SetCommConfig(IntPtr hCommDev, [In] ref COMMCONFIG lpCC,
  uint dwSize);
static extern bool SetCommMask(IntPtr hFile, uint dwEvtMask);
static extern bool SetCommState(IntPtr hFile, [In] ref DCB lpDCB);
static extern bool SetCommTimeouts(IntPtr hFile, [In] ref COMMTIMEOUTS
  lpCommTimeouts);
static extern bool SetComputerName(string lpComputerName);
static extern bool SetComputerNameEx([In] ref COMPUTER_NAME_FORMAT NameType,
  string lpBuffer);
static extern bool SetConsoleActiveScreenBuffer(IntPtr hConsoleOutput);
static extern bool SetConsoleCP(uint wCodePageID);
static extern bool SetConsoleCtrlHandler(ConsoleCtrlDelegate HandlerRoutine,
  bool Add);
```

```
static extern bool SetConsoleCursorInfo(IntPtr hConsoleOutput,
  [In] ref CONSOLE_CURSOR_INFO lpConsoleCursorInfo);
static extern bool SetConsoleCursorPosition(IntPtr hConsoleOutput,
  COORD dwCursorPosition);
static extern bool SetConsoleMode(IntPtr hConsoleHandle, uint dwMode);
static extern bool SetConsoleOutputCP(uint wCodePageID);
static extern bool SetConsoleScreenBufferSize(IntPtr hConsoleOutput,
  COORD dwSize);
static extern bool SetConsoleTextAttribute(IntPtr hConsoleOutput,
  ushort wAttributes);
static extern bool SetConsoleTitle(string lpConsoleTitle);
static extern bool SetConsoleWindowInfo(IntPtr hConsoleOutput, bool bAbsolute,
  [In] ref SMALL_RECT lpConsoleWindow);
static extern uint SetCriticalSectionSpinCount(ref CRITICAL_SECTION
  lpCriticalSection, uint dwSpinCount);
static extern bool SetCurrentDirectory(string lpPathName);
static extern bool SetDefaultCommConfig(string lpszName, [In] ref
  COMMCONFIG lpCC, uint dwSize);
static extern bool SetEndOfFile(IntPtr hFile);
static extern bool SetEnvironmentVariable(string lpName, string lpValue);
static extern uint SetErrorMode(uint uMode);
static extern bool SetEvent(IntPtr hEvent);
static extern void SetFileApisToANSI();
static extern void SetFileApisToOEM();
static extern bool SetFileAttributes(string lpFileName, uint dwFileAttributes);
static extern uint SetFilePointer(IntPtr hFile, int lDistanceToMove,
  IntPtr lpDistanceToMoveHigh, uint dwMoveMethod);
static extern bool SetFilePointerEx(IntPtr hFile, long liDistanceToMove,
  IntPtr lpNewFilePointer, uint dwMoveMethod);
static extern bool SetFileTime(IntPtr hFile, [In] ref FILETIME lpCreationTime,
  [In] ref FILETIME lpLastAccessTime, [In] ref FILETIME lpLastWriteTime);
static extern bool SetHandleInformation(IntPtr hObject, uint dwMask,
  uint dwFlags);
static extern bool SetInformationJobObject(IntPtr hJob,
  JOBOBJECTINFOCLASS JobObjectInfoClass, IntPtr lpJobObjectInfo,
  uint cbJobObjectInfoLength);
static extern void SetLastError(uint dwErrCode);
static extern bool SetLocaleInfo(uint Locale, uint LCType, string lpLCData);
static extern bool SetLocalTime([In] ref SYSTEMTIME lpLocalTime);
static extern bool SetMailslotInfo(IntPtr hMailslot, uint lReadTimeout);
static extern bool SetNamedPipeHandleState(IntPtr hNamedPipe, IntPtr lpMode,
  IntPtr lpMaxCollectionCount, IntPtr lpCollectDataTimeout);
static extern bool SetPriorityClass(IntPtr hProcess, uint dwPriorityClass);
static extern bool SetProcessAffinityMask(IntPtr hProcess,
  UIntPtr dwProcessAffinityMask);
static extern bool SetProcessPriorityBoost(IntPtr hProcess,
  bool DisablePriorityBoost);
```

```
static extern bool SetProcessShutdownParameters(uint dwLevel, uint dwFlags);
static extern bool SetProcessWorkingSetSize(IntPtr hProcess, UIntPtr
  dwMinimumWorkingSetSize, UIntPtr dwMaximumWorkingSetSize);
static extern bool SetStdHandle(uint nStdHandle, IntPtr hHandle);
static extern bool SetSystemPowerState(bool fSuspend, bool fForce);
static extern bool SetSystemTime([In] ref SYSTEMTIME lpSystemTime);
static extern bool SetSystemTimeAdjustment(uint dwTimeAdjustment,
  bool bTimeAdjustmentDisabled);
static extern uint SetTapeParameters(IntPtr hDevice, uint dwOperation,
  IntPtr lpTapeInformation);
static extern uint SetTapePosition(IntPtr hDevice, uint dwPositionMethod,
  uint dwPartition, uint dwOffsetLow, uint dwOffsetHigh, bool bImmediate);
static extern UIntPtr SetThreadAffinityMask(IntPtr hThread,
  UIntPtr dwThreadAffinityMask);
static extern bool SetThreadContext(IntPtr hThread,
  [In] ref CONTEXT lpContext);
static extern EXECUTION_STATE SetThreadExecutionState(EXECUTION_STATE esFlags);
static extern uint SetThreadIdealProcessor(IntPtr hThread,
  uint dwIdealProcessor);
static extern bool SetThreadLocale(uint Locale);
static extern bool SetThreadPriority(IntPtr hThread, int nPriority);
static extern bool SetThreadPriorityBoost(IntPtr hThread,
  bool DisablePriorityBoost);
static extern bool SetTimeZoneInformation([In] ref TIME_ZONE_INFORMATION
  lpTimeZoneInformation);
static extern FilterDelegate SetUnhandledExceptionFilter(FilterDelegate
  lpTopLevelExceptionFilter);
static extern bool SetupComm(IntPtr hFile, uint dwInQueue, uint dwOutQueue);
static extern bool SetVolumeLabel(string lpRootPathName, string lpVolumeName);
static extern bool SetVolumeMountPoint(string lpszVolumeMountPoint,
  string lpszVolumeName);
static extern bool SetWaitableTimer(IntPtr hTimer, [In] ref long pDueTime,
  int lPeriod, TimerCompleteDelegate pfnCompletionRoutine,
  IntPtr lpArgToCompletionRoutine, bool fResume);
static extern uint SignalObjectAndWait(IntPtr hObjectToSignal,
  IntPtr hObjectToWaitOn, uint dwMilliseconds, bool bAlertable);
static extern uint SizeofResource(IntPtr hModule, IntPtr hResInfo);
static extern void Sleep(uint dwMilliseconds);
static extern uint SleepEx(uint dwMilliseconds, bool bAlertable);
static extern uint SuspendThread(IntPtr hThread);
static extern void SwitchToFiber(IntPtr lpFiber);
static extern bool SwitchToThread();
static extern bool SystemTimeToFileTime([In] ref SYSTEMTIME lpSystemTime,
  out FILETIME lpFileTime);
static extern bool SystemTimeToTzSpecificLocalTime(IntPtr
  lpTimeZoneInformation, [In] ref SYSTEMTIME lpUniversalTime,
  out SYSTEMTIME lpLocalTime);
```

```
static extern bool TerminateJobObject(IntPtr hJob, uint uExitCode);
static extern bool TerminateProcess(IntPtr hProcess, uint uExitCode);
static extern bool TerminateThread(IntPtr hThread, uint dwExitCode);
static extern bool Thread32First(IntPtr hSnapshot, ref THREADENTRY32 lpte);
static extern bool Thread32Next(IntPtr hSnapshot, out THREADENTRY32 lpte);
static extern uint TlsAlloc();
static extern bool TlsFree(uint dwTlsIndex);
static extern IntPtr TlsGetValue(uint dwTlsIndex);
static extern bool TlsSetValue(uint dwTlsIndex, IntPtr lpTlsValue);
static extern bool Toolhelp32ReadProcessMemory(uint th32ProcessID,
  IntPtr lpBaseAddress, [Out] byte [] lpBuffer, UIntPtr cbRead,
  IntPtr lpNumberOfBytesRead);
static extern bool TransactNamedPipe(IntPtr hNamedPipe, byte [] lpInBuffer,
  uint nInBufferSize, [Out] byte [] lpOutBuffer, uint nOutBufferSize,
  IntPtr lpBytesRead, IntPtr lpOverlapped);
static extern bool TransmitCommChar(IntPtr hFile, char cChar);
static extern bool TryEnterCriticalSection(ref CRITICAL_SECTION
  lpCriticalSection);
static extern int UnhandledExceptionFilter([In] ref EXCEPTION_POINTERS
  ExceptionInfo);
static extern bool UnlockFile(IntPtr hFile, uint dwFileOffsetLow,
  uint dwFileOffsetHigh, uint nNumberOfBytesToUnlockLow,
  uint nNumberOfBytesToUnlockHigh);
static extern bool UnlockFileEx(IntPtr hFile, uint dwReserved,
  uint nNumberOfBytesToUnlockLow, uint nNumberOfBytesToUnlockHigh,
  [In] ref OVERLAPPED lpOverlapped);
static extern bool UnmapViewOfFile(IntPtr lpBaseAddress);
static extern bool UnregisterWait(IntPtr WaitHandle);
static extern bool UnregisterWaitEx(IntPtr WaitHandle, IntPtr CompletionEvent);
static extern bool UpdateResource(IntPtr hUpdate, string lpType, string lpName,
  ushort wLanguage, IntPtr lpData, uint cbData);
static extern bool VerifyVersionInfo([In] ref OSVERSIONINFOEX lpVersionInfo,
  uint dwTypeMask, ulong dwlConditionMask);
static extern uint VerLanguageName(uint wLang, [Out] StringBuilder szLang,
  uint wSize);
static extern ulong VerSetConditionMask(ulong dwlConditionMask,
  uint dwTypeBitMask, byte dwConditionMask);
static extern IntPtr VirtualAlloc(IntPtr lpAddress, UIntPtr dwSize,
  uint flAllocationType, uint flProtect);
static extern IntPtr VirtualAllocEx(IntPtr hProcess, IntPtr lpAddress,
  UIntPtr dwSize, uint flAllocationType, uint flProtect);
static extern bool VirtualFree(IntPtr lpAddress, UIntPtr dwSize,
  uint dwFreeType);
static extern bool VirtualFreeEx(IntPtr hProcess, IntPtr lpAddress,
  UIntPtr dwSize, uint dwFreeType);
static extern bool VirtualLock(IntPtr lpAddress, UIntPtr dwSize);
```

```
static extern bool VirtualProtect(IntPtr lpAddress, UIntPtr dwSize,
  uint flNewProtect, out uint lpflOldProtect);
static extern bool VirtualProtectEx(IntPtr hProcess, IntPtr lpAddress,
  UIntPtr dwSize, uint flNewProtect, out uint lpflOldProtect);
static extern uint VirtualQuery(IntPtr lpAddress, out MEMORY_BASIC_INFORMATION
  lpBuffer, UIntPtr dwLength);
static extern uint VirtualQueryEx(IntPtr hProcess, IntPtr lpAddress,
  out MEMORY_BASIC_INFORMATION lpBuffer, UIntPtr dwLength);
static extern bool VirtualUnlock(IntPtr lpAddress, UIntPtr dwSize);
static extern bool WaitCommEvent(IntPtr hFile, out uint lpEvtMask,
  IntPtr lpOverlapped);
static extern bool WaitForDebugEvent(out DEBUG_EVENT lpDebugEvent,
  uint dwMilliseconds);
static extern uint WaitForMultipleObjects(uint nCount, IntPtr [] lpHandles,
  bool bWaitAll, uint dwMilliseconds);
static extern uint WaitForMultipleObjectsEx(uint nCount, IntPtr [] lpHandles,
  bool bWaitAll, uint dwMilliseconds, bool bAlertable);
static extern uint WaitForSingleObject(IntPtr hHandle, uint dwMilliseconds);
static extern uint WaitForSingleObjectEx(IntPtr hHandle, uint dwMilliseconds,
  bool bAlertable);
static extern bool WaitNamedPipe(string lpNamedPipeName, uint nTimeOut);
static extern int WideCharToMultiByte(uint CodePage, uint dwFlags,
  [MarshalAs(UnmanagedType.LPWStr)] string lpWideCharStr, int cchWideChar,
  string lpMultiByteStr, int cbMultiByte, IntPtr lpDefaultChar,
  out bool lpUsedDefaultChar);
static extern uint WinExec(string lpCmdLine, uint uCmdShow);
static extern bool WriteConsole(IntPtr hConsoleOutput, string lpBuffer,
  uint nNumberOfCharsToWrite, out uint lpNumberOfCharsWritten,
  IntPtr lpReserved);
static extern bool WriteConsoleInput(IntPtr hConsoleInput,
  INPUT_RECORD [] lpBuffer, uint nLength, out uint lpNumberOfEventsWritten);
static extern bool WriteConsoleOutput(IntPtr hConsoleOutput, CHAR_INFO []
  lpBuffer, COORD dwBufferSize, COORD dwBufferCoord, ref SMALL_RECT
  lpWriteRegion);
static extern bool WriteConsoleOutputAttribute(IntPtr hConsoleOutput,
  ushort [] lpAttribute, uint nLength, COORD dwWriteCoord,
  out uint lpNumberOfAttrsWritten);
static extern bool WriteConsoleOutputCharacter(IntPtr hConsoleOutput,
  string lpCharacter, uint nLength, COORD dwWriteCoord,
  out uint lpNumberOfCharsWritten);
static extern bool WriteFile(IntPtr hFile, byte [] lpBuffer,
  uint nNumberOfBytesToWrite, out uint lpNumberOfBytesWritten,
  [In] ref OVERLAPPED lpOverlapped);
static extern bool WriteFileEx(IntPtr hFile, byte [] lpBuffer,
  uint nNumberOfBytesToWrite, [In] ref OVERLAPPED lpOverlapped,
  WriteFileCompletionDelegate lpCompletionRoutine);
```

```
static extern bool WriteFileGather(IntPtr hFile, [Out] FILE_SEGMENT_ELEMENT []
  aSegmentArray, uint nNumberOfBytesToWrite, IntPtr lpReserved,
  [In] ref OVERLAPPED lpOverlapped);
static extern bool WritePrivateProfileSection(string lpAppName,
  string lpString, string lpFileName);
static extern bool WritePrivateProfileString(string lpAppName,
  string lpKeyName, string lpString, string lpFileName);
static extern bool WritePrivateProfileStruct(string lpszSection,
  string lpszKey, IntPtr lpStruct, uint uSizeStruct, string szFile);
static extern bool WriteProcessMemory(IntPtr hProcess, IntPtr lpBaseAddress,
  byte [] lpBuffer, UIntPtr nSize, IntPtr lpNumberOfBytesWritten);
static extern bool WriteProfileSection(string lpAppName, string lpString);
static extern bool WriteProfileString(string lpAppName, string lpKeyName,
  string lpString);
static extern uint WriteTapemark(IntPtr hDevice, uint dwTapemarkType,
  uint dwTapemarkCount, bool bImmediate);
```

OLE32.DLL

All of these functions should be preceded with the following line when used in source code:

```
[DllImport("ole32.dll")]
```

Most of these methods return an HRESULT. Therefore, rather than using an int return value to represent the HRESULT, you could change it to void and add PreserveSig=false to the DllImportAttribute for functions that don't return multiple success HRESULT values. For example:

```
[DllImport("ole32.dll", PreserveSig=true)]
```

This way, failure HRESULTs cause exceptions to be thrown, which is usually more convenient but at the sake of performance. In the signatures listed, PreserveSig=true is *not* used, so methods that return an HRESULT are listed as returning int.

Notice that the PInvoke signatures for functions in OLE32.DLL are generally longer than the previous signatures, because they use common COM types that the Interop Marshaler doesn't handle by default for PInvoke (such as IUnknown and Unicode strings). The MarshalAsAttribute pseudo-custom attribute is required to use these COM types with PInvoke marshaling. Here are signatures from OLE32.DLL:

```
static extern int BindMoniker(UCOMIMoniker pmk, uint grfOpt,
  [In] ref Guid iidResult, [MarshalAs(UnmanagedType.Interface)] out Object
  ppresult);
static extern int CLSIDFromProgID([MarshalAs(UnmanagedType.LPWStr)] string
  lpszProgID, out Guid pclsid);
static extern int CLSIDFromProgIDEx([MarshalAs(UnmanagedType.LPWStr)] string
  lpszProgID, out Guid pclsid);
```

```
static extern int CLSIDFromString([MarshalAs(UnmanagedType.LPWStr)] string
  lpsz, out Guid pclsid);
static extern int CoAddRefServerProcess();
static extern int CoAllowSetForegroundWindow(
  [MarshalAs(UnmanagedType.IUnknown)] object pUnk, IntPtr lpvReserved);
static extern int CoCancelCall(uint dwThreadID, uint ulTimeout);
static extern int CoCopyProxy([MarshalAs(UnmanagedType.IUnknown)] object
  pProxy, [MarshalAs(UnmanagedType.IUnknown)] out object ppCopy);
static extern int CoCreateFreeThreadedMarshaler(
  [MarshalAs(UnmanagedType.IUnknown)] object punkOuter,
  [MarshalAs(UnmanagedType.IUnknown)] out object ppunkMarshaler);
static extern int CoCreateGuid(out Guid pguid);
static extern int CoCreateInstance([In] ref Guid rclsid,
  [MarshalAs(UnmanagedType.IUnknown)] object pUnkOuter, uint dwClsContext,
  [In] ref Guid riid, [MarshalAs(UnmanagedType.IUnknown)] out object ppv);
static extern int CoCreateInstanceEx([In] ref Guid rclsid,
  [MarshalAs(UnmanagedType.IUnknown)] object pUnkOuter, uint dwClsCtx,
  IntPtr pServerInfo, uint cmq, [In, Out] MULTI_QI [] pResults);
static extern int CoDisableCallCancellation(IntPtr pvReserved);
static extern int CoDisconnectObject([MarshalAs(UnmanagedType.IUnknown)]
  object pUnk, uint dwReserved);
static extern bool CoDosDateTimeToFileTime(ushort nDosDate, ushort nDosTime,
  out FILETIME lpFileTime);
static extern int CoEnableCallCancellation(IntPtr pvReserved);
static extern int CoFileTimeNow(out FILETIME lpFileTime);
static extern bool CoFileTimeToDosDateTime([In] ref FILETIME lpFileTime,
  out ushort lpDosDate, out ushort lpDosTime);
static extern void CoFreeAllLibraries();
static extern void CoFreeLibrary(IntPtr hInst);
static extern void CoFreeUnusedLibraries();
static extern int CoGetCallContext([In] ref Guid riid,
  [MarshalAs(UnmanagedType.IUnknown)] out object ppInterface);
static extern int CoGetCancelObject(uint dwThreadID, [In] ref Guid riid,
  [MarshalAs(UnmanagedType.IUnknown)] out object ppUnk);
static extern int CoGetClassObject([In] ref Guid rclsid, uint dwClsContext,
  IntPtr pServerInfo, [In] ref Guid riid,
  [MarshalAs(UnmanagedType.IUnknown)] out object ppv);
static extern uint CoGetCurrentProcess();
static extern int CoGetInstanceFromFile(IntPtr pServerInfo, [In] ref Guid
  pclsid, [MarshalAs(UnmanagedType.IUnknown)] object pUnkOuter, uint dwClsCtx,
  uint grfMode, [MarshalAs(UnmanagedType.LPWStr)] string szName, uint cmq,
  MULTI_QI [] rgmqResults);
static extern int CoGetInstanceFromIStorage(IntPtr pServerInfo, [In] ref Guid
  pclsid, [MarshalAs(UnmanagedType.IUnknown)] object pUnkOuter, uint dwClsCtx,
  IStorage pstg, uint cmq, MULTI_QI [] rgmqResults);
```

```
static extern int CoGetInterfaceAndReleaseStream(UCOMIStream pStm, [In] ref
  Guid riid, [MarshalAs(UnmanagedType.IUnknown)] out object ppv);
static extern int CoGetMalloc(uint dwMemContext, out IMalloc ppMalloc);
static extern int CoGetMarshalSizeMax(out uint pulSize, [In] ref Guid riid,
  [MarshalAs(UnmanagedType.IUnknown)] object pUnk, uint dwDestContext, IntPtr
  pvDestContext, uint mshtflags);
static extern int CoGetObject([MarshalAs(UnmanagedType.LPWStr)] string pszName,
  [In] ref BIND_OPTS pBindOptions, [In] ref Guid riid,
  [MarshalAs(UnmanagedType.IUnknown)] out object ppv);
static extern int CoGetObjectContext([In] ref Guid riid,
  [MarshalAs(UnmanagedType.IUnknown)] out object ppv);
static extern int CoGetPSClsid([In] ref Guid riid, out Guid pclsid);
static extern int CoGetStandardMarshal([In] ref Guid riid,
  [MarshalAs(UnmanagedType.IUnknown)] object pUnk, uint dwDestContext,
  IntPtr pvDestContext, uint mshlflags, out IMarshal ppMarshal);
static extern int CoGetStdMarshalEx([MarshalAs(UnmanagedType.IUnknown)]
  object pUnkOuter, uint dwSMEXFlags, [MarshalAs(UnmanagedType.IUnknown)]
  out object ppUnkInner);
static extern int CoGetTreatAsClass([In] ref Guid clsidOld,
  out Guid pclsidNew);
static extern int CoImpersonateClient();
static extern int CoInitialize(IntPtr pvReserved);
static extern int CoInitializeEx(IntPtr pvReserved, uint dwCoInit);
static extern int CoInitializeSecurity(IntPtr pVoid, int cAuthSvc,
  SOLE_AUTHENTICATION_SERVICE [] asAuthSvc, IntPtr pReserved1,
  uint dwAuthnLevel, uint dwImpLevel, IntPtr pAuthList, uint dwCapabilities,
  IntPtr pReserved3);
static extern bool CoIsHandlerConnected([MarshalAs(UnmanagedType.IUnknown)]
  object pUnk);
static extern bool CoIsOle1Class([In] ref Guid rclsid);
static extern IntPtr CoLoadLibrary([MarshalAs(UnmanagedType.LPWStr)]
  string lpszLibName, bool bAutoFree);
static extern int CoLockObjectExternal([MarshalAs(UnmanagedType.IUnknown)]
  object pUnk, bool fLock, bool fLastUnlockReleases);
static extern int CoMarshalHresult(UCOMIStream pStm, int hresult);
static extern int CoMarshalInterface(UCOMIStream pStm, [In] ref Guid riid,
  [MarshalAs(UnmanagedType.IUnknown)] object pUnk, uint dwDestContext,
  IntPtr pvDestContext, uint mshlflags);
static extern int CoMarshalInterThreadInterfaceInStream([In] ref Guid riid,
  [MarshalAs(UnmanagedType.IUnknown)] object pUnk, out UCOMIStream ppStm);
static extern int CoQueryAuthenticationServices(out uint pcAuthSvc,
  IntPtr asAuthSvc);
static extern int CoQueryClientBlanket(IntPtr pAuthnSvc, IntPtr pAuthzSvc,
  [MarshalAs(UnmanagedType.LPWStr)] out string pServerPrincName, IntPtr
  pAuthnLevel, IntPtr pImpLevel, IntPtr pPrivs, IntPtr pCapabilities);
```

```
static extern int CoQueryProxyBlanket([MarshalAs(UnmanagedType.IUnknown)]
  object pProxy, IntPtr pAuthnSvc, IntPtr pAuthzSvc,
  [MarshalAs(UnmanagedType.LPWStr)] out string pServerPrincName, IntPtr
  pAuthnLevel, IntPtr pImpLevel, IntPtr ppAuthInfo, IntPtr pCapabilities);
static extern int CoRegisterClassObject([In] ref Guid rclsid,
  [MarshalAs(UnmanagedType.IUnknown)] object pUnk, uint dwClsContext,
  uint flags, out uint lpdwRegister);
static extern int CoRegisterMallocSpy(IMallocSpy pMallocSpy);
static extern int CoRegisterMessageFilter(IMessageFilter lpMessageFilter,
  out IMessageFilter lplpMessageFilter);
static extern int CoRegisterPSClsid([In] ref Guid riid, [In] ref Guid rclsid);
static extern int CoRegisterSurrogate(ISurrogate pSurrogate);
static extern int CoReleaseMarshalData(IStream pStm);
static extern int CoReleaseServerProcess();
static extern int CoResumeClassObjects();
static extern int CoRevertToSelf();
static extern int CoRevokeClassObject(uint dwRegister);
static extern int CoRevokeMallocSpy();
static extern int CoSetCancelObject([MarshalAs(UnmanagedType.IUnknown)]
  object pUnk);
static extern int CoSetProxyBlanket([MarshalAs(UnmanagedType.IUnknown)]
  object pProxy, uint dwAuthnSvc, uint dwAuthzSvc,
  [MarshalAs(UnmanagedType.LPWStr)] string pServerPrincName, uint dwAuthnLevel,
  uint dwImpLevel, IntPtr pAuthInfo, uint dwCapabilities);
static extern int CoSuspendClassObjects();
static extern int CoSwitchCallContext([MarshalAs(UnmanagedType.IUnknown)]
  object pNewObject, [MarshalAs(UnmanagedType.IUnknown)] out object
  ppOldObject);
static extern IntPtr CoTaskMemAlloc(uint cb);
static extern void CoTaskMemFree(IntPtr pv);
static extern IntPtr CoTaskMemRealloc(IntPtr pv, uint cb);
static extern int CoTestCancel();
static extern int CoTreatAsClass([In] ref Guid clsidOld,
  [In] ref Guid clsidNew);
static extern void CoUninitialize();
static extern int CoUnmarshalHresult(UCOMIStream pStm, out int phresult);
static extern int CoUnmarshalInterfaceUCOMIStream pStm, [In] ref Guid riid,
  [MarshalAs(UnmanagedType.IUnknown)] out object ppv);
static extern int CoWaitForMultipleHandles(uint dwFlags, uint dwTimeout,
  uint cHandles, IntPtr [] pHandles, out uint lpdwindex);
static extern int CreateAntiMoniker(out UCOMIMoniker ppmk);
static extern int CreateBindCtx(uint reserved, out UCOMIBindCtx ppbc);
static extern int CreateClassMoniker([In] ref Guid rclsid,
  out UCOMIMoniker ppmk);
static extern int CreateDataAdviseHolder(out IDataAdviseHolder ppDAHolder);
```

```
static extern int CreateDataCache([MarshalAs(UnmanagedType.IUnknown)] object
    pUnkOuter, [In] ref Guid rclsid, [In] ref Guid riid,
    [MarshalAs(UnmanagedType.IUnknown)] out object ppvObj);
static extern int CreateErrorInfo(out ICreateErrorInfo pperrinfo);
static extern int CreateFileMoniker([MarshalAs(UnmanagedType.LPWStr)] string
    lpszPathName, out UCOMIMoniker ppmk);
static extern int CreateGenericComposite(UCOMIMoniker pmkFirst,
    UCOMIMoniker pmkRest, out UCOMIMoniker ppmkComposite);
static extern int CreateILockBytesOnHGlobal(IntPtr hGlobal, bool
    fDeleteOnRelease, out ILockBytes ppLkbyt);
static extern int CreateItemMoniker([MarshalAs(UnmanagedType.LPWStr)] string
    lpszDelim, [MarshalAs(UnmanagedType.LPWStr)] string lpszItem,
    out UCOMIMoniker ppmk);
static extern int CreateObjrefMoniker([MarshalAs(UnmanagedType.IUnknown)]
    object pUnk, out UCOMIMoniker ppMk);
static extern int CreateOleAdviseHolder(out IOleAdviseHolder ppOAHolder);
static extern int CreatePointerMoniker([MarshalAs(UnmanagedType.IUnknown)]
    punk, out UCOMIMoniker ppmk);
static extern int CreateStreamOnHGlobal(IntPtr hGlobal, bool fDeleteOnRelease,
    out UCOMIStream ppstm);
static extern int DoDragDrop(IDataObject pDataObject, IDropSource pDropSource,
    uint dwOKEffect, out uint pdwEffect);
static extern int FmtIdToPropStgName([In] ref FMTID pfmtid,
    [Out, MarshalAs(UnmanagedType.LPWStr)] StringBuilder oszName);
static extern int FreePropVariantArray(uint cVariants, [In] ref PROPVARIANT
    rgvars);
static extern int GetActiveObject(ref Guid rclsid, IntPtr pvReserved,
    [MarshalAs(UnmanagedType.IUnknown)] out Object ppunk);
static extern int GetClassFile([MarshalAs(UnmanagedType.LPWStr)] string
    szFileName, out Guid pclsid);
static extern int GetConvertStg(IStorage pStg);
static extern int GetErrorInfo(uint dwReserved, out IErrorInfo pperrinfo);
static extern int GetHGlobalFromILockBytes(ILockBytes pLkbyt,
    out IntPtr phglobal);
static extern int GetHGlobalFromStream(UCOMIStream pstm, out IntPtr phglobal);
static extern int GetRunningObjectTable(uint reserved,
    out UCOMIRunningObjectTable pprot);
static extern int IIDFromString([MarshalAs(UnmanagedType.LPWStr)] string lpsz,
    out Guid lpiid);
static extern bool IsAccelerator(IntPtr hAccel, int cAccelEntries,
    [In] ref MSG lpMsg, IntPtr lpwCmd);
static extern bool IsEqualGUID([In] ref Guid rguid1, [In] ref Guid rguid2);
static extern int MkParseDisplayName(UCOMIBindCtx pbc,
    [MarshalAs(UnmanagedType.LPWStr)] string szUserName, out uint pchEaten,
    out UCOMIMoniker ppmk);
```

```
static extern int MonikerCommonPrefixWith(UCOMIMoniker pmkThis,
  UCOMIMoniker pmkOther, out UCOMIMoniker ppmkCommon);
static extern int MonikerRelativePathTo(UCOMIMoniker pmkSrc,
  UCOMIMoniker pmkDest, out UCOMIMoniker ppmkRelPath, bool dwReserved);
static extern int OleCreate([In] ref Guid rclsid, [In] ref Guid riid,
  uint renderopt, [In] ref FORMATETC pFormatEtc, IOleClientSite pClientSite,
  IStorage pStg, [MarshalAs(UnmanagedType.IUnknown)] out object ppvObj);
static extern int OleCreateDefaultHandler([In] ref Guid clsid,
  [MarshalAs(UnmanagedType.IUnknown)] object pUnkOuter, [In] ref Guid riid,
  [MarshalAs(UnmanagedType.IUnknown)] out object ppvObj);
static extern int OleCreateEmbeddingHelper([In] ref Guid clsid,
  [MarshalAs(UnmanagedType.IUnknown)] object pUnkOuter, uint flags,
  IClassFactory pCF, [In] ref Guid riid, [MarshalAs(UnmanagedType.IUnknown)]
  out object ppvObj);
static extern int OleCreateEx([In] ref Guid rclsid, [In] ref Guid riid,
  uint dwFlags, uint renderopt, uint cFormats, uint rgAdvf, FORMATETC []
  rgFormatEtc, IAdviseSink pAdviseSink, [Out] uint [] rgdwConnection,
  IOleClientSite pClientSite, IStorage pStg,
  [MarshalAs(UnmanagedType.IUnknown)] out object ppvObj);
static extern int OleCreateFromData(IDataObject pSrcDataObj,
  [In] ref Guid riid, uint renderopt, [In] ref FORMATETC pFormatEtc,
  IOleClientSite pClientSite, IStorage pStg,
  [MarshalAs(UnmanagedType.IUnknown)] out object ppvObj);
static extern int OleCreateFromDataEx(IDataObject pSrcDataObj, [In] ref Guid
  riid, uint dwFlags, uint renderopt, uint cFormats, uint rgAdvf, FORMATETC []
  rgFormatEtc, IAdviseSink pAdviseSink, [Out] uint [] rgdwConnection,
  IOleClientSite pClientSite, IStorage pStg,
  [MarshalAs(UnmanagedType.IUnknown)] out object ppvObj);
static extern int OleCreateFromFile([In] ref Guid rclsid,
  [MarshalAs(UnmanagedType.LPWStr)] string lpszFileName, [In] ref Guid riid,
  uint renderopt, [In] ref FORMATETC pFormatEtc, IOleClientSite pClientSite,
  IStorage pStg, [MarshalAs(UnmanagedType.IUnknown)] out object ppvObj);
static extern int OleCreateFromFileEx([In] ref Guid rclsid,
  [MarshalAs(UnmanagedType.LPWStr)] string lpszFileName, [In] ref Guid riid,
  uint dwFlags, uint renderopt, uint cFormats, uint rgAdvf, FORMATETC []
  rgFormatEtc, IAdviseSink pAdviseSink, [Out] uint [] rgdwConnection,
  IOleClientSite pClientSite, IStorage pStg,
  [MarshalAs(UnmanagedType.IUnknown)] out object ppvObj);
static extern int OleCreateLink(UCOMIMoniker pmkLinkSrc, [In] ref Guid riid,
  uint renderopt, [In] ref FORMATETC pFormatEtc, IOleClientSite pClientSite,
  IStorage pStg, [MarshalAs(UnmanagedType.IUnknown)] out object ppvObj);
static extern int OleCreateLinkEx(UCOMIMoniker pmkLinkSrc, [In] ref Guid riid,
  uint dwFlags, uint renderopt, uint cFormats, uint rgAdvf, FORMATETC []
  rgFormatEtc, IAdviseSink pAdviseSink, [Out] uint [] rgdwConnection,
  IOleClientSite pClientSite, IStorage pStg,
  [MarshalAs(UnmanagedType.IUnknown)] out object ppvObj);
```

```
static extern int OleCreateLinkFromData(IDataObject pSrcDataObj, [In] ref Guid
    riid, uint renderopt, [In] ref FORMATETC pFormatEtc, IOleClientSite
    pClientSite, IStorage pStg, [MarshalAs(UnmanagedType.IUnknown)] out object
    ppvObj);
static extern int OleCreateLinkFromDataEx(IDataObject pSrcDataObj, [In] ref
    Guid riid, uint dwFlags, uint renderopt, uint cFormats, uint rgAdvf,
    FORMATETC [] rgFormatEtc, IAdviseSink pAdviseSink, [Out] uint []
    rgdwConnection, IOleClientSite pClientSite, IStorage pStg,
    [MarshalAs(UnmanagedType.IUnknown)] out object ppvObj);
static extern int OleCreateLinkToFile([MarshalAs(UnmanagedType.LPWStr)] string
    lpszFileName, [In] ref Guid riid, uint renderopt, [In] ref FORMATETC
    pFormatEtc, IOleClientSite pClientSite, IStorage pStg,
    [MarshalAs(UnmanagedType.IUnknown)] out object ppvObj);
static extern int OleCreateLinkToFileEx([MarshalAs(UnmanagedType.LPWStr)]
    string lpszFileName, [In] ref Guid riid, uint dwFlags, uint renderopt,
    uint cFormats, uint rgAdvf, FORMATETC [] rgFormatEtc, IAdviseSink
    pAdviseSink, [Out] uint [] rgdwConnection, IOleClientSite pClientSite,
    IStorage pStg, [MarshalAs(UnmanagedType.IUnknown)] out object ppvObj);
static extern IntPtr OleCreateMenuDescriptor(IntPtr hmenuCombined, int []
    lpMenuWidths);
static extern int OleCreateStaticFromData(IDataObject pSrcDataObj, [In] ref
    Guid riid, uint renderopt, [In] ref FORMATETC pFormatEtc, IOleClientSite
    pClientSite, IStorage pStg, [MarshalAs(UnmanagedType.IUnknown)]
    out object ppvObj);
static extern void OleDestroyMenuDescriptor(IntPtr holemenu);
static extern int OleDoAutoConvert(IStorage pStg, out Guid pClsidNew);
static extern int OleDraw([MarshalAs(UnmanagedType.IUnknown)] object pUnk,
    uint dwAspect, IntPtr hdcDraw, [In] ref RECT lprcBounds);
static extern IntPtr OleDuplicateData(IntPtr hSrc, CLIPFORMAT cfFormat,
    uint uiFlags);
static extern int OleFlushClipboard();
static extern int OleGetAutoConvert([In] ref Guid clsidOld,
    out Guid pClsidNew);
static extern int OleGetClipboard(out IDataObject ppDataObj);
static extern IntPtr OleGetIconOfClass([In] ref Guid rclsid,
    [MarshalAs(UnmanagedType.LPWStr)] string lpszLabel, bool fUseTypeAsLabel);
static extern IntPtr OleGetIconOfFile([MarshalAs(UnmanagedType.LPWStr)]
    string lpszPath, bool fUseFileAsLabel);
static extern int OleInitialize(IntPtr pvReserved);
static extern int OleIsCurrentClipboard(IDataObject pDataObject);
static extern bool OleIsRunning(IOleObject pObject);
static extern int OleLoad(IStorage pStg, [In] ref Guid riid, IOleClientSite
    pClientSite, [MarshalAs(UnmanagedType.IUnknown)] out object ppvObj);
static extern int OleLoadFromStream(UCOMIStream pStm, [In] ref Guid riid,
    [MarshalAs(UnmanagedType.IUnknown)] out object ppvObj);
```

```csharp
static extern int OleLockRunning([MarshalAs(UnmanagedType.IUnknown)] object
  pUnknown, bool fLock, bool fLastUnlockCloses);
static extern IntPtr OleMetafilePictFromIconAndLabel(IntPtr hIcon,
  [MarshalAs(UnmanagedType.LPWStr)] string lpszLabel,
  [MarshalAs(UnmanagedType.LPWStr)] string lpszSourceFile, uint iIconIndex);
static extern int OleNoteObjectVisible([MarshalAs(UnmanagedType.IUnknown)]
  object pUnknown, bool fVisible);
static extern int OleQueryCreateFromData(IDataObject pSrcDataObject);
static extern int OleQueryLinkFromData(IDataObject pSrcDataObject);
static extern int OleRegEnumFormatEtc([In] ref Guid clsid, uint dwDirection,
  out IEnumFORMATETC ppenumFormatetc);
static extern int OleRegEnumVerbs([In] ref Guid clsid, out IEnumOLEVERB
  ppenumOleVerb);
static extern int OleRegGetMiscStatus([In] ref Guid clsid, uint dwAspect,
  out uint pdwStatus);
static extern int OleRegGetUserType([In] ref Guid clsid, uint dwFormOfType,
  [Out, MarshalAs(UnmanagedType.LPWStr)] StringBuilder pszUserType);
static extern int OleRun([MarshalAs(UnmanagedType.IUnknown)] object pUnknown);
static extern int OleSave(IPersistStorage pPS, IStorage pStg,
  bool fSameAsLoad);
static extern int OleSaveToStream(IPersistStream pPStm, UCOMIStream pStm);
static extern int OleSetAutoConvert([In] ref Guid clsidOld,
  [In] ref Guid clsidNew);
static extern int OleSetClipboard(IDataObject pDataObj);
static extern int OleSetContainedObject([MarshalAs(UnmanagedType.IUnknown)]
  object pUnk, bool fContained);
static extern int OleSetMenuDescriptor(IntPtr holemenu, IntPtr hwndFrame,
  IntPtr hwndActiveObject, IOleInPlaceFrame lpFrame,
  IOleInPlaceActivateObject lpActiveObj);
static extern int OleTranslateAccelerator(IOleInPlaceFrame lpFrame,
  [In] ref OLEINPLACEFRAMEINFO lpFrameInfo, [In] ref MSG lpmsg);
static extern void OleUninitialize();
static extern int ProgIDFromCLSID([In] ref Guid clsid,
  [MarshalAs(UnmanagedType.LPWStr)] out string lplpszProgID);
static extern int PropStgNameToFmtId([MarshalAs(UnmanagedType.LPWStr)]
  string oszName, out FMTID pfmtid);
static extern int PropVariantClear(ref PROPVARIANT pvar);
static extern int PropVariantCopy(ref PROPVARIANT pvarDest, [In] ref
  PROPVARIANT pvarSrc);
static extern int ReadClassStg(IStorage pStg, out Guid pclsid);
static extern int ReadClassStm(UCOMIStream pStm, out Guid pclsid);
static extern int ReadFmtUserTypeStg(IStorage pStg, IntPtr pcf,
  [MarshalAs(UnmanagedType.LPWStr)] out string lplpszUserType);
static extern int RegisterDragDrop(IntPtr hwnd, IDropTarget pDropTarget);
static extern void ReleaseStgMedium([In] ref STGMEDIUM pmedium);
static extern int RevokeDragDrop(IntPtr hwnd);
```

```
static extern int SetConvertStg(IStorage pStg, bool fConvert);
static extern int SetErrorInfo(uint dwReserved, IErrorInfo perrinfo);
static extern int StgCreateDocfile([MarshalAs(UnmanagedType.LPWStr)]
  string pwcsName, uint grfMode, uint reserved, out IStorage ppstgOpen);
static extern int StgCreateDocfileOnILockBytes(ILockBytes plkbyt, uint grfMode,
  uint reserved, out IStorage ppstgOpen);
static extern int StgCreatePropSetStg(IStorage pStorage, uint reserved,
  out IPropertySetStorage ppPropSetStg);
static extern int StgCreatePropStg([MarshalAs(UnmanagedType.IUnknown)] object
  pUnk, [In] ref FMTID fmtid, [In] ref Guid pclsid, uint grfFlags, uint
  dwReserved, out IPropertyStorage ppPropStg);
static extern int StgCreateStorageEx([MarshalAs(UnmanagedType.LPWStr)] string
  pwcsName, uint grfMode, uint stgfmt, uint grfAttrs, [In] ref STGOPTIONS
  pStgOptions, IntPtr reserved2, [In] ref Guid riid,
  [MarshalAs(UnmanagedType.IUnknown)] out object ppObjectOpen);
static extern int StgGetIFillLockBytesOnFile([MarshalAs(UnmanagedType.LPWStr)]
  string pwcsName, out IFillLockBytes ppflb);
static extern int StgGetIFillLockBytesOnILockBytes(ILockBytes pilb,
  out IFillLockBytes ppflb);
static extern int StgIsStorageFile([MarshalAs(UnmanagedType.LPWStr)]
  string pwcsName);
static extern int StgIsStorageILockBytes(ILockBytes plkbyt);
static extern int StgOpenAsyncDocfileOnIFillLockBytes(IFillLockBytes ppflb,
  uint grfmode, uint asyncFlags, out IStorage ppstgOpen);
static extern int StgOpenPropStg([MarshalAs(UnmanagedType.IUnknown)] object
  pUnk, [In] ref FMTID fmtid, uint grfFlags, uint dwReserved,
  out IPropertyStorage ppPropStg);
static extern int StgOpenStorage([MarshalAs(UnmanagedType.LPWStr)] string
  pwcsName, IStorage pstgPriority, uint grfMode, IntPtr snbExclude, uint
  reserved, out IStorage ppstgOpen);
static extern int StgOpenStorageEx([MarshalAs(UnmanagedType.LPWStr)] string
  pwcsName, uint grfMode, uint stgfmt, uint grfAttrs, ref STGOPTIONS
  pStgOptions, IntPtr reserved2, [In] ref Guid riid,
  [MarshalAs(UnmanagedType.IUnknown)] out object ppObjectOpen);static extern
int StgOpenStorageOnILockBytes(ILockBytes plkbyt,
  IStorage pStgPriority, uint grfMode, IntPtr snbEnclude, uint reserved,
  out IStorage ppstgOpen);
static extern int StgSetTimes([MarshalAs(UnmanagedType.LPWStr)] string
  lpszName, [In] ref FILETIME pctime, [In] ref FILETIME patime,
  [In] ref FILETIME pmtime);
static extern int StringFromCLSID([In] ref Guid rclsid,
  [MarshalAs(UnmanagedType.LPWStr)] out string ppsz);
static extern int StringFromGUID2([In] ref Guid rclsid,
  [Out, MarshalAs(UnmanagedType.LPWStr)] StringBuilder lpsz, int cchMax);
static extern int StringFromIID([In] ref Guid rclsid,
  [MarshalAs(UnmanagedType.LPWStr)] out string ppsz);
```

```
static extern int WriteClassStg(IStorage pStg, [In] ref Guid rclsid);
static extern int WriteClassStm(UCOMIStream pStm, [In] ref Guid rclsid);
static extern int WriteFmtUserTypeStg(IStorage pStg, CLIPFORMAT cf,
  IntPtr lpszUserType);
```

SHELL32.DLL

All of these functions should be preceded with the following line when used in source code:

```
[DllImport("shell32.dll")]
```

Here are signatures from SHELL32.DLL:

```
static extern IntPtr CommandLineToArgvW(
  [MarshalAs(UnmanagedType.LPWStr)] string lpCmdLine, out int pNumArgs);
static extern int DllGetVersion(ref DLLVERSIONINFO pdvi);
static extern uint DoEnvironmentSubst(StringBuilder pszString, uint cbSize);
static extern void DragAcceptFiles(IntPtr hwnd, bool fAccept);
static extern void DragFinish(IntPtr hDrop);
static extern uint DragQueryFile(IntPtr hDrop, uint iFile,
  [Out] StringBuilder lpszFile, uint cch);
static extern bool DragQueryPoint(IntPtr hDrop, out POINT lppt);
static extern IntPtr DuplicateIcon(IntPtr hInst, IntPtr hIcon);
static extern IntPtr ExtractAssociatedIcon(IntPtr hInst, string lpIconPath,
  out ushort lpiIcon);
static extern IntPtr ExtractIcon(IntPtr hInst, string lpszExeFileName,
  uint nIconIndex);
static extern uint ExtractIconEx(string szFileName, int nIconIndex,
  [Out] IntPtr [] phiconLarge, [Out] IntPtr [] phiconSmall, uint nIcons);
static extern IntPtr FindExecutable(string lpFile, string lpDirectory,
  [Out] StringBuilder lpResult);
static extern void SHAddToRecentDocs(uint uFlags, IntPtr pv);
static extern IntPtr SHAppBarMessage(uint dwMessage,
  [In] ref APPBARDATA pData);
static extern int SHBindToParent([In] ref ITEMIDLIST pidl, [In] ref Guid riid,
  out IntPtr ppv, IntPtr ppidlLast);
static extern IntPtr SHBrowseForFolder(ref BROWSEINFO lpbi);
static extern void SHChangeNotify(int wEventId, uint uFlags, IntPtr dwItem1,
  IntPtr dwItem2);
static extern int SHCreateDirectoryEx(IntPtr hwnd, string pszPath, IntPtr psa);
static extern bool SHCreateProcessAsUserW([In] ref SHCREATEPROCESSINFOW pscpi);
static extern bool Shell_NotifyIcon(uint dwMessage,
  [In] ref NOTIFYICONDATA pnid);
static extern int ShellAbout(IntPtr hWnd, string szApp, string szOtherStuff,
  IntPtr hIcon);
```

```
static extern IntPtr ShellExecute(IntPtr hwnd, string lpVerb, string lpFile,
  string lpParameters, string lpDirectory, int nShowCmd);
static extern bool ShellExecuteEx(ref SHELLEXECUTEINFO lpExecInfo);
static extern int SHEmptyRecycleBin(IntPtr hWnd, string pszRootPath,
  uint dwFlags);
static extern int SHFileOperation([In] ref SHFILEOPSTRUCT lpFileOp);
static extern uint SHFormatDrive(IntPtr hwnd, uint drive, uint fmtID,
  uint options);
static extern void SHFreeNameMappings(IntPtr hNameMappings);
static extern int SHGetDataFromIDList(IShellFolder psf, ref ITEMIDLIST pidl,
  int nFormat, IntPtr pv, int cb);
static extern int SHGetDesktopFolder(ref IShellFolder ppshf);
static extern bool SHGetDiskFreeSpace(string pszVolume, out ulong
  pqwFreeCaller, out ulong pqwTot, out ulong pqwFree);
static extern IntPtr SHGetFileInfo(string pszPath, uint dwFileAttributes,
  out SHFILEINFO psfi, uint cbFileInfo, uint uFlags);
static extern int SHGetFolderLocation(IntPtr hwndOwner, int nFolder,
  IntPtr hToken, uint dwReserved, IntPtr ppidl);
static extern int SHGetFolderPath(IntPtr hwndOwner, int nFolder, IntPtr hToken,
  uint dwFlags, [Out] StringBuilder pszPath);
static extern int SHGetIconOverlayIndex(string pszIconPath, int iIconIndex);
static extern int SHGetInstanceExplorer([MarshalAs(UnmanagedType.IUnknown)]
  out object ppunk);
static extern int SHGetMalloc(out IMalloc ppMalloc);
static extern bool SHGetNewLinkInfo(string pszLinkTo, string pszDir,
  string pszName, out bool pfMustCopy, uint uFlags);
static extern bool SHGetPathFromIDList(ref ITEMIDLIST pidl,
  [Out] StringBuilder pszPath);
static extern void SHGetSettings(out SHELLFLAGSTATE lpsfs, uint dwMask);
static extern int SHGetSpecialFolderLocation(IntPtr hwndOwner, int nFolder,
  IntPtr ppidl);
static extern bool SHGetSpecialFolderPath(IntPtr hwndOwner,
  [Out] StringBuilder lpszPath, int nFolder, bool fCreate);
static extern int SHInvokePrinterCommand(IntPtr hwnd, uint uAction,
  string lpBuf1, string lpBuf2, bool fModal);
static extern int SHIsFileAvailableOffline([MarshalAs(UnmanagedType.LPWStr)]
  string pszPath, out uint pdwStatus);
static extern int SHLoadInProc([In] ref Guid rclsid);
static extern int SHLoadNonloadedIconOverlayIdentifiers();
static extern int SHPathPrepareForWrite(IntPtr hwnd,
  [MarshalAs(UnmanagedType.IUnknown)] object punkEnableModless,
  string pszPath, uint dwFlags);
static extern int SHQueryRecycleBin(string pszRootPath, ref SHQUERYRBINFO
  pSHQueryRBInfo);
```

USER32.DLL

All of these functions should be preceded with the following line when used in source code, unless specified otherwise:

```
[DllImport("user32.dll")]
```

Here are signatures from USER32.DLL:

```
static extern int ActivateKeyboardLayout(IntPtr nkl, uint Flags);
static extern bool AdjustWindowRect(ref RECT lpRect, uint dwStyle, bool bMenu);
static extern bool AdjustWindowRectEx(ref RECT lpRect, uint dwStyle,
  bool bMenu, uint dwExStyle);
static extern bool AllowSetForegroundWindow(uint dwProcessId);
static extern bool AnimateWindow(IntPtr hwnd, uint dwTime, uint dwFlags);
static extern bool AnyPopup();
static extern bool AppendMenu(IntPtr hMenu, uint uFlags, UIntPtr uIDNewItem,
  IntPtr lpNewItem);
static extern uint ArrangeIconicWindows(IntPtr hWnd);
static extern bool AttachThreadInput(uint idAttach, uint idAttachTo,
  bool fAttach);
static extern IntPtr BeginDeferWindowPos(int nNumWindows);
static extern IntPtr BeginPaint(IntPtr hwnd, out PAINTSTRUCT lpPaint);
static extern bool BlockInput(bool fBlockIt);
static extern bool BringWindowToTop(IntPtr hWnd);
static extern int BroadcastSystemMessage(uint dwFlags, IntPtr lpdwRecipients,
  uint uiMessage, UIntPtr wParam, IntPtr lParam);
static extern bool CallMsgFilter([In] ref MSG lpMsg, int nCode);
static extern IntPtr CallNextHookEx(IntPtr hhk, int nCode, UIntPtr wParam,
  IntPtr lParam);
static extern IntPtr CallWindowProc(WndProcDelegate lpPrevWndFunc, IntPtr hWnd,
  uint Msg, UIntPtr wParam, IntPtr lParam);
static extern ushort CascadeWindows(IntPtr hwndParent, uint wHow,
  IntPtr lpRect, uint cKids, IntPtr [] lpKids);
static extern bool ChangeClipboardChain(IntPtr hWndRemove, IntPtr hWndNewNext);
static extern int ChangeDisplaySettings(IntPtr lpDevMode, uint dwFlags);
static extern int ChangeDisplaySettingsEx(string lpszDeviceName,
  IntPtr lpDevMode, IntPtr hwnd, uint dwflags, IntPtr lParam);
static extern IntPtr CharLower(StringBuilder lpsz);
static extern uint CharLowerBuff(StringBuilder lpsz, uint cchLength);
static extern IntPtr CharNext(IntPtr lpsz);
static extern IntPtr CharNextEx(ushort CodePage, IntPtr lpCurrentChar,
  uint dwFlags);
static extern IntPtr CharPrev(IntPtr lpszStart, IntPtr lpszCurrent);
static extern IntPtr CharPrevEx(ushort CodePage, IntPtr lpStart,
  IntPtr lpCurrentChar, uint dwFlags);
static extern bool CharToOem(string lpszSrc, [Out] StringBuilder lpszDst);
```

```
static extern bool CharToOemBuff(string lpszSrc, string lpszDst,
    uint cchDstLength);
static extern IntPtr CharUpper(StringBuilder lpsz);
static extern uint CharUpperBuff(string lpsz, uint cchLength);
static extern bool CheckDlgButton(IntPtr hDlg, int nIDButton, uint uCheck);
static extern uint CheckMenuItem(IntPtr hmenu, uint uIDCheckItem, uint uCheck);
static extern bool CheckMenuRadioItem(IntPtr hmenu, uint idFirst, uint idLast,
    uint idCheck, uint uFlags);
static extern bool CheckRadioButton(IntPtr hDlg, int nIDFirstButton,
    int nIDLastButton, int nIDCheckButton);
static extern IntPtr ChildWindowFromPoint(IntPtr hWndParent, POINT Point);
static extern IntPtr ChildWindowFromPointEx(IntPtr hWndParent, POINT pt,
    uint uFlags);
static extern bool ClientToScreen(IntPtr hWnd, ref POINT lpPoint);
static extern bool ClipCursor(IntPtr lpRect);
static extern bool CloseClipboard();
static extern bool CloseDesktop(IntPtr hDesktop);
static extern bool CloseWindow(IntPtr hWnd);
static extern bool CloseWindowStation(IntPtr hWinSta);
static extern int CopyAcceleratorTable(IntPtr hAccelSrc, [Out] ACCEL []
    lpAccelDst, int cAccelEntries);
static extern IntPtr CopyIcon(IntPtr hIcon);
static extern IntPtr CopyImage(IntPtr hImage, uint uType, int cxDesired,
    int cyDesired, uint fuFlags);
static extern bool CopyRect(out RECT lprcDst, [In] ref RECT lprcSrc);
static extern int CountClipboardFormats();
static extern IntPtr CreateAcceleratorTable(ACCEL [] lpaccl, int cEntries);
static extern bool CreateCaret(IntPtr hWnd, IntPtr hBitmap, int nWidth,
    int nHeight);
static extern IntPtr CreateCursor(IntPtr hInst, int xHotSpot, int yHotSpot,
    int nWidth, int nHeight, byte [] pvANDPlane, byte [] pvXORPlane);
static extern IntPtr CreateDesktop(string lpszDesktop, string lpszDevice,
    IntPtr pDevmode, uint dwFlags, uint dwDesiredAccess, IntPtr lpsa);
static extern IntPtr CreateDialogIndirectParam(IntPtr hInstance,
    IntPtr lpTemplate, IntPtr hWndParent, DialogDelegate lpDialogFunc,
    IntPtr lParamInit);
static extern IntPtr CreateDialogParam(IntPtr hInstance, string lpTemplateName,
    IntPtr hwndParent, DialogDelegate lpDialogFunc, IntPtr dwInitParam);
static extern IntPtr CreateIcon(IntPtr hInstance, int nWidth, int nHeight,
    byte cPlanes, byte cBitsPixel, byte [] lpbANDbits, byte [] lpbXORbits);
static extern IntPtr CreateIconFromResource(byte [] presbits, uint dwResSize,
    bool fIcon, uint dwVer);
static extern IntPtr CreateIconFromResourceEx(byte [] pbIconBits, uint
    cbIconBits, bool fIcon, uint dwVersion, int cxDesired, int cyDesired,
    uint uFlags);
static extern IntPtr CreateIconIndirect([In] ref ICONINFO piconinfo);
```

```
static extern IntPtr CreateMDIWindow(string lpClassName, string lpWindowName,
  uint dwStyle, int X, int Y, int nWidth, int nHeight, IntPtr hwndParent,
  IntPtr hInstance, IntPtr lParam);
static extern IntPtr CreateMenu();
static extern IntPtr CreatePopupMenu();
static extern IntPtr CreateWindowEx(uint dwExStyle, string lpClassName,
  string lpWindowName, uint dwStyle, int x, int y, int nWidth, int nHeight,
  IntPtr hWndParent, IntPtr hMenu, IntPtr hInstance, IntPtr lpParam);
static extern IntPtr CreateWindowStation(string pwinsta, uint dwReserved,
  uint dwDesiredAccess, IntPtr lpsa);
static extern bool DdeAbandonTransaction(uint idInst, IntPtr hConv,
  uint idTransaction);
static extern IntPtr DdeAccessData(IntPtr hData, IntPtr pcbDataSize);
static extern IntPtr DdeAddData(IntPtr hData, byte [] pSrc, uint cb,
  uint cbOff);
static extern IntPtr DdeClientTransaction(byte [] pData, uint cbData,
  IntPtr hConv, IntPtr hszItem, uint wFmt, uint wType, uint dwTimeout,
  IntPtr pdwResult);
static extern int DdeCmpStringHandles(IntPtr hsz1, IntPtr hsz2);
static extern IntPtr DdeConnect(uint idInst, IntPtr hszService,
  IntPtr hszTopic, IntPtr pCC);
static extern IntPtr DdeConnectList(uint idInst, IntPtr hszService,
  IntPtr hszTopic, IntPtr hConvList, IntPtr pCC);
static extern IntPtr DdeCreateDataHandle(uint idInst, byte [] pSrc, uint cb,
  uint cbOff, IntPtr hszItem, uint wFmt, uint afCmd);
static extern IntPtr DdeCreateStringHandle(uint idInst, string psz,
  int iCodePage);
static extern bool DdeDisconnect(IntPtr hConv);
static extern bool DdeDisconnectList(IntPtr hConvList);
static extern bool DdeEnableCallback(uint idInst, IntPtr hConv, uint wCmd);
static extern bool DdeFreeDataHandle(IntPtr hData);
static extern bool DdeFreeStringHandle(uint idInst, IntPtr hsz);
static extern uint DdeGetData(IntPtr hData, [Out] byte [] pDst, uint cbMax,
  uint cbOff);
static extern uint DdeGetLastError(uint idInst);
static extern bool DdeImpersonateClient(IntPtr hConv);
static extern uint DdeInitialize(ref uint pidInst, DdeDelegate pfnCallback,
  uint afCmd, uint ulRes);
static extern bool DdeKeepStringHandle(uint idInst, IntPtr hsz);
static extern IntPtr DdeNameService(uint idInst, IntPtr hsz1, IntPtr hsz2,
  uint afCmd);
static extern bool DdePostAdvise(uint idInst, IntPtr hszTopic, IntPtr hszItem);
static extern uint DdeQueryConvInfo(IntPtr hConv, uint idTransaction,
  ref CONVINFO pConvInfo);
static extern IntPtr DdeQueryNextServer(IntPtr hConvList, IntPtr hConvPrev);
```

```
static extern uint DdeQueryString(uint idInst, IntPtr hsz, StringBuilder psz,
  uint cchMax, int iCodePage);
static extern IntPtr DdeReconnect(IntPtr hConv);
static extern bool DdeSetQualityOfService(IntPtr hwndClient, [In] ref
  SECURITY_QUALITY_OF_SERVICE pqosNew, IntPtr pqosPrev);
static extern bool DdeSetUserHandle(IntPtr hConv, uint id, uint hUser);
static extern bool DdeUnaccessData(IntPtr hData);
static extern bool DdeUninitialize(uint idInst);
static extern IntPtr DefDlgProc(IntPtr hDlg, uint Msg, UIntPtr wParam,
  IntPtr lParam);
static extern IntPtr DeferWindowPos(IntPtr hWinPosInfo, IntPtr hWnd,
  IntPtr hWndInsertAfter, int x, int y, int cx, int cy, uint uFlags);
static extern IntPtr DefFrameProc(IntPtr hWnd, IntPtr hWndMDIClient,
  uint uMsg, UIntPtr wParam, IntPtr lParam);
static extern IntPtr DefMDIChildProc(IntPtr hWnd, uint uMsg, UIntPtr wParam,
  IntPtr lParam);
static extern IntPtr DefWindowProc(IntPtr hWnd, uint uMsg, UIntPtr wParam,
  IntPtr lParam);
static extern bool DeleteMenu(IntPtr hMenu, uint uPosition, uint uFlags);
static extern bool DestroyAcceleratorTable(IntPtr hAccel);
static extern bool DestroyCaret();
static extern bool DestroyCursor(IntPtr hCursor);
static extern bool DestroyIcon(IntPtr hIcon);
static extern bool DestroyMenu(IntPtr hMenu);
static extern bool DestroyWindow(IntPtr hWnd);
static extern IntPtr DialogBoxIndirectParam(IntPtr hInstance, IntPtr
  lpTemplate, IntPtr hWndParent, DialogDelegate lpDialogFunc,
  IntPtr dwInitParam);
static extern IntPtr DialogBoxParam(IntPtr hInstance, string lpTemplateName,
  IntPtr hWndParent, DialogDelegate lpDialogFunc, IntPtr dwInitParam);
static extern IntPtr DispatchMessage([In] ref MSG lpmsg);
static extern int DlgDirList(IntPtr hDlg, StringBuilder lpPathSpec,
  int nIDListBox, int nIDStaticPath, uint uFileType);
static extern int DlgDirListComboBox(IntPtr hDlg, StringBuilder lpPathSpec,
  int nIDComboBox, int nIDStaticPath, uint uFiletype);
static extern bool DlgDirSelectComboBoxEx(IntPtr hDlg, [Out] StringBuilder
  lpString, int nCount, int nIDComboBox);
static extern bool DlgDirSelectEx(IntPtr hDlg, [Out] StringBuilder lpString,
  int nCount, int nIDListBox);
static extern bool DragDetect(IntPtr hwnd, POINT pt);
static extern bool DrawAnimatedRects(IntPtr hwnd, int idAni,
  [In] ref RECT lprcFrom, [In] ref RECT lprcTo);
static extern bool DrawCaption(IntPtr hwnd, IntPtr hdc, [In] ref RECT lprc,
  uint uFlags);
static extern bool DrawEdge(IntPtr hdc, ref RECT qrc, uint edge,
  uint grfFlags);
```

```
static extern bool DrawFocusRect(IntPtr hDC, [In] ref RECT lprc);
static extern bool DrawFrameControl(IntPtr hdc, [In] ref RECT lprc,
  uint uType, uint uState);
static extern bool DrawIcon(IntPtr hDC, int X, int Y, IntPtr hIcon);
static extern bool DrawIconEx(IntPtr hdc, int xLeft, int yTop, IntPtr hIcon,
  int cxWidth, int cyHeight, uint istepIfAniCur, IntPtr hbrFlickerFreeDraw,
  uint diFlags);
static extern bool DrawMenuBar(IntPtr hWnd);
static extern bool DrawState(IntPtr hdc, IntPtr hbr, DrawStateDelegate
  lpOutputFunc, IntPtr lData, UIntPtr wData, int x, int y, int cx, int cy,
  uint fuFlags);
static extern int DrawText(IntPtr hDC, string lpString, int nCount,
  ref RECT lpRect, uint uFormat);
static extern int DrawTextEx(IntPtr hdc, StringBuilder lpchText, int cchText,
  ref RECT lprc, uint dwDTFormat, IntPtr lpDTParams);
static extern bool EmptyClipboard();
static extern bool EnableMenuItem(IntPtr hMenu, uint uIDEnableItem,
  uint uEnable);
static extern bool EnableScrollBar(IntPtr hWnd, uint wSBflags, uint wArrows);
static extern bool EnableWindow(IntPtr hWnd, bool bEnable);
static extern bool EndDeferWindowPos(IntPtr hWinPosInfo);
static extern bool EndDialog(IntPtr hDlg, IntPtr nResult);
static extern bool EndMenu();
static extern bool EndPaint(IntPtr hWnd, [In] ref PAINTSTRUCT lpPaint);
static extern bool EnumChildWindows(IntPtr hwndParent, EnumChildDelegate
  lpEnumFunc, IntPtr lParam);
static extern uint EnumClipboardFormats(uint format);
static extern bool EnumDesktops(IntPtr hwinsta, EnumDesktopsDelegate
  lpEnumFunc, IntPtr lParam);
static extern bool EnumDesktopWindows(IntPtr hDesktop,
  EnumDesktopWindowsDelegate lpfn, IntPtr lParam);
static extern bool EnumDisplayDevices(string lpDevice, uint iDevNum,
  out DISPLAY_DEVICE lpDisplayDevice, uint dwFlags);
static extern bool EnumDisplayMonitors(IntPtr hdc, IntPtr lprcClip,
  EnumMonitorsDelegate lpfnEnum, IntPtr dwData);
static extern bool EnumDisplaySettings(string lpszDeviceName, uint iModeNum,
  out DEVMODE lpDevMode);
static extern bool EnumDisplaySettingsEx(string lpszDeviceName, uint iModeNum,
  out DEVMODE lpDevMode, uint dwFlags);
static extern int EnumProps(IntPtr hWnd, EnumPropsDelegate lpEnumFunc);
static extern int EnumPropsEx(IntPtr hWnd, EnumPropsExDelegate lpEnumFunc,
  IntPtr lParam);
static extern bool EnumThreadWindows(uint dwThreadId, EnumThreadDelegate lpfn,
  IntPtr lParam);
static extern bool EnumWindows(EnumWindowsDelegate lpEnumFunc, IntPtr lParam);
```

```
static extern bool EnumWindowStations(EnumWindowStationsDelegate lpEnumFunc,
   IntPtr lParam);
static extern bool EqualRect([In] ref RECT lprc1, [In] ref RECT lprc2);
static extern int ExcludeUpdateRgn(IntPtr hDC, IntPtr hWnd);
static extern bool ExitWindowsEx(uint uFlags, uint dwReason);
static extern int FillRect(IntPtr hDC, [In] ref RECT lprc, IntPtr hbr);
static extern IntPtr FindWindow(string lpClassName, string lpWindowName);
static extern IntPtr FindWindowEx(IntPtr hwndParent, IntPtr hwndChildAfter,
   string lpszClass, string lpszWindow);
static extern bool FlashWindow(IntPtr hwnd, bool bInvert);
static extern void FlashWindowEx([In] ref FLASHWINFO pwfi);
static extern int FrameRect(IntPtr hdc, [In] ref RECT lprc, IntPtr hbr);
static extern bool FreeDDElParam(uint msg, IntPtr lParam);
static extern IntPtr GetActiveWindow();
static extern bool GetAltTabInfo(IntPtr hwnd, int iItem, out ALTTABINFO pati,
   [Out] StringBuilder pszItemText, uint cchItemText);
static extern IntPtr GetAncestor(IntPtr hwnd, uint gaFlags);
static extern short GetAsyncKeyState(int vKey);
static extern IntPtr GetCapture();
static extern uint GetCaretBlinkTime();
static extern bool GetCaretPos(out POINT lpPoint);
static extern bool GetClassInfo(IntPtr hInstance, string lpClassName,
   out WNDCLASS lpWndClass);
static extern bool GetClassInfoEx(IntPtr hinst, string lpszClass,
   out WNDCLASSEX lpwcx);
static extern uint GetClassLong(IntPtr hWnd, int nIndex);
static extern int GetClassName(IntPtr hWnd, [Out] StringBuilder lpClassName,
   int nMaxCount);
static extern ushort GetClassWord(IntPtr hWnd, int nIndex);
static extern bool GetClientRect(IntPtr hWnd, out RECT lpRect);
static extern IntPtr GetClipboardData(uint uFormat);
static extern int GetClipboardFormatName(uint format, [Out] StringBuilder
   lpszFormatName, int cchMaxCount);
static extern IntPtr GetClipboardOwner();
static extern uint GetClipboardSequenceNumber();
static extern IntPtr GetClipboardViewer();
static extern bool GetClipCursor(out RECT lpRect);
static extern bool GetComboBoxInfo(ref COMBOBOXINFO pcbi);
static extern IntPtr GetCursor();
static extern bool GetCursorInfo(out CURSORINFO pci);
static extern bool GetCursorPos(out POINT lpPoint);
static extern IntPtr GetDC(IntPtr hWnd);
static extern IntPtr GetDCEx(IntPtr hWnd, IntPtr hrgnClip, uint flags);
static extern IntPtr GetDesktopWindow();
static extern int GetDialogBaseUnits();
static extern int GetDlgCtrlID(IntPtr hwndCtl);
```

```
static extern IntPtr GetDlgItem(IntPtr hDlg, int nIDDlgItem);
static extern uint GetDlgItemInt(IntPtr hDlg, int nIDDlgItem, IntPtr
  lpTranslated, bool bSigned);
static extern uint GetDlgItemText(IntPtr hDlg, int nIDDlgItem,
  [Out] StringBuilder lpString, int nMaxCount);
static extern uint GetDoubleClickTime();
static extern IntPtr GetFocus();
static extern IntPtr GetForegroundWindow();
static extern uint GetGuiResources(IntPtr hProcess, uint uiFlags);
static extern bool GetGUIThreadInfo(uint idThread, out GUITHREADINFO lpgui);
static extern bool GetIconInfo(IntPtr hIcon, out ICONINFO piconinfo);
static extern bool GetInputState();
static extern uint GetKBCodePage();
static extern IntPtr GetKeyboardLayout(uint idThread);
static extern uint GetKeyboardLayoutList(int nBuff, [Out] IntPtr [] lpList);
static extern bool GetKeyboardLayoutName([Out] StringBuilder pwszKLID);
static extern bool GetKeyboardState(byte [] lpKeyState);
static extern int GetKeyboardType(int nTypeFlag);
static extern int GetKeyNameText(int lParam, [Out] StringBuilder lpString,
  int nSize);
static extern short GetKeyState(int nVirtKey);
static extern IntPtr GetLastActivePopup(IntPtr hWnd);
static extern bool GetLastInputInfo(out LASTINPUTINFO plii);
static extern int GetListBoxInfo(IntPtr hwnd);
static extern IntPtr GetMenu(IntPtr hWnd);
static extern bool GetMenuBarInfo(IntPtr hwnd, int idObject, int idItem,
  out MENUBARINFO pmbi);
static extern int GetMenuCheckMarkDimensions();
static extern uint GetMenuContextHelpId(IntPtr hmenu);
static extern uint GetMenuDefaultItem(IntPtr hMenu, uint fByPos,
  uint gmdiFlags);
static extern bool GetMenuInfo(IntPtr hmenu, out MENUINFO lpcmi);
static extern int GetMenuItemCount(IntPtr hMenu);
static extern uint GetMenuItemID(IntPtr hMenu, int nPos);
static extern bool GetMenuItemInfo(IntPtr hMenu, uint uItem, bool fByPosition,
  ref MENUITEMINFO lpmii);
static extern bool GetMenuItemRect(IntPtr hWnd, IntPtr hMenu, uint uItem,
  out RECT lprcItem);
static extern uint GetMenuState(IntPtr hMenu, uint uId, uint uFlags);
static extern int GetMenuString(IntPtr hMenu, uint uIDItem,
  [Out] StringBuilder lpString, int nMaxCount, uint uFlag);
static extern bool GetMessage(out MSG lpMsg, IntPtr hWnd, uint wMsgFilterMin,
  uint wMsgFilterMax);
static extern IntPtr GetMessageExtraInfo();
static extern uint GetMessagePos();
static extern int GetMessageTime();
```

```
static extern bool GetMonitorInfo(IntPtr hMonitor, out MONITORINFO lpmi);
static extern int GetMouseMovePointsEx(uint cbSize, [In] ref MOUSEMOVEPOINT
  lppt, [Out] MOUSEMOVEPOINT [] lpptBuf, int nBufPoints, uint resolution);
static extern IntPtr GetNextDlgGroupItem(IntPtr hDlg, IntPtr hCtl,
  bool bPrevious);
static extern IntPtr GetNextDlgTabItem(IntPtr hDlg, IntPtr hCtl,
  bool bPrevious);
static extern IntPtr GetOpenClipboardWindow();
static extern IntPtr GetParent(IntPtr hWnd);
static extern int GetPriorityClipboardFormat(uint [] paFormatPriorityList,
  int cFormats);
static extern bool GetProcessDefaultLayout(out uint pdwDefaultLayout);
static extern IntPtr GetProcessWindowStation();
static extern IntPtr GetProp(IntPtr hWnd, string lpString);
static extern uint GetQueueStatus(uint flags);
static extern bool GetScrollBarInfo(IntPtr hwnd, int idObject,
  out SCROLLBARINFO psbi);
static extern bool GetScrollInfo(IntPtr hwnd, int fnBar, ref SCROLLINFO lpsi);
static extern int GetScrollPos(IntPtr hWnd, int nBar);
static extern bool GetScrollRange(IntPtr hWnd, int nBar, out int lpMinPos,
  out int lpMaxPos);
static extern IntPtr GetSubMenu(IntPtr hMenu, int nPos);
static extern uint GetSysColor(int nIndex);
static extern IntPtr GetSysColorBrush(int nIndex);
static extern IntPtr GetSystemMenu(IntPtr hWnd, bool bRevert);
static extern int GetSystemMetrics(int nIndex);
static extern uint GetTabbedTextExtent(IntPtr hDC, string lpString,
  int nCount, int nTabPositions, int [] lpnTabStopPositions);
static extern IntPtr GetThreadDesktop(uint dwThreadId);
static extern bool GetTitleBarInfo(IntPtr hwnd, out TITLEBARINFO pti);
static extern IntPtr GetTopWindow(IntPtr hWnd);
static extern bool GetUpdateRect(IntPtr hWnd, IntPTr lpRect, bool bErase);
static extern int GetUpdateRgn(IntPtr hWnd, IntPtr hRgn, bool bErase);
static extern bool GetUserObjectInformation(IntPtr hObj, int nIndex,
  [Out] byte [] pvInfo, uint nLength, out uint lpnLengthNeeded);
static extern bool GetUserObjectSecurity(IntPtr hObj, [In] ref uint
  pSIRequested, IntPtr pSD, uint nLength, out uint lpnLengthNeeded);
static extern IntPtr GetWindow(IntPtr hWnd, uint uCmd);
static extern uint GetWindowContextHelpId(IntPtr hwnd);
static extern IntPtr GetWindowDC(IntPtr hWnd);
static extern bool GetWindowInfo(IntPtr hwnd, out WINDOWINFO pwi);
static extern int GetWindowLong(IntPtr hWnd, int nIndex);
static extern uint GetWindowModuleFileName(IntPtr hwnd,
  [Out] StringBuilder lpszFileName, uint cchFileNameMax);
static extern bool GetWindowPlacement(IntPtr hWnd,
  out WINDOWPLACEMENT lpwndpl);
```

```
static extern bool GetWindowRect(IntPtr hWnd, out RECT lpRect);
static extern int GetWindowRgn(IntPtr hWnd, IntPtr hRgn);
static extern int GetWindowText(IntPtr hWnd, [Out] StringBuilder lpString,
  int nMaxCount);
static extern int GetWindowTextLength(IntPtr hWnd);
static extern uint GetWindowThreadProcessId(IntPtr hWnd, IntPtr lpdwProcessId);
static extern bool GrayString(IntPtr hDC, IntPtr hBrush, GrayStringDelegate
  lpOutputFunc, IntPtr lpData, int nCount, int X, int Y, int nWidth,
  int nHeight);
static extern bool HideCaret(IntPtr hWnd);
static extern bool HiliteMenuItem(IntPtr hwnd, IntPtr hmenu, uint uItemHilite,
  uint uHilite);
static extern bool ImpersonateDdeClientWindow(IntPtr hWndClient,
  IntPtr hWndServer);
static extern bool InflateRect(ref RECT lprc, int dx, int dy);
static extern bool InSendMessage();
static extern uint InSendMessageEx(IntPtr lpReserved);
static extern bool InsertMenu(IntPtr hMenu, uint uPosition, uint uFlags,
  UIntPtr uIDNewItem, IntPtr lpNewItem);
static extern bool InsertMenuItem(IntPtr hMenu, uint uItem, bool fByPosition,
  [In] ref MENUITEMINFO lpmii);
static extern bool IntersectRect(out RECT lprcDst, [In] ref RECT lprcSrc1,
  [In] ref RECT lprcSrc2);
static extern bool InvalidateRect(IntPtr hWnd, IntPtr lpRect, bool bErase);
static extern bool InvalidateRgn(IntPtr hWnd, IntPtr hRgn, bool bErase);
static extern bool InvertRect(IntPtr hDC, [In] ref lprc);
static extern bool IsCharAlpha(char ch);
static extern bool IsCharAlphaNumeric(char ch);
static extern bool IsCharLower(char ch);
static extern bool IsCharUpper(char ch);
static extern bool IsChild(IntPtr hWndParent, IntPtr hWnd);
static extern bool IsClipboardFormatAvailable(uint format);
static extern bool IsDialogMessage(IntPtr hDlg, [In] ref MSG lpMsg);
static extern uint IsDlgButtonChecked(IntPtr hDlg, int nIDButton);
static extern bool IsIconic(IntPtr hWnd);
static extern bool IsMenu(IntPtr hMenu);
static extern bool IsRectEmpty([In] ref RECT lprc);
static extern bool IsWindow(IntPtr hWnd);
static extern bool IsWindowEnabled(IntPtr hWnd);
static extern bool IsWindowUnicode(IntPtr hWnd);
static extern bool IsWindowVisible(IntPtr hWnd);
static extern bool IsZoomed(IntPtr hWnd);
static extern void keybd_event(byte bVk, byte bScan, uint dwFlags,
  UIntPtr dwExtraInfo);
static extern bool KillTimer(IntPtr hWnd, UIntPtr uIDEvent);
static extern IntPtr LoadAccelerators(IntPtr hInstance, string lpTableName);
```

```csharp
static extern IntPtr LoadBitmap(IntPtr hInstance, string lpBitmapName);
static extern IntPtr LoadCursor(IntPtr hInstance, string lpCursorName);
static extern IntPtr LoadCursorFromFile(string lpFileName);
static extern IntPtr LoadIcon(IntPtr hInstance, string lpIconName);
static extern IntPtr LoadImage(IntPtr hinst, string lpszName, uint uType,
   int cxDesired, int cyDesired, uint fuLoad);
static extern IntPtr LoadKeyboardLayout(string pwszKLID, uint Flags);
static extern IntPtr LoadMenu(IntPtr hInstance, string lpMenuName);
static extern IntPtr LoadMenuIndirect(IntPtr lpMenuTemplate);
static extern int LoadString(IntPtr hInstance, uint uID,
   [Out] StringBuilder lpBuffer, int nBufferMax);
static extern bool LockSetForegroundWindow(uint uLockCode);
static extern bool LockWindowUpdate(IntPtr hWndLock);
static extern bool LockWorkStation();
static extern int LookupIconIdFromDirectory(byte [] presbits, bool fIcon);
static extern int LookupIconIdFromDirectoryEx(byte [] presbits, bool fIcon,
   int cxDesired, int cyDesired, uint Flags);
static extern bool MapDialogRect(IntPtr hDlg, ref RECT lpRect);
static extern uint MapVirtualKey(uint uCode, uint uMapType);
static extern uint MapVirtualKeyEx(uint uCode, uint uMapType, IntPtr dwhkl);
static extern int MapWindowPoints(IntPtr hwndFrom, IntPtr hwndTo,
   IntPtr lpPoints, uint cPoints);
static extern int MenuItemFromPoint(IntPtr hWnd, IntPtr hMenu,
   [In] ref POINT ptScreen);
static extern bool MessageBeep(uint uType);
static extern int MessageBox(IntPtr hWnd, string lpText, string lpCaption,
   uint uType);
static extern int MessageBoxEx(IntPtr hWnd, string lpText, string lpCaption,
   uint uType, ushort wLanguageId);
static extern int MessageBoxIndirect([In] ref MSGBOXPARAMS lpMsgBoxParams);
static extern bool ModifyMenu(IntPtr hMnu, uint uPosition, uint uFlags,
   UIntPtr uIDNewItem, string lpNewItem);
static extern IntPtr MonitorFromPoint(POINT pt, uint dwFlags);
static extern IntPtr MonitorFromRect([In] ref RECT lprc, uint dwFlags);
static extern IntPtr MonitorFromWindow(IntPtr hwnd, uint dwFlags);
static extern void mouse_event(uint dwFlags, uint dx, uint dy, uint dwData,
   UIntPtr dwExtraInfo);
static extern bool MoveWindow(IntPtr hWnd, int X, int Y, int nWidth,
   int nHeight, bool bRepaint);
static extern uint MsgWaitForMultipleObjects(uint nCount, IntPtr [] pHandles,
   bool bWaitAll, uint dwMilliseconds, uint dwWakeMask);
static extern uint MsgWaitForMultipleObjectsEx(uint nCount, IntPtr [] pHandles,
   uint dwMilliseconds, uint dwWakeMask, uint dwFlags);
static extern void NotifyWinEvent(uint event, IntPtr hwnd, int idObject,
   int idChild);
static extern uint OemKeyScan(ushort wOemChar);
```

```
static extern bool OemToChar(IntPtr lpszSrc, [Out] StringBuilder lpszDst);
static extern bool OemToCharBuff(IntPtr lpszSrc, [Out] StringBuilder lpszDst,
  uint cchDstLength);
static extern bool OffsetRect(ref RECT lprc, int dx, int dy);
static extern bool OpenClipboard(IntPtr hWndNewOwner);
static extern IntPtr OpenDesktop(string lpszDesktop, uint dwFlags,
  bool fInherit, uint dwDesiredAccess);
static extern bool OpenIcon(IntPtr hWnd);
static extern IntPtr OpenInputDesktop(uint dwFlags, bool fInherit,
  uint dwDesiredAccess);
static extern IntPtr OpenWindowStation(string lpszWinSta, bool fInherit,
  uint dwDesiredAccess);
static extern IntPtr PackDDElParam(uint msg, UIntPtr uiLo, UIntPtr uiHi);
static extern bool PaintDesktop(IntPtr hdc);
static extern bool PeekMessage(out MSG lpMsg, IntPtr hWnd, uint wMsgFilterMin,
  uint wMsgFilterMax, uint wRemoveMsg);
static extern bool PostMessage(IntPtr hWnd, uint Msg, UIntPtr wParam,
  IntPtr lParam);
static extern void PostQuitMessage(int nExitCode);
static extern bool PostThreadMessage(uint idThread, uint Msg, UIntPtr wParam,
  IntPtr lParam);
static extern bool PtInRect([In] ref RECT lprc, POINT pt);
static extern IntPtr RealChildWindowFromPoint(IntPtr hwndParent,
  POINT ptParentClientCoords);
static extern uint RealGetWindowClass(IntPtr hwnd, [Out] StringBuilder pszType,
  uint cchType);
static extern bool RedrawWindow(IntPtr hWnd, [In] ref RECT lprcUpdate,
  IntPtr hrgnUpdate, uint flags);
static extern ushort RegisterClass([In] ref WNDCLASS lpWndClass);
static extern ushort RegisterClassEx([In] ref WNDCLASSEX lpwcx);
static extern uint RegisterClipboardFormat(string lpszFormat);
static extern IntPtr RegisterDeviceNotification(IntPtr hRecipient,
  IntPtr NotificationFilter, uint Flags);
static extern bool RegisterHotKey(IntPtr hWnd, int id, uint fsModifiers,
  uint vk);
static extern uint RegisterWindowMessage(string lpString);
static extern bool ReleaseCapture();
static extern int ReleaseDC(IntPtr hWnd, IntPtr hDC);
static extern bool RemoveMenu(IntPtr hMenu, uint uPosition, uint uFlags);
static extern IntPtr RemoveProp(IntPtr hWnd, IntPtr lpString);
static extern bool ReplyMessage(IntPtr lResult);
static extern IntPtr ReuseDDElParam(IntPtr lParam, uint msgIn, uint msgOut,
  UIntPtr uiLo, UIntPtr uiHi);
static extern bool ScreenToClient(IntPtr hWnd, [In] ref POINT lpPoint);
static extern bool ScrollDC(IntPtr hDC, int dx, int dy, IntPtr lprcScroll,
  IntPtr lprcClip, IntPtr hrgnUpdate, out RECT lprcUpdate);
```

```
static extern bool ScrollWindow(IntPtr hWnd, int XAmount, int YAmount,
   IntPtr lpRect, [In] ref RECT lpClipRect);
static extern int ScrollWindowEx(IntPtr hWnd, int dx, int dy, IntPtr prcScroll,
   IntPtr prcClip, IntPtr hrgnUpdate, IntPtr prcUpdate, uint flags);
static extern IntPtr SendDlgItemMessage(IntPtr hDlg, int nIDDlgItem, uint Msg,
   UIntPtr wParam, IntPtr lParam);
static extern uint SendInput(uint nInputs, INPUT [] pInputs, int cbSize);
static extern IntPtr SendMessage(IntPtr hWnd, uint Msg, UIntPtr wParam,
   IntPtr lParam);
static extern bool SendMessageCallback(IntPtr hWnd, uint Msg, UIntPtr wParam,
   IntPtr lParam, SendMessageDelegate lpCallBack, UIntPtr dwData);
static extern IntPtr SendMessageTimeout(IntPtr hWnd, uint Msg, UIntPtr wParam,
   IntPtr lParam, uint fuFlags, uint uTimeout, out UIntPtr lpdwResult);
static extern bool SendNotifyMessage(IntPtr hWnd, uint Msg, UIntPtr wParam,
   IntPtr lParam);
static extern IntPtr SetActiveWindow(IntPtr hWnd);
static extern IntPtr SetCapture(IntPtr hWnd);
static extern bool SetCaretBlinkTime(uint uMSeconds);
static extern bool SetCaretPos(int X, int Y);
static extern uint SetClassLong(IntPtr hWnd, int nIndex, uint dwNewLong);
static extern ushort SetClassWord(IntPtr hWnd, int nIndex, ushort wNewWord);
static extern IntPtr SetClipboardData(uint uFormat, IntPtr hMem);
static extern IntPtr SetClipboardViewer(IntPtr hWndNewViewer);
static extern IntPtr SetCursor(IntPtr hCursor);
static extern bool SetCursorPos(int X, int Y);
static extern bool SetDlgItemInt(IntPtr hDlg, int nIDDlgItem, uint uValue,
   bool bSigned);
static extern bool SetDlgItemText(IntPtr hDlg, int nIDDlgItem,
   string lpString);
static extern bool SetDoubleClickTime(uint uInterval);
static extern IntPtr SetFocus(IntPtr hWnd);
static extern bool SetForegroundWindow(IntPtr hWnd);
static extern bool SetKeyboardState(byte [] lpKeyState);
static extern void SetLastErrorEx(uint dwErrCode, uint dwType);
static extern bool SetLayeredWindowAttributes(IntPtr hwnd, uint crKey,
   byte bAlpha, uint dwFlags);
static extern bool SetMenu(IntPtr hWnd, IntPtr hMenu);
static extern bool SetMenuContextHelpId(IntPtr hmenu, uint dwContextHelpId);
static extern bool SetMenuDefaultItem(IntPtr hMenu, uint uItem, uint fByPos);
static extern bool SetMenuInfo(IntPtr hmenu, [In] ref MENUINFO lpcmi);
static extern bool SetMenuItemBitmaps(IntPtr hMenu, uint uPosition,
   uint uFlags, IntPtr hBitmapUnchecked, IntPtr hBitmapChecked);
static extern bool SetMenuItemInfo(IntPtr hMenu, uint uItem, bool fByPosition,
   [In] ref MENUITEMINFO lpmii);
static extern IntPtr SetMessageExtraInfo(IntPtr lParam);
static extern IntPtr SetParent(IntPtr hWndChild, IntPtr hWndNewParent);
```

E

**PINVOKE
DEFINITIONS FOR
WIN32 FUNCTIONS**

```
static extern bool SetProcessDefaultLayout(uint dwDefaultLayout);
static extern bool SetProcessWindowStation(IntPtr hWinSta);
static extern bool SetProp(IntPtr hWnd, string lpString, IntPtr hData);
static extern bool SetRect(out RECT lprc, int xLeft, int yTop, int xRight,
  int yBottom);
static extern bool SetRectEmpty(out RECT lprc);
static extern int SetScrollInfo(IntPtr hwnd, int fnBar, [In] ref SCROLLINFO
  lpsi, bool fRedraw);
static extern int SetScrollPos(IntPtr hWnd, int nBar, int nPos, bool bRedraw);
static extern bool SetScrollRange(IntPtr hWnd, int nBar, int nMinPos,
  int nMaxPos, bool bRedraw);
static extern bool SetSysColors(int cElements, int [] lpaElements,
  uint [] lpaRgbValues);
static extern bool SetSystemCursor(IntPtr hcur, uint id);
static extern bool SetThreadDesktop(IntPtr hDesktop);
static extern UIntPtr SetTimer(IntPtr hWnd, UIntPtr nIDEvent, uint uElapse,
  TimerDelegate lpTimerFunc);
static extern bool SetUserObjectInformation(IntPtr hObj, int nIndex,
  byte [] pvInfo, uint nLength);
static extern bool SetUserObjectSecurity(IntPtr hObj, [In] ref uint
  pSIRequested, IntPtr pSD);
static extern bool SetWindowContextHelpId(IntPtr hwnd, uint dwContextHelpId);
static extern int SetWindowLong(IntPtr hWnd, int nIndex, int dwNewLong);
static extern bool SetWindowPlacement(IntPtr hWnd,
  [In] ref WINDOWPLACEMENT lpwndpl);
static extern bool SetWindowPos(IntPtr hWnd, IntPtr hWndInsertAfter, int X,
  int Y, int cx, int cy, uint uFlags);
static extern int SetWindowRgn(IntPtr hWnd, IntPtr hRgn, bool bRedraw);
static extern IntPtr SetWindowsHookEx(int idHook, HookDelegate lpfn,
  IntPtr hMod, uint dwThreadId);
static extern bool SetWindowText(IntPtr hWnd, string lpString);
static extern IntPtr SetWinEventHook(uint eventMin, uint eventMax, IntPtr
  hmodWinEventProc, WinEventDelegate lpfnWinEventProc, uint idProcess,
  uint idThread, uint dwFlags);
static extern bool ShowCaret(IntPtr hWnd);
static extern int ShowCursor(int bShow);
static extern bool ShowOwnedPopups(IntPtr hWnd, bool fShow);
static extern bool ShowScrollBar(IntPtr hWnd, int wBar, bool bShow);
static extern bool ShowWindow(IntPtr hWnd, int nCmdShow);
static extern bool ShowWindowAsync(IntPtr hWnd, int nCmdShow);
static extern bool SubtractRect(out RECT lprcDst, [In] ref RECT lprcSrc1,
  [In] ref RECT lprcSrc2);
static extern bool SwapMouseButton(bool fSwap);
static extern bool SwitchDesktop(IntPtr hDesktop);
static extern bool SystemParametersInfo(uint uiAction, uint uiParam,
  IntPtr pvParam, uint fWinIni);
```

```
static extern int TabbedTextOut(IntPtr hDC, int X, int Y, string lpString,
  int nCount, int nTabPositions, int [] lpnTabStopPositions, int nTabOrigin);
static extern ushort TileWindows(IntPtr hwndParent, uint wHow, IntPtr lpRect,
  uint cKids, IntPtr lpKids);
static extern int ToAscii(uint uVirtKey, uint uScanCode, byte [] lpKeyState,
  [Out] StringBuilder lpChar, uint uFlags);
static extern int ToAsciiEx(uint uVirtKey, uint uScanCode, byte [] lpKeyState,
  [Out] StringBuilder lpChar, uint uFlags, IntPtr hkl);
static extern int ToUnicode(uint wVirtKey, uint wScanCode, byte [] lpKeyState,
  [Out, MarshalAs(UnmanagedType.LPWStr)] StringBuilder pwszBuff, int cchBuff,
  uint wFlags);
static extern int ToUnicodeEx(uint wVirtKey, uint wScanCode, byte []
  lpKeyState, [Out, MarshalAs(UnmanagedType.LPWStr)] StringBuilder pwszBuff,
  int cchBuff, uint wFlags, IntPtr dwhkl);
static extern bool TrackMouseEvent(ref TRACKMOUSEEVENT lpEventTrack);
static extern bool TrackPopupMenu(IntPtr hMenu, uint uFlags, int x, int y,
  int nReserved, IntPtr hWnd, IntPtr prcRect);
static extern bool TrackPopupMenuEx(IntPtr hmenu, uint fuFlags, int x, int y,
  IntPtr hwnd, IntPtr lptpm);
static extern int TranslateAccelerator(IntPtr hWnd, IntPtr hAccTable,
  [In] ref MSG lpMsg);
static extern bool TranslateMDISysAccel(IntPtr hWndClient, [In] ref MSG lpMsg);
static extern bool TranslateMessage([In] ref MSG lpMsg);
static extern bool UnhookWindowsHookEx(IntPtr hhk);
static extern bool UnhookWinEvent(IntPtr hWinEventHook);
static extern bool UnionRect(out RECT lprcDst [In] ref RECT lprcSrc1,
  [In] ref RECT lprcSrc2);
static extern bool UnloadKeyboardLayout(IntPtr hkl);
static extern bool UnpackDDElParam(uint msg, IntPtr lParam, out UIntPtr puiLo,
  out UIntPtr puiHi);
static extern bool UnregisterClass(string lpClassName, IntPtr hInstance);
static extern bool UnregisterDeviceNotification(IntPtr Handle);
static extern bool UnregisterHotKey(IntPtr hWnd, int id);
static extern bool UpdateLayeredWindow(IntPtr hwnd, IntPtr hdcDst,
  IntPtr pptDst, IntPtr psize, IntPtr hdcSrc, IntPtr pptSrc, uint crKey,
  [In] ref BLENDFUNCTION pblend, uint dwFlags);
static extern bool UpdateWindow(IntPtr hWnd);
static extern bool UserHandleGrantAccess(IntPtr hUserHandle, IntPtr hJob,
  bool bGrant);
static extern bool ValidateRect(IntPtr hWnd, IntPtr lpRect);
static extern bool ValidateRgn(IntPtr hWnd, IntPtr hRgn);
static extern short VkKeyScan(char ch);
static extern short VkKeyScanEx(char ch, IntPtr dwhkl);
static extern uint WaitForInputIdle(IntPtr hProcess, uint dwMilliseconds);
static extern bool WaitMessage();
static extern IntPtr WindowFromDC(IntPtr hDC);
```

```csharp
static extern IntPtr WindowFromPoint(POINT Point);
static extern bool WinHelp(IntPtr hWndMain, string lpszHelp, uint uCommand,
    uint dwData);
[DllImport("user32.dll", CallingConvention=CallingConvention.Cdecl)]
static extern int wsprintf([Out] StringBuilder lpOut, string lpFmt, ...);
// You need to define separate overloaded methods for wsprintf with
// different numbers of parameters to simulate a variable number of arguments
```

Glossary

ActiveX Assembly   An assembly created by the ActiveX importer that contains .NET class definitions for ActiveX controls. An ActiveX Assembly references an Interop Assembly containing the "raw" type definitions. *See also Interop Assembly.*

ActiveX importer   Also called the ".NET ActiveX Control to Windows Forms Assembly Generator", the ActiveX importer generates an ActiveX Assembly (and possibly the referenced Interop Assembly) from a type library. This functionality is exposed when using a COM component from the toolbox in Visual Studio .NET, or by using the AXIMP.EXE SDK tool. *See also type library exporter.*

apartment   In COM, an apartment is a logical process that contains objects with similar threading requirements. A single-threaded apartment (STA) only has one thread, a multi-threaded apartment (MTA) can contain multiple threads, and a neutral apartment (NA) contains no threads.

application domain   Often abbreviated as AppDomain, it is a lightweight logical container managed by the CLR. It provides the same sort of isolation as an operating system process, but multiple application domains may exist in a single process.

ASP Compatibility Mode   An ASP.NET setting that provides backwards-compatible behavior with ASP. The main use of this is to use STA threads rather than the default MTA threads used by ASP.NET. *See also MTA thread, STA thread.*

assembly   An assembly is the unit of deployment and versioning in the .NET Framework. An assembly contains a manifest, metadata, MSIL, and possibly binary resources. Most assemblies are single files, but an assembly can consist of multiple files, such as DLLs, picture files, and even HTML files. *See also manifest, metadata, and MSIL.*

binary compatibility   Indicates that one COM object can be replaced with another without affecting existing COM clients. This can occur when they have the same CLSID and ProgID, when they both implement the same interfaces, and when they both source the same interfaces. By doing this, their binary specifications are equivalent.

blittable   A blittable data type is one that has the same managed and unmanaged representations. For such data types, the Interop Marshaler pins an instance and exposes it directly to unmanaged code rather than performing a slower copy operation. This performance optimization is not possible for non-blittable types, since one representation must always be copied to the other representation. See Chapter 3, "The Essentials for Using COM in Managed Code," for a list of blittable types.

C-style array   A C-style array is any array type that is simply a pointer to the first element in a list of contiguous elements. The user of such an array must always know its length, otherwise she can easily access meaningless memory. C-style arrays in a type library do not work well with COM Interoperability, and do not have the same self-describing qualities as a COM SAFEARRAY or a .NET array.

CCW   *See COM-Callable Wrapper.*

class interface   A class interface can be exposed by a COM-Callable Wrapper for a .NET class. Such an interface exposes all the COM-visible members of the .NET class and its base classes. By default, .NET classes have an auto-dispatch class interface exposed, meaning that COM clients can only late bind to members not explicitly exposed on an interface. This is the safest option for versioning, but an auto-dual class interface can be exposed instead, or a class interface can be suppressed altogether.

CLR   *See Common Language Runtime.*

CLS   *See Common Language Specification.*

CLSID   *See GUID.*

coclass interface   A coclass interface is an interface produced by the type library importer that has the same name as a coclass in the input type library. A coclass interface derives from the coclass's default interface and possibly an importer-generated event interface. Coclass interfaces are marked with the `CoClassAttribute` custom attribute so languages like C# and VB .NET can enable users to instantiate the interface type as if it's a class type.

COM-Callable Wrapper   A COM-Callable Wrapper (CCW) is a COM object that acts as a proxy for a .NET object. The wrapper forwards calls to the .NET object through its exposed interfaces, enabling .NET-unaware COM objects to use .NET objects in a natural way.

COM marshaling   Marshaling between COM contexts (apartments, processes, or threads). This is the same sort of marshaling that can occur in COM and is unrelated to the .NET Framework. COM components, such as those authored in Visual Basic 6, often use type library marshaling to accomplish COM marshaling, but it could also be done with a MIDL-generated proxy/stub DLL or in a custom fashion. *See also type library marshaling, Interop marshaling.*

COM Interoperability   The technology that enables COM components to be used in .NET and .NET components to be used in COM.

COM visibility   Indicates whether a .NET type or member is accessible from COM. Anything public in .NET is visible to COM unless it's marked with the `ComVisibleAttribute` custom attribute with its argument set to false, or its containing assembly is marked with the attribute with its argument set to false.

Common Language Runtime   The execution engine or "kernel" of the .NET Framework.

Common Language Specification   A subset of language features that should be supported by .NET languages and tools, to enable cross-language interoperability.

connectable object   A COM object that exposes connection points to provide event-like behavior.

custom attribute   A class that can be marked on elements like assemblies, types, members, parameters, and so on, to mark them with custom information. Often simply referred to as "attributes," custom attributes enable arbitrary extensibility of metadata. The .NET Framework makes heavy use of custom attributes to provide semantics that can't be expressed in standard metadata alone. *See also pseudo-custom attribute.*

custom marshaling   In COM Interoperability, custom marshaling refers to using an object that implements `System.Runtime.InteropServices.ICustomMarshaler` that can replace the standard Interop Marshaler when marshaling between managed and unmanaged code is performed. *See also Interop Marshaler, Interop marshaling.*

default constructor   A constructor with no parameters. .NET classes must have a public default constructor in order to be instantiated from COM.

default interface   A coclass's interface marked with [`default`] in a type library, or the first interface listed if none are marked with the attribute. Default interfaces are important when importing a type library since every coclass interface inherits the members of the default interface (but no other implemented interfaces), and parameters or fields of the default interface type may be substituted with the coclass interface type.

delegate   A .NET class representing a method signature that can be used like a type-safe function pointer. .NET applications use delegates for callback functionality.

DISPID   Short for *dispatch identifier*, a DISPID is a number assigned to a member of a dual or dispinterface that is passed to `IDispatch.Invoke` in order to call it. Each member's parameter can also have a DISPID in order to support invocation using named parameters.

dispinterface   A COM interface whose members can only be accessed via the members of `IDispatch`. This is the only type of interface for which COM users don't depend on the layout of its members.

dual interface   A COM interface that derives from `IDispatch` but also exposes its methods for v-table access.

formatted class   A formatted class is a .NET class that has structure layout. This means that it's marked with `StructLayoutAttribute` and either `LayoutKind.Sequential` or `LayoutKind.Explicit`. Such a class is treated like a value type would be when exposed to unmanaged code.

formatted reference type   *See formatted class.*

garbage collection   The act of freeing unused memory ("garbage") whenever appropriate so the users who allocate memory aren't responsible for freeing it themselves. Objects that don't release limited resources until destruction can cause problems in a garbage collection environment, since the garbage collector is unaware of the need to release such an object in a timely fashion unless available memory is low.

Global Assembly Cache A central storage location for strong-named assemblies that are meant to be shared by multiple applications. The Global Assembly Cache (GAC) and its assembly-loading rules are the key to side-by-side installation and execution of assemblies. By default, the Global Assembly Cache resides in the `Assembly` subdirectory of your Windows folder. *See also assembly.*

GUID A 128-bit *globally unique identifier*, sometimes called a *universally unique identifier* (UUID). The `CoCreateGuid` Windows API (exposed as the `System.Guid.NewGuid` method in the .NET Framework) can generate GUIDs that are highly likely to be unique. GUIDs are used in COM to provide unique identity to elements such as classes, interfaces, and type libraries. A GUID used to identify a class is called a CLSID (Class Identifier), a GUID used to identify an interface is called an IID (Interface Identifier), and so on.

HRESULT A 32-bit status code used to convey errors, warnings, or success. Almost all COM members return HRESULTs.

IDispatch A COM interface implemented by most COM objects in order to provide late bound access to its members.

IDL *See Interface Definition Language.*

IID *See GUID.*

IL Assembler The IL Assembler is a utility that is installed with the .NET Framework SDK with the filename `ILASM.EXE`. With it, you can convert source code in a language typically called *IL*

Assembler into an assembly. IL Assembler can be viewed as just another .NET language and compiler like C# or Visual Basic .NET, but at a much lower level. Source files used as input for the IL Assembler usually have a `.il` extension and often originate from files created by the IL Disassembler. This is useful for making changes to an existing assembly by disassembling it, changing the output text file, then re-assembling it, as demonstrated in Chapter 7, "Modifying Interop Assemblies." *See also IL Disassembler, metadata, and MSIL.*

IL Disassembler The IL Disassembler is a utility that is installed with the .NET Framework SDK with the filename `ILDASM.EXE`. With it, you can browse any assembly's metadata and view each member's IL implementation. By default, it runs as a graphical application, but with command-line options it can do additional tasks such as outputting a text file that can be consumed by the IL Assembler. *See also IL Assembler, metadata, and MSIL.*

Interface Definition Language Interface Definition Language (IDL) is a language used to define COM types, typically compiled with MIDL. *See also MIDL.*

Intermediate Language *See MSIL.*

Interop Assembly An assembly, usually produced by the type library importer, that contains definitions of COM types described in metadata. Authors of COM components should create a *Primary* Interop Assembly to prevent duplicate, non-compatible Interop Assemblies from becoming prevalent. *See also Primary Interop Assembly.*

F

Interop Marshaler   A marshaler built-into the CLR that performs the transformations between managed and unmanaged data types. The same marshaler is used for COM Interoperability and for PInvoke, although its default behavior can change depending on the context in which it is used. The Interop Marshaler is not general-purpose, but can be customized using custom attributes such as `MarshalAsAttribute`, `InAttribute`, and `OutAttribute`. *See also Interop marshaling.*

Interop marshaling   The process of converting managed data types to unmanaged data types and vice-versa. Interop marshaling is only done when crossing the managed/unmanaged boundary, and does not take the place of COM marshaling. *See also COM Marshaling.*

IUnknown   A COM interface that must be implemented by an object for it to be considered a COM object. `IUnknown` provides methods for reference counting and for obtaining other interfaces implemented by the object.

JUMP to .NET   The Java User Migration Path to .NET is a collection of technologies, including Visual J# .NET, for migrating and interoperating with existing unmanaged Java components. Java developers are best served by using these technologies rather than using COM Interoperability to use Java-COM components from .NET.

link demand   A .NET security check that occurs during just-in-time compilation and only checks the immediate caller of the member marked with the demand. Members marked with link demands can execute faster than those marked with regular demands because a full stack walk to check every caller's permissions is avoided. Such code is susceptible to luring attacks, however, so great care must be used with them.

managed code   Managed code is code that requires the execution environment of the Common Language Runtime. Compilers emit managed code as IL and metadata. The reason for the name is that the code is *managed* by the CLR and objects are allocated from a heap *managed* by the CLR. *See also unmanaged code.*

manifest   The part of an assembly that describes it identity, lists the files it is comprised of, lists the dependencies on other assemblies, and contains other information such as its required permission set. Every assembly has one manifest, regardless of how many files it contains. The file with the embedded manifest is the one that must be used with tools such as `REGASM.EXE` or APIs such as `Assembly.LoadFrom`.

marshaling   The act of translating data from one representation to another. The Interop Marshaler performs marshaling of managed data types to unmanaged data types, whereas COM marshaling refers to translating data from one context (apartment, process, or thread) to another. *See also Interop Marshaler, Interop marshaling, COM marshaling.*

metadata   Information inside an assembly that describes its types. Metadata is required by .NET compilers for binding, required by the CLR for many of its services, and used by object browsers and IntelliSense to provide a rich programming experience. Metadata is the .NET version of COM type information (as found in a type library), but much more expressive.

MIDL   MIDL stands for *Microsoft IDL Compiler*. It compiles an IDL file and can produce a proxy/stub DLL required for COM marshaling, and/or a type library. *See also COM marshaling, type library.*

MSIL   MSIL, sometimes abbreviated as just IL, is short for *Microsoft Intermediate Language*. MSIL is produced by any .NET compiler, and is *the* language of .NET. At run time, the .NET just-in-time (JIT) compiler converts MSIL into assembly code that's native to the current computer's processor. Since assemblies contain their source code in the form of MSIL (except for mixed-mode C++ assemblies, which also contain unmanaged code), they can be used on any platform with an appropriate JIT compiler without being recompiled from its original source code.

MTA Thread   A thread that runs inside a multi-threaded apartment (MTA). *See also apartment.*

Names file   A file that can be used with the type library exporter (TLBEXP.EXE) and its /names option in order to control the case of exported identifiers. *See also type library exporter.*

pinning   Holding a .NET object in a fixed location in memory, preventing it from being moved or collected by the .NET garbage collector. Any .NET objects whose memory is exposed directly to unmanaged

code must be pinned, because the garbage collector is free to move objects in memory at any time otherwise. Pinning should be done as little as possible and for short amounts of time, because it interferes with the garbage collector and may prevent it from executing optimally.

PInvoke   *See Platform Invocation Services.*

Platform Invocation Services   The technology that enables calling unmanaged DLL entry points directly from managed code, and enables callbacks into managed code. Platform Invocation Services is commonly called PInvoke or Platform Invoke.

Primary Interop Assembly   An assembly containing definitions of COM types that is distributed and digitally signed by the author of the COM component. Visual Studio .NET transparently uses a registered Primary Interop Assembly when a user references its corresponding type library. Primary Interop Assemblies are important because multiple definitions of the same COM types in separate assemblies are treated as unrelated types in .NET. *See also Interop Assembly.*

pseudo-custom attribute   Bits in metadata that are set in source code using custom attribute syntax. Pseudo-custom attributes seem no different than real custom attributes to the programmer marking their code, but they are persisted in metadata differently. The same abstraction is not maintained in reflection, for which pseudo-custom attributes are not discoverable as custom attributes. Instead, some pseudo-custom attribute

F

data can be obtained using specific APIs, whereas other data cannot be obtained from reflection alone. Examples of pseudo-custom attributes discussed in this book are `ComImportAttribute`, `DllImportAttribute`, and `MarshalAsAttribute`. *See also custom attribute.*

RCW   *See Runtime-Callable Wrapper.*

reference type   A data type that is always passed as a reference to the actual instance on the managed heap. In C++ terms, reference types always have an implied pointer. Reference types (except for strings and usually arrays) are marshaled to unmanaged code as interface pointers unless they are marked with sequential or explicit layout using the `StructLayoutAttribute` pseudo-custom attribute.

reflection   The technology that enables the discovery of .NET type information at run time, and dynamic invocation.

Runtime-Callable Wrapper   A Runtime-Callable Wrapper (RCW) is a .NET object that acts as a proxy for a COM object. The wrapper, which is a `System.__ComObject` or derived type, forwards calls to the COM object through its exposed interfaces and handles COM tasks such as reference counting.

SAFEARRAY   The self-describing array type used in COM. Arrays in Visual Basic 6 are `SAFEARRAY`s.

source interface   An interface listed by a coclass that it can call back upon to support event-like behavior in COM. The coclass listing a source interface does *not* implement it. Objects that implement the interface can "register" themselves with the coclass using the COM connection point interfaces.

STA Thread   A thread that runs inside a single-threaded apartment (STA). *See also apartment.*

strong name   An assembly name that includes a public key, sometimes called a shared name. Strong named assemblies have unique names by virtue of the public key information.

type library   A binary file containing type information of COM types; the COM version of metadata. The MIDL compiler creates type libraries from IDL files, and Visual Basic 6 creates type libraries from source code. A type library can be a standalone file (usually with a `.tlb` extension) or embedded as a resource in any other file, like a DLL. *See also MIDL.*

type library importer   Creates an Interop Assembly from a type library. This functionality is exposed when referencing a type library in Visual Studio .NET, or when using the `TLBIMP.EXE` SDK tool.

See also Interop Assembly, Primary Interop Assembly.

type library exporter   Creates a type library from an assembly. This functionality is exposed when using the `Register for COM Interop` option in Visual Studio .NET, or when using the `TLBEXP.EXE` SDK tool.

type library marshaling   COM marshaling done by the OLE Automation marshaler, which uses a registered type library to determine how to marshal the types.

UDT   *See user defined type.*

unmanaged code   Unmanaged code is code that does not use or require the execution environment of the Common Language Runtime. Unmanaged code is outside of the reach of the CLR's security system, garbage collector, and other services. *See also managed code.*

unmanaged code permission   The common term used to describe `SecurityPermissionFlag.UnmanagedCode`, a flag that is a part of `SecurityPermission` (in the `System.Security.Permissions` namespace). Unmanaged code can only be called and run by a .NET application if the application has been granted unmanaged code permission. Due to the nature of unmanaged code, this permission effectively means full trust. *See also unmanaged code.*

unsafe code   A feature in the C# language that lets you use pointers like in C++. Such code must be used in an `unsafe` block, but it's not really "unsafe" to use these features correctly; the term refers to the fact that the CLR can't prove the safety of such code. Also, manipulating pointers can easily lead to buggy code. The use of this feature requires unmanaged code permission since direct manipulation of memory isn't verifiably type safe and could enable a malicious programmer to access resources that would otherwise have been blocked by code access security.

user-defined type   A user-defined type (UDT) is a name typically given to a structure in COM or a value type in .NET.

v-table   Short for *virtual function table*, a v-table is a table of virtual function pointers. This binary structure forms the basis of COM interfaces.

value type   A data type that is a value on the stack, rather than an object on a garbage-collected heap. Value types are marshaled to unmanaged code as structures.

VARIANT   A common COM data type that serves a similar role as .NET's `System.Object` type. A VARIANT is a structure that can contain any primitive type or a pointer to an interface pointer or UDT. It has a `vt` field that describes what kind of type is contained within, set to a constant such as VT_BSTR, VT_DECIMAL, or VT_I4.

F

GLOSSARY

INDEX

A

accessors
  get, 442
  let, 442
  set, 442
Activated event, 625
Activator.CreateInstance method (COM Interoperability), 91
ActiveX
  Assembly, 712
  containers, hosting Windows Forms controls in, 471-477
  controls, 120-121
    converting, 196-198
    referencing in Visual Studio .NET, 121-122
    referencing with .NET Framework SDK, 122-123
    Web browser example, 123, 126
  events, 240-245
  importer transformations, 235-240
ActiveX Control. *See* AXIMP.EXE
ActiveX Data Objects, 92-94
adapter objects
  CCWs, 904-905
  custom marshalers, 901-909
    alternative to, 910-913
    ICustomAdapter interface implementation, 909
  RCWs, 904-906
Add method, 347, 596
Add Reference command (Project menu), 25

addImport parameter
C# definition, 994
VB .NET definition, 994
AddMessage method, 625
**AddNotificationType
method, 285**
**AddRef method (Marshal
class), 1294**
AddressLists dispinterface
IDL representation, 982
.NET Definition in Visual
C++, 982-984
**AddrOfPinnedObject
method (GCHandle
value type), 1275**
addRule parameter
C# definition, 994
VB .NET definition, 994
**add_EventName method,
592**
**ADO (ActiveX Data
Objects), 92-94**
Advise methods, 216
**Alias keyword, customiz-
ing PInvoke function
names, 796**
**Alloc method (GCHandle
value type), 1275**
**AllocCoTaskMem method
(Marshal class), 1295**
**AllocHGlobal method
(Marshal class), 1295**
**AllowMultiple property,
30**
**AllowPartiallyTrusted-
CallersAttribute,
305-307, 419, 473**
**AnimatedEnvelopePicture
class, 1133, 1143, 1146**
**AnimatedEnvelopePicture
method, 1144**

**AnimatedPicture class,
1133, 1139**
fields, 1140
methods, 1140-1143
properties, 1140
**AnimatedPicture method,
1140**
**AnnoyingMessage
method, 206**
**Ansi setting, string
behavior, 797-798**
**Ansi value, CharSet
enumeration, 1256**
**Apartment string value,
276**
**apartment-threaded
components, 277-278**
apartments, 275-277, 733
COM, 276
callbacks from COM
objects to .NET objects,
282-289
choosing states, 277-282
defined, 276
incompatibility, 291-292
MTAs (Multi-Threaded
Apartments), 276-278
NAs (Neutral Apartments),
276-277
STAs (Single-Threaded
Apartments), 276-277
**ApartmentState property,
280-281**
C#, 280-281
starting new threads, 282
Visaul Basic .NET, 281
APIs
ClrCreateManagedInstance,
468-471
CoCreateGuid, 60

GetPrivateProfileSectionN
ames, 789-791
Interactive Interop Tool,
1062-1064
COM+ tab, 1097-1100
*compared to SDK,
1062-1063*
Exporter tab, 1083-1092
Importer tab, 1069-1083
*MainForm class,
1100-1101*
*MiscTypes.cs,
1064-1068*
Register tab, 1092-1097
structure, 1063
Interop, 52
names, 499-502
.NET Visualization API,
1224
*ColorfulVisualization,
1231-1235*
*Dancing Cat
Visualization,
1235-1243*
*SimpleVisualization,
1224-1226*
*WizardVisualization,
1227-1230*
SafeArrayGetVartype, 946
System.Runtime.InteropSe
rvices, versus unsafe C#
code, 250-258
Visualization, 1197, 1201
*BookExamples.Window
sMediaPlayer
assembly, 1201*
*IWMPEffects interface,
1199-1223*
registry keys, 1197-1198
*Visualization Wizard,
1198*

Win32
  *converting data types
    into .NET types to
    define PInvoke
    signatures, 778-781*
  CopyFileEx, 810-815
  *customizing string
    behaviors, 796-799*
  error handling, 800-807
  *GetWindowsDirectory
    function, 784-788*
  MessageBeep, 810
  PInvoke, 772
  PlaySound, 810
  *ReadConsoleInput,
    865-868*
  RegCloseKey, 856
  RegDeleteKey, 860
  RegEnumKey, 856
  RegOpenKey, 856
  *SetVolumeLabel
    function, 783-784*
**AppDomain interface,
  exported methods,
  488-489**
Application object, 646
**ApplicationAccessControl
  Attribute, 584**
**ApplicationActivation-
  Attribute, 584**
**ApplicationCrmEnabled-
  Attribute, 584**
**ApplicationEvents_SinkHe
  lper class, constructor,
  332**
**ApplicationIDAttribute,
  584**
**ApplicationNameAttribute,
  584**

**ApplicationQueuing-
  Attribute, 584**
**applications, .NET frame-
  work sound, 810**
**/appname (REGSVCS.EXE),
  1394-1395**
arcade games. *See* **E-mail
  Attack**
**architecture, custom
  marshaling, 895-896**
  adapter objects, 901-909
  ICustomMarshaler
    interface, 896-898
  MarshalAsAttribute,
    898-901
  marshaling by value versus
    reference, 910-913
arrays, 154, 792-794.
  See also **parameters**
  associative, 1242
  conformant, 160-161
  conformant varying,
    161-162
  custom marshaling,
    943-947
  customizing,
    MarshalAsAttribute,
    549-550
  exposing, 524-527
  fixed-length, 157-158
  frequency, 1199
  nested, 518-519
  parameter
    *method conversions,
      169-171*
    SAFEARRAYs, 717-719
    *single-dimensional,
      719-720*
    zero-bounded, 719

  SAFEARRAYs, 154-156,
    348-351
    *adding size to C-style
      arrays, 349-351*
    *UnmanagedType
      enumeration, 550-552*
  type library transformations,
    440-441
  varying, 158-159
  waveform, 1199
**ArraySubType parameters,
  337, 1343**
**ArrayWithOffset value
  type
  (System.Runtime.Interop
  Services namespace),
  1252-1254**
**AskYesNoQuestion
  method, 1068**
asmFileName,
  setting to string, 1043
  parameter
    (ConvertTypeLibToAsse
    mbly method), 1357
**asmNamespace parameter,
  1046, 1357**
**/asmversion (TLBIMP.EXE),
  1377**
**asmVersion parameter
  (ConvertTypeLibToAssem
  bly method), 1357**
**ASP Compatibility Mode,
  279**
ASP.NET
  aspcompat=true directive,
    280
  COM components, 90-94
  System.STAThreadAttribute,
    279-280

aspcompat=true directive, 280

assemblies, 22. *See also* **components; Interop Assembly**

ActiveX controls, 712

adding methods to modules, 372-373

BookExamples.Windows-MediaPlayer, 1201, 1217, 1223-1224

content modifications, 324-328

  changing data types, 340-342

  custom attributes, 351-366, 370-372

  custom marshalers, 248, 364-366

  errors, 328

  exposing success HRESULTs, 342-348

  key option, 327

  malicious edits, 327

  managed resources, 326

  output file names, 328

  SAFEARRAYs, 348-351

  unmanaged resources, 326

converting, 426

  exported type library, 428

  helpstrings, 427

  LCID, 427

  library names, 427-428

  type library identification, 426-427

  version numbers, 427

ConvertTypeLibTo-Assembly, 1048

creating from type libraries, 1040

  dynamic assemblies, 1042-1046

  GetPrimaryInteropAssembly method, 1047-1048

  saving, 1048-1050

  TypeLibConverter class, 1040-1042

creating type libraries, 1050

  dynamic libraries, 1050-1055

  saving dynamic libraries, 1055

custom attributes. *See* custom attributes

deployment, 532-535

disassembling/reassembling, managed resources, 326-327

dynamic

  creating, 1042-1046

  saving, 1048-1050

global assembly cache. *See* GAC

installing GAC, 392

installing in GAC, 649-650

Interop Assembly, 84-86

  ActiveX control conversions, 196-198

  class conversions, 179-186

  creating, 85

  data type conversions, 143-162

  DISPIDs conversions, 173-176

  enumeration conversions, 193-194

  GetPrimaryInterop-Assembly method, 1047-1048

ILDASM.EXE, 653

  interface conversions, 177-179

  method conversions, 162-171

  module conversions, 187-188

  Primary, 86, 88-90

  property conversions, 171-173

  registering, 297

  signatures, 344

  structure conversions, 189-191

  type library conversion, 141-143

  typedef conversions, 194-196

  union conversions, 191-192

KeywordAttributes, 30

ManagedForm, 923

meta data, reflection, 26-28

Microsoft.VisualBasic, 38, 356-358

mscorlib, 23, 34-35, 38, 71, 463, 522

  exceptions to HRESULT transformations, 1416-1417, 1423, 1429

  HRESULT, 1400, 1406-1407, 1413

  Interop API, 52

MyCustomMarshalers, 365

names, 23-24, 502-503, 533

namespaces, 23
parameter, 1060
partial binding, 91
PIAs
  ActiveX controls, 712
  constants, 709-710
  constructs, 710
  creating, 686
  customizing metadata, 693-694
  defining classes in IDL files, 702-707
  deployment, 694-696
  IDL type libraries, 697-702
  names, 686-687
  naming enums, 707-709
  naming output assembly, 690-693
  opening, 695
  reasons for creating, 684-685
  registering type libraries, 711
  registration, 694-696
  type library references, 687-689
Primary Interop, 1003
referencing, 25
REGASM.EXE, 535
registering, 390-392, 1056
  HRESULTs, 393
  REGASM.EXE, 391-394
  RegistrationServices class, 391, 1056-1058
  TypeLoadException, 392
  VB6.EXE, 392
  WSCRIPT.EXE, 392

signing, 24
spoofing public key token, 61
StringValidator, 381, 392
System, 23, 508
System.Drawing, 28, 34, 365
System.Web, 510
System.Windows.Forms, 50, 427, 1221
System.Xml, 34
TLBEXP.EXE, 535
type libraries. *See* type libraries
versioning, 527-529
Windows Registry, 80
Assembly class, 512
Assembly Registration Utility. *See* REGASM.EXE
Assembly to Type Library Converter. *See* TLBEXP.EXE
Assembly.GetExported-Types method, 1052
Assembly.Load method, 1050
Assembly.LoadFrom method, 1050
AssemblyBuilder.Save method, 1048
AssemblyKeyFileAttribute, 381
AssemblyName.tlb, 426
AssemblyQualifiedName property, 61
AssemblyRegistration-Flags enumeration (System.Runtime. InteropServices namespace), 1056-1057, 1096, 1254

AssemblyVersionAttribute, 530
associative arrays, 1242
ATL COM Wizard (C++), 725
ATL Simple Object Wizard (C++), 726
attributes
custom, 28, 30
  ApplicationAccess-ControlAttribute, 584
  ApplicationActivation-Attribute, 584
  ApplicationCrmEnable dAttribute, 584
  ApplicationIDAttribute, 584
  ApplicationName-Attribute, 584
  ApplicationQueuing-Attribute, 584
  AssemblyKeyFile-Attribute, 381
  AssemblyVersion-Attribute, 530
  AttributeUsageAttribute, 1223
  AutoCompleteAttribute, 585
  AutomationProxyAttrib ute, 581-582, 1254
  C#, 36-38
  C++, 43-45
  ClassInterface(Class-InterfaceType.Auto-Dual), 435
  ClassInterfaceAttribute, 556-560, 1256-1257

CoClassAttribute, 1258
COM interfaces,
  963-964
ComAliasNameAttribute,
  1258
ComClassAttribute,
  560-565, 605-608,
  613
ComConversionLoss-
  Attribute, 1258
ComEventInterface-
  Attribute, 1258-1259
ComponentAccess-
  ControlAttribute, 585
ComRegisterFunction-
  Attribute, 568, 1261
ComSourceInterfaces-
  Attribute, 598-605,
  611, 631, 1261
COMTIIntrinsics-
  Attribute, 585
ComUnregisterFunction-
  Attribute, 568, 1262
ComVisibleAttribute,
  562-565, 1262-1263
ConstructionEnabled-
  Attribute, 585
controlling apartments
  that .NET components
  reside on, 278-280
creating, 29-30
custom marshalers. See
  custom marshaling
customizing structures,
  829-839
DescriptionAttribute,
  359, 585
DispIdAttribute,
  574-578, 601, 651,
  1265-1266

DISPIDs, 366, 370
EventClassAttribute,
  585
EventTrackingEnabled
  Attribute, 585
ExampleAttribute, 354
ExceptionClassAttribute,
  585
exported type libraries,
  428
GetCustomAttributes,
  1220
GuidAttribute, 331,
  427, 574, 1278
helpstring, 358-363
IDispatchImplAttribute,
  660-661, 1282
IDL, 371-372
IISIntrinsicsAttribute,
  585
ILASM.EXE, 351-356
ImportedFromTypeLib-
  Attribute, 331, 1284
InterfaceQueuing-
  Attribute, 585
InterfaceTypeAttribute,
  578-579, 601, 1285
JustInTimeActivation-
  Attribute, 585
KeywordAttribute, 509
LCIDConversion, 583
LCIDConversionAttrib
  ute, 582, 1290-1291
LoadBalancingSupport
  edAttribute, 585
Microsoft.VisualBasic.
  CompilerServices.
  StandardModule-
  Attribute, 356
MustRunInClient-
  ContextAttribute, 585

ObjectPooling-
  Attribute, 585
PresetEnumAttribute,
  1220-1223
PrimaryInterop-
  AssemblyAttribute,
  1348
PrivateComponent-
  Attribute, 585
ProgIdAttribute, 566,
  1349
pseudo, 33
reflection, 31-33
RestrictedAttribute,
  508-509
SecureMethodAttribute,
  585
SecurityPermission-
  Attribute, 305
SecurityRoleAttribute,
  585
STAThreadAttribute,
  1100
SuppressUnmanaged-
  CodeSecurityAttribute,
  308
Synchronization-
  Attribute, 276, 586
System.EnterpriseServi
  ces, 584-586
System.FlagsAttribute,
  1022
System.MTAThread-
  Attribute, 278
System.Reflection.-
  AssemblyDescription
  Attribute, 1067
System.Runtime.
  CompilerServices.
  MethodImplAttribute,
  276

System.Runtime.Interop
    Services namespace,
    1250
System.Security.
    SuppressUnmanagedC
    odeSecurityAttribute,
    308
System.STAThread-
    Attribute, 278-280
TransactionAttribute,
    586
TypeLibFuncAttribute,
    1358
TypeLibTypeAttribute,
    1359
TypeLibVarAttribute,
    1359
usage guidelines, 508-
    510
VB .NET modules,
    356-358
Visual Basic .NET,
    40-42
pseudo-custom
    ComImportAttribute,
    298, 1260
    DllImportAttribute,
    772, 776-777, 795,
    863, 865, 1266-1267
    FieldOffsetAttribute,
    832-833, 1271-1272
    InAttribute, 438,
    553-554, 792-794,
    1284-1285
    MarshalAsAttribute,
    334-340, 541-553,
    651, 834-839,
    898-901, 1222,
    1342-1344

OptionalAttribute,
    583-584, 1345-1346
OutAttribute, 438,
    553-554, 786,
    792-794, 1346-1347
PreserveSigAttribute,
    436, 579, 1347-1348
StructLayoutAttribute,
    270, 554-556,
    829-832, 839-844,
    1354
AttributeUsageAttribute,
    1223
AttributeUsageAttribute
    class, 30
audioTitle field, 1217
Auto setting, string
    behavior, 797-798
Auto value
    CharSet enumeration,
        1256
    LayoutKind enumeration,
        1290
auto-dispatch class
    interface, 398
auto-dual class interface,
    398
AutoCompleteAttribute,
    585
AutoDispatch value,
    ClassInterfaceType
    enumeration, 1257
AutoDual value,
    ClassInterfaceType
    enumeration, 1257
AutomationProxyAttribute
    (System.Runtime.
    InteropServices
    namespace), 581-582,
    1254
AxCoClassName class, 236

AxCoClassNameEvent-
    Multicaster class, 236
AXIMP.EXE, 324, 712,
    1252, 1390-1391
    /?, 1393
    /delaysign, 1391
    /help, 1393
    /keycontainer, 1391
    /keyfile, 1392
    /nologo, 1393
    /out, 1392
    /publickey, 1392
    /silent, 1393
    /source, 1393
    /verbose, 1393
    syntax, 1390
AxImporter class, 1252
AxWebBrowser class, 239
AxWebBrowserEvent-
    Multicaster class, 240

B

back buffer surfaces, 1118
background field, 1150
balloon effect, manually
    defining COM types,
    1033-1036
basic string. *See* **BSTR**
bi-directional
    communication, 202
binary compatibility
    Visual Basic 6, 294-295
    components, 628-633
    instancing, 633-634
binding
    late, 91
        COM components,
        119-120
        .NET members, 119
        unmanaged C++,
        404-407
    partial, 91

**BINDPTR value type
(System.Runtime.Interop
Services namespace),
1255**
**BindToMoniker method
(Marshal class), 1296**
**BIND_OPTS value type
(System.Runtime.Interop
Services namespace),
1255**
**BitConverter.ToString
method, 946**
blittable data types, 98
blittable value types, 792
BonusPicture field, 1120
**BookExamples.Windows
MediaPlayer assembly,
1201,1217, 1223-1224**
**Boolean parameters,
MarshalAsAttribute,
1343**
Both string value, 276
**Both threading model,
733**
**BSTR (basic string),
149-150, 249**
**by-reference null value
types (IntPtr type),
manipulating, 264-265**
**by-reference parameters,
119-120, 518**
   ILASM.EXE, 334
   method conversions,
      164-167
   .NET method transforma-
      tions, 436-438
by-value parameters
   method conversions,
      164-167
   .NET method transforma-
      tions, 436-438

ByValArray
   UnamangedType
      enumeration values, 549
   value, 834
ByValTStr value, 834

C

/c (REGSVCS.EXE), 1395
C#, 34
   ApartmentState property,
      280-281
   callback functionality
      using delegates,
         205-206
      using events, 210-211
   calling GetObjectAttribute
      method, 260
   clients, assembly
      modifications, 345-348
   coclass IDL representation
      of .NET classes, 450-452
   COM View and .NET View
      of an event, 446
      of fields exported as
         properties, 444
      of methods with
         parameter arrays, 441
      of properties, 442
   ComImport-marked class,
      1026
   compiler, 1006
   custom attributes, 29-30,
      36-38
   custom marshalers,
      converting Stream to
      IStream, 901-905
   defining IWMPEffects
      Interface, 971, 973

   definition of IMarshal,
      672-673
   definition of
      IRunningAppCollection,
      976-979
   definitions
      addImport and addRule
         parameters, 994
      C# IHTMLStyleSheet
         interface, 1035-1036
      IHTMLStyleSheet
         interface, 996-998
      IPersist and
         IPersistStream
         Interfaces, 985-987,
         1000-1001
      NetMeeting Coclass
         interface, 1009,
         1016-1018
   enumerations and
      parameters, and the IDL
      representation of
      exported types, 454, 457
   explicit interface
      implementation, 656
   exposing .NET events as
      COM connection points,
      592-593
   Form1.cs. Using Microsoft
      Word Spell Checking
      listing, 128-130, 133-137
   fully qualified names, 61-62
   Hello, World, 36
   ICustomMarshaler
      interface, 896
   IDictionary interface, 746
   ITypeLibImporterNotifySin
      k interface methods,
      1044, 1051

keywords corresponding to System namespace, 35

manual SAFEARRAY marshaling, 273-275

manual variant marshaling, 267, 270-272

marking array parameters with InAttribute and OutAttribute, 792-794

MyWebBrowser.cs. Using the WebBrowser ActiveX Control in C# listing, 123, 126

Non-Static Extern Members feature, 1029-1031

PInvoke, 50, 776-777

raw connections points, 219-222

reflection, 26-28

Register for COM Interop option, 534

RegistrationHelper class methods, 1059

signatures, MarshalAsAttribute, 899-901

StringValidator class, 380-381

syntax for imported C-style array fields, 262

System.Runtime.Interop-Services.UCOMIConnection Point syntax, 676-676, 684

System.STAThreadAttribute, 279

translation of IWMPEffects, 965-966, 1002

TypeLibConverter class, 1040, 1050

unsafe code, 849-852

unsafe code versus System.Runtime.Interop-Services APIs, 250-254
  obtaining value type addresses, 254-255
  obtaining value type sizes, 255-258

using construct, 1218-1220

using statement, 35

writing COM-creatable classes and non-COM-creatable classes, 514

C++

definition of ISupportErrorInfo, 674

ItypeLibImporterNotifySink interface methods, 1044, 1052

late binding, 404-407

RegistrationHelper class methods, 1059

RegistrationServices class methods, 1056

StringValidator class, 385-388

TypeLibConverter class, 1041, 1050

C-style array fields (IntPtr type), manipulating, 262
  imported C# syntax, 262
  imported Visual Basic .NET syntax, 262-264

C-style arrays, adding size to, 349-351

caches, GAC (global assembly cache), 24-25

callbacks

COM, 214-217, 226
  exceptions, 286
  to .NET objects, 282-289

.NET, 202
  delegates, 204-208
  events, 208-214
  interfaces, 202-204

Win32 functions, 810-811
  delegates as function pointers, 811-817
  invoking unmanaged pointers in managed code, 818-821

CALLCONV enumeration, 1255

CallerId
  event, 592-593
  method, 596

CallerIdEventArgs class, 610

CallerIdEventHandler class, 596

calling
  GetObjectAttribute method, 260
  members, .NET objects, 400-403
  methods, COM objects, 101-109
  properties, COM objects, 101-109

CallingConvention (PInvoke), 799-800
  enumeration, 1255-1256
  parameter, DllImportAttribute, 1266

camel casing, 503

Capabilities property, 1220

casing, type libraries, 489-492

casting

QueryInterface, 110-112

to RCW types, 295-297

categories, COM components, 569

CCWs (COM-Callable Wrapper), 69, 71, 394

class interfaces, 397-399

custom marshaling, 880-882

adapter objects, 904-905

deterministic release of resources, 947-952

exposing Stream as IStream, 932-943

Cdecl value, CallingConvention enumeration, 1255

CFileWriter class, 750-759

ChangeFontButton_Click method, 923

ChangeWrapperHandle-Strength method (Marshal class), 1296-1297

channelCount field, 1217

Character class, 1133

fields, 1157

methods, 1158, 1161-1162

private fields, 1158

Character method, 1158

CharSet enumeration, 1256

CharSet parameter

DllImportAttribute, 1266

StructLayoutAttribute, 830

ChatRoomDisplay interface, 204

ChatRoomServer class, 215

CheckForDeath method, 1121, 1133

class interfaces, 741-743

ClassInterfaceAttribute, 556-560

classes. *See also* **coclasses**

AnimatedEnvelopePicture, 1133, 1143-1146

AnimatedPicture, 1133, 1139

fields, 1140

methods, 1140-1143

properties, 1140

ApplicationEvents_ SinkHelper, 332

Assembly, 512

AttributeUsageAttribute, 30

AxCoClassName, 236

AxCoClassNameEvent-Multicaster, 236

AxImporter, 1252

AxWebBrowser, 239

AxWebBrowserEvent-Multicaster, 240

CallerIdEventArgs, 610

CallerIdEventHandler, 596

CFileWriter, 750-759

Character, 1133

fields, 1157

methods, 1158, 1161-1162

private fields, 1158

ChatRoomServer, 215

ClassVisibleToAll, 479

Client, 853

COM, 54

converting, 179-186

manually defining, 1022-1036

COM-creatable, writing in C#, 514

ComFriendlyForm, 611, 621

ComPlusInstaller, 1097-1100

ComVisibleForm, 479

ConsoleDisplay, 204

CorRuntimeHost, 468

creating instances

CreateObject method, 99-101

error detection, 101

new operator, 99

CustomCCW

exposing Stream as IStream, 932-943

MarshalManagedTo-Native, 948-952

CustomRCW, exposing IStream and Stream, 923-932

defining in IDL files, 702-703

default interfaces, 704-707

source interfaces, 703-704

DevTagAction, 635, 643, 645

DevTagRecognizer, 635, 643-644

DINPUT8STRING-CONSTANTS, 356

Display, 206

EmailAttack, 1178, 1182

EmailAttackForm,
  1166-1171
Envelope, 1162
  methods, 1162,
  1165-1166
  public fields, 1162
Environment, 1171
EventNameEventArgs, 609
Exporter, 1083-1084,
  1086-1092
FontMarshaler, 365,
  914-923
Form, 611-612, 1171
formatted, customizing
  classes, 839-844
FrontLayer methods, 1154
Game, 1111, 1119-1121,
  1131-1133, 1154, 1166
  private fields, 1121
  properties, 1121
  public fields, 1120
GCHandle, 250, 270, 306
GroundLayer methods,
  1153
IDL coclass representation,
  450-453
Importer, 1069-1083
INetMeetingEventsEventPr
  ovider, 1017
inheritance, COM,
  311-315
IntroScreen, 1156-1157
Kernel32, 1167
Layer, 1133, 1150
  fields, 1150
  methods, 1150-1152
LoadTypeLibEx, 1066
MainForm, 1100-1101
ManagedIStream, 889-895
Marshal, 250, 263, 270,
  306, 1067

MarshalGetObjectFor-
  NativeVariant method,
  272
members, private, 653
Microsoft.Win32.Registry,
  644
Monitor, 275
MustInherit, 506
Mutex, 275
NumberPicture, 1133,
  1146
  methods, 1147-1150
  private fields, 1147
Object, interface, 439-440
OwnerWindow, 1221
Phone, 592, 596-597
  event handlers, 597
  exposing .NET events
  to COM with CLR,
  602-605
  exposing .NET events
  to COM without CLR,
  594, 596-597
Picture, 1133-1134
  methods, 1136-1139
  properties, 1136
RCW, converting, 182
Register, 1093-1097
Registrar, 1096
registration,
  REGASM.EXE, 568
RegistrationHelper, 1059,
  1252
  InstallationFlags enu-
  meration, 1060-1061
  methods, 1060
  C#, 1059
  C++, 1059
  Visual Basic .NET,
  1059

RegistrationServices, 391,
  1097, 1056-1058
RegistryKey, 853, 856,
  859-860
RegistryKeyEnumerator,
  853, 856
RingEventHandler, 596
Screen, 1133, 1155-1156
Sound, 1133-1136
SourceInterfaceName_
  MethodNameEvent, 236
Stack, late binding, 404
Stream, 889-895
StringValidator, 381
  C#, 380-381
  C++, 385, 387-388
  JScript, 388-390
  Visual Basic 6, 382-384
StructLayoutAttribute, 433
System.Activator, 99
System.Collections.Stack,
  InvalidOperation-
  Exception, 403
System.ComponentModel,
  620
System.Console, 868
System.Drawing.Font,
  custom marshaling, 910,
  912
System.EnterpriseServices.
  ServicedComponent,
  283, 507
System.EventArgs, 608
System.IDisposable, 69
System.IO.Stream,
  methods, 883-889
System.MarshalByRef-
  Object, 295, 507
System.Object, 295,
  741-743

System.Runtime.Interop-
    Services, 620
System.Runtime.Interop-
    Services namespace
    CurrencyWrapper,
        1263-1264
    DispatchWrapper,
        1264-1265
    ErrorWrapper,
        1267-1268
    ExtensibleClassFactory,
        1269-1271
    Marshal, 1292-1342
    RegistrationServices,
        1349-1351
    RuntimeEnvironment,
        1351-1352
    TypeLibConverter,
        1356-1357
    UnknownWrapper,
        1366-1367
System.Runtime.
    InteropServices.Custom
    Marshalers namespace
    EnumerableToDispatch
        Marshaler, 1370
    EnumeratorToEnum-
        VariantMarshaler,
        1371
    ExpandoToDispatchEx
        Marshaler, 1371-1372
    TypeToTypeInfo-
        Marshaler, 1372
System.Runtime.Interop-
    Services.Marshal, 307,
    501, 845
System.Text.Regular-
    Expressions.Regex, 396
System.Threading.Manual
    ResetEvent, 286

System.Type, 26, 99
System.Web.Services.Web
    Service, 507
System.Web.UI.Page, 507
System.Windows.Forms.
    Form, 479, 507, 1221
System.Windows.Forms.
    MainMenu, 507
TAPI, methods, 227-229
type library transforma-
    tions, 449-451
TypeLibConverter, 85, 1052
    creating assemblies
        from type libraries,
        1040-1048
    creating type libraries
        from assemblies,
        1050-1055
    generating type
        libraries, 395
    ResolveRef method,
        1045
UnicodeEncoding, 946
UnmanagedType.LPArray,
    337
UnmanagedType.Safe-
    Array, 337
usage guidelines, versus
    interfaces, 506-508
Util, 1112, 1138-1139
    methods, 1112,
        1118-1119
    public fields, 1112
VB .NET modules,
    356-358
Visualization, 1208-1223,
    1229
INetMeetingEvents
    EventProvider, 1008
INetMeetingEvents
    SinkHelper, 1008

ClassInterface(ClassInterfa
    ceType.AutoDual), 435
ClassInterfaceAttribute
    (System.Runtime.Interop
    Services namespace),
    1256-1257
    ClassInterfaceType
        enumeration, 556-560
ClassInterfaceType enu-
    meration, 556-560, 1257
ClassVisibleToAll class,
    479
CleanUpManagedData
    method
    (ICustomMarshaler
    interface), 897, 1282
CleanUpNativeData
    method
    (ICustomMarshaler
    interface), 897, 1281
Client class, 853
clients
    defining exception types,
        COM, 520-522
    names, 499-502, 505
    .NET Framework
        designing COM compo-
            nents for, 716-728
        designing COM mem-
            bers for, 729-731
        designing COM objects
            for, 731-738
        COM, 53, 403-407
    versioning
        COM, 528-529
        .NET, 527-529
ClippedRectangle
    method, 1136, 1139
Closing event, 622-623

CLR (Common Language Runtime), 15
COM Interoperability. *See* COM Interoperability
core services, 52
exception object properties, 722
exposing COM connection points with, 598
  ComClassAttribute, 605-608
  ComSourceInterfaces-Attribute, 598-600
  defining source interfaces, 600-605
  design guidelines, 608-611
  Phone class, 602-605
  Windows Forms, 611-614, 620-625
hosting, 460-468
IDispatch implementation, 659-660
  compatible, 660-665
  internal, 660-665
IManagedObject, 658
IUnknown implementation, 657
JIT (just-in-time compiler), 21
managed code, 48
releasing COM objects, 109-110
unmanaged code, 48
versioning, 19
ClrCreateManagedInstance API, 468-471
CLS (Common Language Specification), 16, 868-870

CLSIDs
creating COM components in ASP.NET pages, 91
versioning, 530-531
COAUTHINFO structure, 873
CoClassAttribute (System.Runtime.Intero pServices namespace), 1258
coclasses. *See also* **classes**
converting, 180-182
CorRuntimeHost, 460-461
HTMLDocument, 234
HTMLStyleSheet, 1023
interfaces, manually defining, 1003-1009, 1016- 1019
InternetExplorer, 218-222, 231
MultiPurposeObject, 705
NetMeeting, 1007
type library transformations of classes, 449-451
CoCreateGuid API, 60
CoCreateInstanceEx, activating remote COM objects, 871-874
code
luring attacks, 306
managed, 48
  adapter objects, 905-909
  connection points, 218-235
  debugging COM Interoperability calls to unmanaged code, 315-319

  interaction with unmanaged code, 49-53, 69-71
  invoking unmanaged pointers in, 818-821
Registry, adding, 567-569
unmanaged, 48, 72
  adapter objects, 905-909
  debugging COM Interoperability calls from managed code, 315-319
  goals for interaction, 48-49
  interaction with managed code, 49-53, 69-71
  late binding, 404-407
  reflection, 482-488
  security, 49, 304-308
unmanaged StringValidator class
  C++, 385, 387-388
  JScript, 388-390
unsafe (C#), 849-852
code-access security, 21
/codebase (REGASM.EXE), 393-394, 1386
CoEEShutDownCOM, 492
collections
COM enumerations, 114
exposing, 524-527
COM
callbacks, 214-217, 226
classes, 54
  converting, 179-186
  creating instances, 99-101
  inheritance, 311-315

manually defining,
1022-1036
writing in C#, 514
clients, 53
defining exception
types, 520-522
names, 499-502, 505
returned error
codes/messages,
403-407
collections, enumerations,
114
compared to .NET
Framework, 55-57
component locations,
62-64
component names,
59-62
error handling, 66-68
object lifetimes, 68-69
programming model,
57-58
type compatibility, 64
type information, 58-59
type safety, 66
versioning, 64-66
components
apartment-threaded,
277-278
ASP.NET, 90-94
Both threading model,
733
categories, 569
connection points, 202,
214-235
debugging into, 315-319
designing for .NET
clients, 716-728
free-threaded, 277
late binding, 119-120

library names, 142
locations, 62-64
migration to .NET,
684-685
neutral, 277
referencing in Visual
Studio .NET, 78-84
referencing with SDK,
81-84
registration, 460-471
sliced interfaces,
743-747
Windows Registry, 62
core interoperability tools.
See TLBIMP.EXE;
TLBEXP.EXE;
REGASM.EXE
data types
BSTR, 149-150
converting, 143-162
converting .NET data
types into, 429,
432-433
CURRENCY, 148-149
DECIMAL, 148-149
HRESULT, 150-151
LPSTR, 149-150
LPWSTR, 149-150
SCODE, 150-151
Variant, 146-147
DCOM. See DCOM
definitions, manually
defining, 958-959
deploying .NET
applications, 126-137
enumerations, converting,
193-194
enums, manually defining,
1022
event sinks, 623-625

exposing enumerators to,
524-527
exposing events as
connection points
Windows Forms,
611-614, 620-625
with CLR, 598-611
without CLR, 592-597
extended interoperability
tools. See AXIMP.EXE;
REGSVCS.EXE
fonts, custom marshaling,
914-923
interfaces, 57-58, 506-508,
628
converting .NET
interfaces to, 447-449
custom attributes,
963-964
customizations,
998-1003
default implementations,
657-677
definitions, 628-629
dispinterface, 608,
982-984
dual, 58
dual interfaces,
975-981
error handling,
112-114
explicit interface
members, 655-656
HRESULTs, 656
IAmVisibleToAll, 479
IAssemblyCache, 1040
IConnectionPointConta
iner, 675-676
ICorRuntimeHost, 460

ICreateErrorInfo,
  727-728
IDebuggerInfo, 461
IDispatch, 54-55, 58,
  146-147, 654,
  659-672
IDispatchEx, 152-153
IEnumVARIANT,
  152-153
IGCHost, 460
IMarshal, 672-673
Implement Interface,
  option, 651-652
implementation,
  112-114
inheritance, 654-655,
  984-987
IObjectSafety, 676-677
IPersist, 654-656
IPersistStream,
  654-656
IPhoneEventHookup,
  596
IPhoneEvents, 596-597
IProvideClassInfo, 296,
  673-674, 705-706,
  734
IRecordInfo, 271
ISmartTagAction,
  635-636, 643-646, 654
ISmartTagRecognizer,
  635-636, 643-646, 654
IStream, 881, 883, 888
ISupportErrorInfo, 674,
  725-726
ITypeInfo, 152-153, 730
IUnknown, 54, 57, 68,
  70, 146-147, 654,
  657-659

IUnknown-Only
  interfaces, 964-974
IValidator, 461
language limitations,
  988-995, 998
manually defining,
  962-963
method signatures, 652
MultiPurposeObject,
  705
names, 500
non-public, 967
Office XP smart tags,
  634-636, 643-650,
  653-656
parameterized
  properties, 653-654
private members, 653
QueryInterface,
  110-112, 706
selecting members, 651
SetErrorInfo, 728
versioning, 65-66
Visual Studio .NET
  shortcuts, 650-653
invisibility, 477-482,
  562-565
members
  converting for .NET
    object models,
    434-447
  designing for .NET
    clients, 729-731
modules, converting,
  187-188
names, 59-62
.NET types, 678-679
objects, 53
  activating with
    CoCreateInstanceEx,
    871-874

  calling methods,
    101-109
  calling properties,
    101-109
  designing for .NET
    clients, 731-738
  IProvideClassInfo
    interface, 734
  Marshal.ReleaseCom-
    Object, 299-304
  passing, 115-118
  releasing, 109-110
  visualizations, 572
objects created in source
  code,
  Activator.CreateInstance
  method, 91
optional parameters,
  104-105
overview, 53-55
structures
  converting, 189-191
  manually defining,
    1019-1022
testing components from,
  535-536
threading, 275
  apartment states,
    277-282
  apartment types,
    276-277
  callbacks to .NET
    objects, 282-289
  HKEY_CLASSES_ROO
    T\CLSID\{CLSID}
    InProcServer32 string
    values, 276-277
  incompatible
    apartments, 291-292
type libraries, 58-59, 64

type systems, 64
typedefs, converting, 194-196
unions, converting, 191-192
utilities, 55-56
visibility, 477-482, 562-565
Visual Basic 6, 57
visualizations, 1196-1197
COM Interoperability, 51-53, 69-71
    debugging calls from managed code into unmanaged code, 315-319
    goals, 53
    GUIDs, 529
    performance monitoring, 320-321
    versioning, 528-529
COM+
    components, 96
    objects, 309-311
        exposing .NET objects as, 584-586
        installing in Component Services explorer, 309
COM+ Catalog, installation, 1059-1061
COM+ tab (Interactive Interop Tool), 1097-1100
COM-Callable Wrapper. See CCW
COM-compatible components. See binary-compatible components
ComAliasNameAttribute (System.Runtime.Interop Services namespace), 1258
ComClassAttribute, 560-562, 613

ComConversionLoss-Attribute (System. Runtime.InteropServices namespace), 1258
ComEventInterface-Attribute (System. Runtime.InteropServices namespace), 1258-1259
COMException, 728 (System.Runtime. InteropServices name-space), 1259-1260
ComFriendlyForm class, 611, 621, 623
ComImport-marked class, C#, 1026
ComImportAttribute (System.Runtime.Intero pServices namespace), 298, 1260
    COM interface implementations, 658
    custom attribute, 963
ComInterfaceType enumeration, 578-579, 1260
commands
    CLS (clearing Console screen), 868-870
    Project menu, Add Reference, 25
ComMemberType enumeration, 1261
Common Language Runtime. See CLR
Common Language Specification. See CLS
communication, bi-directional, 202
_ComObject, 71, 104, 229-232, 295-298, 422, 696, 734-735

compatibility, Visual Basic .NET, 38
compatible IDispatch CLR implementation, 660-665
compiler, C#, 1006
compilers, managed, 15
ComPlusInstaller class, 1097-1100
Component parameter, 508
Component Services explorer, installing COM+ objects, 309
ComponentAccessControl Attribute, 585
components. *See also* assemblies
    binary-compatible, 628-634
    COM
        apartment-threaded, 277-278
        ASP.NET, 90-94
        Both threading model, 733
        categories, 569
        connection points, 202, 214-235
        debugging into, 315-319
        free-threaded, 277
        library names, 142
        migration to .NET, 684-685
        neutral, 277
        referencing in Visual Studio .NET, 78-84
        referencing with SDK, 81-84

registration, 460-471
sliced interfaces,
743-747
Windows Registry, 62
COM+, 96
designing for .NET clients,
716-717
array parameters, 718,
720
array parmeters,
717-719
error reporting,
720-728
VARIANT parameters,
720
locations
.NET Framework,
62-64
COM, 62-64
names, COM compared to
.NET Framework, 59-62
.NET Framework, 380
C# StringValidator
class, 380-381
C++ StringValidator
class, 385-388
DirectX, 1106
JScript StringValidator
class, 388-390
Visual Basic 6
StringValidator class,
382-384
side-by-side, 18-19
testing from COM,
535-536
version policies, 19
versioning, 527-529
/componly
(REGSVCS.EXE), 1395

ComptibleImpl value,
IDispatchImplType
enumeration, 1283
ComRegisterFunction--
Attribute (System.
Runtime.InteropServices
namespace), 568, 1261
ComSourceInterfaces-
Attribute (System.
Runtime.InteropServices
namespace), 598-600,
611, 631, 1261
defining source interfaces,
600-605
COMTIIntrinsicsAttribute,
585
ComUnregisterFunction-
Attribute (System.
Runtime.InteropServices
namespace), 568, 1262
ComVisibleAttribute
(System.Runtime.Intero
pServices namespace),
562-565, 1262-1263
ComVisibleForm class,
479
concurrency, .NET
Framework, 275
Configure value, 1061
ConfigureComponents-
Only value, 1061
conformant arrays,
160-161
conformant varying
arrays, 161-162
ConformantArray1D
method, 161
connectable objects,
229-235

CONNECTDATA value type
(System.Runtime.I
nteropServices name-
space), 1263
connection points, COM
components, 202,
214-217
connectable objects,
229-235
event handling, 219-222
lazy connection point
initialization, 227-229
managed code, 218-222
type library importer
transformations, 222-227,
235-240
Console
clearing screen, 868-870
input, responding to
immediately, 865-868
ConsoleDisplay class, 204
ConsoleMessage method,
206
constants, 709-710
ConstructionEnabled-
Attribute, 585
constructors
adding to RCW class, 182
usage guidelines, 513-514
constructs, 710
containers, ActiveX
hosting Windows Forms
controls in, 471-477
Control property, 621
controls
ActiveX, 120-121
converting, 196-198
referencing in Visual
Studio .NET, 121-122

referencing with .NET Framework SDK, 122-123
Web browser example, 123, 126
TreeView, 624
WebBrowser, 236
events, 241-242, 244-245
referencing ActiveX controls, 123, 126
Windows Forms, hosting in ActiveX containers, 471-477
ConvertAssemblyToType-Lib method (TypeLibConverter class), 1356
C#, 1050
C++, 1050
converting
assemblies, 426
exported type library, 428
helpstrings, 427
LCID, 427
library names, 427-428
type library identification, 426-427
version numbers, 427
classes, 449-451
COM members for .NET object models, 434
.NET events, 446-447
.NET fields, 444-446
.NET methods, 434-441
.NET properties, 441-444
enumerations, 453-454, 457

.NET data types, 429, 432-433
.NET interfaces to COM interfaces, 447-449
value types, 452-453
ConvertTypeLibToAssembly assembly, 1048
ConvertTypeLibToAssembly method (TypeLibConverter class), 1041-1042, 1356-1357
creating assemblies from type libraries 1042-1044
parameters, 1357
Copy method, Marshal class, 1297-1298
CopyFileEx API, callbacks, 810-815
CorExitProcess, 492-493
CorRuntimeHost class, 468
CorRuntimeHost coclass, 460-461
Counter field, 1112
CreateInstance method, 468
CreateObject method, creating instances, 60, 99-101
CreateRemoteInstance method, 874
CreateSink method, 239
CreateSoundBufferFromFile method, 1112
CreateSurfaceFromFile method, 1112, 1118
CreateTargetApplication value, 1061
CreateTypeInfo method, 1068

CreateWrapperOfType, 298-299, 1298-1299
creating. *See* **writing**
CURRENCY data type, 148-149
CurrencyWrapper, 115, 119, 1263-1264
CurrentAudioTitle property, 1220
CurrentChannelCount property, 1220
CurrentPreset property, 1217, 1229
CurrentSampleRate property, 1220
custom attributes, 28, 30
ApplicationAccessControl Attribute, 584
ApplicationActivation-Attribute, 584
ApplicationCrmEnabled-Attribute, 584
ApplicationIDAttribute, 584
ApplicationNameAttribute, 584
ApplicationQueuing-Attribute, 584
AssemblyKeyFileAttribute, 381
AssemblyVersionAttribute, 530
AttributeUsageAttribute, 1223
AutoCompleteAttribute, 585
AutomationProxyAttribute, 581-582
C#, 36-38
C++, 43-45

ClassInterface(Class-
   InterfaceType.AutoDual),
   435
ClassInterfaceAttribute,
   556-560
COM interfaces, 963-964
   ComImportAttribute,
   963
   GuidAttribute, 963
   InterfaceTypeAttribute,
   964
ComClassAttribute,
   560-562, 605-608, 613
ComImportAttribute, 298,
   658
ComponentAccessControl
   Attribute, 585
ComRegisterFunction-
   Attribute, 568
ComSourceInterfaces-
   Attribute, 598-605, 611,
   631
COMTIIntrinsicsAttribute,
   585
ComUnregisterFunction-
   Attribute, 568
ComVisibleAttribute,
   562-565
ConstructionEnabled-
   Attribute, 585
controlling apartments that
   .NET components reside
   on, 278-280
creating, 29-30
custom marshalers,
   364-366
customizing structures, 829
   FieldOffsetAttribute,
   832-833
   MarshalAsAttribute,
   834-839

StructLayoutAttribute,
   829-832, 839-844
DescriptionAttribute, 359,
   585
DispIdAttribute, 574-578,
   601, 651
DISPIDs, 366, 370
DllImportAttribute, 772,
   795
EventClassAttribute, 585
EventTrackingEnabled-
   Attribute, 585
ExampleAttribute, 354
ExceptionClassAttribute,
   585
exported type libraries, 428
FieldOffsetAttribute,
   customizing structures,
   832-833
GetCustomAttributes, 1220
GuidAttribute, 331, 427,
   574
helpstring, 358-363
IDispatchImplAttribute,
   IDispatch implementation,
   660-661
IDL, 371-372
IISIntrinsicsAttribute, 585
ILASM.EXE, 351-356
ImportedFromTypeLib-
   Attribute, 331
InAttribute
   customizing data flow,
   553-554
   export behavior, 438
   marking array
   paraetmers, 792-794
InterfaceQueuingAttribute,
   585
InterfaceTypeAttribute,
   578-579, 601

JustInTimeActivation-
   Attribute, 585
KeywordAttribute, 509
LayoutKind enumeration,
   829-830
LCIDConversion, 582-583
LoadBalancingSupported-
   Attribute, 585
MarshalAsAttribute, 895,
   898, 1222
   C# signatures, 899-901
   COM interface short-
   cuts, 651
   customizing arrays,
   549-550
   customizing data types,
   541-549, 552-553
   customizing structures,
   834-839
   detecting errors in,
   552-553
   Inherited property, 546
   parameters, 898-900
   syntax, 334-340
   UnmanagedType enu-
   meration, 542-545,
   549-552
   UnmanageType values,
   834
Microsoft.VisualBasic.
   CompilerServices.
   StandardModuleAttribute,
   356
MustRunInClientContext-
   Attribute, 585
ObjectPoolingAttribute,
   585
OptionalAttribute, 583-584
OutAttribute, 786
   customizing data flow,
   553-554

export behavior, 438
marking array
     parameters, 792-794
parameters, 830
PreserveSigAttribute, 436,
     579
PresetEnumAttribute,
     1220-1223
PrivateComponentAttribute,
     585
ProgIdAttribute, customiz-
     ing registration, 566
pseudo, 33
reflection, 31-33
RestrictedAttribute,
     508-509
SecureMethodAttribute,
     585
SecurityPermissionAttribute
     , 305
SecurityRoleAttribute, 585
STAThreadAttribute, 1100
StructLayoutAttribute, 270
     customizing structure
          layout, 554-556
     customizing structures,
          829-832
     LayoutKind enumera-
          tion, 554
SuppressUnmanagedCode
     SecurityAttribute, 308
SynchronizationAttribute,
     276, 586
System.EnterpriseServices
     namespace, 584-586
System.FlagsAttribute,
     1022
System.MTAThread-
     Attribute, 278

System.Reflection.
     lAssemblyDescription-
     Attribute, 1067
System.Runtime.Compiler
     Services.MethodImpl-
     Attribute, 276
System.Runtime.InteropSe
     rvices namespace, 1250
     AutomationProxy-
          Attribute, 1254
     ClassInterfaceAttribute,
          1256-1257
     CoClassAttribute, 1258
     ComAliasNameAttribute
          , 1258
     ComConversionLoss-
          Attribute, 1258
     ComEventInterface-
          Attribute, 1258-1259
     ComRegisterFunction-
          Attribute, 1261
     ComSourceInterfaces-
          Attribute, 1261
     ComUnregisterFunctio
          nAttribute, 1262
     ComVisibleAttribute,
          1262-1263
     DispIdAttribute,
          1265-1266
     GuidAttribute, 1278
     IDispatchImplAttribute,
          1282
     ImportedFromTypeLib-
          Attribute, 1284
     InterfaceTypeAttribute,
          1285
     LCIDConversion-
          Attribute, 1290-1291
     PrimaryInterop-
          AssemblyAttribute,
          1348

ProgIdAttribute, 1349
TypeLibFuncAttribute,
     1358
TypeLibTypeAttribute,
     1359
TypeLibVarAttribute,
     1359
System.Security.Suppress-
     UnmanagedCodeSecurity
     Attribute, 308
System.STAThreadAttribute,
     278
     in ASP.NET, 279-280
     in C#, 279
TransactionAttribute, 586
usage guidelines versus
     interfaces, 508-510
VB .NET modules,
     356-358
Visual Basic .NET, 40-42
**custom marshalers, 248,
364-366, 880, 895-896**
adapter objects, 901-903,
     905-909
     ICustomAdapter inter-
          face implementation,
          909
     marshaling by value
          versus reference,
          910-913
arrays, 943-947
by value, 914
     FontMarshaler class,
          914-918
     .NET Windows Form
          consumer, 918-920
     Visual Basic 6 .NET
          form, 921-923
CCWs, 880-882
     adapter objects,
          904-905

deterministic release of resources, 947-952

exposing Stream as IStream, 932-943

data type transformations without, 882-883

    ComStream adapter class exposing IStream implementation as .NET streams, 883-889

    ManagedIStream class exposing Stream objects through IStream implementation, 889-895

    .NET definition of UCOMIStream in C#, 883, 888

deterministic release of resources, 947-952

FontMarshaler class, 365

ICustomMarshaler interface, 896-898

Interop Marshaler without marshaling, 880

limitations, 952-953

MarshalAsAttribute, 895, 898-901

marshaling between .NET and COM fonts, 914

    FontMarshaler class, 914-918

    .NET Windows Form consumer, 918-920

    Visual Basic 6 .NET form, 921-923

marshaling between System.IO.Stream and IStream, 923-943

.NET class implementation, 909

RCWs, 880-882

    adapter objects, 904-906

    exposing IStream and Stream, 923-932

System.Runtime.Interop-Services, 1252

CustomCCW class

exposing Stream as IStream, 932-943

MarshalManagedToNative, 948-952

customizing

arrays, MarshalAsAttribute, 549-550

C# definitions of IPersist and IPersistStream Interfaces, 986-987

COM interfaces, 998-1003

data flow, 553

    InAttribute, 553-554

    OutAttribute, 553-554

data types, 540-549, 552-553

PIAs, 693-694

registration, 566

    adding arbitrary registration code, 567-569

    custom registration functions, 570-574

    ProgIdAttribute, 566

    System.Guid.ToString, 570

    unregistration functions, 569-570

structure layout, 554-556

structures, 829

    FieldOffsetAttribute, 832-833

    formatted classes, 839-844

    MarshalAsAttribute, 834-839

    StructLayoutAttribute, 829-832

    structure inspection, 844-847

translation of IWMPEffects to C#, 967

CustomRCW class, exposing IStream and Stream, 923-932

D

Dancing Cat visualization, 1235-1243

data flow, customizing, 553

InAttribute, 553-554

OutAttribute, 553-554

data types. *See also* **types**

blittable, 98

COM

    BSTR, 149-150

    converting, 143-162

    converting into .NET, 429, 432-433

    CURRENCY, 148-149

    DECIMAL, 148-149

    HRESULT, 150-151

    LPSTR, 149-150

    LPWSTR, 149-150

    SCODE, 150-151

converting, 143-144, 429, 432-433

    arrays, 433

    combining types, 145-151

    complex types, 152-162

custom marshaling,
   895-896
   adapter objects,
      901-909
   arrays, 943-947
   deterministic release of
      resources, 947- 952
   ICustomMarshaler
      interface, 896-898
   limitations, 952-953
   MarshalAsAttribute,
      895, 898-901
   marshaling between
      .NET and COM fonts,
      914-923
   marshaling between
      System.IO.Stream and
      IStream, 923-943
   marshaling by value
      versus reference,
      910-913
   .NET class implementa-
      tions, 909
   by value, 914-923
customizing, 540-549,
   552-553
ILASM.EXE, 332-333,
   340-342
.NET, 429, 432-433,
   516-517
System.IntPtr, 248-250
transformations without
   custom marshaling,
   882-883
   ComStream adapter
      class, 883-889
   ManagedIStream class,
      889-895
   NET definition of
      UCOMIStream in C#,
      883, 888

usage guidelines, 516
   nested arrays, 518-519
   OLE Automation,
      516-518
   pointers, 518
   user-defined value
      types, 519
Variant, 146-147
Win32, 778-781
DCOM (distributed COM)
objects, 54, 309-311
   creating remote objects,
      309-310
   .NET remoting, 310
   Type.GetTypeFromCLSID
      method, 309
   Type.GetTypeFromProgID
      method, 309
debugging, into COM
components, 315-319
DECIMAL data type,
148-149
Declare statement
   customizing, 795
   PInvoke, 773-775
Declare statement
(PInvoke)
   changing string behavior,
      797-799
   function names, 796
DeclaredOnly flag, 1220
default COM interface
implementations, 657
   IDispatch, 659-665
   IUnknown, 657-659
default interfaces,
defining classes in IDL
files, 704-707
default values, 1061
   language limitations of
      COM interfaces,
      994-995, 998

definitions (.NET), 628
   C#
      addImport and addRule
         parameters, 994
      C# IHTMLStyleSheet
         interface, 1035-1036
      IHTMLStyleSheet
         interface, 996-998
      IPersist and
         IPersistStream
         Interfaces, 985-987,
         1000-1001
      IRunningAppCollection
         , 976-979
      NetMeeting Coclass
         interface, 1009,
         1016-1018
   COM
      interfaces, 628-629
      manually defining,
         958-959
   HTML Object Library,
      1003
   IDL
      IHTMLStyleSheet
         interface, 988-989
      INetMeetingEvents
         dispinterface and
         INetMeeting interface,
         1007-1008
      IPersist and
         IPersistStream
         Interfaces, 985
      IRunningAppCollection,
         975-976
      IWMPEffects interface,
         964
   .NET Framework, 1021
   VB .NET
      addImport and addRule
         parameters, 994

DispHTMLStyleSheet interface and the HTMLStyleSheet coclass interface, 1004-1006
IHTMLStyleSheet interface, 991
IRunningAppCollection, 980-981

/delaysign (AXIMP.EXE), 1391

/delaysign (TLBIMP.EXE), 1377

delegates
as function pointers, 811-812
CopyFileEx, 812-815
SetConsoleCtrlHandler, 815-817
.NET callbacks, 204-208
SourceInterfaceName_
MethodNameEvent-
Handler, 235
System.Runtime.InteropSer
vices namespace, 1345

DeleteSubKey method, 860

deployment, 19-20
assemblies, 532-535
.NET applications, 126-130, 133-137
PIAs, 694-696
XCOPY, 20
zero-impact, 20

Desc property, 644-645
DESCKIND enumeration, 1264
Description property, 1216-1217, 1233
DescriptionAttribute, 359, 585

DESCUNION value type (System.Runtime.Intero pServices namespace), 1264
design
COM components for .NET clients, 716-717
array parameters, 717-720
error reporting, 720-728
VARIANT parameters, 720
COM members for .NET clients, 729
passing error information, 731
passing interface pointers to anything, 729
passing type information, 730-731
COM objects for .NET clients
IProvideClassInfo, 734
naming guidelines, 734-735
performance, 735-738
resource management, 731-733
threading, 733
guidelines for exposing .NET events as COM connection points, 608-611

DestroyStructure method (Marshal class), 1299
DetachSink method, 239
device software, 14
DevTagAction class, 635, 643-645

DevTagRecognizer class, 635, 643-644
diagnotics, PInvoke signatures, 778
dialog boxes, Implement Interface, 748
digital signing.
See signing
digitSpacing field, 1147
DigitWidths field, 1131, 1147
DINPUT8STRING-CONSTANTS class, 356
DINPUT8STRING-CONSTANTS module, 357
DirectMusicPerformance interface, 283-285
directories, System32, 25
DirectX, 1106
Advanced Version of E-mail Attack, 1171-1172
compiling, 1172
DirectX namespace, 1183, 1193-1194
EmailAttack class, 1178, 1182
Win32.cs file, 1172, 1178
E-mail Attack. *See* E-mail Attack
files
heartland.sty, 284
heartland2.sgt, 284
Layer class. *See* Layer class
.NET components, 1106
Screen class. *See* Screen class
type library errors, 294

Visual Basic .NET code
COM callbacks running on threads, 287-289
callbacks on separate threads, 283-286
Web site, 1106
DirectX 7 for Visual Basic Type Library, 284
DirectX for VB, 1106
DirectX namespace, 1111, 1118, 1135, 1138, 1143, 1146, 1183, 1193-1194
dispatch identifiers. *See* **DISPIDs**
DispatchWrapper class (System.Runtime.Interop Services namespace), 1264-1265
DispatchWrapper wrapper, 115
DispHTMLStyleSheet interface, 1004-1006
DispIdAttribute (System. Runtime.InteropServices namespace), 574-578, 601, 651, 1265-1266
DISPIDs (dispatch identifiers), 173, 366, 370
converting, 173-174
DISPID NEWENUM -4, 175-176
DISPID Value 0, 174-175
DispIdAttribute, 574-578
dispinterfaces (COM interfaces), 982-984
Display class, 206
DisplayPropertyPage method, 1201, 1220-1221

Dispose method, 69, 1121, 1131, 1134-1136, 1151-1152, 1155-1156, 1167, 1171
DISPPARAMS value type (System.Runtime. InteropServices namespace), 1266
distributed COM. *See* **DCOM**
"DLL Hell", 16
defined, 17
.NET Framework solution to, 17-18
side-by-side components, 18-19
version policies, 19
DLL/COM redirection, 17
dlldatax.c file, 292
DllGetClassObject method, 392
DllImportAttribute (System.Runtime.Intero pServices namespace), 772, 1266-1267
choosing DLL locations dynamically, 863-865
choosing DLL names dynamically, 863-865
customizing, 795
DllImportAttribute (PInvoke)
ExactSpelling, 799
functio names, 796
GetLastError parameter, 800-801
PreserveSig parameter, 803-807
SetLastError parameter, 800-801
string behavior, 797-799

DllImportAttribute pseudo-custom attribute, 776-777
DLLs
assembly names, 502
choosing locations dynamically, 863-865
choosing names dynamically, 863-865
MSCOREE.DLL, 460, 468
Office.dll, 301
PInvoke signatures, 1432-1433
GDI32.DLL, 1433, 1442
KERNEL32.DLL, 1442, 1461
OLE32.DLL, 1461, 1470
SHELL32.DLL, 1470-1471
USER32.DLL, 1472, 1486
PowerPoint.dll, 301
static entry points, 772
DUMPBIN.EXE, 772
Platform Invocation Services. See PInvoke
do-it-yourself marshaling, 248
BSTR types, 249
C# unsafe code versus System.Runtime.Interop-Services APIs, 250-254
obtaining value type addresses, 254-255
obtaining value type sizes, 255-258
manipulating IntPtr types, 258
by-reference null value types, 264-265

C-style array fields,
   262-264
null pointers, 259
SAFEARRAYs, 273-275
struct, 258-262
variants, 266-267,
   270-272
metadata signatures, 249
System.IntPtr data type,
   248-250
**DownloadBegin interface,
239**
Draw method, 1147-1149
**DrawAt method, 1136,
1139-1140, 1143-1144,
1146**
**DrawSurface method,
1112, 1139**
**dual interfaces (COM
interfaces), 58, 975-979,
981**
**DUMPBIN.EXE, static
entry points, 772**
**DWebBrowserEvents
interface, 226**
**DWebBrowserEvents2
interface, 226**
DX7VB.DLL, 284
**DXCallback method, 285,
289**
dxSurface method, 1136
dynamic assemblies
   creating
      *ConvertTypeLibTo-
      Assembly method,
      1042-1044*
      *ImporterEventKind
      enumeration, 1044*
      *ItypeLibImporterNotify
      Sink interface, 1044*

*ResolveRef method,
   1045-1046*
*setting asmFileName
   to string, 1043*
*TypeLibImporterFlags
   enumeration,
   1043-1044*
saving, 1048-1050
dynamic type libraries
creating, 1050-1055
saving, 1055

E

**E-mail Attack (DirectX
application), 1106**
Advanced Version,
   1171-1172
   compiling, 1172
   *DirectX namespace,
   1183, 1193-1194*
   *EmailAttack class,
   1178, 1182*
   *Win32.cs file, 1172,
   1178*
AnimatedEnvelopePicture
   class, 1143-1146
AnimatedPicture class,
   1139
   fields, 1140
   methods, 1140-1143
   properties, 1140
Character class
   fields, 1157
   *methods, 1158,
   1161-1162*
   private fields, 1158
EmailAttackForm class,
   1166-1168, 1171
enumerations, 1120

Envelope class, 1162
   *methods, 1162,
   1165-1166*
   public fields, 1162
FrontLayer class, 1154
Game class, 1111,
   1119-1121, 1131-1133,
   1166
   private fields, 1121
   properties, 1121
   public fields, 1120
GroundLayer class, 1153
IntroScreen class,
   1156-1157
Layer class, 1150
   fields, 1150
   methods, 1150-1152
NumberPicture class, 1146
   *methods, 1147,
   1149-1150*
   private fields, 1147
Picture class, 1133-1134
   *methods, 1136,
   1138-1139*
   properties, 1136
programmer's perspective,
   1108-1109
   compiling, 1111
   *picture management,
   1111*
   source files, 1109-1111
Screen class, 1155-1156
Sound class, 1133-1136
user's perspective, 1107
Util class, 1112
   *methods, 1112,
   1118-1119*
   public fields, 1112
effects. *See* visualizations
**ELEMDESC value type
(System.Runtime.Interop
Services namespace),
1267**

**E-mailAttack class, 1178,
1182**
**E-mailAttackForm class,
1166-1171**
**E-mailAttackForm
method, 1167**
encapsulation, 209
**EnterFullScreen event,
1217**
entry points
calling conventions,
799-800
exact spelling setting, 799
FunctionName, 796
FunctionNameW, 796
static, 772
callbacks, 810-821
*choosing DLL locations
dynamically, 863-865*
*choosing DLL names
dynamically, 863-865*
*customizing structures,
829-847*
DUMPBIN.EXE, 772
*passing structures,
821-829*
*Platform Invocation
Services. See PInvoke
variable-length s
tructures, 847-849*
**EntryPoint parameter,
1266**
**EntryPoint property, 36,
40, 43**
**EnumConnectionPoints
method
(IConnectionPoint-
Container interface), 216**
**EnumerableToDispatch-
Marshaler class, 1370**

enumerations
AssemblyRegistration
Flags, 1056-1057, 1096
ClassInterfaceType,
556-560
COM, 193-194, 1022
ComInterfaceType,
578-579
E-mail Attack, 1120
ExporterEventKind,
1052-1055, 1068
ImporterEventKind, 1044,
1068
InstallationFlags, 1099
InstallationFlags
enumeration, 1060-1061
IWMPEffects interface,
1204-1208
LayoutKind, 554, 829-830
MessageTypes, 1068
names, 707-709
REGKIND, 1068
System.Runtime.InteropSe
rvices namespace
*AssemblyRegistration-
Flags, 1254*
CALLCONV, 1255
*CallingConvention,
1255-1256*
CharSet, 1256
*ClassInterfaceType,
1257*
*ComInterfaceType,
1260*
ComMemberType, 1261
DESCKIND, 1264
*ExporterEventKind,
1268-1269*
FUNCFLAGS, 1272
FUNCKIND, 1273
GCHandleType, 1277
IDispatchImplType,

1283
IDLFLAG, 1283
*IMPLTYPEFLAGS,
1283*
*ImporterEventKind,
1284*
INVOKEKIND, 1287
LayoutKind, 1290
LIBFLAGS, 1291
PARAMFLAG, 1347
SYSKIND, 1354
TYPEFLAGS, 1355
TYPEKIND, 1355
*TypeLibExporterFlags,
1357*
*TypeLibFuncFlags,
1358*
*TypeLibImporterFlags,
1358*
*TypeLibTypeFlags,
1359*
TypeLibVarFlags, 1359
*UnmanagedType,
1367-1368*
VarEnum, 1369-1370
VARFLAGS, 1370
System.Threading.
ApartmentState, 280
TagTypes, 643-644
type library, 453-454, 457
TypeLibExporterFlags,
1051
TypeLibImporterFlags,
1043-1044
UnmanagedType, 337-338,
542-545, 549-552
usage guidelines, 514-516
VarEnum, 337-338
Verbs, 643
enumerators
COM collections, 114
exposing to COM, 524-527

EnumeratorToEnumVarian tMarshaler class, 1371
Envelope class, 1162
  methods, 1162, 1165-1166
  public fields, 1162
Envelope method, 1162
EnvelopeGrid field, 1120
EnvelopePicture field, 1120
envelopes (E-mail Attack game). *See Game class*
EnvelopeUnderneath property, 1162
envelopeX field, 1158
envelopeY field, 1158
Environment class, 1171
Equals method, 743
ErrorCode, 722
errors. *See also* **troubleshooting**
  assembly content modifications, 328
  creating COM objects, 101
  handling
    COM compared to .NET Framework, 66-68
    interface implementation, 112-114
    Win32 APIs, 800-807
  MarshalAsAttribute, 552-553
  reporting, 720-721
    HRESULTs, 721-722
    setting information, 722-723
    setting information in Visual Basic 6, 723-724
    setting information in Visual C++, 725-728

  returned error codes/ messages
    unmanaged C++, 404-407
    Visual Basic 6, 403-404
  type libraries, 294
ErrorWrapper class (System.Runtime.Intero pServices namespace), 1267-1268
ErrorWrapper wrapper, 115
ERROR_REFTOINVALID-ASSEMBLY value, 1052, 1268
ERROR_REFTOINVALID-TYPELIB value, 1044, 1284
event handling
  ActiveX
    events, 240—245
    importer transforma-tions, 235-240
  connectable objects, 229-235
  hookup, 603-604
  Internet Explorer
    .NET events, 224-227
    raw connection points, 219-222
  lazy connection point initialization, 227-229
  Phone class, 597
  type library importer transformations, 222-227, 235-240
EventClassAttribute, 585
EventNameEventArgs class, 609
events, 592
  Activated, 625
  ActiveX, 240-245

  adding for source interfaces, 186
  CallerId, 592-593
  Closing, 622-623
  COM
    connectable objects, 229-235
    handling in managed code, 218-222
    lazy connection point initialization, 227-229
    type library importer transformations, 222-227
  EnterFullScreen, 1217
  ExitFullScreen, 1217
  exposing as COM connection points
    Windows Forms, 611-614, 620-625
    with CLR, 598-611
    without CLR, 592-597
  handling. *See* event handling
  InputLanguageChanging, 622-623
  manually defining, 1003-1009, 1016-1017, 1019
  MediaChange, 1217, 1220
  members, 229-232
  .NET Framework
    callbacks, 208-214
    handling, 488-489
  NOTIF_TYPE-CONVERTED, 1052
  OnCallerId, 596
  OnRing, 596
  QueryAccessibilityHelp, 623
  Ring, 592-593

sinks, 623-625

type library transformations, 446-447

Validating, 612, 622-623

WebBrowser control, 241-245

WindowResize, 226

EventTrackingEnabled-Attribute, 585

ExactSpelling (entry point name), 799, 1266

ExampleAttribute, 354

/exapp (REGSVCS.EXE), 1395

EXCEPINFO value type (System.Runtime.Interop Services namespace), 1268

ExceptionClassAttribute, 585

exceptions

COMException, 728

defining new exceptions, 520-522

HRESULTs

error information, 404

HRESULT to, 1400, 1406-1407, 1413

to HRESULT transformations, 1416-1417, 1423, 1429

InvalidCastException, 289-299

InvalidOperationException, 403

.NET methods called back from COM, 286

properties, 722

returned error codes/ messages

unmanaged C++, 404-407

Visual Basic 6, 403-404

System.Runtime.Interop-Services namespace

COMException, 1259-1260

ExternalException, 1271

InvalidComObject-Exception, 1286

InvalidOleVariantType Exception, 1286-1287

MarshalDirective-Exception, 1344-1345

SafeArrayRank-Mismatch-Exception, 1352

SafeArrayTypeMismatc hException, 1352-1353

SEHException, 1353

TypeLoadException, 313, 392, 403

user-defined, 521-523

Win32 errors, 803-807

ExitFullScreen event, 1217

ExpandoToDispatchEx-Marshaler class, 1371-1372

ExpectExistingTypeLib value, 1061

explicit members, 655-656

Explicit value, 1290

exported type libraries, 428

Exporter class, 1083-1084, 1086-1092

Exporter tab (Interactive Interop Tool), 1083-1084, 1086-1092

Exporter.cs, 1084, 1086-1092

ExporterEventKind enumeration

(System.Runtime.Interop Services namespace), 1052-1055, 1068, 1268-1269

exporters (type library), 394-397

COM-Callable Wrappers. *See* CCWs

generating type libraries, 395

REGASM.EXE, 395

Register for COM Interop option, 395

TLBEXP.EXE, 395-396

TypeLibConverter class, 395

MarshalAsAttribute C# signatures, 900-901

exportOpenButton_Click method, 1100

ExtensibleClassFactory class (System.Runtime.Interop Services namespace), 1269-1271

ExtensibleClassFactory. RegisterObjectCreation-Callback method, 314

ExternalException (System.Runtime.Interop Services namespace), 1271

/extlb (REGSVCS.EXE), 1395

extraLifeSound field, 1121

F

FACILITY_URT (HRESULTs), 393

FAILED method, 347

failure HRESULTs, 579-580, 721

ErrorCode, 722
setting error information, 722-723
setting error information in Visual Basic 6, 723
FastCall value, CallingConvention enumeration, 1255
/fc (REGSVCS.EXE), 1395
FieldOffsetAttribute (System.Runtime.Interop Services namespace), 832-833, 1271-1272
fields
AnimatedPicture class, 1140
audioTitle, 1217
channelCount, 1217
Character class, 1157-1158
Layer class, 1150
private
Character class, 1158
Game class, 1121
NumberPicture class, 1147
public
Envelope class, 1162
Game class, 1120
type library transformations, 444-446
usage guidelines, versus properties, 510-511
Util class, 1112
File Signing Tool. *See* SignCode.exe
filenames, DLLs, 690
files
DirectX
heartland.sty, 284
heartland2.sgt, 284

dlldatax.c, 292
Win32.cs, 1172, 1178
FILETIME value type (System.Runtime.Interop-Services namespace), 1272
FillRect method, 271
Finalize method, 743
FindOrCreateTargetApplic ation value, 1061
fixed-length arrays, 157-158
flags
DeclaredOnly, 1220
hasTransparentColor, 1138
ImporterEventKind enumeration, 1044
parameter, 1051, 1357
TypeLibImporterFlags enumeration, 1043
FontMarshaler class, custom marshaling, 365, 914-918
.NET Windows Form consumer, 918-920
Visual Basic 6 .NET form, 921-923
fonts, custom marshaling, 914
FontMarshaler class, 914-918
.NET Windows Form consumer, 918-920
Visual Basic 6 .NET form, 921-923
Form class, 611-612, 1171
format specifiers, GUIDs, 570
formatted classes, customizing structures, 839-844

forms
ComFriendlyForm, 623
Visual Basic 6, FontMarshaler custom marshaler, 921-923
Windows Forms
exposing events to COM, 611-614, 620-625
FontMarshaler custom marshaler, 918-920
Interactive Interop Tool, 1100-1101
frameHeight field, 1140, 1146
frames field, 1140
framesInRow field, 1140
framesSinceDeath field, 1158
frameWidth field, 1140
Framework Services Installation Utility. *See* REGSVCS.EXE
Free method (GCHandle value type), 1275
Free string value, 276
free-threaded components, 277
free-threaded marshaler. FTM, 282
FreeBSTR method (Marshal class), 1299-1300
FreeCoTaskMem method (Marshal class), 1300
FreeHGlobal method (Marshal class), 1300
frequency, 1199
frequency field, 1140, 1150
FromGlobalAccessCache method (Runtime-Environment class), 1351

front buffer surfaces, 1118

FrontLayer class, 1154

FTM (free-threaded marshaler), 282

fully qualified names, C#, 61-62

FUNCDESC value type (System.Runtime.Interop Services namespace), 1272

FUNCFLAGS enumeration (System.Runtime.Interop Services namespace), 1272

FUNCKIND enumeration (System.Runtime.Interop Services namespace), 1273

FunctionName entry point, 796

FunctionNameW entry point, 796

functions

GetLastError, 800

GetWindowsDirectory, 784-788

KERNEL32.DLL, 774-777, 797

Microsoft.VisualBasic.Left, 788

PInvoke

case-sensitivity, 774

names, 796

PInvoke signatures, 1432-1433

GDI32.DLL, 1433, 1442

KERNEL32.DLL, 1442, 1461

OLE32.DLL, 1461, 1470

SHELL32.DLL, 1470-1471

USER32.DLL, 1472, 1486

pointers, 810-811

delegates as, 811-817

invoking unmanaged pointers in managed code, 818-821

QueryPerformanceCounter, 774

QueryPerformance-Frequency, 774-777

registration, 570-574

SetConsoleCtrlHandler, delegates as, 815-817

SetVolumeLabel, 783-784

shutdown, MSCOREE.DLL, 492-493

unregistration, 569-570

Win32

GetConsoleScreen-BufferInfo, 821-829

GetLastError, 800

G

GAC (global assembly cache), 24-25, 63

compared to System32 directory, 25

compared to Windows Registry, 64

installing assemblies, 392, 649-650

gacutil.exe, 24, 1040

Game class, 1111, 1119-1121, 1131-1133, 1154, 1166

private fields, 1121

properties, 1121

public fields, 1120

Game method, 1121

Game.Render method, 1171

GameStates enumeration, E-mail Attack, 1120

garbage collection

GC.Collect, 301-302

Marshal.ReleaseComObject, 299-304

PowerPoint, 301-304

Garbage Collector, premature collecting, 852-853, 856, 859-862

GC.Collect, 301-302

GCHandle class, 250, 270, 306

GCHandle value type (System.Runtime.Interop Services namespace), 1273-1275

conversion operators, GCHandle/IntPtr, 1276-1277

methods

AddrOfPinnedObject, 1275

Alloc, 1275

Free, 1275

properties

IsAllocated, 1275

Target, 1276

GCHandle/IntPtr conversion operator, GCHandle value type, 1276-1277

GCHandleType enumeration (System.Runtime.InteropServices namespace), 1277

GDI32.DLL, PInvoke signatures, 1433, 1442

GenerateGuidForType method (Marshal class), 1301

GenerateProgIdForType method (Marshal class), 1301

get accessors, 442

GetActiveObject method (Marshal class), 1301

getBonusSound field, 1121

GetCapabilities method, 1200

GetClassID method, 654

GetComInterfaceForObject method (Marshal class), 1302

GetComObjectData method (Marshal class), 1303

GetComSlotForMethodInfo method (Marshal class), 1303

GetConsoleScreenBufferInfo function, 821-829

GetCurrentPreset method, 1201

GetCustomAttributes, 1220

GetDisplayNameForAssembly method, 1067

GetEndComSlot method (Marshal class), 1303

GetEnumerator method, 440, 524-527

GetExceptionCode method (Marshal class), 1303-1304

GetExceptionPointers method (Marshal class), 1304

GetExportedTypes method, 1097

GetFrequency method, 1225

GetHashCode method, 743

GetHINSTANCE method (Marshal class), 1304

GetHRForException method (Marshal class), 1304-1305

GetHRForLastWin32Error method (Marshal class), 1305

GetIDispatchForObject method (Marshal class), 1305-1306

GetIDsOfNames method, 662

GetInstance method, 897-898

GetITypeInfoForType method (Marshal class), 1306

GetIUnknownForObject method (Marshal class), 1306-1307

GetLastError function, 800

GetLastWin32Error method (Marshal class), 1307

GetManagedCategoryGuid method, 1057, 1349

GetManagedThunkForUnmanagedMethodPtr method (Marshal class), 1307

GetMethodInfoForComSlot method (Marshal class), 1308

GetNativeDataSize method, 897, 1282

GetNativeVariantForObject method (Marshal class), 1308-1309

GetObjectAttribute method
  calling, 260
  .NET signature, 260

GetObjectForIUnknown method (Marshal class), 1309

GetObjectForNativeVariant method (Marshal class), 272, 1309

GetObjectsForNativeVariants method (Marshal class), 1310

GetPresetCount method, 1201

GetPresetTitle method, 1201, 1220, 1225

GetPrimaryInteropAssembly method, 1047-1048, 1357

GetPrivateProfileSectionNames API, 789-791

GetProgIdForType method (RegistrationServices class), 1057, 1350

GetRecordInfoFromTypeInfo method, 271

GetRegistrableTypesInAssembly method, 1057, 1350

GetRuntimeDirectory method (RuntimeEnvironment class), 1351

GetSite
    method, 729
    .NET signature, 729
GetStartComSlot method
    (Marshal class),
    1310-1311
GetSystemVersion
    method
    (RuntimeEnvironment
    class), 1352
GetThreadFromFiberCookie
    method (Marshal class),
    1311
GetTitle method, 1201
GetType method, 511-512
GetTypeCode method,
    118
GetTypedObjectForI-
    Unknown method
    (Marshal class), 1311
GetTypeForITypeInfo
    method (Marshal class),
    1311-1312
GetTypeInfo method, 663
GetTypeInfoName
    method (Marshal class),
    1312
GetTypeLibGuid method,
    1067, 1312
GetTypeLibGuidFor-
    Assembly method
    (Marshal class), 1312
GetTypeLibLcid method,
    1067, 1313
GetTypeLibName method,
    1067, 1313
GetUnderlyingObject
    method
    (ICustomAdapater
    interface), 909

GetUnmanagedThunkFor
    ManagedMethodPtr
    method (Marshal class),
    1313-1314
GetWindowsDirectory
    function, 784-788
Global Assembly Cache
    Utility. See gacutil.exe
GlobalMultiUse setting
    (instancing), 634
GlobalSingleUse setting
    (instancing), 633
GoFullscreen method,
    1201, 1222
Graphics property, 622
GroundLayer class,
    methods, 1153
GuidAttribute, 331, 427,
    574, 1278
GuidAttribute custom
    attribute, 963
GUIDs
    COM Interoperability, 529
    format specifiers, 570
    GuidAttribute, 574
    names, 60-61
    property, 568-570, 1216

H

Handle property, 1171,
    1221
HandleRef instance, 862
HandleRef value type
    (System.Runtime.Intero
    pServices namespace),
    1278-1280
HasAttachment field, 1162
HashCode property, 502

Hashtable key
    IComparer interface
        implementation, 764-766
    IHashCodeProvider
        interface implementation,
        764-766
HasPropertyPage method,
    1232
hasTransparentColor flag,
    1138
hasTransparentColor
    method, 1136
HDC parameter, 1218
heartland.sty file, 284
heartland2.sgt file, 284
Height property, 1136,
    1139-1140, 1143
Hello, World program
    C#, 36
    C++, 43
    Visual Basic .NET, 39-40
/help (AXIMP.EXE), 1393
/help (REGASM.EXE), 1390
/help (REGSVCS.EXE), 1396
/help (TLBEXP.EXE), 1384
/help (TLBIMP.EXE), 1381
HelpLink string, 723
helpstring
    assemblies, 427
    attributes, 358-361, 363
    type libraries, 382
hiding HRESULTs, 162-164
highScore field, 1121
HighScore property, 1121,
    1132
HKEY_CLASSES_ROOT
    registry key, 62
hosts, CLR, 460-468
HResult property, 520

HRESULTs, 67-68, 150-151
caused by .NET exceptions, error information, 404
COM interface implementation, 656
defining, 520
to exception transformations, 1400, 1406-1407, 1413
exceptions to transformations, 1416-1417, 1423, 1429
exposing success, 342-348
FACILITY_URT, 393
failure, 579-580, 721
ErrorCode, 722
setting error information, 722-723
hiding, 162-164
IDispatch implementations, 664-665
.NET interface implementation, 758
.NET method transformations, 434-436
registering assemblies, 393
success, 580, 721-722
HTML Object Library (Microsoft), 234, 1003
HTMLDocument coclass, 234
HTMLDocument interface, 235
HTMLStyleSheet class, 1003
HTMLStyleSheet coclass, 1004-1006, 1023

I

IAmVisibleToAll interface, 479
IAssemblyCache interface, 1040
IChatRoomDisplay interface, 215-216
ICollection interface, 746
IComparer interface, implementation to use COM objects as Hashtable key, 764-766
IConnectionPointContainer interface
implementation, 675-676
methods, 216
ICorRuntimeHost interface, 460
ICreateErrorInfo interface, 727-728
IcreateTypeInfo interface, 1068
IcreateTypeLib interface, 1068
ICustomAdapter interface (System.Runtime.InteropServices namespace), 1280-1281
GetUnderlyingObject method, 909
implementation, 909
ICustomFactory interface (System.Runtime.InteropServices namespace), 1281
ICustomMarshaler interface (System.Runtime.InteropServices namespace), 896-898, 1281-1282
IDASite interface, 731

IDE (Integrated Development Environment), 25
IDebuggerInfo interface, 461
IDictionary interface, 746
IDispatch (COM interfaces), 54-55, 58,103, 146-147, 654, 659
CLR, 659-665
writing, 665-672
IDispatch.Invoke method, 608
IDispatchEx interface, 152-153, 678-679
IDispatchImplAttribute (System.Runtime.Interop Services namespace), 660-661, 1282
IDispatchImplType enumeration (System. Runtime.InteropServices namespace), 1283
IDisposable interface, 732, 750-759, 1131
IDisposable.Dispose method, 493, 1135
IDL (Interface Definition Language), 54
coclasses
IDL representation of .NET classes, 451-453
representation of .NET classes, 451
representation of .NET classes, 450-453
COM data type conversions, 143-144
combining types, 145-151
complex types, 152-162

COM View and .NET
    View
    of an event, 447
    of fields exported as
        properties, 445
    of methods with para-
        meter arrays, 441
    of properties, 443
custom attributes, 371-372
definitions
    IHTMLStyleSheet
        interface, 988-989
    INetMeetingEvents
        dispinterface and
        INetMeeting inter-
        face, 1007-1008
    IPersist and
        IPersistStream
        Interfaces, 985
    IRunningAppCollection,
        975-976
    IWMPEffects interface,
        964
IDispatch (COM interface),
    54-55
IUnknown (COM interface),
    54
.NET View and COM
    View
    of the same methods,
        435
    of the same methods
        by-value and by-refer-
        ence parameters, 437
    of the same overloaded
        methods, 439
optional parameters,
    104-105
representation of the
    AddressLists dispinter-
    face, 982

type libraries, 697-698
    ActiveX controls, 712
    constants, 709-710
    constructs, 710
    defining classes,
        702-707
    naming enums, 707-
        709
    referencingexternal
        types, 698-702
    registering type
        libraries, 711
IDLDESC value type
    (System.Runtime.Intero
    pServices namespace),
    1283
IDLFLAG enumeration
    (System.Runtime.Intero
    pServices namespace),
    1283
IEnumerator interface,
    524, 746
IEnumVARIANT interface,
    152-153, 524-525, 678
IErrorInfo interface,
    723-725, 731
IFont interface, 910-912
IFormattable interface,
    761-764
IFormEvents methods,
    623
IGCHost interface, 460
IHashCodeProvider
    interface, 764-766
IHTMLStyleSheet
    interface
    C# definition, 996-998,
        1035-1036
    IDL definition, 988-989
    VB .NET definition, 991
IIDs, versioning, 531-532

IISIntrinsicsAttribute, 585
IL (Intermediate
    Language), 21
IL Assembler syntax
    metadata listing, 967-971
    structure definitions, 1020
IL Assembler. See ILASM;
    ILASM.EXE
IL Disassembler. See
    ILDASM; ILDASM.EXE
ILASM.EXE (IL Assembler),
    45, 324
    adding methods to modules,
        372-373
    assembly content modifi-
        cations, 324-328
        changing data types,
            340-342
        custom attributes,
            351-366, 370-372
        custom marshalers,
            248, 364-366
        errors, 328
        exposing success
            HRESULTs, 342-348
        key option, 327
        malicious edits, 327
        managed resources, 326
        output file names, 328
        SAFEARRAYs, 348-351
        unmanaged resources,
            326
    syntax, 328-329, 331
        ApplicationEventsSink
            Helper class con-
            structor, 332
        changing data types,
            340-342
        custom attributes,
            351-358

data types, 332-333
exposing HRESULTs, 342-348
input files, 331
MarshalAsAttribute, 334-340
nested types, 334
passing parameters, 334
SAFEARRAYs, 348-351
ILDASM.EXE (IL Disassembler), 45, 307, 324, 512, 653
assembly content modifications, 324-327
changing data types, 340-342
malicious edits, 327
managed resources, 326
unmanaged resources, 326
opening PIAs, 695
IMainMenu interface, 507
IManagedObject interface, 658
IMarshal interface, 672-673
Implement Interface dialog box, 651-652, 748
IMPLTYPEFLAGS enumeration (System.Runtime.InteropServices namespace), 1283
import directive, referencing external types, 698-702
ImportedFromTypeLib-Attribute, 331, 1284
Importer class, 1069-1083
Importer tab (Interactive Interop Tool), 1069-1083

importer transformations (type library)
exposing connection pointers, 222-227, 235-240
IntPtr types. *See* IntPtr types
Importer.cs, 1070-1083
ImporterEventKind enumeration (System.Runtime.InteropServices namespace), 1044, 1068, 1284
importers, type library, 84, 1049-1050
Interop Assembly. *See* Interop Assembly
transformations, 86
importlib directive, 698-702
Imports statement (Visual Basic .NET), 38
in, [out] parameter, method conversions, 167-169
InAttribute (System.Runtime.InteropServices namespace), 1284-1285
customizing data flow, 553-554
export behavior, 438
marking array parameters, 792-794
INetMeeting interface, 1007-1008
INetMeetingEvents dispinterface, 1007-1008
INetMeetingEvents_Event Provider class, 1017
infectSound field, 1121
infrastructure, 14

inheritance
COM
classes, 311-315
interface implementation, 654-656
.NET interfaces, 743-747, 984-985, 987
Inherited property, 30, 546
Initialize method, 227, 1112, 1118
InitializeComponent method, 239
inproc servers, 63
input files (ILASM.EXE), 331
InputLanguageChanging event, 622-623
InputLanguageChanging method, 622
Install method, 1099
Install value, 1061
InstallAssembly method, 1060, 1099
installation
assemblies
GAC, 392
in GAC, 649-650
COM+ objects, 309
serviced components, 1059-1061
InstallationFlags enumeration, 1060-1061, 1099
installFlags parameter, 1060
instances
creating
CreateObject method, 99-101
error detection, 101
new operator, 99

HandleRef, 862
ManualResetEvent, 289
RegistryKey, 856
System.Collections.Array-
    List, 463
System.Collections.Sorted
    List, 461
System._ComObject, 232
VARIANTs, 117-118
**instantiating objects,
    229-235**
**Integrated Development
    Environment.** *See* **IDE**
**Interactive Interop Tool,
    1062, 1064**
    COM+ tab, 1097-1100
    compared to SDK,
        1062-1063
    Exporter tab, 1083-1092
    Importer tab, 1069-1083
    MainForm class,
        1100-1101
    MiscTypes.cs, 1064-1068
    Register tab, 1092-1097
    structure, 1063
**Interface Definition
    Language.** *See* **IDL**
Interface value, 834
**InterfaceIsDual value
    (ComInterfaceType
    enumeration), 1260**
**InterfaceIsIDispatch value
    (ComInterfaceType
    enumeration), 1260**
**InterfaceIsIUnknown
    value (ComInterfaceType
    enumeration), 1260**
**InterfaceName_
    MemberName method,
    663**

**InterfaceQueuing-
    Attribute, 585**
interfaces
    Advise, methods, 216
    AppDomain, 488-489
    ChatRoomDisplay, 204
    CLR-specific, 658
    coclasses, 1003-1009,
        1016-1019
    COM, 57-58, 506-508,
        628
        *converting .NET
            interfaces to, 447-449*
        *custom attributes,
            963-964*
        *customizations,
            998-1003*
        *default implementa-
            tions, 657-677*
        definitions, 628-629
        Dispatch, 70
        *dispinterfaces, 608,
            982-984*
        dual, 58, 975-981
        *error handling, 112-
            114*
        *explicit interface
            members, 655-656*
        HRESULTs, 656
        IAmVisibleToAll, 479
        IAssemblyCache, 1040
        *IConnectionPointConta
            iner, 675-676*
        ICorRuntimeHost, 460
        *ICreateErrorInfo,
            727-728*
        IDebuggerInfo, 461
        *IDispatch, 54-55, 58,
            146-147, 654,
            659-672*
        IDispatchEx, 152-153

        *IEnumVARIANT,
            152-153*
        IGCHost, 460
        IMarshal, 672-673
        *Implement Interface
            option, 651-652*
        *implementation,
            112-114*
        *inheritance, 654-655,
            984-987*
        IObjectSafety, 676-677
        IPersist, 654-656
        *IPersistStream,
            654-656*
        *IPhoneEventHookup,
            596*
        IPhoneEvents, 596-597
        *IProvideClassInfo, 296,
            673-674, 705-706, 734*
        IRecordInfo, 271
        *ISmartTagAction,
            635-636, 643-646, 654*
        *ISmartTagRecognizer,
            635-636, 643-646, 654*
        IStream, 881, 883, 888
        *ISupportErrorInfo, 674,
            725-726*
        ITypeInfo, 152-153, 730
        *IUnknown, 54, 57,
            68-70, 146-147, 654,
            657-659*
        *IUnknown-Only
            interfaces, 964-974*
        IValidator, 461
        *language limitations,
            988-995, 998*
        *manually defining,
            962-963*
        method signatures, 652
        *MultiPurposeObject,
            705*

names, 500
.NET types, 678-679
non-public, 967
Office XP smart tags,
    634-636, 643-650,
    653-656
parameterized
    properties, 653-654
private members, 653
QueryInterface,
    110-112, 706
selecting members, 651
SetErrorInfo, 728
versioning, 65-66
Visual Studio .NET
    shortcuts, 650-652
COM callbacks, source,
    215-216, 226
converting, 177-179
default, defining classes in
    IDL files, 704-707
DirectMusicPerformance,
    283, 285
DownloadBegin, 239
DWebBrowserEvents, 226
HTMLDocument, 235
IChatRoomDisplay,
    215-216
ICollection, 746
IComparer, 764-766
IConnectionPointContainer,
    methods, 216
ICreateTypeInfo, 1068
ICreateTypeLib, 1068
ICustomAdapter
    GetUnderlyingObject
        method, 909
    implementation, 909
    ICustomMarshaler,
        896-898

IDictionary, 746
IDispatch, 103
IDispoable interface,
    750-759, 1131
IEnumerable, 746
IEnumerator, 524
IEnumVARIANT, 524-525
IErrorInfo, 723-725
IFont, 910-912
IFormattable, 761-764
IHashCodeProvider,
    764-766
IMainMenu, 507
ISearch, 360-361, 363
IServicedComponent, 507
ISuportErrorInfo, 726-727
IToolClient, 1068
ITypeLibConverter, 1042
IVSSDatabase, 102
IWin32Window, 1221
IWMPEffects, 1199,
    1202-1204
    enumerations,
        1204-1208
    methods, 1200-1201
    Render method,
        1199-1200
    structs, 1204-1208
    Vizualization class,
        1208-1223
Microsoft Direct
    Animation, IDASite, 731
.NET Framework, 740
    callbacks, 202-204
    class interfaces,
        741-743
    COM, 678-679
    converting to COM
        interfaces, 447-449
    disabling marshaling,
        580-582

HRESULTs, 758
IComparer implementa-
    tion, 764-766
IDispatchEx, 678-679
IDisposable, 732
IEnumVARIANT, 678
IErrorInfo, 731
IHashCodeProvider
    implementation,
        764-766
inheritance, 743-747
InterfaceTypeAttribute,
    578
IReflect, 665-672
ITypeInfo, 678
names, 503-504
System.IConvertible,
    652
Visual Basic 6,
    397-399, 759-764
Visual C++, 747-759
Object class, 439-440
PowerPoint.EApplication,
    366
QueryInterface, failures,
    290-295
source, defining classes in
    IDL files, 703-704
SourceInterfaceName_
    Event, 222
SourceInterfaceName_
    EventProvider, 222
SourceInterfaceName_
    MethodNameEvent-
    Handler, 222
SourceInterfaceName_
    SinkHelper, 222
System.Collections.
    IEnumerable, 740

System.Runtime.Interop-
Services namespace
custom marshaling,
1252
ICustomAdapter,
1280-1281
ICustomFactory, 1281
ICustomMarshaler,
1281-1282
IRegistrationServices,
1287
ITypeLibConverter,
1287-1288
ITypeLibExporterName
Provider, 1288
ITypeLibExporterNotify
Sink, 1289
ITypeLibImporterNotify
Sink, 1289
UCOMIBindCtx, 1360
UCOMIConnectionPoint
, 1360
UCOMIConnectionPoin
tContainer, 1360
UCOMIEnum-
ConnectionPoints,
1360
UCOMIEnum-
Connections, 1361
UCOMIEnumMoniker,
1361
UCOMIEnumString,
1361
UCOMIEnumVARIANT,
1361-1362
UCOMIMoniker,
1362-1363
UCOMIPersistFile,
1363
UCOMIRunningObject
Table, 1363

UCOMIStream, 1364
UCOMITypeComp,
1364-1365
UCOMITypeInfo, 1365
UCOMITypeLib, 1366
System.Runtime.InteropSe
rvices.ITypeLibExporter-
NameProvider, 1054-
1055
C# method, 1054
C++ method, 1054
Visual Basic .NET
method, 1054
TypeInfo, 59
Unadvise, methods, 216
usage guidelines
versus classes, 506-508
versus custom attributes,
508-510

InterfaceTypeAttribute,
578-579, 601, 1285
InterfaceTypeAttribute
custom attribute, 964
Intermediate Language.
See IL
internal IDispatch CLR
implementation, 660-
665
InternalImpl value
(IDispatchImplType
enumeration), 1283
Internet Explorer, han-
dling events
.NET events, 224-227
raw connection points,
219-222
InternetExplorer coclass,
218-222, 231
InternetExplorer.Docume
nt property, 234
Interop API, 52

Interop Assembly, 84-86.
***See also* assemblies;**
Interop Marshaler
ActiveX control conver-
sions, 196-198
adding methods to modules,
372-373
assembling/reassembling,
326-327
class conversions, 179
coclasses, 180-182
RCW class, 182-186
content modifications, 324-
328
changing data types,
340-342
custom attributes,
351-366, 370-372
custom marshalers,
248, 364-366
errors, 328
exposing success
HRESULTs, 342-348
key option, 327
malicious edits, 327
managed resources,
326
output file names, 328
SAFEARRAYs, 348-351
unmanaged resources,
326
creating, 85
data type conversions, 143-
144
combining types, 145-
151
complex types, 152-162
DISPIDs conversions,
173-174
DISPID NEWENUM -4,
175-176
DISPID Value 0,
174-175

enumeration conversions,
193-194
GetPrimaryInteropAssembly
method, 1047-1048
helpstrings, 427
ILDASM.EXE, 653
interface conversions,
177-179
method conversions, 162
*by-value versus by-
reference, 164-167*
*hiding HRESULTs,
162-164*
*in, [out] parameter,
167-169*
*[in] versus [out],
167-169*
*parameter arrays,
169-171*
module conversions,
187-188
Primary, 86-90
property conversions,
171-173
registering, 297
signatures, 344
structure conversions,
189-191
type library conversion,
141-143
typedef conversions,
194-196
union conversions, 191-192
Interop Marshaler, 96-98.
See also Interop
Assembly
do-it-yourself marshaling,
248
BSTR types, 249
*C# unsafe code versus
System.Runtime.
InteropServices APIs,
250-258*

*manipulating IntPtr
types, 258-267,
270-275*
*metadata signatures,
249*
*System.IntPtr data
type, 248-250*
marshaling strings. *See*
strings
without custom marshaling,
880
interoperability
core COM tools. *See*
TLBIMP.EXE;
TLBEXP.EXE;
REGASM.EXE
extended COM tools.
See AXIMP.EXE;
REGSVCS.EXE
IntPtr parameter, 340-341
IntPtr types
defining string parameters
as, 789-791
initializing to null, 259
manipulating, 258
*by-reference null value
types, 264-265*
*C-style array fields,
262-264*
SAFEARRAYs, 273-275
struct, 258-262
*variants, 266-267,
270-272*
IntroScreen class, 1156-
1157
InvalidCastException
exception, troubleshoot-
ing, 289-290
*casting to RCW types,
295-299*
*QueryInterface failure,
290-295*

InvalidComObject-
Exception (System.
Runtime.InteropServices
namespace), 1286
invalidMoveSound field,
1121
InvalidOleVariantType-
Exception (System.
Runtime.InteropServices
namespace), 1286-1287
InvalidOperationException,
403, 477-482, 562-565
Invoke method, 501, 663
INVOKEKIND enumeration
(System.Runtime.
InteropServices name-
space), 1287
InvokeVerb method,
645-646
[in] parameter, method
conversions, 167-169
IObjectSafety interface,
implementation,
676-677
IPersist interface, C#
definition, 985
customizations, 986-987
explicit interface members,
655-656
IDL definition, 985
inheritance, 654-655
IPersistStream interface
C# definition, 985-987
explicit interface members,
655-656
IDL definition, 985
inheritance, 654-655
IPhoneEventHookup
interface, 596
IPhoneEvents interface,
596-597

IProvideClassInfo interface, 296, 673-674, 705-706, 734
IRecordInfo interface, 271
IReflect interface
IDispatch interface implementation, 665-672
members, 665-666
parameters, 671
IRegistrationServices interface (System. Runtime.InteropServices namespace), 1287
IRunningAppCollection dual COM interface, 975-976
definition in C#, 976-979
definition in VB .NET, 980-981
IsAllocated property (GCHandle value type), 1275
IsComObject method (Marshal class), 1314
IsDying field, 1158
ISearch interface, 360-361, 363
IServicedComponent interface, 507
IsInfected field, 1162
ISmartTagAction interface, 635-636, 643-646, 654
IsmartTagRecognizer interface, 635-636, 643-646, 654
ISmartTagRecognizer.get_ Name method, 654
ISmartTagRecognizer.Reco gnize method, 635
IsPhoneNumber method, 381

IsTimeToMove method, 1112, 1118
IStream, 881
IStream interface,
by-reference null value types, 264-265
methods, 883, 888
IsTypeVisibleFromCom method (Marshal class), 1314
ISupportErrorInfo interface, 674, 725-727
IsVisible field, 1162
isVisible parameter, 504
IsVisible property, 504
IsZipCode method, 381, 388
IToolClient interface, 1068
ITreeNode.isVisible property, 504
ITypeInfo interface, 59, 152-153, 678, 730
ITypeInfo.Invoke method, 582
ITypeLibConverter interface (System.Runtime. InteropServices name-space),1042, 1287-1288
ITypeLibExporterName-Provider interface (System.Runtime.Intero pServices namespace), 1288
ITypeLibExporterNotifySin k interface (System. Runtime.InteropServices namespace), 1289
ITypeLibExporterNotify-Sink.ReportEvent method, 1052

ITypeLibImporterNotify-Sink interface, 1044, 1051-1055, 1289
IUnknown (COM inter-faces), 54, 57, 68, 70, 146-147, 654
IDL, 54
implementation, 657
non-reflexive implementa-tion, 292-293
QueryInterface, 658-659
IUnknown-Only interfaces (COM interfaces), 964-974
IUnknown.AddRef method, 109
IUnknown.AddRef object, 68
IUnknown.Release method, 109
IValidator interface, 461
IVSSDatabase interface, 102
IWin32Window interface, 1221
IWMPEffects interface, 1199, 1202-1204
defining in C#, 971-973
defining in VB .NET, 974
enumerations, 1204-1208
IDL definition, 964
methods, 1200-1201
Render method, 1199-1200
structs, 1204-1208
translation to C#, 965-967, 1002
Visualization class, 1208-1223

J

jagged arrays, 518-519
JIT (just-in-time compiler), 21
JScript, StringValidator class, 388-390
JUMP to .NET, 51
just-in-time compiler. *See* JIT
JustInTimeActivation-Attribute, 585

K

Kernel32 class, 1167
KERNEL32.DLL
    functions, 774-797
    PInvoke signatures, 1442, 1461
key option (ILASM.EXE), 327
/keycontainer (AXIMP.EXE), 1391
/keycontainer (TLBIMP.EXE), 1377-1378
/keyfile (AXIMP.EXE), 1392
/keyfile (TLBIMP.EXE), 1378
keyPair parameter (Con-vertTypeLibTo-Assembly method), 1046, 1357
KeywordAttribute, 509
KeywordAttributes assembly, 30
keywords
    Alias, customizing PInvoke function names, 796
    names, 500
    WithEvents, 213-214, 603-604
Kill method, 1133, 1158,

1162
KillPlayer method, 1121, 1133

L

language limitations, COM interfaces, 988-995, 998
languages, 33-34
    C#. *See* C#
    C++. *See* C++
    managed, 15
    Visual Basic .NET. *See* Visual Basic .NET
late binding, 91
    COM components, 119-120
    .NET members, 119
    unmanaged C++, 404-407
Layer class, 1133, 1150
    fields, 1150
    methods, 1150-1152
Layer method, 1150
layers field, 1121
LayoutKind enumeration (System.Runtime.Intero pServices namespace), 1290
    StructLayoutAttribute, 554, 829-830
LCIDConversion, 583
LCIDConversionAttribute (System.Runtime.Intero pServices namespace), 582, 1290-1291
LCIDs (Local Identifier), 529
    assemblies, 427
    methods, 582-583
LDIC (Locate Identifier),

426
leftAligned field, 1147
let accessors, 442
LIBFLAGS enumeration (System.Runtime.Interop Services namespace), 1291
LIBIDs (Library Identifier), 426-427, 529
library identifiers. *See* LIBIDs
lifetimes, 68-69
link demands, 306
listings
    AnimatedEnvelopePicture. cs., 1144, 1146
    AnimatedPicture.cs., 26-28
    C# definition of IHTMLStyleSheet interface, 1035-1036
    C# definition of IMarshal, 672-673
    C# definition of NetMeeting Coclass interface, 1009, 1016-1018
    C# defintion of IHTMLStyleSheet interface, 996, 998
    C# Non-Static Extern Members feature, 1029, 1031
    C# representation of enumerations and enumeration parameters, 454, 457
    C# representation of two interfaces related by inheritance, 448-449
    C# source code demon-

strating how to put
ExampleAttribute on
different elements, 36-38
C++ definition of
ISupportErrorInfo, 674
C++ source code demon-
strating how to put the
ExampleAttribute on dif-
ferent elements, 44-45
Character.cs., 1158,
1161-1162
ChessBoard.cls., 765-766
ColorfulConsole Class
Wraps Win32 APIs for
Printing in Color,
822-829
ColorfulVisualization.cs,
1231-1235
COM Class Implementing
Several Interfaces,
183-184
COM View and .NET
View of an event, 446
COM View and .NET
View of fields exported
as properties, 444-446
COM View and the .NET
View of a Method that
Doesn't Return an
HRESULT, 163
COM View and the .NET
View of a Method with a
Parameter Array, 170
COM View and the .NET
View of Methods with
In-Only and Out-Only
By-Reference
Parameters, 168
COM View and .NET
View of Methods with
Parameter Arrays, 441
COM view and the .NET

View of Parameters, 165
COM View and .NET
View of Properties,
442-444
COM View and the .NET
View of the Same Fixed-
Length Arrays, 157
COM View and the .NET
View of the Same
Methods with a Variety
of String Parameters, 149
COM View and the .NET
View of the Same
Methods with By-Value
and By-Reference
Parameters, 164
COM View and the .NET
View of the Same
Methods with DECI-
MAL and CURRENCY
Parameters, 148
COM View and the .NET
View of the Same
Methods with SCODE
and HRESULT
Parameters, 151
COM View and the .NET
View of the Same
Methods with VARI-
ANT, IUnknown*, and
IDispatch* Parameters,
146
COM View and the .NET
View of the Same Simple
Methods, 162
ComPlusInstaller.cs.,
1098-1100
CopyFileEx Function
Calls Back into Managed
Code, 812-815
ComStream.cs., 883-889

Custom attributes written
in C#, 29-30
CustomCCW Adapter
Class, 932-943
CustomRCW Adapter
Class, 924-932
Custom Marshaler Written
in C++, 907-909
Custom Registration
Required for Plugging
Components into
Windows Media Player,
572-574
D3DCOLORAUX from
Listing 7.9, 373
DancingCatVisualization.
cs, 1238, 1243
defining IWMPEffects
Interface in C#, 971, 973
defining IWMPEffects
Interface in VB .NET, 974
defining source interface,
602-603
DirectX.cs., 1183,
1193-1194
DispHTMLStyleSheet
interface, 1004-1006
DISPIDs for the
EApplication Interface,
366, 370
Disposing an Object on its
Last Release, 948-952
Dynamic PInvoke,
863-865
EmailAttack.cs., 1168,
1171, 1178, 1182
Ensuring that all
PowerPoint RCWs are
Collected, 303-304
Enums.cs., 1120

Envelope.cs., 1162, 1165-1166

Exported Methods for the Seven Events, 488-489

Exporter.cs, 1084, 1086-1092

Exporting an Assembly Containing a COM-Visible Type, 564-565

Exposing .NET events to COM without CLR, 594-597

Exposing Different Default Members than ToString to COM Clients, 575-578

Extracting Type Library Attributes, 1047-1048

FileWriter.cpp., 752-753, 755-759

FileWriter.h., 751-752, 754-755

Form1.cs., 128-137

FormattableClass.cls., 761, 763-764

FrontLayer.cs., 1154

Game.cs., 1121, 1131-1133

GroundLayer.cs., 1153

Handling Variable-Length Structures Using Multiple Definitions, 847-849

Hooking Up Event Handlers to Objects, 233-235

Hosting the CLR and Using .NET Objects in Visual Basic 6 COM Clients, 461-463

Hosting the CLR and

Using .NET Objects in Unmanaged Visual C++ COM Clients, 463-468

IDL custom attribute recognized by type library importer, 692-693

IDL definition of IHTMLStyleSheet interface, 988-989

IDL definition of IRunningAppCollection, 975-976

IDL definition of the IWMPEffects interface, 964

IDL definitions of INetMeetingEvents dispinterface and INetMeeting interface, 1007-1008

IDL representation of the AddressLists dispinterface, 982

IDL Representation of Two Modules, 187-188

IEnumVARIANT parameters transformed to IEnumerator types, 153

implementing System.Reflection.Ireflect, 668-672

implementing two COM interfaces, 636, 643-646

Importer.cs., 1070-1083

Incorrect C# Source Code, 546-547

Instantiating a Remote COM Object, 871, 873-874

Interface Hierarchy

Exported to COM, 744-746

IntroScreen.cs., 1156-1157

Invoking an Unmanaged Function Pointer, 818, 820-821

IPersist and IPersistStream Interfaces in C#, 985-987, 1000-1001

IPersist and IPersistStream Interfaces in IDL, 985

IRunningAppCollection definition in C#, 976-979

IRunningAppCollection definition in VB .NET, 980-981

IWMPEffects.cs., 1202-1204, 1209-1222

Layer.cs., 1151-1152

Making PInvoke Methods Throw Exceptions Upon Failure using PreserveSig, 803-805

ManagedForm.vb, 918, 920

Marking a strongly-type GetEnumerator method with DispIdAttribute, 525-527

Marking an Array Parameter with InAttribute and OutAttribute in C#, 792-794

MarshaledStructInspector. DisplayStruct, 845-847

Metadata Definitions of Documents.Add and Application.Quit, 343-345

Metadata for the ISearch

Interface with Added DescriptionAttributes, 361-363

Metadata Generated by the Type Library Importer for the Recordset. ActiveConnection Property, 992-993

metadata in IL Assembler syntax, 967-971

MiscTypes.cs., 1064-1068

MyWebBrowser.cs., 123, 126

.NET and COM representations of two classes implemented, 636

.NET Definition of AddressLists in Visual C++ .NET, 982-984

.NET Definition of UCOMIStream Shown in C# Syntax, 883, 888

.NET definitions of the RECT and TimedLevel Structures, 1021

.NET interfaces with conflicting capitalization of the same indentifier, 503-504

.NET View and COM View of same methods By-Value and By-Reference parameters, 436-438

.NET View and COM View of the same methods, 434-436

.NET View and COM View of the same overloaded methods, 438-439

.NET view of Conformant

Arrays, 160

NumerPicture.cs., 1147-1150

Object class interface, 439-440

Obtaining an Error String from an Error Code, 802

Performing Manual SAFEARRAY Marshaling in C#, 273-275

Performing Manual VARIANT Marshaling in C#, 267, 270-272

Picture.cs., 1136-1139

PresetEnumAttribute.cs., 1222-1223

ReadConsoleInput, 865-868

Registrar.cs., 1093-1097

Screen.cs., 1155-1156

Simple Struct, 189-191

SimpleVisualization.vb, 1224-1226

Snippets of Word.il, 329, 331

Sound.cs., 1134-1136

StreamMarshaler.cs., 901-903, 905

StringValidator.cs., 380-381

structure definitions, 1020

SupportingType.cs., 1204-1208

System.Reflection.MemberInfo, 490, 492

System.Runtime.InteropServices.UCOMIConnection, 676

System.Runtime.Interop-

Services.UCOMIConnectionPointContainer, 675-676

SetConsoleCtrlHandler Function, 816-817

StringMarshaler Custom Marshaler, 943-947

Traditional ADO, 93-94

translation of IWMPEffects to C#, 965-966

.NET customizations, 1002

customizations, 967

Tricks with COM, 477-482

Two Versions of a C# Client, 345-348

Unmanaged C++ Code, 404-407, 727

Unmanaged Enum and Managed Enum, 193-194

Unmanaged Union Converted to a .NET Value Type, 191-192

Unmanaged Visual C++ Code Using a .NET Class, 385-388

Util.cs., 1112, 1118-1119

VB6Form.frm, 921-923

Win32.cs., 1167, 1172, 1178

Windows Handle Wrapping, 853, 856

WizardVisualization.cs, 1227-1230

LoadAndDisplayAssembly method, 1097

LoadBalancingSupported Attribute, 585

LoadTypeLibEx class, 1066

LoadTypeLibEx method,

1042-1043
Local Identifier. *See* LCID
LocaleID parameters, 644
location of property
  accessors, 990-994
LocationX field, 1158
LocationY field, 1158
lostLifeSound field, 1121
LPArray, UnamangedType
  enumeration values, 550
LPSTR, 149-150
LPStr value, 834
LPTStr value, 834
LPWSTR, 149-150
LPWStr value, 834
luring attacks, 306

M

Main method, 1167, 1171
MainForm class,
  1100-1101
MainForm class
  (Interactive Interop
  Tool), 1100-1101
MakeVisibleAndInfected
  method, 1162, 1166
managed code, 48
  adapter objects, 905-909
  connection points, 218-222
    connectable objects,
    229-235
    lazy connection point
    initialization, 227-229
    type library importer
    transformation,
    222-227
  debugging COM
    Interoperability calls
    to unmanaged code,
    315-319
  interaction with unmanaged

code, 49
  C++ extensions, 50-51
  COM Interoperability,
  51-53, 69-71
  JUMP to .NET, 51
  PInvoke, 49-50
  invoking unmanaged
    pointers in, 818-821
managed compilers, 15
managed extensions,
  C++, 42
managed languages, 15
managed resources,
  assemblies, 326
ManagedForm assembly,
  923
ManagedIStream class,
  889-895
ManualResetEvent
  instance, 289
Marshal class, 250, 263,
  270, 306, 1067,
  1292-1294
  methods
    AddRef, 1294
    AllocCoTaskMem, 1295
    AllocHGlobal, 1295
    BindToMoniker, 1296
    ChangeWrapperHandle
    Strength, 1296-1297
    Copy, 1297-1298
    CreateWrapperOfType,
    1298-1299
    DestroyStructure, 1299
    FreeBSTR, 1299-1300
    FreeCoTaskMem, 1300
    FreeHGlobal, 1300
    GenerateGuidForType,
    1301
    GenerateProgIdForType,
    1301
    GetActiveObject, 1301

    GetComInterfaceFor-
    Object, 1302
    GetComObjectData,
    1303
    GetComSlotForMethod-
    Info, 1303
    GetEndComSlot, 1303
    GetExceptionCode,
    1303-1304
    GetExceptionPointers,
    1304
    GetHINSTANCE, 1304
    GetHRForException,
    1304-1305
    GetHRForLastWin32-
    Error, 1305
    GetIDispatchForObject,
    1305-1306
    GetITypeInfoForType,
    1306
    GetIUnknownForObject,
    1306-1307
    GetLastWin32Error,
    1307
    GetManagedThunkFor
    UnmanagedMethod-
    Ptr, 1307
    GetMethodInfoForCom
    Slot, 1308
    GetNativeVariantFor-
    Object, 1308-1309
    GetObjectForIUnknown,
    1309
    GetObjectForNative-
    Variant, 272, 1309
    GetObjectsForNative-
    Variants, 1310
    GetStartComSlot,
    1310-1311
    GetThreadFromFiber-

Cookie, 1311
GetTypedObjectForI-
    Unknown, 1311
GetTypeForITypeInfo,
    1311-1312
GetTypeInfoName,
    1312
GetTypeLibGuid, 1312
GetTypeLibGuidFor-
    Assembly, 1312
GetTypeLibLcid, 1313
GetTypeLibName, 1313
GetUnmanagedThunk-
    ForManagedMethod-
    Ptr, 1313-1314
IsComObject, 1314
IsTypeVisibleFromCom,
    1314
NumParamBytes, 1314
OffsetOf, 1314-1315
Prelink, 1315-1316
PrelinkAll, 1316
PtrToStringAnsi,
    1316-1317
PtrToStringAuto,
    1317-1318
PtrToStringBSTR, 1318
PtrToStringUni, 1319
PtrToStructure,
    1319-1321
QueryInterface,
    1321-1323
ReadByte, 1323-1325
ReadInt16, 1326
ReadInt32, 1326-1327
ReadInt64, 1327
ReadIntPtr, 1327-1328
ReAllocCoTaskMem,
    1328
ReAllocHGlobal,

1328-1329
Release, 1329-1330
ReleaseComObject,
    1330
ReleaseThreadCache,
    1330
SetComObjectData,
    1331
SizeOf, 1331
StringToBSTR,
    1331-1332
StringToCoTaskMem-
    Ansi, 1332
StringToCoTaskMem-
    Auto, 1332
StringToCoTaskMem-
    Uni, 1333
StringToHGlobalAnsi,
    1333
StringToHGlobalAuto,
    1333-1334
StringToHGlobalUni,
    1334
StructureToPtr,
    1334-1336
ThrowExceptionForHR,
    1336-1337
UnsafeAddrOfPinned-
    ArrayElement, 1337
WriteByte, 1337-1339
WriteInt16, 1340
WriteInt32, 1340-1341
WriteInt64, 1341
WriteIntPtr, 1342
properties
SystemDefaultCharSize
    , 1336
SystemMaxDBCSChar-
    Size, 1336
Marshal.ReleaseCom-

Object, 299-304
**Marshal.ReleaseComObject
    method, 110**
**Marshal.SizeOf method,
    839**
**MarshalAsAttribute, 895,
    898, 1222, 1342-1344**
C# signatures, 899-901
COM interface shortcuts,
    651
customizing arrays,
    549-550
customizing data types,
    541-549, 552-553
customizing structures,
    834-839
detecting errors in,
    552-553
Inherited property, 546
parameters, 898, 900
    ArraySubType, 1343
    Boolean, 1343
    MarshalCookie, 1343
    MarshalType, 1343
    MarshalTypeRef, 1343
    object, 1343
    SafeArraySubType,
        1343
    SafeArrayUserDefined-
        SubType, 1344
    SizeConst, 1344
    SizeParamIndex, 1344
    strings, 1342
syntax, 334-335
    SafeArraySubType
        parameter, 338-340
    UnmanagedType.
        LPArray class, 337
    UnmanagedType.Safe-
        Array class, 337
UnmanagedType enumera-

tion, 542-545, 550-552
ByValArray, 549
LPArray, 550
UnmanagedType values, 834
MarshalCookie parameter (MarshalAsAttribute), 898, 1343
MarshalDirectiveException (System.Runtime. InteropServices namespace), 1344-1345
marshalers. *See* **custom marshalers; Interop Assembly; Interop Marshaler**
MarshalManagedToNative method, 896, 1281
MarshalNativeToManaged method, 896
MarshalType parameter (MarshalAsAttribute), 898, 1343
MarshalTypeRef parameter (MarshalAsAttribute), 898, 1343
Media Player, 1196
custom registration, 572-574
skins, 1196
visualizations, 1196
COM objects, 1196-1197
.NET Visualization API, 1224-1243
Visualization API, 1197-1223
MediaChange event, 1217, 1220
MediaInfo method, 1201,

1220
members
converting for .NET object models, 434
.NET events, 446-447
.NET fields, 444-446
.NET methods, 434-441
.NET properties, 441-444
designing for .NET clients, 729
passing error information, 731
passing interface pointers to anything, 729
passing type information, 730-731
explicit, 655-656
IReflect interface, 665-666
names, 500-501, 505
private, 653
selecting, 651
static, reflection, 482-488
versioning, 527
Menu property, 507
Message string, 722
MessageBeep API, 810
MessageTypes enumeration, 1068
metadata
assemblies, 26-28
customizing PIAs (Primary Interop Assemblies), 693-694
in IL Assembler syntax, 967-971
ISearch interface, 360-363
signature transformations to expose HRESULTs, 344-348
signatures, 249

VB .NET modules, 356-358
Method value (ComMemberType enumeration), 1261
methods
Add, 347, 596
adding to Interop Assembly, 372-373
AddMessage, 625
AddNotificationType, 285
AddRef, Marshal class, 1294
add_EventName, 592
Advise interface, 216
AllocCoTaskMem, Marshal class, 1295
AllocHGlobal (Marshal class), 1295
AnimatedEnvelopePicture, 1144
AnimatedEnvelopePicture class, 1144-1146
AnimatedPicture, 1140
AnimatedPicture class, 1140-1143
AnnoyingMessage, 206
AskYesNoQuestion, 1068
Assembly.GetExported-Types, 1052
Assembly.Load, 1050
Assembly.LoadFrom, 1050
AssemblyBuilder.Save, 1048
BindToMoniker (Marshal class), 1296
BitConverter.ToString, 946
CallerId, 596
calling COM objects, 101-109
ChangeFontButtonClick,

923

ChangeWrapperHandleStre
ngth (Marshal class),
1296-1297

Character, 1158

Character class, 1158,
1161-1162

CheckForDeath, 1121,
1133

CleanUpManagedData
(ICustomMarshaler
interface), 1282

CleanUpNativeData
(ICustomMarshaler
interface), 1281

ClippedRectangle, 1136,
1139

ConformantArray1D, 161

ConsoleMessage, 206

ConvertAssemblyToType-
Lib (TypeLibConverter
class), 1356

converting, 162
by-value versus by-
reference, 164-167
hiding HRESULTs,
162-164
in, [out] parameter,
167-169
[in] versus [out],
167-169
parameter arrays,
169-171

ConvertTypeLibTo-
Assembly, 1041-1042
creating assemblies
from type libraries,
1042-1044
parameters, 1357

ConvertTypeLibTo-

Assembly (TypeLib-
Converter class), 1356-
1357

Copy (Marshal class),
1297-1298

CreateInstance, 468

CreateObject, creating
instances, 99-101

CreateObject (Visual
Basic 6), 60

CreateRemoteInstance,
874

CreateSink, 239

CreateSoundBufferFrom-
File, 1112

CreateSurfaceFromFile,
1118

CreateTypeInfo, 1068

CreateWrapperOfType
(Marshal class),
1298-1299

DeleteSubKey, 860

DestroyStructure (Marshal
class), 1299

DetachSink, 239

DisplayPropertyPage,
1220-1221

Dispose, 69, 1121,
1131-1136, 1151-1156,
1167, 1171

DllGetClassObject, 392

Draw, 1147-1149

DrawAt, 1136, 1139-1140,
1143-1146

DrawSurface, 1112, 1139

DXCallback, 285, 289

dxSurface, 1136

E-mailAttackForm class,
1167-1168, 1171

E-mailAttackForm, 1167

EnumConnectionPoints,

216

Envelope, 1162

Envelope class, 1162,
1165-1166

Equals, 743

exportOpenButton_Click,
1100

ExtensibleClassFactory
class, 1269

ExtensibleClassFactory.
RegisterObjectCreation-
Callback, 314

FAILED, 347

FillRect, 271

Finalize, 743

FreeBSTR (Marshal class),
1299-1300

FreeCoTaskMem (Marshal
class), 1300

FreeHGlobal (Marshal
class), 1300

FromGlobalAccessCache
(RuntimeEnvironment
class), 1351

Game, 1121

Game.Render, 1171

GCHandle value type
AddrOfPinnedObject,
1275
Alloc, 1275
Free, 1275

GenerateGuidForType
(Marshal class), 1301

GenerateProgIdForType
(Marshal class), 1301

GetActiveObject (Marshal
class), 1301

GetClassID, 654

GetComInterfaceForObject
(Marshal class), 1302

GetComObjectData

(Marshal class), 1303
GetComSlotForMethodInfo
(Marshal class), 1303
GetDisplayNameForAssem
bly, 1067
GetEndComSlot (Marshal
class), 1303
GetEnumerator, 440,
524-527
GetExceptionCode
(Marshal class),
1303-1304
GetExceptionPointers
(Marshal class), 1304
GetExportedTypes, 1097
GetFrequency, 1225
GetHashCode, 743
GetHINSTANCE (Marshal
class), 1304
GetHRForException
(Marshal class),
1304-1305
GetHRForLastWin32Error
(Marshal class), 1305
GetIDispatchForObject
(Marshal class),
1305-1306
GetIDsOfNames, 662
GetITypeInfoForType
(Marshal class), 1306
GetIUnknownForObject
(Marshal class),
1306-1307
GetLastWin32Error
(Marshal class), 1307
GetManagedCategoryGuid,
1057, 1349
GetManagedThunkFor-
UnmanagedMethodPtr
(Marshal class), 1307
GetMethodInfoForComSlot

(Marshal class), 1308
GetNativeDataSize
(ICustomMarshaler
interface), 1282
GetNativeVariantForObjec
t (Marshal class),
1308-1309
GetObjectAttribute
calling, 260
.NET signature, 260
GetObjectForIUnknown
(Marshal class), 1309
GetObjectForNativeVarian
t (Marshal class), 272,
1309-1310
GetPresetTitle, 1220, 1225
GetPrimaryInteropAssembl
y (TypeLibConverter
class), 1357
GetProgIdForType, 1057,
1350
GetRecordInfoFromType-
Info, 271
GetRegistrableTypesIn-
Assembly, 1057, 1350
GetRuntimeDirectory
(RuntimeEnvironment
class), 1351
GetSite, 729
GetSite .NET signature,
729
GetStartComSlot (Marshal
class), 1310-1311
GetSystemVersion
(RuntimeEnvironment
class), 1352
GetThreadFromFiberCooki
e (Marshal class), 1311
GetType, 511-512
GetTypeCode, 118
GetTypedObjectFor-

IUnknown (Marshal
class), 1311
GetTypeForITypeInfo
(Marshal class),
1311-1312
GetTypeInfo, 663
GetTypeInfoName
(Marshal class), 1312
GetTypeLibGuid, 1067,
1312
GetTypeLibGuidFor-
Assembly (Marshal
class), 1312
GetTypeLibLcid (Marshal
class), 1067, 1313
GetTypeLibName (Marshal
class), 1067, 1313
GetUnderlyingObject
(ICustomAdapter
interface), 909
GetUnmanagedThunkFor
ManagedMethodPtr
(Marshal class),
1313-1314
GoFullScreen, 1222
GroundLayer class, 1153
HasPropertyPage, 1232
hasTransparentColor, 1136
IConnectionPointContainer
interface, 216
ICustomMarshaler inter-
face, 896-897, 1281-1282
CleanUpManagedData,
897
CleanUpNativeData,
897
GetInstance, 897-898
GetInstance method,
897-898
GetNativeDataSize, 897
MarshalManagedTo-

Native, 896
*MarshalNativeTo-
    Managed, 896*
IDispatch.Invoke, 608
IDisposable.Dispose, 493,
    1135
IFormEvents, 623
Initialize, 227, 1112, 1118
InitializeComponent, 239
InputLanguageChanging,
    622
Install, 1099
InstallAssembly, 1060,
    1099
InterfaceName_
    MemberName, 663
Invoke, 501, 663
InvokeVerb, 645-646
IsComObject (Marshal
    class), 1314
ISmartTagRecognizer.get_
    Name, 654
ISmartTagRecognizer.
    Recognize, 635
IsPhoneNumber, 381
IsTimeToMove, 1112,
    1118
IStream interface, 883, 888
IsTypeVisibleFromCom
    (Marshal class), 1314
IsZipCode, 381, 388
ITypeInfo.Invoke, 582
ITypeLibExporterNotify-
    Sink interface, 1289
ITypeLibExporterNotifySi
    nk.ReportEvent, 1052
ITypeLibImporterNotify-
    Sink interface, 1044,
    1051-1055, 1289
IUnknown (COM inter-

face), 54
IUnknown.AddRef, 109
IUnknown.Release, 109
IWMPEffects interface,
    1199-1201
Kill, 1133, 1158, 1162
KillPlayer, 1121, 1133
Layer, 1150
Layer class, 1150-1152
LCIDs,
    LCIDConversionAttribute
    , 582-583
LoadAndDisplayAssembly,
    1097
LoadTypeLibEx, 1042-
    1043
Main, 1167, 1171
MakeVisibleAndInfected,
    1162, 1166
Marshal class
    AddRef, 1294
    AllocCoTaskMem, 1295
    AllocHGlobal, 1295
    BindToMoniker, 1296
    *ChangeWrapperHandle
        Strength, 1296-1297*
    Copy, 1297-1298
    *CreateWrapperOfType,
        1298-1299*
    DestroyStructure, 1299
    FreeBSTR, 1299-1300
    FreeCoTaskMem, 1300
    FreeHGlobal, 1300
    *GenerateGuidForType,
        1301*
    *GenerateProgIdForType
        , 1301*
    GetActiveObject, 1301
    *GetComInterfaceFor-
        Object, 1302*
    GetComObjectData,

    1303
    *GetComSlotForMethod-
        Info, 1303*
    GetEndComSlot, 1303
    *GetExceptionCode,
        1303-1304*
    *GetExceptionPointers,
        1304*
    GetHINSTANCE, 1304
    *GetHRForException,
        1304-1305*
    *GetHRForLastWin32-
        Error, 1305*
    *GetIDispatchForObject,
        1305-1306*
    *GetITypeInfoForType,
        1306*
    *GetIUnknownForObject,
        1306-1307*
    *GetLastWin32Error,
        1307*
    *GetManagedThunkFor
        UnmanagedMethod-
        Ptr, 1307*
    *GetMethodInfoForCom
        Slot, 1308*
    *GetNativeVariantFor-
        Object, 1308-1309*
    *GetObjectForIUnknown
        , 1309*
    *GetObjectForNative-
        Variant, 1309*
    *GetObjectsForNative-
        Variants, 1310*
    *GetStartComSlot,
        1310-1311*
    *GetThreadFromFiber-
        Cookie, 1311*
    *GetTypedObjectFor-
        IUnknown, 1311*
    GetTypeForITypeInfo,

1311-1312
GetTypeInfoName, 1312
GetTypeLibGuid, 1312
GetTypeLibGuidFor-
  Assembly, 1312
GetTypeLibLcid, 1313
GetTypeLibName, 1313
GetUnmanagedThunk-
  ForManagedMethod-
  Ptr, 1313-1314
IsComObject, 1314
IsTypeVisibleFromCom,
  1314
NumParamBytes, 1314
OffsetOf, 1314-1315
Prelink, 1315-1316
PrelinkAll, 1316
PtrToStringAnsi,
  1316-1317
PtrToStringAuto,
  1317-1318
PtrToStringBSTR, 1318
PtrToStringUni, 1319
PtrToStructure,
  1319-1321
QueryInterface,
  1321-1323
ReadByte, 1323-1325
ReadInt16, 1326
ReadInt32, 1326-1327
ReadInt64, 1327
ReadIntPtr, 1327-1328
ReAllocCoTaskMem,
  1328
ReAllocHGlobal,
  1328-1329
Release, 1329-1330
ReleaseComObject,
  1330
ReleaseThreadCache,
  1330
SetComObjectData,

1331
SizeOf, 1331
StringToBSTR,
  1331-1332
StringToCoTaskMem-
  Ansi, 1332
StringToCoTaskMem-
  Auto, 1332
StringToCoTaskMem-
  Uni, 1333
StringToHGlobalAnsi,
  1333
StringToHGlobalAuto,
  1333-1334
StringToHGlobalUni,
  1334
StructureToPtr,
  1334-1336
ThrowExceptionForHR,
  1336-1337
UnsafeAddrOfPinned-
  ArrayElement, 1337
WriteByte, 1337-1339
WriteInt16, 1340
WriteInt32, 1340-1341
WriteInt64, 1341
WriteIntPtr, 1342
Marshal.ReleaseComObject
, 110
Marshal.SizeOf, 839
MarshalManagedToNative
  (ICustomMarshaler
  interface), 1281
MarshalNativeToManaged
  (ICustomMarshaler
  interface), 1281
MediaInfo, 1220
Microsoft.VisualBasic.
  CreateObject, 646
Microsoft.VisualBasic.
  Interaction.Beep, 810
Move, 1158, 1162

MoveNext, 524
MovePlayer, 1121, 1133
NumberPicture, 1147
NumberPicture class,
  1147, 1149-1150
NumParamBytes (Marshal
  class), 1314
OffsetOf (Marshal class),
  1314-1315
OnChangeUICues, 622
OnClosing, 622
OnEnterFullScreen, 1222
OnEventName, 609,
  622-623
OnKeyDown, 1167, 1171
OnValidating, 622
optional parameters,
  583-584
Picture, 1136
Picture class, 1136,
  1138-1139
Play, 1134-1136
Prelink (Marshal class),
  1315-1316
PrelinkAll (Marshal class),
  1316
PtrToStringAnsi (Marshal
  class), 1316-1317
PtrToStringAuto (Marshal
  class), 1317-1318
PtrToStringBSTR (Marshal
  class), 1318
PtrToStringUni (Marshal
  class), 1319
PtrToStructure (Marshal
  class), 1319-1321
QueryInterface
  (Marshal class),
  1321-1323
  IUnknown implementa-
  tion, 658-659
Read, by-reference null

value types, 264-265

ReadByte (Marshal class),
1323-1325

ReadInt16 (Marshal class),
1326

ReadInt32 (Marshal class),
1326-1327

ReadInt64 (Marshal class),
1327

ReadIntPtr (Marshal class),
1327-1328

ReAllocCoTaskMem
(Marshal class), 1328

ReAllocHGlobal (Marshal
class), 1328-1329

Recognize, 644-645

RegEnumKey, 856

RegisterAssembly, 1350,
1056-1057

RegisterFunction, 644

RegisterObjectCreation-
Callback, Extensible-
ClassFactory class, 1269

RegisterTypeForCom-
Clients, 1058, 1350

RegistrationHelper class,
1060
    C#, 1059
    C++, 1059
    *Visual Basic .NET,
    1059*

RegistrationServices
    *GetManagedCategory-
    Guid, 1349*
    *GetProgIdForType,
    1350*
    *GetRegistrableTypesIn-
    Assembly, 1350*
    RegisterAssembly, 1350
    *RegisterTypeForCom-
    Clients, 1350*

RegistrationServices class,

1056-1058
    *TypeRepresentsCom-
    Type, 1350*
    *TypeRequires-
    Registration, 1351*
    *UnregisterAssembly,
    1351*

Release (Marshal class),
501, 1329-1330

ReleaseComObject
(Marshal class), 110, 1330

ReleaseThreadCache
(Marshal class), 1330

Remove, 596

remove_EventName, 592

Render, 1121, 1133,
1151-1158, 1162,
1217-1218, 1233

RenderComplete, 1112,
1118

RenderFullScreen, 1222

ReportEvent, 1044-1045,
1289

Reset, 1151-1152, 1158,
1162, 1166

ResizeAndDrawAt, 1136,
1140, 1143-1146

ResizeAndDrawSurface,
1112

ResolveRef, 1053-1054
    *creating assemblies
    from type libraries,
    1045-1046*
    implementation, 1045
    *ITypeLibExporterNotify
    Sink interface, 1289*
    *ITypeLibImporterNotify
    Sink interface, 1289*
    *TypeLibConverter
    class, 1045*

Ring, 596

RuntimeEnvironment class
    *FromGlobalAccess-
    Cache, 1351*
    *GetRuntimeDirectory,
    1351*
    *GetSystemVersion,
    1352*

Screen, 1155

SetComObjectData
(Marshal class), 1331

setGUID, 728

SetPosition, 1147, 1149

Shutdown, 227

signatures, 652

size, 1136

SizeOf (Marshal class),
1331

SomeMethod, 479

Sound, 1134

Sound class, 1134-1136

StringToBSTR (Marshal
class), 1331-1332

StringToCoTaskMemAnsi
(Marshal class), 1332

StringToCoTaskMemAuto
(Marshal class), 1332

StringToCoTaskMemUni
(Marshal class), 1333

StringToHGlobalAnsi
(Marshal class), 1333

StringToHGlobalAuto
(Marshal class),
1333-1334

StringToHGlobalUni
(Marshal class), 1334

StructureToPtr (Marshal
class), 1334-1336

System, 1135

System.AppDomain.
Unload, 1049

System.Enum.Format, 646

System.Guid.NewGuid, 60

System.IO.Stream class,
883-889

System.Object class, 743

System.Runtime.Interop-
Services.ItypeLib-
ExporterNameProvider
interface, 1054

System.Runtime.Interop-
Services.Marshal, 845

System.Type.GetType, 68

System.Windows.Forms.
Control.Invoke, 1100

System.Windows.Forms.
Design.PictureBox-
Designer.Initialize, 508

System.Windows.Forms.
MessageBox.Show, 50

TAPI class, 227-229

ThrowExceptionForHR
(Marshal class),
1336-1337

ToString, 743
*IFormattable interface
implementation,
761-764*
*type library
transformation,
439-440*

type library transformations,
434
*by-reference parameters,
436-438*
*by-value parameters,
436-438*
*GetEnumerator method,
440*
HRESULTs, 434-436
overloaded, 438-439
parameter arrays,

440-441
*ToString method,
439-440*

Type.GetTypeFromCLSID,
309

Type.GetTypeFromProgID
, 309

TypeLibConverter class
C#, 1040
C++, 1041
*ConvertAssemblyTo-
TypeLib, 1050, 1356*
*ConvertTypeLibTo-
Assembly, 1356-1357*
*GetPrimaryInterop-
Assembly, 1357*
*Visual Basic .NET,
1041*

TypeRepresentsComType,
1057, 1350

TypeRequiresRegistration,
1058, 1351

Unadvise interface, 216

UnicodeEncoding.
GetBytes, 946

Uninstall, 1100

UninstallAssembly, 1061,
1099

UnregisterAssembly, 1056,
1351

UnregisterFunction, 644

UnsafeAddrOfPinnedArra
yElement (Marshal
class), 1337

usage guidelines, 511-513

Util class, 1112, 1118-
1119

Util.CreateSoundBuffer-
FromFile, 1135

windowsForm_Activated,
625

windowsForm_

ChangeUICues, 625

windowsForm_DragDrop,
625

WriteByte (Marshal class),
1337-1339

WriteInt16 (Marshal class),
1340

WriteInt32 (Marshal class),
1340-1341

WriteInt64 (Marshal class),
1341

WriteIntPtr (Marshal
class), 1342

**methods Screen class,
1155-1156**

**MFC (Microsoft
Foundation Classes), 277**

**Microsoft C Runtime
Library, 15**

**Microsoft Direct
Animation type library,
731**

**Microsoft DirectX. *See*
DirectX**

**Microsoft Foundation
Classes. *See* MFC**

**Microsoft Intermediate
Language. *See* IL**

**Microsoft Telephony API.
See TAPI**

**Microsoft Word, Spell
Checking application
example, 127-137**

**Microsoft.VisualBasic
assembly, 38, 356-358**

**Microsoft.VisualBasic
namespace, 643**

**Microsoft.VisualBasic.Com
pilerServices.StandardM
oduleAttribute, 356**

Microsoft.VisualBasic.

CreateObject method, 646

Microsoft.VisualBasic. Interaction.Beep method, 810

Microsoft.VisualBasic.Left function, 788

Microsoft.Win32 namespace, 1131

Microsoft.Win32.Registry class, 644

MIDL.EXE, 55

MiscTypes.cs (Interactive Interop Tool), 1064-1068

mixed-mode
debugging, 315-319
programming (Visual C++ managed extensions), 50-51

MKTYPLIB.EXE, 55

modules, converting COM, 187-188

Monitor class, 275

monitoring performance, 320-321

Move method, 1158, 1162

MoveNext method, 524

MovePlayer method, 1121, 1133

Moves enumeration, E-mail Attack, 1120

moveSound field, 1121

MSCOREE.DLL, 391, 460, 468, 492-493

MSCOREE.TLB, 460

mscorlib
IL Assembler types, 332-333
registering REGDB_E_ CLASSNOTREG failure, 403

mscorlib assembly, 23,

34-35, 38, 71, 463, 522
exceptions to HRESULT transformations, 1416-1417, 1423, 1429
HRESULT to exception transformations, 1400, 1406-1407, 1413
Interop API, 52

mscorlib.tlb type library, 623

MSHTML.TLB, 234

MSIL. See IL

MSXML, running TLBIMP on, 142

MTA (multi-threaded), 733

MTA value, System.Threading.Apart mentState enumeration, 280

MTAs (Multi-Threaded Apartments), 276-278, 282-289

Multi-Threaded Apartments. See MTAs

MultiPurposeObject coclass, 705

MultiPurposeObject interface, 705

MultiUse setting (instancing), 633

MULTI_QI structure, 873

MustInherit class, 506

MustRunInClientContext-Attribute, 585

Mutex class, 275

MyCustomMarshalers assembly, 365

N

Name property, 645

named_guids directive, 387

names
assemblies, 23-24, 533
clients, 499-502, 505
COM interfaces, 500
components, COM compared to .NET Framework, 59-62
designing COM objects for .NET clients, 734-735
DLL filenames, 690
enums, 707-709
GUIDs, 60-61
libraries, 427-428
members, 501, 505
namespaces, 502-503, 690-693
parameters, 503-504
PIAs (Primary Interop Assemblies), 686-687
PInvoke functions, 796
properties, 504-505
structures, 707-709
type libraries, 141-143
types, 500, 505
V-table binding, 505

/names (TLBEXP.EXE), 1383

/namespace (TLBIMP.EXE), 1379

/namespace option

namespaces, 643
assemblies, 23
DirectX, 1111, 1118, 1135, 1138, 1143, 1146, 1183, 1193-1194
Microsoft.VisualBasic, 643
Microsoft.Win32, 1131
names, 502-503

output assembly, 690-693

Sams.SmartTags, 643

SmartTagLib, 643

System, 35, 52, 620, 643,
887, 894, 1016,
1066-1068, 1079, 1096,
1118, 1131, 1138, 1146,
1149, 1152, 1156, 1171,
1215

  C# keywords, 35

  C++ keywords, 42-43

  IntPtr type, 270

  Visual Basic .NET
    keywords, 39

System.Collections, 596,
743-744, 746-747

System.Diagnostics, 321

System.Drawing, 1215

System.EnterpriseServices,
52, 584-586, 1059, 1099

System.Globalization, 620

System.IO, 887, 894

System.Reflection, 26,
59,,270, 1066, 1096,
1215

System.Runtime.
InteropServices, 52, 218,
250, 297, 391, 596-598,
643, 772, 837, 861, 887,
909, 998, 1016, 1056,
1066-1067, 1118, 1138,
1215, 1250, 1252

  ArrayWithOffset value
    type, 1252-1254

  AssemblyRegistration-
    Flags enumeration,
    1254

  AutomationProxy-
    Attribute, 1254

  BINDPTR value type,

1255

BIND_OPTS value
  type, 1255

CALLCONV enumera-
  tion, 1255

CallingConvention enu-
  meration, 1255-1256

CharSet enumeration,
  1256

ClassInterfaceAttribute,
  1256-1257

ClassInterfaceType
  enumeration, 1257

CoClassAttribute, 1258

ComAliasNameAttribute
  , 1258

ComConversionLoss-
  Attribute, 1258

ComEventInterface-
  Attribute, 1258-1259

COMException
  exception, 1259-1260

ComImportAttribute,
  1260

ComInterfaceType
  enumeration, 1260

ComMemberType
  enumeration, 1261

ComRegisterFunction-
  Attribute, 1261

ComSourceInterfaces-
  Attribute, 1261

ComUnregisterFunctio
  nAttribute, 1262

ComVisibleAttribute,
  1262-1263

CONNECTDATA value
  type, 1263

CurrencyWrapper
  class, 1263-1264

custom attributes, 1250

DESCKIND enumera-
  tion, 1264

DESCUNION value
  type, 1264

DispatchWrapper class,
  1264-1265

DispIdAttribute,
  1265-1266

DISPPARAMS value
  type, 1266

DllImportAttribute,
  1266-1267

ELEMDESC value type,
  1267

ErrorWrapper class,
  1267-1268

EXCEPINFO value
  type, 1268

ExporterEventKind
  enumeration,
  1268-1269

ExtensibleClassFactory
  class, 1269-1271

ExternalException
  exception, 1271

FieldOffsetAttribute,
  1271-1272

FILETIME value type,
  1272

FUNCDESC value
  type, 1272

FUNCFLAGS
  enumeration, 1272

FUNCKIND
  enumeration, 1273

GCHandle value type,
  1273-1277

GCHandleType
  enumeration, 1277

GuidAttribute, 1278

HandleRef value type,
  1278-1280

ICustomAdapter interface, 1280-1281

ICustomFactory interface, 1281

ICustomMarshaler interface, 1281-1282

IDispatchImplAttribute, 1282

IDispatchImplType enumeration, 1283

IDLDESC value type, 1283

IDLFLAG enumeration, 1283

IMPLTYPEFLAGS enumeration, 1283

ImportedFromTypeLibAttribute, 1284

ImporterEventKind enumeration, 1284

InAttribute, 1284-1285

InterfaceTypeAttribute, 1285

InvalidComObjectException exception, 1286

InvalidOleVariantTypeExceptionexception, 1286-1287

INVOKEKIND enumeration, 1287

IRegistrationServices interface, 1287

ITypeLibConverter interface, 1287-1288

ITypeLibExporterNameProvider interface, 1288

ITypeLibExporterNotifySink interface, 1289

ITypeLibImporterNotify

Sink interface, 1289

LayoutKind enumeration, 1290

LCIDConversionAttribute, 1290-1291

LIBFLAGS enumeration, 1291

Marshal class, 1292-1342

MarshalAsAttribute, 1342-1344

MarshalDirectiveException, 1344-1345

ObjectCreationDelegate delegate, 1345

OptionalAttribute, 1345-1346

OutAttribute, 1346-1347

PARAMDESC value type, 1347

PARAMFLAG enumeration, 1347

PreserveSigAttribute, 1347-1348

PrimaryInteropAssemblyAttribute, 1348

ProgIdAttribute, 1349

RegistrationServices class, 1349-1351

RuntimeEnvironment class, 1351-1352

SafeArrayRankMismatchException, 1352

SafeArrayTypeMismatchException, 1352-1353

SEHException, 1353

STATSTG value type, 1353

StructLayoutAttribute, 1354

SYSKIND enumeration, 1354

tool APIs, 1252

TYPEATTR value type, 1355

TYPEDESC value type, 1355

TYPEFLAGS enumeration, 1355

TYPEKIND enumeration, 1355

TYPELIBATTR value type, 1356

TypeLibConverter class, 1356-1357

TypeLibExporterFlags enumeration, 1357

TypeLibFuncAttribute, 1358

TypeLibFuncFlags enumeration, 1358

TypeLibImporterFlags enumeration, 1358

TypeLibTypeAttribute, 1359

TypeLibTypeFlags enumeration, 1359

TypeLibVarAttribute, 1359

TypeLibVarFlags enumeration, 1359

UCOMIBindCtx interface, 1360

UCOMIConnectionPoint interface, 1360

UCOMIConnectionPointContainer interface, 1360

UCOMIEnum-
ConnectionPoints
interface, 1360
UCOMIEnum-
Connections interface,
1361
UCOMIEnumMoniker
interface, 1361
UCOMIEnumString
interface, 1361
UCOMIEnumVARIANT
interface, 1361-1362
UCOMIMoniker
interface, 1362-1363
UCOMIPersistFile
interface, 1363
UCOMIRunningObject
Table interface, 1363
UCOMIStream
interface, 1364
UCOMITypeComp
interface, 1364-1365
UCOMITypeInfo
interface, 1365
UCOMITypeLib
interface, 1366
UnknownWrapper
class, 1366-1367
UnmanagedType enu-
meration, 1367-1368
VARDESC value type,
1368
VarEnum enumeration,
1369-1370
VARFLAGS
enumeration, 1370
wrappers, 115
System.Runtime.
InteropServices, 1135
System.Runtime.

InteropServices.
CustomMarshalers, 1370
EnumerableToDispatch
Marshaler class,
1370
EnumeratorToEnumVar
iantMarshaler class,
1371
ExpandoToDispatchEx
Marshaler class,
1371-1372
TypeToTypeInfo-
Marshaler class,
1372
System.Runtime.
InteropServices.Expando
, 1372-1373
System.Text, 946
System.Text.
RegularExpressions, 381
System.Threading, 275,
288
System.Windows.Forms,
52, 620, 1171, 1215
Win32, 1166-1167, 1171
NAs (Neutral
Apartments), 276, 277
nested arrays, data types,
518-519
nested types, ILASM.EXE,
334
.NET Framework
compared to COM, 55-57
component locations,
62-64
component names,
59-62
error handling, 66-68
object lifetimes, 68-69
programming model,
57-58
type compatibility, 64

type information, 58-59
type safety, 66
versioning, 64-66
components, 15, 380
C# StringValidator
class, 380-381
C++ StringValidator
class, 385-388
DirectX, 1106
JScript StringValidator
class, 388-390
locations, 62-64
Visual Basic 6
StringValidator class,
382-384
converting COM members
for object models, 434
.NET events, 446-447
.NET fields, 444-446
.NET methods, 434-441
.NET properties,
441-444
defined, 14
designing COM compo-
nents for, 716-717
array parameters,
717-720
error reporting,
720-728
VARIANT parameters,
720
designing COM members
for, 729
passing error
information, 731
passing interface point-
ers to anything, 729
passing type informa-
tion, 730-731
designing COM objects for
IProvideClassInfo, 734
naming guidelines, 734-

735
performance, 735-738
resource management,
731-733
features, 16
deployment, 19-20
platform neutrality,
21-22
security, 20-21
version resiliency,
16-19
DLL Hell, 16-17
interfaces, 740
class interfaces,
741-743
COM, 678-679
converting to COM
interfaces, 447-449
disabling type library
marshaling, 580-582
HRESULTs, 758
IComparer implementa-
tion, 764-766
IDispatchEx, 678-679
IDisposable, 732
IEnumVARIANT, 678
IErrorInfo, 731
IHashCodeProvider
implementation,
764-766
inheritance, 743-747
InterfaceTypeAttribute,
578
IReflect, 665-672
ITypeInfo, 678
names, 503-504
System.IConvertible,
652
Visual Basic 6,
397-399, 759-764
Visual C++, 747-759

monitoring performance,
320-321
naming guidelines, 499
names to avoid, 500-502
namespaces, 502-503
Pascal casing, 503-506
SDK
referencing ActiveX
controls, 122-123
referencing COM
components, 81-84
running Office XP
smart tags example,
650
WINCV.EXE, 960, 962
threading, 275
callbacks from COM
objects to .NET
objects, 282-289
COM apartment
incompatibility, 291-
292
COM apartment states,
277-282
COM apartment types,
276-277
COM ThreadingModel
registry value,
276-277
concurrency, 275
usage guidelines, 506
constructors, 513-514
data types, 516-519
enumerations, 514-516
interfaces versus
classes, 506-508
interfaces versus
custom attributes,
508-510
overloaded methods,
511-513

properties versus fields,
510-511
.NET Visualization API,
1224
ColorfulVisualization,
1231-1235
Dancing Cat Visualization,
1235-1243
SimpleVisualization,
1224-1226
WizardVisualization,
1227-1230
NetMeeting Coclass
interface, C# definitions,
1007-1009, 1016-1018
Neutral Apartments.
***See* NAs**
neutral components, 277
Neutral string value, 276
new operator, creating
instances, 99
NewWrapper type, 298
/nologo (AXIMP.EXE),
1393
/nologo (REGASM.EXE),
1389
/nologo (REGSVCS.EXE),
1396
/nologo (TLBEXP.EXE),
1384
/nologo (TLBIMP.EXE),
1381
non-contiguous property
accessors, 992
non-public interfaces
(COM interfaces), 967
non-reflexive IUnknown,
implementations,
292-293
Non-Static Extern
Members feature (C#),

1029-1031
None value
AssemblyRegistrationFlags
enumeration, 1254
CharSet enumeration, 1256
ClassInterfaceType
enumeration, 1257
**/noreconfig
(REGSVCS.EXE), 1395**
**Normal value
(GCHandleType enumer-
ation), 1277**
**notifySink parameter
(ConvertTypeLibToAssem
bly method), 1051, 1357**
**NOTIF_CONVERTWARNING
value, 1044-1045, 1052**
ExporterEventKind
enumeration, 1269
ImporterEventKind
enumeration, 1284
**NOTIF_TYPECONVERTED
events, 1052**
**NOTIF_TYPECONVERTED
value, 1045, 1052**
ExporterEventKind
enumeration, 1269
ImporterEventKind
enumeration, 1284
**no_namespace directive,
387**
**NumberPicture class,
1133, 1146**
methods, 1147-1150
private fields, 1147
**NumberPicture method,
1147**
numBonuses field, 1121
**NumBonuses property,
1121, 1132**

numLives field, 1121
**NumLives property, 1121,
1132**
**NumParamBytes method
(Marshal class), 1314**

O

**Object class, interface,
439-440**
**Object Definition
Language.** *See* **ODL**
**object parameters,
MarshalAsAttribute,
1343**
**ObjectCreationDelegate
delegate
(System.Runtime.Intero
pServices namespace),
1345**
**ObjectPoolingAttribute,
585**
objects
adapter
alternative to, 910-913
CCWs, 904-905
*custom marshalers,
901-909*
RCWs, 904-906
Application, 646
COM, 53
*activating with
CoCreateInstanceEx,
871-874*
*calling methods, 101-
109*
*calling properties,
101-109*
*IProvideClassInfo
interface, 734*
*Marshal.ReleaseCom-
Object, 299-304*
passing, 115-118

releasing, 109-110
*visualizations, 572,
1196-1197*
COM+, 309-311
*exposing .NET objects
as, 584-586*
*installing in Component
Services explorer, 309*
DCOM, 309-311
*creating remote objects,
309-310*
.NET remoting, 310
*Type.GetTypeFromCLSI
D method, 309*
*Type.GetTypeFromProg
ID method, 309*
designing for .NET clients
IProvideClassInfo, 734
*managing resources,
731-733*
*naming guidelines, 734-
735*
performance, 735-738
threading, 733
IUnknown.AddRef
(COM), 68
lifetimes, COM compared
to .NET Framework,
68-69
.NET Framework
*calling members,
400-403*
creating, 399-400
*exposing as COM
objects, 584-586*
performance, 320-321
**ODL (Object Definition
Language), 54**
**Office XP, smart tags,
634-636, 643-646**
explicit interface members,

655-656
HRESULTs, 656
inheritance, 654-655
parameterized properties,
  653-654
running example using
  .NET Framework, 650
running example using
  Visual Studio .NET,
  646-650
Office.dll, 301
**OffsetOf method
(Marshal class),
1314-1315**
OLE Automation, 516-518
IDispatch implementations,
  665
LoadTypeLibEx method,
  1042
SAFEARRAY parameters,
  517
VARIANTs, 517
**OLE/COM Object Viewer.
See OLEVIEW.EXE**
**OLE32.DLL, PInvoke
signatures, 1461, 1470**
**OLEVIEW.EXE, 55-56, 291,
427, 535-536, 688**
**OLE_COLOR parameter,
194, 341-342**
OnCallerId event, 596
**OnChangeUICues
method, 622**
OnClosing method, 622
**OnEnterFullScreen
method, 1222**
**OnEventName method,
609, 622-623**
**OnKeyDown method,
1167, 1171**
OnRing event, 596

OnValidating method, 622
**operators, creating new
instances, 99**
**optional parameters, 104,
583-584**
COM, 104-105
.NET Framework, 105-109
**OptionalAttribute
(System.Runtime.Intero
pServices namespace),
583-584, 1345-1346**
Options property, 1099
**ordering property acces-
sors, language limita-
tions of COM interfaces,
990-994**
/out (AXIMP.EXE), 1392
/out (TLBEXP.EXE), 1384
/out (TLBIMP.EXE), 1378
**OutAttribute
(System.Runtime.Intero
pServices namespace),
786, 1346-1347**
customizing data flow,
  553-554
export behaviors, 438
marking array parameters,
  792-794
**outgoing interface. See
source interface (COM
callbacks)**
outproc servers, 63
output
C# code demonstration, 28
assembly content modifi-
  cations, 328
creating PIAs (Primary
  Interop Assemblies), 690
discovering custom
  attributes with reflection,
  32-33

method conversions,
  167-169
namespaces, 690-693
**OutputDirectory property,
1079**
**overloaded methods, 438-
439, 511-513**
**OwnerWindow class,
1221**

P

**Pack parameter,
StructLayoutAttribute,
830**
padding field, 1147
page flipping, 1118
**PARAMDESC value type
(System.Runtime.Interop
Services namespace),
1347**
**parameter arrays, method
conversions, 169-171**
**parameters. See also
arrays**
arrays, 717
  SAFEARRAYs, 717-719
  *single-dimensional,
    719-720*
  *type library transfor-
    mations, 440-441*
  zero-bounded, 719
ArraySubType, 337
asmNamespace, 1046
assembly, 1060
by-reference, 119-120, 518
  ILASM.EXE, 334
  *method conversions,
    164-167*
  .NET method transfor-

mations, 436-438
by-value
  method conversions,
   164-167
  .NET method transfor-
   mations, 436-438
Component, 508
ConvertTypeLibToAssembly
  method, 1357
flags, 1051
ILASM.EXE, 334
in, [out]
  method conversions,
   167-169
installFlags, 1060
IntPtr, 340-341
[in], 167-169
IReflect interface, 671
isVisible, 504
keyPair, 1046
language limitations of
  COM interfaces,
  994-995, 998
LocaleID, 644
MarshalAsAttribute, 898,
  900
  ArraySubType, 1343
  Boolean, 1343
  MarshalCookie, 1343
  MarshalType, 1343
  MarshalTypeRef, 1343
  object, 1343
  SafeArraySubType,
   1343
  SafeArrayUserDefined-
   SubType, 1344
  SizeConst, 1344
  SizeParamIndex, 1344
  strings, 1342
names, 503-504
notifySink, 1051
OLE_COLOR, 194,

341-342
optional, 104, 583-584
  COM, 104-105
  .NET Framework,
   105-109
[out], 167-169
PInvoke,
  DllImportAttribute,
  1266-1267
PInvoke signatures
  arrays, 792-794
  CallingConvention,
   799-800
  Declare statement,
   796-799
  default marshaling, 782
  DllImportAttribute,
   796-807
  strings, 782-791
ppAttributeEntries (struct
  type), 259
properties, 653-654
publicKey, 1046
RecognizerSite, 645
Render method, 1218
SafeArraySubType,
  338-340
SmartTagID, 645
strTypeLibName, 1050
StructLayoutAttribute, 830
System.Type, GUID
  property, 568-570
throwOnMissingSubKey,
  569
tlb, 1060
Type,
  ComSourceInterfaces-
  Attribute, 600
VARIANT, 720
VerbID, 645
**PARAMFLAG enumeration
(System.Runtime.Intero
pServices namespace),**

1347
**/parname (REGSVCS.EXE),
1395-1396**
partial binding, 91
**Pascal casing (naming
guidelines), 503-506**
passing
  error information, 731
  interface pointers, 729
  objects, COM, 115-118
  structures, 821-829
  type information, 730-731
pauseScreen field, 1121
performance
  designing COM objects for
   .NET clients, 735-738
  monitoring, 320-321
permissions
  reflection, 304
  serialization, 304
  unmanaged code, 304
Phone class, 592, 596-597
  event handlers, 597
  exposing .NET events to
   COM with CLR,
   602-605
  exposing .NET events to
   COM without CLR,
   594-597
**PIAs (Primary Interop
Assemblies), 86-90, 684**
  creating, 686
   customizing metadata,
    693-694
   names, 686-687
   naming output assembly,
    690-693
   type library references,
    687-689
  deployment, 694-696
  IDL type libraries, 697-698
   ActiveX controls, 712

constants, 709-710
constructs, 710
defining classes,
    702-707
naming enums, 707-709
referencing external
    types, 698-702
registering type
    libraries, 711
opening, 695
reasons for creating,
    684-685
registration, 694-696
Picture class, 1133-1134
methods, 1136-1139
properties, 1136
Picture method, 1136
**pictures, E-mail Attack,
1111**
**Pinned value,
GCHandleType enumera-
tion, 1277**
PInvoke, 49-50
**Pinvoke (Platform
Invocation Services), 49,
772**
C#, 50, 776-777
choosing DLL locations
    dynamically, 863-865
choosing DLL names
    dynamically, 863-865
delegates as function
    pointers, 811
    CopyFileEx, 812-815
    SetConsoleCtrlHandler
        function, 815-817
DLL entry points, 772
functions
    case-sensitivity, 774

KERNEL32.DLL,
    774-777
names, 796
invoking unmanaged
    function pointers in
    managed code, 818-821
parameters,
DllImportAttribute,
    1266-1267
responding to console
    input, 865-868
signatures, 1432-1433
arrays, 792-794
calling conventions,
    799-800
changing exact
    spelling, 799
converting data types,
    778-781
Declare statement,
    795-796
default marshaling for
    parameters, 782
diagnostics, 778
error handling,
    800-807
GDI32.DLL, 1433,
    1442
KERNEL32.DLL, 1442,
    1461
OLE32.DLL, 1461,
    1470
premature garbage
    collecting, 852-853,
    856, 859-862
SHELL32.DLL,
    1470-1471
strings, 782-791,
    796-799
USER32.DLL, 1472,
    1486
unsafe C# code, 849-852

Visual Basic .NET,
    773-775
Win32 APIs, 772
**pixelsOffscreen field,
1150**
**Platform Invocation
Services. *See* PInvoke**
platforms, 21-22
Play method, 1134, 1136
Player field, 1120
PlayerPicture field, 1121
PlaySound API, 810
**pointer to string. *See*
LPSTR**
**pointer to wide-character
string. *See* LPWSTR**
pointers, 810-811
customizing structures,
    829
    FieldOffsetAttribute,
        832-833
    formatted classes,
        839-844
    MarshalAsAttribute,
        834-839
    StructLayoutAttribute,
        829-832
    structure inspection,
        844-847
data types, 518
delegates as, 811-812
    CopyFileEx, 812-815
    SetConsoleCtrlHandler,
        815-817
invoking unmanaged
    pointers in managed code,
    818-821
passing structures, 821-829
**PowerPoint, garbage
collection, 301-304**
PowerPoint.dll, 301

PowerPoint.Eapplication interface, 366

ppAttributeEntries parameter (struct type), 259

Prelink method (Marshal class), 1315-1316

PrelinkAll method (Marshal class), 1316

PreserveSig parameter, 803-807, 1267

PreserveSigAttribute (System.Runtime.Interop Services namespace), 436, 579, 1347-1348

PresetCount property, 1221

PresetEnumAttribute, 1220-1223

/primary (TLBIMP.EXE), 1379

Primary Interop Assembly. *See* PIAs

PrimaryInteropAssembly-Attribute (System. Runtime.InteropServices namespace), 1348

private fields
    Character class, 1158
    Game class, 1121
    NumberPicture class, 1147

private members, 653

Private setting (instancing), 633

PrivateComponent-Attribute, 585

problems, COM interface implementations
    explicit interface members,

655-656
    HRESULTs, 656
    inheritance, 654-655
    parameterized properties, 653-654

ProgId property, 644-645

ProgIdAttribute (System.Runtime.Intero pServices namespace), 566, 1349

ProgIDs, 63-65

programming models, COM compared to .NET Framework, 57-58

Progress property, 1068

ProgressMaximum property, 1068

Project menu commands, Add Reference, 25

projects, binary-compatible components. *See* binary-compatible components

properties
    AllowMultiple, 30
    AnimatedPicture class, 1140
    ApartmentState, 280-281
    C#, 280-281
    starting new threads, 282
    Visual Basic .NET, 281
    AssemblyQualifiedName, 61
    calling COM objects, 101-109
    Capabilities, 1220
    COM interface language limitations, 990
    location and ordering

    of property accessors, 990-994
    optional parameters and default values, 994-995, 998
    Control, 621
    converting, 171-173
    CurrentAudioTitle, 1220
    CurrentChannelCount, 1220
    CurrentPreset, 1217, 1229
    CurrentSampleRate, 1220
    Desc, 644-645
    Description, 1216-1217, 1233
    EntryPoint, DllImportAttribute, 36, 40, 43
    EnvelopeUnderneath, 1162
    exception objects, CLR, 722
    Game class, 1121
    GCHandle value type
    IsAllocated, 1275
    Target, 1276
    Graphics, 622
    GUID, 568-570, 1216
    Handle, 1171, 1221
    HashCode, 502
    Height, 1136, 1139-1140, 1143
    HighScore, 1121, 1132
    HResult, 520
    Inherited, 30, 546
    Instancing, 633
    InternetExplorer.Document, 234
    IsVisible, 504
    ITreeNode.isVisible, 504
    Marshal class

SystemDefaultCharSize, 1336
SystemMaxDBCSChar-Size, 1336
Menu, 507
Name, 645
names, 504-505
NumBonuses, 1121, 1132
NumLives, 1121, 1132
Options, 1099
OutputDirectory, 1079
parameterized, 653-654
Picture class, 1136
PresetCount, 1221
ProgId, 644-645
Progress, 1068
ProgressMaximum, 1068
Rectangle, 622
Score, 1121, 1132
SmartTagCaption, 645
SmartTagCount, 644-645
SmartTagDownloadURL, 645
SmartTagName, 645
State, 1121, 1132
System.Windows.Forms. Form.Menu, 507
SystemConfigurationFile (RuntimeEnvironment class), 1351
SystemDefaultCharSize (Marshal class), 1336
SystemMaxDBCSCharSize (Marshal class), 1336
TextBoxFont, 923
Title, 1216-1217, 1233
Type, 502
type library transformations, 441-444

usage guidelines, versus fields, 510-511
VerbCaptionFromID, 645
VerbCount, 645
VerbID, 645
VerbNameFromID, 646
Width, 1136, 1139-1140, 1143
PropGet value, ComMemberType enumeration, 1261
PropSet value, ComMemberType enumeration, 1261
pros and cons, manually defining COM defini-tions, 958-959
pseudo-custom attributes, 33
DllImportAttribute, 776-777
choosing DLL locations dynamically, 863, 865
choosing DLL names dynamically, 863, 865
System.Runtime. InteropServices namespace
ComImportAttribute, 1260
DllImportAttribute, 1266-1267
FieldOffsetAttribute, 1271-1272
InAttribute, 1284-1285
MarshalAsAttribute, 1342-1344
OptionalAttribute, 1345-1346
OutAttribute,

1346-1347
PreserveSigAttribute, 1347-1348
StructLayoutAttribute, 1354
PtrToStringAnsi method (Marshal class), 1316-1317
PtrToStringAuto method (Marshal class), 1317-1318
PtrToStringBSTR method (Marshal class), 1318
PtrToStringUni method (Marshal class), 1319
PtrToStructure method (Marshal class), 1319-1321
public fields
Envelope class, 1162
Game class, 1120
Util class, 1112
public key, assemblies, 61
public properties, Game class, 1121
/publickey (AXIMP.EXE), 1392
/publickey (TLBIMP.EXE), 1379
publicKey parameter (ConvertTypeLibToAssem bly method), 1046, 1357
PublicNotCreatable setting (instancing), 633

Q
QueryAccessibilityHelp event, 623

QueryInterface, 706, 110-112
failures, 290-291
incompatibile apartments, 291-292
non-reflexive IUnknown implementations, 292-293
type library errors, 294
Visual Basic 6 projects without binary compatability, 294-295
method (Marshal class), 658-659, 1321-132,3
QueryPerformanceCounter function, 774
QueryPerformance-Frequency function, 774-777
/quiet (REGSVCS.EXE), 1396

R

RandomNumber field, 1112
raw_interfaces_only directive, 387
RCW (Runtime-Callable Wrapper), 69-71
class, 182-186
custom marshaling, 880-882
adapter objects, 904, 906
exposing IStream and Stream, 923-932
types, 295-304
Read method, 264-265
ReadByte method (Marshal class), 1323-1325

ReadConsoleInput API, 865-868
ReadInt16 method (Marshal class), 1326
ReadInt32 method (Marshal class), 1326-1327
ReadInt64 method (Marshal class), 1327
ReadIntPtr method (Marshal class), 1327-1328
ReAllocCoTaskMem method (Marshal class), 1328
ReAllocHGlobal method (Marshal class), 1328-1329
Recognize method, 644-645
RecognizerSite parameter, 645
/reconfig (REGSVCS.EXE), 1396
ReconfigureExistingApplication value, 1061
Recordset. ActiveConnection property, 992-993
RECT parameter, 1218
RECT structure, 1021
Rectangle property, 622
/reference option (TLBIMP.EXE), 1045, 1380
referencing
ActiveX controls
with .NET Framework SDK, 122-123
in Visual Studio .NET, 121-122
Web browser example, 123, 126

assemblies, 25
COM components
SDK, 81-84
in Visual Studio .NET, 78-84
reflection, 26
C# code, 26-28
custom attributes, 31-33
Reflection Emit, 26
static members, 482-488
reflection permission, 304
REGASM.EXE, 296, 385, 535, 694-696, 1040, 1056, 1062-1063, 1385-1386
/?, 1390
/codebase option, 393-394
/codebase, 1386
generating type libraries, 395
/help, 1390
/nologo, 1389
/regfile, 573, 1386-1387
/registered, 1387
registration, 568
assemblies, 391-394, 532
Interop Assemblies, 297
/silent, 1389
syntax, 1385
/tlb, 1387-1389
/tlb option, 1057
/tlb switch, 571
/u option, 569
/unregister, 1389
/verbose, 1390
RegCloseKey API, 856
REGDB_E_CLASSNOTREG failure, 403
RegDeleteKey API, 860

REGEDIT.EXE, 55
REGEDT32.EXE, 55
RegEnumKey API, 856
RegEnumKey method,
856
/regfile (REGASM.EXE),
573, 1386-1387
Register class, 1093-1097
Register for COM Interop
option, 390, 395, 649
   C#, 534
   Visual Basic .NET, 534
   Visual Studio .NET, 535
Register tab (Interactive
Interop Tool), 1092-1097
Register value, 1061
RegisterAssembly method
(RegistrationServices
class), 1056-1057, 1350
/registered
(REGASM.EXE), 1387
RegisterFunction method,
644
RegisterObjectCreation-
Callback method, 1269
RegisterTypeForComClients
method
(RegistrationServices
class), 1058, 1350
Registrar class, 1096
registration, 460
   assemblies, 390-392,
     532-535, 1056
     HRESULTs, 393
     REGASM.EXE, 391,
      393-394
     RegistrationServices
      class, 391, 1056-1058
     TypeLoadException, 392
     VB6.EXE, 392

WSCRIPT.EXE, 392
ClrCreateManagedInstance
   API, 468-471
customizing, 566
   adding arbitrary regis-
     tration code, 567-569
   custom registration
     functions, 570-574
   ProgIdAttribute, 566
   System.Guid.ToString,
     570
   unregistration functions,
     569-570
hosting CLR, 460-468
Interop Assemlies, 297
mscorlib, 403
PIAs, 694-696
REGASM.EXE, 568
type libraries, 711
Registration Utility.
REGASM.EXE, 385
RegistrationHelper class,
1059, 1252
   InstallationFlags
     enumeration, 1060-1061
   methods, 1060
     C#, 1059
     C++, 1059
     Visual Basic .NET, 1059
RegistrationServices class
(System.Runtime.Intero
pServices namespace),
391, 1097, 1349
   methods, 1056-1058
     GetManagedCategory-
      Guid, 1349
     GetProgIdForType,
      1350
     GetRegistrableTypesIn
      Assembly, 1350
     RegisterAssembly, 1350
     RegisterTypeForCom-

     Clients, 1350
     TypeRepresentsCom-
      Type, 1350
     TypeRequires-
      Registration, 1351
     UnregisterAssembly,
      1351
Registry
   adding additional entries,
     567-569
   assemblies, 80
   HKEY_CLASSES_ROOT\
     CLSID\{CLSID}\
     InProcServer32 key,
     276-277
   registering assemblies in.
     See registration
   Visualization API,
     1197-1198
RegistryKey class, 853,
856, 859-860
RegistryKey instance, 856
RegistryKey.DeleteSubKey,
569
RegistryKeyEnumerator
class, 853, 856
REGKIND enumeration,
1068
RegOpenKey API, 856
REGSVCS.EXE, 1040, 1060,
1252, 1394
   /?, 1396
   /appname, 1394-1395
   /c, 1395
   /componly, 1395
   /exapp, 1395
   /extlb, 1395
   /fc, 1395
   /help, 1396
   /nologo, 1396

/noreconfig, 1395
/parname, 1395-1396
/quiet, 1396
/reconfig, 1396
syntax, 1394
/tlb, 1396
/u, 1396
REGSVR32.EXE, 55, 271, 291
Release method (Marshal class), 501, 1329-1330
ReleaseComObject method (Marshal class), 110, 300, 1330
ReleaseThreadCache method (Marshal class), 1330
releasing COM objects, 109-110
remote DCOM objects, creating, 309-310
remote servers, 63
remoting (.NET), 310
Remove method, 596
remove_EventName method, 592
Render method, 1121, 1133, 1151-1156, 1158, 1162, 1199-1200, 1217-1218, 1233
RenderComplete method, 1112, 1118
RenderFullScreen method, 1200, 1222
ReportEvent method (ITypeLibExporterNotify-Sink interface), 1044-1045, 1289
ReportEvent method (ITypeLibImporterNotify

Sink interface), 1289
reporting errors, 720-721
HRESULTs
failure, 721
success, 721-722
setting information, 722-728
ReportWarningsToConsole value, 1061
Reset method, 1151-1152, 1158, 1162, 1166
ResizeAndDrawAt method, 1136, 1140, 1143-1144, 1146
ResizeAndDrawSurface method, 1112
ResolveRef method (ITypeLibExporterNotify Sink interface), 1053-1054, 1289
creating assemblies from type libraries, 1045-1046
implementation, 1045
ITypeLibImporterNotify-Sink interface, 1289
TypeLibConverter class, 1045
resources
management, 731-733
unmanaged, 326
RestrictedAttribute, 508-509
Ring event, 592-593
Ring method, 596
RingEventHandler class, 596
role-based security, 21
running object tables, 1301
runtime environment, 15

Runtime-Callable Wrapper. *See* **RCW**
RuntimeEnvironment class, 1351-1352
methods
FromGlobalAccess-Cache, 1351
GetRuntimeDirectory, 1351
GetSystemVersion, 1352
properties, 1351

S

safe mode, 19
SAFEARRAY parameters, 517
SafeArrayAsSystemArray flag, 1043
SafeArrayGetVartype API, 946
SafeArrayRankMismatch-Exception (System. Runtime.InteropServices namespace), 1352
SAFEARRAYs, 154-156, 348-351, 717-719
adding size to C-style arrays, 349-351
custom marshaling .NET string, 943-947
UnmanagedType enumeration values, 550-552
variants containing structures, 273-275
SafeArraySubType parameter, 338-340, 1343
SafeArrayTypeMismatch-Exception (System. Runtime.InteropServices namespace), 1352-1353

SafeArrayUserDefinedSub Type parameters, 1344

Sams.SmartTags namespace, 643

saving
assemblies, 1048-1050
dynamic type libraries, 1055

SCODE data type, 150-151

score field, 1121

Score property, 1121, 1132

ScorePicture field, 1121

screen (Console), clearing, 868-870

Screen class, 1133, 1155-1156

Screen method, 1155

SDK (Software Developer Kit), 15, 33-34, 78
COM utilities, 55-56
compared to Interactive
Interop Tool, 1062-1063
referencing ActiveX
controls, 122-123
referencing COM
components, 81-84
running Office XP smart
tags example, 650
tools, 960-962

SecureMethodAttribute, 585

security, 20
code-access, 21
link demands, 306
role-based, 21
unmanaged code, 49, 304-308

security identifier. *See* **SID**

SecurityPermission-Attribute, 305

SecurityRoleAttribute, 585

SEHException (System.Runtime.Intero pServices namespace), 1353

Sequential value, 1290

serialization permission, 304

servers
inproc, 63
outproc, 63

serviced components, installation, 1059-1061

services, Web, 14

set accessors, 442

SetCodeBase value, 1254

SetComObjectData method (Marshal class), 1331

SetConsoleCtrlHandler function, 815-817

SetCurrentPreset method, 1201

SetErrorInfo interface, 728

SetGUID method, 728

SetLastError parameter, 800-801, 1267

SetPosition method, 1147-1149

SetVolumeLabel function, 783-784

shared names, 23-24

SHELL32.DLL, 1470-1471

shutdown functions, 492-493

Shutdown method, 227

SID (security identifier), 847-848

side-by-side components, 18-19

sideEdge field, 1147

signatures (.NET), 729
C#, 899-901
GetObjectAttribute
method, 260
GetSite, 729
Interop Assembly, 344
metadata, 249
methods, 652
premature Garbage
Collection, 852-853, 856, 859-862
unsafe C# code, 849-852
variable-length, 849

signatures (PInvoke), 1432-1433
arrays, 792-794
calling conventions, 799-800
changing exact spelling, 799
converting data types, 778-781
Declare statement, 795-796
default marshaling for
parameters, 782
diagnostics, 778
error handling, 800
error codes, 800-802
exceptions on failure, 803-807
GDI32.DLL, 1433, 1442
KERNEL32.DLL, 1442, 1461
OLE32.DLL, 1461, 1470
SHELL32.DLL, 1470-1471
strings, 782
customizing behavior,

796-799

System.IntPtr, 789-791

System.String, 783-784, 787-788

System.Text. StringBuilder, 783-786

USER32.DLL, 1472, 1486

SignCode.exe, 24

signing

  assemblies, 24

  SignCode.exe, 24

/silent (AXIMP.EXE), 1393

/silent (REGASM.EXE), 1389

/silent (TLBEXP.EXE), 1384

/silent (TLBIMP.EXE), 1381

Simple Object Access Protocol. *See* **SOAP**

Single string value, 276

single-dimensional arrays, 719-720

Single-Threaded Apartments. *See* **STAs**

SingleUse setting (instancing), 633

sink helper class (NetMeeting coclass interface), 1016

size, adding to C-style arrays, 349-351

size method, 1136

Size parameter, 830

SizeConst parameters, 1344

SizeOf method (Marshal class), 1331

SizeParamIndex parameters, 1344

skins (Media Player), 1196

smart tag

  explicit interface members, 655-656

  HRESULTs, 656

  inheritance, 654-655

  parameterized properties, 653-654

smart tags, 634-636, 643-648

smart tagsrunning example

  .NET Framework SDK, 650

  Visual Studio .NET, 649-650

SmartTagCaption property, 645

SmartTagCount property, 644-645

SmartTagDownloadURL property, 645

SmartTagID parameter, 645

SmartTagLib namespace, 643

SmartTagName property, 645

SN.EXE (Strong Name Utility), 380

SOAP (Simple Object Access Protocol), 14

software, 14

Software Development Kit. *See* **SDK**

SomeFormattedClass table entry, 433

SomeMethod method, 479

Sound class, 1133-1136

Sound method, 1134

sounds, 810

/source (AXIMP.EXE), 1393

source files, 1109-1111

source interfaces (COM callbacks), 215-216

  defining classes in IDL files, 703-704

  DownloadBegin, 239

  DWebBrowserEvents, 226

  DWebBrowserEvents2, 226

  IChatRoomDisplay, 216

  IConnectionPointContainer, 216

Source string, 722

SourceInterfaceName_ Event interface, 222

SourceInterfaceName_ EventProvider interface, 222

SourceInterfaceName_ MethodNameEvent class, 236

SourceInterfaceName_ MethodNameEvent-Handler delegate, 235

SourceInterfaceName_ MethodNameEvent-Handler interface, 222

SourceInterfaceName_ SinkHelper interface, 222

Spell Checking application, 127-130, 133-137

SQL Distributed Management Objects. *See* **SQLDMO**

SQLDMO (SQL Distributed Management Objects), 293

STA value, 280, late binding, 404

StackTrace, 723
STAs (Single-Threaded Apartments), 276-277, 282-289
state field, 1121
State property, 1121, 1132
statements
Declare
  changing string behavior, 797-799
  customizing, 795
  function names, 796
  PInvoke, 773-775
  #import, 502
  Imports (Visual basic .NET), 38
  using (C#), 35
STAThreadAttribute, 1100
static entry points, 772
  callbacks, 810-821
  choosing DLL locations dynamically, 863-865
  choosing DLL names dynamically, 863-865
  customizing structures, 829
    FieldOffsetAttribute, 832-833
    formatted classes, 839-844
    MarshalAsAttribute, 834-839
    StructLayoutAttribute, 829-832
    structure inspection, 844-847
  DUMPBIN.EXE, 772
  passing structures, 821-829
  Platform Invocation Services. *See* PInvoke
  variable-length structures,

847-849
static members, reflection, 482-488
STATSTG value type (System.Runtime.Intero pServices namespace), 1353
status codes, HRESULTS, 67-68
StdCall value, 1255
STDOLE2.TLB, 194
Stream class, 889-895
/strictref (TLBIMP.EXE), 1380
strings, 782
  BSTR, 149-150
  customizing behavior, 796-799
  help, 382
  HelpLink, 723
  LPSTR, 149-150
  LPWSTR, 149-150
  MarshalAsAttribute, 1342
  marshaling to SAFEARRAYs, 943-947
  Message, 722
  Source, 722
  System.IntPtr, 789-791
  System.String, 783-784, 787-788
  System.Text.StringBuilder, 783-786
StringToBSTR method (Marshal class), 1331-1332
StringToCoTaskMemAnsi method (Marshal class), 1332
StringToCoTaskMemAuto method (Marshal class), 1332

StringToCoTaskMemUni method (Marshal class), 1333
StringToHGlobalAnsi method (Marshal class), 1333
StringToHGlobalAuto method (Marshal class), 1333-1334
StringToHGlobalUni method (Marshal class), 1334
StringValidator assembly, 381, 392
StringValidator class, 381
  C#, 380-381
  C++, 385, 387-388
  JScript, 388-390
  Visual Basic 6, 382-384
Strong Name Utility. *See* SN.EXE
strong names, assemblies, 23-24
strTypeLibName parameter, 1050
struct (IntPtr type), manipulating, 258-262
StructLayoutAttribute (System.Runtime.Interop Services namespace), 270, 433, 1354
  customizing structure layout, 554-556
  customizing structures, 829-832
  formatted classes, 839-844
  LayoutKind enumeration, 554, 829-830
  parameters, 830
structs, IWMPEffects interface, 1204-1208

structures

COAUTHINFO, 873

COM, converting, 189-191

customizing, 829

FieldOffsetAttribute,
832-833

formatted classes,
839-844

MarshalAsAttribute,
834-839

StructLayoutAttribute,
829-832

structure inspection,
844-847

layout, customizing,
554-556

MULTI_QI, 873

names, 707-709

passing, 821-829

variable-length, 847-849

variants, 266-267, 270-275

StructureToPtr method
(Marshal class),
1019-1022, 1334-1336

success HRESULTs,
342-343, 580, 721-722

metadata changes, 344-348

SuppressUnmanagedCode
SecurityAttribute, 308

SynchronizationAttribute,
276, 586

syntax, ILASM.EXE,
328-329, 331

ApplicationEvents_
SinkHelper class
constructor, 332

changing data types,
340-342

custom attributes, 351-358

data types, 332-333

exposing HRESULTs,
342-348

input files, 331

MarshalAsAttribute,
334-340

nested types, 334

passing parameters, 334

SAFEARRAYs, 348-351

/sysarray (TLBIMP.EXE),
1380

SYSKIND enumeration
(System.Runtime.Intero
pServices namespace),
1354-1355

System namespace, 35

System assembly, 23, 508

System method, 1135

System Monitor, 320-321

System namespace, 52,
620, 643, 887, 894, 1016,
1066-1068, 1079, 1096,
1118, 1131, 1138, 1146,
1149, 1152, 1156, 1171,
1215

C# keywords, 35

C++ keywords, 42-43

IntPtr type, 270

Visual Basic .NET key-
words, 39

System.Activator class, 99

System.AppDomain.
Unload method, 1049

System.Collections name-
space, 596, 743-747

System.Collections.
ArrayList instance, 463

System.Collections.
Ienumerable interface,
740

System.Collections.Sorted
List instance, 461

System.Collections.Stack
class, 403

System._ComObject, 71,
104, 229-232, 295-298,
422, 696, 734-735

System._ComObject
instance, 232

System.ComponentModel
class, 620

System.Console class, 868

System.Diagnostics
namespace, 321

System.Drawing assembly,
28, 34, 365

System.Drawing name-
space, 1215

System.Drawing.dll type
library, 396

System.Drawing.Font
class, 910-912

System.EnterpriseServices
namespace, 52, 584-586,
1059, 1099

System.EnterpriseServices
.ServicedComponent
class, 283, 507

System.Enum.Format
method, 646

System.EventArgs class,
608

System.FlagsAttribute
custom attribute, 1022

System.Globalization
namespace, 620

System.Guid.NewGuid
method, 60

System.Guid.ToString, 570

System.IConvertible
interface, 652

System.IDisposable class,
69

System.IntPtr, 789-791

System.IntPtr data type,
248-250

System.IO namespace,

887, 894
System.IO.Stream class, 883-889
System.MarshalByRef-Object class, 295, 507
System.MTAThread-Attribute, 278
System.Object class, 295, 741-743
System.Reflection name-space, 26, 59, 270, 1066, 1096, 1215
System.Reflection.AssemblyDescription-Attribute, 1067
System.Runtime.CompilerServices.MethodImplAttribute, 276
System.Runtime.InteropServices name-space, 52, 218, 250, 297, 391, 596-598, 643, 772, 837, 861, 887, 909, 998, 1016, 1056, 1066-1067, 1118, 1138, 1215, 1250-1252
  APIs, versus unsafe C# code, 250-254
    obtaining value type addresses, 254-255
    obtaining value type sizes, 255-258
  classes, 620
    CurrencyWrapper, 1263-1264
    DispatchWrapper, 1264-1265
    ErrorWrapper,

1267-1268
ExtensibleClassFactory, 1269-1271
Marshal, 1292-1342
RegistrationServices, 1349-1351
RuntimeEnvironment, 1351-1352
TypeLibConverter, 1356-1357
UnknownWrapper, 1366-1367
custom attributes, 1250
  AutomationProxy-Attribute, 1254
  ClassInterfaceAttribute, 1256-1257
  CoClassAttribute, 1258
  ComAliasName-Attribute, 1258
  ComConversionLoss-Attribute, 1258
  ComEventInterface-Attribute, 1258-1259
  ComRegisterFunction-Attribute, 1261
  ComSourceInterfaces-Attribute, 1261
  ComUnregister-FunctionAttribute, 1262
  ComVisibleAttribute, 1262-1263
  DispIdAttribute, 1265-1266
  GuidAttribute, 1278
  IDispatchImplAttribute, 1282
  ImportedFromTypeLib-Attribute, 1284
  InterfaceTypeAttribute,

1285
  LCIDConversion-Attribute, 1290-1291
  PrimaryInterop-AssemblyAttribute, 1348
  ProgIdAttribute, 1349
  TypeLibFuncAttribute, 1358
  TypeLibTypeAttribute, 1359
  TypeLibVarAttribute, 1359
custom marshaling interfaces, 1252
delegates, 1345
enumerations
  AssemblyRegistration-Flags, 1254
  CALLCONV, 1255
  CallingConvention, 1255-1256
  CharSet, 1256
  ClassInterfaceType, 1257
  ComInterfaceType, 1260
  ComMemberType, 1261
  DESCKIND, 1264
  ExporterEventKind, 1268-1269
  FUNCFLAGS, 1272
  FUNCKIND, 1273
  GCHandleType, 1277
  IDispatchImplType, 1283
  IDLFLAG, 1283
  IMPLTYPEFLAGS, 1283
  ImporterEventKind,

1284

INVOKEKIND, 1287

LayoutKind, 1290

LIBFLAGS, 1291

PARAMFLAG, 1347

SYSKIND, 1354

TYPEFLAGS, 1355

TYPEKIND, 1355

TypeLibExporterFlags,
1357

TypeLibFuncFlags,
1358

TypeLibImporterFlags,
1358

TypeLibTypeFlags,
1359

TypeLibVarFlags, 1359

UnmanagedType,
1367-1368

VarEnum, 1369-1370

VARFLAGS, 1370

exceptions

COMException,
1259-1260

ExternalException,
1271

InvalidComObject-
Exception, 1286

InvalidOleVariantType-
Exception, 1286-1287

MarshalDirective-
Exception, 1344-1345

SafeArrayRank-
MismatchException,
1352

SafeArrayType-
MismatchException,
1352-1353

SEHException, 1353

interfaces

ICustomAdapter,

1280-1281

ICustomFactory, 1281

ICustomMarshaler,
1281-1282

IRegistrationServices,
1287

ITypeLibConverter,
1287-1288

ITypeLibExporterName
Provider, 1288

ITypeLibExporterNotify
Sink, 1289

ITypeLibImporterNotify
Sink, 1289

UCOMIBindCtx, 1360

UCOMIConnection-
Point, 1360

UCOMIConnection-
PointContainer, 1360

UCOMIEnum-
ConnectionPoints,
1360

UCOMIEnum-
Connections, 1361

UCOMIEnumMoniker,
1361

UCOMIEnumString,
1361

UCOMIEnumVARIANT,
1361-1362

UCOMIMoniker,
1362-1363

UCOMIPersistFile,
1363

UCOMIRunningObject
Table, 1363

UCOMIStream, 1364

UCOMITypeComp,
1364-1365

UCOMITypeInfo, 1365

UCOMITypeLib, 1366

pseudo-custom attributes

ComImportAttribute,
1260

DllImportAttribute,
1266-1267

FieldOffsetAttribute,
1271-1272

InAttribute, 1284-1285

MarshalAsAttribute,
1342-1344

OptionalAttribute,
1345-1346

OutAttribute,
1346-1347

PreserveSigAttribute,
1347-1348

StructLayoutAttribute,
1354

tool APIs, 1252

value types

ArrayWithOffset,
1252-1254

BINDPTR, 1255

BIND_OPTS, 1255

CONNECTDATA, 1263

DESCUNION, 1264

DISPPARAMS, 1266

ELEMDESC, 1267

EXCEPINFO, 1268

FILETIME, 1272

FUNCDESC, 1272

GCHandle, 1273-1277

HandleRef, 1278-1280

IDLDESC, 1283

PARAMDESC, 1347

STATSTG, 1353

TYPEATTR, 1355

TYPEDESC, 1355

TYPELIBATTR, 1356

VARDESC, 1368

wrappers, 115

System.Runtime.

InteropServices.Custom
Marshalers namespace
classes
  EnumerableToDispatch-
    Marshaler, 1370
  EnumeratorToEnumVariant
    Marshaler, 1371
  ExpandoToDispatchEx-
    Marshaler, 1371-1372
  TypeToTypeInfoMarshaler,
    1372
System.Runtime.
  InteropServices.Expando
  namespace, 1372-1373
System.Runtime.
  InteropServices.ItypeLib
  ExporterNameProvider
  interface, 1054-1055
  C# method, 1054
  C++ method, 1054
  Visual Basic .NET method,
    1054
System.Runtime.
  InteropServices.Marshal
  class, 307, 501, 845
System.Security.Suppress
  UnmanagedCodeSecurit
  yAttribute, 308
System.STAThread-
  Attribute, 278
  in ASP.NET, 279-280
  in C#, 279
System.String, 783-784,
  787-788
System.Text namespace,
  946
System.Text.
  RegularExpressions
  namespace, 381
System.Text.

RegularExpressions.
  Regex class, 396
System.Text.StringBuilder,
  783-786
System.Threading
  namespace, 275, 288
System.Threading.
  ApartmentState
  enumeration, 280
System.Threading.Manual
  ResetEvent class, 286
System.tlb type library,
  623
System.Type class, 26, 99
System.Type parameter,
  568-570
System.Type.GetType
  method, 68
System.Web assembly,
  510
System.Web.Services.Web
  Service class, 507
System.Web.UI.Page
  class, 507
System.Windows.Forms
  assembly, 50, 427, 1221
System.Windows.Forms
  namespace, 52, 620,
  1171, 1215
System.Windows.Forms.
  Control.Invoke method,
  1100
System.Windows.Forms.
  Design.PictureBox-
  Designer.Initialize
  method, 508
System.Windows.Forms.
  dll type library, 396
System.Windows.Forms.
  Form class, 479, 507,
  1221
System.Windows.Forms.

Form.Menu property,
  507
System.Windows.Forms.
  MainMenu class, 507
System.Windows.Forms.
  MessageBox.Show
  method, 50
System.Windows.Forms.
  tlb type library, 623
System.Xml assembly, 34
System.Xml.dll type
  library, 396
System32 directory, 25
SystemConfigurationFile
  property
  (RuntimeEnvironment
  class), 1351
SystemDefaultCharSize
  property (Marshal class),
  1336
SystemDefinedImpl value,
  1283
SystemMaxDBCSCharSize
  property (Marshal class),
  1336

T

tables, running object,
  1301
TagTypes enum, 643-644
TAPI (Microsoft Telephony
  API), 227
  methods, 227-229
Target property
  (GCHandle value type),
  1276
testing components from
  COM, 535-536
TextBoxFont property, 923

ThisCall value, 1255
threading, 275, 733
ApartmentState property,
 280
 C#, 280-281
 starting new threads,
 282
 Visual Basic .NET, 281
Both model, 733
COM, 275
 apartment states,
 277-282
 apartment types,
 276-277
 callbacks to .NET
 objects, 282-289
 *HKEY_CLASSES_*
 ROOT\CLSID
 {CLSID}\InProc-
 Server32 key string
 values, 276-277
 incompatible
 apartments, 291-292
MTA (multi-threaded), 733
.NET Framework, 275
 callbacks from COM
 objects to .NET
 objects, 282-289
 COM apartment incom-
 patibility, 291-292
 COM apartment states,
 277-282
 COM apartment types,
 276-277
 COM ThreadingModel
 registry value, 276-
 277
 concurrency, 275
threadsafe, 275
ThreadingModel registry

value, 276-277
threadsafe, 275
ThrowExceptionForHR
 method (Marshal class),
 1336-1337
throwOnMissingSubKey
 parameter, 569
TimedLevel structure,
 1021
Title property, 1216-1217,
 1233
titleScreen field, 1121
/tlb (REGASM.EXE),
 1387-1389, 1057
/tlb (REGSVCS.EXE), 1396
tlb parameter, 1060
tlb switch (REGASM.EXE),
 571
TLBEXP.EXE, 426, 535,
 1040, 1062, 1382
 /?, 1384
 converting assemblies, 426
  exported type library,
  428
  helpstrings, 427
  LCID, 427
  library names, 428
  type library
  identification, 426-
  427
  version numbers, 427
 converting classes,
  449-451
 converting COM members,
  434
  .NET events, 446-447
  .NET fields, 444, 446
  .NET methods, 434-441
  .NET properties,

  441-444
 converting enumerations,
  453-454, 457
 converting .NET data
  types, 429, 432-433
 converting .NET interfaces
  to COM interfaces,
  447-449
 converting value types,
  452-453
 generating type libraries,
  395-396
 /help, 1384
 /names, 1383
 /nologo, 1384
 /out, 1384
 /silent, 1384
 syntax, 1382
 /verbose, 1384
TLBIMP.EXE, 1040,
 1062-1063, 1376-1377
 /?, 1381
 /asmversion, 1377
 creating PIAs, 686
  customizing metadata,
  693-694
  names, 686-687
  naming output
  assembly, 690-693
  reasons for, 684-685
  type library references,
  687-689
 /delaysign, 1377
 /help, 1381
 /keycontainer, 1377-1378
 /keyfile, 1378
 /namespace, 1379
 /nologo, 1381
 /out, 1378
 /primary, 1379

/publickey, 1379
/reference, 1045, 1380
referencing COM
    components with SDK,
    81-84
registering PIAs, 694-696
running on MSXML.DLL,
    142
/silent, 1381
/strictref, 1380
syntax, 1376
/sysarray, 1380
troubleshooting, 167
/unsafe, 1380-1381
/verbose, 1381
writing IDL type libraries,
    697-698
        constants, 709-710
        constructs, 710
        defining classes,
            702-707
        naming enums, 707-709
        referencing external
            types, 698-702
        registering type
            libraries, 711
topEdge field, 1147
ToString method, 743
    IFormattable interface
        implementation, 761-764
    type library transforma-
        tions, 439-440
TransactionAttribute, 586
transformations, 86
    ActiveX controls, 196-198
    classes, 179
        coclasses, 180-182
        RCW, 182-186
    data types, 143-144
        combining types,
            145-151

complex types, 152-162
DISPIDs, 173-174
    DISPID NEWENUM -4,
        175-176
    DISPID Value 0,
        174-175
enumerations, 193-194
HRESULTs, 1400,
    1406-1407, 1413,
    1416-1417, 1423, 1429
interfaces, 177-179
methods, 162
    by-value versus
        by-reference, 164-167
    hiding HRESULTs,
        162-164
    [in, out] parameter,
        167-169
    [in] versus [out],
        167-169
    parameter arrays,
        169-171
modules, 187-188
properties, 171-173
structures, 189-191
type libraries, 141-143
typedefs, 194-196
unions, 191-192
**transformations (data
types).** *See also* **type
libraries**
    custom marshaling,
        895-896
        adapter objects,
            901-903, 905-909
        arrays, 943-947
        by value, 914-923
        deterministic release of
            resources, 947-952
        ICustomMarshaler
            interface, 896-898
        limitations, 952-953
        MarshalAsAttribute,

895, 898-901
        marshaling between
            .NET and COM fonts,
            914-923
        marshaling between
            System.IO.Stream and
            IStream, 923-943
        marshaling by value
            versus reference,
            910-913
        .NET class implementa-
            tions, 909
    without custom marshal-
        ing, 882-883, 883-895
TreeView control, 624
troubleshooting. *See also*
errors
    InvalidCastException,
        289-290
        casting to RCW types,
            295-299
        QueryInterface failure,
            290-295
    TLBIMP.EXE, 167
**tryAgainScreen. field,
1121**
type libraries, 262, 426.
See also **transformations
(data types)**
    casing, 489-490, 492
    COM, 58-59, 64
    converting, 141-143
        assemblies, 426-428
        classes, 449-451
        COM members for
            .NET object models,
            434-447
        enumerations, 453-454,
            457
        .NET data types, 429,

432-433
.NET interfaces to COM interfaces, 447-449
value types, 452-453
creating assemblies from, 1040
dynamic assemblies, 1042-1046
GetPrimaryInteropAssembly method, 1047-1048
saving, 1048-1050
TypeLibConverter class, 1040-1042
creating from assemblies, 1050
dynamic libraries, 1050-1055
saving dynamic libraries, 1055
disabling marshaling, 580-582
dynamic
creating, 1050-1055
saving, 1055
errors, 294
exported, 428
exporter, 394-397
COM-Callable Wrappers. See CCWs
generating type libraries, 395-396
helpstring, 382
importer transformations to create IntPtr types. *See* IntPtr types
importer transformations to expose connection points, 222-227, 235-240

importing in separate application domains, 1049-1050
LCID (Local Identifier), 529
loading, 1043
MarshalAsAttribute C# signature exportation, 900-901
marshaling, 291
Microsoft Direction Animation, 731
mscorlib.tlb, 623
names, 141-143
OLEVIEW.EXE, 535
references
creating PIAs (Primary Interop Assemblies), 687-689
OLEVIEW.EXE, 688
referencing in Visual Studio .NET, 79-81
searching for, 662
System.Collections class interface transformations, 743-747
System.Drawing.dll, 396
System.tlb, 623
System.Windows.Forms.dll, 396
System.Windows.Forms.tlb, 623
System.Xml.dll, 396
TLBEXP.EXE, 426
VBA, 64
versioning, 529
Windows Registry, 65
writing IDL, 697-698
ActiveX controls, 712
constants, 709-710

constructs, 710
defining classes, 702-707
naming enums, 707-709
referencing external types, 698-702
registering type libraries, 711
type library importer. See Interop Assembly
Type Library to Assembly Converter. See TLBIMP.EXE
Type parameter, 600
Type property, 502
type safety, .NET Framework, 66
type systems, 64
Type.GetTypeFromCLSID method, 309
Type.GetTypeFromProgID method, 309
TYPEATTR value type (System.Runtime.InteropServices namespace), 1355
typedefs, 194-196
TYPEDESC value type (System.Runtime.InteropServices namespace), 1355
TYPEKIND enumeration (System.Runtime.InteropServices namespace), 1355
TYPELIBATTR value type (System.Runtime.InteropServices namespace), 1356
TypeLibConverter class, 85, 1052, 1356

creating assemblies from
   type libraries, 1040
   C# methods, 1040
   C++, 1041
   dynamic assemblies,
      1042-1046
   GetPrimaryInterop-
      Assembly method,
      1047-1048
   ITypeLibConverter
      interface, 1042
   Visual Basic .NET
      methods, 1041
creating type libraries from
   assemblies, 1050-1055
generating type libraries,
   395
methods
   ConvertAssemblyTo-
      TypeLib, 1356
   ConvertTypeLibTo-
      Assembly, 1356-1357
   GetPrimaryInterop-
      Assembly, 1357
   ResolveRef method, 1045
TypeLibExporterFlags
   enumeration (System.
   Runtime.InteropServices
   namespace), 1357, 1051
TypeLibFuncAttribute
   (System.Runtime.Interop
   Services namespace),
   1358
TypeLibFuncFlags enumer-
   ation (System.Runtime.
   InteropServices name-
   space), 1358
TypeLibImporterFlags
   enumeration (System.
   Runtime.InteropServices
   namespace), 1043-1044,
   1358
TypeLibTypeAttribute

(System.Runtime.Intero
   pServices namespace),
   1359
TypeLibTypeFlags enu-
   meration
   (System.Runtime.
   InteropServices name-
   space), 1359
TypeLibVarAttribute
   (System.Runtime.Intero
   pServices namespace),
   1359
TypeLibVarFlags enumera-
   tion (System.Runtime.
   InteropServices name-
   space), 1359
TypeLoadException, 313,
   392, 403
TypeRepresentsComType
   method (Registration-
   Services class), 1057,
   1350
TypeRequiresRegistration
   method
   (RegistrationServices
   class), 1058, 1351
types. *See also* data types
   IntPtr, 789-791
   names, 500, 505
   RCW. *See* RCW types
   System.Runtime.Interop-
      Services namespace. *See*
      System.Runtime.Interop-
      Services namespace
TypeToTypeInfoMarshaler
   class, 1372

U

/u (REGSVCS.EXE), 1396
/u option (REGASM.EXE),
   569
U1 value, 834
U2 value, 834

UCOMIBindCtx interface,
   1360
UCOMIConnectionPoint
   interface, 1360
UCOMIConnectionPoint-
   Container interface, 1360
UCOMIEnumConnection-
   Points interface, 1360
UCOMIEnumConnections
   interface, 1361
UCOMIEnumMoniker
   interface, 1361
UCOMIEnumString inter-
   face, 1361
UCOMIEnumVARIANT
   interface, 1361-1362
UCOMIMoniker interface,
   1362-1363
UCOMIPersistFile inter-
   face, 1363
UCOMIRunningObjectTable
   interface, 1363
UCOMIStream interface,
   1364
UCOMITypeComp inter-
   face, 1364-1365
UCOMITypeInfo interface,
   1365
UCOMITypeLib interface,
   1366
Unadvise interface, 216
Unicode setting, 797-798
Unicode value, 1256
UnicodeEncoding class,
   946
UnicodeEncoding.GetBytes
   method, 946
Uninstall method, 1100
UninstallAssembly
   method, 1061, 1099
unions, 191-192
Unknown value, 280

UnknownWrapper class
(System.Runtime.Interop
Services namespace),
1366-1367
UnknownWrapper
wrapper, 115
unmanaged code, 48, 72
    adapter objects, 905-909
    debugging COM
        Interoperability calls
        from managed code,
        315-319
    errors, 404-407
    goals for interaction, 48-49
    interaction with managed
        code, 49
        C++ extensions, 50-51
        COM Interoperability,
        51-53, 69-71
        JUMP to .NET, 51
        PInvoke, 49-50
    permission, 304
    reflection, 482-488
    security, 49, 304-308
    StringValidator class
        C++, 385-388
        JScript, 388-390
UnmanagedType enumer-
ation (System.Runtime.
InteropServices name-
space), 337-338,
1367-1368
    MarshalAsAttribute,
        542-545
        ByValArray, 549
        LPArray, 550
        SAFEARRAY element
        types, 550-552
UnmanagedType.LPArray
class, 337
UnmanagedType.
  SafeArray class, 337

UnmanageType values,
834
/unregister
(REGASM.EXE), 1389
UnregisterAssembly
method
(RegistrationServices
class), 1056, 1351
UnregisterFunction
method, 644
unregistration functions,
569-570
/unsafe (TLBIMP.EXE),
1380-1381
unsafe code (C#), 849-852
UnsafeAddrOfPinned-
ArrayElement method
(Marshal class), 1337
UnsafeInterfaces flag,
1043
usage guidelines, 506
    constructors, 513-514
    data types, 516
        nested arrays, 518-519
        OLE Automation,
        516-518
        pointers, 518
        user-defined value
        types, 519
    enumerations, 514-516
    interfaces versus classes,
        506-508
    interfaces versus custom
        attributes, 508-510
    overloaded methods,
        511-513
    properties versus fields,
        510-511
useBonusSound field,

1121
user experience, 14
user input, 865-868
user-defined data types,
519
user-defined exceptions,
521-523
USER32.DLL, 1472, 1486
using construct (C#),
1218-1220
using statement (C#), 35
Util class, 1112, 1138-1139
    methods, 1112, 1118-1119
    public fields, 1112
Util.CreateSoundBuffer-
FromFile method, 1135

V

V-table binding, 505
Validating event, 612,
622-623
value types
    IntPtr. *See* IntPtr types
    type library transforma-
        tions, 452-453
    unsafe C#
        obtaining addresses,
        254-255
        obtaining sizes,
        255-258
VARDESC value type
(System.Runtime.Interop
Services namespace),
1368
VarEnum enumeration
(System.Runtime.Interop
Services namespace),

337-338, 1369-1370

VARFLAGS enumeration (System.Runtime.Interop Services namespace), 1370

variable-length signatures, 849

variable-length structures, 847-849

variants

data type, 146-147

instances, 117-118

OLE Automation, 517

parameters, 720

structures, 266-267, 270-275

varying arrays, 158-159

VB .NET

definitions

addImport and addRule parameters, 994

DispHTMLStyleSheet interface and the HTMLStyleSheet coclass interface, 1004-1006

IHTMLStyleSheet interface, 991

IRunningAppCollection, 980-981

IWMPEffects Interface, 974

modules, 356-358

VB6.EXE, registering assemblies, 392

VBA (Visual Basic for Applications), 64

VerbCaptionFromID property, 645

VerbCount property, 645

VerbID parameter, 645

VerbID property, 645

VerbNameFromID property, 646

/verbose (AXIMP.EXE), 1393

/verbose (REGASM.EXE), 1390

/verbose (TLBEXP.EXE), 1384

/verbose (TLBIMP.EXE), 1381

Verbs enum, 643

version numbers, assemblies, 427

versioning, 64-66, 527-529

assemblies, 527-529

clients

COM, 528-529

.NET, 527-529

CLSIDs, 530-531

IIDs, 531-532

LIBIDs, 529

members, 527

.NET Framework, 16

CLR, 19

DLL Hell, 17-18

policies, 19

resiliency, 16

side-by-side components, 18-19

ProgIDs, 65

visibility (COM), 477-482, 562-565

Visual Basic .NET, 38

ApartmentState property, 281

callback functionality using delegates, 206-208

callback functionality using events, 212-214

coclass IDL representation of .NET classes, 450-452

code to handle COM callbacks on another thread, 287-289

code with COM callbacks on separate threads, 283-286

COM View and .NET View

of an event, 446

of methods with parameter arrays, 441

of properties, 442

of the same methods, 147

ComClassAttribute, 560-562

compatibility, 38

ComVisibleAttribute, 562-565

custom attributes, 40-42

definition of IProvideClassInfo, 673-674

explicit interface implementation, 656

Hello, World, 39-40

IObjectSafety, 677

ItypeLibImporterNotifySink interface methods, 1044, 1052

keywords corresponding to System namespace, 39

.NET View and COM View

of the same methods, 435, 437

of the same overloaded

methods, *438*
PInvoke, 773-775
Register for COM Interop option, 534
RegistrationHelper class methods, 1059
RegistrationServices class methods, 1056
strings, 787-788
syntax for imported C-style array fields, 262-264
TypeLibConverter class, 1041, 1050

Visual Basic 6
class interfaces, 397-399
coclass IDL representation of .NET classes, 452
COM, 57
COM View and .NET View
of an event, 447
of fields exported as properties, 445
of properties, 442
compiling projects without binary compatability, 294-295
errors, returned error codes/messages, 403-404
forms, custom marshaling, 921-923
IPhoneEvents interface, 597
.NET interfaces, 759-764
.NET View and COM View
of the same methods, 435-437
of the same overloaded methods, 439
optional parameters, 105

setting error information, 723-724
StringValidator class, 382-384
Visual Basic for Applications, 64
Visual Basic Runtime, 15
Visual C++, 42
custom attributes, 43-45
Hello, World, 43
keywords corresponding to System namespace, 42-43
managed extensions, 42, 50-51
.NET definition of AddressLists dispinterface, 982-984
.NET interfaces, 747-759
setting error information, 725-728
Visual Studio .NET
COM interface shortcuts, 650
custom attributes, 652
members, 653
selecting Implement Interface,, 651-652
selecting members, 651
syntax changes, 652-653
mixed-mode debugging, 315-319
referencing ActiveX controls, 121-122
referencing COM components, 78, 83-84
Register for COM Interop option, 535
running Office XP smart tags example, 646-650
Visualization API, 1197,

1201
BookExamples.WindowsMediaPlayer assembly, 1201
IWMPEffects interface, 1199, 1202-1204
enumerations, 1204-1208
Render method, 1199-1201
structs, 1204-1208
Vizualization class, 1208-1223
registry keys, 1197-1198
Visualization Wizard, 1198
Visualization class, 1208-1223, 1229
Visualization Wizard, 1198
visualizations (Media Player), 572, 1196
COM objects, 1196-1197
.NET Visualization API, 1224
ColorfulVisualization, 1231-1235
Dancing Cat Visualization, 1235-1243
SimpleVisualization, 1224-1226
WizardVisualization, 1227-1230
Visualization API, 1197, 1201
BookExamples.WindowsMediaPlayer assembly, 1201
IWMPEffects interface, 1199-1223

registry keys,
1197-1198
Visualization Wizard,
1198

W

waveform array, 1199
Weak value
(GCHandleType enumer-
ation), 1277
WeakTrackResurrection
value (GCHandleType
enumeration), 1277
Web services, 14
Web sites, DirectX, 1106
WebBrowser control, 236
    events, 241-245
    referencing ActiveX
        controls, 123, 126
Width property, 1136,
1139-1140, 1143
Win32
    APIs
        CopyFileEx, 810-815
        data types, converting
            into .NET types to
            define PInvoke s
            ignatures, 778-781
        error handling, 800-
            807
        MessageBeep, 810
        PlaySound, 810
        ReadConsoleInput,
            865-868
        RegCloseKey, 856
        RegDeleteKey, 860
        RegEnumKey, 856
        RegOpenKey, 856
    functions
        customizing string
            behaviors, 796-799

GetConsoleScreen-
    BufferInfo, 821-829
GetLastError, 800
GetWindowsDirectory,
    784-788
SetVolumeLabel,
    783-784
namespace, 1166-1167,
    1171
PInvoke, 772
Win32.cs file, 1172, 1178
Winapi value,
CallingConvention
enumeration, 1256
WINCV.EXE tool
(Windows Forms Class
Viewer tool), 960-962
WindowResize event, 226
Windows Explorer, GAC,
24
Windows Forms
    controls, 471-477
    exposing events to COM,
        611
        COM event sink,
            623-625
        .NET event source,
            611-614, 620-623
    FontMarshaler custom
        marshaler, 918-923
    Interactive Interop Tool,
        1100-1101
Windows Forms Class
Viewer tool. *See*
WINCV.EXE tool
Windows Media Player.
See **Media Player**
Windows Registry
    COM components, 62
    compared to GAC, 64
    ProgIDs, 63
    type library versions, 65

windowsForm_Activated
method, 625
windowsForm_ChangeUIC
ues method, 625
windowsForm_DragDrop
method, 625
WINMM.DLL, 810
WithEvents keyword, 603
    automatic event handler
        hookup, 604
    callback functionality
        using events in Visual
        Basic .NET, 213-214
wizards
    ATL COM (C++), 725
    ATL Simple Object (C++),
        726
    Visualization, 1198
Word, Spelling Checking
application, 127-130,
133-137
wrappers
    CCW, 69, 71
    CurrencyWrapper, 115,
        119
    DispatchWrapper, 115
    ErrorWrapper, 115
    RCW, 69-71
    System.Runtime.InteropSe
        rvices namespace, 115
    UnknownWrapper, 115
WriteByte method
(Marshal class),
1337-1339
WriteInt16 method
(Marshal class), 1340
WriteInt32 method
(Marshal class),
1340-1341
WriteInt64 method
(Marshal class), 1341

**WriteIntPtr method
  (Marshal class), 1342**
writing
  custom attributes, 29-30
  IDispatch implementations,
    665-672
**WSCRIPT.EXE, registering
  assemblies, 392**

X–Z

XCOPY deployment, 20
zero-bounded arrays, 719
**zero-impact deployment,
  20, 1008**